GLOBAL AMERICANS

For our Parents, Teachers, Professors,
and all Global Americans

GLOBAL AMERICANS

VOL 2: since 1865

A History of the United States

Maria E. Montoya
New York University

Laura A. Belmonte
Oklahoma State University

Carl J. Guarneri
Saint Mary's College of Californina

Steven W. Hackel
University of California, Riverside

Ellen Hartigan-O'Connor
University of California, Davis

Lon Kurashige
University of Southern California

Cengage

Australia • Brazil • Canada • Mexico • Singapore • United Kingdom • United States

Cengage

Global Americans: A History of the United States
Maria E. Montoya / Laura A. Belmonte / Carl J. Guarneri / Steven W. Hackel / Ellen Hartigan-O'Connor / Lon Kurashige

Product Director: Paul Banks

Product Manager: Joseph Potvin

Managing Content Developer: Anais Wheeler

Content Developer: Erika Hayden

Associate Content Developer: Andrew Newton

Product Assistant: Emma Guiton

Senior Marketing Manager: Valerie Hartman

Senior Content Project Manager: Carol Newman

Senior Art Director: Cate Barr

Manufacturing Planner: Fola Orekoya

IP Analyst: Alexandra Ricciardi

IP Project Manager: Erika Mugavin

Production Service / Compositor: SPi Global

Text Designer: Jeanne Calabrese

Cover Designer: Nilou Moochhala /NYM Design

Cover Image: (left to right): Jane Addams (*Library of Congress Prints and Photographs Division[LC-USZ62-10598]*), Wovoka (*The Granger Collection*), Dith Pram (*Jerry Soloway/Corbis*), Paul Robeson (*Alfred Eisenstaedt/The Life Picture Collection/ Getty Images*), Ernie Pyle (*Everett Collection Inc/ Alamy*), Clara Lemlich (*The Kheel Center for Labor-Management Documentation and Archives in the ILR School at Cornell University*)

Library of Congress Control Number: 2016951291

Student Edition:
ISBN: 978-1-337-10112-7
Loose-leaf Edition:
ISBN: 978-1-337-10124-0

Cengage
200 Pier 4 Boulevard
Boston, MA 02210
USA

Printed at CLDPC, USA, 03-23

Brief Contents

Contents

25 The Vietnam War Era, 1965–1975 740

26 The Global Conservative Shift, 1975–1988 772

Maps & Features

History Without Borders

Global Americans

Timelines

Preface

Global Americans embodies a new, internationalized approach to American history. In their form and content, most textbooks portray the United States as a national enterprise that developed largely in isolation from the main currents of world history. In contrast, this textbook speaks to an increasingly diverse population of students and instructors who seek to understand the nation's place in a constantly changing global, social, and political landscape. It incorporates a growing body of scholarship that documents how for five centuries North America's history has been subject to transnational forces and enmeshed in overseas activities and developments.

American history was global in the beginning, and it has been ever since. We therefore present a history of the United States and its Native American and colonial antecedents in which world events and processes are central features, not just colorful but peripheral sidelights. Our narrative is meant to show how at each stage of its unfolding, the American story was shaped by exchanges of goods, people, and ideas with others, and in turn how Americans exerted growing influence abroad. This enlarged American history is intended to break down curricular walls that discourage connections between U.S. and world history. Its globally informed narrative also aims to capture more accurately how Americans have actually experienced their lives in the past as well as the present.

Students today face a world that is rapidly changing with stepped-up exchanges of ideas and goods that reshape the economy; new technologies that transform work and communication; global conflicts over ideologies and religions; and political and economic developments that challenge the United States' role in the world. We believe that history students need a narrative that recovers the global contexts of America's past and helps them understand the origins of the interconnected world in which we live. *Global Americans* weaves together stories, analysis, interpretation, and visual imagery from across time and place to craft a new American history that develops in relation to events and peoples across this continent and beyond. While integrating this enlarged geographic coverage into our narrative, we have taken care not to sacrifice the detailed coverage of domestic events that are keys to the nation's history and to include consideration of the distinctive features and ideas that have shaped that history.

World history narratives sometimes neglect the human element in favor of describing economic systems and impersonal forces. *Global Americans* instead focuses on people. Our narrative is committed to integrating the experiences of Americans whose stories are often omitted from U.S. history courses because they are somehow deemed foreign or because they represented minority voices. We also cast new light on familiar figures and events by placing them in a global or transnational context. *Global Americans* reflects our belief that different groups of people have had, and still have, claims to being American and part of U.S. history. The narrative of American history is enriched by exploring the world of Native Americans prior to their contact with Europeans and Africans, as well as examining the full range of Spanish, French, Dutch, and English colonial projects for trade and settlement. Just as we do not see global contexts as incidental to this history, we do not portray the period prior to the founding of the United States as simply a prelude to nationhood. The colonial history of North America is the story of a place laid claim to by various peoples and governments. Including its diversity of actors and aspirations adds contingency to a national story that is often told as if destined or preordained. After the United States achieved independence, its history similarly underwent a process of conflict and experiment in the context of international and local events and people. The nation's territorial spread, its mix of peoples, and its global position were forged in the crucible of powerful domestic and international influences. Today's Americans experience the effects of both the local and the global as they work, play, worship, consume, travel, and wage war or peace. We have aimed to construct a historical narrative that does justice to the dramatic conflicts, diverse peoples, and myriad connections that have created our American world.

What's New About This Textbook?

A global perspective informs the presentation of the essential social, economic, religious, and political themes of American history.

Global Context

U.S. history textbooks have traditionally conceptualized American history as distinct and standing apart from the rest of the world, with events beyond its borders acknowledged almost solely through U.S. foreign policy and wars. Yet recent scholarship has emphasized how the United States has considered global social, economic, and cultural factors, and historians have highlighted the role of the United States in the world. Engaging this expanded notion of U.S. history requires a new look at the United States as a nation with a web of worldwide connections.

We build on this scholarship by suggesting that borders have historically been porous and fluid and that demographics have constantly shifted from the precolonial era to the present. We show that the early history of North America was created by the intersections of Atlantic, Pacific, Indian, and African history, as well as one element in Europe's expansion during the early modern era. Thus, the experiences of Indians, the Spanish, the French, the Dutch, and the English all figure prominently in the early chapters. We consider transatlantic slavery and the diaspora of African peoples as part of a thousand-year saga that is not limited to the history of North America or the United States. We continue the focus on migration and diverse populations throughout the nineteenth- and twentieth-century chapters, and we give special attention to commerce and trade and the ways in which technology, culture, and ideas are transmitted across national boundaries. With a global perspective, the narrative of U.S. history connects to the rest of the world not only through the actions of presidents, generals, and diplomats, but also through the experiences of business leaders, social activists, missionaries, workers, immigrants, refugees, athletes, musicians, artists, tourists, and consumers.

At the same time, the core narrative of American political, economic, and social history constitutes the spine of *Global Americans*. Our work covers all the major domestic trends and events and highlights all the familiar players. Presidents and presidential elections serve to mark eras and change over time. Students will always know that they are situated in the broadly familiar terrain of U.S. history. But the traditional narrative looks different within a global context, and this informs the other themes that run through the book.

A Continental Nation

Global context necessitates a continental orientation. Our work takes seriously that the history of all parts of the nation and its territories matters, not just the regions formally incorporated into the United States during the Revolutionary War. What happened before the United States became a nation had important consequences for the society that would later develop. For example, we want our students to understand how California Indians experienced the Franciscan missions, how Spanish soldiers and settlers reacted to life in this distant frontier, and how North American regions settled by Spain differed from New France or British North America. We also want our students to understand how the peoples and lands of the trans-Mississippi West were and were not incorporated into the United States during the nineteenth and twentieth centuries. Our focus on the American West, on the nation's continental borderlands, and on its territories, including Alaska and Hawai'i, provides new perspectives on westward migration, the slavery controversy, railroads and industrialization, and the centrality of California to modern American culture.

One of the most important recent intellectual developments in history has been the move to view the Atlantic World as a loosely integrated region with connections that transcend nation-states and national boundaries. Just as we chronicle the integration of the Americas into an Atlantic system of politics, commerce, and culture during the Age of European Expansion, we similarly treat the Pacific Ocean and the lands adjacent to it as an integrated region that has long affected American history. Seeing the U.S. East and West coasts as elements within their respective oceanic communities reinforces our global integration framework.

Diversity in Global and Continental Contexts

Global integration and a continental orientation allow a fresh look at issues of race, class, and gender. In recent decades, historians and their textbooks have given much consideration to racial and ethnic minorities, the lives of working people, and the roles of women, yet they have been slower to advance an interpretive framework that presents U.S. history from their varying points of view and acknowledges multiple perspectives within these groups. In contrast, we examine what it looked like to live through events in U.S. history from different perspectives; we explore diversity *within* the categories of race, ethnicity, and class; and we situate movements for women's rights and LGBT rights within national and transnational contexts. For example, we discuss the very different impact the diffusion of European consumer goods in the eighteenth century had on the lives and politicization of free women, enslaved women, and Cherokee women. In an example from the nineteenth century, we describe the roles played by the *Californio*, *Tejano*, and New Mexican *Hispano* elite in the economic and political conquest of the Southwest by the United States during the 1830s and 1840s, and we examine the ways colonialism affected women and families in this region. During the twentieth century, we place World War II in the context of worldwide, concurrent racial ideologies and situate the U.S. civil rights movement in the context of global struggles for human rights. We also look at the rise of politically conservative Christian activity in light of rising religious fundamentalism worldwide.

Format for Each Chapter

Global Perspective

Each chapter deliberately embeds a global framework in the text and in the features. The opening vignette sets the focus by making global connections, and the chapter introduction deliberately surveys the global context of the chapter's time frame. This global context is reinforced in presentation of events and people throughout the chapter text and reiterated at the end of the chapter in a summary and globalized timeline. The strategy for achieving a global perspective derives from what we have come to call, during the book's development, the Five Cs: comparisons, connections, concepts, contexts, and consequences. Different national experiences are *compared. Connections* among international social movements are examined as are theories and models concerning, for example, revolutions, nation building, industrialization, imperialism, feminism, and racism. We look at the broad international *contexts* for what seem to be internal developments, such as the American Revolution and Progressivism. We track worldwide *consequences* for what seem to be American events—plantation slavery and commercial cotton, for example, or Henry Ford's moving assembly line—as well as the impacts of international ideas and events on America's history.

Opening Vignette

Each chapter opens with a story of an individual who has crossed borders—in geography, national boundaries, culture, or identity—and whose experience exemplifies the book's global integration framework.

Visual Headings

Each section within a chapter opens with an image that signals the content that follows. These photos, cartoons, paintings, and objects of material culture prompt students to connect, understand, and remember major points and ideas. An informative caption directs interpretation of the image and promotes visual learning. For example, in the book's first chapter, the "Open Hand" symbol of the Eastern Woodlands peoples can be read as either a welcome or a warning. In the chapter on the American Revolution, an eyewitness watercolor depicting four different soldiers in the Continental forces at Yorktown—a black soldier, a New England militiaman, a backcountry rifleman, and a French officer—demonstrates not only the diversity among fighting men but also the different motives for fighting the American War for Independence. Furthermore, in the chapter on the New Deal, we use an image of Franklin Roosevelt broadcasting a "fireside chat" to signal his innovations in connecting the presidency to the people through technology and his efforts to explain his administration's policies in everyday language.

Focus Questions and Subheading Clues

At the end of each visual heading is a focus question that guides students in absorbing and interpreting the information in the subsections that follow. For example, the major section on the U.S. Constitution asks:

- As you read, focus on the ways in which the relationship between local and federal power was central to the framing of the Constitution and the debates over its ratification. Which side won the debate initially? Ultimately?

Each subheading in that section is then annotated with a brief statement of core content intended both to cue understanding and aid in review.

- The Constitutional Convention rethinks the new nation's political structure.
- The new Constitution creates a stronger central government.
- The debates over ratifying the Constitution center on federal powers and the nature of a republic.
- The continuing importance of protecting individual rights against a powerful central government reflects the Revolution's legacy.

Together, these clues build toward an informed, comprehensive answer to the focus question that opened the section. In conjunction with the focus question, the clues are designed to support departmental and campuswide learning objectives and assessment programs.

Key Terms

Within each chapter, approximately forty specialized terms are boldfaced for students' attention with brief definitions appearing on the same page. Terms highlighted include concepts, laws, treaties, movements and organizations, legal cases, and battles. Unlike other textbooks, *Global Americans* also includes specialized terms relating to world events that affected Americans, such as *Revolutions of 1848* and *blitzkrieg*. The key terms thus highlight the connections between U.S. history and developments around the globe.

Global Americans Portraits

Each chapter features three portraits—brief biographies and often an image—of individuals whose lives or careers cross borders or were affected by international events. These portraits also highlight the various ways people experienced the social, economic, and political turmoil discussed in the chapter narrative. The familiar (e.g., Harriet Tubman) and less familiar (e.g., Medicine Snake Woman and Dith Pran) are both represented. Collectively, the portraits aim to challenge preconceptions and offer surprising new insights into people as diverse as Daniel Boone, who joined both sides of the American Revolution and ended up a local official in Spanish North America, and Hedy Lamarr, who is best-known as a Hollywood starlet, but who was also a self-taught inventor who made a major contribution to the wireless communication revolution.

History Without Borders

Each chapter includes a global feature highlighting an issue, idea, product, or material object that was not constrained by political borders. A brief essay, images, and a world or hemisphere map trace the global path of ideas and goods. Often this feature reveals something not well known by Americans on a topic not typically included in a U.S. history textbook, such as the Iroquois' adoption of Chinese vermilion as body paint, Japan's antinuclear movement in the 1950s, and the impact of artificially created nitrogen fertilizer on world food production. Critical thinking questions help students place American events or trends in a larger, global context. This feature is not merely global decoration but rather an extension of an already globalized text.

Summary and "Thinking Back, Looking Forward"

The core text of each chapter ends with a summary that revisits the focus questions to establish large-scale generalizations and promote a synthetic understanding of U.S. history and its connections to the world. The "Thinking Back, Looking Forward" element directs students to see long-term trends and recurring themes that appear across chapters.

Timeline

A timeline at the end of each chapter is intended to help students review by visualizing chronology and events' cause and effect. Timelines conventionally list the most important events covered in the chapter. In our chapters, timelines incorporate international events to reinforce the book's global framework and use maps to correlate the regions of the world with events in the timeline.

Resources

A list of secondary and Internet sources appears in each chapter. These are the resources that we believe are useful to both students and instructors who want to dig deeper into the content of the chapter. They are not meant to be comprehensive but rather to suggest the richness of the field.

Note on Terminology

As authors we have grappled with the challenge of finding the appropriate term for a specific ethnic or racial group during a particular period in history. These terms are not fixed, but in fact shift over historical periods, adding even more complexity. The terms we have chosen to use in each of the chapters are deliberate and reflect our understanding of both the historiography and contemporary uses. Our intention is not to make a final determination about the use of specific ethnic and racial labels, but rather to help teachers suggest that these terms can be used as a basis for discussion regarding the importance of names and who gets to decides various labels.

Note on Images

The images in *Global Americans* have been thoughtfully chosen to help students engage with the text on a visual level as well as a reading comprehension level. We encourage instructors to have their students "read" the images carefully and ask questions about each of them. We have also selected some images that are quite disturbing, such as an image of the lynching of Will Brown in Chapter 18 and the liberation of Jews from a World War II concentration camp in Chapter 21. We debated the pros and cons of using these images, deciding to do so because we believe that they reflect important historical moments with which we want students to engage and interpret.

MindTap

MindTap Instant Access Code: ISBN – 9781337114677
MindTap Printed Access Card: ISBN – 9781337116107

MindTap for *Global Americans* is a personalized, online learning platform that provides students with an immersive learning experience to build and foster critical thinking skills. Through a carefully designed chapter-based learning path, MindTap allows students to easily identify learning objectives; draw connections and improve writing skills by completing unit-level essay assignments; read short, manageable sections from the e-book; and test their content knowledge with map- and timeline-based critical thinking questions.

MindTap allows instructors to customize their content, providing tools that seamlessly integrate YouTube clips, outside Websites, and personal content directly into the learning path. Instructors can assign additional primary source content through the Instructor Resource Center and Questia primary and secondary source databases that house thousands of peer-reviewed journals, newspapers, magazines, and full-length books.

The additional content available in MindTap mirrors and complements the authors' narrative, emphasizing the global forces and dynamics that have been central to the history of the United States. It also includes primary source content and assessments not found in the printed text. To learn more, ask your Cengage Learning sales representative to demonstrate it for you—or go to www.Cengage.com/MindTap.

Instructor Resources

The Instructor's Companion Website, accessed through the Instructor Resource Center (login.cengage.com), houses all of the supplemental materials you can use for your course. This includes a Test Bank, Instructor's Manual, and PowerPoint Lecture Presentations. The Test Bank, offered in Microsoft® Word® and Cognero® formats, contains multiple-choice, identification, true or false, and essay questions for each chapter. Cognero® is a flexible, online system that allows you to author, edit, and manage test bank content for Global Americans, 1e. Create multiple test versions instantly and deliver through your LMS from your classroom, or wherever you may be, with no special installs or downloads required. The Instructor's Resource Manual includes chapter summaries, suggested lecture topics, map exercises, discussion questions for the primary sources, topics for student research, relevant websites, suggestions for additional videos, and online resources for information on historical sites. Finally, the PowerPoint Lectures are ADA-compliant slides collate the key takeaways from the chapter in concise visual formats perfect for in-class presentations or for student review.

Acknowledgements

The development and writing of *Global Americans* has taken almost a decade. Along the way, we have indebted ourselves to some very fine editors and scholars who helped us find our collective voice as well as the will to continue on what has been an enormous project. We would like to thank Irene Biber and Sally Constable who first approached us about writing such a textbook. Along the way, we had the great fortune to work with Ann West and Jean Woy who both helped shape the book in the early stages. We were also lucky enough to have Clint Attebery guide the team through a critical juncture. Our biggest debt, however, goes to Ann Grogg, an exceptional editor, who worked closely with each of us to translate our knowledge into a readable and usable text for college students. We are all better writers from having her skillful touch on our prose.

We also owe a debt of gratitude to each other for the years of hard work as we each read and edited chapters that were often far afield from our own special area of expertise. Throughout the long process of writing and editing, we coauthors have held lively biweekly conference calls in which every stage of every chapter was discussed in detail. *Global Americans*, therefore, is the outcome of countless hours of shared discussions about American history and how it should be presented to a new generation of students.

We are also indebted to many colleagues who voiced their encouragement, read draft chapters, and provided helpful suggestions for improvement.

Alexander Haskell, *University of California, Riverside*
James Huston, *Oklahoma State University*
Ann M. Little, *Colorado State University*
Peter Mancall, *University of Southern California*
Lisa Materson, *University of California, Davis*
Andrew Needham, *New York University*
Marcy Norton, *George Washington University*
Gregory E. O'Malley, *University of California, Santa Cruz*
Lorena Oropeza, *University of California, Davis*
Thomas J. Osborne, *Santa Ana College (emeritus)*
Robert C. Ritchie, *Henry E. Huntington Library*
Susanah Shaw Romney, *New York University.*
Virginia Scharff, *University of New Mexico*
Carole Shammas, *University of Southern California*
Terri Snyder, *California State University, Fullerton*
Michael Witgen, *University of Michigan*

We want to thank all the scholars who were contracted by Cengage as expert reviewers of the text at various stages. Their critiques were thoughtful and much appreciated.

Thomas Adam, *The University of Texas at Arlington*
Ian Aebel, *University of Iowa*
Brian Alnutt, *Northampton Community College*
Rick Ascheman, *Rochester Community and Technical College*
Shelby Balik, *Metropolitan State University of Denver*
Evan Bennett, *Florida Atlantic University*
Katherine Benton-Cohen, *Georgetown University*
Angela Boswell, *Henderson State University*
Blanche Brick, *Blinn College*
Rachel Buff, *University of Wisconsin*
Brian Casserly, *Bellevue College*
Tonia Compton, *Columbia College*

Cynthia Counsil, *Florida State College at Jacksonville*
David Dalton, *College of the Ozarks*
Bruce Daniels, *The University of Texas at San Antonio*
Wendy Davis, *Campbellsville University*
Rodney Dillon, *Palm Beach State College*
Shaughnessy Doyel, *Saint Charles Community College*
Shannon Duffy, *Texas State University*
Mark Elliott, *University of North Carolina at Greensboro*
Richard Filipink, *Western Illinois University*
Kristen Foster, *Marquette University*
Jennifer Fry, *Moravian College*
Joshua Fulton, *Moraine Valley Community College*
Bryan Garrett, *The University of Texas at Arlington*
Matthew Garrett, *Bakersfield College*
Diane Gill, *North Lake College*
Aram Goudsouzian, *University of Memphis*
Larry Grubbs, *Georgia State University*
Elisa Guernsey, *Monroe Community College*
David Hamilton, *University of Kentucky*
Kristin Hargrove, *Grossmont College*
Aimee Harris-Johnson, *El Paso Community College*
Justin Hart, *Texas Tech University*
Mary Ann Heiss, *Kent State University*
Robin Henry, *Wichita State University*
Warren Hofstra, *Shenandoah University*
Thomas Humphrey, *Cleveland State University*
Matthew Hutchinson, *Kennesaw State University*
Sheyda Jahanbani, *University of Kansas*
Ely Janis, *Massachusetts College of Liberal Arts*
Volker Janssen, *California State University, Fullerton*
Patricia Knol, *Triton College*
Tim Lehman, *Rocky Mountain College*
Carmen Lopez, *Miami Dade College*
Frances M. Jacobson, *Tidewater Community College*
Eric Mayer, *Victor Valley College*
Suzanne McFadden, *Austin Community College*
Mark Mengerink, *Lamar University*
Robert O'Brien, *Lone Star College-CyFair*
Deirdre O'Shea, *University of Central Florida*
Stephen Patnode, *Farmingdale State College*
Darren Pierson, *Blinn College*
David Raley, *El Paso Community College*
Monica Rankin, *The University of Texas at Dallas*
Nik Ribianszky, *Georgia Gwinnett College*
Ayesha Shariff, *Saint Paul College*
John Smolenski, *University of California, Davis*
Diane Vecchio, *Furman University*
Felicia Viator, *University of California, Berkeley*
Elwood Watson, *East Tennessee State University*
William Whisenhunt, *College of DuPage*
Vibert White, *Bethune Cookman University*
Scott Williams, *Weatherford College*
Mary Wolf, *University of Georgia*

We are indebted to the following for creating the instructor and student resources for *Global Americans*: Elizabeth Bischof, University of Southern Maine; Christopher

Jillson, New York University; Carmen Lopez, Miami Dade College; Sarah Nytroe, DeSales University; Jacqueline Shine, University of California, Berkeley; and Mary Montgomery Wolf, University of Georgia.

We appreciate the following for their helpful feedback on the MindTap for *Global Americans*: Milan Andrejevich, Ivy Tech Community College of Indiana; Michelle Barsom, Bainbridge State College; Jordan Bauer, University of Alabama at Birmingham; Timothy Buckner, Troy University; Carlos Contreras, Grossmont-Cuyamaca Community College District; Richard Filipink, Western Illinois University; Kristen Foster, Marquette University; Jason Friedman, Wasatch Academy; Matthew Garrett, Bakersfield College; Aimee Harris-Johnson, El Paso Community College; Leslie Heaphy, Kent State University; Karen Huggin, Georgia Highlands College; Ely Janis, Massachusetts College of Liberal Arts; Kathryn Johnson, Northern Michigan University; Stephen Katz, Community College of Pennsylvania; Jeremy Lehman, McLennan Community College; Denise Lynn, University of Southern Indiana; Dustin Mack, University of Oklahoma; Mark Mengerink, Lamar University; Brian Miller, Mission College; Caryn Neumann, Miami University Middletown; Anne Paulet, Humboldt State University; David Raley, El Paso Community College; Mark Sample, Monroe County Community College; Kelly Shannon, Florida Atlantic University; Camille Walsh, University of Washington; and Thomas Wirth, State University of New York at Cortland.

We are also happy to have this opportunity to express our gratitude to the great folks at Cengage who have shepherded this project through the process that took words on a manuscript page and made them into the vibrant text and online resources that you see here, especially Paul Banks, product director; Joe Potvin, product manager; Carolyn Lewis, executive director of development; Anais Wheeler, content development manager; Lauren MacLachlan, production manager; Carol Newman, senior content project manager; Cate Barr, senior art director; Valerie Hartman, senior marketing manager; Erika Hayden, content developer; Andrew Newton, associate content developer; Rob Alper, senior learning design author/consultant; Charlotte Miller, art editor; Emma Guiton, product assistant; Erika Mugavin, intellectual property project manager; and Alexandra Ricciardi, intellectual property analyst.

Finally, we are so appreciative of our families who have hung in there with us as we drafted chapters, slogged through rewrites, sat through too many conference calls while on vacation, and rejoiced as it all came together. It does not go without saying that we could not have done this without all of their support. Thank you.

About the Authors

Maria E. Montoya earned her B.A at Yale University in 1986 and Ph.D. at Yale in 1993. She is Associate Professor of History at New York University as well as the Dean of Arts and Science at New York University, Shanghai. She was previously Associate Professor of History at the University of Michigan where she also served as the Director of Latina/o Studies. Her articles include works on western, labor, Latina/o, and environmental history, and they have appeared in the *Western Historical Quarterly, The Journal of Women's History*, and *American Quarterly*. She is the author of *Translating Property: The Maxwell Land Grant and the Conflict over Land in the American West, 1840-1900* (University of California Press, 2002). She has taught the U.S. History survey for more than twenty years and has worked on the AP U.S. History Development Committee and consulted with the College Board.

Laura A. Belmonte earned her B.A. at the University of Georgia and her Ph.D. at the University of Virginia in 1996. She is Department Head and Professor of History at Oklahoma State University. A specialist in the history of U.S. foreign relations, she is the author of *Selling the American Way: U.S. Propaganda and the Cold War* (University of Pennsylvania Press, 2008) and numerous articles on cultural diplomacy. Belmonte is editor of *Speaking of America: Readings in U.S. History* (Cengage, 2nd edition, 2006), and she is concurrently working on books on U.S. global policy on HIV/AIDS and the history of the international LGBT rights movement (Bloomsbury, forthcoming 2017). She is a member of the U.S. Department of State's Historical Advisory Committee on Diplomatic Documentation. After participating in the 2005 National Endowment for the Humanities summer institute "Rethinking America in Global Perspective," she began teaching undergraduate and graduate courses with a transnational focus, including "America in International Perspective" and "HIV/AIDS in Transnational Perspective."

Carl J. Guarneri earned his B.A. at the University of Pennsylvania, M.A. at the University of Michigan, and his Ph.D. at Johns Hopkins University in 1979, and he is Professor of History at Saint Mary's College of California, where he has taught since then. He has also been a visiting professor at Colgate University and the University of Paris. A historian of nineteenth-century America, Guarneri has won national fellowships for his research and published books and articles on reform movements, utopian socialism, the Civil War, and American cultural history, which include *The Utopian Alternative: Fourierism in Nineteenth-Century America* (Cornell University Press, 1991) and two edited collections: *Religion and Society in the American West* (University Press of America, 1987), and *Hanging Together: Unity and Diversity in American Culture* (Yale University Press, 2001). He is currently writing a book on the Civil War career of Charles A. Dana, an influential New York journalist and Assistant Secretary of War. Through his publications and presentations, Guarneri has also been a leading voice in the movement to globalize the study and teaching of U.S. history. He has codirected institutes for the National Endowment for the Humanities on "Rethinking America in Global Perspective." His survey-course reader, *America Compared: American History in International Perspective* (Cengage, 2nd ed., 2005), and his brief textbook, *America in the World: United States History in Global Context* (McGraw-Hill, 2007) are seminal undergraduate texts, and his anthology, *Teaching American History in a Global Context* (M.E. Sharpe, 2008), offers a globalizing "toolkit" for U.S. history instructors.

Steven W. Hackel earned his B.A. at Stanford University and his Ph.D. at Cornell University in 1994. From 1994 to 1996, he was a postdoctoral fellow at the Omohundro Institute of Early American History and Culture and a visiting Assistant Professor at the College of William and Mary. He taught at Oregon State University from 1996 to

2007 and is now Professor of History at the University of California, Riverside. Within the larger field of early American history, Hackel's research focuses on the Spanish Borderlands, colonial California, and California Indians. Hackel is especially interested in Indian responses to Spanish colonialism, the effects of disease on colonial encounters, and new ways of visualizing these processes through digital history. His first book, *Children of Coyote, Missionaries of Saint Francis: Indian-Spanish Relations in Colonial California*, 1769-1850, was published by the Omohundro Institute of Early American History and Culture (2005) and garnered numerous national prizes. His most recent book, *Junípero Serra: California's Founding Father* (Hill and Wang, a division of Farrar, Straus and Giroux, 2013), was named a top-ten book for 2013 by Zócalo Public Square and the best book of the year on early California by the Historical Society of Southern California. He has edited two volumes of essays and published nearly two dozen scholarly essays and has been awarded fellowships from the National Endowment for the Humanities and many other agencies.

Ellen Hartigan-O'Connor earned her B.A. at Yale University and Ph.D. at the University of Michigan in 2003. She is Associate Professor of History at the University of California, Davis, where she teaches courses on gender, American social and cultural history, and the histories of colonialism and capitalism. She is the author of *The Ties That Buy: Women and Commerce in Revolutionary America* (University of Pennsylvania Press, 2009) as well as articles and book chapters on gender and economy in the eighteenth and nineteenth centuries. With support from the National Endowment for the Humanities, she is currently completing a project on auctions and market culture in early America, tracing the economic and cultural power of a widespread but little-studied institution. She became interested in globalizing U.S. history through her expertise in Atlantic world and transnational women's and gender histories. She is coeditor of the *Oxford Handbook of American Women's and Gender History* (Oxford University Press, forthcoming), and a board member of Women and Social Movements. A founding and Standing Editor of *Oxford Bibliographies—Atlantic History*, Hartigan-O'Connor is also a speaker with the Organization of American Historians' Distinguished Lectureship Program.

Lon Kurashige earned his B.A. from the University of California, Santa Barbara and his Ph.D. from the University of Wisconsin-Madison in 1994. Since 1995, he has taught at the University of Southern California, where he is Associate Professor of History. He is author of *Two Faces of Exclusion: The Untold History of Anti-Asian Racism in the United States* (Chapel Hill: University of North Carolina Press, 2016) and *Japanese American Celebration and Conflict: A History of Ethnic Identity and Festival, 1934-1990* (University of California Press, 2002). He was the winner of the History Book Award from the Association for Asian American Studies in 2004. He coedited "Conversations in Transpacific History," a special edition of *Pacific Historical Review* (2014) and *Major Problems in Asian American History*, 2nd ed. (Cengage Learning, forthcoming 2017). His article "Rethinking Anti-Immigrant Racism: Lessons from the Los Angeles Vote on the 1920 Alien Land Law" won the Carl I. Wheat prize for best publication to appear in the *Southern California Quarterly* between 2012 and 2014. His other publications include articles published in the *Journal of American History, Pacific Historical Review*, and *Reviews in American History*. Kurashige has been awarded fellowships from the Fulbright Program, Social Science Research Council, Rockefeller Foundation, the National Endowment for the Humanities, and other funding agencies.

14

Reunion and Retreat: Reconstruction

1865–1877

The son of immigrants from Haiti and Cuba, Rodolphe Desdunes worked throughout his life for equal rights for people of color in Louisiana. This included organizing support for Homère Plessy, the plaintiff in the landmark *Plessy v. Ferguson* case, which ultimately upheld segregation and proved a deep disappointment to Desdunes.

For Louisiana people of color like Rodolphe Desdunes, emancipation was a transnational movement and a multigenerational commitment. Carried by slaves and other migrants, the ideal of racial equality coursed across the Atlantic and stretched in time from the French and Haitian Revolutions of the 1790s to the American antisegregation campaigns a century later. Desdunes's parents were from Haiti and Cuba; he grew up in the New Orleans community of Creoles or "free coloreds" whose French language associations protested racial restrictions and advocated abolition. When federal troops occupied New Orleans during the Civil War, many Creole men joined the Union army, cementing their claim to full citizenship. After the war, Louisiana's new Constitution of 1868 guaranteed "equal civil, political and public rights" to all citizens. Six years of Republican rule built freed people's schools, enlisted blacks in the state militia, and elected dozens of American-born and Caribbean-origin blacks to office.

Louisiana Division/City Archives

Desdunes was too young to vote for the 1868 Constitution, but he defended it when black civil rights came under attack by violent white-supremacist groups. Serving on the New Orleans Metropolitan Police, Desdunes was wounded in 1874 when more than three thousand armed White Leaguers, mostly Confederate veterans, stormed city hall and the statehouse. They withdrew only after President Grant rushed federal troops to the city.

As the rights of people of color were assailed, Desdunes began studying law to take their grievances to the federal courts, where postwar constitutional amendments could be used to challenge state laws. When Louisiana mandated racial segregation on railroads, Desdunes enlisted his son to test the statute and won a verdict that integrated interstate trains. Because railroad travel *within* Louisiana remained segregated, Desdunes organized support for Homer (born Homère) Plessy, another Creole of Haitian descent, to mount a legal challenge that climbed to the U.S. Supreme Court. *Plessy v. Ferguson* (1896), which upheld Louisiana's segregationist practices, broke the promise of Louisiana's 1868 constitution and signaled the final unwinding of Reconstruction. Heartbroken, Desdunes withdrew from public life to write a history of black Creole activism in New Orleans meant to inspire future generations to renew the struggle.

Desdunes's post-Civil War experience had unique features that stemmed from Louisiana's Afro-French community and its cosmopolitan outlook. Still, Louisiana blacks played an important role outside the state as prominent advocates for civil equality. Moreover, the struggle in Louisiana broadly resembled the course of postwar debates elsewhere in the nation. What political and social rights would be guaranteed to emancipated African Americans? How far would the northern victors and newly empowered freed people restructure southern society and politics to embody those rights? How would the former Confederate states be restored to the Union, and who would control that process? How much authority should the federal government exert over the states?

How do the experiences of Rodolphe Desdunes reflect the struggle of Louisiana blacks and the role that they played as prominent advocates for civil equality?

Go to MindTap® to watch a video on Desdunes and learn how his story relates to the themes of this chapter.

The answers to such questions were hotly debated among different political, economic, and racial groups. Control over events veered between the president and Congress, the states and the federal government. All knew that the outcome was as important as the Civil War's battles, for it was possible to win the war and lose the peace. The questions themselves implied a dilemma: Rapid and lenient restoration of Rebel states to the Union would mean letting go of transforming the South and enforcing racial equality, whereas determination to revolutionize the South's economic and racial order would mean a long, costly, and potentially bloody struggle.

Of the two main postwar tasks Americans faced—restoring political relations with former rebels and reshaping southern life after slavery—the first was the residue of civil war, and the second was the aftermath of emancipation. Viewed in a global context, the postwar political settlement resembled national unification in countries such as Italy and Germany, where the northern victors dominated the national government but North-South differences remained and regional resentments festered. The struggle over emancipation was also a familiar global theme. Around the world, other slaveholding nations, including Spain (in Cuba), Britain (in Jamaica), and Brazil, faced similar conflicts over emancipating slaves and defining justice once they were liberated. Emancipation during the Civil War gradually undermined the existence of slavery elsewhere, including Cuba and Brazil. Yet the abandonment of the North's Reconstruction program indicated that for the time being, the United States would follow a conservative path similar to that of other postemancipation societies in the Americas, which retreated from equality, limited the rights won by freed people, and appeased their former masters.

14-1 Wartime Origins of Reconstruction

As the Civil War ended, the Freedmen's Bureau, northern charities, and former slaves collaborated to construct local schools in the South. This photograph shows the Freedmen's School and its students on James Plantation in North Carolina.

Examine the photograph and the placement of its subjects. Who is the woman on the left? What can we learn from the varied heights and two sexes of the pupils? What can this photograph tell you about freedmen's schools and black Southerners' attitudes toward education? ▶

The Granger Collection, New York

Reconstruction began long before the Civil War ended. When the federal army occupied areas in Louisiana, Tennessee, and Virginia, local Unionists made preparations to rejoin the federal government. Before and after President Lincoln's Emancipation Proclamation, hundreds of thousands of runaway slaves migrated behind Union lines, seeking freedom and enlisting as federal soldiers or hospital workers. Wartime debates in Congress over readmitting rebellious states, addressing freed people's aspirations for land and labor, and adopting Union policies to meet the needs of the refugee influx provided a rehearsal for the postwar struggle over Reconstruction.

☞ As you read, consider how the Union's actions during wartime helped to set up conflicting expectations for postwar reconstruction. Were Union policies meant to raise former slaves' economic status or to keep them as farm laborers?

14-1a Lincoln versus Congress

The president and congressional Republicans quarrel over Reconstruction.

In his Proclamation of Amnesty and Reconstruction of December 1863, President Lincoln set lenient terms to entice Confederates back to the Union. While holding firm on emancipation, the president offered pardons and restoration of property to Confederates (except to high military and civil officials) who would swear an oath of allegiance to the United States. According to Lincoln's **Ten-Percent Plan**, as soon as 10 percent of those who had voted in 1860 took the oath, new state governments could be formed. He imposed no requirements for freed people's civil and political rights.

Most congressional Republicans criticized Lincoln's plan of "restoration" and favored a more thorough "reconstruction" of the South. Republican radicals, about one-third of the party's congressmen, wanted to "revolutionize Southern institutions, habits, and manners," according to spokesman Thaddeus Stevens. Moderates favored less drastic changes but agreed that Congress, not the president, should control reconstruction. The gap between Lincoln and **Radical Republicans** was exposed in the struggle over reconstruction in Louisiana, where the new state constitution of 1864, ratified by only 10 percent of Louisiana's adult white males, rejected black suffrage. In response, Congress denied admission to Louisiana's representatives.

In July, Republicans in Congress countered Lincoln's plan with the **Wade-Davis Bill**. It required 50 percent of voters to take an oath of allegiance to the Union and mandated that new state constitutions be drawn up by delegates elected by those who had never supported the rebellion. Lincoln, fearing that this bill would halt the process underway in Louisiana and Arkansas, killed the legislation by using a pocket veto, refusing to sign it before Congress's session ended.

Lincoln's reelection in 1864 paved the way for passage of a measure that the president and Republican radicals agreed on: the **Thirteenth Amendment**, abolishing slavery nationwide. Republicans feared that Lincoln's Emancipation Proclamation would be overturned by the courts in peacetime or reversed by new state governments in the South. The solution was to amend the federal constitution. Fall elections in 1864 gave the Republicans a strong congressional majority, and in January 1865, the House of Representatives passed the Thirteenth Amendment after several wavering Democrats were wooed by Republican lobbyists to their side. When the amendment was ratified by three-quarters of the states, emancipation became the law of the land in December 1865.

14-1b Emancipation on the Ground

Northern volunteers and the Union government assist the freed people.

In regions far from the invading Union armies, most black Southerners did not learn about emancipation until the spring of 1865. *Juneteenth*, the official announcement of emancipation in the holdout state of Texas on June 19, 1865, became a special day of celebration for African Americans. Long before that, slaves in coastal regions and the upper South had taken steps to free themselves. More than a million fled the South's plantations during the war, and half ended up in Union-occupied areas.

Union army officers' response to the influx of freed people was shaped by the desire to maintain order and agricultural production more than humanitarian motives. Herded into makeshift camps, some freed people were supplied rations and hired by the army and navy for meager wages as laborers, cooks, or hospital workers. Others were contracted to work on plantations seized by Union armies and leased to loyal southern whites or Yankee entrepreneurs.

For freedmen intent on staying in the agricultural South, leasing or buying confiscated lands was the preferred alternative. By the end of the war, nearly one-fifth of the farmland in areas under Union occupation was being worked by independent black families. When General Sherman passed through coastal Georgia and South Carolina in January 1865, local black leaders persuaded him to draft **Field Order No. 15** to give each freed family provisional title to forty acres of land confiscated from slaveholders. Union officials settled more than forty thousand freed people there. Elsewhere in the South, small pockets of freed people had been able to purchase land during the war.

Freed people's thirst for education was quenched more readily than their hunger for land. Freedmen's aid societies formed in the North sent more than one thousand teachers to the South during the war, and the influx increased after Appomattox. Three-quarters were women and perhaps one-fifth were black. Charlotte Forten, a young African American woman who journeyed from Philadelphia to teach in South Carolina's Lowcountry, told her

Ten-Percent Plan Lincoln's lenient wartime program to restore pacified Confederate states to the Union.

Radical Republicans Party faction intent on ensuring civil rights for former slaves and transforming the South's society and economy during Reconstruction.

Wade-Davis Bill Congressional measure that required stiff loyalty tests for readmitting former Confederate states but that Lincoln pocket vetoed.

Thirteenth Amendment Constitutional addition outlawing slavery in the United States that was ratified eight months after the Civil War ended.

Field Order No. 15 Sherman's 1865 decree setting aside land confiscated from slaveholders in coastal South Carolina, Georgia, and Florida for settlement by freed people.

Freedmen's Bureau Federal agency created under the War Department to oversee education, labor contracts, and welfare of former slaves.

students about "the noble Toussaint [L'Ouverture]," the black liberator of Haiti, so that they "should know what one of their own color could do for his race." Teachers like Forten promoted basic literacy and numeracy but also strove to help freed people "unlearn the teachings of slavery" by promoting pride, self-discipline, and the dignity of work.

Higher education for freed people was offered in seminaries, colleges, and "normal schools" (teacher training institutions) that were founded by northern charitable organizations and biracial missionary societies. Howard University in Washington, D.C., Fisk University in Tennessee, and Hampton Institute in Virginia trace their origins to Reconstruction; all were named after or led by prominent Civil War generals.

Congress assisted these philanthropic ventures and independent schools through the **Freedmen's Bureau**, established in March 1865. Run by the War Department, the bureau allocated one-third of its budget to schools from primary education to colleges such as Howard and Fisk. It took over the Union army's wartime mandate to provide relief to refugees and to enforce labor contracts between planters and former slaves.

Prevailing stereotypes and ideologies compromised most types of help available to the freed people, whether it was provided by the federal government or private volunteers. Many army supervisors and Unionist whites envisioned southern blacks as permanent farm workers, not owners. Free-market practices meant that whites often outbid former slaves who had scraped together money to buy land. And the free-labor ideology decreed that blacks should be left to fend for themselves after a short period of aid and tutelage. These assumptions persisted and undermined Northerners' plans to reconstruct the South.

14-2

Postwar Conditions and Conflicting Agendas

Library of Congress Prints and Photographs Division

Thomas Nast's widely distributed cartoons in *Harper's Weekly* magazine both shaped and reflected northern views of Reconstruction. This cartoon of August 5, 1865, features contrasting episodes. On the left panel titled *Pardon*, Columbia, a symbol of the United States, wonders "Shall I trust these men?" referring to the prostrate figures of Robert E. Lee, Jefferson Davis, and other former Confederate leaders. On the right panel called *Franchise*, Columbia clasps the shoulder of a disabled black Union veteran and asks, "And not these men?" The globe-shaped object on the pedestal is a ballot box.

How does the cartoonist contrast President Johnson's plan to pardon former Confederate leaders with mainstream Republicans' program to give voting rights to male African Americans? Which position does the cartoonist favor, and how does his portrayal indicate it? ▶

Go to MindTap® to practice history with the Chapter 14 **Primary Source Writing Activity: Responses to Reconstruction.** Read and view primary sources and respond to a writing prompt.

At the end of the Civil War, white Southerners were demoralized and resentful while the region's blacks looked forward to free and independent lives. All realized that postwar life would require changes, and each group developed its own agenda. Dramatic divisions formed among white and black Southerners, political parties, the president, and Congress over restoring the Union and defining the role of former slaves. The debate over Reconstruction paralleled struggles that followed the emancipation of slaves and other unfree laborers in overseas lands, but control by congressional Republicans seemed to promise a more equitable outcome than elsewhere.

☞ As you read, consider the agendas of different political groups in the North and South for postwar Reconstruction. How did the varied positions of former slaves, southern whites, President Johnson, and the Republican-dominated Congress lead to conflict, and over which issues?

14-2a Freedom in Action

African American families reunite and organize to secure equal rights.

At the war's end, slavery was gone and the Confederacy dissolved, but no new social or political system emerged to take their place. Despite the initial confusion, the lines were quickly drawn between southern blacks and whites over the fundamental issues of land, labor, and political power.

Former slaves had firm ideas about what they expected from freedom. For many, the first task was to reunite families who had been separated by slavery or the war. Freed people used their communal grapevine to locate relatives and took to the roads to find them. They enlisted help from the Freedmen's Bureau or paid for newspaper advertisements. Some relatives were never found, but most families broken by slavery were mended in the postwar years, and by 1870, the two-parent household became the norm.

Reconstituted African American families had to decide where to live. Some returned to the familiar surroundings of their old plantation, but many others fled the places where they had labored. As one slave told her former owner, "If I stay here I'll never know I'm free." Thousands moved to cities, believing that life would be freer there and Union troops would provide protection. The black population of major southern cities doubled in the five years after the war. Urban black enclaves were segregated "across the tracks" from whites, and occupational choices were restricted by prejudice. The majority of males became unskilled manual laborers and women were hired as maids, washerwomen, or seamstresses. Still, their neighborhoods provided precious space where African Americans established schools, clubs, benevolent societies, and other community institutions.

Whether in towns or the countryside, African Americans organized and built separate Protestant churches. Predominantly Baptist and Methodist, they became focal points for religious life and other community activities from educational classes and festivals to political meetings. Black women played prominent roles in these events, and male ministers emerged as respected community leaders who dispensed political as well as spiritual guidance.

In an agricultural society, economic independence entailed access to land. Stimulated by the Freedman's Bureau, "forty acres and a mule" became the rallying cry for freed people who demanded a portion of the lands they had worked for generations. They were deeply disappointed when "Sherman's lands" were restored to white owners and various proposals to confiscate and redistribute Rebel plantations failed to win passage in Congress.

The majority of newly emancipated blacks had little choice but to work on plantations for wages. Determined to get their full worth, blacks bargained hard over wages and hours and turned to the Freedmen's Bureau for help in enforcing annual contracts with white employers. Many African American women refused to return to full-time fieldwork, eager to raise their children and tend their own households. Labor shortages gave freedmen bargaining power, but they hated working in gangs, which reminded them of slavery, and distrusted their former masters as employers.

Freedmen realized that political organizing was necessary to demand equal rights. Even before the war ended, freedmen had joined Union Leagues, Republican clubs that had been organized in occupied districts, and used them to call for the rights of "all loyal men, without distinction of color." In the summer and fall of 1865, freedmen's conventions assembled in most former Confederate states,

Dressing for the Carnival In the 1870s, northern artist Winslow Homer captured this image of a freed Virginia family preparing for the Afro-Caribbean festival of Jonkonnu, a celebration that former slaves merged with the Fourth of July. In the painting, two women sew colorful shards on a man dressing like a harlequin, while children look on, one holding a lowered American flag. Homer celebrated the freed people's creative mix of cultures while subtly contrasting hopes for Reconstruction with its harsh realities. ◄

several in black churches. Delegates addressed petitions to white-dominated constitutional conventions, demanding equal participation and the right to vote. The new white governments ignored these demands, indicating how far apart former masters and former slaves stood at the dawn of the new era.

14-2b White Resistance

In defeat, white Southerners are devastated but defiant.

The war's physical and economic devastation demoralized white Southerners, who had controlled the region's resources. Much of Atlanta, Charleston, and Richmond lay in ruins. Slave emancipation and farms destroyed by marching armies diminished planters' wealth, and the wartime deaths of one in five white southern men deprived households of traditional heads. With no new legal system in place, crime rates rose sharply.

Many former Confederates feared being subject to occupying troops who had recently killed the South's soldiers. White Southerners especially dreaded reprisals from their former slaves, who might claim former masters' possessions or even murder them. In late 1865, rumors of a pending Christmas insurrection of violent freedmen, stirred by recollections of a similar revolt in Jamaica, sent chills through the South's white communities. A South Carolina planter's wife foresaw "the foulest demonic passions of the negro, hitherto so peaceful & happy, roused into being & fierce activity by the devilish Yankees."

Paranoia about potential black violence prompted immediate attacks by whites. The Civil War left a legacy of guerrilla warfare, racial hatred, and gun carrying in the South that continued to fuel violence after Appomattox. On Christmas Eve 1865, a group of Confederate veterans gathered in Pulaski, Tennessee, to organize the **Ku Klux Klan**. This secret vigilante group pledged to suppress all freedmen's assertions of equality and restore white supremacy by intimidation and violence. Its membership grew rapidly in the following year as it allied with opposition to black voting. Even white Southerners who renounced the Klan's tactics could not imagine peaceful coexistence of the two races under legal equality.

Southern whites especially worried about losing the cheap and disciplined labor of African American slaves on their farms. In the summer of 1865, white-dominated state legislatures passed restrictive **Black Codes** designed to return freed people to conditions as close to slavery as possible. They forbade blacks from owning guns, consuming alcohol, and marrying whites. Vagrancy laws forced black men and women to carry permits and mandated fines or imprisonment for the unemployed. The Black Code in South Carolina required freedmen to pay hefty fees to set up businesses, and Mississippi's made it illegal for blacks to own or lease farmland. These codes announced that southern whites' immediate postwar agenda was to reestablish social and economic dominance over African Americans.

Ku Klux Klan White supremacist secret society organized by former Confederates that terrorized southern blacks and their supporters during Reconstruction.

Black Codes Restrictive laws passed by Democratic-controlled southern states that denied civil rights and economic advancement to former slaves.

14-2c Johnson's Reconstruction Plan

President Johnson seizes the initiative and conciliates former Confederates.

Ex-Confederates' aspirations were bolstered by the new president, Andrew Johnson, who developed a surprisingly lenient Reconstruction plan.

In some ways, Johnson was a worthy successor to the slain president. Like Lincoln, he was born in humble circumstances in the upper South's backcountry, had little formal education, and rose through hard work. Johnson was also an ardent Unionist. A Democrat and the only senator from the South to remain in Congress after secession, he had been appointed military governor of occupied Tennessee and inserted as Lincoln's running mate in 1864 on a bipartisan Union ticket. Johnson once owned slaves but during the war supported emancipation, mainly as way to punish the South's aristocrats, whom he resented. At the war's end, he declared repeatedly that "treason is a crime and must be made odious." Some Radical Republicans who had criticized Lincoln's generous reconstruction terms saw Johnson as a potential ally.

Yet as a former southern Democrat with states' rights leanings and unreconstructed racial views, Johnson had as much in common with the war's vanquished as its victors. His plan, introduced in May 1865, called for swift restoration of the Rebel states, which he claimed had never legally left the Union. Nearly all Southerners who swore an oath of allegiance to the Union would regain their political and property rights. Confederate civilian and military officers and those owning more than $20,000 in property had to obtain a presidential pardon. Except for having southern states ratify the Thirteenth Amendment, the plan was silent on civil or voting rights for the freed people.

Over the summer of 1865, Johnson dropped his call to punish Confederate leaders and granted more than thirteen thousand pardons to wealthy former Confederates. Meanwhile, southern states largely accepted Johnson's mild conditions and created new governments little different from prewar regimes. Some refused to ratify the Thirteenth Amendment or repudiate their Confederate debts. No reorganized southern state allowed black votes, and the former Confederates who led those states adopted harsh Black Codes. To underscore their defiance, white Southerners sent Alexander Stephens, the former Confederate vice president, to the U.S. Congress along with ten Confederate generals and fifty-eight former Confederate congressmen. Eight months after the war's end, Republican leaders wondered aloud who had actually won it.

14-2d Congressional Response

When Congress reconvened in December 1865, angry Republicans refused to seat representatives from the former Confederate states. Moderates agreed that the former slaves' civil rights should be protected, and most Republicans believed that southern states should not be readmitted until they renounced secession and repudiated Confederate debts. Many worried that unrepentant southern Democrats might undo Republican wartime legislation. Emancipation had nullified the constitution's clause that African Americans represented three-fifths of a person or citizen. Because freedmen were then counted as one whole person, southern states stood to gain as many as two dozen representatives in Congress. These concerns moved congressional Republicans toward extending voting rights to the former slaves on political as well as moral grounds.

Congress opposes Johnson and forges an alternative Reconstruction program.

Taking aim at the Black Codes, Congress in early 1866 reauthorized the Freedman's Bureau, directing it to prosecute state officials who violated blacks' civil rights. President Johnson vetoed the bill. Clinging to old racial fears, he was convinced that efforts to empower freedmen would come at poor whites' expense. Congress next sought to broaden its protection of freed people by passing the **Civil Rights Act of 1866**, a landmark bill that specified that blacks enjoyed the same rights guaranteed to other U.S. citizens. It directly aimed to overturn the Supreme Court's *Dred Scott* decision of 1857. Again, Johnson vetoed the measure, denouncing its expansion of federal power as well as its assertion of equal rights. In both cases, the president's refusal to compromise helped to unite his Republican opponents, who mustered the two-thirds majority necessary to override his veto.

To counter white Southerners' opposition, Republican leaders sought constitutional protection for equal rights. In June 1866, Congress passed the **Fourteenth Amendment**, which absorbed the new Civil Rights Act into the federal charter. It declared that all persons born or naturalized in the United States (except Native Americans) were citizens entitled to due process and equal protection of the law. When ratified by the states in 1868, this sweeping provision established a policy of **birthright citizenship**, automatic granting of citizenship to those born within the nation's borders. This policy was later adopted by nearly all Western Hemisphere republics—most immediately, Argentina in 1869—but was resisted by European nations that relied on ties of language or blood lineage to bind their nationality.

Civil Rights Act of 1866 Law that recognized citizenship rights of former slaves and gave the federal government power to enforce them.

Fourteenth Amendment Constitutional addition ratified by the states in 1868 that gave citizenship to nearly all persons born or naturalized in the United States, including former slaves, and penalized states that restricted male suffrage.

birthright citizenship Automatic provision of citizenship to children born within a nation's borders or territories, which became common practice in the Americas after U.S. adoption.

Other sections of the Fourteenth Amendment repudiated the Confederate debt and disqualified Confederate officeholders from state and national positions. Rather than give black people the vote outright, the amendment specified that states denying suffrage to black men would have their representation in Congress reduced proportionally. Many Republicans represented northern states that denied blacks the vote and balked at mandating universal male suffrage. Some hoped that Johnson would accept the amendment as a compromise and a minimum condition for Reconstruction.

Johnson flatly opposed the Fourteenth Amendment and encouraged white Southerners and northern conservatives to remain defiant. In the summer of 1866, he launched an unprecedented speaking tour across the

Memphis Riots, May 1866 Three days of violence erupted after a white policeman tried to arrest a black Union veteran. Memphis's whites, who resented policing by black Union soldiers and competition with former slaves for jobs, attacked a black shantytown, shooting at will and setting buildings ablaze. Forty-six blacks and two whites died and one hundred buildings were burned, but no arrests were made. Accounts of the riot influenced passage of the Congressional Reconstruction Act. ▶

SCENES IN MEMPHIS, TENNESSEE, DURING THE RIOT—SHOOTING DOWN NEGROES ON THE MORNING OF MAY 2, 1866.—[SKETCHED BY A. R. W.]

Tennessee State Library and Archives

Print Collector/Hulton Archive/Getty Images

Global Americans The son of a Cuban schoolmaster, **Ambrosio Gonzales** was educated in New York and returned to Havana to earn a law degree and teach languages. There he joined a secret organization that advocated U.S. annexation of Cuba without ending slavery. In 1849 and 1850, Gonzales helped organize two failed filibusters to invade Cuba from the United States. Through these activities he became associated with prominent southern planters, and in 1856, he married into a wealthy South Carolina slaveholding family. During the Civil War, Gonzales served as a Confederate artillery chief under General P.G.T. Beauregard, his former schoolmate in New York. Reconstruction turned Gonzales's privileged plantation life upside down. The family estate languished when black workers departed and cotton prices fell, and Gonzales's Caribbean import business in Charleston was destroyed in a race riot. An experiment in hiring Chinese and European contract laborers for his sawmill ended in bankruptcy. In 1869, the family sailed to Havana, counting on wealthy relatives and the legality of Cuban slavery to escape the reversals of Reconstruction. Less than a year later, Gonzales's wife died of yellow fever. Returning to the United States in the 1870s, he scraped together a living by teaching in various cities and repeatedly urged Grant and others to annex Cuba. Although his Cuban background was unusual for the South's planter elite, Gonzales's career embodied their Caribbean connections, expansionist dreams, and resistance to emancipation and Reconstruction.

northern states to rally public support for his resistance to equal rights legislation. Scheming to bypass Republicans and forge a new centrist coalition, Johnson labeled his congressional opponents traitors who should be hung.

These crude attacks alienated the North's public. Meanwhile, two bloody race riots that broke out in southern cities suggested the violence Johnson's stand appeared to encourage. In May 1866, a mob of whites stormed a freed people's neighborhood in Memphis, killing nearly fifty and burning schools and churches. Three months later, armed whites in New Orleans attacked a black parade for voting rights; nearly eighty citizens were killed or wounded, most of them African Americans. These outrages prompted a backlash against Johnson and his policies. The 1866 congressional elections returned a veto-proof Republican majority to Congress. Republicans were poised to replace the president's discredited program of "restoration" with a more sweeping "reconstruction" agenda.

14-2e Reconstruction in a Global Perspective

During the Reconstruction years, Americans battled over the aftermath of civil war and the meaning of emancipation. Viewed in global perspective, neither struggle was unique. In the mid-nineteenth century, many countries faced continued turmoil after civil wars and emancipations. Their histories served as important points of influence and comparison for U.S. developments.

> The United States stands out among postemancipation societies in granting freed slaves the right to political equality.

Former Confederates complained that Reconstruction was unduly harsh on the South, but most groups defeated in nineteenth-century civil wars were treated more brutally. The victorious Chinese imperial forces who suppressed the Taiping Rebellion (1850–1864) executed more than 1 million captives. Defeated spokesmen for the 1848 revolutions in Europe, when not imprisoned, were forced into exile. After the failed Hungarian revolt, Louis Kossuth never returned to his native land, and thousands of his fellow secessionists languished in Austrian prisons.

Some Confederate partisans who refused to accept defeat went into voluntary exile. Confederate cabinet member Judah Benjamin fled to England, where he began a successful second career as a barrister. Colonies of Confederate expatriates were formed in Mexico, Cuba, and British Honduras (now Belize). About twenty thousand whites from the Deep South migrated to Brazil, whose emperor offered subsidized transport and cheap land and where slavery was still legal. These *Confederados* established cotton plantations and introduced Baptist Christianity to the region north of Sao Paolo.

In comparison to conquerors in civil wars elsewhere, victorious Unionists were remarkably lenient. A few Radical Republicans declared that "the leaders of this rebellion must be executed or banished," yet neither Jefferson Davis nor Robert E. Lee was tried for treason and the victors imposed no exile or mass imprisonments. Federal laws disfranchised a small number of high-ranking Confederates, but pardons and amnesty acts restored their property and political rights.

In contrast to this relatively mild political punishment, many Republicans favored wholesale social changes in the conquered South. Compared to emancipation elsewhere in the Western world, postwar Reconstruction made possible a more abrupt break with the past. In Russia, where Czar Alexander II emancipated the serfs, and in the British Caribbean and Brazil, where plantation slavery was abolished gradually, masters were compensated for losing their human property and strongly influenced the terms of emancipation. When Confederates rejected President Lincoln's offer of compensated emancipation, they triggered his Emancipation Proclamation—the largest confiscation of property in the nation's history. The Union's military victory meant that in the postwar period Congress excluded former masters from setting the terms of the new order.

In most plantation societies in the Americas, landed white elites retained the upper hand after emancipation and used it to keep political power and force former slaves back to work. In Jamaica, for example, freed people had to accept a four- to six-year apprenticeship working for their former masters without wages. Although full civil rights were supposed to follow, freed slaves were prevented from voting by prohibitive property requirements and eventually outright exclusion. Reconstruction in the United States got off to a more promising start. When the Republican-dominated Congress passed laws guaranteeing civil and political rights regardless of race, the United States became unique among postemancipation societies in granting freed slaves the right to political equality.

Morant Bay Rebellion Uprising in Jamaica by freedmen asserting their right to land to which whites retaliated by killing more than four hundred blacks and revoking colonial self-rule.

As Americans debated Reconstruction, they looked for lessons as emancipation unfolded in the Caribbean. In October 1865, freed black farm workers in Jamaica rose up to protest lack of access to land. The **Morant Bay Rebellion** was brutally suppressed, and Jamaican whites returned control of the colony to Britain. When news of the rebellion reached North America, the South's newspapers warned that demands for land and similar "incendiary teachings" would produce violent uprisings among former slaves. Meanwhile, northern abolitionists such as Lydia Maria Child compared the Jamaican freed peoples' restrictions to the South's Black Codes, declaring that such schemes for "legislating the blacks back into slavery" must be stopped.

14-3

Congressional Reconstruction

This political cartoon was published during the impeachment trial of President Andrew Johnson in 1868 when Republicans in Congress charged him with obstructing enforcement of the Constitution and recent Reconstruction laws. "This little boy would persist in handling books above his capacity," the caption reads. "And this was the disastrous result." The cartoon reflects Republicans' confidence that Johnson would be convicted.

Why would political opponents portray Johnson as a "little boy" involved in matters "over his head"? Why is it significant that Johnson is shown crushed by "Vol. 14" of the Constitution? ▶

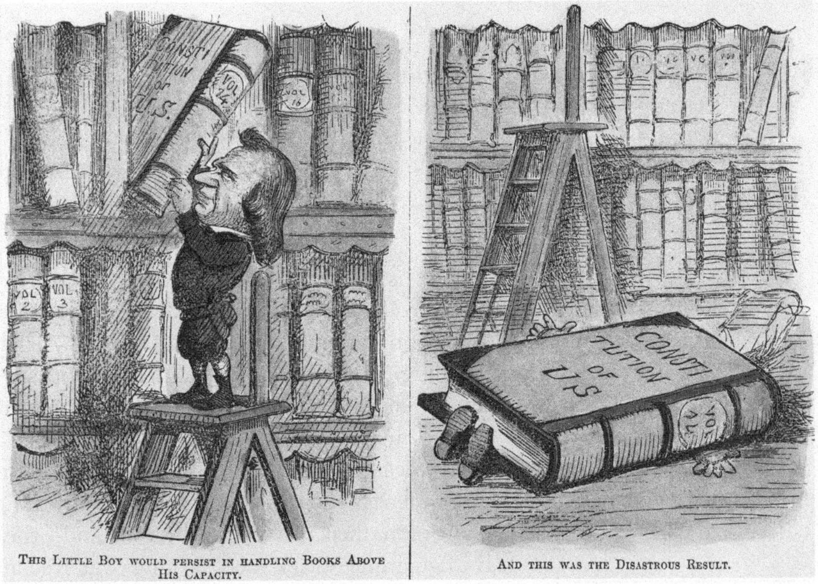

CONSTI TUTION OF U.S.
VOL 14
VOL 2
VOL 3
THIS LITTLE BOY WOULD PERSIST IN HANDLING BOOKS ABOVE HIS CAPACITY.
CONSTI TUTION OF U.S.
AND THIS WAS THE DISASTROUS RESULT.

The Granger Collection, New York

Under "radical" Reconstruction, congressional Republicans used their strong majority to impose plans to restore the Union and reconstruct the South politically. Their program did not distribute land to freed people; it did not enfranchise women or prevent indirect disfranchisement of African Americans. But it amended the constitution to make voting rights colorblind and federally protected. And it installed loyal Republican governments in the former Confederate states. This expansion of federal power paralleled the growth of national influence abroad following the Union's victory in the Civil War.

☞ As you read, think about how the Union victory in the Civil War and growing federal powers reconfigured sectional relations in the United States as well as foreign relations in North America. How did Congressional Reconstruction attempt to make over the South politically and socially? How did expanding U.S. power redraw the map of North America?

14-3a Military Occupation and Impeachment

Congress takes charge of Reconstruction during a constitutional crisis.

After debating several proposals, Congress drew up a comprehensive blueprint for overhauling the South's political framework. The

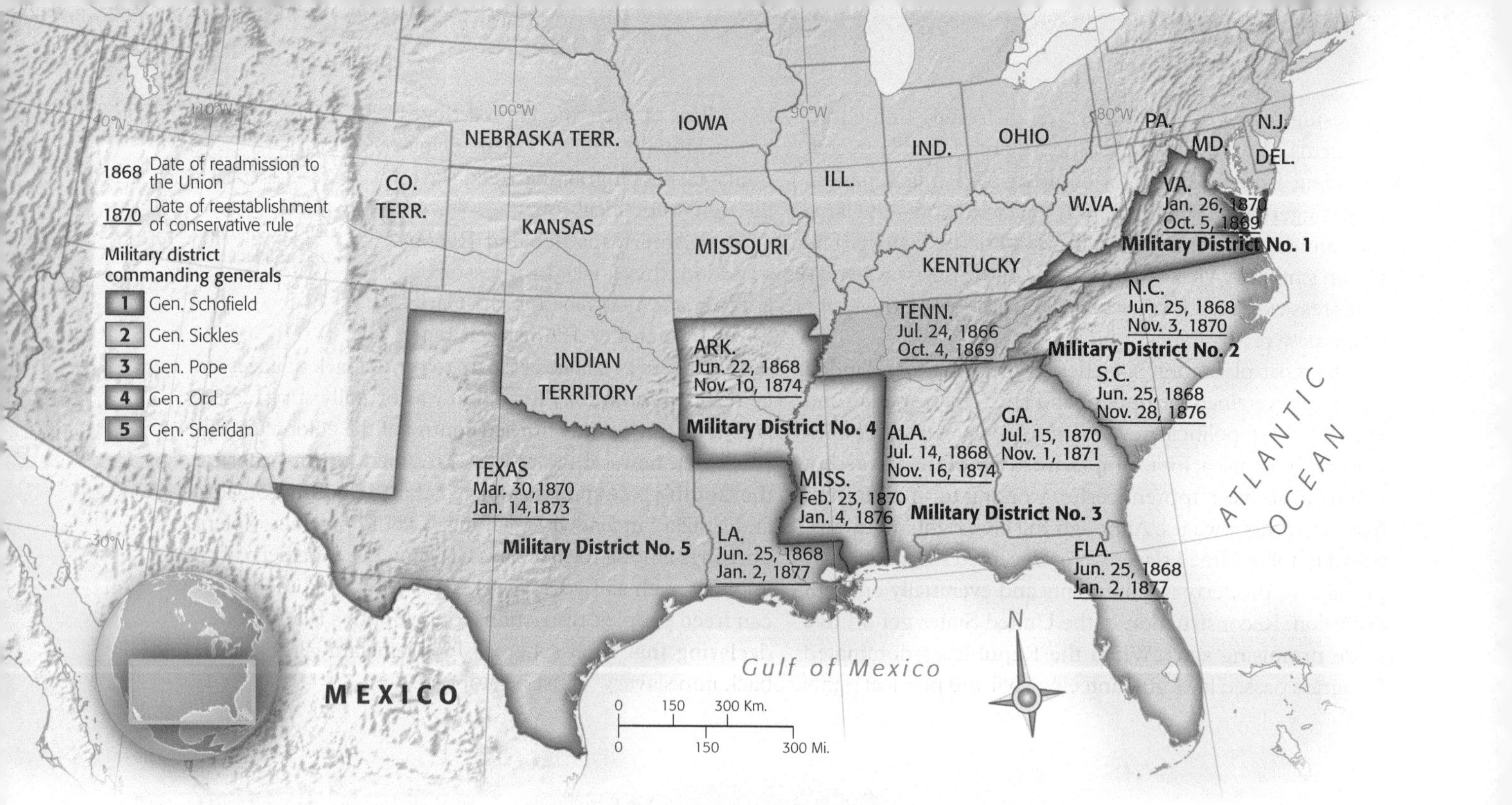

Map 14.1 Course of Reconstruction This map shows the five military districts established when Congress passed the Reconstruction Act of 1867. As the dates within each state indicate, by 1870 all southern states had been readmitted to the Union. Almost immediately, however, conservative Democratic forces began regaining control of state governments, and so-called radical Reconstruction was in retreat. ▲

Reconstruction Act of 1867 rolled back the restoration process begun under Johnson. It divided ten former Confederate states—excluding Tennessee, which ratified the Fourteenth Amendment—into five military districts overseen temporarily by the Union army (see Map 14.1). These states were required to call constitutional conventions with delegates elected by blacks and whites. For states to win readmission to the Union, their new constitutions had to guarantee black men's voting rights, Congress had to approve the new charters, and the states had to ratify the Fourteenth Amendment. Congressional Reconstruction met Republicans' call for freedmen's rights, loyal southern governments, and federal control of the process.

Expecting Johnson to oppose their plans, Republicans passed laws to limit his power. The **Tenure of Office Act**, which prohibited the president from removing cabinet members and other high officials without the Senate's consent, became the focus of conflict. It was designed to protect Secretary of War Edwin Stanton, a Radical Republican who supervised military occupation in the South. Johnson, believing the law unconstitutional, fired Stanton in February 1868. Congress responded immediately by initiating the first **impeachment** of a U.S. president. By a vote of 126 to 47, the House approved eleven articles of impeachment. Nine centered on the Tenure of Office Act; the others accused Johnson of insulting Congress and—the crux of the matter—holding up enforcement of its Reconstruction laws.

In the Senate trial in May 1868, Johnson escaped removal from office by a single vote short of the two-thirds required. A handful of Republicans who held the balance of power hesitated. Some believed that Johnson's political tussling with Congress fell short of the "high crimes and misdemeanors" required by the Constitution. Others distrusted Radical Republican senator Benjamin Wade, who was next in line for the presidency and a crude, combative figure much like Johnson himself.

Johnson remained publicly defiant after his narrow acquittal, granting amnesty to more Confederates and pardons to Jefferson Davis and Robert E. Lee. During the trial, however, Republicans obtained his private promise to accept the Reconstruction Act. The disgrace of impeachment ensured that Johnson would be a one-term president.

Reconstruction Act of 1867 Legislation that returned former Confederate states to military rule and set conditions for readmission, including new constitutions and ratification of the Fourteenth Amendment.

Tenure of Office Act Law passed in 1867 to prevent Johnson from firing cabinet members without Senate approval.

impeachment Constitutional process of bringing federal officials to trial in the Senate for "high crimes and misdemeanors" that requires a two-thirds vote to remove them from office.

14-3b Completion of Congress's Plan

Americans elect Grant and Congress finalizes Reconstruction legislation.

Only six months intervened between Johnson's impeachment trial and the election of 1868. The Republicans turned to Civil War hero Ulysses S. Grant as their nominee. Although he lacked political experience, Grant had won Republicans' respect by eagerly enlisting black soldiers and backing Congress in its dispute with Johnson. The Republican platform, however, placated conservatives by leaving the question of black suffrage in the loyal North to the states. Between 1865 and 1868, white voters in the North had rejected equal suffrage amendments in eight states, passing them only in Iowa and Minnesota.

The Democrats nominated former New York governor Horatio Seymour, who had opposed emancipation and wartime expansion of federal power. The party's platform denounced Congressional Reconstruction as a "military despotism" designed to secure "negro supremacy." The party used openly racist appeals in the North and furtive violence in the South, where the Ku Klux Klan and other white supremacist groups tried to prevent black and white Republicans from voting. Violence succeeded in a few states, including Louisiana, where armed whites negated black voting rights granted by the constitution of 1868 (see this chapter's introduction). But African American votes helped Grant win five southern states, ensuring his strong victory (214 to 80) in the Electoral College.

In February 1869, the Republicans used their large majority in both houses of Congress to impose a new Reconstruction requirement. The **Fifteenth Amendment**, adopted in direct response to voter suppression in the recent election, outlawed denial of the vote "on account of race, color, or previous condition of servitude." The amendment's language left open a loophole for literacy, property, or other restrictions. To boost the amendment's chances, Congress required three as yet unreconstructed states—Mississippi, Texas, and Virginia—to ratify it before readmission.

In February 1870, the Fifteenth Amendment became law. Although its language was not airtight, it was a landmark addition to the Constitution. African American men were guaranteed the vote in states where they had recently been slaves. Ironically, they were also given the vote for the first time in fourteen northern states where racial prejudices remained strong. The amendment's adoption sealed the readmission of all former Confederate states to the Union, almost all with Republican-dominated legislatures. Congressional Republicans had restored the southern states and, they believed, reconstructed southern politics.

In the process, these Republicans expanded the scope and power of the federal government over states in ways that they believed necessary but that many Americans found troubling. Reconstruction continued the nationalizing process begun during the Civil War. In 1870, Democratic politicians and the conservative majority on the Supreme Court began responding by reasserting state prerogatives. Before that, the Court handed congressional Republicans an important victory in *Texas v. White* (1869). The case hinged on the legality of Confederate state war bonds, which the justices invalidated, declaring that the South's unilateral secession had been unconstitutional. It was too late to save seven hundred thousand soldiers' lives, but the ruling codified the Union's victory in law.

14-3c Women's Suffrage and Electoral Reform

Feminists enter voting rights debates in the United States and Great Britain.

The post-Civil War battle in the United States over black voting rights took place at the same time that the British Parliament debated extending suffrage to most male workers. The example of radical Reconstruction influenced Britain's Reform Act of 1867, which lowered property requirements for voting. In both nations, women's rights advocates demanded to be included in electoral reform.

American feminists were angered by the Reconstruction amendments. The Fourteenth Amendment guaranteed voting rights only to male citizens, and the Fifteenth Amendment permitted denial of the vote on grounds of sex. Women's rights advocates, who had actively supported emancipation and the Union, felt betrayed. Elizabeth Cady Stanton vowed to oppose the Fourteenth Amendment unless the word "male" was deleted, but Republican leaders gave priority to racial justice over "the lesser question of sex." Even Frederick Douglass, a longtime women's rights supporter, argued that Reconstruction was "the Negro's hour." Mainstream Republican leaders believed that endorsing female suffrage would jeopardize the immediate task of enfranchising African American men.

Stanton and Susan B. Anthony next opposed the Fifteenth Amendment, whose passage, they claimed, would establish an "aristocracy of sex." By 1869, the dispute over Reconstruction amendments split women's rights advocates into rival organizations. Moderates in the **American Woman Suffrage Association** such as Lucy Stone and Julia Ward Howe cooperated with the Republican Party, supported the Fifteenth Amendment, and focused on winning the vote through state-level campaigns. The more radical **National Woman Suffrage Association**, led by Stanton and Anthony, attacked

Fifteenth Amendment Constitutional addition that became law in 1870, prohibiting states and the federal government from denying the vote on grounds of skin color or prior condition of servitude.

American Woman Suffrage Association Organization formed after women's rights advocates split over the Fifteenth Amendment and that supported black voting rights despite women's exclusion.

National Woman Suffrage Association Organization formed by a splinter group of women's activists who opposed Fourteenth and Fifteenth Amendments and other discriminatory laws.

Library of Congress, Prints & Photographs Division, [LC-USZ62-2023]

Women Press Congress for the Vote, 1871 Joined by Susan B. Anthony (second from the right in the foreground), Victoria Woodhull presented a petition to the House Judiciary Committee in January 1871 claiming that the Fourteenth Amendment gave women as citizens the right to vote—an argument that the committee rejected. Woodhull ran for president the following year as the candidate of the Equal Rights Party, becoming the first woman to do so. ◄

discrimination more broadly and pushed for a federal women's suffrage amendment.

Women's suffrage advocates in England watched U.S. developments closely, but they divided over class, not race. Moderates advised winning the vote incrementally beginning with educated and propertied women, whereas radicals pushed immediately for equal rights for all women. Parliament put off the former proposal and roundly rejected the latter in 1867 when the philosopher-politician John Stuart Mill introduced it.

Suffrage advocates won small victories in 1869 and 1870 when two western U.S. territories, Wyoming and Utah, enfranchised women, in part to attract female migrants. Elsewhere the state-by-state strategy met with strong opposition from traditionalists as women's suffrage proposals failed in New York and Kansas. The federal government also proved hostile to gender equality. When Susan B. Anthony voted in the 1872 presidential election, a federal marshal arrested her. Missouri suffragist Virginia Minor, who attempted to follow her example, sued the registrar who had blocked her, claiming that the Fourteenth Amendment's guarantee of citizenship enfranchised women. In ***Minor v. Happersett*** (1875), the Supreme Court ruled that national citizenship did not compel states to grant women the vote. American feminists' defeats during Reconstruction and British feminists' rejection in Parliament indicated that a long struggle would be necessary before the "women's hour" arrived in the Anglo-American world.

14-3d Reconstruction of the Nation's Borders

Union victory expands U.S. territory and influence in North America.

Increased federal power at home under Reconstruction was complemented by reaffirmed U.S. prowess in North America. The Civil War had threatened to remake the continent's borders and reshuffle its deck of players, but U.S. leaders used the Union's victory to restore, and even enhance, the nation's continental preeminence.

Deploying troops freed by the war's end, U.S. officials helped Mexican liberals overthrow the French-imposed regime of Emperor Maximilian (see Chapter 13). Far north of the U.S. border, Americans seized an opportunity to extend the nation's reach into the Pacific by purchasing the vast territory of Alaska from Russia.

The imperial Russian-American Company had attempted to monopolize the fur trade, but it lacked the resources to colonize Alaska or to thwart the westward push of Britain's Hudson's Bay Company across Canada. To keep Alaska out of Britain's hands, Russia offered to sell it to the United States, and Secretary of State William Seward readily agreed. He had long championed a U.S. continental empire, and purchasing Alaska would end one more European power's presence in North America. Confederate attacks on Yankee whaling ships had convinced him that the nation needed advanced outposts in the northern Pacific. In the spring of 1867, the U.S. Senate ratified Seward's treaty, purchasing Alaska for $7.2 million.

Skeptics mocked the **Alaska Purchase** as "Seward's Folly." Although Americans did not organize a territorial government there until 1884, Seward was vindicated when a major gold deposit was discovered in the Yukon in 1896. Meanwhile, Alaska's Aleutian Islands, which stretched twelve hundred miles westward toward Japan, provided a safe harbor for American whaling boats, naval vessels, and merchant ships bound for Asia. For similar reasons, Seward authorized the navy to occupy the uninhabited Midway Islands eleven hundred miles west of Hawai'i in 1867, the nation's first seizure of overseas lands.

Some Americans saw purchasing Alaska as the prelude to annexing British Columbia, which Seward's deal sandwiched between two U.S. landmasses. Officials in

United States Coast Guard

Global Americans One of ten children of Michael Morris Healy, an Irish immigrant planter in Georgia, and his wife, Mary Eliza Smith, a mixed-race African American woman who had been his slave, blue-eyed **Michael Healy** "passed" for white. Because racial intermarriage was illegal in Georgia and the Healy children were technically born into slavery, they were sent to northern states and Canada to be educated in Catholic schools. Most pursued careers in the church, but free-spirited Healy signed aboard a U.S. clipper ship bound for Calcutta. During the Civil War, he entered the U.S. Revenue Marine Service (later the Coast Guard) and in 1868, cruised to the newly purchased Alaska Territory. Soon commanding his own cutter, Healy represented the U.S. government in Alaska for two decades, informally called "king" but acting as policeman, judge, rescuer, and medical officer to whaling crews, merchant seamen, and Alaskan natives. In the 1880s, Healy took the renowned naturalist John Muir on several scientific voyages. When commercial fishermen overhunted seals and whales, Healy steamed to Russia's Siberian coast and returned with herds of reindeer, which became an essential source of food and clothing for Alaska natives. "Hell Roaring Mike" was a hard drinker and larger-than-life figure, beloved and feared by subordinates and recognized as the dominant U.S. authority on the North Pacific rim. Not until Healy died in 1904 did his African American ancestry become public knowledge.

Canada eyed the United States suspiciously, aware of Americans' annexationist dreams and fearing reprisals for Canadian aid to Confederates. British Canadians were alarmed when the **Fenians**, a secret brotherhood pledged to promote Irish nationhood, launched raids in 1866 across the U.S. border intended to dismember Britain's empire. Joined by hundreds of Irish-American Union veterans, the Fenians aspired to conquer Canada and exchange it with England for Ireland's independence.

When Britain captured two Irish-American Fenians and charged them with treason, Congress responded with the Expatriation Act (1868), which denied other countries' claims that naturalized U.S. citizens still owed them allegiance. This law and the **Bancroft treaties** that the United States signed with dozens of foreign countries after 1868 struck a decisive blow for voluntary citizenship against the feudal doctrine of "perpetual allegiance" to monarchs. The same conflict underlay the impressment controversy that had sparked the War of 1812, but increased naval power allowed U.S. naturalization policies to prevail after the Civil War.

In response to threats from Fenians and U.S. annexationists, Britain took steps to unite its Canadian colonies under a single government. The **British North America Act** of 1867 created a federal Dominion of Canada that stretched from the Maritime Provinces to western Ontario, and four years later to British Columbia. Confederation was designed to fortify Canada against U.S. pressure to invade or annex it and to take the Civil War's lesson that a stronger government might prevent internal secessions.

Tensions over Canada added to difficult Anglo-American negotiations over Civil War damages. Americans recalled the wartime attacks on Union ships by the *Alabama* and other Confederate raiders built in Britain, and some demanded Canadian territory as reparation. Claims and counterclaims hummed over the undersea transatlantic cable, which, ironically, had begun operating in 1866 with friendly telegrams between Queen Victoria and President Johnson. Eventually, diplomats moderated their demands, and in 1871, the two nations signed the **Treaty of Washington**. The *Alabama* claims and others were submitted to a five-nation arbitration commission, which awarded the United States $15.5 million and England about half that sum. The treaty also resolved a standoff over the San Juan Islands, which occupied the Puget Sound between Vancouver Island and the Pacific Coast. This final U.S.–Canada boundary settlement fixed the northern U.S. border and put to rest the question of annexation.

Minor v. Happersett Supreme Court decision declaring that citizenship rights were separate from voting rights and used by states to justify outlawing women's suffrage.

Alaska Purchase U.S. acquisition of Alaska Territory from Russia, designed to promote continental expansion and overseas trade.

Fenians Members of an Irish republican organization founded in the United States whose raids into Canada in 1866 aimed to coerce Ireland's independence from Britain.

Bancroft treaties Agreements between the United States and other nations signed after 1868 that recognized naturalized citizens as long as they resided in their new countries.

British North America Act Parliamentary law creating the federal Dominion of Canada from three British colonies to strengthen transcontinental ties and fend off U.S. expansion.

Treaty of Washington Pact that fixed the U.S.–Canadian border and addressed claims for Civil War damages between Britain and the United States.

MOTHER BRITANNIA.—" Take care, my child!"
UNCLE SAM.—" Oh! never mind, if she falls I'll catch her!"
McCord Museum

Canadian Confederation In this British cartoon of 1870, Mother Britannia exults that her child Canada can stand alone, while Uncle Sam urges "Oh! Never mind, if she falls I'll catch her!" The image reflects British anxiety about potential U.S. annexation of Canada after the Civil War, which might be disguised as economic assistance or protection against foreign "interference." ◀

14-4

Reconstruction and Resistance in the South

This lithograph, entitled *The First Vote*, was published in a northern magazine in 1867. It pictures the uniquely American—although temporary—postemancipation enforcement of equal political rights for former slaves under the terms of Congressional Reconstruction.

Whom does the artist portray as representative African American male voters in the South? Which party would they likely support? Why are they under an American flag? What problems might voting in public view create? ▶

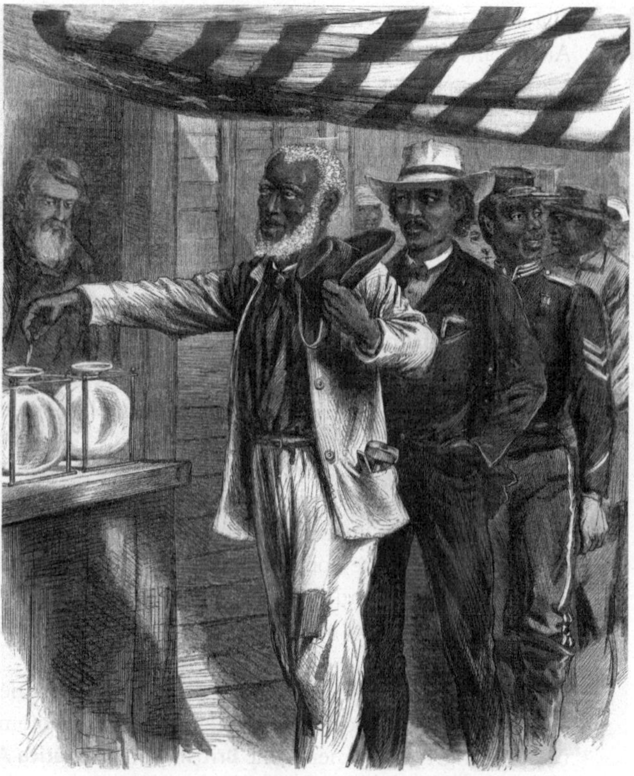

Many Northerners were confident that with new laws and constitutional amendments, the South was being reconstructed as well as restored to the Union. Southerners, however, knew that a long struggle lay ahead. Ex-slaves and former masters argued over access to land and terms of labor, evolving the compromise system of sharecropping. Relying heavily on black voters, the South's Republican Party built a coalition that formed new state governments and enacted programs for education and economic development. But white Southerners refused to accept the Republican regimes and their challenge to the old order. Mobilizing through the Democratic Party and violent paramilitary groups, angry whites fought to reverse Reconstruction's gains for blacks and retake political control.

☞ As you read, consider the key issues under dispute in the postwar South. What important changes did Reconstruction bring to the South's politics and society? How were these changes contested and eventually reversed?

14-4a Transition to Sharecropping

The majority of the South's freed people aspired to become independent farmers, but this was a dream deferred. By 1867, federal authorities had restored almost all confiscated lands to planters, and several land redistribution bills had died in Congress. The **Southern Homestead Act** of 1866, modeled on the earlier national law, gave African Americans and loyal whites access to public lands in five states in plots of eighty or one hundred sixty acres. The law was not well publicized, however, and the acreage was often unsuitable for tilling. In the end, only a thousand free blacks were granted land certificates.

Postwar land and labor systems limit freed people's rise.

In some areas, the number of black farm workers dwindled to half its prewar total because freedmen migrated elsewhere and freedwomen withdrew from fieldwork. To relieve the shortage, southern states established agencies to encourage immigration. But as the result of local prejudices against Asian and Caribbean immigrants and opposition by the federal government, the effort to import cheap substitutes for the South's former slaves floundered.

Gradually, **sharecropping** and other forms of tenant farming evolved as the most widespread alternative to wage labor for freed people or contracts for imported workers. Landlords divided plantations into parcels of twenty-five to fifty acres, allowing families to settle on the land. In return, the owner received a share of the annual crop, usually half (see Map 14.2). In tenant farming, a variant that involved more poor whites than blacks, households received the crop's proceeds but used them to pay rent and to reimburse the landlord for the outlay of equipment and animals.

In theory, sharecropping and tenant farming represented a reasonable compromise between planters and former slaves. Planters gave up daily supervision of freedmen, who lived in separate cottages and set their own hours. Freed people rented land but hoped to accrue enough crop surpluses to buy their own farm. Both parties avoided outlays of cash, which was in short supply in the South. In practice, sharecroppers and tenants got the short end of the bargain. Unscrupulous landlords raised rents, cheated in weighing the crop, or evicted independent-minded tenants. Rural merchants (often planters themselves) advanced food, clothing, and other supplies to tenants on credit at interest rates as high as 50 percent. Under the **crop-lien system**, the landlord and merchant secured their

Southern Homestead Act Legislation that opened public lands in the South for settlement by free blacks and loyal whites initially, and later all Southerners, but was repealed in 1876.

sharecropping System of tenant farming by which renters worked a plot of land in return for paying half or more of the crop to landlords.

crop-lien system Legal restriction by which landlords and other creditors asserted priority rights to tenant farmers' crops.

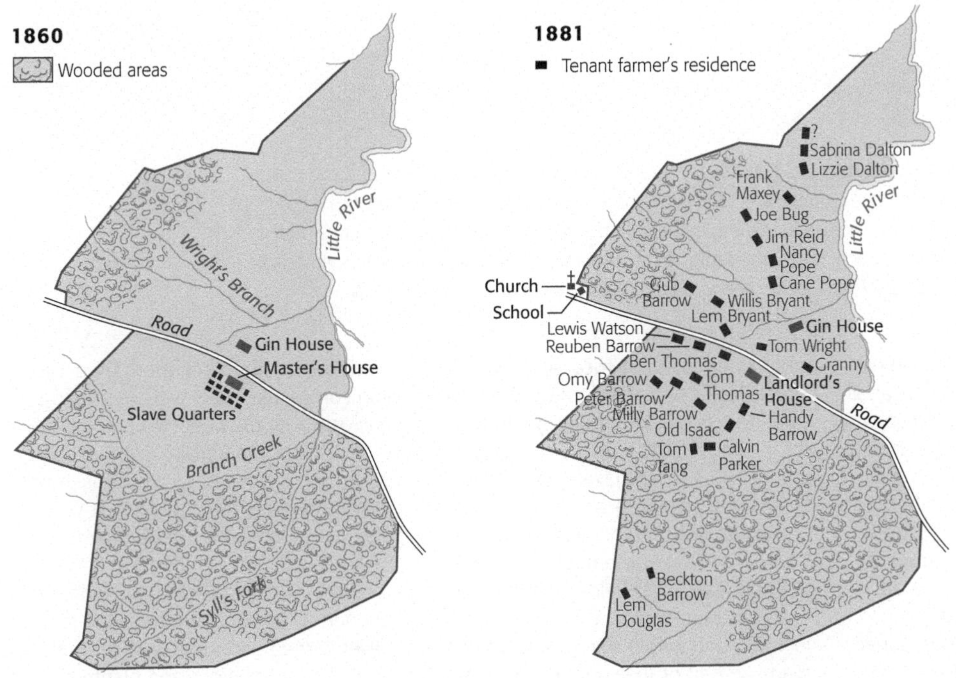

Map 14.2 From Plantation to Sharecropping Maps of the Barrow plantation in Georgia in 1860 and 1881 illustrate the postwar transformation of southern agriculture. In 1860, about one hundred thirty-five slaves lived in quarters behind the master's house. After the Civil War and a brief interlude of growing cotton for wages, freed people moved to cottages on rented farms of twenty-five to thirty acres on plantation lands. The former master had become their landlord. Note the presence of some female-headed households as well as a church and school established by African Americans. ◀

History without Borders

After Slavery: Debt Bondage in Sugar and Cotton

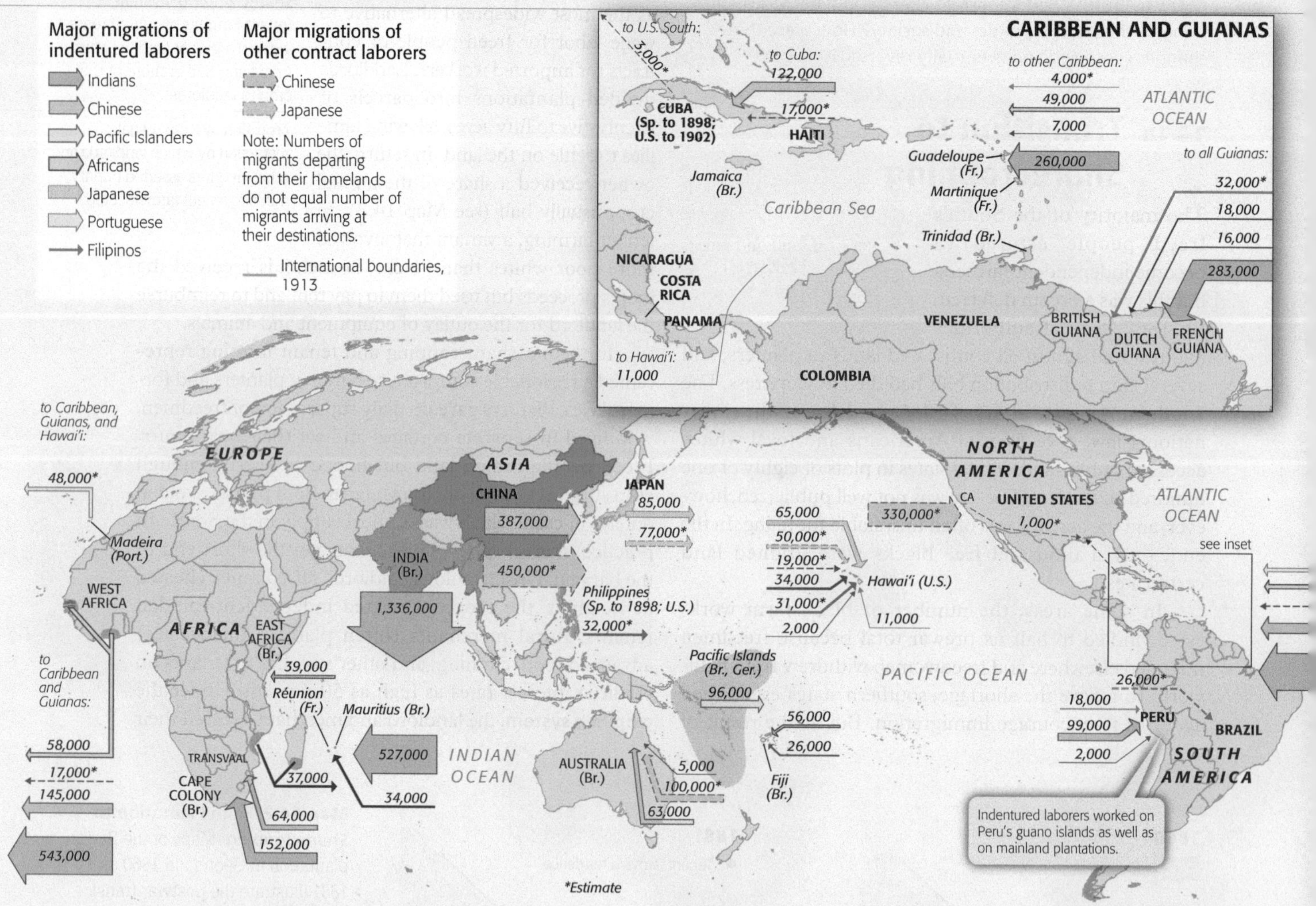

Major Overseas Indentured Migrations, 1834–1919 Millions of workers from Asia, Africa, and the South Pacific were recruited overseas to replace emancipated slaves. Some were bound by strict indenture agreements while others worked under simple wage contracts. Whereas the majority of indentured laborers from Africa and Asia harvested sugar and similar plantation crops, other migrant workers were employed building railroads in the United States, mining gold in South Africa, or shoveling guano (valuable as fertilizer) in Peru. ▲

For millions of agricultural workers across several continents, the abolition of slavery led not to prosperity but to a subtler form of bondage based on indebtedness rather than ownership of persons. Looking for ways to boost production after emancipation, planters and merchants tied to the growing global market for cash crops created new forms of dependent labor.

To replace newly freed slaves, sugar planters worldwide recruited contract laborers from Asia, Africa, and the South Pacific. Great Britain opened the trade for *coolies* (a Tamil-origin term for hirelings) to its Indian Ocean sugar islands in 1834. As slave emancipation spread, Indian laborers were sent to Fiji and South Africa to harvest sugar, and Chinese and Japanese migrants worked in Caribbean sugar fields. The first Chinese contract workers arrived in Hawai'i in 1852, and within thirty years, they made up half of the sugar plantation workforce. Altogether, more than 1 million contract laborers were recruited to harvest sugar between 1865 and 1885.

Customary indenture contracts compelled these workers to work for several years and repay the cost of their voyage. In practice, this arrangement was often brutal, and workers had little legal recourse. Some of them were kidnapped or coerced to sign contracts, and many never earned enough to pay off their debt. Such conditions and planters'

Historic New Orleans Collection

Chinese Contract Laborers in Louisiana
In 1867, hundreds of Chinese laborers were brought from Cuba to Louisiana to harvest sugar cane. Some cotton farmers were eager to follow suit to boost production and reassert white supremacy. "Give us five million Chinese laborers in the valley of the Mississippi," wrote a planter's wife, "and we can furnish the world with cotton and teach the negro his proper place." ◀

Universal History Archive/Getty Images

Cotton Cultivators in Egypt In this 1873 illustration, Egyptian farm workers deliver cotton in bags to a mercantile house, where it is weighed before packing and shipment overseas. By the 1870s, large landowners, small farmers, and tenants expanded Egypt's and India's cotton exports to more than triple their pre-Civil War total. But many peasant cultivators incurred debts to local moneylenders, suffered from declining cotton prices, and lacked access to food crops, resulting in regional food shortages and even famines. ◀

use of impoverished Asian workers to replace African slaves in tropical lands led critics to charge that a new form of racial slavery had emerged. When abuses were publicized and local protests erupted against "coolie labor," Britain and the United States restricted its trade in the 1880s. Latin American governments gradually followed, but the practice continued in modified forms elsewhere into the twentieth century.

Cotton growers chose a different option. During and after the Civil War, production of cotton went global, stimulated initially by the Confederacy's cutoff of shipments. Around the world, farm workers aspired to become growers and shunned picking cotton for wages. In contrast to sugar, cotton was increasingly produced by cultivators who worked their own small farms or rented land using family labor and outside capital.

In the U.S. South, planters and former slaves developed the sharecropping system, which dominated cotton production. In other lands, tenants and small farmers predominated and financial elites encouraged them to abandon subsistence crops to grow cotton for the world market. In India and Brazil, farmers used advances from European capitalists and local merchants to plant cotton. After 1860, cotton exports from India, Brazil, and Egypt increased dramatically. But whether they were landowners, sharecroppers, or tenants, small farmers depended on merchants and landlords, who were backed by harsh lien laws. Vulnerable to price fluctuations, subject to punitive laws, and politically marginalized, small cotton growers were technically free but often trapped in debt.

To indentured sugar workers and small cotton farmers, the postemancipation global economy appeared to offer opportunities for advancement. But the global market's demands for commodities and profits translated into new forms of exploitation. Historians disagree when comparing migrant contract laborers to slaves, but most agree that indentures often led to agricultural "debt bondage." The United Nations Supplementary Convention on the Abolition of Slavery outlawed indentured labor in 1956. The practice continues, however, in South Asia, and the recent wave of globalization has resulted in the rise of other varieties of forced migrant labor.

Critical Thinking Questions

▶ How did the abolition of slavery transform global sugar and cotton production? What factors led to the establishment of indentured migrants and tenant farmers as dependent farm laborers?

▶ In what ways was agricultural debt bondage similar to slavery? How was it different?

Carpetbaggers Derisive term for Northerners who moved to the South after the Civil War and became active Republicans and whom southern Democrats saw as interlopers.

Scalawags Derogatory term for white Southerners who backed the Republican Party during Reconstruction and were marked as turncoats by southern Democrats.

advances by placing a legal claim on the farmer's next crop. The system guaranteed payouts for creditors but not their victims, and most tenants and sharecroppers fell into chronic debt.

By 1880, the division of plantations into tenant and sharecropping tracts encompassed the majority of farms in the cotton belt and nearly three-quarters of the South's black farmers. Because lienholders made borrowers grow cotton, which was easy to sell, the South's small farmers turned from diversified or subsistence farming to growing a single crop for the national and global market. Cotton production recovered to surpass prewar levels, but prices declined (see Table 14.1). Caught in a perfect storm of low cotton prices, spiraling debt, and reduced access to food crops, the South's freed people saw their dreams of economic independence fade. By the end of Reconstruction, few black sharecroppers had graduated to owning their own farms.

Table 14.1 U.S. Cotton Production and Exports, 1860–1880

After severe wartime declines and the adjustment to tenant farming and sharecropping, the South's production of cotton recovered in the mid-1870s to surpass prewar levels. U.S. cotton exports gradually approached their pre-Civil War share of the global market. At the same time, prices fell to half the immediate postwar level.

Year	Cotton Produced (Thousands of Bales)	Price (Cents per Pound)	U.S Share of British Cotton Imports (Percentage)
1860	3,841	12	80
1861	4,491	15	65
1862	1,597	30	4
1863	449	51	8
1864	299	53	9
1865	2,094	45	20
1866	2,097	25	38
1867	2,520	20	42
1868	2,366	16	43
1869	3,011	19	38
1870	4,352	18	54
1871	2,974	13	49
1872	3,933	15	35
1873	4,168	14	47
1874	3,836	13	49
1875	4,631	13	50
1876	4,474	12	57
1877	4,773	11	62
1878	5,074	12	73
1879	5,756	11	71
1880	6,606	12	71

14-4b Republican Governments in the South

Fragile Republican Party coalitions bring change to reconstructed southern states.

Freed people's political status improved under Congressional Reconstruction. Between 1867 and 1869, all states in the former Confederacy adopted new constitutions as required by Congress. These charters brought progressive changes to the South's electoral system, but the Republican coalitions that won the first statewide elections found it difficult to forge a common platform and even harder to win acceptance from southern whites.

The coalition was made up of three groups. **Carpetbaggers**, or transplanted Northerners, were caricatured by southern whites as transient opportunists, but most contradicted the stereotype. Their numbers included former Union soldiers who stayed in the South after the war along with businessmen, Freedmen's Bureau agents, and teachers. **Scalawags**, another derisive name invented by political opponents, were southern whites who joined the Republicans. Some were small farmers who had been wartime Unionists, others represented the South's business and financial elites, and a few others were planters who wagered that cooperating with Republicans was the best route to postwar recovery or personal gain.

African Americans were the third and by far the largest component of the South's Republican alliance. Their votes were essential for the party to control state governments. After the ordeal of slavery and years of political mobilization, they were eager to participate. "It is the hardest thing in the world to keep a negro away from the polls," a white Alabamian admitted as he watched former slaves respond to voter registration drives.

White Southerners opposed to Reconstruction stigmatized it as "Negro Rule." Taken literally, this charge was exaggerated. Fourteen blacks served during Reconstruction in the U.S. Congress and two in the Senate. South Carolina had a black majority in its House of Representatives, led by former slave and Union naval hero Robert Smalls. Yet African Americans held no major offices in Alabama, Georgia, North Carolina, or Texas. Despite providing four-fifths of the South's Republican votes, blacks received less than one-fifth of the offices, mostly local positions. Carpetbaggers and scalawags were determined to dominate Reconstruction politics.

If Reconstruction was not "negro rule," it was still a startling reversal of status for blacks and whites. Black mayors, sheriffs, town councilmen, and justices of the peace ran many small southern communities. Perhaps most galling to former Confederates, African Americans dominated the state militias called out to suppress local riots and protect black voting rights. The rise of the Ku Klux Klan and other white supremacist groups created an increasingly militarized environment, and there were not enough federal troops to patrol the entire South.

Beset by violent white opponents, the South's Republican Party also suffered internal tensions. Party supporters had divergent agendas. Moderates courted southern whites by promoting compromise whereas radicals relied on black voters. Yankee carpetbaggers pushed to modernize the South's economy while freedmen concentrated on voting rights, debt relief, and public schools. Poor whites sought economic relief but opposed racial integration. Each group had to make concessions, but all came to realize that most white Southerners would never join the Republicans. The party's continued rule depended on the national government.

While they lobbied for federal support, Republican leaders in the South enacted important changes in civil rights, public welfare, and economic development. New state laws empowered African American men to serve on juries and in police and fire departments. Reorganized southern states built public orphan and insane asylums and enacted laws against child abuse. Continuing the assault on illiteracy begun by freedmen's schools, Republican regimes set up public educational systems in every state in the South. Black leaders accepted segregated schools, often reluctantly, as the price for this improvement. Despite substandard facilities and shortages of funds, the literacy rate in 1875 among southern blacks had risen to more than 30 percent, three times the figure at the war's end. Educational gains were the most notable achievement of Republican rule in the South.

Republicans' economic programs were less successful. Seeking to diversify the South's economy and expand its markets, white Republican leaders chartered hundreds of new banks and encouraged construction of factories. Above all, state leaders promoted railroads, believing them an almost magical key to prosperity. According to one Tennessee Republican, "a free and living Republic [will] spring up in the track of the railroad . . . as surely as grass and flowers follow in the spring." Track mileage increased by 40 percent, a pace that outran farmers' needs and saddled state governments with huge debts.

Generous charters and subsidies for bonds led to a building spree. The construction boom overwhelmed southern state budgets. Republican lawmakers addressed deficits by raising taxes to levels unseen in the tax-hating prewar South. Soaring tax bills alienated landowners already reeling from the loss of $2.4 billion in slave "property" and spurred charges of waste and corruption. Some southern states had honest governments, but in others, such as South Carolina, Louisiana, and Florida, bribery, embezzlement, and profiteering were rampant. Political corruption was probably no more prevalent in the postwar South than in the North, but it lent a strong impetus to southern Democrats and others determined to end Republican rule.

14-4c Conservative White Resurgence

Using politics and terror, southern Democrats restore white supremacy.

The high taxes and blatant corruption of some Republican regimes gave southern Democrats potent campaign issues. In reality, they had never considered Republicans legitimate participants in the South's politics. Many white Southerners saw Reconstruction as a foreign occupation, with the former slaves controlled by white Republicans who ruled with the backing of nearby federal troops.

Such attitudes sanctioned any form of resistance, from ballots to bullets. If policy differences failed to rouse the white public, racial hatred worked. Just as a shared belief in white supremacy had united prewar slaveholders and nonslaveholding whites, postwar Democrats used race baiting and violence to energize white voters. Violence against African Americans escalated as former slaves entered politics and served in local militias. White paramilitary groups spread spontaneously to punish "uppity" African Americans, sometimes after false accusations that they had raped or dishonored white women. The

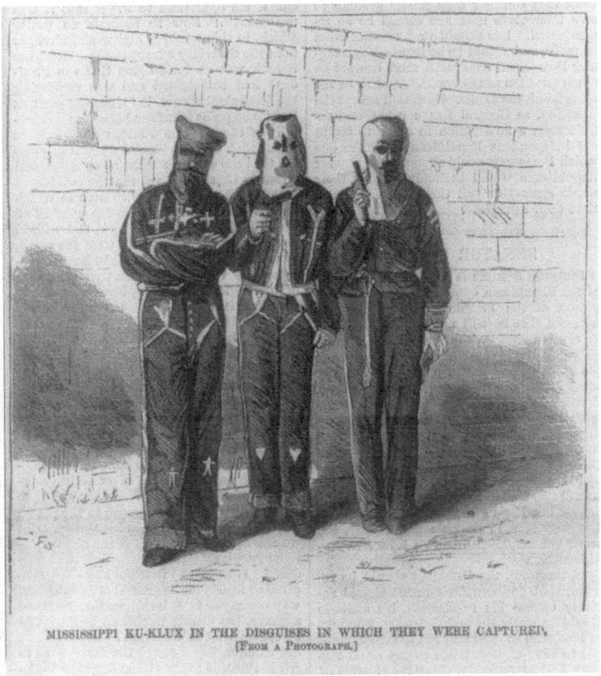

MISSISSIPPI KU-KLUX IN THE DISGUISES IN WHICH THEY WERE CAPTURED.
[FROM A PHOTOGRAPH.]

Library of Congress Prints and Photographs Division

Ku Klux Klan in Mississippi, 1871 Mississippi Klan members pose for a photograph in the disguises they wore when they were arrested by federal authorities for attempted murder. None is wearing a pointed hood or white clothes, regalia that the Klan adopted in the early twentieth century. Enforcement of federal anti-Klan laws in the early 1870s netted hundreds of arrests, but violent resistance to black voting and office holding persisted among a variety of secret white supremacist organizations in the South. ▲

Redeemers Self-description of southern Democrats who rebelled against Reconstruction and restored Democratic rule and white dominance in the 1870s.

convict lease system Legal practice of hiring out convicts to employers for low wages that was combined with vagrancy laws to reduce many black Southerners to semislaves.

Ku Klux Klan, the most notorious of these groups, conducted night raids clad in costumed disguise, murdering dozens of blacks and several white Republican leaders before Congress sanctioned a campaign against it.

The Klan and its imitators served as the terrorist wing of the South's Democratic Party. Other Democrats adopted more subtle means of controlling black voters. In an era before the secret ballot, the party supervised polling places to identify Republican voters as potential targets of intimidation or retaliation. Employers required workers to sign contracts barring participation in political meetings, and landlords threatened politically active tenants with eviction.

One by one, southern states fell to conservative Democrats, who called themselves **Redeemers**. The counterrevolution succeeded first in 1869 in Virginia and Tennessee, upper South states whose black population was too small to sustain Republican electoral victories. In the Deep South, more violence was required to suppress Republican voters. In 1875, the White Line movement in Mississippi mobilized Democratic supporters to break up Republican meetings, patrol voter registration sites, and march in military formation through black neighborhoods. Republican governors hesitated to call out black-dominated state militias to restore order, fearing it would enrage whites further or spark all-out race war. By 1876, the Democrats had toppled Republican regimes in all but three Deep South states.

Redeemer governments wasted no time in their effort to erase Reconstruction. Once in power, southern Democrats slashed taxes on land and state spending on schools and social services. Poll taxes, long-term residency requirements, and other restrictions not expressly forbidden by the Fifteenth Amendment were adopted to curtail black voting. Unable to reverse constitutional emancipation, the South's Democrats employed an arsenal of legal tactics to "re-enslave the colored race," as Texas Republicans charged in 1876. Toughened criminal codes restricted hunting and fishing and meted out prison terms for trespassing or petty theft. Redeemer legislators revived the Black Codes' vagrancy laws to imprison unemployed or loitering blacks. From overcrowded prisons, the **convict lease system** rented black inmates to private contractors for work on chain gangs harvesting crops, mining coal, or building railroads. Conditions were so bad that death tolls among prisoners averaged 15 percent annually and reached 41 percent in Alabama in 1870. Protesting this system, a Tennessee convention of freedmen in 1875 called it a "condition of servitude scarcely less degrading than that endured before the late civil war."

14-5 Abandonment of Reconstruction

Frank Leslie's Illustrated Newspaper. Image courtesy of Wikimedia.

A series of scandals damaged Grant's presidency. In the Crédit Mobilier affair, U.S. lawmakers accepted shares of stock for allowing payments to a phony railroad company. None were charged with crimes. In this cartoon, Uncle Sam, backed by public opinion, directs senators implicated in the scheme to commit hari-kari, or ritual suicide. In Japanese tradition, when a person is condemned to hari-kari, the victim's best friend stands by to complete the work.

Why would the cartoonist suggest suicide as the appropriate fictional punishment for the Crédit Mobilier conspirators? Why is Senator Roscoe Conkling, a spokesman for Grant, shown unsheathing a sword? How might Americans have learned about hari-kari in this era? ►

White Southerners' violent return to power succeeded in part because Northerners abandoned their commitment to Reconstruction. After a decade of turmoil, many Northerners were impatient to leave the "Southern question" behind. Northern voters were preoccupied by the booms and busts of the national economy, distracted by overseas adventures, and frustrated by the difficulty of transforming southern ways. The Republicans were weakened by corruption and factionalism within their party and joined voters in turning against Reconstruction. The contested presidential election of 1876 completed the process by which the former Confederate states were restored without being truly reconstructed.

☞ As you read, consider the impact that political changes and economic fluctuations had on the federal government's enforcement of Reconstruction. What factors, attitudes, and events led Northerners to abandon Reconstruction?

14-5a "Grantism" and the Gilded Age

Political scandals and unchecked corporate influence herald a new era.

Grant moved into the White House pledging both to uphold Congressional Reconstruction and to restore sectional peace. This agenda was daunting and perhaps contradictory. Grant made a good-faith effort to assist embattled freed people in the South and even to reform federal Indian policy, but his prospects were hurt by the growing taint of fraud and corruption that surrounded his administration.

To sustain black voting rights, Grant worked hard to pass the Fifteenth Amendment, whose adoption he believed "the most important political event since the nation came into life." To protect Native Americans from further dispossession and bring peace to federal-Indian relations, Grant overhauled reservation appointments and policies (see Chapter 15). Finally, to atone for his notorious wartime order expelling Jews (whom he stigmatized as cotton speculators) from his military district on the Mississippi River, he appointed several prominent Jews to government positions.

Yet Grant made serious mistakes with other appointments. Although scrupulously honest as a soldier, he had a lower standard concerning civilians. Some of his advisees and cabinet members were mediocre men, bumbling relatives, and wartime cronies to whom Grant remained loyal after their incompetence or deceptions were exposed.

Partly as a result, a string of scandals weakened his administration and fixed the label "Grantism" on political corruption. On "Black Friday" in September 1869, the price of gold plummeted after financier Jay Gould and his partner Jim Fisk tried to corner the market. They had involved Grant's brother-in-law in the scheme. In 1872, Grant's vice president, Schuyler Colfax, was reportedly among the thirty federal officeholders given shares in **Crédit Mobilier**, a phony construction company formed by the directors of the Union Pacific Railroad to multiply profits. Colfax was dropped from the Republican ticket that year, but the scandals continued. Grant's private secretary Orville Babcock was indicted in 1875 for allowing federal agents to accept bribes from whiskey distillers to avoid excise taxes. The next year, a House investigation revealed that Grant's secretary of war, William Belknap, sold rights to trading posts in Indian Territory. He was impeached, but Grant allowed him to resign to avoid conviction. Grant's later cabinet appointees were able men who attacked corruption in the Interior, Treasury, and Justice Departments. But the damage to the president's relationship with Congress and the public had already been done.

The wave of scandals in railroads, finance, and government contracts showed that opportunities for illicit gain were legion during the postwar era's surge of economic growth. Industrial production nearly doubled during Reconstruction as did the number of workers in manufacturing and construction. Railroads, lavishly subsidized by federal and state governments, reached from coast to coast and incorporated new southern lines. The National Mineral Act of 1866 granted mining companies free access to millions of acres of public land.

Crédit Mobilier Grant administration scandal in which railroad companies generated fraudulent profits and distributed shares of stock to government accomplices.

political machine Powerful political organization in which a party boss or elite rewards loyal supporters with jobs, money, or contracts, often acquired illegally.

Tammany Hall New York City's Democratic Party political machine, named after its headquarters and controlled by Boss William M. Tweed from 1869 to 1873.

Gilded Age Term coined in 1873 to critique an era of political corruption and economic inequality that stretched to 1900.

To gain subsidies, win contracts, and avoid regulation, promoters of railroads and oil and mining corporations wooed politicians with shares of stock, appointments to boards, or outright bribes. Ethical standards were low and conflict of interest laws nonexistent. One wag wrote that John D. Rockefeller of the Standard Oil Company could do everything he wanted with the Pennsylvania legislature except refine it. Republican leaders increasingly catered to big business interests instead of tending to farmers' aspirations or freed peoples' rights.

Republicans were not alone in pocketing cash. The nation's mushrooming cities provided enticing opportunities for politicians who awarded contracts or distributed patronage. Many big-city bosses ran **political machines**. In New York City, Democratic boss William M. Tweed and his ring of operatives stole tens of millions of dollars from the city treasury through embezzlement, inflated contracts, and bribes. Tweed's headquarters, **Tammany Hall**, became a national byword for corrupt city government. One Tammany leader's epitaph, "I seen my opportunities and I took 'em," could serve as a motto for the frenzied speculation and flagrant corruption of an era that novelist Mark Twain and his coauthor Charles Dudley Warner labeled the **Gilded Age**.

14-5b Influence and Opportunities Overseas

As postwar business booms, Americans seek influence in Latin America and Asia.

As Reconstruction waned, American policy makers refocused on gaining markets and raw materials in Latin America and strengthening

Virginia Baptist Historical Society.

Global Americans Born into a family of wealthy Virginia planters, **Charlotte "Lottie" Moon** and her sisters were given an unusually fine education. At first a nonbeliever, she underwent a religious awakening at age eighteen through revivals on her college campus. During the Civil War, Moon took teaching positions at various Virginia schools; after the war, she settled into a teaching career but felt called to overseas missionary work. Treaties with China opened the country to foreign missionaries, and in 1872, the Southern Baptists reversed their policy against sending single women abroad. The next year, Moon left for the treaty port of Tengchow, beginning a forty-year ministry in China. In 1885, she gave up teaching and evangelized full-time in China's interior. During her missionary career, Moon faced famine, plague, revolution, and war and responded with practical assistance to natives. (Here she is shown with students in Japan after fleeing China's Boxer Rebellion.) Moon's time in Asia coincided with renewed U.S. overseas expansionism after the Civil War and enlarged public roles for women. By 1900, 60 percent of American overseas missionaries were women. Missionaries spread Western religion and middle-class values, believing them superior to native peoples' ways. Moon advocated a similar paternalism of racial "uplift" for southern blacks. But Moon and other U.S. missionaries also fostered women's education abroad, introduced Americans to other cultures, and sometimes criticized colonial policies.

the nation's position in the Caribbean. Yet the issues of slavery and race continued to influence U.S. policies in complex ways. On the one hand, emancipation hastened the end of bondage in two New World societies where plantation slavery still thrived. In 1866, Emperor Dom Pedro II suggested that Brazil consider abolishing slavery, and five years later, a law declared that the children of slaves born thereafter would be freed. The Thirteenth Amendment also energized abolitionists in Cuba, many of whom sought U.S. assistance in winning the island's independence from Spain. On the other hand, Reconstruction disputes often spilled into foreign affairs, and motives of national interest competed with moral considerations in the struggle to define U.S. diplomacy.

Grant proved an inconsistent champion of both U.S. expansion and local freedom struggles in the Caribbean. Shortly after acquiring Alaska from Russia, Secretary of State Seward negotiated a treaty to purchase for $7.5 million two islands of the Danish West Indies (later called the *Virgin Islands*) to be used as naval stations. But President-elect Grant was hostile and the U.S. Senate, hounded by critics of the Alaska deal and preoccupied with the Johnson impeachment crisis, refused to act.

When Cuban colonists rose up against Spanish rule in 1868, Grant favored assisting them, but he feared war with Spain or a costly diversion from Reconstruction. Guided by cautious Secretary of State Hamilton Fish, Grant called the revolt "premature," accepted Spanish rule, and urged Madrid to adopt reforms. Even when Spain seized a hired American ship that transported supplies to the rebels and executed fifty-three persons aboard, the United States remained a bystander. The Ten Years' War, the Cuban struggle for independence and emancipation, ended in 1878. Spain freed slaves who had fought in the war (but not others) and enacted financial reforms but maintained its colonial rule. Not until 1886 did Spain decree freedom for all of Cuba's slaves. Some Cuban rebels, including the young nationalist writer José Martí, refused to surrender and continued plotting from U.S. soil to free their homeland.

Burlingame Treaty U.S.–China pact promoting cooperation that recognized China's territorial sovereignty and rights of Chinese immigrants except for U.S. citizenship.

Although Grant hesitated over Cuba, he made strenuous efforts to acquire the small Caribbean republic of Santo Domingo (later the Dominican Republic), whose corrupt president, Buenaventura Báez, was willing to exchange annexation for debt relief. The U.S. navy, eager for Caribbean bases, coveted the island's protected Samaná Bay. Grant believed that the tropical land could become a refuge for the South's persecuted freed people, and he convinced Frederick Douglass that this would increase southern blacks' leverage at home. But opposition arose from many sides. U.S. newspapers derided the project as a financial risk, and some warned against "adding to our population nearly a million of creoles and West Indian negroes." Charles Sumner, Republican chair of the Senate Foreign Relations Committee, opposed annexation as the plot of unsavory speculators and a threat to neighboring Haiti. When the annexation treaty came before the Senate in June 1870, it fell short of the necessary two-thirds approval.

Across the Pacific, the reunified United States continued to seek trade concessions similar to those won by aggressive European powers. U.S. diplomacy veered between conciliation and force. The nation's minister to China, Radical Republican Anson Burlingame, saw parallels between Reconstruction's program of racial equality at home and respect for Asian peoples abroad. The **Burlingame Treaty**, ratified in 1868, recognized China's control of its territory and declared discriminatory anti-Chinese legislation in California illegal. But it did not remove the ban on naturalizing Chinese immigrants to the United States, and it reaffirmed the rights of American missionaries to China granted ten years earlier.

In Japan, the United States again sought a leading role, although the Civil War limited its ability to enforce the unequal treaties of the 1850s. Subdued by a flotilla of European ships that included a lone U.S. gunboat, Japan's Shogun agreed in 1864 to pay indemnities and allow Westerners access to local traders. Popular resentment of this national humiliation helped precipitate the Shogun's overthrow in the **Meiji Restoration** of 1868. Asserting power over samurai warriors and regional lords, the young emperor Meiji and his ministers embarked on a crash program to modernize Japan by abolishing feudal privileges, developing industry, and creating an efficient government bureaucracy.

Americans viewed this revolution as a potential bonanza for U.S. producers and traders, but the Japanese were determined to copy modern industrial methods without becoming subject to Western domination. During a seven-month "knowledge-seeking" mission to the United States in 1873, Japanese envoys paid special attention to new technologies and political reforms. Disappointed American political humorist Finley Peter Dunne complained through his Irish alter ego, "Mr. Dooley": "the throuble is whin the gallant Commodore [Perry] kicked open th' door, we didn't go in. They come out."

Still, more than three hundred U.S. experts were recruited in the 1870s to assist Japan's modernization. They taught scientific farming and brought new breeds of livestock to northern Japan. U.S. educators designed a college-level science curriculum and helped draw up Japan's blueprint for universal schooling. In 1873, Horace Wilson, a Union army veteran, introduced baseball at elite schools in Tokyo. Within two decades, the game had captivated the Japanese as it had the Americans.

Americans resorted to violence to pry open the Kingdom of Korea, which strongly resisted foreign trade. In 1866, a heavily armed U.S. merchant vessel, the *General Sherman*, landed at Pyongyang to impose a trade agreement. Angry Koreans set fire to the ship and killed its fleeing crew. In retaliation, the Grant administration sent a squadron of warships in 1871. Fired on as they approached Seoul, the Americans landed a squad of marines who killed some three hundred Koreans before departing. Eventually, the U.S. navy secured China's help to reach a pact with Korea in 1882 that granted concessions to American merchants and missionaries.

14-5c Republicans in Retreat

Despite Grant's reelection, Congress and the courts back away from Reconstruction.

By the time Grant's first term ended, a Republican splinter movement had formed to voice several grievances against party policies. First, congressional expansion of federal power during Reconstruction worried such reformers, who subscribed to the **laissez-faire** doctrines that were gaining traction with transatlantic industrialists and intellectuals. Adopting as a model Britain's Liberal Party, whose leader William Gladstone became prime minister in 1868, the **Liberal Republicans** advocated limited government, free trade, and unfettered enterprise. These policies, they argued, would create prosperity and reduce taxes and corruption. Liberals also called for a **civil service system** to replace appointed spoilsmen with professional managers. Finally, the Liberals opposed continued federal intervention to support black Southerners and prop up the region's Republican governments. Further progress, the Liberals declared, was up to freed people themselves. This retreat from Reconstruction allied them with southern white opponents of Reconstruction. The Liberals proposed a general amnesty for unreconstructed Southerners and a return to self-government by the "best men" among former Confederates.

The rise of the Liberal Republicans temporarily shook up existing party alignments. Unable to convert Republican "regulars," they formed an alliance with Democrats and nominated Horace Greeley, longtime editor of the *New York Tribune*, for president. Greeley, who had earlier supported Congressional Reconstruction, urged Americans to put the Civil War behind them and "clasp hands across the bloody chasm." Grant, running for a second term, defeated Greeley easily. Drawing on his reservoir of goodwill among the northern public and a high turnout among the South's black voters, Grant amassed 56 percent of the popular vote and carried all but six southern states.

The Liberal Republican revolt ended with the election but brought changes. Grant signed the nation's first civil service law in 1871 to select federal employees on merit, not political connections. Responding to Greeley's call for reconciliation, Congress passed the Amnesty Act, which allowed almost all former Confederates to hold office. More generally, the Liberal split forecast increased impatience among Republicans with their party's reconstruction program.

Toward the end of his first term and into his second, Grant remained committed to radical Reconstruction. When the South's Republicans clamored for protection from violent attacks, Congress responded with strong measures. To protect black voters, the **Ku Klux Klan Act** of 1871 and related enforcement acts authorized the government to prosecute members of groups that denied citizens' civil rights. Although these laws did not end racial violence, they resulted in hundreds of convictions of Klan members. Grant sent federal troops to South Carolina to break up the Klan and dispatched army units to North Carolina, Mississippi, and Louisiana to quell white supremacist insurrections. Congress

Meiji Restoration Rise to power of Japan's Emperor Meiji after widespread protests against unequal treaties, leading to modernization program for Japanese government, army, and industry.

laissez-faire Doctrine opposing government regulation or intervention in economic matters beyond a necessary minimum.

Liberal Republicans Party faction that favored limited government, free trade, and conciliation of southern whites and bolted to the Democratic ticket in 1872 under Greeley.

civil service system Arrangement for hiring and promoting government employees by professional merit rather than personal or political connections.

Ku Klux Klan Act Legislation also known as the Third Enforcement Act that allowed the president to impose martial law to combat attacks by the Klan and other white supremacist organizations.

followed with the Civil Rights Act of 1875, which banned racial discrimination in theaters, hotels, and other public places.

Before long, however, Congress realized that many Northerners had grown tired of southern tumult and the "negro question." Northern businessmen sought order and stability in the South to secure trade and investment. The number of Union soldiers in the South dwindled as they and Civil War generals such as O. O. Howard, the former head of the Freedmen's Bureau, were reassigned to the West to enforce the government's new reservation policy for Native Americans.

White Republicans who had supported African American rights primarily for partisan political advantage never shed their racial prejudice. In the 1870s, many northern Republicans swallowed tales of "black rule" and "barbarism" told by journalists touring the South. Increasingly, former supporters of black suffrage blamed southern violence and Republican losses on black voters, whom they condemned as ignorant and easily corrupted by Democrats.

Republicans who stood firm on African American rights suffered a major defeat when the Supreme Court, uneasy about Reconstruction's expansion of federal powers, restricted the government's authority to enforce civil rights. In its first ruling on the Fourteenth Amendment, the so-called **Slaughterhouse Cases** of 1873, the Court declared that freedom of speech, the right to a fair trial, and most other civil rights derived from state, not national, citizenship and were controlled by state law.

Another damaging decision concerned the **Colfax Massacre**, the bloodiest instance of racial violence during Reconstruction. In 1873, an armed mob of white Louisiana Democrats attacked a courthouse that was held by newly elected Republican officeholders (mostly black) and defended by the state militia. More than one hundred African Americans were killed, many while fleeing or surrendering. Prosecutors secured the conviction of only three men for murder and conspiracy. Reviewing their appeal, the Supreme Court ruled in ***U.S. v. Cruikshank*** (1876) that the Reconstruction amendments gave Congress the power to outlaw acts of discrimination only by state governments, not private individuals. This ruling was solidified in the Civil Rights Cases of 1883, when the Court declared the antidiscrimination strictures of the Civil Rights Act of 1875 unconstitutional. These decisions undermined federal protection of equal rights and gave a tacit go-ahead to white supremacist organizations in the South.

Radical Republicans began to lose in Congress as well as the courts. In the 1874 elections, the Democrats gained control of the House for the first time since the 1850s, proof that support for Reconstruction had dwindled. Grant cared about southern blacks' rights, but he understood which way the political winds were blowing. Responding to a call from South Carolina to suppress a massacre of black militiamen in 1876, Grant deplored the incident but weakly appealed to "the better judgment and co-operation of citizens of the State" to bring the offenders to justice "without aid from the Federal Government."

Slaughterhouse Cases Supreme Court ruling that weakened the Fourteenth Amendment by declaring that state, not federal, laws covered most civil rights.

Colfax Massacre Murderous attack by armed whites on black officeholders and state militia defending a county courthouse in Louisiana.

U.S. v. Cruikshank Supreme Court decision concerning the Colfax Massacre that exempted private individuals from federal prosecution for civil rights violations.

Panic of 1873 International financial crisis that led to U.S. economic depression, weakening Republican control and eroding support for Reconstruction.

14-5d Panic and Compromise

An economic crisis and a contested election end Reconstruction.

The North's shift away from Reconstruction accelerated when the postwar economic boom slid into a deep depression. Like earlier U.S. financial crises, the **Panic of 1873** originated in Europe. After its victory in the Franco-Prussian War (1870–1871), an increasingly powerful Germany demanded payments to it in gold rather than silver. This decree spurred bank failures in Vienna that spread through financial networks to northern Europe and North America. The U.S. economy was especially vulnerable because of speculation and overbuilding of railroads. The influential investment firm Jay Cooke and Company shut down, sparking a chain reaction among

The Library of Congress

Bank Panic, 1873 The run on the Union Trust Company in New York City was among those on hundreds of banks that had to suspend operations in the Panic of 1873. Founded as savings banks, trust companies were virtually unregulated and prone to speculative schemes. Dramatic scenes of bank runs predominated in magazine depictions of the panic and depression. Such male-dominated images overlooked the depression's devastating effects on unemployed women and families. ▲

banks and businesses. Over the next five years, one of four American railroads failed, hundreds of banks folded, and many businesses closed. Unemployment reached 15 percent, and those who hung onto their jobs faced seasonal layoffs and severe wage cuts.

For working-class victims of the depression, the crisis exposed the inadequacy of Republicans' free-labor ideology to the new industrial era. Unemployed workers in New York and other cities demanded that government officials create jobs or at least finance public relief. But Republican spokesmen and business leaders denounced such programs as interfering with the free market and discouraging hard work. According to laissez-faire tenets, workers in the North, like southern blacks, enjoyed mobility and civil rights and had to rise by their own efforts. As Reconstruction evolved, it hardened, rather than tempered, the creed of middle-class individualism that Republicans had fashioned in the 1850s.

The lingering economic depression and the Grant administration's continuing scandals gave the Democrats momentum going into the 1876 presidential campaign. They nominated Governor Samuel J. Tilden of New York, a reformer renowned for prosecuting the Tweed Ring in New York City. In addition to "corrupt centralism" in Washington, Tilden promised to end "carpetbag tyrannies" in the South. The Republicans nominated Rutherford B. Hayes, a former Civil War general with a clean record as governor of Ohio, who promised to crack down on graft and voiced conciliatory sentiments toward southern whites.

Tilden received 250,000 more popular votes than Hayes, but in the Electoral College, his total was 184, one shy of the number required for victory (see Map 14.3). Hayes received 166, but the votes of one Oregon elector and three southern states were disputed. South Carolina, Louisiana, and Florida were the only remaining Republican governments in the South. The contest there was marred by fraud, and both parties claimed victory.

Faced with this unprecedented situation, Congress created a fifteen-member commission composed of senators, representatives, and Supreme Court justices to examine the disputed returns. The commission voted eight to seven along strict party lines to give Hayes all the contested electoral votes and with them the presidency. Outraged Democrats threatened to block Hayes's victory in the House of Representatives. The impasse was broken when Democrats and Republicans appeared to negotiate a series of back-room deals just two days before the inauguration. The arrangement became known as the **Compromise of 1877**. In return for the Democrats' acceptance of Hayes as president, the Republicans agreed (among other concessions) to provide federal subsidies for a southern transcontinental railroad (the northern line had been completed in 1869). Most importantly, the Republicans pledged to withdraw federal troops that bolstered the remaining Republican regimes in the South.

The Compromise of 1877 broke down so rapidly that some historians question whether it was forged at all. The most important feature held, however: Shortly after Hayes was inaugurated, he removed federal troops stationed in the three contested states. Without the army to support them, the South's Republicans ceded control of Louisiana, South Carolina, and Florida to the Democrats. This closed the long sectional struggle over whether the postwar South would simply be restored to the Union or thoroughly reconstructed. Sectional peace returned, but at the price of relinquishing Reconstruction's transformational agenda. By abandoning the pledge of civil and political equality recently inscribed in the Fourteenth and Fifteenth Amendments, the North and South were reunited.

Compromise of 1877 Political deal that resolved the disputed election of 1876 by ceding electoral votes to Republican candidate Hayes in exchange for ending Reconstruction.

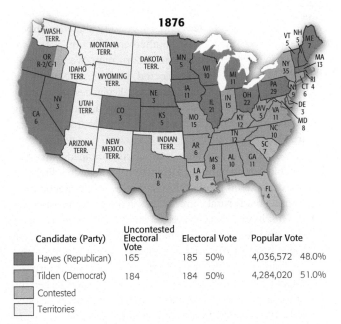

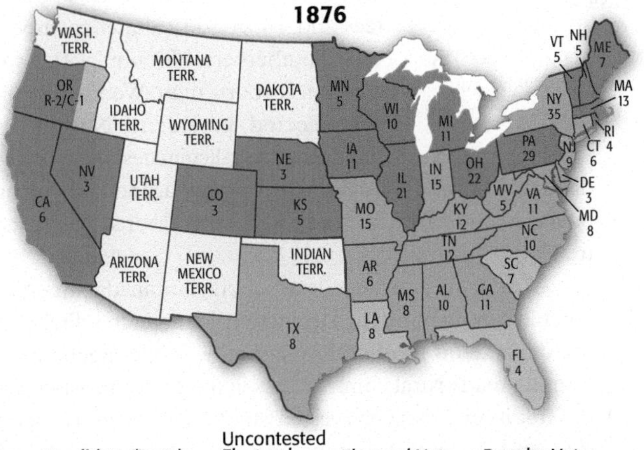

Candidate (Party)	Uncontested Electoral Vote	Electoral Vote	Popular Vote
Hayes (Republican)	165	185 50%	4,036,572 48.0%
Tilden (Democrat)	184	184 50%	4,284,020 51.0%
Contested			
Territories			

Map 14.3 Election of 1876 and Compromise of 1877 Democratic gains in the North and the collapse of Reconstruction governments in the South gave Samuel Tilden the majority of popular votes. However, Republican Rutherford Hayes captured the presidency after a special commission gave him all the disputed Electoral College votes and a private agreement assured Democrats that Reconstruction was over. ▲

14-5e Reconstruction's Troubled Legacy at Home and Abroad

Home rule in the South isolates it politically and entrenches racist practices.

The end of Reconstruction had important consequences for relations between the South and the nation. Relinquishing rule to the South's large landowners enabled them to recapture their regional power and set the terms of southern race relations, but they no longer controlled national politics. Before the Civil War, white Southerners dominated the presidency, Supreme Court, and other federal leadership positions; afterward, the sectional balance of power was reversed. In the next fifty years,

Lost Cause Nostalgic praise of the plantation South and Confederate bravery voiced by white Southerners who were opposed to Reconstruction and racial equality.

only 7 of 31 Supreme Court appointees and 14 of 133 cabinet members were Southerners. Not until 1912 was a southern-born man, Woodrow Wilson, elected president. Nationally, political party allegiances were evenly divided, but the Republicans' economic agenda, including banking, land, tariff, and tax policies that favored the industrial North, prevailed.

Meanwhile, wartime destruction combined with unfavorable conditions in the international market to inflict lasting damage on the South's economy. While mechanized farming made rural communities in the North prosperous, the traditional hand-harvested staples of cotton, tobacco, rice, and sugar still dominated southern agriculture. All these crops suffered from global overproduction and declining prices. Industrialization and diversified farming might ensure future prosperity, but Southerners lacked the home-grown capital to make changes, and many resisted industry as an alien way of life. Southerners emerged from Reconstruction dependent on the North's banks, factories, and corporations to offset diminishing returns from staple crops. The South's subordination in the national government and its lagging economic development resembled the outcome of national consolidation in countries such as Italy and Germany, where north-south disparities continued to divide nations that were unified politically in midcentury.

Shaken by their declining status, southern whites idealized the prewar plantation economy, lamented the Confederacy's **Lost Cause**, and demonized their alleged oppressors during radical Reconstruction. Once the South's Republican regimes were toppled, white politicians launched systematic campaigns to disfranchise, intimidate, and segregate African Americans. To justify discrimination against blacks and nonwhite immigrants, white commentators and academics in both the North and South developed elaborate racial theories based on ideas of Anglo-Saxon superiority, immutable racial traits, or the evolutionary "backwardness" of nonwhite peoples.

By providing fodder for such racial theories, the abandonment of Reconstruction had damaging international repercussions. According to James Bryce, Britain's ambassador to the United States and a respected authority on American society, postwar turmoil in the South showed "the risk a democracy runs when the suffrage is granted to a large mass of half-civilized men." British imperialists in lands such as Australia and South Africa cited Bryce's view that Reconstruction was a mistake as proof that nonwhite peoples were incapable of self-rule. Such views produced segregation laws, racial exclusion from voting, literacy tests, and similar methods of disfranchisement in Britain's so-called white dominions that were based on models from the U.S. South.

Blacks in the American South, like their global counterparts, did not let such views go unchallenged. Beginning in the mid-1870s, emigration movements recruited heavily in the cotton belt. Perhaps 30,000 southern blacks left for Kansas in the so-called Exoduster movement (see Chapter 15) and another 4,000 sought new lives in Liberia. The vast majority remained in their adopted land, struggling to make a living and fighting for their rights. Despite legal restrictions and physical threats, the South's African Americans continued to vote in large numbers into the 1880s. When in the next decade southern states passed laws restricting voting and mandating segregation, people of color, including Louisiana's Rodolphe Desdunes and his friend Homère Plessy, reasserted equal rights against all odds.

Summary

Americans entered the post-Civil War era with conflicting agendas for restoring peace and distributing justice. Emancipated slaves sought political rights and economic independence. Former Confederates insisted on the freedom to retain regional power and racial dominance. Republicans in Congress held the balance of political power and debated plans for the postwar settlement. The contest between revolutionizing the South and restoring the prewar status quo galvanized the nation when the Republicans impeached their renegade president and framed a program to reconstruct southern life as a precondition to reunion. Congressional Reconstruction strengthened the federal government's domestic power at the same time that the purchase of Alaska confirmed the nation's continental dominance. In 1867, the United States became the only postemancipation society in the Americas committed to guaranteeing former slaves full civil and political rights.

Reconstruction shook southern society to its foundations as Republican state governments elected with African American votes enacted sweeping changes in politics, education, and public welfare. But in the South, as in postemancipation societies in Caribbean islands, white planters who had resisted emancipation led determined efforts to maintain their racial and economic supremacy after slavery's end. Using the Democratic Party and secret paramilitary groups, angry white Southerners arose to take control of their states. As political winds shifted, industrial upheavals and overseas expansion drew the public's attention, and the North's Republicans retreated from their commitment to enforce racial equality.

By the time Reconstruction officially ended in 1877, an informal settlement emerged by which Northerners dominated the newly powerful national government and traditional white elites regained control over the postwar South's politics, agriculture, and race relations. As in most nations undergoing unification struggles, sectional integration was incomplete and cultural and ideological rifts lingered. The North returned to peace, prosperity, and expansion, the South assumed a subordinate relationship in national politics, and the Union's promise of full freedom to the former slaves was sacrificed. Instead of serving as a model of political equality for other postemancipation societies, Americans provided examples of racial segregation and political disfranchisement amid glimpses of progress.

Thinking Back, *Looking Forward*

As you review this chapter, think about how Reconstruction transformed American politics, the national economy, and social relations in the South. Which changes endured, and which were temporary? Did the North win the Civil War but lose the postwar peace? Why did Americans retreat from their unique pledge of postemancipation equality between races? How complete was U.S. national unification compared to that of other nations? In the next chapters, look for the lasting consequences of Reconstruction's battles. What did the South's segregationist regime mean for Reconstruction's legacy? What were the consequences of Reconstruction for Native Americans, immigration, and U.S. citizenship?

To make your study concrete, review the timeline and reflect on the entries there. Think about their causes, consequences, and connections. How do they fit with global trends?

Additional Resources

Books

Beckert, Sven. *Empire of Cotton: A Global History*. New York: Knopf, 2014. ▶ Documentation of the worldwide switch to tenancy and small-farm production after the U.S. Civil War.

Cook, Adrian. *The Alabama Claims: American Politics and Anglo-American Relations, 1865–1872*. Ithaca, NY: Cornell University Press, 1975. ▶ Scholarly history of U.S.–Great Britain relations during Reconstruction.

Dubois, Ellen Carol. *Feminism and Suffrage: The Emergence of an Independent Women's Movement in America, 1848–1869*. Ithaca. NY: Cornell University Press, 1978. ▶ Account of the break of women's rights' advocates from their abolitionist roots to focus on the vote.

Foner, Eric. *Reconstruction: America's Unfinished Revolution, 1863–1877*. New York: HarperCollins, 1988. ▶ The best single-volume history of the period.

Hahn, Steven. *A Nation under Our Feet: Black Political Struggles in the Rural South from Slavery to the Great Migration*. Cambridge, MA: Harvard University Press, 2005. ▶ Exploration of the hidden history of black political organizing during and after Reconstruction.

Hunter, Tera W. *To 'Joy My Freedom: Southern Black Women's Lives and Labors after the Civil War*. Cambridge, MA: Harvard University Press, 1997. ▶ Retelling of urban black women's lives and struggles as domestics.

Litwack, Leon. *Been in the Storm So Long: The Aftermath of Slavery*. New York: Vintage Books, 1980. ▶ Classic account, based on participants' testimony, of how blacks experienced freedom.

Scott, Rebecca J. *Degrees of Freedom: Louisiana and Cuba after Slavery*. Cambridge: Belknap Press, 2005. ▶ Comparison and contrast of emancipation and race relations in two sugar plantation societies.

Simpson, Brooks D. *The Reconstruction Presidents*. Lawrence: University Press of Kansas, 1998. ▶ A comparative assessment that rehabilitates Grant's reputation.

Stewart, David O. *Impeached: The Trial of President Andrew Johnson and the Fight for Lincoln's Legacy*. New York: Simon & Schuster, 2009. ▶ A dramatic narrative that criticizes Johnson for squandering Lincoln's hopes for emancipation.

Trelease, Allen. *White Terror: The Ku Klux Klan Conspiracy and Southern Reconstruction*. Baton Rouge: Louisiana State University Press, 1995. ▶ A comprehensive, state-by-state history of Klan activities during Reconstruction.

Go to the MindTap® for **Global Americans** to access the full version of select books from this Additional Resources section.

Websites

Andrew Johnson Impeachment Trial. (http://www.law.umkc.edu/faculty/projects/ftrials/impeach/impeachmt.htm). ▶ A collection of documents, information, and links about the impeachment.

Freedmen and Southern Society Project. (http://www.history.umd.edu/Freedmen/). ▶ Essays and primary source documents related to emancipation, land, and labor.

Freedmen's Bureau Online. (http://www.freedmensbureau.com/) ▶ State-by-state reports and documents, many capturing African American voices.

***Harper's Weekly*. (http://blackhistory.harpweek.com/default.htm).** ▶ Collection of reports on Black America 1857–1874 that includes editorials, news stories, and cartoons on Reconstruction from the popular northern magazine.

Ohio State University Libraries. (http://cartoons.osu.edu/digital_albums/thomasnast/index.htm). ▶ Extensive portfolio of Thomas Nast's political cartoons, which reflect changing Republican attitudes during Reconstruction.

Reconstruction: The Second Civil War. (http://www.pbs.org/wgbh/amex/reconstruction/index.html). ▶ Background information, documents, and access to two PBS documentary films about Reconstruction.

MindTap®

Continue exploring online through MindTap®, where you can:

- **Assess your knowledge with the Chapter Test**
- **Watch historical videos related to the chapter**
- **Further your understanding with interactive maps and timelines**

Reunion and Retreat: Reconstruction

1863

December

Lincoln's Proclamation of Amnesty and Reconstruction outlines lenient plan for restoring rebellious states to the Union.

1864

July

Lincoln pocket vetoes congressional Wade-Davis bill imposing strict terms for readmission to the Union.

1865

March

Congress establishes Freedmen's Bureau to assist former slaves.

April

Lincoln is assassinated and is succeeded by Vice President Andrew Johnson .

May

Johnson announces plan to disfranchise Confederate leaders and quickly restore former Confederate states.

Summer

White governments in restored southern states adopt Black Codes restricting freed people's rights.

October

Morant Bay Rebellion in Jamaica stiffens southern whites' resistance to freedmen's rights.

December

Thirteenth Amendment is ratified, outlawing slavery in United States.

Ku Klux Klan is organized in Tennessee to terrorize freed people.

1866

April

Civil Rights Act extends citizenship and accompanying rights to all persons born in the United States, including former slaves.

May–June

Fenian Brotherhood launches invasion of Canada aimed at securing Irish independence.

July

Armed U.S. merchant ship *General Sherman* is attacked and destroyed in Korea.

1867

March

United States purchases Alaska territory from Russia to promote continental expansion and Pacific trade.

Reconstruction Act returns former Confederate states to military rule and sets congressional requirements for readmission.

British North America Act creates Canadian Confederation in response to threat of U.S. expansion.

August

Reform Act in Britain expands voting rights to double the electorate but rejects women's suffrage.

1868

January

Japan's Meiji Restoration initiates modernization and increases U.S. influence in its industry and educational system.

February

Bancroft Treaties spread recognition of naturalized citizenship, beginning with pact between German states and the United States.

March

Johnson impeached but not convicted by Congress in dispute over Reconstruction policies.

July

Fourteenth Amendment gives citizenship to African Americans and establishes birthright citizenship as U.S. policy.

Burlingame Treaty between U.S. and China proclaims mutual respect and continues Chinese immigration to United States.

October

United States stays neutral as the Ten Years' War erupts in Cuba over abolition and colonial independence from Spain.

November

Republican candidate and Civil War hero Ulysses Grant is elected president.

1869 – 1870

April
In *Texas v. White*, the Supreme Court declares secession unconstitutional without consent of the United States.

May
Debate over Reconstruction amendments splits U.S. women's suffrage activists.

March
Fifteenth Amendment bans denial of vote on grounds of race.

June
U.S. Senate rejects annexation of Santo Domingo.

1871

January
Women's suffrage advocates appear before Congress to press their claims.

May
Treaty of Washington resolves U.S.–Britain disputes over Civil War claims and Canadian border.

June
U.S. expedition to Korea avenges *General Sherman* incident but fails to open trade relations.

September
Brazil, influenced by prior British and U.S emancipation, adopts a gradual emancipation law.

1872

September
Crédit Mobilier scandal rocks Grant administration, eroding support for Republican Party.

November
Grant is reelected president as Liberal Republican revolt fails.

1873

April
White Southerners murder black officeholders in Louisiana's Colfax Massacre.

U.S. Supreme Court weakens Fourteenth Amendment in Slaughterhouse Cases ruling.

September
Bank Panic in Europe triggers U.S. economic crisis and six-year global depression.

1874

November
Democrats win control of House of Representatives for the first time since the Civil War.

1875

March
U.S. Supreme Court rejects women's suffrage in *Minor v. Happersett.*

1876

March
U.S. v. Cruikshank drastically limits federal oversight of freed people's civil rights.

November
Republican Rutherford Hayes and Democrat Samuel Tilden deadlock in disputed presidential election.

1877

March
Electoral College and congressional compromise declare Hayes president and officially end Reconstruction.

Go to MindTap® to engage with an interactive version of the timeline. Analyze events and themes with clickable content, view related videos, and respond to critical thinking questions.

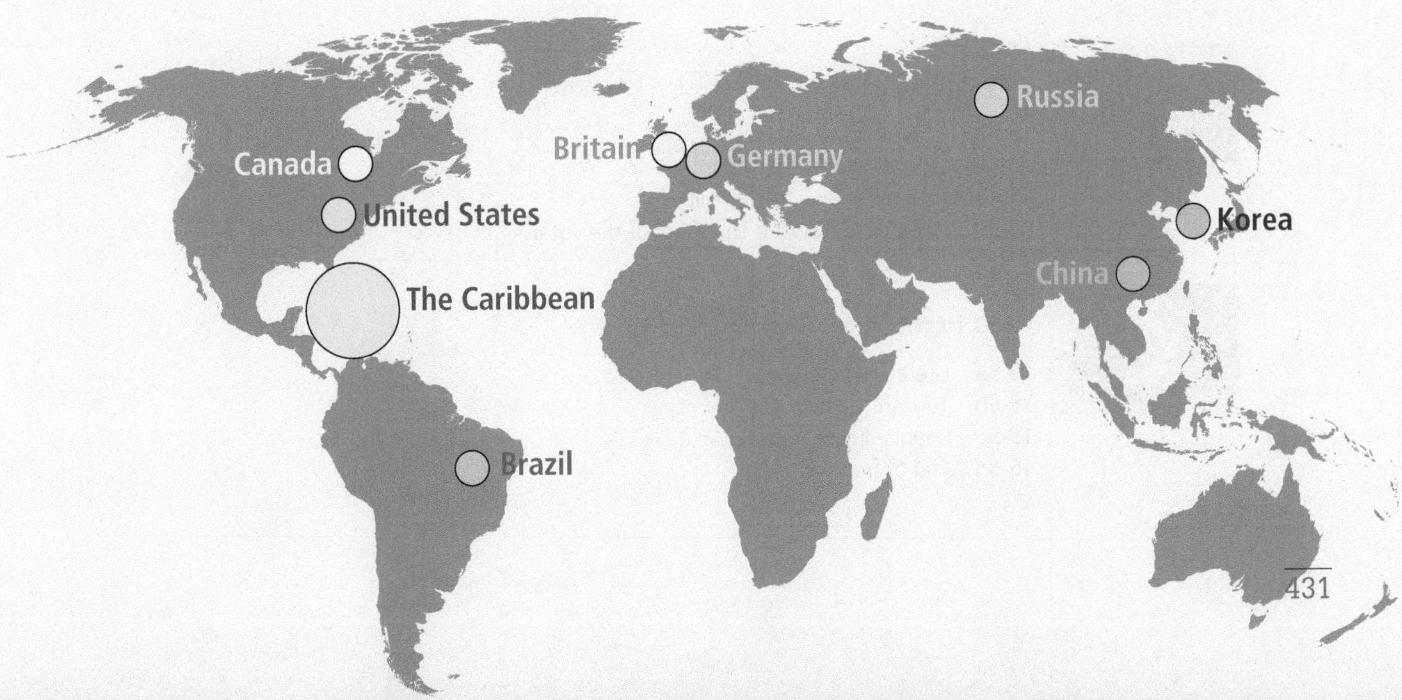

15

Incorporation of the U.S. West

1862–1917

In the aftermath of the Sand Creek Massacre, the U.S. government removed Black Kettle and the remainder of his group to a reservation in Indian Territory along the Washita River in present-day Oklahoma. Black Kettle's story reveals the dangers Indians faced when they opted for peace with the U.S. government.

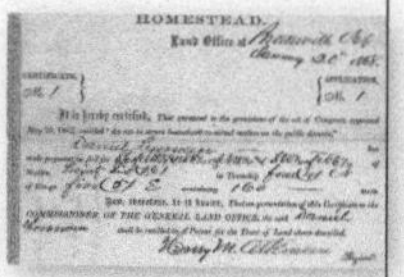

Black Kettle, a leader of the Cheyennes who advocated accommodation with the U.S. military and white society, left his home at Sand Creek, Colorado, and made his way to Fort Lyon. There, on September 26, 1861, he signed a peace treaty and surrendered. He asked Major Scott Anthony if he and his people could overwinter in the fort for safety and receive government food rations. Because the fort was already at capacity with other Cheyennes, Anthony told Black Kettle to return to his camp thirty miles away, where they could hunt for winter game and wait for further instructions. Anthony assured Black Kettle that his people would be safe despite U.S. military campaigns against other Indians nearby.

Bosse, Left Hand, White Wolf, Black Kettle, White Antelope, Bull Bear, Neva: (b/w photo), American Photographer, (19th century)/Denver Public Library, Western History Collection/The Bridgeman Art Library

Chiefs of the Arapahoe, Sioux, Cheyenne, and Kiowa tribes, circa 1860–1868. Black Kettle is the figure seated on the far left side of the front row.

Not all Cheyennes accepted Black Kettle's surrender. The Dog Soldiers, a group of young men who had separated themselves to create a warrior culture, opposed accommodations to whites that almost always ended in Indian land loss and the suppression of Indian culture. During the Plains Wars of the mid-nineteenth century, increasing numbers of young men abandoned the Cheyenne leaders to join the Dog Soldiers. In Colorado, they were preparing to fight Colonel John M. Chivington as he and his regiment of seven hundred left Denver to attack the Cheyennes and Arapahoes.

It was a time of violence. Half a continent away, in the same month that Black Kettle moved to Sand Creek, Union general William T. Sherman conquered Atlanta. He marched through Georgia, destroying anything useful to the Confederacy. The Civil War's legitimization of force against civilians was perpetuated in the West where the U.S. military continued to use force to subjugate Indian peoples. Similar migrations and violent encounters were occurring in Australia, Argentina, and South Africa where European settlers pushed aside native peoples to take control of natural resources.

Early on the morning of November 29, 1864, Chivington, who was aware of the peace agreement, attacked Black Kettle's sleeping camp. Only a few men were present to mount a defense, so women and children scattered or burrowed into the ground to protect themselves from gunfire. By mid-afternoon, more than one hundred fifty Cheyennes lay dead. Miraculously, Black Kettle and his wife survived. The white fur trader, George Bent, living at Sand Creek, and other traders with mixed-race families tried to negotiate a peace, but Chivington's men burned the camp and then pushed on to destroy other Indian villages.

In the aftermath, the U.S. government removed Black Kettle and the remainder of his group to a reservation in what was known as *Indian Territory* (present-day Oklahoma). Four years later, in the winter of 1868, Colonel George Armstrong Custer attacked Black Kettle's encampment. This time neither Black Kettle nor his wife survived. Black Kettle's experiences reveal the dangers that Indians faced when they opted for peace with the U.S. government.

How do Black Kettle's experiences with warfare on the Great Plains reflect the dangers that Indians faced when they opted for peace with the U.S. government?

Go to MindTap® to watch a video on Black Kettle and learn how his story relates to the themes of this chapter.

Once southern members had vacated Congress during the Civil War, the overwhelmingly Republican majority was free to plan the future of the trans-Mississippi territories without the obstacle of southern slaveholders. In quick succession, Republicans passed three pieces of legislation that changed the West forever. The Pacific Railroad Acts funded the building of transcontinental railroads, the Homestead Act granted land to settlers who would improve it, and the Morrill Act encouraged land sales to establish state universities specializing in agricultural science and engineering. Together, these acts, which suggested the federal government's increasing power after the Civil War, opened the West to commercial development and a wave of white settlement.

In the decades following the Sand Creek Massacre, warfare on the Great Plains peaked and then subsided as the U.S. military destroyed Indian settlements and broke down resistance. By the 1890s, the U.S. government had placed the last of the Indian leaders—Sitting Bull, Chief Joseph, and Geronimo—on reservations and decimated the great herds of bison that had supported Indian life for centuries. The land was then enclosed into ranches and farms settled by white Americans and European immigrants. Railroads transported people and products to eastern factories and cities. Commerce and communications knit the continent and connected it across the Pacific to China and Japan, which opened new markets for U.S. goods and created opportunities for new immigrants. New markets, new agricultural methods, and new technologies united the nation and made the West less distinctive. In reality and in Americans' imagination, the West had been tamed and brought into the nation. As the violence that had begun with the arrival of the Spanish conquistadors faded into history, Americans romanticized the development of the West into a story of progress.

15-1 Ties of Commerce

John Gast completed *American Progress* in 1872. Notice the city on the right in the sunshine and the rugged mountains and darkness on the left. Find the horsemen, farmers, fleeing bison and Indians, and the train puffing black smoke. The crowned and classically garbed figure carries a book and trails a telegraph wire behind her as she floats, beneficently, over the landscape.

What do you think the floating female figure represents? How does Gast use light and imagery to tell a story about progress? ▶

American Progress, 1872 (oil on canvas), Gast, John (b.1842-d.?)/Private Collection/Photo © Christie's Images/The Bridgeman Art Library

The economic development of the West intensified with the growth of the railroads, which were built across the trans-Mississippi frontier in advance of most commerce and white settlement. Americans' desire for commercial ties linking the nation with western ports for trade with Japan and China was the driving force behind railroad development. Transcontinental railroad projects were immense and expensive undertakings made possible only by the federal government, whose economic and political power surpassed that of the largest private corporations. The federal government also sponsored the establishment of state universities specializing in agriculture and engineering. These produced the managers and engineers who planned the railroad routes and directed these projects. But the work of carving rail lines into the landscape was accomplished by the labor of millions of men, often immigrants willing to take grueling and dangerous jobs.

☞ As you read, consider ways in which the transcontinental railroad knit the nation together. What problems did railroad development cause?

15-1a The Transcontinental Railroad

Building a transcontinental railroad was a dream of business and political leaders before the Civil War. After the war, underwritten by the federal government, it became a reality. The Pacific Railroad Acts (1862, 1864) financed the project through **land grants** from the public domain amounting to 174 million acres, larger than the size of Texas (see Map 15.1). The Union Pacific built west from Omaha, Nebraska, and the Central Pacific built east from Sacramento, California. Each received ten sections (sixty-four hundred acres) along the right of way for each mile of track laid. That incentive later increased to twenty, and then forty, sections per mile. The railroads sold these lands to settlers and speculators who built towns and created business that required rail traffic for the new lines.

The transcontinental railroad draws the nation together through commerce.

Because of the magnitude of the transcontinental line, the federal government also financed the railroad by selling bonds that promised a return of 6 percent to the investors. Ultimately, the government advanced about $77 million

land grants Awards of public domain lands by Congress to railroad companies and to states to support the development of railroads and schools.

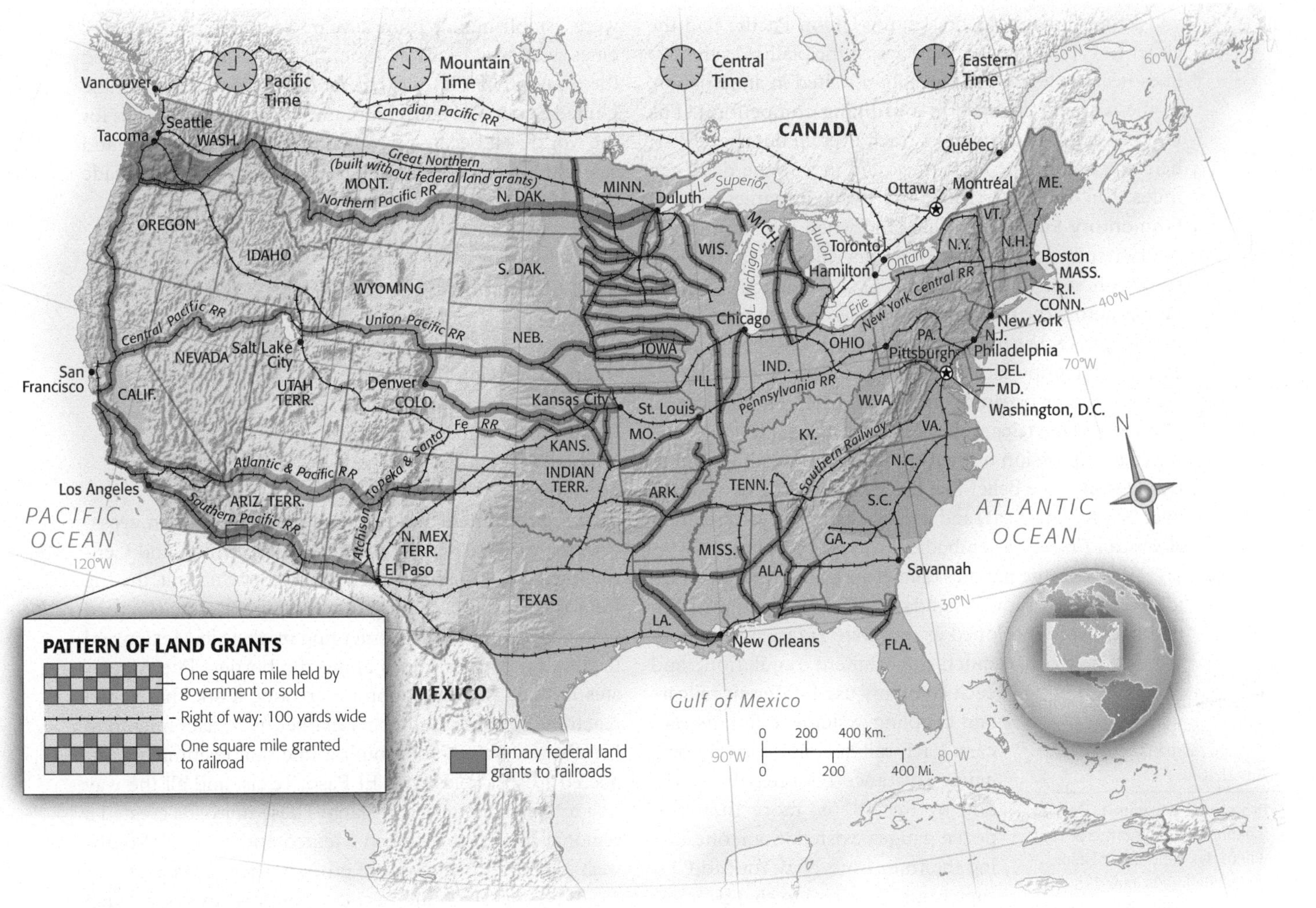

Map 15.1 Federal Land Grants Given to Railroads Building railroads after the Civil War would not have been possible without immense federal subsidies of land. Taken from Native Americans, who were increasingly confined to reservations, these lands were turned over to railway companies that sold them to raise revenue. While homesteaders could get "free" land, many who could afford it chose to pay a premium price to have easy access to the railroad, which opened a global market to them. ▲

in bonds to the railroad companies, which they were supposed to repay over the next thirty years, but in fact they repaid only a fraction of what was owed. The government also covered about $43 million in deferred interest payments to the railroads' bondholders. The magnitude of this infrastructure project succeeded only because of these massive government subsidies to private corporations.

The Central Pacific Railroad (CPRR) started the first transcontinental line in Sacramento, California, and began laying track east across and through the Sierra Nevada mountains and out onto the high plateaus of the interior West. A group of powerful tycoons financially underwrote the railroads. Known as the **Big Four**, Leland Stanford, Collis P. Huntington, Mark Hopkins, and Charles Crocker bought and sold the government-backed bonds to finance the railroad, amassing a huge profit. With the exception of timber, all of the materials—rails, equipment, and engines—had to be shipped from the East Coast to the West via the Isthmus of Panama or through Cape Horn on the southern tip of South America. The cost was enormous in terms of material, labor, and time.

From Omaha, Nebraska, the Union Pacific had the easier task, pushing westward across the plains. As the two lines neared each other, the nation waited in anticipation, as the workers engaged in a gripping competition. The Union Pacific laid the most track overall, but the CPRR held the record for most track laid in a single day—ten miles. On May 10, 1869, the two companies met at **Promontory Summit** in Utah, and when the hammer hit the last spike at 12:32 P.M., joining the two railroads, a telegraph sent to Washington, D.C., declared "Done." People across the nation celebrated as one newspaper columnist wrote that this was the marriage of "the gorgeous east and the imperial west of America, with the indissoluble seal of inter-oceanic commerce." The transcontinental railroad and the telegraph wire strung alongside it were the physical expression of the U.S. fascination with its Manifest Destiny (the belief that the U.S. was ordained to rule over North America), and its more benevolent version of *American Progress* as embodied in Gast's painting.

Although the nation's rail network had expanded rapidly, very little of it was standardized or compatible. Each line had been developed as a private enterprise without much government regulation, and each company used different railcars and coupling systems to link its railcars. Each rail line also used its own gauge (distance between the rails), and by the 1870s, more than two dozen gauges existed. Someone taking the train from New York to Chicago would have had to change trains and transportation companies at least three times. Freight had to be transferred by hand from one railway line's railcars to those of the next company as it moved through the system, driving up shipping costs. The Pacific Railway Acts codified a standard gauge for the entire transcontinental railroad to avoid these problems. This type of standardization spread throughout the railroad industry after the Civil War to provide efficiency and convenience amid fierce competition and cutthroat practices among rival companies.

Big Four Businessmen, also known as the *Associates*, who used unscrupulous tactics to develop railroads across North America.

Promontory Summit The meeting point in northern Utah where the Central and Union Pacific Railroads joined to create the first transcontinental railroad.

standard time Synchronized time within designated zones conforming to one standard time rather than a local one.

Until 1883, when the railroads adopted the policy of **standard time**, people in North America operated on "local time" or simply had an approximate sense of what time it was. With the advent of railroads and the need to coordinate transfers and rail use precisely, this practice had to change. Since the eighteenth century, mariners had used Greenwich Mean Time (GMT), based on the established longitude of zero degrees at Greenwich, England, to help navigate the seas. In 1847, British railroads had adopted GMT, which became known as *railway time*, to synchronize their schedules. Britain eventually adopted GMT as its legal time in 1880. Then in 1883, on the "day of two noons," railroad stations across the United States set their clocks to railway standard time, and time zones were established. Within a year, 85 percent of all U.S. cities were using railway time. In 1918, Congress passed the Standard Time Act that set official time zones in the United States. Globally, railroads literally set the clocks for the world as it became essential in terms of efficiency and safety to make sure that the trains ran on time and made their posted connections, particular at rail crossings.

15-1b Railroad Expansion at Home and Abroad

Railroads and transportation networks link the world together.

Railroad development in the 1860s went far beyond building the first transcontinental railroad. Once it was finished, other rail lines competed to access government funding and create their own cross-country roads. After the meeting of the Union and Central Pacific Railroads rails at Promontory Summit, the Big Four turned to developing the Southern Pacific Railroad Company to tap into the emerging markets in Mexico and to develop copper mines along the border. The Associates focused their attention on creating a line that would reach the growing California market from Sacramento to Los Angeles. They then built a line that eventually connected Los Angeles with El Paso, Texas, and all the way east to New Orleans, Louisiana. These railroads created a regional market that linked Mexico and the U.S. Southwest into an intricate web of cross-border commerce.

The southern line had the potential to draw much larger and international markets as they tapped into the Gulf of Mexico and Mississippi River trade that drew goods from the Caribbean and Central and South America. Under President Porfirio Diaz, Mexico had its own railroad boom. Because of his favoritism to

Everett Collection Historical/Alamy Stock Photo

Global Americans **J.J. Hill** was born in Ontario, Canada, in 1838. At the age of eighteen, he saw an opportunity in the expanding transportation markets along the upper Mississippi River and moved to St. Paul, Minnesota, to work first on steamboats and then the railroad. In 1870, he started the Red River Transportation Company, which hauled coal, fuel, and passengers on steamboat lines from St. Paul to Winnipeg, developing cross-border commerce between Canada and the United States. A relentless worker, Hill had the motto "Work, hard work, intelligent work, and then more work." He was one of the very few who profited from the Panic of 1873 by buying a bankrupt railroad. During the Panic of 1893, when his competitors were failing, he stayed in business by lowering rates and extending credit to his customers. In 1879, he bought the St. Paul, Minneapolis, and Manitoba Railway with cash. Unlike all other railway owners, Hill never took government land grants, bonds, or loans to finance his businesses. He was the only railway owner never to go into bankruptcy. But in order to make his railways profitable, he created markets. He opened immigration offices in Germany and Scandinavia to encourage farmers to migrate to the upper Midwest. He also introduced hybridized wheat from Russia, which was hardier and could grow in the harsh Dakota winters. Hill was a globalized businessman who realized the advantages of open immigration and free markets. He was an early and strong proponent of free trade, always opposing any tariff bills that would inhibit his companies' profits.

U.S. businessmen, the Mexican government granted $32 million in subsidies to U.S. companies that would build railroads. Five railroad companies eventually constructed more than twenty-five hundred miles of track that ran south to north. In August 1884, Mexican Central Railway completed an international, transcontinental railroad that linked Mexico City with El Paso, Texas, and the Atchison, Topeka, and Santa Fe Railway. The road eventually went as far north as Santa Fe, New Mexico. Railroad **boosters** created an even more lucrative *Camino Real* than the one the Spanish had created in the colonial period. By 1910 and the Mexican Revolution, U.S. companies held almost 90 percent of all investments in Mexican railroads and owned fifteen thousand miles of track south of the border.

Railroad owners realized that trade did not end at the shores of the Pacific Ocean. They gambled that the transcontinental railroad combined with Pacific steamship service from San Francisco would make the United States a conduit for trade between Europe and Asia, serving as a constructed Northwest Passage, the imagined all-sea route that had enticed early European explorers. Their hopes were dashed when the **Suez Canal** opened in 1869 just after the railroads had been joined in Utah, providing a sea route between Europe and Asia that cut off the long trip around Africa. Nevertheless, railroad investors such as the Big Four saw potential growth in trade between the East Coast and Asia by means of the Pacific Mail and the Occidental and Oriental Steamship Companies, which provided bimonthly service between the West Coast and various ports in Asia. The United States exported cotton, wheat, silver, and opium whereas Asian countries shipped tea, silk, spices, porcelain, and laborers to California ports for distribution throughout the United States.

15-1c Railroad Workers

An international labor force builds the railroads.

Railroad development happened because of the engineers who planned the routes and the physical labor of thousands of men who did the day-to-day work. As industrialization proceeded, the need for a new class of technical experts knowledgeable in the design and operation of machines emerged. The military had long trained engineers to build fortifications. But now, an entirely new array of engineers—mechanical, mining, and later chemical and electrical engineers—emerged. Many received training at the new land-grant institutions established under the Morrill Act. This act supported technical education by granting 30,000 acres of public domain land that could be used to fund agricultural, mechanical, and technical schools. Some states, such as Wisconsin, put the money into their existing educational systems; others, such as Michigan, created a new school, Michigan State University. These schools gave students the skills necessary to develop the nation's infrastructure and extract its natural resources. Such schools created a managerial class who oversaw the work of laborers and thus contributed to the class hierarchies evolving in industrializing America.

At the other end of the labor spectrum were the day laborers who did the arduous work of cutting the timber, preparing and shipping the rail ties, mining the coal that fueled the trains, laying the track, and then maintaining the entire system once it was in place. Like the urban areas of

boosters Local businessmen who wanted to draw settlers to their community by boasting of its advantages.

Suez Canal Sea-level canal that linked the Mediterranean and Red Seas, opening a trade route between Europe and the Middle and Far East.

the East Coast in the United States in this period, the U.S. West was an industrializing landscape that drew thousands of immigrants from around the world (see Figure 15.1). Chinese men worked on the northern and western lines, and Mexicans for the most part built the southwestern rail lines. African Americans made up the majority of the workers on the southern railroads. By the 1890s, women were also working for railway companies as clerks, machinists, and laborers in the roundhouse and on the tracks. The Northern Pacific employed more than two thousand women by the early twentieth century.

Not everyone who worked on the railroad was a new immigrant. When the Union Pacific started building west from Nebraska, it turned to the Irish, who made up more than half of its workforce. Irish immigrants had been coming to the United States since the early nineteenth century when they fled the famines in their home country. They found work as laborers in East Coast cities and later along the growing transportation routes as diggers for the Erie Canal and tracklayers for the emerging railroads across the interior of the nation.

In California, the CPRR turned to Chinese labor when white workers went on strike. It employed ten thousand Chinese laborers who constituted 90 percent of its workforce. The Northern Pacific employed fifteen thousand Chinese railroad construction workers, which was a majority of its workers. The Chinese, many of whom had come during the gold rush in the early 1850s, worked for $31 a month (or about $870 in 2014), which was much less than the white workers earned. Although they were given housing—usually in old boxcars—they had to pay for their meals from their wages. The work was difficult for these laborers who dug and dynamited the tunnels that went through the Sierra Nevada. Some men hung from baskets as they bored holes into the side of a mountain, stuffed nitroglycerin in the holes, and lit the fuse after which they were quickly whisked upward. Chinese laborers struck to protest low pay and dangerous conditions, but they were in the middle of nowhere and the company reduced their rations, and so the strike ended quickly.

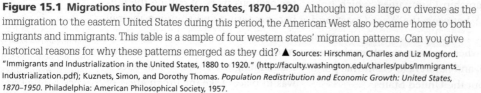

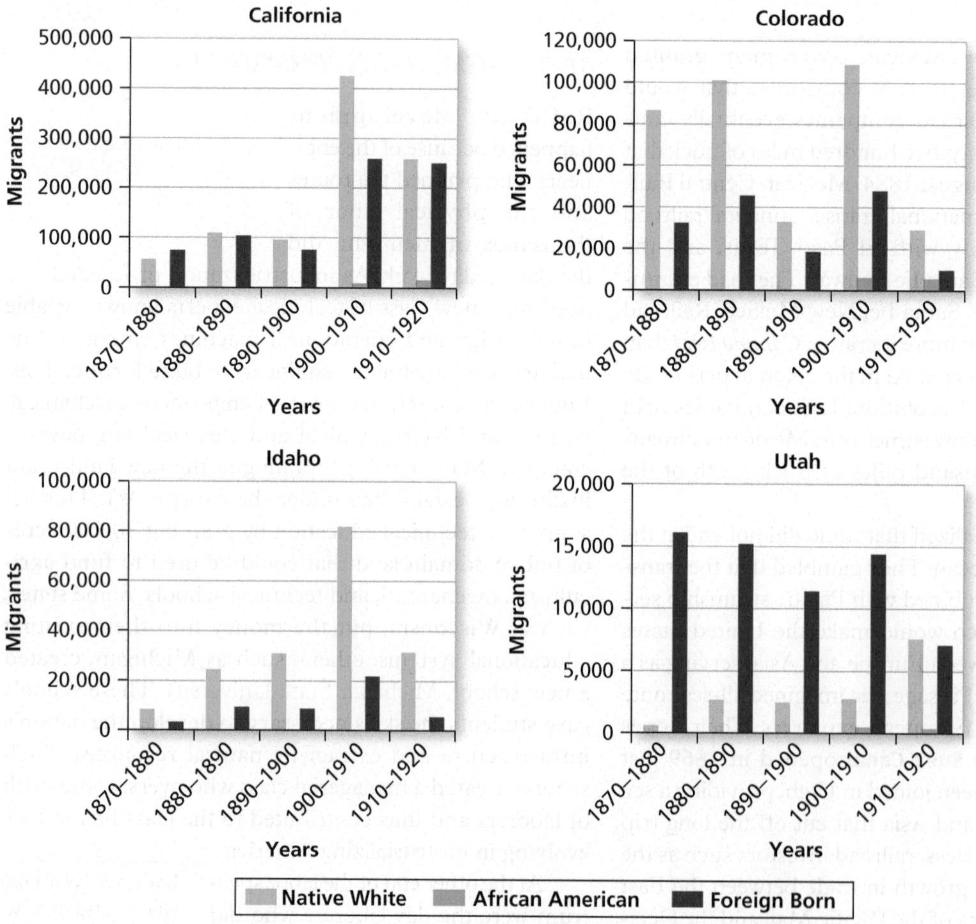

Figure 15.1 Migrations into Four Western States, 1870–1920 Although not as large or diverse as the immigration to the eastern United States during this period, the American West also became home to both migrants and immigrants. This table is a sample of four western states' migration patterns. Can you give historical reasons for why these patterns emerged as they did? ▲ Sources: Hirschman, Charles and Liz Mogford. "Immigrants and Industrialization in the United States, 1880 to 1920." (http://faculty.washington.edu/charles/pubs/Immigrants_Industrialization.pdf); Kuznets, Simon, and Dorothy Thomas. *Population Redistribution and Economic Growth: United States, 1870–1950*. Philadelphia: American Philosophical Society, 1957.

Topham/The Image Works

Chinese Workers on the Union Pacific Railroad, circa 1869 Regardless of race or ethnicity, life as a railway worker was difficult, low paying, and dangerous. Workers had to follow the track as they were laying it. They lived in makeshift shacks or abandoned railway cars and cooked meals over an open fire. Some brought their families, but most were single men who hoped to make enough money before returning home to settle down. ◀

Throughout the latter decades of the nineteenth century, railroads continued to employ both Chinese and Irish workers, while Mexicans began to make up a larger proportion of the railroad workforce. Because of the massive U.S. investment and development in Mexico, its economy began to shift from a subsistence to an export-driven market. The creation of the railroads that connected the two nations also made migration easier. Mexican men began leaving their homes in rural communities and moving to Mexico's urban centers, which were becoming overcrowded and could not provide enough work for all. Consequently, Mexican workers kept moving north along the railroad until they crossed the border, which had few barriers, and found work. Eventually families followed. Many settled in the emerging urban areas such as El Paso, Los Angeles, and Albuquerque. Some moved along with the railroad expansion, living in old boxcars that were pulled along behind the advancing track lines.

The railroad transformed the U.S. economy by drawing settlers and workers into the West. Many of these newcomers were Americans in search of economic opportunity. Many were foreign-born immigrants from all over the world, mostly from Asia, Mexico, and southern Europe, who hoped to start a new life. The railroad transformed U.S. trading relations with foreign countries such as Mexico, Canada, and Asia. The railroad was often the first step in drawing these markets and people into the U.S. orbit.

15-2

A Strong Federal Role

Daniel Freeman's Homestead certificate for one hundred and sixty acres of the U.S. public domain was issued January 20, 1868. Such certificates were the means by which the U.S. government distributed public domain land to heads of households.

What does this document suggest about the authority of the federal government to transfer land and organize society? Who benefited and who did not? ▶

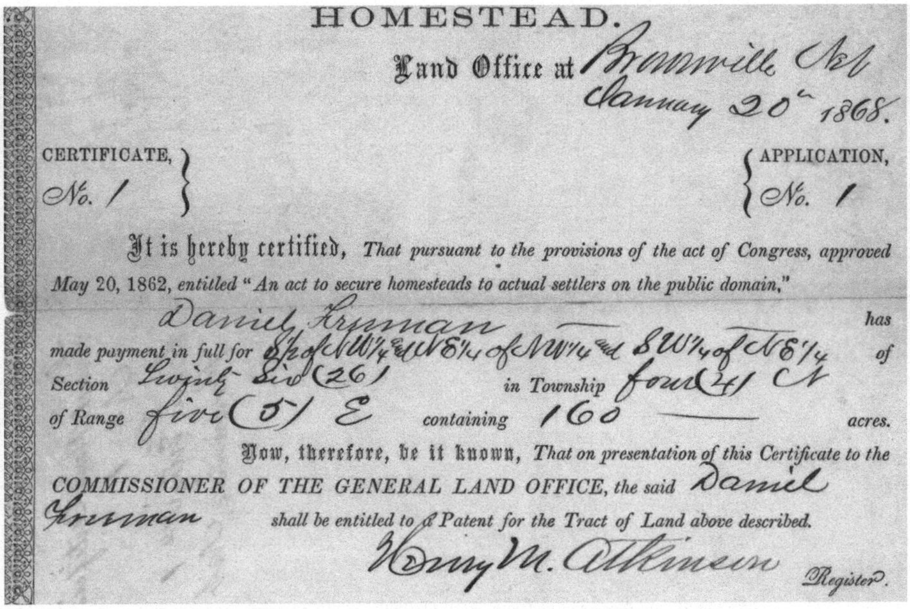

HOMESTEAD.

Land Office at Brownville Neb
January 20th 1868.

CERTIFICATE, No. 1

APPLICATION, No. 1

It is hereby certified, *That pursuant to the provisions of the act of Congress, approved May 20, 1862, entitled "An act to secure homesteads to actual settlers on the public domain,"* Daniel Freeman has *made payment in full for* S½ of NW¼ & NE¼ of NW¼ and SW¼ of NE¼ of *Section* twenty six (26) *in Township* four (4) N *of Range* five (5) E *containing* 160 *acres.*

Now, therefore, be it known, *That on presentation of this Certificate to the COMMISSIONER OF THE GENERAL LAND OFFICE, the said* Daniel Freeman *shall be entitled to a Patent for the Tract of Land above described.*

Henry M. Atkinson *Register.*

National Archives and Records Administration

U.S. Geological Survey (USGS) Federal agency created from the earlier General Survey to explore the West so that its lands could be developed for industrial and other uses.

Homestead Act Congressional act that provided citizens and immigrants 160 acres of free land.

Timber Culture Act Congressional act allowing homesteaders to acquire another one hundred sixty acres, in addition to land obtained from the Homestead Act, if they planted one-quarter of the new parcel with trees.

In addition to the Pacific Railway Acts and the Morrill Act, the Civil War Congresses also promoted the development of the West through a program of land distribution that attracted rapid settlement. Later legislation advanced the development of timber and mining resources. As federal troops left the South after the war, the military turned its attention to the West and reacting to the increasing conflicts between Indians and settlers. For the first time, the federal government was able to exert a consistent influence over the region. On the nonmilitary side, the federal government sent scientists through the **U.S. Geological Survey (USGS)**, founded in 1879, to map the West's natural resources. This information helped settlers, speculators, and developers to transform the West's economy, which provided the raw resources for the nation's continued economic development. Finally, the federal government politically incorporated the areas in and peoples of the West.

☞ As you read, consider how the federal government extended its power across the American West.

15-2a Land Distribution

The federal government passes a variety of laws to distribute western lands.

Since the 1830s, the federal government had been distributing public domain land, all of it taken from Native Americans, to U.S. citizens and immigrants. The Free-Soil Party and later, in the 1850s, the new Republican Party promoted this distribution. In 1862, under the **Homestead Act**, anyone—a citizen or someone intending to become a citizen—who was twenty-one years old and head of a family could file for a quarter section (one hundred sixty acres) of land (see Table 15.1). Women who were heads of households or were single could file a claim. If the person lived on the land for five years and improved it by building a house, digging a well, plowing ten acres, and fencing at least part of it, the land was his or hers to keep for free. Those who wanted to own their land sooner could pay $1.25 an acre and forgo these requirements. This process of acquiring free or cheap land by settling on it and improving it was known as *homesteading*. Between 1870 and 1930, more than 270 million acres of land (10 percent of the United States) were given out to more than 1 million people who had completed their claims and received their land. In 1873, under the **Timber Culture Act**, people could also file for another one hundred sixty acres if they agreed to cultivate timber.

These acts did not deliberately discriminate. Some Indians and Mexican Americans who had lost land, freedmen, and some women had direct access to the Homestead Act and gained landholdings in the trans-Mississippi West. In 1866, Congress passed the Southern Homestead Act, which gave Southerners, even former members of the Confederate Army, the same rights to homestead land. In 1890, the Morrill Act was extended to include former Confederate states, where it funded state schools for African Americans that provided agricultural and technical education. The act also funded tribal colleges for Native Americans. Nevertheless, although the federal government distributed 250 million acres to the U.S. public, the system had faults. Only about one of every six acres distributed by the Homestead Act went directly into the hands of small farmers.

Table 15.1 Civil War and Reconstruction Legislation Related to the Development of the West

Historians tend to focus on this period as a time when the federal government was preoccupied with reintegrating the U.S. South into the nation. The government simultaneously passed a number of laws and signed two treaties that stimulated the economic development of the West. In addition to the two treaties, the legislation gave land that had formerly belonged to Indians to railroads, state governments, and individuals who created infastructure and businesses.

Date	Legislation	Summary
May 1862	Homestead Act	Allowed immigrants and citizens to claim and eventually own one hundred sixty acres of land
July 1862	First Pacific Railway Act	Authorized selling bonds and granting lands to finance railroad development
July 1862	First Morrill Act	Granted large parcels of land to state governments to raise funds for public higher education
June 1866	Southern Homestead Act	Opened 43 million acres to black and white farmers in former Confederate states
April 1868	Fort Laramie Treaty	Signed by the U.S. government and Lakotas, Dakotas, and Arapahoes to secure small reservations and prohibit further white settlement
May 1872	General Mining Act	Authorized and regulated mining on federally held lands
March 1873	Timber Culture Act	Allowed homesteaders to acquire another one hundred sixty acres if they planted one-quarter of it with trees
May 1875	Reciprocity Treaty with Hawai'i	Free trade agreement with Hawai'i that also ceded land to the United States for a military base

The rest was acquired by land speculators and by railroad companies through the Pacific Railway Acts.

Land development was just one aspect of the federal government's allocation of natural resources to individuals and private corporations. Through the Mining Act of 1872, individuals and corporations could purchase government lands for anywhere between $2.50 and $5.00 per acre to mine for gold, silver, platinum, copper, coal, oil, or uranium. Once the land was purchased, mineral rights could be freely developed without encumbrances. Purchasers did not have to pay royalties to the federal government or the state on any profit they made from the mine.

15-2b Land Surveys

The federal government sponsors surveys to explore and map the West.

The post-Reconstruction period in the West experienced a shift from an age of exploration to an age of surveying and mapping. On May 11, 1869, the day after the final spike was driven for the transcontinental railroad, John Wesley Powell joined the Colorado River Exploratory Expedition, which he was to command. Powell, a scientist and Civil War veteran who had lost most of his right arm at the Battle of Shiloh, was the first Euro-American to explore the Grand Canyon. Although less celebrated than the completion of the transcontinental railroad, the work done by Powell, his expedition, and, later, the USGS transformed the way Americans thought about the West and their use of the nation's natural resources. Under the central organization of the USGS, expeditions led by Powell and others created detailed maps that settlers could use to find the choice parcels of land for farming or ranching.

Powell spent three months floating down the Colorado River, mapping its geology, and noting abandoned buildings and campsites everywhere. Simultaneously, three other surveyors—Clarence King, Ferdinand Hayden, and George Wheeler—also mapped and surveyed portions of the West. Each worked under contracts from private institutions and state governments with some federal funding appropriated by Congress or the Department of War. The days of government-sanctioned but loosely organized expeditions such as those by Lewis and Clark and Zebulon Pike gave way to a much more centralized mapping and cataloging of the West. No longer were such people sent to "discover" the West and its peoples; they were to write reports that detailed rainfall, mineral deposits, soil conditions, and waterways.

Some surveyors, such as Powell, also conducted ethnographic research on Indians, but for the most part government surveys assumed that Indians would disappear as immigrants moved westward. Surveys also were used by European and American speculators who wanted to exploit the West's mineral wealth such as coal, copper, silver, and gold, which had become much more accessible since the completion of the transcontinental railroad. This period also started the federal government's control over the West's natural resources that could be marketed.

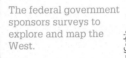

Bettmann/Corbis

Clarence King King, first director of the U.S. Geological Survey, lived among the most elite in New York City but had a double life. In 1887, he met Ada Copeland, a former slave, and fell in love. He told her that his name was James Todd and that he was a Pullman porter. She believed he was African American. They raised five children and lived in a common-law marriage until his death. He never revealed his true identity to her. ◄

Some USGS staff pandered to western congressional delegations and business boosters. For example, Ferdinand Hayden falsely touted the West as a well-watered and fertile place where Americans could settle and thrive. Powell thought differently. What Powell saw on his 1869 expedition convinced him that the West was so arid in comparison to the eastern United States that it could not be settled in the same way. He argued that the Homestead Act and U.S. land policy, based on an assumption that all of North America received as much rainfall as the land east of the Mississippi River, would not work because in most western regions "160 acres could barely support a field mouse." Powell was ignored because neither bureaucrats nor boosters wanted to hear this realistic assessment. Instead, they based both land and development policy on an overly optimistic vision of the West.

15-2c States and Citizens

Statehood evolves slowly in the West.

Before the Civil War, the nation had expanded to the Pacific, but questions regarding statehood and citizenship had been tabled during the war. After the war and despite the process laid out in the Northwest Ordinance of 1787, most of the West's inhabitants endured exceptionally long periods in territorial status. Alaska's lasted ninety-two years. New Mexico and Arizona, with majority Mexican American

polygamy The practice of one man marrying multiple women that Joseph Smith declared in 1831 to be a tenet of the Mormon Church.

Reynolds v. United States U.S. Supreme Court decision that outlawed polygamy because religious belief did not exempt a person from criminal acts.

Edmunds-Tucker Act Legislation that unincorporated the Mormon Church and ended the Perpetual Emigration Fund.

The Manifesto Mormon Church's statement that polygamy was no longer a practice endorsed by the church.

Buffalo Soldiers African American cavalry regiments formed after the Civil War and stationed in the West to assert federal power and fight Indians.

populations, waited for sixty-two years before becoming states in 1912. Oklahoma, which had the largest Indian population, had become a state only five years earlier in 1907. Utah, with its majority Mormon population, waited forty-eight years. These states had populations not considered to be in the mainstream of U.S. society and so languished in the territorial period while Congress debated about how to incorporate them, an issue that would also arise with the Spanish-American War in 1898 (see Chapter 19). The exception was California, which had a similar mixed population but had been granted statehood in 1850.

Because residents of territories did not enjoy full citizenship rights, they were not represented in Congress and could not vote in presidential elections. Their governors were appointed, not elected, and like staffing decisions made in British and Dutch colonial settings, presidential appointments did not always reflect the interests of territorial residents. Governorships might be political plums, although some found them to be political death. General Lew Wallace, for example, was so disappointed at being sent to Santa Fe as governor of New Mexico that he locked himself in his office and focused more on writing the famous novel, *Ben Hur* (1880), than on governance. The consequences of territorial status were not only a lack of representation, about which residents complained bitterly to newspapers and Congress, but also lagging political and economic development.

Utah, largely settled by Mormons, reflected the nation's apprehension about incorporating outsiders. Most Americans regarded the Mormon practice of **polygamy** as immoral and un-Christian, and by the Republican Party as, a "relic" of "barbarism." Brigham Young, the first territorial governor, had married at least twenty women, and other leaders in the Mormon community likewise practiced polygamy. But federal law prohibited bigamy. The U.S. Supreme Court ruled in ***Reynolds v. United States*** (1879) that the First Amendment protected religious belief but not practice. Congress then passed a series of laws restricting the practice of polygamy. The most extensive law, the **Edmunds-Tucker Act** (1887), not only prohibited polygamy but also unincorporated the Mormon Church and the Perpetual Emigration Fund, and dissolved the Mormon militia. As one of the most sweeping pieces of legislation since Reconstruction, the act sought to reorder Mormon society and bring it into the mainstream of U.S. culture.

Known polygamists went into hiding or were arrested and their wives were forced to testify against them. Their considerable assets were frozen, placing individuals, families, and communities in jeopardy. Finally, Wilford Woodruff, the president and a prophet of the Mormon Church, issued **The Manifesto** in 1890, telling his followers that God had revealed to him that U.S. law should be obeyed. With that official recognition of polygamy's illegality, the barriers to statehood for a population that was otherwise prosperous and politically powerful were removed. Utah became a state in 1896. Still, the following year, the federal government sent the **Buffalo Soldiers** to Salt Lake City to ensure that Mormons were obeying the order. As in the Reconstruction South, the U.S. government used its military power to enforce federal law.

Polygamy did not end immediately among Mormon families. It was difficult to unravel such complex social, economic, and emotional relationships. Many polygamous families stayed together because federal authorities were then much less likely to pursue cases following renunciation. Mexico and Canada provided havens for polygamous families who still believed in the covenant. The Mormon

Buffalo Soldiers These all-black federal forces were stationed in the U.S. West and most often dealt with problem populations such as strike breakers, Indians and Mormons. The soldiers were known for their horsemanship, dedication, and loyalty. They aided the federal government in opening territory so that settlement could continue, westward. ▶

Time Life Pictures/Time & Life Pictures/Getty Images

Church purchased more than one hundred thousand acres just across the border in Mexico to settle polygamous families in 1885. Charles Card escaped custody on his charge of practicing polygamy and fled across the Canadian border into Alberta, where he founded the town of Cardston. Until the early twentieth century, polygamy remained a national issue. One Mormon congressman was refused his seat on grounds that he was a polygamist, and Utah senator Reed Smoot came under intense scrutiny before he was seated in 1903.

The long period of territorialism in the West points to the fluid nature of how people thought about their relationship to the federal government and their citizenship. Although Americans who left the eastern United States retained citizenship once they headed into the territories, the extent of their political rights often remained unclear. The lack of a strong federal presence along the national borders complicated the issues of citizenship. As people crossed freely from both Canada and Mexico into the United States, they made communities among themselves, ignoring international boundaries along the **borderlands**. These areas were filled with families, often of mixed ethnicity and race. Mexican border towns such as El Paso, Texas, and San Diego, California, developed an economy and society allowing people to pass freely between the borders to go to school, work, and shop. As a result of this fluidity, people tended to think more about affiliations with their small towns or regions than with their identity as U.S. citizens. In these communities, persons who otherwise were marginalized in the national political scene worked at the local level, electing school boards, mayors, and council members to represent their interests.

borderlands Communities along international borders that have more in common with their neighbors across the border than they do with the majority population of their own nation.

White women found more opportunity in the West and made inroads into political office in the western states, where opposition to suffrage was much lower. In 1869, the Wyoming legislature granted equal and complete suffrage for its thousand female inhabitants, hoping to lure more to the territory. Susanna M. Salter was the first woman ever elected to political office in the United States when she won the election for mayor in Argonia, Kansas, in 1887. And in 1890, when Colorado women won the right to vote, journalist Caroline Nichols Churchill declared that the West "Shall be the Land for Women!" National citizenship and identity were complex issues that remained in flux for the many Americans living on the western edges of the United States.

15-3 Indian Resistance and Resettlement

This photograph was taken on Pine Ridge Reservation in 1890, just after the Wounded Knee Massacre. Note that most of the household items, including the tent, were government-issued to this family.

As you look at the photo, consider what the meaning of home is in the photo? Can you identity items that would have been traditionally used and items that were more modern, and issued by the U.S. government? Can you speculate as to why there is only one adult male in this photo? Who do you think took the photo and why? ▶

The Sioux Reservation at Pine Ridge, South Dakota, c.1890 (b/w photo)/American Photographer, (19th century)/PETER NEWARK'S PICTURES/Private Collection/Bridgeman Images

Go to MindTap® to practice history with the Chapter 15 **Primary Source Writing Activity: Indian Resistance.** Read and view primary sources and respond to a writing prompt.

During the Civil War and into Reconstruction, conflict among Native American groups and violence between Indian and white settlers or U.S. troops disrupted life on the Great Plains. By the mid-1870s, violence had escalated as settlers pushed west and Indians competed for dwindling land and natural resources. In an effort to protect the western immigrants, the Department of War established a system of forts and increased military presence along the trails. These forts provided protection for travelers and created trading opportunities for those settlers eager to supply the troops. Even with this new effort to secure the trails, however, the U.S. military simply did not have enough personnel to cover all of the trouble spots in the West. By 1887, as a result of escalating violence, the federal government passed laws meant to move all Indians onto reservations and educate them in the ways of sedentary farming. Indians both resisted and accommodated the new regime, which lasted well into the twentieth century.

☞ As you read, reflect on the late nineteenth century as a turning point for Native Americans as they adjusted to westward expansion, industrialization, and technological developments. What forms did their adjustments take?

15-3a Settlement, Indians, and Bison

Migrants to the West confront and displace American Indians and bison.

Violence escalated dramatically after the close of the Civil War all across the West as newcomers to the region put everyone in competition for land and resources. After the Sand Creek Massacre, violence on the Plains grew to such an extent that most U.S. troops felt they were penned inside the forts without enough soldiers to suppress the various Plains groups. When a young lieutenant, William Fetterman, ignored the orders from his superiors not to go beyond the boundaries of Fort Phil Kearny in Dakota Territory in 1866, he was ambushed by a group of Cheyennes, Arapahoes, and Sioux, who were waging Red Cloud's War against the U.S. troops. These Plains Indians had allied to keep settlers and the U.S. cavalry out of the Powder River Valley in Wyoming. Fetterman and his eighty-one men were entirely wiped out. The ambush made it clear to the U.S. public and the federal government that Indian warfare had to be dealt with forcefully by an increased military presence.

In 1868, President Grant ran for reelection using the slogan, "Let Us Have Peace," which referred to both the South's Reconstruction and hostilities with Indians in the West. **Grant's Peace Policy** between 1868 and 1876 encouraged making treaties in an effort to bring Native Americans under U.S. control. By the late nineteenth century, the U.S. government realized that it could no longer just move Indians to places farther West but had to confine them on small parcels of land called *reservations*. The Grant Administration signed the **Treaty of Fort Laramie of 1868** with Lakotas, Dakotas, and Arapahoes, ending Red Cloud's War, promising to give Lakotas the entirety of the Black Hills, which was only a small part of their reservation, and closing it to white settlement. Under the Grant Peace Policy, reservations were run by religious organizations, particularly Quakers, who were supposed to help Indians incorporate into U.S. society. The federal government promised an ideal form of reservation life: private property, education, and the tools necessary to move from a hunting society to a settled (and supposedly) prosperous agricultural life that would conform to a Jeffersonian ideal of farming. But by the late 1870s, violence perpetuated by whites in tandem with inadequate supplies from the federal government and poor governance meant that the Peace Policy was a failure.

Grant's Peace Policy Set of policies initiated by a group of reformers who persuaded the federal government to take a more benevolent approach toward Indians.

Treaty of Fort Laramie of 1868 Treaty between the United States and the Lakotas (among others) who agreed to move onto a reservation in the Black Hills but that white settlers violated.

accommodation A political and cultural stance in which a group agrees to blend in with the dominant society rather than resist it.

The U.S. military moved Indians onto reservations while simultaneously depleting their most important resource—bison. There has been much historical debate about how the near extinction of the bison happened in such a short period of time. To some extent, Indians themselves were partially responsible for the depletion as they became entwined in the developing market economy that placed a premium price on bison hides and tongues and consequently put pressure on the ecosystem and bison survival. Native groups competed with one another for the best hunting grounds and for access to the American and European traders who set up posts and forts in strategic locations.

White western migrants also helped decimate bison herds by overhunting them for the market and for sport. Buffalo hunters sought to exploit the abundant resource by indiscriminately killing vast herds, skinning them where they dropped, carrying off the hides and tongues, and leaving the open Plains littered with decaying waste. Finally, the western army realized that the main reason that Indians stayed on the Plains and away from the forts and reservations was that they could sustain themselves on their traditional economy that relied on bison. Therefore, the U.S. government sought to destroy the remaining bison to force Indians off the Plains and onto reservations where they could not hunt and would have to subsist on government rations. All these factors combined to create a desolate environment where few bison survived and Indians' options dwindled as the U.S. government's actions forced them to raid white settlements or move to the reservations.

15-3b Indian Wars

Indian removal takes on its most violent phase in the late nineteenth century.

While the federal government advanced a policy of containment and removal, Native Americans imagined a different future for themselves. Even as new migrants pushed into their territories, many Native Americans thought it possible to live next to settlers as long as each side would leave the other alone and respect the other's rights. But as it became clear that settlers would never coexist with Indians, two factions arose within Indian communities, each side using different strategies to survive the onslaught. **Accommodationists** were leaders such Black Kettle who willingly cooperated with whites and lead their people into reservations or forts where they would be under the watchful eye of the U.S. government.

On the other side were those, like the Dog Soldiers, who refused to be brought into the reservation system and fought all efforts by the U.S. military to subdue them (see Map 15.2). Until the late 1870s, Indians had significant success in resisting U.S. policies and pushing back the military. The greatest defeat of U.S. forces came against General George Armstrong Custer and the Seventh Cavalry. Custer was part of a larger military force that had been sent to the Black Hills of South Dakota to take the area for U.S. settlement in violation of the 1868 Treaty of Fort Laramie. Miners had been rushing into the area after gold was discovered. Boomtowns such as Deadwood required military protection if they were to survive.

Custer and his commanders set out to attack the encampment along the Greasy Grass River, which held the Sioux as well as their Cheyenne and Arapahoe allies. The U.S. military underestimated the size of the group encamped and attacked headlong into the middle of the camp, which held more than 3,000 people, including many survivors from Sand Creek. Custer ignored directions to wait until he had support from Major Marcus Reno and sent his men into the heart of the camp to engage them on the **Little Bighorn River**. The fight lasted "no longer than it takes a hungry man to eat his lunch." and when it was over, not one of Custer's 268 men survived. Ironically, news of the Seventh Cavalry's complete defeat reached the east coast around July 4, 1876, just as the nation was celebrating the 100th anniversary of the signing of the Declaration of Independence. While Americans celebrated the birth of their republic, its future and security were not yet entirely certain.

Little Bighorn River Location in present-day Montana where Custer and his men were defeated by a coalition of Plains Indians.

After the defeat of Custer, the U.S. military launched an all-out effort to secure the West for settlement and mineral extraction by sending in thousands of troops. Two of the three leaders of the Lakotas (Sitting Bull and Gall) who had defeated Custer and his men retreated across the border to Canada to avoid pursuit by an enraged U.S. Cavalry. Crazy Horse, however, stayed in the area around the Little Big Horn and battled General Nelson Miles, who pursued Crazy Horse's forces throughout the winter. The constant military harassment as well as the dwindling bison population eventually forced Crazy Horse's group to surrender in May 1877. Gall stayed out until January 1881, when he brought his group into the Poplar River agency to surrender. Sitting Bull lived in Canada and rebuffed offers by the U.S. government to surrender until July 1881, when he finally agreed to come into the reservation at Standing Rock.

Map 15.2 Selected U.S.– Indian Battles, 1860–1890 Violent conflicts on the Great Plains were a constant background as Euro-American settlers pushed onto Indian lands and displaced families. After the Civil War, U.S. policy makers realized that Indians could no longer be pushed west and forcibly contained them on reservations. However, by 1887 with the passage of the Dawes Act, these reservations were further reduced by allotment. Violence, as depicted in this map, was then replaced with policy and law in an effort to further contain Indians. ▼

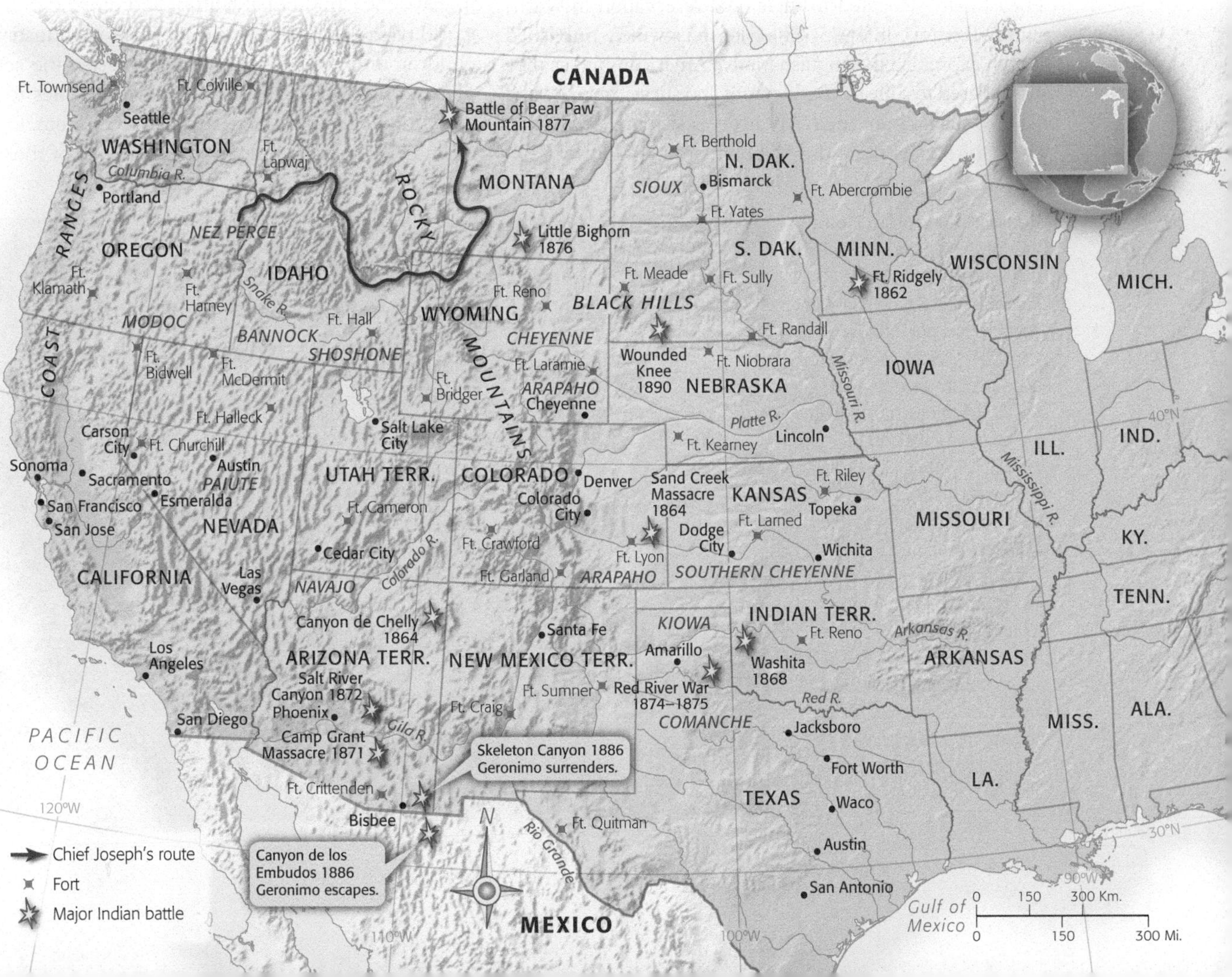

General Allotment Act, or Dawes Act Congressional act that allotted land, provided a path to U.S. citizenship, and set up schools for Native Americans.

The Sioux were not the only group who resisted placement on reservations. The borders between the United States with Canada and Mexico became important barriers and protections for those fleeing the U.S. military. Both Mexicans and Americans were pushing Apaches from their lands along the border between Sonora and Arizona. The Apaches constantly fought to maintain their land and to keep their families safe. After the Civil War, violence escalated as the U.S. military sought to quell border violence, and capturing or killing Geronimo became their main goal. Between 1858 and 1886, Geronimo and his group evaded the cavalry and became notorious nationwide for their attacks on both sides of the border. Slowly and steadily, both the Mexican and U.S. militaries, including the Buffalo Soldiers, pressured Geronimo's followers into increasingly smaller territory where they were barely able to survive. He surrendered at Skeleton Canyon, Arizona, in September 1886. Until his death in 1909, he was a prisoner of war held on various military installations.

In eastern Oregon, Chief Joseph (Hin-mah-too-yah-lat-kekt) led his group of Nez Perce along a 1,170-mile trek in an attempt to escape U.S. troops in 1877. For more than three months, seven hundred fifty Nez Perce moved across the Pacific Northwest and the upper West before the Cavalry captured them. The group was taken to Fort Leavenworth, Kansas, and then to a reservation in Indian Territory. They finally relocated to their own reservation in Washington Territory in 1885. Chief Joseph's widely published speech expressed the anguish Native Americans felt as they surrendered to a life of confinement and surveillance: "Hear me, my chiefs! I am tired. My heart is sick and sad. From where the sun now stands I will fight no more forever."

15-3c Dawes Act and Indian Resistance

An allotment program aims to assimilate Indians and make reservations obsolete.

Passed in 1887, the **General Allotment, or Dawes Act**, was the culmination of governmental policies that had been enacted after the failure of Grant's Peace Policy as a response to the brutality of the Indian Wars. As part of a moral reform movement that found its origins in abolitionism and in Reconstruction, a group of northeastern Republican reformers pushed for a government-sponsored project that would assimilate Indians into mainstream society, economy, and culture. These Republicans viewed reservations as obsolete and as barriers to Indians' progress and urged the federal government to break them up into individual plots of private property.

One of the most forceful reformers, Captain Richard Pratt, called for Indian children to be taken from their families and placed in boarding schools where they would be educated in the U.S. tradition. In 1879, Pratt began opening schools such as the Carlisle Industrial Training School in Pennsylvania—which borrowed ideas from Reconstruction schools for newly freed blacks such as Hampton Institute and the training programs developed by Booker T. Washington at Tuskegee Institute. Pratt believed his educational institutions would prepare Indian children to leave their traditional culture and move into a modern world where they could farm or work in industry. Indian children and their families, however, saw the schools as places where their culture, language, and ties to kin and community networks were stripped from them. Pratt's idealism never matched the lived experience of those Indian

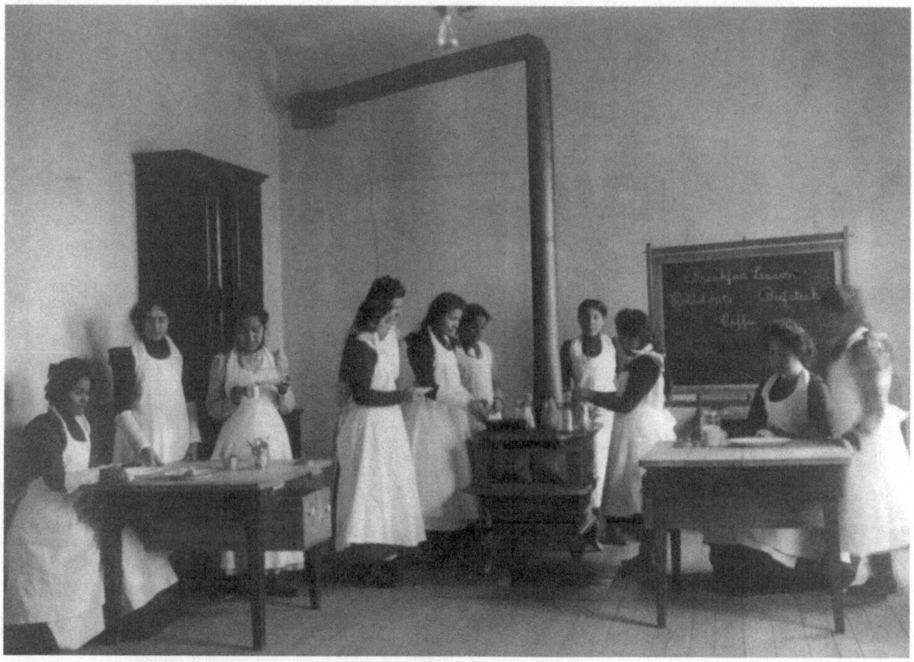

Breakfast Lesson in Home Economics Class, Carlisle Indian School, 1901 At Carlisle Indian School, Captain Richard Pratt put into practice his motto, "Kill the Indian, and save the man" or, as in the case of the photo, the woman. These schools were intent on "civilizing" Indian children, which first meant removing them from their families and homes and sending them to boarding schools such as this one. The curriculum forced isolated children to abandon their native language, foods, and customs and then adopt what Pratt believed to be the modern and progressive way of Euro-Americans. ▶

Johnston, Frances Benjamin, 1864–1952, photographer

The Granger Collection, New York

Global Americans **Wovoka** was a member of the Northern Paiutes born around 1856 in Smith Valley, Nevada, in what was then Utah territory. While growing up, he worked for a white couple, David and Abigail Wilson. When dealing with whites, Wovoka often used the name Jack Wilson and later in life used it exclusively. The Wilsons were devout Christians who taught Wovoka various Bible passages and infused him with Christian theology. He was also exposed to Mormon theology as that group was migrating into and setting up communities near him. On January 1, 1889, during a solar eclipse, Wovoka had a vision from which he later prophesized three events: all whites would leave the U.S. West, allowing Indians to live in peace and prosperity; the bison, which were disappearing, would reappear as would the Indian dead; and Indians would be protected from bullets fired by whites. For this to happen, Wovoka said, believers had to perform the Ghost Dance and live righteous lives. He explicitly linked the prophecy with salvation for believers. Wovoka's prophecy mirrored other millenarian movements of the time such as Mormonism and Christian evangelicalism. His teachings spread throughout the North American West. In Saskatchewan, among Canadian Sioux who were refugees from the 1882 Dakota War, it became the New Tidings Congregation. Others, such as Lakotas, sent representatives via train to visit and learn from Wovoka. They then returned to their homelands, sometimes on reservations, where they spread Wovoka's message of salvation and spiritual renewal and taught the Ghost Dance. Until the massacre at Wounded Knee abruptly ended the movement, it was part of a broader religious awakening across North America.

children who were sent to his schools. A similarly tragic story played out in Canada, Australia, and New Zealand, where white governments established modified versions of U.S. Indian boarding schools to forcibly assimilate native peoples.

Passage of the Dawes Act came at the same moment that the last of the Reconstruction reforms in the South were receding in the face of virulent racism. The act had three broad provisions. First, it decreed that the remaining acres within the reservations would be allotted to Indian families in a system that duplicated that of the Homestead Act, forcing them to give up their communal reservation lands and become sedentary farmers. Once Native American families had chosen their land plots, the rest of the reservation land would be open to white settlement and sold at market rates. In theory, the monies generated from these land sales would be used for farming tools, seeds, and education to help Indians make the transition to farmers. The act's second policy provided more funding for expanding the educational system that Pratt had begun a decade earlier. Finally, it established a clear path to citizenship, promising it to those Indians who agreed to have land allotted to them and work toward becoming assimilated into U.S. culture. However, citizenship was not granted to Native Americans until 1924.

Although there was some opposition to the Dawes Act among Congress and Americans, most wanted to embrace a program that would assimilate and acculturate Indians into the U.S. mainstream. On the other hand, Native Americans were not entirely willing to embrace this new set of policies that stripped them of their land base, economy, culture, and, in many cases, their children. Most Indians accepted the act's terms and suffered terribly as a result. However, a few groups, notably Navajos and Senecas, resisted the Dawes Act. In 1881, Indian reservation lands totaled some 155 million acres; by 1900, as a result of allotment, the figure had fallen to 78 million acres. Allotment remained U.S. policy until 1934 when Indians had lost 60 percent of their reservation lands.

The most dramatic reaction to the Dawes Act and the power of the federal government came in the form of a religious movement, the **Ghost Dance**. In 1889, Wovoka, a Paiute leader, revived a religious movement that had long been a part of Native American culture. He preached that if his followers performed the Ghost Dance, the depredations they had suffered would turn into triumphs. This message was a powerful and hopeful antidote to the reality of Native Americans' day-to-day experience of privation and hunger on the reservation. The Ghost Dance swept across the U.S. West as Indian leaders traveled to see Wovoka and then returned to their reservations to teach the dance and its meaning to followers. U.S. officials, who believed it to be a war ceremony, viewed the Ghost Dance with unease. They speculated that Indians would rise up against the army and Indian agents policing the reservations.

In December 1890, an inexperienced Indian agent at the Pine Ridge Reservation feared that the Ghost Dancers were turning violent as they repeatedly performed the ritual. Tensions came to a crisis point when the reservation's residents found out that Sitting Bull had been killed during his arrest at nearby Standing Rock Reservation. Indian agents there were convinced that Sitting Bull had been encouraging the Ghost Dance and other forms of resistance. When another leader, Big Foot, brought his band from the Cheyenne River Reservation toward Pine Ridge, the Seventh Cavalry (formerly Custer's

Ghost Dance Native American religious movement that preached salvation for believers who were morally upright and practiced the dance.

Wounded Knee Tragic event in which the Seventh Cavalry gunned down Indian families at the Pine Ridge Reservation.

Indian Question "Question" that concerned how best to deal with Indians and their place in U.S. society.

unit) stopped them near Wounded Knee Creek. On the morning of December 29, the unit's commander ordered Big Foot's band to surrender. When a shot rang out, the cavalry unleashed its full force and fired indiscriminately into the camp, gunning down 146 Sioux, including forty-five women and eighteen children. Other deaths were accounted for later, bringing the Sioux death toll to more than 250. The officers were later disciplined, and there was some public outcry about the massacre of subdued Indians and innocent women and children. **Wounded Knee** has come to symbolize the tragedy and brutality of U.S. Indian policy.

By the end of the nineteenth century, laws and military action contained Native Americans and brought them under the tutelage of reformers and the U.S. government, leaving them very little physical space or legal room to maneuver and create self-sustaining lives. Answers to the **Indian Question** changed as reformers worried—not if Indians could survive in the twentieth century but what their roles would be as integrated U.S. citizens. Indians in the twentieth century moved their resistance to U.S. courtrooms and, public arenas where Indians and their advocates would push for fair treatment and equal rights.

15-4 Development of the West as a Market

Lake County Museum/Curt Teich Postcard Archives/Getty Images

Postcard of the Chicago Union Stockyards, 1910 Here immigrant laborers processed unfathomable numbers of animals so that every last piece of an animal could be made into an edible product, from steaks, to hot dogs, to dog food. The leftovers were used to make gelatin, leather, and other by-products. One observer noted, "From the snout to the tail—everything but the squeal."

Notice the relationship between the city, the railcars, and the animals. Describe the journey that these animals took from the Great Plains to this stockyard. How did the railroad connect the city and countryside? ▶

Even before the Indian Question was settled, Americans saw the West as a place that they could safely invest in and develop. The completion of the transcontinental railroad as well as the development of the smaller intertwined rail systems created new markets. The new economic opportunities lured farmers, ranchers, and miners west. Through the end of the nineteenth century, people pushed into the Midwest and West by the thousands, but unlike pre-Civil War migrants, they came by train, not by horseback, pushcart, or covered wagon. Through their labor, these people continued the development of the West by selling their goods in global markets. Their crops, animal products, and minerals could be exported by rail to the east, for consumption or to export to Europe, across the border into Mexico, and to the Pacific Coast for trade with China, where demand for U.S. agricultural products had increased dramatically. Farmers populated the Great Plains and began planting cash crops. Cattlemen moved north and onto the recently opened ranges on the Plains. By the end of the century, Americans looked beyond the boundaries of the continental United States to exploit the trade opportunities in Hawai'i and Alaska.

☞ As you read, identify the commodities and markets that emerged in the West. How were they tied to the industrialization of the eastern United States?

15-4a Commercial Agriculture

Farmers use emerging technologies to expand large-scale agriculture.

Once the nation realized the limitations, if not the failures, of Reconstruction, many Americans looked west for the potential to rebuild their lives with more promising opportunities. Union soldiers who took pay in land scrip were allowed to homestead under fewer restrictions than those that applied to other homesteaders. After 1866, southern farmers and former Confederate soldiers were allowed to take homesteads, and many left war-torn southern landscapes and the unstable labor conditions.

Former slaves with no land and few resources were also eager to leave the South, especially because Ku Klux

Klan violence threatened their lives and the return of white supremacy closed economic opportunity. Under the leadership of men such as Benjamin "Pap" Singleton, thousands of African Americans—by 1881 about fifty thousand—moved west, primarily to Kansas, to become farmers. Called **exodusters**, they packed what little they had and walked to the Mississippi River, where they caught steamboats going upriver toward Kansas. There they built new communities, mostly separated from white settlers. All-black towns such as Nicodemus, Kansas, had their own schools, markets, and churches. Although such communities never provided a huge haven for former slaves, the West and independent farming did offer an alternative to sharecropping. For people of varied backgrounds, the West held promise and hope.

Immigrants from around the world made their way to the Midwest to farm and create homes for their families. Railroads set up emigration offices in Scandinavian and German cities to entice successful farmers, who they believed would be potential clients. These immigrants, along with Bohemians, populated the upper Midwest as they fled economic downturns, landlessness, and political instability in their home countries. They built **sod homes** since there was no hard wood left on the Great Plains. Families tolerated these dark dwellings, which rarely had windows, but which kept them protected from both the harsh winters and summers.

With railroads, farmer's business methods became entwined in the global economy and relied on corporations to transport and market their goods. Corn and wheat could be stored, graded, and shipped from **grain elevators**. Grain was loaded and unloaded by steam power onto railroad cars and steamships. The grading system allowed for a futures market in agricultural products to develop into a commodities exchange centered in Chicago. Innovations in irrigation, windmill technology, and drought-resistant seeds transformed U.S. agriculture from primarily a local affair of trade and consumption and trade to a burgeoning national and international market.

Perhaps even more transformative than railroads and grain elevators was the mechanical **combine** that not only cut wheat but also raked it and bound it into bales. Benjamin Holt made improvements on Cyrus McCormick's earlier reaper, and both men launched the machines into mass production in the 1870s. With a combine, the time it took to harvest an acre of wheat dropped from sixty-one hours in the 1840s to just under three hours by 1890. When Holt and McCormick saturated the U.S. market, including New England and the South—which were the last places to adopt the combine—their companies began promoting combine sales to overseas markets such as China, Africa, and the Caribbean.

Despite geography, experience, and John Wesley Powell's dire warning about western aridity, farmers put as many fields into wheat and other grains as possible to meet expanding market demands. They ignored the twenty-year drought cycle on the Great Plains and instead followed the old adage that "rain follows the plow." Moreover, boosters aided by railroads, grain elevators, and the combine, encouraged farmers to invest in mechanized equipment even if it meant going into debt in order to survive in the competitive market economy.

15-4b Expanding the Cattle Range

Technologies and global capital expand ranching and exterminate the bison.

The development of ranching in the trans-Mississippi West also depended on the railroad, expanding markets, and technological innovations. Patented in 1867, barbed wire allowed ranchers to fence large tracts of land. Prior to the late nineteenth century, cattlemen and families let their animals run freely across the open range. People branded their animals to signify which ones belonged to them. Each year, roundups sorted cattle by owner after which they were taken to market. Barbed wire also allowed farmers to enclose their own agricultural lands and protect them from animals that might destroy the crops. This relatively inexpensive fencing solved many problems and helped grow the market, but it also exacerbated conflicts between competing ranchers who quickly, and often illegally, tried to enclose land. These **range wars** led to violence, property destruction, and sometimes death, as in the case of the 1892 Johnson County War in Wyoming. The violence was so intense that President William Henry Harrison called in the Ninth Regiment of Buffalo Soldiers to keep the peace, and it remained as an occupying force for a year.

Prior to the railroad, cattle and pigs—key sources of protein—were driven "on the hoof" short distances to the local butcher. Chances were that the cow or pig that a town dweller saw alive by the side of the road was the "dressed" meat he or she would buy from the local butcher next week. People were intimately acquainted with the food they ate. With the advent of railroads, however, cattle that had been grazing on the open range were rounded up, branded, and then driven hundreds of miles to "cow towns" such as Dodge City, Kansas, or Fort Worth, Texas. These towns were known for their stockyards where animals were rested, fed, and watered before they were loaded and shipped by railroad to places such as Chicago. There, the live animals were slaughtered and butchered for mass consumption.

exodusters Groups of African Americans who migrated from the U.S. South to the Midwest looking to start farms.

sod homes Solid and warm, but damp, houses built by stacking squares cut from prairie grass, which had a deep root structure.

grain elevators Technological innovation that allowed grain to be deposited into a silo without bagging and where it was graded, mixed, and sold in large lots.

combine Machine that combined reaping and binding wheat into one machine, saving time in the harvesting process.

range wars Confrontation between ranchers over the use of private property and government lands to graze cattle.

History without Borders

Wheat

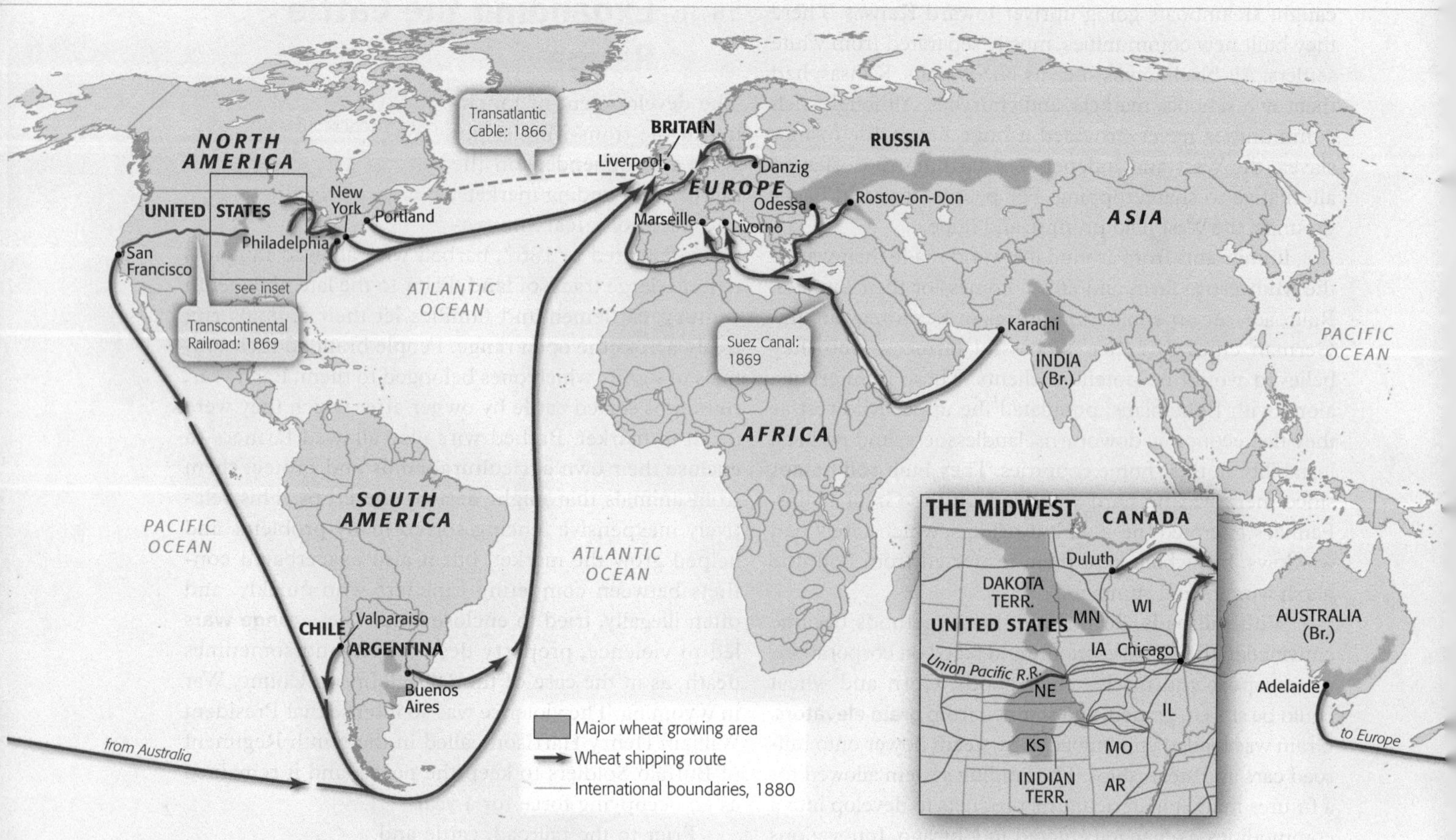

Cultivation and Distribution of Wheat around the World Grains such as wheat developed into commodities that pulled the world closer together through trade and migration. The regions indicated on the map indicate the "bread baskets" that provided food to large portions of the globe's population. The availability of commercially grown and traded grains helped bolster the world's population. Immigrants brought seed varietals to their new homes, which helped develop new areas such as the Bonanza wheat farms in the upper Midwest of the United States.

Wheat, like all food commodities, weaves the globe together through trade, immigration, and technology transfer. Wheat production began around 8000 BCE in an area of the Middle East called the *Fertile Crescent*. It spread north to Europe and west to China and was introduced into North America during the Columbian Exchange. Cultivation of the grain began in the middle colonies of British North America. As settlers pushed west across the Appalachian Mountains, they took their cultivation techniques with them. Most of the grain they grew was for the local market, but after the development of road and canal systems during the early nineteenth century, for various other parts of the nation.

Technological innovations transformed the market for wheat. The invention of the reaper and later the combine, which "combined" cutting the wheat and removing its kernels, dramatically reduced the number of person hours needed to grow and harvest a bushel of the grain. Its market expanded with the invention of grain elevators, which allowed wheat to flow freely rather than be bagged and to be graded by quality. Finally, the expansion of rail and steamship networks allowed the grain to travel all over the nation and to be put on boats to Europe, Russia, and China, which became the largest customers for it. When the Chicago Board of Trade allowed contracts of "futures" to be bought and sold in 1864, a full-fledged commodity trading in wheat opened to national and global markets. By 1900, the United States produced 25 percent of the world's wheat and was being called the global "bread basket."

Hulton Archive/Getty Images

McCormick Machines Are the Best in the World, 1901 Advertisements like this one appeared in magazines all over the world and in dozens of languages. Note how it uses the image of an attractive woman to draw the reader's attention and then shows the practical uses in the smaller images. Other companies such as Kellogg's and Karo Syrup also used foreign language advertisements to increase their market share and to entice foreigners to purchase American foodstsuffs such as cereal and corn syrup. ▲

Detroit Publishing Co., publisher

Grain Elevator in Buffalo, New York, 1900 This grain elevator was located in a central location on the border between the United States and Canada, where steamships could easily load and unload grains for shipment to regional and global markets. Technological innovations, such as the grain elevator, combine, and railroad, in conjunction with marketing and the rise of business practice efficiencies, made the United States the largest exporter of grain at the turn of the century. ▲

bonanza farms Large acreage farm that used labor, mechanization, and hybrid seeds to produce huge yields for a global market.

Because wheat was farmed across the world, U.S. wheat exports had global effects. In Italy, cheap U.S. wheat undersold local farmers, prompting unemployed peasants to migrate to the Americas. Immigrant farmers from northern Europe brought different growing methods and seeds to the United States. Some were hybrids that had been cross-bred to thrive in colder climates, which was perfect for the upper Midwest. These immigrants created the **bonanza farms** (large acreage farms that used labor and mechanization to produce huge yields) in the Red River Valley. They fueled the production and export of wheat from the end of the nineteenth century through World War I. Flour producers, such as General Mills, distributed cookbooks in different languages, particularly Chinese, to stimulate demand for wheat, flour, and other wheat-based products in foreign countries.

New technologies associated with the Green Revolution in the late twentieth century ensured that global wheat production kept pace with that of rice and corn, although corn surpassed it around the beginning of the twenty-first century. Wheat has the highest protein content of any vegetable-based grain, still making it one of the most demanded food products around the world.

Critical Thinking Questions

▶ What made the North American landscape viable for wheat growing and exportation?

▶ What social, economic, and political forces helped develop the wheat market?

Goodnight-Loving Trail Path used by cattle drives from Texas to move the animals to markets in the upper Midwest where they could be placed in railroad cars.

vaqueros Herdsman or cowboy in North America and term from which *buckaroo* is derived.

At its peak production, the Union Stockyard could process twenty-one thousand cattle, seventy-five thousand pigs, twenty-two thousand sheep, and two hundred horses daily. With the advent of refrigerated cars (filled with ice cut from the Great Lakes), the animal flesh could be transported from Chicago to major cities as dressed meat, which urban consumers could purchase at the local butcher or corner store. By the end of the nineteenth century, most city dwellers had no idea where their meat originated. The railroads and the production of animal flesh had severed peoples' connection to food and nature.

Cowboys who worked the range and drove the cattle to the railroads came from a variety of ethnic backgrounds. Many had some sense that their work was tied to these larger markets. Most cowboys worked for large organizations run by men such as Charles Goodnight, who, with Oliver Loving, first opened the cattle market by driving thousands of cattle from Texas north to New Mexico and west to California, establishing the **Goodnight-Loving Trail** in the 1860s (see Map 15.3). Cowboys were a diverse group of workers who reflected the immigrant culture of the West. Many were ***vaqueros*** from Mexico where the cowboy culture originated, Indians who had left the reservations, and African Americans such as Nat Love.

Foreign businessmen from Scotland, England, and the Netherlands owned many of the large cattle ranching outfits. They found owning a cattle operation in the U.S. West to be a romantic adventure (see Figure 15.2). No doubt they wanted to make money, but few of these enterprises were very profitable. Ranching was a volatile business with high turnover in personnel (cowhands) and overwhelming obstacles (rain, drought, diseases) in getting animals from the range into the stockyards.

Map 15.3 Mining and Ranching Enterprises in the West, 1860–1890 In the late nineteenth century, the U.S. West developed economically at a phenomenal pace. All of these enterprises—whether ranching and mining as depicted here or farming, cutting timber, or other extractive endeavors—depended on the railroads. By the late nineteenth century, these enterprises also depended on money from the East Coast or foreign banks and investors. This infrastructure and investment capital connected the West intimately to the global economy. ▼

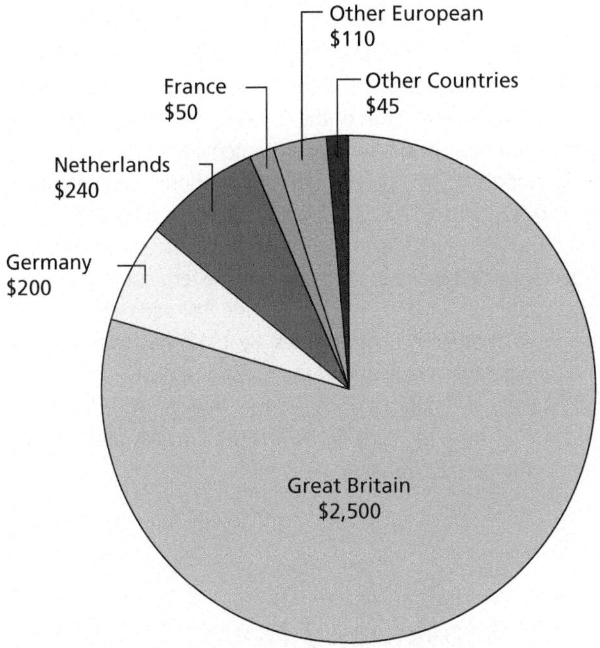

Figure 15.2 Sources of Foreign Investment in the United States in 1899 (Millions) This chart provides some sense of the extent to which the United States and the West, in particular, depended on investment from foreign capital markets. These investors were lured by the scope of development and put their money into building railroads, buying land, running cattle ranches, and extracting mineral wealth from the United States. ▲ *Source:* Davis, Lance E., and Robert J. Cull. *International Capital Markets and American Economic Growth, 1820–1914*. Cambridge, UK: Cambridge University Press, 1994.

15-4c Mineral Resources and Mines

Outside investment and immigrants lead to the intense extraction of mineral resources.

Like farming and ranching, mining depended on the developing markets created by the railroad. All three activities changed the western landscape, and all were tied to the growth of the East Coast in the post-Civil War era. As factories produced more goods and more people moved to cities, the demand increased for the products of ranching, agriculture, and mineral resources.

Whereas earlier mineral booms in the West had focused on precious metals such as gold and silver, by the late nineteenth century, the emphasis was on extracting minerals essential to industrialization. Coal played a vital role in the nation's development as it fueled homes and industry. Copper, primarily found in the southern half of Arizona and northern Mexico, was in high demand for wiring used in telegraphs and later telephones. Both copper and coal mining reshaped labor relations as well as people's relationship to the environment.

Industrial mining demanded immense amounts of capital, which was supplied by eastern bankers and industrialists, such as John D. Rockefeller, who was interested in diversifying his oil empire. He invested in the iron rich properties of the Mesabi Range in Minnesota and in the coalfields of Colorado. Both ventures involved teaming with other industrialists—including Andrew Carnegie to develop the iron fields and Jay Gould to develop the coal fields—to control not only the resources but also the railroad lines that took them to market. Massive capital investment from these eastern investors incorporated the West into the national and global economy.

Coal Miners Underground, circa 1910 Mining camps were some of the most multicultural and diverse communities in the nation. Miners from all over the world came to these camps to find work. Their work was dangerous and difficult, and a miner was in constant jeopardy of injury or death. As a result, union organization moved sporadically across these western enclaves as men and their families sought to create a better life and gain a fair wage and safe workplace from their employers. ▶

Detroit Publishing Co., publisher/Library of Congress

Utah State Historical Society

Global Americans **Leonidas Skliris**, a native of Sparta, Greece, emigrated and in 1897 set up a labor agency in the heart of "Greektown" in Salt Lake City, Utah, near the rail yards. He became successful and powerful, with offices in many towns where new immigrants flocked to find work. Known as the "Czar of the Greeks," he sent agents to Greece to recruit even more workers and ran a series of advertisements there and other places abroad. Skliris used his old-world skills as a *padrone* to recruit laborers. He charged each man for whom he found work $20 and a $1 to $2 monthly fee for as long as the laborer worked at that job. Skliris was accused of taking kickbacks from the companies to which he supplied laborers, especially strikebreakers, to the largest western companies, such as Carbon Coal Mines and the Denver and Western Rio Grande Railroads. He was adept at playing ethnicities against each other in labor disputes. By 1912, however, even his own countrymen tired of his manipulative ways, and in the midst of a nasty labor dispute between the United Mine Workers of America and the copper miners, the workers, including his countrymen, threw out Skliris as their leader. He left Utah quickly and eventually moved to Mexico where he purchased part ownership in a mine.

Immigrants and migrants formed the majority of the work force used in mining across the West. Until the 1890s, most of the miners were Irish, Italian, English, Welsh, and Mexican. They made their way into the West from other mining fields in North America, such as those in Kentucky, the upper peninsula of Michigan, and northern Mexico. By the turn of the century, workers from southern Europe, Japan, and China joined this initial group of immigrants. Mining camps across the West were multicultural work areas where laborers learned to work with one another on the job and in their personal associations. Management opposed the development of unions or camaraderie among workers because a divided labor pool kept wages as low as possible. Consequently, the U.S. West experienced some of the worst industry violence and the emergence of some of the most radical unions from the Knights of Labor to the Industrial Workers of the World (the IWW, or Wobblies.)

Even with the advent of rail transportation, much the West was remote from urban centers, and mining camps were isolated. Women who followed their husbands as they sought mining work often found substandard housing, few groceries, and a dangerous landscape on which to raise their children. Mining was not steady work, and for long periods, mines could lie idle and men were laid off. Most women adapted to the harsh economic and physical environment by growing vegetables, raising small animals, such as goats and chickens, and keeping a vigilant eye on their children who played on mining slag heaps or walked along the railroad tracks.

As a result of these harsh conditions, recruiting workers was difficult and retaining them more difficult. One solution that management employed to address this problem was to hire immigrant labor agents who recruited workers in their home country. Known as *patrons, padrones*, or *coyotes*, depending on the ethnic group, these agents shared the common purpose of persuading their countrymen to leave their homes, take a boat or train to the United States, and work for a mining company.

15-4d Alaska and Hawai'i: The West of the Future

U.S. business looks even farther west to new markets.

As the nineteenth century progressed, U.S. business interests looked farther west to Alaska and across the Pacific for new opportunities. In 1867, as part of his vision of an expansive U.S. commercial empire across the Pacific, Secretary of State William Seward purchased Alaska from the Russian empire, which opened the region for U.S. exploration. In 1896, gold was discovered in the Klondike region of Canada's Yukon Territory and then, in 1899, in Nome, Alaska. These gold rushes brought more than one hundred thousand immigrants from around the world who established new comunities and put millions of dollars into the North American economy. The Nome rush alone produced more than one hundred twelve metric tons of gold ore, approximately one-third of the amount mined during the California Gold Rush.

After the Civil War, Hawai'i gained geostrategic importance as another crucial part of U.S. designs for commercial empire in the Pacific. In 1875, the United States and the Hawaiian Kingdom signed a trade agreement that allowed Hawaiian sugar to enter the U.S. market duty free and barred Hawai'i from extending territorial or economic concessions to any other nation. As a result, the sugar industry in the islands grew rapidly. Americans who owned the majority of the sugar plantations in Hawai'i built irrigation projects and imported Chinese and Japanese laborers. Production of Hawai'ian sugar increased tenfold while native islanders—their population severely depleted by epidemics—lost much of their political and economic autonomy. In addition to commanding Hawaii's economy, Americans also controlled its politics after 1887, when the Hawai'ian monarch was forced to agree to a new constitution that took away much of his authority. The naval station that the United States acquired at Pearl Harbor in 1875 provided coal to U.S. transpacific steamers and military vessels patrolling the Pacific to ensure the free flow of travel and trade.

15-5

West in the American Imagination

This painting, *Yosemite Valley*, was completed by Albert Bierstadt in 1866.

What mood is Bierstadt trying to invoke in his audience? Why did he paint in such a romantic style? What would someone who had never been to the West think about the place? ▶

Buyenlarge/Getty Images

In the 1890s, three events marked the incorporation of the American West into the nation. First, after the massacre at Wounded Knee, violent Indian resistance appeared to be coming to an end. Second, the Buffalo Bill Show, which set up just outside the gates at the Chicago World's Fair in 1893, presented both the West and Indians as entertainment for those who might never see the region in person. Finally, in Chicago that same year, a young historian named Frederick Jackson Turner pondered the significance of the closing of the western frontier, articulating ideas that would have a profound influence on U.S. thought for generations afterward. The confluence of these three factors allowed Americans to imagine the West—Indians on the land and white settlers moving westward—as part of the country's past and to begin to create idealized notions about what the West had been.

☞ As you read, consider why boosters, artists, and writers created mythical images about the U.S. West. What purposes did such images serve?

15-5a Literature and Art

> American and European novelists and popular artists create images of the western past.

The West had always held an important place in American literature and popular culture. Beginning with James Fenimore Cooper's leatherstocking tales in the early nineteenth century, which told of a "West" in upstate New York that existed just over the edge of eastern settlement, Americans became fascinated with stories of the U.S. frontier. In the late nineteenth century, writers such as Mark Twain (Samuel Clemens) chronicled the development of the West.

Twain, who grew up along the banks of the Mississippi River, understood the impulses that pushed people west. In the first paragraph of *Huckleberry Finn*, Twain described his young hero's inability to settle down and be "sivilized" by the Widow Douglas. Instead Huck "lit out" for the country where he could be "free and satisfied." Twain based some of his work on his travels west to California and then back to New York across the Isthmus of Panama, and he told easterners about the western world that was opening up to them. His novels portrayed a frontier society filled with characters capable of pushing the boundaries of language, etiquette, and racial norms set by eastern society.

Western literature and travel journal articles by popular authors such as Mary Halleck Foote and Bret Harte appeared in popular magazines including *National Geographic, Colliers, Harper's, and Scribner's*. These writers introduced their readers to the sights, landscapes, and peoples of the West. Some of these were truthful accounts, but most embellished on real life there.

Another popular way of portraying the U.S. West was through grand paintings that found large public audiences in the East and Europe. The most popular images were painted by the **Rocky Mountain School** painters, German-born Albert Bierstadt and Thomas Moran. They painted dramatic, almost unreal, mountain vistas and breathtaking landscapes. Bierstadt first went west with the Frederick West Lander Expedition, which was engineering an emigrant trail from Nebraska to Oregon in 1859. Bierstadt convinced Lander to provide an escort for him as he explored and painted. Bierstadt took the techniques and styles from his earlier work within the Hudson River School and began

Rocky Mountain School Group of painters who were known for their majestic landscapes of U.S. western scenery.

applying them to the spectacular western landscapes of the Rocky Mountains. The paintings were huge, literally and figuratively. Bierstadt painted on canvasses that took up an entire wall of a large room. He always chose sweeping vistas with dramatic light as his subject.

Thomas Moran also gained his first exposure to the West and to what became Yellowstone National Park through a government-sponsored geological expedition led by Ferdinand V. Hayden. Moran first saw the Yellowstone region (northwestern Wyoming bordering Idaho and Montana) in 1870 and took this landscape as the subject of many of his dramatic paintings. He made field sketches and quick watercolors of the landscape while he was surveying the region and then returned to his studio to create the vast canvasses. Neither Bierstadt nor Moran made his home in the West but both were taken with its inspirational landscapes. Their work came to epitomize Americans' image of the West to such an extent that Congress appropriated tens of thousands of dollars to purchase some of their largest works.

15-5b Tourism to the West

Boosters lure tourists to the West to see the natural beauty.

Literature, travelogues, magazine articles, and paintings piqued the curiosity of Americans about the landscapes and peoples of the West. However, the greatest purveyors of the U.S. West as a tourist destination were the railroad companies, which were anxious to fill their trains with tourists and potential settlers to the region. Railroads advertised the dry and warm climates of the U.S. Southwest for those suffering from asthma, consumption, and gout in the damp eastern climate. The companies packaged and advertised the natural and spectacular beauty of places such as Yellowstone, the Grand Canyon, and Yosemite as destinations for wealthy Americans who could afford to vacation. Railroad advertisers made Native Americans into spectacles to be gazed on by tourists who sought to have an authentic experience by visiting reservations. Marketers relied on government surveyors such as Hayden and King to boost the image of the West as a place to be preserved, revered, and visited for the sheer emotional uplift of experiencing its landscape.

Yellowstone, which was made the first national park in 1872, fascinated Americans as they learned about the boiling cauldrons of sulfurous water and "Old Faithful" geyser, which blew a twenty-two-foot plume of water out every ninety-one minutes. Bierstadt's paintings of Yosemite in California made the park even more popular with his dramatic interpretations of the valley floor and the mountain peaks. The first tourists visited there in 1855, and by 1864, the region had so much commercial traffic that President Lincoln signed an act allowing for the Yosemite Valley and the nearby Mariposa Grove of giant sequoia trees to "be held for public use, resort, and recreation . . . inalienable for all time" (see Table 15.2). This act inspired other states to seek federal protection for their special lands. In 1890, Congress authorized the second national park, Yosemite, which epitomized to Americans the need to preserve wilderness areas to be enjoyed in their natural beauty.

Table 15.2 National Reserves and Parks Created, 1832–1916

The Organic Act, which set aside lands for national parks and created the United States Park Service was signed in August of 1916. But this was not the first time that the federal government had set aside land for preservation. Prior to that legislation, these thirteen sites were protected by Congress or the president to make sure that the areas were not developed for commercial use but instead could be enjoyed by visitors.

Date Protection Enacted	Site of Reserve or Park	State
April 1832	Hot Springs	Arkansas
March 1872	Yellowstone	Wyoming, Montana, Idaho
September 1890	Sequoia	California
October 1890	Yosemite	California
March 1899	Mount Rainier	Washington
May 1902	Crater Lake	Oregon
January 1903	Wind Cave	South Dakota
June 1906	Mesa Verde	Colorado
May 1910	Glacier	Montana
January 1915	Rocky Mountain	Colorado
August 1916	Haleakalā	Hawai'i Territory
August 1916	Lassen Volcanic	California
August 1916	Denali	Alaska Territory

15-5c Popular Images of the West

Western images appeal to the masses as well as the elite and middle class.

Although railroad literature, travelogues, paintings, and advertising reached a large audience, they were geared toward the middle class, encouraging them to visit the West. Other forms of entertainment were targeted more specifically at the mass of Americans who would never be able to afford to travel west. The drama of the West was brought to them by dime novels and popular traveling shows. Inspired by such tales and traveling theatrics, European authors such as Germany's Karl May wrote about a West they had never seen and told extremely popular tales of adventure.

Dime novels became increasingly popular in the United States and in England, where they were called *penny dreadfuls*. The rise in literacy opened a new mass market of readers. Dime novels were sold at newsstands as part of the popular "rag" literature movement that targeted young working-class men and women who toiled in urban factories. Although the genre covered a wide array of subjects from detective fiction to tales of urban outlaws and working girls, some of the most popular series were westerns. Series about Nat Love (the black cowboy also known as Deadwood Dick), Jesse James (the infamous outlaw), and Buffalo Bill Cody (a scout for the U.S. military) were some of the most popular, aimed at young boys who lived in urban areas and could only dream of going west, being a cowboy, and fighting Indians.

Another popular venue portraying the West was **Buffalo Bill's Wild West Show**. Like popular shows presented by the showman and entrepreneur P.T. Barnum, Bill Cody drew millions into the world he created. In his two-hour show, which included hundreds of animals; sharpshooters, such as the ever-popular Annie Oakley; and Indians, such as Sitting Bull, Cody portrayed the winning of the West by white Americans over subdued Indians. Popular skits included the family homestead attacked and burned down by marauding Indians with Cody and the cavalry saving them from certain disaster, a staged buffalo hunt with real animals and Indians in pursuit, and, perhaps the most popular scene, a reenactment of the Battle of Little Big Horn.

Cody was able to portray the Indians as victorious because by the late nineteenth century, they appeared to be on an irreversible retreat in the face of U.S. expansion. Cody's show sought to re-create a fantastic West that had at least some basis in history and reality. Hundreds of Native Americans, called *show Indians*, toured with the Wild West Show. It played to huge audiences in the United States and across Europe. It was so popular that in 1887, Queen Victoria, who rarely was seen in public while mourning her husband, Prince Albert, came to a special showing that Cody arranged for her. Delighted by the dramatic display of western scenes, she encouraged her subjects to attend.

15-5d End of the Frontier

Myth making about the West depends on the fiction that the frontier had closed.

Frederick Jackson Turner began his presentation at the Chicago World's Fair in 1893 with the statement that, according to the 1890 census, "Up to and including 1880 the country had a frontier of settlement, but at present the unsettled area has been so broken by isolated bodies of settlement that there can hardly be said to be a frontier line." With that statement, Turner's provocative analysis of the American character declared the frontier closed. American identity had been so influenced by the movement west, he wondered how it would continue to develop when migrants would no longer be able to remake themselves and create new opportunities in the wide-open frontier. In so doing, he created a mythologized West that charted the progressive states of development that the U.S. frontier underwent. Starting with the era of "savagery" when Indians dominated the American continent, progressing through fur trading, ranching, farming, and eventually mercantile society, Turner connected frontier history to the stages of human history since prehistoric times. At the same time, he told a story of U.S. national development that was the direct product of Manifest Destiny and portrayed vividly in Gast's painting, *American Progress*.

The **frontier**, of course, never closed, and Indians did not disappear from the western landscape. During the remainder of the nineteenth century and well into the twentieth century, Americans and immigrants from around the world continued to press into the West and to create new homes in what was increasingly becoming one of the most multiethnic and diverse regions in the world. Indians continued to live and work in the country although within constricted political, economic, social, and educational boundaries established by the Dawes Act and the reservation system. Together, old settlers and new immigrants had created a new West based on the region's ties to eastern and global markets.

Buffalo Bill's Wild West Show Traveling variety show portraying the West of the United States that entertained thousands across the country and Europe.

frontier Region beyond Anglo-European settlements and control.

Summary

The end of the Civil War allowed Americans to look westward again. They and thousands of immigrants from around the world moved into the West to expand farming, ranching, and mining. Completion of the first transcontinental railroad, which was followed by other cross-continent lines, made possible the development of national and global markets. The railroad also drew a diverse group of laborers who found ample opportunity despite difficult working conditions.

Federal officials asserted power over western lands and the people who settled there. They incorporated them into the nation through land surveys, property distribution, and, ultimately, statehood, although residents in some regions were denied full rights as citizens for unusually long periods. Some who found their status as citizens questioned used the international borders of Canada and Mexico to create their own local communities or to flee the U.S. military. White women, however, found the West a more hospitable place than the rest of the nation for their political ambitions of equality and suffrage.

Incorporation also highlighted the legacy of the U. S. relationship with Native Americans who lived on these western lands. Violence was often the most common solution, and these groups were pushed onto reservations and forced to make accommodations to U.S. laws and customs. Despite strong resistance, by the end of the nineteenth century, Indians seemingly had been incorporated through the Dawes Act. In response to these changes, Americans began to indulge in a nostalgic fondness for the western past. They painted ethereal images, wrote novels, and created tourist destinations that recalled a distant romantic history. Most of these images were misleading or emphasized an idealized past, reassuring settlers about the West's development and progress, and providing escapism for East Coast or European city dwellers.

<Thinking Back, *Looking Forward*>

As you review this chapter, think about the ways that the U.S. West was transformed by violence, migration, and capital investment. How does this transformation compare to the changes in the West during the antebellum period? What role did immigrants and foreign capital play in the development of the West? As you read the next chapter, think about how changes in the West were driven by the industrialization of the eastern United States.

To make your study concrete, review the timeline and reflect on the entries there. Think about their causes, consequences, and connections. How do they fit with global trends?

Additional Resources

Books

Cronon, William. *Nature's Metropolis: Chicago and the Great West, 1848–1893*. New York: WW Norton, 1991. ▶ Sweeping study of the U.S. West's economic ties to Chicago and points farther east.

Isenberg, Andrew C. *The Destruction of the Bison: An Environmental History, 1750–1920*. New York: Cambridge Press, 2001. ▶ Argues that white and Indian participants in the growing hide market caused the near extinction of the bison.

Lukas, J. Anthony. *Big Trouble*. New York: Simon & Schuster, 1997. ▶ Readable narrative of industrial violence at the turn of the century, focusing on the IWW.

Pasco, Peggy. *What Comes Naturally: Miscegenation Law and the Making of Race in America*. New York: Oxford Press, 2009. ▶ Comprehensive look at how laws regulating sexuality and race shaped the way Americans dealt with racism and segregation.

Sandweiss, Martha A. *Passing Strange: A Gilded Age Tale of Love and Deception Across the Color Line*. New York: Penguin Press, 2009. ▶ Gripping narrative about Clarence King, head of the USGS, and the secret life he led passing as a black man.

St. John, Rachel. *Line in the Sand: A History of the Western U.S. Mexico Border*. Princeton, NJ: Princeton Press, 2012. ▶ Comprehensive history of how the border was formed, maintained, and crossed between 1848 and 1940.

Scharff, Virginia. *Twenty Thousand Roads: Women, Movement and the West*. Berkeley: University of California Press, 2002. ▶ Biographies of six women illuminate the influence of women in the development of the West.

Warren, Louis. *The Rising of God's Red Son: The Making of an American Religion and the Road From Wounded Knee*. 2017. ▶ Discussion that places the Ghost Dance movement within the context of America's religious traditions and shows its international implications.

West, Elliott. *Contested Plains: Indians, Goldseekers, and the Rush to Colorado*. Lawrence: University of Kansas Press, 1998. ▶ Gripping narrative about the multiethnic world of the Great Plains that involved competing groups struggling to control their futures.

White, Richard. *Railroaded: The Transcontinentals and the Making of Modern America*. New York: WW Norton, 2011. ▶ Comprehensive economic and political history of how railroads were financed and built during the Gilded Age.

Go to the MindTap® for **Global Americans** to access the full version of select books from this Additional Resources section.

Websites

Keeping History: Plains Indian Ledger Drawings. (http://americanhistory.si.edu/documentsgallery/exhibitions/ledger_drawing_2.html). ▶ Based on a Smithsonian exhibit, a good introduction to the system of recording Plains life.

National Park Service. (www.nps.org). ▶ Excellent resource from which to gather accurate and concise histories of particular places protected by the National Park Service.

Shadows at Dawn. (http://brown.edu/Research/Aravaipa/). ▶ Primary and secondary sources that help students understand the multiple perspectives of the Camp Grant Massacre in Arizona.

Women of the West Museum. (www.theautry.org). ▶ Primary and secondary sources regarding the experiences of women, particularly an important exhibit on suffrage.

MindTap®

Continue exploring online through MindTap®, where you can:

- **Assess your knowledge with the Chapter Test**
- **Watch historical videos related to the chapter**
- **Further your understanding with interactive maps and timelines**

Incorporation of the West

1862

May

Lincoln signs the Homestead Act.

July

Lincoln signs the Pacific Railroad Act.

Lincoln signs the First Morrill Act.

1863–1864

June 1864

Lincoln signs law protecting Yosemite.

September 1864

Black Kettle signs Treaty of Fort Lyon.

October 1864

General Sherman's march to the sea.

November 1864

Indians are killed in the Sand Creek Massacre.

1865–1867

April 1865

Barbed wire is patented.

June 1866

Goodnight-Loving Trail is established.

June 1866

Congress passes the Southern Homestead Act.

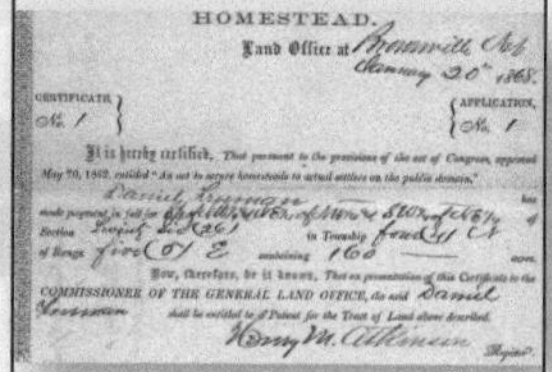
HOMESTEAD.

Land Office at Brownville, Neb. January 20th 1863.

CERTIFICATE, No. 1

APPLICATION, No. 1

It is hereby certified, That pursuant to the provisions of the act of Congress, approved May 20, 1862, entitled "An act to secure homesteads to actual settlers on the public domain,"

Daniel Freeman has made payment in full for [illegible] of Section Twenty Six (26) in Township four (4) N of Range five (5) E containing 160 acres.

Now, therefore, be it known, That on presentation of this Certificate to the COMMISSIONER OF THE GENERAL LAND OFFICE, the said Daniel Freeman shall be entitled to a Patent for the Tract of Land above described.

Henry M. Atkinson, Register.

December 1866

U.S. cavalrymen are killed in the Fetterman Massacre.

March 1867

United States purchases Alaska from Russia.

1868–1870

April 1868

Fort Laramie Treaty is signed.

November 1868

Battle of Washita takes place in Oklahoma.

May 1869

Transcontinental railroad is completed.

John Wesley Powell explores the Grand Canyon.

November 1869

Suez Canal is completed.

1871–1873

January 1872

Gast paints *American Progress.*

May 1872

Congress passes the General Mining Act.

June 1872

The combine is patented.

March 1873

Congress passes the Timber Culture Act.

1874–1879

May 1875

United States and Hawai'i sign the Reciprocity Trade Treaty.

July 1876

Custer and his men are killed at the Battle of Little Big Horn.

by the Sioux and their allies.

October 1877

Chief Joseph surrenders.

January 1879

U.S. Supreme Court issues ruling in *Reynolds v. United States.*

1880–1885

July 1881

Exoduster migration to Kansas reaches its peak.

November 1883

Railroads begin adopting standard time.

August 1884

Mexico completes its transcontinental railroad.

February 1885

Huckleberry Finn is published in the United States.

1886–1889

September 1886

Geronimo surrenders to the U.S. army.

February 1887

Congress passes the Edmunds-Tucker Act.

Congress passes the Dawes Act.

July 1887

Hawaiian king is forced to cede powers to the United States.

January 1889

Wovoka has vision and encourages the Ghost Dance.

1890

January 1890

Census Bureau data suggests the frontier closed.

August 1890

Congress Passes the Second Morrill Act.

September 1890

The Mormon Church issues The Manifesto.

December 1890

Massacre at Wounded Knee leaves more than two hundred and fifty dead.

1891–1910

April 1892

Johnson County war erupts in Wyoming.

December 1893

Turner presents "The Significance of the Frontier" at the Chicago World's Fair.

August 1896

Gold is discovered in the Klondike.

September 1898

Gold is discovered in Nome in Alaska.

November 1910

Mexican revolution begins.

Go to MindTap® to engage with an interactive version of the timeline. Analyze events and themes with clickable content, view related videos, and respond to critical thinking questions.

16

The Making of Industrial America

1877–1917

Mary Harris Jones immigrated to Toronto as a child to escape famines in her birthplace of County Cork, Ireland. Her life as a wife and mother took her to Tennessee. Later, she returned to Chicago and helped found the growing labor movement there.

16-1
Age of Steel

16-1a International Advances in Technology and Manufacturing
16-1b New Business Practices
16-1c Risk and Economic Volatility

16-2
Growth of Cities

16-2a Local and Global Migrations
16-2b Urban Infrastructures
16-2c Cities and Their Countrysides

16-3
Life in Industrialized America

16-3a Inequality
16-3b Ethnic Segregation and Racial Divisions
16-3c Recreation and Entertainment in the City

16-4
Industrial Violence and the Rise of Unions

16-4a Transformation of Work
16-4b Knights of Labor
16-4c Age of Strikes
16-4d Labor Organization in the West

Barely thirty years old, Mary Harris Jones sat alone in her darkened home wondering how her life had become so undone. Just a week earlier, she had been the wife of George Jones, an iron molder, and the mother of four small children. Now all five were dead from the yellow fever epidemic that swept through Memphis in 1867.

National Photo Company Collection (Library of Congress)

Mother Jones Speaking to President Coolidge, 1924 ▲

Jones had been a migrant all her life. She was born in County Cork, Ireland, in 1837 and immigrated as a child, first to Canada and then to Michigan and Chicago before settling with her husband in Memphis. She had worked as a teacher in Michigan and a seamstress in Chicago. And, although she took in sewing work while in Memphis, she focused on being a mother and wife in a working-class family.

With nothing left for her in Memphis, Jones returned to Chicago, where she settled in a small apartment and began work as a dressmaker for wealthy Lake Shore Drive clients. Her business thrived, but in 1871 she lost everything in the great fire that burned much of Chicago to the ground. With no money, no family, and very little hope, she embraced the growing labor movement in Chicago and joined the Knights of Labor, becoming an organizer. That choice provided the stepping stone that launched her career as one of the foremost labor leaders of the late nineteenth and early twentieth centuries.

The Knights' policy of organizing all workers regardless of gender, race, or occupation appealed to Jones. She quickly rose through the ranks and earned a reputation as a passionate speaker and compassionate advocate who was best when drawing women and children to labor's cause. Jones became increasingly radicalized with each strike. She rallied workers and their families at some of the most notorious strikes, including the Ludlow strike against the Colorado Fuel & Iron Company in 1914, which earned her a stay in federal prison. She became an outspoken advocate, who, as she aged, looked more like a dear grandmother than an anticapitalist hell-raiser. Yet her ability to incite workers earned her the moniker, "the most dangerous woman in America" from a U.S. attorney general who prosecuted her.

In 1905, Jones became one of the founding members of the Industrial Workers of the World (IWW) along with William D. ("Big Bill") Haywood and Eugene V. Debs. The IWW brought together a coalition of immigrants and workers who pushed for changes that affected all workers, not just skilled ones, and sought to reorder the relationship between the laboring and capitalist classes. The *Wobblies*, as they were called, built on their U.S. experiences and their interactions with union leaders, socialists, and Marxists from Europe and Russia.

"Mother" Jones had contradictory ideas about the place of women in society and in the world of work. She was known to use her grandmotherly persona to persuade men such as John D. Rockefeller Jr. and Theodore Roosevelt of the necessity to protect workers and families.

In what ways does the journey of Mary Harris Jones—from immigrant, wife, and mother to laborer and workers' advocate—illustrate the turbulence brought on by immigration, industrialization, and urbanization at the turn of the century?

Go to MindTap® to watch a video on Jones and learn how her story relates to the themes of this chapter.

She believed that men needed to earn a decent wage so that women could stay home and tend to their children. She reasoned that parental absenteeism was the single largest cause for juvenile delinquency, a problem that she thought dangerous to society and the fabric of the family. She also opposed women's suffrage, arguing that a woman did not need the franchise in order to "raise a little hell." Her campaign against child labor was meant to keep young girls out of the workplace and in the confines of their home with their families.

Jones was part of a massive immigration movement that uprooted families across the world. When she settled in the United States, she encountered immigrant workers from all over the globe and was influenced by the ideas of intellectual labor leaders from Europe. Given the tragedies she had experienced in early life, it is not surprising that Jones dedicated herself to advocating for the sanctity of the family, the right of men to earn a decent living, and the opportunity for children to have wholesome childhoods. Jones lived through turbulent times for families, women, and ethnic minorities, who felt the deep impact of the changes brought by immigration, industrialization, and urbanization at the turn of the century. In advocating for workers and their families, she faced global economic upheaval on the local level.

16-1

Age of Steel

The Bessemer process, as portrayed in this British painting, enabled molten pig iron to be turned into steel by blowing extremely hot air through it. The Bessemer Steel Converter made steel cheaper and stronger, leading to robust production that drove the global economic expansion of the late nineteenth century.

What does this image reveal about the labor conditions for factory workers? What were the dangers? ▶

SSPL/Getty Images

The end of the nineteenth century saw an unprecedented growth in technology and business innovation that transformed the way people worked and lived. Steel enabled the construction of high-rise buildings that became the hallmark of dense cities, which drew people into closer proximity with one another. Steamships became larger and faster as global trade expanded and immigrants poured into the United States, greatly increasing the pace of urbanization. Industrialists, such as Andrew Carnegie, John D. Rockefeller, and J.P. Morgan, capitalized on scientific breakthroughs to boost the consumption of their products and profits using new legal and business practices to consolidate their corporations and expand market share. This business expansion, however, was tempered by economic instability and a major economic downturn in 1893 that hurt not only the rich and powerful but also workers, immigrants, and farmers as the nation struggled to adjust to economic cycles of boom and bust.

☞ As you read, think about the specific ways in which technological innovation and business consolidation transformed the global economy. How did the economic cycles of boom and bust affect business owners, workers, and farmers?

16-1a International Advances in Technology and Manufacturing

The marriage of theoretical science and its practical application in the late nineteenth century prompted what observers later described as the **Second Industrial Revolution**. Building on the major technological advances in British manufacturing made earlier in the nineteenth century, businesses capitalized on new technologies in industrial chemistry and the production of steel and electricity. These innovations combined with advances in railroad transportation after the Civil War created a synergy in which global markets in steel, grains, petroleum, and fertilizers flourished. This growth was most rapid in the United States, Great Britain, northwestern Europe, and Japan, but the effects were felt throughout the global economy (see Figure 16.1).

Electricity and steel production drive new types of industrial development.

U.S. businessmen applied scientific research emerging in European universities to industrial markets. By the early twentieth century, more than one hundred fifty U.S. companies, such as U.S. Steel, DuPont, and Standard Oil operated research facilities that hired foreign scientists. These companies found practical uses for theoretical innovations in chemistry, engineering, and physics for consumer use. The companies also engaged in what is now called *patent trolling*, the practice of buying any new patents to lessen competition. The three most transformative technologies during this period were electricity, Bessemer steel, and the automobile.

Second Industrial Revolution Late nineteenth-century period of industrialization driven by technological innovations and advances in chemistry.

Of these innovations, electricity had the most dramatic initial impact in people's day-to-day lives by stimulating new types of inventions. In 1876, Thomas Alva Edison created the first U.S. commercial research lab in Menlo Park, New Jersey. Among the dozens of inventions that Edison produced over his lifetime, the first practical incandescent bulb transformed daily life. Although a number of inventors across Europe and the United States developed the bulb itself, Edison made it marketable by creating the first commercially successful electrical system in New York City in 1882. Streets, factories, and many homes were lit using electricity instead of gas. Edison declared, "We will make electricity so cheap that only the rich will burn candles."

By 1887, the United States had 121 generating plants that distributed electricity through Edison's direct current (DC). Meanwhile, George Westinghouse, another U.S. inventor, developed alternating current (AC), which was more practical because it allowed electricity to travel long distances at high voltage via transformers and then be transformed to low voltage for civic, commercial, and home use. After intense competition, AC current eventually became the voltage used in the United States. Able to run electrical machines around the clock, businesses then instituted both day and night shifts and extended the workday.

Communication also transformed rapidly at the end of the nineteenth century. In the 1840s, engineers in Russia, Germany, and the United States had developed the electric

Figure 16.1 Highest Steel- and Wheat-Producing Countries, 1860–1900 (in metric tons)
Production of steel and wheat is a good indicator of a country's economic development and participation in the global market. Initially, steel production in the United States lagged behind that of both Great Britain and Germany but by 1900 almost matched the two combined. The United States was a leader in wheat production and exports throughout this period; by 1890, Japan and India, in addition to the countries shown here, had also begun producing wheat for their own consumption. ▼
Sources: Mitchell, B.R. *International Historical Statistics: Europe, 1750–2005*. New York: Palgrave Macmillan, 2007; *International Historical Statistics: The Americas, 1750–2005*. New York: Palgrave Macmillan, 2007; *International Historical Statistics: Africa, Asia, and Oceania, 1750–2005*. New York: Palgrave Macmillan, 2007.

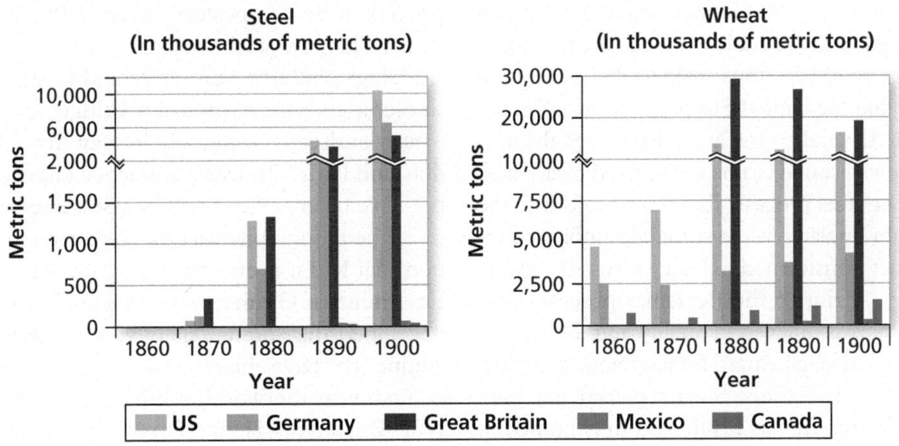

Exposition Universelle or World's Fair, Paris, 1900 Panorama of the gardens of Trocadero and Champ-de-Mars. World's Fairs like this one and the Chicago World's Fair of 1893 were created to bring countries together to share ideas, inventions and to show off for others. The 1900 Fair was meant to celebrate the turn of the twentieth century and praised the trends in modernism and *Art Noveau.* ▲

telegraph that increased the speed of communication. In 1851, the United States and Europe had adopted Samuel Morse's patented telegraph and coded alphabet. By the middle part of the century, telegraph wires and poles had covered much of North America. The first transatlantic telegraph cable between Ireland and Newfoundland was laid in 1858, but broke after a month, and its investors lost confidence. A second cable weighing one ton per nautical mile laid in 1866 proved more durable. By the end of the nineteenth century, British, French, German, and U.S. telegraph companies had laid multiple cables that could carry more than one message at a time, thus making the connection between Europe and the United States closer. In 1876, the Scottish emigrant Alexander Graham Bell patented the telephone, which allowed sounds to be transmitted over wires.

The **Bessemer steel process**, first introduced into the United States from England, was a second technology during this period that transformed industry across the globe. Prior to the Bessemer process, steel was uneven in quality and too expensive to be used for anything other than small tools. Steel replaced pig iron, which was brittle and thus limited in its uses. After a conversation with Napoleon III, Emperor of France, about the poor quality of pig iron for manufacturing armaments, Sir Henry Bessemer improved his oxidation experiments that rid pig iron of its impurities. Convinced that the process had commercial potential, Bessemer patented it in 1856. The resulting steel was much stronger, 80 percent cheaper, took less time to manufacture, and was less labor intensive than manufacturing pig iron.

Bessemer steel process
Industrialized manufacturing of steel that used oxidation to produce a strong steel quickly and cheaply, revolutionizing machinery and construction.

In 1873, Andrew Carnegie introduced the Bessemer process at his Homestead plant in Pittsburgh, Pennsylvania. The new steel transformed almost every industry. Buildings could be built taller and bridges made longer. Skyscrapers and suspension bridges began to dot the urban landscape, especially in New York, Chicago, London, and Paris. The transcontinental railroad system would not have been possible without Bessemer steel.

The automobile was the third technological innovation that had a profound impact on the global economy. Karl Benz of Germany, the inventor of the automobile, developed the commercially viable internal combustion engine. By 1896, his was the largest car manufacturing company in the world, selling a modest 596 units that year. But it was Henry Ford in the United States who mastered mass assembly, drawing on techniques such as

Classic Image/Alamy Stock Photo

Singer Sewing Machine Ad, *Revista Popular*, 1880
Advertisement for Singer sewing machines to be bought on credit system. The ad appeared in the1880 edition of the Spanish publication *Revista Popular de Conocimientos Utiles*. Ads for U.S. companies such as Singer, Coca Cola, and International Harvester reveal the extent of U.S. commercial influence. ▲

using interchangeable parts, developed during the First Industrial Revolution of the early nineteenth century in England and Massachusetts. Ford pioneered a new system of production by using machines and moving assembly lines to dramatically increase the speed of production. By 1914, Ford had cut the time to make an automobile from more than twelve hours to ninety-three minutes. The efficiency saved money as well as time, allowing Ford to slash the price of his popular Model T car from $950 in 1909 to $290 in 1924. Rapid technological and commercial innovation during the late nineteenth century reinforced a feeling of **modernity** among many Americans.

16-1b New Business Practices

> Organizational innovations make corporations more efficient and successful.

In addition to applying technological innovations, businesses also transformed operations and marketing. **Industrial capitalism** fully replaced eighteenth-century economic views about merchant capitalism, as **surplus labor**, and goods entered the global market. One of the most useful concepts that industrialists applied to their enterprises was **vertical integration**, which allowed a company to control each part of the **supply chain**, from natural resources through production and delivery, to marketing and sales.

Andrew Carnegie was one of the first U.S. businessmen to perfect this system. He acquired iron and coal mines, as well as the coke ovens that produced the high-quality fuel needed to produce steel. He either owned or made close alliances with railroad lines that would ship and deliver his products. By controlling the entire supply chain, Carnegie maximized efficiencies and cost savings. Both reformers and workers, however, protested the immense power concentrated in vertically integrated corporations.

American businesses also used monopolies, which had been used by colonial governments and were the basis of the transatlantic economy. A true **monopoly** exists when one firm or a group of firms exerts total control over the supply of a good or service in order to control its price. Even though it did not reach that benchmark, John D. Rockefeller's Standard Oil owned 88 percent of all oil-refining facilities in the country, practically shutting out all other competition. Rockefeller then used vertical integration to control other parts of the oil supply chain. Until the Supreme Court ruled in 1911 that his company was an unfair monopoly, Standard Oil was the largest corporation in the nation.

Rockefeller's near-monopoly created a **holding company** that allowed Standard Oil to control many other corporations. This legal device allowed the board (or trustees) of one firm to govern dozens of others, ensuring that they did not compete with one another. During the **great merger movement** between 1895 and 1905, manufacturers of everything from paper bags to tin merged small businesses into gigantic holding companies. More than eighteen hundred firms disappeared and were replaced by consolidated firms prefaced with brand names connoting nationwide power, such as American, Standard, Union, or General. Many consolidated firms, such as Otis Elevator and International Harvester, controlled 70 percent or more of their respective industries. The reasons for the mergers remain controversial among historians. One reason could have been that the industries were trying to suppress competitive price wars by buying out competitors. Another reason could have been that the industries were simply trying to

modernity Term used to distinguish a historical era as "modern" based on the convergence of new technologies, lifestyles, and personal independence.

Industrial capitalism Economic system based on a free market in which all enterprises are privately owned.

surplus labor Farm workers whose labor was not needed year-round for household subsistence. Some found wage work that added security and comfort.

vertical integration Business practice that encourages ownership of all aspects of production from the natural resources to the delivery of the finished product.

supply chain System of organizations, people, activities, information, and resources needed to provide materials to manufacture a product for customers.

monopoly Also termed *horizontal integration*, exclusive control of ownership of every outlet for a good or service, thus allowing it to set the price.

holding company Entity that exists for the sole purpose of holding shares/stock of other companies, allowing a few people to control many companies.

great merger movement Period in U.S. economic history when companies consolidated into larger corporations.

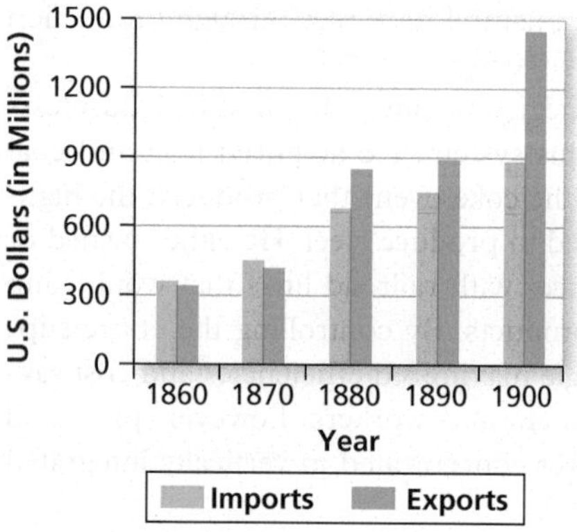

Figure 16.2 U.S. Exports and Imports, 1860–1900 During the latter half of the nineteenth century, the United States became increasingly enmeshed in the global economy by importing and exporting goods. The United States had a fairly even trade balance in 1870, but by 1880, its exports had surpassed imports. By the turn of the twentieth century, the value of exports was nearly double that of imports, indicating U.S. companies' ability to export wheat, steel, and finished manufactured goods, such as combines and sewing machines. ▲ Source: Mitchell, B.R. *International Historical Statistics: The Americas, 1750–2005*. New York: Palgrave Macmillan, 2007.

become more efficient through scale economies in transportation or capital investment.

These business practices and improved efficiency not only provided U.S. consumers a new array of choices but also expanded U.S. exports (see Figure 16.2). The Singer Sewing Machine Corporation, for example, had been selling its machines since the early nineteenth century. Innovations in marketing and production enabled Singer to begin exporting on a scale that would have been unimaginable earlier. By the early twentieth century, U.S. industrialized consumer products from typewriters and cameras to razor blades and packaged cereals had become popular items in Asia, Europe, and Latin America.

The global economy expanded dramatically in the late nineteenth century with every industrialized country seeing significant growth in productivity, exports, and imports. But even among this phenomenal growth, the United States stood out. The U.S. economy quintupled in size and accounted for 25 percent of global economic growth in the period between the end of the Civil War and the turn of the century. The U.S. economy was the largest in the world and was more than twice the size of the next largest economic powerhouses, Germany and the United Kingdom. These two economies had grown because of their access to new markets with the opening of the Suez Canal. U.S. growth depended on the extraction of the West's resources and the immigrant labor that was flooding into the country and providing the human power to develop those resources and markets.

boom-bust cycles Economic process typified by expanding and then contracting business activity that typified the U.S. economy in the late nineteenth century.

Panic of 1893 Economic depression brought on by the failure of railroads and banks, business bankruptcies, and high unemployment.

16-1c Risk and Economic Volatility

Cycles of prosperity and depression destabilize the global economy.

After 1865, the global economy grew as the United States built railroads and established new markets and European powers developed their colonial possessions. But two periods of economic depression were interspersed in this generally upward trend. These **boom-bust cycles** triggered dramatic upswings and downward spirals and contributed to income inequality. In 1873, both sides of the Atlantic experienced an economic depression brought on by the collapse of railroad expansion and the demonetization of silver (see Chapter 14). Banks in the United States, Germany, and Great Britain shuttered, and companies shut down production, laid off workers, and declared bankruptcy. The New York Stock Exchange closed for twenty days, and more than one hundred U.S. railroad lines failed or were in bankruptcy by 1874. In the United States, the depression lasted until 1877. Great Britain fared even worse and endured twenty years of economic downturn called the *long stagnation*.

In 1893, after almost a decade of economic growth in the United States, an economic depression again engulfed global markets. The downturn began in France in 1889, and Great Britain and Germany felt the recession by the following year. The collapse of speculative projects in European colonial outposts in South Africa, Australia, and Latin America caused both European and U.S. banks that had financed the speculation to falter. Like the 1873 depression, as the market became saturated, rampant railroad speculation and then railway failures also triggered the **Panic of 1893**. Many of these railroads had been financed by British banks, which were overly leveraged with bad debt. At the peak of the depression, fifteen thousand companies and five hundred banks in the United States had failed, and almost 20 percent of Americans were unemployed. Workers in the cities fared much worse. Unemployment reached nearly 35 percent in New York City. Europe did not fully recover from the recession until 1896. The worldwide depression showed just how interdependent the European and U.S. economies were. Both were also intertwined with the global speculative and growing markets. A downturn in one part of the world could trigger panic and decline in other markets.

Such economic volatility made life precarious for businessmen, workers, and their families. Small farms and businesses were particularly vulnerable to downturns. Those with more money and economic stability were able to better weather the crises. Mark Twain labeled this period the *Gilded Age* because a thin veneer of opulent wealth for the few gilded the problems, corruption, and inequalities associated with industrialization, urbanization, and immigration that accompanied such rapid growth.

16-2 Growth of Cities

This photograph, taken between 1900 and 1910, shows laundry hanging above the yard between tenement buildings in Manhattan. Many city dwellers left the crowded living conditions on the southern end of New York City. They spread north as a result of both the growing immigrant population and the desire of wealthy families to live uptown on Park Avenue and Central Park West, away from the masses.

What does the photograph suggest about the ways that families adapted to such crowded living situations? ▶

Detroit Publishing Company Photograph Collection

The technological innovations that drove the spectacular growth of the world economy also drove people to reconsider how and where they wanted to live. One of the most dramatic shifts at the end of the nineteenth century was the global migration of peoples to other countries and cities to take advantage of new economic and social opportunities. During this period, millions of people left their rural homes and made their way across international borders, oceans, and sometimes just across the state to find a new life in the emerging cities. The period between the end of the Civil War and the beginning of World War I saw the largest migration of peoples to date within the borders of the United States as well as from other nations.

☞ As you read, consider how the influx of these new migrants transformed cities. What types of infrastructure did cities have to create to accommodate them? How did living in urban areas reshape people's social lives?

16-2a Local and Global Migrations

> Immigrants from around the world and migrants from the countryside transform U.S. cities.

The efficiencies created by technological advances—including the development of the combine, which required less demand for manual labor, and the railroads—allowed Americans to leave their farms in unprecedented numbers. Drawn to urban areas by jobs in manufacturing, sales, and distribution, people flocked to U.S. cities seeking jobs, homes, and the consumer goods associated with living there. Although families often moved, young rural single men and women made up the majority of the internal migrants. The urban population of the United States increased by seven times in the last half of nineteenth century.

Western cities also grew rapidly, although they did not match the size or pace of eastern urban areas. Port cities such as San Francisco, Los Angeles, Portland, and Seattle became commercial centers that processed, marketed, and sold the natural resources of the U.S. West internally and to rest of the world. Interior hub cities such as Denver, Fort Worth, and Kansas City processed wheat and livestock and were connected by an expanding railroad system that tied rural America to the rest of the nation.

Although the South remained largely rural throughout this period with only 17 percent of its population living in cities, the region also felt the impact of internal migration (see Map 16.1). In addition to the freedmen who moved to both southern and northern cities, rural whites also took advantage of the new urban opportunities. Black and white women found new work as domestic servants as well as in factories. Migration to southern cities was part of an economic expansion pushed by southern elites in the wake of Reconstruction's end. Leaders such as Henry W. Grady, editor of the *Atlanta Constitution*, hailed the **New South** as the place where increased industrialization and an influx of capital would lift the region out of its economic devastation. This vision of economic uplift for the South, however, was not based on

New South Term used to describe the industrializing southern United States in the period between the end of Reconstruction and World War I.

Jim Crow Type of law put in place after the end of Reconstruction that intended to limit the rights and mobility of African American citizens.

new immigrants Religiously and ethnically diverse newcomers to the United States, mostly from southern and eastern Europe.

pogrom An organized, often state-sponsored, massacre of a singled out ethnic or religious group. Term is most often associated with the expulsion and killing of Jews.

Ellis Island Immigration station in New York's Upper Bay that processed more than 12 million immigrants.

Angel Island Immigration station in San Francisco Bay that processed more than 1 million immigrants, mostly from Asia, to the United States.

racial equality because the Southern elite continued to believe in white supremacy and saw **Jim Crow** laws as a part of this new regime.

The movement of rural peoples into U.S. cities only partly explains the unprecedented pace of urbanization. The key factor that made cities grow rapidly and more diverse was the wave of immigrants who arrived between 1870 and 1920. Earlier immigrants were largely German, British, Irish, and Scandinavian sojourners who tended to arrive with skills and some capital to start a business. More than half of those from Germany traveled west to start farms using the Homestead Act, but the remainder stayed in the cities where they built tightly knit communities.

By the 1880s, the immigrant flow shifted to arrivals of the **new immigrants** from eastern and southern Europe, who were young—between the ages of fifteen and forty-five—and were mostly Catholic or Jewish. Seventy percent were young men looking for economic opportunity. Unlike earlier waves, these men were unskilled laborers who worked some of the dirtiest and most difficult jobs in the industrial economy. They left their countries of origin for a variety of reasons, including economic upheaval from the global depressions of the 1870s and 1890s and religious persecution from **pogroms**. The most prevalent factor, however, was the lure of employment in the expanding U.S. economy. Migrants who had been "pushed" from their homeland by famine or persecution came to start a new life. Those "pulled" by job possibilities often planned a temporary stay, but most settled permanently. The two major immigration stations, **Ellis Island** (1890–1964) in New York harbor and **Angel Island** (1910–1940) in San Francisco Bay together processed more than 13 million immigrants (see Map 16.2).

Although most immigrants to the United States in this era were Europeans, western cities took in thousands who came from Asia and Mexico. Immigrants from China and Japan and to a lesser extent Korea, India, and the Philippines came to West Coast ports on transpacific steamer ships that carried goods and people. Prior to 1924, Mexican immigrants easily crossed back and forth across the U.S.–Mexico border, which was unpatrolled in most places. These people lived and worked in the growing industries of mining, ranching, and agriculture in the West.

The confluence of migration and urbanization occurred worldwide. In Japan, the industrialization in Tokyo and secondary cities such as Osaka triggered tremendous growth driven by internal migration from the countryside. Berlin (Germany) and Sao Paulo (Brazil) grew at faster rates than Chicago during this period. Argentina, where 30 percent of the population was foreign

Map 16.1 Global Immigration Patterns, 1900 Immigrants from both Asia and Europe pressed into the Americas to make homes and find work in these booming economies. Notice that in this period, as opposed to the early nineteenth century, more immigrants came from southern, rather than northern, Europe. Consider what both pushed and pulled these immigrants to relocate. Notice that other places in the Americas also received large immigrant populations. Was the U.S. immigrant experience unique? ▼

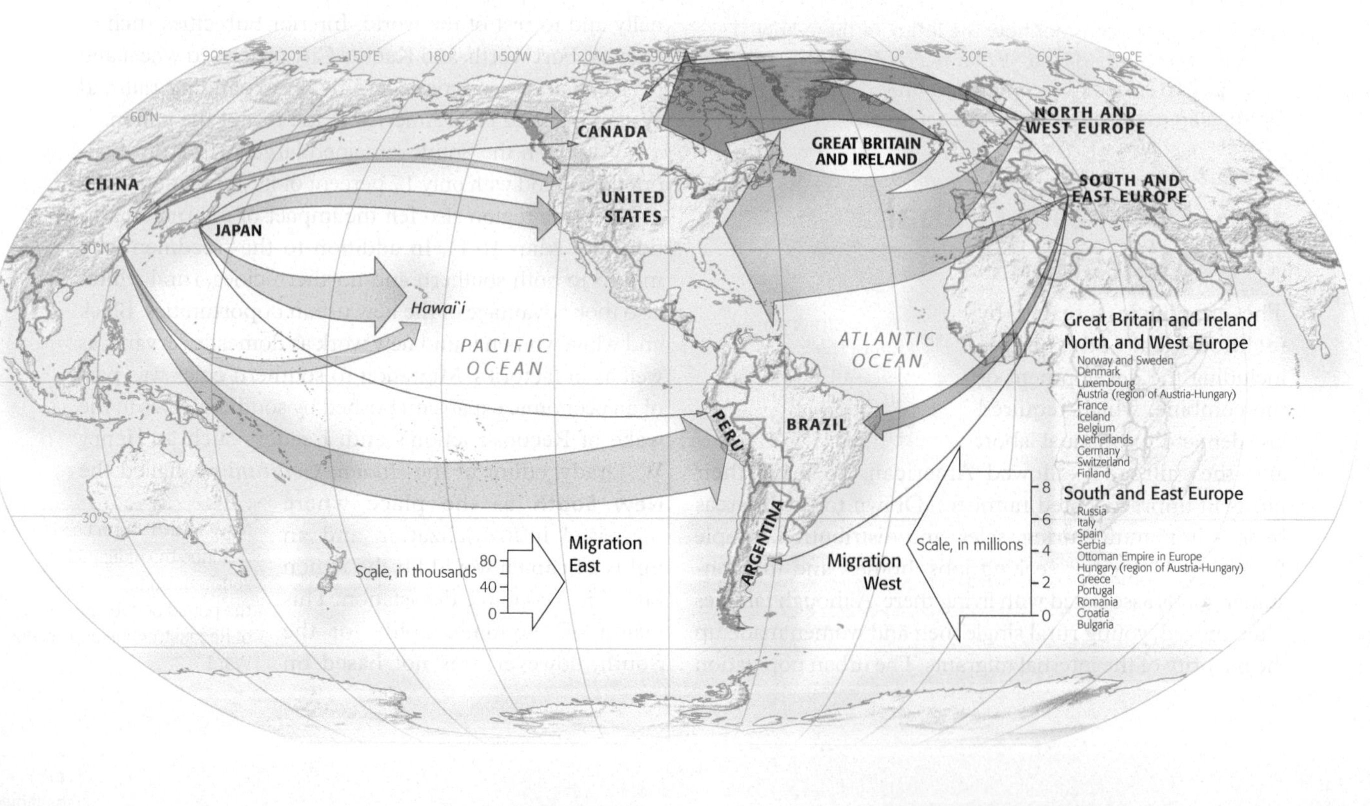

born, had an immigrant experience most similar to that of the United States. By 1914, the proportion of immigrants in Buenos Aires (70 percent) rivaled that of New York City, but they came from a more limited range of countries such as Spain and Italy. Labor markets, cultural preferences, ease of citizenship, and migration "chains" set up by relatives who preceded them influenced immigrants' destination choices. For many, migration within Europe or Asia preceded an overseas move.

The massive global migrations in the late nineteenth and early twentieth centuries affected the United States in two unique ways. First, it received more immigrants than any other country. From the 1830s to 1930, the United States took in 60 percent of all immigrants from Europe. Canada, in second place, received 12 percent. The ability to absorb so many foreigners reflected the availability of land and the rapid industrial growth in the United States. Second, the nation received a much broader diversity of newcomers than other countries. Canada's immigrants came mainly from Great Britain, and those to South America were overwhelmingly Iberian and Italian. Immigrants to the United States, however, came from all over the world. Arriving in U.S. cities, these diverse newcomers created ethnic neighborhoods (Little Italy, Little Tokyo, Greektown, Chinatown, etc.) that were often sealed off from each other and from mainstream society by heritage, language, culture, food, and social customs. Yet the new immigrants found themselves working side-by-side with people from other immigrant communities and together created civic organizations, unions, and religious communities that cut across ethnic lines. Such experiences and institutions advanced the process of assimilation through which immigrants developed common forms of communication and understanding while still maintaining distinct ethnic identities and practices. To the optimist, the merging of global, ethnic, and linguistic differences exemplified the United States as a **melting pot**, a timely metaphor drawn from a blast furnace, which forged different elements into solid metal.

melting pot Metaphor relating to a society's ability to assimilate newcomers who gradually make one community.

Map 16.2 U.S. Immigration and Urbanization, 1890–1900 Millions of immigrants spread across the United States to find economic opportunity in both rural and urban locations. The orange-shaded areas in the U.S. West show where immigrants flocked to work in the mining and agricultural industries. In the Northeast, immigrants were more concentrated in cities, with Chicago, New York, and Philadelphia totaling a million people, making them some of the largest and most vibrant cities globally. ▼

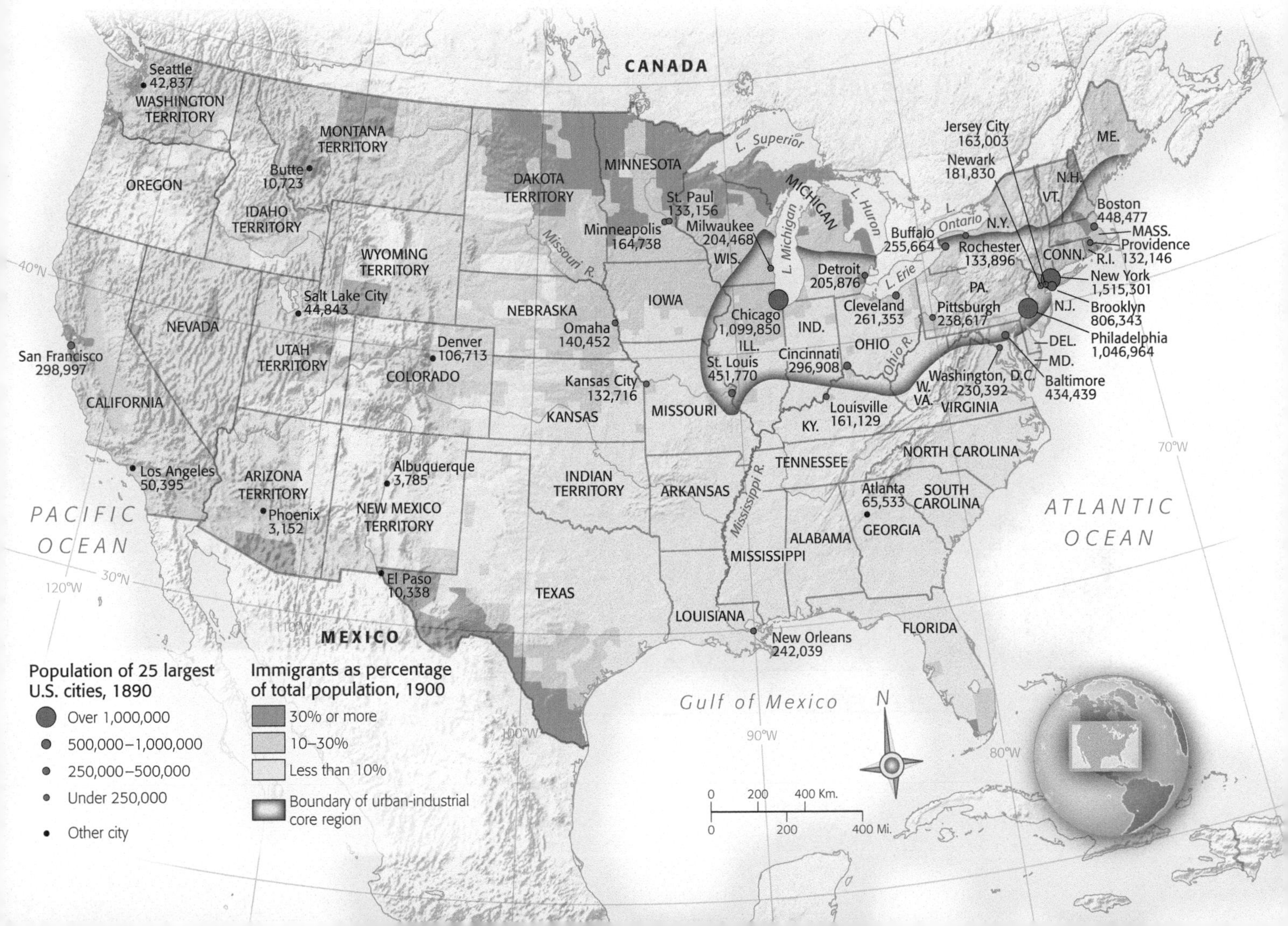

16-2b Urban Infrastructures

> Electricity and other technological innovations transform the urban landscape.

Thousands of people moving into such concentrated masses in the cities required local governments to build infrastructures that kept cities running efficiently and cleanly by addressing the most urgent problems: transportation and public health.

Prior to the Second Industrial Revolution, people in cities relied on their bodies (by walking) and horses (by riding in omnibuses or wagons) to move themselves and their goods. The crowding and the piles of animal waste on the streets convinced officials that horse-drawn transportation was not workable in this dense environment. After an outbreak of equine influenza that killed thousands of horses, it became clear that cities needed to find a new energy source for transportation.

In the early 1880s, a number of city governments such as those in Scranton, Pennsylvania, Richmond, Virginia, and Newark, New Jersey, experimented with public transportation powered by electricity. By the late 1880s, San Francisco, Chicago, and New York riders were using electric or cable trolley cars that moved along embedded rail lines laid in the middle of roads. There was also a surge in building elevated rail lines and, in 1897, Boston built the nation's first urban transportation system consisting of both subways and above-ground trains. By the beginning of the twentieth century, thousands of miles of subways, elevated trains, cable cars, and improved roads had been constructed in the nation's cities. These improvements enabled shorter travel times, allowing people to live farther from their workplaces.

Chicago frame Building term referring to the development of a structure's skeleton steel frame by Chicago architects that enabled construction of skyscrapers.

The cheaper and stronger steel made possible by the Bessemer process produced a surge in civil engineering projects, building rail lines, bridges, and skyscrapers that transformed the nation's cities. The 1883 opening of the Brooklyn Bridge, which connected Manhattan and Brooklyn, then the fourth largest city in the United States, was celebrated as one of the great engineering feats of the century and expanded commerce between two thriving downtown areas. In the mid-1880s, architects and engineers developed the **Chicago frame**, which took advantage of steel rather than stone or brick to build lighter and taller structures. The earlier 1852 invention of the elevator had made skyscrapers practical. The new buildings, in turn, allowed for increased urban density as cities rose skyward, packing more people into fewer square feet of land. The price of this land shot up because a new building such as a high-rise apartment complex could house many more rent-paying tenants. Fortunes were made in urban real estate that rivaled those made in western land speculation.

The Granger Collection, New York

Map of Chicago's Elevated Trains, 1897 This illustrated map shows the elevated train lines of the Chicago, Rock Island and Pacific Railroad in Chicago, Illinois. Also note the infrastructure of the city in term of the roads laid out in a grid, and the Chicago River, which had been reengineered to flow backwards so that the industrial waste of the city and the stockyards would flow away from the city center and into Lake Michigan. ◄

City officials created intricate water and sewer systems to deal with public health issues in addition to building public transportation systems, bridges, and skyscrapers. Overcrowding made it dangerous for families to dump their **night soil** onto the streets or to dig outhouses in the back of apartment buildings. The United States had suffered a series of cholera, typhoid, and yellow fever epidemics because of poor sanitation systems. Mother Jones's family had been victims of such an epidemic in Memphis. The first sewer systems were built in London as the result of a devastating cholera outbreak in 1858. The first sewage treatment plant in the United States was built in Worcester, Massachusetts, in 1890. In one of the greatest hydraulic engineering feats of the time, the city of Chicago in 1887 changed the course of the Chicago River so that it could more effectively deal with its sewage problem from both humans and the Union Stockyards on Chicago's south side.

Public officials also lived in constant fear of a great catastrophe. The 1871 Great Chicago Fire killed three hundred people and burned almost the entire city's downtown. The fire that swept through Boston a year later burned sixty-five acres, caused $73.5 million in damages, and killed thirty people. These two fires prompted municipalities across the nation to make sure that there was ample public water available to fight fires and inspired the creation of city-funded professional firefighter services. But even this planning could not prevent the impact of natural disasters such as the 1906 San Francisco earthquake. In the quake and fires that ensued, more than three thousand people died and 80 percent of the city burned to the ground.

16-2c Cities and Their Countrysides

Transportation technologies bring rural and urban spaces together.

Urbanization transformed the cities as well as the surrounding countryside, drawing rural places into the economic orbit of cities. Agriculture and transportation systems developed rapidly to meet the demands of the cities, which did not have the physical ability to feed their growing populations. Moreover, as urban populations exploded, more affluent residents moved out of city centers. To escape the crowds in lower Manhattan, New York's wealthiest families moved farther north up Fifth Avenue, and after Central Park was finished in 1858 and transportation lines expanded, they moved to the Upper West Side. In the late nineteenth century, the rise of the popular streetcar and railroad allowed people to commute to the **suburbs**, such as the North Shore of Chicago, Brookline just outside of Boston, and Westchester north of New York.

Although boosters of suburban communities espoused the idea that the countryside was separate from the teeming masses and dirty streets that epitomized the U.S. city, in reality, the two were intimately connected. These early suburbs were "bedroom" communities that housed middle-class workers who still depended on the city for their economic survival. Men traveled to work each day on the newly expanded commuter train lines. People depended on the city to provide their consumer demands. Department stores such as Bullocks in Los Angeles, Marshall Fields in Chicago, and Macy's in New York provided fancy clothes and household goods that could be purchased in the city centers and moved to new homes in the suburbs.

More subtly, and perhaps in ways that most city dwellers did not realize, the success of the cities depended on the countryside for their survival. They also depended on public funds, rather than private corporations, to build urban infrastructure projects. Cities utilized not only technological advances and public funding to create waterworks and sewers but also nearby natural resources to supply their fresh drinking water. New York built the forty-one-mile Croton Aqueduct to bring ample fresh water to holding lakes in Central Park and under today's New York Public Library. It was then distributed to a series of fresh-water fountains throughout the city for public use. (Piped indoor plumbing would not come to most city dwellers until the early twentieth century.) San Francisco completed one of the most ambitious public water works projects when it brought water 167 miles in a gravity-driven system from a newly built dam in Yosemite National Park. The controversy over damming the Hetch Hetchy River in California pitted President Theodore Roosevelt against John Muir, one of the earliest environmentalists and the founder of the Sierra Club in 1892, sparking the beginning of the modern environmental movement.

Burgeoning cities depended on the countryside for food as well as water. City dwellers provided almost no food for themselves because of the crowded conditions and lack of gardens. The rural areas closest to the cities provided eggs, milk, and fresh produce that could be trucked in daily. With the advent of better transportation and wide use of refrigerated train cars in the 1880s by companies such as Armour and Company, U.S. city dwellers could have clean, dressed beef shipped to their local stores. Grain grown in the countrysides was also delivered to cities. By the end of the nineteenth century, most city dwellers could expect to find most of the foods they needed at their local grocery or on the carts that lined city streets. That availability of these products depended on the intricate balance between technology, transportation, the market, and the countryside.

night soil Euphemism for human waste that people threw out of their windows or dumped into the street before indoor plumbing.

suburbs Community built outside the city limits primarily for families looking to escape the crowded urban areas.

16-3 Life in Industrialized America

This 1890 photo of an Italian immigrant family was taken by photographer and social reformer Jacob Riis. This family was living in a one-room apartment on New York's Lower East Side. Riis exposed the way poor and immigrant familes lived and worked during the late nineteenth century.

What does Riis's photograph reveal about this family and how its members could benefit from attempts at social reform? Why would this family pose for him? ▶

Go to MindTap® to practice history with the Chapter 16 **Primary Source Writing Activity: Life in Industrialized America.** Read and view primary sources and respond to a writing prompt.

Robber Barons Disparaging name given to wealthy industrialists who dominated corporate United States in the late nineteenth century.

Disparities in class and racial divisions in the United States became more apparent as the century came to a close. The concentration of wealth in the hands of a few people increased after the Civil War and by the end of the century, a small percentage of individuals controlled a majority of the nation's wealth, creating class divisions. Many Americans, however, interpreted this accumulation of wealth as something positive for the nation, a source for inspiration and aspiration. In this way, the working classes admired the rags-to-riches stories of commanding business leaders such as Andrew Carnegie because they held out hope that they too could become rich and powerful. At the same time, these stories, supported by interpretations of Charles Darwin's theory of evolution, taught Americans that their own limitations and failures—not the structure of the economy—prevented them from climbing out of poverty. Such theories, together with violent state repression, stymied reform efforts seeking to improve the conditions for millions of poor Americans and their families.

☞ As you read, think about the kinds of economic and racial tensions that emerged within a rapidly industrializing and urbanizing society filled with a range of new immigrants and internal migrants.

16-3a Inequality

Economic inequalities lead to class divisions and explanations for those divisive disparities.

Accelerating technological innovation created vast amounts of cash and capital as the global economy grew. Consumers purchased new goods and services, which created more jobs and wealth. This increased wealth, however, was not evenly distributed. Capitalists, who were derisively called **Robber Barons** because of the opulent way they displayed their wealth and their apparent disregard for the working classes, accumulated wealth at a far higher rate than workers. James Bryce, an Englishman talking about the U.S. elite, noted in 1897 that "those who deem themselves ladies and gentlemen draw just the same line between themselves and the multitude as is drawn in [aristocratic] England, and draw it in much the same way." Americans, who liked to distinguish between their democratic republic and old world feudalism, found Bryce's comparisons offensive. Yet wealthy New Yorkers proved his point at the annual 1898 Christmas dinner they sponsored for the poor in Madison Square Garden. The elite came and sat in the galleries and watched twenty thousand of the city's poor line up to eat at the tables below them.

In fact, many of America's burgeoning elite often wanted to be like Europe's nobility. It became fashionable to take transatlantic ocean liners to visit famous sites and purchase art. Women returned from these trips dressed in the latest Parisian fashions. Some American elite also married their daughters off to European nobility in an attempt to gain an aristocratic pedigree. For example, Consuelo Vanderbilt, granddaughter to the railroad magnate Cornelius Vanderbilt, married Charles Spencer Churchill, the ninth Duke of Marlborough in England and the heir to Blenheim Palace. The $2.5 million from her wedding dowry kept the estate running. These *dollar princesses*, as they came to be known, were popular. By 1915, there were 42 American-born princesses, 17 duchesses,

Library of Congress Prints and Photographs Division Washington[LC-USZ62-102808]

Andrew Carnegie (Far Right) with Booker T. Washington and Others at the Tuskegee Institute's 25th Anniversary

Global Americans

Andrew Carnegie was born in Scotland where his father was a skilled weaver but struggled to provide for his family. In 1848, the Carnegies emigrated to Allegheny, Pennsylvania. At thirteen, he found work as a bobbin boy for $1.20 a week. Two years later, he found a job as a messenger boy for a telegraph company. Self-educated, Carnegie found another job as a secretary when he was eighteen at Pennsylvania Railway Company and began his upward climb into corporate America. During the Civil War, he worked to open rail and telegraph lines for the North, earning an excellent wage and making lucrative investments. By the end of the war, Carnegie recognized that real wealth and growth lay in the development of the steel industry to supply the expanding railways. He opened his own steel works, and eventually purchased the rival Homestead Steel Works in 1888. The introduction of Bessemer steel into the U.S. economy caused dramatic growth and development of the nation's infrastructure. By 1901, when Carnegie sold his interest to J.P. Morgan, U.S. Steel became the first $1 billion company. Carnegie faced criticism for his labor policies that included brutal strike breaking. In his later career, however, based on his teachings from "The Gospel of Wealth," he funded thousands of libraries both in the United States and abroad and endowed cultural institutions and recreational facilities for working families. During the Spanish-American War, which he opposed, he joined the Anti-Imperialist League and became an outspoken critic of U.S. imperial ambitions in both the Caribbean and the Pacific.

33 viscountesses, 33 marchionesses, 46 ladies, 64 baronesses, and 136 countesses.

American popular culture revered self-made men like Cornelius Vanderbilt. They were the heroes of popular novels by the prolific author Horatio Alger, who wrote almost one hundred books during his career. The formulaic narratives told the rags-to-riches stories of young, poor boys who worked hard and were thrifty and honest—virtues that led to their inevitable climb into the comfortable middle class. Wealth and success were tied to moral uprightness whereas poverty was ascribed to laziness and moral failings. Such views of rich and poor were backed by new but pseudoscientific theories, such as **Social Darwinism**, which argued that Darwin's theory of evolution as outlined in his famous *Origin of Species* (1859) could be applied to human societies. While Darwin limited his concept of **natural selection** to biological contexts, highly regarded English social thinkers, including Herbert Spencer and Darwin's half-cousin Francis Galton, ranked various groups in society based on evolutionary notions of the "survival of the fittest." In the United States, Social Darwinists such as William Sumner of Yale University applied the theory of evolution to the emerging U.S. industrialized society. In 1883, Sumner argued in his pamphlet "What the Social Classes Owe Each Other" against social reforms to help the poor because society worked best when it was left alone (laissez-faire) to let the strongest survive. He warned that the government must stay out of social and economic affairs and focus instead on individual rights and protections.

Unlike Social Darwinists, the powerful business leader Andrew Carnegie believed that the rich were duty bound to return capital to the working class. One of the wealthiest men in America, Carnegie embodied the Horatio Alger hero who was transformed from rags to riches. In decrying the new class of wealthy industrialists who lived opulently with no regard to the workers they employed, he developed a philosophy called the *gospel of wealth* that extolled his paternalistic vision of the obligations of the wealthy classes to the laboring poor. He favored Britain's high estate tax that penalized what he called "selfish and greedy" men who died wealthy and left their riches to their families. Carnegie believed that men of wealth needed to engage in paternalistic philanthropy, give away the majority of their money, and thus help guide the poor to live rewarding lives. He lived by his creed by donating $10 million to found the Carnegie Endowment for International Peace (which still exists today), the largest gift at the time to support harmonious global relations.

Carnegie had a very clear vision of those he believed to be worthy of his largesse. To advance educational opportunities, he built more than twenty-five hundred libraries across the world (sixteen hundred of them in the United States), endowed schools that eventually became the Carnegie Institute of Technology (later Carnegie-Mellon University), erected concert halls, and gave money to institutions that he believed would help working peoples improve their lives. He did not believe in charity or welfare but maintained that the poor were lazy and needed to be taught skills to improve their lives. The

Social Darwinism Popular theory at the end of the nineteenth century applying Darwin's theory of natural selection to human societies.

natural selection Biological process through which the strongest traits of a given species survive and thrive.

collective bargaining Negotiation process between a company and its workers in which a group, not individual workers, present demands.

de jure Legitimate or legal, often used to describe segregation that is established and enforced by law.

de facto In fact or reality, whether legal or not, often used to describe segregation that is not necessarily legal but enforced by customs and practices.

philanthropist's largesse also did not extend to the thousands of workers at his own companies whose requests for **collective bargaining** he denied repeatedly. As a result, the workers educated themselves about the power of organized labor, which much to Carnegie's chagrin, led to many contentious strikes.

One great irony of the late nineteenth century is that while industrialists fought off the ever-looming threat of unionization, the gospel of wealth created a space for workers to develop their own class identity. Whether it was while sitting in a library endowed by Carnegie or working under the ever-present watchful eye of the foreman, employees came to see themselves as a distinctive economic class from their employers.

16-3b Ethnic Segregation and Racial Divisions

Although the Civil War ends slavery, conflicts over race and ethnicity continue.

Racial segregation became the pattern in most U.S. cities during the late nineteenth and early twentieth centuries. For example, ethnic groups, such as the Bohemians, Poles, and Slavs, congregated into neighborhoods close to their industrial jobs at the Chicago stockyards where they worked on the killing floors of the Swift and Armour meatpacking plants. They joined earlier Irish and German immigrants, making up the multiethnic, neighborhood-centric cities that came to symbolize U.S. urbanism. Mexicans and African Americans remained segregated in less desirable locations farther from work. In many cases, their urban neighborhoods became institutionalized as *barrios* and segregated neighborhoods for racial minorities. In addition to experiencing urban segregation in southern cities after the end of Reconstruction in 1877, African Americans faced restrictions on their voting rights. Ten of the eleven former confederate states passed new state constitutions that disenfranchised blacks. The laws inhibited blacks' ability to resist the imposition of discriminatory (albeit legal) Jim Crow laws and practices, which in many cases were reapplications of antebellum slave codes (see Table 16.1). Much of the anxiety that provoked Jim Crow was the fear of African American mobility and the loss of their labor. African American families began leaving their rural homes and moved to emerging southern cities such as Memphis, Atlanta, and Birmingham or north to the booming industrial centers of New York, Chicago, and Philadelphia. These migrations set the pattern for the largest black outflow from the South that started during World War I.

Even before Reconstruction officially ended, white Southerners returned to power and enacted laws prohibiting the equal treatment of blacks and whites, creating legal (**de jure**) racial classifications. All across the South "Whites Only" signs appeared as private businesses enforced new laws requiring racial segregation by refusing to serve African Americans. Public facilities and transportation, schools, theaters, restaurants, and bathrooms were separated into different spaces for blacks and whites. While this type of racial segregation occurred less frequently outside the South, local governments in the North and West practiced **de facto** racial segregation and discrimination rooted in common practices rather than overtly racist laws.

African Americans in the South contested the imposition of the new Jim Crow regime. After Louisiana passed the Separate Car Act in 1890, which stipulated that all public transportation would be segregated by race, a group of concerned citizens challenged the

Table 16.1 Select Jim Crow Laws

The term *Jim Crow* first was used in the early 1890s to describe laws that segregated blacks from whites in restaurants, schools, and public transportation. It regulated all aspects of African Americans' lives. This table gives a sense of how encompassing these restrictions were for black Americans.

State	Area Restricted	Restriction
Alabama	Health care	White nurses allowed to deny care to black patients
Arizona, Maryland, Wyoming	Marriage	Marriage between a Caucasian and a Negro, Mongolian, Malay, or Hindu declared null and void
Georgia	Burial	Whites and blacks separated by law in cemeteries
New Mexico	Education	Black and white children segregated in schools
North Carolina	Education	Black and white children not allowed to share the same textbooks
Oklahoma	Public utilities	Separate telephone booths for blacks and whites maintained by telephone companies
Texas	Public institutions	Public libraries segregated

MANDARIN YUNG WING.

The Granger Collection, New York

Global Americans In 1854, **Yung Wing** was the first Chinese man to earn a Bachelor of Arts degree at Yale University. He had come to the United States in 1847, accompanying the missionary Reverend S.R. Brown who was returning to the United States from his mission in southern China, where Yung and his family lived on a small farm. Yung became a naturalized U.S. citizen in 1852. After graduating, he returned to China where he found work in the government. After the signing of the Burlingame Treaty (see Chapter 14) that permitted Chinese immigration to the United States, Yung developed an educational program in China that enabled Chinese students to study in the United States for four years. He also founded the Chinese Education Mission, which eventually sent more than one hundred students to the United States who returned to China as engineers, teachers, and doctors. While running the program, he married Mary Kellogg and had two sons with her. In 1876, Yale granted him an honorary Doctor of Laws degree.

When Empress Dowager Cixi came to power 1898, she decided to end connections with the West. She was suspicious of Yung, who fled to Hong Kong. In 1902, he petitioned the United States to return to Connecticut, but the Department of State had revoked his citizenship as a result of the passage of the Chinese Exclusion Act of 1882 so that he could not legally reenter the United States. With the help of friends and his family, however, Yung returned illegally, just in time to see his youngest son graduate from Yale. He lived the rest of his life in Hartford, Connecticut. A portrait of him hangs at Yale, and PS 124 in Chinatown, New York City, is named after him.

law. This group included New Orleans editor and civil rights activist Rodolphe Desdunes (see Chapter 14) who enlisted Homer Plessy, an octoroon (seven-eighths white but categorized as "colored" under the law), to purchase a first-class ticket and board the Whites Only car on a New Orleans tram. Plessy had the blessing of the tram company, which opposed the law because of the high cost of separating blacks and whites. Local police immediately arrested him when he refused to leave the white section of the tram. The incident spurred a series of court rulings that led to an 1896 U.S. Supreme Court decision.

At issue in *Plessy v. Ferguson* was the plaintiff's claim that Louisiana's segregation of tram riders by race deprived him of the equal protection of the laws guaranteed by the Fourteenth Amendment and imposed involuntary servitude on him, a violation of the Thirteenth Amendment. In a seven-to-one decision, the Supreme Court held that Louisiana law could segregate citizens by race into separate physical spaces so long as those spaces were equal in quality and comfort because such segregation did not "stamp . . . the colored race with a badge of inferiority." In his lone dissent, Justice John Marshall Harlan, a Southerner familiar with Jim Crow practices, argued that Louisiana's law "put the brand of servitude and degradation upon a large class of our fellow citizens," because, regardless of the equal quality of the tramcars, "the real meaning of such legislation" was that "colored citizens are so inferior and degraded that they cannot be allowed to sit in public coaches occupied by white citizens."

Although discriminatory laws were directed primarily against blacks, Asian immigrants became the first targets of exclusionary immigration laws. Congress enacted the Chinese Exclusion Act in 1882, which for a ten year-period barred laborers of Chinese ancestry from entering the United States. Despite attempts by Radical Republicans to naturalize the Chinese, they continued to be banned by a 1790 statute limiting U.S. citizenship to whites. Capitalists, such as the Central Pacific Railroad's Big Four, benefited from Chinese labor, which was hard to find in the sparsely populated West, and often paid them less than whites. Although a combination of industrialists and supporters of Pacific trade ensured that the door to Chinese migration remained opened, western laborers and workingmen's organizations had long pressed Congress to shut it.

The Chinese were discouraged from creating stable families as the immigration of women was all but prohibited by the Page Act (1875). The law barred only prostitutes from entering the United States, but its enforcement came to exclude most Chinese women. Only 2 percent of Chinese immigrants were female in 1855 and by 1890, that number had risen to just 4 percent. Asian exclusion policies were not unique to the United States in this era. Canada, Australia, and New Zealand, as well as other societies of British origin on the Pacific Rim, passed similar laws restricting the flow of first Chinese, and then Japanese, workers.

The exclusion of the Chinese initially focused on laborers (the vast majority of immigrants) but armed with further restrictions from Congress, immigration officials expanded the reach of exclusion to include the so-called exempt classes of Chinese (merchants, teachers, students, and travelers). By 1904, the ten-year period of exclusion (which had already been twice renewed) had been extended in perpetuity. The situation was dire for Chinese immigrants, but one bright spot was that their children were able to retain their U.S. citizenship. In *United States v. Wong Kim Ark* (1898), the U.S. Supreme Court protected immigrant rights under the Fourteenth Amendment's guarantee of citizenship. Customs officials had barred Wong Kim Ark from re-entering the United States after he had visited China because he was the son of Chinese nationals, even though Wong was born and had lived his entire life in California. The Court's decision allowed him to return to the United States and held that the Fourteenth Amendment's guarantee of citizenship to "all persons born . . . in the United States and subject to the jurisdiction thereof" applied to Wong, because, unlike a foreign ambassador's child, he was governed by U.S. laws when he was born on American soil. Since the *Wong Kim Ark* decision, all children born on U.S. soil who are subject to U.S. laws have been regarded as natural-born citizens, regardless of the nationality of their parents.

The *Plessy* and *Wong Kim Ark* decisions occurred against a backdrop of violence toward African Americans and Chinese. Between 1892 and 1901, whites **lynched** at least one hundred African Americans each year in racially motivated crimes. In 1892 alone, two hundred thirty blacks were murdered, mostly in the South. Sometimes racist whites acted as a mob and sometimes as individuals in what they believed to be vigilante justice. Each case had its own specific circumstances but tended to follow a pattern. White men would perceive some sort of behavior on the part of African American men as offensive. It might have been that a black man had become successful by opening a shop in town, had talked back to a white person, or perhaps had looked at or spoken with a white woman. These perceived transgressions of racial, economic, and sexual boundaries happened as people lived and worked among one another and often led to horrific race-based violence.

Ida B. Wells witnessed such brutality, and its impact transformed her life. She became an outspoken advocate for racial justice. Born a slave in Mississippi, Wells became responsible for the family after her parents died in a yellow fever epidemic in 1876 and she moved her five siblings to Memphis. Even at a young age, she was known for outspoken views on racial equality as the columnist for a local paper. In 1892, her world was turned upside down when a white mob attacked three of her friends who owned the Peoples Cooperative Grocery Store, which competed against a white-owned store. The mob set the store on fire and in the ensuing melee, three white men were shot but not killed. The police arrested Wells's three African American friends. While they were in jail, a second white mob attacked it, took them out, and lynched them.

lynched Extralegal public execution meant to intimidate a particular minority group.

In response, Wells called for African Americans to boycott white-owned establishments and even suggested that they leave Memphis where their property and bodies could not be protected. She then worked tirelessly to expose the evils of lynching, specifically that of her friends. She published the pamphlet "Southern Horrors: Lynch Laws in All Its Phases." This earned her the wrath of local whites who threatened her with violence and caused her to flee to Chicago, where she began working for the *Chicago Conservator*, a well-established African American-owned newspaper. From this platform, Wells broadened her campaign against lynching. She traveled across the North and even to England where huge crowds heard powerful evidence about the failures of Reconstruction and African American quest for racial equality.

While blacks faced racial persecution in the South, Chinese people suffered mob violence throughout the West. In 1871, more than five hundred whites invaded Los Angeles's Chinatown and killed eighteen people in retaliation for the murder of a white police officer who had intervened in violence among rival Chinese groups. The hostility was fueled by a deadly combination of white supremacist racial views and economic fears that Chinese immigrants were stealing jobs from white men. Pressured by the depressions of the late nineteenth century, white laborers took out their frustrations on Chinese immigrants.

Although violence was widespread throughout the West, one of the region's most horrific attacks occurred in1885 at Rock Springs, Wyoming, where twenty-eight Chinese were murdered. The thousand or so Chinese people who lived in Wyoming had come to work on the Union Pacific railroad and stayed to work in the company's coal mines. They also found jobs as cooks, laundry owners, and various other service workers. The railroad paid Chinese laborers less than others and used them as strikebreakers against Cornish, Irish, and Welsh miners who belonged to the Knights of Labor. Encouraged by local Knights members, whites burned the Chinese camp and attacked fleeing residents. Federal troops had to be called in to quell the violence, and the next year at the urging of the U.S. secretary of state, Congress paid a large indemnity to China as compensation to the victims' families without accepting responsibility for the crime.

16-3c Recreation and Entertainment in the City

Cities create entertainment opportunities for all classes.

Amid spectacular growth, race riots, segregation, and an epidemic of urban squalor, philanthropists such as Andrew Carnegie and John D. Rockefeller sponsored recreation centers to uplift the poor and calm labor and racial tensions. Rockefeller sponsored the first U.S. branch of the Young Men's Christian Association (YMCA) in 1885. Founded in London in 1844, it provided wholesome activities and safe short-term housing for working-class youth of "healthy mind, body, and sprit." The organization began as an evangelical outlet for Protestantism but over time welcomed youth of all Christian faiths and peoples from every continent. YMCA leaders focused on issues of moral uplift, good citizenship, and the redeeming values of athletic competition and recreation.

The Salvation Army was another organization seeking to uplift workers and immigrants from the drudgery of urban life. Methodists William and Katherine Booth founded the organization in England in 1865. They preached "soup, soap, and salvation" as the antidote for the ills suffered by alcoholics, drug users, prostitutes, and the poor. As an advancing "army of Christians," the organization came to the United States in 1880 and set up operations in urban immigrant communities.

Another form of moral and social uplift came from Catholic charities tied to neighborhood dioceses. At a time when government did not aid the poor and needy through social welfare programs, religious organizations, such as Catholic charities, joined with the YMCA and Salvation Army, forming the frontline of urban social services. These faith-based institutions provided a place where working people found companionship, recreation, and entertainment amid the alienating culture of the late nineteenth century city.

In addition, most immigrant communities provided mutual aid that benefited members of their own ethnic and national groups. Mexican Americans formed *mutualista* societies whose dues provided modest unemployment insurance, burial insurance, job references, and even personal counseling to families. Almost every small town or community group living in large urban centers had a group such as the *Sociedad Proteccion Mutua de Trabaiadores Unidos (SPMDTU)*. Chinese immigrants depended on their own benevolent societies (*huiguan*), and in 1882, the Chinese Consolidated Benevolent Association, also known as the Six Companies, was incorporated. It supported immigrants by emphasizing moral living and hard work, opposed anti-Chinese legislation and vigilante violence, and encouraged ties to their home provinces and villages.

Not all leisure and recreation in cities was organized or institutionalized. Increased transportation combined with new leisure time and cash in working people's pockets led to the emergence of an entertainment economy. In New York, working people could take the outbound train to **Coney Island** to enjoy what by the 1880s had become the largest amusement park area in the country. They also headed to the Bowery where they could dance, drink, and socialize among their peers. Chicagoans went to the lakeshore to swim or to visit sites such as the newly built **Field Museum of Natural History**. In southern California, people took the electric train to Coronado and Balboa Islands.

Coney Island Amusement park and boardwalk in Brooklyn, New York, on the Atlantic Ocean where working-class people spent leisure time and found entertainment.

Field Museum of Natural History Building from the World's Columbian Expedition held in Chicago in 1893 that presents scientific knowledge about the world and is named for its founder, department store magnate Marshall Field.

The impact on old-world immigrant families and young women transformed the way a generation of young working-class people interacted with the opposite sex, families, and workplaces. Women negotiated their newfound freedom and economic resources. Young people could more freely mingle in public with one another. Because the homes of many workers were crowded, many individuals spent their leisure time in the streets, in public parks, or at local diners and saloons where they could meet without being under the watchful eyes of their families. Single men and women were able to go to nickelodeon shows or dance halls together, which meant more intimacy between the sexes in public places.

The cities' elite also found new forms of entertainment. Often mimicking the European culture, benefactors created libraries, concert halls, opera houses, and museums. These cultural institutions became the pet projects of the rich and elevated their own social status and in some cases provided cultural venues for the working class. The Metropolitan Opera in New York was founded in 1880 and included the Vanderbilts, Roosevelts, and Morgans among its first subscribers.

By the end of the nineteenth century, much of the country was in upheaval, as the effects of migration, immigration, industrialization, and urbanization pressured people in their daily lives. This phenomenal interaction of people allowed for both the potential for understanding as well as the very real possibility of conflict, some of it violent. Although many fed that friction for numerous reasons including fear or prejudice, many others worked to solve the problems by joining reform movements and advocating for their causes. Nowhere were these frictions more apparent and more violent than in the upheaval that was caused by the industrialization of the U.S. workplace.

History without Borders

Baseball

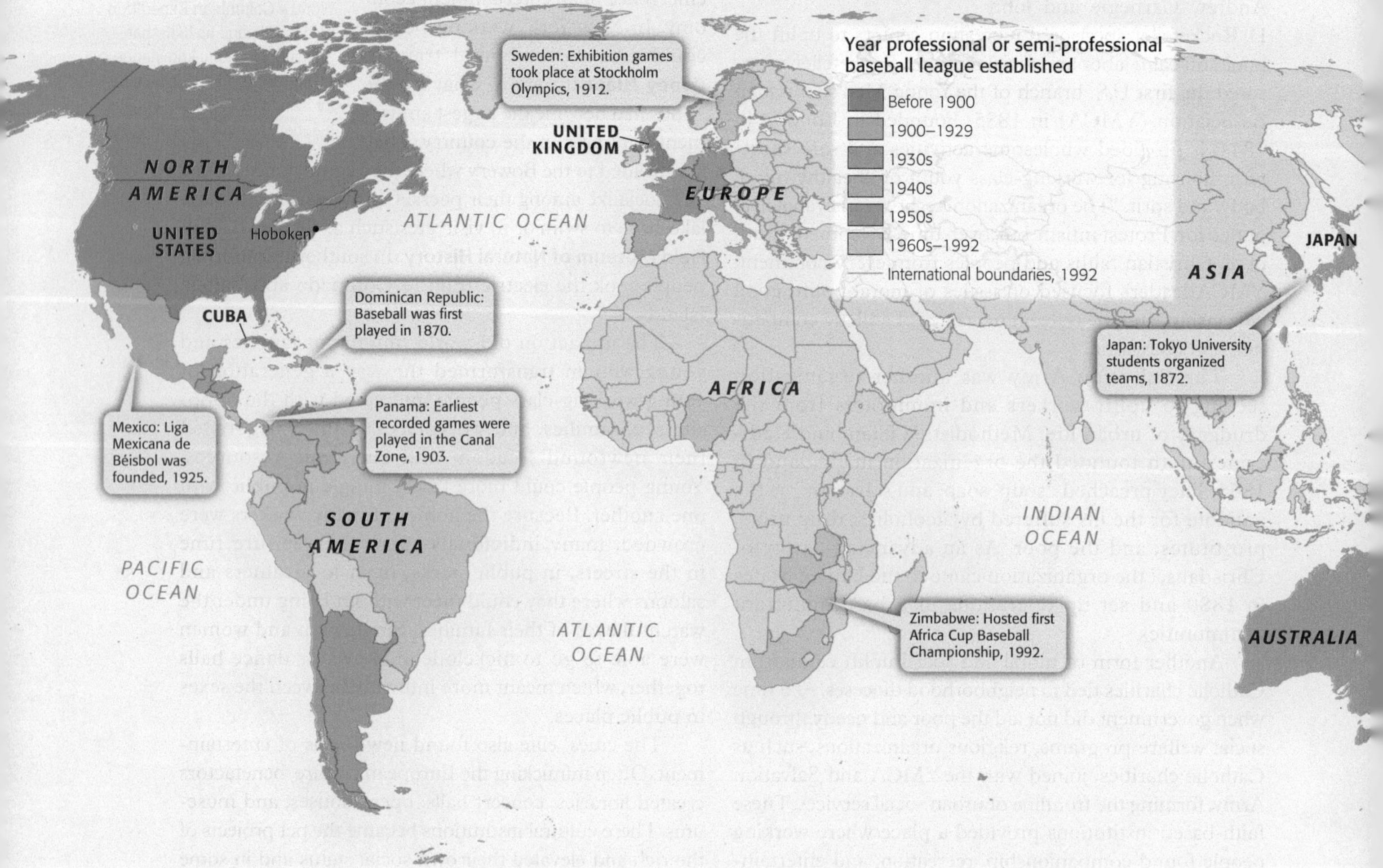

Baseball Organizations, 1870–1992 Baseball is considered the most American of all sports. Yet baseball found its origins in a game called rounders that emerged from England and may have been a derivative of cricket. Since its inception in the late nineteenth century, baseball has become a global phenomenon that has entertained both men and women. Increasingly, Major League Baseball, which is the largest professional league in the world, reflects the globalization of the sport as athletes from around the world come to compete in the United States.

Baseball has been called "America's Pastime," but it in fact originated in England and then spread around the globe. Nevertheless, it is still most closely associated with the United States, which is the most lucrative market for Major League Baseball (MLB).

Baseball is derived from a game called *rounders*, which was played in England during the late eighteenth century and may also have been a precursor to cricket. By the early nineteenth century, Americans in the Northeast—both men and women—were playing some form of baseball as a leisure activity after work. In 1845, the New York Knickerbockers, a club of elite men, formalized the rules of what is now considered modern baseball. The first professional game was played in Hoboken, New Jersey, in 1846. However, almost ten years later in 1855, the New York sports pages were still devoting more space to coverage of cricket than that of baseball.

By the late nineteenth century, baseball had taken off as a major leisure time sport among both urban and rural youth. Groups like the YMCA created youth leagues in order to provide activities for boys after school or work. John D. Rockefeller Jr. financed a baseball league in his Colorado mines. The league boasted state-of-the-art facilities, with scoreboards, spectator stands, and uniforms and stipends for the players. Mine superintendents would "trade" miners between various camps to ensure they had a championship team.

With the advent of the railway system, a professional national league developed where city teams could compete with one another despite long

The Granger Collection, New York

Engraving of a Baseball Game Between the Cincinnati Red Stockings and the Brooklyn Atlantics, 1870 This image captures the early years of baseball, in which professional teams would travel long distances in order to compete in front of ever increasing audiences. The rise in the popularity of baseball marked a moment when American workers began to have leisure time as well as extra money that they could spend to entertain themselves purely for pleasure. Baseball along with city parks, dances, and amusement parks like Coney Island provided public spaces for freedom and entertainment. ▲

National Photo Company Collection (Library of Congress)

Osaka Mairuchi Baseball Players Visit the White House, 1925 At the peak of the U.S.-Japanese trans-Pacific baseball exchange, the Osaka Mairuchi baseball players were invited to appear at the White House to visit with President Calvin Coolidge. ▲

Library of Congress Prints and Photographs Division, LC-USZC4-3227

Advertisement for Baseball Game, 1867 This poster advertised a match for the Cuban All Star Club team, which played in Havana. ▲

distances. In the 1870s, professional baseball was being played up and down the East Coast and across the Midwest. Blacks were allowed to play until 1888, when the league owners signed an agreement that imposed Jim Crow on baseball.

Black baseball leagues had been in existence since the Civil War and thrived alongside white teams, often playing them, even during the Jim Crow era. In 1887, the National Colored Baseball League, known as the Negro League, was formally founded. Meanwhile, baseball was also emerging as a national sport in Cuba. In 1889, the mixed-race team, the All Cubans, toured the United States playing both Negro-league and MLB teams. These leagues developed simultaneously and spread the sport throughout the Caribbean diaspora. Finally, in April of 1947, baseball was once again desegregated when the Brooklyn Dodgers signed and played Jackie Robinson.

During the same time period, Japan was also discovering the joys of playing baseball. In 1878, Hiroshi Hiraoka returned from his studies in the United States and introduced the game to his colleagues at the Japan national railways. In Japan, baseball was played predominately at the college level. Players were amateurs but trained with an intensive physical regimen. In 1905, the MLB in conjunction with Japanese baseball leaders organized a tour of Japanese players through the United States to play semi-pro and college teams. The group collaborated on these trans-Pacific exchanges until World War II. In 1934, Japan created its first professional baseball league, now known as the *Nippon Baseball League*.

Baseball has also been the place of some of the most important contract decisions in U.S. labor history. In 1969, Curtis Flood challenged his trade from the St. Louis Cardinals to the Philadelphia Phillies. The MLB had a reserve clause that forced a player to stay with his team throughout his career, and only the team's management could decide where a player could play. Flood's case went all the way to the Supreme Court where he lost. However, it shed light on the labor of baseball players who, through their union, won the right of free agency and the ability to leave a team at the end of their contracts.

Critical Thinking Questions

▶ What aspects of baseball have made it such a globally accepted game?

▶ How did the development of baseball reflect the contemporary attitudes about nationalism and racism?

16-4

Industrial Violence and the Rise of Unions

This cover from Frank Leslie's *Illustrated* in July 1892 depicted one of the nation's most violent strikes in Homestead, Pennsylvania, which pitted the Amalgamated Association of Iron and Steel workers against the Carnegie Steel Company.

What is happening in this image? Why are women and children so prominently displayed? Does the illustration side with the workers or the company? ▶

Library of Congress Prints and Photographs Division[LC-USZ62-75205]

craft unions Organization whose members have the same craft or trade and that did not believe in organizing all workers.

The Second Industrial Revolution that drew people from the countryside to rapidly expanding cities also transformed their workplaces and relations with their employers. A large urban industrial labor force emerged in which strangers from different ethnicities, races, and nationalities, speaking different languages, labored shoulder to shoulder. This new work environment was not just diverse; it was also communal. This was very different from farm work that was usually done alone or with just a few family members.

This gathering of workers in urban factories enabled them to find common causes against their employers. Companies were stubbornly resistant, sometimes violently, to workers' demands. Emerging labor unions struggled for legal recognition. The courts constantly ordered unions to stop organizing workers and cease disrupting their workplaces with strikes and other forms of protest. High rates of immigration, high unemployment, and the erratic economy during the depressions of 1873 and 1893 created a "reserve army of workers" of desperate people willing to work at almost any wage. Although the surplus hurt labor organization, advocates worked tirelessly on behalf of the nation's industrial workers, forming the basis for the dynamic growth of the U.S. labor movement.

☞ As you read, consider why creating a strong union movement in the United States was so difficult. What challenges did they face? What benefits were accrued?

16-4a Transformation of Work

Labor shifts from small-scale craft work to large-scale industrialized work.

Prior to the Civil War, **craft unions** or guilds were the predominant form of work-based organizations. Shoemakers, typesetters, and workers in many other crafts labored alone or in small workshops, providing goods and services to local communities. These workers rarely considered the condition of those not in their professional guild. Master craftsmen trained young people in a particular craft during a long apprenticeship. Most major cities had more than fifty craft unions. The craft system of production, however, collapsed with industrialization, which transformed the way work was done. Unskilled workers who had no training in a particular craft performed simple, repetitive, mechanized jobs that required little training and no apprenticeship.

Unskilled work was demanding and remade the ways that men, women, and their families organized their lives. Men worked in the large factories that had emerged during the Second Industrial Revolution. Women, who had been the early industrial workforce in the United States, working in the antebellum textile industry, were also drawn into these new settings in the form of sewing shops and textile factories. Children also worked in the new factories, since high school was not mandatory and there were as yet no protective labor laws to prevent them from being exploited. Industrial labor was repetitive, often boring, and in many cases, dangerous. The workday was long, sometimes up to twelve hours, with few, if any, breaks. In most cases, workers had Sunday off, and sometimes their bosses closed shops early on Saturday, so that there would be time for doing errands, enjoying leisure, and taking rest. Workers had no safety net if they were fired, had their hours or pay reduced, or suffered injuries or extended illness. Employers could fire workers without hesitation and replace them from the reserve army of workers in the labor market.

Factory owners looked not only for low-wage workers but also for methods to boost their productivity, which was measured by the time it took to make goods at a set quality level. In the 1880s, Frederick Taylor decided not to attend Harvard College but to apprentice himself as a patternmaker. He observed his fellow laborers' work inefficiencies that cost the company both time and money. As Taylor worked his way up to become a foreman, he experimented with a wide variety of ways to increase laborers' productivity through a system that became known as **scientific management**, or Taylorism. His careful studies, the most famous of which broke down worker movements into discrete and timed tasks, became the basis of new work routines that greatly increased production across industries.

Although highly profitable for business owners, scientific management increased the pace of work and reduced any control that workers had over their labor. To raise profits, capitalists sought to keep wages low, the workday long, and the workplace devoid of expensive safety precautions. In the face of these working conditions, unions emerged in industrialized nations around the world. Treated like expendable cogs in the wheels of industrial profit, workers responded by turning to labor unions that negotiated for better wages, hours, and work conditions. Strikes, which were illegal at the time, were among the few tools that gave workers leverage against owners. U.S. labor leaders drew inspiration from British and European intellectuals and working-class reformers.

Three ideologies imported from across the Atlantic gained particular hold among U.S. workers. **Anarchism**, a broad set of radical ideas that pushed for a stateless society in which workers would govern themselves and not be subject to profit-seeking capitalists, appealed to the most radical workers. **Syndicalism**, which was associated with anarchism, advocated that workers organize themselves into small confederations and resist state power and the capitalist class. **Socialism**, in opposition to the other two ideologies, called for the state to cooperatively own industries and manage them collectively. First in Paris and then in London, the German émigré Karl Marx with Friedrich Engels developed widely influential theories about the role of economics and the class conflicts in world historical development. Engels published *Das Kapital, Volume II* espousing those theories. Many European immigrants were exposed to anarchist, syndicalist, and socialist ideas in their homelands and provided a key constituency for radical movements in the United States. With the exception of socialism, however, radical alternatives to capitalism did not win a mass following, and most Americans remained wedded to democratic and republican ideals.

16-4b Knights of Labor

The labor movement becomes a national economic and political force.

The first nationwide confrontation between labor and capital came during the Great Railroad Strike of 1877. In the wake of the Panic of 1873 and the Hayes-Tilden contested presidential election of 1876, tensions ran high as Americans struggled financially and were uneasy about the partisan conflict that had wracked the Union. Since 1874, there had been strikes and labor violence throughout the country as the depression caused businesses to reduce workers' hours, cut wages, and ultimately lay off employees. At least eighteen thousand companies failed during the depression, including 89 percent of the nation's 364 railroad firms. In July 1877, workers at the Baltimore and Ohio (B&O) railroad in Martinsburg, West Virginia, went on strike spurred by the third in a series of pay cuts. B&O workers in Maryland stopped working and joined the West Virginians in the strike. The shipping of freight across the country came to a halt as newly elected President Rutherford B. Hayes called in the U.S. military to protect the nation from "insurrection." In Baltimore, federal troops fired on a crowd of protestors, killing eleven and leaving forty injured (see Map 16.3).

Hayes's heavy-handed response enraged workers and the public at large. Within weeks, the strike spread to railroad workers in Pennsylvania, Illinois, and Missouri. The peak of violence occurred in Pittsburgh where federal troops opened fire on strikers and their families, killing twenty people, including one woman and three small children. As news of the deaths spread through the town, Pittsburgh was thrown into turmoil. Striking workers set the Pennsylvania Railroad on fire. By morning, the roundhouse was burned to the ground, and twenty residents and five soldiers lay dead. In just over twenty-four hours, almost forty people had been killed in Pittsburgh.

After forty-five days, the Great Railroad Strike ended without any tangible gains for the workers. Yet it revealed the ability of unions to reach across local and state regions in their labor disputes. It also generated deep concerns about the threat of labor cooperation to the nation's economy among government officials and the U.S. public in general. Some worried that ideas from European labor movements, particularly the **Paris Commune of 1871**, a brief takeover of the French government by anarchists, would spread to the United States. Consequently, much of the nativist rhetoric against immigrants often focused on labor movements as conduits for the influx of radical ideas about politics and labor rights.

scientific management System driven by efficiency concerns intended to increase labor productivity.

anarchism Political theory that advocates a stateless society governed by independent and autonomous communities.

syndicalism Political theory associated with anarchism that advocated organizing governments around syndicates or confederations rather than a central government.

socialism Political theory that called for the state to cooperatively own the means of production and manage the economy for the benefit of all citizens.

Paris Commune of 1871 Revolutionary socialist action against the government in France whose success many Americans feared.

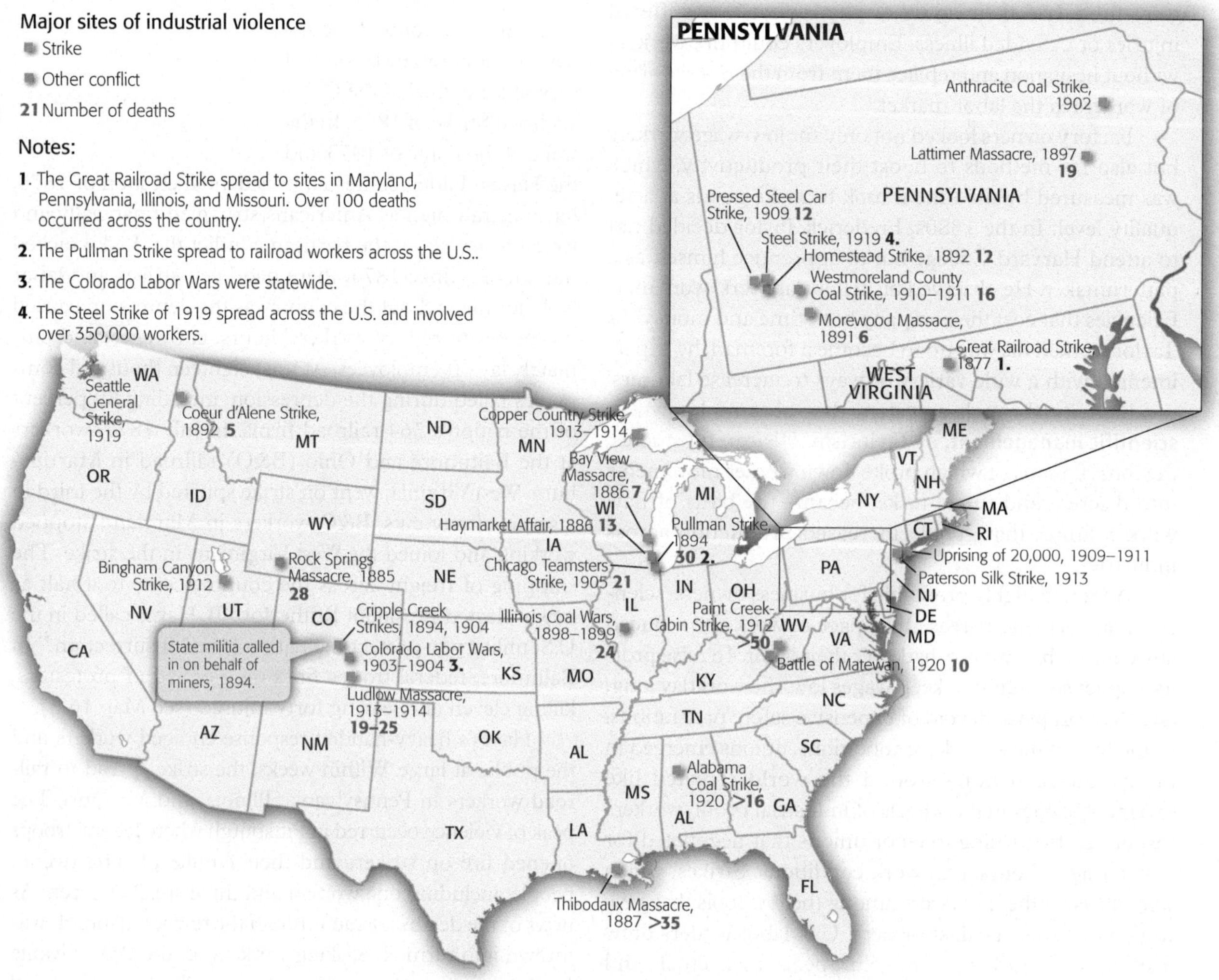

Map 16.3 Sites of Industrial Violence in the United States Between the 1890s and the 1920s, major—and often violent—labor conflicts erupted throughout the United State's industrial centers. These strikes and uprisings attained only limited reforms. ▲

One of the most successful labor unions in the late nineteenth century was the Knights of Labor, first founded in Philadelphia in 1869. (It was also the first union that Mother Jones joined.) The Knights' power and membership increased significantly under the dynamic leadership of Terence V. Powderly, who became the union's grand master workman in 1879. Under Powderly, the union organized workers regardless of race, gender, nationality, occupation, or skill level, which was in direct contrast to craft unions. At the same time, the Knights were not beyond pushing Congress to exclude Italian, Hungarian, and especially Chinese immigrants.

The power and influence of the Knights continued through the early 1880s and peaked in 1886. That year, the union boasted almost a million workers as it advocated for better wages and safer working conditions. The Knights also joined the nationwide push to shorten the workday to eight hours, which would have given workers more rest and free time outside the rigidly controlled workplaces. The union used the slogan "Eight Hours for What We Will." U.S. workers did not want to be "wage slaves" to capitalist employers.

The struggle over the eight-hour day came to a peak in Chicago in May 1886. On May 1, Albert Parsons, a leading labor and anarchist thinker, and his wife Lucy Parsons led a group of eighty thousand marchers through the streets of Chicago demanding the eight-hour workday. The demonstration was without incident. But two days later, when the protesters gathered in Haymarket Square outside the McCormick Reaper Works, violence broke out when police beat workers and fatally shot two men. Protesting the killings, Albert Spies, editor of a local working-class newspaper, called for a gathering on Haymarket Square the following night. The crowd was relatively small, but as people were leaving, a bomb exploded, killing seven policeman and four civilians. In the violence that ensued, dozens were injured.

In the aftermath of the Haymarket bombings, the police arrested eight anarchists including Spies and

Archive Photos/Getty Images

Battle after the Explosion of a Bomb at Haymarket Square, Chicago, May 4, 1886 This image appeared in a Chicago newspaper just days after the violence in Haymarket Square. Note how the engraving conveys the sense of confusion and chaos. The Haymarket bombing was a turning point for labor organizing in the United States, as the Knights of Labor, although they had nothing to do with the bombing, came to be viewed by the American public as too radical. Not until the Industrial Workers of the World (IWW) emerged in 1905 was there such a broadly based union moement. ◀

Parsons on charges of conspiracy to commit murder. After a trial in which no evidence was presented that linked the eight men to the actual bomb, they were all convicted and sentenced to death. Four of them, including Spies and Parsons, were hanged and one committed suicide. But, in 1893, the governor of Illinois pardoned the remaining three men.

Although there was significant doubt about the guilt of the accused Haymarket bombers, the damage had been done. The radical labor movement, symbolized by the Knights of Labor, became unpopular. Americans refused to embrace a labor movement that could turn violent and seemingly had ties to radical Communist, anarchist, and even socialist political views, all of which seemed foreign and un-American. The United States had little room for a union movement that was not enmeshed in the republican and democratic principles of the nation. Any hint of European radical influence doomed any labor organization.

Local, state, and federal government stepped up their efforts to suppress labor agitation by increasing local police forces, state militias, and national guard units. Business owners responded by opposing the eight-hour-a-day movement and hiring private police forces such as the **Pinkerton Detective Agency** to undermine labor organizing. Reaction to the Haymarket bombing resulted in anti-labor, anti-immigrant, and anti-Communist rhetoric that was often associated with critiques of the working classes. Even though the Knights of Labor denounced the use of violence and disassociated themselves from Parsons and the others, the union suffered from anti-union efforts, and its numbers declined radically. By 1890, the Knights' membership had plummeted from almost 1 million in the 1870s to one hundred thousand.

16-4c Age of Strikes

Labor conflict continues and peaks through a series of new strikes.

Into the void left by the collapse of the Knights of Labor stepped the American Federation of Labor (AFL). Founded in 1886 by Samuel Gompers, an English-born cigar maker, it was the umbrella organization for numerous craft unions of skilled workers. Gompers distrusted government officials, who, he argued, served the interests of capitalists through legislation, tax breaks, the use of federal troops, and, most troublesome, court injunctions against strikes. A much more conservative union than the Knights, the AFL divided, rather than united, workers across trades, skill levels, and races. It excluded blacks, Chinese, and other nonwhite workers from its ranks and never organized women. The AFL was not interested in creating one big union to revolutionize society, choosing instead to advocate only for the "bread and butter" issues for the benefit of its own members. This type of conservative unionism was known as **business unionism**. The AFL was not opposed to going on strike and challenging the capitalist system to improve wages and work conditions, but it rejected radical ideas about overthrowing the capitalist system or establishing a worker's democracy that displaced business owners.

The true test of the AFL's power came in 1892 at Andrew Carnegie's Homestead Steel Works in Pittsburgh. The Amalgamated Association of Iron and Steel Workers (the Amalgamated) was a powerful union that three years earlier had secured wages that were one-third higher than the

Pinkerton Detective Agency Private agency hired by corporations to break strikes and intimidate workers.

business unionism A nonradical form of unionism that did not advocate socialist takeover but believed that unions should be run as business enterprises.

prevailing wages in the industry and increased the wages of nonunionized unskilled workers. From Amalgamated's perspective, the labor situation at Homestead was the best that workers could expect: work in a thriving industry, a fair and steady wage, and an owner who was known for his more enlightened ("Gospel of Wealth"), if paternalistic, thinking about giving workers opportunities to raise their standard of living. Despite this seemingly ideal situation, Carnegie and his associate Henry Clay Frick were not willing to share decision-making power with the Amalgamated by engaging in collective bargaining. In June 1892, as Carnegie headed to his summer estate in Scotland, he empowered Frick to break the union at Homestead.

Frick canceled contract renewal negotiations with the Amalgamated, declaring that he would negotiate only with individual workers. He then hired three hundred Pinkerton agents to patrol the mill's perimeter, which he had lined with three miles of twelve-foot steel fence topped with barbed wire. The workers labeled the mill Fort Frick. On July 2, Frick locked out the workers, closed the mill, and stated that he would reopen it with nonunionized labor. The Amalgamated, which was part of a tight-knit community in Pittsburgh, mobilized the entire town against Frick, barring strikebreakers and resources from entering or exiting the mill. Frick reacted by sending heavily armed Pinkertons who arrived on barges from the river to take over the mill. In the twelve-hour battle that ensued, nine strikers and three Pinkerton agents were killed. Scores more were injured when the strikers' families fought back against the Pinkertons, who eventually surrendered.

The win at Homestead was short lived because Frick, with the aid of the Pennsylvania militia, by November 1892 had secured the mill and resumed production without union labor. By Christmas of that year, the union had surrendered to the inevitable. Frick cabled Carnegie: "Our Victory is now complete and more gratifying. Do not think we will ever have any serious labor trouble again." The defeat was devastating to not only the Homestead community but also the national labor movement (see Table 16.2). What chance did other smaller, less-organized, and poorly funded unions have against corporations such as Carnegie Steel if Amalgamated could not stand up to them?

Table 16.2 Selected Unions Worldwide, to 1925

As indicated in this table, the drive to unionize workers was a global movement throughout the nineteenth and early twentieth centuries. Early unions, such as the Stonemasons in Australia and the guilds in the United States, organized according to the type of work. Later unions, beginning with the Knights of Labor and Great Britain's International Workingmen's Association, were organized regardless of type of work and coalesced around ideas of a laboring class that opposed the capitalist class and management. Leaders in labor unions across the globe were in contact and shared ideas and tactics about how to advance labor's cause.

Year	Country	Name
1855	Australia	Stonemasons Society
1864	Great Britain	International Workingmen's Association
1869	United States	Knights of Labor
1886	United States	American Federation of Labor
1890	United States	United Mine Workers of America
1892	Germany	Generalkommission der Gewerkschaften Deutschlands
1893	United States	American Railway Workers Union
1897	Japan	Metalworkers Union
1900	United States	International Ladies Garment Workers Union
1905	United States	International Workers of the World
1925	China	All-China Federation of Trade Unions

The American Railway Union (ARU) under the leadership of Eugene V. Debs built itself on the base of the Knights of Labor. In 1893, it was the fastest-growing union with increasing political power. The ARU's opportunity came when workers at the Pullman Palace Car Company struck. Pullman was well known for its **company town** just south of Chicago that housed its workers and their families in a controlled environment that included curfews and payment of goods from company-owned stores in company scrip, not cash. Although some people admired the high quality of housing and schooling for children, many workers resented the company's oversight on their lives. One worker complained, "We are born in a Pullman house, fed from the Pullman shop, taught in the Pullman school, catechized in the Pullman church, and when we die we shall be buried in the Pullman cemetery and go to the Pullman hell." In April 1894, George Pullman, in response to global depression, laid off 33 percent of his workforce and reduced wages by 25 to 40 percent for those fortunate enough to retain their jobs. However, he did not reduce the rents or the prices charged at the company store. Workers responded by going on strike. They asked the ARU to support them and in response, its leader Debs asked that railway workers nationwide refuse to handle any trains that had Pullman cars. More than a quarter of a million workers across the nation complied and practically stopped train traffic.

company town Community whose land and houses where workers lived as well as its businesses and roads were owned by a corporation that had workers under constant surveillance.

The railroad companies responded by getting a federal court injunction against the ARU for impairing interstate delivery of mail, which effectively outlawed the strike. Debs went to jail for six months for ignoring the injunction, and the U.S. Supreme Court ruled in the 1895 case, *In re Debs*, that the federal government did indeed possess the power to regulate interstate commerce by ordering the ARU to call off the strike. Labor unionists then had a deep distrust of the federal government. It seemed to them that both the executive and judicial branches were willing to bend the law to destroy unions. By July, federal troops backed by U.S. marshals, state militias, and local governments began attacking the Pullman strikers. In mid-July, violence erupted in twenty-six states, practically making the strike a war between workers and capitalist interests. The Depression of 1893, combined with

The Kheel Center for Labor-Management Documentation and Archives int he ILR School at Cornell University

Global Americans In 1903, seventeen-year-old **Clara Lemlich** and her family fled a Ukrainian pogrom and immigrated to the United States. She grew up speaking Yiddish, a Germanic language written in Hebrew, but taught herself to read Russian and became well read in radical and revolutionary literature. By the time she immigrated to New York, she was a committed socialist. She eventually joined the U.S. Communist Party.

In New York, her family settled in the Lower East Side, and she quickly found work in one of the shirtwaist factories as a seamstress. She became involved in labor, joined the International Ladies Garment Workers Union (ILGWU), and was elected to its executive board. She was a vigorous and fearless leader. After a strike in 1909 when she had been beaten by police, suffering two broken ribs, she was arrested but returned the next day to the picket line.

In November 1909, thousands of shirtwaist workers and supporters gathered at The Cooper Union to discuss striking. After listening to the American Federation of Labor (AFL) leader speak, Lemlich was literally lifted to the stage and stated, "I have listened to all the speakers, and I have no further patience for talk. I am a working girl, one of those striking against intolerable conditions. I am tired of listening to speakers who talk in generalities. What we are here for is to decide whether or not to strike. I make a motion that we go out in a general strike." The crowd responded enthusiastically to call the strike, which became known as the Uprising of the Twenty Thousand.

changing technologies that allowed companies to reduce their labor force and the overwhelming tendency of state governments to side with businesses, hampered labor's ability to obtain reform.

By the turn of the century, as more women entered the workforce, they began to form their own unions and fight their own battles to secure safer conditions and higher wages. A coalition of women garment workers, most of whom were recent immigrants from southern Europe and Russia and many of whom were Jewish, founded the International Ladies Garment Workers Union (ILGWU) in 1900. All of these women, regardless of their background, worked in extremely difficult and unsafe conditions. They often brought their experiences with trade unionism and socialism from their home countries. In 1903, the Women's Trade Union League (WTUL), which had been founded in Great Britain thirty years earlier, was started in the United States as an affiliate of the AFL. The WTUL was often considered the more conservative of the two unions, but together they led the largest and most successful strikes.

The unions slowly gained membership but did not grow rapidly until 1909 when a general strike swept New York City. The workers were responding to protests by garment workers at the Triangle Shirtwaist Factory. A young Jewish activist, Clara Lemlich, spoke to a packed house at The Cooper Union and called for a general strike of garment workers. More than twenty thousand workers heeded her call and walked off their jobs for more than fourteen weeks. The long conflict was difficult because the police brutalized the strikers and arrested them. The brutality eased only when the **mink brigade**, a group of wealthy and middle-class women who included Anne Morgan, the daughter of banking magnate J.P. Morgan, and Frances Perkins, joined the picket line. The strike resulted in a contract for the unionized workers. One of the few holdouts was the Triangle Shirtwaist Company, which refused to sign a union contract.

mink brigade Upper-class New York women reformers who joined striking shirtwaist workers during the Uprising of the Twenty Thousand.

A little more than a year later, the Triangle Shirtwaist Company was again the center of labor agitation. On a beautiful spring afternoon, a fire broke out on the ninth floor of the building. The flames spread so rapidly that few of the women were able to escape. Dozens of them died when they jumped from the windows to the pavement as horrified onlookers watched, unable to help. Within an hour, 146 people died, 123 of whom were women. The youngest victims were fourteen years old. It became known later that the women had been locked into the shop, which was a common practice meant to keep workers from taking breaks. The next week, in one of the largest parades in the city's history, New Yorkers mourned the workers' deaths and agitated for reform. In response to the tragedy, New York City created a committee on public safety and passed laws to protect workers and improve building conditions.

16-4d Labor Organization in the West

Organizing labor in the West had its own particular challenges and opportunities because of its geographical isolation and the lack of industrial development

Western labor unions concentrate on mining.

company unions Organization established by a company to represent workers in labor disputes and contract negotiations.

in mining. That business required a concentration of capital, which made attracting and keeping labor much more difficult than in the Northeast. Although labor radicalism was declining there and in the Midwest, it had a stronger following in the West where the IWW, led by Big Bill Haywood and Joe Hill, pushed the radical idea of creating "one big union" to represent all workers regardless of skill level, race, ethnicity, or gender. Although the IWW was considered the most radical of all unions, its message appealed to many of the rank and file workers in the western extractive industries. Unlike the AFL, the IWW and its less radical counterpart in the West, the United Mine Workers of America (UMWA), pushed for a broad coalition of workers that included African Americans in the South and Mexican Americans in the West.

The UMWA created a coalition of skilled and unskilled laborers from all over the world. By 1910, it had organized almost one-third of all miners across the United States, which had been a herculean task given the scope of workers involved. Tensions between mine owners and workers ran high throughout the turn of the century in places such as Bingham Canyon, Utah, and Cripple Creek, Colorado, but the conflict climaxed in Ludlow, Colorado, in 1913.

John D. Rockefeller's Colorado Fuel and Iron Company (CF&I) had resisted union organization throughout the early part of the twentieth century. Despite CF&I's best efforts, the UMWA under the leadership of John R. Lawson and Mother Jones launched a successful union organizational drive and called a strike against Rockefeller's network of coal mines throughout Colorado, New Mexico, and Wyoming. The UMWA also shut down his Minnequa Steel works in Pueblo, Colorado. In retaliation, Rockefeller's managers in Colorado evicted workers and their families from their homes in the middle of winter. The UMWA then leased a piece of land at Ludlow to set up a tent colony for the displaced workers, who continued the strike.

On a cold April morning in 1914, a coalition of company men, Pinkerton agents, and the Colorado national guard surrounded the tent encampment. An armed battle ensued throughout the day, and a fire swept through the worker's temporary homes. The fire killed eighteen women and children. The nation was outraged at the site of dead women and children who had been cowering in a dug-out cellar trying to escape the violence. CF&I and the Rockefeller family in particular were vilified, which prompted Congress to scrutinize the family and its labor practices. Although no major legislation came out of the tragedy, Rockefeller pushed fellow business leaders such as Henry Ford and E.I. DuPont to reconsider the relationship between labor and capital. They implemented **company unions** and reforms to improve working conditions for their employees and living conditions for their families while maintaining paternalist control and denying workers the right to engage in collective bargaining.

Summary

The late nineteenth and early twentieth centuries were transformative periods for U.S. workers and their families. Fueled by technological changes and unprecedented access to capital investment, the economy grew dramatically but did not favor everyone equally. Industrialization led to class divisions and inequality that were only exacerbated by the harsh global depressions in the 1870s and the 1890s during which millions lost their jobs.

All Americans felt the impact of economic growth, whether they stayed on farms and met increased demands for their products brought on by urbanization or moved to the cities. Meanwhile, tens of millions of immigrants from around the world chose the United States as their destination. Europeans, Latin Americans, and, to a lesser extent, Asians (whose journeys were cut short by race-based exclusionary laws) immigrated and made the nation's population one of the most diverse collections of peoples ever. The immigrants and internal migrants from the countryside met in urban neighborhoods, workplaces, and entertainment halls and—through their often unsettling and sometimes violent encounters—created a new idea of what it meant to be an American.

This comingling of people and ideas reordered individuals' relationships with their fellow workers, bosses, physical work, and home spaces. At the end of the nineteenth century, union activity increased, and some of the most violent strikes in U.S. history occurred but attained only limited reforms.

Thinking Back, *Looking Forward*

As you review this chapter, compare the nature and impact of the nation's Second Industrial Revolution with its first one in the nineteenth century. What new technologies emerged later in the century, and how did they transform the global economy and U.S. labor relations? Thinking back to Chapter 15, how did the development of the U.S. West impact the development of cities? How did industrialization create a common bond or experience across the nation, and how did it extend these bonds across the world? In the next chapter, look for ways in which progressive reformers sought to moderate the inequalities wrought by industrialization.

To make your study complete, review the timeline and reflect on the entries there. Think about their causes, consequences, and connections. How do they fit with global trends?

Additional Resources

Books

Andrews, Thomas G. *Killing for Coal: America's Deadliest Labor War*. Cambridge, MA: Harvard University Press, 2010. ▶ Environmental and labor history of the Colorado coal fields that culminated in the tragedy at Ludlow.

Beckert, Sven. *Monied Metropolis: New York City and the Consolidation of the American Bourgeoisie, 1850–1896*. New York: Cambridge Press, 2001. ▶ Analysis of the development of class divisions and status in New York.

Brands, H. W. *American Colossus: The Triumph of Capitalism, 1865–1900*. New York: Anchor Press, 2010. ▶ Popular narrative of the period with a gripping style that brings this period to life.

Gorn, Elliott J. *Mother Jones: The Most Dangerous Woman in America*. New York: Hill and Wang, 2001. ▶ Definitive biography of this labor activist whose career spanned decades.

Levy, Jonathan. *Freaks of Fortune: The Emerging World of Capitalism and Risk in America*. Cambridge, MA: Harvard University Press, 2012. ▶ A sweeping narrative about nineteenth-century capitalism and the development of the idea of risk and how to mitigate it.

Orleck, Annelise. *Common Sense and a Little Fire: Women and Working Class Politics in the United States*. Charlotte: University of North Carolina Press, 1995. ▶ Classic book about the power of women's political and labor organizing in this period.

Montgomery, David. *The Fall of the House of Labor: The Workplace, the State, and American Labor Activism, 1865–1925*. New Haven, CT: Yale Press, 1988. ▶ Still the definitive examination of the rise and fall of U.S. labor movements prior to the New Deal.

Peiss, Kathy. *Cheap Amusements: Working Women and Leisure in Turn-of-the-Century New York*. Philadelphia: Temple Press, 1986. ▶ Narrative about New York City leisure practices among the city's working classes.

Stilgoe, John R. *Borderland: Origins of the American Suburb, 1820–1939*. New Haven, CT: Yale University Press, 1989. ▶ Theoretical and historical look at how the earliest U.S. suburbs developed amid growing urbanization.

Go to the MindTap® for **Global Americans** to access the full version of select books from this Additional Resources section.

Websites

Gilder Lehrman Institute of American History. https://www.gilderlehrman.org ▶ Excellent repository of documents and analytical essays about U.S. history.

Illinois Labor History Society. http:/www.illinoislaborhistory.org/resources.html ▶ Exploration of Illinois' labor history.

Museum of Chinese in America. http://www.mocanyc.org/collections ▶ Comprehensive collection that covers the experiences of Chinese immigrants to the United States.

The Statue of Liberty—Ellis Island Foundation, Inc. http://www.libertyellisfoundation.org/passenger ▶ Exploration of more than 51 million passenger records of immigrants who passed through Ellis Island.

MindTap®

Continue exploring online through MindTap®, where you can:

- **Assess your knowledge with the Chapter Test**
- **Watch historical videos related to the chapter**
- **Further your understanding with interactive maps and timelines**

The Making of Industrial America

1869–1875

December 1869
Knights of Labor is founded.

March 1871
Paris Commune comes to power.

June 1871
Charles Darwin's *Descent of Man* is published.

October 1871
Great Chicago Fire destroys most of the city.

August 1875
Andrew Carnegie introduces Bessemer steel process in United States.

1876–1882

July 1877
Great Railway Strike begins.

November 1879
Thomas Edison is issued patent for incandescent bulb.

May 1882
Congress passes the Chinese Exclusion Act.

July 1882
Chinese Consolidated Benevolent Association is founded.

December 1882
First electrical plant in New York City opens.

1883–1884

May 1883
Brooklyn Bridge is completed.

October 1883
Metropolitan Opera House opens in New York City.

1885

February
Congress passes the Alien Contract Labor Law.

May
Friedrich Engels publishes *Das Kapital, Volume II* from Karl Marx's notes.

September
Anti-Chinese riot breaks out at Rock Springs, Wyoming.

First YMCA opens in New Jersey.

1886–1889

January 1886
Karl Benz patents first gasoline-powered automobile.

May 1886
Haymarket Riots erupt in Chicago.

American Federation of Labor is founded.

June 1889
Andrew Carnegie publishes "The Gospel of Wealth."

1890–1892

July 1890
New Croton Aqueduct for New York City is completed.

October 1890
Louisiana state legislature passes Separate Car Act.

December 1890
First sewage system in United States opens in Worcester, Massachusetts.

January 1892
Ellis Island in New York harbor opens to immigrants.

May 1892
John Muir founds the Sierra Club in San Francisco.

June 1892
Workers strike against Carnegie at Homestead Steel Works.

1893–1896

May 1894
Railway workers nationwide begin Pullman Strike.

May 1895
Supreme Court issues decision for *In re Debs*.

May 1896
Supreme Court issues decision for *Plessy v. Ferguson*.

July 1896
Mercedes Benz begins production of its automobile.

1897–1900

September 1897
First subway in Boston opens for operation.

June 1900
International Ladies Garment Workers Union (ILGWU) founded in New York City.

November 1900
Paris World's Fair opens to an international crowd.

1901–1909

November 1903
Women's Trade Union League (WTUL) is founded.

August 1906
San Francisco earthquake sets off a massive fire.

November 1909
Twenty thousand shirtwaist workers strike in New York City in what becomes known as the Uprising.

1910–1914

January 1910
Angel Island opens as immigration processing center in San Francisco.

March 1911
Triangle Shirtwaist Factory fire occurs.

April 1914
Ludlow Massacre occurs at Rockefeller's coal mine in Colorado.

Go to MindTap® to engage with an interactive version of the timeline. Analyze events and themes with clickable content, view related videos, and respond to critical thinking questions.

17

Politics of Reform

1877–1917

After his wife Alice died in childbirth, Roosevelt headed to the American West to recover. His time in Dakota Territory transformed him, and throughout his life Roosevelt would turn to the wilderness for clarity and work for its preservation.

17-1
Party System in an Industrial Age

17-1a Big Business and Government
17-1b Party Loyalty and Ideology
17-1c Voting and Disenfranchisement

17-2
Early Reform Attempts

17-2a Farmers and Railroad Regulation
17-2b Urban Professionals and Civil Service Reform
17-2c Evangelicals Challenge Threats to the Home
17-2d Workers and Politics

17-3
Economic Crisis and the Populist Party

17-3a Republican Coalition of Pensioners and Business
17-3b Emergence of the Populists
17-3c Panic of 1893 and Its Political Aftermath

17-4
Limitations and Triumphs of Progressivism

17-4a Progressive Era Anti-Immigrant Measures
17-4b Roosevelt's Control over Monopolies
17-4c Progressive Victories and Their Limits
17-4d Grassroots Progressive Movements

17-5
Progressivism and National Politics

17-5a Divisions in the Republican Party
17-5b Progressive Party
17-5c Wilsonian Progressivism

Theodore (Teddy) Roosevelt and his brother Elliott hung out the window that overlooked Union Square in New York City and watched the flag-draped casket of President Abraham Lincoln followed by the Invalid Brigade pass beneath their window. The Invalid Brigade, Civil War veterans who had been maimed in the war, particularly touched six-year-old Teddy. He revered those veterans with "the empty sleeve" who had given a part of themselves to save the Union. Teddy was a weak child who suffered from asthma; his mother remembered that he loved to dress up as a wounded soldier and play that he had lost his arm in glorious battle.

The Granger Collection, New York

After attending Harvard and marrying, Theodore Roosevelt was elected as the youngest member of the New York State Assembly and served three terms. He sponsored a bill, backed by the Cigar Makers Union, which regulated the manufacturing of cigars in homes because of the poor living conditions in tenements. The bill passed but was struck down by the New York courts. "It was this case which first waked me to [social] injustices," Roosevelt wrote, "and the Courts were not the best judges . . . they knew legalisms, but not life." From his early career, he pushed for reform.

While he was an assemblyman, however, tragedy struck. In the course of twenty-four hours, he became a new father, a widower, and an orphan. His wife Alice died in childbirth and his mother died of typhoid fever. Roosevelt sent his daughter to live with his sister, put the family house up for sale, and headed to the American West to recover. Throughout his life, the wilderness would be a space where he would find clarity, and its preservation became a top priority during his presidency. His experience in Dakota Territory transformed him. Returning east, he married again and began a long political career during which he spread his belief that an activist government should be a positive force in its citizens' lives.

Roosevelt's faith in an activist government entered mainstream U.S. political thought in the early years of the twentieth century. Decades earlier, European reformers and politicians had begun to use the power of government to address economic inequalities and dangerous working and living conditions wrought by industrial capitalism. Since the 1870s, cities such as London, Glasgow, and Berlin had used municipal government and scientific expertise to solve their infrastructure needs through sanitation, expansion of utilities, and centralized city planning. Roosevelt combined ideas about reform at home with a vision of America's place in the world. When he called the United States the "most belated of nations" in 1907 for not adopting European-style workers' compensation, he worried that Americans were falling behind in a world that was expanding government's role and adopting reforms to solve societal ills.

Teddy Roosevelt believed that an activist government should be a positive force in its citizens' lives. How would these ideas, and the European models they were inspired by, come to transform political thought and actions at the turn of the century?

Go to MindTap® to watch a video on Roosevelt and learn how his story relates to the themes of this chapter.

Germany had passed workmen's compensation laws in 1884, Austria in 1887, and Britain in 1897. Given the industrial violence and hardship that U.S. workers faced, looking to such nations for models of reform and humane alternatives to class warfare made sense.

17-1

Party System in an Industrial Age

Library of Congress Prints and Photographs Division [LC-DIG-ppmsca-15785]

This 1874 Thomas Nast illustration shows a braying ass (which represents the Democratic Party) in a lion's coat with a *New York Herald* collar frightening other animals in the forest. A giraffe (*New York Tribune*), a unicorn (*New York Times*), and an owl (*New York World*) represent other politically partisan newspapers. An elephant (which represents the Republican Party) stands near broken planks "Inflation" and "Reconstruction" over a pit labeled "Southern Claims. Chaos, Rum."

What does this cartoon suggest about the nature of partisan politics in the Reconstruction era? What was the role of newspapers, as suggested by Nast, in their political debates? ▶

During the late nineteenth century, politics and business were inextricably bound as government at all levels aided businessmen to secure financing (on railroads), suppress worker unrest (in Homestead and Ludlow), and pass business-friendly legislation. Many reformers and the general public complained about and worked to reform this cozy relationship at both the state and national levels. One of the most striking aspects of politics since the end of Reconstruction in 1877 had been how evenly balanced the two major parties were. The Republicans held the presidency for three terms and the Democrats for two. Presidents rarely had the luxury of their party having a majority in both the House and the Senate. The result was general stagnation in national governance, which provided an opening for reformers and third-party movements to push for changes.

☞ As you read, consider the sources of political stagnation. How did it affect different groups of Americans?

17-1a Big Business and Government

As a result of the government's laissez-faire economic policies and expanding global markets, business magnates gained tremendous wealth during this period. A market that lacked oversight or regulation from local, state, or federal government agencies made this possible. Business leaders were eager to protect their gains and keep a cooperative government in place. Few government officials, and certainly no private citizens, had the power to curb the dominance over the consolidated corporations on the U.S. economy and political arena.

Governments are unwilling to regulate businesses because of their close relationship to them.

A wealthy class intent on preserving its own power dominated government at all levels. Businessmen made alliances with state and federal officials who could protect their interests and defend them against the rising tide of reform that began to sweep the nation in the 1890s. For example, John D. Rockefeller Jr., the heir to his father's vast fortune as the head of Standard Oil, married Abby Aldrich, the daughter of Senator Nelson Aldrich and sister to Congressman Richard Aldrich. Senator Aldrich and his cohort of Republicans were known for their ties to business and fierce protection of those interests. Businessmen such as J.P Morgan and Jay Gould were disappointed when Theodore Roosevelt turned out to be such a progressive reformer during his presidency. His background and political pedigree made businessmen believe that he would protect their interests. When he began prosecuting Rockefeller for violating antitrust laws, however, Henry Clay Frick, Andrew Carnegie's business partner, complained, "We bought the son-of-a-bitch and then he didn't stay bought." They saw his reforms as treachery to their common class interests.

Roosevelt represented a new constituency in U.S. politics: college-educated, middle-class professionals calling for government by impartial experts rather than party bosses or capitalists. Often trained in new social sciences such as statistics, the new constituency called for a larger government role in controlling industry and a smaller role for party politicians in controlling government. While the ideal of these professionals was government by public-spirited experts, they were suspicious of popular politics that emphasized popularity over expertise and civic virtue. These people pressed for reforms to protect vulnerable groups such as workers and women. Their brand of moralistic, nonpartisan, expertise-based government would come to be called *Progressivism*, and Teddy Roosevelt would be their champion.

17-1b Party Loyalty and Ideology

Voters tend to make decisions based on party loyalty, not beliefs or issues.

From the end of Reconstruction until the 1896 presidential election, U.S. political parties emphasized group loyalty over ideology. This is not to say that each did not have a coherent program. In general, Republicans continued to promote the commercial and industrial development of the nation through governmental support for railroads and corporations. They also worked to protect the morals and customs of native-born evangelical Protestants. Republicans favored a high tariff to protect domestic manufactured goods from foreign competition, and they sponsored laws to forbid state aid to church (primarily Catholic) schools, to require English to be the primary language of instruction in all schools, and to ban alcoholic beverages (temperance). Democrats, in contrast, favored a more laissez-faire agenda. They advocated low tariffs to reduce prices for consumers, supported states' rights, and opposed any governmental aid to corporations. Democrats denounced the Republican program of moral legislation, such as temperance as a paternalistic invasion in people's lives, which they believed was biased toward a New England Protestant sensibility.

These political agendas, however, were not the primary political drivers. Voters made **standing decisions** to favor a party based on their ethnic and religious backgrounds more than on their policy stances (see Table 17.1). Brand Whitlock, mayor of Toledo from 1906–1914, remembered that belonging to the Republican Party in his community in Ohio was "not a matter of intellectual choice, it was a matter of biological selection," an "elemental" fact of life. Native-born Protestants, especially those descended from New Englanders in the Northeast and upper Midwest, voted consistently for Republicans. Irish Catholics and other immigrant groups tended to favor the Democrats, a party that had long mobilized them.

The **Solid South** was made up of the sixteen southern states and the District of Columbia, which consistently voted for the Democratic candidate in presidential elections between Reconstruction and World War I. New York and Ohio were swing states that could tilt either way. Consequently, an inordinate number of presidential nominees came from Ohio as party leaders sought an advantage there in the general election. Republican politicians "waved the bloody shirt" by recalling the wounds inflicted on Union soldiers by the Democrat-led Confederacy. Southern Democrats responded by warning that Republicans would destroy white supremacy with "black rule" as they allegedly had done during Reconstruction. These raw Civil War memories led Thomas Nast, the New York cartoonist, to portray the Democrats as a stubbornly rebellious donkey and Republicans as an elephant who never forgets—symbols about past history and regional loyalties rather than particular policy positions.

Because of these strong feelings, voter turnout was extraordinarily high until the end of the century, routinely bringing out 80 to 90 percent of eligible voters, meaning males in the North and West and, increasingly, only white males in the South. Competition between the two parties was so fierce that between 1877 and 1897, each party won undivided control of the national government only for two years (the Republicans,

Table 17.1 U.S. Party Affiliation by Religion, Late Nineteenth Century

Religion and political affiliations often mapped onto one another, and politicians and political movements exploited those connections. Regional attachments and immigration status also influenced political affiliations.

Religion	Democrat (%)	Republican (%)
Immigrant		
Irish Catholic	80	20
Total Catholic	70	30
German Lutheran	65	35
Norwegian Lutheran	20	80
British Protestant	35	65
Northern Native Born		
Quaker	5	95
Congregational	25	75
Methodist	25	75
Baptist	35	65
Presbyterian	40	60
Episcopal	45	55
Southern Native Born		
Disciples of Christ	50	50
Presbyterian	70	30
Baptist	75	25
Methodist	90	10

Source: Paul Kleppner, *The Third Electoral System, 1853–1892* (1979).

standing decisions Political choice made by voters based on their family history and background rather than issues.

Solid South Block of sixteen southern states and the District of Columbia that consistently voted Democrat in national elections.

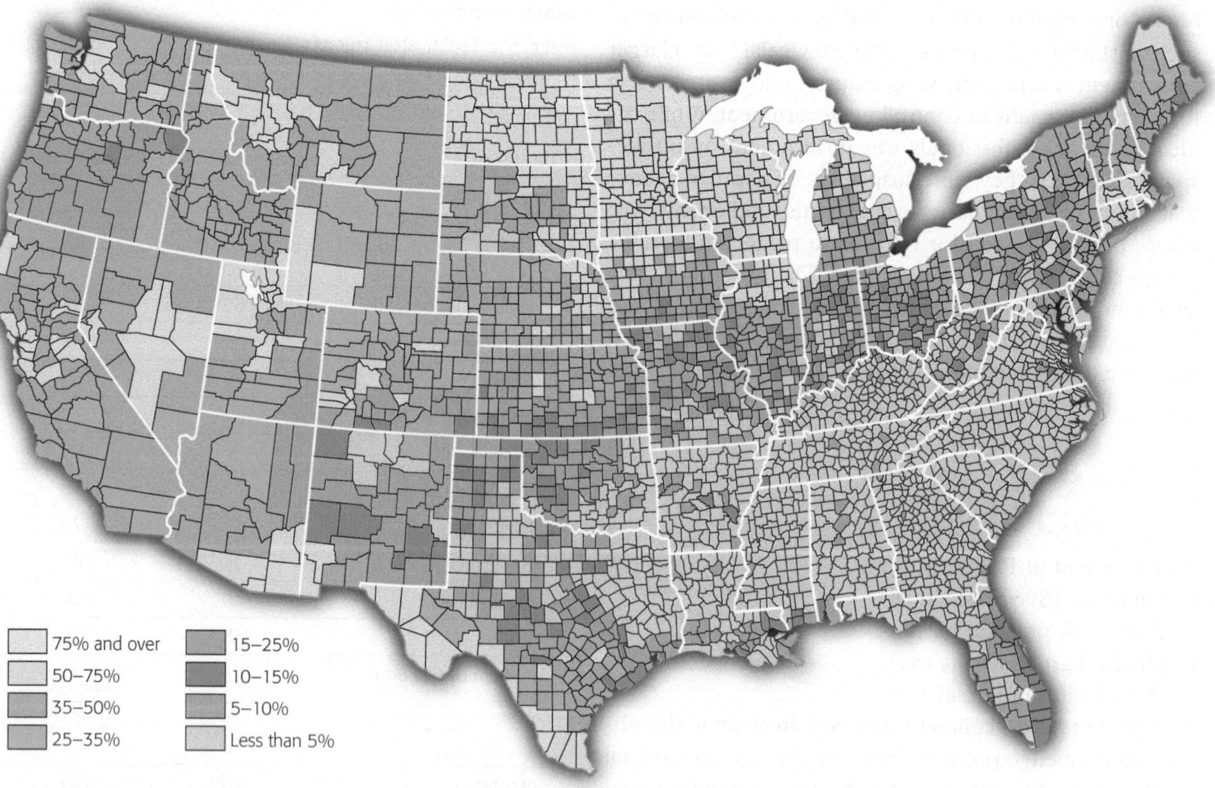

Map 17.1 Percentage of Foreign-Born People by County, 1910 Political parties paid close attention to the immigrant status of their constituencies and attempted to make political inroads with specific communities by meeting their particular political demands. Note the places where foreign-born people tended to concentrate. Obviously, cities like Los Angeles, Chicago, and Boston had high concentrations. However, rural areas such as the upper Midwest and the United States-Mexico borderland were also home to a majority of foreign-born populations. ▲

1889–1891 and the Democrats, 1891–1893). Between 1876 and 1892, no president received a majority of the popular vote. As a consequence, the entire executive branch tended to be weak and underfunded by Congress.

Voters' commitments to a party were not easily changed, so elections turned on mobilizing the party's supporters rather than changing undecided voters' minds. Parties relied heavily on professional organizers to whip up supporters' enthusiasm with spectacles such as torchlight parades, brass bands, bonfires, and campaign souvenirs, including clay pipes, ribbons, and matchboxes emblazoned with their candidate's image. Until the 1890s, there were no officially printed ballots, so voters simply filled out brightly colored ballots and handed them to party organizers at the polls, making it easy for party poll watchers to see how people had voted.

spoils system Political patronage system in which the winning party dismisses government workers and replaces them with its own loyal party members.

political machines Political organization, usually urban, that supports candidates who pushed its constituents' agenda.

The organizational politics of parades and mass turnout cost time and money. Each party induced its supporters to contribute money and energy to campaigning with the lure of governmental jobs. Such "spoils" of electoral "war" required the winning party to fire thousands of incumbent civil servants and replace them with party loyalists. Under the **spoils system**, presidents spent much time handing out thousands of clerical jobs. Grover Cleveland and Benjamin Harrison each fired up to forty thousand post office employees, one of the few large organizations that the federal government operated, to make room for their own supporters. In return, the parties "assessed" jobholders a percentage, sometimes as much as 10 percent of their salaries, to hold their positions.

17-1c Voting and Disenfranchisement

Political machines and discrimination limit democracy in the United States.

For parties and politicians to protect their power, they had to control the electorate (see Map 17.1). In the growing northern industrial cities, **political machines** drew their power from appeals to recent immigrants, especially Catholics, whom

Protestant natives despised. Local ward bosses provided services to newly arrived immigrants, helping them to settle into their new lives. In return, they expected party loyalty and a high turnout on election day. William "Boss" Tweed's Tammany Hall in New York City was for a time the most successful political machine. Tweed was able to hand out patronage to loyal voters while making money for himself, actions satirized by cartoonists such as Thomas Nast, who looked for ways to curb the machines' influence.

In the rural South, disenfranchisement played a significant role in controlling the electorate. In the post-Reconstruction period in violation of the original intention of the Fifteenth Amendment, whites gradually stripped African American men of their right to vote by requiring measures such as paying a poll tax and meeting literacy requirements. Between 1890 and 1908, southern state legislatures passed new constitutions, amendments, and laws that made registration and voting more difficult for black citizens as well as many poor whites. In the U.S. West, Mexican Americans were also limited in participating in elections because of de facto practices and intimidation that kept them away from the polls.

At the federal level, Native Americans and Chinese immigrants were denied citizenship and therefore the right to vote. Because of the 1790 statute reserving citizenship to "free white persons," Chinese and other Asian immigrants could not become citizens and had no standing to vote regardless of how long they had lived in the United States. Numerous treaties and the Dawes Act had promised Native Americans a path toward citizenship once they had accommodated to U.S. culture, but enforcement was weak. The Fifteenth Amendment did not apply to Indians, and they were not granted citizenship until 1924. Even then, some states prohibited Indians from voting. By the end of the twentieth century, only white men had a secure constitutional right to exercise the vote and have a say in how the country was governed.

17-2 Early Reform Attempts

Members of a Woman's Christian Temperance Union branch that marched on Washington, D.C., pose in this 1909 image. Under the leadership of Frances Willard, the WCTU advocated for more than temperance extending its reform movement to include women's suffrage, labor unions, clean municipal government, and free education for children. Willard's motto was to "Do everything" (petition, protest, and lobby) possible to create real reform of U.S. society.

What do you notice about the class, gender, and race of the people in this photograph? What do you conclude from your observations? By reading their banners, can you tell what reforms they advocated? ▶

Topical Press Agency/Hulton Archive/Getty Images

Because the Democrats and Republicans did not sufficiently address issues of enfranchisement, corruption, and government regulation, there was an opening for challengers. Farmers, middle-class professional men and women, evangelical reformers (many of them women), and workers built social movements that defied party loyalty and instead pursued each group's particular area of concern. These groups believed they needed to work outside the party system in order to have government officials take up their cause. Although none succeeded in winning control of Congress or the presidency, all influenced public discourse—and ultimately the major political parties—to bring about reform at the national and local levels.

☞ As you read, consider how reform movements challenged the entrenched party system. What were their motives, and what was the nature of their challenges?

17-2a Farmers and Railroad Regulation

Farmers' organizations advocate and win regulations that bring railroads under public control.

Because national parties focused primarily on party loyalty and patronage, they paid little attention to problems that plagued farmers and rural workers caused by competition from an expanding global market. Farmers organized to demand fair treatment against railroad and grain monopolies. They initially petitioned state governments but ultimately came to believe that only the federal government could exercise control over corporate monopolies. Farmers protested the railroads' practice of **pooling** and giving **rebates** to shippers who used a particular line exclusively. Farmers also objected to the lower rates that large enterprises received for sending goods long distances rather than the short hauls that farmers and small businesses used more frequently.

In the South, the Civil War had destroyed industrial infrastructure such as mines, machinery, railroads, and telegraphs. In the 1890s, most southern counties reported a per capita real estate value of between $100 and $200 in comparison to the $637 national average and $970 in New York City. After Reconstruction, southern Democratic state governments repudiated the debts incurred by their Republican predecessors, so northern banks were hesitant to lend further funds to rebuild the region. As a result, the South lagged far behind the rest of the country in economic development. Describing a southern farmer's funeral in the late 1880s, one observer bitterly noted that everything from the marble of the headstone to the nails in the coffin had been imported from the North: "The South didn't furnish a thing for that funeral but the corpse and the hole in the ground."

The Midwest and West had higher per capita investments in buildings, slaughterhouses, breweries, railroads, telegraphs, mines, and other industrial infrastructure, but capital was frequently owned by nonresident investors, many of them foreign. One-third of Minnesota's banks, for instance, were owned by nonresidents, compared with less than 10 percent of New England banks. The control over the economy exercised by eastern capitalists left Westerners feeling that they were an internal colony of eastern interests.

Organizations such as **The National Grange of the Order of Patrons of Husbandry** advocated for farmers. In the wake of the Panic of 1873, the Grange challenged the owners of railroads and grain elevators by starting **cooperatives**, which provided an alternative outlet for farmers' grain sales by pooling harvests and holding out for higher prices. Critics derided these "co-ops" as socialism. Under pressure from local Granges, however, midwestern state legislatures passed laws that regulated railroads and grain elevators in an attempt to keep pricing fair. In 1876, the Supreme Court upheld these Granger Laws in *Munn v. Illinois*. The Court said that because Munn, a grain elevator owner, operated a business that was invested with a public interest, it could be regulated by state, as could railroads.

Farmers responded to corporate control and government collusion by forming economic and political coalitions that often resulted in **third-party** runs for state and national offices. In 1884, the Anti-Monopoly Party ran candidates in eleven midwestern and western states on a platform that included antitrust legislation, direct election of senators, and a graduated income tax. The party was short lived because it merged with the Greenback Party. Since the end of Reconstruction, the Greenbacks had been pressing the federal government to issue paper money that was not tied to the **gold standard**, which encouraged high inflation. An inflationary economy based on greenbacks benefited farmers who typically carried heavy debts (see Figure 17.1).

The strongest coalition emerged from the **Farmers Alliance**, which eventually supplanted the Grange as the most outspoken advocate for farmers. Local chapters created cooperatives that sold grain and purchased supplies in bulk to save money for their members. They also formed small banks to ensure farmers' control over their money. The Colored Farmer's Alliance, the Women's Alliance, and the Southern Alliance each catered to its members' particular concerns. Eventually, the coalition realized that it needed national laws to curb nationally

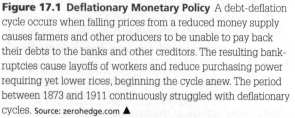

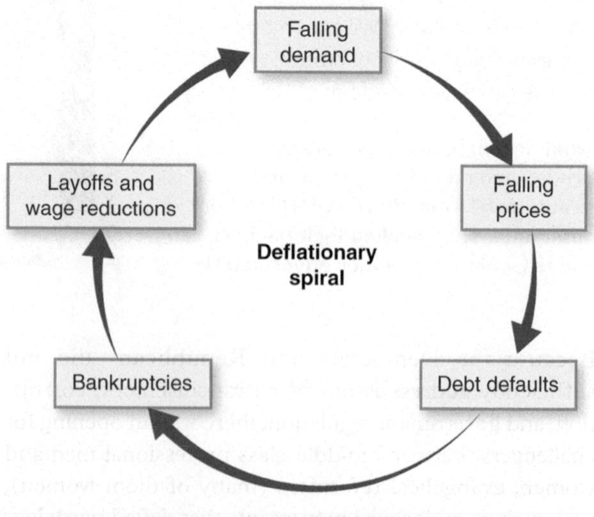

Figure 17.1 Deflationary Monetary Policy A debt-deflation cycle occurs when falling prices from a reduced money supply causes farmers and other producers to be unable to pay back their debts to the banks and other creditors. The resulting bankruptcies cause layoffs of workers and reduce purchasing power requiring yet lower rices, beginning the cycle anew. The period between 1873 and 1911 continuously struggled with deflationary cycles. Source: zerohedge.com ▲

pooling Practice used by railroads to minimize competition and set favorable rates among themselves.

rebates Money given back, in this case, to companies that shipped their goods on railroads exclusively, thus giving those companies a hidden discount and advantage.

The National Grange of the Order of Patrons of Husbandry Support group for farmers that focused on sociability and education, which eventually transformed into a political advocacy group.

cooperatives Group of individuals who come together to create a nonprofit entity to pool their resources to purchase goods in bulk and/or to create a sales outlet for their goods.

third-party Political party in the United States that challenged the Democrats and Republicans in a general election.

gold standard A monetary policy that ties the amount of currency in circulation directly to the amount of gold that a government holds in its treasury.

Farmers Alliance Outgrowth of the Grange made up of northern and southern branches that advocated for farmers at the national level.

scaled industries. In 1892, the alliances joined the Knights of Labor, and both eventually joined the People's and then the Populist parties.

When alliance members gained traction politically and were bolstered by the decision in the *Granger Cases*, businessmen lobbied recently elected President James A. Garfield to nominate an ally to the Supreme Court. In 1881, Garfield named Stanley Matthews, a probusiness Ohio senator. Aided by Matthews's vote, the Court in *Wabash v. Illinois* reversed its earlier decision in the *Granger Cases*, holding that state regulation of railroad traffic was unconstitutional because the Constitution granted exclusive jurisdiction over interstate commerce to Congress, not the states.

The *Wabash* decision placed 85 percent of railroad traffic beyond state control. Seeking federal regulation, a coalition of New York merchants, small oil producers in Pennsylvania, and farmers pressed for passage of the Interstate Commerce Act in 1887. Supporters argued that since railroads crossed state lines and were therefore engaged in interstate commerce, making them subject to the legal jurisdiction of Congress under the **Commerce Clause**. The Interstate Commerce Act's passage enabled the creation of the first-ever federal regulatory agency, the Interstate Commerce Commission, to enforce its provisions. The law's definition of illegal rate discrimination, however, was left deliberately vague until the 1906 Hepburn Act because of disagreements between shippers and railroads about what constituted a reasonable rate.

17-2b Urban Professionals and Civil Service Reform

Progressive urban reformers take lessons from abroad to institute changes.

A growing class of urban professionals—accountants, lawyers, middle managers, and engineers—claimed that the right to government jobs should be based on education and expertise, rather than the spoils system. These reformers contrasted their predicament with the British and German civil service systems, which hired educated professional experts from those nations' elite universities. In the United States, this professional class disproportionately came from Protestant New England families who were losing influence to newer ethnic groups through the political machines.

Many middle-class advocates of civil service reform were suspicious of universal suffrage, believing that elections dominated by Irish Catholic Democrats in northern cities and the newly enfranchised Republican-leaning freedmen in the South would result, in Charles Francis Adams's words, "government of ignorance and vice" controlled by "a . . . Celtic proletariat on the Atlantic coast; an African proletariat on the shores of the Gulf; and a Chinese proletariat on the Pacific." Finding common cause with white Southerners seeking to disenfranchise the freedmen, these northern middle-class reformers also abandoned efforts to protect the black vote. The group opposed Massachusetts Senator Henry Cabot Lodge's 1890 Election Bill (which white Southerners derisively called the *Force Bill*) that would have protected southern blacks' voting rights with federal election monitors.

These reformers' nobler objective was transforming government administration along "scientific" lines with policy implemented by properly trained experts rather than party loyalists who pursued office for their own self-interest. Founded in 1881, the National Civil Service Reform League pressed for a law banning partisan hiring and firing of government workers. Both parties, however, ridiculed civil service reformers as ineffectual, elitists, even effeminate dreamers—"snivel service reformers"—who did not understand the organizational realities of mobilizing voters.

Despite this resistance, civil service reformers in the Republican Party succeeded in nominating the "good-government" congressman, James A. Garfield, in the 1880 presidential race. He won the election, but it was an assassin's bullet that pushed Congress to act. On July 2, 1881, as Garfield boarded a train in Washington, D.C., Charles Julius Guiteau, a mentally unstable man who believed that his earlier support for Garfield had earned him an ambassadorship, shot Garfield. He suffered from his wounds for more than two months before dying, making Vice President Chester Alan Arthur the next president.

The press proclaimed Garfield a martyr to civil service reform, and, in 1883, Congress passed the **Pendleton Civil Service Reform Act**. It established the Civil Service Commission to administer appointments to federal jobs based on merit. Modeled explicitly on the British system, the act required office seekers to demonstrate their qualifications by taking a written exam. In the beginning, the commission administered only about 10 percent of federal jobs. By the end of the nineteenth century, more than 50 percent of federal jobs had come under its jurisdiction. The system also created good-paying professional jobs for women. In the 1890s, almost half of the applicants who passed the exam were women.

The good government reformers shifted the tone of presidential politics. The 1884 Democratic presidential nominee, Grover Cleveland, was chosen because of his efforts to promote "educational" political campaigns as well as his hostility to government spending for partisan purposes. When Republicans nominated James Blaine, a **stalwart** supporter of the Republican party, which favored machine politics and

Commerce Clause Article 1, Section 8 of the U.S. Constitution gives Congress the right to regulate trade with foreign countries as well as between the states and Native Americans.

Pendleton Civil Service Reform Act Law that required federal jobs to be awarded on the basis of merit, not party loyalty, and instituted the Civil Service Exam.

stalwart Marked by loyalty, reliability, and hard work that describes the more conservative branch of the late nineteenth-century Republican Party, which favored machine politics rather than civil service reform.

Vintage Collection/The Granger Collection, New York

Frederic Howe (Center) Pictured with a Group of Hindu and Parsee Immigrants from India on Ellis Island, New York.

Global Americans The career trajectory of **Frederic Howe** was emblematic of the transatlantic world of Progressive reformers at the turn of the twentieth century. He lived at Toynbee Hall in England and studied in Germany with some of the leading urban reformers. He brought his knowledge to Cleveland, Ohio, where he became a leader in municipal reform as Cleveland successfully addressed the problems of rapid urban growth under the leadership of its mayor, Tom Johnson. Howe also shared his expertise with nationally known urban reformers. He was most concerned with the fairness of taxation and how to fund government infrastructure projects. He was one of the earliest proponents of tax reform and Henry George's single tax, which advocated taxing only undeveloped land rather than wages. Throughout his career, Howe traveled back and forth to Europe to meet with city managers and urban planners. Based on his meetings and observations with European municipal reformers, particularly in Denmark, Germany, and England, Howe published *The City: The Hope of Democracy* in 1905.

Howe's own political alliances as a progressive-minded reformer mirrored those of the time period. He began his career as a Republican but switched to the Democratic Party just as most Progressives shifted with the changes in the national parties. In 1914, President Wilson appointed Howe, who had since moved to New York, the Commissioner of Immigration of the Port of New York. He ended his career working for the New Deal in the Department of Agriculture.

patronage rather than civil service reform, many middle-class professionals left the Republican Party to support Cleveland.

17-2c Evangelicals Challenge Threats to the Home

Moral reformers push for temperance legislation in the name of preserving home and family.

Like farmers and middle-class professionals, evangelicals, particularly evangelical women, felt that the two major parties ignored their issues. **Evangelical Christians** believed that personal reformation and public advocacy should protect the home from what they regarded as destructive male behaviors—drinking alcohol, visiting prostitutes, gambling, and fighting. Evangelicals also built coalitions with other reform groups such as the farmer alliances and civil service reformers.

Evangelical Christians Religious believers who stress that personal transformation accompanies conversion, offering a vision of individual self-respect.

Woman's Crusade Loose coalition of women's groups that protested the sale of liquor by picketing saloons and bars and was a precursor to the Women's Christian Temperance Union (WCTU).

Inspired by sermons denouncing alcoholic beverages, women in Ohio launched the **Woman's Crusade** in 1873. Their tactics included occupying saloons while singing hymns and praying to stop liquor sales. In smaller towns dominated by Yankee Protestants, these women were often successful. In cities with large immigrant-born communities, their campaigns stalled when urbanites resisted attacks on the saloons that were their social gathering places. The crusade, dominated by white middle-class women, denounced the sellers of alcohol in class-based terms. One temperance journalist was shocked that "the fine, old, respectable city of Chillicothe, Ohio" could "vomit forth such a crowd," a "masculine crowd" of "low-browed, stubby-haired sons of humanity," including one man with "a roaming red nose, pig eye, and soap-fat chin."

Inspired by the Woman's Crusade, Midwesterners formed the Woman's Christian Temperance Union (WCTU) in 1873 dedicated to protecting the home from male vices. The WCTU soon became an international organization with branches in Australia, England, Canada, and Japan. It joined forces with the Prohibition Party to push for legislation and to sponsor national candidates. Together they advocated a ban on the consumption and manufacture of alcoholic beverages. Led by Frances Willard, a charismatic evangelical woman who took control of the WCTU in 1881, the organization eventually moved beyond anti-alcohol measures to call for banning prostitution, "impure" (sexually explicit) literature, and child labor. The WCTU also lobbied for the eight-hour workday and suffrage for women and joined political coalitions to further their causes.

The common element in all of these reforms was the protection of the home as a safe haven from materialistic commercial values and male sinfulness. By focusing on maternal roles, WCTU activists could move from domestic settings to engage in public speaking, lobbying for legislation, and occupying demonstrations at taverns and saloons. As the WCTU broadened its agenda, however, its leadership in the anti-alcohol movement yielded to the Anti-Saloon League, which was dominated by male leaders.

New York Illustrated Times

Ann Lohman Arrested by Anthony Comstock, *New York Illustrated Times* Anthony Comstock, arrested Ann Trow Lohman, also known as Madame Restelle, on charges that she performed abortions, which were illegal in New York, and provided birth control to women through the mail. Comstock pursued women like Lohman, Margaret Sanger, Victoria Woodhull, and Emma Goldman who advocated for a woman's right to use birth control. He was derided by sexual progressives such as George Bernard Shaw who mocked his vigilance against sexuality and vice as "Comstockery." ▲

Alcohol and domestic abuse were only two aspects of urban life that motivated reformers. Another was vice. Anthony Comstock, a New York dry goods clerk affiliated with the YMCA, persuaded evangelically inclined wealthy merchants to create the **New York Society for the Suppression of Vice**. In 1876, prodded by Comstock's lobbying, Congress enacted the Comstock Act, banning from the mails not only "obscene, lewd, lascivious" materials but also information about contraception and related products. Comstock himself was appointed the postal service's special agent in charge of inspecting the mails for obscene materials. He brought hundreds of criminal cases against pornographers and reformers who mailed pamphlets advocating contraception or revision of marriage and divorce laws.

By the mid-1880s, some evangelical reformers expanded their political agenda to include attacks on economic inequality and poverty through what became known as the **Social Gospel**. Strong in midwestern centers of evangelical reform, the movement had its origins in the earlier abolitionist movement. Richard Ely, an American economist, argued that sinful behaviors such as drinking and visiting prostitutes were the direct result of industrial capitalism's mass unemployment, low wages, and poor working conditions. Blaming the corporate elite for un-Christian behavior toward workers, Ely argued that sin was social as well as individual, and that widespread economic well-being was a safeguard for Christian morality. The Social Gospel movement owed its intellectual origins to **Christian socialism**, a movement that made alliances with the secular Fabian Society in order to effect change in Great Britain. In Britain and in France and Germany, a coalition of socialists had influenced local and national governments to take direct action to alleviate poverty, improve housing, and create safe working conditions. U.S. reformers such as Frederic Howe and Frances Willard had direct and long-term interaction with their European counterparts to share ways to improve the quality of life for the masses.

New York Society for the Suppression of Vice Group founded to enforce laws that prohibited the sale and transport of lewd and obscene materials.

Social Gospel Christian principle focusing on the application of virtues, such as charity and forgiveness, to social problems such as poverty and vice.

Christian socialism Political ideology based on Christian belief that capitalism is rooted in greed, a mortal sin.

Toynbee Hall Toynbee Hall was England's first settlement house and was representative of the larger social reform movement. The same year, 1884, the Fabian Society was founded in London by a group of socialist reformers including Sidney and Beatrice Webb. Its logo was the tortoise, which reflected the reform movements' belief in slow and steady reform, rather than the revolutionary movements associated with Marxism and communism. The Fabian Society's and Toynbee Hall's influence extended internationally. Both European and U.S. reformers adopted their views and pushed for similar kinds of socialist agendas gained through moderate and slow reforms. ▶

Toynbee Hall, illustration from 'The Builder', February 14th, 1885 (litho), English School, (19th century)/Private Collection/The Bridgeman Art Library

17-2d Workers and Politics

Workers challenge existing political parties.

Both political parties claimed to represent industrial workers, but the leaders of the most important labor unions refused to endorse either one. Federal intervention on the side of corporations, such as during the Pullman and Homestead strikes, made workers distrustful of government. Samuel Gompers, head of the AFL, was reluctant to ask his members to back either party. He wanted the parties to pledge that government, especially the courts, would not interfere with unions' efforts to organize workers. Neither political party endorsed this principle, and consequently the labor movement looked elsewhere for a political home.

single tax Taxation system of mainly or exclusively one tax based only on unimproved land, not workers' wages that was popularized by Henry George in the United States.

United Labor Party Third party formed by a coalition of socialists, labor leaders, and single-tax advocates.

Thousands of workers worldwide were drawn to the concept of a **single tax** proposed by Henry George, a journalist who had published the phenomenally successful *Progress and Poverty* in 1879. According to George, economic injustice could be eliminated through a single tax imposed on land that was equal to its unimproved value. Such a tax would eliminate wealth not attributable to labor and encourage landowners to sell vacant land to those who could make productive use of it. Around the world, workingmen were attracted to George's message that wealth not based on labor was illegitimate. Groups fighting "landlordism" and clamoring for land redistribution in China, Australia, and Ireland warmed to George's single-tax remedy. He appealed directly to Irish immigrants in a pamphlet praising the Irish Land War, which was a popular movement to transfer land to tenant farmers from landlords, particularly absentee ones.

In 1886, George ran for mayor of New York City under the **United Labor Party**, declaring that "the use of the land belongs to the entire people," and "[e]veryone should be entitled to share in it." The Farmers Alliance and the liberal wing of the WCTU joined this third party. Frightened by George's mass appeal, business interests and Tammany Democrats united behind Abraham Hewitt, a wealthy owner of ironworks. Hewitt narrowly defeated George and a distant third-place finisher, Theodore Roosevelt. George's 1886 mayoral campaign marked the high tide of labor's influence for the next decade, and his ideas remained influential for the rest of the century, inspiring hundreds of single-tax clubs and proposals to nationalize railroads and utilities. A U.S. supporter, Elizabeth Magie, invented The Landlord's Game, a board game designed to demonstrate George's principles that over the decades evolved into Monopoly.

17-3 Economic Crisis and the Populist Party

Picture History/Newscom

This 1894 photo of Coxey's Army, also known as the *Army of the Commonwealth of Christ*, depicts the unemployed men who left their homes across the nation and marched to Washington, D.C. They demanded that the federal government spend more on relief efforts in the wake of the 1893 depression.

How would you describe the men in this photo? What do their dress and demeanor suggest to you? Why were they displaying two American flags? ▶

The political stalemate that characterized late nineteenth-century politics shifted dramatically in response to the largest economic crisis to hit the nation. The depression following the Panic of 1893 caused reformers to come together, and third-party coalitions rose to challenge the Democrats and Republicans to answer the needs of the U.S. electorate. The most successful was the Populist Party, which united the interests of farmers, evangelicals, and industrial workers for a short time. Although the Populists never won the presidency, they shifted the balance of political power to the Republican Party, which, along with the Democrats, ultimately co-opted some of their issues to broaden their bases.

☞ As you read, trace the rise and eventual decline of the Populist Party. Why did it fail to survive in the national political arena? Which of its ideas survived, and how?

17-3a Republican Coalition of Pensioners and Business

Republicans struggle to build a national coalition.

Republicans had a difficult time creating a winning coalition at both the national and state levels. Grover Cleveland's single-minded focus on lowering tariffs aroused fears in the industrial Northeast and cost him the election in 1888, although he won the popular vote. With dour Civil War general Benjamin Harrison in the presidency, Republicans initially pressed a program of Protestant piety. Following several Republican defeats in Midwest state elections in 1889, however, the national Republican leadership decided in 1890 to emphasize economic issues over the cultural issues favored by evangelical reformers.

Shepherded through Congress by Representative William McKinley of Ohio, the Tariff of 1890 imposed high tariffs on imported goods, winning support from some farmers as well as businesses and their employees who feared competition from cheap imports. But the tariff required importers to send scarce gold to the U.S. Treasury to pay the fees, creating a cash shortage. To win additional support and disburse the accumulated cash, Congress also enacted the Dependent and Disability Pension Act, which authorized pensions for disabled veterans and widows of Union soldiers who had served at least 90 days during the Civil War. At its peak, the Pension Act disbursed more than $135 million annually for 970,000 veterans. The law ultimately cost $8 billion. By 1900, pensions consumed 40 percent of the federal budget.

F.B. Opper/The Granger Collection, New York

Income Tax Cartoon, 1895 With few exceptions, American agricultural products did not compete with imports, giving farmers little benefit from high tariffs. This caused the economic burden of the tariff to fall on the farming regions. Wealthy individuals, in contrast, paid income taxes. In this cartoon, which appeared in *Puck*, Uncle Sam demands millionaire tax-dodgers to settle their outstanding tax bills to cover the U.S. Treasury deficits. ▲

The Republicans, in short, hoped to hold power with a coalition of business leaders and their employees, a few groups of farmers, and Union veterans. But the combined tariff-pension policy had the drawback of imposing extraordinarily high prices on consumers. Derided by Democrats as the **Billion-Dollar Congress**, Republicans chipped away at their probusiness image by enacting the Sherman Antitrust Act of 1890, which attempted to end monopolies but was ultimately judged as weak in its enforcement.

In an additional effort to win western farmers' support, the Republican-controlled Congress enacted the Sherman Silver Purchase Act, which required the federal government to purchase millions of ounces of silver from western mines and issue bonds repayable in either gold or silver coin. This took U.S. currency off the gold standard. By buying up virtually all the output of silver mines in Nevada, Colorado, and Montana, Republicans also hoped to win support from western silver producers.

17-3b Emergence of the Populists

Third-party Populists influence the tone and content of the national debate over monetary policy and government regulation.

Neither the Sherman Silver Purchase Act nor the Sherman Antitrust Act was sufficient to win agrarian or middle-class support for the Republican Party. The Antitrust Act's language was so vague that in the first suit brought under it, *United States v. E.C. Knight Co.* (the Sugar Trust Case), the Supreme Court construed the Commerce Clause to apply only to the transportation of goods across state lines, not to manufacturing monopolies. The Silver Purchase Act permitted bondholders to be repaid in either gold or silver coin, and they predictably preferred the more valuable metal, reducing the U.S. Treasury's supply of gold currency to dangerously low levels. The tariff burdened farmers by increasing the costs of farming equipment and other manufactured goods.

In response, the Grange, Farmers Alliance, remnants of the Union Labor Party, and other agrarian organizations formed the People's or **Populist Party**, charging that both major parties ignored the interests of workers and farmers in favor of the "sham issue" of the tariff. Meeting in Omaha, Nebraska, on July 4, 1892, the new third party adopted a platform that outlined the reforms that

Billion-Dollar Congress The fifty-first Congress, which was the first to pass a billion dollar budget, leading critics to deride it for what they saw as excessive spending.

Populist Party One of the most successful third parties in the history of the United States composed of a coalition of farmers and workers that the two parties ignored.

History without Borders

Feminism

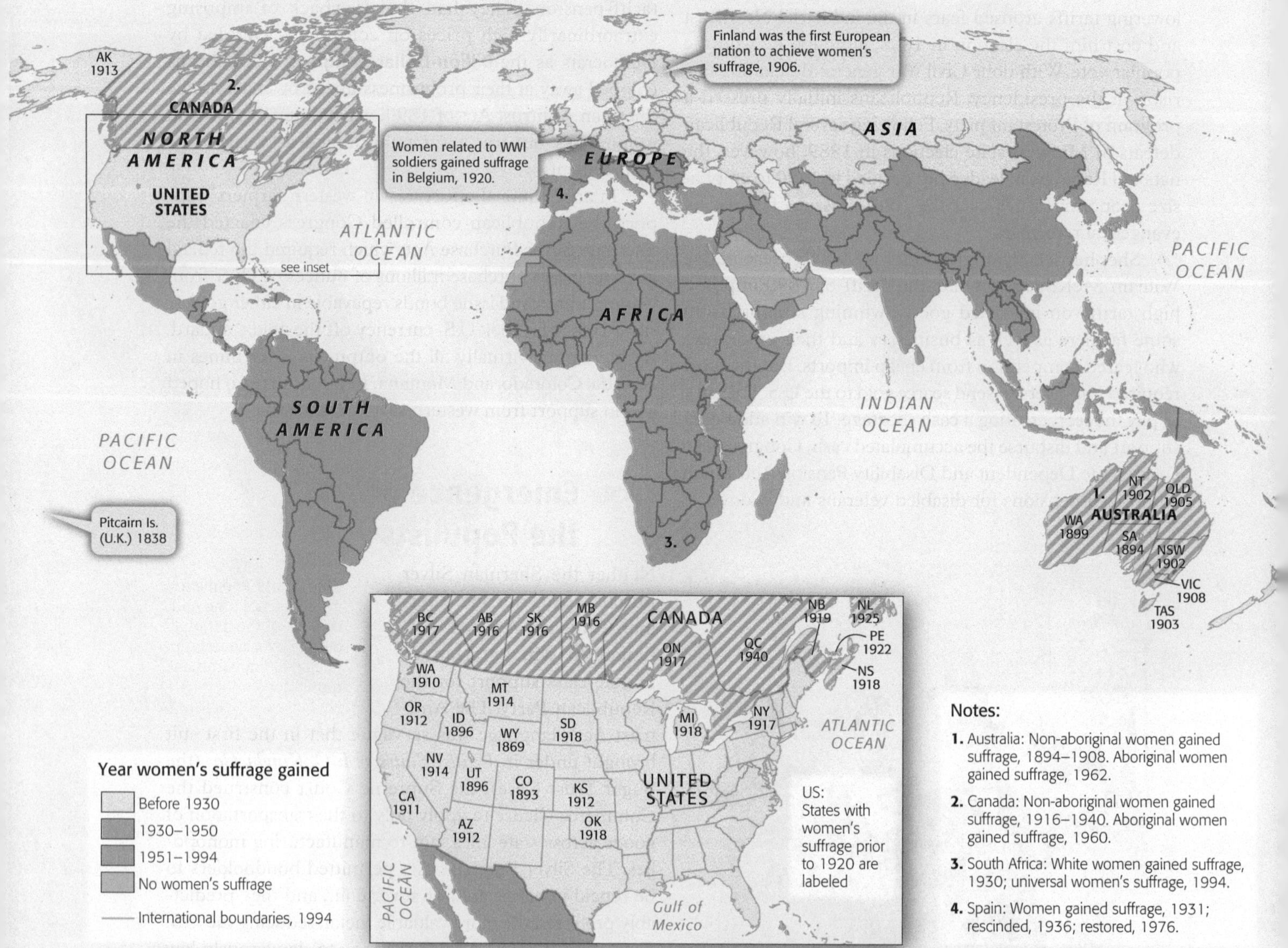

Suffrage Laws Globally 1838–1994 This map shows when women gained the right to vote across the world. The United States along with a handful of other countries were relatively early in granting suffrage to women. Note that in 1994 women in Saudi Arabia could not vote; they were finally granted the right in 2015. ▲

Feminism's origins date back centuries. In the seventeenth and eighteenth centuries, the "woman question" fueled public debate in Europe about the worth of women relative to that of men in terms of moral, spiritual, and intellectual capacity. In 1792, Englishwoman Mary Wollstonecraft made the case for men's and women's equality in the famous *A Vindication of the Rights of Women*, and revolutionaries in France and the United States pushed for expanded female education. French suffragist Hubertine Auclert first used the word feminism or *feminisme* in the 1880s. By the first decade of the twentieth century, it was a concept celebrated in the United States as something new and modern: "All feminists are suffragists, but not all suffragists are feminists." Feminism, an ideology far broader than the movement for voting rights, is based on three principles: First, women and men are fundamentally equal. Second, women's status is shaped by society, not determined by God or nature, and therefore is changeable. Finally, women and men who are feminists perceive themselves as part of a shared social grouping although there is lively debate over how much is shared.

Corbis

Seneca Falls This painting portrays Elizabeth Cady Stanton speaking during the first Woman's Rights Convention, held in the Wesleyan Methodist Chapel in Seneca Falls, New York. The very act of speaking in public in a mixed gender audience with men would have been, in and of itself, a radical act. Advocating for woman's equality even more so. ▲

Hulton Archive/Getty Images

Beatrice Webb Webb, a leader in the Fabian Society, was a historian, sociologist and economist. She is often credited with coining the term "collective bargaining," which is used to describe the negotiations that union leaders make on behalf of their members. Webb, along with her husband Sidney Webb, founded the London School of Economics. ▲

Educated free women in the early nineteenth century built a "woman movement" characterized by ideas of shared domesticity and motherhood, calling out the perils of bad marriages, alcoholism, and abuse by husbands. Even for reformers who focused on equality, the family was a major focus. Transatlantic socialist movements experimented with family arrangements based on equality, which, they claimed would elevate the position of women. Irish reformers William Thompson and Anna Wheeler wrote in 1825 that only when "women cease to be dependent on individual men for their daily support" could there be "perfect equality and entire reciprocity of happiness between women and men." Margaret Fuller, the first woman allowed to use Harvard's library, wrote "let them be sea-captains, if you will."

The revolution of 1848 in Europe raised questions of expanded political rights, fueling demands that women, should have the right to vote. In the United States, this demand was included in the 1848 Seneca Falls *Declaration of Sentiments*. Suffrage was a focus for the first international women's congress in Paris in 1878.

At the same time, the emergence of welfare states in Europe and the Progressive movement in the United States fostered maternalist movements claiming an expanded political role for women based in their roles as mothers. Urban reformers both in England and the United States such as Beatrice Webb and Jane Addams took these ideas and applied them to the settlement house movement, which provided not only services for immigrants and the poor but also careers for women to work outside the home and spread ideas about equality.

Several strands of feminism coalesced at the turn of the twentieth century around the New Woman who was educated, individualistic, and emancipated. Publications with *New Woman* in their titles emerged in Egypt, Japan, China, and Korea, promoting the idea that women had to be freed from a "savage" past that included practices like sati, veiling, polygamy, concubinage, harems, and foot binding. In Asian contexts, the New Woman was linked with the "modernizing" required to throw off imperialism.

Woman suffrage became the law in the United States in 1920, but feminism took divergent paths. In 1923, in an attempt to write full equal rights for women into the Constitution, Alice Paul introduced the Equal Rights Amendment (ERA). In 1972, Congress finally passed the ERA with a resounding majority. Ratification, however, failed — just three states short of the 38 needed. Feminists worked for equal wages, access to birth control, prosecutions of rape, and Lesbian, Gay, Bisexual, Transgender (LGBT) rights.

☞ Critical Thinking Questions

▶ How and where has suffrage for women been granted around the world? Which countries were latecomers to granting suffrage? Which countries granted suffrage to women based on race?

▶ In the United States, what factors do you suppose contributed to women's suffrage being recognized earlier in the western states than in the eastern states?

Go to MindTap® to engage with an interactive version of **History without Borders: Feminism**. Learn from an interactive map, view related video, and respond to critical thinking questions.

free silver Economic policy that advocates basing currency on both gold and silver, thereby making more currency available for circulation in the economy.

fusion Synthesis; in this case, a coalition of a third party and a dominant political party to create a joint campaign or political ticket.

each group had been calling for since the early 1880s. To attract workingmen, the Populist Party endorsed the eight-hour day for government work, restrictions on "undesirable immigration," and support for the Knights of Labor. Perhaps most controversially, Populists called for a more inflationary monetary policy known as **free silver**.

The Omaha Platform was one of the most strident attacks on the excesses of wealth and big business in U.S. history. The Populists' radicalism went beyond their platform. In Georgia, Populist Tom Watson tried to organize a biracial coalition of black and white farmers, declaring to racially mixed audiences that "[y]ou are made to hate each other because upon that hatred is rested the keystone of the arch of financial despotism which enslaves you both." Populists also endorsed feminism not only in the form of women's suffrage but also by sponsoring charismatic female orators such as Kansas lawyer and lecturer Mary Elizabeth Lease, who urged farmers to "raise less corn and more hell." The highly visible participation of female speakers in the Populist campaign attracted angry denunciations from conservatives shocked by women engaged in rough-and-tumble debate.

The Populist Party did surprisingly well in the 1892 elections, capturing eleven seats in Congress, several governorships, and the state legislatures of Kansas, Nebraska, and North Carolina. Their presidential candidate, James Weaver, a Civil War general and former Greenbacker, received more than a million popular votes and twenty-two electoral votes from four states, Colorado, Kansas, Idaho, and Nevada. This success was especially impressive because the major political parties used their influence over the electoral system to minimize Populist gains, especially in the South.

The Democratic Party avoided contentious issues such as monetary policy and government takeover of railroads and nominated former president Grover Cleveland. Campaigning almost solely against the McKinley tariff, Cleveland won a narrow victory over President Benjamin Harrison. The Democrats also made a special appeal to housewives, who were presumed to be "the most important factor" in the election because "in their shopping excursions. . . [they] found a rise in prices explained as due to the McKinley bill" and "went home and told their husbands."

17-3c Panic of 1893 and Its Political Aftermath

Economic upheaval sets the stage for changes within the two major parties.

Cleveland's second presidency was doomed before it even began. Ten days before his inauguration, the Philadelphia & Reading Railroad declared bankruptcy, triggering the Panic of 1893, the nation's most severe depression until the Great Depression in 1929. In 1894, several "armies" of unemployed workers, such as Coxey's Army, left their homes to march on Washington, demanding that the federal government fund public works projects and hire workers to relieve unemployment. Labor unrest gripped the nation as workers headed the American Railway Union's call to honor the Pullman strike (see Chapter 16). Farm product prices plummeted, leading to a rash of farm foreclosures across the nation.

The Cleveland administration responded to these crises with probusiness policies. Convinced that the Silver Purchase Act had helped trigger the financial panic by depleting the gold supply, Cleveland called for its repeal and strenuously resisted any expansion of the money supply, including modest efforts to issue silver coin. Cleveland also was confronted by a rush of bondholders who wanted to redeem their notes for gold coin, an action that would threaten the U.S. government with the risk of defaulting on the bonds. To stave off such a disaster, Cleveland enlisted the financier J.P. Morgan to persuade fellow bankers to cease redeeming bonds for gold and to lend $65 million in gold coin to the federal government in exchange for federal bonds that promised to pay 4 percent interest. Although the effort staved off federal default, the deal (on which Morgan earned a handsome commission) also gave the impression that private bankers dictated federal monetary policy.

Voters blamed the Cleveland administration for the depression, and Democrats at the 1896 Chicago convention rejected its probusiness policies in favor of a less radical version of the Populist Party's agrarian program. William Jennings Bryan, a representative from Nebraska, delivered a fiery call for silver currency at the convention, declaring, "We shall answer their demands for a gold standard by saying to them: you shall not press down upon the brow of labor this crown of thorns. You shall not crucify mankind upon a cross of gold." The delegates enthusiastically nominated Bryan and called for unlimited coinage of silver. Eastern Democrats—including Cleveland Democrats who had embraced him as a symbol of middle-class professional reform—deserted the Democratic Party, disgusted by what they regarded as a demagogic appeal for inflation. Cleveland himself sat out the election, refusing to endorse Bryan, but Democrats won new support from the West and South when the Populist Party endorsed Bryan's **fusion** candidacy.

Republicans nominated William McKinley, who was backed by a coalition of wealthy businessmen. The most powerful of these was Mark Hanna from Ohio who spent much of his own money and raised large sums from wealthy supporters to ensure that the McKinley campaign was the best funded. The Republicans painted Bryan as a demagogic radical who would save debt-ridden farmers by inflicting an inflated currency on the nation. To counteract McKinley's campaign war chest, Bryan frenetically toured the nation in an effort to win support from eastern workers as well as western and southern farmers. In eastern cities, however, his appeal was limited because workers saw little to be gained from inflation, and Catholic and Jewish immigrants were suspicious of his evangelical style. In response to Bryan's calls for workers to make common cause with farmers, Samuel Gompers pointed out that farmers were also employers. McKinley defeated both Bryan and the idea of economic radicalism. For a generation, sectional distrust and economic prosperity buried the idea of a unified farmer-labor alliance of producers (farmers and workers) against capitalists.

McKinley's first term was as blessed by good fortune as Cleveland's had been cursed by depression. By the late 1890s, the depression of 1893 had begun to dissipate. As farm prices rose, agrarian discontent diminished. The 1898 war against Spain (see Chapter 18) contributed to a sense of national unity and pride that benefited the incumbent administration. In the 1900 campaign, McKinley again faced Bryan, but this time with Theodore Roosevelt running as McKinley's vice president to win middle-class reformers' support. Bryan supplemented his old message, denouncing monopolies with a new message attacking overseas expansion in the Philippines and the subsequent bloody struggle against Filipino guerillas as a brutal act of imperialism. But his anti-imperialist campaign was handily defeated by McKinley's slogan, "four more years of the full dinner pail," made credible by the return of economic prosperity.

The elections of 1896 and 1900 made it clear that no party could win national elections in an urbanizing and industrializing nation with the support of farmers alone. Winning the support of middle-class professionals, urban workers, and farmers was essential for national success, but assembling such a coalition proved to be elusive in a sectionally divided economy. Democratic efforts to woo the professional middle class alienated farmers. Bryan's appeal to farmers alienated the professional middle class. Workers refused to endorse either party. Bryan's failure to create a winning national coalition paved the way for Republican dominance, and, for the next sixteen years, Republicans held undivided control of the presidency and Congress. In 1901, Leon Czolgosz, an anarchist and unemployed factory worker, assassinated McKinley. As a result, Roosevelt, the man Mark Hanna had derided as "that cowboy," was president.

17-4

Limitations and Triumphs of Progressivism

This cartoon, which appeared in *Puck*, a New York humor magazine, portrays an infant President Roosevelt as the Greek hero, Hercules. He wrestles with the unwieldy serpents J.P. Morgan and John D. Rockefeller, the titans of U.S. finance and industry.

Why is Roosevelt portrayed as a baby Hercules? What was the cartoonist trying to convey by portraying Morgan and Rockefeller as serpents? ▶

Go to MindTap® to practice history with the Chapter 17 **Primary Source Writing Activity: Brands of Progressivism.** Read and view primary sources and respond to a writing prompt.

Library of Congress Prints and Photographs Division Washington, D.C. [LC-DIG-ppmsca-26061]

Following McKinley's assassination, intense antiradical sentiment swept the nation because Czolgosz was linked to European anarchists. As radical political programs associated with anarchism, socialism, and communism became more popular in Europe, Americans became increasingly suspicious of immigrants, who might spread such ideas. Anti-immigrant legislation became a key Progressive reform. Theodore Roosevelt, however, also assured Americans that his solutions, adapted from European middle-class reformers, were meant to stop any potential socialist threat to the United States. In many western industrializing nations, new political coalitions wedged themselves between socialists on the left and the barons of land and industry on the right. Calling themselves New Liberals in Britain, radicals in France, social liberals in Chile, and Progressives in the United States, each group tried to steer government on a stable middle course that would avoid revolts by the poor or rule by the rich. Roosevelt practiced a top-down form of Progressive reform, aggressively asserting unilateral presidential power to control big business. At the same time, he exhibited little hostility toward either business or bigness. In contrast, grassroots-level reformers who continued to advocate for more sweeping reforms increasingly pressured lawmakers.

☞ As you read, try to understand the complexity of ideas that constituted Progressivism and why Roosevelt believed that his brand of it was the best one. What groups opposed Roosevelt's vision?

17-4a Progressive Era Anti-Immigrant Measures

Progressive reformers embrace anti-immigrant legislation.

Fear of immigrants had been a part of U.S. politics since the American Party's nativism against Irish and German immigrants during the 1850s. After the Civil War, however, anti-immigrant politics got a boost from pseudoscientific theories often linked to Darwin's theory of natural selection. Immigration controls became a popular means for protecting Americans from non-Anglo Saxon ethnic groups believed by many to be inferior. By 1905, anti-immigrant measures against new waves of immigrants from southern and eastern Europe became politically popular.

Formed in 1894, the Immigration Restriction League (IRL) argued that "Indians, Negroes, Chinese, Jews, and Americans cannot all be free in the same society." The IRL pressed for the exclusion of all immigrants who could not read twenty-five words of the U.S. Constitution—a test similar to the one used to bar blacks from voting in the South. The Democratic Party, however, had resisted such limits on immigration by styling itself as the champion of Irish Catholics and other immigrants. It won support by resisting evangelical efforts to ban saloons and giving aid to parochial schools and foreign language classes. During the 1890s, Democratic President Cleveland continued this pro-immigrant stance, vetoing the IRL's literacy test for immigrants and denouncing the "radical departure" from the generous and free-handed policy" of "welcom[ing] all who came to us from other lands." Cleveland's veto of the exclusion bill was bolstered by pro-immigrant Southerners, a key Democratic constituency, who wanted cheap labor to build up the South's new textile industry.

The debate against immigrants, however, began to change after 1905. Gompers of the AFL was persuaded that his membership's interest in higher wages required restricting competition from immigrant labor. Racial fears of Japanese were stoked both by a spike in Japanese immigration into California as well as the Japanese Navy's decisive defeat of the Russian Empire in 1905, a victory that called into question the racial supremacy of white Europeans. Southerners increasingly saw the exclusion of migrants from southern and eastern Europe as part of their policy of white supremacy. Oscar Underwood, an Alabama senator, called for a literacy test for immigrants to protect "the great Celtic and Teutonic races" from immigration that would "contaminate our blood with an inferior race." Procedural maneuvering prevented the passage of the 1906 literacy test for immigrants.

In place of a literacy test, Congress created the Dillingham Commission, named for the anti-immigrant chair of the House Immigration Committee, to report on the peoples migrating to the United States. The Commission studied the British colonial settler nations of Australia, New Zealand, and Canada. Supporters and opponents of immigration testified before the Commission, often focusing on the supposed biological qualities of different ethnic groups. "The question before us is a race question," declared Robert deCourcy Ward of the IRL to the Dillingham Commission: "It is a question of what kind of babies shall be born." The Immigrant Protective League was formed by Chicago's Hull House to resist anti-immigrant measures and offer support

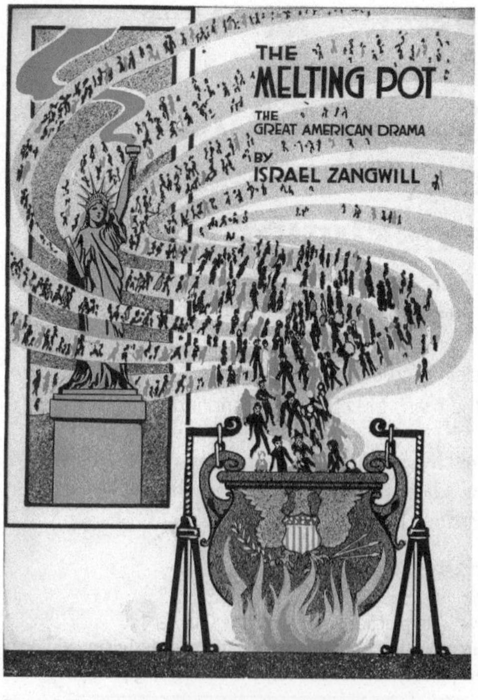

Library of Congress

Israel Zangwill, *The Melting Pot* Zangwill's 1908 play popularized the term *melting pot*. It told the story of a Russian-Jew who had fled the 1903 Kishinev pogrom in Russia. Wanting to make a new life in America, he composed *An American Symphony*, which praises the haven that the United States represents. At the climax of the play, the protagonist says, "What is the glory of Rome and Jerusalem where all nations and races come to worship and look back, compared with the glory of America, where all races and nations come to labour and look forward!" ▲

to recently arrived European immigrants. Grace Abbott, the League's chief, argued that industrial exploitation, not racial inferiority, caused broken families and crime among new immigrants. In 1910, the Dillingham Commission issued a forty-one-volume report laden with statistics and urging restrictions on immigrants that were eventually enacted in 1917 and 1924.

Fears about immigration also influenced Congress's domestic legislation. In 1910, Congress voted for the so-called White Slavery Act, prohibiting the transportation of women across state lines "for any immoral purpose." The law was passed in the wake of reports, often spurious, that brothels said to be owned by Chinese, Italians, and Jews, were kidnapping white women—"white slaves"—and forcing them into prostitution. "Shall we defend our American civilization . . . or lower our glorious flag to the most despicable foreigners—French, Irish, Italians, Jews, and Mongolians?" asked antiwhite slavery activist Ernest Bell. After Congress passed the White Slavery Act, its was often enforced against women themselves for entering into what federal prosecutors regarded as "immoral" relationships, such as interracial romance.

17-4b Roosevelt's Control over Monopolies

The president's "gentlemen's agreements" with corporations begin to curb their excesses.

Theodore Roosevelt approached the problem of big business cautiously. As a reformer, he recognized that monopolies were unfair and had to be controlled. The wave of mergers even disturbed conservative businessmen. When in 1901, J.P. Morgan organized the purchase of Andrew Carnegie's steel company and its merger with several other steel manufacturers to form U.S. Steel, he created the world's first billion-dollar firm and roused small businesses' fears that a tiny cabal of financial elites controlled industry. Fearing that they could not survive against such goliaths, these smaller businesses formed the **National Association of Manufacturers (NAM)** to lobby for more aggressive enforcement of the Sherman Antitrust Act to preserve competition. The NAM also opposed trade unions, calling them the "Labor Trust" on the grounds that unions operated like a monopoly in labor. Federal and local governments tended to agree with the NAM's characterization of unions.

Roosevelt did not, however, object to all large-scale businesses. For example, he endorsed the view that interstate railroads could not survive without pooling to control price wars. Instead of stopping all mergers, he believed that the federal government should closely supervise them. In 1902, Morgan attempted a second giant consolidation by negotiating with railroad titans J.J. Hill and E.H. Harriman to merge the Northern Pacific, the Great Northern, and the Chicago, Burlington, and Quincy railroads. Roosevelt instructed his attorney general to prosecute the company for violation of the Sherman Antitrust Act. In *United States v. Northern Securities*, the Supreme Court upheld the prosecution, saying that the Commerce Clause could apply to railroad regulation. Roosevelt boasted that "the most powerful men in the country were held to accountability before the law."

National Association of Manufacturers (NAM) Coalition of small- and medium-sized companies that came together to lobby out because they feared major corporations.

Roosevelt used this accountability not to prohibit mergers but to ensure that they did not abuse consumers or competitors. He believed that mergers should be governed by informal meetings between titans of industry and titans of politics—that was, by himself. In 1903, Roosevelt secured congressional approval to create the Department of Commerce and Labor and, within it, the Bureau of Corporations. Under his plan, businesses seeking to consolidate would apply to the Bureau for preapproval of the deal. In return for assurances that the consolidated firm would act in a socially responsible manner, Roosevelt would give it immunity from antitrust prosecution. The leaders of U.S. Steel, Standard Oil, and International Harvester met with officials from Roosevelt's Departments of Justice and Commerce, opening their books to secure "gentlemen's agreements" that would relieve them from fear of antitrust prosecution.

17-4c Progressive Victories and Their Limits

The president and Congress pass a series of Progressive legislation.

With the nation prosperous and ascendant in world affairs, Roosevelt easily won a landslide victory in 1904, beating the Democratic nominee, Alton Parker, a New York judge who was honest but dull. The election's turnout was low and rhetoric was mild because the two main candidates were largely indistinguishable from each other. The two probusiness New Yorkers agreed on most issues, from colonizing the Philippines to their dislike of trade unions. The excitement in the election was that Eugene V. Debs, former head of the American Railway Union, who had been imprisoned for his labor activism, ran as the Socialist Party candidate, polling almost half a million votes.

Buoyed by his victory, Roosevelt was able to pass several important pieces of legislation through a Republican Congress despite the opposition of conservatives, who distrusted his excessive fondness for governmental intervention and regulation. The legislation shared a common feature: It delegated broad policy-making discretion to bureaucratic experts qualified not by their party loyalty but by special training.

For example, in 1905, Congress enacted the Forest Transfer Act, which gave the National Forest Service headed by Gifford Pinchot supervision over 150 million

Map 17.2 Early National Park System Environmentalists such as John Muir, the founder of the modern conservation movement, opposed the policy of using natural resources for economic gain. He urged that wilderness areas be preserved in their natural state as game preserves and recreational areas. President Roosevelt added 150 million acres to the national forests, created fifty-one federal bird sanctuaries, four national game reserves, five national parks, and eighteen national monuments. ▲

acres of federal forest land formerly managed by the General Land Office (see Map 17.2). Pinchot, a pioneer in forestry, was a close personal friend of Roosevelt's. After studying at the French National Forestry School, he returned to the United States and established scientific stewardship of natural resources by government experts. Convinced that there would never be any constituency in favor of natural resource preservation unless it could be made to pay for itself, Pinchot urged that federal lands be opened for ranchers and timber companies to use so long as management practices guaranteed a "sustained yield."

In 1906, Congress enacted the Pure Food and Drug Act, which prohibited the interstate shipment or sale of polluted or mislabeled foods and drugs, and the Federal Meat Inspection Act, which ensured that meat was sanitarily processed. Support for the acts followed the publication of *The Jungle* by Upton Sinclair, a socialist tied to Progressive causes. Sinclair wrote an exposé about the miserable working conditions in Chicago's stockyards, but the public focused on the few pages that described in disgusting detail the unsanitary conditions in which meat was processed. Sinclair mournfully noted, "I aimed at the public's heart, and by accident I hit it in the stomach." His story about a radical agenda watered down to create modest reform symbolized Progressivism's middle-class limitations. He and journalists such as Ida Tarbell practiced a new kind of investigative reporting termed **muckraking** that took aim at government and corporate corruption and unfair practices, but their efforts brought only modest reforms.

muckraking Investigating possible political, corporate, and social corruption used by journalists such as Ida B. Tarbell and Upton Sinclair who wrote exposés on corporations and politicians.

Urged by Roosevelt, Congress enacted the Hepburn Act (1906), which gave the Interstate Commerce Commission the power to set maximum railroad rates on interstate routes. The legislation pleased no one. Railroad owners darkly warned that rate setting by bureaucrats would drive railroads into bankruptcy. Farmers were disappointed by the complex, lengthy, and expensive proceedings the act required, preferring simpler rules such as uniform per mile prices or even outright government ownership. Nevertheless, the Supreme Court deferred to the Commission's experts and upheld the act.

During this period of rapid reform, labor policy remained an unresolved area of the law. In 1905, the U.S. Supreme Court decided in *Lochner v. New York* that the state had only limited power to regulate employees' work

Underwood & Underwood/Corbis

Global Americans **Florence Kelley** grew up in an abolitionist household in Philadelphia. Her father, William D. Kelley, was a U.S. congressman and had been one of the founders of the Republican Party. She graduated from Cornell University in 1882 and then left for Zurich, Switzerland, to join other Americans who were interested in learning from European social theorists. There she became friends with Friedrich Engels and worked on an English translation of his book, *The Condition of the Working Class in England*, which was published in the United States in 1887.

In Zurich, Kelley met and married Socialist Labor Party member Lazare Wischnewetzky with whom she had three children. They divorced, and she and the children moved to Chicago's Hull House. Kelley devoted her career to reforming labor conditions for U.S. workers and remained a committed socialist. She was appointed as Illinois's first inspector of factories and pushed through legislation that limited women and child labor to eight hours a day. In 1899, she formed the National Consumers League, an advocacy group that informed consumers about how goods were manufactured to enable them to make informed choices, and lobbied for fair labor standards. She worked closely with Louis Brandeis on his brief for *Muller v. Oregon*, supplying research. In keeping with her Quaker and abolitionist upbringing, Kelley was one of the founding members of the National Association for the Advancement of Colored People (NAACP).

hours. Lochner, a bakery owner, sued and asked for relief from the state law that mandated a ten-hour work day and a six-day workweek for bakers. The Court held that baking was not a dangerous job requiring such protections.

Three years later, however, the Court made an exception to this ruling. Influenced by a legal brief written by Louis Brandeis, the Court in *Muller v. Oregon* (1908) decided that a state did have an interest in regulating the work hours of women. The Court did not overturn *Lochner* but instead relied on the **Brandeis brief**, which distilled scientific and social scientific evidence about the ill effects on women's health and homes when they worked long hours. Some feminists, however, were dismayed by the assumption that women were weaker than men.

Despite the growth of its bureaucracy, the federal government still lacked a central bank. The system was vulnerable to panics and collapse. In 1906, the earthquake and fire that destroyed one-third of San Francisco forced insurance companies to ship millions of dollars to cover claims in the West. The resulting shortfall of money in the East produced a panic when a speculator attempting to corner the copper market could not repay his loans. Rumors of the default started a run on the banks as jittery citizens worried that withdrawals would cause the banks to fail. The run threatened even healthy banks, triggering a freeze on credit and a massive business slowdown known as the Panic of 1907.

As in 1894, Morgan stepped in to save the financial system. Gathering New York's most important bankers in his private library, he pressured them to pledge their deposits to rescue banks threatened by runs. Morgan personally pledged to buy $30 million of New York City's bonds to save the city, and he organized committees of bankers to urge the clergy and press to reassure citizens. Prodded by Morgan, the U.S. Treasury promised to use federal revenues to help avert panic.

To stave off the bankruptcy of an investment bank, Morgan asked Roosevelt to promise antitrust immunity if U.S. Steel purchased a company held by the bank, and the president agreed. Although a business slowdown followed the crisis, a massive recession was averted. But Morgan's general management of the crisis suggested how completely a tiny group of bankers controlled the economic life of the nation, and the private bargain between Roosevelt and Morgan later produced a major rift within the Republican Party.

Brandeis brief A statement of a client's case that in this case used research on topics such as history, sociology, and statistics rather than legal citations to convince a court to make a decision based on a particular opinion or version of a case.

Although Roosevelt and his administration pushed for reform on the national level and looked favorably on regulation and reform at the local and state levels, they were by no means radical in their ideas or deeds. Roosevelt and his wing of the Progressive movement wanted to regulate business but only within certain narrow limits that allowed businesses such as those held by Morgan to thrive.

17-4d Grassroots Progressive Movements

After the Panic of 1893, Progressive reforms spread to all levels of society.

In opposition to the top-down views of national leaders, a series of reforms percolated from the bottom up, often initiated by those whose interests were not represented in national politics. Many of the reforms emerged from the activities of women, who were still denied the vote in most of the country but were determined to engage in the work of social and political reform.

Although African American men had been granted the right to vote with the passage of the Fifteenth Amendment, all women were specifically excluded. The struggle to gain women's right to vote was a long one although women in many western states had been successful (see Chapter 15.) In 1890, the National American Woman Suffrage Association (NAWSA) elected Elizabeth Cady Stanton as its president. Lucy Stone was the head of its executive committee, but Susan B. Anthony was its most public face, eventually becoming president when Stanton stepped down. Their sole focus was the expansion of voting rights for women, and they pressed for the vote state-by-state while lobbying for a constitutional amendment to guarantee the right for women. Some of the group's younger and more radical members, such as Alice Paul, broke away to pursue additional causes, such as a more general equal rights amendment, that were deemed distracting to the NAWSA. Paul, who had spent time with the British suffrage movement, was considered too outspoken and radical for the NAWSA.

Progressives passed legislation to amend state constitutions to challenge the power of the two major parties and to attain direct democracy. Citing the precedent of Australia, they pushed for the **secret ballot** that would have the government print ballots with the names of all candidates on which voters could cast in secret at polling places. All states had adopted this practice by 1891. Some states, particularly western and southern ones, also instituted the initiative (right of voters to initiate legislative action), referendum (submission for popular vote of a measure passed or proposed by a legislative body), and recall (the right of citizens to vote to remove an official). These three direct democratic interventions were intended to make their elected representatives more directly answerable to their constituents. In 1913, the Progressives' scored their biggest victory for direct democracy with ratification of the Seventeenth Amendment, which moved the right to elect U.S. senators from state legislatures to individual voters.

African American Progressive reformers concerned themselves particularly with the elimination of segregation and discrimination. Booker T. Washington dominated the conservative end of the reform spectrum, advocating for occupational training for young African Americans. He built the Tuskegee Institute in Alabama, which he had helped found in 1881 with the labor of his students: They laid the bricks, glazed the windows, and painted the walls. Washington believed in the principle of equality for all but thought that campaigning for social equality was "extremist folly." Instead, he believed that if African Americans could prove themselves as worthy citizens through hard work, moral behavior, and economic uplift, white America would openly embrace, or at least not resist, some semblance of equality. In his speech at the 1895 Cotton States and International Exhibition, Washington called on white Southerners to "cast down your buckets where you are" and to hire blacks, rather than new immigrants, to work in their factories.

secret ballot Practice of keeping a citizen's vote private, also known as the *Australian ballot*.

talented tenth Concept championed by W.E.B Dubois that emphasized the need for higher education in order to develop leadership capacity among the most able 10 percent of African Americans.

Other African American leaders such as Ida B. Wells and W.E.B. Du Bois criticized Washington's approach and instead advocated forcefully for total equality under the law. Du Bois also suggested that African Americans resist Washington's industrial education model, which emphasized technical skills for the trades. Instead, he advocated for the liberal education of the **talented tenth** of African Americans, whom he thought would be competitive and respected if given access to colleges and universities. From this group, leaders would emerge who could be effective spokespeople for African American rights. Dubois and Washington did not always agree or work together, but they were two sides of an effective reform movement that pushed forward on economic and social rights for blacks in America.

One of the most vocal groups of race reformers met in 1905 and formed the Niagara Movement. They directly repudiated Booker T. Washington's accommodationist approach, demanding instead equality under the law and full civil rights protections for African Americans. The Niagara Movement believed that only confrontational politics to force federal and state governments to implement the Fourteenth and Fifteenth amendments would truly secure African Americans' rights and economic advancement. As their influence grew, they sought white

Eartha M.M. White Collection, University of North Florida, Thomas G. Carpenter Library, Special Collections and Archives

National Association of Colored Women's Clubs In July 1896, a group of women including Harriet Tubman, Ida B. Wells-Barnett, and Mary Church Terrell founded the National Association of Colored Women's Clubs (NACWC). Adopting the motto, "Lifting as We Climb," they worked to end Jim Crow Laws, lynching, and also advocate for suffrage for all women, regardless of race. The national organization's many branches worked within local communities to provide social and educational services. By 1918, the organization had a membership of more than 300,000. ▲

allies, including Jane Addams and Florence Kelley. In the wake of one of the worst race riots in Atlanta, a national meeting of race reformers met in New York City. They founded the **National Association for the Advancement of Colored People (NAACP)** in 1909. Hiring lawyers and using both the courts and legislative process, the NAACP pushed for voting rights, educational opportunities, and an end to Jim Crow laws. One of its major public protests came when *Birth of a Nation* was first screened in 1915. The movie, which depicted the rise of the Ku Klux Klan and racist depictions of blacks, was so popular that Woodrow Wilson held a public screening in the White House.

The problems that faced immigrants influenced young, unmarried, educated women to transplant the **settlement house movement** from England to the United States. These women, mostly college graduates, moved into urban homes in immigrant enclaves to work directly with newcomers to help them adjust to their new lives. The settlement movement had begun at Toynbee Hall, a pioneering social settlement in the East End of London founded in 1884, and was closely associated with English universities and the Christian socialism movement. Progressives from Gifford Pinchot to Lillian Wald and Frederic Howe visited and worked at Toynbee Hall. Jane Addams, after working with reformers there, returned to Chicago to open Hull House in 1889.

Settlement house staff and its backers across the United States, like Hull House, gave time and money to helping immigrants. Staff organized English language classes, intervened with exploitative landlords, provided public kitchens and baths and day care services for children, and homeless shelters for new immigrants. At the same time, they gathered data about the lives of the poor to be used in setting social policy. Settlement house workers, who were mostly women, became the first social workers who used their education to solve day-to-day problems associated with poverty and to push policy and legislative solutions. By the early 1920s, there were almost five hundred settlement homes across the country, serving mostly urban immigrant communities.

National Association for the Advancement of Colored People (NAACP) Legal and social advocacy group that lobbies for advancing the rights of African Americans.

settlement house movement Reform based on improving the lives of urban immigrant families by working intimately with them, providing relief and practical education.

eugenics Field of scholarship seeking to identify and engineer the perfect blending of human genes in order to create healthy, intelligent, and internally compatible populations.

These Progressives battled against the anti-immigrant movement in U.S. politics. In 1894, a group of Boston intellectuals founded the Immigration Restriction League. These people believed that the New Immigrants were of moral, social, and biological inferior stock and threatened the supposed purity of Americans. At the same time, the **eugenics** movement was also gaining traction in the United States. Based on the theories of British biologist, Francis Galton, eugenicists believed that Americans could control their biological destiny through mate selection, anti-immigration measures, and antimiscegenation laws. Neither academics nor the public scorned their position.

17-5

Progressivism and National Politics

This 1916 photo shows young workers advocating for the passage of legislation that would outlaw child labor. Notice the way that they are dressed.

Judging from the photo, would you surmise that this is an organized demonstration or a spontaneous one? If organized, which adults do you think organized them? Why would they wear their best clothes to a protest? ▶

Library of Congress

In the first two decades of the twentieth century, progressive ideas prevailed in reform movements and politics. The Democrats, Republicans, and a new third party, the Progressive Party, claimed to be progressive but had very different ideas about what that term meant. In the elections of 1912 and 1916, the parties battled over how to balance the needs of business, urban dwellers, educated professionals, workers, and farmers. Increasingly, the Democratic Party's vision of Progressivism prevailed, and Congress enacted protections for labor, an income tax, and lower tariffs during a productive legislative session before the turmoil that would engulf the nation in World War I.

☞ How did elements of Progressivism change as major political parties adopted them? What elements were left out?

17-5a Divisions in the Republican Party

Issues of reform split the Republicans and create an opening for the Democrats.

In the wake of the 1907 panic and resulting business slowdown, Democrats saw an opportunity to retake the White House in the 1908 election. Running for a second time, William Jennings Bryan, a pioneer in modern political campaigning, had built a formidable political organization by then. Although probusiness Democrats such as the newspaper publisher Joseph Pulitzer tried to stop him, Bryan easily secured the Democratic nomination. Realizing that he could not win with farmer support alone, Bryan worked hard to win labor by courting Gompers and the AFL. The normally nonpartisan Gompers was brought over by the unusually prolabor Democratic platform of 1908, which called for an eight-hour day, a separate Department of Labor, an income tax to replace revenues from the tariff, and an end to federal court interference with strikes and boycotts.

Voters, however, did not embrace the Democrats' message of economic equality in 1908. As in 1896, Bryan lost eastern states soundly because Gompers could not deliver workers' votes. Bryan's evangelical style and support for prohibition alienated immigrant workers. Meanwhile, William Howard Taft, the Republican nominee, picked up support of middle-class professionals because he had Roosevelt's support. Despite that support, Taft rejected Roosevelt's advice on tariff reform, endorsing a probusiness platform with only vague promises for farmers. Taft's victory, however, seemed to confirm that support for business stability trumped social reform and equality in the majority of the voters.

Taft's handling of antitrust cases further alienated Roosevelt and Progressives. In 1911, Taft's attorney general charged U.S. Steel with violating antitrust laws despite the 1908 gentlemen's agreement between Morgan and Roosevelt. The case alleged that U.S. Steel officials had deceived Roosevelt. The insinuation that Roosevelt was unaware of his own administration's actions humiliated him. Vigorously denying this, Roosevelt accused Taft of deception and incompetence. What had begun as such a close political relationship was torn apart by Taft's very public rejection of Roosevelt and his brand of Progressivism.

rule of reason Order based on a "gentlemen's agreement" between government and corporations as to who could form monopolies that benefit the consumer.

The split between Taft and Roosevelt over the *U.S. Steel* case did not reflect disagreement about the substance of antitrust policy but about whether such policy should be carried out judicially or presidentially. Both Roosevelt and Taft supported a **rule of reason** in antitrust cases under which courts allowed businesses to engage in monopolistic operations out of economic necessity for the public benefit. In 1911, the U.S. Supreme Court adopted the rule of reason in *Standard Oil Co. of New Jersey v. United States* holding that only combinations and contracts that unreasonably restrained trade violated the Sherman Act, so monopolies were not inherently illegal. The rule of reason, however, further alienated farmers from the Republican Party because they regarded corporations as inherently undemocratic threats to their economic and political autonomy.

17-5b Progressive Party

The Progressives create one of the most successful third-party movements in U.S. politics.

Having lost Roosevelt's support, Taft faced new rules and familiar challengers when he decided to run for president again in 1912. He. As a result of Progressive lobbying, some states used direct primary elections to select delegates to presidential conventions rather than, for example, caucuses of state legislators. Taft was challenged for the nomination by the charismatic Roosevelt, who won nine primary victories by a landslide, and by Progressive Senator Robert LaFollette, who won the primaries in Wisconsin and Ohio, Taft's home state. Nevertheless, the Republican National Committee awarded enough contested delegates to Taft to secure his nomination.

Campaign Flyer for the Progressive Party, 1912 The party nominated Hiram Johnson, governor of California, as Roosevelt's running mate. Johnson was one of the most progressive governors in the nation, and under his leadership, the state legislature passed laws that allowed for the direct election of senators and the initiative, referendum, and recall. The voting reforms gave California citizens unprecedented access to direct democracy. ▶

Corbis

Bain News Service, publisher

Global Americans Born in 1877 to a Jewish family in Budapest, Hungary, **Rosika Schwimmer** began advocating for feminist causes at an early age. During the 1890s, she helped found the Hungarian Feminist Association, the Hungarian National Council of Women, and the Women's Trade Union. In 1913, she became the corresponding secretary for the International Woman Suffrage Association (IWSA). She became close friends with suffragists in the United States and toured with Carrie Chapman Catt through Europe and the United States, pushing for women's suffrage.

After the outbreak of World War I, Schwimmer could not return home to her war-torn nation. She helped form the Women's Peace Party in the United States and became a lifelong pacifist who lobbied President Wilson directly to establish an international peace commission to stop the war. Schwimmer worked with Henry Ford to fund the Peace Ship that sailed with relief workers and supplies to Stockholm. After the war, she became vice president of the International League for Peace and Freedom. In 1919, when the Communists briefly took over Hungary, Schwimmer fled and settled in Chicago, but she was denied U.S. citizenship because of her pacifist beliefs. Her case went to the Supreme Court in 1929. She told the Court: "My cosmic consciousness of belonging to the human family is shared by all those who believe that all human beings are the children of God." The U.S. government allowed her to stay in the country, but she died without citizenship in any country.

Roosevelt's followers angrily denounced Taft's nomination as brazen theft and bolted the convention to found the **Progressive Party**, which nominated Roosevelt for president and Governor Hiram W. Johnson of California for vice president. This third party had a base broad enough to threaten the two major parties because it had finally united middle-class and Social Gospel reformers in a reform tradition dating back to the abolitionist movement. The conservative (and Democratic) *New York Times* described the convention as "an assemblage of religious enthusiasts . . . a Methodist camp meeting." After singing "Onward Christian Soldiers!" the delegates were ecstatic when Roosevelt thundered, "We stand at Armageddon, and we battle for the Lord." Roosevelt electrified the convention with his appearance because he had just recently survived an attempt on his life. He declared at the convention that he was "as fit as a Bull Moose" to run for president. A new political mascot joined the donkey and elephant.

Democrats were also deeply divided between the pro-business and pro-immigrant East and the more evangelical and agrarian West and South. Leading the latter was the "Great Commoner," William Jennings Bryan. Having been defeated three times, however, he was an unlikely nominee for a party that could smell victory in Republican dissension. Instead, Champ Clark of Missouri assumed an early lead among the delegates. The eastern and conservative Democrats campaigned for Woodrow Wilson, the recently elected governor of New Jersey, former president of Princeton University, and a political newcomer.

The pious son of a Presbyterian minister, Wilson grew up in Virginia and Georgia and had strong southern sympathies. He was the first Southerner to run for and win the presidency since before the Civil War, marking a seeming reconciliation between North and South. He had spent most of his career as a professor of political science, first at Johns Hopkins and later at Princeton. In his writings, Wilson championed themes popular with middle-class reformers, advocating government by well-qualified experts and a professional civil service free from patronage politics. Wilson's antimachine stance had made him an ideal candidate for governor of New Jersey in 1910 when the Democratic Party was looking for someone to challenge the Republicans whose lax regulatory policies, which Lincoln Steffens, another muckraking journalist, had titled "traitor state." Wilson's victory in New Jersey gave him a national reputation without much political baggage. Bryan saw in him a possible unifier of the eastern and western wings of the party. Attracted both by Wilson's dislike of political machines and his Protestant piety, Bryan threw his support behind Wilson, who narrowly defeated Clark for the nomination.

Progressive Party Reform that would improve society by using the power of the federal government to distribute wealth and regulate businesses.

Wilson had the Democratic nomination but not much of a program. His real opponent was not Taft—who had no chance of victory—but Roosevelt with his progressive track record. Wilson discovered a way to differentiate himself from Roosevelt and the Progressive Party by working with Louis Brandeis, a Boston labor lawyer (*Mueller v. Oregon*) and social reformer who became Wilson's most important campaign adviser. Brandeis advised Wilson to champion small businessmen and farmers in opposition to Roosevelt's "New Nationalism," supporting bureaucratically managed monopolies. Calling Wilson's program the "New Freedom," Brandeis helped him craft

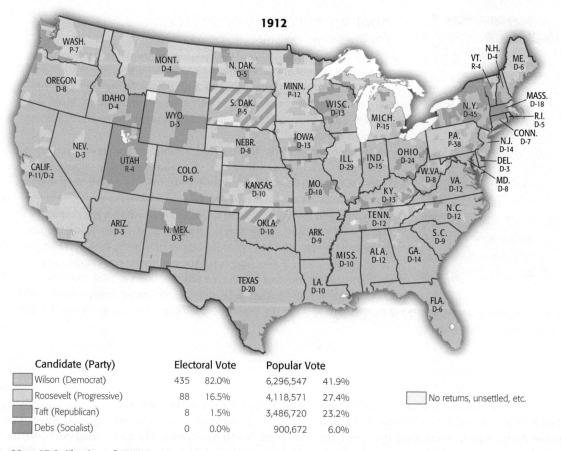

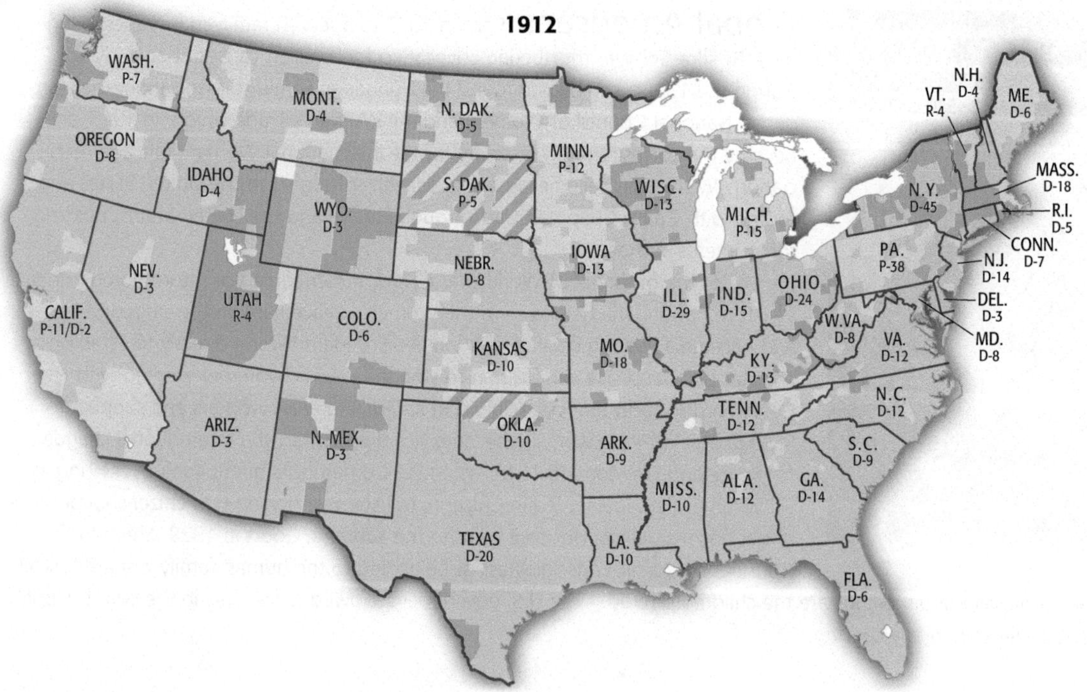

Candidate (Party)	Electoral Vote		Popular Vote	
Wilson (Democrat)	435	82.0%	6,296,547	41.9%
Roosevelt (Progressive)	88	16.5%	4,118,571	27.4%
Taft (Republican)	8	1.5%	3,486,720	23.2%
Debs (Socialist)	0	0.0%	900,672	6.0%

No returns, unsettled, etc.

Map 17.3 Election of 1912 In this election, Wilson narrowly won a plurality of the popular vote with 42 percent against Roosevelt's 27 percent and Taft's 23 percent. Of electoral votes, Wilson had 435 against Roosevelt's 88 and Taft's meager 8. Eugene Debs, running on the Socialist ticket, took 6 percent of the popular vote. ▲

a policy of breaking up monopolies, creating a publicly accountable banking system, and regulating railroads for the benefit of farmers and small shippers. This policy was attuned to Bryan's agrarian ideology, but because it was championed by an Easterner with a southern background and sympathies, Wilson's program unified the party more than Bryan ever could. Wilson won the 1912 election (see Map 17.3).

17-5c Wilsonian Progressivism

Wilson's presidency is bolstered by congressional Progressive legislation.

In the election of 1912, the Democrats won control of the Senate and maintained their majority in the House of Representatives, so they had complete control over the federal government for the first time since 1894. With a mandate from the voters to control big business, Democrats used their new power to reduce tariffs, regulate banking, and impose new controls over monopolies (see Table 17.2).

During the spring of 1912, Democrats in the House had set up a committee to investigate the "money trust." The Pujo Committee interrogated leading bankers, including the aging Morgan, and in early 1913 issued a report confirming that a small group of bankers linked to him controlled numerous manufacturing and transportation companies. Public outcry over such concentrated financial power demanded a major overhaul of the banking system, but the Democrats quickly divided over how much control the federal government should exercise. For populist agrarians like Bryan, then Wilson's secretary of state, it was essential that the government, not private bankers, control the money supply. Brandeis also urged the president to end private bankers' power over monetary policy.

The Federal Reserve Act created the seven-person Federal Reserve Board whose members the president would nominate and the Senate confirm as well as twelve private regional Federal Reserve banks, each with its own board of directors and branches. All nationally chartered banks were required to buy stock in and deposit reserves with their regional reserve bank in return for which that bank would give its member banks access to loans and dividends. By lending money to member banks according to the rules adopted by the Federal Reserve Board, the Federal Reserve banks could avert runs such as those that had occurred in all of the prior depressions.

Table 17.2 Legislation Passed during the Wilson Administration

Legislation passed during the Wilson administration was the culmination of Progressive reforms that had percolated at the local and state levels. Some regulated the economy and corporation, and others helped particular constituencies such as farmers, workers, and temperance advocates. This legislation revealed the Progressive belief that the federal government had an important and active role in regulating all aspects of society.

Date	Name	Description
1912	Federal Reserve Act	Created Federal Reserve Board and regulated monetary policy for the nation
March 1913	Webb-Kenyon Act	Prohibited interstate shipment or transportation of alcoholic beverages between states
October 1913	Revenue (Underwood) Act	Imposed an income tax and lowered tariff rates from 40% to 25%
October 1914	Federal Trade Commission Act	Regulated unfair trade practices and protected consumers as the result of the reforms begun with the Sherman Antitrust Act
	Clayton Antitrust Act	Regulated price discrimination, mergers, and acquisitions and prevented one person from being a director of two or more competing businesses
July 1916	Federal Farm Loan Act	Created a loan board and increased credit to rural families
July 1916	Federal Aid Road Act	Provided first federal highway funding
August 1916	National Park Service Organic Act	Created an agency to oversee and manage U.S. national parks and monuments
September 1916	Adamson Act	Established eight-hour day and overtime for interstate railroad workers
September 1917	Keating-Owen Child Labor Act	Prohibited the interstate sale of goods made by factories that employed children under 14 but was declared unconstitutional in 1918

In addition to creating the Federal Reserve system, Wilson signed legislation for other financial reforms. In 1913, Congress sent the Sixteenth Amendment, legalizing a federal income tax, to the states for ratification. Congress then passed the Revenue (Underwood) Act in 1913, which cut all tariffs substantially. To placate farmers who were skeptical about the centralized control of the Federal Reserve Act, Democrats enacted the Federal Farm Loan Act that allowed the federal government to loan funds secured by crops in warehouses to farmers. Congress also steeply increased the income tax rates on the highest incomes and created a workers' compensation program for federal employees.

The New Freedom had called for the breakup of corporate monopolies, but Wilson's antimonopoly laws were much less sweeping. At his urging, Congress passed the Federal Trade Commission Act and the Clayton Antitrust Act, which he signed in 1914. The first measure created the Federal Trade Commission, a regulatory agency charged with investigating unfair trade practices and mergers above a specified size as well as certain anticompetitive practices. The Clayton Act exempted union activities such as boycotts and strikes from injunctions by federal judges but did not overrule the Supreme Court's rule of reason, nor did it mandate the breakup of all monopolies. Samuel Gompers praised the measure as the "magna carta for labor."

Workers got part of what they wanted from the Wilson Administration and the Democratic Congress. Congress enacted the Keating-Owen Child Labor Act, which banned the interstate transportation of goods made with child labor. The measure was strongly backed by Social Gospel reformers and labor unions, hoping to prevent child exploitation. Labor unions wanted to eliminate competition by child laborers who worked for low wages. Faced with a national railroad strike, Congress also passed the Adamson Act, setting a maximum eight-hour day for railroad workers on interstate routes. In dealing with federal workers, Wilson took executive action and bowed to the wishes of his southern cabinet officials and instituted the segregation of the federal government. Most blacks who had the few federal government jobs available to them were fired and replaced with white workers. Women such as Mary Church Terrell and the NAACP voiced loud opposition but to no avail.

Because Wilson had won his first term as a result of the Republican split, many doubted whether he could win reelection against a united Republican Party. His legislative successes weakened the Progressive Party's appeal. Roosevelt declined to run again as a Progressive and instead sought the Republican Party nomination. Angered by his previous defection to the Progressives, however, Republican stalwarts instead chose Charles Evans Hughes, the former governor of New York and associate justice of the U.S. Supreme Court. Hughes's reputation as a strict regulator of business gave him sufficient credibility among Progressive Party members so that they endorsed the Republican ticket. Roosevelt fell in line and campaigned for Hughes.

In the 1916 presidential contest between Wilson and Hughes, two issues dominated the debate. First, the Democrats were firmly identified as the party of labor. Hughes attacked laws such as the Adamson Act and the Keating-Owen Act as detrimental to business. He also advocated something more akin to Roosevelt's New Nationalism as a means of regulating corporations as opposed to the more aggressive Wilsonian policies.

Second, the candidates also had to directly confront the Great War that had commenced in Europe in 1914 between France, England, and Russia on one side and Germany and Austria-Hungary on the other. Hughes accused Wilson of neglecting preparations for war in case the United States was dragged into the conflict. Germany's submarine strikes against neutral shipping and passenger liners made some Americans seek a more aggressive stand against Germany. Wilson, however, campaigned on the slogan, "He kept us out of war," a position popular with both Bryan's agrarian followers and voters of Irish and German descent who were hostile to England or sympathetic to Germany. Wilson's coalition of workers, farmers, and middle-class reformers was fragile, but it was enough for him to win reelection. This coalition and its progressive reform agenda, however, soon took a back seat as the war in Europe loomed menacingly over Americans' lives.

Summary

At the beginning of the Gilded Age, business and government interests were intricately and corruptly intertwined. Political parties were evenly matched, and consequently stagnation permeated national governance. Furthermore, a vast number of Americans, including all women as well as Asian, including the Oxford, African and Native Americans, were prevented from participating in democratic governance. Reform movements, however, emerged from a grassroots level as middle-class professionals, farmers, moral reformers, and workers sought the government's help in improving their lives.

Farmers organized against railroad monopolies, and urban workers formed unions and short-lived labor parties. Middle-class professionals sought to mitigate the worst effects of industrial capitalism and chaotic urban growth by promoting reform measures adopted from European precedents, ranging from civil service reform and city planning to unemployment insurance and workers' compensation. When small movements coalesced, national third-party organizations such as the Populists and the Progressives gained enough political strength to influence the Democrats and the Republicans.

Two strains of Progressivism, one touted as Roosevelt's New Nationalism and the other as Wilson's New Freedom, became integral to party politics. Progressivist management of government and social problems by educated experts combined with their desire to create better communities and uplift citizens became a hallmark of the Democratic Party. The legacy of these local grassroots movements, culminating in the Progressive movement, had long-term effects into the twentieth century.

<Thinking Back, *Looking Forward*>

As you review this chapter, think about how reform movements emerged in the United States in response to the vast changes brought by industrialization, immigration, and urbanization discussed in this and the two previous chapters. How did U.S. efforts compare to movements abroad? How did race and gender influence both the reform movements and those targeted for reform? In the next great era of reform—the 1930s—look, too, for the influence of race and gender. Identify which reforms came from the bottom up and which from the top down. How did Progressive ideas continue to shape reform including the New Deal and the Great Society into the twentieth century?

To make your study concrete, review the timeline and reflect on the entries there. Think about their causes, consequences, and connections. How do they fit with global trends?

Additional Resources

Books

Addams, Jane. *Twenty Years at Hull House*. Urbana-Champaign: University of Illinois Press, 1990. ▶ First-person, intimate account of life inside the settlement house movement; originally published in 1910.

Amar, Akhil Reed. *America's Constitution: A Biography*. New York: Random House, 2005. ▶ An overview of U.S. constitutional history that applies history, sociology, and legal reasoning to interpret each clause of the Constitution.

Bender, Thomas. *A Nation Among Nations: America's Place in World History*. New York: Hill & Wang, 2006. ▶ A study that makes the case for considering U.S. history in the context of global history by using the Progressive movement as a prime example.

DuBois, Ellen Carol. *Woman Suffrage & Women's Rights*. New York: New York University Press, 1998. ▶ A collection of essays that looks at the history of the suffrage movement and its complex legacy for other groups seeking the vote.

Edwards, Rebecca. *New Spirits, 1865–1905*. New York: Oxford University Press, 2006. ▶ A readable overview of the period with excellent examples and analyses of how corruption and reform were intimately tied.

Hahn, Steven. *A Nation Under Our Feet: Black Political Struggles in the Rural South from Slavery to the Great Migration*. Cambridge, MA: Harvard University Press, 2004. ▶ Pulitzer Prize-winning book that traces the way African Americans actively worked to preserve their rights during the Jim Crow era.

Rogers, Daniel. *Atlantic Crossings: Social Politics in a Progressive Era*. Cambridge MA: Harvard University Press, 1998. ▶ Presentation of the Progressive Era internationally with documents related to the transit of urban and social welfare reforms from Europe to the United States.

Sinclair, Upton. *The Jungle*. ▶ A 1906 novel that follows the lives of immigrant meat-packing workers and their families in the shadows of Chicago's stockyard.

Tyrrell, Ian. *Reforming the World: The Creation of America's Moral Empire*. Princeton, NJ: Princeton University Press, 2010. ▶ Review of the way the United States used cultural and military and economic influence globally to achieve its foreign policy goals.

Go to the MindTap® for **Global Americans** to access the full version of select books from this Additional Resources section.

Websites

Documenting the South. http://docsouth.unc.edu/ ▶ University of North Carolina collection of primary sources that examine U.S. history from a southern perspective.

In Motion: The African American Migration Experience. http://www.inmotionaame.org/home.cfm;jsessionid=f83047852144998 7328734?bhcp=1 ▶ Schomburg Center overview of the major African American migrations with primary and secondary sources.

Oyez IIT Chicago-Kent College of Law. https://www.oyez.org/ ▶ Multimedia archive that explores the history of the Supreme Court of the United States.

MindTap®

Continue exploring online through MindTap®, where you can:

- **Assess your knowledge with the Chapter Test**
- **Watch historical videos related to the chapter**
- **Further your understanding with interactive maps and timelines**

Politics of Reform

1873–1877

October 1873

President Grant signs the Comstock Act.

December 1873

Woman's Christian Temperance Union is founded in Ohio.

March 1876

U.S. Supreme Court upholds *Munn v. Illinois.*

January 1877

United Labor Party is formed.

1878–1881

May 1879

Henry George publishes *Progress and Poverty.*

November 1880

James A. Garfield is elected president.

August 1881

National Civil Service Reform League is founded.

September 1881

Chester Alan Arthur becomes president after Garfield is assassinated.

1882–1884

January 1883

Arthur signs the Pendleton Civil Service Act.

May 1884

Anti-Monopoly Party is founded and nominates Benjamin Butler for president.

November 1884

Grover Cleveland is elected president.

December 1884

Toynbee Hall is founded in London, England.

Germany adopts workmen's compensation laws.

1885–1889

October 1886

U.S. Supreme Court decides *Wabash v. Illinois.*

February 1887

Cleveland signs the Interstate Commerce Act.

November 1888

Benjamin Harrison becomes president.

September 1889

Hull House opens in Chicago.

1890

June

Harrison signs the Dependent and Disability Pension Act.

July

Harrison signs the Sherman Antitrust Act.

October

Harrison signs the Sherman Silver Purchase Act.

Harrisons signs the McKinley Tariff.

1891–1893

July 1892
Populist Party adopts the Omaha Platform.

February 1893
Panic of 1893 begins.

September 1893
New Zealand becomes the first country in which women have the right to vote.

1894–1900

April 1894
Coxey's Army reaches Washington, D.C.

January 1895
U.S. Supreme Court decides *U.S. vs. E.C. Knight, Co.*

November 1896
William McKinley is elected president.

April 1898
U.S. declares war on Spain in the Spanish-American War, with battles fought in the Caribbean and in the Pacific.

1901–1904

April 1901
J.P. Morgan creates U.S. Steel.

September 1901
Leon Czolgosz assassinates McKinley, and Roosevelt becomes president.

February 1903
Department of Commerce and Labor is created.

March 1904
U.S. Supreme Court *decides U.S. v. Northern Securities.*

November 1904
Roosevelt wins reelection.

1905–1908

April 1905
U.S. Supreme Court decides *Lochner v. U.S.*

July 1905
Niagara Movement is founded.

February 1906
Upton Sinclair publishes *The Jungle*.

February 1908
U.S. Supreme Court decides *Muller v. Oregon*.

November 1908
William Howard Taft elected president.

1909–1914

February 1909
National Association for the Advancement of Colored People is founded.

November 1910
Mexican Revolution begins.

May 1911
U.S. Supreme Court decides *Standard Oil Co. of New Jersey v. United States* case.

May 1912
Congress forms the Pujo Committee.

November 1912
Woodrow Wilson is elected president.

February 1913
Sixteenth Amendment, instituting an income tax, goes into effect.

May 1913
Seventeenth Amendment allowing direct election of senators goes into effect.

18 Projecting Power

1875–1920

In 1900, W.E.B. Du Bois joined black leaders and intellectuals from Britain, the West Indies, and Africa, at the Pan-African Congress in London, where he delivered an "Address to the Nations of the World" on the dangers of racism to the ideals of justice and freedom.

18-1
Roots of the U.S. Empire

18-1a Commerce and National Pride
18-1b Protectorate over Latin America
18-1c West across the Pacific

18-2
War, Insurrection, and the Challenges of Empire

18-2a War with Spain
18-2b Debates on Empire and Response to Insurgents
18-2c Political Nuances and the Question of Citizenship

18-3
Economic Imperialism in the Pacific and in the Americas

18-3a Protection of U.S. Interests in East Asia
18-3b Construction of the Panama Canal and Domination of Latin America
18-3c Intervention in Mexico

18-4
The Great War

18-4a U.S. Neutrality
18-4b America Enters the War
18-4c Combat in Europe

18-5
Home Front Mobilization for the War and the Peace Settlements

18-5a Government Expansion and Control
18-5b Dissent and Resistance
18-5c Politics of Peacemaking

In July 1900, W.E.B. Du Bois, thirty-two-year-old African American professor of history and economics at Atlanta University, traveled to London to attend the first Pan-African Congress. He joined black leaders and intellectuals from Britain, the West Indies, and Africa with a shared commitment to improving the status of African people around the world. Slavery in the United States had ended only thirty-five years before, and thus far Du Bois's academic study had focused on the history of African Americans and the economic and social conditions in which they lived. At the Congress, he had an opportunity to place African Americans into an international context. At the closing session of the Congress, he delivered the "Address to the Nations of the World" in which he declared: "The problem of the twentieth century is the problem of the color line, the question of how far differences of race . . . will hereafter be made the basis of denying to over half the world the right of sharing to their utmost ability the opportunities and privileges of modern civilization." He also predicted that the continued mistreatment of people of color would imperil "the high ideals of justice, freedom, and culture" enshrined in European civilization. Over the next sixty years, Du Bois would become a persistent critic of racism. A renowned intellectual, he understood that U.S. race relations were not simply a domestic social problem but a manifestation of deep-seated racial attitudes whereby white people justified the exploitation of peoples of color.

Scurlock Studio Records, ca. 1905–1994, Archives Center, National Museum of American History

In the late nineteenth century, European powers had divided Africa among themselves and consolidated their holdings in Asia and the Pacific. By 1900, Belgium, France, Great Britain, Germany, Italy, the Netherlands, Portugal, and Spain were extracting the African continent's raw materials—gold, diamonds, copper, rubber, ivory, and palm oil, as well as cocoa transplanted from Latin America—for the benefit of European consumers. But those who mined, cultivated, and prepared these resources were Africans working in conditions resembling slavery. Only two African nations remained independent—Abyssinia (Ethiopia), which had recently beaten back Italian aggressors, and Liberia, founded in 1821 by Americans as a haven for former slaves. In Asia, Europeans ruled or dominated India, Burma, Singapore, Malaya, Indochina (Vietnam, Laos, and Cambodia), the East Indies, the Pacific islands, Australia, and New Zealand. The Philippines, formerly a Spanish colony, had just come under U.S. control. China—the age-old empire that had long controlled the region—was severely weakened by European trade policies and territorial concessions.

Du Bois criticized the intersection of racism and capitalism—the need for raw materials as nations industrialized and competed for markets and profits—that drove European domination and exposed tensions in his own nation's rise to global prominence. Some Americans admired the colonial empires that European nations had built in Africa and Asia

W.E.B. Du Bois understood that race relations were a manifestation of deep-seated racial attitudes whereby white people justified the exploitation of peoples of color. How do Du Bois's views on the dangers of racism to the ideals of freedom relate to the growing economic imperialism of the U.S. and Europe?

Go to MindTap® to watch a video on Du Bois and learn how his story relates to the themes of this chapter.

and believed that the United States needed its own foreign territories to guard its economic and strategic interests and to export its products as well as its political and cultural ideals. Others pointed to the ironies of a democratic nation imposing U.S. rule on people in faraway lands. Still others feared that colonialism might encourage the immigration of people of color who were perceived as racially inferior. Between 1875 and 1920, America's projection of international power—economic, military, and political—generated tremendous economic growth and national pride, but it also sparked wars in Cuba and the Philippines, interventions in Central America and Mexico, and entry into a European war with profound global ramifications.

18-1 Roots of the U.S. Empire

Drawn in 1888, this U.S. cartoon depicts the British Empire. By the late nineteenth century, the British had colonial possessions in Africa, the Asian subcontinent, and the Far East. To protect their vast territorial holdings from competing colonial powers like France and Germany, they built the world's largest navy. Aided by an extensive network of civil servants and soldiers, the British maintained a firm grip on the diverse foreign peoples under their rule.

Does this image portray British colonialism positively or negatively? What does this image's appearance in a American publication suggest about U.S. attitudes toward imperial expansion in the late nineteenth century? ▶

Go to MindTap® to practice history with the Chapter 18 **Primary Source Writing Activity: Roots of the U.S. Empire.** Read and view primary sources and respond to a writing prompt.

The Granger Collection, New York

Although the United States lacked formal overseas colonies before 1898, it had become a continental empire long before. Through purchase, war, and treaty settlements, the U.S. government had extended the nation's boundaries. Americans and new immigrants moved west to settle new lands and pursue commercial opportunities. They embraced the idea of Manifest Destiny, a belief first articulated in the 1840s that U.S. territorial expansion across North America was inevitable and justified.

Almost since the beginning of the republic, U.S. leaders had sought to develop the country's economy without becoming embroiled in foreign wars and political controversies. In his 1796 farewell address, President George Washington asserted, "The great rule of conduct for us in regard to foreign nations is in extending our commercial relations, to have with them as little political connection as possible." Although the U.S. government did not hesitate to wield its power in negotiating commercial treaties or defending its international economic interests, it did not join Europeans in occupying foreign territories.

Americans had an uncomfortable relationship with the concept of empire. From its founding, they had distinguished their country from nations driven by greed and the desire to subjugate foreign peoples. Although they recoiled at the violence and domination displayed in the European scramble for territory in Africa and Asia,

Americans also acquired land and displaced other peoples. Fusing economic, political, religious, and racial motives, white Americans conquered much of North America and began to project U.S. power globally. Although its path to empire differed from those of its European counterparts, the United States became an empire nonetheless.

☞ As you read, consider how and why the United States began to engage the wider world more extensively in the late nineteenth century. What were some of the most important domestic and international factors that drove the United States to expand its power internationally?

18-1a Commerce and National Pride

Economic, political, religious, and racial factors propel an increased international role for the United States.

As the United States rapidly industrialized, its policy makers worried that their failure to challenge European **imperialism**—the cultural, political, and economic domination of foreign peoples—would have serious economic consequences. By the 1870s, despite a rapidly growing population, the United States was producing more foodstuffs and manufactured goods than its domestic markets could absorb. Without additional consumers abroad, U.S. leaders worried that markets would remain glutted, prices would plummet, and labor unrest would intensify. Such concerns became particularly strong during the economic depressions that rocked the United States during the Panics of 1873 and 1893. Eager to find a safety valve to defuse domestic tensions, government officials, farmers, and businessmen began vigorously pursuing foreign markets. U.S. exports increased from $526 million in 1876 to more than $1 billion a year by the late 1890s.

imperialism Policy or practice of controlling a foreign territory or people through territorial acquisition or political, economic, or cultural domination.

As the United States became a dominant force in global trade, Europeans invested heavily in the nation's industries and railroads (see Chapter 15). American entrepreneurs borrowed extensively from British bankers. The financial risks paid off spectacularly and U.S. economic growth soared. On the eve of World War I, the United States generated nearly 20 percent of the world's economic output (see Figure 18.1).

This stunning economic success triggered European anxieties about a possible "Americanization" of the world. In 1902, when the British Empire encompassed one-fifth of the globe and one-quarter of its population, English writer F.A. McKenzie worried about the cultural impact of U.S. commercial power. In *The American Invaders*, McKenzie decried the proliferation of U.S. products in British daily life: "The average citizen wakes in the morning at the sound of an American alarm clock; rises from his New England sheets, and shaves with his New York soap, and a Yankee safety razor. He pulls on a pair of Boston boots over his socks from West Carolina, fastens his Connecticut braces, slips his Waterbury watch into his pocket, and sits down to breakfast. . . . [He] eats bread made from prairie flour, tinned oysters from Baltimore, and a little Kansas City bacon." Although foreign consumers eagerly purchased U.S. goods, many remained wary of U.S. influence and of Americans themselves.

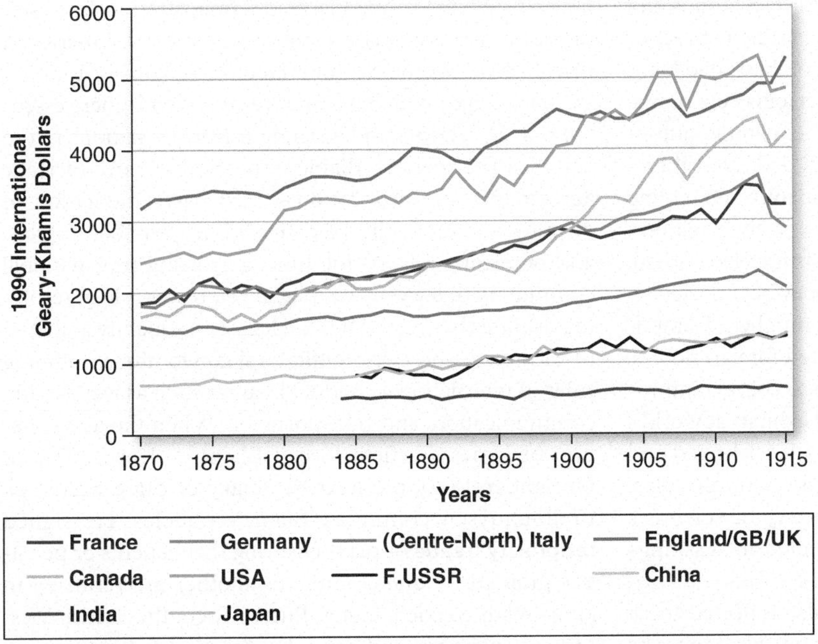

NOTE: Precise economic statistics are not available for the eras of Indian, Chinese, and Russian history where data is not listed.

Figure 18.1 Gross Domestic Product of Major Economies, 1870–1915 Measuring the total value of all the goods produced and services provided in a single year, gross domestic product (GDP) is an important indicator of a nation's economic performance. This chart documents the spectacular economic growth the United States experienced from 1870–1915. The Geary–Khamis dollar (more commonly known as the *international dollar*) is a benchmark used to estimate the purchasing power of the U.S. dollar at different points in time. ◄ Sources: https://en.wikipedia.org/wiki/US-GNP-per-capita-1869–1918.png; Angus Maddison, The University of Groningen, Netherlands, 2006, http://www.ggdc.net/maddison/Historical_Statistics/horizontal-file_02–2010.xlsmethodology

Americans were also conflicted about their nation's growing interconnections to the wider world. The telephone, telegraph, and transatlantic cable made them more aware of international politics, culture, and wars. As Americans imported millions of foreign goods, their homes and clothes became more cosmopolitan. But however much they may have enjoyed Japanese art or French fashion, most Americans did not view foreigners as equals. They expected millions of immigrants moving to the United States to assimilate and resented competing with them for jobs in the industrializing U.S. workforce. As the United States expanded its involvements abroad, many Americans believed that exposure to U.S. institutions of government, manufactured goods, and culture would elevate underdeveloped societies. They adopted transatlantic philosophies and pseudoscientific theories justifying the domination of the world's supposedly weaker races by peoples defined as "white."

Josiah Strong was an avid proponent of these ideas. As a Congregationalist minister, he traveled through the West working for the Home Missionary Society. His experiences inspired him to write *Our Country: Its Possible Future and Its Present Crisis*. Published in 1885, *Our Country* called for the expansion of U.S. power and trade. Led by missionaries working abroad to spread Protestant Christianity and consumerism, white Americans could uplift foreign peoples and prevail in a "final competition of races" that would "move down upon Mexico, down upon Central and South America, out upon the islands of the sea, over upon Africa and beyond." Voicing many of the attitudes fueling popular support for an increased international role for the United States, Strong became a national celebrity.

As the United States became more globally prominent, Americans left their imprint on many foreign societies, and foreigners shaped U.S. attitudes and daily life. Businesspeople pursued international markets for U.S. goods and overseas resources critical to the industrializing U.S. economy. Financiers from the United States orchestrated loans and banking practices that fueled spectacular economic growth, sometimes at the expense of other nations' autonomy. Missionaries and moral reformers dedicated themselves to converting foreigners to Christianity and ending prostitution, alcoholism, and opium use in their nations. Wealthy U.S. tourists traveled abroad. Flush with new money but rejected by local high society, a number of American heiresses married foreign nobles. Through exposure to college anthropology courses and exhibits at World's Fairs, Americans both celebrated and degraded non-European peoples. Published by a society of scientists and explorers founded in Washington, D.C., in 1888, *National Geographic* magazine also reflected these tensions. Its vibrant photographs presented indigenous peoples authentically, but images of bare-breasted native women both intrigued and scandalized readers in an age of taboos against nudity. As U.S. military, economic, and cultural power grew, so did the complexities and contradictions of American imperialism.

arbitration Resolution of disputes through third-party legal negotiations.

multilateral convention Also called *multilateral treaty*, legal agreement binding three or more sovereign states to identical regulations and terms.

reciprocity treaties Agreement between two nations providing equal benefits and mutually binding rules and obligations.

18-1b Protectorate over Latin America

For ideological and economic reasons, U.S. officials expand their involvement in Latin America.

In the aftermath of the Civil War, U.S. policy makers took tentative steps away from policies opposing foreign entanglements. In response to a rapidly changing global landscape, the United States acquired its first offshore territories and searched for ways to protect its unique qualities while increasing its political, economic, and cultural influence internationally. Although domestic opposition to direct colonialism constrained these efforts, the United States began more aggressively challenging its European rivals.

Both idealism and prejudice shaped U.S. anti-imperialism. Many Americans took pride in their country's tradition of government with the consent of the governed and thought colonialism violated that principle. Some objected to the large navy and high costs that overseas territorial acquisition required. Others perceived the United States as a white, Protestant nation and opposed adding colonies with large nonwhite populations who did not share America's dominant religious faith. These views transcended party lines, and members of the same party often strongly disagreed on overseas expansion and its possible impact on issues like tariffs, immigration, and currency reform.

These limitations did not prevent Secretary of State James G. Blaine in the Garfield administration from significantly increasing U.S. involvement in Latin America. A firm believer in the Monroe Doctrine—James Monroe's 1823 message proclaiming the Western Hemisphere essential to U.S. security and warning European nations not to colonize the region—Blaine advocated the use of trade agreements and **arbitration**—third-party mediation of disputes—to undercut the nation's European commercial and political rivals. At the time, a growing transnational community of lawyers was playing a greater role in resolving disputes between states. Delegates frequently gathered to formulate and sign **multilateral conventions** outlining rules of international conduct in areas such as war, health, communication, and transportation. When the assassination of James Garfield forced Blaine to leave office in December 1880, the next Secretary of State Frederick Frelinghuysen continued Blaine's policies. He signed **reciprocity treaties**—pacts ensuring that benefits or penalties granted by one country to another are returned in kind—with Mexico, Cuba, Puerto Rico, the British West Indies, Colombia, and Santo Domingo.

In 1889, Blaine began a second term as secretary of state under new president Benjamin Harrison. Still determined to cultivate closer ties between the Americas, Blaine organized the first Inter-American Conference. In early 1890, representatives from nineteen nations negotiated several trade pacts. Hoping to strengthen cultural and scientific exchanges throughout the region, the delegates established the International Bureau of the American Republics, later renamed the Pan-American Union. But the spirit of cooperation evident in the meeting proved short lived.

18-1c West across the Pacific

Americans debate acquisition of Pacific territories and modernize their navy to protect trade.

Throughout this era, as the United States secured trade concessions in the Pacific and continued attempts to broaden access to overseas markets in China, foreign peoples sometimes resisted these endeavors. In 1887, wealthy U.S. landowners in Hawai'i forced King Kalakaua to sign the so-called Bayonet Constitution, which stripped the Hawaiian monarchy of its authority and bestowed suffrage rights not only on naturalized citizens but also on foreign resident aliens. Hawaiian, American, and European men who met property and literacy requirements were permitted to vote, but Asians' voting rights were abolished.

In the early 1890s, a number of events triggered a U.S. attempt to annex Hawai'i. In 1890, the McKinley Tariff ended the special status given to Hawaiian sugar and enabled U.S. domestic sugar producers to sell at prices lower than their foreign competitors. The decision devastated the Hawaiian sugar industry. In 1891, after the ineffective King Kalakaua died, his sister Lili'uokalani assumed the Hawaiian throne. Fiercely nationalistic, the new queen instituted a new constitution restoring political power to the indigenous majority. In early 1893, disgruntled white elites assisted by U.S. Minister to Hawai'i John L. Stevens and 162 marines overthrew Queen Lili'uokalani. U.S. officials and the newly created provisional government signed an agreement annexing Hawai'i to the United States, thus ensuring that Hawaiian sugar would be classified as domestic rather than imported. With only two weeks remaining in his term, President Benjamin Harrison presented the treaty to the U.S. Senate.

But Grover Cleveland, Harrison's successor, withdrew the treaty only five days after taking office. A probusiness Democrat, Cleveland supported commercial expansion but believed that the annexation and administration of underdeveloped tropical areas would necessitate a large federal bureaucracy and jeopardize U.S. ideals of self-governance. After investigators concluded that the United States had acted illegally in Hawai'i, Cleveland demanded that Queen Lili'uokalani be reinstated. The provisional government refused and instead created the Republic of Hawai'i. Outmaneuvered, Cleveland reluctantly recognized Hawai'i as an independent nation. The contentious issue of whether Hawai'i should be annexed to the United States remained unresolved for the time being.

In other areas in the world, the United States began clashing with European powers. In 1878, the country extended its range into the Pacific from Hawai'i and Midway Island by acquiring a coaling station on a group of fourteen volcanic islands called Samoa. Rivalry for control over it soon arose. Germany and the United States were on the brink of war until a typhoon scuttled the fleets of both nations. At the Berlin Conference of 1889, Britain, the United States, and Germany split Samoa into a tripartite protectorate. A decade later, the United States and Germany officially divided Samoa into colonies and compensated Britain with other Pacific territories.

Alarmed by the growing sea power of its commercial rivals, the United States began modernizing and expanding its naval capabilities. In *The Influence of Sea Power upon History* (1890), Alfred Thayer Mahan, a lecturer at the Naval War College, argued that a nation's greatness was inextricably connected to its naval strength. Because industrialization generated vast surpluses of manufactured and agricultural goods, foreign markets for the excesses were essential. Protecting those markets necessitated a large merchant marine to carry the goods and long-range steel battleships that could be deployed all over the globe. Such a force required a network of colonies to be used for coaling, making repairs, and obtaining raw materials. In addition to this string of strategic bases, Mahan called for the construction of a canal bisecting Central America and linking the Atlantic and Pacific Oceans. Mahan's ideas greatly influenced policy makers in the United States and several other countries, including fast-militarizing Japan. U.S. Secretary of the Navy Benjamin F. Tracy significantly expanded the U.S. battleship fleet and by 1900, the U.S. Navy ranked second in the world behind Great Britain. The Imperial Japanese Navy began challenging Russian naval expansion in the Far East.

In 1899, after thousands of private citizens urged their governments to address the escalating arms race, delegates from twenty-six countries gathered in The Hague, Netherlands, for an historic peace conference on disarmament and rules of war. Although the representatives did not agree to arms limitations, they adopted multilateral treaties on wartime conduct, ground and naval combat, and the use of certain weapons. The delegates' acceptance of a convention creating the Permanent Court of Arbitration set an important precedent for the League of Nations created after World War I.

18-2

War, Insurrection, and the Challenges of Empire

The "White man's burden," a phrase coined by British poet Rudyard Kipling, referred to the duty of the white race to uplift and Christianize peoples perceived as primitive and inferior. Such attitudes played a key role in justifying the acquisition of foreign territories in the late nineteenth and early twentieth centuries. This 1899 cartoon from the U.S. satire magazine *Judge* depicts Uncle Sam and John Bull as symbols of American and British colonization.

In this cartoon, what do the concepts etched into the rocks on the upward climb to "civilization" and the images of the Egyptian, Sudanese, Chinese, Indian, and Zulu in John Bull's basket and the Cuban, Hawaiian, Filipino, Puerto Rican, and Samoan in Uncle Sam's basket suggest about the artist's attitudes toward foreign peoples and his views of British and U.S. annexations of foreign territories? ▶

"The White Man's Burden (Apologies to Rudyard Kipling)." Victor Gillam, *Judge*, April 1, 1899.

reconcentration policy Relocation of native rural populations to enclosed compounds in urban areas, often instituted as a means of undercutting popular support for insurgents.

yellow journalism Term originating in the 1890s to describe a style of news reporting emphasizing sensationalism and exaggeration over objective fact.

In the late 1890s, following decades of resistance to an overseas empire, the United States catapulted into the ranks of formal colonial powers after defeating Spain in a brief war. Sympathetic to Cubans seeking independence from Spanish rule and determined to guard American interests on the island, U.S. officials demanded that Spain accord Cuba more autonomy. Struggling to retain the remnants of its once-great empire, Spain resisted and political tensions escalated. After the Spanish-American War erupted, the United States expanded its power in the Pacific and gained improved access to Asian markets by annexing Hawai'i and seizing the Spanish-controlled Philippine Islands. At the same time, U.S. ground troops captured Spain's territories in the Caribbean.

These events forced Americans to confront challenges and contradictions. At home, they debated the economic, political, and racial implications of the new U.S. empire. Abroad, U.S. officials and soldiers attempted to govern, manage, and defend foreign peoples with different cultures and often fierce determination to resist U.S. domination.

☞ As you read, pay close attention to the causes and consequences of the U.S. pursuit of overseas territories. How did Americans differ in their attitudes about governing foreign peoples? How and why did foreign peoples' responses to U.S. control vary?

18-2a War with Spain

The United States intervenes in a Cuban revolt against Spanish rule.

From 1868 to 1878, U.S. officials keenly observed, but did not intervene in, the Ten Years War, a failed Cuban revolt against more than four centuries of Spanish imperialism and slavery. Although Spain abolished slavery in 1886, it did not institute economic or political reforms. U.S. capitalists heavily invested in the island's sugar, mining, and tobacco industries and persuaded many Cuban planters to exchange their lands for stock or jobs in U.S.-owned firms. In 1895, after a new U.S. tariff imposed duties on imported sugar and Spain retaliated by restricting Cuban sugar shipments to the United States, the Cuban economy crashed and the insurgents rose again. The rebels hoped to win American backing for their struggle against Spain but not at the price of U.S. annexation of Cuba.

Determined to crush the uprising, Spanish governor-general Valeriano y Nicolau Weyler instituted a ruthless **reconcentration policy** that divided Cuba into districts and forced five hundred thousand civilians into fortified compounds. Rancid food, overcrowding, and terrible sanitation led to the deaths of approximately two hundred thousand people. At the same time, Weyler's troops ravaged the countryside, targeting rebels and their supporters and destroying livestock, crops, and water supplies. Vying for readers, American tabloids printed sensationalized accounts of Spanish atrocities that sparked calls for U.S. intervention. But such **yellow journalism** failed to sway U.S. policy makers. They were unwilling to provoke a war with Spain that could jeopardize American economic interests in Cuba and did not believe that Cubans—whom they considered backward and racially inferior—could rule themselves. Rejecting calls to buy or annex Cuba, President Cleveland instead declared U.S. neutrality, a policy reaffirmed by his successor, William McKinley.

But when renewed unrest in Cuba threatened U.S. citizens and investments, McKinley deployed the battleship *Maine* to Havana Harbor. On February 15, 1898, it exploded and sank, killing 266 Americans. Most Americans immediately blamed the Spanish, but McKinley tried to defuse the crisis by ordering an investigation. Advocates of intervention accused McKinley of cowardice and a lack of manhood. Assistant Secretary of the Navy Theodore Roosevelt proclaimed that McKinley had "no more backbone than a chocolate éclair."

In late March, after investigators attributed the sinking of the *Maine* to an undersea mine of undetermined national origin (recent studies blame a spontaneous explosion of coal dust), pressure for war against Spain intensified. Deferring to the bellicose public mood, McKinley won congressional approval for $50 million in emergency defense expenditures and sent Spain his final terms. But the Spanish would not accept a U.S.-brokered peace process or Cuban independence. Dissatisfied, the president sent Congress a message asking for the authorization of U.S. military intervention to stop the Spanish-Cuban war and to protect U.S. property and trade. Convinced that the Cubans were not yet suited for self-government, McKinley did not request diplomatic recognition of the "so-called Cuban Republic."

On April 19, 1898, Congress issued a joint resolution authorizing the use of force and declaring Cuba independent (without recognizing the rebels). To emphasize their anti-imperialist intentions, Congress also passed the **Teller Amendment** stating that the United States did not intend to annex Cuba. On April 21, Spain severed diplomatic ties with the United States and the next day, the United States began blockading Cuba. By April 25, the two nations were officially at war.

McKinley then deployed U.S. forces to Cuba and to the Philippines, a chain of Pacific islands colonized by Spain since the late 1500s. On May 1, 1898, implementing pre-existing plans drafted by the Naval War College, Admiral George Dewey led his Asiatic Squadron to Manila Bay and crushed the Spanish fleet in a single day, losing only one U.S. sailor (who died of heatstroke). By late June, U.S. ground troops in Cuba were poised outside Santiago, a critical Spanish stronghold. On July 1, U.S. soldiers—including Teddy Roosevelt, who had resigned from the Navy Department to lead a volunteer regiment called the *Rough Riders*—joined Cuban rebels in a victorious assault on San Juan Hill and secured Santiago. Two days later, U.S. naval forces defeated the Spanish naval squadron when it made a desperate effort to escape Santiago Harbor and reach open waters. With its battle fleet in ruins, Spain surrendered. Capitalizing on Spain's weakness, U.S. forces quickly seized Spain's nearby colony, the island Puerto Rico.

By mid-August, Spain had capitulated in the Philippines. Attempting to salvage its pride after yet another loss, Spain surrendered only to the United States, not to the Filipino nationalists who had been fighting for independence since 1896. Americans rejoiced at their overwhelming victory. Although 5,463 U.S. troops perished during the four-month conflict, only 379 died in battle. The others died in accidents or from diseases such as yellow fever and malaria.

The brief war against Spain provided McKinley a pretext for acquiring Hawai'i. Asserting that the islands were vital to the U.S. naval effort in the Philippines, he urged the Senate to approve an annexation treaty he had negotiated with the white-dominated Hawaiian government months earlier. Circumventing the constitutional requirement of a two-thirds Senate vote approving treaty ratification, McKinley asked for a joint resolution requiring only a majority vote. On July 7, 1898, both houses of Congress voted in favor of U.S. annexation of Hawai'i.

18-2b Debates on Empire and Response to Insurgents

U.S. occupation of the Philippines sparks intense domestic debates and a Filipino revolt.

In the 1898 **Treaty of Paris** that ended the war, Spain recognized Cuban independence, assumed Cuba's debts, and ceded Guam, Puerto Rico, and the Philippines to the United States in exchange for $20 million. Even before the president sent the treaty to the U.S. Senate for ratification, a heated political debate erupted. Although most Americans accepted overseas commercial expansion, many were horrified at the occupation of Cuba, Puerto Rico, and the Philippines by U.S. troops. In June 1898, prominent individuals including former Democratic president Cleveland, steel magnate Andrew Carnegie, pacifist Lucia True Ames Mead, union leader Samuel Gompers, reformer Jane Addams, and writer Mark Twain formed the **Anti-Imperialist League** to protest possible annexation of the Philippines. Their platform declared that "imperialism is hostile to liberty" and vowed to defend the ideals enshrined in the Declaration of Independence.

Despite their shared commitment to republicanism, members of this diverse coalition had varied reasons for opposing the annexation of the Philippines. Some sought to guard U.S. society from the immigration of peoples considered racially inferior. Opposing the subjugation of foreign people as a violation of cherished

Teller Amendment Congressional resolution added to the U.S. declaration of war on Spain proclaiming that the United States would not permanently occupy or annex Cuba.

Treaty of Paris Agreement ending hostilities between Spain and the United States and granting the United States the former Spanish colonies of Cuba, Guam, and the Philippines.

Anti-Imperialist League Diverse coalition founded in opposition to the U.S. annexation of the Philippines.

American principles, U.S. Senator George Hoar, a Republican from Massachusetts, warned that the United States was about "to be transformed from a Republic . . . into a vulgar, commonplace empire, founded upon physical force." Labor leaders across the political spectrum voiced fears that workers imported from the Pacific would undercut U.S. wages. Participation in the anti-imperialist cause inspired thousands of American men and women to build a peace movement that shaped discourse on U.S. foreign policy for years afterward.

Linking notions of masculinity and militarism, the imperialists mocked their opponents as "unmanly aunties" (a pun on *antis*) and extolled the strategic and economic advantages of expanding U.S. territorial holdings. They argued that the United States had a duty to spread "civilization" and to uplift morally and racially inferior foreigners. Protestant missionaries wanted to convert non-Christians and to bring sanitation, education, and health care to "backward" regions. Rudyard Kipling exhorted the United States to join Great Britain in assuming the **"White man's burden"** of governing an empire and "new-caught, sullen peoples, half devil and half child." Senator Albert Beveridge, a Republican representing Indiana, proclaimed that God intended Americans to be the "master organizers of the world" who could transfuse "the blood of government" into the veins of the Filipinos.

Such triumphalist rhetoric rankled Emilio Aguinaldo, leader of the Filipino resistance movement. After Admiral Dewey dispatched a ship to retrieve Aguinaldo from exile in Hong Kong, he and his comrades joined the ongoing U.S. war against Spain. Proclaiming an independent Philippine Republic in June 1898, the Filipino insurgents soon controlled most towns and appointed officials to lead them. But U.S. officials ordered them out of Manila and insulted Filipinos with racial epithets like "*gu gu*" (the antecedent of "*gook*," a term later used by U.S soldiers in the Korean and Vietnam wars). Determined to govern themselves and unwilling to submit to U.S. authority, the Filipinos drafted a constitution in late January 1899. Shortly thereafter, the rebels attacked U.S. troops stationed on the islands.

News of the insurrection intensified continuing debates over the Treaty of Paris. Anti-imperialists published accounts of U.S. war atrocities committed against the Filipino nationalist forces, stimulating cries to reject the treaty. Senator Henry Cabot Lodge, a Republican from Massachusetts, warned that if they rejected the pact, Americans would be "branded as a people incapable of taking rank as one of the greatest of world powers." On February 6, 1899, after defeating an amendment granting the Filipinos independence once they established a stable government, the Senate narrowly ratified the Treaty of Paris. The United States now had a territorial empire but also faced another war.

"White man's burden" Taken from the name of a poem by Rudyard Kipling, a description of the presumed moral duty of the white race to govern and educate nonwhite peoples.

commonwealth Nation with local governmental autonomy but voluntarily united to another country.

The Philippine-American War proved more bloody and difficult than the preceding conflict in Cuba. With significant popular support, the Filipinos launched guerilla assaults and then hid in the jungles. U.S. soldiers retaliated by destroying villages deemed friendly to the insurgents. Echoing the brutal tactics used by General Weyler in Cuba, American forces rounded up civilians and herded them into prison camps, where tens of thousands soon died from malnutrition and disease. After Filipino soldiers cut off captives' ears and noses or buried them alive, U.S. troops subjected prisoners to the "water cure," a torture technique that simulated drowning. By the time the war ended in 1902, 126,000 U.S. troops had fought in the $160 million conflict and the death toll included 4,165 of them, sixteen thousand Filipino insurgents, and two hundred thousand Filipino civilians.

Following his reelection in 1900, McKinley dispatched a special commission headed by William Howard Taft to the Philippines. Over the next several months, the commissioners issued 499 laws and established a judicial system. In March 1901, after U.S. soldiers captured him, Aguinaldo signed a decree urging the rebels to surrender. Some refused and the fighting continued for another year. On July 4, 1901, Taft became the civil governor of the islands. While suppressing Philippine resistance through censorship and jailing dissidents, U.S. officials tried to win the loyalty of elite Filipinos by introducing programs for education, road and bridge construction, tax reforms, sanitation, and vaccinations. These officials also sent scores of Filipino students to the United States to pursue higher education. The new colonial leaders promoted exports of agricultural products and raw materials to the United States, a model of trade that made the Philippines depend heavily on U.S. capital and imports of finished goods for decades afterward.

American leaders took steps to ensure that their governance of the islands would be temporary and would not make Filipinos U.S. citizens. In 1902, Congress allowed the Filipinos to create a bicameral legislature under the supervision of the U.S. War Department. Fourteen years later, the Jones Act formally committed the United States to granting the Philippines independence once a stable government was established. In 1935, it became a self-governing **commonwealth**, but the Japanese occupation of the islands during World War II forced the Filipino regime into temporary exile in the United States. On July 4, 1946, eleven months after Japan surrendered, the Philippines finally became an independent nation.

18-2c Political Nuances and the Question of Citizenship

The acquisition of foreign possessions forces U.S. policy makers to confront a number of difficult questions.

How would the United States govern these colonies? Would their inhabitants enjoy the same rights as U.S. citizens? Whereas some Americans believed that "the Constitution follows the flag," others contended that people residing in overseas territories owned or controlled by the United States should not necessarily be accorded constitutional protections. Another group sought to extend citizenship and basic civil rights such as trial by jury and voting rights but to withhold special privileges such as using U.S. currency and running for president.

To resolve these complicated issues, Congress created new legal frameworks for U.S. foreign possessions and their inhabitants. In 1900, the lawmakers designated Hawai'i an **incorporated territory** and made all white and indigenous Hawaiians—but not Asian residents—U.S. citizens with a U.S.-appointed governor and an elected legislature. In 1912, Alaska became a territory with a similar structure. These moves put Hawai'i and Alaska on the path to eventual statehood followed in earlier U.S. land acquisitions on continental North America.

But U.S. officials instituted different policies for territories recently acquired from Spain. In 1900, the Foraker Act made Puerto Rico an **unincorporated territory** subject to U.S. laws. In a series of important decisions between 1901 and 1904 known as the **Insular Cases**, the U.S. Supreme Court ruled that residents of Guam, Puerto Rico, and the Philippines were not automatically entitled to all of the rights and protections guaranteed by the U.S. Constitution. Although residents of these unincorporated territories were subject to U.S. laws, they were not U.S. citizens, nor were they granted voting representation in Congress or the Electoral College. These political nuances allowed the United States to govern possessions it did not intend to make states.

While resolving these legal complexities, U.S. policy makers quickly organized their new empire but in contrast to European imperial powers did not create large colonial bureaucracies. Small teams of U.S. administrators—often in collaboration with local inhabitants—forged creative solutions to the problems they encountered abroad. These teams took inspiration from territorial management policies in North America and in British-held colonies like Burma and Egypt but also pioneered new practices in policing, public health, agriculture, environmental management, and drug control. Through education, they sought to promote the values of U.S. democracy and to persuade foreign peoples of the superiority of Anglo-American culture and the English language.

Reactions to U.S. control differed. Unlike the Filipinos, Puerto Ricans readily accepted American rule and McKinley quickly withdrew U.S. troops. In 1900, the United States established a civilian government in Puerto Rico without extending U.S. citizenship. In March 1917, the Jones-Shafroth Act granted the island's residents U.S. citizenship and the right to create a locally elected bicameral legislature. But Congress could block any law passed by the Puerto Rican lawmakers, and the U.S. government retained control over the island's economy, defenses, and other matters. When the United States entered World War I shortly thereafter, Puerto Ricans were subject to conscription.

Cuba presented a far more complex situation. Having vowed not to annex the island in the Teller Amendment, the United States had promised to rule Cuba only until its inhabitants could form a successful government of their own. In 1900, General Leonard Wood, commander of U.S. forces in Cuba, supervised a census and organized delegate elections for a constitutional convention. In exchange for a U.S. pledge to end its military occupation, Cuba amended the resulting constitution. The **Platt Amendment** made Cuba a U.S. protectorate; it restricted Cuba's ability

incorporated territory Land acquisition directly governed by the United States but that has lower political and legal status than states.

unincorporated territory Areas controlled by the U.S. government but accorded only limited constitutional rights and privileges and lacking statehood status.

Insular Cases Series of Supreme Court decisions declaring that areas under U.S. control are not automatically entitled to full constitutional rights.

Platt Amendment U.S. policy asserting the right to intervene in Cuba in defense of Cuban independence and to ensure "protection of life, property, and individual liberty."

"School Begins," 1899
American racial views and previous experience with continental expansion shaped U.S. policies toward newly acquired foreign territories. Many Americans felt it was a moral duty to educate and uplift peoples perceived to be ignorant and inferior. This 1899 image links America's interactions with African Americans, Native Americans, and Chinese immigrants to its success in putting continental territories on the path to statehood and the belief that foreign peoples needed supervision and instruction before transitioning to self-government. ◄

History without Borders

The 1904 Louisiana Purchase Exposition

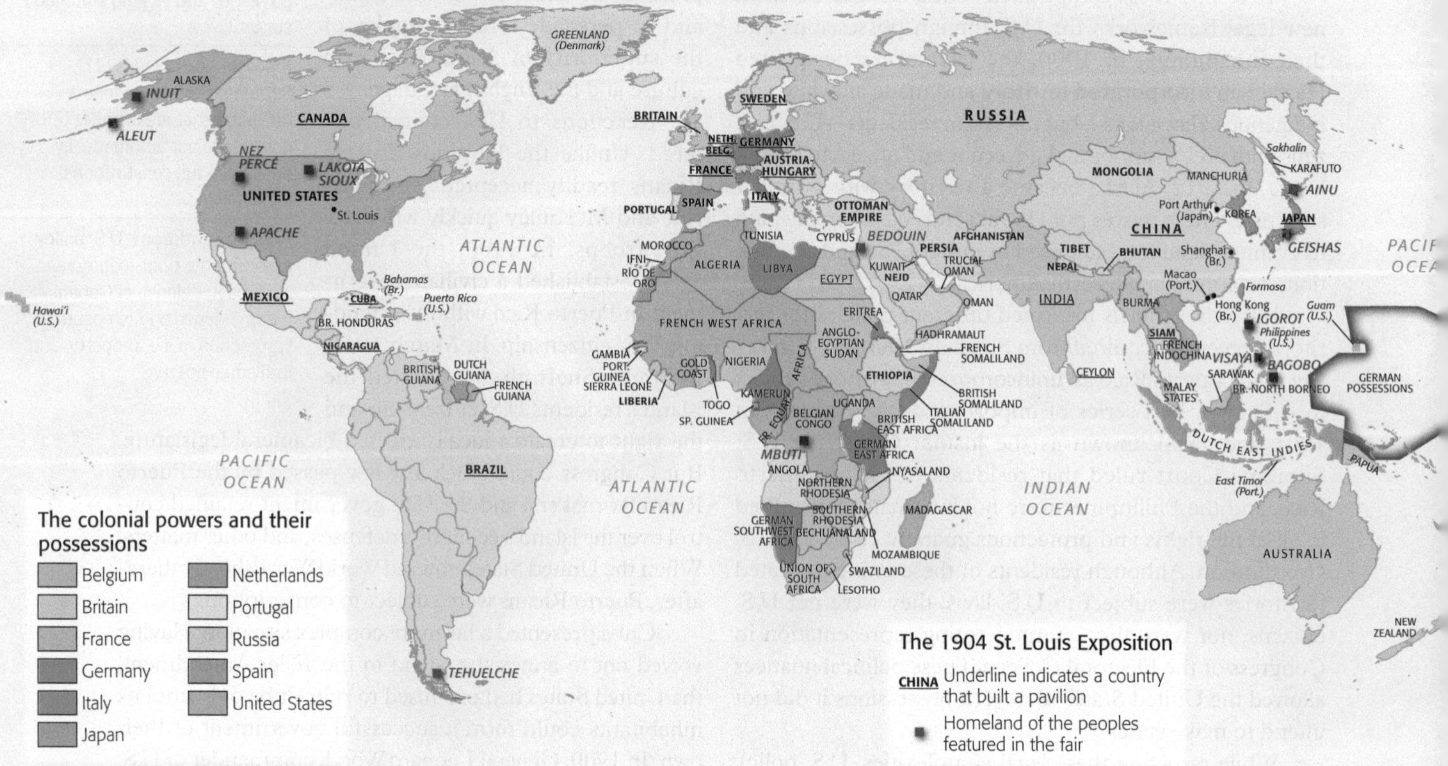

Global Imperialism Driven by a combination of economic, political, and cultural motives, Belgium, Great Britain, France, Portugal, the United States, Spain, Japan, Germany, Italy, Netherlands, and Denmark maintained imperial control over foreign territories in 1900. Beginning with the Great Exhibition held in London in 1851, world's fairs and exhibitions became important venues for imperial powers to demonstrate their products, culture, and the diversity of the peoples living under their rule. ▲

On April 30, 1904, an international exposition commemorating the one hundredth anniversary of the Louisiana Purchase opened in St. Louis. Delayed by a year in order to allow participation from more nations, the exposition filled twelve hundred acres with fifteen hundred buildings connected by seventy-miles of roads and paths. Sixty-two countries and forty-three of the forty-five U.S. states highlighted their industrial, scientific, and cultural achievements. Over the next seven months, nearly 20 million people streamed through the exhibits and amusements of the largest world's fair to date. Many got their first opportunity to try Dr. Pepper, peanut butter, cotton candy, and ice cream cones.

Held shortly after the U.S. victory in the Spanish-American War, the exposition celebrated America's continental empire and its recent acquisitions of Hawai'i, Guam, Cuba, Puerto Rico, and the Philippines. Organizers presented the Louisiana Purchase and overseas expansion as inevitable results of the nation's Manifest Destiny. Reflecting prevailing theories about race and "civilization," its creators pointed to the U.S. political system, economic success, and technological prowess as evidence of the inferiority of nonwhite, "barbarous" or "semi-barbarous" peoples.

Anthropological displays of more than two thousand indigenous peoples exemplified this fusion of imperialism and racism. Living ethnological exhibits featured Ainu aborigines from Japan, Patagonian giants from Argentina, and a Congolese *Mbuti* pygmy named Ota Benga. The exposition's most popular exhibit featured one thousand Filipinos re-enacting their daily lives on a

Philippine exposition, World's Fair, St. Louis, 1904

Poster Advertising the Philippine Exposition, The Louisiana Purchase Exposition, St. Louis, 1904 Organizers isolated the Philippine Exposition and further divided it to highlight different levels of societal advancement among the Filipinos as evidenced by the contrast between the constable and the Moro chief depicted here. ▲

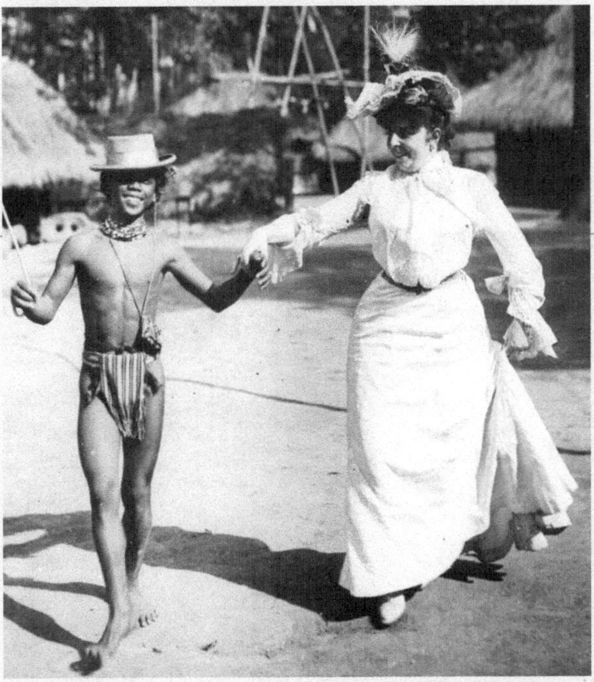

Missouri History Museum

A Filipino Boy and a Fairgoer, The Louisiana Purchase Exposition, St. Louis, 1904 A woman identified as "Mrs. Wilkins" teaches an "Igorot" boy the cakewalk, a dance first appearing among slaves in the plantation South. The photo reflects prevailing ideas about whites "civilizing" people of darker races but also hints at some of the erotic tensions created by the Filipinos' comfort in displaying the body and white Victorian taboos against nudity and sexuality. By dancing with this scantily clad boy, Mrs. Wilkins was exercising her white privilege but also challenging notions of appropriate behavior for upper-class white women. ▲

forty-seven acre site featuring mock villages, a man-made lake, a replica of the Walled City of Manila, and displays of traditional art, agricultural products, and weapons.

To simplify the complexities of Filipino society, organizers invented religious and racial groupings that did not exist and identified Igorot, Negrito, Moros, Bagobos, and Visayans "tribes." The Igorot Village housed one hunded twelve indigenous peoples from the Philippines and featured a stone fireplace in which the Igorot killed, roasted, and ate dogs as part of a ritual ceremony. Fairgoers erroneously assumed that the "savage" Igorot consumed dogs as part of their regular daily diet. Rumors of canines disappearing from St. Louis neighborhoods spread like wildfire, and derogatory characterizations of Filipinos as dog eaters persisted for decades. Afraid that the sight of Igorot in native breechcloths would offend delicate Victorian sensibilities, the Roosevelt administration demanded that they wear "bright-colored silk trousers" but withdrew the request after anthropologists complained that the directive would compromise the authenticity of the exhibit.

On "Receiving Day," the Igorot greeted American Indians including Chief Joseph, Geronimo, and Quanah Parker. Neither group knew that the two shared a common bond as peoples who had borne the sometimes devastating price of America's territorial conquests. U.S. policies had uprooted Native Americans from their tribal lands and had placed Filipino civilians in fortified reconcentration camps to prevent them from aiding armed rebels resisting U.S. occupation. Tens of thousands died from starvation and disease in these relocations. Such were tragic legacies of American imperialism that endured long after most of the buildings of the exposition were dismantled.

Critical Thinking Questions

▶ Why do you think that world's fairs and international exhibitions became so popular when nations were vying for global territories and markets?

▶ How do you think the experience of being a U.S. fairgoer compared to that of being one of the indigenous people on display at the 1904 St. Louis Exposition? What are some of the positive and negative ways these encounters might have shaped the fairgoers' views of foreign peoples and foreign peoples' views of Americans?

Go to MindTap® to engage with an interactive version of **History without Borders: The 1904 Louisiana Purchase Exposition.** Learn from an interactive map, view related video, and respond to critical thinking questions.

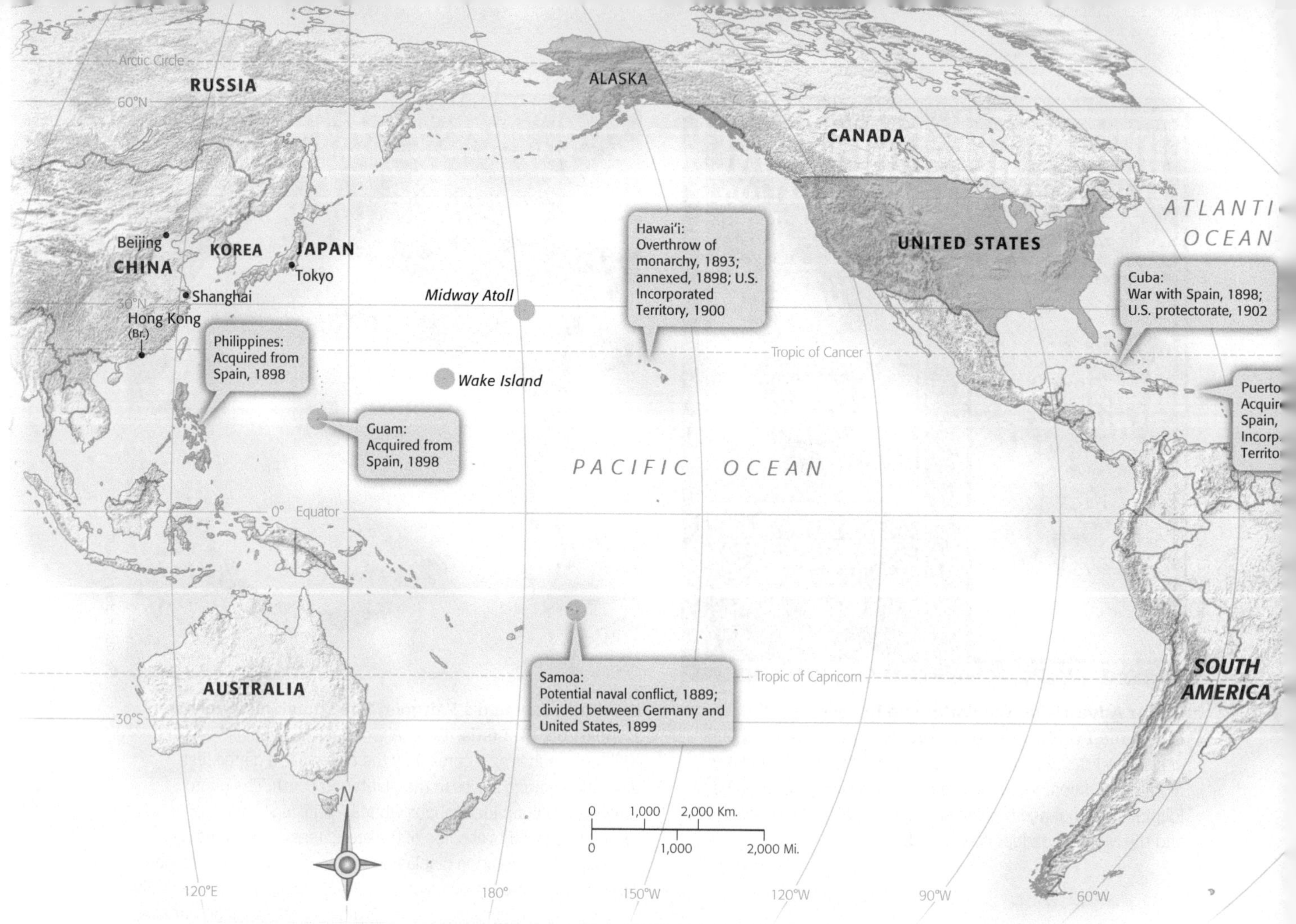

Map 18.1 U.S. Overseas Expansion, 1893–1902 In the years following the Civil War, the United States began acquiring territories beyond continental North America in a quest to expand its military, economic, and cultural power. A series of federal acts and judicial rulings determined whether specific territories would become states and outlined the citizenship status, rights, and responsibilities of foreign peoples living under U.S. governance. ▲

to sign treaties or accrue debts, gave the United States the right to lease naval bases such as Guantánamo Bay, and permitted U.S. intervention if the Cuban government failed to protect "life, property, or individual liberty." Before departing in 1902, the U.S. military government rebuilt war-torn communities, constructed roads and bridges, and eradicated yellow fever. Cuba was superficially independent, but the United States dominated its economy and militarily intervened several times over the next two decades (see Map 18.1).

18-3

Economic Imperialism in the Pacific and in the Americas

In this drawing, Louis Dalrymple, a cartoonist renowned for his political satire, captures the blend of threats and mediation that punctuated President Theodore Roosevelt's interventionist approach to global affairs in the early twentieth century.

Why are Roosevelt's size and location in the cartoon important? What does the image suggest about the changing international role of the United States in the years immediately following the Spanish-American War? ▶

Cartoon of President Roosevelt portrayed as a giant policeman astride two continents/Private Collection/Bridgeman Images

From 1898 to 1914, as U.S. overseas investments increased from $445 million to $2.5 billion, U.S. policy makers defended, controlled, and expanded the country's new territorial and commercial empire. The United States clashed with other imperial nations and put down protests by peoples who resented American influence and power. In East Asia, U.S. officials pushed for expanded access to China and closely monitored Japan's rising military and economic capabilities. In Latin America, Roosevelt promised to "speak softly and carry a big stick" as he vigorously promoted U.S. interests in the region where its investments were sometimes so extensive and its corporations so powerful that they could undermine national autonomy. William Howard Taft, Roosevelt's successor to the presidency and a fellow Republican, adopted a less confrontational approach, using U.S. financial power to protect commerce and ensure national security. After winning the presidency in 1912, Woodrow Wilson, a Democrat, announced his intention to moderate the aggressive stance of his predecessors but then escalated their interventionist policies to protect U.S. lives, investments, and property.

☞ As you read, consider the tactics that U.S. policy makers used to defend, control, and expand the U.S. empire in this era. How and why did U.S. policies in the Western Hemisphere often differ from those pursued elsewhere in the world?

18-3a Protection of U.S. Interests in East Asia

The United States competes with other imperialist powers in pursuit of greater engagement with China.

The annexation of the Philippines deepened long-standing U.S. interest in China. Protestant missionaries hoped to spread Christianity there. Between 1890 and 1900, the number of U.S. missionaries in China doubled from 513 to more than 1,000. U.S. business leaders wanted to expand the nation's tiny share of the huge Chinese market, but Britain, Germany, Russia, and France had already divided China into **spheres of influence** with exclusive trading privileges. Following its quick victory in the Sino-Japanese War of 1895, Japan, too, had secured interests in China and established military control of the Korean peninsula that would lead to its annexation in 1910.

To avoid being blocked out of the China market, the McKinley administration had developed the **Open Door policy** calling for an end to foreign control of Chinese trade. In September 1899, Secretary of State John Hay sent diplomatic notes to Britain, Germany, Russia, France, Italy, and Japan requesting that they permit all nations to trade freely in their spheres of influence. Aware that the United States lacked the military or economic power to open international trade barriers, the six nations responded ambivalently. Nonetheless, in March 1900, Hay boldly announced that all the powers had accepted the principle of the Open Door.

But the eruption of a nationalistic revolt in China soon tested the policy. In June 1900, the Boxers, members of a secret society, demanded the expulsion of all foreigners and murdered hundreds of Christian missionaries and their Chinese converts. In Peking (now Beijing), terrified foreigners barricaded themselves in their respective diplomatic legations. Hoping to prevent a vindictive counterattack on the Chinese, McKinley, without congressional approval, redeployed 2,500 U.S. troops from the Philippines to China to join 15,500 from other countries in suppressing the **Boxer Rebellion**. On July 3, 1900, Hay issued another Open Door note proclaiming U.S. determination to guard the lives and property of its citizens, preserve Chinese sovereignty, and guarantee "equal and impartial trade." Nevertheless, the foreign powers that quelled the uprising forced the Chinese government to pay $300 million in damages. The United States used its portion to fund scholarships for Chinese students to attend American schools. The program became a model for the Fulbright international educational exchanges established after World War II.

In 1904, the United States again intervened in East Asia after Japan launched an attack on Russia over competing interests in Manchuria in northeast China. As Japan won a string of victories in the Russo-Japanese War and Russian authorities quashed protests in St. Petersburg that challenged the absolute rule of Tsar Nicholas II, Roosevelt sought to guard U.S. interests in the Pacific. In August 1905, he invited Russian and Japanese diplomats to Portsmouth, New Hampshire. After hammering out several territorial concessions, the delegates signed an armistice that won Roosevelt the Nobel Peace Prize. In Atlanta, W.E.B. Du Bois observed that Japan's triumph over Russia was proof that nonwhite people could successfully challenge white dominance of natural resources and political power.

Roosevelt understood that the victory made Japan the strongest force in East Asia. Although doing so violated the Open Door policy, the United States officially recognized Japan's colonization of Korea in exchange for the Japanese pledge not to invade the Philippines. Controversies generated by Japanese immigration to the United States proved more difficult to resolve. In 1907, after he failed to persuade the city of San Francisco not to segregate Japanese schoolchildren, Roosevelt brokered a **Gentlemen's Agreement** in which Japan voluntarily agreed to restrict emigration to the United States in return for U.S. elimination of anti-Japanese segregation. To ensure that Japan did not misinterpret his diplomacy as weakness, Roosevelt bolstered American defenses in the Pacific and expanded the navy. As a show of force,

spheres of influence Area outside a nation's territory but still under its control; in the case of empires, lands that conceded trading and other rights to imperial powers.

Open Door policy U.S. policy calling for an end to foreign control of Chinese trade and respect for Chinese territorial sovereignty.

Boxer Rebellion Anti-imperialist uprising led by nationalists attempting to expel Christian missionaries and all foreigners from China.

Gentlemen's Agreement 1907 pact under which Japan voluntarily restricted emigration to the United States in exchange for President Theodore Roosevelt's pledge to combat school segregation in San Francisco.

Source: Library of Congress (http://www.loc.gov/item/hec2008002821/)

Global Americans **William C. Gorgas** (1854–1920) was a groundbreaker in the fields of public health and tropical medicine. His sanitation efforts were key elements of the U.S. occupation of Cuba and the successful completion of the Panama Canal. After graduating from medical school in 1879, Gorgas entered the U.S. Army Medical Corps. In July 1898, he became chief sanitary officer for U.S.-occupied Cuba. Inspired by Walter Reed's work in identifying mosquitos as carriers of disease, Gorgas implemented mosquito control efforts that eliminated yellow fever in the Havana area by late 1901. That same year, the U.S. government appointed him the sanitary expert on its new Panama Canal project. Initially, yellow fever outbreaks seriously hindered progress on the canal. But after winning cooperation from his superiors, canal employees, and Panamanians, Gorgas instituted measures that led to a steep decline in yellow fever cases. At the invitation of the Rockefeller Foundation, he later worked as an international public health consultant, first in Africa and then in Central and South America.

In January 1914, Gorgas was appointed U.S. Army surgeon general and promoted to major general soon after. When U.S. troops mobilized for World War I, he ensured that army camps had appropriate sanitation practices, and soldiers' deaths from disease significantly declined as compared to previous wars. After retiring from the army in October 1918, he spent two years investigating international outbreaks of yellow fever. He died of complications from a stroke in 1920.

dollar diplomacy Foreign policy promulgated by President William Howard Taft aimed at promoting financial stability in foreign countries deemed essential to U.S. commercial interests.

he sent sixteen new U.S. battleships—the "Great White Fleet"—around the world with a stop in Tokyo in October 1908. Shortly thereafter, the United States and Japan negotiated a pact promising to respect each other's Asiatic territories and reaffirming a commitment to the Open Door policy and Chinese independence.

The accord soon unraveled, and Japanese immigrants again faced racism in California when in 1913 the state restricted them from owning farmland (a law that was reinforced in 1920). Illustrating how U.S. commerce could be a tool of international power, a policy known as **dollar diplomacy**, President Taft encouraged private U.S. investments in the Manchurian railroad, infuriating Japan, Russia, and Britain. But the eruption of a revolution in China in May 1911 defused these tensions. Taft's successor Woodrow Wilson extricated the United States from the railroad deal and recognized the new Chinese Republic. Having reaffirmed the U.S. commitment to the political integrity of China, Wilson hoped to restore harmony in U.S.-Japanese relations.

18-3b Construction of the Panama Canal and Domination of Latin America

The United States builds the Panama Canal and expands its interventions in the Western Hemisphere.

Determined to consolidate U.S. power in the Caribbean and Central America, Roosevelt pushed for the construction of a canal that would link the Atlantic and Pacific Oceans with obvious commercial advantages for trade with China and protection of U.S. interests in the Pacific. Europeans and Americans had long advocated such a waterway as a means of dramatically boosting America's global commerce and travel. In 1880, eleven years after successfully completing the Suez Canal in Egypt, the French started a canal project in Panama. But design flaws, epidemics, and financial mismanagement forced them to abandon it in 1893.

Roosevelt was determined to succeed where the French failed. Through the Hay-Pauncefote Treaty of 1901, the United States and Britain agreed to exclusive U.S. control over any Central American canal, voiding an earlier treaty that had promised shared access. After a site selection committee chose a fifty-mile route through Panama (then part of Colombia), Secretary of State Hay and Colombian chargé d'affaires Tomás Herrán signed an agreement granting the United States a ninety-nine-year lease on a six-mile wide canal zone in exchange for $10 million and a $250,000 annual leasing fee. But the Colombian Senate unanimously rejected the treaty, objecting to the loss of sovereignty over the zone and hoping for a higher payment. Incensed, Roosevelt considered ordering a U.S. invasion of Panama. Instead, he supported Panamanians in a revolt against Colombia and announced U.S. recognition of the Republic of Panama. Two weeks later, Panama and the United States signed the Hay-Bunau-Varilla Treaty granting U.S. control over a ten-mile wide canal zone. In exchange, the United States guaranteed Panamanian independence and paid the same fees originally offered to Colombia.

In August 1914 during Wilson's presidency, the first ship traveled through the new $375 million U.S. canal, a stunning feat of engineering enacted through the labors of tens of thousands of workers from Asia, Europe, Latin

Hulton Archive/Getty Images

Global Americans Born in 1845, **Elihu Root** became one of the most influential figures in the history of U.S. foreign relations. After a highly successful career in corporate law, he served as secretary of war from 1899 to 1904. Playing a major role in the administration of U.S. territories newly acquired from Spain, Root formulated plans for eventual self-governance in Cuba and the Philippines and abolished U.S. tariffs on goods imported from Puerto Rico. In 1905, at the invitation of President Roosevelt, Root became secretary of state. To curtail cronyism, he placed the consular service under the U.S. Civil Service. In 1907, he negotiated the Gentlemen's Agreement for restricting Japanese emigration to the United States.

After serving in the U.S. Senate from 1909 to 1915, Root remained active in global affairs well into his eighties, heading a special U.S. diplomatic mission to Russia in 1917 and helping to craft naval disarmament proposals at the Washington Naval Conference of 1921–1922.

Convinced that international law could be a tool for preserving world peace, Root was an impassioned advocate of arbitration. He was the leading architect of the Central American Court of Justice in 1907. In 1910, he became the first president of the Carnegie Endowment for International Peace and won the 1912 Nobel Peace Prize in recognition of his efforts to promote negotiation as an alternative to war. In 1920, he joined the League of Nations committee that established the Permanent Court of International Justice. Much to Root's disappointment, the United States opted not to join.

America, and primarily the West Indies. The workers battled torrential rains, venomous snakes, and segregation based on race and skill level. In 1922, the United States paid Colombia $25 million but did not apologize for seizing the canal. Many of the West Indians who worked on the canal later migrated to the United States, mostly to New York City.

As U.S. investments in the Caribbean and South America expanded, U.S. policy makers worried about Latin American countries defaulting on loans made by European governments and banks. In 1904, Roosevelt had become alarmed when the Dominican Republic veered near financial collapse and it appeared that Germany would invade to collect its debts. An economic powerhouse with one of the world's largest navies, Germany could easily threaten U.S. interests. On December 6, 1904, to warn Europe to stay out of the Western Hemisphere and to justify U.S. dominance of the region, Roosevelt issued a bold expansion of the Monroe Doctrine. The **Roosevelt Corollary** threatened U.S. intervention in Latin American nations that engaged in "chronic wrongdoing, or an impotence which results in a general loosening of the ties of civilized society . . . ." Convinced that the Dominicans lacked the ability or temperament to resolve their own affairs, U.S. officials seized control of the nation's customs collections. In 1912, after rebels from neighboring Haiti attacked customs houses, Taft sent a commission bolstered by seven hundred fifty marines to restore order. The commission redrew the border between Haiti and the Dominican Republic and forced out a corrupt Dominican president. Four years later, Wilson established a U.S. military occupation of the Dominican Republic that continued until 1922. Dominicans greatly resented these measures.

The United States played an equally intrusive role in Haiti. Although U.S. investment in the nation was minimal, French and German nationals controlled most of its banks. When World War I erupted in Europe in 1914, U.S. policy makers worried that Germans would seize the port of Môle Saint Nicholas as a base for aggressive actions in the Caribbean. Accordingly, when Haitians began protesting their government the following year, Wilson sent two thousand marines to restore order. The U.S. occupation of the first independent black republic in the Western Hemisphere outraged activists such as Du Bois: "SHAME ON AMERICA!" he raged. The situation deteriorated as the United States took control of Haiti's finances and forced the election of a pro-U.S. president who instituted racial segregation, press censorship, and forced labor. In the 1920s, after a peasant revolt against these measures, U.S. officials began training Haitians to take control of their government but did not end the occupation until 1934.

Roosevelt Corollary Addition to the Monroe Doctrine asserting a U.S. right to intervene in Latin American nations at risk of European intervention or occupation.

18-3c Intervention in Mexico

Revolution in Mexico creates unrest in the American Southwest and strains U.S.-Mexican relations.

Upon assuming office in 1913, Wilson declared, "The force of America is the force of moral principle." He intended to create a more humane, open, and peaceful world in the face of instability, militarism, and imperialism. Yet in most cases, Wilson pursued policies that differed little from those of his predecessors.

Wilson's responses to the Mexican Revolution embodied these contradictions. In 1910, rebels in northern Mexico began violently resisting Porfirio Diaz, Mexico's dictatorial ruler for the previous thirty-four years. The upheaval troubled U.S. officials who feared the bloodshed might spread north to the borderlands where Mexicans and Mexican

Plan of San Diego
Anonymous manifesto circulated during the Mexican Revolution calling for nonwhite peoples to seize six U.S. states and create a new republic.

Americans far outnumbered Anglos and much of the local population supported the revolutionaries. After Diaz's ouster in 1911, Francisco I. Madero, a liberal reformer, took power but faced challenges to his authority from elite landowners, the Catholic Church, and the military. In 1913, troops led by General Victoriano Huerta imprisoned and then executed Madero. Denouncing Huerta's "government of butchers," Wilson withheld recognition of the rebels despite $1.5 billion in U.S. investments in Mexico. Strongly influenced by emerging doctrines of international law, Wilson explained that legitimate regimes must be "based upon law, not upon arbitrary or irregular force."

Such pious assertions did not, however, stop Wilson from orchestrating Huerta's overthrow. When diplomatic meddling did not work, Wilson sent U.S. ships to patrol Mexico's coastline. In 1914, after the brief detention of several U.S. sailors purchasing supplies in the port of Tampico, U.S.-Mexican tensions escalated. On April 20, Wilson discovered that a German arms shipment intended for Huerta was heading to Veracruz and asked Congress for authority to use force. Before receiving a response, Wilson ordered U.S. ships to bombard the harbor. The following day, eight hundred U.S. marines landed and captured the city despite ferocious resistance. Wilson did not withdraw the troops until November 23, 1914.

U.S. intervention did little to stop continuing unrest. After Huerta fled the country, a power struggle erupted between the forces of Venustiano Carranza and Pancho Villa. Civilians endured food shortages. Refugees flooded across the U.S. border into southwestern states. Mexican rebels in Texas drafted the **Plan of San Diego**, a manifesto calling for Mexican nationals, Mexican Americans, and African Americans to "free" Texas, New Mexico, Arizona, California, and Colorado from U.S. control. Although the proposed race war never materialized, it alarmed U.S. and Texas officials. Clashes between the Texas Rangers and Mexican raiders continued after Carranza supporters organized thirty guerilla raids in the lower Rio Grande Valley. Preoccupied with German U-boat attacks on neutral U.S. ships sailing the Atlantic Ocean, Wilson reluctantly acknowledged the Carranza regime's control of Mexico and blocked arms sales to opposing Mexican factions.

In retaliation, Pancho Villa led a March 1916 attack on Columbus, New Mexico, that left seventeen Americans and more than one hundred Mexicans dead. On Wilson's orders, General John J. Pershing and seven thousand U.S. troops quickly pushed three hundred fifty miles into Mexico in an unsuccessful hunt for Villa. The United States and Mexico teetered on the brink of war. In February 1917, in preparation for formal U.S. entry into World War I, Wilson abandoned the search and recalled Pershing and his troops (see Map 18.2).

Map 18.2 U.S. Interventions in Central America, 1898–1941 To guard its economic interests and expand its political power in the region, the United States intervened in Central America many times after entering the Spanish-American War in 1898. These interventions took numerous forms including business investments, financial oversight, construction projects, military occupations, and wars. ▼

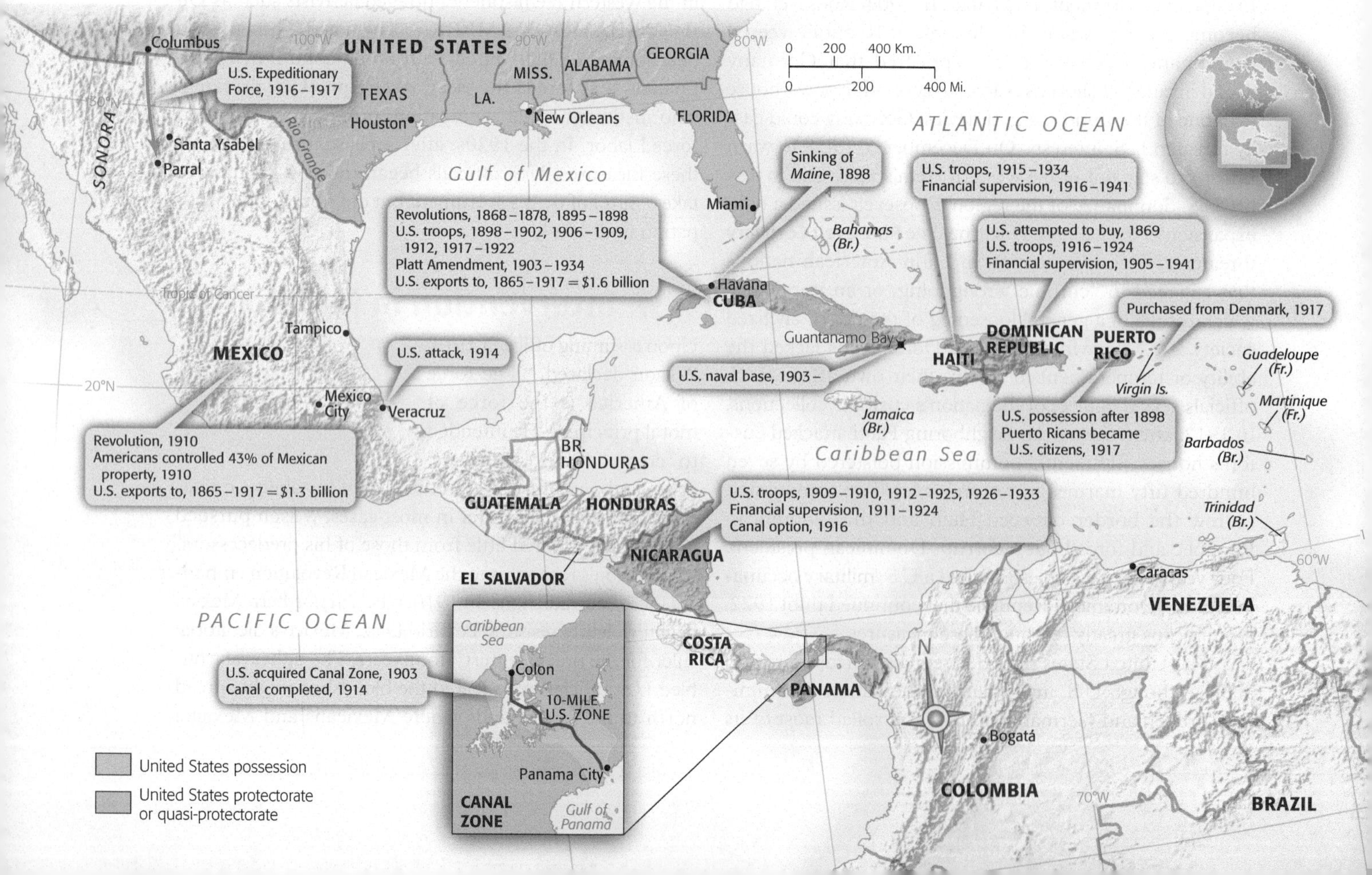

Aultman, Otis A. [Mexican Revolution Refugees]. The Portal to Texas History. http://texashistory.unt.edu/ark:/67531/metapth63330/. Accessed December 23, 2015.

Arrival of Refugees of the Mexican Revolution at Fort Bliss, Texas Between 1910 and 1920, approximately 890,000 Mexicans legally entered the United States, most to escape the chaos and violence of the Mexican Revolution. Some continued to support different factions vying for power in their home country. Others permanently assimilated into extant Mexican American communities. Some returned to Mexico when peace was restored. ◀

18-4
The Great War

Throughout the Great War, later called World War I, the fusion of traditional combat tactics and modern military innovations like tanks, poison gas, and flamethrowers had horrific results. In this image, a U.S. Cavalry officer and his horse prepare for chemical warfare. An estimated 9 million soldiers and 8 million horses on all sides died during the war, the last conflict where mounted troops were used in battle on a wide scale.

What does this image suggest about the ways that this war marked a departure from earlier conflicts and how it affected those who fought it? ▶

Hirz/Getty Images

Beginning in June 1914, events across the Atlantic dwarfed the skirmishes on the U.S.–Mexican border. A four-year, worldwide conflict called the Great War (later World War I) toppled empires and killed millions. Although the assassination of the heir to the Austro-Hungarian throne by a Serbian nationalist was its immediate trigger, the war's root causes were much more complicated (see Table 18.1). Rivalries over colonies, raw materials, and markets had set the nations of Europe against each other and drawn them into local conflicts for half a century. Countries forged mutual defense alliances and militarized at a breathtaking pace. Nationalist Slavs, Hungarians, Poles, and other minorities agitated for independence from Austrian, Russian, and Ottoman rule. Once war began, each belligerent fielded huge armies—70 million soldiers in total—who faced carnage inflicted by new technologies of warfare, such as submachine guns, fragmentation shells, and poison gas. They fought in Africa, where British and French troops seized German colonies. In East Asia, Japan seized German colonies too. In France, the armies soon barricaded themselves in trenches, where soldiers endured cold, mud, rats, lice, and the stench of dead comrades. Such realities shattered idealized notions of heroic warfare widely held prior to the conflict.

The most important question for the United States was whether to stay out of Europe's war and its entanglements. But the Wilson administration pursued policies that greatly favored Britain and France over Germany. German attacks on U.S. merchant ships and vessels bearing American passengers drew the United States into the conflict. After the United States formally declared war on Germany, U.S. troops played an important part in the Allies' final defeat of the Central Powers.

☞ As you read, consider the evolution of the U.S. response to the Great War and the impact of the conflict on those fighting against the Central Powers. How and why did Americans experience the Great War differently than their European allies did?

18-4a U.S. Neutrality

When war engulfs Europe, the United States declares neutrality but favors the Allies.

On July 28, 1914, in retaliation for a Serb nationalist's assassination of Archduke Franz Ferdinand the previous month, Austria-Hungary declared war on Serbia, setting in motion a series of actions based on defensive pacts and secret alliances. Germany backed Austria-Hungary. Russia, the protector of Slavic nations, mobilized to support Serbia. Germany then declared war on Russia and its ally France and launched the **Schlieffen Plan**, a military strategy for the quick defeat of the French followed by a concentrated assault on the Russians. But on August 4, when the Germans invaded neutral Belgium on their way to Paris, Great Britain declared war on Germany, defying German assumptions that the British would not join a continental war. Within weeks, Japan joined the Allies, as Britain, France, and Russia were now designated, while the Ottoman Empire allied itself with the Central Powers led by Germany and Austria-Hungary. Italy reneged on its treaty with Germany and joined the Allies. Europe's alliances, intended to maintain a balance of power, had imploded.

Schlieffen Plan Formulated by General Count Alfred von Schlieffen, strategy for German forces invading and occupying France before Russia, France's ally, could mobilize its troops.

When the war in Europe began, Wilson declared the United States neutral "in thought, as well as action." Because "the people of the United States are drawn from many nations, and chiefly from the nations now at war," he explained, fighting on either side would alienate millions of Americans. Wilson believed that the United States had a moral duty to remain the "one great nation at peace" and to mediate among the warring powers.

Most Americans supported Wilson's decision. Although some felt culturally and historically bound to the Allies, others had direct family ties to the Central Powers. Many Irish-Americans who opposed British control over Ireland and Jewish-Americans who had fled Russian religious persecution also sided with the Central Powers. Progressive reformers feared that U.S. involvement in the

Table 18.1 Origins of World War I

In July 1914, a combination of immediate and long-term causes contributed to the outbreak of a devastating global conflict. Mutual defense alliances, imperialism, militarism, nationalism, and the assassination of Archduke Franz Ferdinand of Austria-Hungary and his wife Sophie by a Serb nationalist were among them. The latter set off a chain of events that plunged Europe into a war that forever reshaped the continent and global politics.

Date	Event
June 28, 1914	Serbian nationalist Gavrilo Princep assassinates Franz Ferdinand, heir to the Austria-Hungarian throne, and his wife Sophie in Sarajevo
July 23, 1914	Austria-Hungary sends an ultimatum to Serbia, demands response in 48 hours
July 24, 1914	Germany declares its support for Austria-Hungary Serbia begins mobilizing for war Russia, a Serbian ally, masses troops along the Austrian border
July 28, 1914	Austria-Hungary declares war on Serbia
July 29, 1914	Great Britain warns Germany that it will not remain neutral in the burgeoning European conflict Germany prepares for war Great Britain asks France and Germany to pledge to support Belgian neutrality. France agrees, but Germany does not respond Germany asks France whether it will remain neutral in the event of war between Germany and Russia
July 30, 1914	Russia begins mobilizing for war
August 1, 1914	Germany declares war on Russia, and France begins mobilizing for war
August 2, 1914	Ottoman Empire (Turkey) and Germany forge a secret alliance
August 3, 1914	Germany declares war on France and invades Belgium. Britain begins mobilizing for war
August 4, 1914	Great Britain declares war on Germany
August 6, 1914	Russia and Austria-Hungary declare war
August 10, 1914	Austria-Hungary invades Russia
August 12, 1914	Great Britain declares war on Austria-Hungary

Sources: "How Did the First World War Start?" *The Week*, November 5, 2014, http://www.theweek.co.uk/world-news/first-world-war/59782/how-did-the-first-world-war-start; "Countdown to War: The Events That Triggered WWI," ITV *News*, July 21, 2014, http://www.itv.com/news/2014-07-21/countdown-to-war-the-events-that-triggered-ww1/

Hulton Archive/Getty Images

Women's Peace Parade, late 1910s In August 1914, more than fifteen hundred women marched down Fifth Avenue in New York City in a silent protest against the hostilities in Europe. The march inspired the creation of the Women's Peace Party (WPP) in January 1915. Under the leadership of Jane Addams, WPP played a major role in transnational women's peace activism. Critics found their public demonstrations unpatriotic and mocked the slogan "Real Patriots Keep Cool" by countering with "Real Patriots Fight Hard." ◄

European war would undermine their quest for improved working and living conditions at home.

Pacifists organized against the war. In April 1915, more than one thousand women from warring and neutral nations attended an International Congress of Women for Peace and Freedom in The Hague, Netherlands. With Jane Addams presiding, it adopted a proposal drafted by Rosika Schwimmer (see Chapter 17), a Hungarian feminist who called for belligerent nations to attend a mediation conference and formed a permanent committee. Later that year, Schwimmer persuaded automaker Henry Ford to send an antiwar delegation to Europe. On December 4, 1915, the Peace Ship sailed from Hoboken with one hundred forty activists and dozens of journalists aboard. After arriving in Norway, the delegates lobbied foreign diplomats in several countries but did not achieve their goal of arranging a cease-fire by Christmas.

Wilson discovered that maintaining strict neutrality was exceedingly difficult. Although international law decreed that neutral nations could trade nonmilitary goods with nations at war, Great Britain mined the North Sea and began stopping and searching neutral merchant vessels for contraband items useful to the enemy. Wilson repeatedly protested these violations of U.S. neutrality. The British, seeking to retain American goodwill, usually returned the goods or promised to compensate U.S. shippers after the war.

The balance of commerce further undermined American neutrality. U.S. factories and farms increased production to meet European needs, but they overwhelmingly sent war matériel, consumer products, and food to the Allies. After Wilson overrode Secretary of State William Jennings Bryan's opposition to private loans to belligerent nations, U.S. financiers also demonstrated bias toward the Allies, loaning them $2.3 billion while advancing the Central Powers only $27 million. After lending millions of dollars to European combatants, the United States shifted from debtor nation to creditor nation. In 1914, Americans owed foreigners $3 billion; by 1919, foreigners owed Americans $10 billion (see Figure 18.2).

In the face of British naval superiority and U.S. economic bias toward the Allies, Germany introduced the *Unterseeboot* (U-boat). International law dictated that any naval vessel firing on another must first warn its adversaries

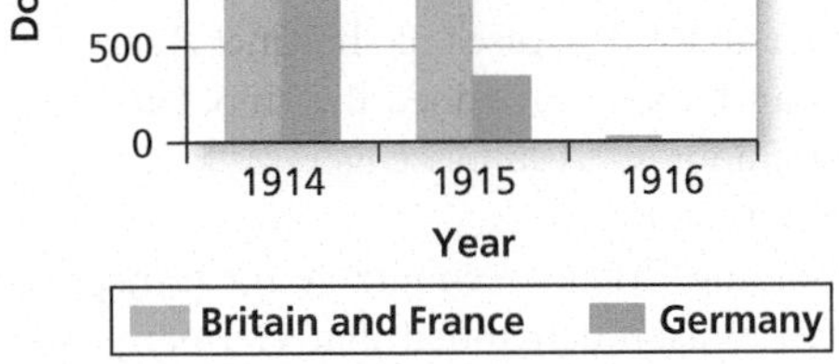

Figure 18.2 U.S. Trade with Europe, 1914–1916 Despite its proclamation of neutrality when war erupted in Europe in 1914, the United States adopted trade policies that greatly favored Britain and France over Germany—a trend that made the German government question U.S. impartiality. ▲ *Source:* Thomas G. Paterson et al. *American Foreign Relations*, vol. 2 (Boston: Wadsworth, 2010), p. 78.

Library of Congress

Global Americans Born in 1860, **Jane Addams** was one of the most renowned women in the world in the early twentieth century. In 1887, while traveling in Europe with her friend Ellen G. Starr, she visited Toynbee Hall, a settlement house in London's East End. The visit inspired them to open a similar facility called Hull House in an impoverished part of Chicago. While raising funds and enlisting volunteers, they organized a kindergarten, classes, club meetings, a library, a public kitchen, and more. Hull House earned widespread acclaim and was emulated across the nation.

Ascribing to a world view interweaving social justice, democracy, and peace, Addams strongly supported women's suffrage and was very active in domestic and transnational peace movements. In 1898, she joined the Anti-Imperialist League, a coalition opposing U.S. annexation of the Philippines. In January 1915, following the outbreak of World War I in Europe, she became the national chair of the newly created Women's Peace Party (WPP). Three months later, she was elected president of the permanent committee created at the International Congress of Women in The Hague, which became the Women's International League for Peace and Freedom (WILPF) in 1919. Addams served as the organization's president for a decade. Many U.S. newspapers deemed her pacifist activities unpatriotic and the Daughters of the American Revolution expelled her. Undeterred, she worked as an assistant for Herbert Hoover's wartime relief efforts for women and children. In 1931, after becoming the first U.S. woman to win the Nobel Peace Prize, Addams donated the prize money to WILDF.

and then allow all passengers and crew to evacuate prior to any attack. But submarines were small and vulnerable. British ships often rammed or fired on U-boats whose commanders tried to comply with the rules.

In February 1915, Germany struck back by announcing the creation of a war zone around Great Britain. The Germans warned neutral ships to stay out of the area to avoid being mistaken for enemy vessels and urged people not to travel on enemy passenger ships. When Bryan begged Wilson to bar Americans from entering the war zone, the president claimed that neutrality accorded Americans the right to travel wherever they wished. Although Great Britain was violating international law by arming merchant vessels obtaining supplies at neutral ports, Wilson excused Britain's actions while denouncing Germany's submarine warfare.

Wilson's response to Germany's sinking of the British liner *Lusitania* highlighted these contradictions. On May 1, 1915, the *Lusitania* departed New York with 1,257 travelers and a crew of seven hundred two. It also transported contraband including 4.2 million rounds of rifle ammunition and 1,250 cases of shrapnel shells. On May 7, a German U-boat torpedoed the ship, sinking it in only eighteen minutes: 1,198 passengers, 128 of whom were Americans, drowned.

Without holding Britain accountable for transporting war matériel, Wilson demanded that Germany stop attacking passenger ships and pay for U.S. losses. After the president rejected Bryan's calls for a simultaneous protest of British violation of rules regarding contraband, he resigned. Although the German government apologized for the deaths of Americans and offered compensation, it refused to modify its submarine strategy. Now convinced that Germany posed a grave threat to global democracy, Wilson sent presidential adviser Colonel Edward House on several unsuccessful missions to negotiate a peace settlement among the warring European factions.

In March 1916, a German sub mistook the French steamer *Sussex* for a minesweeper and fired a torpedo, injuring several passengers including four Americans. Wilson warned Germany that if it failed to cease its attacks on passenger and cargo vessels, the United States would sever diplomatic relations. Reeling from the recent loss of five hundred thousand troops in the unsuccessful German assault on Verdun, Kaiser Wilhelm II decided not to risk war with the United States and agreed to Wilson's demands. His *Sussex* pledge temporarily eased tensions with the Wilson administration. Great Britain, meanwhile, was boycotting eighty U.S. companies that traded with the Central Powers.

18-4b America Enters the War

The United States abandons neutrality and joins the war against the Central Powers.

While trying to maintain U.S. neutrality, Woodrow Wilson confronted an American public bitterly divided about the war. Advocates like Roosevelt condemned Wilson's failure to bolster the nation's defenses. Pacifists decried any steps toward improving military readiness. When a popular antiwar song declared, "I Didn't Raise My Boy to Be a Soldier," their opponents retorted with the ditty "I Didn't Raise My Boy to Be a Slacker." Caught in the middle, Wilson embarked on a program of "moderate preparedness" and asked Congress for large increases in troops for the army and navy.

Campaigning on the slogan "He kept us out of war," Wilson defeated Republican Charles Evans Hughes in the 1916 presidential election.

Having won a second term, Wilson renewed his efforts to negotiate peace. On the verge of defeating Russia on the Eastern Front and anticipating victory on the Western Front, the Germans expected to gain territories in eastern Europe, Africa, Belgium, and France—terms that the British, the French, and their allies would mightily resist. Certain that a punitive settlement would spark another catastrophic war, Wilson proposed a new vision of international relations. In an address to the U.S. Senate on January 22, 1917, he outlined a "peace without victory" based on "the equality of nations," consent of the governed, freedom of the seas, arms limitation, and a community of power. Such a peace would mark a stark departure from previous conflicts in which the victors humiliated their opponents by stripping them of territory and imposing harsh indemnities. Wilson's peace would replace fragile, secretive alliances and destructive arms races with a system in which all nations—whatever their size, strength, or wealth—worked collectively to maintain open trade and security.

Even as Wilson spoke, Germany was preparing to launch a major offensive to end the war before the United States could mobilize and send troops to Europe. On January 31, Germany announced that U-boats would attack *all* vessels—passenger or merchant, enemy or neutral—that entered waters near England or France. With the *Sussex* pledge now violated, Wilson severed diplomatic relations with Germany.

In late February, the exposure of a telegram from Arthur Zimmermann, the German foreign minister, pushed the United States closer to a declaration of war. Intercepted by British intelligence agents monitoring the transatlantic cable, the **Zimmermann telegram** asked Mexico to ally with Germany in case of war with the United States, promising financial assistance and help in regaining the former Mexican territories of Arizona, New Mexico, and Texas. Ironically, Wilson had withdrawn U.S. troops from Mexico and formally recognized the Carranza regime as Mexico's legal government less than a month earlier. When confronted with evidence of German plotting against the United States, Wilson asked Congress for the authority to arm merchant ships to thwart U-boat attacks. When the U.S. Senate filibustered his request, he issued an executive order arming the merchant vessels. But the measure did not prevent Germany from quickly sinking five U.S. ships. By late March, Wilson and his cabinet unanimously concluded the time for war had arrived.

On April 2, 1917, Wilson addressed a special joint session of Congress and asked for a declaration of war against Germany, arguing that the Germans' unrestricted submarine warfare and the Zimmermann telegram insulted America's national honor and imperiled U.S. economic interests. Hopeful that the Russians would adopt a democratic government similar to those of the other Allies, Wilson welcomed a partnership with the provisional regime that had recently deposed the autocratic Tsar Nicholas II. Insisting that the United States fought for principles like liberty, not for material gain, Wilson declared, "The world must be made safe for democracy." On April 4, the Senate voted 82 to 6 in favor of declaring war. Two days later, the House approved the measure 373 to 50. Representative Jeannette Rankin, a Montana Republican who was the first woman to serve in Congress and a pacifist, was among those voting "no."

Zimmermann telegram German proposal urging Mexico to attack the United States in exchange for the return of territory lost during the Mexican-American War (1846–1848).

18-4c Combat in Europe

The U.S. mobilizes its troops, revolution rocks Russia, and the Allies force Germany to surrender.

When the United States declared war, the Allies were perilously close to defeat. Wilson selected John J. Pershing, leader of the recent U.S. incursion in Mexico, to command the American Expeditionary Force. With only one hundred thirty thousand active-duty troops (many of whom were poorly trained) and outdated equipment, the army was not ready for war in Europe. To build military strength as quickly as possible, Congress passed the Selective Service Act in May 1917. It required all men ages twenty-one to thirty (later expanded to eighteen to forty-five) to register for conscription. By the time the war ended in November 1918, more than 2.8 million conscripts of a pool exceeding 24 million had been inducted into the armed forces. Unwilling to place U.S. soldiers under the command of the European generals responsible for the slaughter of millions, Wilson and Pershing insisted that American units remain separate and independent. Desperate for reinforcements, the Allies acquiesced, and the first battalion of U.S. soldiers arrived in France on July 4, 1917.

While the United States mobilized for war, some troops contracted a virulent strain of influenza. U.S. soldiers first carried the disease from their home bases to Europe in the spring of 1918, but few victims died. When the disease resurfaced in the fall, it was deadly. Some victims died only hours after developing symptoms. Ravaging young and old alike, the virus soon infected one-fifth of the world's people. By the spring of 1919, an estimated 50 million people had died in the worst pandemic ever witnessed.

U.S. troops also carried American racism to Europe. Eager to demonstrate their patriotism, more than four hundred thousand African Americans enlisted in the army. W.E.B. Du Bois, then working in New York as editor of *The Crisis*, declared, "Let us, while this war lasts, forget our special grievances and close ranks." But the marines refused entirely to accept blacks, and the navy allowed them to serve only in menial capacities. Although the army did not technically bar African Americans from combat roles, most worked as laborers. The exclusion prompted

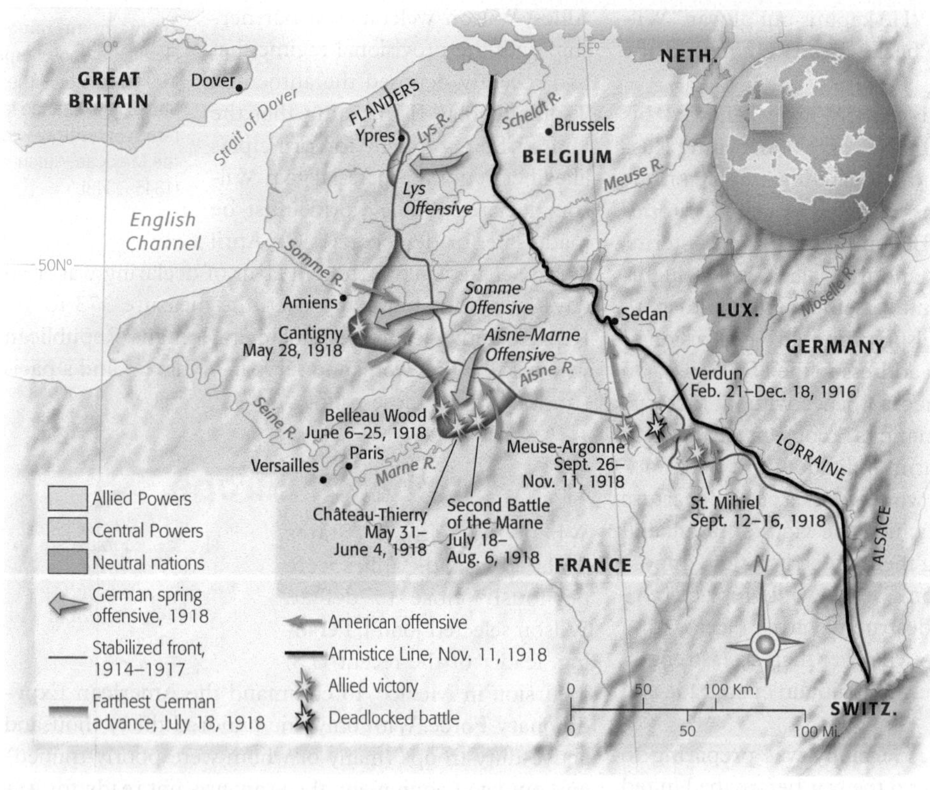

Map 18.3 The Western Front Throughout the fifty-one months of World War I, there was continuous action on the Western Front—a 435-mile line of trenches, shelters, and fields stretching from Switzerland to the North Sea. Most battles were fought in France and Belgium, and none occurred in Germany. Although France and Britain contributed the most soldiers and equipment of the more than twenty nations fighting for the Allies, the United States played a vital role in the conflict's last stages. ▲

genocide Deliberate and systematic destruction of all or part of an ethnic, religious, racial, or cultural group.

such an outcry from black communities that the War Department created two black combat units, the 92nd and 93rd Divisions, both sent into battle in France. Like the Buffalo Soldiers before them, these black soldiers rarely received equal treatment. In 1917, after a riot broke out on a military base near Houston leaving seventeen whites and two blacks dead, the army convicted one hundred ten black soldiers in the biggest court martial in U.S. history, but white soldiers and civilians escaped prosecution. The irony of fighting to make the world "safe for democracy" while facing discrimination at home did not escape African American soldiers.

Throughout 1917, political instability in Russia had profound ramifications on the Great War. In October 1917, the Bolsheviks, Communists committed to abolishing private property and imperialism, ousted the provisional government and honored their pledge to take Russia out of the conflict. In the Treaty of Brest-Litovsk, signed in March 1918, the Russians ceded one-quarter of their prewar population and arable land and half their coal fields and iron manufacturing to the Germans. After Russia's capitulation on the Eastern Front, Germany launched a major offensive in western Europe. By May, German forces were encamped on the Marne River, only fifty miles outside Paris. U.S. troops saw their first action there. The following month, American forces stopped the Germans at Château-Thierry and in July, pushed them out of Belleau Wood.

After crushing a second German attempt to capture Paris, the Allies launched a counteroffensive. In late September 1918, more than 1 million U.S. troops joined French and British units in six weeks of fighting in the Meuse-Argonne (see Map 18.3). More than twenty-six thousand Americans died, and nearly ninety-six thousand sustained wounds. As the German army retreated, the Allies sank U-boats on the Atlantic, freeing supply lanes for the first time in months.

In early October, the German chancellor concluded the war was lost and asked Wilson for peace terms. Bulgaria, Turkey, and Austro-Hungary surrendered in quick succession. After forcing Kaiser Wilhelm II to abdicate, members of the new German government signed an armistice on November 11, 1918. The German, Austro-Hungarian, and Ottoman empires had collapsed, and 16 million people had died, including 6.8 million civilians and more than 1 million Armenian victims of a **genocide** orchestrated by Turks (see Figure 18.3).

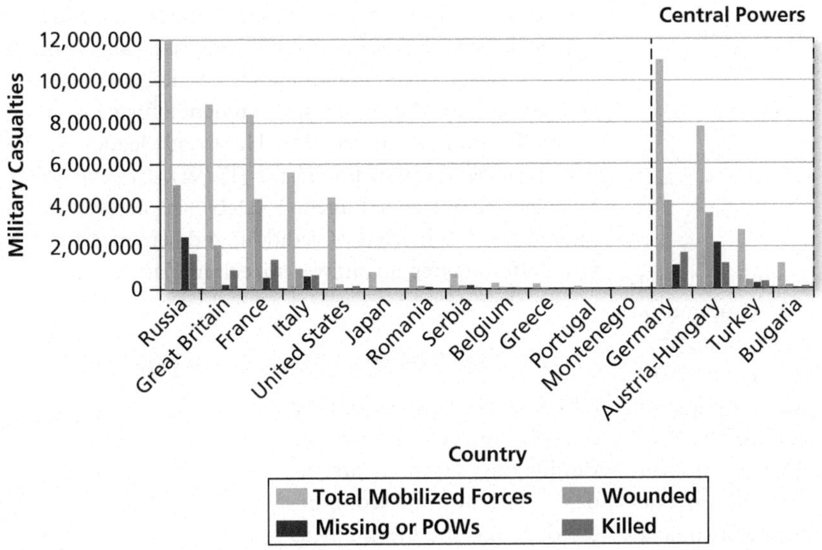

Figure 18.3 Estimated WWI Military Casualties A collision of nineteenth-century battlefield tactics with twentieth-century technologies contributed to high military casualties in World War I. Powerful, mobile artillery inflicted grave damage on enemy positions. Exploding shells and shrapnel were responsible for killing more soldiers than any other military innovation during the conflict. The continued use of infantry charges during trench warfare proved a particularly senseless tactic as waves of soldiers were often mowed down with modern weapons. ◀

Sources: WWI Casualty and Death Tables, http://www.pbs.org/greatwar/resources/casdeath_pop.html; Daily Chart, Remembrance, *The Economist*, November 11, 2013, http://www.economist.com/blogs/graphicdetail/2013/11/daily-chart-4

18-5

Home Front Mobilization for the War and the Peace Settlements

Hopps, Harry R., 1869–1937/Library of Congress Prints and Photographs Division Washington, D.C.[LC-DIG-ds-03216]

To mobilize Americans for war against the Central Powers, the Committee on Public Information produced thousands of propaganda posters like this one. Notice that "militarism" is inscribed on the ape's helmet and "kultur" is etched on his club as he steps on the shoreline identified as "America." Consider the possible symbolism of the woman the ape is carrying.

Why did U.S. officials portray their German foes in this manner, and how might such images have contributed to the deep divisions the war generated among Americans? ▶

U.S. entry into the Great War triggered great changes on the home front. Aided by a stronger and larger federal bureaucracy, business leaders and government officials worked closely to coordinate production. Workers seized new economic opportunities. Race riots, labor unrest, and political repression highlighted societal divisions. In the turmoil of wartime, Progressive reformers worked to advance causes such as racial equality, women's suffrage, and prohibition. European leaders' intransigence and domestic partisan politics derailed Wilson's ambitious plan to reshape foreign relations through open diplomacy, free trade, disarmament, and international cooperation. But the United States entered the 1920s as the world's leading economic, military, and cultural power.

☞ As you read, consider how U.S. entry into World War I shaped life on the home front while President Wilson articulated a new framework for international relations. What were the key elements of Wilson's vision for the postwar world? Was he able to realize these aims at the Paris Peace Conference? Why or why not?

18-5a Government Expansion and Control

The U.S. government mobilizes for war, tries to build public support, and restricts civil liberties.

To mobilize for war, the Wilson administration greatly expanded the size and power of the U.S. government. Almost five thousand newly created federal agencies coordinated manufacturing, transportation, and agriculture. Increased cooperation between government and business tripled corporate profits and boosted U.S. industrial output 20 percent by 1919. The War Industries Board purchased war supplies, set production quotas, and allocated raw materials. The Food Administration, led by future president Herbert Hoover, ensured that U.S. troops had adequate diets. To encourage Americans to save vital supplies, Hoover instigated "meatless" and "wheatless" days and urged them to plant "victory gardens." Other agencies managed fuel, railroad traffic, shipping, and trade.

To maintain production and avoid strikes, the War Labor Board mediated disputes between employers and workers. The Wilson administration also supported Progressive reforms such as eight-hour workdays, improved wages and working conditions, and collective bargaining. Such policies strengthened organized labor, and union membership almost doubled during the war.

When the United States declared war in April 1917, Americans were still bitterly divided in their opinions of the Allies and the Central Powers. To generate popular support, Wilson created the **Committee on Public Information (CPI)**. Headed by former journalist George Creel, CPI used pamphlets, speeches, films, and advertising in dozens of different languages to shape public views of the war and to encourage patriotic sacrifice among America's varied ethnic populations.

Determined to curtail pro-German activity in the United States, Wilson persuaded Congress to pass the **Espionage Act of 1917**. It imposed penalties of up to $10,000 and twenty years in prison for anyone convicted of aiding the enemy, obstructing military recruitment, or encouraging disloyalty. The act also empowered the postmaster general to seize materials deemed treasonous. The following year, the **Sedition Act** expanded the law to encompass "disloyal, profane, scurrilous, or abusive language" about the U.S. government, the American flag, or the armed forces. More than fifteen hundred people were arrested for alleged violations of the laws. Acting on long-standing animosities toward immigrants and political radicals, law enforcement officials used the Espionage Act and the Sedition Act to arrest prominent leftists including journalist John Reed and Bill Haywood, leader of the Industrial Workers of the World (IWW). In June 1918, Socialist Party leader Eugene V. Debs was arrested for a second time, convicted of sedition, and sentenced to ten years after making an antiwar speech in Canton, Ohio.

Committee on Public Information (CPI) U.S. propaganda agency created to generate public support for U.S. entry into World War I.

Espionage Act of 1917 U.S. federal law updating and expanding antispy statutes, criminalizing opposition to the draft, and giving postal officials authority to censor mail and newspapers.

Sedition Act Amendment to the Espionage Act outlawing criticism of the Constitution, the U.S. government, the U.S. armed forces, or the American flag in time of war.

Eighteenth Amendment Constitutional amendment prohibiting the manufacture, sale, and transportation of alcohol, later repealed by the Twenty-First Amendment in 1933.

Nineteenth Amendment Constitutional amendment signed into law on August 26, 1920, that prohibits denying a U.S. citizen the right to vote on the basis of sex.

18-5b Dissent and Resistance

The war sparks political repression of some Americans while providing opportunities for others.

CPI fueled a wave of intense anti-German sentiment. Publicizing German atrocities in Belgium, the committee depicted the Germans as "Huns, rapists, and pillagers." Schools stopped teaching German language courses and banned books by German authors such as the eighteenth-century writer and literary critic Johann Wolfgang von Goethe. Orchestras refused to play works by J.S. Bach, Ludwig van Beethoven, and Johannes Brahms. Restaurants renamed hamburgers "liberty sandwiches" and sauerkraut "liberty cabbage."

Exploiting the anti-German atmosphere, prohibition proponents emphasized the prominent role of German immigrants in operating breweries and saloons. Having succeeded in getting half of the states to ban alcohol prior to 1917, the Anti-Saloon League pushed for a constitutional amendment outlawing the manufacture, transportation, and sale of alcohol nationally. These xenophobic (antiforeigner) appeals combined with wartime demand for grains used in alcoholic beverages led to ratification of the **Eighteenth Amendment** in January 1919.

Despite the political discord it unleashed, the war also enabled some groups to make gains. Because Wilson opposed women's suffrage, Alice Paul and her fellow activists picketed outside the White House, emulating the confrontational tactics of the suffragists that Paul had witnessed in England. When the United States entered the war, some Americans considered the demonstrations unpatriotic and onlookers harassed and physically attacked the picketers. Police arrested the suffragists for obstructing traffic. While some women spent only a few days in jail, others were sentenced to seven-month terms. News of the protesters' mistreatment by prison officials outraged the public. Wilson used the incident to call for a federal women's suffrage amendment in recognition of women's vital contribution to the war effort. In June 1919, the Senate passed the measure by one vote and sent it to the states for ratification. On August 26, 1920, when Tennessee became the thirty-sixth state to adopt it, the **Nineteenth Amendment** went into effect.

After a labor shortage arose as men were drafted, employers began to hire women, African Americans, and Mexican Americans. Although the number of women working for wages did not significantly increase, some

Lawrence, Jacob (1917-2000)/The Phillips Collection, Washington, D.C., USA/ Acquired 1942/Bridgeman Images

Jacob Lawrence, *Migration Series, Panel No. 1,* 1940–1941 By late 1919, with the influx of at least four hundred fifty thousand southern African Americans drawn by the prospect of better-paying wartime jobs, the black population of many major northern cities soared. Having moved to Harlem with his family in 1930 at age thirteen, Jacob Lawrence did not experience these events personally, but in 1940–1941, he depicted them in sixty paintings collectively entitled *Migration Series.* The series won national acclaim, and he became a celebrated artist. ◄

female workers moved into better-paying positions in defense plants. In most cases, however, women received less pay than their male coworkers.

African Americans also sought to take advantage of opportunities for industrial work. Starting in 1916, the exodus of southern blacks that began after Reconstruction spiked dramatically, and four hundred fifty thousand of them joined a **Great Migration** from the South to cities such as St. Louis, Chicago, and Detroit before the war's end. Many found better wages and living conditions, but tensions with whites often exploded. In mid-1917, a race riot erupted in East St. Louis, Illinois, that left nine whites and almost forty blacks dead. During the **Red Summer** of 1919, racial unrest swept more than three dozen U.S. cities including a thirteen-day riot in

Great Migration Movement of approximately 6 million African Americans from the rural South to northern urban areas beginning in 1916.

Red Summer Wave of intense racial unrest occurring across the United States from May to October 1919, the largest of which occurred in Chicago, Washington, D.C., and Elaine, Arkansas.

Will Brown, a Lynching Victim in Omaha, Nebraska, 1919 After World War I ended, racial hostilities escalated greatly and a wave of lynchings and race riots swept the country. In September 1919, more than ten thousand whites in Omaha, Nebraska, stormed and then burned the county courthouse, demanding the release of Will Brown, a black man accused of raping a white woman. After hanging Brown and burning his body, the mob destroyed more than $1 million of property before federal troops could restore order. ▼

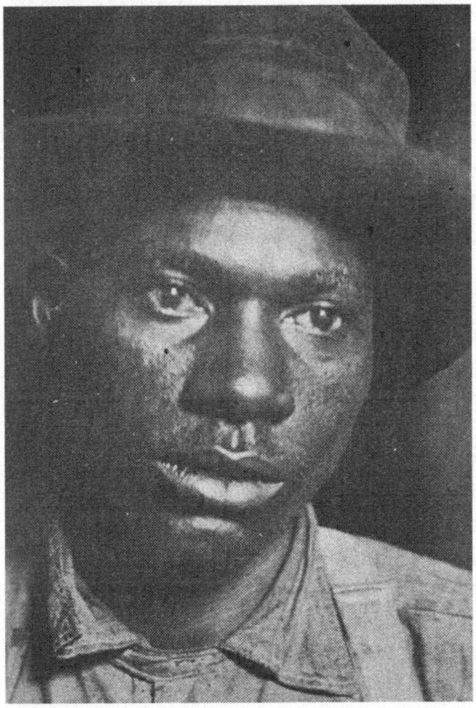

Nebraska State Historical Society

Chicago. Between 1914 and 1920, 382 African Americans were lynched. Incensed by the violence, W.E.B. Du Bois and other activists called for a federal antilynching law and an end to segregation. Many African American veterans were embittered by the second-class treatment they received from the countrymen they had fought to defend.

Mexican Americans had similar experiences. Wartime labor shortages prompted some to move to cities for defense jobs. Many congregated in barrios similar to ethnic enclaves created by other minorities. After the Immigration Act of 1917 relaxed immigration restrictions on Mexico (while adding a literacy requirement for emigrants from other nations), more than one hundred thousand Mexicans eager to escape the upheavals of the Mexican Revolution and to pursue wartime economic opportunities migrated to the Southwest. Although racism was endemic, many built better lives in the United States.

18-5c Politics of Peacemaking

Wilson's new framework for international relations meets Allied resistance and domestic political opposition.

Even before the United States entered the war, Wilson envisioned a postwar world that transcended the imperialist rivalries, militarism, and destructive nationalism that triggered the conflict. In late 1917, after the Bolsheviks began publishing secret Allied agreements for dividing the Central Powers' colonies, Wilson and a group of experts drafted a proposal offering a global alternative to both imperialism and communism.

On January 8, 1918, Wilson presented his **Fourteen Points** to Congress. The first five points called for open diplomacy, freedom of the seas, arms limitation, free trade, and "impartial adjustment of all colonial claims." The next eight points proposed **self-determination** for national minorities in Europe. The final and most important point recommended the establishment of the **League of Nations**, an international organization that would mediate disputes peacefully and guarantee "political independence and territorial integrity to great and small states alike."

Fourteen Points Proposal offered by President Woodrow Wilson that became a framework for peace negotiations following World War I.

self-determination Freedom of the people of a state or territory to choose their own government.

League of Nations International organization first proposed by Wilson in 1918 and founded in 1920 to promote global cooperation and to preserve peace, disbanded in 1946.

Pan-African Congress Originating in the mid-nineteenth century, an ideology and movement calling for all peoples of African descent to unite to further economic, political, and social aims.

To promote the Fourteen Points, the CPI launched one of the world's first international advertising campaigns. Its representatives around the world received the message via radio and transatlantic cable and then disseminated posters and handbills promoting the information. In battle zones, artillery shells filled with leaflets were lobbed over enemy lines. Colonized peoples responded enthusiastically, but the Allies, eager to avenge the catastrophic losses they were suffering in the war, were skeptical. In October 1918, after Wilson threatened to sign a separate peace with Germany, the British, French, and Italians reluctantly accepted his plan. On November 11, all combatant nations signed an armistice ending the war.

In an unprecedented move, Wilson announced that he personally would represent the United States at the Paris Peace Conference. Energized after winning control of both houses of Congress in the recent midterm elections, Republicans attacked the president's refusal to rely on the diplomat corps who usually conducted U.S. foreign policy abroad and his failure to include any prominent Republicans in the American delegation. These decisions had grave domestic political consequences, but the cheering crowds that greeted Wilson when he arrived in Europe led him to believe he could dominate the peace process and gain universal acceptance of his Fourteen Points.

W.E.B. Du Bois was among the millions inspired by Wilson. He rushed to Paris and organized a **Pan-African Congress** to be held in conjunction with the peace negotiations. When the meeting began in February 1919, fifty-seven delegates from fifteen nations attended and immediately declared their support for global racial equality and anti-imperialism. The participants applauded the Japanese government's decision to share its concerns at the official proceedings of the Paris Peace Conference.

The meetings at the palace of Versailles got off to a rocky start. In the face of British and French resistance, Wilson repeatedly capitulated in order to save the League of Nations. Jettisoning his demands for open diplomacy and equality of nations, he agreed to conduct most of the talks in secret and to bar Germany and the Bolsheviks from the discussions. The United States, Great Britain, France, and Italy (The "Big Four") dictated terms presented to the other twenty-eight national delegations.

Transferring more than 1.1 million square miles of territory formerly controlled by Russia, Austro-Hungary, and Germany, delegates redrew the map of Europe. France regained Alsace-Lorraine, lost in the punitive settlement of the 1871 Franco-Prussian War. Italy annexed South Tyrol and Trieste. In an effort to grant self-determination to diverse peoples once under Austro-Hungarian rule, delegates made Austria, Hungary, Czechoslovakia, Romania, and Yugoslavia independent nations. Similarly, but also to intensify the political isolation of the Bolsheviks, the Allies recognized Poland, Finland, Estonia, Latvia, and Lithuania—all formerly parts of the Russian Empire—as independent states.

The delegates also addressed the issue of colonies. Long angered by white claims that nonwhites were inferior, the Japanese proposed a racial equality clause for the League of Nations Covenant. It would have guaranteed "equal and just treatment in every respect making no distinction, either in law or in fact, on account of their race or nationality." But representatives from Great Britain, South Africa, Australia, and New Zealand zealously opposed the proposal. So did Wilson.

The delegates' white supremacist views also shaped the **mandate system** created for governing colonies and regions previously controlled by the defeated German and Ottoman empires. "Peoples not yet able to stand by themselves under the strenuous conditions of the modern world," were placed under the "tutelage" of "advanced nations" in preparation for independence and economic self-sufficiency. In the Middle East, delegates created several new nations and mapped their boundaries. France was granted mandates for Syria and Lebanon, and Britain received Iraq, Trans-Jordan, and Palestine, where according to the **Balfour Declaration** (1917), a Jewish homeland was to be established—a **Zionist** goal not realized until Israel was founded in 1948. In the Pacific, the Japanese acquired mandates for some of Germany's islands as well as Shandong, a portion of China with 30 million inhabitants. In effect, the mandate system maintained colonialism.

These maneuvers outraged colonized people who had embraced the Fourteen Points' message of self-determination. Nationalist movements erupted in China, Tunisia, Indonesia, Egypt, India, and elsewhere. At the Paris Peace Conference, a Vietnamese who took the name Nguyen Ai Quoc (Nguyen the Patriot, later known as Ho Chi Minh) called for Indochina's independence from France and challenged Wilson to grant self-determination to all people, not just Europeans. Confident that the League of Nations would eventually resolve problems arising from imperialism, Wilson ignored such pleas.

Wilson's faith in the League also informed his decision to accept harsh peace terms against Germany. Britain and France pushed for high reparations and a "war guilt" clause that made Germany solely responsible for the conflict. Certain that the League would prevent excessive vengeance, Wilson agreed. It proved a major miscalculation. In 1921, an international commission presented Germany a $33 billion bill that had shattering economic and political consequences.

In February 1919, Wilson briefly returned to the United States to get feedback on a draft treaty that contained both the peace terms and the covenant creating the League of Nations. Polls indicated that most Americans supported the League, but Wilson encountered strong opposition from Congress, where leading senators such as Republican Henry Cabot Lodge feared the League would compromise U.S. sovereignty. To placate his critics, the president stormed back to Paris and secured Allied approval of amendments that safeguarded the Monroe Doctrine, removed the United States from the mandate system, prohibited League intervention in domestic disputes, and allowed nations to leave the League with two years' notice. On June 28, 1919, the Allies presented Germany the extremely vindictive **Versailles Treaty**.

In July, Wilson submitted the treaty to the U.S. Senate and expected quick ratification. Instead, the senators continued their barrage of criticisms. Many believed that **Article X**, the **collective security** provision of the League covenant obligating all members to come to the defense of a member facing external attack, would force U.S. troops to act as international police. Others claimed the treaty encroached on congressional war-making powers.

mandate system Policy that granted authority to member states of the League of Nations to govern territories formerly under German or Ottoman rule.

Balfour Declaration British declaration of support for the establishment of a Jewish homeland in Palestine, later included in the League of Nations mandate for Palestine.

Zionist Political movement calling for the creation of a sovereign Jewish homeland in Israel, also called Palestine, Canaan, or the Holy Land.

Versailles Treaty Post-World War I agreement imposing extremely punitive Allied penalties on Germany including loss of colonies and territory, demilitarization, and payment of reparations.

Article X Provision in the Covenant of the League of Nations obligating members to defend a fellow member facing external aggression.

collective security Arrangement among nations under which an attack on one participating nation is met by all countries bound by the pact.

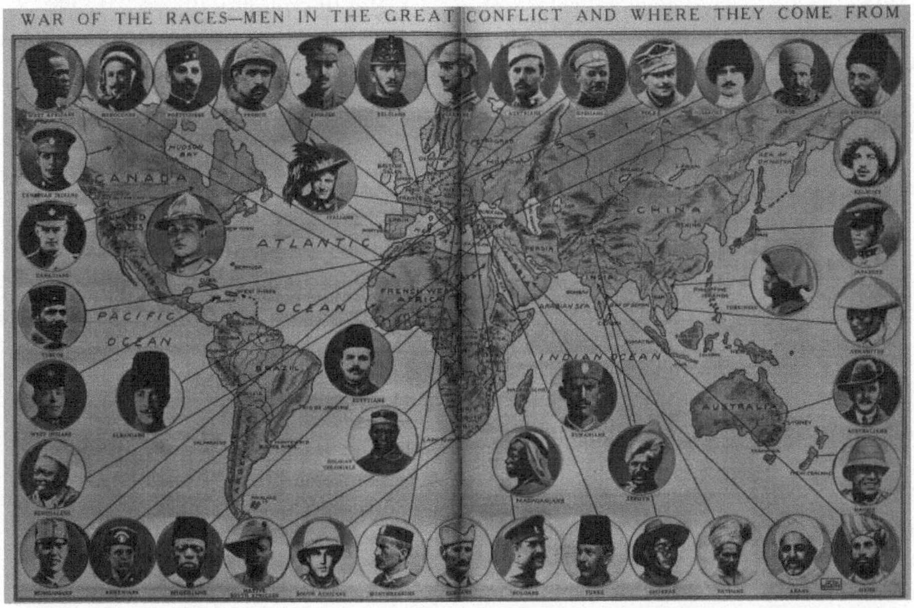

"War of the Races—Men in the Great Conflict and Where They Come From," 1919 As shown in this map that originally appeared in the *New York Times*, soldiers of many races fought for both the Allies and the Central Powers. Colonized peoples and racial minorities hoped wartime sacrifices would be rewarded with independence and equality. While some European ethnic minorities were made part of newly created nation-states, many peoples living under imperial rule were bitterly disappointed by postwar negotiations and launched movements for self-determination. ◀

Library of Congress, Serials and Government Publications Division

Unmoved, Wilson refused to alter any provisions of the treaty and embarked on a national tour during which he vigorously defended the League. A few days after giving an impassioned speech, he suffered a massive stroke that paralyzed his left side. In the following weeks, Edith Bolling Galt Wilson, the president's wife, handled her husband's political affairs and prevented his advisers from seeing him.

With Wilson incapacitated, the U.S. Senate resoundingly defeated the Versailles Treaty in two separate votes. In July 1921, Congress finally passed a joint resolution ending the war. The following month, the United States accepted the Versailles Treaty—but not the provisions on the League. In a tragic irony, the United States did not participate in the new international organization for which Wilson had fought so intensely.

Summary

In the years following Reconstruction, Americans expanded their continental empire abroad. A fusion of geostrategic, commercial, political, religious, and racial motives drove U.S. efforts to gain foreign territories. Although they claimed to reject the harsh methods of European imperialists, Americans engaged in brutal wars and economic exploitation while expanding their nation's international reach. From 1899 to 1902, U.S. troops battled nationalist insurgents in the Philippines, a first glimpse of the ferocious resistance that American interventionism sometimes provoked. At home, anti-imperialists alleged that imperialism endangered democracy, undercut U.S. workers, and jeopardized the white race. Imperialists countered by emphasizing the superiority of American political institutions and values and the economic necessity of securing markets and raw materials in an age of industrialization and international rivalries.

In the early twentieth century, the United States vigorously defended, controlled, and expanded its new empire. Despite their paternalism toward foreign peoples, U.S. officials, businessmen, missionaries, and moral reformers ushered in positive changes including public health initiatives, sanitation, road and bridge construction, and economic opportunities. U.S. policy makers instituted a variety of legal structures to govern new colonies. Through coercive policies such as the Platt Amendment and the Roosevelt Corollary, they subjugated Central Americans. Dollar diplomacy and the Open Door policy became additional tools for protecting U.S. commercial and security interests abroad. American interference in the Mexican Revolution brought the two nations to the brink of war.

Initially neutral when a world war began in 1914, the United States entered the conflict in April 1917. More than 2 million U.S. soldiers arrived in Europe before the armistice of November 1918. Although they played a critical role in the war's final stages, U.S. losses paled in comparison to those of other combatants. Determined to quash the Allies' desires for revenge against their German adversaries and eager to provide an alternative to worldwide Communist revolution, Woodrow Wilson put forward the Fourteen Points as a framework for a new era in international relations. Although he was able to win support for some of his aims at the Paris Peace Conference, he encountered intense political resistance at home. Congressional rejection of the Versailles Treaty ensured that the United States would not be a part of the League of Nations that Wilson believed would end destructive global conflicts.

The war triggered significant political and economic changes in the United States. Business and finance boomed. Workers won economic gains. Reformers advanced prohibition and women's suffrage. But the war also unleashed race riots, political repression, and labor unrest. Despite the tumult, the United States emerged from the war as the world's leading economic, political, and cultural power.

Thinking Back, *Looking Forward*

As you review this chapter, consider the evolution of U.S. expansion beyond North America into foreign territories. How did U.S. acquisition of an overseas empire affect Americans and foreign peoples? Why did U.S. interactions with European imperialist powers change? How did the Great War shift global economic and political dynamics? In the next chapters, consider how World War I affected interaction among nations. What new institutions and treaties arose? How did the war impact American society and the postwar U.S. economy? What forces united Americans in the 1920s? What issues divided them?

To make your study concrete, review the timeline and reflect on the entries there. Think about their causes, consequences, and connections. How do they fit with global trends?

Additional Resources

Books

Hogansen, Kristen. *Fighting for American Manhood: How Gender Politics Provoked the Spanish-American and Philippine-American Wars*. New Haven: Yale University Press, 2000. ▶ Pioneering assessment of intersections of gender and imperialist politics.

Katz, Friederich, and Loren Goldner. *The Secret War in Mexico: Europe, the United States, and the Mexican Revolution*. Chicago: University of Chicago Press, 1981. ▶ Groundbreaking study placing the Mexican Revolution in international context.

Keegan, John. *The First World War*. New York: Vintage, 2000. ▶ Gripping account of the war's battles by a noted military historian.

Kennedy, David M. *Over Here: The First World War and American Society*. New York: Oxford University Press, 1980. ▶ Pulitzer Prize-winning account of the U.S. home front during the Great War.

Kramer, Paul A. *The Blood of Government: Race, Empire, the United States, and the Philippines*. Chapel Hill: University of North Carolina Press, 2006. ▶ Groundbreaking examination of the intersections of racial and imperial politics.

LaFeber, Walter. *The New Empire: An Interpretation of American Expansion, 1860–1898*. Ithaca: Cornell University Press, 1963. ▶ Classic text arguing that economic factors were the primary motivation for U.S. imperialism.

Manela, Erez. *The Wilsonian Moment: Self-Determination and the Origins of Anti-Colonial Nationalism*. New York: Oxford University Press, 2009. ▶ Exploration of the resonance of the anti-imperialist message of the Fourteen Points among colonized peoples worldwide.

McWhirter, Cameron. *Red Summer: The Summer of 1919 and the Awakening of Black America*. New York: St. Martin's Griffin, 2012. ▶ Narrative account of the wave of lynchings and race riots that engulfed the United States post-World War I.

Rydell, Robert W. *All the World's a Fair: Visions of Empire at American International Exhibitions, 1876–1916*. Chicago: University of Chicago Press, 1987. ▶ Examination of the racial and imperialistic dimensions of world's fairs by a noted expert.

Zahniser, J.D., and Amelia R. Fry. *Alice Paul: Claiming Power*. New York: Oxford University Press, 2014. ▶ Definitive biography of the acclaimed suffrage activist.

Go to the MindTap® for **Global Americans** to access the full version of select books from this Additional Resources section.

Websites

The Great War and the Shaping of the 20th Century. (http://www.pbs.org/greatwar/). ▶ Multipart documentary accompanied by online videos, images, and oral histories.

In Motion: The African-American Migration Experience. (http://www.inmotionaame.org/migrations/landing.cfm;jsessionid=f8302884821440133616962?migration=8&bhcp=1). ▶ Schomburg Museum's collection of texts, images, and maps on the Great Migration.

The National World War I Museum and Memorial. (https://theworldwar.org/). ▶ Global materials on the conflict that include a searchable database.

PBS American Experience: Woodrow Wilson. (http://www.pbs.org/wgbh/amex/wilson/). ▶ Collection of photos, primary sources, interviews, and teaching materials.

The World of 1898: The Spanish-American War. (http://www.loc.gov/rr/hispanic/1898/index.html). ▶ Collection offering interdisciplinary and multinational perspectives on the conflict.

MindTap®

Continue exploring online through MindTap®, where you can:

- **Assess your knowledge with the Chapter Test**
- **Watch historical videos related to the chapter**
- **Further your understanding with interactive maps and timelines**

Projecting Power

1878

U.S. acquires a coaling station on Samoa.

1885

Josiah Strong publishes *Our Country: Its Possible Future and Its Present Crisis.*

1887

July

U.S. landowners in Hawai'i force King Kalākaua to sign the so-called Bayonet Constitution.

1890

Alfred Thayer Mahan publishes *The Influence of Sea Power upon History.*

January–April

First Inter-American Conference is held in Washington, D.C.

1893

January

U.S. forces help overthrow the Hawaiian monarchy.

1898

April

U.S. Congress adopts the Teller Amendment, pledging not to annex Cuba.

June

Anti-Imperialist League forms in opposition to U.S. annexation of the Philippines.

1899–1905

May-July 1899

Delegates from twenty-six nations convene in The Hague, Netherlands, to consider disarmament and rules of war.

1899–1901

Boxer Rebellion erupts in China and is suppressed by a multinational force.

1899–1902

Filipinos wage guerilla war against U.S. occupation.

July 1900

First Pan-African Congress meets in London.

Hawai'i becomes a U.S. territory.

August 1900

United States wins the Spanish-American War, gaining control of Puerto Rico, Cuba, and the Philippines.

March 1903

Platt Amendment makes Cuba a U.S. protectorate.

September 1905

Japan defeats Russia in the Russo-Japanese War.

1910–1915

November 1910

Mexican Revolution begins.

1911–1912

Revolution erupts in China, Chinese Republic established.

June 1914

Gavrilo Princep assassinates Archduke Franz Ferdinand of Austria.

August 1914

Panama Canal opens for shipping.

The Great War erupts in Europe, United States declares neutrality.

April 1915

International Congress of Women for Peace and Freedom convenes in The Hague.

May 1915

German submarine sinks the *R.M.S. Lusitania*, drowning 1,128 people.

July 1915

U.S. occupation of Haiti begins.

1916–1918

1916

Great Migration of southern blacks to northern U.S. cities begins.

March 1916

U.S. forces invade Mexico in pursuit of Pancho Villa.

May 1916

U.S. occupation of the Dominican Republic begins.

November 1916

Wilson wins reelection.

April 1917

United States enters World War I.

June 1917

Congress passes the Espionage Act.

October 1917

Bolshevik Revolution begins in Russia.

1918

Spanish flu pandemic begins, killing 50 million people.

January 1918

Wilson proposes the Fourteen Points.

November 1918

Armistice ending World War I is signed.

1919–1920

January 1919

Delegates convene at Paris Peace Conference.

February 1919

Pan-African Congress convenes in Paris amid peace conference ending World War I.

May-October 1919

Red Summer wave of racial violence sweeps the United States.

June 1919

Treaty of Versailles imposes severe punishments on Germany and redraws European borders.

August 1920

Nineteenth Amendment granting women the right to vote is ratified.

September 1920

Mohandas Gandhi launches noncooperation movement in India.

19

Managing Modernity

1919–1929

Charles Lindbergh's 1927 solo nonstop flight from New York to Paris made him the most famous person in the world. He became an instant symbol of the triumph of modern technology, a hero in an era of mass consumption that seems to have invented the very idea of "celebrity."

Early on the morning of May 20, 1927, a 25-year-old pilot from Minnesota pushed the throttle of his tiny single-engine plane and took off toward New York's Long Island Sound. *The Spirit of St. Louis* was so heavy with fuel that it barely cleared the telephone wires at the end of the muddy runway. Charles Lindbergh was trying to do what more than a dozen aviators had failed to do—fly nonstop, solo, from New York to Paris. If he succeeded, he would win $25,000, but more acclaimed flyers had crashed, been injured, and died.

NY Daily News Archive/Getty Images

Lindbergh flew northeast toward Nova Scotia. As he headed out over the open ocean, darkness fell, and fog so thick enveloped the plane that he was forced to skim just ten feet above the waves. "Which way is Ireland?" he shouted to a fishing boat when the fog cleared in the morning. As darkness fell a second time, he was over the coast of France. At 10:00 P.M. Paris time, he first saw the city's lights, and he circled the Eiffel Tower. Twenty minutes later, he landed to the cheers of wildly enthusiastic fans who lifted him to their shoulders and shouted "Vive!" Radio transmitted the news, and at that moment, Charles Lindbergh, the "Lone Eagle," was the most famous person on Earth. Millions turned out to see him in England and Canada as he made his way back to a hero's homecoming in the United States. New York City officials closed public schools and shuttered the Wall Street stock exchange to stage the city's largest ever ticker tape parade for "Lindbergh Day." President Calvin Coolidge presented Lindbergh the Distinguished Flying Cross, and in 1928 *Time* magazine named him its first ever "Man of the Year."

Lindbergh was beloved, an instant symbol of the triumph of modern technology, a hero in an era of mass consumption that seemed to have invented the very idea of celebrity. Yet he was uncomfortable with much about contemporary society. His rugged individualism, as well as his racism against immigrants and non-whites, seemed to fit the nineteenth century better than the twentieth. Change was happening too fast. He was not alone in worrying about the downside to modernity—crowded, crime-ridden, and vice-ridden cities filled with immigrants and racial minorities that seemed to have no place for tradition and morality. The Great War had made the United States the world's leading economic, military, and cultural power; like many Americans, however, Lindbergh recoiled from global responsibility. When facing another emerging world war, he opposed U.S. involvement and sympathized with racist Nazi leaders in Germany.

The Great Aviator's perplexities reflected the contradictions that shaped the United States in the 1920s. How did a decade marked by modern developments in technology, economic activity, urban life, and global power give rise to a national mood seemingly opposed to the very concept of change? Since the middle of the nineteenth century, the word *modernity* had captured the welcoming embrace of new social, economic, cultural, and political trends that distinguished the present from past traditions and looked forward to the future. Most Americans, like Lindbergh, did not reject modernity so much as to seek to tame or manage its excesses. They yearned for social cohesion, law

Charles Lindbergh was a symbol of the triumph of modern technology, yet he was apprehensive of contemporary society. How do these perplexities reflect the contradictions that shaped the United States in the 1920s?

Go to MindTap® to watch a video on Lindbergh and learn how his story relates to the themes of this chapter.

and order, and a perfection of the social and political reforms of the Progressive Era. If they participated in global affairs, they wanted to do so on their own terms. While most of Europe was in turmoil, struggling to recover from the Great War and to stem the spread of Communist revolution, the United States experienced remarkable prosperity and social stability. Yet Americans were uneasy about their place in the world.

Nor was the U.S. economy so stable as it seemed. Farmers faced declining crop prices, wages remained stagnant, and many families took on debt to purchase the automobiles, radios, and new household appliances that now seemed to be necessities. Advertisers pushed consumer goods, which were produced in great volume by new efficiencies in management and production and made available through credit, another innovation of the 1920s. Overproduction in the domestic market and economic insecurities overseas were bad omens for the global economy that relied disproportionately on U.S. output and loans.

The rejection of Europe and its problems exemplified in 1919 by the refusal of Congress to join the League of Nations extended into the 1920s when there emerged a widespread rejection of foreigners. New laws severely limited the number of immigrants admitted each year, and some groups were excluded altogether. Many Americans associated immigrants with radicalism and with racial and religious minorities who were unwelcome in a republic that the majority defined as white, Protestant, and English or at least northern European in character. Intolerance and cultural conformity marked the decade. At the same time, however, diverse peoples pushed back, aligning themselves with a more inclusive vision of citizenship. Popular culture promised liberation and free expression, and consumer products offered a taste of the good life to a broad sweep of Americans.

19-1 Aftermath of World War I

This 1919 British graphic depicts the League of Nations as a flower blossoming from the graves of World War I, representing the massive human cost of the war. The dark sky at top, depicting the world's uncertain future, stands in contrast to the League of Nation's angelic white figure who appears to float upward toward a Christian notion of heaven.

How might have persons in the United States, disillusioned by the war and wanting to retreat from the problems of Europe, responded to this image? ▶

The Star/Associated Newspapers Ltd./Solo Syndication/British Cartoon Archive

The carnage and destruction of World War I was so great that for at least a decade after it ended, preventing another global bloodletting was high on the world's agenda. Reaching this goal was the main purpose of the League of Nations, which the United States did not join. But it did participate in major arms control agreements and joint international efforts to topple the newly founded Soviet Union and thwart its mission to foment a world Communist revolution. Fears of Communist takeover in Italy, Germany, and Spain fed an aggressive militarism in those countries, posing a threat to global peace. In the United States, a burst of labor and radical protests inspired in part by the Soviet mission provoked government crackdowns on radical activists and their organizations. The horrors of the Great War followed by the threat of class warfare pushed the majority of Americans to favor homespun Americanism rooted in small-town values, Protestantism, law and order, and racial and cultural homogeneity. This "return to normalcy" was evident in the fulfillment of Progressive Era reform movements for women's suffrage and temperance. At the same time, federal interventions on behalf of labor and the working classes ceased as the economy turned prosperous.

☞ As you read, consider the impact of World War I and its aftermath on U.S. politics and international relations. In what ways did it curb U.S. global intervention? In what ways did it compel it?

19-1a Communism and the Red Scare

The Communist revolution in Russia intensifies class conflict at home and around the world.

Russian Communists started on the wrong foot vis-à-vis the United States and other leading capitalist nations. After coming to power during the Great War, Communist revolutionaries led by Vladimir Lenin fought and won a difficult civil war. Twelve nations, including the United States, Britain, and Japan, sent aid to anti-Communist forces and dispatched their own troops to defeat the revolutionaries (see Map 19.1). In 1922, Lenin founded the Soviet Union, a federation of Russian, Transcaucasian, Ukrainian, and Byelorussian republics. Beginning in 1925, Lenin's successor, Joseph Stalin, engaged in a series of political purges that sought to cleanse the new nation of supposed political enemies through execution or removal to forced labor camps.

Stalin, who remained in power for nearly three decades, never forgot the Allied "imperialist invasion" during his country's civil war. Equally antagonistic, the Allies withheld diplomatic recognition of the Soviet Union and did not invite the new country to join the League of Nations for some years. The Soviets responded by hosting a series of congresses known as the **Communist International (Comintern)** attended by people from around the world (including the United States) to create revolutionary parties answering to Moscow. Although there were no sustained Soviet-inspired revolutions during the 1920s, Communists rose up in Germany and Hungary in the immediate aftermath of World War I, and the Communist Party modeled after Lenin's movement flourished in China, where the Chinese Communist Party was founded in 1921.

In Italy, postwar Communist and socialist labor strikes gave strongman Benito Mussolini and his right-wing paramilitary units the chance to seize power. Mussolini, known as Il Duce (The Leader), became prime minister in 1922 and promised stability through **fascism**. This political and economic system was characterized by dictatorial leadership, economic regimentation, and restrictions on civil liberties. Mussolini ruthlessly suppressed opponents, dismantled labor unions, instituted a one-party rule, and mandated state control of business and banking. A dramatic, even bombastic speaker, he vowed to make Italy "great, respected, and feared." In 1923, he bombed and occupied the Greek island of Corfu and in so doing revealed the weakness of the League of Nations in protecting its weak members such as Greece.

In the United States, fears of revolutionary disruptions grew out of widespread labor unrest occurring during the nation's postwar economic slump. Triggering fear were acts of terror committed by anarchists seeking to undermine the capitalist order. In April 1919, thirty-six mail bombs were sent to state officials responsible for cracking-down on political dissent through policies such as the Espionage Act, Sedition Act, and the Immigration Act of 1917. Two months later, much larger bombs were delivered to eight different targets, including U.S. attorney general A. Mitchell Palmer, who escaped harm. The terrorist attacks culminated on September 16, 1920, with the explosion of bombs at the heart of New York's financial district on Wall Street, killing thirty-eight persons and seriously injuring more than one hundred forty.

Fears of labor and radical agitation erupted into what was later called the **Red Scare**. From late 1919 to mid-1920, Palmer orchestrated raids in twenty-three states, arresting more than eight thousand suspected radicals. Many were subjected to illegal searches and imprisoned without being formally charged. The United States deported approximately five hundred "alien enemies" (mainly Russian and Jewish immigrants), including the anarchist Emma Goldman, well known for her antidraft activities during the war and who fled to the Soviet Union, and socialist labor organizer Eugene V. Debs (see Chapter 18). The actions damaged the Industrial Workers of the World (IWW), one of the nation's most radical and violent labor unions that sought to unite all workers regardless of skill, industry, race, or gender.

In response to Red Scare persecutions, Roger Nash Baldwin, a conscientious objector who went to prison during the Great War, settlement house leader Jane Addams, and Helen Keller, the well-known advocate for the deaf and blind, joined in founding the American Civil Liberties Union (ACLU) to provide legal aid to radicals persecuted during the Red Scare and safeguard constitutional protections. The ACLU championed Debs's release as did many cities across the nation where amnesty zones for free speech were established. The organization also provided defense counsel to Nicola Sacco and Bartolomeo Vanzetti, Italian immigrant anarchists

Communist International (Comintern) Gathering of socialists from across the world organized by the Soviet Union in 1919 to oppose capitalism and install Soviet-style rule.

fascism Authoritarian and ultra-nationalist system of government led right-wing conservatives.

Red Scare Fear of communism and anarchism that gripped the United States, manifest in domestic terrorism, government suppression, and violations of civil liberties.

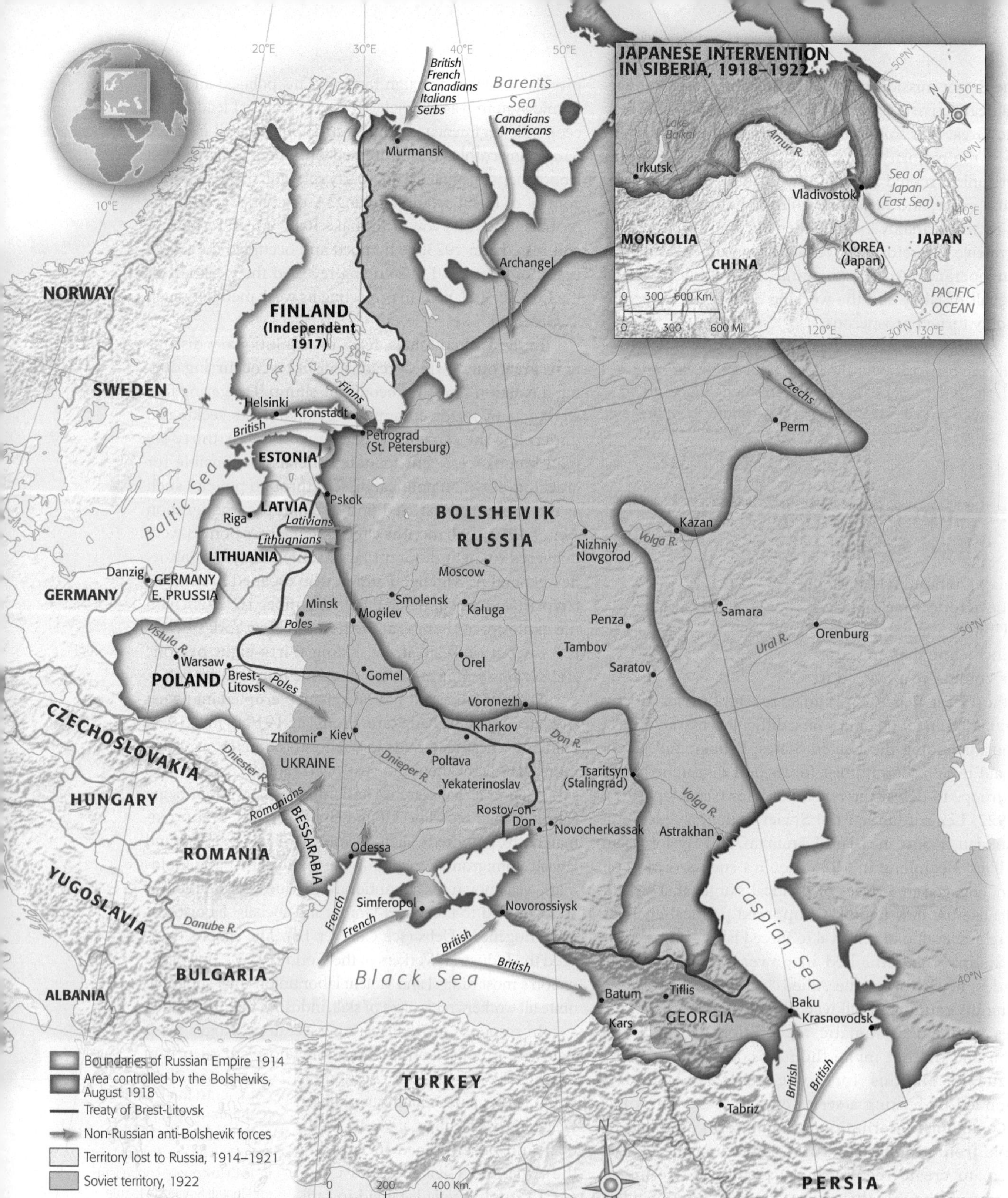

Map 19.1 Foreign Intervention in Russian Civil War Communist control over Russia, beginning in 1917, was not secure until 1922 when the Bolsheviks won a brutal civil war. Foreign countries, including the United States, Great Britain, France, and Japan, sent troops in a failed attempt to oust the Communists. The seventy thousand Japanese troops who entered Russia through Vladivostok (see map insert) were the largest foreign contingent. The Bolsheviks remained wary and suspicious of these "foreign imperialist" nations long after the civil war ended. ▲

arrested outside Boston in May 1920 for allegedly murdering two men as part of an armed robbery. The stolen money, it was said during trial, had contributed to the Wall Street bombing that had occurred later that year. Sacco and Vanzetti were convicted of murder and received the death sentence. Their case elicited strong opposition from radicals and others who believed that the court's view of the two men had been biased by the climate of nativism and the Red Scare. Their execution in August 1927 provoked domestic unrest and anti-American protests around the world.

19-1b "Normalcy" at Home and Abroad

The search for domestic stability leads to the promotion of international peace.

The 1920 presidential election—the first in which women could vote—marked a moment of reflection for Americans after a global war, a controversial peace treaty, and a tumultuous postwar period marked by labor unrest, recession, and the Red Scare. What the country most wanted, said the Republican candidate Warren G. Harding, was to close the chapter on the World War I era: "America's present need is not heroics, but healing; not nostrums, but normalcy, not revolution, but restoration." Harding won the election over fellow Ohioan, Democrat James M. Cox, by a record margin, receiving more than 60 percent of the popular vote and more than 76 percent of the electoral vote. Debs, the Socialist Party candidate, garnered 1 million votes despite being in prison.

The Harding administration ended debate about whether the United States should join the League of Nations and set the federal government on a course featuring sharp reductions in spending, increased cooperation with private business, and tax relief for the wealthy. Despite opposing Woodrow Wilson's internationalism, state-sponsored social reform, and organized labor, Harding was more forward looking than he seemed. The new president put an end to the raids by Attorney General Palmer, eased Federal Bureau of Investigation surveillance of radicals, oversaw the repeal of the Sedition Act, and commuted the sentences of Debs and other political prisoners. The British author H. G. Wells praised Debs's release as an indication the nation had realized that "the attempt to shout down and suppress unpopular opinions and to create panics of hostility against minority views is unworthy of the general greatness of American life."

The Harding administration also made historic inroads to securing international peace. His opposition to joining the League of Nations did not make him an **isolationist** in terms of global efforts to prevent war. He did urge the nation to join the Permanent Court of International Justice, which beginning in 1921 operated as the World Court for the League of Nations. Harding's efforts, however, were blocked by the "irreconcilable" senators who opposed joining the League of Nations. They saw World Court membership as a backdoor into the League. He had more luck in convening the **Washington Naval Conference** (1921–1922) to avoid the arms race that had preceded World War I. The conference produced the Five-Power Naval Limitation Treaty that restricted warship tonnage by means of a ratio (5:3:1.75) that allowed the United States and Britain (which maintained both Atlantic and Pacific fleets) the highest tonnage, Japan the next highest, and France and Italy the lowest. The five powers also agreed to a ten-year "naval holiday" during which there would be no construction of new battleships and aircraft carriers. Meeting the treaty requirements, said Secretary of State Charles Evans Hughes, meant scrapping 1.8 million tons of naval vessels. One newspaper proclaimed that "Hughes sank in thirty-five minutes more ships than all the admirals of the world have sunk in a cycle of centuries."

The success of the Washington Conference was not repeated. Further attempts to control arms in Geneva (1927) and London (1930) failed to ease the global arms race in submarines, destroyers, and cruisers, vessels that were not included in the Washington treaties. The United States (and Japan) refused to sign an international agreement banning poison gases, deeply disappointing Jane Addams and other members of the Women's International League for Peace and Freedom, which had advocated strongly for the agreement. The ultimate futility of U.S., attempts to build on the success of the Washington treaties was evident in the U.S.,-backed Kellogg-Briand Pact (1928), a much celebrated although unenforceable global renunciation of war.

A final international challenge stemmed from the increasing discontent of colonized and subordinated peoples around the world, who had been encouraged by the message of self-determination in President Wilson's Fourteen Points. These peoples were subsequently disappointed that neither the Versailles Treaty nor the League of Nations opposed empire building or white supremacy. The League established a *mandate* system that transferred colonies from the defeated powers of Germany and the Ottoman Empire to mainly England and France. Japan received German possessions in the Pacific, but it was more concerned with its existing colony in Korea when in March 1919 as many as 2 million Koreans demanded liberation from Japanese rule. Although the uprising failed—hundreds of protesters were killed and tens of thousands imprisoned—it galvanized support for Korean independence, especially from Korean immigrants in the United States and Hawai'i. A month earlier in February 1919, Du Bois re-energized the Pan-African Congress, which proceeded to meet three more times in a span of eight years after the Great War. Pan-Africanism sought the liberation of Africa and African peoples around the world as part of a global movement against racism and colonialism.

isolationist Term for a person who opposed allowing the United States to join the League of Nations.

Washington Naval Conference International gathering in Washington, D.C., in which the world's major powers agreed to a naval tonnage limitation.

History without Borders

International Organizations and the Construction of a Global Community

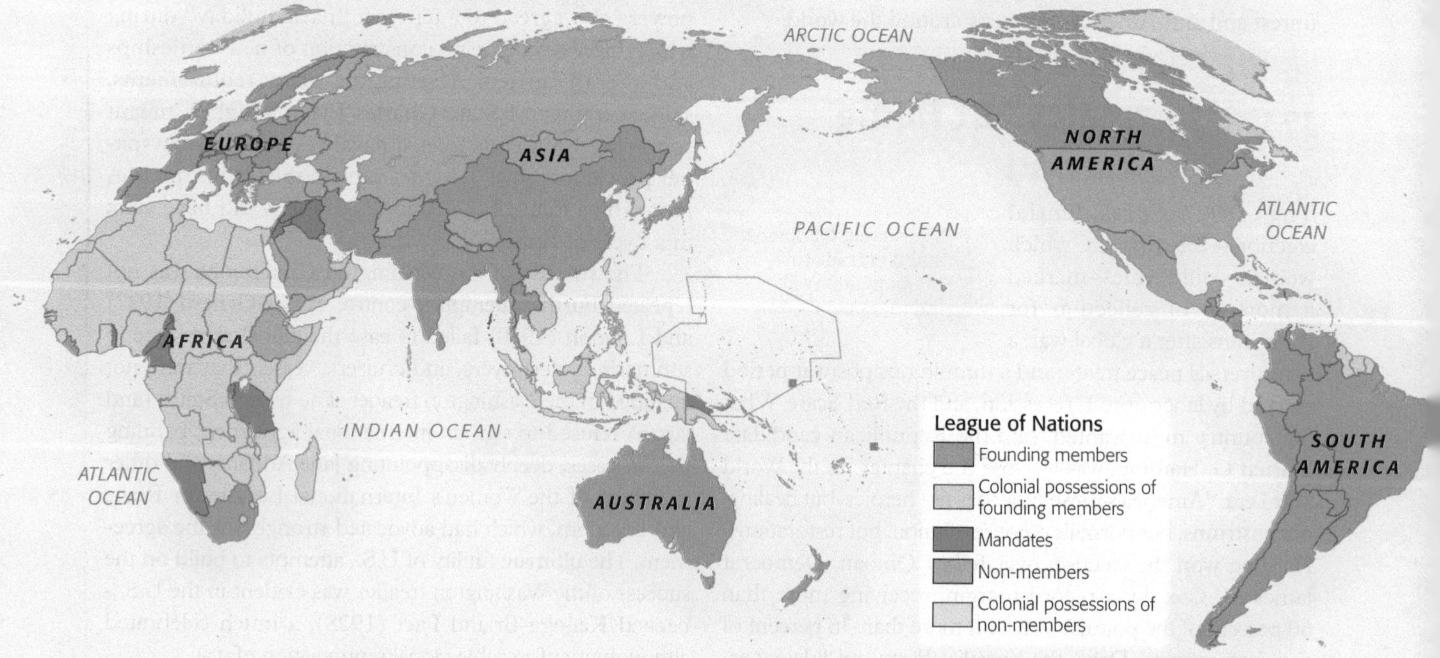

League of Nations Founding Members, 1920 The nations that founded the League of Nations and their colonies and mandates covered most of the world in 1920. The number of member nations would grow for many years. ▲

During the 1920s, a significant expansion of international organizations raised awareness of global problems without being obligated to the interests of any one nation-state. The two types of these organizations were intergovernmental organizations (IGOs), such as the League of Nations, which functioned through collective actions among nation-states, and nongovernmental organizations (NGOs), such as the International Red Cross, which relied on support from groups and individuals who did not represent governments. Both types continued a process begun in the nineteenth century to build a global community.

The League of Nations was a foundational step toward global intergovernmental cooperation. Headquartered in Geneva, Switzerland, it had three main branches. The Executive Council included the leading powers and assumed the major responsibility for preventing war. Council measures needed majority consent from the Assembly, the second branch of League governance, in which each member nation-state had one vote. Once approved by the Council and Assembly, the League Secretariat, the body's third branch, administered and implemented its policies. The Secretariat consisted of more than six hundred officials who engaged in peacekeeping and a wide variety of League programs. Affiliated with the League was the Permanent Court of International Justice, which opened in 1922 in The Hague, Netherlands. Popularly known as the *World Court*, its purpose was to adjudicate disputes between League member nations.

As important as the League was for advancing intergovernmental cooperation, it had even a greater impact by encouraging the the proliferation of NGOs. Ninety percent of the 478 international organizations listed by the League of Nations in 1929 were NGOs. They included various bodies to establish international regulations for air traffic,

Corbis

League of Nations Members Discuss Disarmament, 1924 The League of Nations created protocols to prevent war by seeking to enforce collective security and mandatory arbitration of international disputes. Even though the United States did not join the League, this intergovernmental organization was the most important of its kind during the 1920s, spawning the rapid proliferation of a global community through both intergovernmental and nongovernmental organizations. Americans played an active role in the latter, and the United States sent representatives to observe the League's proceedings. ◄

Archive Photos/Getty Images

Ambulance Driving Class for the American Red Cross, 1920 The Red Cross pioneered and epitomized the humanitarian spirit of nongovernmental organizations that enabled many concerned peoples, including Americans, to participate in ameliorating a wide variety of global challenges. In this case, trainees in Washington, D.C., were being taught about an ambulance motor. ◄

undersea cable communications, audio technology, and others to promote friendship among students worldwide and the international preservation of birds.

Two NGOs embodied the creation of a truly global community that extended beyond the Euro-American orbit to include areas in Asia-Pacific, Africa, and the Middle East. The Institute of Pacific Relations (IPR) was established in 1925 to establish representative bodies from every nation in the Pacific including the Soviet Union and colonies such as Korea and the Philippines. Begun in Hawai'i under the auspices of the YMCA, the IPR brought people from the vast and increasingly important Pacific region together to engage in joint research projects on problems threatening peace and on advancing international and cross-cultural understanding. The International Alliance of Women, created before World War I, mainly comprised European and North American members seeking to broaden women's suffrage in their nations. During the 1920s the Alliance greatly expanded its global campaign to include women from Argentina, Brazil, Egypt, India, Jamaica, Japan, Syria, and Turkey.

Critical Thinking Questions

▶ The growth of international organizations in the 1920s coincided with the intensification of nationalism in the United States, Germany, Italy, Japan, and elsewhere. How was it possible for internationalism and nationalism to coexist at this time? In what ways did the love of country conflict with the love for humanity?

▶ Today there are roughly forty thousand international NGOs around the world. Name the ones you know about. What do they do? To what extent were their general goals anticipated by international organizations during the 1920s? Explain.

From the perspective of many whites, colonial empires and racial hierarchies were bedrocks of Western civilization. In a widely regarded book, Lothrop Stoddard warned about *The Rising Tide of Color Against White World Supremacy* (1920). The Harvard-educated scholar claimed that the Great War was actually a terrible civil war among the ruling white races that damaged their power to control the "lesser" peoples of the world, particularly the Japanese, who seemingly posed the most significant threat to the United States. Stoddard's views resonated with many white Americans who blamed urgent social problems on the immigrant masses and the war on changing racial demographics through which Anglo-Saxons—the supposed makers of Western civilization—were being displaced by lesser peoples. In contrast, the well-known young writer F. Scott Fitzgerald parodied Stoddard's racial alarmism as that of an older, self-satisfied generation more interested in preserving the status quo than in embracing the modern world.

19-1c Women's Activism

Women' political influence increases, although suffrage fails to bring equal rights.

In August 1920, the ratification of the Nineteenth Amendment granted American women the right to vote, fulfilling the aims of the suffrage movement. Many women in the U.S. West already had the right to vote in state and local elections as did women in the Soviet Union and in industrialized democracies such as the United Kingdom, Germany, New Zealand, Australia, and Canada. Six months before the amendment's ratification, Carrie Chapman Catt's National American Woman Suffrage Association established the **League of Women Voters**, a nonpartisan organization designed to encourage newly enfranchised women to assume a greater role in civic affairs. The 1920 presidential election was the first federal election in which all qualified adult U.S. citizens could vote. To the surprise of some activists in the League of Women Voters, the amendment did not result in a political revolution. Women went to the polls in far fewer numbers than men and when they did were not united as women. Women's reform issues did not make an impact except where they melded with the nation's general desire to eradicate crime, corruption, and immorality in American life and politics. Activists such as labor radical Mary Harris "Mother" Jones opposed women's suffrage because they saw it as a cause for privileged women and that a public role for women put in jeopardy vital child-raising responsibilities. Jones said, "You don't need the vote to raise hell!"

League of Women Voters Nonpartisan organization that arose in 1920 with the granting of women's suffrage to advance the political interests of women as a group.

equal rights amendment Failed effort by women's activists in the 1920s to embed equal treatment of women and men into the Constitution.

Prohibition U.S. public policy that banned the manufacturing, sale, and interstate transportation of alcoholic beverages.

Although the Nineteenth Amendment did not produce a national revolution in politics, it did expose other gender-based inequalities. Alice Paul's National Woman's Party sought to use it as a step for achieving an **equal rights amendment** that would guarantee women equal rights, much as the Fourteenth Amendment had been designed to guarantee equal treatment under the law for all individuals regardless of race. Congress did not consider the amendment. In 1922, Congress did approve the Cable Act, which eliminated nativist immigration laws that caused American women to lose their own citizenship upon marrying a foreigner. The new law, however, bowed to pressure from western states to make an exception for marrying Asians. Until the law was changed in 1931, U.S. citizens marrying Asian immigrant men lost their citizenship. Meanwhile, southern African American women mobilized successful voter registration drives through networks of churches, fraternal societies, women's clubs, and voluntary associations, but despite success in the 1920 elections, they were disenfranchised by whites who quickly closed loopholes for women under Jim Crow segregation.

Activists for women's rights, or "feminists" as they were called, were more successful at lobbying for issues supported by the increasing number of working women who typically opposed the equal rights amendment because it would have overturned special labor protections for women secured by the *Muller* decision in 1908. Working-class advocates, such as Jane Addams, Florence Kelley, and Margaret Sanger, and labor activists in the Women's Trade Union League focused on women's rights in the workplace and to birth control. A victory for these labor feminists came in 1921 when Congress provided modest funding for nurse training programs to improve care for infants and pregnant mothers in the Sheppard-Towner Act. The act's supporters pointed with alarm to a 1917 U.S. Children's Bureau study ranking the nation seventeenth of twenty nations in maternal morality and eleventh in infant mortality. The American Medical Association, in contrast, opposed Sheppard-Towner as a Communist plan in which the state reached into private business; by 1929, the association convinced Congress to stop funding the program, but it was later restored.

19-1d Prohibition

State authority over alcohol consumption expands greatly even though it is undermined by a sharp rise in criminal activity.

Women had long played a leading role in the temperance movement, which since the nineteenth century had sought to end urban crime and family instability by outlawing alcohol. The social experiment of **Prohibition** was not entirely new. Thirty-four states (almost entirely in the South and West) already had laws that either banned or severely regulated the sale of alcohol. Prohibition was not limited to the United States. Finland, which long had

Global Americans The daughter of immigrant parents, **Margaret Sanger** grew up in a large Irish Roman Catholic family. Her mother endured eighteen pregnancies (eleven of which led to live births) in twenty-two years before dying at age forty-nine. As an adult, Sanger studied nursing and became involved in free-thinking socialist politics. She saw enough crude abortions and suffering among poor women to be convinced that contraception was essential for women's health. In the early twentieth century, however, contraceptives and abortion were illegal in the United States and most developed nations. Inspired by the radical Emma Goldman, Sanger began to publish writings that challenged the laws preventing the distribution of information about contraceptives. She popularized the term *birth control*, opened the first U.S. birth control clinic, and argued that in minimizing the possibility of getting pregnant, liberated women could enjoy the pleasures of sexual intercourse.

After the Great War and Red Scare, Sanger's influence peaked as she moved away from left-wing organizations to gain support from the mainstream eugenics movement whose goal was to reduce the birthrate of persons deemed inferior. In 1921, she established the American Birth Control League. By this time, the Soviet Union had become the first nation to legalize abortion and endorse birth control. Germany and Great Britain sanctioned birth control as a means of aiding poor families. During the 1920s, Sanger spread the birth control movement to China, Korea, and Japan. ◀ Library of Congress Prints and Photographs Division [LC-USZ62–29808]

been influenced by the U.S. temperance movement, followed suit.

Prohibition reduced alcohol consumption among Americans by one-third, and medical statistics from the 1920s reveal that this decline had positive health effects. In Massachusetts, the admission rate for patients with alcohol-related illnesses fell from 14.6 per one hundred thousand in 1910 to 7.7 in 1929. In New York, the rate was cut nearly in half, falling from 11.5 in 1910 to 6.5 in 1931. Nationwide, the death rate from alcohol-related illness, such as cirrhosis of the liver, dropped from 14.8 per one hundred thousand in 1907 to no more than 7.5 for every year in the 1920s.

Yet more apparent at the time was Prohibition's negative impact on law and order. The experiment initiated the largest expansion in federal authority since Reconstruction, continuing state interventions in the economy and society from the Progressive Era, and even so it was nearly impossible to enforce. The modest allocation of federal agents was not enough to secure the nation's wide-open borders, shutter illicit **speakeasy** bars, and otherwise win the war against alcohol. The journalist Herbert Asbury noted that those who expected Prohibition to create a more perfect U.S. society "were met by a horde of bootleggers, moonshiners, rumrunners, hijackers, gangsters, racketeers, trigger men, venal judges, corrupt police, crooked politicians, and speakeasy operators, all bearing the twin symbols of the Eighteenth Amendment—the tommy gun and the poisoned cup." Prohibition's enforcement difficulties put the great experiment in jeopardy. It gave rise to organized crime syndicates led by infamous gangsters such as Al Capone, and it diminished respect for governmental authority because millions of otherwise law-abiding Americans regularly violated that amendment.

speakeasy Illegal establishment where alcoholic beverages were sold and consumed during Prohibition.

19-2

Economic Boom

Photographed in 1927, Ford Motor Company's massive River Rouge plant in Dearborn, Michigan, was more than a mile long and a mile and one-half wide. Henry Ford took automobile manufacturing to a new level of self-sufficiency. He owned and controlled all stages of production from the raw materials and their transportation to the manufacture of automobile parts and their assembly. The plant also produced its own electricity.

Notice the river running through the plant. What advantages were gained by locating an automobile manufacturing plant on a river? ▶

Library of Congress Prints and Photographs Division [LC-D414-K3461]

After World War I, the United States was the leading global economic power. The nation's rise had occurred during the war when it served as the Allies' main source of food, munitions, and manufactured goods and provided much needed loans to them to pay for these items. The end of the war did not alter U.S. leadership while Britain, France, and Germany struggled to revive their economies. Already blessed with an abundance of raw materials and a huge consumer market, U.S. firms during the 1920s intensified labor management and innovated marketing strategies that together gave a tremendous boost to both production and sales. The automobile industry led the way, powering much of the nation's prosperity and global economic success. For the first time, automobiles and other large consumer products such as washing machines, refrigerators, and radios became widely available, and their production propelled the nation's economy. Improvements in the nation's infrastructure—roads, electricity, and communication networks—spread access to goods. A new emphasis on marketing increased sales at home and abroad. Hopeful that U.S. business innovations and success would produce lasting prosperity, the nation's political leaders unleashed big corporations from the trust busting and regulations they had faced during the Progressive Era. The "roaring twenties" was a time when business reigned supreme in U.S. politics and culture.

☞ As you read, look for the ways that World War I and its aftermath stimulated business and consumer trends that boosted the national economy. In what ways did the economy grow and transform?

19-2a Nation's Business

Harding's close relationship with big businesses, his critics charged, spawned political corruption. Starting in 1922 and continuing well after his death in office the following year, congressional investigators uncovered scandals involving the administration's issuance of oil contracts in Elk Hills, California, and Tea Pot Dome in Wyoming. Calvin Coolidge, the man elevated to the presidency after Harding's death, continued the former president's business relationships. Although as governor of Massachusetts, Coolidge had supported labor protections and other state interventions in the economy, he and Secretary of Commerce Herbert Hoover were adamant that such regulations were beyond the powers of the federal government. Contrary to social reformers, Coolidge followed a laissez-faire view of government that trusted rather than criticized private corporations. Banker Andrew Mellon, one of the richest men in the United States, served as his secretary of the treasury. "The chief business of the U.S. people is business," Coolidge said. "They are profoundly concerned with producing, buying, selling, investing and prospering in the world."

The federal government prioritizes economic growth.

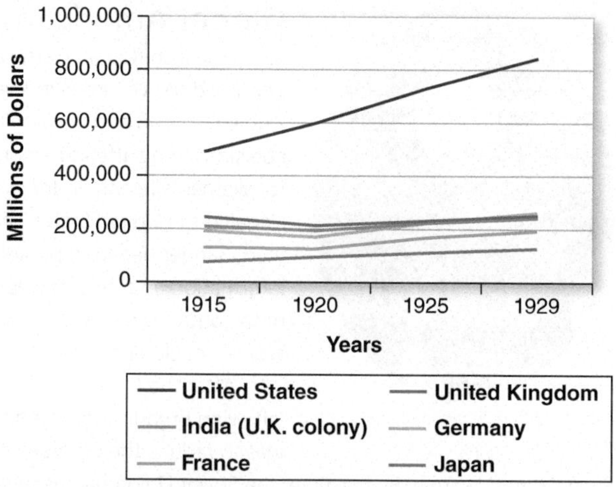

NOTE: Figures represent millions in 1990 dollars.

Figure 19.1 GDP by Nation, 1915–1929 America's gross domestic product (GDP) led the world in 1915 and had nearly doubled by 1929. Although the GDP of the United Kingdom remained far behind that of the United States, the significant GDP of India, its colony, provides a sense of the might of the British empire—and why the British strongly resisted Indian independence. ▲ Source: Maddison Project. (www.ggdc.net/maddison/Historical_Statistics/horizontal-file_02-2010.xls).

With the federal government's support, the nation's businesses built upon the gains made during World War I. Although leading the world in gross domestic product (GDP) before World War I, the United States far surpassed all nations after the war (see Figure 19.1). Central to this postwar economic boon in the United States was the automobile, which during the 1920s changed from an extravagance for wealthy persons to a necessity for masses of people. By the 1930s, the automobile industry was the nation's third largest employer and highest in average pay, a great rise from 1917 when it ranked fifteenth and seventh, respectively. Car and truck sales tripled during the 1920s, and by 1929, the United States produced nearly 90 percent of the world's automobiles.

The automobile bonanza reshaped much of the U.S. economy. It led to new and thriving industries for automobile parts and service as well as the tourist business. Gasoline production moved to the center of the U.S. oil industry, and mammoth orders for tires and windshields boosted rubber and glass manufacturing. The automobile industry increased overall manufacturing output in the United States by 50 percent during the 1920s. In 1929, the nation produced 40 percent of the world's coal, 70 percent of its gasoline, and 50 percent of its steel.

19-2b Fordism and Labor

What enabled the explosive increase in automobiles in the United States was Henry Ford's innovations in mass production that generated

New efficiencies of production developed by Ford transform the nature of work.

Handout/Getty Images News /Getty Images

Global Americans Born of immigrant parents in 1863, **Henry Ford**, like most Americans of his day, was not a major world traveler. Yet by the 1920s, his automobiles were being shipped to six continents, and he had established assembly plants in Britain, Canada, France, Germany, Australia, and India. Ford's columns for his newspaper, *The Dearborn Independent*, drew praise in Germany from Adolf Hitler for exposing the supposed Jewish conspiracy for global domination. Hitler idolized Ford, who was the only American named in the German's autobiographical manifesto, *Mein Kampf* (*My Struggle*). Hitler singled him out for maintaining independence from the Jewish-led "controlling masters of the producers in a nation of one hundred and twenty millions."

Another example of Ford's global reach was Fordlandia, the company's massive rubber plantation the size of Connecticut. Started in 1928, the project that cut supplies from Brazil's Amazon rainforest was intended to supply the only major element missing from Ford's vertically integrated production process. Fordlandia was also a great experiment in welfare capitalism. The plantation resembled a U.S. company town where Brazilian workers were required to adopt not just Ford's work routines but also his standards of living, dress, diet, leisure, and social relations. The experiment failed. Workers resisted the imposition of U.S. culture, the Amazonia environment—particularly rubber plant pests—proved too much to manage, and synthetic rubber replaced the need for natural stocks. The plantation later closed before it could supply the rubber for even one automobile tire.

high-quality goods on a larger scale and at a lower cost than ever before. The genius of **Fordism**, a term of the time, was that it applied the mid-nineteenth century factory system of production (interchangeable parts and deskilling of labor) to automaking and with the application of electricity to industry greatly increased the scale of production. In 1914, Ford shocked his competitors by more than doubling the lowest worker's wage from $2.34 to $5.00 while shortening the workday from nine hours to eight. By 1923, he estimated that nearly 80 percent of manufacturing jobs in his company required no more than one week to learn. The compensation Ford offered for the **deskilling** of labor was higher pay and shorter hours. In 1926, he eliminated Saturday from the workweek by adopting the five-day, forty-hour standard that is still in effect today. Ford Motor Company paid African Americans and women equal pay to that of their white male counterparts, although African American men worked on more dangerous jobs. In the end, most workers had little choice but to accept the bargain of high wages for repetitive work because the spread of Fordism to other industries meant the decline of skilled jobs everywhere. To manufacturers, the **wage bargain** was a win–win proposition. The higher wages and shorter hours appeased labor demands while enabling workers to buy the products they made.

In seeking to ensure peaceful labor relations, Ford and fellow business leaders such as John D. Rockefeller offered workers benefits including sick leave, pensions, stock ownership, employee representation in management decisions, personnel services, and recreation programs. Advocates of these changes described

Archive Photos/Getty Images

Assembly Line, 1927 Workers in New York City operate a machine that filled bottles with salad dressing. "Mass production," said Henry Ford, "lightens work, but increases its repetitive quality." To its critics, Fordism stripped workers of their skills and creativity by turning them into human machines who had to keep pace with the moving assembly line. Doing the same small task again and again, hour after hour, brought no pride or satisfaction. Like parts, workers, too, were interchangeable. ▲

Fordism Streamlined and profitable manufacturing process based on Ford's development of fast assembly of parts leading to repetitive work that did not require skilled labor.

deskilling Process in which the skills once needed to perform work were rendered obsolete by either machines or new work routines.

wage bargain Trade-off experienced by workers in which higher wages (welcomed by workers) came with less pride and ownership of labor (which was not).

such worker benefits as **welfare capitalism**, and saw them as a sign of corporate social conscience. Yet such programs were not available to the vast majority of workers in private industry. Few companies, for example, offered pension plans, and those that did had only a fraction of workers who met the requirements needed to collect benefits. Critics charged that welfare capitalism in the long run hurt workers by forestalling unionism and efforts for a fairer and more reliable system of government-sponsored welfare.

The spread of Fordism led to the addition of white-collar managers, designers, researchers, and clerical staff to companies. Ford explained that in his system of production, the "mental load is shifted from men in production to men in designing." During the 1920s, the number of managers in the United States increased at a rate (29 percent) twice that of manual workers (14 percent). Universities created programs to meet the growing need for managers, and companies established their own research facilities, such as AT&T's Bell Labs, which opened in 1925. The number of research professionals nationwide increased nearly fourfold, from 2,775 in 1921 to 10,927 in 1933. Clerical work also expanded with the new emphasis on white-collar jobs and was redefined as a job for women rather than men. By 1920, more than 90 percent of stenographers who used a stenograph machine to take shorthand notes were women.

19-2c Mass Consumption

Increased production expands a culture of consumption.

The driving force for prosperity stemmed as much from mass consumption as it did from mass production. The wage bargain propelled consumer spending by putting more money into the pockets of workers. Sociologists Robert and Helen Lynd published a study depicting how consumption had become a universal fact of life in the "typical" U.S. city of Muncie, Indiana. Ball Corporation, a leading manufacturer of glass jars for canning, was located there. In the 1890s, Muncie residents had grown their own food, sewed their own clothing, and pumped water from their own wells. They moved about by horse, and because only 1 percent of homes had electrical service, their light came from candles and kerosene lamps. In the 1920s, when Ball was making not only canning jars but also glass insulators for electrical wiring and automobile engines, workers purchased groceries, ready-made clothing, and automobiles. At that time, 95 percent of homes had electrical service, and residents bought both electricity and water from the city. The Lynds documented a clear example of the spread of modernity.

welfare capitalism Alternative to labor unions whereby businesses took responsibility for the well-being of workers, including their wages, safety, health, housing, and general happiness.

marketing Business strategies including product differentiation, pricing, distribution, and advertising designed to increase the sales of goods and services.

Another sign of the modern consumer age was the use of **marketing** by U.S. firms. Although production involved making products, marketing addressed the best ways to inform consumers about them and to distribute them. Marketing experts relied on product differentiation, pricing, distribution, and, especially, advertising to make their products attractive and desirable. Marketing bolstered the demand for products to keep pace with the increasing supply. Ford learned about the importance of marketing the hard way. In the 1920s, rival General Motors surpassed Ford Motor Company in sales by offering a variety of car colors and appealing to different income levels through its five brands. In 1938, *Fortune* magazine described these as "Chevrolet for *hoi polloi*,. . . Pontiac for the poor but proud, Oldsmobile for the comfortable but discreet, Buick for the striving, Cadillac for the rich." Although the original Model-T had come in various colors, Ford limited it to black from 1914 until the end of its production in 1927 to speed production.

The beverage company Coca-Cola, which dominated the U.S. soft drink market by the 1920s, also attested to the importance of marketing. Unlike Ford, Coca-Cola had no production advantages over its competitors because many companies produced good-tasting cola drinks. What distinguished its product was marketing. The company sent an army of sales agents throughout the country to lock the

Coca-Cola Advertisement Testifying to the power of marketing is the fact that Coca-Cola and other leading brands of the 1920s remain widely recognized today, including Kellogg breakfast cereals, Del Monte canned fruit, Wrigley chewing gum, Gold Medal flour, Life Saver candies, Gillette razors, Crisco shortening, Ivory soap, Campbell soups, Lipton tea, Goodyear tires, and Colgate toothpaste. ▼
Archive Photos/Getty Images

nation's bottling manufactures and retail soda fountains in exclusive contracts preventing them from working for competitors or supplying their products. In addition to this massive distribution system, Coca-Cola engaged in intensive and costly advertising that gave its drink brand recognition by displaying the company symbol on lighted signs, billboards, bottle openers, clocks, and many other everyday objects.

Many national brands became internationally recognized during the 1920s through increasing exports, especially of automobiles. By 1928, more than 70 percent of all cars and trucks exported worldwide were made in the United States. Japan at that time bought almost all of its automobiles from the United States, and the Soviets invested heavily in Ford tractors. Meanwhile, U.S. news services, the Associated Press (AP) and United Press International (UPI), expanded their global reach, and U.S. films surpassed European ones in international popularity. U.S. films constituted 95 percent of those shown in Britain, 70 percent in France, and 80 percent in Latin America. These films, like the globalization of U.S. products, spread the nation's culture and lifestyles around the world.

19-3 Market Expansion

Among the many fads sweeping the United States during the 1920s was mahjong, a Chinese board game similar to the card game gin-rummy but with a more elaborate set of rules.

What does this photograph of the women playing mahjong suggest about international linkages at this time? What does it reveal about the expanding popularity of leisure activities? ▶

Library of Congress Prints and Photographs Division Washington, D.C. 20540 USA

Emergence of new forms of mass production and consumption made far-reaching changes in the nation's electrical and transportation networks, leisure culture, and business of loans and credit. The increase in consumer products, especially automobiles, undergirded the transformation of each area. New electrical power plants made it possible for more Americans, especially those outside cities, to enjoy vacuum cleaners and washing machines. Highway construction changed transportation by automobile. The expansion of leisure activities—such as organized sports and movies—and the increase of credit resulted from the efforts of businesses to create new domestic and global markets for their products.

☞ As you read, identify the impact of economic innovations and prosperity on U.S. society and culture. What types of products and leisure activities became popular? How did people get access to credit?

19-3a Infrastructure for Wires and Roads

{ Infrastructure improvements raise living standards and enable consumption.

Major improvements in the nation's infrastructure fueled consumerism. Breakthroughs in electrical technology expanded the capacity of central power stations to provide universal service to entire cities. Combined with the growth of indoor plumbing, electricity brought millions of new customers into the market for electrical appliances such as washing machines and refrigerators. Technological improvements in communication infrastructure also generated a robust market for radios and telephones, and the construction of gasoline pipelines hundreds of miles long ensured that automobile drivers would have a steady and inexpensive supply of fuel.

The nation's investment in highway construction literally paved the way for the expansion of automobile ownership. In 1916, 1921, and 1925, Congress increased funding for road improvement and created the numbered national highway system using the symbol of the shield. Federal involvement doubled the amount of paved highways from 257,291 miles in 1914 to 521,915 miles in 1926. Paved roads encouraged the growth of the trucking industry, which for the first time could compete for business with railroads. Farmers, who had long suffered under monopolistic railroad rates, were the first to rely extensively on trucking. Many other businesses used trucks and the highway system to grow from local to regional and even national companies. Milk sellers (dairies), for example, used refrigerated trucks and good roads to greatly expand their customer base by providing home deliveries.

The national highway system also made it easier and faster for people to move around the country, especially to the sparsely populated regions of the U.S. West opened by U.S. **Route 66**. Known as the "mother road," this highway began in Chicago where it connected hundreds of rural farm communities to the metropolis. It then followed an almost entirely paved "all-weather" road through the Great Plains and Southwest to end on the Pacific Ocean near Los Angeles, California. The new highway fed the population explosion in Los Angeles. The city doubled in size between 1920 and 1930, moving from tenth place to fifth on the list of the largest U.S. urban centers. Another major city that expanded with the automobile and highways was Houston, Texas. It more than doubled in size in the 1920s, moving from forty-fifth to twenty-sixth of the nation's largest cities. The expansion was caused by the many oil companies based in Houston, including what would become Texaco, Gulf, and Exxon, that supplied the increased consumer demand for gasoline.

Eastern cities, designed for getting around by foot and streetcar, had to adjust to new modes of transportation. Massive road construction linked them to each other and to surrounding communities. Cities such as New York City and Boston transformed the look and function of their streets by constructing wide boulevards and thoroughfares to accommodate automobile traffic.

19-3b Leisure and Popular Culture

> Businesses capitalize on the shorter workweek to expand commercialized culture and recreation.

The forty-hour workweek created the "weekend," a two-day break that gave workers time to engage in leisure activities previously reserved for wealthy individuals. In the late 1920s, a government committee led by Secretary of Commerce Herbert Hoover investigated the nation's recent social trends and found that Americans spent almost $10.25 billion per year on "leisure and recreation," equal to roughly 13 percent of the nation's total budget. The Hoover committee noted that in the 1920s, "the conception of leisure as 'consumable' began to be realized upon in business in a practical way and on a broad scale," which meant that fun, entertainment, and play had become a major market.

Expanding leisure time boosted urban entertainment in places such as bars, restaurants, nightclubs, and dance halls that catered to the increasing number of office workers, both men and women, who had more time for social activities. Unlike the utilitarian working-class saloons in the nineteenth century, these up-scale establishments were places where dress, manners, and dancing skills mattered. A population going out Friday night needed department stores, dance studios, and beauty parlors to get them ready, generating an extensive leisure economy.

Technological innovations and advertising built the radio and motion picture industries. The nation's radio infrastructure mushroomed virtually overnight from one station in 1920 to 623 at the decade's end. By 1929, 12 million Americans could tune in to music, sports, sermons, children's shows, and political speeches sponsored by advertisers eager to promote new products with this modern tool. Wireless radio was a marvel of technology that dramatically reduced distances and isolation among people in the United States and around the world.

At the same time, the audience for films more than doubled. In 1930, movie houses welcomed over 100 million patrons each week, out of a total U.S. population of only 123 million. As in the case of automobiles, Americans transformed films from artifacts of elite European culture to products of mass production and consumption. Silent films captivated audiences and established the first cohort of international movie stars including Charlie Chaplin,

Route 66 Transnational highway from Chicago to Los Angeles that boosted migration to urban centers and other parts of the West.

Movie Poster of *The Jazz Singer* (1927) The allure of movies took on an added dimension in 1927 when the combination of sound recordings and moving images created the first "talkie," *The Jazz Singer*, which starred Jewish American Al Jolson in a dramatic musical about the breakdown of religious traditions in a contemporary Orthodox Jewish immigrant family. The film's content, which included Jolson in "blackface," embodied the racial mores of the day. ▼

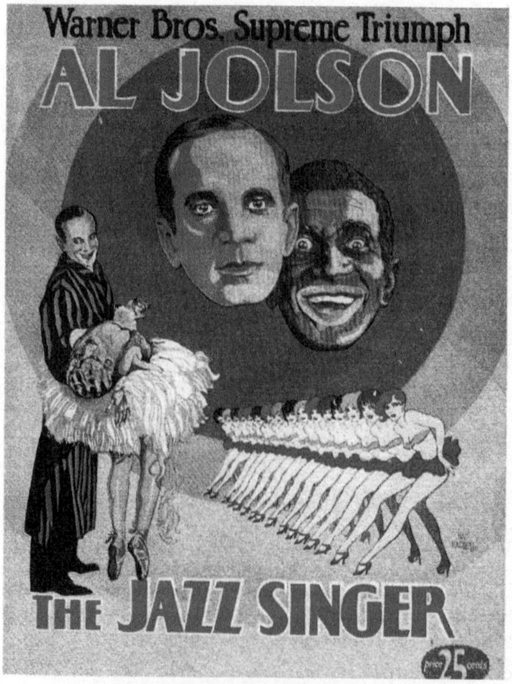

GAB Archive/Redferns/Getty Images

Mary Pickford, Douglas Fairbanks, Rudolf Valentino, and Sessue Hayakawa. The U.S. film industry was centered in the Los Angeles suburb of **Hollywood** where land was affordable, and the sunny climate made filming outdoors all year long possible.

Public money in the form of massive investments in popular recreation joined private money in expanding popular culture. The total acreage of city parks more than tripled during the first decades of the twentieth century, much of the growth occurring in the 1920s. During this decade, the number of golf courses and tennis courts tripled, and manufacturers of sporting goods experienced explosive success. The Rawlings Company reaped huge rewards when it had major league pitcher Bill Doak design the modern baseball glove by separating the thumb and forefinger with a few strands of rawhide leather. A rival company, Wilson, also innovated baseball equipment but became better known for creating the modern, double-stitched, valve-inflated leather football with the help of legendary Notre Dame University football coach Knute Rockne.

The use of celebrity advisers such as Rockne and Doak indicated the growing popularity of college and professional sports. During the 1920s, the audiences for and revenue from college football outpaced those of professional baseball. Celebrity players such as home-run hitter Babe Ruth led major league baseball to reach a new level of national interest. Radio broadcasts of baseball games created the new profession of sports reporting, and reporters and fans alike created a new language of statistics such as batting averages, pitcher's earned run average, and records for home runs in a season. Radio broadcasts and sports marketing developed further with the birth of the American Professional Football Association in 1920, which became the National Football League two years later.

In the late nineteenth century, wealthy Americans had toured the nation by rail, but the automobile revolution coupled with the expansion of leisure time transformed tourism into a mass phenomenon. Tourism often cultivated nostalgia for the past. Urbanites traveled to national and state parks to experience the great outdoors they had known on farms in their youth. With increased automobile access, attendance rates at national and state parks more than tripled. Hoover's committee on social trends calculated that nearly one-fourth of automobile use was for recreational purposes, leading to the emergence of road maps, guidebooks, roadside curio shops, diners, and motels. Curiosity about the past fueled a burst of museum building and historical projects such as the full-scale restoration of Virginia's Colonial Williamsburg started in 1926. In cities, ethnic enclaves such as Chinatowns, Little Tokyos, and Mexican barrios reinvented themselves as tourist markets, allowing white Americans to experience cultures that seemed frozen in time—pristine and untouched by the corrupting influence of modern, industrial society.

19-3c Credit and Crisis

The excess purchases of consumer goods leads to a revolution in the credit system.

Personal loans made possible the explosion of consumption during the 1920s. Banks had always loaned money to wealthy clients, and they began to do so to working-class people during this time. But when a worker was sick, injured, unemployed, or faced a family or household emergency, the only source of money was a pawnbroker or **loan shark**, who might charge 10 percent interest a month (185 percent per year) although the practice was illegal. To counteract loan sharking, twenty-five states, encouraged by social reformers, had passed consumer loan protection laws by 1928. Under these laws, interest was limited to 3.5 percent per month on loans under $300 and was charged only on the loan's unpaid balance. New retail loan businesses capitalized on the proliferation of automobile sales to expand their customer base beyond emergency payday lending. The stunning profits made in car loans enticed automobile makers and even conservative banks to follow suit. By 1927, more than 60 percent of automobiles had been bought on **installment plans**, as opposed to almost no such purchases in 1919. The extension of credit spread to many consumer goods from furniture to radios to washing machines. The expansion transformed the idea of personal debt for many Americans from a mark of immorality to a way to equalize class differences. As one truck driver put it, "with his radio receiving set the workman can now listen to grand opera singers whose voices formerly were heard only by the socially elect."

The democratization of credit also allowed more Americans, although rarely the working classes, to invest in the stock market. The center of global finance shifted after World War I from London to New York City. Soaring stock prices for U.S. firms attracted increasing numbers of investors, including banks, corporations, affluent people, and middle-class individuals who engaged in **buying on the margin**. They paid as little as 20 percent down and borrowed the rest from a broker. One historian calls the stock boom of the 1920s "massive, exhilarating, and foolish." Both investors and brokers made money as long as the market was up, but when stock prices dropped, those who had bought on margin lost their down payment and still owed interest and transaction fees.

The sector of the U.S. economy that suffered the most from credit problems during the 1920s was agriculture. Skyrocketing crop prices during World War I had pushed farmers

Hollywood Suburb of Los Angeles where movie studios began to concentrate in the early twentieth century.

loan shark Person loaning money at exceedingly high (and often illegal) interest rates and who took advantage of the most desperate classes.

installment plans Type of loan that boosted consumption by allowing a buyer to pay for products purchased over a given period of time.

buying on the margin Purchasing stock market securities by paying a fraction of the price and borrowing the rest from a stock broker.

to buy land to increase production, amassing debts. When agricultural prices fell sharply after the war—by 1921, the prices of wheat, corn, and hogs had fallen to less than half of their value in 1918—a farm crisis ensued (see Figure 19.2). Farmers' share of national income dropped from 16 percent in 1919 to less than 9 percent in 1929. Congress sought to resolve the farm crisis by approving the McNary-Haugen relief bill, which provided price supports for farm commodities. But price supports were controversial, and in 1927 and 1928, Coolidge vetoed the measure as violating the principles of laissez-faire. Farmers also failed to receive the same level of tariff protection from foreign imports given to manufacturers under the Fordney-McCumber tariff of 1922.

Despite agricultural depression, the outlook for the U.S. economy was bright in the 1920s compared to that for Europe. In Germany, war reparations contributed to hyperinflation that erased personal savings by reducing the value of the country's currency to virtually zero. This led sociologist Robert Lynd to lament the middle-class men and women in Berlin he saw lining up for free meals at soup kitchens. Large U.S. banks led by Morgan and Company supplied billion-dollar loans to Germany under the 1924 Dawes Plan and 1929 Young Plan that enabled Germany to pay its debts. In the late 1920s, U.S. loans and investments in Europe totaled more than $10.3 billion per year, contributing to the Americanization of European cities where U.S. consumer goods, foods, and fashions were widely advertised and in abundance. "Paris," reported the historian Charles Beard, "was plastered with American signs."

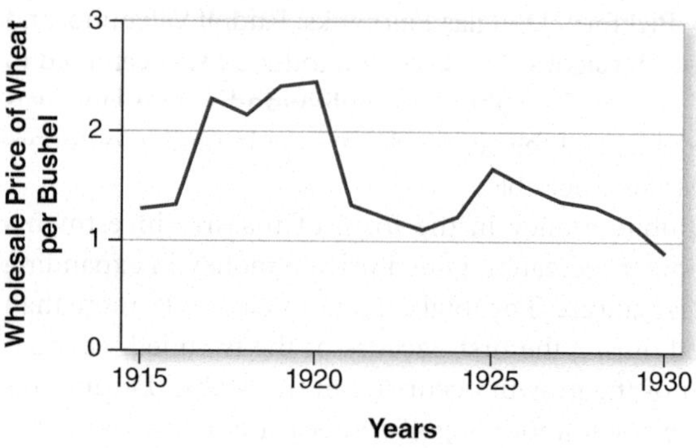

Figure 19.2 U.S. Wheat and Stock Prices, 1915–1930
The precipitous fall in wheat prices after World War I and throughout most of the 1920s created instability in U.S. agriculture. To compensate for the collapse in prices, farmers planted more crops, plowing up native prairie grasses and exposing the thin topsoil of the Great Plains to the ever-present wind. This created an environmental disaster in the making, especially in a season of drought. ▲ Source: U.S. Bureau of the Census. *Historical Statistics of the United States, Colonial Times to 1957.* Washington, D.C., 1960, 122–123.

19-4 Americanization

MPI/Getty Images

This cartoon, entitled "The Only Way to Handle It," appeared in the *Providence Journal* in 1921 when Congress considered restricting immigration by means of a quota system. What does the funnel represent? Recall the immigration flows into the United States in the late nineteenth century and the means by which progressives had attempted to deal with these newcomers.

Why were immigrants considered a problem that had to be "handled," and by what means did the United States erect a "gate" to limit them? ▶

In addition to rejecting the League of Nations and radicalism, the majority of Americans sought to remove foreign influence by painting the United States as a white, Anglo-Saxon Protestant nation. Major targets of this Americanization movement were new immigrants who were seen as inclined to radicalism, given to practicing strange religions, and spoke foreign tongues. Congress rejected the notion of the United States as a melting pot for the world's peoples, and for the first time limited European immigrants by national origin while excluding Asians completely. The restrictionist policies fit with a groundswell of conservative reform movements defending Prohibition, opposing ethnic and racial minorities, and promoting what were known as "traditional" values associated with small towns, white skin, Anglo-Saxon ancestry, and the Protestant faith. The rise of Fundamentalist Christianity and resurgence of the Ku Klux Klan were the more visible aspects of intolerance and cultural conformity that attracted many who were disillusioned by war, afraid of radicalism, and threatened by the dramatically increased numbers of African Americans and foreigners in U.S. cities.

☞ As you read, think about ways in which the drive for Americanization was consistent with the politics and economics of "normalcy." What did fears of immigrants, racial minorities, and secularization have in common?

19-4a Immigration Restriction

The nation ends unrestricted European immigration.

Evident during World War I, the momentum for immigration restriction gained strength after the peace. The causes were the Red Scare and fears that war-torn Europe would send boatloads of refugees and displaced persons to the United States. For the first time, immigrants were required to pass a literacy test. Southern and eastern Europeans and especially Asians were considered difficult, if not impossible, to Americanize, supposedly the result of immutable racial traits. Many of these immigrants were Jews and Catholics deemed incompatible with U.S. institutions and culture. In this context, restrictionists cast off the notion of America as a melting pot where peoples from all over the world were transformed into a common type and gradually made one community. On the one hand, Americans had been exposed to popular scientific theories in eugenics that seemed to prove that immigrants could degrade the U.S. racial stock (see Chapter 17). Eugenicists argued that in mixing with the older Anglo-Saxon stock of Americans, new immigrants had **mongrelized** the nation by lowering the quality of the intelligence, health, and propensity for democracy of its people. On the other hand, restrictionists condemned new immigrants not because they melted down, or assimilated, with Americans, but because they retained their foreign languages, cultures, and religions. Thus, immigrants were damned for contradictory reasons: because they blended in and because they did not.

During the postwar economic slump in 1921, Congress passed the Emergency Quota Act, which temporarily imposed the nation's first limit on total immigration, set at three hundred fifty thousand people per year, or about half the number of arrivals in that year. To restrict immigration from southern and eastern Europe even further, the act established a 3 percent quota for each nationality resident in the United States in 1910. Three years later, Congress replaced the temporary restrictions with the more severe **Immigration Act of 1924**, which reduced the annual limit by more than half to one hundred fifty thousand and further lowered the proportion of southern and eastern Europeans by setting national origins quotas to 2 percent of the nationalities resident in 1890, which was before the great surge of immigrants from those regions. The act also ended the Gentlemen's Agreement by disallowing, with minor exceptions, Japanese and any other "aliens ineligible to citizenship" from entering the United States (see Table 19.1). National origins quotas given to all nations

mongrelized Process that would result in a negative outcome if the introduction of "inferior" elements into a melting pot lowers the quality of a population.

Immigration Act of 1924 Legislation decreasing immigration to the United States that discriminated against southern and eastern Europeans as well as Asians.

Table 19.1 U.S. Immigration Restrictions, 1875–1924

Although the restriction of immigrants beginning in 1917 applied broadly to many groups based on literacy or national origins, most of the nation's restrictionist policies (including the 1917 and 1924 immigration acts) targeted Asian immigrants and other unwanted groups such as contract laborers, criminals, and persons likely to become a public charge.

Date	Law	Provisions
1875	Page Act	Prohibits immigration of Asian laborers forced into service, prostitutes, and convicts
1882	Chinese Exclusion Act	Prohibits immigration of Chinese laborers for a period of 10 years; renewed in 1892 and 1902, and made permanent in 1904
1882	Immigration Act	Imposes a head tax of 50¢; excludes "convicts, lunatics, idiots, or any person unable to take care of himself or herself without becoming a public charge"
1885	Alien Contract Labor Act	Prohibits importation of contract laborers but exempts professionals and skilled and domestic laborers
1907–1908	Gentlemen's Agreement	Ends immigration of Japanese laborers by agreement between President Roosevelt and Japanese officials
1917	Immigration Act	Establishes a literacy test requiring those over age 16 required to read 30–40 words in English or a language or dialect of their choosing, including Hebrew and Yiddish; 1 Asian exclusion by establishing an Asiatic Barred Zone (Japan exempted); expands excluded "undesirables" to include anarchists, epileptics, alcoholics, those with tuberculosis and other contagious diseases, polygamists, and prostitutes
1921	Emergency Quota Act	Sets quota[a] of 357,000 immigrants per year and limits numbers of each nationality to 3 percent of the number of that nationality in the census of 1910
1924	Immigration Act	Cuts quota[a] by more than half to 164,447, and recalculates numbers of each nationality to 2 percent of that nationality represented in the census of 1890. After July 1, 1927, quota[a] is 150,000 to be divided between countries in proportion to population in the census of 1920; Japanese immigrants excluded

[a]Quota laws do not apply to immigrants from Canada or Latin America.

and approved in 1929 favored those in western and northern Europe (see Map 19.2). The **National Origins System** required a new, complex immigration bureaucracy to track quota levels and waiting lists and to grant entrance visas to qualified applicants. To ease the overseas screenings, U.S. consular staff merged with the nation's diplomatic corps to form the modern Foreign Service. This change had a negative impact on black migration from English-speaking Caribbean islands (West Indies), which had flowed through a pipeline to New York City after the completion of the Panama Canal in 1914, enabling West Indian workers to follow their bosses back to the United States. Even though the national origins system did not restrict West Indians, U.S. officials in the Caribbean all but ended their migration by refusing to grant visas to nonwhites. As with Prohibition, immigration restriction was a conservative reform that greatly expanded the size and responsibilities of the federal government.

National Origins System Arrangement that established discriminatory quotas determining the number of immigrations per year for all nations and excluding all Asians.

So-called backdoor migration from within the Americas remained unrestricted. As had been true in the past, the largest number of these migrants came from Canada, and Mexicans joined the influx to U.S. cities, many as refugees fleeing the nation's prolonged civil war. Mexican immigrants went where work was available—to the steel mills of Pennsylvania and Indiana, the meatpacking houses of the Midwest, cement plants, railroad lines, and sugar beet farms in Colorado, Nebraska, and Michigan. Most ended up in the Southwest, where they had already worked as seasonal agricultural laborers in newly irrigated regions of Texas, Arizona, and southern California. In addition, Mexican immigrants became a major source of labor in the Texas cotton belt as landowners shifted from tenant sharecropping to temporary migrant labor. Filipino immigrants, whose status as U.S. colonial subjects allowed them to enter, unlike other Asians, came through a backdoor to fill Western farmers' labor shortages.

Native Americans, who had a much longer and more complicated history of being "wards of the state" than did Filipinos, received U.S. citizenship in 1924 as a reward for their service during the Great War and to encourage their assimilation to the U.S. culture and protection of tribal lands. Although some indigenous people already had received citizenship through the Dawes Act or by joining the U.S. military or marrying white U.S. men, the Indian Citizenship Act gave citizenship to three hundred

Map 19.2 U.S. Immigration Quotas by World Areas, 1929 The racial basis of U.S. immigration policy was evident according to which countries had an immigration quota, and of those that did, which had the highest quotas. The largest were given to Great Britain and Northern Ireland. Southern and eastern Europe received much lower quotas than northern and western Europe, and all of Asia, with the exception of the U.S. colony of the Philippines, was excluded. Blacks from the West Indies faced informal exclusion. Independent nations and League of Nations mandates were eligible for quotas, but not colonies. ▼

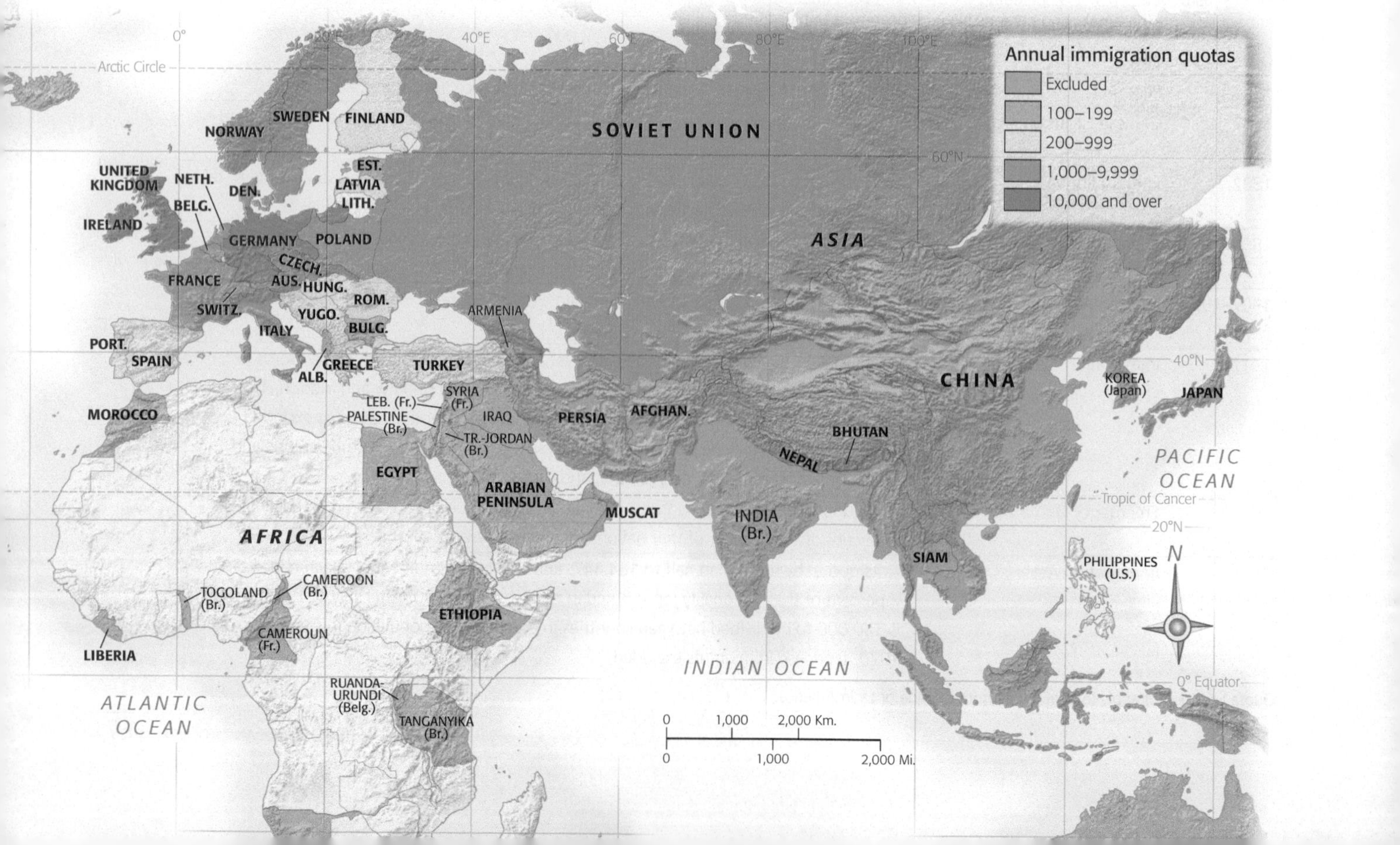

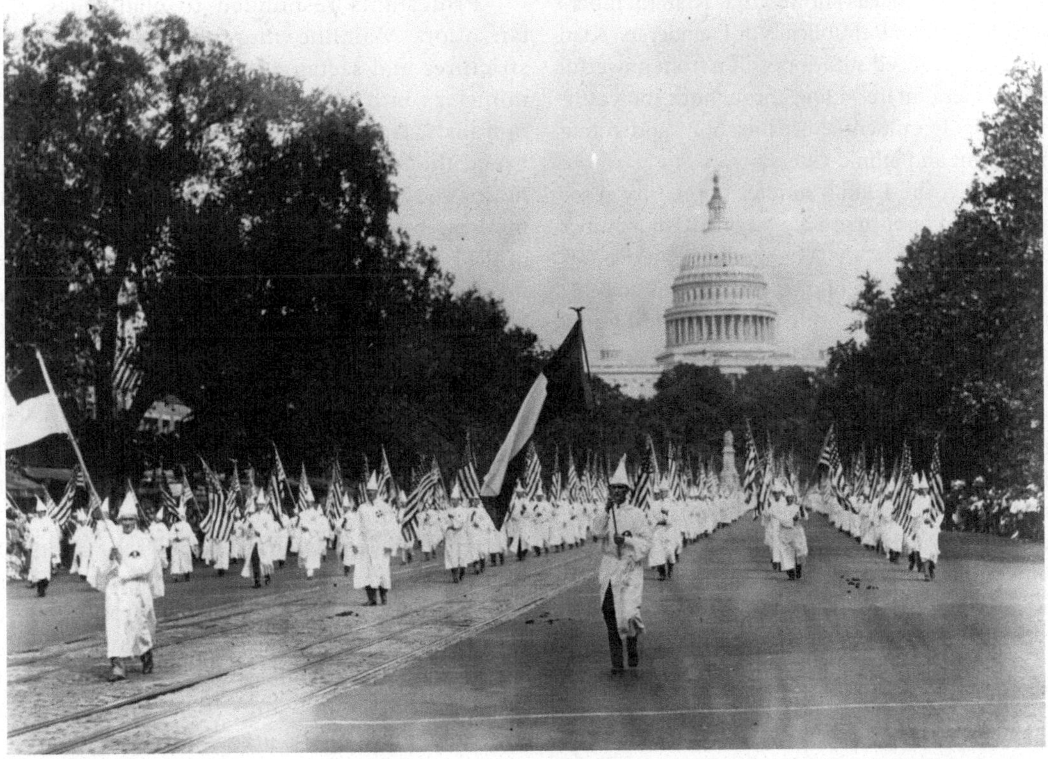
Topical Press Agency/Getty Images

Klan Marching in Washington, D.C., 1925 The rebirth of the Ku Klux Klan drew inspiration from Hollywood's first feature-length film, *Birth of a Nation* (1915). President Wilson had given his approval to this film adaptation of a novel and play, *The Clansman*, that portrayed Reconstruction as a criminal mistake and the KKK as the savior of both southern civilization and national reconciliation. The new Klan enjoyed major political success outside the South before it declined after 1925. ▲

thousand more individuals. But not all wanted to become American if this put in question their tribal sovereignty and citizenship.

19-4b Ku Klux Klan and Conservative Politics

Rural and small-town white Protestants fear displacement by foreigners and racial minorities.

Immigration restriction, business-friendly politics, and Prohibition were emblematic of a broad-based populism that galvanized white Protestant unity across sectional, class, and partisan divisions. Unlike the radical agrarianism of the late-nineteenth century Populist Party, this movement was concerned about cultural rather than economic displacement. Its leading symbol was the rebirth of the Ku Klux Klan during the late 1910s and early 1920s. Joined by as many as 5 million men and women, the **second Ku Klux Klan** spread beyond the South to the Midwest and was especially strong in Indiana. Klan members defended Prohibition and immigration restriction as the way to take back the country from "wets," foreigners, radicals, Catholics, and Jews.

Ku Klux Klan (second) Revival of racist domestic terror organization that grew outside the South and gained national recognition as a force in mainstream politics.

The Klan continued to use violence and terror, especially in the South. It also became a mainstream political force because a wide array of middle-class reformers, intellectuals, and elected officials who were not Klan members shared its brand of nativist conservatism. For example, U.S. icons such as Henry Ford and Charles Lindbergh also wished for a homogeneous white, Protestant nation and advocated theories of engineering a superior race of Anglo-Saxons. After the kidnapping and murder of his oldest child, Lindbergh fled his homeland to live in voluntary exile abroad, where his ambivalence about the modern United States became manifest as criticism of its low morals, high crime rates, drunkenness, and sexual impropriety.

Similar to the nativist Know-Nothings in the mid-nineteenth century, the second Klan suddenly burst on to the national political stage in the early 1920s to control state governments in Indiana, Colorado, Oregon, Oklahoma, and Alabama; and it also quickly collapsed. The momentum of the Klan declined after 1925 when its leader in Indiana was convicted of murder. Also, its members became disappointed when scandals involving the organization's public officials showed that Klan members were no more moral than Republicans or Democrats. Klan politicians in Indiana faced stiff opposition from powerful Republican business interests and throughout the country from increasingly influential organizations and voting blocs of immigrant and ethnic voters.

Internationally, the Klan's sudden popularity resonated with the rise of fascism in Italy. As one Klan member put it, the organization was "the Mussolini of America," as the result of the "vast volume of discontent in this country with things as they are." In both Italy and the United States, the growth of labor radicalism and the Communist Party stimulated the rise of conservative nationalism. Similarly, in postwar Germany, a small, right-wing fringe group, the **National Socialist German Workers' Party**, sought in 1923 to seize power in the German city of Munich. Led by the spellbinding orator Adolf Hitler, the Nazis, as they were called, sought to repair Germany's troubled economy and restore its national pride by reclaiming the nation from Communists, Jews, and liberals.

19-4c Secularization and Fundamentalist Christianity

Americans respond in different ways to the modernization of Protestantism.

Transformation of America's religious environment was another factor in the conservative groundswell. The horror of World War I had disillusioned many to the seemingly naïve message of universal brotherhood. The explosion of business and consumer cultures accentuated pleasure and materialism to an extent that was inconsistent with most Protestant practices. The nation's **secularization** was evident in the huge decrease in volunteers to serve as foreign missionaries (from twenty-seven hundred in 1920 to just two hundred twenty-five in eight years). The study of Muncie by the Lynds found that Methodists, Baptists, Congregationalists, Presbyterians, and other mainline faiths maintained a hold, especially on the working class, but church attendance (in general, 11 percent for men and 18 percent for women) was low. The Lynds placed part of the blame on leisure activities that took time away from church. In Muncie, the middle classes ranked the social status of ministers below that of the business and professional class.

National Socialist German Workers' Party German political party whose eventual leader, Adolf Hitler, promoted fascism as an alternative to communism.

secularization Process of decreasing the influence of religion and religious institutions in society.

fundamentalist churches Religious movement focusing on the literal meaning of the Bible and the second coming of Jesus Christ.

interdenominational Relating to more blurring lines between religious sects or denominations, such as between Methodists and Baptists.

Scopes trial Legal proceeding that found high school teacher John Scopes guilty of violating the Tennessee state law against teaching Darwinian evolution.

Protestants responded to challenges of secularization. Mainline churches loosened theological strictures and sectarian differences and transformed ministers into helpful counselors rather than stern moralists. Advertising executive Bruce Barton published the best-selling book, *The Man Nobody Knew*, noting the humanity of Jesus Christ as the "founder of modern business" who created and marketed one of the biggest organizations of all time. Henry Emerson Fosdick, a leading Protestant modernizer, looked beyond sectarian differences in stressing the need to make Christianity relevant to the times by emphasizing the Social Gospel movement. Fosdick ascended the pulpit of New York City's mammoth Riverside Church, an **interdenominational** bastion of liberal Christianity, when it opened through the financial graces of John D. Rockefeller Jr.

Opposing the liberals was a wide variety of conservative evangelical Protestants emphasizing the literal interpretation of the Bible and the second coming of Christ. Catering especially to the white and black working classes, the evangelicals flourished in the 1920s with the spread of Pentecostal and **fundamentalist churches**—many operating from homes and storefronts. In Los Angeles, evangelical faith healer Aimee Semple McPherson enjoyed a huge following including Hollywood celebrities who enjoyed her elaborate "illustrated sermons" complete with professionally designed sets, actors, and musicians. Church records claimed that 40 million visitors came to her Angelus Temple within seven years of its founding in 1923, and even larger audiences listened to her radio broadcasts.

Fundamentalists rejected modern science, specifically Charles Darwin's theory of evolution, which contradicted the Bible's version of human creation, and they succeeded in banning the teaching of evolution in public schools in Oklahoma, Florida, and Tennessee. In 1925, schoolteacher John Scopes became the center of a widely followed trial for teaching Darwin's theory in Dayton, Tennessee. William Jennings Bryan, former secretary of state and populist legend, was the prosecutor in the **Scopes trial**. Defending Scopes was renowned lawyer and avowed agnostic Clarence Darrow, who was assisted by the American Civil Liberties Union. Although Scopes was convicted and had to pay a $100 fine, the main attention focused on Darrow's questioning of Bryan's faith in the veracity of Biblical miracles. The U.S. and international press mocked Bryan's literal interpretation of the Bible, and the famed orator's death shortly thereafter seemed to his opponents to confirm the weakness of his claims. Yet the law against teaching evolution remained in Tennessee for more than forty more years.

19-5
Cultural Pluralism

Archibald Motley's *Octoroon Girl* portrays a beautiful, well-dressed woman in an elegant setting. Notice the leather gloves she is holding and the way she looks confidently at the viewer with calm grace. The only evidence of blackness is in the title of the painting: *Octoroon* denotes a person with one-eighth African ancestry.

Why do you think the artist choose the title *Octoroon Girl*? How did his choice embody his view of racism as well as the importance of combating class and gender stereotyping? ▶

Michael Rosenfeld Gallery

Go to MindTap® to practice history with the Chapter 19 **Primary Source Writing Activity: Cultural Pluralism.** Read and view primary sources and respond to a writing prompt.

Americanism was a conservative reaction to the nation's growing religious, cultural, and racial diversity that, in turn, prompted many Americans to reject intolerance and cultural conformity. According to the opponents of Americanism, the United States was like a jazz ensemble that emphasized spontaneity and freedom of expression in music rather than a marching band moving in lockstep to the same musical score. Novelist F. Scott Fitzgerald saw the impulse to reject old traditions and embrace new freedoms in the 1920s as indicative of what he called the **Jazz Age**. A generation of creative artists, urbanites, and youth embraced the 1920s as the time when the distance between strangers shrank and moral strictures relaxed. The "cultural pluralists" welcomed the continuation of migrations from the South that established the modern multiracial city with large populations of blacks, whites, and immigrants. Such urban centers gave rise to immigrant rights organizations and expressions such as *New Negro* and *New Woman* that sought liberation from the racial, sexual, and nativist policies perpetrated by conservatives. Thus, the opposition to conservative Americanization embraced a vision of the nation as a mosaic consisting of many peoples who would not and should not be melted down into one national culture.

☞ As you read, think about the concept of cultural pluralism. Who thought it was a positive attribute, and why?

19-5a Internal Migrations and the Multiracial City

Continued southern migrations generate new racial demographics in the nation's cities.

By cutting off immigration, the Great War and its subsequent restrictive legislation stimulated internal migration. During the war, northern industries sent labor recruiters south to fill jobs formerly taken by immigrants. Although jobs were plentiful in the North, Southerners also were pushed to migrate because of shaky cotton prices and a boll weevil infestation that threatened the crop's future. In 1920, the census recorded that for the first time, the majority of Americans lived in cities with a population of at least twenty-five hundred. More proof of a great urban migration came a decade later when it was revealed that one-tenth of all farmers (a total of 1 million people) had moved to town (see Figure 19.3).

African American migrants especially wanted to escape Jim Crow segregation. By 1930, more than 1 million of them had arrived in northern industrial cities, the continuation of the Great Migration begun during World War I (see Map 19.3). In that year, 21 percent of African Americans, including the writer Richard Wright, lived in the North, double the percentage in 1910. Wright had left Mississippi for Chicago in 1927 to be free of the religious strictures of his grandmother and the racism that dogged him at school and work. He recalled in his autobiography, "My sustained expectation of violence had exhausted me. My preoccupation with curbing my impulses, my speech, my movements, my manner, my expressions had increased my anxiety. . . . I could not make subservience an automatic part of my behavior."

African Americans from the South as well as immigrants from the Caribbean, Mexico, and Asia laid the foundations for the multiracial

Jazz Age Period characterized by the social and cultural freedoms epitomized by young adult Americans during the 1920s.

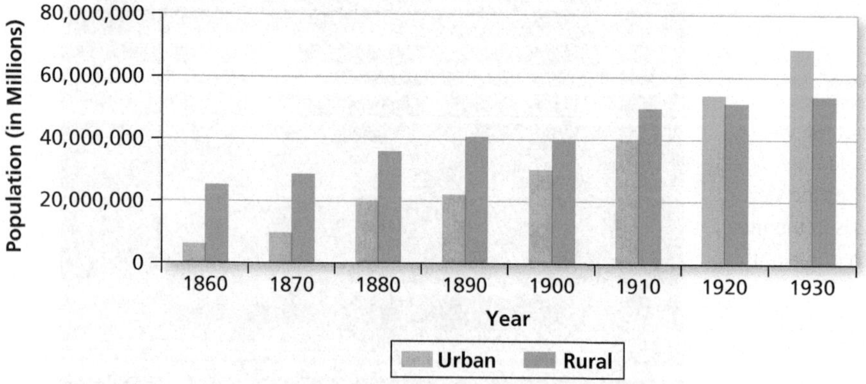

Figure 19.3 U.S. Urban and Rural Population, 1860–1930 This graph reveals the urbanization of the United States, showing that by 1920, the urban population had surpassed that of the rural population—and the disparity continued to increase during the 1920s. ◀

Source: U.S. Census

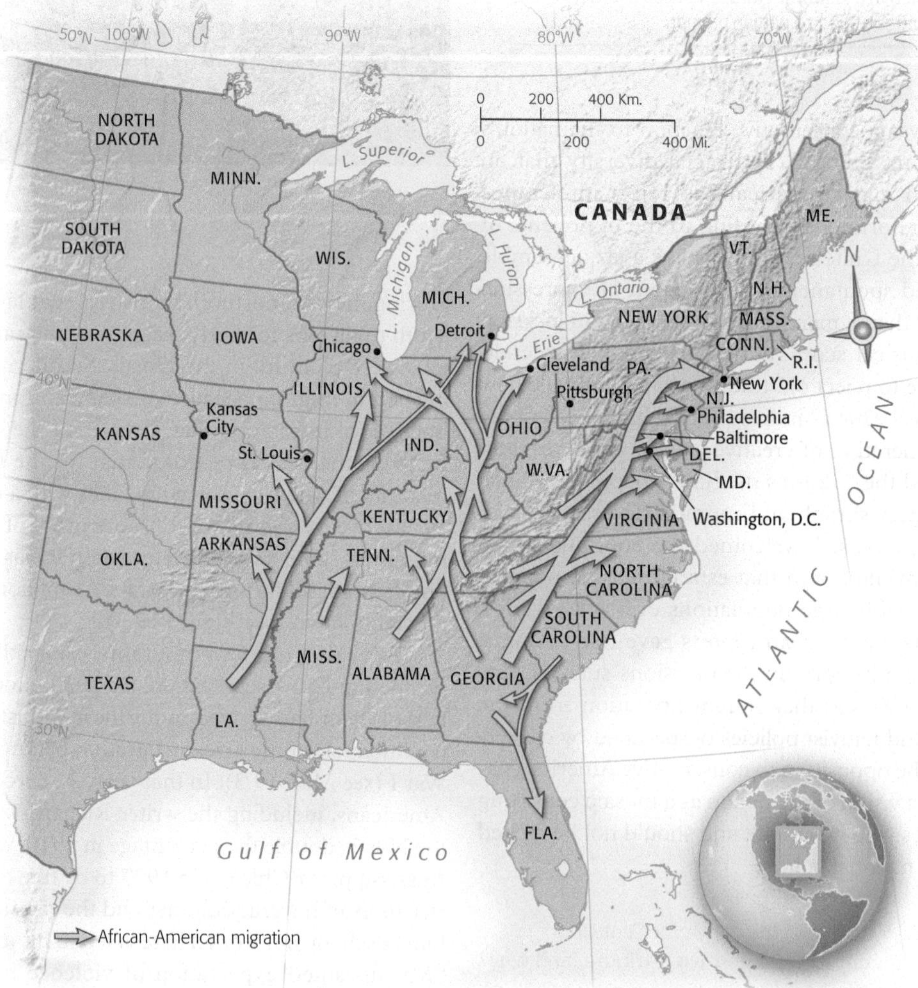

Map 19.3 Great Migration Migration pipelines channeled African Americans largely from the South to the North during and after World War I. To recruit blacks, a Cleveland factory official assured them that they would not be relegated to unskilled positions: "We have [black] molders, core makers, chippers, fitters, locomotive crane operators, melting furnace operators, general foremen, foremen, assistant foremen, clerks, timekeepers[;] in fact, there is no work in our shop that [you] cannot do and do well, if properly supervised." ▲

Keystone-France/Getty Images

Global Americans Born in St. Louis, Missouri, in 1906, **Josephine Baker** was raised in poverty by a single mother struggling to make a living in show business. By age thirteen, the young Baker dropped out of school and lived on the streets, scavenging for food in the garbage. Two years later, she was discovered dancing on street corners and became a performer in a stage show. From there, Baker went to New York City, where the Harlem Renaissance generated opportunities for her to perform in popular Broadway revues featuring all-African American casts, such as *Chocolate Dandies* in 1924. The next year she traveled to Paris to join a similar all-black revue. She was an immediate hit and became celebrated for her erotic style of dancing. Her breakout performance featured her dancing topless, clad only in a string of fake bananas dangling from her waist. A crucial part of Baker's persona embodied "primitive" African themes, which fit the modernist artistic movement that valued the supposed purity of nonwestern peoples unspoiled by capitalism and the modern world. She frequently danced on stage with her pet cheetah and could be seen walking it down the fashionable Champs-Elysee. Baker became the most popular American performer in Paris and a source of inspiration for the Lost Generation of expatriates. Ernest Hemingway called her "the most sensational woman anyone ever saw."

city. For the first time, nonwhite migrants rather than European immigrants became a growing and dynamic force in U.S. cities. But migrants of color were not always welcomed as the race riots of the Red Summer had attested. On the West Coast, immigrants from India and the Philippines endured forms of racist violence similar to those that African Americans suffered in the urban North, particularly concerning issues of housing. White residents relied on home owners' associations, real estate developers, bank lending policies, and urban planning to restrict nonwhite populations to the least desirable parts of a city. **Racial covenants**—private agreements that prevented owners from selling their homes to specific groups—also made moving into white neighborhoods difficult for racial minorities. The result was a concentration of ethnic groups in distinctive neighborhoods that developed unique subcultures.

The U.S. territory of Hawai'i had a different multiracial population: a small white planter oligarchy that ruled a labor force consisting of workers from Japan, the Philippines, Korea, China, Portugal, and Puerto Rico and oversaw an indigenous population of Hawaiians. In campaigning to make Hawai'i a state, planters sought to persuade a skeptical nation that the territory was a racial melting pot and members of its majority Asian population were capable of becoming good Americans. Congress, however, remained unconvinced. The workers on the islands took issue with the planter description of Hawai'i's "racial paradise" and accused the planters of pitting Japanese and Filipino workers against each other. In 1920, these groups overcame their antagonism to unite in the Great Hawai'i Sugar Strike that eventually led to increased wages and better labor conditions. Economic cooperation in this case proved stronger than racial division.

19-5b New Negro and Harlem Renaissance

African Americans assert race consciousness in cultural expression, economic endeavors, and politics.

The epicenter of urban black Americans became Harlem in New York City. It was not merely a large residential community for black migrants from the South and Caribbean but also a home to an ethnic infrastructure that included black-owned newspapers, local businesses and professional services, religious institutions, and various types of political organizations. Harlem advanced an assertive, unapologetic black identity that in 1925 Howard University philosopher Alain Locke dubbed the **New Negro**. In Harlem, as well as in Chicago's Bronzeville and many other black enclaves, New Negroes put a racial twist on mass consumption by buying and selling products, such as Madame C. J. Walker's hair-straightening agents, that reinforced race pride and solidarity. Black music, film productions, professional baseball leagues, and famous athletes such as world heavyweight boxing champion Jack Johnson were in their own ways expressions of the New Negro in a black world that provided its own identity, aesthetic, cultural symbols, and leisure activities.

In addition to being a center for jazz music, Harlem was home to an explosion of black expression in literature, the arts, dance, and scholarship. Culture makers of the

racial covenants Clause in property purchase agreements that maintained racial segregation by preventing the owner from selling the home to nonwhite racial groups.

New Negro African American identity during the Harlem Renaissance featuring the assertion of racial pride and the celebration of black history, culture, diaspora, and political power.

Harlem Renaissance addressed what it meant to be both American and black by engaging with what National Association for the Advancement of Colored People (NAACP) leader W.E.B. Du Bois called "two-ness": "two souls, two thoughts, two unreconciled strivings; two warring ideals in one dark body, whose dogged strength alone keeps it from being torn asunder." Writers, poets, and painters explored southern folk culture, the history of racism and its resistance, and persistent connections with Africa. Performers such as Josephine Baker took the New Negro identity to Paris, and her risqué cabaret act made her one of the most popular black stars overseas.

Du Bois and the NAACP focused on the natural leadership of the "talented tenth" of middle-class, educated African Americans in their push for civil rights reforms. In contrast, A. Philip Randolph, a black socialist and union leader, focused on the black working class. He organized black railroad porters into the Brotherhood of Sleeping Car Porters, a union that gained the favor of the Communist and Socialist Parties for its stand against exploitation that demanded "Fight or be Slaves." Nor did some artists, writers, and scholars of the Harlem Renaissance, including highly regarded jazz poet Langston Hughes, always agree with Du Bois. Although much of his poetry appeared in the NAACP's news organ, *The Crisis*, Hughes rejected the talented tenth strategy by appreciating the black "lowlife," including agricultural and industrial workers as well as their folk traditions. Hughes exposed what he perceived as a longing for whiteness among middle class blacks: "And so the word white comes to be unconsciously a symbol of all virtues. It holds for the children beauty, morality, and money. The whisper of 'I want to be white' runs silently through their minds."

Adored by millions during the 1920s, the most popular black leader was Marcus Garvey, a racial nationalist whose United Negro Improvement Association (headquartered in Harlem) advanced black economic empowerment. One of its ventures, the Black Star shipping line, offered African Americans transportation "back to Africa." Known for his **black nationalism**, the philosophy that saw blacks (not whites) as the global standard for civilization, Garvey proclaimed: "When Europe was inhabited by a race of cannibals, a race of savages, naked men, heathens and pagans, Africa was peopled with a race of cultured black men, who were masters in art, science, literature; men who were cultured and refined; men, who, it was said, were like gods." In truth, Garvey, the "black Moses," did not expect to lead a massive exodus of blacks from the United States, but his organization's promotion of black self-confidence and pride drew 4 million members worldwide.

Harlem Renaissance Explosion of African American creative expression centered in Harlem (New York City), Chicago's "black belt," and other urban centers.

black nationalism Expression of African American identity and pride that in extreme forms took precedence over U.S. nationalism.

Du Bois and Randolph criticized Garvey's Afrocentrism, deeming that the advocacy of black separatism was at odds with their aims of civil and economic rights. They were furious when Garvey met with Klan leaders to ask their support. Du Bois, Randolph, and other black leaders pushed Attorney General Palmer to expedite existing charges accusing Garvey of mail fraud related to his shipping line. In 1923, a federal court found him guilty and sentenced him to five years in jail. A year before he was to be released, President Coolidge commuted his sentence upon which Garvey was deported back to Jamaica. Although his back-to-Africa plans did not materialize, his Afrocentrism and racial separatism left a deep imprint in black America.

Library of Congress Prints and Photographs Division

Marcus Garvey Delivers "Constitution for Negro Rights," 1920 A migrant from Jamaica, Garvey preached that the highest achievement of black pride and culture was for African Americans to go back to Africa not figuratively through literature and art but by actually leaving the United States and establishing a new nation in Africa. He developed a huge following by catering to the often unschooled and unskilled masses whereas leaders such as W.E.B. Du Bois focused on the black elite and A. Philip Randolph on organized workers. ▲

19-5c Jazz Age Liberation

New musical styles reject cultural traditions.

Jazz, an entirely new type of popular music, emerged in the 1920s from a blending of African American musical traditions—West African call-and-response patterns, slave spirituals, gospel, blues, and ragtime—with Western classical music and marching band arrangements. More than just music, jazz was notorious

Corbis

Races Mix at Nightclub in Harlem, 1929 Nightclubs in urban centers such as New York City became places of interracial mingling during the 1920s. White youth flocked to Harlem and other black communities to hear live jazz music performed by African American musicians. ▲

for its sensuality and racial impropriety as a form of "black music" that delighted white audiences. No one embodied the spirit of jazz more than Louis "Satchmo" Armstrong. Born poor and fatherless in 1901, he possessed natural musical gifts that developed as he sang for money on the streets of New Orleans, played gigs in the city's red-light district, and received music lessons at a home for black juvenile delinquents. By the early 1920s, Armstrong came under the tutelage of Joe "King" Oliver, then one of the best musicians in New Orleans who would be drawn to the emerging jazz mecca of Chicago. Armstrong followed and soon shuttled back and forth between Chicago and New York City playing and recording with the leading jazz bands and singers. His own gravelly voice and virtuoso trumpet playing became widely recognized. In 1929, his rendition of the popular song "Ain't Misbehaving" proved a crossover hit that helped to catapult jazz into the orbit of mainstream music.

A younger generation of white Americans—writers, artists, and musicians—were drawn to the rhythms and culture of jazz. During the Jazz Age, a younger generation of writers, including F. Scott Fitzgerald and Ernest Hemingway, fled to Paris, where they gathered with other American expatriates and drew inspiration from modern European writers, artists, and intellectuals. Hemingway, who had volunteered as an ambulance driver for the Red Cross during World War I, typified the "lost generation" that he portrayed in *The Sun Also Rises* (1926). Once attracted by the notion of heroism, these young people were disillusioned by the reality of war. Scarred, even disfigured, they struggled to find meaning to their lives outside the United States.

Other members of the postwar generation sought the cultural liberation that cities offered. The New Woman embraced independence and individual freedom, exemplified in the extreme by the **flapper**, a middle-class, often college-educated woman who dressed daringly, cut her hair short, listened to jazz, smoked, drank alcohol, and claimed sexual autonomy and pleasure. Fitzgerald depicted flappers as rebels who refused to be domesticated wives and mothers. The author's wife and muse, Zelda Sayre Fitzgerald, was a prominent flapper, as were screen stars Louise Brooks and Clara Bow and poet Edna St. Vincent Millay, each of whom was known for flaunting sexual norms. More generally, the decade celebrated a youth culture. Since the beginning of the twentieth century, the nation's birth rate had declined steadily, and with fewer youth under pressure to enter the job market, the period of adolescence expanded. New compulsory education laws kept young people in school through high school, increasing enrollments by 650 percent between 1900 and 1930, with most of the growth coming during the 1920s. For the first time, the vast majority of American teenagers went to school, and an increasing percentage of them continued on to college. In their study of Muncie, Indiana, the Lynds found that public schools, most of which were coeducational and had a wide

flapper Cultural rebel during the 1920s who opposed feminine conventions and expectations through dress, speech, writing, personal style, interracial relations, and sexuality.

Ernest Hemingway and Sylvia Beach infront of the 'Shakespeare and Company' bookshop, Paris, 1928 (b/w photo)/ Bridgeman Images

Lost Generation in Paris A young generation of U.S. artists and writers including F. Scott Fitzgerald and Ernest Hemingway gathered in Paris and other places outside the United States during the 1920s to partake in artistic, ideological, and racial freedoms not possible at home. In this 1928 photo Hemingway (far right) appears with Sylvia Beach (second from right) and others outside of Beach's Shakespeare and Company bookstore in Paris. ▲

range of socioeconomic classes, had become the central meeting places for young men and women, who engaged in new rituals such as going on "dates," "petting," seeing movies, and taking drives in automobiles. Yet premarital sexual intercourse remained taboo.

So too did same-sex erotic relations, which were banned by sodomy laws throughout the states. The term *homosexual* had been coined in the late nineteenth century by a German psychologist, and during this time some doctors sought to "cure" people of same-sex desires. Jazz Age freedoms extended as well to sexual minorities, who mixed freely within the heterosexual spaces of Harlem and other sites of social experimentation. The concentration of bars, restaurants, and dance clubs that drew gay, lesbian, transgendered, and bisexual clientele amounted to **"gay ghettos"** in New York City's Times Square and Greenwich Village, Chicago's Southside, and San Francisco's North Beach neighborhoods. To find these communities, one often needed a special guidebook, or word of mouth, and in this way, they thrived in the semisecretive world of the speakeasy where people defied Prohibition by drinking alcoholic beverages.

gay ghettos Hidden bars, restaurants, nightclubs, or speakeasies in which gay men, lesbians, and other sexual minorities gathered and socialized.

19-5d Immigrant Generations and the Election of 1928

Catholics and Jews promote cultural pluralism.

Like Protestants, Catholics faced a growing division between new and older immigration groups as Church leadership—which was dominated by the Irish, Germans, and other older immigrant groups—responded to World War I by embracing Americanization and seeking to homogenize ethnic differences among congregations. In contrast, new Catholic immigrants, including Italians, Poles, Slovaks, and Mexicans, sought to maintain their own religious traditions. Jewish temples faced a similar division as the older and more established wave of German Jews pushed a liberal Reform faith against the wishes of the more Orthodox new immigrants from eastern Europe. These newcomers whose Yiddish language, working-class identity, and tendency toward labor radicalism exacerbated the theological conflict. Jews were also split by differences over Zionism, the quest for a Jewish homeland. In addition, both Catholics and Jews experienced a generational split as the sons and daughters of immigrants sought independence from their homeland traditions.

The Ku Klux Klan targeted new immigrants as much as blacks, a fact that gave Jews and Catholics cause to organize their own efforts on behalf of ethnic identity, pride, and self-defense. Harvard-trained philosopher Horace Kallen provided an overarching rationale for these new immigrants' resistance to Americanization. A German Jewish immigrant himself, Kallen advanced the notion that democracy in the United States did not require a melting pot in which everyone shared one culture. He argued instead that "in society each ethnic group is the natural instrument, its spirit and culture are its theme and melody, and the harmony and dissonances and discords of them all make the symphony of civilization." Amid the controversy over immigration in 1924, Kallen called the democratic harmonizing of differences "cultural pluralism."

Campaigns for immigration restriction also united Catholics and Jews. Established in 1919, the National Catholic Welfare Council brought various ethnic churches together to oppose Prohibition, immigration restriction, and education laws that disadvantaged parochial schools. New Jewish immigrants formed the American Jewish Congress in 1918 to compete with the older German Jewish-led American Jewish Committee. But both organizations, as well as a third, B'nai B'rith's Anti-Defamation League, opposed the Klan's anti-Semitism and eugenic preference for white Nordic peoples. The organizations opposed Henry Ford's weekly newspaper, the *Dearborn Independent*, for the same reason. Speakers at a New York Jewish forum in 1924 denounced "Fordism, Nordism, and Klanism."

The clash between white Anglo-Saxon Protestant (WASP) conformity and cultural pluralism came to a head in the presidential election of 1928, which pitted Herbert Hoover, Coolidge's secretary of commerce, against the Democrat Al Smith. The first Catholic presidential candidate to be nominated by a major political party, Smith campaigned against Prohibition and for progressive social reforms that he, as New York's long-standing governor, had championed. Republicans countered by underscoring the nation's booming economy and benefited from popular fears that if elected, Smith would take his orders from the Pope. In the end, Hoover won by a landslide with more than 58 percent of the popular vote and more than 83 percent of the electoral vote. The Republicans, for the first time, made inroads into the solidly Democratic South. One reporter noted that Smith was defeated by the three Ps: "Prohibition, Prejudice, and Prosperity."

Summary

The United States in the 1920s was marked by Fordism, Nordism, and Klanism as well as the rise of the New Woman, New Negro, and new consumer culture, the latter of which built domestic and global markets for consumer goods and credit. Although each of these developments including that of the League of Nations had important roots in the years before World War I, they blossomed in the decade after the Treaty of Versailles. The horrors of the Great War caused Americans to retreat from the wartime vow to "make the world safe for democracy." Although the United States became a leader in international arms control and in economic and financial global integration, the nation turned inward, first to manage threats from radicalism and then to install a conservative, probusiness ethic that countered Communist calls for social equality with the realities of prosperity and consumer freedoms. Republican presidents Harding and Coolidge celebrated mass production and consumption that were epitomized by the popularity and profitability of the automobile.

The nation also managed modernity by advancing Progressive causes such as Prohibition and immigration restrictions that were designed to suppress the nation's ethnic, cultural, and religious diversity. The influx of black and white Southerners to northern and western cities and migrations of Mexicans, West Indians, and Asians created multiracial demographics that induced a conservative popular movement in which millions joined the new Ku Klux Klan to assert the primacy of white Protestant power. Charles Lindbergh went into exile disgusted by what he considered to be the dangerous mix of radicals, criminals, and anti-Prohibition "wets". Many free-thinking artists and writers disillusioned by the Great War also left the United States because it was too conservative, not too chaotic.

Meanwhile, an array of groups championed a new assertiveness and pride for women as well as ethnic, racial, religious, and sexual minorities. The Harlem Renaissance and flappers were expressions promoting cultural liberation from racist and Victorian traditions. Jim Crow segregation, immigration restriction, and Prohibition were contested by a variety of ethnic and religious organizations including the NAACP, Garvey's United Negro Improvement Association, the National Catholic Welfare Council, and the Anti-Defamation League. But the election of the Republican Herbert Hoover as president in 1928 revealed the continued strength of conservatism in the midst of rising demands for cultural pluralism.

<Thinking Back, *Looking Forward*>

As you review this chapter, trace the roots of U.S. economic, political, and international developments during the 1920s to the widespread impact of industrialization during the late nineteenth and early twentieth centuries. How were the 1920s influenced by U.S. businesses, labor relations, immigration, and progressive attempts to humanize the excesses of industrialization? In the next chapters, pay attention to how the developments of the 1920s were responsible for the origins of economic catastrophe and another world war.

To make your study concrete, review the timeline and reflect on the entries there. Think about their causes, consequences, and connections. How do they fit with global trends?

Additional Resources

Books

Baldwin, Davarian L. *Chicago's New Negroes: Modernity, the Great Migration, and Black Urban Life*. Chapel Hill: University of North Carolina Press, 2007. ▶ Studies black consumption, entrepreneurship, and celebrities in 1920s Chicago.

Dumenil, Lynn. *The Modern Temper: American Culture and Society in the 1920s*. New York: Hill and Wang, 1995. ▶ Classic account covering the major topics of the decade.

Grandin, Greg. *Fordlandia: The Rise and Fall of Henry Ford's Forgotten Jungle City*. New York: Metropolitan Books, 2009. ▶ A journalist's examination of an intriguing, though failed, attempt to spread Fordism to the Brazilian rainforest.

Gregory, James N. *The Southern Diaspora: How the Great Migrations of Black and White Southerners Transformed America*. Chapel Hill: University of North Carolina Press, 2005. ▶ Original analysis of the major demographic shifts during the 1920s.

Hyman, Louis. *Debtor Nation: The History of America in Red Ink*. Princton, NJ: Princeton University Press, 2011. ▶ Book that explains the origins of the widespread emergence of credit during the 1920s.

Iriye, Akira. *Global Community: The Role of International Organizations in the Making of the Contemporary World*. Berkeley: University of California Press, 2004. ▶ Discussion by a prominent international historian of the origins of today's global community.

Lauren, Paul Gordon. *Power and Prejudice: The Politics and Diplomacy of Racial Discrimination*, 2nd ed. Boulder, CO: Westview, 1996. ▶ Broad global history that examines racial politics in the League of Nations and other institutional bodies during the 1920s.

Lynd, Robert Staughton, and Helen Merrell Lynd. *Middletown: A Study of American Culture*. New York: Harcourt Brace, 1929. ▶ Classic study of life in the average U.S. town of Muncie, Indiana.

MacLean, Nancy. *Behind the Mask of Chivalry: The Making of the Second Ku Klux Klan*. New York: Oxford University Press, 1995. ▶ Analysis of the rise of the Klan in the 1920s with some comparisons of movements in Europe.

Ngai, Mae M. *Impossible Subjects: Illegal Aliens and the Making of Modern America*. Princeton, NJ: Princeton University Press, 2004. ▶ Important study of U.S. immigration law and politics that starts with the Immigration Act of 1924.

Rosenberg, Emily. *Spreading the American Dream: American Economic and Cultural Expansion, 1890–1945*. New York: Hill and Wang, 1982. ▶ Time-tested account of expanding U.S. consumer and cultural influence around the world between the world wars.

Go to the MindTap® for **Global Americans** to access the full version of select books from this Additional Resources section.

Websites

The Great Gatsby at New Student Reading Project, Cornell University. (http://reading.cornell.edu/reading_project_06/gatsby/jazz_age.htm). ▶ Collection of many resources regarding the famous book, its author, and the period.

Harlem Renaissance at the Library of Congress. (http://www.loc.gov/teachers/classroommaterials/primarysourcesets/harlem-renaissance/). ▶ Outstanding collection of primary sources including songs, literary works, and images.

League of Nations Photo Archive. (http://www.indiana.edu/~librcsd/nt/db.cgi?db=ig&do=search_results&mh=12&sb=Notes&Cat=Secretariat). ▶ Information and photographs about this important organization.

Monkey Trial at PBS. (http://www.pbs.org/wgbh/amex/monkeytrial/index.html). ▶ Website for film devoted to the Scopes trial with primary sources, songs, and an opinion poll about teaching evolution in public schools.

The Roaring Twenties at the Gilder Lehrman Institute of American History. (https://www.gilderlehrman.org/history-by-era/progressive-era-new-era-1900-1929/roaring-twenties). ▶ Primary sources and essays about the era written by prominent historians.

MindTap®

Continue exploring online through MindTap®, where you can:

- **Assess your knowledge with the Chapter Test**
- **Watch historical videos related to the chapter**
- **Further your understanding with interactive maps and timelines**

Managing Modernity

1919

January

Eighteenth Amendment is ratified, beginning Prohibition.

February

Pan-African Congress meets in Paris amidst peace conference ending World War I.

March

Communist International is established to counter capitalism around the world.

June

League of Nations is established.

Marcus Garvey's organization establishes Black Star shipping line to return American blacks to Africa.

November

U.S. Attorney General A. Mitchell Palmer begins three-month crackdown on suspected domestic terrorists.

1920

January

Japanese, Filipino, and other workers unite in the Great Hawai'i Sugar Strike.

August

Nineteenth Amendment is ratified, giving women the right to vote.

September

Anarchists explode bomb on Wall Street, killing thirty-eight.

November

Harding (Republican) wins presidential election, and socialist Eugene V. Debs garners more than 1 million votes.

1921

May

Emergency Quota Act imposes first limit to immigration to the United States, enacting restrictions based on national origin.

July

Chinese Communist Party founded in Shanghai, China.

November

Harding signs Sheppard-Towner Act funding maternity and health care services.

1922

Louis Armstrong moves from New Orleans to Chicago to play in a popular jazz band.

February

Five-Power Naval Limitation Treaty agreement is reached during Washington Naval Conference.

September

Fordney-McCumber tariff increases U.S. protectionism against foreign competition in farm and industrial products.

October

Benito Mussolini becomes prime minister of Italy.

December

Soviet Union is founded with Vladimir Lenin as head of state.

1923

January

Angelus Temple opens, housing Aimee Semple McPherson's exciting brand of international Christian evangelism.

July

Federal court imposes five-year sentence on black leader Garvey for mail fraud.

August

Coolidge (Republican) becomes president after Harding's death.

August–September

Italy bombs Greek island of Corfu.

1924

Ford Model-T automobile sells for lowered price of $290.

January

Joseph Stalin becomes leader of the Soviet Union.

April

Fitzgerald and his wife Zelda Sayre Fitzgerald become part of the "Lost Generation" in Paris.

May

Immigration Act further reduces immigration by lowering annual quotas. Japanese immigrants excluded.

November

Ku Klux Klan wins control of state governments in Indiana and Colorado.

1925

Alain Locke declares the "New Negro."

Archibald Motely unveils *Octoroon Girl* exposing injustice of antiblack prejudice.

July

John Scopes is tried for teaching Darwinian evolution, and is found guilty after a dramatic defense.

1926

Ford Motor Company cuts workweek to five days.

November

U.S. Route 66 becomes one of the first roads within the U.S. highway system.

1927–1928

The Jazz Singer, starring Al Jolson, becomes the first feature-length "talkie" film.

May 1927

Charles Lindbergh is the first to fly solo across the Atlantic.

August 1927

Execution of convicted murders Nicola Sacco and Bartolomeo Vanzetti provokes anti-American protests around the world.

August 1928

Germany, France, and the United States sign toothless Kellogg-Briand treaty.

November 1928

Hoover (Republican) defeats Al Smith (Democratic) in presidential election.

1929

U.S. proportion of global production is coal (40%), steel (50%), gasoline (70%), and automobiles (90%).

July

Armstrong records popular cross-over hit "Ain't Misbehaving."

Go to MindTap® to engage with an interactive version of the timeline. Analyze events and themes with clickable content, view related videos, and respond to critical thinking questions.

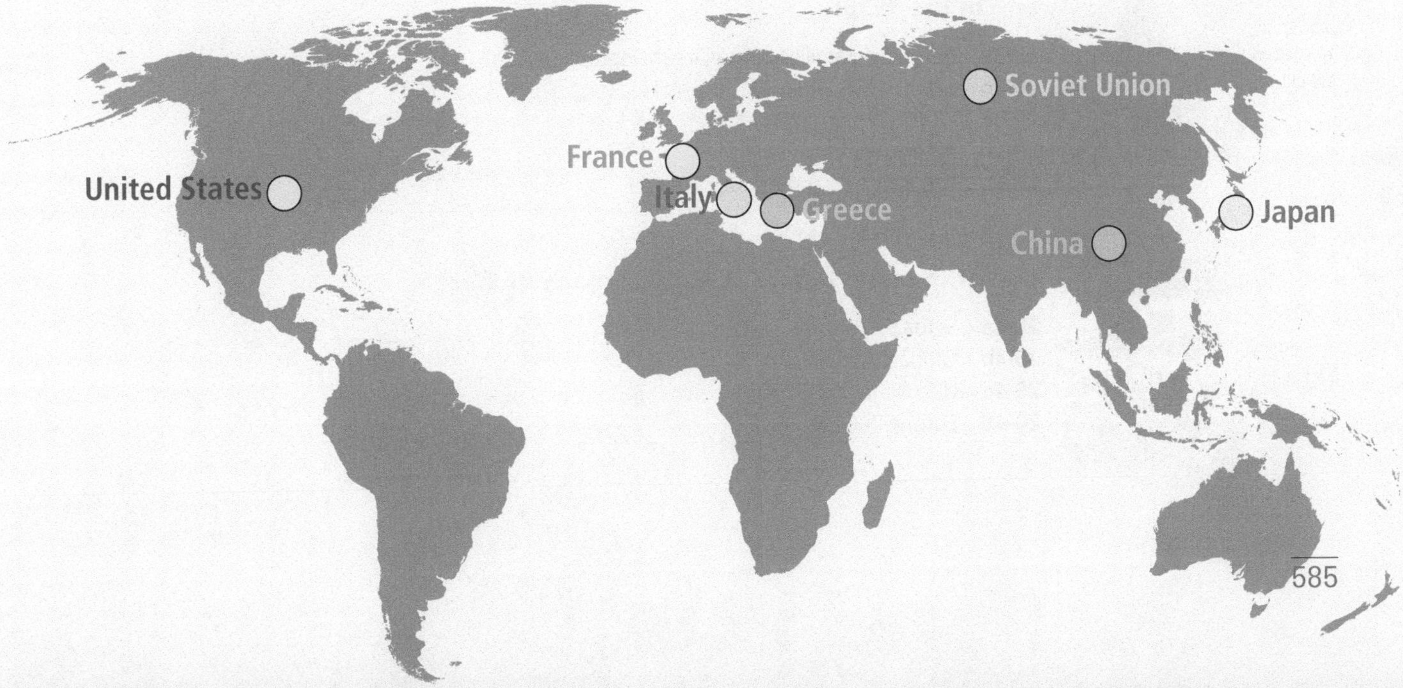

20 Great Depression, New Deal, and Impending War

1929–1939

As a federal relief worker, Fabiola Cabeza de Baca crossed many social and cultural borders and drove thousands of miles, all within Santa Fe County.

When thirty-five-year-old Fabiola Cabeza de Baca began her job as a home demonstration agent in 1929, she set out on the great adventure of her life. Her job was to aid New Mexico farmers and their families, but she could not have known how impoverished they would be as the world plunged into the most severe economic depression of all time. Through the food she cooked and garden clubs she organized, she taught white, Hispano, and Pueblo farm women how to stretch their meager resources—the pickings from a garden, the last sheep for butchering, a bolt of cloth for winter clothes. She promoted good home management, helped women obtain canning equipment and sewing machines, and found a way for women's traditional weaving and needlework to reach a growing tourist market.

Traveling alone, she drove thousands of miles across mountains and deserts that lacked modern roads. The job and its demands were immense. "A home demonstration agent," she later recalled, "started her day no later than six o'clock in the morning and returning home as late as midnight at times." When she was at her busiest in 1932, she was in an accident. Her car stalled on a railroad track where it was hit by a train, severing her leg and leaving her face permanently disfigured. But by 1934, she was driving again and back at work.

Fabiola Cabeza de Baca, Gilbert Photograph Collection, Center for the Southwest Research, University of New Mexico

Fabiola Cabeza de Baca in Front of a New Mexican Schoolhouse, circa 1920s ▲

In these years, Cabeza de Baca crossed social and cultural borders, all within Santa Fe County. Her work bridged the divide between white governmental reformers from the East and the world of rural New Mexicans. She wrote weekly newspaper columns in Spanish and spoke the native languages when she visited Pueblo homes. She brought modernity to a society still deeply rooted in historic practices. The encounter was sometimes difficult, because her clients did not always want to be Americanized or to accept modern ways of cooking and housekeeping. At the same time, the government bureaucracies, both state and federal, had no means of accommodating the complexity of Hispano and Indian cultures. Cabeza de Baca tried to bridge the two worlds. In her later life, she wrote cookbooks with recipes that used the traditional ingredients and practices she had observed in her home demonstration work but also incorporated the use of modern kitchen technology such as pressure cookers to save time and preserve food.

For Cabeza de Baca and those who worked for or benefited from state and federal relief agencies during the Great Depression, the experience transformed their lives. Many were absolutely destitute. Following the stock market crash in 1929, U.S. financial institutions and industries collapsed. Millions lost their jobs, savings, farms, and homes—literally everything they had. Private charities could not cope with the crisis, and the federal government, through programs established under President Franklin D. Roosevelt, took on the well-being of citizens as a federal responsibility. For the first time, the federal government played a major role in the economic, social, and cultural lives of ordinary Americans. Following a rush of legislation to stop the economy's downward spiral, Roosevelt implemented structural reforms

How does Fabiola Cabeza de Baca's service during the Great Depression reflect a shift in the role the federal government played in the lives of ordinary Americans?

Go to MindTap® to watch a video on Cabeza de Baca and learn how her story relates to the themes of this chapter.

in the nation's labor relations and welfare system to ensure stability. Government intervention in the economy regulated markets and created jobs but did not end the Depression. Toward the end of the decade, however, national attention was increasingly diverted by conflicts in Europe and Asia.

The United States was not the only nation in crisis in the 1930s. The severe downturn caused European economies to collapse, and many of the fragile new democracies established after World War I did not survive. Dictators took over—most notably in Italy, Germany, and Spain—reshaping national economies to militaristic purposes. Their societies under total government control were not unlike that of the Soviet Union, where another dictator under the banner of communism also directed the economy and subordinated the rights of citizens to the needs of the state. In Asia, the rising power of Japan led by a military faction similarly threatened the nations of East Asia. By 1939, aggression in Europe and Asia had engulfed much of the world—but not yet the Western Hemisphere—in war.

20-1 Enduring Economic Collapse

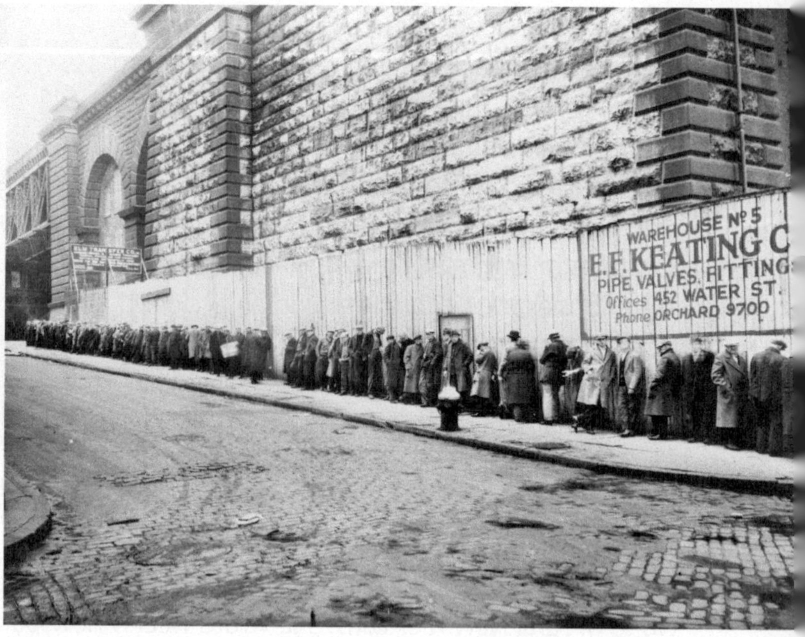

The Granger Collection, New York

In the early 1930s, bread lines formed in cities and small towns, wherever private charities offered free food. This one is in Manhattan, New York, under the Brooklyn Bridge.

What events compelled these people to join the line? How did receiving aid influence people's ideas about self-reliance? ▶

Go to MindTap® to practice history with the Chapter 20 **Primary Source Writing Activity: Experiences of the Depression.** Read and view primary sources and respond to a writing prompt.

In 1929, the U.S. economy collapsed, sending the nation into a deep economic depression from which it would not recover for more than a decade. From rural hamlets to urban centers, Americans suffered a loss of jobs, income, and wealth. The Depression quickly spread through Europe, Asia, and Latin America, which were linked to the United States by trade and finance. The Hoover administration took steps to cushion the impact of the economic downturn, but they were not enough. The Depression grew worse. In 1932, voters were ready for new leadership and elected Franklin Delano Roosevelt, a Democrat to the presidency. He promised bold programs to boost the economy into recovery and pledged "a new deal for the American people."

☞ As you read, assess the relationship between the U.S. and global economies. Why and how and did the Great Depression engulf so many nations around the world?

20-1a Stock Market Crash and Its Impact

Although the 1920s seemed prosperous, in reality wealth was unequally distributed, stocks were overvalued, and the global economy as a whole was unstable. Farmers both at home and abroad who had overproduced during World War I and its aftermath faced declining demand and agricultural prices. They could not meet their increasing debts and began to default on loans and leave their farms. Production of consumer goods soared during the 1920s, but the wages of the workers who produced them did not. Few could buy what they made. As consumer goods were stockpiled and demand dropped, the economy softened. Farmers and most workers did not realize the gains of the roaring twenties. The gap between the rich and the poor increased. As the national and global economies began to teeter at the end of the decade, Americans were the first to feel the impact.

Americans feel the first effects of the economic downturn.

Then, on October 24, 1929, Black Thursday, a massive stock sell-off began at the New York Stock Exchange. Brokers sold millions of shares. At the end of the day, twenty-five Wall Street brokerage houses issued a statement saying that the "worst has passed" in an attempt to calm the market. But the next day, the sell-off continued. Investors panicked and dumped their stocks for any price. Those who had bought on the margins—that is, borrowed money to purchase stocks—frantically sold to pay their creditors. Five days later, on Tuesday, October 29, the bubble burst for good when 3 million shares were sold in the first thirty minutes of trading. More than 16 million shares changed hands that day, a volume that would not be reached again for almost forty years. Since early September, the value of the leading industrial stocks had declined by almost 40 percent. Stock losses for just the month of October 1929 totaled some $50 billion, an amount exceeding what the United States had spent in waging World War I.

The **stock market crash** did not cause the **Great Depression**. In fact, only about half a million people owned stocks. For almost a year after the crash, few Americans felt its direct impact or understand its implications. But by 1932, every American was painfully aware of the magnitude of the downward spiral. Its effects were felt across the country in every sector of the economy at every level of society.

As the value of stocks plummeted, businesses began to fail, companies laid off workers, and workers cut back on purchasing. Reduced demand for consumer goods caused more businesses to fail and more workers to lose their jobs. By the early 1930s, some 14 million Americans—one-quarter of the workforce—were out of work and another 40 million in a population of 123 million did not have sufficient income to meet their obligations. Between 1929 and 1932, families lost more than 30 percent of their income. For the nation's minorities, the situation was worse. A survey of one hundred six cities reported that half of African Americans were jobless.

The falling value of stocks also meant that banks called in their loans. As homeowners and farmers fell behind in mortgage payments, foreclosures hit an all-time high. In the South, shrinking cotton and tobacco markets squeezed sharecropping families. One Texas cotton picker explained: "I picked all week and made 85 cents. I can starve sitting down a lot easier than I can picking cotton." Although the economy had endured cycles of boom and bust for more than a century, this depression was unprecedented in its severity.

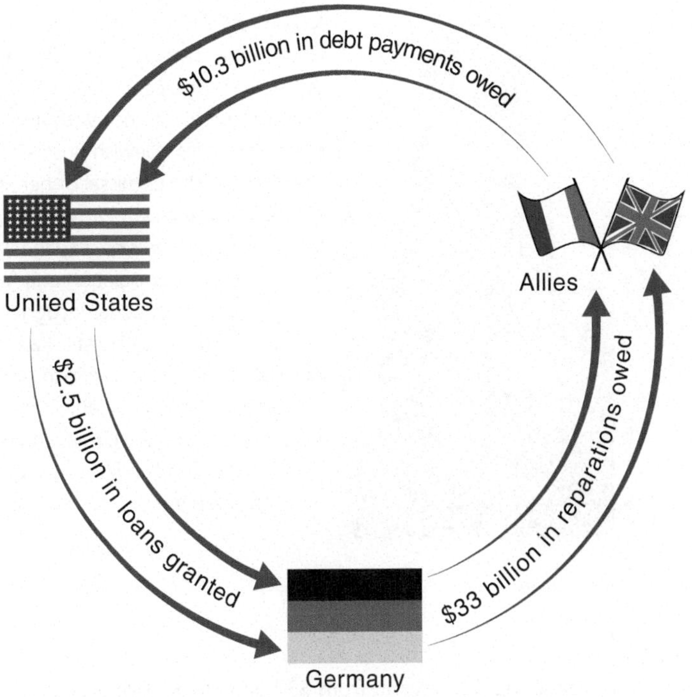

Figure 20.1 International Financial System between the End of World War I and the Great Depression After World War I, world financial markets became deeply intertwined by loans and debt. In 1924, after Germany ceased reparations payments to the Allies, former U.S. budget director Charles G. Dawes developed a payment plan that included U.S. loans to Germany. Dawes won the Nobel Peace Prize for his efforts, but the plan ultimately failed, and in 1932, Germany stopped reparations payments altogether. Allied war loan repayments to the United States had also ceased; only Finland paid its debt promptly. In 2010, Germany made the last of its reparations and debt payments under the Dawes Plan. ▲ Source: Leonard Gomes, *German Reparations, 1919–1932: A Historical Survey*. New York: Palgrave Macmillan, 2010.

20-1b Global Economic Crisis

> As the depression spreads, people all over the world feel the effects.

Because U.S. and European financial markets were interconnected, the U.S. economic crisis quickly spread to Europe. For the first time in its history, the United States was a creditor nation. U.S. banks and financiers had loaned European allies $10 billion during and after World War I and since the mid-1920s had been sending loans to Germany so it could make its reparations payments. This flow of money had helped to stabilize European economies **(see Figure 20.1)**. But when U.S. banks demanded repayment of loans to cover stock market losses, Europe, too, suffered a wave of bank failures. The most devastating was that of Austria's Kreditanstalt in 1931. Foreign investment in European industry also plummeted, and by 1931, the level of U.S. investment in Europe was zero. The withdrawal of U.S. money from European markets produced a shock, because throughout the 1920s, the United States had played a major role in European finance. As banks and factories closed in Europe, unemployment also soared, to 22 percent in Britain and more than 30 percent in Germany.

With credit cut off and the European economy crashing downward, the value of U.S. exports also declined from $5.4 billion in 1929 to $2.1 billion in 1933. To protect U.S. manufacturers from foreign competition, Congress passed the **Hawley-Smoot Tariff** in 1930, which taxed imported goods at the highest rates in U.S. history. Other industrialized counties retaliated with their own protectionist tariffs. Germany, for example, imposed a 50 percent tariff on all entering goods. As trade barriers went up, global trade slowed, declining by a

stock market crash Sudden plunge in stock prices that is made worse by panic and more selling. The crash of 1929 signaled the onset of the Great Depression.

Great Depression Deep and decade-long economic collapse, beginning with the U.S. stock market crash in 1929, which soon engulfed nations throughout the world.

Hawley-Smoot Tariff Tariff law passed in 1930 that raised import taxes to their highest levels ever. By suppressing trade, it heightened the impact of the Great Depression globally.

Image of postcard. Courtesy of Cathleen Cahill. Trieste, Italy.

Global Americans In 1931, an aspiring singer from Oklahoma arrived in Berlin to study opera. **Tessie "Lushanya" Mobley** had been born in 1906 to a white father and a mother of Chickasaw descent. Her studies in Berlin coincided with the rise of Adolf Hitler and the Nazi Party, and her journals are rich with first-person accounts of the experience. She described the National Day of Boycott against Jewish businesses, April 1, 1933, shortly after Hitler assumed dictatorial powers; she recorded the dismissal of her Jewish professors and reflected on a close friend's decision to leave school to join the Nazi Party. Her April 28, 1933, entry concludes, "I believe that always the majority people will be victims or scapegoats of those who lead. . . . I am wondering what this next year will bring." Despite her isolation and fear, Mobley never hid her Chickasaw heritage, and the next years brought her international recognition as the "Songbird of the Chickasaws." In 1937, when she made her operatic debut at Trieste, Italy, she answered three hours of curtain calls before falling down in exhaustion. Her starring role in *Aida* (shown in this postcard) made her famous, and she repeated her success at La Scala in Milan. This image suggests that although Mobley was a renowned singer, she was often cast in ethnic roles that reflected her indigenous background. For example, at the Royal Albert Hall in London, she played Minnehaha in *Hiawatha*. Her career spanned decades, and while she often lived in Paris, she always maintained close family and tribal ties.

staggering 62 percent, from $3 billion to $1 billion. Japan's exports dropped by 50 percent. Britain's weekly newspaper *The Economist* blamed the Hawley-Smoot Tariff for turning "a stock market collapse into a crippling, decade-long Depression" (see Map. 20.1).

The repercussions were worldwide. When U.S. automakers stopped importing rubber for ties, the rubber industry in Malaya, Indochina, and the Dutch East Indies fell apart. Japan, devastated by the collapse of the silk trade, prohibited the importation of rice. Latin American exports of sugar, coffee, wool, copper, tin, silver, and petroleum almost ceased. Furthermore, as U.S. banks went into crisis, they stopped financing the Latin American projects that U.S. companies such as Ford and United Fruit had undertaken. No country escaped the impact of the Great Depression, and as each country walled off imports and tried to solve its own financial problems, international tensions increased.

Efforts at international cooperation faltered. In June 1931, President Hoover proposed a one-year **moratorium** on German reparations and on Allied war debt payments to the United States. But when the moratorium ended, all debtor nations except Finland defaulted. Germany stopped paying reparations altogether. In 1933, sixty-six nations, including the United States, came together at the **London Economic Conference** to find a way to revive international trade and stabilize international currencies. Although the participants agreed on the devastating effects of the Depression, none could agree on how to end it. With this failure, nations turned inward, seeking individual, often nationalistic solutions rather than collaborative efforts that they feared would embroil them in their neighbors' economic problems.

moratorium Authorized delay in debt payment. In 1931, Hoover proposed a one-year moratorium for war debts and reparations.

London Economic Conference International meeting in 1933 that tried but failed to coordinate efforts to ease the global depression and stabilize national currencies.

totalitarianism Single-party political system in which the state has almost complete control over all aspects of civil society. An example is Nazi Germany.

20-1c International Responses to Global Depression

National solutions involve varying degrees of government intervention.

For many, the unprecedented economic crisis seemed to signal that capitalism had failed. In some European parliamentary democracies, disagreements between the left and right wings of the socialist parties actually paralyzed governments and made them unable to enact programs of social welfare. Socialist leaders influenced by Marxist theories were reluctant to embrace any reforms short of total nationalization of industry. On the other hand, middle-class reform parties fearful of Communist revolution refused to form coalitions with socialists. As a result, elected leaders could not maintain stable governments. In France, for example, between 1931 and 1936, ten different premiers formed twelve different governments, one lasting only a week.

It is not surprising that some European nations turned to authoritarian solutions. One model for a new type of economy came from Italy, where since the 1920s, Benito Mussolini's fascism had protected capitalists from strikes and revolution through total state power over the economy. In 1933, Germany turned to a similar solution when Adolf Hitler's Nazi Party took control of the economy and subordinated the individual to the state by glorifying militarism and nationalism. Hitler's **totalitarian** dictatorship was also overtly racist. He pledged to rid the country of Jews, Communists, homosexuals, and others

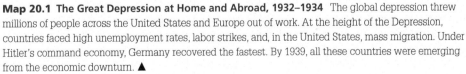

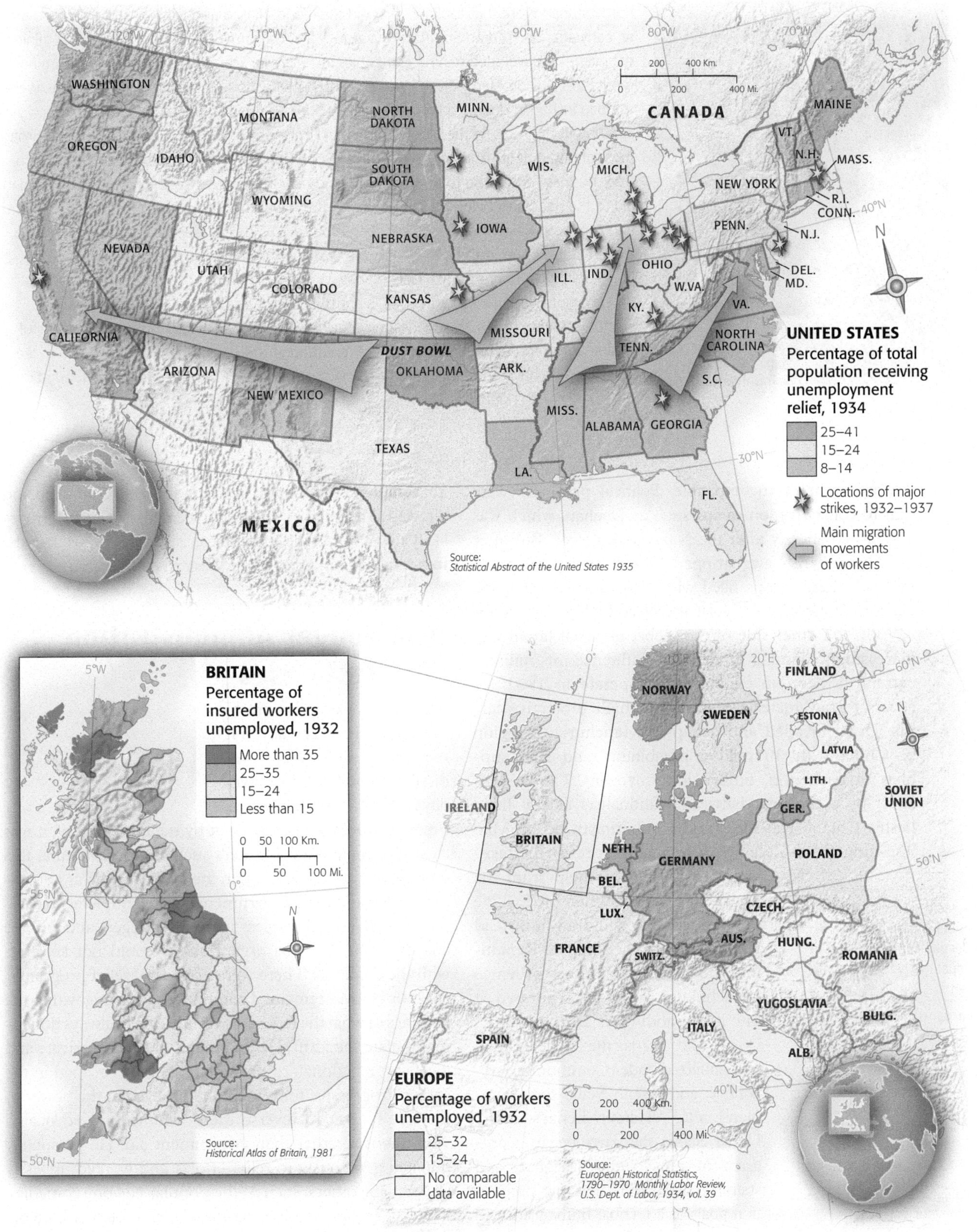

Map 20.1 The Great Depression at Home and Abroad, 1932–1934 The global depression threw millions of people across the United States and Europe out of work. At the height of the Depression, countries faced high unemployment rates, labor strikes, and, in the United States, mass migration. Under Hitler's command economy, Germany recovered the fastest. By 1939, all these countries were emerging from the economic downturn. ▲

AP Images

Global Americans As a young man, **Herbert Hoover** pursued a career and humanitarian work that took him around the world. Raised as a Quaker and orphaned at an early age, he entered Stanford University's first class in 1891 and graduated as a mining engineer. He developed mining companies in Australia, South Africa, and China, earning a reputation as a problem solver. When he and his wife, Lou, also a Stanford graduate, were trapped in Tianjin during China's Boxer Rebellion, his fluent Chinese helped U.S. troops evacuate foreigners. By the time World War I broke out in Europe, Hoover had lived abroad most of his adult life and amassed a fortune of $4 million. The war prompted him to turn from business enterprise to public service, and he worked tirelessly to provide humanitarian aid to the people of Belgium. At the height of the war, his Commission for Belgian Relief and American Relief Association supplied food to 10.5 million people every day. After the United States entered the war, he ran the U.S. Food Administration. During the Harding and Coolidge administrations, Hoover was secretary of commerce, overseeing programs that promoted open trade agreements and U.S. businesses abroad. When he was elected president in 1928, Americans were confident that his background as a successful businessman and a humanitarian with a reputation for efficiency had prepared him to lead the nation. "I have no fear for the future of our country," Hoover said at his inauguration. "It is bright with hope."

deemed unfit or incompatible. Political prisoners were sent to **concentration camps** such as Dachau, which was established shortly after the Nazis took power. But after the Nuremberg Laws stripped Jews of their civil rights in 1935, these camps filled with those accused of being enemies of the state for racial, moral, and religious reasons.

On the other side of the globe, imperial Japan was increasingly coming under the influence of military extremists bent on expansion. Desperate in 1931 for access to raw materials because of high protective tariffs, Japan invaded and occupied Manchuria, a region of China with 30 million inhabitants and rich supplies of coal, iron, timber, and soybeans. China, torn apart by a civil war between Nationalists led by Jiang Jieshi (Chiang Kai-shek) and Communists led by Mao Tse-tung (Mao Zedong), was unable to resist the takeover but did ask for help from the League of Nations. When the League ordered Japan to withdraw, it instead withdrew from the League. Renaming the former Chinese province Manchukuo, Japan incorporated it into its expanding Asian empire.

In the 1920s, the Soviet Union had stabilized under Communist Party control, and Joseph Stalin took command after Vladimir Lenin's death. Under Stalin, the party began a program of rapid industrialization and state-run agriculture that met production goals at a terrible human cost. In the winter of 1932–1933, an estimated 7 million peasants starved to death in the Ukraine, and later in the decade, Stalin's purges of state enemies and the Red Army officer corps killed millions. Yet **command economies**, in which the state controlled and directed all aspects of production, seemed to many to be more likely to withstand the economic crisis of the 1930s than the **free-market** economies of the Western democracies.

concentration camp Isolated and enclosed location where political and/or ethnic undesirables were relocated to separate them from civil society.

command economy State-run economy with little or no participation from private firms or free competition.

volunteerism Practice of relying on charitable agencies and private sector cooperation rather than government action to provide relief.

Reconstruction Finance Corporation (RFC) Independent agency established in 1932 that distributed billions in loans to banks and railroads to stabilize the economy.

20-1d Hoover Administration Responses

Hoover's reforms and aid prove inadequate.

After the stock market crash, President Hoover at first remained optimistic, predicting recovery in just sixty days. New York Governor Franklin Roosevelt agreed. But by the end of 1929, it was clear to state and local leaders such as Roosevelt that this depression was far worse than the post-World War I downturn. State and local governments were completely unprepared to deal with joblessness and hunger, and private charities and religious organizations could not keep up with the demands. There were no federal relief programs.

Yet Hoover remained committed to staying within the confines of what the federal government had always done—manipulate the tariff. He continued to call for private and local, not a national, response to the crisis. Steeped in the earlier Progressive movement, he believed in the power of the free market to reverse the downturn and advocated **volunteerism** rather than government aid. He personally donated generously to relief efforts and worked tirelessly to persuade others, such as the popular cowboy comedian Will Rogers, to promote charitable giving. Yet while giving was at an all-time high, it was not enough.

By January 1932, as banks failed, industries closed, and unemployment soared, Hoover realized that government action was needed. He asked Congress to create the **Reconstruction Finance Corporation (RFC)**, which

Sueddeutsche Zeitung Photo/Alamy Stock Photo

Bonus Marchers at the Capitol, Summer 1932 World War I veterans and their supporters traveled across the United States to pressure Congress to require immediate payment of the bonuses by passing the Bonus Bill. Proponents believed this would help alleviate the economic hardship of the global depression. Despite political pressure, the bill was defeated. Peaceful demonstrations, like the one depicted here, turned violent when the U.S. Army and local police dispersed the veterans' encampments. ▲

made loans to banks, railroads, and insurance companies to keep them afloat. In July, with the crisis deepening, the Emergency Relief and Reconstruction Act authorized the RFC to make loans directly to farmers, states, and public works projects. Yet Hoover insisted on a very conservative set of guidelines. RFC loans carried high interest rates (to avoid competing with private lenders) and collateral requirements. Nevertheless, the loans totaled almost $2 billion in the RFC's first year, enough to delay a banking catastrophe but not enough to inspire an upturn.

To those who were suffering, Hoover seemed harsh and uncaring. Mocking him, homeless people forced to live under bridges and in tents and shacks called their new communities Hoovervilles. His reaction to the poverty-stricken veterans who straggled into Washington in the summer of 1932 branded him as uncaring. In 1924, Congress had granted a bonus to those who had served in World War I to be paid in 1945 as an insurance policy or pension. But the hardships of the Depression caused veterans to ask Congress for the bonus early. Starting in Oregon in the spring of 1932, they marched east, and by the time they arrived in Washington, they were known as the **Bonus Army**. More than 20,000 veterans and their families set up camp on Anacostia Flats, near the U.S. Capitol. In Congress, the bonus bill was defeated, and most veterans left. Washington police sought to evict those remaining, and when violence erupted, Hoover called in federal troops under General Douglas MacArthur to restore order. In a display of force, MacArthur sent tanks and soldiers with drawn bayonets to remove the veterans and to burn the camp. During these attacks on the Bonus Army, two veterans were killed, two infants died from asphyxiation, and more than a thousand people were exposed to tear gas. The spectacle of MacArthur's troops attacking unarmed veterans and their families shocked Americans and led them to oppose a president who seemed incapable of dealing with the crisis.

Nevertheless, the Republicans nominated Hoover for a second term. The Democrats had no clear front-runner although Governor Roosevelt was attracting attention. Republicans and more conservative Democrats feared he would take the country in the direction of European democratic socialism. Others saw him as shallow. "An amiable boy scout," quipped journalist Walter Lippmann. The Democratic convention was a free-for-all as candidates jockeyed for the nomination, but after four ballots, Roosevelt won. As he campaigned, he promised Americans a **New Deal** to end the Depression but did not outline specific policies. Yet he won the general election with 57 percent of the popular vote to Hoover's 40 percent.

Adolf Hitler and Franklin Roosevelt assumed the leadership of their countries within one month of each other in early 1933. Both Germans and Americans were looking for a forceful leader who could provide a clear path for economic recovery. Although Hitler and Roosevelt each provided charismatic leadership, they took radically different approaches. Hitler, following a fascist model, became a dictator who suppressed his critics and initiated a military buildup as a means of strengthening the economy. Roosevelt, in contrast, had to fend off doubts about his leadership sown during the election as well as critics from both the left and the right. Nevertheless, the democratic solution to economic crisis that he pursued endured, and, as the rise of militarist regimes in Asia and Europe portended global conflict, Roosevelt sought to insulate the United States from international tensions.

Bonus Army World War I veterans who marched on Washington in 1932 to demand that promised cash bonuses be paid immediately but were refused.

New Deal Roosevelt's program for providing relief during the Great Depression and reforming the nation's economy and financial institutions.

20-2

The New Deal

Roosevelt was the first president to speak regularly to Americans by radio. His broadcasts masterfully allayed fears and rallied Americans to face and endure the difficulties of both the Great Depression and international conflicts.

How did regular radio broadcasts from the president change the relationship between the federal government and Americans? ▶

Marie Hansen/Time Life Pictures/Getty Images

Although Roosevelt entered office in March 1933, determined to bring relief to Americans, the only consistent theme of his administration's first days was frenetic activity. Roosevelt himself lacked a unified philosophy of government, and his advisers sometimes gave conflicting advice about how to handle the crisis. He knew only that he needed to experiment constantly until the Depression ended. Some policies worked, but others did not. Although the Supreme Court overturned much of what Roosevelt set in motion in those first heady months of his presidency, he persisted with major reforms in labor legislation and in social welfare that restructured the U.S. economy.

☞ As you read, think about the goals of the New Deal. What impeded its success?

20-2a A Modern Presidency

Franklin and Eleanor Roosevelt transform the American presidency.

Franklin Delano Roosevelt grew up wealthy and protected on his family's Hyde Park estate in New York. At the age of 14, he was sent to Groton, an elite boarding school in New England. He then entered Harvard, where he was a class officer and editor of the Harvard *Crimson*. During this time, he dated his distant cousin Eleanor Roosevelt, the niece of President Theodore Roosevelt. Both were devoted to reform and public service, and they can be considered the first modern political couple. Roosevelt was assistant secretary of the navy under President Wilson and the Democratic Party vice presidential nominee in 1920. The Democrats lost to Republican Harding, and the next year, Franklin contracted polio, which left him paralyzed from the waist down. He was determined not to be an invalid. Both he and Eleanor believed that he should re-enter public life. Despite her personal shyness, Mrs. Roosevelt promoted her husband's place in New York and national politics. Increasingly, she spent less time as his nursemaid and more time tending to his political fortunes in the public spotlight. This was an arrangement that would serve the couple throughout his governorship and presidency.

Brains Trust Term used to describe Roosevelt's policy advisers, chosen for their expertise rather than their personal association with the president.

fireside chats Roosevelt's radio addresses to Americans in which he explained in clear language how his administration was addressing pressing issues.

Following his election to the presidency in 1932, Roosevelt assembled what came to be known as the **Brains Trust**. These advisers were known for their policy specialties rather than their personal friendship with the president and shared his belief that an active government could solve the nation's economic problems. Deeply influenced by the Progressive movement, they envisioned the New Deal as the legacy of President Theodore Roosevelt's New Nationalism and President Wilson's New Freedom. Roosevelt saw his role as picking and choosing from among the policies his advisers presented even if the result lacked a coherent ideology. "Take a method and try it," Roosevelt said. "If it fails, admit it frankly, and try another. But above all, try something." Roosevelt's willingness to take action reassured Americans during the first months of his presidency. As his presidency proceeded, he enacted relief, reform and recovery programs that would have a lasting impact on the nation.

Both Franklin and Eleanor reached out to Americans in a way that personalized the presidency. Just eight days after his inauguration, Roosevelt went on the radio to explain in everyday language what his administration was doing to end the banking crisis. These radio messages came to be called **fireside chats**. Frances Perkins, secretary of labor and the first woman ever to serve in the cabinet, remembered that when the president began speaking into the radio microphone "his face would smile and light up as though he were actually sitting on the front porch or in the parlor with them. People felt this, and it bound them to him in affection." Eleanor Roosevelt also made a personal connection to Americans through her daily newspaper column, **"My Day."** One Nebraska woman said she had come to think of Eleanor Roosevelt as a personal friend because she knew so much about her from the columns.

20-2b First Hundred Days

Roosevelt administration takes decisive action to improve the economy.

The pressing crisis that Roosevelt faced immediately upon his inauguration was the failure of hundreds of banks. As panicked depositors withdrew their savings and some hoarded cash, banks without adequate reserves called in outstanding loans and foreclosed on farms and homes, evicting many from their property. When banks still could not keep pace with withdrawals, they defaulted, and depositors lost all their money. Although a few states suspended bank operations to stem the crisis, there had been no coordinated, federal response by the Hoover administration.

Roosevelt's first act in office was to declare a **Bank Holiday**. He closed all banks for four days (later extended to eight days), and no withdrawals were allowed. Under the Emergency Banking Act, passed on March 9, banks that were solvent reopened while the federal government guided those that were in trouble toward solvency. This action gave people confidence and ended the panicked withdrawals. The Bank Holiday was followed by the Glass-Steagall Act, which provided a long-term solution to bank failures. It created the Federal Deposit Insurance Corporation (FDIC), which insured individual deposits up to $2,500. It also prohibited banks from dealing in stocks and thus ended practices that put depositors' savings at risk.

Other financial reforms quickly followed. To stabilize the stock market, the Securities Act required sellers to disclose to investors information about the value of the stock. Taking the United States off of the **gold standard**, Roosevelt instructed the Treasury to print more money than was backed up by actual gold reserves held by the government. This move provided extra cash that could be directed to relief and jobs programs. The Roosevelt administration thus engaged in **deficit spending**, an approach recommended by the British economist John Maynard Keynes. **Keynesian economic theory** advocated centralized economic planning and government spending on public works to stimulate the economy, ideas that would eventually guide Roosevelt's program of economic recovery.

To stimulate production and trade, Roosevelt supported repeal of prohibition, which was accomplished by constitutional amendment in 1933. He also recognized the Soviet Union and signed a trade agreement designed to increase U.S. exports. Ford sold tractors to Soviet collective farms, and skilled U.S. workers went to the Soviet Union to help build new factories and train technicians.

NRA Cartoon, "In It Together," July 1933 This cartoon depicts Uncle Sam as a coalition builder between employers and their employees to bolster the sagging economy. Hugh Johnson, Administrator of the NRA, was sympathetic to Mussolini's ideology of corporatism, which meant that the government would broker and enforce a consensus between labor and management about how to make industry work for both sides. Corporatism, as embodied in Johnson's NRA, promised no more strikes and fair working conditions. ▲

In addition to alleviating the financial crisis, the Roosevelt administration provided direct relief to individuals and families. The new Home Owners' Loan Corporation helped those who had defaulted on mortgages to keep their family homes. To get money into the hands of consumers so they could spend it, Roosevelt created the Federal Emergency Relief Agency (FERA), which provided work programs and direct cash payments to those with no other means of support. FERA was only a temporary measure, however, because both Roosevelt and Harry Hopkins, secretary of commerce, preferred to stimulate the economy by providing incentives for creating jobs rather than direct aid.

Two programs—the National Industrial Recovery Act (NIRA) and the Agricultural Adjustment Act (AAA)—best represent the approach Roosevelt took early in his administration. The NIRA established the National Recovery Administration (NRA), which negotiated with both

"My Day" Newspaper column written by Eleanor Roosevelt that ran six days a week between 1935 and 1962, describing her thoughts on events and issues.

Bank Holiday Roosevelt's first act in office, closing banks for four (later eight) days to prevent panic withdrawals and ensure that banks had adequate funds to cover deposits.

gold standard Monetary system in which the government can print and circulate only the amount of paper money backed by actual gold held in government vaults.

deficit spending Government policy of spending more on services than it collects in tax revenues and other income. This policy creates national debt.

Keynesian economic theory Economic policy advocated by British economist John Maynard Keynes in which monetary inputs by government keep the economy in balance.

business and labor to regulate wages, production quotas, and ceilings and floors on prices for consumer goods. Theoretically, it had the power to enforce these regulations but preferred voluntary compliance. Businesses had an incentive to agree to the NRA's codes because compliance exempted them from antitrust laws. Labor was granted the first federal protection for unions and the right of **collective bargaining** for wages and working conditions. Roosevelt's choice to head the NRA, Hugh Johnson, led a national campaign urging businesses to "do their part." Those that complied could display the Blue Eagle, the symbol of the NRA, as a way to attract clients and customers. New York City's largest parade in history was held to promote the Blue Eagle.

The NIRA also established the Public Works Administration (PWA). Under the direction of Secretary of the Interior Harold Ickes, the PWA implemented Keynesian ideas about "priming the pump" of the U.S. economy. The PWA was initially authorized to spend up to $3.3 billion on large infrastructure projects such as dams, schools, hospitals, airports, roads, and sidewalks. For every person the PWA employed directly, two additional workers were hired by private companies. Again, the idea was to provide jobs, not aid.

The Tennessee Valley Authority (TVA) undertook a massive infrastructure program to bring electricity, flood control, and land restoration to one of the poorest regions in the nation. Throughout the country, the government put unemployed young men to work in the newly created Civilian Conservation Corps (CCC), which engaged in reforestation projects, dam construction, and infrastructure improvements in national parks.

The AAA did for agriculture what the NIRA did for industry. It encouraged voluntary cooperation in ending overproduction—a major cause of the global depression—by paying farmers subsidies in return for letting their land lie fallow or slaughtering their animals. Although Americans suffering from want were shocked to see farmers killing piglets and dumping thousands of gallons of milk onto the ground, farm prices and farm income did stabilize and begin to rise. Meanwhile, the Farm Credit Administration worked to prevent foreclosures and increased the availability of credit.

During Roosevelt's first months in office—what came to be called the **Hundred Days**—a wide range of New Deal programs sought to address the nation's economic crisis (see Table 20.1). Some were successful, some not, and most had to be bolstered with additional legislation. But together they announced that the government was taking a new and active role in the economy by using public works to stimulate job creation and encouraging cooperation from business, workers, and farmers in nationwide economic planning. These steps were unprecedented in the United States, but they fell far short of the command economies implemented by force in the Soviet Union, Italy, and Germany, where Hitler's programs reduced unemployment by almost half in 1934. Although none of the New Deal programs brought an immediate end to the Depression, they did alleviate suffering, and they laid the foundation for a modern federal bureaucracy that addresses the well-being of people directly.

But not all Americans benefited equally. In southern states, the prevailing system of Jim Crow meant that African Americans hired for federal work programs were systematically placed in lower status jobs and paid less than white workers. By the second year of the NRA, not one African American held the rank of clerk or its equivalent, and the black press asserted that the NRA really stood for "Negro Removal Act." The farm subsidies, meant to be passed down from independent farmers to tenants and sharecroppers, never made it into the hands of those who needed the money most.

collective bargaining Right of workers represented by a union to negotiate wage and workplace issues with management, first recognized by law during the New Deal.

Hundred Days Term for Roosevelt's first three months in office during which Congress passed fifteen major laws addressing relief and economic recovery.

Share Our Wealth Huey Long's program for redistributing wealth more equally among the American people.

20-2c Limits and Critics

The New Deal faces many critics and crucial setbacks.

By early 1935, Roosevelt's New Deal confronted its limitations and vocal criticism from both the left and the right. Despite some success, the NIRA had become unpopular in some circles, and Congress was reluctant to renew it. On one hand, small businesses complained that the codes of competition favored big corporations, and a review board set up by Roosevelt denounced the legislation for promoting monopolies. On the other hand, consumers and workers thought it did not do enough to protect them from low wages and high prices, and unions protested that the Roosevelt administration had been too cooperative with business interests.

Critics charged that the New Deal did not go far enough to relieve the crisis. In 1934, Senator Huey Long, former governor of Louisiana, launched **Share Our Wealth**, a program that proposed to liquidate the wealth of every American who held more than $1 million in assets and distribute this money to the poor so that every family could purchase a home, a car, and a radio. The elderly would receive pensions, workers would earn a minimum wage, and deserving young men would be sent to college for free. From Royal Oak, Michigan, Father Charles Coughlin used his weekly radio show to attack Roosevelt's friendly dealings with banking and financial establishments in language that scarcely disguised his anti-Semitism. A third challenge came from Dr. Francis Townsend of Long Beach, California, who advocated a plan to secure the welfare of the country's senior citizens by taxing business transactions to fund pensions. These critics drew many vocal followers. Together, they signaled a trend toward experimentation with radical political ideologies that rejected capitalism.

Table 20.1 **New Deal Agencies, Laws, and Programs**

During the first two terms of the Roosevelt administration, Congress passed a series of laws meant to regulate the economy, stimulate economic growth, and provide both short-term aid and long-term entitlements to U.S. citizens.

Year	Legislation	Description
1933	Emergency Banking Act	Closed most U.S. banks to prevent further panic, allowed the Federal Reserve to direct cash to stable banks, and provided federal insurance to depositors
1933	Home Owners Loan Corporation (HOLC)	Provided refinancing assistance to those homeowners who had defaulted on their mortgages
1933	Banking Act (Glass-Steagall Act)	Created the Federal Deposit Insurance Corporation (FDIC) to insure individual bank deposits and limited banks' ability to engage in securities trading
1933	Farm Credit Act	Created the Farm Credit Administration (FCA) to make credit more available for agricultural production and help farmers refinance farm mortgages
1933	Securities Act	Superseded state laws and required disclosure to investors
1933	Federal Emergency Relief Act (FERA)	Gave federal grants to states for relief efforts but was later replaced by the Works Progress Administration (WPA)
1933	National Industrial Recovery Act (NIRA)	Established the National Recovery Administration, which regulated businesses in an effort to stabilize the economy and the Public Works Administration (PWA), which the Supreme Court overturned in 1935
1933	Agricultural Adjustment Act (AAA)	Created to limit agricultural products in order to raise prices and pay farmers subsidies not to grow crops but was overturned by the Supreme Court in 1936
1933	Tennessee Valley Authority (TVA)	Created as a regional economic development agency to provide aid and jobs by using centralized planning to prevent river flooding, generate electricity, manufacture fertilizer, and sponsor social programs
1933	Civilian Conservation Corp (CCC)	Assigned young men between the ages of 18 and 25 to public works projects, providing wages that most workers sent home to their families
1934	Securities and Exchange Act	Created the Securities and Exchange Commission, which regulated the trading of stocks and bonds
1934	National Housing Act (NHA)	Created the Federal Housing Authority (FHA), which insured loans made by banks or private lenders
1934	Indian Reorganization Act (IRA)	Reversed many provisions of the Dawes Act and gave Native Americans more control over their governance and assets, particularly land
1935	Works Progress Administration (WPA)	Provided work to millions of Americans through such programs as the National Youth Administration (NYA), the Farm Securities Administration (FSA), and the Federal Theatre Project
1935	National Labor Relations Act (Wagner Act)	Guaranteed workers the right to organize into trade unions freely and to engage in collective bargaining with their employers
1935	Social Security Act	Provided a social safety net for those most in need through such programs as Aid to Families with Dependent Children (AFDC) and the Old-Age Reserve Account, which provided a pension to elderly Americans
1938	Fair Labor Standards Act (Wages and Hours Bill)	Established the 44-hour work week and a national minimum wage and guaranteed "time-and-a-half" for overtime

History without Borders

International Communism in the 1930s

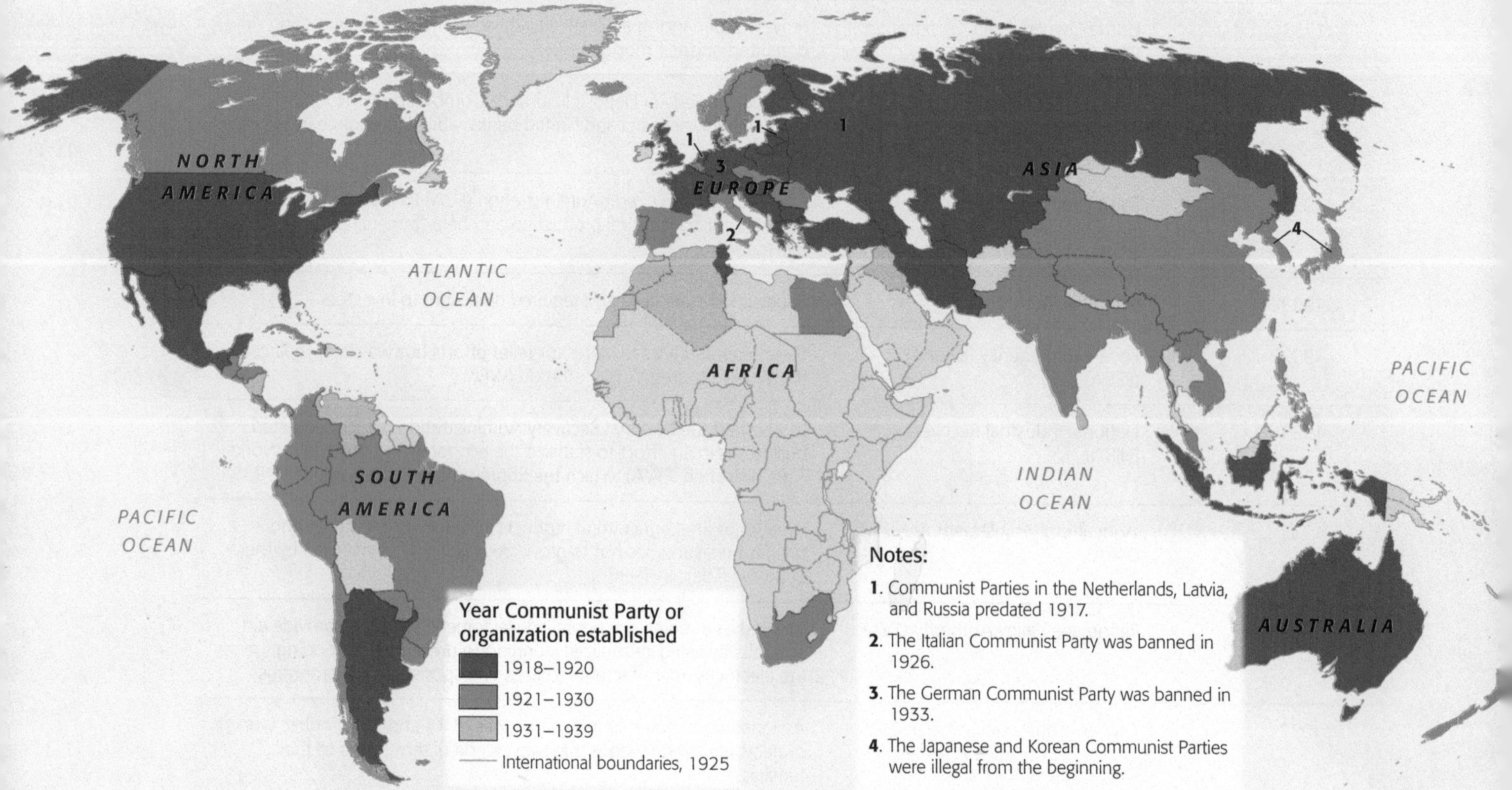

International Communism, 1905–1939 After the 1917 Russian revolution, Communist parties emerged rapidly in other nations. The Communist Party of the United States (CPUSA), established in 1919, was one of the earliest. By the height of the Depression, Communist parties were forceful political voices in suggesting ways to solve the economic downturn. Communism remained a strong political and economic ideology throughout the post-World War II period before declining in popularity. ▲

The global Great Depression gave Communists their best chance to win adherents worldwide since the Russian Revolution of 1917. As trade declined and factories closed, the Communist program of common ownership of production and the ideal of a classless society had a new, almost urgent appeal while capitalism seemed to be faltering. The Communist International (Comintern), a Soviet-led international organization, promoted communism throughout the Western world. In Britain, Communists made gains in trade unions and recruited spies at Cambridge University. In France, the Communist Party attracted workers, artists, and intellectuals.

In the United States, the Communist Party (CPUSA, founded in 1919), together with the Socialist and Socialist Labor parties, drew more than 1 million votes in the 1932 presidential election. The party's membership increased sevenfold from seven thousand five hundred in 1930 to fifty-five thousand in 1940 and, with its much larger following of "fellow travelers" and left-wing liberals, had significant influence in parts of the federal government, the labor movement, and Hollywood. Although the CPUSA gave up its fundamental opposition to capitalism, it continued to cooperate directly with the Soviet Union, and Soviet intelligence received secret reports from at least two hundred agents.

As the Depression deepened, the Communist Party stepped up its appeals to labor unions, university elites, and African Americans, whom the Comintern recognized as an oppressed national group. The party condemned the Scottsboro Trials as a sham and raised funds to appeal the convictions. It backed the Tenants Union, which organized white, African American, and Mexican American sharecroppers to protest the unfair terms and poor living conditions in the South.

But Communist activism also inspired a right-wing reaction. Benito Mussolini's fascist government suppressed Italian Communists, and German Chancellor Adolf Hitler used Communist conspiracies to claim the emergency powers that

AP Images/John Rider-Rider

May Day Rally in London, 1936 Socialists, Communists, and Popular Front organizations rallied together to show their support for labor rights, socialism, and other progressive issues. Students like those shown in this photo dressed in their finest clothes to publicly push the government to enact policies that would help end the Depression, equalize wealth, institute national health care, and give fair rights to workers. These were not fringe or radical organizations but groups that emerged from earlier progressive movements such as the Fabians. ◄

FPG/Archive Photos/Getty Images

Female Communists Protest Germany in New York, 1938 Many Americans, particularly Communists, supported the Spanish Republicans, who fought to keep Francisco Franco's right-wing government from coming to power. Some, like these women carrying the Spanish flag in defiance of German intervention, publically protested. Others, like those who joined the Lincoln Brigade, went to fight alongside the Republicans, although the U.S. government prohibited it. These fighters thought of themselves as preserving a republican government against fascist aggression. ◄

made him dictator. By 1935 for capitalist democracies everywhere, fascist dictatorships seemed a more immediate threat than communism. The Communists recognized the threat as well, and the Comintern tempered its aims for world revolution to urge alliances with democratic parties called Popular Fronts. In France, the *Front Populaire* formed a liberal government that countered fascist factions. In China, the United Front joined nationalists and Communists to fight Japanese military aggression. In Spain, when fascist-backed forces attacked the *Frente Popular*, Communists from many countries joined international brigades to put down this right-wing revolt.

Most unexpected was the alliance between Western democracies and the Communist Soviet Union, which was sealed with Hitler's invasion during World War II. But to Americans who had rallied to the Communist banner in the 1930s, including African Americans Langston Hughes, Richard Wright, and Paul Robeson, the postwar climate was chilling. In the context of Cold War hostility between the Soviet Union and the West, many who had fought against injustice at Scottsboro and against fascists in Spain were charged with "un-Americanism." In 1938, the House Un-American Activities Committee began holding hearings in an effort to find supposed Communist agitators. In 1954, Congress outlawed the CPUSA and made it a crime to be a member.

Critical Thinking Questions

► Why did the Soviet Union and the Comintern believe that they could gain adherents in capitalist democracies, such as the United States, during the 1930s?

► Why were Popular Front alliances among Communists, liberals, and "fellow travelers" so important to the fight against fascism?

Go to MindTap® to engage with an interactive version of **History without Borders: International Communism in the 1930s**. Learn from an interactive map, view related video, and respond to critical thinking questions.

Communist Party of the United States (CPUSA) Political party advocating centralized government control of the economy as opposed to capitalism.

House Un-American Activities Committee (HUAC) House of Representatives committee created in 1938 to investigate disloyalty and subversive organizations.

National Labor Relations Act (Wagner Act) Law passed in 1935 that protected American workers and allowed them to unionize freely.

Social Security Act New Deal legislation passed in 1935 that protected the elderly, disabled, widowed women, and orphaned children from economic insecurity.

unemployment insurance Payments made by the government to workers who have lost their jobs. The New Deal solidified this entitlement for American workers.

entitlements Government programs, enacted by legislation, that give a defined benefit to a specified group.

Some who challenged the New Deal joined the **Communist Party of the United States (CPUSA)**, which during the Great Depression became the leading leftist organization in the United States. The party courted African Americans with promises of social equality and unemployed workers with promises of economic equality. Unlike the domestic critics of the New Deal, the Communists had international ties. As global tensions mounted, those who sympathized with Communist ideology came under increasing suspicion. Later in the decade, some suspected Communists were called before an early incarnation of the **House Un-American Activities Committee (HUAC)**, where their loyalty to the United States was called into question.

But it was the Supreme Court—not Congress or Roosevelt's critics—who decided the fate of the NIRA and ultimately much of the early New Deal. In May 1935, the Court, in its unanimous decision in *Schechter Poultry v. U.S.*, struck down the NIRA as unconstitutional, citing its centralizing tendencies. Then in early 1936, in a six-to-three decision, the Court struck down the AAA as unconstitutional with much the same reasoning. The London *Daily Express* ran the headline: "America Stunned; Roosevelt's Two Years' Work Killed in Twenty Minutes."

20-2d Second New Deal

The Roosevelt administration puts long-term reforms in place.

The London newspaper's view was an exaggeration. Despite the Supreme Court decisions invalidating sections of early New Deal legislation, Roosevelt and Congress were working on even more radical legislation that the Supreme Court would ultimately uphold. Midterm elections in 1934 gave the Democrats control of Congress. Under pressure from his advisers and politicians in his own party, such as New York's senator Robert Wagner, Roosevelt made changes. He abandoned his attempts to cooperate with business and turned his attention to the plight of workers, the unemployed, and the poor. In his State of the Union address for 1935, he reiterated his commitment to placing "the security of the men, women and children of the Nation first." That spring, he used an executive order to create the Works Progress Administration (WPA), which put unemployed individuals to work in federally funded infrastructure, social, and cultural projects. In summer, he kept Congress in session to pass two landmark laws, the **National Labor Relations Act (Wagner Act)** and the Social Security Act.

The NIRA had given the federal government the authority to regulate prices and wages and had recognized the right of unions to organize and engage in collective bargaining, but there had been no means of enforcement. The Wagner Act provided that means through the National Labor Relations Board, which was given the authority to supervise the election of union representatives and to force employers to bargain in good faith with them. It also outlawed unfair labor practices, among them the company-sponsored unions that industrialists such as John D. Rockefeller Jr. had used to suppress worker-organized unions. The act gave workers power against management and control over their working conditions. It also stimulated rapid growth in union organizing.

The **Social Security Act** sought to alleviate the hardships arising from unemployment, poverty, the death of the family breadwinner, and old age. It had taken shape under the guidance of the Committee on Economic Security chaired by Francis Perkins. Like the earlier Progressive reformers, New Dealers were open to learning from social welfare programs being tried in Europe. The committee spent the summer of 1934 researching European social insurance programs and listening to the ideas of Sir William Beveridge, a British economist who helped shape his nation's social insurance plan.

One provision of the new Social Security law helped fund state programs managing **unemployment insurance**, temporary cash payments to workers who lost their jobs through no fault of their own. Several states had already established these programs, funded largely by taxes on employers. By 1937, all states had similar **entitlement** programs. Another provision provided grants to states to assist blind individuals. The Aid to Dependent Children program was a similar state–federal partnership, providing $1 of federal money for every $2 of state money to help children who had lost one or both parents. The program was an outgrowth of earlier state programs that helped widowed mothers raise their children without having to enter the workforce full-time. On average, each recipient received $18 a month, but because states set benefit amounts, they varied considerably. Southern and western states paid the least. African American and Mexican American children who were concentrated in these regions received lower payments than white children on average.

The main provision of the Society Security Act was an arrangement under which payroll taxes, paid by employers and employees, funded an Old-Age Reserve Account that beginning in 1942 would pay benefits to workers over age 65 who no longer worked. When they began, payments averaged $33 a month although they varied according to how long a worker had been employed. Much to the chagrin of Perkins, the definition of *employment* excluded workers in agriculture, domestic service in a private home, and "casual labor," meaning day labor. Thus, like the Aid to Dependent Children program, Social Security operated in a way that at first largely excluded African Americans and Mexican Americans, who were more likely than white Americans to hold such jobs. It was also a **regressive tax** in that the proportion of wages to be paid into the system was highest for those who made the least.

regressive tax Tax applied uniformly, like a sales tax, that disproportionately burdens the poor; also tax rate that decreases as the amount being taxed increases.

The Roosevelt administration was careful to portray Social Security as a social insurance program. Although welfare programs in Britain and France were funded by general revenues, Social Security was funded entirely by employers and workers. The arrangement blunted criticism from conservatives that the New Deal was instituting a welfare state, and Social Security proved to be enormously popular. Townsend Plan supporters lobbied for its passage in the belief that Social Security would preserve people's dignity and save them from starvation and homelessness when they aged and left the workforce. The Social Security Act was watershed legislation, implementing a federal responsibility for the well-being of the nation's citizens (see Figure 20.2).

20-2e Election of 1936

Roosevelt solidifies his democratic base as he expands New Deal reforms.

As election year approached, a third-party challenge by followers of Roosevelt's critics Long, Coughlin, and Townsend largely disintegrated after Long was assassinated in September 1935 in the Louisiana state capitol. The Republicans nominated Alf Landon, a candidate with $14 million in campaign funds but no clear program to challenge Roosevelt. In fact, Roosevelt was extraordinarily popular because most Americans felt they were better off than they had been in 1932. He won a landslide victory, capturing 60.8 percent of the popular vote and all but two states in the electoral vote.

The victory was also the result of Roosevelt's explicit bid to solidify his support among minorities and the working class. His reelection marked a political realignment that lasted for decades. Influenced by Mrs. Roosevelt and Ickes, Roosevelt placed African Americans in high-level posts. He named Mary McLeod Bethune, head of the National Council of Negro Women, director of Negro affairs for the WPA's National Youth Administration, which provided assistance and training for unemployed youth. Ickes created a new post, Director of Negro Economics, to help distribute New Deal aid among African American communities. Although they had long supported the party of Lincoln and Emancipation, African Americans shifted their allegiance to the Democrats. Labor leaders, who had worked closely with Labor Secretary Perkins and Senator Wagner to pass the Wagner Act, were also firmly behind Roosevelt. When United Mine Workers (UMW) leader John L. Lewis, a lifelong Republican, switched his allegiance to Roosevelt, he brought union votes with him. Roosevelt owed much of his success to this new coalition.

Figure 20.2 Public Expenditures on Social Welfare, 1890–1940 This graph shows how dramatically expenditures on social welfare programs increased both at the federal, state, and local levels. However, only in 1936 did the federal government spend more money than state and local governments combined. This was a trend that would last until 1967, when federal spending exceeded state and local expenditures. That pattern continued through the end of the twentieth century. ▼ Source: Carter, Susan B., Scott Sigmund Gartner, Michael R. Haines, Alan L. Olmstead, Richard Sutch, and Gavin Wright, eds. *Historical Statistics of the United States*, millennial ed. © Cambridge University Press, 2006.

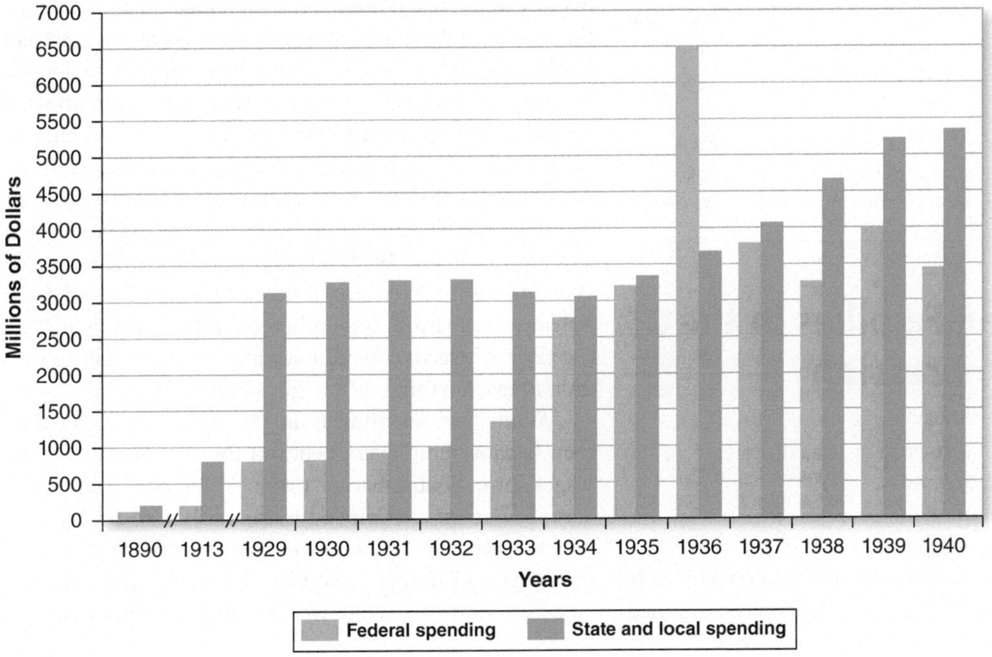

Good Neighbor Policy Roosevelt's policy of noninterference in Latin American affairs to repair relations and build hemispheric solidarity.

The beginning of Roosevelt's second term marked the high point of the New Deal. The Democratic Party was united behind the president, whose bold spending and liberal policies appeared to be pulling the nation out of the Depression. In his second inaugural address, Roosevelt committed his administration to continuing its concern for those in need. "I see one-third of a nation," he stated, "ill-housed, ill-clad, and ill-nourished." He also affirmed the capacity of democratic government "to protect its people against disasters once considered inevitable, to solve problems once considered unsolvable."

Roosevelt also addressed growing concerns about international tensions and sought to shore up allies in the Western Hemisphere by his **Good Neighbor Policy**. In describing the United States as peaceful and "a good neighbor among the nations," he not only referred to his efforts in improving relations with Latin America but also implicitly contrasted U.S. democracy with aggressive military regimes in Europe and Asia. A government that does the will of the people, he affirmed, will be "strong among the nations in its example of the will to peace." Roosevelt's second administration would not match the lofty rhetoric of his inaugural address, but, in an increasingly threatening world, his first administration had proved that democracy could prevail.

20-3 Life in the 1930s

During the Great Depression, men who had formerly taken pride in their jobs and their families became tramps—hobos wandering on roads and "riding the rails" in search of work and a free meal. Severed from community and family, they concerned President Roosevelt and other reformers.

Study the man in the photograph. What narrative would you tell about him and how he found himself at this juncture in his life? ►

Everett Historical/Shutterstock.com

The economic crisis of the Great Depression caused social and cultural upheaval throughout the nation. Families were torn apart by economic hardship and, in some cases, government policies that failed to help them stay together in their homes and on their farms. Although the Wagner and Social Security acts began to bring some measure of stability to workers and families, labor organizing created conflict. Yet Americans were resilient, appreciating what they did have and enjoying new forms of popular entertainment such as movies and radio.

☞As you read, consider the ways in which Americans were both displaced and drawn together in the 1930s. What programs brought stability, and what movements and events created strife?

20-3a American Families in the Great Depression

Families face overwhelming challenges.

The Depression took a heavy toll on family life. Men thrown out of work often had to leave their families in search of work elsewhere, and some simply walked out on their responsibilities. The Majewski family in Chicago is one example. After Mr. Majewski abandoned his wife and five children, Mrs. Majewski scrubbed floors. She lost her job, and when she found another, it paid half her former wages. One daughter went to work as a domestic servant. By 1931, the family was making do on their wages and $5 of aid a week from a local private charity. Like many families in the Great Depression, they endured separation. Tensions in families also occurred when extended families had to move in together to save on rent and avoid eviction. Birth rates dropped. Suicide rates rose (see Figure 20.3). Louis Banks, who had moved from Arkansas to Detroit, remembered, "I'd see 'em floatin' on the river where they would commit suicide because they didn't have anything. White guys and colored."

White women often found getting work easier than men because employers believed they could pay women wages lower than what a "primary" breadwinner would accept. Women also moved more easily into poorly paid jobs traditionally defined as female work, such as clerical positions and domestic service. In taking domestic service jobs, however, white women often displaced African

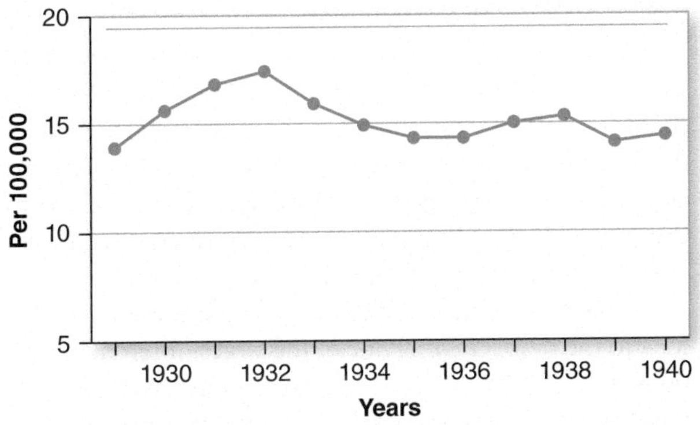

Figure 20.3 Suicides in the Great Depression, 1929–1940
In 1932, at the peak of the Great Depression, the suicide rate in the United States climbed to the highest point (17.4 per 100,000) that it ever had been or would be in the nation's history. In 2013 the suicide rate in the United States was 12.6 per 100,000, having climbed a bit since the recent low in 2000, when it was 10.4 per 100,000. ▲ Source: Carter, Susan B., Scott Sigmund Gartner, Michael R. Haines, Alan L. Olmstead, Richard Sutch, and Gavin Wright, eds. *Historical Statistics of the United States*, millennial ed. © Cambridge University Press, 2006.

American women, who could rarely get any work. Yet for both African American and white families, females were often the sole breadwinner, supporting not only young children but also older relatives. Most elderly people lived in poverty. For those who suffered most in the Great Depression, the New Deal programs that offered relief and jobs, such as Social Security, the CCC, WPA, and NYA, saved and changed lives. They also created new connections between government and the people that gave the most vulnerable, such as the rural New Mexicans whom Cabeza de Baca instructed, a means for sustaining their homes and families.

20-3b Dislocations and Racial Tensions

Extreme economic hardship pushes people from their homes and into conflict.

In March 1931, African American and white teenage boys were "riding the rails" together in a boxcar in Alabama when a fistfight broke out. The white youngsters jumped off the train and complained that a black gang had attacked them. At the next stop, two white women who had also been on the train accused the black teenagers of rape. Nine black teens were arrested and jailed. A mob formed, and only the bravery of the local sheriff kept them from being lynched. The prisoners were moved to the nearby town of Scottsboro for the first of a series of trials that would capture national and international attention.

In the first of the **Scottsboro Trials**, all but one (a thirteen-year-old) were convicted of rape and sentenced to death. Although the NAACP and ACLU denounced the hasty trial, the Communist Party took the case as its own and, through its legal arm, the International Labor Defense (ILD), appealed the verdicts and publicized the cases internationally. The party also used the Scottsboro Trials as a way to appeal to African Americans who were sympathetic to its support for workers, antiracist stance, and strong defense of the young men. Two cases went to the Supreme Court, which ruled that the defendants had not received fair trials because effective legal defense had not been provided and because African Americans were routinely excluded from juries. Ultimately, four were acquitted, but five served various prison terms. The racism of the U.S. legal system had been exposed to worldwide condemnation.

Scottsboro Trials Series of trials in Alabama from 1931 to 1937 in which nine black youths were unjustly convicted of rape. The trials drew worldwide condemnation of racial injustice.

repatriation Process of returning people to their home country. In the 1930s, Mexican Americans were forcibly repatriated to reduce relief rolls in the Southwest.

Scarcity increased racial tensions not only in the South but everywhere. In the cities of the Northeast, Puerto Ricans faced discrimination in the distribution of relief, and between 1929 and 1934, more than ten thousand of them returned to the island in search of work and aid. Although the federal government had created relief and reconstruction administrations for Puerto Rico, their programs were underfunded and could not meet the overwhelming needs of the island's population.

In southern California during the 1930s, the presence of the many Mexican Americans on relief rolls created tensions. Although most were citizens, Los Angeles officials proposed their **repatriation** across the border to

Mexican Family on the Road, 1936 This photo by Dorothea Lange shows Mexican American family members with a broken-down car as they look for work picking peas in California. Mexican American families faced not only the threat of deportation or removal across the border but also discrimination, which often prevented them from attaining the few jobs available during the Depression. Like the Okies fleeing the Dust Bowl, Mexican American families were forced onto the road to look for work. ▲ Library of Congress Prints and Photographs Division [LC-USZ62-131733].

Dust Bowl Severe dust storms on the Great Plains in the 1930s caused by drought and harmful farming practices. Thousands lost their farms and homes.

general strike Work stoppage in one union or industry that workers in other industries join in sympathy.

Mexico. In the beginning, the city offered free train tickets or cash to those families willing to move. When this policy proved ineffective, local law enforcement agencies with the help of Anglo vigilantes began forcible roundups. In one incident, local police and federal agents closed off a park that had drawn many Mexican American families to its green spaces and then asked each person for proof of citizenship. Of the four hundred people in the park that day, more than a dozen were deported to Mexico. Well-publicized incidents such as this had a chilling effect on all Mexican Americans, who wondered if they would be next. Between 1929 and 1945, more than half a million people, including many U.S. citizens, were moved across the border to Mexico.

Tensions over relief to people in California were further complicated by the mass migration of farmer families from the Great Plains, driven from their homes by drought and dust storms. The drought was most severe in the region that came to be known as the **Dust Bowl** (see Map 20.2). Starting in 1930, the rain stopped, crops dried up, and livestock and people baked and died. In 1936, a year in which *Newsweek* described the country as "a vast simmering cauldron," more than forty-five hundred people died from heat and dehydration. Financial losses associated with the drought in 1934 alone amounted to half of what the nation had spent on World War I. In 1936, the drought was costing farmers $25 million a day, and 2 million farm families were on relief.

Compounding the impact of the drought were strong winds that swept the desiccated soil up into the jet stream and transported it as far away as the North Atlantic. The dust storms lasted from 1931 until 1937, but the worst ones came in 1935. Black Sunday, April 14, 1935, started out as a clear spring Sunday morning, but by afternoon a monstrous dark blizzard appeared on the northern horizon. The dust storm trapped people in their cars, in stranger's homes, and in any makeshift shelter they could find.

Unable to farm or even to stay in their homes, families took to the road, creating one of the largest internal migrations in U.S. history. Some moved as individuals, some as families, and sometimes whole communities picked up and resettled as did five hundred families from the eastern plains of Colorado. The most desperate and adventurous set out for California, moving along Route 66 toward what they hoped would be paradise. In one year, more than eighty-six thousand people resettled in California, more than had arrived in the two years after the gold rush of 1849. But even in California, there were no jobs and no relief monies for them. Like Mexican Americans and other minorities, these "Okies" and "Arkies" from Oklahoma and Arkansas were despised and feared.

20-3c Industrial Conflict

Workers are emboldened by New Deal reforms to push for better conditions and higher pay.

The Wagner Act gave laboring men and women protections they had never had, and probably had been passed just in time to stave off both labor violence and the appeal of communism. Although trade unions in Europe had at times been powerful enough to call **general strikes**, involving workers in many industries

Map 20.2 The Dust Bowl, 1934–1940 While most of the country suffered from drought, these twelve midwestern states experienced the lowest precipitation on record. With the drought came intense heat with temperatures above 110 degrees. Accompanying dust storms wiped out almost 5 million acres of wheat: half of the crop in Kansas, one-quarter in Oklahoma, and all in Nebraska. These storms blew away twice as much earth as had been removed to create the Panama Canal. ►

Rapport Press/Newscom

Flint Sit-Down Strike, 1936 These men, members of the United Auto Workers (UAW), went out on strike during the 1936 Christmas season. By refusing to work or to physically leave the Fisher Body Plant Number 1, which contained the dyes for GM's 1937 models, this small group of workers almost completely halted GM production. News of this successful strike spread through the auto industry and ushered in a new era of powerful unions. ▲

that shut down regions or even a nation, labor in the United States had not been so well organized. During the first years of the Depression, most workers had endured layoffs and firings without protest. But in 1934, West Coast longshoremen turned militant under the leadership of Harry Bridges, an Australian unionist with ties to the Communist Party. They went out on strike on May 9, 1934, blockading the transport of goods from the docks by rail. When in July the Industrial Association, a coalition of business owners, sought to break the strike by moving goods by truck, violence erupted; dozens were severely wounded and two men killed. The Teamsters and other powerful unions in the Bay Area then joined the longshoremen in a general strike that shut down commerce in San Francisco for four days before both sides agreed to arbitration.

Following passage of the Wagner Act, unions renewed their organizing efforts. The increase in union membership and power was dramatic. Soon Lewis's UMW made sure that more than 90 percent of the nation's coal was mined under union contracts. He also took the lead in founding the **Congress of Industrial Organizations (CIO)**, which challenged the American Federation of Labor (AFL) by organizing workers by industry instead of by trade and opening its ranks to women and ethnic minorities. The increasing power of industrial labor was dramatically symbolized in a fistfight at an AFL convention, when Lewis punched the leader of the carpenters' union and sent him writhing on the floor.

The CIO rapidly unionized workers in the steel and automobile industries and began to organize transnationally into Latin America, particularly Mexico. In Flint, Michigan, a city dominated by General Motors, the local United Auto Workers (UAW) counted only one hundred twenty-two members when it launched a **sit-down strike** in December 1936. Instead of calling on the National Guard to break the strike, as happened so often in the nineteenth century, Michigan's governor called out the National Guard to protect the striking workers. In February 1937, GM agreed to negotiate with the workers, and Chrysler soon followed. Within a few months, the UAW's membership grew from 98,000 to 400,000 workers. The success of the strike showed reluctant workers the immense power of unions, which could win higher wages and better working conditions for them. At no other time in U.S. history were workers as free to organize unions as they were then, protected by federal legislation that allowed them to bargain fairly with their employers. Nevertheless, the Roosevelt administration remained cool to the pressures of the CIO, which it regarded as potentially threatening to the New Deal's more moderate agenda for labor. In the 1940 election, Lewis publically withdrew his support from Roosevelt.

20-3d A New Deal for Indians

Reforms benefit Indian communities.

Indians in general, and in particular the groups that Cabeza de Baca served, had been in a precarious economic situation since the end of the nineteenth century. Long before the Depression began, they suffered the highest poverty level, the worst health, and the highest unemployment of any Americans. Although they had made significant population gains since their nadir in 1891, when the federal government had removed most of them to reservations, they had the highest infant mortality rate and suffered from tuberculosis, whooping cough, and other communicable diseases at proportions far above the national average. Almost one-third of Indians lived in poverty in 1930, with no means of support.

New Deal policies regarding Indians highlighted arguments that had been raging among Washington bureaucrats as well as among Indians themselves about how they should be incorporated into the modern world. Since the 1887 Dawes Act, Indians had struggled to find a way to modernize while maintaining their ties to tradition. Meanwhile, the federal policy of assimilation, including the Indian Citizenship Act of 1924, had forced many onto reservations and small parcels of land so they

Congress of Industrial Organizations (CIO) Umbrella organization of unions founded in 1935 representing workers, often unskilled, by industry rather than by trade.

sit-down strike Work stoppage in which workers stay at their work stations but refuse to work until their demands are met, preventing management from hiring strikebreakers.

could be farmers. The New Deal for Indians reversed this decades-long policy. Under the Indian Reorganization Act of 1934 (IRA), allotment, boarding schools, and assimilation as a goal were replaced by a program that fostered local control, encouraged the scientific management of land and water resources, and put governance in the hands of tribal councils, although many decisions were still subject to approval by the Department of the Interior. By the end of the New Deal, one hundred seventy-four tribes (about one hundred thirty-two thousand people) had passed referendums voting for reorganization and created constitutions to govern themselves.

John Collier, Roosevelt's choice to head the Bureau of Indian Affairs, spearheaded the legislation and took funds from existing New Deal programs to cobble together the Indian New Deal. Collier had been advocating on behalf of Native Americans for a decade before his appointment, and the IRA was his way of bringing those progressive changes to completion. He redirected more than $5 million from the CCC budget to provide for infrastructure projects on reservations that employed young Indian men. States also allocated monies for cooperative extension programs that directed aid to Native American communities, such as the one for which Cabeza de Baca worked in New Mexico. The seventy-three tribes (about seventy-eight thousand people) that rejected the IRA continued to operate under the federal government's previous terms.

20-3e Public Works and Popular Culture

> The New Deal encourages the creation of public goods that all Americans can enjoy.

With the Wagner and Social Security acts, the federal government touched the lives of ordinary Americans as never before. So did a series of projects that dammed and transformed America's rivers, created reservoirs, brought electricity to rural Americans, and changed agriculture through irrigation. Through monies that came from Hoover's RFC, the PWA, the TVA, and later New Deal legislation, the federal government spearheaded the largest public works projects in the nation's history, building sewers, bridges, schools, airports, and highways and making improvements in national parks.

With RFC funding, Boulder (later renamed Hoover) Dam, whose construction had begun under the Hoover administration, best exemplifies the planning, labor practices, consolidation of capital, and government intervention that marked these dam-building projects in the West. Costing $114 million and employing more than five thousand people over the course of the project, the fifty-story-high structure managed the Colorado River's erratic flow and generated four times the hydroelectric power of Niagara Falls. A group of ambitious businessmen, the Six Companies, won the bid for the project, and although none had ever managed such a large endeavor, they finished the dam in 1936, two years ahead of schedule and under budget, epitomizing the benefits of massive centralized government investment.

Perhaps no area was transformed as much as the South following the establishment of the TVA in May 1933 (see section 20-2b). It was part of a regional planning project that combined water resource management through dams with rural electrification, fertilizer production, and, reforestation, and aid for the rural poor. Before the TVA, less than 5 percent of farms in the region had electricity, but eventually, more than 90 percent had it. Families also had access to educational programs similar to those Cabeza de Baca offered in New Mexico. Men found work on the major dam projects and in facilities producing nitrate fertilizers at Muscle Shoals, Alabama. New Dealers saw projects such as the TVA, the Columbia Basin River project, and the dams along the Missouri River in the upper Midwest as a way to bring prosperity and comforts to farmers and rural Americans.

In the course of their work, many WPA writers and artists critiqued both the capitalist system that had allowed the Depression to occur and the federal government's response to the crisis. For example, filmmaker Pare Lorentz's visually stunning short film, *The Plow That Broke the Plains,* held capitalism, global demand for wheat, and overuse of the land responsible for the Dust Bowl. Dorothea Lange, one of the most prolific photographers employed by the Farm Security Administration, produced thousands of images depicting a cross-section of Americans. Whether it was a photograph of a Mexican American family being repatriated or a defeated migrant mother nursing her child in a labor camp, Lange put a real face on poverty in the United States. She wanted people to see themselves in these haunting images, and the Roosevelt administration used them to rally support for the New Deal's more liberal and redistributive aspects.

Art commissioned for private collectors sometimes had a different fate. A mural created by the Mexican artist Diego Rivera for New York City's Rockefeller Center was covered and then destroyed when Nelson Rockefeller objected to the Communist themes and the likeness of Lenin. Rivera returned to Mexico to create a smaller version of the mural, *Man at the Crossroads* with its praise for labor and Communist ideas. His mural for the Detroit Institute of Arts was also an ode to America's multiracial workforce. Edsel Ford, whose family had funded the institute and the mural, defended Rivera's work.

While artists such as Lange and Rivera critiqued capitalism, most Americans found comfort in popular culture. They flocked to movie theaters to see Hollywood films that, for a few hours, allowed them to escape the difficulties in their own lives. Charlie Chaplin and the Marx

Alfred Eisenstaedt/The Life Picture Collection/Getty Images

Global Americans

Paul Robeson, son of an escaped slave, football All-American at Rutgers University, Phi Beta Kappa, and class valedictorian, seemed destined for success. He gravitated to the theater and, during the heyday of the Harlem Renaissance, became famous as an actor and singer known for his gift for oration and his resonating voice. At a time when few serious roles were open to African Americans, he starred in Eugene O'Neill's *Emperor Jones* and sang "Ol' Man River" in the musical *Showboat,* both later made into popular movies. During the 1920s and 1930s, Robeson often lived and performed in London, where he starred in *Othello,* a role he could not have performed in the United States. In London, he associated with leftist radicals, became interested in Africa, and was drawn to anticolonialism and communism. Visiting the Soviet Union in 1934, he extolled the lack of racial bias. "Here I am not a Negro but a human being," he remarked. "Here, for the first time in my life I walk in full human dignity." But in the United States, Robeson's Communist ties made him suspect. In the 1940s, he was investigated by the Federal Bureau of Investigation and the House Un-American Activities Committee and was blacklisted in Hollywood. In the 1950s, the State Department refused to renew his passport, thus preventing him from touring internationally. Although these restraints were later lifted, Robeson's career seemed tarnished in the United States even as he was welcomed abroad.

Brothers emerged from the silent era, and new stars such as Claudette Colbert and a young Katherine Hepburn introduced the age of romantic comedies. Americans also listened to the radio. The soap opera emerged in this era, taking its name from sponsors selling soaps, such as Palmolive and Procter & Gamble. First broadcast in 1937, *The Guiding Light* became a staple for millions of American women who turned on the radio. When it moved to television in 1956, its audience seamlessly followed the Spaulding and Bauer families in the fictional town of Springfield. Through movies, radio, and best-selling novels, such as *Gone with the Wind,* Americans across the country began to share a common culture that crossed class and racial boundaries.

Diego Rivera, *Man, Controller of the Universe,* Mexico 1934 This is a re-creation of Rivera's mural at Rockefeller Center in New York City. Abby Aldrich Rockefeller was an admirer of Rivera, one of the most famous artists of his time. However, Rivera's depiction of Vladimir Lenin and other anticapitalist imagery in the mural proved controversial. Amid protests, the mural was destroyed and replaced by *American Progress*, a mural featuring Abraham Lincoln. ▼

Artepics/Alamy Stock Photo

20-4

End of the New Deal and the Approach of War

In this cartoon titled "Isn't This What We Really Want?" the editorial cartoonist known as Herblock humorously depicts the debate over U.S. neutrality as world conflict increases. He suggested that the Roosevelt administration was attempting to solve all kinds of problems and to appease people both domestically and abroad.

What does the image suggest about the complexities and contradictions of U.S. neutrality policies in this era? ▶

Isn't This What We Really Want?

DO NOT DISTURB
A NEUTRALITY ACT THAT WILL KEEP US OUT OF ANY WAR,
WILL INSURE THE CONTINUITY OF AMERICAN COMMERCE,
WILL ACT TO CURB THE POWER OF THE DICTATORSHIPS,
AND WILL SCRUB FLOORS AND DO THE DISHES IN ITS SPARE TIME.

Library of Congress Prints and Photographs Division[LC-DIG-ppmsc-03387]

After the landslide victory in 1936, the Roosevelt administration appeared to have unlimited power to push more programs for recovery. Moreover, Roosevelt and his advisers believed that because the economy was on the upturn, they could attempt to balance the budget and reduce their reliance on deficit spending, which the president had never liked or intended as a long-term solution to the economic crisis. They misjudged, however, and the administration made a number of strategic mistakes that put presidential authority and the economy in jeopardy. Moreover, as hostilities engulfed both Europe and Asia, the Roosevelt administration and Americans in general had to confront the prospect of war.

☞ As you read, consider the national and international concerns that Roosevelt faced in his second term. How did the economic turmoil of the 1930s contribute to the rising conflict in Europe and Asia?

20-4a Setbacks to the New Deal

Roosevelt makes missteps as he seeks to increase his presidential powers.

Roosevelt worried most about what he called his "Court problem"—the Supreme Court rulings that had invalidated much of the early New Deal legislation. He wanted more influence, if not control, over future Court decisions to ensure the permanence of his legislative agenda. Less than two weeks after his 1937 inauguration, he shocked Congress and the public with a proposal for reorganizing the judicial branch of government, citing the need for efficiency and the principle of mandatory retirement. He proposed that the president appoint a new justice when one who had served for ten years did not retire within six months of turning seventy. This would also apply to judges of lower federal courts. Under this plan, Roosevelt would have been able to appoint six new justices to the Supreme Court immediately.

Court-packing plan Roosevelt's 1937 attempt to reorganize the judicial branch so that the constitutionality of New Deal laws would be decided by a more favorable set of judges.

It was not only the content of the bill that angered its opponents but also the imperious way in which Roosevelt presented it, without consultation. Opponents, many of them Democrats, saw what they called his **Court-packing plan** as an attack on the judicial branch that overstepped the constitutional boundaries of the presidency. Chief Justice Charles Evans Hughes composed a scathing letter to Roosevelt detailing the working of his court and revealing Roosevelt's "efficiency" argument as a sham.

The legislation lagged in Congress, and, in the meantime, the Court made some adjustments of its own. In a series of five-to-four decisions in the spring of 1937, the Court began to validate key pieces of New Deal legislation, such as the Wagner Act. Then on May 18, Justice Willis Van Devanter announced his retirement, and Roosevelt nominated Hugo Black to the bench. Eventually, retirements enabled Roosevelt to appoint five justices during his second term, and the plan for judicial reorganization died, but the New Deal coalition that had emerged during the 1936 presidential election had been damaged. Subsequently, the Democrats found it difficult to pass liberal reform legislation. They abandoned a plan to take up universal health care in 1937, although they did pass the Fair Labor Standards Act in 1938 that established a minimum wage and maximum number of work hours.

In the midst of the political crisis over the Court-packing plan, the nation experienced another economic downturn in the fall of 1937. Earlier that year, the economy had pulled above 1929 levels of output, and, as complete recovery seemed imminent, Roosevelt began to cut funding to balance the federal budget. He slashed

AP Images

Paul G. Hallett Looking for Work, 1937 The plight of men such as that of Mr. Hallett during the Roosevelt Recession unnerved Americans who worried about both the sagging economy and tensions abroad. The renewed depression was caused by the federal government's attempts to balance the budget by cutting back spending programs. The growth in the global economy caused by the buildup to war, however, stimulated growth both at home and abroad as companies sought to meet the emerging wartime demands. ▲

the budget of the WPA and eliminated whole programs. Quite suddenly, the economy sank. Because the $2 billion collected in taxes for the new Social Security program was also withdrawn from the economy, one critic noted, "Not only is the government not priming the economic pump, they are taking some water out of the spout." This so-called **Roosevelt Recession** was not as severe as the 1929 downturn, but it unnerved Americans.

In 1938, 19 percent of Americans were out of work, 5 percent higher than in 1936. Between October 1937 and the spring of 1938, applications for WPA jobs soared 194 percent in Toledo and 434 percent in Detroit. In Cleveland, sixty-five thousand people were on the relief roles, unable to find food or housing. Children rummaged through garbage cans looking for spoiled produce. Many compared Roosevelt to Hoover, offering little more than a calculated and conservative response to an immense crisis.

The combination of the Court-packing plan and the recession left Roosevelt unable to work with Congress because Democrats distanced themselves from him. For the next three years, federal action on the economy stalled, and some suggested that having 5–9 million people out of work might be the new "normal" economy. In the end, however, the Depression ended not so much because of government intervention but by events in Europe and Asia that stimulated a massive military buildup.

20-4b Global Dangers

Threats from militarist regimes worry Americans and the Roosevelt administration.

Centralized economic planning had pulled Germany out of depression by the mid-1930s, aided by increased military spending following Hitler's renunciation of the Treaty of Versailles's disarmament clauses in May 1935. The next year, his troops marched into the Rhineland in defiance of the treaty, which had established that region between Germany and France as a demilitarized zone. In October 1935, Mussolini's Italian troops invaded Ethiopia, the East African nation that had resisted an Italian takeover in 1896. This time, with superior weapons and planes that sprayed outlawed poison gas on civilians, the Italians easily overpowered the Ethiopians. It was clear to Roosevelt that the fascist dictatorships were embarking on dangerous military aggressions (see Map 20.3), especially after Italy and Germany signed a treaty of friendship in 1936 that Mussolini called the Rome-Berlin Axis. In 1937, Mussolini withdrew Italy from the League of Nations as Germany and Japan had already done (see Table 21.1).

The League was clearly weakened by such defections, and its response to Italy's takeover of Ethiopia only highlighted its lack of power. Although it briefly imposed economic sanctions on Italy, it did not provide collective security for Ethiopia. In May 1936, Haile Selassie, emperor of Ethiopia, fled the country. A month later, he implored the League to denounce the Italian invasion of his country: "It is us today. It will be you tomorrow." But the plea was ignored, and when Mussolini made Ethiopia an Italian colony, only six nations, including the United States and China, refused to recognize its status.

Then in July 1936, Spain plunged into a civil war that further aggravated the growing hostilities in Europe. The Nationalists—a coalition of conservative Catholics, landowners, soldiers, and businessmen—rebelled against the leftist Republican government and sought to institute a fascist state. They received troops and military equipment from Germany and Italy as in order to expand fascism and intimidate Britain and France. The Soviet Union and Mexico sent military assistance to the Republicans. In April 1939, the Nationalists prevailed, and General Francisco Franco established a long-lasting right-wing dictatorship.

Roosevelt Recession Economic downturn of 1937–1938 believed to have been caused by government's pullback on deficit spending and the implementation of Social Security.

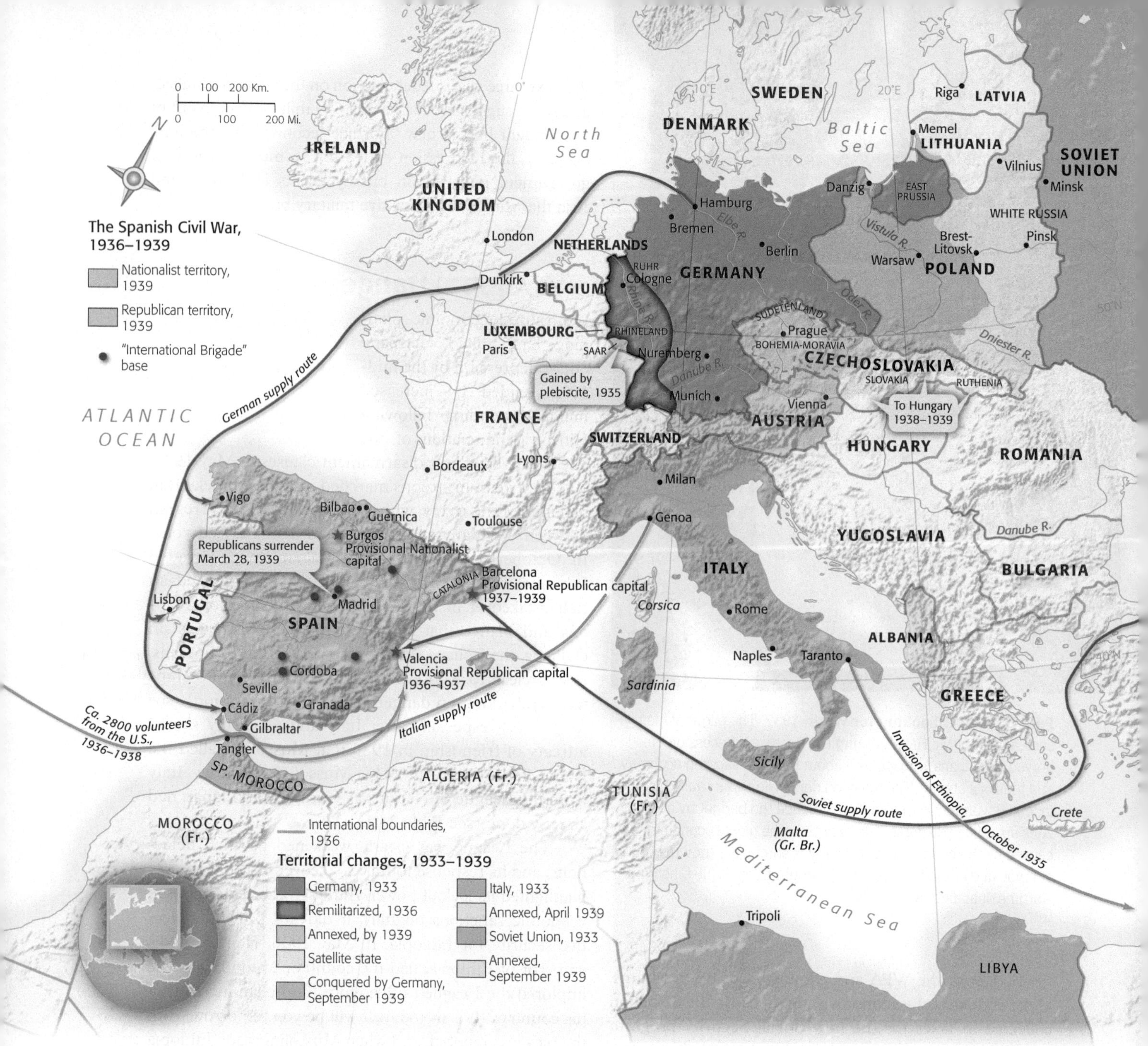

Map 20.3 Axis Aggression in Europe, 1933–1939 In the midst of the global depression, the militarized regimes of Benito Mussolini in Italy and Adolf Hitler in Germany pushed aggressively to acquire more territory. During this time period, Mussolini seized Ethiopia and Albania and Hitler annexed Austria and Czechoslovakia. Both supported the establishment of a fascist regime in Spain. This military expansion went unanswered by Britain and France until Hitler menaced Poland. His invasion there brought declarations of war from the Western democracies and began World War II. ▲

In July 1937, the Japanese launched an undeclared war on China, capturing Shanghai, Peking (now Beijing), and Nanjing before the end of the year. In Nanjing, obeying orders to "kill all captives," Japanese soldiers massacred more than three hundred thousand civilians and raped eighty thousand women. By the end of 1938, the Japanese held most of China's seaports and seemed intent on regional domination (see Map 20.4).

U.S. policy makers responded cautiously to the crisis in China. With ongoing global economic instability, Roosevelt did not want to jeopardize U.S. trade with either China or Japan. In an October 1937 speech, he had called for a "quarantine" of aggressor states. He was privately considering economic sanctions against Japan but took no further action and accepted a Japanese apology for bombing the U.S. gunboat *Panay* on the Yangtze River while it was evacuating Americans from Nanjing. Despite the massacre of Chinese civilians, Roosevelt was certain the Americans would not support going to war against Japan at this time. While helping the Chinese Nationalists buy U.S. military equipment to use against both the Communists and the Japanese, U.S. officials continued supplying Japan with nearly half of its imports, including oil, cars, iron, and steel. This delicate balance of political interests and economic imperatives proved impossible to sustain.

20-4c U.S. Neutrality

As world conflict intensifies, most Americans want to remain neutral.

Recognizing the volatile international situation and convinced the United States would need more allies in the event of war, Roosevelt had already sought to improve U.S.–Latin American relations and promote hemispheric solidarity through the Good Neighbor Policy. This arrangement renounced the military interventionism that had punctuated U.S. actions in the region for decades. In 1934, U.S. officials had repealed the Platt Amendment, which had authorized U.S. meddling in Cuban affairs since 1901. By 1936, all U.S. troops had been removed from the Caribbean, although U.S. officials retained control over customs collections and some military bases. U.S. companies still dominated local production of sugar, cotton, coffee, and bananas. To improve trade, Secretary of State Cordell Hull launched the Export-Import Bank to extend credit for foreign purchases of American products. In 1938, when the Mexican government confiscated the properties of foreign oil companies, Roosevelt overruled calls for U.S. intervention in favor of a negotiated settlement. These changes proved economically beneficial. From 1933 to 1938, the value of U.S. exports to Latin America increased from $244 million to $642 million.

Although most Americans supported close ties with Latin America, they also opposed engagement in overseas conflicts, remembering the sacrifices of the Great War. Influenced by the best seller, *Merchants of Death* (1934), many people interpreted U.S. participation in that war as manipulated by the industrialists and bankers who profited from it. Congressional hearings led by Republican senator Gerald Nye of North Dakota called on the financier J. P. Morgan Jr. and the industrialist Pierre du Pont to account for their roles as businessmen in World War I. With little evidence to substantiate its allegations, the Nye Committee concluded that U.S. bankers and munitions makers had dragged the United States into war in pursuit of profit. Already disdainful of business leaders because of the economic crisis, most Americans accepted these accusations, reinforcing the general isolationist sentiment, strong since the 1920s.

Determined not to replicate the same errors that had entangled the United States in World War I, Nye introduced a bill outlawing arms sales to nations at war and warning Americans traveling on combatants' ships that they did so at their own risk. In August 1935, Congress passed his **Neutrality Acts** and extended it in February 1936, adding a ban on loans and credits to belligerents. In May 1937, Congress made the first two acts permanent, expanding them to cover civil wars and prohibiting U.S. ships from transporting passengers or cargo to combatant states. Private U.S. citizens were also forbidden to travel on belligerent ships.

Roosevelt signed the Neutrality Acts and invoked them to prevent arms and ammunition shipments to either side during the Ethiopian crisis and the Spanish Civil War. But U.S. neutrality also drew criticism from constituencies sympathetic to belligerents in both conflicts. In 1935, W.E.B. Du Bois described Italy's seizure of Ethiopia as one more instance of white imperialism and aggression against "the dark peoples." He also warned that Japan "is regarded by all colored peoples as their logical leader, the one non-white nation that has escaped forever the dominance and exploitation of the white world." Leftist supporters of Spain's Republican government also charged that Roosevelt had betrayed democracy, and some three thousand Americans volunteered to fight for Spain's defense. Vocal congressional leaders, on the other hand, were outraged when Roosevelt did not invoke the Neutrality Acts in Japan's war against China but continued to trade with both belligerents.

Whereas economic and geopolitical imperatives shaped Roosevelt's approach to neutrality, he privately wanted to aid Britain and France should war break out in Europe. With the long view in mind and on the advice of Bernard Baruch, in 1937 he convinced Congress to amend the Neutrality Acts to include a two-year "cash-and-carry" provision that permitted the sale of nonmilitary items to combatants as long as they paid cash for the items and transported them. It was clearly intended to benefit Britain and France, which could meet these terms, over Germany, which could not. In 1939, the act was made permanent.

Neutrality Acts Series of laws passed in the late 1930s to prevent direct U.S. involvement in international conflicts.

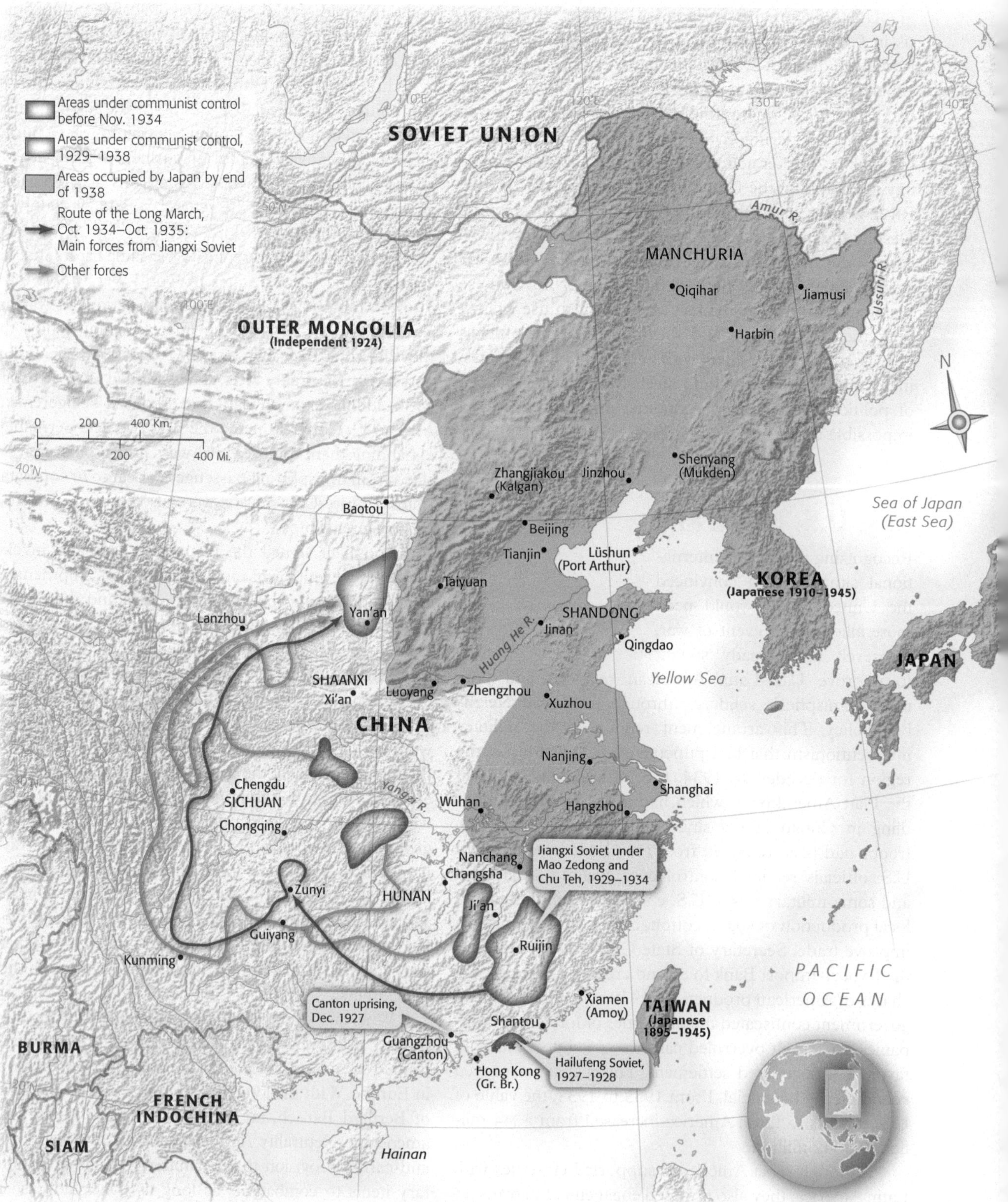

Map 20.4 Japanese Invasion of China, 1934–1938 The militarist regime in Japan seized Manchuria from China in 1931 and in 1937 launched a full-scale attack on China. Japan's expansionist program aimed to secure natural resources and dominate East Asia. During their occupation of China, the Japanese set up large farming and industrial operations and forced millions of Chinese to work in these enterprises. The Chinese people suffered harsh treatment and brutal conditions, and hundreds of thousands were massacred at Nanjing. ▲

Keystone/Getty Images

Jewish Refugees Disembarking from the *SS St. Louis*, Belgium, 1939 Two weeks earlier, these passengers had been turned away from Cuba as they sought to escape the Nazis. Most possessed visas, but Cuba had changed its laws while the boat was at sea. Captain Gustav Schroeder negotiated with both the Cuban and U.S. governments to allow the ship to discharge its passengers. The boat sailed along the Florida coast but was not allowed to dock and returned to Europe. Historians estimate that about 250 of the 937 passengers died in the Holocaust. ◄

20-4d Europe in Crisis

Nazi Germany persecutes Jews and embarks on conquest.

In the late 1930s, Hitler intensified his campaign to rid Germany of Jews. Yet Jews who were desperate to leave Germany and Austria found that few nations would receive them. Unwilling to accept immigrants who might be an additional burden on the already fragile economy, U.S. officials did not adjust the 1924 immigration quotas to permit entrance of these refugees. These quotas, combined with pervasive anti-Semitism in the State Department, made it difficult for Jews to obtain U.S. visas. In July 1938, Roosevelt convened (but did not attend) a conference to address the growing Jewish refugee crisis. Delegates from thirty-two nations met at Évian-les-Bains, France, but most of the represented countries refused to accept large numbers of refugees.

In September, after a young Jewish refugee murdered a German diplomat in Paris, the Nazis escalated their attacks. On November 9–10, later known as *Kristallnacht* (Night of Broken Glass), they destroyed Jewish property throughout Germany and Austria, fined Jews $400 million for the damage, and sent thirty thousand Jews to concentration camps at Buchenwald and Dachau. News of the violence and detentions swept the world, but Western nations were still reluctant to take more Jewish émigrés.

Emboldened by the lack of a concerted global response to his remilitarization efforts and his intervention in Spain, Hitler launched an ambitious plan to conquer Europe. Seeking first to absorb nations with large populations of ethnic Germans, he had seized neighboring Austria in 1938. He then demanded to annex the Sudetenland, a province of Czechoslovakia with 3 million people of German descent. Meeting in Munich in September 1938, British and French leaders acceded to this demand in exchange for a promise that Hitler would not annex any more Czech territory. The Czech government was not invited to the proceedings.

Upon returning to England, British prime minister Neville Chamberlain announced that the Munich agreement ensured "peace in our time." But the strategy of what came to be known as **appeasement** backfired when just six months later, Hitler seized the rest of Czechoslovakia. In April 1939, Mussolini invaded Albania. The following month Germany and Italy—the **Axis Powers**—formalized their military alliance. A new crisis in Poland soon erupted when Hitler demanded Danzig, a free city under the protection of the League of Nations. Determined not to surrender their access to the Baltic Sea, the Polish government resisted Hitler's desire to control the port. The British and French, recognizing that appeasement had failed, vowed to support Poland.

Fearing German expansionism and dismayed when the British and French rebuffed his attempts to form alliances, Soviet premier Stalin directed his foreign minister to get guarantees from Germany. Despite their diametrically opposed political ideologies, the two nations signed a nonaggression pact on August 23, 1939. It included secret protocols that divided Romania, Poland, Lithuania, Latvia, Estonia, and Finland into German and Soviet spheres of influence. On September 1, German troops invaded Poland. Two days later, Britain and France declared war on Germany. On September 17, Soviet troops invaded Poland from the east. World War II was under way, and the U.S. commitment to neutrality was to be severely tested.

appeasement Diplomatic policy that makes concessions to an aggressive foreign power in order to avoid military conflict.

Axis Powers Alliance of Germany, Italy, and Japan that fought in World War II against the Allied nations of the United States, Britain, France, Poland, and later the Soviet Union.

Summary

Although the crash of the U.S. stock market in October 1929 was the most dramatic signal of a global depression, it was only one aspect of the worldwide economic downturn. Americans, as well as Europeans, Asians, and Latin Americans, faced the loss of jobs, homes, and lifetime savings as industrial production and trade declined and nations turned inward in search of security.

In the United States, families suffered from the Depression in differing degrees, based on whether they lived in cities or in rural areas, were old or young, were male or female, or were white or people of color. Although the New Deal never met the expectations of the liberal reformers who wanted a complete restructuring of the economy and a redistribution of wealth, it was not the radical overhaul that conservatives feared.

In the end, the New Deal was a set of moderate reforms that provided relief, shored up the economy, and kept Americans from turning to more radical solutions that were evident elsewhere, such as national socialism in Germany, communism in the Soviet Union, and militarism in Japan. The New Deal also put in place a set of programs such as Social Security, protections for workers and unions, farm supports and subsidies, and infrastructure projects that would have a long-term impact on the economy and individual lives. These pieces of New Deal legislation were the foundation for the modern welfare state, entitlements for individuals, and government contracts that would come to dominate twentieth-century American life.

The end of the Second New Deal and the Roosevelt Recession of 1937 raised questions about the effectiveness of New Deal reforms. At the same time, overseas conflicts strengthened Congress's resolve that the United States should remain neutral. Roosevelt cautiously tried to preserve U.S. neutrality even as German, Italian, and Japanese aggression made another world war seem inevitable.

<Thinking Back, *Looking Forward*>

As you review this chapter, think about the role of the federal government in bringing about reforms that regulated markets and aided struggling Americans. What made the New Deal so different from earlier attempts at reform, such as those in the Progressive era? Why did the New Deal mark a turning point in how Americans viewed their relationship with the federal government? Keep New Deal reforms in mind when you study the Great Society reforms of the 1960s in later chapters. How was the New Deal different from economic programs to end the Depression in other parts of the world?

To make your study concrete, review the timeline and reflect on the entries there. Think about their causes, consequences, and connections. How do they fit with global trends?

Additional Resources

Books

Brinkley, Alan. *Voices of Protest: Huey Long, Father Coughlin, and the Great Depression.* New York: Vintage Press, 1982. ▶ Award-winning book examining the opposition to Roosevelt's New Deal.

Cohen, Lizabeth. *Making a New Deal: Industrial Workers in Chicago, 1919–1939.* New York: Cambridge University Press, 1991. ▶ Engaging study about the families who struggled during both the "roaring twenties" and the Great Depression.

Gilmore, Glenda Elizabeth. *Defying Dixie: The Radical Roots of the Civil Rights Movement, 1919–1950.* New York: Norton, 2008. ▶ Compelling stories of those who worked within radical organizations such as the CPUSA to push for civil rights.

Gordon, Linda. *Dorothea Lange: A Life Beyond Limits.* New York: Norton Press, 2009. ▶ Award-winning biography of perhaps the greatest U.S. photographer and the historical context in which she worked.

Katznelson, Ira. *Fear Itself: The New Deal and the Origins of Our Time.* New York: Norton, 2013. ▶ Argument that the New Deal was based on a general sense of fear in order to pull the nation through the Great Depression and World War II.

Kelly, Robin D. G. *Hammer and Hoe: Alabama Communists during the Great Depression.* Chapel Hill: University of North Carolina Press, 1990. ▶ Argument that the CPUSA was the most effective agent for social change in the U.S. South.

Kennedy, David. *Freedom from Fear: The American People in War and Depression, 1929–1945.* New York: Oxford University Press, 1999. ▶ Pulitzer-Prize-winning book that gives a clear and general overview of the period.

O'Neill, Colleen. *Working the Navajo Way: Labor and Culture in the Twentieth Century.* Lawrence: University of Kansas Press, 2005. ▶ Compelling narrative about how the Navajos adapted to the changes brought on by the Depression and New Deal policies.

Sanchez, George. *Becoming Mexican-American: Ethnicity, Culture and Identity in Chicano Los Angeles, 1900–1945.* New York: Oxford University Press, 1993. ▶ Consideration of how both long-time residents and recent immigrants to Los Angeles found work, created families, and endured through the Great Depression

Worster, Donald. *The Dust Bowl: The Southern Plains in the 1930s.* 25th anniv. ed. New York: Oxford University Press, 2004. ▶ Most comprehensive and gripping narrative about the Dust Bowl and its impact.

Go to the MindTap® for **Global Americans** to access the full version of select books from this Additional Resources section.

Websites

American Life Histories: Manuscripts from the Federal Writers Project, 1936–1940. (http://www.loc.gov/collection/federal-writers-project/about-this-collection/) ▶ Almost three thousand stories of people collected from twenty-four states during the late 1930s.

Franklin Delano Roosevelt Presidential Library and Museum. (http://www.fdrlibrary.marist.edu/library/) ▶ Repository of the personal papers of Franklin and Eleanor Roosevelt's as well as those of many of their colleagues and friends.

Museum of Modern Art (MOMA): Dorothea Lange Collection. (http://www.moma.org/collection/artist.php?artist_id=3373) ▶ Collection of thirty-five images Lange produced for the Farm Security Administration.

New Deal Network. (http://newdeal.feri.org/) ▶ Database of more than two hundred thousand primary sources including newspapers, letters, and advertisements.

Slave Narratives from the Federal Writers Project: American Memory (http://memory.loc.gov/ammem/snhtml/snhome.html). ▶ Most comprehensive repository of oral history testimonies from former slaves.

MindTap®

Continue exploring online through MindTap®, where you can:

- **Assess your knowledge with the Chapter Test**
- **Watch historical videos related to the chapter**
- **Further your understanding with interactive maps and timelines**

Great Depression, New Deal, and Impending War

1929

October

Stock market crashes, indicating a global economic crisis.

1930

June

Hawley-Smoot protective tariff suppresses global trade.

1931

March

Scottsboro trials of black youths draw international condemnation.

June

Hoover proposes moratorium on reparations and war debt payments.

September

Japan seizes Manchuria from China.

1933

January

Adolf Hitler becomes chancellor of Germany and shortly assumes dictatorial powers.

March

Roosevelt is inaugurated president.

June

London Economic Conference fails to revitalize international trade.

December

Twenty-First Amendment is ratified, ending Prohibition.

Good Neighbor Policy seeks to improve U.S. relations with Latin America.

1934

April

Nye Committee hearings on munitions profits in World War I heightens skepticism.

July

Longshoremen launch a general strike in San Francisco.

1935

April

Dust Bowl storms destroy crops, leave thousands homeless.

May

Hitler renounces disarmament clauses of the Treaty of Versailles.

Supreme Court strikes down much of the Hundred Days legislation.

July

Wagner Act gives protections to labor.

August

Social Security Act provides for the unemployed, poor, and elderly.

Neutrality Acts begin to define U.S. neutrality as international tensions rise.

September

Nuremberg Laws deprive German Jews of civil rights.

October

Italy invades and shortly conquers Ethiopia.

1936

July

Spanish Civil War begins.

September

Hoover Dam is completed, controlling water flow and generating electricity.

November

Benito Mussolini announces the Rome-Berlin treaty between Axis powers.

Roosevelt wins second term in landslide.

December

Flint sit-down strike begins.

1937

February

Roosevelt's Court-Packing Plan proves unpopular.

July

Japan launches attack on China.

Isn't This What We Really Want?
A NEUTRALITY ACT THAT WILL KEEP US OUT OF ANY WAR,
WILL INSURE THE CONTINUITY OF AMERICAN COMMERCE,
WILL ACT TO CURB THE POWER OF THE DICTATORSHIPS,
AND WILL SCRUB FLOORS AND DO THE DISHES IN ITS SPARE TIME.

October

During Roosevelt Recession, profits and production decline and unemployment rises.

November

Japan occupies Nanjing and begins massacre of civilians.

1938

March

Germany annexes Austria.

June

Fair Labor Standards Act establishes minimum wages and maximum hours.

September

Germany negotiates agreement to annex Czechoslovakia's Sudetenland.

November

During anti-Jewish riots called *Kristallnacht*, Nazis destroy Jewish property.

1939

March

Germany seizes the rest of Czechoslovakia.

April

Italy invades Albania.

May

Germany and Italy form a military alliance.

August

Germany and the Soviet Union sign a nonaggression pact.

September

Germany invades Poland, World War II begins, and the Soviet Union invades Poland.

21

The World at War

1939–1945

Albert Einstein left Hitler's Germany in 1933 and settled in Princeton, New Jersey, becoming a U.S. citizen in 1940.

In 1940, Albert Einstein became a U.S. citizen. Having witnessed firsthand the rise of fascism and anti-Semitism in Europe, he celebrated the freedoms found in the United States. America, he explained, protected the "right of individuals to say and think what they pleased" and fostered creativity and upward mobility.

Library of Congress Prints and Photographs Division [LC-DIG-ppmsca-05649]

Albert Einstein accepts his U.S. citizenship certificate from Judge Philip Forman on October 1, 1940.

Einstein was the most famous physicist in the world, and his renunciation of German citizenship was Germany's loss. In 1905, his so-called miracle year, he had published four internationally renowned papers on the photoelectric effect, Brownian motion, special relativity, and the equivalence of matter and energy (expressed in the equation $E = mc^2$). During World War I, while a research professor at Humboldt University in Berlin, he revolutionized physics with his theory of general relativity.

After the war, the intensification of German anti-Semitism caused Einstein to embrace his Jewish identity, though he had been raised as a non-observant Jew. He did not join or worship at a synagogue, but he supported Zionism, the movement for the establishment of Jewish settlements in Palestine. In June 1922, Einstein was devastated when far-right extremists assassinated his close friend Walter Rathenau, a wealthy Jew who was serving as Germany's foreign minister. Although threatened by members of the fledgling National Socialist (Nazi) Party because of his Jewish identity, Einstein remained in Germany until 1933 when Adolf Hitler became the German chancellor. Moderating his strict pacifist views, he urged Western nations to prepare for war. After the Nazis barred Jews from holding any official positions, Einstein emigrated to America and accepted an appointment at the Institute for Advanced Study in Princeton, New Jersey. In January 1936, he filed his Declaration of Intention to become a U.S. citizen. Reflecting the racialized thinking that permeated Western democracies as well as authoritarian governments at the time, the form required Einstein to identify his color (white), complexion (fair), race (Hebrew), and nationality (German). Under Nazi policies, Einstein's racial identification disqualified him from participation in civic life. In the United States, his color did not, but wartime social change accelerated movements for equality that would challenge discrimination against those whose color identification was not white.

Throughout the 1930s, Einstein communicated with other physicists who had emigrated to the United States to escape Nazi persecution. In the summer of 1939, just weeks before World War II began in Europe, Leo Szilard, a refugee nuclear physicist from Hungary, alerted Einstein to the potential military uses of chain reactions triggered by the fission of uranium. Together, they wrote a letter to President Franklin Roosevelt warning that German scientists might develop an atomic weapon and encouraging the president to launch a U.S. program of atomic research. Roosevelt acted on their recommendation, and the program he established produced the world's first atomic bombs with the help of other refugees from Nazi persecution and scientists from Canada and Great Britain.

How do the circumstances of Einstein's emigration to America and his support of atomic bomb research and development reflect the grave threats posed by totalitarianism and racial ideologies?

Go to MindTap® to watch a video on Einstein and learn how his story relates to the themes of this chapter.

Einstein was only one of millions of people whose lives were irreparably changed by history's most destructive conflict. After Germany invaded Poland on September 1, 1939, democratic nations could no longer ignore the grave threats posed by potential Nazi domination of western Europe, Japanese aggression in Asia, and Italian incursions in Africa and Albania. Fusions of totalitarianism and racial ideology imperiled the political freedoms and economic viability of the democratic capitalist world. At the same time, they highlighted the contradictions posed by the colonialism and segregation practiced by nations ostensibly committed to freedom. By August 1945, when the six-year worldwide conflagration ended, more than 60 million people had died—an average of twenty-seven thousand deaths per day. The conflict transformed warfare, displaced millions, sparked anti-imperialist and civil rights movements, and left most of Europe and much of Asia in ruins.

Although fighting a war on two fronts, the United States was spared this destruction and chaos. In fact, the war catapulted the country out of the Great Depression and ushered in a period of economic growth that continued until the late 1960s. As the nation mobilized, economic opportunities for American workers abounded. Cities swelled as people migrated from rural areas in pursuit of defense jobs. Altogether 16 million U.S. men and women served in the armed forces over the course of the war. Traditionally underrepresented groups enjoyed new visibility and opportunities. When the conflict concluded, the United States was indisputably the world's strongest military and economic power.

21-1 From Neutral to Belligerent

The Granger Collection, New York

This 1939 editorial cartoon titled, "The Only Way We Can Save Her," reflects popular and congressional debates over how the United States should respond to the outbreak of war in Europe.

What is the core message of this cartoon? Does it advocate intervention or neutrality? How might someone with an opposing view have challenged the cartoon's claims? ▶

The September 1, 1939, German invasion of Poland shattered the illusion that Adolf Hitler was a leader who could be restrained through appeasement and triggered a six-year global war. Intent on building a German empire (the Third Reich) based on ideas about the racial superiority of the Germanic peoples, Hitler believed that because Britain and France had acquiesced to his recent seizure of Czechoslovakia, neither nation would honor its agreements to defend Poland. To his surprise, Britain and France declared war on Germany on September 3. Undaunted, German troops plunged onward toward Warsaw, and on September 17, their Soviet allies attacked Poland from the east, following the plan of the nonaggression pact signed the month before.

Throughout much of the 1930s, international tensions had run high (see Table 21.1), and the outbreak of war in Europe created serious political challenges for President Roosevelt. Although constrained by the Neutrality Acts passed by Congress to keep the United States out of another European war, he took steps to guard U.S. security and to aid the British and French. These actions sparked intense public debates. At the same time, U.S.–Japanese relations collapsed after negotiations and economic sanctions failed to resolve a diplomatic crisis in Asia. After the Japanese launched a surprise attack on Pearl Harbor, a U.S. naval base in Hawai'i, the United States finally joined the battle against the Axis Powers.

☞ As you read, pay attention to how the changing international situation affected U.S. policies. Why and how did the Roosevelt administration begin moving away from neutrality once war erupted in Europe?

Table 21.1 The Rise of Militarist Regimes and the Coming of World War II

During the 1930s, repressive regimes in Italy, Germany, Japan, and the Soviet Union began to rise. While Soviet leaders brutally suppressed internal political enemies, Italian, German, and Japanese leaders militarized and embraced expansionism as a means of realizing nationalistic, economic, and racial aims. In 1939, despite their diametrically opposed political philosophies, the Soviets and Germans forged an alliance and attacked Poland, triggering World War II.

Year	Italy	Germany	Japan	Soviet Union
1922	Fascists march on Rome			Union of Soviet Socialist Republics (Soviet Union) is established
1923	Benito Mussolini establishes a fascist state	Adolf Hitler tries to overthrow Bavarian government but fails and is imprisoned		
1924				Vladimir Lenin dies; Joseph Stalin becomes Communist Party leader
1925		In *Mein Kampf,* Hitler outlines his plans for the future of Germany		
1928				Stalin's first Five-Year Plan calls for rapid industrialization and the collectivization of agriculture
1931			Japanese forces seize Manchuria from China, set up puppet government Japan withdraws from the League of Nations	
1932				Failure of collectivization results in two-year famine in Ukraine, 7 million people die
1933		Hitler becomes chancellor of Germany and soon assumes dictatorial powers Nazis begin imprisoning political enemies in concentration camps Nazis eliminate opposition parties Germany withdraws from the League of Nations		
1935	Italy invades Ethiopia, and the next year makes it an Italian colony	Hitler begins rearming Germany, reintroduces conscription Nazis announce Nuremberg Laws that restrict the civil rights of Jews		
1936	Italy supports military uprising against the Spanish Republic Italy signs Rome-Berlin Axis Treaty with Germany	Germany supports military uprising against the Spanish Republic Germany signs Rome-Berlin Axis Treaty with Italy Germany signs Anti-Comintern Pact with Japan	Military faction comes to power Japan signs Anti-Comintern Pact with Germany	Show trials of individuals deemed to be state enemies begin in Moscow, and defendants found guilty are sent to labor camps or executed Soviet Union sends aid to Spanish Republic
1937	Italy withdraws from the League of Nations		Japan launches all-out assault on China, captures Peking (now Beijing) and Shanghai At Nanjing, Japanese troops kill 300,000 civilians	Stalinist purge of the leadership of the Red Army and Military Maritime Fleet begins

(continued)

Table 21.1 The Rise of Militarist Regimes and the Coming of World War II *(continued)*

Year	Italy	Germany	Japan	Soviet Union
1938	Manifesto of Race declares Italians to be descendants of the Aryan (Germanic) race Italian racial laws restrict the civil rights of Jews, and laws target Africans in Italian colonies	Germany invades and annexes Austria Germany annexes Czechoslovakia's Sudetenland In anti-Jewish riot called *Kristallnacht*, Nazis kill and destroy property	Japan issues plan to dominate East Asia	After an estimated 1.5 million detentions and nearly 700,000 executions, the Great Purge ends
1939		Germany annexes the rest of Czechoslovakia Germany signs a nonaggression pact with the Soviet Union Germany invades Poland		Soviet Union signs a nonaggression pact with Germany Soviet Union invades Poland Soviet Union attacks Finland

21-1a War in Europe

The Axis Powers and the Soviet Union initially score victories in Europe and Africa.

Fiercely nationalistic, the Poles tried to stop the onslaught of the ***Wehrmacht***, Germany's combined ground, naval, and air forces. Using the tactic ***blitzkrieg*** (lightning war), the Nazis aimed to create disarray among enemy troops and to score a quick victory with minimal loss of life and equipment. Although Poland had the fourth largest army in Europe, its outdated equipment and airplanes were no match for the *Wehrmacht,* and its allies Britain and France—unwilling to send ill-prepared troops into battle—never contributed to Poland's defense. After the Soviets invaded from the east, Poland succumbed, and on October 6, following the secret protocols of the nonaggression pact they had concluded, Germany and the Soviet Union divided the country between them.

Wehrmacht Unified armed forces of Germany from 1935 to 1945, consisting of the *Heer* (army), the *Kriegsmarine* (navy), and the *Luftwaffe* (air force).

blitzkrieg German for lightning war, a method of warfare in which highly mobile, mechanized infantry supported with air forces use short, rapid maneuvers to destabilize the enemy.

Allies Countries that opposed the Axis Powers during World War II; sought to stop German, Japanese, and Italian aggression.

In the months to come, the Soviets arrested and held captive approximately 1.5 million Poles. Of these, three hundred fifty thousand eventually died, including twenty-five thousand murdered by the Soviet secret police (the NKVD) and buried in mass graves in the forests near Katyn and other sites. Some seven hundred thousand Polish solders were taken as German prisoners of war (POWs). Compared to other European countries later occupied by Germany, there was little collaboration between the Poles and the Nazis. Approximately one hundred fifty thousand Poles fled westward, the largest exodus of all of the nations that fell under German domination. Some Polish soldiers and pilots eventually fought with the **Allies**, as the nations fighting the Axis Powers came to be called. Polish refugees in London established an unelected Polish government in exile to which hundreds of thousands Poles pledged their loyalty as they waged an armed struggle against their German and Soviet occupiers. It became the largest underground resistance movement in Europe.

Deeply alarmed by these events, President Roosevelt feared that the Germans would now conquer Europe, isolate the United States politically and economically, and then launch military strikes in the Western Hemisphere. Accordingly, he adopted cautious—and sometimes duplicitous—methods to circumvent the Neutrality Acts and aid the Allies. On September 21, 1939, three weeks after Germany invaded Poland, he asked Congress to lift the arms embargo as a means of keeping the United States out of the European conflict. Allowing the British and French to buy U.S. weapons and war matériel on a "cash-and-carry" basis would also safeguard against the tensions created by U.S. loans and supply shipments to both sides during World War I. In early November, Congress approved the president's proposal. Eager to avoid being drawn into another world war and sympathetic to the Allies, most Americans supported these measures.

Roosevelt also took steps to ensure security in the Western Hemisphere. In the fall of 1939, the United States and several Latin American nations signed the Declaration of Panama, proclaiming their neutrality and establishing a coastal security zone closed to belligerent navies.

U.S. officials convinced Latin American colleagues to limit or end their trade with Germany and its ally Italy. The following year, Roosevelt established an Office of Inter-American Affairs headed by Nelson Rockefeller. Through radio programs, publications, and Hollywood films such as *The Three Caballeros* (1944), the office sought to improve hemispheric relations. Despite persistent anxieties about U.S. imperialism in the region, all Latin American countries eventually joined the Allies, although Chile and Argentina waited until the conflict's final weeks to do so.

While U.S. policy makers fostered hemispheric unity, the Allies anxiously awaited the Nazis' next move. Following Poland's quick collapse, many in Britain and France concluded that their governments had committed them to waging an unwinnable war, and some politicians called for a negotiated settlement with Hitler. Neither nation had ground or air forces capable of defeating the *Wehrmacht*. Hoping to buy enough time to rearm and mobilize, the Allies bolstered defenses on France's eastern border while imposing a naval blockade off the German coast.

With the Allies' attention focused on Germany, Stalin grabbed more territory. In October 1939, Soviet troops invaded Finland and met ferocious resistance. On March 12, 1940, with their supplies depleted and no significant military assistance from Britain or France forthcoming, the Finns signed an armistice ceding 10 percent of their land. Determined to regroup after losing more than one hundred twenty-five thousand soldiers, Stalin allowed the Finns to retain their independence and turned his energies toward modernizing the Red Army and rebuilding an officer corps weakened by the political purges of the late 1930s.

In April 1940, the Nazis launched another *blitzkrieg*, and waves of German soldiers supported by tanks, artillery, and bombers seized Norway and Denmark. After the British military failed in an attempt to assist the Norwegians, Prime Minister Neville Chamberlain lost the support of many fellow Conservatives and resigned. Winston Churchill, a more bellicose leader with a gift for inspiring the masses, became his successor. At the same time, the Nazis began marching westward. They quickly captured Holland, Luxembourg, and Belgium and advanced on France. As French defenses collapsed, 8 million people fled their homes, the largest mass migration in western European history. German troops sped toward Paris, and to rescue British, French, Dutch, and Belgian troops trapped behind their lines at Dunkirk, the British sent almost nine hundred civilian and military vessels across the English Channel. In nine days, they evacuated nearly three hundred forty thousand men but abandoned huge stores of ammunition, weapons, and military vehicles that took months to replace.

On June 14, the Germans marched into Paris, and on June 22, France signed an armistice with Germany. The newly formed **Vichy French** state collaborated with the Nazis in exchange for a pledge that France and its colonies would not be divided among the Axis Powers. Although many French citizens supported the Vichy regime's efforts to maintain French territorial sovereignty, others resisted the German occupiers and backed the **Free French** movement led by General Charles de Gaulle, then exiled in London.

Meanwhile, the Soviets seized Bessarabia and the Baltic States of Latvia, Estonia, and Lithuania. Unwilling to miss out on the spoils from an Axis victory, Benito Mussolini brought Italy into the war, and Italian troops soon invaded France, Sudan, Kenya, British Somaliland, and Egypt. Reactions in Africa were mixed. Some Africans hoped that the fascists would liberate them from decades of British and French colonial rule whereas others fought for the British but were disillusioned by salaries and conditions inferior to those of their white comrades in arms.

Great Britain was now the only major European democracy not under German occupation. To weaken it in preparation for a land invasion, the ***Luftwaffe*** began bombing British cities, soon with nightly raids known as the *blitz*. Contrary to Hitler's expectations, the bombings only stiffened British resolve, and German pilots met intense resistance from the Royal Air Force (RAF) in battles over the English Channel.

21-1b U.S. Support for the Allies

As German victories mount, Roosevelt leads the United States toward intervention.

Certain that a Nazi-dominated Europe would imperil U.S. economic and political interests, Roosevelt vowed to help the British and started preparing the nation for war. He persuaded Congress to increase the defense budget from $2 billion to $10 billion. In September 1940, he transferred fifty World War I–era destroyers to England in exchange for rights to build or lease bases on eight British territories in the Western Hemisphere. He also signed the Selective Service Act requiring all men between the ages of twenty-one and forty-five to register for conscription, the first peacetime draft in U.S. history.

These measures outraged advocates for neutrality. Organized as the America First Committee, they denied that Hitler posed a threat to the United States and warned that participating in Europe's war would permanently militarize U.S. life. At its peak, the committee had more than eight hundred thousand members. In response, interventionists formed the Committee to Defend America by Aiding the Allies. Rejecting claims that the war in Europe did not endanger the United States, the group defended Roosevelt's policies and advocated all measures to help the Allies short of direct U.S. participation in the war.

At the same time, the war escalated. On September 27, Germany, Italy, and Japan—hoping to dissuade the United States from entering the war on the side of the Allies—signed the **Tripartite Pact**, an agreement in

Vichy France Authoritarian regime that governed France and collaborated with the Axis after the Axis took control of the country in July 1940 to the Allied liberation in August 1944.

Free French Individuals and military units that joined the resistance founded by Charles de Gaulle from exile in London to fight Axis and Vichy troops.

Luftwaffe Aerial warfare branch of the *Wehrmacht* from 1935 to 1945.

Tripartite Pact Treaty signed by Nazi Germany, fascist Italy, and imperial Japan in Berlin on September 27, 1940, established the Axis Powers.

Eileen Tweedy/The Art Archive/Art Resource

America First Poster, circa 1940 The views of Americans were quite divided on the appropriate U.S. response to war in Europe. This poster was used by the America First Committee, the largest noninterventionist group. At its peak, the organization's eight hundred thousand members included film producer Walt Disney, aviator Charles Lindbergh, and future U.S. president Gerald Ford. While Lindbergh openly declared Nazi sympathies, other members claimed that intervention would permanently militarize daily life and undermine civil liberties. ▲

which they pledged to defend one another from attack by any nation not already involved in the European conflict or the ongoing war between China and Japan. In October, Italy invaded Greece.

After carefully avoiding additional steps toward war while campaigning in the 1940 presidential race, Roosevelt won an unprecedented third term and resumed his efforts to assist the British and their allies. In a fireside chat, he called for the United States to become "the great arsenal of democracy." To prevent German world domination, he announced his intention to manufacture and supply the Allies with "the implements of war, the planes, the tanks, the guns, and the freighters that will enable them to fight for their liberty and for our security."

In his State of the Union address on January 6, 1941, Roosevelt built on these themes and recommended that the United States loan or rent supplies to the Allied nations whose war efforts were depleting their national treasuries. Without such measures, he argued, the world risked losing **Four Freedoms** essential to humanity: freedom of speech, freedom of religious worship, freedom from want, and freedom from fear. Over the next two months, he urged Americans to support **Lend-Lease** as a means of protecting the democracy they cherished and keeping the United States out of the conflict. In March 1941, after a heated political battle, Congress approved the bill authorizing the president to "sell . . . exchange, lease, lend, or otherwise dispose of" war matériel "to any country whose defense the President deems vital to the defense of the United States." Starting with an initial $7 billion appropriation, the United States eventually provided more than $50 billion in interest-free Lend-Lease aid. Britain alone received more than $31 billion.

Although the legislation provided critically needed financial aid to the British, it did nothing to guard their vessels from German submarines (U-boats) that were sinking Allied and U.S. merchant ships carrying five hundred thousand tons of cargo per month. Determined to help, Roosevelt ordered the U.S. Navy to patrol the North Atlantic. U.S. troops occupied Greenland as part of the president's expanded defense of the Western Hemisphere.

In June 1941, after months of Allied–Axis battles confined to the Balkans and Africa, World War II took a dramatic turn when the Germans invaded the Soviet Union, thus violating the nonaggression pact. This action catapulted the Soviet Union—Germany's ally in the division of Poland—into the Allied camp. Setting aside Americans' traditional antipathy toward communism (and hoping that the Soviets would weaken the German war machine), Roosevelt began sending Lend-Lease aid to the Soviet Union. Nothing could stop the *Wehrmacht*, however, which quickly overran Belorussia and the Ukraine and was soon besieging Leningrad and Moscow.

Convinced that it was only a matter of time before the United States would join the battle against the Axis Powers, President Roosevelt and Prime Minister Churchill met to outline postwar aims. Aboard a ship off the coast of Newfoundland, U.S. and British teams spent four days drafting a statement of goals. They renounced territorial aggrandizement and called for the self-determination of nations, free trade, global cooperation, disarmament, and a peace that allowed people everywhere to "live out their lives in freedom from fear and want." Formally issued on August 14, the **Atlantic Charter** echoed Roosevelt's Four Freedoms as well as Woodrow Wilson's Fourteen Points.

To persuade a still wavering public of the need for direct intervention, Roosevelt allowed the U.S. Navy to take steps certain to provoke German retaliation that would, he anticipated, outrage Americans. On September 4, after a German submarine fired two torpedoes that narrowly missed the U.S. destroyer *Greer*, the president revealed in a fireside chat that he had ordered U.S.

Four Freedoms Liberties that President Roosevelt argued "everyone in the world" ought to have: freedom of speech, freedom of religion, freedom from want, and freedom from fear.

Lend-Lease U.S. program that supplied Allied nations with $50.1 billion of weapons and supplies during World War II.

Atlantic Charter Statement of postwar aims drafted by Roosevelt and Churchill in August 1941.

naval commanders to shoot German submarines on sight and authorized naval convoys to go as far as Iceland. His description of the attack on the *Greer* as unprovoked omitted the fact that the *Greer* had tracked the German submarine for more than three hours. In two incidents in October, German submarines sank U.S. ships—the *Kearney* and the *Reuben James*—killing more than one hundred U.S. sailors. In November, Roosevelt asked for repeal of the sections of the Neutrality Act that prohibited the arming of merchant vessels and barred such ships from war zones. Congress agreed, acknowledging the public's shift toward intervention. Roosevelt's strategy had worked, and the United States was inching closer to war.

21-1c Path to Pearl Harbor

Japan attacks Pearl Harbor and captures territories throughout Asia and the Pacific.

Ironically, events in Asia, not Europe, triggered the U.S. entry into the war against the Axis Powers. While still fighting in China, the militant Japanese government sought to capture Indochina and the Dutch East Indies, the Asian colonies of recently defeated France and the Netherlands. In a radio broadcast on June 29, 1940, the Japanese regime called for the creation of a Greater East Asia Co-Prosperity Sphere, an economically self-sufficient "bloc of Asian nations led by the Japanese and free of Western powers." A few weeks later, the Vichy French allowed the Japanese to seize northern Indochina. The recently formed Viet Minh (Vietnamese nationalists), later backed by China and the United States, ferociously opposed their Vichy and Japanese occupiers.

Elsewhere, Japanese propagandists used slogans like "Asia for the Asiatics!" and disseminated pamphlets celebrating pan-Asian unity. In actuality, the Japanese militarists held racially supremacist views similar to those of the Nazis and secretly planned to dominate their Asian neighbors. Although some Asians initially welcomed Japanese troops who drove out their European rulers, the subsequent brutality of the Japanese military and the sexual enslavement of so-called **comfort women** forced to serve as prostitutes for the Japanese Army persuaded many that Japanese colonialism was even worse than Western imperialism.

Confronted with a global totalitarian threat, Roosevelt attempted to deter Japanese aggression by increasing aid to Nationalist China and using economic sanctions against Japan. The United States halted sales of aviation fuel, scrap metal, and steel but initially continued oil sales for fear that a petroleum embargo would trigger a war. But after Japan and the Soviet Union signed a neutrality agreement and Japanese troops marched into southern Indochina, Roosevelt halted all trade, including the sale of American oil, and froze Japanese assets held in U.S. banks. The Dutch government, then in exile in London, took similar actions.

U.S. and Japanese diplomats attempted to defuse the crisis. On November 20, the Japanese offered to withdraw from Indochina if the British, Dutch, and Americans stopped aiding the Chinese and lifted their economic sanctions. Six days later, U.S. officials rejected the proposal and insisted that Japan withdraw from China without conditions—a demand that was unacceptable to Prime Minister Hideki Tojo and the militarists dominating the Japanese government. Facing serious shortages as a result of the U.S. embargo and convinced that further talks would be futile, Japan decided to attack the United States. Because U.S. cryptographers had broken the Japanese diplomatic code, the Roosevelt administration knew that a Japanese attack on U.S. forces in the Pacific was being planned but not exactly where or when.

On December 7, 1941, Japanese planes launched from six aircraft carriers struck the U.S. naval base at Pearl Harbor, Hawai'i. In this surprise attack, 2,403 Americans died, eight U.S. battleships were sunk or damaged, and 188 planes destroyed, most while still on the ground. Axis leaders rejoiced at news of the attacks on the United States, a nation they viewed as degenerate and described by Mussolini as "a country of Negroes and Jews."

The following day, Roosevelt appeared before Congress. "Yesterday, December 7, 1941—a date that will live in infamy"—he announced, the United States "was suddenly and deliberately" attacked by Japan, and he asked for a declaration of war. The vote was nearly unanimous. Only Congresswoman Jeannette Rankin of Montana, a pacifist who had also voted against U.S. entry into World War I, voted no. Three days later, Germany and Italy honored the Tripartite Pact and declared war on the United States.

During his speech to Congress, Roosevelt also announced that the Japanese had invaded the Philippines. Because of damages to U.S. air forces stationed in Hawai'i, U.S. naval forces had lacked aerial protection and retreated. In March 1942, Douglas MacArthur, commander of the U.S. Army forces in the Far East, fled to Australia, vowing "I shall return." A month later, seventy-six thousand U.S. and Filipino defenders on Bataan surrendered, including seventy-eight army and navy nurses, the largest group of American women ever captured by an enemy. The Japanese forced the male POWs to walk eighty miles, and thousands perished on what came to be known as the "Death March," a notorious atrocity that exemplified the Japanese government's official policy of showing no mercy to its enemies. During the ensuing three-year Japanese occupation, Filipino guerillas, supplied and reinforced by MacArthur's troops, maintained control of 60 percent of the islands. Motivated by U.S. guarantees of independence and outraged by the Japanese use of their fellow citizens as forced laborers and sexual slaves, most Filipinos remained loyal to the United States.

Within weeks of striking Pearl Harbor, Japan also captured the oil-rich Dutch East Indies and Britain's colonies Malaya, Burma, Hong Kong,

comfort women Women and girls forced to serve as prostitutes for the Japanese Imperial Army during World War II.

Underwood Archives/Getty Images

Mohandas K. Gandhi and Jawaharlal Nehru Discuss Indian Concerns During World War II, many Indians, Arabs, and Africans protested the disjuncture between the Allied governments' democratic ideals and the injustices of life under British and French imperial rule. ▲

Quit India movement
Nonviolent resistance campaign launched in India in August 1942 that called for an end to British rule.

and Singapore. As their defenses in Southeast Asia collapsed, the British concentrated their forces in the Middle East where the Nazis had support among many Arab nationalists who shared their anti-Zionist views and wished to free themselves from British and French imperialism. This decision had terrible consequences for the people in Britain's Asian colonies because the fleeing British generals and colonial administrators did not orchestrate a general evacuation—a betrayal of the imperial ideal that colonial masters protected their subjects. In Burma, as Japanese troops swept across the country to close off the Burma Road—the Allied supply route to China—fifty thousand Indians who worked for the British died of exposure, disease, and starvation. In India, Jawaharlal Nehru and Mohandas Gandhi pointed to the British failure to provide humanitarian aid as another justification for their **Quit India movement**, a nonviolent campaign calling for the orderly withdrawal of the British from their nation. To quash the independence movement, the British government imprisoned Gandhi, Nehru, and more than thirty thousand Quit India supporters until 1945. In 1942, Britain had more troops maintaining internal control of India than it had fighting the Japanese. In a harbinger of the decolonization and civil rights movements that swept the postwar era, Gandhi warned Roosevelt that any Allied proclamation about "fighting to make the world safe for freedom of the individual and for democracy sounds hollow, so long as India and, for that matter, Africa are exploited by Great Britain, and America has the Negro problem in her own home."

While Japan won a string of victories in Asia and occupied islands throughout the Central Pacific, Germany scored gains elsewhere. By the spring of 1942, German troops had penetrated far into Soviet territory, holding all or part of nine Soviet Republics, and were poised to capture valuable oil fields in the Caucasus Mountains. In North Africa, German forces threatened the Suez Canal, a waterway critical to maintaining Allied supply lines. To many, a total Axis victory seemed imminent.

21-2 First Challenges to Axis Power

War posters/Alamy Stock Photo

This poster, created in 1942 by the U.S. Office of Facts and Figures, includes the flags of the twenty-six nations opposing the Axis Powers. Other countries later joined the coalition.

What is the core message of this propaganda poster? Why would U.S. officials consider it important to impart such a message to Americans? ▶

The Japanese government hoped that Americans would be so demoralized by the Pearl Harbor attacks that they would elect not to go to war and acquiesce to Japanese expansionism in Southeast Asia. This proved a grave miscalculation. The raids outraged Americans and obliterated any significant isolationist sentiment. Determined to defeat the Axis Powers and to protect their nation,

Americans mobilized for war and U.S. leaders coordinated political aims and military strategies with the Allies. By mid-1942, the Allies began winning critical battles that turned the tide of the war in Europe and the Pacific. Although not always in agreement on proposed tactics or plans for the postwar world, the Allies put their enemies on the defensive.

☞ As you read, set aside your knowledge of the outcome of World War II and consider the formidable obstacles the Allies had to surmount to defeat the Axis. What challenges did the United States and its allies face in the early stages of the war? In what ways did the Allied coalition both help and complicate the war effort against the Axis Powers?

21-2a Allies and Adversaries

The Allies formulate strategies for defeating the Axis and try to reconcile differing views on tactics and war aims.

On January 1, 1942, twenty-six countries signed the **Declaration by the United Nations** calling for "complete victory" over the "savage and brutal forces seeking to subjugate the world." The United Nations, commonly called the Allies, agreed that the defeat of the authoritarian powers ruling Germany, Italy, and Japan was essential to the preservation of human rights and pledged to uphold the Atlantic Charter. By the end of the war, several additional countries had endorsed these principles and joined the coalition. This unity of purpose gave the Allies a significant advantage over their enemies. Whereas the Allies coordinated their strategies and diplomatic objectives, Germany and Japan—the major Axis Powers—did not jointly plan their military operations or political aims.

The United States and Great Britain formed the closest Allied partnership. Roosevelt and Churchill spoke or wrote virtually every day until Roosevelt's death in 1945. In late December 1941, top U.S. and British military leaders agreed that Germany posed a greater global threat than Japan and that victory in the European theater must therefore be first priority.

But Allied relations were sometimes difficult. Roosevelt and Churchill disagreed over the future of Britain's colonies. Roosevelt argued that colonized peoples have the right to govern themselves, but Churchill resisted the idea of dismantling the British Empire. China, at war with Japan since 1937, was displeased by the "Europe First" strategy. Although the Nationalists hoarded supplies instead of fighting their Japanese occupiers, the Roosevelt administration was eager to make China one of the world's "Four Policemen." The United States continued to prop up the government of Chinese Nationalist leader Jiang Jieshi (Chiang Kai-shek) in anticipation of resuming the suspended civil war against the Communists led by Mao Tse-tung (Mao Zedong). At the same time, U.S. cooperation with the Vichy French rankled Charles de Gaulle, leader of the Free French government-in-exile.

Relations among the British, Americans, and the Soviets—**The Big Three**—were the most contentious. With his forces singlehandedly fighting more than two hundred divisions of the *Wehrmacht* and sustaining enormous losses, Stalin wanted the Allies to open a second front in western Europe that would force the Germans to split their armed forces. Although Roosevelt tried to placate him with personal flattery and a stream of Lend-Lease aid ($11 billion total), Stalin believed—with much justification—that the Americans and British were intentionally allowing the Soviets to bear the largest burden in fighting Germany. Roosevelt and Churchill's delays saved U.S. and British soldiers' lives but created distrust that had long-term ramifications for relations with the Soviet Union.

21-2b End of the German Offensive

After critical victories, the Allies prepare to invade France and envision the postwar world.

Conquest of the lands around the Mediterranean was not part of Hitler's initial strategy, but his maladroit Italian allies forced him to change course. Mussolini invaded the Balkans and North Africa in the hope of securing territorial gains in the soon-expected Axis victory, but British, Australian, New Zealander, and Indian troops defeated Italian forces in East Africa, Egypt, and Libya. To prevent more Italian losses, the Germans sent troops into North Africa and won victories in Yugoslavia, Greece, and Crete.

But the tide began turning against the Axis when U.S. and British forces landed in Algeria and Morocco in November 1942 and began to push back German gains. To assuage Stalin's anxieties about the delayed opening of the second front, Roosevelt and Churchill met in Casablanca in January 1943 and committed to a policy of unconditional surrender, rejecting the possibility of making a separate peace with any of Germany's allies. But with German submarines still inflicting losses on Allied vessels in the Atlantic, they continued to delay plans for an invasion of northwestern France until the United States could reach maximum troop levels and war production. Instead, they opted to try to push Italy out of the war and force the Germans to divert troops from the Soviet Union to Italy.

On July 9, 1943, British, American, and Canadian amphibious forces landed on Sicily. Two weeks later, Benito Mussolini—discredited by his

Declaration by the United Nations Document signed by twenty-six Allied nations January 1, 1942; term "United Nations" became a synonym for the Allies.

The Big Three Colloquial term describing the three most prominent Allied leaders: U.S. President Franklin Roosevelt, British Prime Minister Winston Churchill, and Soviet Premier Joseph Stalin.

Map 21.1 Axis and Allied Military Actions in Europe, North Africa, and the Soviet Union, 1941–1945 Early in the war, the Germans occupied many western and eastern European nations and made great gains in North Africa and the Soviet Union. But in 1942, the tide turned. After the D-Day landings in June 1944, the Allies retook France and began pushing German forces back into Germany while Soviet troops pushed at them from the east. In May 1945, Germany surrendered. ▲

disastrous military campaigns—was ousted and imprisoned by a new Italian government. Although German special forces soon broke him out of prison, Mussolini did not escape the wrath of his countrymen. In April 1945, he was captured and executed by Italian partisans. The new Italian government soon surrendered to the Allies, but German troops and Italians who remained loyal to the Axis fought with fierce determination to slow the Allied advance north from Naples to Rome toward the Alps. Fighting in Italy continued even after the fall of Berlin in May 1945. In the interim, the task of caring for Italy's devastated civilian population fell to the Allies (see Map 21.1).

Battle of Stalingrad Pivotal Soviet victory over German troops following a protracted siege from August 23, 1942, to February 2, 1943; the turning point of World War II.

By the time the Allies invaded Sicily, the tide had turned against the Axis in the east as well. At the **Battle of Stalingrad**, where nearly 2 million people died in a protracted siege, the German Sixth Army was forced to surrender when the Red Army encircled it. This loss forced the Germans to withdraw from the east and put them on the defensive for the remainder of the war. But the German invasion had decimated the Soviet Union: 1,700 cities and towns, more than 70,000 villages, and 31,000 factories had been demolished. Millions of acres of croplands and tens of millions of farm animals were destroyed. This devastation combined with memories of Russia's catastrophic losses in World War I and suspicions left by the failed Allied intervention in the Russian Civil War intensified Stalin's determination to protect his nation from another invasion. Accordingly, as the Red Army marched west into eastern Europe, he vowed to hold power in the

Interfoto/Alamy Stock Photo

The Battle of Stalingrad, 1942–1943 After losing the protracted siege at Stalingrad, German forces withdrew and never regained the offensive on the vast Russian front. A major strategic miscalculation, the German invasion of the Soviet Union left more than 10 million Soviet soldiers, 2 million German soldiers, and 17 million civilians dead as a result of battles, atrocities, mistreatment of POWs, food and medicine shortages, and the mutual use of scorched earth tactics that left millions homeless and starving. ◄

region, to expand Soviet borders to encompass the Baltic States and eastern Poland, to ensure pro-Communist governments ruled in key eastern European states, and to punish Germany through demilitarization, deindustrialization, and high reparations.

In October 1943, American, British, and Soviet diplomats gathered in Moscow to plan the next phase of the war. They created a council to coordinate Allied policy in Italy and a European Advisory Commission to formulate recommendations for peace agreements. In a significant departure from the U.S. rejection of collective security in the aftermath of World War I, Secretary of State Cordell Hull persuaded the delegates to commit to a postwar replacement for the defunct League of Nations.

A few weeks later, Roosevelt, Churchill, and Stalin met in Tehran. Emphatically rejecting a British proposal for an amphibious landing in the Balkans, Stalin demanded a firm commitment on the long-delayed invasion of France. He also proposed territorial adjustments after the war that would guarantee Soviet security by creating a protective buffer against Germany, but Roosevelt rejected Stalin's contention that the Baltic States were now Soviet Republics. Although Stalin reaffirmed his pledge to enter the war against Japan after Germany surrendered, the meeting highlighted the Allies' differences over territorial concessions, an issue hotly contested after the war.

21-2c End of the Japanese Offensive

Allied forces begin advancing on Japan.

The Allies faced a daunting task in defeating the Japanese across the vast Pacific theater. While implementing their "Europe First" strategy in the early stages of the war, they sought to prevent Japan from seizing additional territories. Before attacking Japan itself, the Allies planned to recapture Japanese-held islands in the Pacific (a strategy called *island-hopping*) and Japan-occupied Southeast Asia.

In June 1942, U.S. forces stopped the Japanese advance at Midway, an island northwest of Hawai'i held by the United States since 1867. A turning point, the victory put the Japanese navy on the defensive for the remainder of the war. Thereafter, Allied forces under MacArthur's command won back the Solomon Islands, Guadalcanal, and New Guinea. In Burma, 450,000 mostly Indian troops under British command held the line against 300,000 Japanese soldiers. By early 1943, American, Australian, and New Zealander troops were moving northward in preparation for a strike on the Philippines (see Map 21.2).

While Allied forces took the offensive throughout Southeast Asia, the Japanese still occupied much of China. U.S. officials in China complained about the corruption and incompetence of Jiang Jeishi and his generals, but the Roosevelt administration continued to support the Nationalist's in hope that China would someday become the leading capitalist democracy in Asia. At a November 1943 conference in Cairo, Roosevelt and Churchill met with Jiang and pledged that the Chinese territories "stolen by Japan" would be restored after the war. The following month, as a gesture of respect to China, Congress repealed the Chinese Exclusion Act, which had barred Chinese laborers from the United States since 1882. The repeal allowed only one hundred five Chinese to emigrate, but it also enabled Chinese already in the United States to become U.S. citizens. In 1946, in a similar overture to India and the Philippines, Congress ended the exclusion of these peoples and allowed them to naturalize.

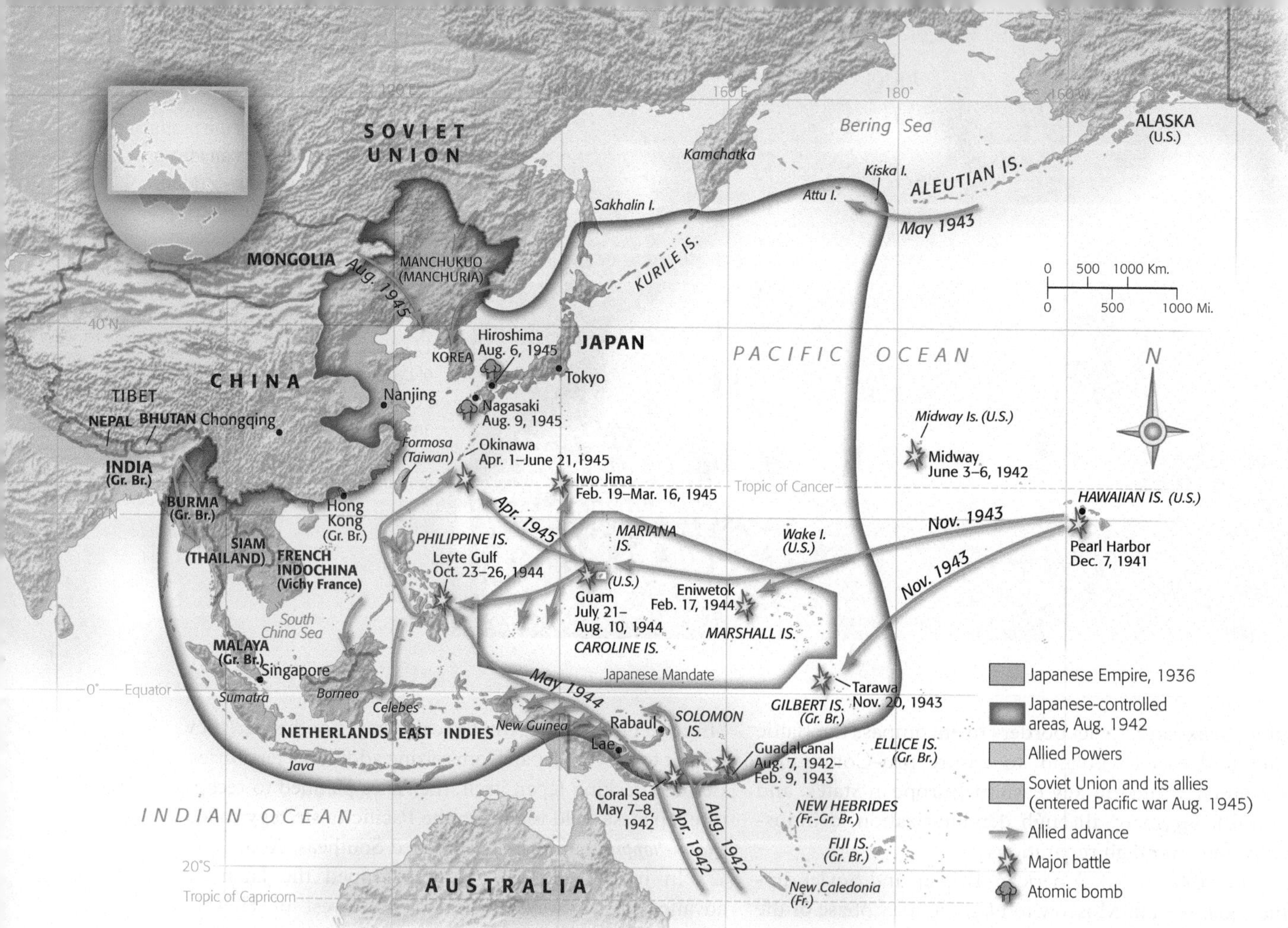

Map 21.2 Major Military Engagements in the Pacific Theater, 1941–1945 By early 1942, Japanese forces had control of the Central Pacific and the Philippines, Burma, Singapore, the Dutch East Indies, and parts of the Solomon Islands, the Gilbert Islands, and New Guinea. At the Battle of Midway in June 1942, the Allies stopped the Japanese advance and began winning back Japanese strongholds. In August 1945, after the atomic bombings of Hiroshima and Nagasaki, the Japanese surrendered. ▲

21-3
On the Home Front

In this March 1942 photograph by Dorothea Lange, a Japanese American store owner in Oakland, California, demonstrates his patriotism in the aftermath of the Pearl Harbor attacks. He was soon forced to abandon his business and sent to an internment camp after Roosevelt mandated the relocation of one hundred ten thousand Japanese Americans living along the West Coast.

How does this photograph reflect some contradictions in U.S. democracy that were highlighted during the war? What were some of these injustices, and how did different groups attempt to combat them? ▶

Library of Congress Prints and Photographs Division[LC-USZ62-23602]

While combat and occupation devastated much of Europe and Asia, the war affected the United States differently. Wartime production ended the Great Depression as factories retooled and increased hiring to meet the nation's defense needs. Farmers increased their yields and sold crops at a profit. Many Americans earned good incomes, and historically underemployed groups entered the paid workforce in record numbers. The war sparked mass migration as men and women who joined the armed forces moved to military bases and families left rural communities for urban defense jobs. At the same time, the war against fascism abroad forced Americans to confront racism at home.

☞ As you read, consider ways the United States changed during World War II. How did the government mobilize the nation for war? What opportunities and challenges did the war create?

21-3a Mobilization for War

Mobilization alters the U.S. economy, the federal bureaucracy, and the civilian workforce.

Upon entering World War II, the United States had to build its armed forces, jump-start a stalled economy, and win a two-front war. To expedite the process of U.S. military expansion begun in 1940, Roosevelt set staggering war production goals. Draftees were required to serve for the duration of the war instead of the previous twelve-month obligation. Throughout 1942, the army increased from 1.5 million to 5.4 million soldiers. By 1945, the United States had more than 8 million men and women in uniform, more than half the number who served in the wartime armed forces (see Figures 21.1 and 21.2).

Figure 21.1 Estimated Number of Combatants per Nation, 1939–1945 This figure illustrates the populations of several major combatant nations in 1939 and the number of citizens who served in each country's armed forces over the course of the war. Consider how the numbers of combatants compare to the overall national populations. How and why do the percentages of combatants differ?

▶ Sources: World War II Casualties, http://en.wikipedia.org/wiki/World_War_II_casualties; Historical Statistics for the World Economy, 1–2003 AD, www.ggdc.net/maddison/historical_statistics/horizontal-file_03-2007.xls

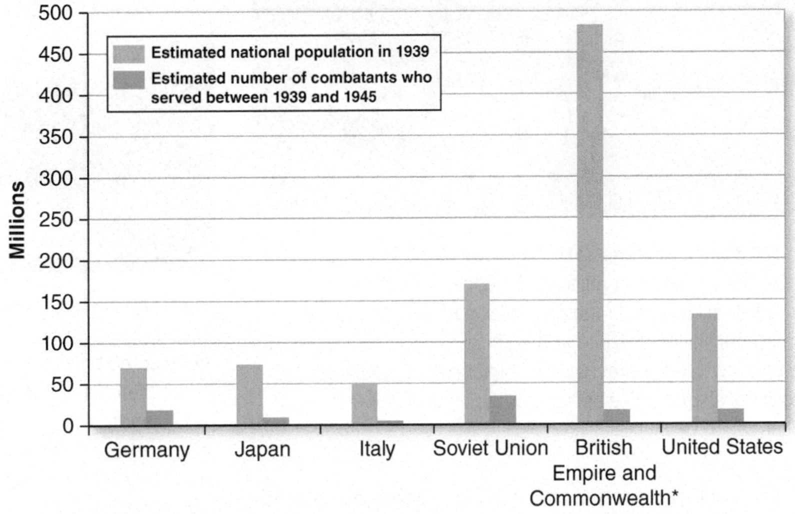

*British Empire and Commonwealth includes United Kingdom, Canada, Australia, New Zealand, South Africa, India, Singapore, Malta, Malaya, and Burma.

Figure 21.2 Strength of the Armed Forces, 1939–1944 As the war progressed, the major combatant nations mobilized their armed forces to the maximum level their populations and economies could support. What might account for different force sizes at different points of the war? ▶ Sources: Dear, I. C. B., and M. R. D. Foot, *The Oxford Companion to World War II* (Oxford, 2003), 2014 online ed., http://www.oxfordreference.com/view/10.1093/acref/9780198604464.001.0001/acref-9780198604464-e-1566?p=emailAWogkKzU5LJo2&d=/10.1093/acref/9780198604464.001.0001/acref-9780198604464-e-1566

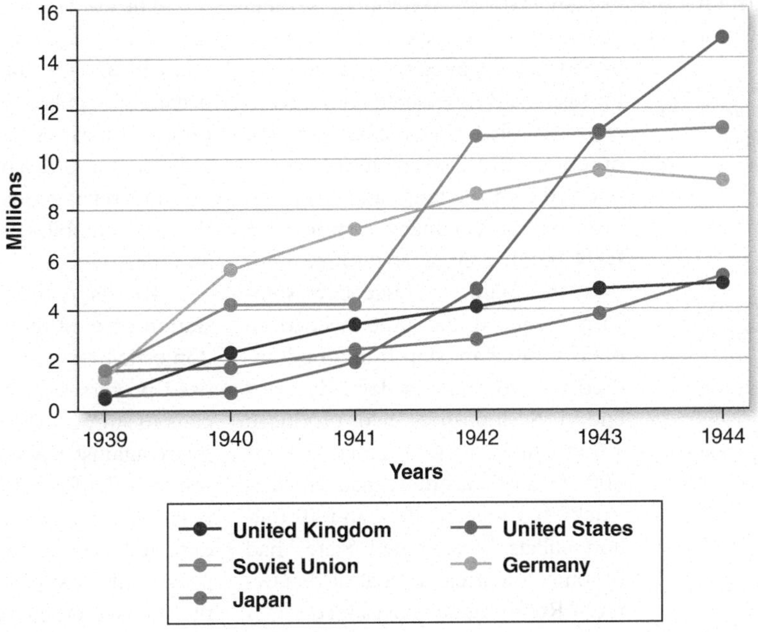

When you ride ALONE
you ride with Hitler!
Join a
Car-Sharing Club
TODAY!

Galerie Bilderwelt/Getty Images

Office of Price Administration Poster, 1943 Throughout the war, the U.S. government relied on Americans' patriotism and voluntarism in enforcing rationing of supplies vital to the war effort. Americans were urged to "Use it up, wear it out, make it do, or do without." This poster aims to help citizens understand the necessity of sharing rides because of the three-gallon-per-week gasoline ration. ▲

MATERIAL
CONSERVATION
"JAP TRAP"

Mooziic/Alamy Stock Photo

U.S. Information Service Propaganda Poster, 1941–1945 Aware that many Americans held racist views of the Japanese and wanted to avenge the Pearl Harbor attacks and the Bataan Death March, the U.S. government played on these sentiments in propaganda posters designed to motivate defense workers and soldiers. Such materials may have contributed to the savagery of the Pacific theater where U.S. soldiers frequently retaliated for enemy atrocities by mutilating the corpses of Japanese troops. ▲

To meet production needs, the nation needed big business, a target of frequent criticism during the Great Depression. Motivated by patriotism and generous economic incentives, industrialists accepted federal defense contracts. Thousands became "dollar-a-year men," serving on government commissions and agencies for $1 a year, often while retaining their private sector salaries. Businessmen and bureaucrats retooled the nation for war production. In Detroit, auto factories retooled to make tanks and airplanes. Ford Motor Company completed a B-24 bomber every sixty-three minutes. In California, huge new shipyards reduced the time needed to build a merchant ship from one hundred four to fourteen days. By war's end, U.S. industries had produced 1,500 ships, 88,000 tanks, almost 300,000 airplanes, more than 2 million trucks, 6.5 million rifles, and 40 million bullets. The United States had become "the great arsenal of democracy" Roosevelt had envisioned.

War Production Board (WPB) U.S. government agency established in 1942 and charged with supervising production of materials and supplies for the war effort.

Office of Price Administration (OPA) U.S. government agency that instituted rent and price controls and rationed items essential to the war effort.

Office of War Information (OWI) U.S. government agency whose domestic and overseas branches delivered propaganda though radio broadcasts, publications, posters, films, and other media.

The war elevated the prestige of corporate America and further expanded the size and power of the federal government. In January 1942, the new **War Production Board (WPB)** began to regulate production and allocate materials. To prevent shortages of vital military materials and to control inflation, the **Office of Price Administration (OPA)** set prices on most retail goods and rationed scarce supplies such as tires, automobiles, shoes, nylon, sugar, gasoline, coffee, and meats.

To shape public attitudes, the Roosevelt administration created the **Office of War Information (OWI)**. Its domestic branch coordinated the release of war news and used posters and radio broadcasts to encourage Americans to support the war effort, join the armed forces, and guard against espionage and sabotage. Overseas, OWI disseminated information about the Allies' war aims and propaganda about the Axis Powers. The Nazis were usually depicted as caricatures of Hitler, while the Japanese were portrayed as superhuman killing machines or as myopic, buck-toothed rats or monkeys. Echoed throughout

Silver Screen Collection/Hulton Archive/Moviepix/Getty Images

Global Americans Born in Vienna in 1914, Hedy Keisler was an intellectually curious girl, and her father taught her about the mechanics of machinery. She became an actress and married Friedrich Mandl, a half-Jewish munitions manufacturer with close ties to the fascist governments of Italy and Germany. When they entertained, her husband and his associates discussed secret military technologies, assuming beautiful Hedy could not understand. Mocking such sexism years later, she declared, "Any girl can be glamourous. All you have to do is stand still and look stupid." Escaping her controlling husband, Hedy fled to Paris and then to Los Angeles, where she began making films under the name **Hedy Lamarr**. Bored by Hollywood socializing, she took up inventing as a hobby, setting up a bench and drafting tools in a corner of her drawing room. In 1940, when German submarines attacked British ships evacuating children to Canada to escape Nazi bombing raids, she decided to use her technical skills to help her adopted nation (though she was still an enemy alien who did not become a naturalized U.S. citizen until 1953). In 1941, Lamarr and composer George Antheil developed frequency-hopping technology that prevented jamming of radio signals used to control torpedoes. U.S. officials kept the innovation top-secret and did not use it until 1962. Because their patent expired, Lamarr and Antheil earned no royalties, but they are now recognized for essential contributions to the development of Wi-Fi, Bluetooth, and other elements of the wireless communication revolution.

American public culture, these deeply entrenched racial stereotypes may have contributed to the decision to intern Japanese Americans and to use atomic weapons on Japan.

Hollywood worked closely with the government in promoting war aims and raising morale. Studios made films featuring ethnically diverse soldiers with shared devotion to democracy. Cartoons showed beloved characters like Bugs Bunny and Daffy Duck doing their part to support the war effort. Not wishing to highlight contradictions in U.S. democracy or to undermine Allied unity, government censors ensured that films sent abroad did not depict the nation's racial segregation, suggest that the United States was solely responsible for victories, or present U.S. allies as imperialists.

Government-sponsored research became a major new industry during the war. To counter Germany's scientific and technological superiority, Roosevelt created the Office of Scientific Research and Development. Its most ambitious undertaking was the $2 billion **Manhattan Project**, the top-secret venture to build an atomic bomb. Federal funds also supported the development of napalm (jellied gasoline), flame throwers, and rockets. The government financed medical research that produced penicillin and plasma, both of which contributed to a 50 percent decrease in the death rate of wounded soldiers compared with that of World War I. New pesticides and antimalarial drugs protected soldiers in tropical environments from insect-borne diseases.

The huge increase in federal spending—from $9 billion in 1940 to $98 billion in 1944—had a ripple effect throughout society. The United States reached full employment, and the standard of living rose. Despite high income taxes on the wealthy (up to 90 percent) and new income taxes on the middle and lower classes, U.S. workers' average annual per capita income increased from $373 in 1940 to $1,074 in 1945. The war created 17 million new civilian jobs. As millions of married women entered the paid workforce, many families had two incomes for the first time. Traditionally underemployed groups such as racial minorities, teenagers, senior citizens, and disabled people found work. Although federal wage controls limited salary increases, many factory workers doubled or even tripled their paychecks with overtime pay. Because consumer goods such as radios and toasters were in short supply, most Americans saved rather than spent.

Despite a thriving economy, many Americans resisted increased government intervention. Manufacturers and farmers disliked price controls. Labor leaders criticized wage freezes. Although unions pledged not to strike during the war, inflation and wage restrictions triggered unauthorized "wildcat" strikes. Although most strikes ended quickly and did not undermine wartime production, some Americans viewed them as unpatriotic. In 1943, Congress overrode Roosevelt's veto to pass the Smith-Connally Act, which banned strikes in defense industries, granted the president the right to seize plants critical to the war effort, and limited unions' political activity. These provisions represented a bipartisan backlash against New Deal liberalism.

Although the Democrats maintained a narrow majority in Congress after the 1942 midterm elections, Republicans believed that they could win the 1944 presidential election. They nominated New York governor Thomas Dewey, who supported Roosevelt's direction of the war effort but opposed additional expansion of federal programs. Despite his failing health, Roosevelt waged a vigorous campaign that was boosted by his proposal for veterans' benefits. The Servicemen's Readjustment Act, better known as the **G.I. Bill of Rights**, offered every man

Manhattan Project U.S. government-sponsored research collaboration that produced the first atomic bombs.

G.I. Bill of Rights U.S. law passed in 1944 granting returning veterans benefits for home ownership, business start-ups, and education.

and woman who served honorably in the armed forces access to low-cost mortgages, business loans, educational assistance, and unemployment compensation. Mindful of the mistreatment of U.S. veterans in the Bonus Army during the Great Depression, Congress unanimously passed the bill in March 1944, and the promises it held helped Roosevelt win an unprecedented fourth term.

21-3b Migration and Social Changes

Women and minorities challenge the United States to fulfill its democratic ideals.

Over the course of World War II, one in every five Americans moved to a different county. Military volunteers and recruits left their homes for training camps and overseas deployments. Heading mostly south and west, rural families moved in pursuit of jobs at defense plants and shipyards, signaling a geographic shift in the U.S. population that would continue after the war (see Map 21.3).

New migrants created housing shortages and overburdened schools, social service agencies, and recreational facilities. Racial tensions increased as urban whites (many themselves emigrants from rural areas) resisted sharing spaces and jobs with newly arrived African Americans. In June 1943, a three-day race riot in Detroit left twenty-five blacks and nine whites dead and caused $2 million in property damage. Similar racial violence occurred among U.S. troops in England. Clashes between black and white soldiers at Bamber Bridge, Launceston, and Leicester resulted in deaths, injuries, and courts-martial.

In addition to new migration patterns, the war years sparked social changes. Marriage and birth rates rebounded after hitting all-time lows during the Great Depression. Before men left for war, many couples conceived "good-bye babies" born nine months later. As wartime separations and experiences tested marriages, divorce rates also increased.

On the home front, the war greatly affected women's lives. Many volunteered at Red Cross chapters or entertained troops at United Service Organizations (USO) clubs. Many more entered the paid workforce, replacing men who were serving in the military. The number of women with paid jobs rose by 57 percent from 12 million in 1940 to 20 million by 1945. For the first time in U.S. history, a majority of married women worked outside the home. Although more than one-third of American women

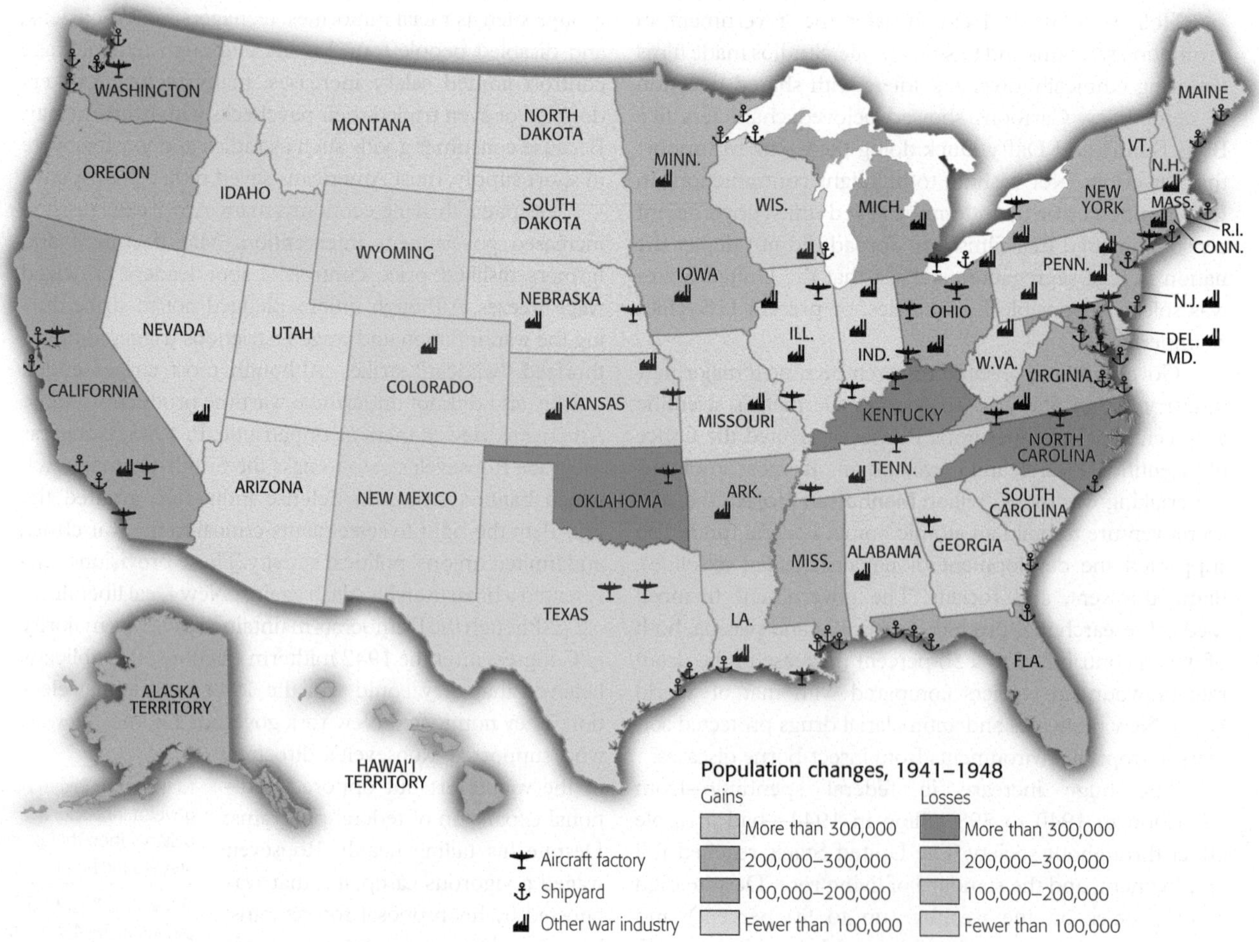

Map 21.3 Wartime Migration Patterns Defense industry jobs played a key role in shaping wartime migration patterns in the United States. ▲

Pvt. Joe Louis says_
"We're going to do our part ... and we'll win because we're on God's side"

Library of Congress Prints and Photographs Division [LC-USZC4-1334]

Global Americans The son of Alabama sharecroppers, the great-grandson of a slave, and the great-great-grandson of a white slave owner, **Joe Louis** attained fame and wealth unprecedented for African Americans of his era. While he held the heavyweight boxing championship from 1937 to 1949 (a record that still stands), two of his fights had particular resonance at a time of rising international tensions. In June 1935, many, especially African Americans, cheered Louis's victory over Italian Primo Carnera while Mussolini's armies invaded Ethiopia. A year later, the Nazis touted Max Schmeling's victory over Louis as proof of Germanic superiority. But in the rematch in June 1938, Louis knocked out Schmeling in the first round as nearly 100 million people worldwide listened on the radio. Louis became an international inspiration for those who opposed fascism, and Americans of all races embraced him as a symbol of democratic values and racial unity. He enlisted in the army right after Pearl Harbor, and rather than sending him into combat, the army used him for morale-boosting boxing exhibitions and recruitment campaigns aimed at African Americans. He donated tens of thousands of dollars from his matches to war relief efforts. At one exhibition, Louis declared, "We're going to do our part and we'll win 'cause we're on God's side," a phrase that U.S. propagandists quickly used in their campaigns. Privately, Louis challenged the military's racist practices. After the war, he struggled financially due to back taxes and unscrupulous managers. When he died broke in 1981, Schmeling, Louis's friend and former adversary, paid part of his funeral costs.

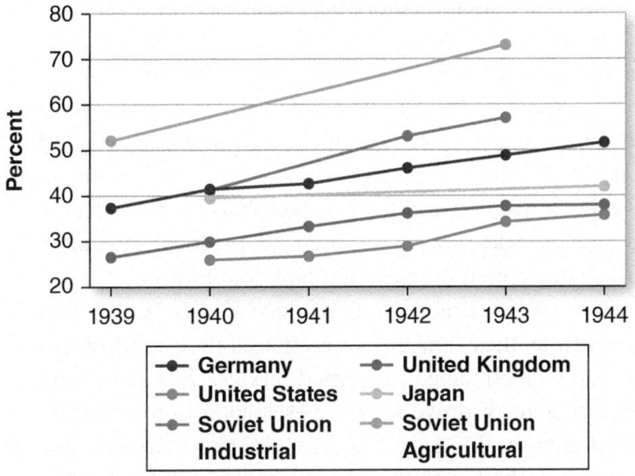

NOTE: No data available for United States, 1939; Soviet Union Industrial, 1939, 1941, 1944; Japan, 1939, 1941–1943; Soviet Union Agricultural, 1940–942, 1944.

Figure 21.3 Women Workers as a Percentage of the Civilian Workforce, 1939–1944 More than one-third of American women joined the civilian workforce during World War II, but this proportion was smaller than that of their British and Soviet counterparts, some of whom were involuntarily conscripted. Although the Nazis placed special emphasis on women's roles as wives and mothers, hundreds of thousands of German women served in auxiliaries of the armed forces and worked in hospitals, offices, and factories. Despite patriarchal cultural norms, Japanese women played vital roles in war production and agriculture. ▲ Source: Dear, I. C. B., and M. R. D. Foot, *The Oxford Companion to World War II* (Oxford, 2003), 2014 online ed, http://www.oxfordreference.com/view/10.1093/acref/9780198604464.001.0001/acref-9780198604464-e-1566?p=emailAWogkKzU5LJo2&d=/10.1093/acref/9780198604464.001.0001/acref-9780198604464-e-1566

worked for wages for all or part of the war, higher percentages of German, Japanese, British, and Soviet women were part of the wartime workforce (see Figure 21.3).

Some American women took traditionally "male" jobs such as welding. **Rosie the Riveter** became a patriotic symbol of women working in defense industries, although few women were actually trained as riveters. But women sometimes paid a price for their new economic independence. Many struggled to find adequate child care. Recruiters stressed that female employees were needed "only for the duration."

U.S. women also joined the armed forces. Each branch of the military organized women's auxiliary units with special uniforms, officers, and pay equal to that of male soldiers. By 1945, more than 350,000 women had joined the Women's Army Corps (WACs), the U.S. Navy's Women Accepted for Volunteer Emergency Service (WAVES), the Women's Auxiliary Service Pilots (WASPs), the Army and Navy Nurses Corps, the Coast Guard (SPARs), and the Marines.

World War II was a transformative era for African Americans. Continuing the Great Migration that had begun in the early twentieth century, 700,000 additional southern blacks moved north during the war. More than 2 million worked in defense jobs, but ongoing wage and housing discrimination limited their wartime gains. To call attention to these problems, in the spring of 1941, labor leader A. Philip Randolph and the National Association for the Advancement of Colored People (NAACP) threatened to stage a march on Washington, D.C., protesting discrimination at defense plants and in federal employment and calling for the integration of the armed services. Worried about the implications of such a demonstration, Roosevelt made a deal. In exchange for the organizers' canceling the march and dropping their demand for integration in the military, the president issued an executive order banning discrimination in defense industries and establishing the Fair Employment Practices Committee (FEPC). By the end of the war, the number of African American federal employees had risen from 60,000 in 1941 to 200,000. Although the understaffed and poorly funded FEPC was less successful in striking down inequities in the private sector, FDR's actions were a historic step toward racial equality.

Rosie the Riveter Cultural icon representing American women who worked in factories during World War II, many in defense industries.

The nearly 1 million African Americans in the military served in segregated units that were mostly relegated to noncombat assignments. For most of the war, the marines excluded blacks entirely and the navy accepted them only for kitchen duties. The army created separate black regiments commanded by mostly white officers. The Red Cross even segregated its blood supply.

These injustices prompted tremendous growth in civil rights activities during the war. Black organizations embraced the **Double V Campaign**, calling for victory over fascism abroad and over segregation and discrimination at home. Membership in the NAACP rose from 18,000 to almost 500,000. In May 1942, the Fellowship of Reconciliation organized one of the nation's earliest sit-ins to protest a Chicago diner's refusal to serve blacks. Other African Americans joined the newly established Congress of Racial Equality (CORE). At a 1944 CORE demonstration in Washington, D.C., participants challenged segregation and carried signs asking, "Are You for Hitler's Way or the American Way?"

Mexican Americans also benefited from the booming wartime economy, and many found industrial work that offered an escape from migrant farm work. Patriotism temporarily overrode cultural mores that discouraged Mexican American women from working outside the home, and they took jobs in offices, hospitals, and defense plants. When the demand for manual labor exceeded the available domestic workforce, the federal government established the ***bracero* program** allowing Mexicans to enter the United States as guest agricultural or railroad workers.

Almost 400,000 Latinos served in the U.S. armed forces, the highest proportional representation of any ethnic group in the United States. Hundreds of Latinas joined the WACs, WAVES, and other women's military auxiliary branches. Puerto Rican soldiers guarded the Panama Canal and the Caribbean. More than 9,000 Latinos died in combat.

Although Mexican Americans were categorized by the U.S. government as white and served in integrated military units, they still experienced discrimination. In the summer of 1943, white sailors stationed in the Los Angeles area clashed with Latino youths wearing zoot suits, colorful and loose garments worn with long key chains and pork-pie hats. The suits violated WPB regulations limiting the amount of fabric that could be used in clothing, but a network of bootleg tailors continued to produce them. Racism combined with anger about the youths' flouting of federal rationing rules triggered the **Zoot Suit riots**, a series of episodes in which sailors physically assaulted Mexican American youths, stripped them, burned their clothing, and cut their ducktail-styled hair. Ordered not to arrest any of the servicemen, police arrested more than five hundred Latinos. The episodes triggered similar attacks on Latinos in Beaumont, Chicago, New York, San Diego, and Philadelphia.

Double V Campaign Launched by the *Pittsburgh Courier*, a black newspaper, demanded that African Americans fighting abroad be granted full citizenship rights at home.

***bracero* program** Spanish for "one who uses his arms"; agreement that allowed for the temporary importation of contract workers from Mexico into the United States.

Zoot Suit riots Series of clashes between Mexican American youth and white sailors in Los Angeles in 1943; police response triggered outrage among Latinos.

World War II had a mixed effect on Native Americans, bringing some into contact with whites, often for the first time. Approximately twenty-five thousand Native Americans served in the military. A select group of soldiers, mostly Navajos, worked as "code talkers," soldiers who used their native languages in military communications. Enemy forces were unable to break those codes, and they proved invaluable in operations in the Pacific theater. For Native Americans who stayed on reservations, the war years were difficult. There were few defense jobs nearby, and government subsidies dwindled as federal funds were diverted to the war effort.

Asian Americans were especially attentive to the Pacific theater of the war because Chinese, Korean, and Filipino immigrants sent money and supplies to their homelands to defeat the Japanese. Many members of these ethnic groups enlisted in the U.S. military, seeing action in both Europe and the Pacific. Those who remained in the United States benefited from nondiscriminatory policies in U.S. war industries.

Although few Americans noticed at the time, World War II was a crucial turning point in the formation of gay communities nationwide. The mobility of the war years created many venues where gay men and women could find others like themselves. As they moved from small towns to gay subcultures in places such as New York, San Francisco, and Los Angeles, many experienced personal liberation. With so many men overseas, lesbians could travel or go out together without attracting much notice. Driven by the same patriotism as their straight counterparts, thousands of gay men and women joined the armed services. Some men did so in order to disprove stereotypes linking homosexuality and effeminacy. Most easily passed the psychological tests the Pentagon had instituted to identify gays prior to enlistment. Although military regulations outlawed sodomy, many commanders refused to report gays who served their units well. Expulsion from the armed services could have grave consequences. A dishonorable discharge not only disqualified one from receiving G.I. Bill benefits but also contained a code alerting potential employers to the reason for dismissal. At a time when homosexuality was illegal in all fifty states and considered a mental illness by the medical profession, many companies refused to knowingly hire gay people.

21-3c Civil Liberties

The war triggers opposition to as well as demands for incarceration of those perceived to be disloyal.

Whereas World War I had divided Americans and triggered severe repressions of civil liberties such as the 1918 Sedition Act, World War II had broad-based popular support and did not spark repressive laws. The 1940 Alien Registration Act (better known as the *Smith Act*), which criminalized speech advocating the overthrow of the U.S. government, was not frequently applied during the war, although it was later used to prosecute U.S. Communists. When FBI director J. Edgar Hoover concluded that Albert Einstein's lifelong associations with pacifist and socialist organizations violated the Smith Act and recommended deportation, the State Department overruled him. Einstein quickly became a U.S. citizen, and as a gesture of loyalty to his newly adopted country, he donated a handwritten copy of his 1905 paper on special relativity to be auctioned at a war bond drive. It sold for $6.5 million.

With German Americans constituting nearly one-quarter of the U.S. population by 1940, the OWI carefully avoided the tactics of World War I's Committee on Public Information, which demonized anything or anyone German. In that era, Socialist Party leaders had gone to jail for denouncing the 1917 conscription law, but in 1941, after Germany attacked the Soviet Union, the Communist Party of the United States backed the campaign to defeat Nazism and fascism. U.S. Communists enlisted in the armed forces, sold war bonds, collected burn dressings, and enforced blackouts.

The war effort united Americans across religious lines, transcending long-standing divisions among Catholics, Jews, and Protestants. Almost everyone viewed the war against fascism as a "just war," a conflict that is morally necessary to defeat a larger evil. Many soldiers found prayer essential to surviving the horrors of combat and forged close bonds with comrades of different faiths. Soldiers' increasing religiosity contributed to a great rise in church attendance and overseas missionary work in the postwar era.

There were, however, Americans who opposed World War II on ethical and religious grounds. Nation of Islam leader Elijah Muhammad, a black separatist, advised his followers to resist the draft and was subsequently jailed for violating the Selective Service Act. Quakers and Mennonites were among those who refused to violate peace traditions of their churches. World War II marked the first time that Congress legally recognized **conscientious objector (CO)** status. Under the law, objectors could fulfill their military obligation by accepting noncombat roles in the armed forces or civilian jobs with "national importance." Many pacifists served as military ambulance drivers or medics. Others volunteered as smoke jumpers fighting forest fires or as guinea pigs in dangerous medical experiments. But 6,000 of the 72,345 Americans who applied for CO status refused to support the war in any way and went to prison. They were often derided as unpatriotic and cowardly.

Although government authorities arrested 14,000 Italian and German potential security risks living in North and South America during the war, only 5,000 Italian and German enemy aliens and U.S. citizens were held in detention camps. Japanese immigrants and Japanese Americans faced far greater curtailment of civil liberties. Following the Pearl Harbor attacks, Hawai'i—then a U.S. territory—instituted martial law, and military police arrested several hundred suspected Japanese spies and saboteurs. None was found to have committed an offense. Military officials considered but decided against interning the island's 100,000 residents of Japanese descent because they constituted almost half of Hawai'i's population and played a critical role in the local economy.

People of Japanese descent on the mainland were treated much more harshly. A tiny percentage of the U.S. population and socially isolated, people of Japanese descent drew the ire of Americans long hostile to Asian immigrants and eager to avenge the Pearl Harbor attacks. Although the U.S. government arrested approximately 2,000 potential subversives with Japanese ancestry, it found none guilty of crimes. In February 1942, Roosevelt nonetheless issued Executive Order 9066, establishing a defense zone along the entire West Coast. More than 110,000 Japanese Americans were evacuated to makeshift "assembly centers," at least two-thirds of them ***Nisei***, native-born U.S. citizens of Japanese extraction. From the assembly centers, Japanese Americans were sent to ten **internment camps** in remote parts of the West and South (see Map 21.4). Living conditions and medical care were basic at best. Armed guards patrolled the fortified compounds.

About thirty-five thousand detainees found ways to leave the camps after they pledged loyalty to the United States and promised to obey a law prohibiting return to their homes within the West Coast defense zone. Some accepted jobs in labor-deprived industries or received college scholarships provided by churches and philanthropies. Around 1,300 Nisei men, about 5 percent of the draft-eligible individuals in the internment camps, volunteered for the all-Nisei 442 Combat Team, which consisted primarily of Japanese Americans from Hawai'i. This unit won more than 1,000 citations for bravery and lost more than 500 men in battle, one of the army's highest casualty rates. Despite an edict from Emperor Hirohito declaring them traitors who should be executed upon capture, a small contingent of Nisei from the internment camps volunteered to serve as military translators in the Pacific.

The Supreme Court confirmed the constitutionality of the Japanese American internment in two decisions handed down in December 1944. Both ***Korematsu v. United States*** and ***Endo, Ex Parte*** upheld the federal government's right to detain Japanese residents on the West Coast as a means of ensuring national security. But the *Endo* decision ruled that the War Relocation Authority had not proven the disloyalty of a Nisei internee named Mitsuye Endo and therefore ordered that she be released and allowed to return to the West Coast. Anticipating the ruling, military authorities proclaimed one day before it was announced that it was

conscientious objector (CO) Individual who refuses military service on the basis of religious or ethical beliefs.

Nisei Japanese term used to describe second-generation children born to immigrants in a new country, as opposed to the first-generation immigrants called *Issei*.

internment camps Ten camps in isolated locations in seven U.S. states used as prisons to which more than one hundred ten thousand Japanese and Japanese Americans were relocated from the Pacific Coast.

Korematsu v. United States U.S. Supreme Court ruling in 1944 upholding the constitutionality of the internment of Japanese Americans during World War II, regardless of citizenship.

Endo, Ex Parte Unanimous 1944 U.S. Supreme Court decision that led to the reopening of the West Coast for resettlement by Japanese American citizens following their internment.

Map 21.4 Internment Camps for Japanese Americans, 1942–1945
Under the internment policy imposed in 1942, the U.S. government gave one hundred ten thousand Japanese Americans living along the West Coast seventy-two hours to close their businesses, find custodians for their farms and pets, and vacate their houses prior to their evacuation to ten isolated compounds scattered across seven states. Most were forced to surrender their property permanently. Others returned months later to homes that had been burglarized or destroyed. ▶

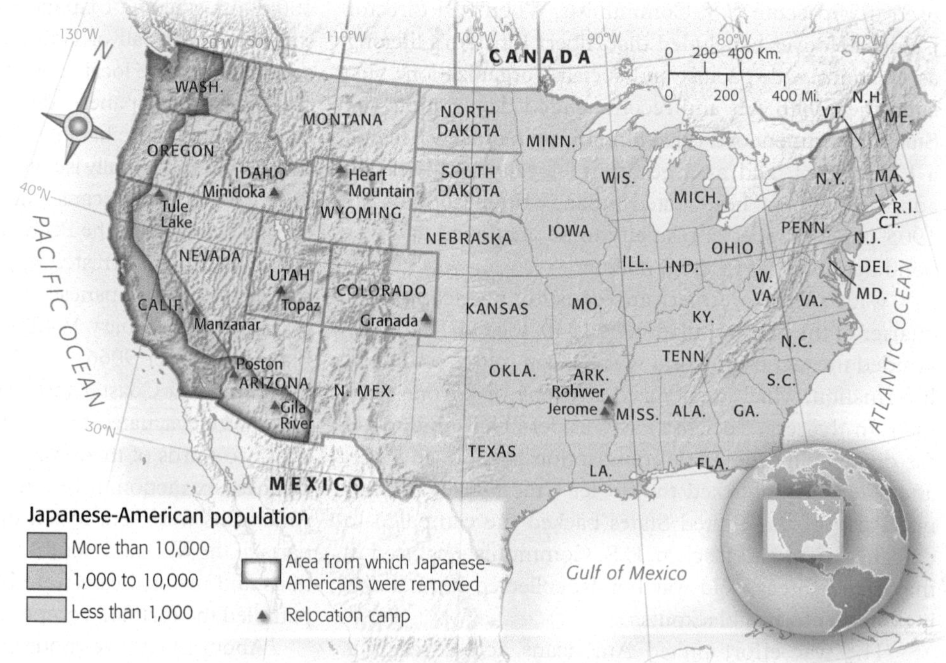

no longer necessary to detain the West Coast Japanese and ordered the release of approved internees starting January 2, 1945.

The internment disillusioned many detainees. After the war, 5,000 renounced their U.S. citizenship and moved to Japan. Although the evacuations had cost those Japanese affected an estimated $400 million in lost property, Congress provided only $37 million in reparations in 1948. Forty years later, federal lawmakers officially apologized for its wartime violation of Japanese American civil liberties and voted to give each of the 60,000 surviving detainees a $20,000 indemnity.

21-4
Road to Victory

On August 14, 1945, the Japanese surrendered. In this U.S. Army photograph taken the following day, American servicemen and women gathered in front of the "Rainbow Corner" Red Cross club in Paris to celebrate the end of World War II.

Examine the faces of the American men and women in this photograph, and imagine how members of the armed forces in Allied and Axis nations might have responded to the end of the war. How had race and gender shaped wartime experiences? ▶

McNulty/American Military Activity/National Archives

Go to MindTap® to practice history with the Chapter 21 **Primary Source Writing Activity: The Road to Victory.** Read and view primary sources and respond to a writing prompt.

After gaining the offensive in 1943, the Allies implemented a two-stage strategy to defeat the Axis. After first defeating the Germans in the European theater, the Allies turned to defeating the Japanese in the Pacific theater. The war's latter months witnessed brutal battles, revealed the horrors of the Holocaust, and marked the beginning of the atomic age. Determined not to repeat the punitive treaties that ended World War I, American, Soviet, and British policy makers planned for peace. They were unable, however, to resolve some issues which had serious ramifications in the postwar era. Inspired by Atlantic Charter objectives, racial minorities and colonized peoples were ready to fight for inclusion and independence.

☞ As you read, compare and contrast the final stages of combat in the European and Pacific theaters. Explain why American, Soviet, and British policy makers differed in their respective peace aims.

21-4a Defeat of Nazi Germany

Following the opening of a second front in France, Allied and Soviet forces push into Germany.

On June 6, 1944—known as **D-Day**—the Allies under the command of U.S. general Dwight D. Eisenhower opened the long-delayed second front in northwestern France. Facing minimal threat from the *Luftwaffe*, which had been weakened by severe losses in air battles and Allied bombings of defense plants, a vast flotilla of 160,000 (ultimately 3 million) troops crossed the English Channel in the first wave. A few hours earlier, paratroopers had dropped behind German lines. At dawn, British, American, and Canadian troops had made amphibious landings at six different points on the coast of Normandy. After meeting strong resistance and incurring heavy casualties, the troops secured the beachhead and began pushing the German defense back. A month later, certain that defeat was imminent, several German military commanders tried to assassinate Hitler to secure peace terms that would spare Germany from invasion, but their plot failed. Hitler retaliated by having 4,000 people executed.

On July 25, after a devastating aerial and artillery assault, the Allies opened a path for their armies to pursue the Germans across France. By August 25, U.S. and Free French troops had liberated Paris. After their successful eastward push through France, the Allies' front lines stretched from the Netherlands in the north to Switzerland in the south.

Aiming to recapture the valuable port at Antwerp before the Allies could resupply and use their superior airpower, Hitler ordered a risky counteroffensive in Belgium. In mid-December, mechanized German divisions broke through weak Allied lines in the Ardennes Forest and then struck Bastogne, a small town where seven major roads converged. But a much smaller U.S. force managed to defend the vital crossroads in a week-long siege. After reinforcements arrived and the weather improved, the Allies defeated the Germans in the **Battle of the Bulge**. Having used most of their reserves and left the western part of Germany vulnerable, the Germans knew that their last gamble had failed.

Within weeks, the Allies crossed into Germany itself. In mid-January 1945, Soviet troops advanced westward across the Oder River and headed toward Berlin. In March, American forces crossed the Rhine River and secured the industrial Ruhr region. In late April, U.S. and Soviet troops met at the Elbe River. On April 30, as the Red Army neared the outskirts of Berlin, Hitler committed suicide by taking a cyanide capsule and then shooting himself in the head. On May 7, his successor unconditionally surrendered to General Eisenhower, and on May 8 people all over the world participated in Victory in Europe Day—**V-E Day**—celebrations.

21-4b The Holocaust

U.S. and Allied leaders struggle to comprehend and confront reports of unprecedented Nazi genocide.

As U.S. and Soviet troops advanced through Germany in 1945, they liberated concentration camps and found incontrovertible evidence of the Nazis' atrocities against Jews, political dissidents, the Roma, Soviet POWs, and others. As many as 500,000 Nazis and Nazi collaborators had identified, deported, enslaved, and killed more than 11 million people at approximately 42,000 facilities in Germany and German-occupied territories. But the Allies had been slow to respond to the **Final Solution**, the Nazis' secret plan to exterminate all of the Jews in Europe formalized in January 1942. During the war, escapees from the camps had informed U.S. and British officials and the Polish government in exile of the mass executions and the Nazis' use of poison gas and crematoria. However, Allied officials had difficulty grasping the enormity of the genocide. In December 1942, the United Nations issued a joint declaration denouncing the Nazis' "bestial policy of cold-blooded extermination" and vowing that war criminals would be prosecuted after the war. The Allies could do little else during the war because the Germans occupied most of Europe.

D-Day June 6, 1944, the day of Allied landings on the Normandy coast, in which the first wave of 160,000 Allied troops challenged heavily fortified German forces along fifty miles of coastline.

Battle of the Bulge Failed German offensive in December 1944 in the Ardennes region, costliest battle of the war in terms of U.S. casualties.

V-E Day (Victory in Europe Day) Public holiday celebrated on May 8, 1945, to mark the Allies' formal acceptance of Nazi Germany's unconditional surrender.

Final Solution Nazi plan formulated in January 1942 following years of severe Nazi discrimination against Jews to systematically exterminate the Jewish people in Nazi-occupied Europe.

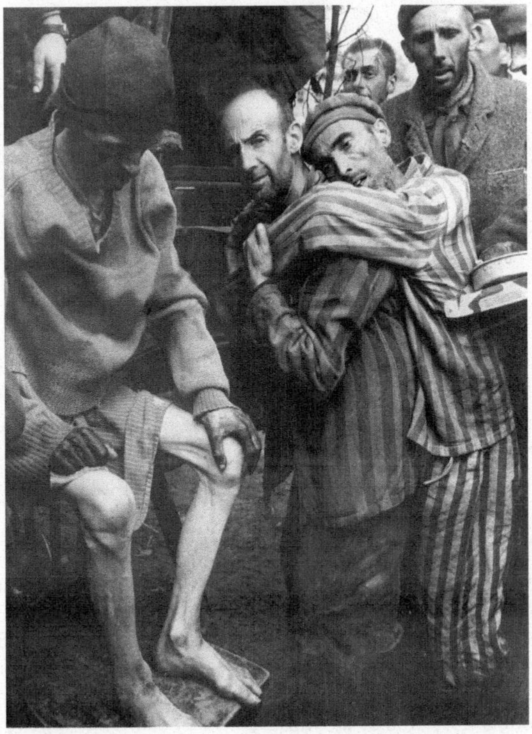

AP Images/Dpa/picture-alliance

The Liberation of Concentration Camps In November 1944, American troops rescue the emaciated and exhausted survivors of the concentration camp Woebbelin. Like all who liberated the camps, they were horrified by the magnitude of Nazi atrocities. Images of mass graves, gas chambers, and ovens used as killing machines and the emaciated, haunted survivors shocked the world and convinced millions of the evil nature of Nazism and the need for global action to prevent the recurrence of such human rights abuses forever. ▲

History without Borders
Eugenics

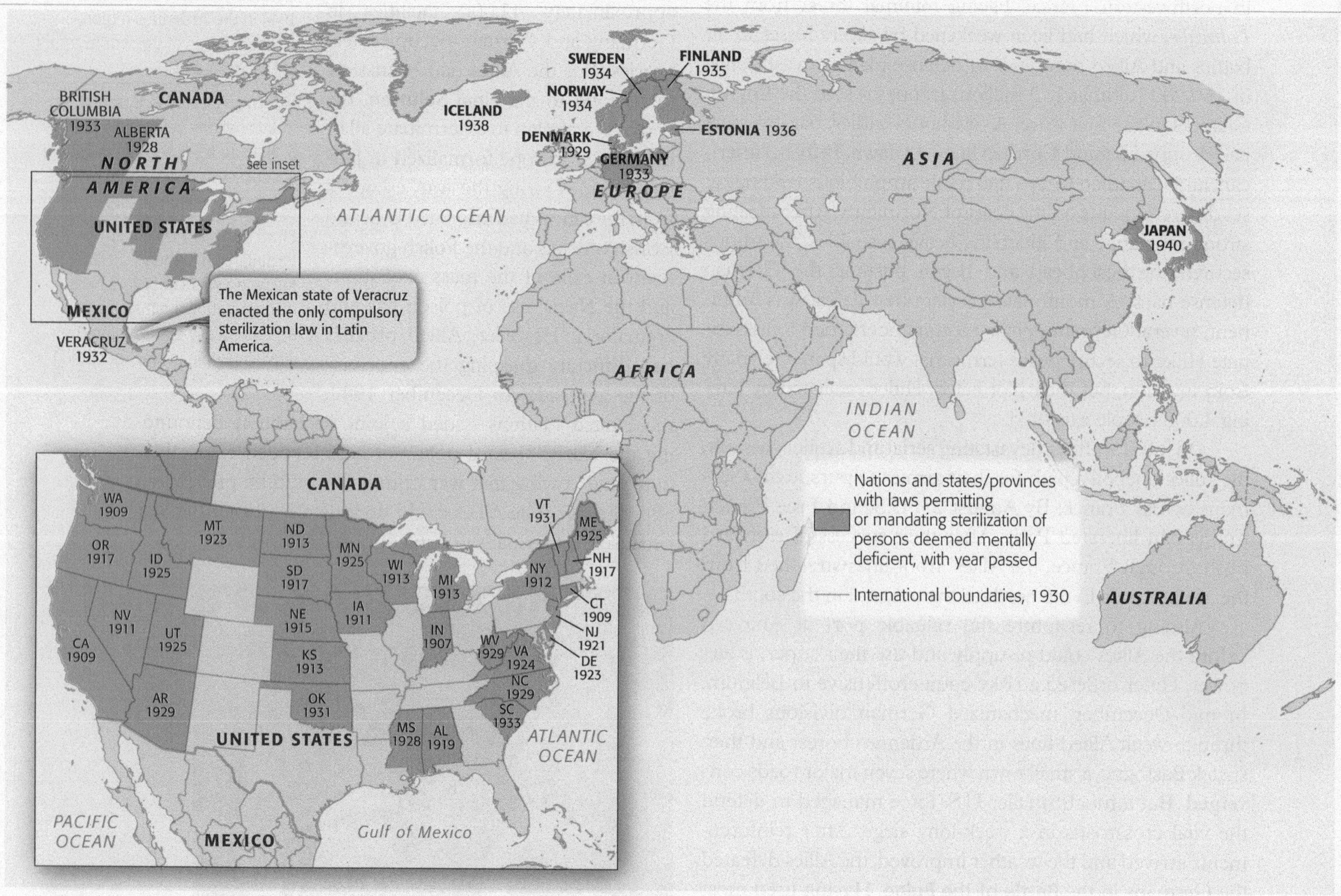

Nations and States with Sterilization Laws, 1907–1940 Eight nations, provinces and states in Canada and Mexico, and thirty-one U.S. states adopted laws permitting or mandating the sterilization of people found to be "mentally deficient" by authorities. Although some jurisdictions required the voluntary consent of those being sterilized, such consent was sometimes obtained through coercive means. In many places, state-sanctioned sterilizations were not discontinued until the mid-1970s. ▲

The Nazis' glorification of a white, blond, blue-eyed "master race" and persecution of Jews and others deemed genetically inferior were grounded in a transnational movement called *eugenics*. Some of the most prominent social scientists in the West contributed to its development, including Thomas Malthus, Herbert Spencer, Charles Darwin, and Gregor Mendel. Sir Francis Galton, a British intellectual, built on their ideas of human population, natural selection, and inherited characteristics to begin the modern field of eugenics in the 1880s. He argued that the human race could be improved by selective breeding amplifying physical health, intelligence, and high moral character. Thus, he advocated early marriage for the production of children among genetically superior people, whom he equated with the British upper classes, an approach known as *positive eugenics*. In the United States, scientists such as the zoologist Charles Davenport flipped Galton's ideas to promote *negative eugenics*. To suppress disease, imbecility, and criminality, Davenport advocated limiting the fertility of those deemed genetically inferior through marriage prohibitions, involuntary sterilization, and even euthanasia.

Backed by Carnegie Institution and the Rockefeller Foundation, Davenport and his researchers collected hereditary data and tried to identify the genetically

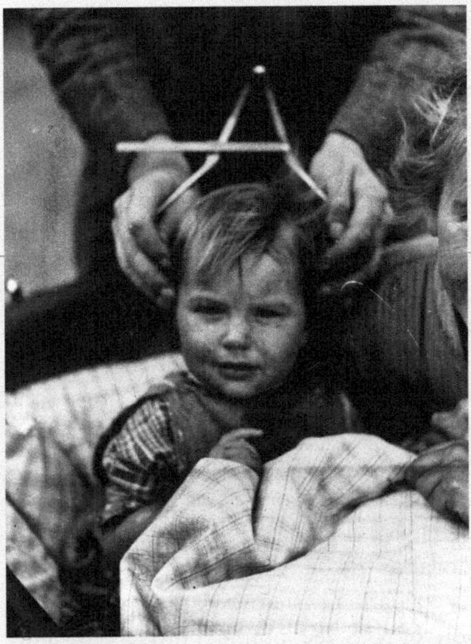
Ullstein Bild/The Granger Collection, New York

A University of Kiel Researcher Measures the Skull of a Child in a German Village, 1932 Developed by German physician Franz Joseph Gall in 1796, phrenology extrapolated personality traits from measurements of the human skull. Although the principles behind phrenology had been largely debunked by the end of the nineteenth century, the pseudoscience was adopted by eugenicists, notably the Nazis, in attempts to provide scientific evidence of Aryan superiority. ▲

CBW/Alamy Stock Photo

Nazi Propaganda Poster, 1938 This 1938 poster promoting Nazi Germany's Aktion T4, a Nazi program of forced euthanasia, reads: "This person suffering from hereditary defects costs the community 60,000 Reichsmark during his lifetime. Fellow German, that is your money, too."▲

desirable and undesirable. Prominent scientists, reformers, and social workers embraced eugenics as a humane and progressive means of addressing social ills.

In the early twentieth century, more than thirty states enacted statutes prohibiting the mentally ill from marrying and requiring their sterilization, a practice upheld by the Supreme Court in *Buck v. Bell* (1927). Between 1907 and 1964, approximately 64,000 Americans were sterilized, primarily in prisons and state-run insane asylums. In 1924, eugenics policy informed the Immigration Act that placed strict quotas on the number of immigrants from eastern and southern Europe, believed to be of racial stock genetically inferior to that of northern Europeans.

U.S. eugenics inspired similar movements throughout Europe, Latin America, and Asia. From 1934 to 1975, Sweden forcibly sterilized more than 62,000 people. In Brazil, the government backed efforts to increase the white population while reducing the fertility of descendants of African slaves and Asian immigrants. Canadian officials legalized the forcible sterilization of First Nation peoples. Australia adopted policies removing mixed-race Aboriginal children from their parents. Japan's National Eugenic Law (1940) authorized the sterilization of criminals and those with genetic diseases such as colorblindness, hemophilia, albinism, mental illness, or epilepsy.

Eugenics fed notions of race purity and Aryan superiority. Adolf Hitler studied American eugenics, using it to justify his call to rid Germany of the polluting influence of Jews. After taking power in 1933, Nazi officials hand selected victims for sterilization and euthanasia. By 1937, they had forcibly sterilized 400,000 people and killed thousands of the institutionalized disabled through programs like Aktion T4. After the war began, gassing victims proved more efficient than lethal injections, a lesson applied to the creation of gas chambers for the mass exterminations of the Holocaust. The Nazis also instituted positive eugenics programs that rewarded Aryan women who gave birth to several children and that placed "racially valuable" children from Nazi-occupied countries with German families.

In the Nazi racial program, eugenics pushed to its extreme in genocide provoked global revulsion. The trajectory of race science changed course from creating categories and hierarchies to rejecting them. Eugenics was renamed *genetics*, a field that now concentrates on the mechanism of heredity, not its social or political application.

Critical Thinking Questions

▶ What factors do you think explain why eugenics became a transnational movement in the early twentieth century? How did Nazi Germany's application of eugenics differ from that of other nations?

▶ What long-range ramifications did eugenics have? How do contemporary ideas about genetics differ from those common in the early twentieth century?

War Refugee Board (WRB) U.S. government agency, established in January 1944, charged with rescuing European Jews and other victims of Nazi persecution.

Bretton Woods economic system First-ever negotiated monetary order governing currency relations among sovereign states; created in 1944 and operated until the early 1970s.

World Bank UN international financial institution founded in 1944 that provides loans and technical assistance to developing nations; aims to reduce global poverty.

International Monetary Fund (IMF) International organization created in 1944 that promotes global monetary and exchange stability and the expansion of world trade.

developing nations Countries seeking to foster economic growth, diversification, and industrialization, often heavily reliant on the export of a few agricultural crops.

United Nations (UN) International organization that promotes global peace and human rights, established on October 24, 1945, as a replacement for the League of Nations.

Yalta Conference Meeting in February 1945 in the Crimea during which Roosevelt, Stalin, and Churchill planned the next phase of the war and discussed the postwar world.

Jewish leaders in the United States, such as Rabbi Stephen Wise, implored President Roosevelt to stop the mass murders. Despite his deep sympathies for the Jews and victims of Axis-sponsored terror, the president was constrained by anti-Semitic and xenophobic sentiments in Congress and among the American public. Many found it difficult to believe that the Nazis were capable of committing the heinous crimes being described by eyewitnesses. In April 1943, U.S. and British officials met in Bermuda to discuss possible solutions, but after the British refused to allow Jewish refugees to emigrate to Palestine, the delegates concluded that the best way to help the refugees was to end the war as quickly as possible. Some Zionists in Palestine and the United States feared helping Jews escape from Nazi Germany would undermine political support for the postwar creation of a Jewish state.

Secretary of the Treasury Henry Morgenthau, the only Jew in Roosevelt's cabinet, disagreed. After an aide submitted *Report to the Secretary on the Acquiescence of This Government in the Murder of the Jews,* a scathing indictment of the U.S. State Department's obstruction of rescue efforts for European Jews, Morgenthau used the report to persuade Roosevelt to create the **War Refugee Board (WRB)**. Established in January 1944, the board enlisted foreign governments and nongovernmental organizations (NGOs) to provide for the evacuation and relief of refugees. But U.S. military commanders, unwilling to divert American planes from key Allied military operations and still unsure that reports of the mass executions were accurate, rejected the WRB's calls to bomb the notorious Auschwitz death camp and its feeder rail lines. By the end of the war, the WRB had rescued approximately 200,000 Jews and 20,000 non-Jews.

21-4c Plans for Postwar Peace

Allied policy makers establish institutions to secure economic and political stability in the postwar world.

In late 1943, as they went on the military offensive in Europe, the Allies accelerated their planning for the postwar era. In contrast to Wilson's rigidity and obsession with the League of Nations, Roosevelt was an adept compromiser who supported the creation of several new international organizations that would reshape postwar politics and economics.

In July 1944, representatives from forty-four countries convened in Bretton Woods, New Hampshire, to establish regulations on global monetary policy, later known as the **Bretton Woods economic system**. Seeking to avoid the economic protectionism of the interwar period, the delegates committed their nations to free trade and open borders. To promote economic stability and growth, they created the International Bank for Reconstruction and Development, known as the **World Bank**, and the **International Monetary Fund (IMF)** to issue short- and long-term loans to **developing nations** to promote their stability and growth. Providing over one-third of $9 billion of original capital and holding one-third of each board's votes, the United States dominated the institutions. The use of the U.S. dollar as the benchmark for the new international currency valuation system became an especially potent illustration of U.S. economic power. Unwilling to surrender its state-centered economic system or give capitalist countries access to its finances, the Soviet Union refused to join either the World Bank or IMF, a decision reflecting growing tensions among the Big Three.

From August to October 1944, U.S., British, Soviet, and Chinese officials met in Washington, D.C., to draft a charter for the **United Nations (UN)**. Renouncing the ideologies of the Axis Powers, the charter's preamble decried "the scourge of war" and reaffirmed "faith in fundamental human rights, in the dignity and worth of the human person, in the equal rights of men and women and of nations large and small." It pledged to uphold international law and "to promote social progress and better standards of life in larger freedom."

The UN delegates created a Security Council comprised of five permanent members (the United States, the Soviet Union, Great Britain, China, and France) and a much larger General Assembly. To address the failings of the League of Nations, the Security Council was charged with maintaining international peace and security through peacekeeping operations, sanctions, and military intervention. Each permanent member of the Security Council could veto any proposed action. In April 1945, two hundred eighty-two UN delegates from fifty countries convened for the first time in San Francisco. On July 28, in a significant contrast to its refusal to join the League of Nations after World War I, the U.S. Senate voted 89-2 to ratify the UN charter. In the postwar era, the United States strongly embraced the principles of collective security that it had previously rejected, and the United Nations built its headquarters in New York City on land donated by the Rockefeller family.

In February 1945, Winston Churchill, Franklin Roosevelt, and Joseph Stalin met for the last time at **Yalta**, a resort town on the Crimean Sea. In ten days of hard bargaining, the Big Three decided to include France in postwar governance of Germany and to require Germany to pay reparations, the amount to be determined later. The question of how to deal with the defeated or liberated nations of Eastern Europe* dominated the conference. With the Red Army already entrenched in much of the region and acutely aware of the Soviets' disproportionate military sacrifices, Churchill and Roosevelt were reconciled to a temporary Soviet sphere of influence there. Accordingly, they accepted Stalin's demands regarding the location of Poland's borders in exchange for a guarantee of free elections. But they hoped that Stalin would make future concessions in exchange for U.S. aid in rebuilding his shattered country.

There was some reason for optimism. The Big Three issued a Declaration on Liberated Europe calling for democratic elections in Eastern Europe. Stalin also promised that the Soviet Union would enter the war against Japan three months after Germany surrendered. In exchange, Roosevelt and Churchill granted the Soviets concessions in Manchuria and Sakhalin Island, thus restoring territories lost in the 1905 Russo-Japanese War. Stalin then pledged to support Jiang Jieshi and the Chinese Nationalists, not their Communist opponents led by Tse-tung (Mao Zedong). Although the delegates were confident that they had made good compromises based on political and military realities, the ambiguity of several agreements made at Yalta later sparked heated debates.

But Roosevelt would not live long enough to defend those decisions or to resolve the issues left unaddressed. On April 12, during a trip to Warm Springs, Georgia, where he had established a polio treatment center, he had a fatal stroke. Vice President Harry S. Truman, a former senator from Missouri with little foreign policy expertise, would now have to lead the United States to victory over Germany and Japan and deal with Soviet demands for the peace.

Everett Collection Inc/Alamy Stock Photo

Joe Rosenthal, *Raising the Flag on Iwo Jima on Mount Suribachi*, March 1945 This photograph is one of the war's most iconic images. Marines Harlon Block, Franklin Sousley, and Michael Strank were killed in action soon after the photo was taken. The three surviving flag raisers, Marines Rene Gagnon and Ira Hayes (a Pima Indian) and sailor John Bradley were celebrated as national heroes and helped sell billions of dollars of war bonds. Each, however, was deeply scarred by his wartime experiences and conflicted about participating in the photograph. ▲

21-4d Defeat of Imperial Japan

Fierce fighting in the Pacific ends with the first combat uses of atomic weapons.

In late 1944, the Allies launched their Pacific offensive and quickly won a series of battles. By February 1945, they had control of the Gilbert, Marshall, and Caroline Islands as well as New Guinea and the Philippines. In October 1944, the U.S. Navy defeated the Japanese at Leyte Gulf, the largest naval battle in history. Japanese human wave assaults called ***Banzai*** charges, civilian suicides at Saipan, and ***kamikaze*** attacks in which pilots deliberately crashed themselves and their planes into American battleships at Leyte, intensified U.S. soldiers' and sailors' hatred for an enemy whose culture they found difficult to understand. On January 20, 1945, Emperor Hirohito approved *Ketsu-Go*, a plan calling for the Japanese soldiers and civilians to fight to the death if the Americans invaded Japan.

On February 19, 1945, U.S. marines landed on Iwo Jima, an island six hundred fifty nautical miles south of the Japanese mainland. Although they outnumbered the Japanese almost four to one, they met ferocious resistance from 22,060 Japanese troops, only 216 of whom survived the thirty-five-day battle. Meanwhile, a campaign of intensive bombing began. On March 9, three hundred B-29s flying at low attitude dropped enough incendiary bombs and napalm to destroy sixteen square miles of Tokyo, killing approximately 83,000 people in less than three hours and leaving 1 million homeless. The previous month, the Allies had carried out a similar fire-bombing of the German city of Dresden. Both attacks exemplified the ways that World War II had shattered distinctions between combatants and noncombatants. This was a **total war** in which millions of people—soldiers and civilians alike—were war targets and war casualties.

Such brutality was evident in the Battle of Okinawa. After Allied troops landed on the island on April 1, they fought Japanese forces holed up in caves. At the same time, Japanese *kamikaze* pilots struck the U.S. Fifth Fleet off the coast of Okinawa, and the Japanese navy sent the battleship *Yamato* on a suicide mission. U.S. naval and air forces sank it, killing 3,000 Japanese sailors. On Okinawa, more than 95,000 Japanese and 12,000 Allied soldiers died in the eighty-four-day battle, the bloodiest of the Pacific theater. Tens of thousands of Okinawan civilians were also killed, wounded, or took their own lives.

Banzai Shortened form of Japanese exclamation "Tenno Heika Banzai" ("Long live the Emperor"), and Allied term for the Japanese infantry's human wave attacks in the Pacific.

kamikaze Japanese for "spirit wind," suicide attacks made by Japanese aviators on Allied naval vessels in the last stages of World War II.

total war Warfare in which every human and material resource is used for defense or targeted offensively.

* NOTE: When capitalized, Eastern and Western Europe indicate the post-World War II political division of Europe. When not capitalized, eastern and western Europe indicate geographical regions.

Everett Collection Inc/Alamy Stock Photo

Global Americans **Ernie Pyle** was an American journalist best known for his columns about World War II. In 1940, after spending seven years traveling the United States writing newspaper stories, Pyle journeyed to England to report on the Battle of Britain. In 1942, he began covering America's involvement in the war, reporting on Allied operations in North Africa, Sicily, Italy, and France. Instead of recounting battlefield maneuvers or actions of heroic generals, Pyle usually wrote from the perspective of the common soldier, an approach that won him great popularity and the Pulitzer Prize for journalism. "I love the infantry because they are the underdogs," he wrote. "They are the mud-rain-frost-and-wind boys. They have no comforts, and they even learn to live without the necessities. And in the end they are the guys that wars can't be won without." In 1944, in response to one of Pyle's columns, Congress authorized $10 a month "fight pay" (a 50 percent salary increase) for combat infantrymen similar to the "flight pay" given to airmen. On April 18, 1945, while covering the invasion of Okinawa, Pyle was killed in a Japanese machine gun attack on the island Iejima (formerly Ie Shima). He was among the few U.S. civilians killed during the war to be awarded the Purple Heart, and a monument in his honor stands on Okinawa. Pyle's columns remain a valuable source on the combat experience in World War II. He is also the subject of *The Story of G.I. Joe*, a feature film released shortly after his death.

The plan for the invasion of the Japanese main islands called for an attack on Kyushu in November 1945 and on Honshu in March 1946. American commanders expected to incur hundreds of thousands of U.S. casualties. But these plans did not take into account the tremendous power of the new atomic bomb. On July 16, while attending a diplomatic meeting of the Big Three in **Potsdam**, Germany, Truman received word that the first test of the atomic bomb in Alamogordo, New Mexico, had been successful. Bolstered by the news and eager to demonstrate his strength to his Soviet counterpart, the president told Stalin that the United States had developed a weapon of "unusual destructive force." Having already received reports from Soviet spies who had infiltrated the Manhattan Project, Stalin showed no special interest. But neither leader fully trusted the other.

Nevertheless, over the next two weeks, the American, British, and Soviet delegations attempted to resolve several lingering disputes. They agreed on new borders for Germany and Poland. Rejecting earlier calls to weaken Germany permanently through high reparations and territorial divisions, they called for four zones of occupation and economic rehabilitation. Each of the four occupying powers (the Soviet Union, the United States, Great Britain, and France) could extract reparations only from its zone. The delegates agreed to prosecute Nazi war criminals. They also established a Council of Foreign Ministers that would address unresolved issues such as the withdrawal of Allied troops from Iran and the fate of Italian colonies. In a declaration issued on July 26, 1945, the United States and Great Britain (the Soviet Union was not yet at war with the Japanese) demanded Japan's unconditional surrender and threatened its "prompt and utter destruction" if it did not comply.

Japan's failure to respond had immediate consequences. Determined to end the war quickly to save American lives and prevent possible gains by the Soviet Union in an attack on the Japanese in Manchuria, the Truman administration commenced with its plans. On August 6, an American B-29 bomber dropped an atomic bomb on the midsized industrial city of Hiroshima. The bomb obliterated six square miles and instantly killed more than 60,000 people. Approximately 75,000 perished later as the result of the effects of radiation. On August 8, Stalin, worried that the United States would renege on the Asian territorial concessions promised at Yalta, ordered 1.5 million Soviet troops into Manchuria and quickly captured it. The following day, hoping to make the Japanese capitulate before the Soviets made additional gains in Asia, the United States used a second, larger atomic bomb on Nagasaki, killing 40,000 people and destroying one-third of the city. On August 14, with Japan reeling from two atomic attacks and the Soviet Union's entry into the Pacific war, Emperor Hirohito defied Allied expectations and persuaded his deadlocked cabinet to accept an unconditional surrender. Victory over Japan—**V-J Day**—celebrations erupted all over the world. On September 2, the Japanese formally capitulated in a ceremony held aboard the USS *Missouri*.

After six years, the most devastating war in history was over. Approximately 65 million people had died—nearly 27 million in the Soviet Union alone; 6 million in both Poland and Germany; at least 15 million in China; 3.1 million in Japan; and millions more in Yugoslavia, Indonesia, Vietnam, and elsewhere (see Table 21.2). Approximately 11 million people died as a result of Nazi atrocities, including 6 million Jews. Although the United States lost more than 407,000 soldiers in the war, its physical landscape was virtually untouched by the conflict, and its economy was booming. By contrast, much of Europe and Asia lay in ruins and economic desolation. With the United States unquestionably the world's strongest power, an unprecedented global reconstruction effort and a major reordering of world politics lay ahead.

Potsdam Meeting in July 1945 at which British, American, and Soviet officials discussed punishment for Germany, strategies for defeating Japan, and plans for the postwar era.

V-J Day (Victory over Japan Day) Public holiday marking Japan's unconditional surrender to the Allies on August 14, 1945.

Table 21.2 Estimated Military and Civilian Casualties of World War II (in Thousands)

More people died in World War II than in any other military conflict. Although it is impossible to have precise numbers because of the challenges of record keeping in time of war, historians estimate that between 50 and 80 million soldiers and civilians died worldwide from battlefield injuries, strategic bombings, accidents, starvation, war crimes, disease, and poor treatment during captivity.

AXIS Powers	Military Deaths	Civilian Deaths	Total Deaths
Germany	4,400	1,400–2,400	5,800–6,800
Japan	2,120	1,000	3,120
Romania	300	160	460
Hungary	300	280	580
Italy	301.4	153.2	454.6
Austria (German controlled)	260	120	380
Finland	95	2	97
AXIS Totals	**7,776.4**	**3,115.2–4,115.2**	**10,891.6–11,891.6**

Allied Powers	Military Deaths	Civilian Deaths	Total Deaths
Albania	30	2	32
Australia	39.7	12	51.7
Belgium	12	76	88
Brazil	1	1	2
Bulgaria	22	3	25
Burma (British colony)	22	250	272
Canada	45.4		45.4
China	3,000–4,000	12,000–16,000	15,000–20,000
Cuba		0.1	0.1
Czechoslovakia	25	300	325
Denmark	2.1	1.1	3.2
Dutch East Indies		3,000–4,000	3,000–4,000
Ethiopia	5	95	100
France	200	350	550
French Indochina		1,000–2,000	1,000–2,000
Greece	20–35.1	300–600	320–635.1
Guam	1–2		1–2
Iceland		0.2	0.2
India (British colony)	87	1,500–2,500	1,587–2,587
Iran	0.2		0.2
Iraq	0.5		0.5
Luxembourg	2		2
Malaya (British colony)		100	100

(continued)

Table 21.2 Estimated Military and Civilian Casualties of World War II (in Thousands) *(continued)*

Allied Powers	Military Deaths	Civilian Deaths	Total Deaths
Malta (British colony)		1.5	1.5
Mexico		100	100
Netherlands	17	284	301
New Zealand	11.9	2	13.9
Norway	6.4	6.5	12.9
Philippines (U.S. territory)	57	500–900	557–957
Poland	240	5,800	6,040
Singapore (British colony)		50	50
South Africa	11.9		11.9
Soviet Union	8,700–13,850	13,000–18,000	21,800–28,000
United Kingdom (England, Scotland, Wales, and Nortern Ireland)	383.8	67.1	450.9
United States	407	12	419
Yugoslavia	300–446	1,400	1,700–1,846
Allied Totals	**13,649.9**	**40,113.6**	**53,763.5**
Overall Totals	**21,426.3**	**43,228.8–44,228.8**	**64,655.1–65,655.1**

Sources: For examples of how estimates of World War II deaths vary, see World War II Casualties, http://en.wikipedia.org/wiki/World_War_II_casualties; By the Numbers, World War II Deaths, http://www.nationalww2museum.org/learn/education/for-students/ww2-history/ww2-by-the-numbers/world-wide-deaths.html; and Estimated War Dead World War II, http://warchronicle.com/numbers/WWII/deaths.htm

Summary

After war erupted in Europe in 1939, Roosevelt tried to bolster the Allies in resisting German aggression without eroding his domestic political support or impeding America's economic recovery. His decisions positioned the United States for a leading role in international political, economic, and military affairs for decades afterward. Yet, domestically, those decisions generated an intense political debate among Americans who were reluctant to become involved in Europe's wars again. But after the Japanese attacked Pearl Harbor in December 1941, Americans were united in going to war against the Axis Powers. The postwar world envisioned by Roosevelt and Churchill earlier that year aimed for stability and security, self-government, and an end to the use of force. But the possibility of such a world receded as the Axis Powers conquered much of Europe and Asia, enslaving and exterminating captured peoples. By mid-1942, however, the Allies had seized the offensive, and their policy makers met repeatedly to coordinate military strategies. At times, they struggled to reconcile differing objectives and to face the contradictions of their own colonialism, racial discrimination, and political repression.

With the devastation of the war confined largely to Europe and Asia, the United States prospered throughout the conflict. The federal government pumped billions of dollars into war production and instituted strict controls on goods, wages, and prices. Business owners and workers alike benefited from a thriving economy. Traditionally underemployed groups seized unprecedented job opportunities. Millions of Americans left their communities as a result of military enlistments or in pursuit of economic advancement. Women and minorities demonstrated their patriotism and sought expanded civil rights. Marriage and birth rates rebounded from the historic lows of the Great Depression. As communities struggled to deal with burgeoning new populations, racial and class tensions sometimes exploded. More than one hundred ten thousand Japanese Americans were forced into internment camps.

Brutal battles were waged in the Atlantic and Pacific theaters during the war's final two years. As German strongholds collapsed, the Allies became aware of the full magnitude of Nazi atrocities against Jews, political dissidents, and others. After defeating Germany in May 1945, the Allies prepared for a long campaign to defeat the Japanese. But in August 1945, the use of the world's first atomic bombs brought World War II to a close, forever changing international relations and the nature of warfare.

<Thinking Back, *Looking Forward*>

As you review this chapter, consider how legacies of World War I contributed to a second global conflict. How did economic weaknesses and national grievances generate the rise of military dictatorships and ideologies that boasted of racial superiority? As the world went to war again, how did the changing nature of warfare strengthen international support for self-government, world cooperation, and human rights? In coming chapters, look for new international organizations and laws that sought to promote justice and preserve peace. What issues rooted in World War II contributed to the subsequent Cold War and to anti-imperialist upheavals in Europe's colonies and civil rights movements in the United States?

To make your study concrete, review the timeline and reflect on the entries there. Think about their causes, consequences, and connections. How do they fit with global trends?

Additional Resources

Books

Adams, Michael C. C. *The Best War Ever: America and World War II,* 2nd ed. Baltimore, MD: Johns Hopkins Press, 2015. ▶ Synthesis that demythologizes the war and describes its impact on soldiers and civilians.

Alvarez, Luis. *The Power of the Zoot: Youth Culture and Resistance in World War II.* Berkeley: University of California Press, 2009. ▶ Exploration of Zoot Suit culture among racial minorities nationwide.

Bérubé, Allan. *Coming Out Under Fire: The History of Gay Men and Women in World War Two.* New York: Free Press, 1990. ▶ Path-breaking study of gay Americans in the armed forces and on the home front.

Breitman, Richard. *FDR and the Jews.* Cambridge, MA: Harvard University Press, 2013. ▶ Balanced account of the constraints that limited Roosevelt's ability to aid victims of Nazism.

Dear, I. C. B., and M. R. B. Foot, eds. *The Oxford Companion to World War II.* Oxford University Press, 2001 print, 2003 online. ▶ Single-volume reference work commemorating the fiftieth anniversary of the war.

Dower, John. *War without Mercy: Race and Power in the Pacific War.* New York: Pantheon, 1987. ▶ Award-winning examination of racism in the war between Japan and the United States.

Frank, Richard B. *Downfall: The End of the Imperial Japanese Empire.* New York: Penguin, 2001. ▶ Exhaustive analysis of Japanese resistance in the last stages of the war.

Hastings, Max. *Inferno: The World at War, 1939–1945.* New York: Knopf, 2011. ▶ Highly readable narrative of the global war and its participants.

Reeves, Richard. *Infamy: The Shocking Story of the Japanese American Internment in World War II.* New York: Henry Holt, 2015. ▶ Best-selling author's account of the origins and impact of the internment.

Walker, J. Samuel. *Prompt and Utter Destruction: Truman and the Use of Atomic Bombs against Japan,* rev. ed. Chapel Hill: University of North Carolina Press, 2005. ▶ Brief overview of U.S. motives for using atomic weapons on Japan.

Go to the MindTap® for **Global Americans** to access the full version of select books from this Additional Resources section.

Websites

The Institute on World War II and the Human Experience. (http://ww2.fsu.edu/) ▶ Repository of more than six thousand collections from U.S. and non-U.S. participants in the war.

The National World War II Museum. (http://nationalww2museum.org/) ▶ Collection of many learning resources and artifacts.

Researching World War II Records. (http://www.archives.gov/research/military/ww2/) ▶ Comprehensive overview of extensive collection of textual, audiovisual, and photographic records held at the National Archives.

United States Holocaust Memorial Museum. (http://www.ushmm.org/) ▶ Collection of many resources for academic researchers and educators.

World War II Documents. (http://avalon.law.yale.edu/subject_menus/wwii.asp) ▶ Multinational primary source collection created by the Avalon Project at Yale University.

MindTap®

Continue exploring online through MindTap®, where you can:

- **Assess your knowledge with the Chapter Test**
- **Watch historical videos related to the chapter**
- **Further your understanding with interactive maps and timelines**

The World at War

1939

November

Congress approves "cash and carry" plan to assist Britain.

1940

April

Germany seizes Norway and Denmark.

May–June

British evacuate Allied forces from Dunkirk.

June

Germany defeats France.

Japan calls for the creation of a Greater East Asia Co-Prosperity Sphere.

1940

September

Germany begins bombing British cities.

Roosevelt arranges destroyer deal to aid Britain.

Germany, Italy, and Japan sign Tripartite Pact.

U.S. stops sales of scrap metal and steel to Japan.

November

Roosevelt wins unprecedented third term as president.

1941

March

Congress approves Lend-Lease to aid Britain.

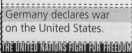

April

Japan and the Soviet Union sign a neutrality pact.

June

Germany invades the Soviet Union, violating the Nonaggression Pact.

1941

July

Japan invades Indochina.

U.S. halts trade with Japan and freezes Japanese assets.

August

Winston Churchill and Roosevelt issue the Atlantic Charter, stating peace goals.

December

Japan attacks Pearl Harbor and the Philippines.

U.S. declares war on Japan.

Germany declares war on the United States.

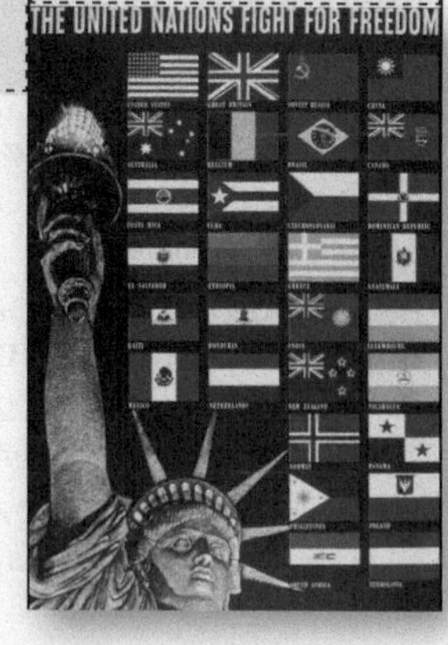

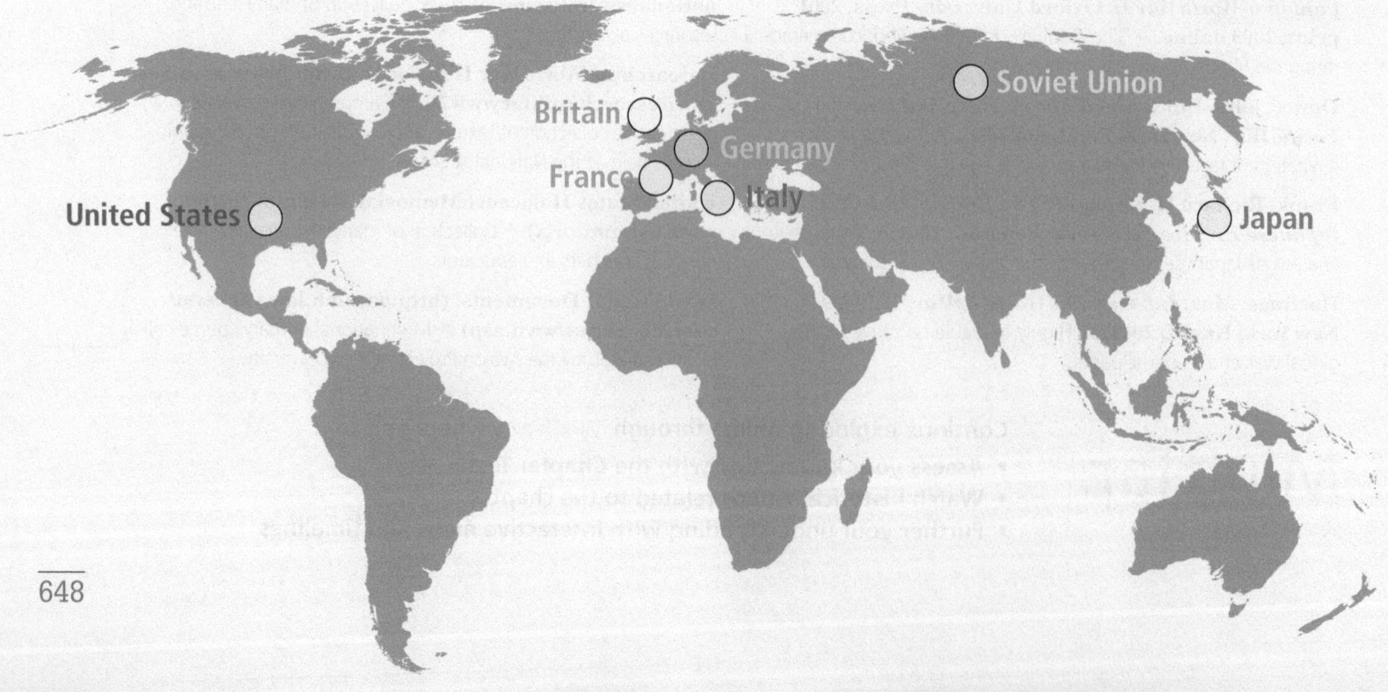

1942

January
Nazis formalize the Final Solution.

January
Roosevelt issues an executive order relocating Japanese Americans on the West Coast to internment camps.

April
Japan conquers the Philippines; U.S. and Filipino POWs die on forced Death March.

June
U.S. naval and air forces defeat the Japanese fleet in the Battle of Midway.

1943

January
In Casablanca, Roosevelt and Churchill announce policy of unconditional surrender.

February
Soviets defeat German forces at the Battle of Stalingrad.

June
Three-day race riot erupts in Detroit.

July
Allied invasion of Sicily begins, and Benito Mussolini is captured.

December
Congress repeals the Chinese Exclusion Act.

1944

March
Congress unanimously passes the G.I. Bill of Rights.

June
Allies launch D-Day landings at Normandy.

July
Allied nations meet in Bretton Woods to craft a new global monetary system.

August
U.S. and Free French troops liberate Paris.

November
Roosevelt wins fourth term as president.

December
Allies prevail against German counteroffensive in the Battle of the Bulge.

1945

February
Roosevelt, Churchill, and Joseph Stalin meet at Yalta to plan the postwar world.

March
U.S. marines defeat the Japanese at the Battle of Iwo Jima.

April
Roosevelt dies, and Truman becomes president.

Delegates from fifty Allied nations convene in San Francisco to establish the United Nations.

Mussolini is executed.

Hitler commits suicide.

1945

May
Germany surrenders.

July
American, British, and Soviet policy makers meet at Potsdam.

August
U.S. drops atomic bombs on Hiroshima and Nagasaki.

Japan surrenders.

Go to MindTap® to engage with an interactive version of the timeline. Analyze events and themes with clickable content, view related videos, and respond to critical thinking questions.

22 The Cold War

1945–1965

Although based in Washington, D.C., Willis Conover was familiar to millions in the Soviet Bloc thanks to his Voice of America radio shows.

22-1
From Allies to Enemies

22-1a Legacies of War
22-1b Reconstruction of Europe
22-1c Occupation of Germany
22-1d U.S. Occupation of Japan

22-2
Militarization of the U.S.–Soviet Conflict

22-2a Nuclear Arms Race
22-2b Communist China
22-2c Partition of Korea and Outbreak of Civil War

22-3
Cold War at Home

22-3a Spies and Scares
22-3b National Security State
22-3c Cold War Culture

22-4
Superpower Crisis and Diplomacy

22-4a Eisenhower and the Arms Race
22-4b Cultural Diplomacy
22-4c Kennedy and the Cuban Missile Crisis
22-4d Peace Movements

22-5
Cold War in the Third World

22-5a Newly Independent Nations and Foreign Aid
22-5b Middle East and Africa
22-5c Latin America
22-5d Southeast Asia

In 1959, a crowd of curious Soviet citizens gathered on the streets of Moscow to ask visiting Americans about life in the United States. One wanted to know the price of U.S. automobiles, another about the nation's unemployment rate, and a third wondered what Americans thought of Willis Conover. This final question stumped the visitor—Harvard University's head reference librarian. He had never heard of Willis Conover, and he was not alone.

AP Images

Willis Conover Hosting the Radio Show "Jazz Hour," 1959. Conover was an international celebrity whom few Americans knew. ▲

Few Americans knew about Conover because the source of his popularity, a Voice of America (VOA) radio show with 30 million listeners in more than eighty nations, was not broadcast in the United States.

Begun during World War II, the VOA was—and continues to be—the federal government's direct channel of communication to the world. After the great jazz musician Duke Ellington completed a successful tour of the Soviet Union in 1954, the VOA hired Conover, a Washington, D.C., disc jockey, to create and host a jazz show. An army brat and veteran, Conover proved to be a valuable cultural soldier. "People in other countries love jazz because they love freedom," he explained, making a connection between jazz—the United States' contribution to great music—and American democracy. Conover's show, as the Harvard librarian discovered, was surprisingly popular in the Soviet Union and other Communist countries that had banned jazz because it was seen as typifying capitalist decadence and corruption.

Conover's effort to subvert the jazz ban was one tiny element of the titanic global conflict between the United States and Soviet Union known as the *Cold War*. Although not inevitable, this conflict stemmed from core ideological differences that had begun after the Russian Revolution in 1917. It pitted the U.S. mission to spread democracy and free-market capitalism (an "empire of liberty") against the Soviet Union's mission to spread socialist revolution and broad-based economic equality (an "empire of justice"). The conflict erupting after World War II was "cold" because their mutual hostility and suspicion, although intense, stopped short of a "hot" military showdown between the two rivals. Instead, it produced a massive nuclear weapons buildup and arms race, an unprecedented division of the world into two camps, ferocious propaganda attacks and ideological repression, and military actions in Korea, Vietnam, and other places that took the lives of at least 4.5 million people. The total financial costs of the Cold War are not known, but for nuclear weapons alone, the United States spent $1 trillion to build 37,737 devices between 1951 and 1965, according to one estimate.

The Cold War lasted more than forty years, but it formed over three phases in the two decades covered in this chapter. Allies during World War II, U.S. and Soviet officials prepared for postwar conflict soon after the United States revealed its superior military technology in dropping atomic bombs on Japan. The alliance crumbled as the two powers clashed

What does the surprising popularity of Willis Conover's show in the Soviet Union and other Communist countries reveal about U.S.-Soviet relations during the Cold War era?

Go to MindTap® to watch a video on Conover and learn how his story relates to the themes of this chapter.

over rebuilding war-torn Europe and controlling the eastern Mediterranean. Ideological conflict, especially in Europe, highlighted the first phase of the Cold War and proved a mainstay of U.S.–Soviet relations. The Cold War's second phase, begun in 1949, became increasingly focused on the military as the Soviets produced their own atomic bomb and the United States countered by rapidly upgrading its nuclear arsenal. At the same time, the conflict intensified in East Asia with the Communist Revolution in China and the Korean War between Communist North Korea and UN-backed South Korea. The militarization of the Cold War generated a culture and politics of military preparedness. In the United States, a pervasive fear of Communists promoted political repression, cultural conformity, and the search for spies, especially in the federal government and labor organizations. In the Soviet Union, military preparedness prolonged war-era economic sacrifices and justified the continued persecution of ideological enemies.

The death of Soviet leader Joseph Stalin in 1953 marked the beginning of the Cold War's third phase as U.S.–Soviet relations reached the brink of war in Cuba and then modestly improved. The return of dialogue between the two nations emboldened peace groups to press for arms control and enabled cultural exchanges, including Willis Conover's radio show. But even as Americans and Soviets found common ground, the Cold War raged in Asia, Africa, the Middle East, and the Caribbean, where scores of economically underdeveloped and newly independent nations proved testing grounds for the U.S.–Soviet conflict. Both sides competed to gain a footing in poor and unstable developing nations that played one superpower off against the other.

22-1 From Allies to Enemies

In this cartoon, published in France in 1949, Uncle Sam and Soviet Premier Stalin stare warily at each other across a pair of conjoined twins. The French caption, which has not been printed here, reads: "My Dear, your sister has some strange friends."

Why is there tension between the two national figures, and what do the conjoined twins represent? ▶

The Granger Collection, New York

World War II marked the height of cooperation between the United States and the Soviet Union. The Allies downplayed ideological differences and conflict over military strategy to be unified in fighting the Axis Powers and to plan a postwar world in which each nation received a sphere of influence. But, at the end of the war, distrust deepened over U.S. possession of atomic weapons, which, to the Soviets, created a dangerous imbalance of military might. Exacerbating the tension was the U.S. booming wartime economy, which as the war ended gave the United States both economic and military supremacy over the Soviet Union where cities and factories lay in ruin. Stalin used the Red Army's occupation of eastern Germany to rebuild the Soviet economy and protect the nation from future attack. Problems arose when U.S. officials sought to counter Soviet influence in Europe by advocating democratic governments and free markets whereas Stalin insisted on protecting Soviet borders by controlling neighboring countries.

☞ As you read, focus on the way the U.S.–Soviet alliance, forged during World War II, dissolved into an intense international rivalry. What soured U.S.-Soviet relations, and what were the major effects of this conflict?

22-1a Legacies of War

The outcome of World War II transforms the global order and puts the United States and the Soviet Union on a collision course.

Both Americans and Soviets hoped to continue their functioning partnership after the war. Despite persistent disagreement as allies, especially over the opening of a second front in Western Europe, the two powers negotiated agreements for the postwar world at the Yalta and Potsdam conferences. The establishment of the United Nations, in which both the United States and Soviet Union played a crucial role, was another basis for prolonged cooperation.

But within less than two years of V-J Day, U.S.–Soviet cooperation unraveled, devolving into an intense, if not entirely new, ideological struggle that marked the first phase of the **Cold War**. The two powers had clashed since the 1917 Communist Revolution in Russia despite a shared antipathy to European power politics and the nineteenth-century imperial order. While the Soviets saw America's faith in free-market capitalism as producing global inequality and perpetuating poverty, Americans considered the Soviets' command economy, single-party system, and suppression of personal freedoms as a violation of basic human rights. Added to these core differences were unrealistic fears on both sides that each was bent on destroying the other.

Another reason for the collapse of the wartime alliance went beyond ideology. For the first time, the United States had become actively involved in the internal affairs of European nations during peacetime. There were three reasons for this reversal of U.S. foreign policy principles in place since the Monroe Doctrine of 1823. First, the development of long-range bombers (and later missiles) shattered forever the protection provided by the Atlantic and Pacific Oceans. Second, because U.S. officials believed that the origins of World War II lay in the worldwide depression in the 1930s, they pushed to rebuild war-torn Europe to prevent another economic collapse. Third, the war taught U.S. officials about the need to stand up early and forcefully to aggressive expansionists such as Adolf Hitler. In 1945, for example, Secretary of the Navy James Forrestal warned that Stalin's desire to control Eastern Europe should not be appeased. "We tried that once with Hitler," he said. "There are no returns on appeasement."

The sustained U.S. involvement in European affairs, something that Stalin did not expect, set it on a collision course with the Soviet Union. An important source of U.S.–Soviet conflict involved the reconstruction of the world's economy under the Bretton Woods economic system, which was designed to ensure open borders and free trade. The Americans welcomed these arrangements that aligned with the nation's manufacturing preeminence, but the Soviets refused to place the free market above the socialist goal of economic equality. The Soviets also recognized that their nascent industrial economy could not withstand free competition with U.S. manufacturers.

Another source of U.S.–Soviet friction involved nuclear weapons. Although Stalin had expressed little interest in the new weapon that President Harry Truman had revealed to him at Potsdam, Soviet officials reacted with alarm at the prospect of a U.S. monopoly on atomic weapons. They feared that it could be used as blackmail to threaten their nation with nuclear destruction. U.S. officials, in turn, faced pressures from within and outside the nation to prevent the further development of nuclear technology by turning over its atomic weapons and technology to the newly established UN Atomic Energy Commission, which sought to safeguard atomic energy development and use. Yet Truman, along with Secretary of State James Byrnes, made the fateful decision to oppose sharing atomic secrets or relinquishing control over the U.S. nuclear arsenal.

The main U.S.–Soviet conflict in the months after World War II involved the political status of Eastern Europe and occupied Germany. Although agreements reached at Yalta required free elections in Soviet-occupied Eastern Europe, Stalin had never intended to give up control. Having been invaded by Germany twice in the twentieth century, he sought a protective buffer that would guarantee Soviet security. In addition, Stalin sought compensation for what World War II had cost the Soviet people: nearly 27 million soldiers and civilians dead, more than 10 percent of the nation's total population. For every two Americans killed in the war, the Soviets lost one hundred. Moreover, Stalin's firm grip on Eastern Europe was immensely popular with the Soviet people, who revered him as the champion of what they called the *Great Patriotic War* and who blamed the United States for compromising the nation's hard-won security.

22-1b Reconstruction of Europe

The first phase of the Cold War centers on competing U.S. and Soviet visions of postwar Germany and Eastern Europe.

The impasse over Eastern Europe set the stage for a shift in U.S. policy toward the Soviet Union that came to be called **containment**. In February 1946, George F. Kennan, a leading U.S. diplomat in Moscow and a historian of Russia, sent a secret "long telegram" to the secretary of state reporting that U.S.–Soviet cooperation was not possible. Instead, he recommended a strategy focusing on rebuilding the industrial centers of Western Europe and Japan and doing everything short of war to restrain Soviet designs on promoting a world Communist revolution. The next month, Winston Churchill described an "**iron curtain**" descending across the continent of Europe, "from Stettin in the Baltic to Trieste in the Adriatic," behind which the nations of Eastern

Cold War Major U.S.–Soviet Union diplomatic and ideological conflict producing massive arms buildup and regional wars but no direct military conflict between the two powers.

containment U.S. national security strategy emerging with the Cold War designed to thwart the spread of real or perceived Soviet-sponsored communism around the world.

iron curtain Churchill's metaphor, first expressed in March 1946, characterizing a Europe divided between the West and Soviet-controlled Eastern European nations.

Europe were subject to "control from Moscow." This warning was intended for President Truman, who had invited Churchill to speak at Westminster College in his home state of Missouri and was in the audience.

Europe was not the only region in which U.S. and Soviet plans for the future clashed. In Iran, which was divided into British and Soviet occupation zones, Stalin sought to retain control of the country's northern oil fields and to keep the British and Americans away from his nation's southern border. But Britain, the United States, and the United Nations pressured him to remove Soviet troops from the country. Stalin sought to gain access to the Mediterranean through Turkey's Sea of Marmara, an ambition that reached back to Czarist Russia, but here, too, he met stiff U.S. opposition. Greece was a different matter because Stalin relied on Yugoslavian Communists to foment socialist revolution in its southern neighbor.

Truman knew that Communist victories in Greece and Turkey would destabilize the oil-rich Middle East, home to two-thirds of the world's reserves. Whoever held the eastern Mediterranean, he worried, could cut off the vital oil supply to Western Europe and Japan. Formerly, the British had controlled vast regions of the Middle East as well as the Suez Canal, but after World War II, they could no longer afford to sustain their empire and stopped supplying anti-Communist forces in Greece and Turkey. Truman committed the United States to assuming Britain's burden.

In March 1947, the president addressed a joint session of Congress to articulate a sweeping vision of a bipolar world in which those who favored freedom and democracy stood against the supporters of totalitarian repression (he concealed concerns about Middle Eastern oil). Although not naming the Soviet Union, Truman warned that without U.S. aid, Communist victory was assured in Greece, and "like apples in a barrel infected by one rotten one, the corruption of Greece would infect Iran and all to the east." This was an early version of the **domino theory**, an explanation for how a Communist revolution in one nation sets up a chain reaction that spreads, toppling one regime after another. To prevent this from happening, the president asked for and received \$400 million from Congress to provide economic and military aid to the governments of Greece and Turkey. In what came to be known as the **Truman Doctrine**, he committed the nation to "support free peoples who are resisting attempted subjugation by armed minorities or by outside pressures." This was the hard-line stance against the spread of Soviet influence that Churchill, Kennan, and others had been advocating.

domino theory U.S. Cold War assumption that if one country became Communist, others in the region would "fall" like dominoes to communism.

Truman Doctrine Foreign policy strategy in March 1947 promising economic and financial aid to "free peoples" fighting communism anywhere, specifically in Greece and Turkey.

Marshall Plan Massive economic aid to rebuild war-torn Europe, remove trade barriers, and blunt the appeal of communism by restoring Europe to prosperity.

The soft side of U.S. Cold War policy came in the form of massive economic aid that reasserted the Four Freedoms by combatting "freedom from want." Also in 1947, Truman's secretary of state, General George C. Marshall, called on the United States to take a bold step to fight "not against any country or doctrine but against hunger, poverty, desperation, and chaos" in postwar Europe. Reconstructing European economies, Marshall claimed, was necessary to diminish the appeal of communism, especially in France and Italy, by permitting "the emergence of political and social conditions in which free institutions can exist." The **Marshall Plan's** aid of more than \$13 billion (\$103 billion in 2014 dollars) from 1948 to 1952 required a degree of economic integration that laid the foundation for the European Common Market (established in 1958), and it carried the bonus of benefiting U.S. manufacturers by enabling European nations to purchase goods from the United States.

The Marshall Plan drove a final wedge between the Americans and Soviets, dividing Europe into eastern and western spheres of influence known as "blocs." Although the Soviets desperately needed American money to recover from the war, U.S. planners did not expect Stalin to agree to the free-trade principles of Bretton Woods, a requirement for receiving aid. Stalin indeed rejected aid and forbade Eastern European nations from accepting much-needed reconstruction funds. Instead, he launched the Council for Mutual Economic Assistance (COMECON) in 1949 as an eastern bloc alternative to the Marshall Plan. More importantly, the prospect of massive U.S. aid pushed Stalin to take bolder, more overt measures to shore up the Soviet sphere, including an overthrow of Czechoslovakia's elected government in February 1948 and the installation of a Communist regime. Stalin also took a hard line in Germany.

22-1c Occupation of Germany

The reconstruction of Germany brings the United States and Soviet Union into direct conflict.

Occupied Germany was the epicenter of Cold War Europe. The defeated nation was divided into four zones, controlled by the Soviet Union, United States, Great Britain, and France. All agreed that although Germany should eventually be reunited, it must first be stripped of Nazi influence and held responsible for its actions. The process of de-Nazification included trials of suspected war criminals that took place in Nuremberg, Germany, from 1945 to 1949. The Allies had a much harder time agreeing about the future of Germany's political and economic systems. Stalin sought heavy war reparations from Germany and relocated much of its industrial capacity from the Soviet zone to the Soviet Union. Truman, in contrast, sought to restore Germany's economy and bring it squarely within the orbit of the Western democracies. By 1948, the British, Americans, and French had combined their zones, making it three against one. Berlin, Germany's former capital, was likewise divided into two occupation zones, although it sat like an international island one hundred miles inside Germany's Soviet zone, accessible to the West only through designated roads, rail lines, canals, and air corridors.

In June 1948, seeking to push the Western nations out of Berlin altogether as a precondition for German reunification, Stalin cut off Western road, rail, and canal access to the city. The blockade was provocative, but he did not want war. Truman, although giving serious thought to resolving the Berlin crisis with atomic weapons, also wanted to avoid military conflict. Instead, he opted for a massive airlift that for one year flew thirteen thousand tons of supplies per day to West Berlin. Stalin did not challenge the **Berlin airlift** and ended the blockade in May 1949.

The blockade and airlift made the division of Germany inevitable because the occupation zones hardened into separate countries. The Federal Republic of Germany (West Germany) was established in September 1949 as a capitalist democracy. The Soviet zone became the German Democratic Republic (East Germany), a socialist state in the Soviet bloc. Berlin and Germany remained divided for the next forty-one years, a constant source of U.S.–Soviet friction. East Germany suffered under heavy Soviet war reparations and restrictions while West Germany, the beneficiary of Marshall Plan aid, became the economic powerhouse of Europe.

AP Images/Charles Gorry

Japanese Women Visiting Lincoln Memorial, 1951
The U.S. occupation of Japan resolved wartime conflict with Japan serving as the junior partner to the victorious Americans. The women in this photograph are advertising the first Hollywood film, *Tokyo File 212*, set in postwar Japan. Approved by SCAP leader General MacArthur, the plot reflects the fear of losing Japan to communism. ▲

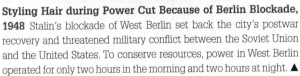

AP Images/dpa DENA

Styling Hair during Power Cut Because of Berlin Blockade, 1948 Stalin's blockade of West Berlin set back the city's postwar recovery and threatened military conflict between the Soviet Union and the United States. To conserve resources, power in West Berlin operated for only two hours in the morning and two hours at night. ▲

22-1d U.S. Occupation of Japan

Massive U.S. aid ensures Japan's stability and pro-Western stance.

Unlike Germany, the United States took sole possession of Japan. The Soviet Union had joined the war against Japan right after the atomic destruction of Hiroshima, but against the spirit of the Potsdam declaration, the United States excluded the Soviets from the occupation, although it allowed them to reclaim territories in Manchuria and Sakhalin Island. The future of Japan thus served as an early pivot toward the Cold War. The massive economic aid the United States gave Japan to reconstruct its economy and reintegrate it into the global economy was similar to what would come later with the Marshall Plan. U.S. officials saw a stable and prosperous Japan as an essential counterbalance to Soviet, and later Chinese, expansionism in East Asia.

General Douglas MacArthur was named Supreme Commander of the Allied Powers (SCAP). He and several hundred U.S. civil servants and three hundred fifty thousand troops, governed Japan, in the words of one

Berlin airlift U.S. military operation, June 1948–May 1949, to bypass Soviet blockade of West Berlin by using a convoy of airplanes.

reverse course Policy change, beginning in 1947 for the U.S. occupation of Japan, from purging wartime leaders and business conglomerations to restoring them as a bulwark against communism.

historian, "as neocolonial overlords, beyond challenge or criticism, as inviolate as the emperor and his officials had ever been." MacArthur's orders to "demilitarize and democratize" Japan had been spelled out at Potsdam. As in occupied Germany, the Americans established a military tribunal for prosecuting suspected war criminals, including Prime Minister Hideki Tojo and those responsible for the Nanjing massacre in 1937. MacArthur spared Emperor Hirohito from trial against the protests of Japan's victims because the revered leader's cooperation was crucial to winning the hearts and minds of the Japanese people.

SCAP initiated a revolution from above that included breaking up concentrations of big businesses, such as the Mitsubishi conglomerate, maker of the well-known Zero fighter plane. The transformation also included democratizing land ownership, severing ties between religion and the state, ensuring women's rights, and writing a new constitution that prevented Japan's ability to make war. But MacArthur could not always control the reform process. Faced with rampant inflation, unemployment, and no legitimate market economy, the public sought alternatives to capitalism and increasingly flocked to Japan's newly legalized Communist Party. As U.S.–Soviet relations dissolved, the new U.S. objective for Japan, like the Marshall Plan for Western Europe, was to combat "freedom from want" by quickly rebuilding the nation's considerable industrial capacity. Beginning in the winter of 1947, SCAP initiated a **reverse course**, removing labor advocates, Communists, and other leftists from official positions while relying on right-wing business and political leaders who had supported the old imperial regime. The right-wingers, in turn, worked with SCAP to generate stability and prosperity through a conservative, U.S.-backed political order. Thus, the foundation was laid for Japan's postwar "economic miracle" that propelled it, along with West Germany, to become one of the world's leading economic powers.

22-2 Militarization of the U.S.–Soviet Conflict

AP Images/Kim Chon-Kil

Two middle school girls commemorate the death of General MacArthur in April 1964 by placing a wreath with the name of their school written in Chinese characters at his statue in Jayu (Freedom) Park in South Korea. Since it was erected in 1957, the statue has been a popular sightseeing destination in the city of Incheon, where it marks the site of a historic offensive during the Korean War.

Consider why people in other countries would build statues to Americans. How is this monument to a U.S general connected to "freedom"? ▶

At the onset of the Cold War, the United States held distinct military advantages over the Soviet Union. Despite Stalin's planned industrialization, his nation remained largely agricultural, relying on government control of the economy to turn its abundant natural and human resources into military might. This plan was almost entirely land based, for the Soviets had yet to develop commanding air and sea power. The United States, by contrast, possessed the world's leading navy and air force, sustained by the most productive and technologically advanced economy in human history—advantages that helped break the Soviet blockade in Berlin and rebuild Western Europe and Japan. Moreover, the United States had the atomic bomb and did not hesitate to remind the Soviets about this "winning weapon" to gain diplomatic advantage. In 1949, however, U.S. fortunes changed as the Soviets developed their own atomic bomb, and China, the world's most populous nation and a crucial U.S. ally, became Communist. In addition to these "twin shocks" came the outbreak of a civil war in Korea that quickly drew Chinese and U.S. troops into combat.

☞ As you read, focus on the factors that pushed the Cold War beyond its first phase of ideological antagonism. How and why did the Cold War become more dangerous? What were the characteristics of its second, military, phase?

the U.S. nuclear arsenal and the creation of much more powerful "thermonuclear" or **hydrogen bombs**. The Soviet threat was then seen as mainly military—not just ideological—and events in China and Korea brought that threat home to the American public.

22-2a Nuclear Arms Race

The stockpiling of nuclear weapons begins the second phase of the Cold War as military strategy and conflict move to the forefront.

U.S. possession of atomic weapons spurred the Soviets to build their own atomic bomb. Like those of the Americans, Soviet efforts relied in part on German scientists who in this case served as captured labor. In addition, the Soviet team had the advantage of being second by using a vast spy network able to steal secrets from the Americans. Klaus Fuchs, a German physicist who defected to Britain and was assigned to the Manhattan Project, gave Soviet intelligence thousands of pages of documents, including a detailed picture with measurements of the atom bomb dropped on Nagasaki. A longtime Communist, Fuchs was convinced that the Soviet Union was the world's best hope for resisting antidemocratic regimes and improving the plight of the poor and working classes.

The successful test of a Soviet atomic bomb in August 1949 came ten years earlier than U.S. officials had predicted. Now there were two **superpowers**, each possessing military power far greater than all other nations. The United States lost its atomic monopoly in the same year that Germany became partitioned. The heightened Communist challenge was countered by a new U.S. defense strategy based on military alliance with Britain and European partners. The **North Atlantic Treaty Organization (NATO)**, signed in April 1949, was based on the principle that an attack against any member nation was tantamount to an attack on all and would be retaliated. NATO reversed the long U.S. tradition of avoiding "entangling alliances." Whereas U.S. allies gained protection from the perceived Soviet threat, the United States gained the chance to build up Western Europe's military defenses, access to strategic locations from which to strike the Soviet Union, and the flexibility of not having to rely on the UN Security Council to check Soviet expansionism. The Soviets responded to NATO in May 1955 by combining eight Communist states in Eastern and Central Europe then firmly under Soviet control into the **Warsaw Pact** (see Map 22.1).

The stockpiling of atomic weapons in Europe signaled the militarization of U.S. Cold War policy and a more aggressive anti-Communist stance. Epitomized by an April 1950 secret National Security Council Study known as **NSC 68**, this new strategy continued the policy of containment but placed more emphasis on building up military defenses and weaponry, including

22-2b Communist China

The Chinese Communist Revolution intensifies U.S.–Soviet conflict in East Asia.

Civil war in China resumed at the end of World War II as the shaky wartime alliance between Jiang Jieshi's Nationalist government and Mao Zedong's Communist Party fell apart. The United States provided $2.5 billion in aid, mostly military, to bolster Jiang's regime even as Truman sent General Marshall to bring the Nationalists and Communists together. Although there was mixed opinion among America's China experts regarding the outcome of the civil war, Truman sided with Jiang because it was difficult to walk away from the tremendous investment already made in his regime. Containment policy also made it almost impossible to see Mao as anything other than a Stalin ally antagonistic to U.S. interests. As it turned out, the United States backed the losing side in the **Chinese Communist Revolution**. Jiang's army disintegrated as Mao's forces, which had gained the support of millions of peasants, marched to Beijing and in October 1949 declared the People's Republic of China (PRC). The Soviet Union was the first to recognize the PRC, and in the subsequent Sino-Soviet pact, Stalin sent $300 million in aid to the new nation. China became the top recipient of Soviet foreign aid, receiving 7 percent of the Soviet Union's national income for much of the 1950s until the two Communist powers split and became bitter rivals. The United States had little choice but to continue supporting Jiang, who fled with his army and 1.3 million civilian supporters to the island of Taiwan off China's southeastern coast. Truman immediately recognized Jiang's regime as China's only legitimate government and made sure it retained China's seat in the UN Security Council. Taiwan relied on the U.S. Seventh Fleet for protection from Mao's threatened invasion.

superpower A nation possessing supreme power and influence, referring especially to the United States and the Soviet Union during the Cold War.

North Atlantic Treaty Organization (NATO) U.S.–led military alliance established in 1949 to provide collective security to nations in Western and Central Europe in opposition to Soviet power.

Warsaw Pact Soviet-led military alliance established in 1955 that countered NATO by providing collective security for Soviet satellite states in Eastern Europe.

NSC 68 A hardening of the Truman Doctrine, national security policy advancing permanent military strategy to thwart communism anywhere in the world.

hydrogen bomb Nuclear weapon, first tested by the United States in 1952 and the Soviet Union in 1953 with far greater destructive capacity than atomic bombs.

Chinese Communist Revolution Overthrow of Nationalist regime in October 1949 by the Chinese Communist Party led by Mao Zedong.

Map 22.1 Divided Europe, 1946–1965 The Cold War divided Europe by an "iron curtain" into eastern and western blocs. United by the Warsaw Pact and Council for Mutual Economic Assistance (COMECON), the East was held together by socialist ideology and, at times, Soviet force. Socialist Yugoslavia, led by Josip Broz Tito, would prove an exception. The West countered with NATO and the beginnings of the European Common Market undergirded by massive U.S. economic aid via the Marshall Plan. ▲

land redistribution State-led transfer of agricultural estates from landowners to landless peasants.

Mao's success in China compelled the United States to place even more significance on Japan as the bulwark against the spread of communism throughout Asia. The "reverse course" that MacArthur's occupation forces had begun following the Truman Doctrine accelerated as the United States rebuilt Japan's industrial capacity and supplied it with billions of orders for goods. The U.S. occupation of Japan ended in 1952 with the understanding, confirmed in the U.S.–Japan Security Treaty in 1960, that U.S. protection of Japan required a vast network of permanent military bases on its soil.

22-2c Partition of Korea and Outbreak of Civil War

Civil war in Korea becomes the Cold War's first military conflict.

Unlike Japan's four main islands, which were under sole U.S. occupation, Korea became subject to Soviet as well as U.S. influence when the two powers hastily and arbitrarily divided the country along the 38th parallel. North of the dividing line, the Soviets encouraged the growth of socialism through **land redistribution**, which appropriated large estates from the wealthy and gave them to landless peasants.

Myron Davis/The LIFE Picture Collection/Getty Images

Global Americans Born Yi Su·ng-man in 1875, **Syngman Rhee** was raised in a Christian mission school in Korea, and he converted to Methodism while imprisoned for reform activities forbidden by the autocratic kingdom of Korea. Upon release from jail in 1904, he came to the United States to advocate for Korea's sovereignty and to study, eventually earning a Ph.D. from Princeton University. In 1910, Rhee returned home to head the Seoul YMCA but within two years fled back across the Pacific after Japan formally annexed Korea. For nearly four decades, Rhee lived in the United States where he mobilized Korean immigrants and pressed Western nations to support Korea's independence. In 1933, Rhee lobbied in Geneva for the League of Nations. Rhee married Austrian immigrant Francesca Donner. After World War II, U.S. officials returned him to Seoul as the president of the Korean government in exile, and in October 1950, he became the first president of South Korea, serving until 1960. Some people revere Rhee as a George Washington figure liberating his people from Japanese and then North Korean tyranny. Others revile him as an iron-fisted dictator whose anti-Communist purges made McCarthyism seem benign. Yet most overlook the fact that Rhee was also a U.S. immigrant who spent almost half of his life outside of his homeland. His final days were spent in Hawai'i, where he died in 1965. His many transpacific migrations revealed the confluence of exile, immigration, and international relations.

In the South, the United States imposed an authoritarian regime that opposed land distribution in order to protect private property. Koreans on both sides of the divide hoped for a quick reunification of their country, but the ideological differences imposed by the two occupying powers became fixed in 1948. The country became two sovereign nations, the Democratic People's Republic of Korea (North Korea) and the Republic of Korea (South Korea). Syngman Rhee, long-standing Korean exile in the United States, became the first president of South Korea, and war hero Kim Il Sung became the North's champion.

After repeated cross-border conflicts between the two Koreas, the North launched a major offensive in June 1950 to reunite the Korean people. Mao and Stalin approved the attack, although Stalin did not pledge troops. Kim planned to defeat the South in a matter of days, hoping the United States would not actively intervene as it had not during the Chinese Revolution. He badly miscalculated. After losing its atomic monopoly to the Soviets and China to Mao's Communists, Truman refused to accept another global embarrassment. Wary of opposition in Congress to U.S. involvement in foreign wars he took his case to the UN Security Council, which—unlike the League of Nations—enforced its collective security commitment by sending troops to defend South Korea against the North's aggression. The expected Soviet veto did not happen because Stalin was boycotting the Security Council to protest its refusal to seat the PRC instead of Jiang's regime. Truman appointed General MacArthur to lead a UN force composed of troops from sixteen nations, including many NATO members and allies in Asia, Africa, and South America, but most troops were South Korean and American.

akg-images

U.S. Soldiers Marching into Battle, South Korean Refugees Fleeing the Other Way, 1950 Before MacArthur's successful landing at Incheon in September 1950, North Korean troops were on the verge of victory, having gained control of almost all of the South and sending millions of civilians fleeing for safety as is shown in this photograph. The Americans were instrumental in reclaiming the South, but civilian security remained uncertain on both sides of the Korean divide until 1953. ▲

In the first stage of the **Korean War**, the North Koreans wiped out half of the South's army and pinned the remainder, as well as tens of thousands of UN troops, far down the Korean peninsula at the southern port of Pusan. In a stroke of tactical brilliance, MacArthur launched an assault behind enemy lines at

Korean War Civil war between North and South Korea, 1950–1953, in which UN troops led by the United States fought with the South and Chinese forces supported the North.

limited war Warfare in which a party cannot use every weapon available in its military arsenal; during the Cold War this meant fighting without the use of nuclear weapons.

Incheon and proceeded to reclaim the nearby capital of Seoul. With his troops sandwiched and cut off from supplies, Kim retreated far to the north near the Chinese border. In September 1950, Americans were elated with victory.

But the United States was next to blunder. Truman ordered MacArthur to invade North Korea, arguing that the South's ultimate security required the elimination of communism on the Korean peninsula. UN forces quickly occupied North Korea's capital of Pyongyang and pressed beyond to finish off Kim's army. With their supply lines stretched thin, MacArthur's troops marched into a trap as hundreds of thousands of fresh Chinese soldiers crossed the Yalu River and quickly pushed U.S. forces back across the 38th parallel. The Chinese then crossed into South Korea and occupied Seoul. Secretary of State Dean Acheson called this "the worst defeat of U.S. forces since Bull Run" during the Civil War. UN forces regrouped, however, and were able to recapture Seoul and push the Sino-Korean forces back across the 38th parallel.

The United States was then in an undeclared war with China, a rising military power with a massive army. After the Chinese offensive began, President Truman noted, "I've worked for peace for five years and six months and it looks like World War III is here. I hope not—but we must meet whatever comes—and we will." It was in this context that U.S. officials relied on superior air power to lay waste to every major military installation, factory, city, and village in North Korea. Truman and his officers considered using more lethal chemical and nuclear weapons but in the end did not (see Map 22.2).

Meanwhile, MacArthur became convinced that a complete victory demanded a naval blockade of Chinese ports and the bombing of China's industrial capacity. Truman strongly opposed these actions, fearing a Soviet declaration of war. In April 1951, he relieved the hero of the Philippines and Korea of his command, but, when MacArthur returned to the United States to much adulation, it seemed that the public supported the push for total victory in Korea. The idea of a **limited war** in which the military could not use every weapon in its arsenal and the goal was something short of total victory was a new and strange concept. But it was an inescapable reality for both the United States and the Soviet Union in the age of nuclear weapons. Although the Korean War had reached an effective stalemate by the time of MacArthur's departure, it took two more years to reach a ceasefire in July 1953. By that time, at least 2.2 million North and South Koreans, 600,000 Chinese, and 36,500 Americans had been killed. North and South Korea remained divided at the 38th parallel by a 160-mile long and 2.5-mile wide demilitarized zone, a heavily fortified buffer between the two nations. The end of the Korean War did not bring peaceful relations. Both Koreas stood prepared to resume the fight at a moment's notice for the next sixty years while the hostility between the superpowers intensified.

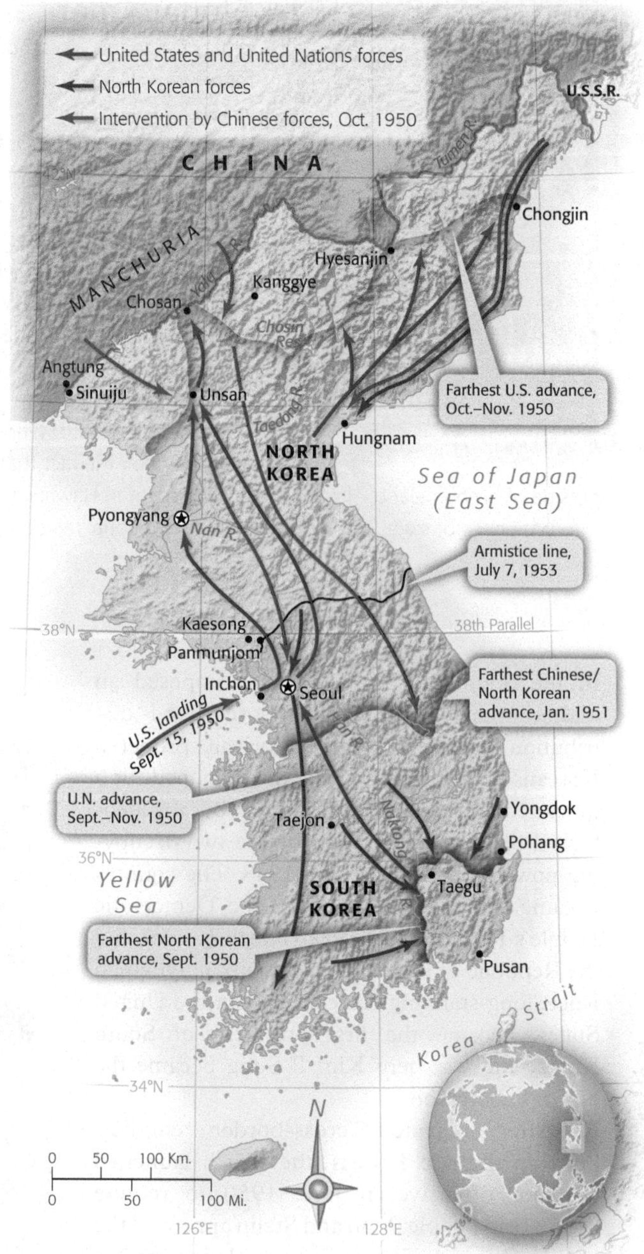

Map 22.2 Korean War, 1950–1953 The North Korean army controlled almost the entire Korean peninsula by the end of summer 1950, but MacArthur's September landing at Incheon gave UN and South Korean troops the upper hand until the Chinese entered the war in October. North Koreans and the Chinese pushed back into the South. The 1953 armistice restored the status quo boundary line at the 38th parallel. ▲

22-3

Cold War at Home

Films such as *I Married a Communist* released in 1949 reflected Americans' fear that Soviet spies had infiltrated the United States, and no one—not even family members—could be trusted. In this movie, the threat comes from a seductive woman involved in labor organizing whose "one mission is to destroy."

What gender and sexual stereotypes does this film poster draw on to portray fears about communism? ▶

Moviestore Collection Ltd/Alamy Stock Photo

The combination of the Soviet atomic bomb, Chinese Communist Revolution, and the Korean War unleashed a wave of fear about national security *within* the United States. It targeted not only members of the Communist Party but also a wide variety of political dissidents and cultural outcasts. The threat of nuclear devastation and the consequent emphasis on national security and military buildup forever changed the U.S. economy and society, whereas survival strategies and new genres of entertainment contributed to anxiety about the future.

☞ As you read, pay attention to efforts made to protect Americans from Communist threats. What did the government do? What roles did the movie studios and other branches of entertainment have? What impact did these actions have on the lives of ordinary Americans?

22-3a Spies and Scares

The shocking discovery of Soviet spies induces a wave of anti-Communist fear that targets dissident or vulnerable social groups.

Fear of communism unleashed a **Second Red Scare** more pervasive than the one following World War I. The Communist Party of the United States (CPUSA) was founded in 1919. As a branch of Vladimir Lenin's movement for socialist world revolution, it had been the leading leftist organization in the United States during the 1930s and found a new legitimacy during the wartime U.S.–Soviet alliance. But it operated more like a secret society than a political party. It is known that some two hundred party members passed U.S. military secrets to Moscow.

Nevertheless, the party's actual influence became greatly exaggerated by J. Edgar Hoover, the director of the Federal Bureau of Investigation (FBI). He committed his powerful agency to an obsessive anti-Communist campaign. Motivating the FBI was the shocking exposure in September 1945 that a network of more than eighty Communist spies had infiltrated the federal government. The most important was Alger Hiss, a rising star in the State Department who had served as an assistant to Roosevelt at Yalta and participated in the creation of the United Nations. Because the FBI had no hard evidence against the left-leaning Hiss, the burden was put upon the House Un-American Activities Committee (HUAC) to establish a case. Led by freshman representative Richard Nixon, HUAC in August 1948 produced Whittaker Chambers, a former Communist Party member, who accused Hiss of being a Soviet operative and produced incriminating evidence to back up his claim (which decoded Soviet intelligence documents later confirmed). In January 1950, a federal jury convicted Hiss of perjury for falsely claiming that he did not know Chambers, but he escaped the charge of espionage because the statute of limitations had expired on acts allegedly committed in the late 1930s.

A second spy case that riveted the nation involved a network of Soviet agents working on the Manhattan Project. The 1948 arrest of Klaus Fuchs, the Manhattan Project scientist who had turned secret documents over to the Soviets, led the FBI to a cadre of Communist engineers in New York City. The agency charged the leader of the group, Julius Rosenberg, with passing crude sketches of atomic technology to Soviet intelligence (a crime also subsequently confirmed by decoded Soviet cables). Unlike Fuchs, Rosenberg refused to confess to being either a spy or a Communist. The FBI sought to coax cooperation from him by arresting his wife Ethel on charges of espionage (which have yet to be confirmed). Both husband and wife were tried, convicted, and sentenced to death. They were executed in June 1953 despite worldwide protests.

Pressured by the Republican congressional victory in 1946 and repeated charges by political rivals that he was "soft on communism," Truman in March 1947 instituted a **Loyalty Program**, subjecting federal

Second Red Scare Fear of Communist infiltration that in the 1950s led to widespread, publically sanctioned, and often unjustified violations of civil liberties.

Loyalty Program First extensive security screening by the U.S. government, subjecting federal employees to investigations for suspicious activities ranging from spying to Communist Party membership.

employees to loyalty oaths and background checks that over nine years resulted in two thousand seven hundred dismissals. Even more Americans were subjected to loyalty tests implemented by state and local governments, universities, school districts, and private companies. Congress updated sedition legislation and placed restrictions on Communist-led labor unions, and immigration officials arrested and deported two hundred fifty foreign-born Communists and ex-Communists for violating immigration statues. Meanwhile, in October 1949, a federal criminal court convicted eleven Communist Party leaders for violating the 1940 Smith Act, which banned speech that advocated the violent overthrow of the U.S. government.

In this climate of fear, the undistinguished junior senator from Wisconsin, Joseph McCarthy, shocked the nation by declaring that he had a list of two hundred five Communist agents working in the State Department. In retrospect, McCarthy's claims were groundless, but at the time, many found him credible. He charged that Secretary of State Dean Acheson and other "striped pants diplomats" were susceptible to communism because they had been made effeminate by the genteel world of wealth and privilege. To the Wisconsin senator, effeminacy was a sign of homosexuality, and homosexuality in turn made a person even more susceptible to communism. Real men, he argued, worked their way up in society from the bottom rather than "being born with a silver spoon in their mouths." Ironically, McCarthy himself fell victim to the taint of homosexuality when the media latched on to the suspicion that two of his closest aides were gay men. The senator's charade came to an end in 1954 following televised hearings in which he was humiliated. With President Dwight D. Eisenhower's support, the Senate censured McCarthy, mainly for ethics violations by a vote of sixty-seven to twenty-two. McCarthy lost his audience and three years later died from complications due to heavy drinking.

Yet McCarthy was not alone in connecting gay bashing and anti-communism. The Second Red Scare relied on stereotypes of gender and sexuality to create a profile of disloyalty. Although anti-Red crusaders after World War I had identified dangerous radicals by their ethnicity (often Jewish or Italian), their post–World War II counterparts used homosexuality as a telling mark of disloyalty. Gays and lesbians were seen as emotionally susceptible to communism. Disguising their sexuality could make them vulnerable to blackmail by Communist agents seeking secret information.

In this way, the Second Red Scare generated a moral panic. Under Eisenhower in 1953, the State Department legitimized what has been subsequently called a **Lavender Scare** by increasing the dismissal of its gay and lesbian employees. By the 1960s, it had purged one thousand employees because of suspected homosexuality. A formal Senate investigation and subsequent security programs under Eisenhower expanded the persecution of gays and lesbians to all branches of the federal bureaucracy. Such measures netted far more homosexuals than Communists and roused calls for gay and lesbian civil rights that were amplified in the late 1960s.

Lavender Scare Part of the Second Red Scare targeting sexual minorities as particularly vulnerable to Communist influence, resulting in widespread violations of civil liberties.

National Security Act of 1947 Law that reorganized federal agencies to increase U.S. capacity to make and prepare for war.

Central Intelligence Agency (CIA) Federal agency responsible for gathering secret information about foreign threats to the United States.

22-3b National Security State

> The Cold War boosts defense spending and programs to a degree unprecedented during peacetime.

It is easy to dismiss the Red and Lavender Scares as the work of demagogues such as McCarthy, but doing so risks failing to grasp the major challenges to U.S. national security that policy makers faced after World War II. Advances in weapons technology coupled with the Soviet threat made clear that the United States needed to strengthen its defense. One element was the reorganization of foreign policy decision making to include the military, the principal goal of the **National Security Act of 1947**. This act also created the **Central Intelligence Agency (CIA)**, the permanent version of a temporary World War II intelligence bureau, to gather information on which government officials based their recommendations for national security. To address

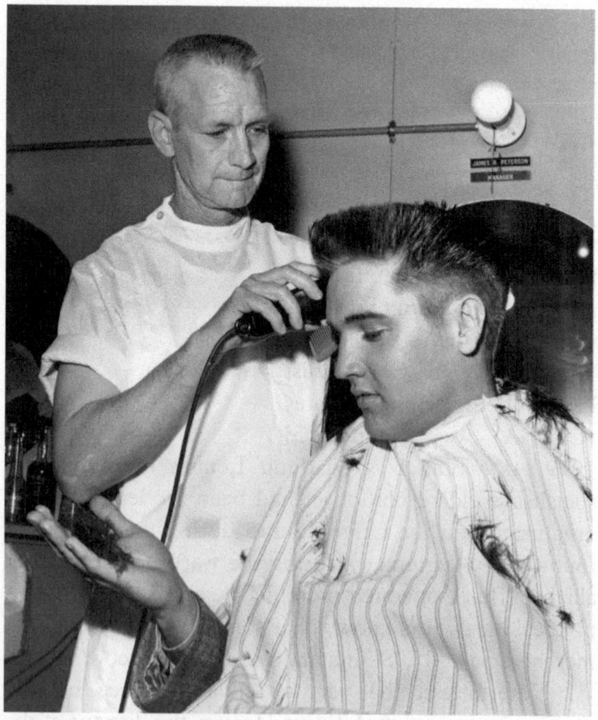

Bettmann/Corbis

Elvis Presley Getting a Haircut on His First Day in the U.S. Army In contrast to the period before World War II, Americans during the early Cold War were more likely to support foreign wars, military expenditures, overseas alliances, and sacrifices to civil liberties due to national security concerns. Military conscription, though unusual during peacetime, became a normal part of American youth during the 1950s. ▲

AP Images/Denis Paquin

Global Americans **Wilma L. Vaught** grew up in a small, midwestern farming town and earned a bachelor of science degree from the University of Illinois in 1952. After graduation, she joined the corporate world only to realize that there were no opportunities for women to rise into management positions. But the newly created U.S. Air Force was different. "I'd always wanted a job that would let me be in charge," she told an interviewer, "so as soon as I found out I could get a direct commission as a second lieutenant, I chose to join." As it turned out, the air force even allowed women to serve with men in integrated noncombat units. Despite the persistence of gender stereotypes and discrimination, Vaught became one of a handful of women who were able to climb the military chain of command. Like millions of other Americans with military careers, Vaught benefited from the unprecedented growth in the nation's armed forces, and she served in Spain, Guam, and Vietnam. U.S. global influence spread through an expanding web of military bases and alliances as well as covert and overt operations. In this way, the Cold War provided women in the United States such as Vaught increasingly equal opportunities.

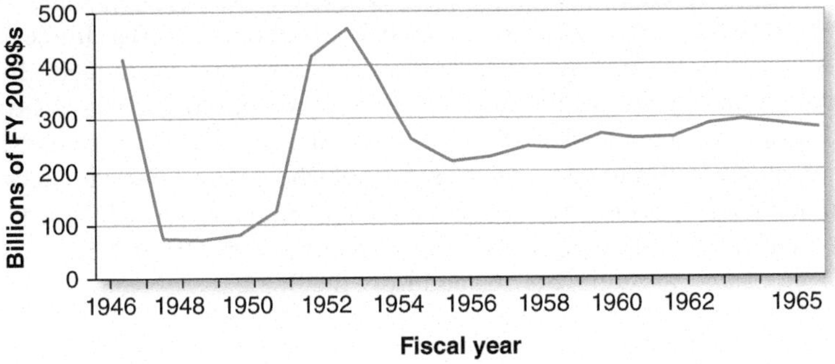

Figure 22.1 U.S. Military Budget, 1949–1965 The U.S. military budget reflects the emphasis on military preparedness that dominated the Cold War. After a huge decline following World War II, spending shot up during the Korean War and remained at 6 percent to 11 percent of GDP, which at least doubled the 1 percent to 3 percent rate before World War II. An average of 2.3 million Americans served in the military between 1946 and 1957; this was eight times the figure from the 1920-1940 period. ◀ Source: Center for Strategic and Budgetary Administration, March 2008. Based on Office of Management and Budget and Department of Defense data.

the new nature of warfare, the act elevated the air force, formerly under the direction of the army, to a third military branch and combined it with the army and navy in the newly created Department of Defense (replacing the Department of War).

The National Security Act also established the National Security Council (NSC), the president's main advisory team whose NSC 68 policy in 1950 permanently militarized U.S. Cold War strategy. Although the Truman Doctrine had recognized the Soviet sphere of influence and tolerated setbacks in less industrialized parts of the world, the new policy painted the Communist threat in even bolder terms. Now armed with the atomic bomb, the Soviet threat, said NSC 68, posed a military challenge everywhere in the world.

The sudden rise of the Cold War also pushed Congress to restore the military draft just one year after it had been suspended. The 1948 Selective Service Act—the second peacetime draft in U.S. history—required every male turning eighteen to register with a local draft board. Even celebrities such as rock star Elvis Presley and baseball great Willie Mays were inducted into the army. The draft increased the armed forces from 1.5 million troops in 1950 to more than 3.6 million in 1952. The number declined after the Korean War, but the nation's troop level remained unusually high until it increased again in 1965 with the Vietnam War.

Military spending was also high (see Figure 22.1), and the most concerning aspect of the national security state was the increasingly close, and thus potentially corrupt, relationship between the federal government and private weapons manufacturers. In his farewell address in 1961, Eisenhower labeled this relationship the **military-industrial complex** and warned that the "conjunction of an immense military establishment and a large arms industry is new in the American experience. The total influence—economic, political, even spiritual—is felt in every city, every statehouse, every office of the federal government."

The reach of the national security state extended into schools and private life through the Federal Civil Defense Administration, which, starting in 1950, mapped evacuation routes and sponsored campaigns to inform Americans about how to protect themselves in the event of a nuclear attack. At school, children practiced "duck and cover" drills, quickly crawling under desks and covering their eyes lest they be melted away during a nuclear blast. Families built backyard bomb shelters stocked with canned food, water, and supplies so they could stay underground until radiation levels had dropped. In this way, fears about the nation's defense touched the daily lives of millions of students, families, and communities: No one seemed to be safe.

military-industrial complex Eisenhower's name for conjoining military and private business interests that he warned in 1961 threatened democratic institutions.

22-3c Cold War Culture

Entertainment industries fuel anti-Communist fears.

The climate of fear created by the threat of Communists and nuclear annihilation was evident in culture and entertainment, and HUAC investigated Hollywood, concerned that Communists were spreading their ideology through films. The committee found no Communist plot, but in November 1947, it cited ten people—the Hollywood Ten—for refusing to testify about their past and present connection to the Communist Party. HUAC's investigation benefited from friendly witnesses such as actor and Screen Actors Guild president Ronald Reagan. To remove even the hint of impropriety, film studios created a **blacklist** of suspected Communists who were banned from employment in Hollywood, including actor and singer Paul Robeson. The studios also began producing movies that portrayed communism as a dangerous menace. Starting in 1953, the British writer Ian Fleming began a celebrated series of books featuring the anti-Communist secret agent James Bond. In addition, films such as *I Was a Communist for the FBI* (1951) and *Big Jim McClain* (1952) celebrated the U.S. agents who exposed traitorous spy rings, while others such as *I Married a Communist* (1949), *The Fearmakers* (1958), and the television show *I Led Three Lives* (1953–1956) warned that even trusted loved ones could actually be Communists in disguise.

blacklist List of persons not charged with a crime but who were not to be employed by the entertainment industry because of their radical beliefs—usually associated with communism and labor organizing.

During this time, the genre of science fiction was directly related to the fear of Communist infiltration and threat of nuclear holocaust. Films such as *It Came from Outer Space* (1953) and especially *Invasion of the Body Snatchers* (1956) used space creatures invading Earth as a metaphor for a Communist plot to conquer the United States. In *Body Snatchers*, Americans in a small town are killed and replaced by a species of "pod people" who look exactly like them but lack emotions and the ability to think for themselves. The novel *1984* (1949) by British author George Orwell achieved great popularity in the United States for its critique of communism by imagining a future Soviet-style society in which the state (Big Brother) keeps track of an individual's every move or thought. In contrast, the Academy-Award-nominated *Dr. Strangelove* (1964) satirized Cold War fears through black comedy. About an insane U.S. general who orders a nuclear attack on the Soviet Union, the film's subtitle captured the general's dangerously absurd point of view: "How I Learned to Stop Worrying and Love the Bomb."

22-4 Superpower Crisis and Diplomacy

"Let's Get A Lock For This Thing"
NUCLEAR WAR
HERBLOCK
©1962 THE WASHINGTON POST CO.

Library of Congress Prints and Photographs Division Washington, D.C.[LC-DIG-ppmsca-19978]

This political cartoon, published in *The Washington Post* in November 1962, shows Soviet Premier Nikita Khrushchev and President John F. Kennedy trying desperately to "lock" away the beast of nuclear war. Their worried looks as well as the unclosed lid revealed the difficulty of achieving this goal.

Compare this cartoon to the one depicting Stalin and Uncle Sam in Section 22-1. How has the Cold War become more dangerous? What is at stake? ▶

Go to MindTap® to practice history with the Chapter 22 **Primary Source Writing Activity: Cold War Prospectives.** Read and view primary sources and respond to a writing prompt.

Stalin's death in 1953 initiated the third phase of the Cold War in which the two foes resumed dialogue and eventually signed arms control agreements but not before pushing the world to the brink of nuclear destruction. Even as they engaged in a nuclear arms race, Soviet and U.S. leaders encouraged opportunities for their peoples to understand each other's culture and society. The relatively improved atmosphere drew strong support from American peace advocates, who since the end of World War II had promoted nuclear arms control.

☞ As you read, pay attention to efforts made to de-escalate the Cold War. What did U.S. and Soviet leaders do to create a more solid foundation for U.S.–Soviet diplomacy? What were the outcomes of these efforts?

22-4a Eisenhower and the Arms Race

U.S.–Soviet competition intensifies with new military strategies and more dangerous weaponry.

Dwight D. Eisenhower, the supreme allied commander of World War II, was elected president in 1952 in part because of his pledge that "I will go to Korea" to end what had become an unpopular war in the United States. The Korean War ceasefire and Stalin's death the next year presented Eisenhower dramatically altered circumstances that enabled the old wartime allies to come together at a **summit meeting** in Geneva, Switzerland, in 1955, the first time leaders of the two nations had met since Potsdam a decade earlier. That Eisenhower and the two new leaders of the Soviet Union, Nikolai Bulganin and Nikita Khrushchev, met at all was cause for hope, but the only real agreement reached was to engage in cultural exchanges. Eisenhower dismissed Soviet calls to end NATO, remove U.S. troops from Europe, and ban the production and use of nuclear weapons, whereas the Soviet leaders ignored his request for free elections in East Germany and arms reduction. The world delighted in the peaceful "spirit of Geneva," but U.S.–Soviet relations continued along the dangerous path of militarization.

Despite his friendly face and big smile, Eisenhower was an ardent cold warrior, who along with Secretary of State John Foster Dulles, believed that Soviet expansionism could be held in check by the threat of massive U.S. bombing of Soviet targets from military bases in Europe. The plan of **massive retaliation** was at the heart of the president's military strategy and led to the stockpiling of nuclear weapons and an emphasis on air supremacy over the use of ground troops. Khrushchev, who took sole control of the Soviet Union, also had two faces: one calling for liberalizing Soviet control over Eastern Europe and another crushing Hungary's attempt to break free from Soviet control in 1956. Khrushchev called Stalin's purges "vile" and "monstrous" and instituted "de-Stalinization" to provide more freedoms for his people, but he had no inclination and was in no position as a new premier to retreat from the nation's revolutionary ideology. Under Eisenhower and Khrushchev, the Cold War generated an arms race spiraling out of control in which the superpowers sought to outdo each other in increasing the production and strategic placement of nuclear weapons. The United States put missiles aimed at the Soviet Union in Turkey, which had joined the NATO alliance in 1952, as had Greece, both recipients of Truman Doctrine aid and firmly in the West's camp.

The successful launch of the Soviet satellite **Sputnik** October 1957 opened outer space to superpower conflict. It was the first human-made satellite to orbit the Earth, a historic achievement revealing Soviet superiority in missile and space technology. In response, Eisenhower established the National Aeronautics and Space Administration (NASA), which quickly launched America's own orbiting satellite and under President John F. Kennedy, NASA set sights on the moon. More pragmatically, space flight gave birth to intercontinental ballistic missiles (ICBMs), which each superpower armed with hydrogen bombs and pointed at each other's major cities.

Bettmann/Corbis

U.S. Nike Anti-aircraft Missiles Protect Washington, D.C., 1954 The development of threats from the air removed U.S. natural ocean protections and generated a greater need for missile defense. This photograph shows one of seventeen missile defense sites surrounding the nation's capital. The United States also deployed offensive missiles in Turkey and other sites to threaten the Soviet Union. ▲

As Americans were recovering from the Sputnik shock amid fears that the United States had fallen behind in missile technology, Khrushchev maneuvered to take control of West Berlin in part to stem defections—3 million since 1949—from impoverished and politically repressive East Berlin. As with the Berlin airlift, the United States in 1958 stood united with its Western European allies in refusing to give up the western half of the city, and Khrushchev temporarily backed off.

For his part, Eisenhower sought to defuse the second Berlin crisis by inviting Khrushchev to the United States. During the visit, Eisenhower proposed a number of arms control agreements, but only one, a multilateral agreement banning nuclear weapons testing in the Antarctic, reached fruition. Khrushchev's famous temper was on display when he was told he could not visit Disneyland and when he banged his shoe on the podium at the UN General Assembly, denouncing a representative from the Philippines as a "toadie of American imperialism." The Soviet leader's lack of subtlety and tact contributed to the fear that his foreign policy was overly aggressive, even reckless.

summit meeting Talks between two or more superpowers designed to improve relations and reduce conflict or the threat of war.

massive retaliation U.S. national security strategy under Eisenhower to deter enemy attack by amassing enough weapons to ensure "mutually assured destruction" in an immediate counterattack.

Sputnik First of its kind, Earth-orbiting satellite made and launched by the Soviet Union.

22-4b Cultural Diplomacy

Cultural exchanges between the United States and the Soviet Union open new chances for cooperation.

Khrushchev's outbursts aside, superpower tension seemed to relax, most notably through **cultural diplomacy** in which each side engaged in wide-scale public relations to promote its interests. The State Department encouraged scholarly exchanges and established U.S. centers around the world that offered English lessons and books and magazines about the way of life in the United States. The Voice of America broadcast news, music, and other programs in nearly every language, including twenty spoken in the Soviet Union. Disc jockey Willis Conover built a following for U.S. jazz, and jazz greats Louis Armstrong, Duke Ellington, and Dizzy Gillespie toured Europe and Africa as cultural ambassadors for the United States. The Soviets sought to counter the popularity of U.S. cultural diplomacy by sending their best orchestras, ballet troupes, and folk dancers for exhibitions in the United States.

The most celebrated U.S.–Soviet cultural exchange was the 1959 U.S. exposition in Moscow. The event featured displays of U.S. automobiles, cosmetics, and sporting goods, as well as free samples of Pepsi-Cola, which Khrushchev liked so much that he allowed it to be bottled and sold in the Soviet Union. A special highlight was a full-scale suburban ranch-style home complete with a washing machine, dishwasher, and other modern labor-saving devices. Escorting the Soviet premier through the display, Vice President Richard Nixon engaged Khrushchev in what became known as the "kitchen debate." "We don't have one decision made at the top by one government official," said Nixon. "We have many different manufacturers and many different kinds of washing machines so that the housewives have a choice." Khrushchev did not deny the superiority of American technology and consumer goods but praised his nation's ability to "overtake our American partners in peaceful economic competition."

cultural diplomacy Foreign relations strategy of building goodwill among people in rival or neutral states by exchanging ideas and programs in art, music, sports, literature, and other fields.

Sovfoto/Getty Images

Nixon and Khrushchev Hold "Kitchen Debate" in Moscow, 1959
Nixon, a hard-charging anti-Communist, became Eisenhower's vice president as the result of recognition he won as a leader of the House Un-American Activities Committee. Khrushchev, a Stalinist stalwart with only four years of formal education, climbed the ranks of the Communist Party to become Soviet premier. Their "debate" about the merits of consumer capitalism was a historic meeting even though neither changed the other's mind. ▲

Soviet citizens may have flocked to see American consumer goods, but their suspicions of the United States were reinforced in 1960 when a U.S. spy plane over Soviet territory crashed. Eisenhower claimed it was conducting weather research. He did not know at the time that the Soviets had recovered the plane with its cameras and photographs of secret Soviet military installations and that the pilot, who survived, had confessed to being a CIA agent. Caught in a major cover-up, Eisenhower made a historic address to Americans in which he admitted to U.S. espionage regarding the Soviet Union. The incident ruined a long-planned Paris summit meeting, and whatever good cultural diplomacy the two nations had generated seemed to be lost.

22-4c Kennedy and the Cuban Missile Crisis

Pushed to the brink of war over Cuba, the United States and the Soviet Union begin to emphasize cooperation.

In the 1960 presidential election, the Democratic candidate John F. Kennedy, a handsome war hero, won a narrow victory over Richard Nixon by blaming Republicans for not keeping pace with Soviet advances, citing the Sputnik shock and the much-feared "missile gap." The youngest president elected to office, Kennedy brought a fresh optimism to U.S. foreign policy. Although every bit as much a cold warrior as his predecessor, he distinguished himself from Eisenhower by criticizing the strategy of massive retaliation for posing an unnecessary risk of nuclear destruction. Kennedy's plan was to provide the United States with "flexible options" enabling it to defeat the Soviets using either conventional or nuclear weapons. Yet, ironically, the new president soon confronted a series of crises that pushed the world to the brink of nuclear war.

Kennedy inherited an Eisenhower plan for overthrowing the new Communist regime in Cuba. As in much of Latin America, the United States regularly supported military dictators capable of suppressing communism, but in 1959, Fidel Castro, a young lawyer advocating land redistribution, led a revolution that ousted dictator Fulgencio Batista, a U.S. ally, and seized $1 billion worth of property belonging to U.S. corporations. Although not a Communist at first, Castro quickly gravitated toward the Soviet Union, proclaiming Cuba to be part of the worldwide Communist revolution and pledging to paint Latin America red. In April 1961, Kennedy implemented Eisenhower's plan for a secret CIA expedition that would land at the Bay of Pigs and ignite an uprising of the Cuban people. The expedition landed, but the uprising did not happen. It was only the first of the **covert operations** aiming to unsettle Cuba's Communist regime and assassinate Castro, but it was a great embarrassment for the new president and placed him in a weak position going into the next crisis over Berlin.

In 1958, Khrushchev had backed down from his threat to go to war over West Berlin, but in June 1961, he repeated it, hoping to bully the shaken president into giving up control over the western half of the city. Kennedy stood firm, however, and the Soviets then built a concrete wall that sealed off the border between East and West Berlin to halt defections altogether. The **Berlin Wall** became an enduring symbol of the Cold War.

Berlin and the divided Germanys remained a superpower standoff, but the next crisis was closer to the United States and the closest that Americans and Soviets ever came to nuclear war—the **Cuban Missile Crisis**. In 1962, Castro agreed to install Soviet missiles in Cuba that would be aimed at the United States and just eight minutes from launch to the White House. For Khrushchev, the missiles offset the U.S. atomic weapon advantage (seventeen to one) and checkmated the U.S. missiles installed in Turkey. When aerial photographs by CIA spy planes confirmed the construction of launch sites, Kennedy went on nationwide TV to declare a U.S. naval blockade of Cuba to prevent the delivery of nuclear warheads. On October 24, the world held its breath as twelve Soviet ships approached the islands, only to make a U-turn at the last moment. After four uncertain days, the world finally exhaled as Khrushchev agreed to remove the missiles from Cuba and Kennedy promised to cease menacing the Castro regime and, more important though not publicized, to remove U.S. missiles in Turkey.

The missile crisis proved an embarrassment for the Soviet Union, toppling Khrushchev and necessitating a huge rearmament campaign to close the nuclear weapons gap with the United States. The arms race continued for nearly two more decades, but what was called **brinkmanship** between the two superpowers subsided. Both agreed to be connected by a private teletype "hotline" to improve communication and prevent future nuclear conflict. Moreover, the near miss pushed them to agree in 1963 to the **Limited Test Ban Treaty**, which prohibited nuclear weapons tests in the atmosphere, outer space, and underwater—all of which could be easily monitored by the more than one hundred signatory nations. Although the treaty did not cover underground tests, a major shortcoming, it paved the way for more extensive arms control agreements between the superpowers in the late 1960s and early 1970s.

22-4d Peace Movements

Nuclear threats reinvigorate international peace activism.

Superpower conflict and crises with the threat of nuclear war revived the U.S. peace movement, which had declined during World War II despite the presence of conscientious objectors. In the aftermath of Hiroshima and Nagasaki, scientists became the most conspicuous group to join traditional pacifists and religious leaders in speaking out against the use of atomic weapons. Albert Einstein was among them, observing that if World War III were waged with nuclear weapons, World War IV would be fought "with sticks." Einstein helped found the Federation of Atomic Scientists, which lobbied the government for peace and the safeguarding of nuclear weapons. Its bestseller *One World or None* (1948) described what would happen if an atomic bomb were dropped on New York City, and its *Bulletin of the Atomic Scientists* still features a Doomsday Clock with hands indicating how many minutes to midnight—the end of the world. After the signing of the Limited Test Ban Treaty, the clock was moved back, to 23:48, and Americans gained confidence that superpower diplomacy was reducing the threat of nuclear holocaust. A 1959 poll had suggested that 64 percent of Americans considered nuclear war the nation's most urgent problem, but by 1964, that figure had fallen to 16 percent.

National and international movements continued to warn of the dangers of nuclear war and the health and environmental hazards of nuclear testing. The logo for Britain's Campaign for Nuclear Disarmament became the international symbol for peace, and in the United States, the National Committee for a Sane Nuclear Policy (SANE) founded in 1957 garnered celebrity endorsements for its lobbying and educational campaigns. The activist Women Strike for Peace, founded in 1961, engaged white middle-class mothers in street demonstrations that called out "End the Arms Race—Not the Human Race."

covert operations Secret, state-sponsored tactics used in a foreign country, usually to prop up an existing government or to promote regime change that the CIA had routinely used since 1947.

Berlin Wall Highly militarized and patrolled cement wall erected by Soviets in 1961 to prevent an embarrassing stream of defections from East Berlin.

Cuban Missile Crisis U.S.–Soviet showdown in 1962 over the placement of Soviet missiles in Cuba that was resolved but pushed the world to the brink of nuclear war.

brinkmanship Security strategy used during Cold War to win a global dispute by pushing the stakes to the brink of nuclear destruction.

Limited Test Ban Treaty Global agreement signed by the United States, the Soviet Union, and other nations, which provided the first limitation on nuclear testing.

History without Borders

Nuclear Testing

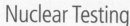

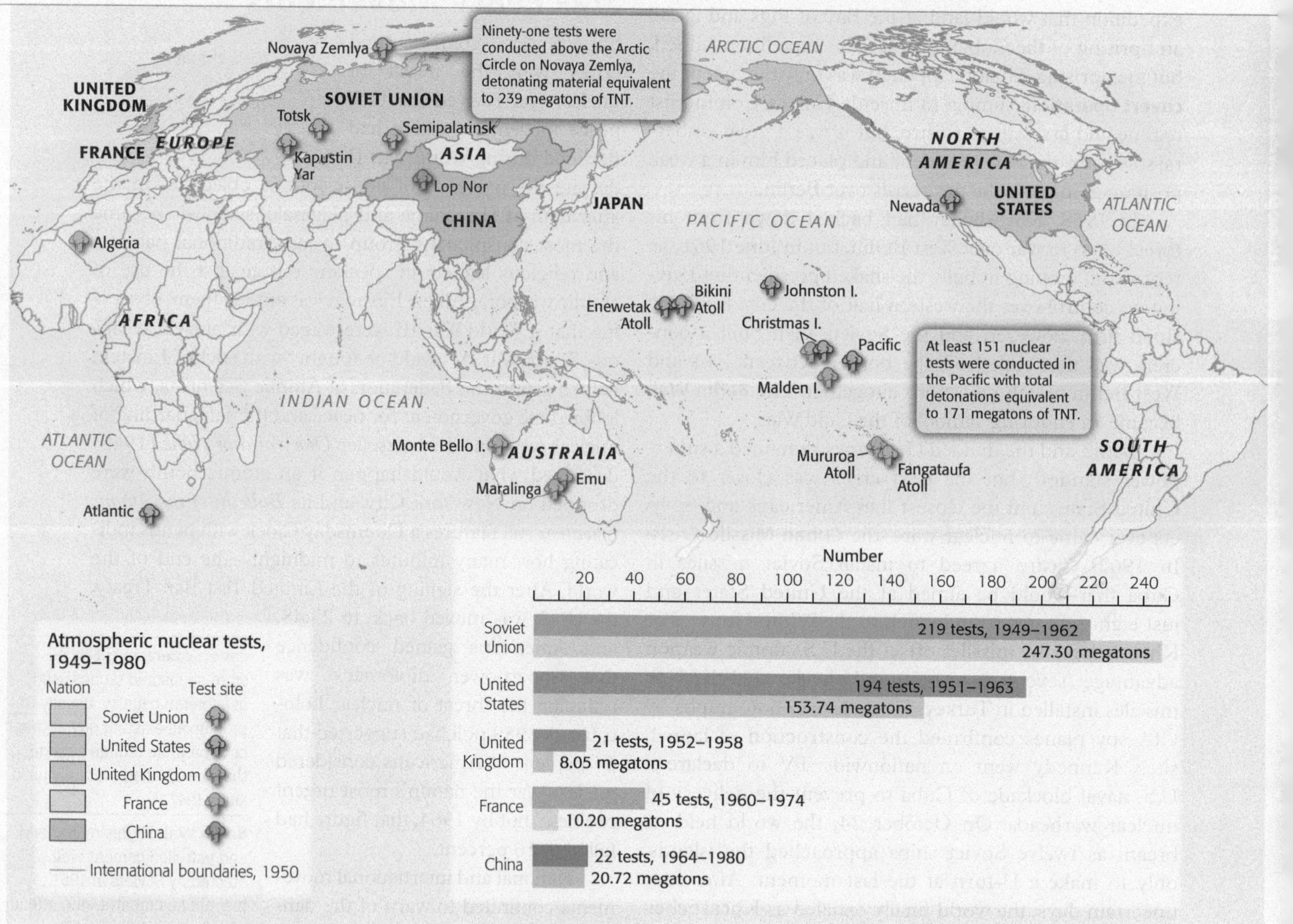

Major Test Sites for Atmospheric Nuclear Weapons, 1949–1980

The twenty test sites on this map spanned the globe with only South America and Antarctica excluded. No spot on Earth was spared nuclear fallout because ever more powerful tests spewed radioactive material into the stratosphere where it could remain for several years and disperse globally. ▲ Sources: Steven L. Simon, André Bouville, and Charles E. Land. "Fallout from Nuclear Weapon Tests and Cancer Risks: Exposures 50 Years Ago Still Have Health Implications Today That Will Continue into the Future." *American Scientist*, (January–February 2006), p. 50. United Nations Scientific Committee on the Effects of Atomic Radiation, *UNSCEAR 2000 REPORT Vol. I: SOURCES AND EFFECTS OF IONIZING RADIATION*, "Annex C: Exposures from man-made sources of radiation."

On March 1, 1954, twenty-three Japanese fishermen on the *Diago Fukuryu Maru* (*Lucky Dragon*), some eighty-five miles from the Bikini atoll in the South Pacific, were stunned by a brilliant flash of light, thunder claps, and then a ball of fire that lit up the sky. Two hours later, a shower of white ashes rained down, and soon every one of them was ill from acute radiation poisoning. That day, the United States exploded a hydrogen bomb at Bikini Atoll that was 750 times more powerful than the one that destroyed Hiroshima. Later, one member of the *Lucky Dragon*'s crew died. The ship's entire haul of fish was contaminated with nuclear fallout.

The *Lucky Dragon* was not the only Japanese fishing boat to suffer from nuclear testing. The nuclear arms race between the Soviets and Americans led to repeated tests of newer and more explosive weapons that posed health risks to life forms across the planet. By December 1954, more than eight hundred other Japanese fishermen had been exposed to radioactive fallout, leading to the destruction of 490 tons of "A-bomb tuna" caught by these fishermen. A "radiation scare" swept Japan, the only nation to have suffered a nuclear attack. Japanese scientists found radioactive material in the smallest sea creatures around Bikini, raising fears that nuclear fallout was being passed on through the food chain. The public, including

AP Images

Japanese Fishing Boat *Daigo Fukuryu Maru* (*Lucky Dragon*), 1954 From 1946 to 1958, the United States detonated twenty-three nuclear devices at the Bikini Atoll in the central Pacific. Hundreds of residents were relocated. In addition to contaminating their home environment with radioactivity, the tests' fallout irradiated the *Lucky Dragon* (and other fishing boats) eighty-five miles away. The poisonous effects of radiation have remained despite the return of residents to Bikini. ◀

Andrea Ferrari/Photoshot

Still from *Godzilla, King of the Monsters,* 1954 Wakened by nuclear tests, Japan's cinematic monster Godzilla embodied global nuclear fears in the wake of the *Lucky Dragon* incident. The aquatic dinosaur-like monster was cast as a metaphor of nuclear destruction with "atomic breath" that destroys cities and rough, scaly skin resembling the scars seen on survivors of the Hiroshima and Nagasaki blasts. ◀

the Japanese emperor, stopped eating fish, and fish markets across the country closed. The Japanese were also concerned about fallout from Soviet nuclear tests in Siberia, and the government warned housewives to wash vegetables in case they contained radioactive residue.

In response to the *Lucky Dragon* incident, the United States paid $2 million as compensation for the medical expenses of the irradiated fishermen, but neither Eisenhower nor the U.S. press gave credence to the widespread radiation scare in Japan. No one seemed concerned about dangers from radioactive fallout from Soviet nuclear tests near the Arctic Circle or U.S. tests in Nevada. The head of the U.S. Atomic Energy Commission contradicted the findings of Japanese scientists, proclaiming that fallout from nuclear tests had a negligible effect on sea life. But movements for arms control beginning in Japan and spreading to many nations indicated the depth of ordinary people's concern.

One of the most unusual expressions of the arms control spirit was the release of *Godzilla, King of the Monsters* in late 1954, the first in a series of more than twenty films made in Japan featuring the mutant, fire-breathing creature. The *Lucky Dragon* influence was apparent from the start of the film when an atomic test sinks a number of Japanese fishing boats and awakens Godzilla from his prehistoric sleep to embark on a path of destruction leading to Tokyo. Publicizing the negative impact of nuclear testing through Godzilla movies enabled the Japanese to get around their government's policy of remaining silent on this issue.

Critical Thinking Questions

▶ What factors encouraged the United States, the Soviet Union, and other nuclear powers to test hundreds of nuclear weapons above ground during the Cold War?

▶ Why was convincing authorities of the dangers of nuclear fallout difficult?

Go to MindTap® to engage with an interactive version of **History without Borders: Nuclear Testing.** Learn from an interactive map, view related video, and respond to critical thinking questions.

22-5

Cold War in the Third World

Prime Minister Kwame Nkrumah (center) waves to the cheering crowd as newly independent Ghana replaced the British colony known as Gold Coast. In attendance were Vice President Richard Nixon and a host of prominent African Americans, including Martin Luther King, Jr., A. Philip Randolph, and Ralph Bunche.

What interests might the United States have had in Ghana? Why did African Americans in particular embrace the country? What is the political implication of Prime Minister Nkrumah wearing African dress instead of a conventional coat and tie? ▶

Bettmann/Corbis

decolonization Process through which colonies gain political, economic, cultural, and psychological independence and autonomy from colonial rulers.

nonaligned movement Alternative to taking sides during Cold War advanced by newly independent nations, especially in Asia and Africa.

Third World Cold War era classification given to developing nations, largely in Africa and Asia, that were not firmly aligned with U.S.-influenced developed nations (First World) or Soviet-influenced nations (Second World).

As superpower relations stabilized, Cold War tensions erupted in former colonies around the world that were gaining independence. With 70 percent of the world's population in 1950, these emerging nations taken together posed a significant alternative to the U.S. and Soviet spheres of influence. Many pledged to stay out of the Cold War and to advance their own collective interests instead. But they also approached one or both of the superpowers when they needed economic and military aid, sometimes playing the Americans and Soviets against each other. To stop what was believed to be the spread of communism, the United States intervened in the internal affairs of nations in the Middle East, Africa, and Southeast Asia as well as the traditional U.S. sphere of influence in Latin America.

☞ As you read, focus on how the Cold War in its third phase spread to the developing world. How did fears about a worldwide Communist revolution influence U.S. responses to the emergence of newly independent nations?

22-5a Newly Independent Nations and Foreign Aid

Independence for former colonies brings new players into world politics.

Within two decades after World War II, the vast majority of colonies achieved independence, a global process known as **decolonization** (see Map 22.3). The age of imperialism with few exceptions had ended as European empires could no longer afford to maintain colonies, especially in the context of Soviet and Chinese support for independence movements. The largest number of the newly independent nations was in Africa, and in 1960, seventeen of them joined the United Nations. Others of these countries were in Asia and the Middle East. The largest new nations—India, Egypt, and Indonesia (with China's support)—led an international movement to establish an alternative to the bipolar politics of the Cold War. Meeting at Bandung, Indonesia, in 1955, the **nonaligned movement** articulated a third way to engage global affairs that addressed the largest but least powerful populations in what came to be known as the **Third World**. Although the United States and its NATO and Pacific allies represented the First World and the Soviet Union and its Warsaw Pact allies constituted the Second World, the Third World encompassed the remaining nations that were typically less economically and militarily developed.

Despite the spirit of the Bandung Conference, the political and economic realities of decolonization worked against the nonaligned movement. The leaders of newly independent nations often found it easier to claim freedom than to manage a country, and some were military dictators who squashed hopes for democracy and provoked a cycle of armed response and regime change. The Cold War further inflamed conflicts internal to these nations as the Soviets and Chinese actively nurtured Communist revolution within them and the Americans sought to counter Communist moves by backing undemocratic regimes, sowing discord, and staging coups.

Applying the model used in the reconstruction of Japan and the Marshall Plan, U.S. officials spurred the

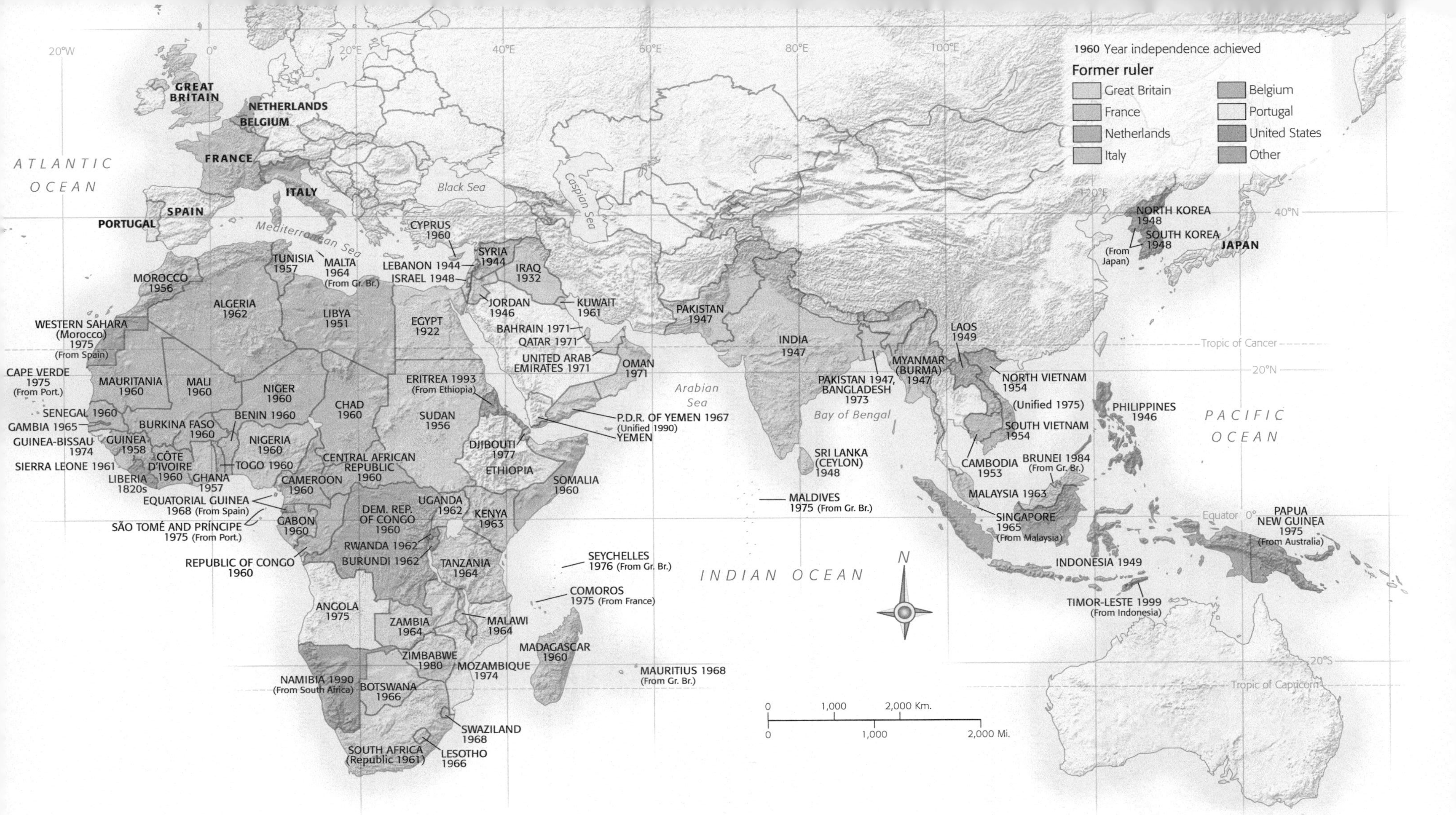

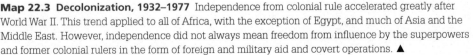

Map 22.3 Decolonization, 1932–1977 Independence from colonial rule accelerated greatly after World War II. This trend applied to all of Africa, with the exception of Egypt, and much of Asia and the Middle East. However, independence did not always mean freedom from influence by the superpowers and former colonial rulers in the form of foreign and military aid and covert operations. ▲

Keystone-France/Getty Images

Global Americans Born of humble origins in Detroit, **Ralph Bunche** arrived in Los Angeles with his grandmother in 1918. He attended high school and then UCLA, where he excelled at debating, starred on the basketball team, and was valedictorian when he graduated in 1927. He went on to get a Ph.D. at Harvard University and to teach political science at Howard University, a historically black university in Washington, D.C. Bunche was a critic of colonialism and imperialism, which he attributed to capitalism. During World War II, he served as an Africa expert in the Office of Strategic Services. After the war, the United Nations became his passion. He was a member of the U.S. delegation at the San Francisco Conference that drafted its charter, and he assisted in the development of its Universal Declaration of Human Rights. In the late 1940s, he was a UN peace negotiator in Africa and the Middle East, and he earned the Nobel Peace Prize for brokering the end of the Arab–Israeli War in 1949. During the Suez Crisis in 1956, Bunche established the first UN peacekeeping force and later supervised subsequent forces in Lebanon, Cyprus, and the Congo. Committed to civil rights and nonviolent protest, he marched with Martin Luther King Jr., and in 1965 contributed to the success of the Voting Rights Act. Bunche's life's work embodied the connection between civil rights struggles in the United States and global efforts for human rights and international peace.

economic development of Third World nations to create conditions favorable to the growth of free-market capitalism and to winning the hearts and minds of Third World peoples. In some cases, this process was dictated by U.S. business interests, but most aid from the United States had more to do with political control than economic markets. **Developmentalism** is an economic theory associated with these ideological aims that prioritized a nation's economic and political stability as well as its participation in the Bretton Woods economic system above that country's democratic rule and social equality. Critics see developmentalism as a disguised form of colonialism in which the recipients of foreign aid are "client states" or "puppet regimes" controlled by the United States, but the defenders of foreign aid underscore its humanitarian motivations and faith in free markets.

Kennedy was even more interested than Eisenhower in using foreign aid and cultural diplomacy to spread the American way of life around the world. The program that came to symbolize these goals was the **Peace Corps**, a volunteer service organization established in 1961 that, like missionary work, sent idealistic, mostly young Americans to live and work in developing nations "to promote world peace and friendship." Kennedy's inaugural address had issued a call for public service. "Ask not what your country can do for you," he declared, "ask what you can do for your country." And he told those "citizens of the world" listening on VOA radio to "ask not what America will do for you, but what together we can do for the freedom of man."

Developmentalism Theory applied to the Third World that emphasizes the significance of free-market economic development and participation in the global capitalist system.

Peace Corps U.S. international social service organization established to fight poverty and aid in the economic development of less-advantaged nations and to counter Communist influence.

22-5b Middle East and Africa

The United States succeeds European nations as the key Western power in these regions.

Complicating efforts by both the United States and the Soviet Union to win allies in the Middle East was the issue of Israel, a long-promised homeland for Jews, especially for survivors of the Holocaust. A UN resolution in 1947 recommended the establishment of separate Jewish and Arab states with control over the contested city of Jerusalem placed under international trusteeship. Jewish representatives in Palestine accepted the partition plan, but their Arab counterparts did not. When Britain relinquished control over its Palestine mandate in 1948 and the independent State of Israel was proclaimed, eight neighboring Arab nations sent troops to aid the Palestinian Arabs in an attack that sought to reclaim the land they believed was theirs. The ensuing Arab–Israeli War lasted a year before a UN cease-fire agreement enlarged the boundaries of Israel but permitted Jordan to annex the West Bank, including East Jerusalem, and Egypt to take the Gaza Strip.

Neither the United States nor the Soviet Union sent troops to the Arab–Israeli War because each recognized the State of Israel and supported UN partition for its own reasons. Stalin sought to divert attention from his anti-Semitic policies and to use the thorn of Israel to galvanize Arab opposition to Western imperialists. Truman expressed sympathy for Holocaust survivors, believed that the transplanted European Jews brought stability and civilization to the Middle East, and, to a lesser extent, sought Jewish American votes. Yet his support for Israel cost him a chance to bring Arab nations into a NATO-like alliance against the Soviet Union.

Superpower tensions were more evident in Iran, where they had already clashed in 1946. In 1951, parliament forced the pro-U.S. Shah Muhammad Reza Pahlavi to accept the new prime minister Mohammed Mossadeq and his intention to nationalize Iran's oil fields. U.S. officials suspected Soviet intervention, and two years later Eisenhower authorized CIA-led covert operations that ousted the nation's democratically elected government, leaving the nation's oil in the hands of British and increasingly U.S. companies.

Cold War tensions also influenced relations with Egypt, a former British colony and the most populous Arab nation. To gain Egypt's favor, U.S. and British officials agreed to work with the World Bank to build the Aswan High Dam, a flood-control and electric power project that the country's socialist leader Gamal Abdel Nasser deemed essential for his nation's economic development. Yet Eisenhower withdrew from the project to punish Nasser for maintaining ties with the Soviets. In response, Nasser in 1956 seized the Suez Canal from Britain only to have British, French, and Israeli forces take it back. In a surprising turn of events, the United States and Soviet Union joined to pressure the invading nations to withdraw. Egypt suffered huge war losses but won a diplomatic victory over the West and convinced the Soviet Union to fund the Aswan High Dam to its completion in 1971.

Following this Suez Crisis, in 1957 Eisenhower vowed to increase the U.S. military role in the Middle East through the **Eisenhower Doctrine**, which announced a commitment to defend the region from "any nation controlled by International Communism." It rested on domino theory fears about the importance of stopping communism and led to interventions in the internal affairs of Jordan, Syria, and especially Lebanon, to which Eisenhower sent fifteen thousand U.S. troops in 1958 to calm political unrest.

U.S. strategy in Africa varied by country but generally involved the combination of economic incentives, covert operations, and foreign aid. The inaugural group of Kennedy's Peace Corps volunteers went to Ghana, the first black African nation to proclaim independence, led by the visionary pan-African organizer Kwame Nkrumah. He had studied in the United States at Lincoln University in Pennsylvania, where he developed close relations with socialists and African American activists such as W.E.B. Du Bois, who spent his final days in Ghana and died there. As the new nation's first prime minister, Nkrumah focused on the development and liberation of Africa rather than taking sides in the Cold War. Like Nasser, he came under suspicion by U.S. officials, who distrusted his nonaligned position and were concerned about socialist connections from his college days. In 1966, while Nkrumah was visiting North Vietnam and China, the CIA arranged a coup that toppled him from power and forced his exile.

Another U.S. covert operation occurred in central Africa where in 1960, Patrice Lumumba, a labor organizer and independence leader, won election as the first prime minister of the newly independent Republic of Congo. During the struggle to free the central African colony from Belgium, Lumumba had articulated a vision of independence for his people: "We are going to institute social justice together and ensure everyone just remuneration for his labor. We are going to show the world what the black man can do when he works in freedom, and we are going to make the Congo the focal point for the development of all of Africa." As prime minister, Lumumba appealed to the Soviet Union for help in resolving a bitter civil war within the Congo but made it clear that he did so as an African nationalist who was not aligned with either side in the Cold War. This stance proved dangerous, because U.S. officials, who often equated nationalism with communism, did not trust Lumumba and in 1960 worked with Belgian operatives to arrange his murder. The new Congolese president, Joseph Mobutu, was a staunch U.S. ally who received millions in U.S. aid, military equipment, and, at his own request, parachute training in the United States at Fort Benning and at the Special Warfare School at Fort Bragg.

22-5c Latin America

The United States struggles to maintain control over the Western Hemisphere amid Communist-influenced democratic movements.

Latin America was more important to U.S. officials than Africa because of its proximity to the United States and the long-standing practice of U.S. intervention throughout the region. By the 1950s, U.S. officials sought to keep Latin American nations' dependence on the United States. An example was Nicaragua, whose exports of sugar, cocoa, and coffee to the United States were so critical to the Nicaraguan economy that one local official could claim his nation "served the dessert at the imperialist dining table."

U.S. economic domination, however, was serious business. In 1954, when Guatemala sought to nationalize the huge landholdings of U.S. firm United Fruit Company, Eisenhower had the CIA overthrow the democratically elected government of Jacobo Árbenz Guzmán in the name of anticommunism. The coup ignored the support of the Guatemalan people for land redistribution and the fact that Guzmán was tied neither to communism nor to the Soviet Union. The new military government, a U.S. ally, reclaimed United Fruit Company's banana plantations and ruled the nation for the next three decades.

The result of U.S. dominance was the **underdevelopment** of Latin American economies, a see-saw process in which rising profits for U.S. firms (and low food costs for American consumers) led directly to the declining economic independence of Latin American nations. Although U.S. influence made the

Eisenhower Doctrine Foreign policy under which the United States supports Middle East nations in resisting Soviet and Communist influence.

underdevelopment Process through which the rising economic fortunes of wealthy nations or classes contributes directly and indirectly to the declining economic fortunes of poorer nations or classes.

nations in the Western Hemisphere far more economically and politically stable than newly independent nations in Africa, this stability reinforced a huge gap between rich and poor that pushed millions to migrate to the United States.

Stability most often meant dictatorial rule, and the United States supported military regimes in Argentina (1946–1955), Venezuela (1952–1958), Chile (1973–1989), Nicaragua (1937–1956), the Dominican Republic (1930–1961), Brazil (1964–1985), and Cuba until Castro's revolution of 1959. The contradiction between U.S. Cold War rhetoric about freedom and democracy and its support of military dictators angered those who suffered under repressive rule. In 1958 on an official visit to Venezuela, Vice President Nixon and his wife narrowly escaped harm. In 1961, Kennedy sought to counter anti-Americanism—and isolate Communist Cuba—by creating the **Alliance for Progress**, a program of $20 billion in aid. The money did not usually reach the region's poor, however, because the military regimes diverted it and were forbidden to use it for land redistribution or other programs the State Department considered Communistic.

22-5d Southeast Asia

The United States struggles to prevent Communist victory in Vietnam.

The region that drew increasing attention from the United States was Southeast Asia, which had been divided since the nineteenth century into French, British, and Dutch colonies. Japan seized the region during World War II, and after the war, Britain and the Netherlands granted their colonies independence. But the French chose to hold onto Indochina—Vietnam, Cambodia, and Laos—for its resources of rubber, tungsten, and rice. Yet they could not suppress Vietnamese independence fighters who rose to power under the leadership of Ho Chi Minh ("the enlightened one"). Ho exemplified the complicated blending of communism and nationalism exhibited by Mao, Kim Il Sung, Castro, Nkrumah, and Lumumba. The revered freedom fighter was first and foremost a Vietnamese patriot who, as a young man, tried to convince President Wilson at the Paris Peace Conference in 1919 that Vietnam deserved self-determination. Failing this, Ho turned to communism as the vehicle for national liberation. In August 1945, he proclaimed the establishment of the Democratic Republic of Vietnam (DRV) to cheering crowds in the capital city of Hanoi. But the French did not accede.

The war between the French and the DRV that began the next year was embroiled in the emerging Cold War conflict (see Map 22.4). The Soviets supported Hanoi with China also contributing after Mao came to power. The United States backed the French, paying for 80 percent of war expenses in 1950 but not sending troops. Following a disastrous French defeat at Dien Bien Phu in 1954, a Geneva peace treaty recognized the DRV victory and called for the withdrawal of French troops. The treaty granted independence to the neighboring colonies of Cambodia and Laos but partitioned Vietnam at the 17th parallel, postponing the question of reunification for two years when popular elections were to be held. Hanoi retained control over northern and central Vietnam, and the French-backed emperor Bao Dai was reinstalled in the South.

The agreed-upon elections never took place. Even before the peace treaty was signed, U.S. officials moved to establish a permanent anti-Communist regime in South Vietnam that could resist a North Vietnamese takeover. The U.S. choice to head this new regime was the Vietnamese nationalist Ngo Dinh Diem, who had the support of Vietnam's Catholic, land-holding elite and the nearly 1 million people pushed out of the north by land redistribution and crackdowns on dissent. Within a year, Diem deposed the emperor and became head of the newly established Republic of Vietnam whose capital was Saigon. To protect Diem's regime, U.S. officials in 1954 formed the **Southeast Asia Treaty Organization (SEATO)**, a collective security alliance including the United States, Britain, France, Australia, New Zealand, Pakistan, Thailand, and the Philippines.

The emergence of South Vietnam had profound political repercussions in Hanoi. By 1960, Vietnamese Worker's Party head Le Duan and his right-hand man Le Duc Tho had taken control, and they shamed Ho and his supporters into submission for agreeing to the North–South partition and for failing in land redistribution. Ho followed a "North-first" strategy to advance socialist revolution, whereas Le Duan changed to a "South-first" plan seeking military conquest through the combination of a general offensive (GO) from the North and general uprising (GU) within the South. The **GO-GU plan** relied on the emergence of the National Liberation Front, which served as Hanoi's covert military arm in the South.

The execution of Hanoi's GO-GU plan in the early 1960s propelled Kennedy to rapidly increase the number of military advisers sent to South Vietnam. In June 1963, Buddhist monks and nuns began to set themselves on fire to protest the Diem regime's religious intolerance. The world gasped in horror upon seeing photographs of their burning bodies. The self-immolations convinced Kennedy that Diem had become a liability, and so in August 1963, the president authorized the CIA to dispose of him. Three months later, South Vietnamese military officers toppled Diem's government and murdered its leader. Not long after this, Kennedy himself was assassinated, and the direction of the U.S. involvement in Vietnam fell to a new president, Lyndon Johnson.

Alliance for Progress Program of U.S. economic aid to Latin America to ward off Cuba's Communist influence.

Southeast Asia Treaty Organization (SEATO) U.S.-led military alliance established to counter Communist influence in the region.

GO-GU plan North Vietnamese military strategy that combined a general offensive (GO) against South Vietnam and a general uprising (GU) of insurgents in South Vietnam.

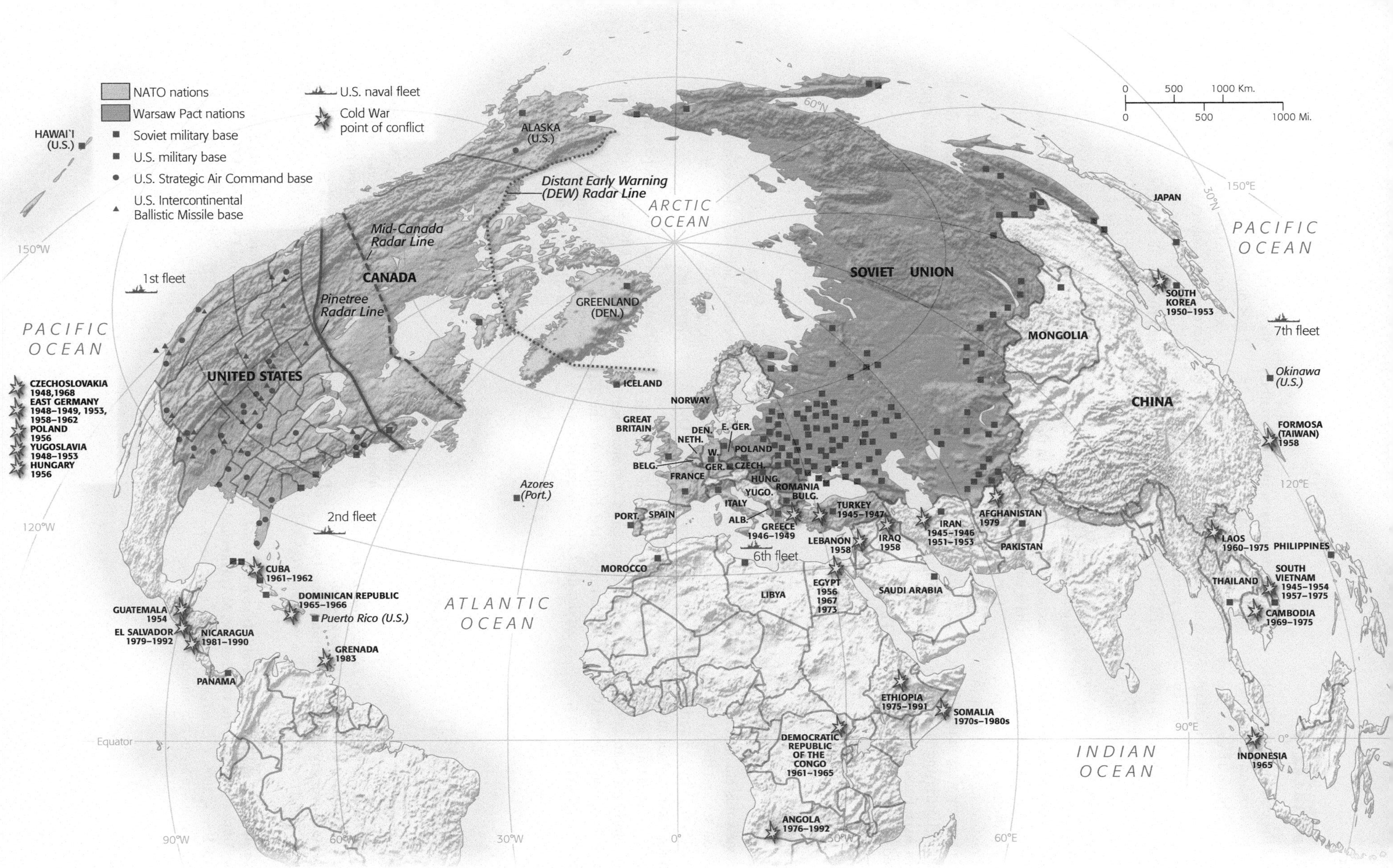

Map 22.4 Cold War Confrontations and Military Presence, 1945–1992
Conflict between the United States and the Soviet Union played out around the world in episodes of conflict and vast networks of military installations, which were far greater in number considering cooperative agreements providing superpower access to allied facilities (not shown on map). Also not shown on the map was the extensive global reach of intelligence gathering by the CIA and its Soviet counterpart, the KGB. ▲

Summary

Following the end of World War II, the United States and the Soviet Union became bitter rivals. Beginning as a struggle to gain ideological control in Europe, this rivalry intensified through the formation of security alliances and the emergence of a nuclear arms race. Although the United States and the Soviet Union avoided direct military conflict, Americans fought in Korea against Communist forces that included hundreds of thousands of Chinese troops. The two superpowers also engaged in proxy wars in the Middle East, Africa, Latin America, and Southeast Asia. Each superpower channeled aid and military support to opposite sides of internal conflicts within newly independent states. In the unstable politics of Third World nations, U.S. officials often confused the nationalism and nonalignment of Third World leaders with support for a world Communist revolution. Thus, the ideological conflict that began the first phase of the Cold War added a military dimension in the second phase and then in the third phase spread to the Third World.

The Cold War crisis on the U.S. home front produced the Second Red Scare and for the first time transformed sexual orientation into a major issue of national security. The impact was the persecution of thousands of U.S. citizens on the basis of their ideological beliefs or sexual orientation. Although high-level policy makers and military leaders played the key roles in shaping the overall patterns of the Cold War, peace activists, novelists, and the entertainment industry influenced how Americans understood these patterns in seeking to avert the potential nightmare of nuclear war. The fear of a nuclear attack combined with the nation's worst era of political repression ended, for the time being, U.S. interest in socialism and communism that began during the Great Depression.

<Thinking Back, *Looking Forward*>

As you review this chapter, think about the causes and the legacy of the Cold War. Why did anti-Communist fears explode in the United States at this time, and how did the Second Red Scare compare to the Red Scare that followed World War I? In the coming chapters, look for the Cold War's impact on the U.S. economy, civil rights, and subsequent war in Vietnam. Did the Cold War ultimately suppress progressive reforms as Americans looked for security in materialism, conformity, God, family, and the flag, or did the Cold War generate a new political activism advocating equality, dissent, and the power of popular participation?

To make your study concrete, review the timeline and reflect on the entries there. Think about their causes, consequences, and connections. How do they fit with global trends?

Additional Resources

Books

Boyer, Paul. *By the Bomb's Early Light: American Thought and Culture at the Dawn of the Atomic Age.* Chapel Hill: University of North Carolina Press, 1994. ▶ Original account of the response to nuclear weapons in U.S. culture.

Craig, Campbell, and Fredrik Logevall. *America's Cold War: The Politics of Insecurity.* Cambridge, MA: Harvard University Press, 2009. ▶ Good overview focusing on domestic politics in the United States that influenced the Cold War.

Cumings, Bruce. *The Korean War: A History.* New York: Modern Library, 2011. ▶ Insight into North Korean regime and U.S. atrocities by a recognized expert on Korean history.

Dower, John W. *Embracing Defeat: Japan in the Wake of World War II.* New York: Norton, 1999. ▶ Extensive examination of the U.S. occupation of Japan.

Gaines, Kevin K. *American Africans in Ghana: Black Expatriates and the Civil Rights Era.* Chapel Hill: University of North Carolina Press, 2006. ▶ Pioneering analysis of the role played by African Americans in African decolonization.

Pells, Richard. ***Not Like Us: How Europeans Have Loved, Hated, and Transformed American Culture since World War II.*** **New York: Basic Books, 1997.** ▶ Path-breaking study of the Americanization of Europe during the Cold War.

Schrecker, Ellen. ***The Age of McCarthyism: A Brief History with Documents*****, 2nd ed. New York: Palgrave, 2002.** ▶ Updated classic overview of the Second Red Scare.

Von Eschen, Penny M. ***Satchmo Blows Up the World: Jazz Ambassadors Play the Cold War.*** **Cambridge, MA: Harvard University Press, 2006.** ▶ Study of U.S. cultural diplomacy during the Cold War.

Westad, Odd Arne. ***The Global Cold War: Third World Interventions and the Making of Our Times.*** **Cambridge, UK: Cambridge University Press, 2007.** ▶ Important study of the significance of the developing world to the Cold War.

Zubok, Vladislav M. ***A Failed Empire: The Soviet Union in the Cold War from Stalin to Gorbachev.*** **Chapel Hill: University of North Carolina Press, 2007.** ▶ Insightful analysis from the Soviet perspective based on recently opened Soviet archives.

Go to the MindTap® for **Global Americans** to access the full version of select books from this Additional Resources section.

Websites

Cold War International History Project at Woodrow Wilson Center. (http://www.wilsoncenter.org/program/cold-war-international-history-project) ▶ Excellent compilation of international historical documents and resources related to the Cold War.

Foreign Relations of the United States at the U.S. Department of State. (https://history.state.gov/historicaldocuments) ▶ Official historical records of U.S. foreign policy decision making since World War II arranged by presidential administration.

Hibakusha: Atomic Bomb Survivors at UN Office for Disarmament Affairs. (http://www.un.org/disarmament/content/slideshow/hibakusha) ▶ Repository of links to Websites, videos, and testimonials related to the experience of atomic bomb survivors and their struggle for nuclear disarmament.

The National Security Archive. (http://nsarchive.gwu.edu/) ▶ Nongovernmental repository for declassified documents including those addressing CIA involvement in Europe, Asia, and the developing world.

Preparatory Commission for the Comprehensive Nuclear-Test-Ban Treaty Organization. (http://www.ctbto.org) ▶ Good historical information and video about international efforts since World War II to ban nuclear weapons tests, by the UN treaty organization.

MindTap®

Continue exploring online through MindTap®**, where you can:**

- **Assess your knowledge with the Chapter Test**
- **Watch historical videos related to the chapter**
- **Further your understanding with interactive maps and timelines**

The Cold War

1946

February
United States formulates policy of containment to counter Soviet threat.

March
Churchill describes Soviet sphere as an "iron curtain" dividing Europe.

May
Soviets seek to control Iran's oil fields, provoking U.S. opposition.

August
Soviet ambitions in the eastern Mediterranean push Turkey into U.S. sphere.

1947

March
Truman Doctrine commits United States to containing communism.

Truman initiates loyalty tests to remove Communists from federal government.

September
National Security Act lays foundation for national security state.

November
Congress investigates Communists in entertainment industry.

Winter
U.S. reconstruction of Japan reverses course to fight communism.

1948

February
Soviets overthrow Czechoslovakian government.

April
Marshall Plan aid begins to reconstruct European economy.

May
State of Israel is established, Arab–Israeli War begins.

June
Soviets blockade West Berlin, United States begins airlifting supplies.

August
Hiss trial enhances fears of Communist spies in U.S. government.

1949

April
NATO reverses longtime U.S. policy of avoiding overseas alliances.

August
Soviets' successful test of atomic bomb changes U.S. diplomatic strategies.

October
Success of Chinese Communist Revolution transforms Cold War in East Asia.

1950

February
Joseph McCarthy's claim of Communists in the State Department intensifies climate of fear and repression.

April
NSC 68 initiates an increasingly militaristic stance toward the Soviet Union.

June
Korean War begins; the first U.S. combat against Communist forces during Cold War.

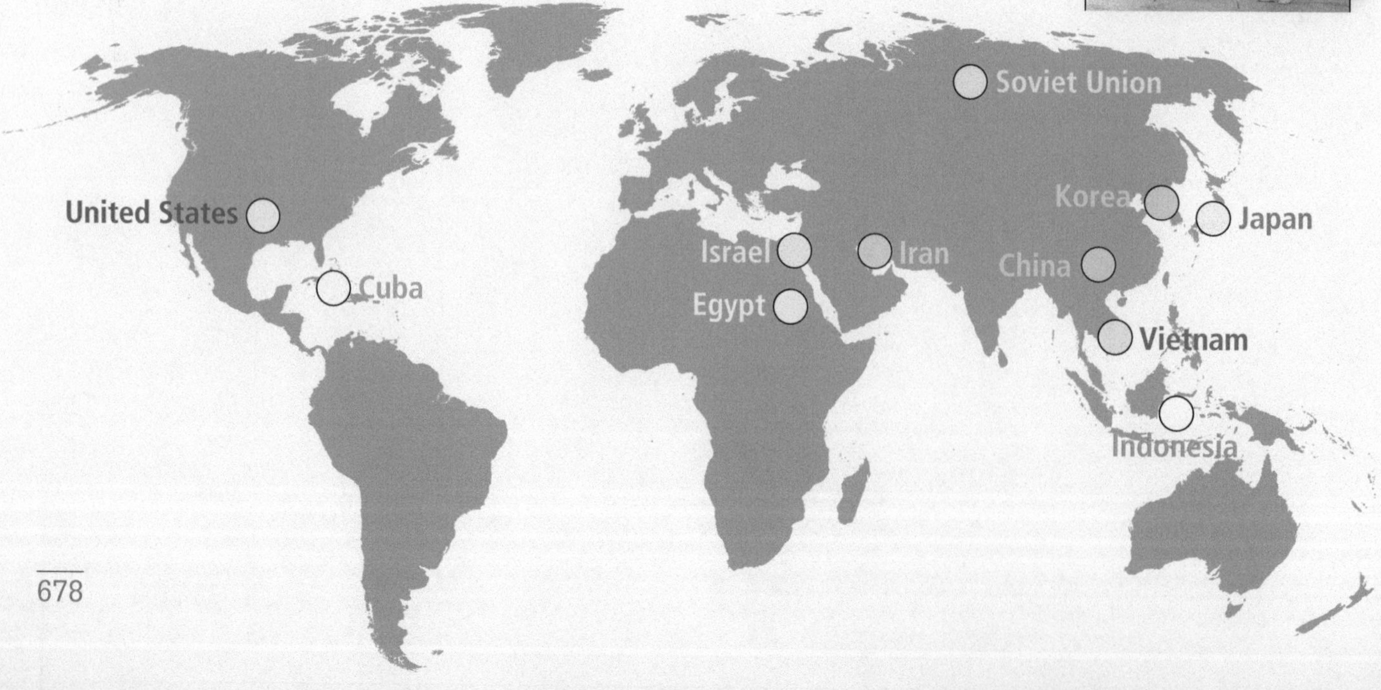

1952–1953

November 1952
Eisenhower is elected president, promising to end the Korean War.

April 1953
State Department legitimizes Lavender Scare by dismissing homosexual employees.

March 1953
Joseph Stalin dies, creating new opportunities for superpower dialogue.

June 1953
Julius and Ethel Rosenberg are executed for spying despite international protests.

July 1953
Korean War ends in stalemate with a ceasefire but no official treaty.

August 1953
CIA deposes Iran's prime minister to prevent nationalization of its oil fields.

1954–1955

May 1954
French lose to Vietnamese independence fighters and withdraw from Indochina.

CIA deposes Guatemala's president to prevent land redistribution from U.S. companies to peasants.

April 1955
Asian–African Conference at Bandung reveals nonalignment option during Cold War.

May 1955
Soviets establish Warsaw Pact to counter NATO.

1956–1959

July 1956
Gamal Abdel Nasser's nationalization of Suez Canal shows rising significance of developing world.

October 1957
Success of Soviet *Sputnik* evokes great fear in United States over "missile gap."

July 1959
"Kitchen debate" between Nixon and Khrushchev reveals ideological importance of consumer products.

1960–1962

Seventeen African nations join the UN.

January 1960
U.S.–Japan Security Treaty guarantees U.S. military force in East Asia.

November 1960
Kennedy is elected president, promising tough Cold War stance.

March 1961
Kennedy establishes Peace Corps, increases aid to developing nations.

October 1962
Cuban Missile Crisis pushes United States and Soviet Union to the brink of nuclear war.

"Let's Get A Lock For This Thing"
NUCLEAR WAR
HERBLOCK

1963

July
Limited Test Ban Treaty reduces superpower tension.

November
Kennedy is assassinated, and Johnson becomes president.

23 Prosperity and the Cold War Economy

1945–1965

In 1957, Los Angeles Mayor Norris Poulson engineered the relocation of the Brooklyn Dodgers from their original, legendary home at Ebbets Field. When the new Dodger Stadium opened in Los Angeles in 1962, one sportswriter called it the "most modern baseball temple in the world."

23-1
Government and Prosperity

23-1a Transition from Total War
23-1b Commercial Innovation
23-1c Consumer Revolution

23-2
Cold War Economic Growth

23-2a Politics and the Middle-Class Nation
23-2b Education and Defense Spending
23-2c United States and the World Market

23-3
Social and Cultural Trends

23-3a White-Collar Work
23-3b Migration, Population Shifts, and New Highways
23-3c Growth of Suburbs
23-3d Suburbia, Central Cities, and Segregation
23-3e Suburban Culture and the Rise of Television

23-4
Family-Centered Culture in an Uncertain World

23-4a Baby Boom and the Nuclear Family
23-4b Companionate Household
23-4c Children of Plenty
23-4d Beginnings of the Sexual Revolution

23-5
New Social Divisions

23-5a Critics of Prosperity
23-5b Costs of Suburban Development
23-5c Agricultural Labor and Mexican Migration
23-5d Rural Transformations

When Mayor Norris Poulson welcomed Soviet Premier Nikita Khrushchev to Los Angeles in September 1959, he had a strong message for the Russian. "You shall not bury us and we shall not bury you." He was referring to a widely circulated remark Khrushchev had made in 1956 directed to the United States, "We will bury you." Khrushchev explained to Paulson that he had not meant nuclear war but the inevitable victory of communism over capitalism. The mayor, however, was determined to demonstrate capitalism's achievements.

The LIFE Picture Collection/Getty Images

Dodger Stadium in Los Angeles, 1962, a ballpark for the automobile and suburban age.

There was no better showcase of capitalism in the United States than Los Angeles. The production of the city's aircraft, auto, and defense industries that had spurred growth during World War II had increased afterward, fueling a population boom, sprawling suburban development, and hundreds of miles of new freeways. As mayor, Poulson, a great city promoter, oversaw the expansion of Los Angeles Harbor, the construction of Los Angeles International Airport, and, dearest to his heart, the building of Dodger Stadium.

In 1957, Poulson had engineered the relocation of the Brooklyn Dodgers, the legendary baseball team based in Brooklyn, New York that played in Ebbets Field, a state-of-the-art stadium when it opened on a streetcar line in 1913. The name "Dodgers" derived from the streetcars that locals were skilled at dodging. But by the 1950s, Ebbets Field was obsolete, and many of its fans had left the gritty streets of Brooklyn for the green suburbs of Long Island. So when Los Angeles offered to build the team a dream ballpark, owner Walter O'Malley agreed. The Dodgers' move to Los Angeles was unprecedented, but then cross-town rival New York Giants relocated to San Francisco.

Dodger Stadium opened in April 1962 with space for twenty thousand more fans, convenient freeway access, abundant parking, and picturesque views of the downtown skyline. One sportswriter called it the "most modern baseball temple in the world." The new stadium catered to middle-class suburbanites whose love of professional sports was matched only by their enchantment with Hollywood (which Khrushchev visited) and Disneyland (which he did not because of safety precautions).

The Soviet premier's famous temper flared in being denied a visit to Disneyland. "Is there an epidemic of cholera there or something?" he blasted, or "have gangsters taken hold of the place that can destroy me?" A few months earlier during the kitchen debate at the U.S. Moscow exhibition, Khrushchev had boasted to Vice President Richard Nixon that his country would soon build better consumer products than the Americans. But he was being excluded from seeing the ultimate display of modern American lifestyles and consumer ingenuity. Such was the United States' mid-century allure; a nation whose wealth, prosperity, and innovations attracted even the leader of the Communist

How does the relocation of the Dodgers from Brooklyn to Los Angeles reflect the major transformations in the U.S. economy and society in the mid-twentieth century?

Go to MindTap® to watch a video on Los Angeles Mayor Norris Poulson and learn how this story relates to the themes of this chapter.

world—to say nothing of millions around the world who also longed to experience Disneyland and the nation's abundant consumer pleasures. Although the Soviets rivaled U.S. military might, no country at that time came close to matching its productive capacity and the social and cultural influence associated with unrivaled economic power. This was the apex of American global influence.

The relocation of professional baseball teams reflected a major transformation in the nation's economy and society that was moving the center of production away from manufacturing and historic urban centers, toward service and information industries as well as newer urban and suburban locales, largely in the South and West. Massive Cold War spending and assiduous preparedness plans propelled these economic and social trends and underwrote the longest era of prosperity in U.S. history. The good times shaped a new version of the American Dream: a home in the suburbs, a college education, and a professional job. Federal dollars supported home ownership, too, and higher education for the children of prosperity. But not everyone was prosperous. As obsolete factories closed and old manufacturing jobs disappeared, unemployment and poverty marked declining central cities, and the poor were disproportionally people of color. In Los Angeles, many lived in three Mexican American communities where the city went back on its promise to build affordable public housing, and instead displaced residents and destroyed their homes as part of the deal to attract the Dodgers. Those residents who struggled with police before bulldozers razed their homes were branded socialists. Others still remember: "What they did to me . . . was the biggest and worst thing of all."

23-1

Government and Prosperity

Special Collections Research Center, North Carolina State University Library

This photograph depicts a North Carolina State University classroom in 1954 after the federal government extended educational benefits to veterans of the Korean War. Many of the students here were able to go to college as the result of a government program for veterans.

What do you notice about the students and how they are dressed? What factors could explain the gender and racial makeup of the class? ▶

Although adjusting from World War II was not easy, the nation's economy eventually righted itself and entered a period of prosperity, consumer spending, and high employment that Americans had not experienced since before the Great Depression. The global context favored the United States because of the war's devastating impact on the world's leading economic powers including Great Britain, Germany, France, and Japan. Americans also benefited from new technology developed during the war that afterward contributed to the growth of airlines, pharmaceuticals, and a host of innovations in industrial research sparking an explosion of new commercial products and services. The federal government played a major role in facilitating this consumer revolution by actively boosting home ownership through low-interest loans to veterans. In this way, the Korean War, which required a high level of military personnel, continued the nation's historic expansion of the middle class.

☞ As you read, focus on economic recovery of the United States as well as the rise of new industries and types of work. What impact did the nation's involvement in World War II, and the Cold War especially, have on these economic trends?

23-1a Transition from Total War

The nation's economic recovery from World War II is difficult for consumers and workers.

Following the attack on Pearl Harbor in December 1941, U.S. war production went into overdrive, so the sudden shift into peacetime, a process known as **reconversion**, was destined to be bumpy. Consumers got a taste of hard times when the cost of living skyrocketed after President Harry Truman abruptly halted wartime rationing and price controls. Inflation in meat prices at the end of summer 1946 prompted the *New York Daily News* to declare: "PRICES SOAR, BUYERS SORE—STEERS JUMP OVER THE MOON." The shortage of housing was even more desperate. After a boom in home construction in the 1920s, the real estate industry dried up for sixteen years through depression and war. Although housing was scarce during the war, the shortage reached crisis level with the demobilization of troops. In 1947, 6 million Americans doubled up with relatives or friends, and half a million lived in converted army barracks and other forms of temporary housing. Playing on an old campaign slogan, the *Kansas City Star* described the situation as "Two Families in Every Garage."

The demobilization of nearly 11 million U.S. troops within two years of the war's end also exacerbated labor relations as veterans re-entered a job market that was already adjusting to reconversion. Organized labor emerged from the war stronger than ever. Both union membership rates (15 million nationwide, or one-third of all nonfarm labor) and the range of unionized industries were at record highs. A remarkable 70 percent of all workers in manufacturing were covered by collective bargaining arrangements with prospects for union expansion into the growing white-collar professional and service sectors (see Figure 23.1). Yet the end of the war brought new tensions between workers and management. Businesses cut hours, wages, and overtime pay with the drastic drop in defense spending. Workers suffered further because inflation diminished their real earnings; they responded by going on strike. The climax of the strike wave came in May 1946 when railroad workers brought the nation's rail system to a standstill for two days before Truman was able to settle the strike. All told, 5 million workers marched on picket lines in 1946, more than any year during the peak of labor protest in the 1930s.

reconversion Transition from special economic circumstances under total war to a peacetime economy in which governments remove controls on businesses and millions serving in the military return to the civilian labor force.

But absent from labor protests were most of the 4.7 million women who had taken jobs outside the home during World War II. Many "Rosie the riveters" happily handed over their hard hats to returning veterans, but those who were the main wage earners in their families and others who had enjoyed being in the workforce did so with great reluctance. Congress provided no unemployment assistance to working women and ignored pleas to ensure gender equality in the workplace. Those fortunate to keep their jobs during reconversion saw their wages almost cut in half, from 90 to 50 cents per hour.

23-1b Commercial Innovation

The rise of new or formerly marginal industries spurs economic recovery.

Surprisingly, the U.S. economy recovered quickly from its postwar readjustment because of domestic supply and demand. The supply grew out of a remarkable degree of commercial innovation. World War II had induced more scientific breakthroughs than had any previous U.S. military conflict, and many of these innovations stimulated the subsequent growth of commercial products. The most immediate impact was on the production of airplanes, pharmaceuticals, plastics, and other industrial chemicals. The war almost overnight had established the modern U.S. aircraft industry as the nation's production of airplanes rose sixteen times from 5,865 units in 1939 to 95,672 by 1944. At the same time, jet engines made the leap in 1958 from military to commercial use. The extensive use of large jet airliners such as the Boeing 707 enabled the commercial airline industry, which had begun in the 1930s, literally to take off in

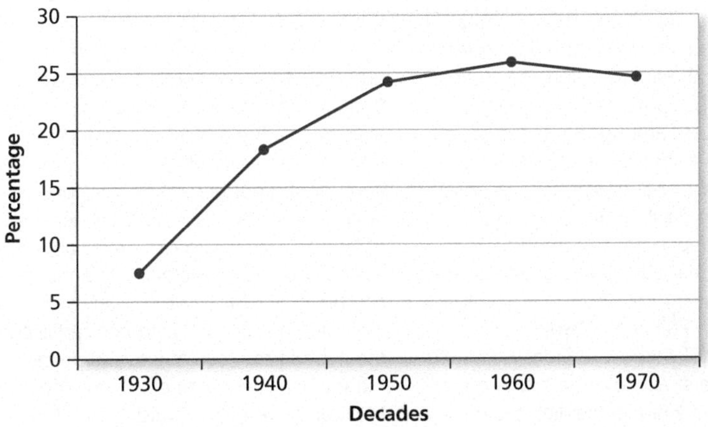

Figure 23.1 Percentage of Union Membership among Employed Workers in the United States, 1930–1970 Labor union membership grew rapidly in the United States after having won collective bargaining rights during the Great Depression and continued to grow through World War II and into the postwar era. ◀ Source: Meyer, Gerald, *Union Membership Trends in the United States*. Washington, DC: Congressional Research Service, 2004, http://digitalcommons.ilr.cornell.edu

History without Borders

Norin 10 and the Worldwide Green Revolution

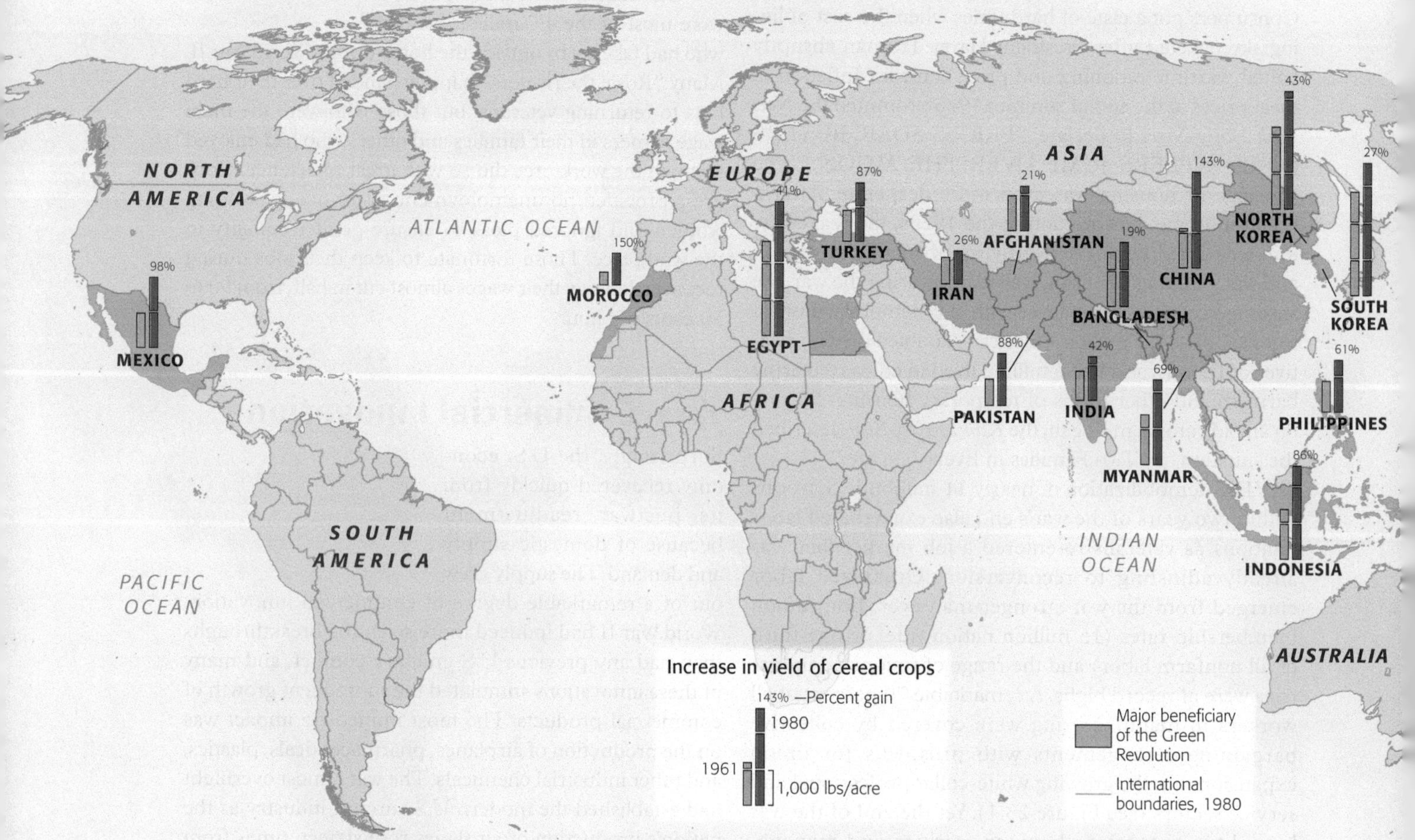

Major Beneficiaries of the Green Revolution, 1961–1980 New technologies in fertilizers and strains of wheat and other cereal grains produced robust increases in the production of agricultural staples, which especially influenced the developing world. This map shows the nations that benefited the most from the Green Revolution during the 1960s and 1970s. ▲

Although new technologies bolstered prosperity in the United States after World War II, their role in promoting a worldwide *Green Revolution* proved even more historically significant. *Green Revolution* is a term that describes the modernization of agriculture, promoted largely by the United States, enabling many developing nations to dramatically increase their production of staple crops such as wheat, corn, and rice. This rapid growth of food supply in poor countries was seen as a key to ending world hunger and promoting Third World economic development.

Another important factor for the Green Revolution was artificially created nitrogen, a chemical that when mixed with natural manure became a cheaply produced but potent fertilizer. Scientists in Japan were among the first to experiment with a shorter variety of wheat that would respond well to large doses of nitrogen fertilizer. In 1946, a U.S. adviser in Japan noticed unusual "semi-dwarf" wheat and sent a sample to the United States to be studied. Agricultural scientists in Pullman, Washington, combined one of them, known as *Norin 10*, with native strains of wheat to produce a significantly higher-yielding grain used with spectacular results by farmers in the Pacific Northwest.

In 1953, a Pullman scientist passed samples of the new grain to Norman Borlaug, an American conducting research for the Rockefeller Foundation on increasing wheat production and fighting hunger in Mexico. Borlaug crossed the Washington varieties of Norin 10 with Mexican grains and within two years developed a winning combination of the two. When used with high amounts of nitrogen fertilizer, the hybrid produced at least 50 percent more wheat per hectare of land. The Mexican government quickly adopted

Art Rickerby//Time Life Pictures/Getty Images

Norman Borlaug in the Field Norman Borlaug, a U.S. scientist whose research was instrumental in generating the Green Revolution, is shown here holding stalks of wheat designed to be disease resistant and to produce maximum yields. ◀

Gamma-Rapho/Getty Images

Rice Fields By 1980, when women in this photograph worked rice fields in West Bengal, India, the country's total yield of cereal grains had increased by 42 percent since 1961. ◀

the high-yielding grain, and within a decade, Mexico no longer confronted shortages of wheat. Instead, its farmers generated a surplus that was exported abroad.

In 1963, scientists in India, aware of Borlaug's success in Mexico, asked him to study the prospects for Norin 10 there. He then sent samples of the Mexican varieties to India, which were well received by the Indian officials. In 1966 with funding from the Rockefeller Foundation, the Indian government imported a large amount of Mexican wheat seeds. The subsequent increase in Indian wheat production played a major role in enabling India to become self-sufficient in food production. Indian varieties of Norin 10 went on to boost wheat production in Pakistan, Afghanistan, Turkey, and other developing countries. For his crucial role in greatly expanding the world's food supply, Borlaug received the Nobel Peace Prize.

The effects of the Green Revolution, however, were not uniformly positive. The huge rise in wheat production in Mexico by medium and larger farms wiped out the livelihood of millions of small farmers, forcing them to relocate to the cities. There they provided the cheap labor needed for the industrial revolution in Mexico. In addition, the dependence on chemical supplements hindered poor developing nations when the price of nitrogen fertilizers dramatically increased in the early 1970s. Another problem was the reliance on artificially produced pesticides to keep insects from destroying crops. Such chemicals were linked to health problems in field-workers and a host of environmental ills. Finally, solving food supply shortages did not end world hunger. Starvation and malnutrition exist because people are too poor to afford a good diet, even in wealthy countries. Thus, the increased production of crops around the world did not mean that nations were able to distribute the resulting food to the people in need or that those in need were able to purchase it.

Critical Thinking Questions

▶ In what ways did the Green Revolution reveal the importance of international cooperation in the production of staple crops?

▶ Why was the Green Revolution unable to end starvation around the world?

Go to MindTap® to engage with an interactive version of **History without Borders: Norin 10 and the Worldwide Green Revolution.** Learn from an interactive map, view related video, and respond to critical thinking questions.

Levittown, New York, 1955 A new method for building houses after World War II mirrored the approach of the assembly line for automobiles. By 1950, Levitt and Sons had manufactured a four-room house every sixteen minutes for a fraction of the cost of custom-built homes. The average price for a two-story home ($7,900) was often more affordable than renting an apartment in the city. ▶

Hulton Archive/Archive Photos/Getty Images

the 1950s. The number of air passengers doubled during that decade with more Americans traveling by air than railroad.

The emergence of the modern pharmaceutical industry was as impressive as the rise of large-scale air travel. The federal government's investment in the production of antibiotics such as sulfa and penicillin during the war was a huge boon to the commercial drug industry. After the war, Merck, Pfizer, Squibb, and other large drug companies introduced a wide range of antibiotics, antihistamines, steroids, and other pharmaceuticals based on their experience producing drugs for the military. The new drugs, which were much more complex than previous ones, stimulated the emergence of the modern pharmaceutical industry. It no longer simply mixed and mass-produced over-the-counter remedies but engaged in expensive, cutting-edge scientific research. Such innovation resulted in the ability to cure or manage tuberculosis (TB), pneumonia, malaria, and other diseases. The postwar explosion of drug and medical treatments formed the basis of what has been called the **therapeutic revolution**.

The production of these new drugs was part of large breakthroughs in the field of industrial chemistry that had developed significantly from the shortage of natural rubber supplies during the war. The military's need for artificially created, or synthetic, rubber opened the door to a wave of chemically fabricated materials that produced substitutes for metal, wood, paper, and almost every other type of commonly used industrial material. Neoprene, for example, substituted for rubber, nylon for silk, and Plexiglas for natural glass.

therapeutic revolution Explosion of new drug research and treatments that produced cures for polio, whooping cough, diphtheria, and other devastating illnesses.

Green Revolution Major increase in food production, most noticeably in poor countries, as the result of the application of agricultural and chemical research in the 1950s to produce high-yield grains.

A leading postwar scientist was the African American chemist Percy Julian, whose research with soybeans paved the way for water-based (latex) paint, linoleum, plywood glue, and other products that would become household staples. His work with artificial sex hormones (namely progesterone, testosterone, and cortisone) created breakthroughs in the field of steroid medicine that garnered him both scientific fame and material fortune. The revolution in industrial chemicals also had agricultural applications with the development of more effective fertilizers and pesticides that expanded the world's food supply, contributing to the **Green Revolution** that dramatically increased the production of staple crops such as wheat, corn, and rice.

23-1c Consumer Revolution

Consumers and the expansion of mass consumption undergird sustained economic growth.

The most important factor for America's postwar prosperity was the rapid and sustained growth of consumer spending. The combination of high household savings, renewed availability of consumer products, and pent-up demand for these goods after doing without them during the Depression and the war fueled the dramatic rise in consumption. The federal government, which had urged citizens to save money during the war, encouraged them to spend to stimulate the economy. Walt Disney animators supported government efforts. Although Mickey Mouse had symbolized the nation's fighting spirit, a cartoon character named Scrooge McDuck, introduced in 1947, embodied the noble pursuit of wealth and its consumer rewards.

The demand for automobiles, radios, washing machines, and other household goods boomed after the war. But real estate proved the most important single force for postwar recovery. Given the nation's severe housing shortage, William Levitt, a builder of barracks and war workers' housing, innovated home construction by abandoning the standard practice of constructing houses one at a time. Instead, he proved that it was more efficient and profitable to mass-produce an entire community or tract of homes. Between 1947 and 1951, Levitt and Sons transformed four thousand acres of farmland on New York's Long Island into a planned community of curved streets and 17,450 look-alike homes. Furthermore, the developer racially segregated **Levittown**, another selling point for whites disgruntled with the increasing presence of racial minorities in the central city. Levittown's success paved the way for a revolution in U.S. home ownership because real estate developers across the country joined the tract housing revolution. By 1960, one of every four homes standing in the United States had been built in the 1950s. As a result of the affordability and supply of new houses, 62 percent of white Americans were home owners in 1960, compared to 44 percent in 1940—the largest increase recorded in the nation's history. This is when home ownership became an essential element of the American Dream.

The federal government contributed to the home owner revolution by providing a home loan benefit to World War II veterans in the G.I. Bill passed in 1944. Congress extended this benefit to Korean War veterans in 1952. The G.I. Bill included low-cost home and business loans, three years of free college tuition or vocational training with paid living expenses, lifetime medical coverage, and preferential treatment when applying for federal government jobs. The $14.5 billion spent on veterans' benefits during the G.I. Bill's first decade was part of the federal government's commitment to boost consumption by expanding access to credit, a process initiated by automobile loans during the 1920s. The federal government through the Veterans Administration (VA) provided home loans to one-fifth of the nation's single-family households between 1945 and 1966, half of whom lived in California and other states in the fast-growing Southwest. These VA loans coincided with Federal Housing Administration (FHA) programs designed to transform the private home loan industry from an exclusive boutique for the well-to-do to a supermarket for common folk. The FHA democratized credit in three ways: It encouraged private banks to lend money to middle- and low-income applicants by ensuring that the government would pay defaulted loans. It also made the cost of home loans more affordable by lowering the minimum required down payment from 30 to less than 10 percent of the house price ($50,000 savings on a typical house today) and by increasing the payment period from ten to thirty years ($15,000 savings per year on a typical house today). Together, the FHA and VA provided crucial access to credit enabling the huge expansion of home ownership in the United States.

Levittown First mass-produced residential community featuring quickly produced and affordable tract housing.

The G.I. Bill was a milestone in the postwar expansion of the U.S. middle class. Its package of economic and educational benefits for veterans was so popular that its support programs quickly moved beyond the realm of partisan politics to become an untouchable political issue, much like Social Security today. In this way, the measure was an extension of the New Deal state. But the G.I. Bill also continued the New Deal's discrimination against women and racial minorities. Former soldiers got preference for jobs and college admission over nonveterans, most of whom were women. Married female veterans did not receive unemployment benefits and had their educational stipends reduced unless they could prove they were the main breadwinner in their household. Finally, racist policies at universities, banks, and new housing tracts like Levittown prevented a large number of veterans of color from using their G.I. Bill benefits. A black veteran in Corpus Christi, Texas, noted that "all the districts that we [Negro veterans] may choose to live have been ruled out" and in this situation, "NO NEGRO VETERAN is eligible for a loan."

23-2

Cold War Economic Growth

The construction in 1965 of the Vehicle Assembly Building at NASA's Kennedy Space Center was a major achievement in U.S. space exploration. This building, the tallest in Florida at the time, was used to assemble and launch rockets into space.

Why would the United States invest in space flight technology during the Cold War? ▶

Steven Siceloff/NASA

Taft-Hartley Act Also known as the *Labor Management Relations Act*, Republican-sponsored legislation that limited the rights of labor unions and discriminated against Communists and other radicals.

right to work laws State measures that prevented organized labor from requiring workers to join a union, which would have increased unions' power against management.

In the late 1940s, no one could have imagined that postwar prosperity would continue for two decades, the longest period of high-level economic growth in U.S. history. During this extended prosperity, the United States for the first time became a largely middle-class nation, propelled by billions of dollars of Cold War defense-related spending. The federal government cooperated closely with big industrialists as if the country were in a permanent state of war. The Cold War economy contributed to the development of information and service industries that became increasingly important even as industrial manufacturing remained a vital economic sector. At the same time, U.S. businesses faced little competition from foreign competitors in Europe and Japan who were preoccupied with postwar recovery. The United States dominated global markets.

☞ As you read, pay attention to how and why the U.S. economy continued to grow and information and service industries continued to rise. How did Cold War developments further these economic trends?

23-2a Politics and the Middle-Class Nation

Truman sustains labor rights, welfare legislation, and the New Deal coalition.

U.S. politics after World War II embarked on a new type of business–government cooperation rooted in the goals of sustaining economic growth and individual social mobility. To meet these ends, the Employment Act of 1946, a compromise measure between Democrats and Republicans, established the federal government as the nation's main vehicle for economic planning including stabilizing inflation and unemployment. Postwar politics also embodied the assumption that private industry—not only government—could be relied on to take care of the working classes in a reprise of welfare capitalism from the 1920s.

Nowhere was the idea of corporate caretaking more evident than in the Labor Management Relations Act approved in June 1947. Better known as the **Taft-Hartley Act**, this legislation rolled back important gains that unions had made since the 1930s and encouraged the widespread fear that Communists had hijacked the labor movement. This legislation allowed states to pass **right to work laws** outlawing the closed shop that required workers to join the local union. In response to the national railway strike in 1946, the act also empowered the president to prohibit strikes deemed against the national interest and to order strikers back to work during labor negotiations. Reflecting Cold War fears, Taft-Hartley excluded Communist-led unions, largely the Congress of Industrial Organizations (CIO), from National Labor Relations Board protections and required union officials to sign affidavits forswearing allegiance to the Communist Party or another "subversive" group. Although the unions vigorously opposed Taft-Hartley as a "slave labor bill," leading labor organizations such as the American Federation of Labor (AFL) accepted the exclusion of Communist unions and jettisoned grand visions of workers' authority over management in order to survive, and even thrive, during the Cold War. The AFL and the now non-Communist CIO merged in 1955 as labor unions centralized and became legitimate power brokers in U.S. politics. As such, they were able to raise the level of real wages more in one postwar decade than during the previous half century. The strength of organized labor in the United States, however, paled in comparison to some other developed countries (see Figure 23.2).

Like mainstream labor unions, Truman was more interested in sustaining prosperity than in elevating worker authority over management. To him, economic growth was necessary in order for the government to expand social support programs. This thinking opened the doors of his administration to conservative, probusiness groups such as the National Association of Manufactures (NAM). Another pressure on Truman was the resurgence of the Republican Party. Taft-Hartley never would have passed if the Republicans had not reclaimed both houses of Congress in the 1946 midterm elections, the first time they had been in power since the Hoover administration. The act's major sponsor, Senator Robert Taft, was an outspoken critic of the New Deal and subsequent social programs.

Figure 23.2 Percentage of Worldwide Union Membership for Wage and Salary Workers, 1960 U.S. labor union membership increased significantly from the Depression to the postwar era and commanded about the same percentage of workers as many other developed countries. However, it did not match the number of unions in the United Kingdom, Australia, Norway, and other nations where unionized workers represented between 40 to 60 percent of the workforce. ▲ Source: Visser, Jelle. Data Base on Institutional Characteristics of Trade Unions, Wage Setting, State Intervention and Social Pacts, 1960–2011 (ICTWSS), vers 4.0. April 2013.

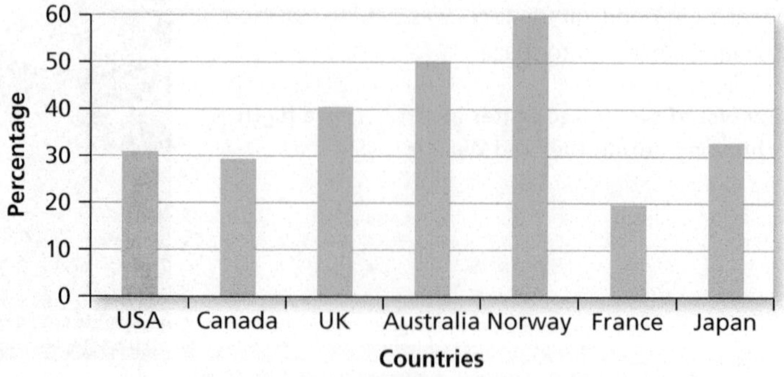

The LIFE Picture Collection/Getty Images

Walter Reuther Testifies at Senate Committee Hearing, 1958 A left-wing labor organizer during the 1930s, Reuther, as head of the United Automobile Workers, proved instrumental after World War II in removing Communists from the CIO. He became the first president of the merged AFL-CIO in 1955. ◄

Son of President William Howard Taft, the Ohio senator led the Republican revival asserting, "We have got to break with the corrupting idea that we can legislate prosperity, legislate equality, legislate opportunity."

But as much as Taft and the Republicans sought to eradicate the New Deal, they simply could not. Instead of dismantling it, they had to settle for shifting the burden of social welfare from government to private businesses. The dramatic presidential race in 1948 in which Truman stumbled but ultimately defeated the Republican candidate Thomas Dewey indicated that whereas Republicans had gained political clout in the postwar era, the New Deal state was there to stay. In the end, the coalition of Democratic voters who had backed FDR stayed with Truman and in the election virtually ignored the more radical platform of longtime New Dealer Henry Wallace who ran on the Progressive Party ticket and the segregationist campaign of southerner Strom Thurmond.

23-2b Education and Defense Spending

The federal government responds to the Cold War by fueling explosive growth in higher education and defense industries.

While commercial innovation and consumer demand continued to fuel prosperity, massive Cold War defense spending also sustained the nation's economic growth. It was no coincidence that the long and unprecedented period of economic growth in the United States corresponded to an equally long and unprecedented period of war production. Following a sharp decline after V-J Day, the nation's defense budget spiked during the Korean War and afterward remained unusually high for peacetime. The bulk of money went to private corporations engaged in military research and development. Consequently, **defense-contracting firms** swelled with profit and power as their business interests became intertwined with winning the Cold War. Although extensive public–private collaboration had occurred during both world wars, it did not become a permanent feature of politics in Washington, D.C., until after World War II. At that time, a triumvirate among military officials, Congress, and large defense firms emerged—which Eisenhower had dubbed the *military-industrial complex*.

American universities benefited tremendously from the prolonged military buildup. During its peak usage in 1947, the G.I. Bill funded half of the nation's 2 million college students. In 1930, less than 8 percent of college-age people were enrolled in higher education, whereas in 1965, the figure had more than tripled to nearly 30 percent (see Figure 23.3). The Soviet launch of Sputnik in 1957 pushed the federal government to expand its support for higher education. **The National Defense Education Act**, approved in September 1958, established programs for low-interest student loans (later known by the name *Perkins*) and direct assistance for instruction in the sciences, mathematics, foreign languages (especially but not limited to Russian), and other areas that could benefit national security. At the same time, the government increased research funding through federal agencies such as the National Science Foundation (NSF), the Atomic Energy Commission (AEC), the Office of Naval Research (ONR), and the National Institutes of Health (NIH). The budgets of many universities in the United States came to rely on these agencies. Starting in 1945, 80 percent of all federally funded industrial research involved military applications. When the

defense-contracting firms Private businesses, usually large corporations, whose primary customer is the Department of Defense or other military-related parts of the federal government.

The National Defense Education Act Legislation that dramatically increased the federal government's financial assistance and commitment to making higher education affordable.

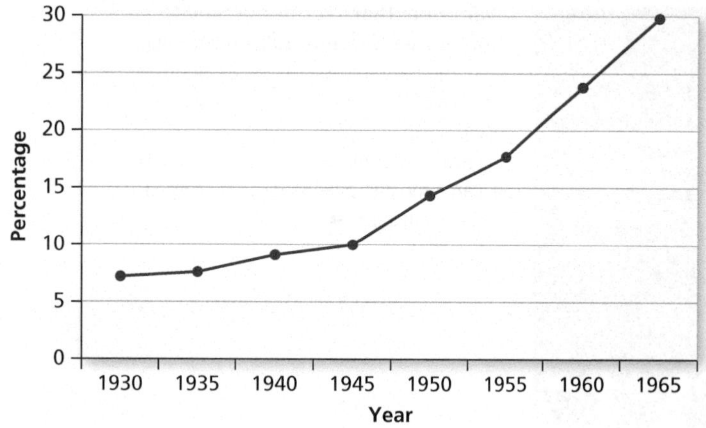

Figure 23.3 Percent of Americans Ages Eighteen to Twenty-Four Enrolled in Higher Education by Year, from 1930–1965 To increase production, expand the nation's middle class, and win the Cold War with new high-tech weaponry, the U.S. expanded its commitment to higher education. It offered research funds to colleges and universities and grants and loans to students. The result was explosive growth in the nation's colleges and universities that allowed more Americans than ever to take advantage of higher education. ◀

Source: Snyder, Thomas D., ed. *120 Years of American Education: A Statistical Portrait.* Washington, DC: National Center of Education Statistics, U.S. Department of Education, January 1993.

Korean War erupted in 1950, there were fifteen thousand of these military research projects. A decade later, the number had increase more than five times to eighty thousand.

23-2c United States and the World Market

U.S. businesses take advantage of favorable international circumstances to dominate global manufacturing and trade.

The United States was the only industrial powerhouse left standing after World War II. Europeans and the Japanese relied on massive U.S. funds and U.S. manufacturers to rebuild their economies, which took about a decade to complete. One sign that the global economy was ready to take off again was the creation in March 1957 of the **European Economic Community (EEC or common market)**, to promote ease of investment and trade among six western European nations including West Germany and France. A series of **General Agreement on Tariffs and Trade (GATT)** rounds followed the creation of the EEC to ease trade barriers around the world, not just in Europe. Another sign that the global economy had recovered was that by December 1958, most European currencies had returned to convertibility, meaning they were freely bought and sold on the world market. The combination of trade agreements and unrestricted currency exchange marked the full-fledged functioning of the Bretton Woods system.

European Economic Community (EEC or common market) Agreement among European nations to form an economic alliance that would prevent the protectionist policies that had contributed to the Great Depression and would enable European businesses to better compete with large nations such as the United States.

General Agreement on Tariffs and Trade (GATT) International accord resulting from UN negotiations to lower tariffs and boost trade around the world.

U.S. corporations were poised to take full advantage of new global opportunities given their technological advantages, managerial efficiencies, and high worker productivity. The world demand for U.S. products from sewing machines to automobiles to soft drinks was so great that the United States enjoyed a highly favorable balance of trade for more than two decades after World War II. In the mid-1950s, the United States, a nation consisting of 6 percent of the world population, produced 50 percent of the world's manufactured goods, including 75 percent of automobiles, 60 percent of telephones, and 30 percent of radios and televisions. At the same time, the emergence of the common market encouraged Americans to set up overseas offices and manufacturing plants to reap the benefits of doing business within the walls of this economic pact. The number of U.S.-based multinational corporations dramatically increased as direct investment in Europe became more important than capturing a global market share.

The influx of U.S. businesses and products generated mixed reactions abroad. For the first time, Europeans embraced mass consumption in clamoring for U.S. fashions such as blue jeans and leather jackets, tastes such as Coca-Cola, and household appliances such as washing machines. After a 1960 visit to Stockholm, Sweden, African American writer James Baldwin noted that he had seen ubiquitous posters of a movie idol from the United States seated on a motorcycle accompanied by a "masochistic girlfriend." At the same time, critics in Europe warned about the shallowness of U.S. culture and consumerism and the threat that U.S. economic power posed to traditional European businesses, products, and lifestyles. Protests in 1949 by beverage companies and the Communist Party in France pushed the government to ban Coca-Cola in part because it was said to be addictive and rot children's teeth. The beverage was also seen as a threat to the local wine industry. Although Coke prevailed, in no small part because of U.S. State Department influence to keep France's market opened to Americans, European businesses learned to adapt to the new consumer market, enabling them to better compete with Coke and other U.S. goods.

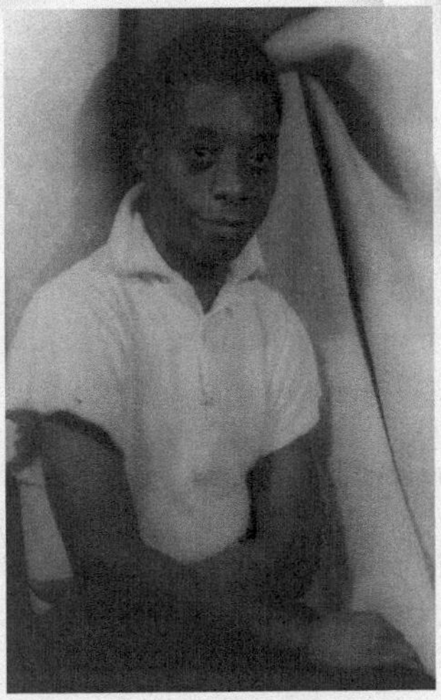

Library of Congress Prints and Photographs Division[LC-USZ62-42481]

Global Americans After emerging as a promising young African American writer, **James Baldwin** moved in 1948 to France, where his writing flourished in a cultural atmosphere far removed from the conformity, racism, and homophobia of Cold War America. "Once I found myself on the other side of the ocean," Baldwin told *The New York Times*, "I could see where I came from very clearly, and I could see that I carried myself, which is my home, with me. You can never escape that. I am the grandson of a slave, and I am a writer. I must deal with both." Among American expatriates in Paris, he was free to explore the ghosts of his own African American past and to reveal himself as a gay man. His published literary criticism and his first novel, *Go Tell It on the Mountain* (1953), established Baldwin as a major literary talent, innovator of gay fiction, and keen observer of U.S. race relations. Largely autobiographical, the book centers on the struggles of a young black man who comes to challenge his stepfather's dictatorial authority and in the process explores his own budding sexuality. Baldwin's expatriation to Europe reveals the obstacles faced by racial and sexual minorities in the United States. He returned to the United States in 1957 and became a participant and shrewd observer of the nation's struggles over civil rights and racial equality.

23-3

Social and Cultural Trends

AP Images

This photograph taken on July 17, 1955, provides an aerial view of the entrance to Disneyland flanked by a massive parking lot. The theme park was erected close to a major interstate freeway to provide access for automobiles. Building Disneyland required removing groves of orange trees, the remainder of which can be seen beyond the park, in the photograph's upper right corner.

Why was freeway access and automobile parking considered important to the success of Disneyland? How did Disneyland compare to Dodger Stadium in these ways? ▶

Go to MindTap® to practice history with the Chapter 23 **Primary Source Writing Activity: Changes in Work, Society, and Culture.** Read and view primary sources and respond to a writing prompt.

Prosperity and the upturn of the Cold War economy resulted in major changes in the nature of work, society, and culture. The United States witnessed a rapid increase in professional careers and white-collar jobs in office and service work. The historic expansion of white-collar jobs coincided with the greatest movement of Americans across city and state lines in U.S. history. Like the Brooklyn Dodgers, people and businesses left cities in the nation's historic urban centers and migrated either to nearby suburbs or across country to newly developed areas in the South and West that had largely been designed for middle-class white Americans. The migrants were seeking cheaper, safer, less crowded, and often more racially homogeneous places where a modern, automobile-based society that was heralded as a welcome step beyond the traditional city emerged. The suburban ideal begun in the United States at this time was celebrated in the new medium of television as well as in other forms of popular entertainment and leisure culture such as Disneyland. The movement to the suburbs also influenced a revival among the major religions in the United States as centers of worship provided important sources of community that reflected the overall interest in wholesome, middle-class values throughout the postwar era.

☞ As you read, pay attention to the increase in white-collar work and suburban communities. What factors caused this growth? How did both of these trends influence new forms of consumption, developments in entertainment, leisure culture, and religious life? How did they perpetuate and create new forms of racial inequality?

23-3a White-Collar Work

New economic conditions stimulate expansion of office and professional employment.

The two postwar decades continued a fundamental shift in the nation's economy beginning in the 1920s with a steep rise in the **information and service economy** that contained a wide range of white-collar jobs from secretaries to engineers to high-level managers. Federal and state governments played a key role in furthering this economic transformation. Blue-collar industrial jobs in the United States began to lose ground to clerical, intellectual, and managerial work in corporations and fast-expanding government bureaucracies. A white-collar society emerged fully blown by 1970 when nearly half of all U.S. jobs were in this category (a growth of more than 65 percent since 1930), whereas blue-collar jobs constituted 37 percent (a slight decline from 40 percent in 1930). The most striking decline was in the agricultural sector, falling from more than 21 percent of jobs in 1930 to just over 3 percent in 1970.

information and service economy The result of a shift from an industrialized economy based in manufacturing to one based in information technology and services.

pink ghettos Environment that offered low-paying office work limited to women.

Whereas before World War II most American men hoped to obtain a secure factory job, after the war, they set their sights on white-collar work. Instead of performing manual labor in factories, millions of men earned college degrees and became mid-level managers in corporations and government bureaucracies. The predominance of managerial work required them to pay attention to the supposed "feminine" virtues of appearance, manners, communication skills, and social graces. Women, in turn, became more "manly" by leaving the home and filling positions at the bottom of the corporate ladder. Just as during World War II, labor shortages and restricted immigration created a huge demand for both single and married women in the workplace. The result was the growing trend of middle-class mothers who engaged in part-time work, usually in low-paid work in the growing **pink ghettos** of office labor. Yet being in the working world gave women an independence from the home that went beyond their domestic role.

Joseph Scherschel//Time Life Pictures/Getty Images

Pan Am Stewardesses Pan American World Airways was the first airline to replace male stewards with beautiful stewardesses to attract customers in the increasingly competitive commercial airline industry. Pan Am provided women with corporate prestige and a rare opportunity to see the world. However, many stewardesses also experienced sex and racial discrimination, harassment, and exploitation. ▲

23-3b Migration, Population Shifts, and New Highways

Extensive highway construction promotes migration to the West and South.

In the two decades after World War II, a major demographic shift occurred. The nation's population dispersed from the Northeast and Midwest to the South and West (see Map 23.1). A look at the nation's one hundred largest cities in 1940 and 1960 reveals the rapid population growth in California and Texas especially. During this period, Los Angeles moved from being the fifth largest U.S. city to the third, and San Diego jumped from the forty-third to eighteenth. Houston broke into the top ten, and Dallas moved from thirty-first to fourteenth. Phoenix, Arizona, which was not counted in 1940, leaped to twenty-ninth. As the population shifted to the South and West, so too did Major League baseball teams such as the Dodgers. Before 1950, there were no teams west of St. Louis or south of Washington, D.C.; by 1965, there were six (and in 2008, there would be fourteen).

The shift to the warm climates of the **Sunbelt** corridor stretching from California to Florida had much to do with the widespread use of central air conditioning in business and home construction starting in the 1950s. But if technology made it comfortable to live and work in the Sunbelt, the federal government provided the infrastructure for moving there by constructing a comprehensive national highway system. Franklin Roosevelt had sought to create such a system in the 1930s to spur the Depression-era economy, and Congress had passed a number of highway proposals in the late 1940s and early 1950s. But it took Eisenhower's leadership and concerns about troop movements and evacuations of cities in the event of a nuclear attack to pass the **Interstate Highway Act** in June 1956. Hailed as one of the greatest public works projects in U.S. history, this act allocated $31 billion also to improve the safety and efficiency of automobile travel. The system linked all cities with a population of more than fifty

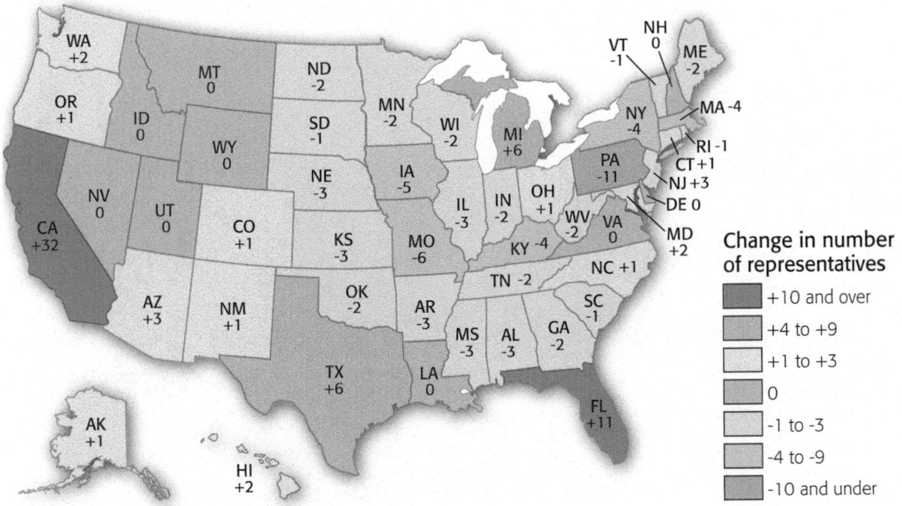

Map 23.1 House of Representatives Reapportionment, 1920–1970 The number of seats apportioned to each state in the House of Representatives represents the sweeping shift of the U.S. population from the Northeast and Midwest to the South and West. The share of seats in the West more than doubled whereas the slight decline in the South did not reflect the growth in Florida, which more than tripled. The Northeast and Midwest experienced the sharpest declines. ▲

thousand in a network of "interstate and defense" highways that stretched for more than forty-two hundred miles (see Map 23.2). These highways enabled the trucking industry to surpass railroads as the nation's predominant means for hauling goods, and businesses catering to the needs to domestic travelers flourished. Consequently, the United States led the world in automobile ownership. In 1960, Los Angeles County alone had more cars than in all of South America or Asia.

23-3c Growth of Suburbs

The Cold War economy and highway system enable suburban communities to flourish.

The Highway Act also was a boon to **suburbanization** because freeway construction between cities and suburbs constituted the bulk of its total expenditures. The suburban population swelled as millions of Americans fled central cities and businesses followed them to take advantage of lower taxes, cheaper land, and a skilled and educated workforce that resulted from the white middle classes that had left the central cities. Between 1947 and 1960, the number of suburbanites increased 100 percent, and by 1960, one-third of the nation's population was living in suburbia (see Figure 23.4). Ten years later, the number of suburban dwellers would surpass those living in the central city. Consequently, the nation's population fanned out over huge conglomerations of urban and suburban areas that linked large parts of the nation into an endless series of **strip cities**. The U.S. census counted thirteen of these areas in 1960, including the corridors connecting San Francisco with San Diego, linking Boston, New York, and Washington, D.C., and joining Dallas, Fort Worth, San Antonio, and Houston.

The federal government further accelerated internal migration and suburbanization through Cold War militarization. The major share of defense spending went to California and Texas, but every western state benefited disproportionately including Alaska and Hawai'i, both of which joined the union in 1959. One study estimated that more than half of California's economic growth from 1947 to 1957 was due to the defense industry and that without this support, its migration would have been cut in half. Cold War funds created a synergy between military bases and defense contracting firms that boosted suburban growth. For example, military air stations in California's Orange County attracted a host of defense contractors that, in turn, produced astronomical suburban growth for twenty years starting in 1950: Fullerton's population rose fivefold, from 13,958 to 85,826, and its neighbor Anaheim (home to Disneyland) grew more than ten times, from 14,556 to 166,701. In 1960, two of every three manufacturing jobs in Orange County were tied to military contracts. This same pattern of military-driven economic and suburban development occurred in the San Francisco Bay Area

Sunbelt Area with warm climate in southern and western regions of the United States that had large population growth and economic development in the second half of the twentieth century.

Interstate Highway Act Legislation that dramatically expanded the system of highways in the United States.

suburbanization Process in which population shifts from central cities to nearby suburbs, that are connected by highways.

strip cities Combinations of urban and suburban communities that form a large, continuous mass of development.

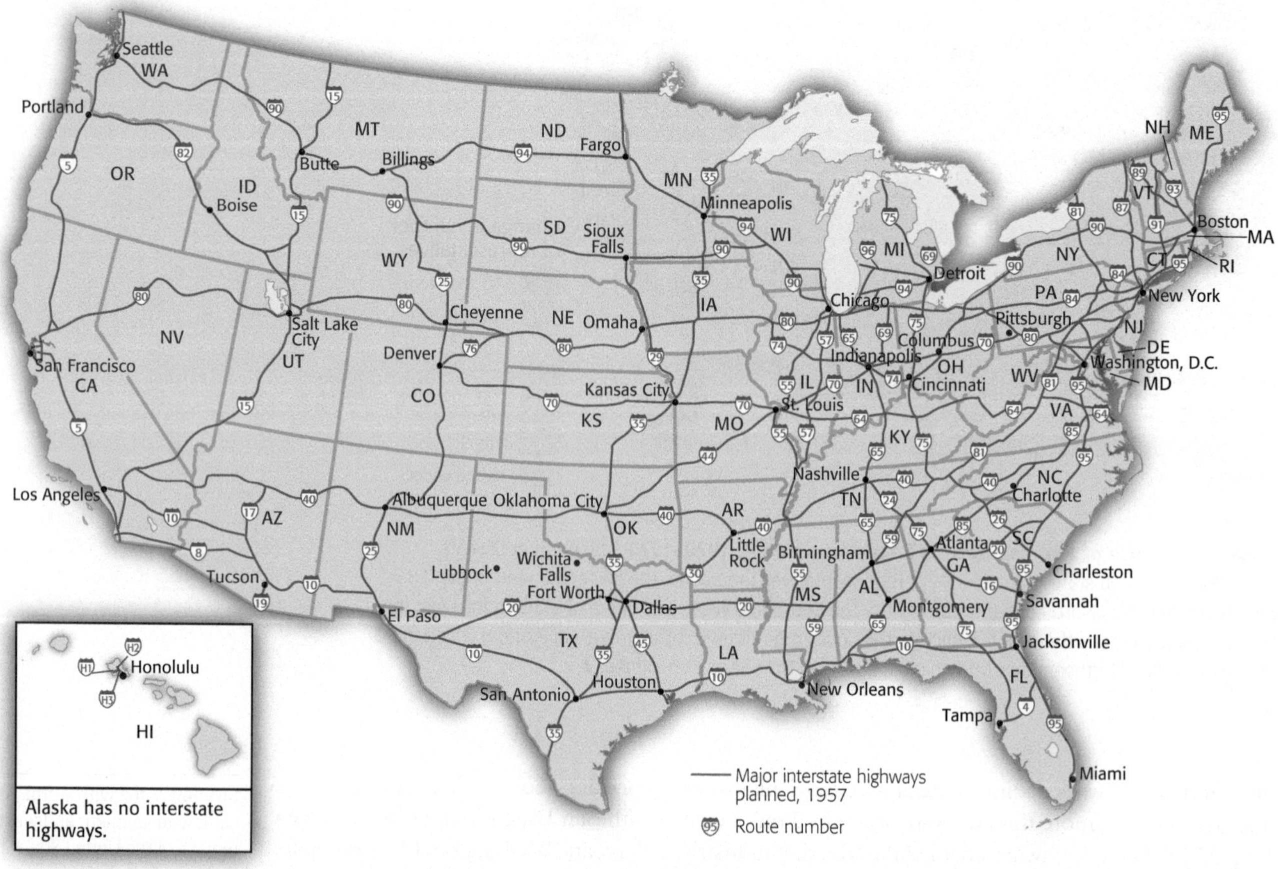

Map 23.2 Major Interstate Highways Planned, 1957 Designed in part for defense reasons under Eisenhower, this highway plan greatly expanded the ability for sales agents, truck drivers, suburban commuters, and tourists to get where they needed to go without using railroads or public transportation. The red, white, and blue numbered signs marking interstate highways came to stand for the world's most modern and extensive highway infrastructure. ▲

triple melting pot Fusion among the nation's three great religious faiths.

with Moffitt Field; in Tucson, Arizona, with the Davis-Monthan Air Force base as the hub; and in Colorado Springs with the combination of Fort Carson Air Force Base, the Air Force Academy, and North American Aerospace Defense Command (NORAD) headquarters.

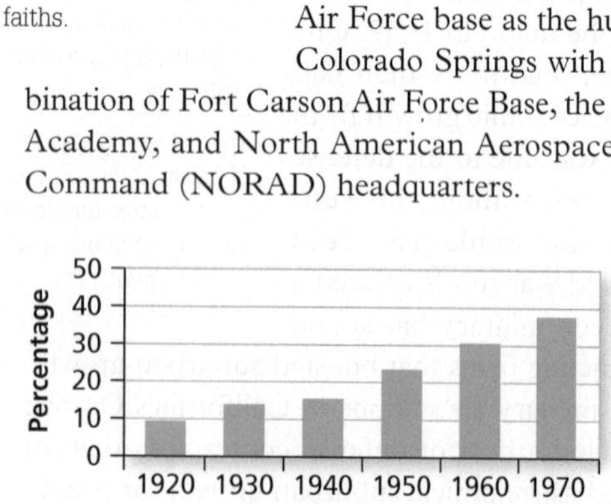

Figure 23.4 Suburban Population, 1920–1970 Highway expansion and the movement of industries and other businesses to the suburbs enabled the dramatic rise in suburban dwellers who often migrated from central cities. ▲ Source: Decennial Census of Population, 1920–1970. Washington, DC: U.S. Census Bureau, 1920–1970.

23-3d Suburbia, Central Cities, and Segregation

Suburbs accept ethnic, cultural, and religious differences but contribute to racial segregation.

Many ethnic and cultural strains from the great influx of European immigrants during the late nineteenth and early twentieth centuries had come together in a middle-class melting pot. Suburbanization also induced assimilation as revealed by the breakdown of once forbidding religious barriers. After World War II, adherents of the nation's three largest religions, Protestantism, Catholicism, and Judaism, were increasingly intermarrying in what one scholar called the **triple melting pot**. Despite continuing religious bigotry, there was a growing and historic level of tolerance among these faiths. Catholics reached a new level of mainstream acceptance with John F. Kennedy's presidency, and Jews achieved something similar through the nation's support for Israel. Protestant evangelicals achieved the same kind of recognition through the rising celebrity of Billy Graham, the radio preacher who became a welcomed guest in the White House for every president beginning with Harry Truman.

An overall surge in the nation's religious attendance resulted to some extent from the mainstreaming of Catholicism, Judaism, and Protestantism. Although 43 percent of Americans had attended a place of worship before World War II, nearly 70 percent did so by the late 1950s. Compared to the economic hard times during the Great Depression, the prosperity of the postwar era boosted the size of congregations, leading to the construction of a historic number of churches, temples, and other religious institutions across the country. Most of this new construction was in suburbs, where religion was stripped of its connection to "old-world" traditions and infused with the sensibilities of middle-class American life. Suburban religious institutions became important centers of community formation for people uprooted from family and ethnic ties.

Meanwhile, the central cities increasingly were composed of racial minorities as whites fled to suburbs that, like Levittown, made racial segregation a major part of their appeal. The use of nefarious tactics, such as charging higher housing costs, discouraged racial minorities from moving into the suburbs. Most damaging to racial minorities, including those seeking to use G.I. Bill benefits, was the practice of **redlining**, which became another way to perpetuate racial segregation. Using this practice, banks drew a red line around minority neighborhoods identified on city maps to designate places where they would not offer home or business loans, ostensibly because of the financial risk involved. Such practices did not technically discriminate on the basis of race but limited equal opportunities to much-needed credit for African Americans and other racial minorities.

23-3e Suburban Culture and the Rise of Television

New forms of leisure and entertainment emerge that maintain old notions about race.

The growth of suburban communities generated new ways of living such as the "drive-in" society that developed with the extensive use of the automobile. In August 1952, the owners of Holiday Inn opened the first of many clean, inexpensive, and respectable motels convenient to highways. Theater chains catered to this new culture by creating drive-in theaters where customers remained in their automobiles, attached a speaker to their car window, and watched movies on a towering outdoor screen. The proliferation of "fast-food" restaurants was another characteristic of suburbia. The iconic story here concerned two brothers, Maurice and Richard McDonald, who in 1948 sought to perfect the fast and efficient assembly of hamburgers in their southern California restaurant. Their business model took off under the control of Ray, Kroc who obtained the rights to establish McDonalds franchises across the country from the brothers. In 1955, Kroc opened the first of these restaurants in Des Plaines, Illinois, and by 1965, he had bought out the McDonald brothers and built their brand into the nation's leading fast-food chain, which was listed on the New York Stock Exchange. Although the McDonald brothers had been uncertain whether fast-food would catch on with the American public, Kroc knew that it fit well with the changing lifestyles and tastes generated in the suburbs.

Disneyland, the famously successful amusement park that opened in July 1955 in southern California, also embodied the growing significance of suburban culture. Built in the suburb of Anaheim, Disneyland also celebrated lifestyles built around the automobile. To the park's visionary Walt Disney, automobiles were a marvel of modern transportation that made it possible to live a more peaceful life in the suburbs outside of crowded, dirty, and hostile cities. This explains why Disneyland's Autopia, the park's major ride featuring automobiles, could be found in the futuristic part of the park known as Tomorrowland. Beyond his faith in technology and urban planning, Disney's overall vision for the amusement park was to underscore the importance of capitalism and democracy for creating orderly, middle-class environments conducive to the animator's brand of creativity and imagination.

Walt Disney also became part of the television medium that embraced suburban middle-class culture and promised a more wholesome and efficient lifestyle. Delayed because of World War II, television technology became standardized in the late 1940s and by the 1950s, it had begun to replace radio as the nation's primary form of entertainment. Sales of television sets skyrocketed from 16,000 in 1947 to 11 million in 1959. Nearly every home had at least one set by the late fifties. Disney created a series of television programs, such as *Wonderful World of Color,* that presented wholesome entertainment reinforcing the values and attractions of his amusement park. The most popular programs were situation comedies (sitcoms) that addressed the lives of white middle-class suburbanites such as the Nelsons of *The Adventures of Ozzie and Harriet*, the Andersons of *Father Knows Best*, and the Cleavers of *Leave It to Beaver*. The most successful sitcom was ***I Love Lucy***, starring Lucille Ball and Desi Arnez. Married in real life, they played a middle-class housewife and Cuban band leader who lived in a New York City apartment, slept in separate beds, and eventually moved to a bucolic suburban home. A January 1953 episode in which Lucy had a baby drew 44 million viewers, twice the number that had watched President Eisenhower's inauguration that same month.

Although racial minorities were scarce on television, *Amos 'n' Andy*, a popular radio show featuring heavily

redlining Practice of designating areas of the city (usually racial minority areas) where banks would not provide home and business loans.

I Love Lucy Popular television comedy that revealed and enacted middle-class lifestyles and gender roles in the middle of the twentieth century.

stereotyped African American characters, made the transition to television in 1951, revealing the connection of early sitcoms to black-faced minstrelsy. Even though *Amos 'n' Andy* showcased an all-black cast, its reputation prompted African American protests leading to its prime-time cancellation, but this did not halt its syndication. Reruns aired on twice as many television stations in 1954. The show's boycott, ironically, also made television producers and sponsors wary of hiring black actors until the mid-1960s.

23-4 Family-Centered Culture in an Uncertain World

NBC Television/Courtesy of Getty Images

This photograph of the cast of *Father Knows Best*, a popular television comedy series from 1954 to 1967, epitomizes the wholesome entertainment that celebrated modern, white middle-class families amid Cold War fears. Despite the show's title, the wife and children typically undermined the father's traditional male authority.

How does the photo represent the typical American family in terms of race and gender roles? How does their clothing reinforce gender and cultural norms? ▶

The rise of the Cold War economy produced new forms of family-centered culture. More than at any time in the twentieth century, Americans celebrated the institution of family, not merely as an economic unit but as source of ultimate happiness and refuge from fears of communism and nuclear destruction. In this way, the American Dream, as expressed by Nixon in his kitchen debate with Khrushchev and by U.S. cultural propaganda spread throughout the world, came to center on the suburban home as a cure for individual, national, and global problems. Many Americans in the suburbs believed that they could achieve a modern type of family in which husbands did not dominate but shared responsibilities with their wives and parents worked together to create an educationally stimulating and psychologically fulfilling environment for their children. Although some celebrated the mutual sexual fulfillment of married couples, they condemned sex between unmarried partners and examined the diversity of human sexual behavior.

As you read, note changes in the American family after World War II. How did these reflect new trends in gender relations and sexuality emerging at mid-century?

23-4a Baby Boom and the Nuclear Family

After World War II, the birthrate in the United States rose sharply during a twenty-year **baby boom**.

The sudden increase in the nation's birthrate generates attention to family life.

Newly married couples and those who had postponed having children during the Depression and the war, had a record number of children. By 1957, the U.S. birthrate had reached its twentieth-century highpoint of 3.7 babies per woman, double the rate from the 1930s and higher than the vast majority of high-income countries in Europe and Asia, although Canada's birthrate was slightly higher than that of the United States. Like postwar economists, demographers could not have predicted that unprecedented prosperity would change the Depression-era pattern in which Americans had postponed marriage and limited family size (see Table 23.1).

The baby boom was part of a larger cultural shift in which families were seen as the main source of happiness and fulfillment. The sudden change from Depression and wartime uncertainties to the postwar faith in unlimited economic growth encouraged Americans to seek fulfillment in marriage and large families. The availability of good-paying jobs and affordable housing after the war enabled women to marry at younger ages (the average was 20 years). These factors also enabled couples to live separately from parents and relatives, causing a decline in the number of extended family households. The independent, self-contained **nuclear family** living in a suburban home came to symbolize mid-century American culture. The immediate family, moreover, served as a sanctuary in a world riddled with Cold War anxieties about atomic destruction.

Table 23.1 Global Birthrates, 1950–1970

Although an expanding population was the normal pattern in low-income countries, Britain and most other high-income nations experienced only a slight increase in births. Canada was one of the few other industrialized nations that experienced a baby boom on par with that in the United States. In Japan, however, the rate sharply declined.

	1950–1955	1955–1960	1960–1965	1965–1970
High-income countries	3.0	3.0	3.0	2.6
Low-income countries	6.4	6.5	6.5	6.6
United States	3.3	3.7	3.4	2.6
Canada	3.7	3.9	3.7	2.6
United Kingdom	2.2	2.5	2.9	2.6
France	2.8	2.7	2.8	2.6
Soviet Union	2.9	2.8	2.6	2.0
Germany	2.1	2.3	2.5	2.4
Japan	3.0	2.2	2.0	2.0

Source: United Nations

Estimated total fertility (children per woman).

23-4b Companionate Household

> Changes in gender relations increase women's authority in the family and their domestic responsibilities.

At the center of the family culture was a more equal partnership between husbands and wives. Middle-class men who held the white-collar managerial values of cooperation and consensus carried them home, and the entrance of their wives into the permanent workforce made it increasingly difficult for them to perform their "womanly" duties. As a result, the postwar generation embraced the theory of **companionate marriage**, which, according to *Reader's Digest*, meant that the "dominating husband and submissive wife are things of the past." In the modern postwar marriage, husbands and wives shared decision making. According to a 1959 study by the U.S. Department of Labor, marketers had become aware that husbands and wives were shopping together, and, as a result, advertisers began to target men for food, household goods, and other products that had been bought primarily by women. The image of the softer, family-oriented man appeared regularly in television comedies. Shows such as *Leave It to Beaver, Father Knows Best*, and *The Adventures of Ozzie and Harriet* regularly poked fun at notion of the domineering men as king of the family. In one *Ozzie and Harriet* episode, Ozzie, the husband, grew a mustache to symbolize his manly authority. But his sons pretended to be intimidated by the mustache, and his wife Harriet cut off half the mustache while he slept because she worried that his new manliness would attract other women. In the end, Ozzie learned that maintaining a harmonious household is more important than clinging to traditional notions of masculine appearance.

The ideal of companionate marriage, however, did not mean that men and women shared an equal burden of childrearing and household duties. After all, 70 percent of all households in 1960 were nuclear families with a stay-at-home mother (this percentage varied for racial minorities). Some women, such as Congresswoman Coya Knutson, who worked outside the home confronted heavy pressure to make their husbands and children their primary focus. Knutson's political career as Minnesota's first female representative, was cut short in the 1958 congressional election by a vicious campaign in which her estranged husband accused her of neglecting her "womanly" duties as wife and mother. The publication of a letter in which her husband pleaded, "Coya, Come Home" was a large part of her loss.

Another problem for women was not necessarily being homemakers but managing homes. Postwar housewives faced new challenges related to their **domesticity**. The combination of the baby boom and the rise of the nuclear family meant that women had more children to raise with less help from grandparents and other family members who earlier might have lived in the home. Despite the promises of "labor-saving" appliances, such as washing machines, housewives also spent more time than ever doing domestic chores.

baby boom Period of significant increases in birthrates.

nuclear family Common and desirable family structure focused on immediate family members (the nucleus) of a single household, usually in the suburbs.

companionate marriage Union characterized by increased equality between husbands and wives and lesser roles for the autocratic males.

domesticity Having to do with home or family, which can include housework and child care.

The Granger Collection, New York

TV Dinner, 1954 As more married women entered the labor market during the 1950s, C. A. Swanson & Sons created the frozen dinner as a quick and easy substitute for preparing a full-course meal. The company sold 10 million of these heat-and-eat frozen foods in their first year on the market ▲.

AP Images/Horst Ossinger

Original Barbie Doll

Global Americans The most popular toy in the United States after its introduction in 1959 was **Barbie**, the first adult-looking doll mass-marketed to children. Before the Mattel Corporation created Barbie, dolls were mainly toy babies that girls took care of as mothers in training. Barbie, however, was more babe than baby. Modeled after Lilli, a sexy adult doll popular among German bachelors, she appealed to the grown-up aspirations of teenage girls interested in dating, having a career, and, above all else, shopping for clothes, accessories, and even a dream house. The original Barbie featured a pony-tail hairstyle, black and white zebra-striped bathing suit, sunglasses, and earrings. Buyers for toy stores were not interested in the doll at first, fearing that parents would look askance at her sex appeal and curvaceous body. But they were wrong, and soon enough Barbie was flying off the shelves across the country. Mattel sold three hundred fifty-one thousand dolls in the first year of production, and soon Barbie became the most popular and profitable doll ever sold in the United States. The Barbie franchise adapted with the times, introducing her boyfriend Ken in 1961 and her sister Skipper four years later. A sexy doll for girls that encouraged fantasies of not just marriage and children but career and personal growth, Barbie influenced and was influenced by the youth-centered focus of parenting and consumer culture that arose amid the postwar baby boom.

New technology had raised the bar of expectations that encouraged homemakers, like industrial managers, to seek higher levels of efficiency and productivity that meant more, not less, work. Finally, the role of women in the household expanded to providing full-time counseling services for all family members, not only caring for the family's basic needs (food, clothing, and shelter). Postwar psychologists replaced the Freudian assumption that a person's personality was set in stone in early childhood with the idea that an individual develops in stages throughout that person's entire life. For housewives, this meant facing the never-ending challenge of creating a fulfilling, educational, emotionally satisfying home environment that catered to the life stage needs for each family member.

23-4c Children of Plenty

Children and youth receive new attention and have influence in the expanded consumer society.

At no time before were Americans more optimistic about their children's future. A great deal of this optimism stemmed from medical breakthroughs that conquered devastating childhood diseases such as polio, whooping cough, and diphtheria. The first polio vaccine, developed by Jonas Salk in April 1952, was a stunning achievement because this paralyzing childhood disease had reached epidemic proportions after World War II. The future looked bright for a generation that was immune to polio. In addition, parents had growing confidence that experts such as pediatrician Benjamin Spock better understood the keys to children's emotional development than the previous generation of experts. Spock's famous child-raising manual, *The Common Sense Book of Baby and Child Care* (1946), emphasized the need for parents to listen to their children and to discipline them with flexible rather than strict rules. Armed with the latest psychological theories, American parents were excited at the prospect of creating a perfect generation of children. Given the nation's overall prosperity, baby boomers were assumed to exceed their parents' remarkable social mobility, pushing the nation to greater heights of achievement and power.

These rosy expectations coupled with prosperity fueled the development of a commercial culture centered on the health and happiness of children. Nowhere was this trend more evident than in the skyrocketing sales of toys: The $84 million spent in 1940 had increased to $1.25 billion by 1960. Popular culture, too, came to center increasingly around baby boomer consumption. The boomers were the first generation to grow up with television, and in many ways TV proved a powerful engine for youth spending. The news spread about the latest "must-have" toy from television commercials during *Howdy Doody*, the *Mickey Mouse Club*, and other popular children's shows. Print media also tapped into the youth market through the expanded production of educational books, such as Dr. Seuss's *Cat in the Hat* series, and periodicals, including the irreverent and satirical *Mad Magazine*.

The creation of a thriving youth market meant that marketers had a vested interest in accelerating the maturity of young consumers. The suburban context also encouraged youth to grow up faster by placing them in adult situations much earlier in life. A community of single-family homes provided youth with more privacy than had living with one's relatives in homes and central city apartments in previous generations. The proliferation of automobiles gave young people more chances to get away from adult authority. As a result of their newfound independence, the baby boomers pushed beyond the traditional boundaries of youth, generating national conversations about problems of juvenile delinquency, gang fighting, drag racing, violent comic books, and teenage sex.

In the 1950s, Hollywood glamorized anxieties about the nation's youth through the emergence of teen-oriented cinema such as *The Wild Ones* (1953), *Teenage Rebel* (1956), *Untamed Youth* (1957), *Reform School Girl* (1957), and *Riot in Juvenile Prison* (1959). The most legendary film was *Rebel without a Cause*, starring the young, enigmatic actor James Dean. The 1955 film featured three white, suburban middle-class teenagers who "tick . . . like a bomb" because of childhoods riddled with misunderstanding, loneliness, parental abandonment, overprotection, and divorce. In the film, Dean's character survives a "manly" car race that kills his high school rival. But tragically and ironically, Dean died in real life while speeding his roadster on a California highway before the movie made him an international symbol of youth rebellion.

The media that became most closely tied to youth culture was commercial radio. The hottest genre of popular music, **rock 'n' roll**, originated in the U.S. South where in the early 1950s, a critical mass of radio disc jockeys and record producers began to experiment with mixing together African American blues and gospel music with white country and folk music. One of the most celebrated of these early pioneers was Sam Phillips, owner of Sun Records in Memphis, Tennessee. An avid lover of black music, he searched for ways to share it with a broad white audience. The discovery of young Elvis Presley in 1954 gave him a golden opportunity to blend his favorite types of music. According to Phillips, Elvis "sings Negro songs with a white voice which borrows in mood and emphasis from the country style, modified by popular music." The young man jetted to popular music stardom, becoming the center of a youth craze for the combined black-white musical styles of rock 'n' roll. Elvis's appearance on the Ed Sullivan Show in 1956 became the most watched moment in TV history up to that time. The performer's bodily gyrations earned him the nickname Elvis "the pelvis," and his brazen sexuality stirred protests against the "devil's music." Alarmed by Elvis's pelvic thrusts, network censors permitted the Ed Sullivan Show to film the singer only from the waist-up.

Although Elvis almost never performed outside North America, his music spread around the world. Most famously, four youths in Liverpool, United Kingdom, grew up idolizing the king of rock 'n' roll, one of them (John Lennon) stating, "Before Elvis, there was nothing." In August 1965, on their second U.S. tour as the Beatles rock band, they finally met their idol in his Hollywood home, which in retrospect was the passage of the old guard to a new generation of rockers fueled to a great extent by the British and other foreigners.

23-4d Beginnings of the Sexual Revolution

Men and women embrace the new freedom of sexual expression, but the results are not necessarily liberating.

A point of contention within the family-centered culture was the assertion that the United States was no longer a place for "real men." Although television characters such as Ozzie Nelson adapted to the new "feminized" nature of work and family life, cultural critics extolled the virtues of rugged individualism and resistance to authority and rejected the ideal of companionate marriage. One critic was Hugh Hefner, a midwesterner from a conservative family who began a men's magazine that cast bachelorhood, not family life, as the pinnacle of male fulfillment. Begun in December 1953, *Playboy* magazine took the daring step of featuring nude photographs of attractive women. The magazine sold out its entire first print run of 70,000 copies showcasing the Hollywood sex symbol Marilyn Monroe. According to one sociologist, the main target of Hefner's rebellion was not conservative sexuality but the institution of marriage itself. "From the beginning," she wrote, "*Playboy* loved women—large-breasted, long-legged, young women . . . —and hated wives." The magazine said that marriage for men was "the biggest mistake of their lives" because it tied them down to one woman and prevented them from exercising their sexual freedom.

The **sexual revolution** made possible the popularity of *Playboy*, diminishing social pressures to form traditional families and interrupting polite silences about human sexuality. Alfred Kinsey's *Sexual Behavior in the Human Male* (1948) paved the way for this revolution and made a believer of Hugh Hefner. In a neutral, scientific voice, Kinsey revealed that 37 percent of men in his study had experienced orgasm with another man. He also noted that 15 percent of the time, married men, reached orgasm with women other than their wives and men and through masturbation and nocturnal emissions. Kinsey's book (followed in 1953 by a companion study on American women) became one of the rare scientific studies to become a best seller.

Kinsey's nonjudgmental approach to human sexuality and separation of morality from normal behavior assisted in removing the stigmas against prolonged bachelorhood. Traditional family values viewed men who did not become husbands, fathers, and breadwinners as failures. One psychoanalyst who studied homosexuality created an equation conveying the logical connections associated with these "failed" men: *I am a failure = I am castrated = I am not a man = I am a woman = I am a homosexual.* This was a shorthand description of the heterosexual ideal that justified discrimination against women, gays and lesbians, and "feminized" men. As with *Playboy*, the Kinsey findings were a factor in the sexual revolution that undermined the traditional ideal for heterosexual men by giving them options to marriage and family life.

A major breakthrough in birth control enabled millions of women to join in the sexual revolution by freeing themselves from the connection between sex and procreation. As in

rock 'n' roll Popular American musical form emerging from the mixture of Southern country music with African American blues and gospel that would spread rapidly around the world and evolve as foreigners (especially the British) innovated new styles.

sexual revolution Rebellion having to do with human sexuality and its popular expression as normal and healthy, not sinful and immoral.

birth control pill Innovation in medical technology that enabled women to prevent pregnancy by taking a simple and effective tablet.

the early days of the birth control movement, the impetus came from social activist Margaret Sanger. By the 1940s, medical doctors were increasingly embracing her efforts to prevent women from becoming pregnant, and the law tolerated them. In 1942, Planned Parenthood, a new organization emerged to lead the U.S. birth control movement and four years later encouraged the establishment of an international organization with the same name. Sanger headed both organizations, arguing that birth control was necessary because babies were healthier when planned by the mother and conceived in love. More controversially, Sanger turned to theories of eugenics in supporting the sterilization of those with severe learning disabilities. She also prodded researchers and philanthropists to create the first **birth control pill**, which, after its approval by the Food and Drug Administration (FDA) in May 1960, soon became the most popular form of contraceptive in the United States. In the 1965 *Griswold v. Connecticut* decision, the Supreme Court upheld the legality of birth control clinics in introducing and distributing the pills and other contraceptive devices.

23-5 New Social Divisions

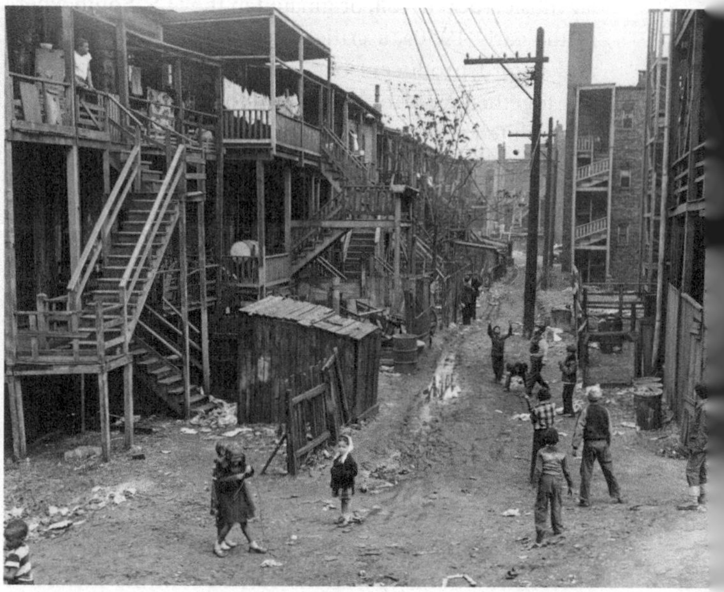

Archive Photos/Getty Images

This photograph, taken in 1951, shows children playing in a muddy Chicago alley on the city's south side. This part of the city experienced tremendous redevelopment and the closure of major factories, such as those dedicated to meatpacking, during the two decades after 1945.

How does this photograph square with the rapid expansion of wealth taking place throughout the United States? What historical factors can explain the conditions depicted in the photograph? ▶

affluence Possession of great wealth that in the 1950s some critics saw as a great weakness for the United States.

Not everyone embraced—or was embraced by—the prosperity and opportunities created by the new economy. Prominent intellectuals, artists, and youth railed against the materialism, conformity, and alienation accompanying the new suburban American dream. Meanwhile, certain industries that had been top performers in the U.S. economy before World War II were becoming obsolete as the result of overseas competition and the depletion of once abundant domestic natural resources. These collapses led to increased unemployment that hurt the most vulnerable classes of industrial workers who were left few opportunities in the Cold War economy. Most of these workers were racial minorities who during and after World War II had migrated to northern industrial cities. Their persistent unemployment became part of a cycle of poverty that generated a growing sense of urban crisis. Nor did rural communities share equally in U.S. prosperity, and labor shortages in agriculture resulted in an immigration conflict between Mexico and the United States.

☞ As you read, focus on the social and economic costs of the nation's postwar prosperity. Why did some Americans question the impact of prosperity? How and why did information and service industries disadvantage certain social groups?

23-5a Critics of Prosperity

Scholars, artists, and activists warn Americans about the downside to economic growth.

Not everyone celebrated technological progress and prosperity as unambiguous achievements. Scientists issued dire warnings about possible consequences of nuclear technology, and social scientists began to uncover problems related to economic developments. John Kenneth Galbraith, one of the nation's most respected economists, argued that the economic goal of maximum production was no longer relevant and the resulting **affluence** actually was hurting U.S. society. His best-seller *The Affluent Society* (1958) targeted the advertising industry for creating unnecessary consumer desires. To Galbraith, prosperity would be better spent on public services that improved everyone's quality of life. Other critics, such as sociological thinkers David Reisman and William H. Whyte, turned a discerning eye toward white-collar work and the suburbs. Riesman's best-selling *The Lonely Crowd: A Study of the Changing American Culture* (1950) distinguished between the self-reliant "inner-directed" personality of the nineteenth century and the conformist "other-directed" type that was characteristic of postwar Americans. Whyte's best seller, *The Organization Man* (1956), bemoaned the managerial revolution in the U.S. corporate world that had replaced the values of ambition and inventiveness with a new emphasis on teamwork, obedience, and loyalty to the firm. Conformity, to him, had replaced the self-reliance that Ralph Waldo Emerson and other nineteenth-century American philosophers had idealized.

Creative artists joined the revolt against the dispiriting influences of postwar prosperity. Some of the best-known nonconformists of the 1950s were the **Beat poets** Allen Ginsburg and Jack Kerouac who raged against materialism, pioneering what was later called "new-age" spirituality in search for deeper inspirations through Buddhism and other non-Western religions. The men stood at the forefront of a movement of young, urban, and mostly white bohemians gathering in New York City's Greenwich Village and San Francisco's North Beach neighborhoods. In its art and lifestyle, the Beat movement also absorbed "hipster" language, sexual freedom, and the drug and alcohol lifestyle of jazz culture. The stereotypical "beatnik" called men "daddy-o," women "chicks," and uttered words such as "far-out" and "groovy." Males wore untrimmed goatees, sandals, turtlenecks, and jeans, and females donned black leotards, short skirts, black eye shadow, and black tights.

Beat poets Cultural nonconformists in the 1950s who wrote poetry, gathered in urban neighborhoods, and assumed the characteristics of jazz musicians, Asian religions, and other alternative groups.

In 1959, *Life* magazine negatively characterized the Beats as unwashed, uneducated, unmotivated, and unprincipled. But the same could not be said of the white middle-class college students who revived folk music of the Great Depression era. They, too, rejected the values of the suburbs in searching for more authentic expressions of the American spirit. Young folk musicians rediscovered the protest songs of Popular Front singers such as Woody Guthrie, Huddie "Leadbelly" Leadbetter, and Pete Seeger, all of whom were closely identified with the political left. In a stark contrast to rock 'n' roll, folk music rejected commercialism, favoring the unpretentious over the faddish and the intellect over bodily passions. The launch of the Newport Folk Festival in July 1959 gave shape to the folk music revival, introducing Joan Baez, Woody Guthrie's son Arlo, and the incomparable Bob Dylan. Born Robert Zimmerman to middle-class Jewish American parents, Dylan dropped out of the University of Minnesota to learn and perform folk music. A self-declared "Woody Guthrie jukebox," he more than anyone else was able to translate

Bettmann/Corbis

Beatniks in Greenwich Village, New York City, 1959 One of the prominent forms of youth rebellion during the 1950s was the Beatnik who embraced Beat poetry that adopted idioms of jazz culture and the spirituality of Eastern religions and pushed the boundaries of sexual freedom. ◄

the protest spirit of Depression-era folk music into political anthems for the baby boom generation. By 1964, Dylan reigned as king of the international folk music movement, galvanizing a generation with the antiwar sensation "Blowing in the Wind" and the youth manifesto "The Times They Are a-Changin'."

23-5b Costs of Suburban Development

Suburban migration exacts heavy costs on urban communities.

Suburbanization and the rise of the Sunbelt carried immediate and long-term costs for central cities as corporations moved manufacturing plants to new locations, decreasing much-needed city tax revenues. U.S. automobile makers led the way as they cut high-paid union wages by downsizing and closing old factories and building new ones in states (almost always outside the central cities) that had lower-cost labor because they constrained labor union organizing through right to work laws made possible by the Taft-Hartley Act. Another problem for unions was **automation**, a process by which firms reduced labor costs by replacing workers with machines (see Chapter 19). Between 1947 and 1958, the big three automakers (General Motors, Ford, and Chrysler) built twenty-five new plants in Detroit, all of them in the suburbs. The corporations leapt at the opportunity to build larger single-story factories in the suburbs, and cost-saving labor concerns influenced decisions to downsize or close central city plants. During the same time period, Detroit lost more than one hundred twenty thousand manufacturing jobs. This especially hurt African Americans and young people who were often last hired and first fired because of their lack of seniority. Deindustrialization in the 1950s and 1960s began to affect other industries and spread throughout the urban Midwest from Milwaukee to Chicago, Detroit, Cleveland, Pittsburgh, and other cities that came to be known as the **rust belt** because of these economic trends.

automation Business process that seeks to save money, streamline production, or subvert labor unions by using machines to do the work of people.

rust belt Former industrial heartland, centered in the urban upper Midwest but including other areas, suffering from postwar flights of industrial production to other regions and countries.

urban redevelopment Process of transforming central city neighborhoods ostensibly to remove blight and slum conditions that often displaced and disadvantaged working-class people and communities while benefiting city governments, private businesses, and the middle classes.

Housing Act Legislative support for widespread urban redevelopment and creation of new public housing.

public housing Government-subsidized housing designed to benefit poor and working-class people but often were incubators of crime, disorder, and poverty.

America's central cities not only faced alarming levels of unemployment but had a vast and growing population of racial minorities who were often unable to find jobs or housing in the suburbs. Southern migrations beginning during World War I had continued during the 1940s and 1950s when more than 2.5 million African Americans left the rural South to live in urban communities, often New York, Chicago, and Los Angeles. Michael Harrington, a socialist writer, revealed many of the problems that the African American migrants faced in his best-selling exposé of the nation's poverty, *The Other America*, published in 1962. He revealed the disturbing fact that one of every five Americans (40 million) was poor. This high rate of poverty was puzzling: Why was there extensive poverty amid a historic period of prosperity? The cause, argued Harrington, was that the new economy obliterated the economic usefulness of large sectors of American workers, often replacing them with machines. Suburbanization made matters worse by isolating the middle classes from the problems of poverty, leaving them blissfully ignorant of the crises that raged in rural America and African American urban communities. In short, Harrington maintained that key engines that had powered postwar prosperity (the Cold War economy and suburbanization) also had produced racial segregation and poverty.

The relationship between suburban prosperity and central city poverty also resulted from the good intentions of government officials and social reformers involved in **urban redevelopment**. The process began in July 1949 with the federal **Housing Act**, which authorized the demolition of slums to make way for eight hundred thousand new housing units throughout the nation. The goal was to help the increasing number of African American central city residents by replacing old and substandard housing. Problems, however, occurred when local governments that had accepted $13 billion in federal funds for urban redevelopment handed over cleared slum land to private real estate developers. With few incentives or requirements to supply housing for the poor, the developers instead built more profitable commercial projects and middle-class housing. In the case of Dodger Stadium, the city of Los Angeles gave three Mexican American communities to a privately owned baseball team instead of fulfilling its plan to build new public housing units. Most cities across the nation also chose to use slum-clearance funds for commercial purposes that would bring tax revenues rather than construct housing for low-income residents. Between 1949 and 1968, only one of every three housing units destroyed through redevelopment was replaced. As a result, the majority of affected residents did not receive new housing but were relocated to nearby and growing slums.

Moreover, cities often used federal highway construction funds to remove central city residents in order to build freeways and interchanges. With commercial and highway construction and middle-class housing taking up most of the cleared land downtown, **public housing** often took the form of hastily planned high-rise complexes packing as many as twelve thousand residents into small urban spaces. The largest concentration of these communities was on a four-mile corridor of sixteen-story identical buildings on the south side of Chicago. Known as the "projects," these

AP Images

Housing Projects in Chicago before 1965 Housing projects, like this one on the south side of Chicago, stemmed from egalitarian impulses to ensure decent housing for everyone. But soon living in "the projects" became synonymous with seemingly permanent class and racial inequality that became an endemic part of the new economy. ▲

forms of public housing that segregated the poor from mainstream society quickly became centers of vandalism, drug use, and violent crime.

The origin of urban problems in postwar Oakland, California, represents the process of central city decay. Like nearly all West Coast cities, this port city across the bay from San Francisco experienced a major boom in industry and population during World War II. But in the two following decades, Oakland lost both as nearby suburban cities such as San Leandro, Hayward, and Fremont raided its industrial base and drew away its white residents. As was the case in Levittown, the G.I. Bill and federal highway funds laid the groundwork for much of the white flight. What was left in Oakland was an expanding working-class black population competing for a diminishing number of industrial jobs and even for low-paying, dead-end jobs in the service sector, such as maintenance and garbage collection. In addition, federally backed redevelopment (slum-clearance) programs as well as the construction of the Nimitz freeway and Bay Area Rapid Transit (BART) destroyed established African American neighborhoods, uprooting hundreds of families and businesses, usually without transplanting them elsewhere. The new transit network created a pipeline between Eastbay suburbs and the city of San Francisco that enriched these two ends but enabled only modest construction of high-rise office buildings in downtown Oakland.

If San Francisco and the Eastbay suburbs benefited from a concerted process of urban and suburban development, the plight of Oakland can be said to have resulted from a related process of **underdevelopment**. This can be seen as the dark side of postwar prosperity through which stable central city communities such as Oakland turned into poverty-ridden ghettos. For nearly a week in August 1965, a local conflict between African American residents in the south-central Los Angeles community of Watts and local police erupted into a devastating conflagration of destruction, violence, and street protest. During what were known as the **Watts riots**, clashes between ten thousand residents and more than thirteen thousand California guardsmen left thirty-four (mostly African Americans) dead, more than four thousand arrested, and six hundred buildings destroyed or damaged. The Watts riots were the first in a series of urban protests that would rock the nation and increase the pressure for racial and class reform if not a social revolution. The riots accelerated suburban migration by pushing whites in the central cities to sell their homes and flee to the presumed safety and racial homogeneity of the suburbs. Enhancing this **white flight** were unscrupulous real estate agents and hustlers who promoted fears of black invasion in order to profit from panicky whites selling their homes. In this way, the division between white suburbia and black and brown central cities hardened as the latest white suburban migrants divested themselves of inner city communities.

underdevelopment Side effect or unintended consequence of economic development in which poor and working class people are often disadvantaged by the types of development that benefit the middle and upper classes.

Watts riots Violent uprisings of urban African Americans in Los Angeles County triggered by police harassment and prolonged and systemic poverty.

white flight Process of whites leaving central cities and moving to the suburbs as the result of a combination of incentives for suburban living, such as affordable and spacious housing, and disincentives for urban living, such as crowds, noise, crime, and large populations of racial minorities.

23-5c Agricultural Labor and Mexican Migration

Growers push the federal government to import foreign workers during an age of immigration restriction.

The steady stream of rural migration to the cities led to shortages of agricultural labor, particularly for crops that were not easily mechanized, such as cotton and fruits. During World War II, U.S. growers had resorted to the long-standing practice of using low-cost foreign workers by pressuring the federal government to form an agreement with Mexico to bring two hundred thousand bracero guest workers into the country. Conflict erupted after the war when Mexican officials pushed for higher wages and better living conditions for the braceros but their U.S. counterparts responded by opening the nation's border, allowing growers to avoid braceros altogether and hire cheaper undocumented workers who were also from Mexico. After the two nations solved their differences and renewed the

Registering Braceros at Labor Center in Hidalgo, Texas, 1959

Bettmann/Corbis

Global Americans A married couple, **Ezekiel** and **Rosaura Perez** were born and raised in an area of Jalisco, Mexico, that traditionally sent migrants to the United States. Both their fathers had come in the late 1920s. Ezekiel came in 1947, six years after he married Rosaura and they had three children. From his perspective, he was fortunate to enter as a bracero guest worker in a program operated by the U.S. government. He picked sugar beets and harvested wheat and beans for ten months in Billings, Montana. Not long after returning to Mexico, Ezekiel tried four times to cross into the United States without formal papers. He was caught each time and sent back. But on his fifth try, he and seventeen others led by a paid guide were successful. Ezekiel worked for three years throughout California picking various crops and in a restaurant. He gradually began to shake the constant fear of being caught and deported. But then loneliness for family and home overcame the excitement of being in a new and wealthy country. Meanwhile, Rosaura was making do back home, thankful that her husband, unlike others who went north, was consistently sending money to her. When he returned for good, they had enough money to purchase parcels of land and send their then seven children to school. The experience of this family reveals both the challenges and benefits of migration to the United States for peoples from less wealthy countries.

Operation Wetback Federal government program to halt the migration of undocumented workers who often were responding to inefficiencies in U.S. guest worker programs.

agribusinesses Large, often multinational, corporations in agricultural industries whose economies of scale often doomed family farming.

guest worker program in 1954, the U.S. border patrol implemented **Operation Wetback**, a campaign that detained and deported at least fifty-seven thousand undocumented Mexicans from California alone. This resulted in huge drops in the number of undocumented immigrants in the United States while raising concerns about the fairness of the nation's immigration policies.

In theory, the bracero program was designed to benefit both Mexico and the United States, but in reality, most of the benefits remained north of the border. A survey of more than six thousand returning guest workers in the Mexican state of Jalisco revealed that the program had utterly failed to achieve its stated goals of teaching the workers new skills in the United States and paying them enough to uplift their rural economies. These failures had a devastating impact, especially on the humble Mexican families who had borrowed money to pay for bracero expenses and went into further debt when the main breadwinner was picking crops across the border. To make ends meet, the wives and children of braceros worked long hours in Mexico. When they still could not earn enough, they scattered throughout the country, taking low-paying, exploitative work. Families were torn apart with little prospect for improving their lot. In addition, thousands of men who did not meet the bracero program's strict requirements crossed the border illegally to fill the huge demand for low-paid migrant labor. Nine of ten males in one Jalisco rural town ended up migrating one way or another to the United States.

23-5d Rural Transformations

Prosperity covers up long-term reductions in family farming and major unemployment in mining.

The bracero experience reflected the broader transformation of rural U.S. areas where large agricultural corporations made earning a decent living difficult for everyday people. As had industrial factories, corporate **agribusinesses** took advantage of their size by investing in new labor-saving technologies enabling them to produce more and better products at faster and cheaper rates. In addition, a number of federal government assistance programs, such as agricultural subsidies, favored big farms because policy makers were more interested in protecting the nation's food supply than the tradition of family-owned farms. The result was a long-term migration of rural families, including Native Americans, to the cities beginning in the 1920s, increasing with the Dust Bowl in the 1930s, and continuing through the height of agribusiness consolidation after World War II. By 1960, the soaring costs of farming, as the result of the scale required to make a profit, had nearly eliminated Native American agriculture. Between 1945 and 1960, these farmers declined from 45 to 10 percent of the total tribal population in the United States. As a consequence, Indian reservations experienced some of the worst poverty rates in rural America.

The depletion of the nation's once abundant natural resources resulting from World War II needs and the extended postwar economic boom also had a negative impact on jobs in rural America. By 1949, the United States was importing more oil from abroad (particularly

AP Images

Native American Poverty on the Reservation, before 1965 Native Americans did not share equally in the benefits of the Cold War economy either as migrants to central cities or, as in this photo, residents of a reservation. This photo shows a dwelling on the Havasupi reservation near the south rim of the Grand Canyon in Arizona. ◄

the Middle East) than it generated domestically. The country's supply of timber declined as forests were cut down at a faster rate than they could be replenished to meet the insatiable demands for lumber from the housing boom. The nation's depletion of its mineral resources was especially acute. Its reliance on foreign cooper and bauxite (for making aluminum) increased significantly over the next twenty years. Corporations were able to offset the loss of native mineral deposits by using inexpensive foreign imports—but workers suffered widespread unemployment. The area hardest hit was Appalachia, a nine-state mountainous region stretching from eastern Pennsylvania to Alabama. The area suffered when the coal industry drastically reduced its labor force by downsizing and automation. Another devastated region was the Mesabi iron range, spanning the northern parts of Minnesota and Wisconsin and upper Michigan. This area once contained the nation's largest deposits of iron ore used for making steel. The depletion of its high-quality ore by the early 1960s caused massive unemployment as mining companies closed, downsized, and retooled to compete against foreign competition.

Summary

Two decades of tense U.S.–Soviet relations after World War II transformed the U.S. economy as well as the nation's military, government, society, and culture. Information and service industries had a powerful and far-reaching impact on American life during the early stages of the Cold War. The transformation did not happen overnight but emerged through five simultaneous and interconnected developments so that by 1970 white-collar jobs represented almost half of all jobs in the nation, far surpassing the number of blue-collar jobs. One reason is that federal policies advanced consumer spending, which in concert with Cold War spending sustained overall prosperity. Another is that through highway construction and labor union limitations, the federal government enabled the nation's manufacturing base to relocate away from central cities. A third reason is that suburbanization and internal migration to the South and West affected the nature of work, community life, and urban development. Also, changing gender roles resulting from the increase of white-collar work and women's employment affected all family members. Finally, the Cold War economy had negative consequences for central cities, racial minorities, and the most vulnerable classes of industrial and agricultural workers. The emergence of the information and services economy created an urban crisis that deepened as deindustrialization accelerated after 1965. Thus, the historic prosperity generated by the U.S. Cold War economy did not become a golden age. Instead it became a transitional era in which the nation and its culture began to emerge from a system of manufacturing rooted in the urban Northeast and upper Midwest. The postindustrial information and service industries housed outside the urban centers of the old economy characterized the nation's economy in the late twentieth century

<Thinking Back, *Looking Forward*>

As you review the Cold War economy, recall the superpower conflict with the Soviet Union as well as global crises occurring in places such as Berlin, China, and Egypt. Decisions made by U.S. officials expanded the U.S. economy and encouraged the growth of suburbs, service and information industries, and higher education. In the coming chapters, look for the impact of the Cold War on movements for civil rights and the U.S. war in Vietnam.

To make your study concrete, review the timeline and reflect on the entries there. Think about their causes, consequences, and connections. How do they fit with global trends?

Additional Resources

Books

Avila, Eric. *Popular Culture in the Age of White Flight: Fear and Fantasy in Suburban Los Angeles*. Berkeley: University of California Press, 2004. ▶ Examination of the postwar transformation of a prominent western city with attention to Hollywood, Disneyland, and the building of Dodger Stadium.

Cobble, Dorothy Sue. *The Other Women's Movement: Workplace Justice and Social Rights in Modern America*. Princeton, NJ: Princeton University Press, 2004. ▶ Penetrating analysis of the history of working women and their struggles for social justice during the twentieth century.

Cohen, Lizabeth. *A Consumers' Republic: The Politics of Mass Consumption in Postwar America*. New York: Vintage Books, 2003. ▶ Path-breaking study of the nation's explosion in consumer spending and its ironic consequences for social inequality.

Gilbert, James. *Men in the Middle: Searching for Masculinity in the 1950s*. Chicago, IL: University of Chicago Press, 2005. ▶ Original study of changing roles for men in the emerging postindustrial economy.

Gillett, Charlie. *The Sound of the City: The Rise of Rock and Roll*. 1970. Reprint, New York: De Capo Press, 1996. ▶ One of the best examinations of the early history of rock music.

Harrington, Michael. *The Other America: Poverty in the United States*. 1962. Reprint, New York: Touchstone, 1997. ▶ Analysis of the problems that the War on Poverty sought to resolve.

Katznelson, Ira. *When Affirmative Action Was White: An Untold History of Racial Inequality in Twentieth-Century America*. New York: Norton, 2005. ▶ Innovative rethinking of affirmative action policies, such as the G.I. Bill, that targeted white people.

May, Elaine Tyler. *Homeward Bound: American Families in the Cold War Era*. New York: Basic Books, 1988. ▶ Classic account of changing gender roles after World War II.

Ngai, Mae M. *Impossible Subjects: Illegal Aliens and the Making of Modern America*. Princeton, NJ: Princeton University Press, 2004. ▶ Important historical analysis of U.S. immigration law and politics that address postwar policies including the bracero program.

Segrue, Thomas J. *The Origins of the Urban Crisis: Race and Inequality in Postwar Detroit*. Princeton, NJ: Princeton University Press, 1996. ▶ Award-winning study of the historical factors contributing to the degeneration of a major American city.

Go to the MindTap® for **Global Americans** to access the full version of select books from this Additional Resources section.

Websites

A Guide to Beat Poets. (https://www.poets.org/poetsorg/text/brief-guide-beat-poets). ▶ Selection of poems, videos of poets reading their work, and biographies of key poets in the Beat movement.

America on the Move: City and Suburb. (http://amhistory.si.edu/onthemove/exhibition/exhibition_15_1.html). ▶ Online interactive exhibit with images, text, and videos about American suburban life in the 1950s.

America on the Move: On the Interstate, 1956–1990. (http://amhistory.si.edu/onthemove/exhibition/exhibition_16_1.html). ▶ Online interactive exhibit with images, text, and videos about highway construction along Interstate 10 spanning the Southwest from California to Texas to Florida.

Bittersweet Harvest: The Bracero Program 1942–1964. (http://americanhistory.si.edu/bracero/introduction). ▶ Extensive coverage of the bracero guest worker program with images and firsthand perspectives from migrants.

The Pan-Am Historical Foundation. (http://www.panam.org/enter). ▶ Video, audio, and textual sources related to a U.S. airline that became an icon of global air travel.

MindTap®

Continue exploring online through MindTap®, where you can:

- **Assess your knowledge with the Chapter Test**
- **Watch historical videos related to the chapter**
- **Further your understanding with interactive maps and timelines**

Prosperity and the Cold War Economy

1946

Benjamin Spock publishes *The Common Sense Book of Baby and Child Care*.

May

Railroad strike shuts down major U.S. transportation system.

November

Republicans claim both houses of Congress for first time since 1932.

1947

G.I. Bill funds half of all college students in its peak year.

March

Levittown tract home community opens in New York.

Truman Doctrine commits United States to containing communism.

June

Congress enacts Taft-Hartley Act.

1948–1949

1948

Alfred Kinsey publishes *Sexual Behavior in the Human Male*.

November 1948

Truman wins second term as president.

1949

U.S. oil imports begin to exceed domestic production.

Protests erupt against Coca-Cola in France.

July 1949

Housing Act authorizes widespread slum clearance.

August 1949

Soviet Union conducts successful test of atomic bomb.

1950–1953

April 1950

NSC 68 initiates an increasingly militaristic stance toward the Soviet Union.

August 1952

Holiday Inn opens first highway convenience hotel.

January 1953

Record 44 million television viewers watch episode of *I Love Lucy*.

December 1953

Playboy magazine begins.

1954–1955

1954

Operation Wetback begins to detain and deport undocumented Mexicans.

1955

Rebel Without a Cause makes James Dean a global symbol of youth rebellion.

April 1955

McDonald's restaurant chain opens in Chicago suburb.

May 1955

Soviets establish Warsaw Pact to counter NATO.

July 1955

Disneyland opens on converted farmland in Anaheim, California.

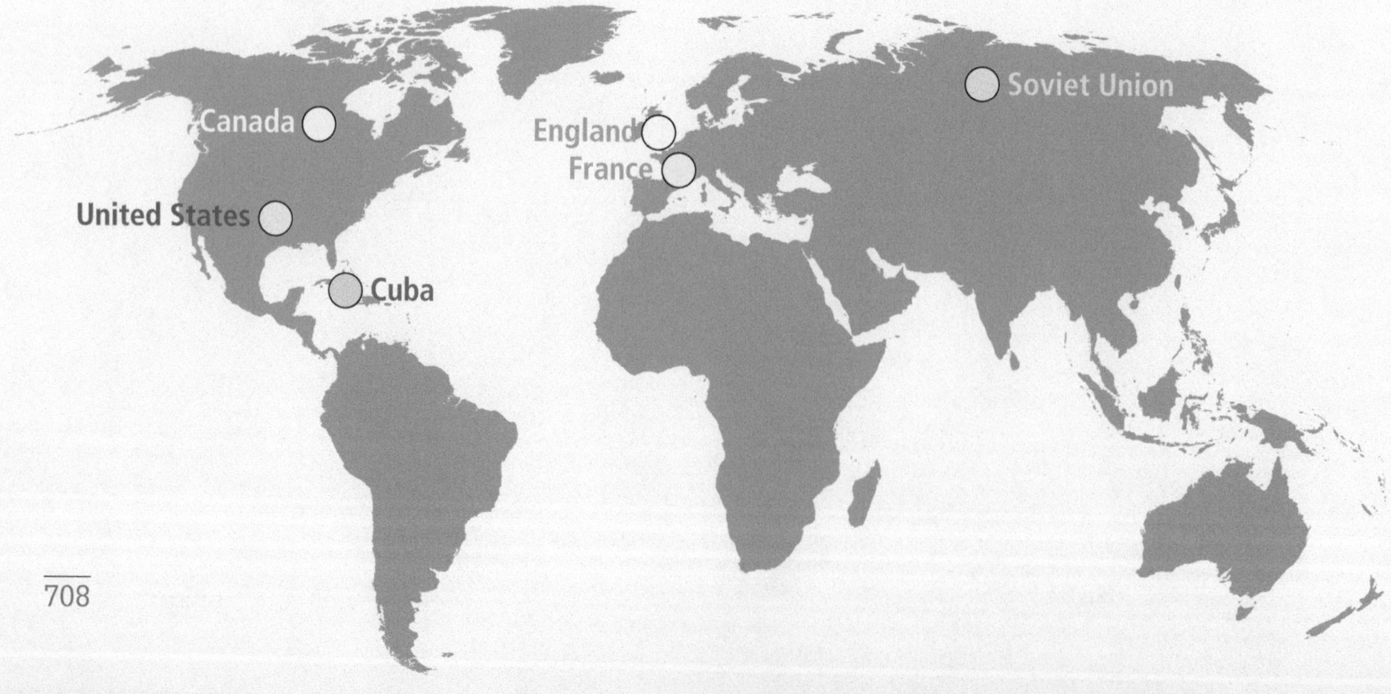

1956–1957

June 1956

Congress passes Interstate Highway Act.

September 1956

Program featuring Elvis Presley has largest television audience.

1957

U.S. baby boom reaches twentieth-century high point (3.7 babies per woman).

Brooklyn Dodgers move to Los Angeles.

Beat poet Jack Kerouac publishes *On the Road*.

October 1957

Success of Soviet Sputnik evokes great fear in United States over "missile gap."

1958

Pan American World Airlines flies first fleet of commercial jet airplanes.

Bretton Woods global economic system becomes fully operational.

John Kenneth Galbraith publishes *The Affluent Society*.

July

United States establishes NASA to compete with Soviet space missions.

September

Congress approves National Defense Education Act.

1959–1960

July 1959

Bob Dylan performs at first Newport Folk Festival.

September 1959

Nikita Khrushchev visits the United States.

1960

U.S. Census counts thirteen "strip cities."

U.S. suburban population doubles from that in 1947.

May 1960

U.S. government approves first birth control pill.

1961–1962

1961

Canada's baby boom peaks at nearly four babies per woman.

January 1961

Eisenhower warns about "military-industrial complex."

Michael Harrington publishes *The Other America*.

April 1962

Dodger Stadium opens in Los Angeles, California.

October 1962

Cuban Missile Crisis pushes United States and Soviet Union to the brink of nuclear war.

1963–1965

February 1964

The Beatles embark on first tour of the United States.

August 1965

Racial uprising erupts in Watts, California.

24

Civil Rights and Human Rights

1945–1965

Rejected from the University of North Carolina and Harvard University because of her race and gender respectively, Pauli Murray nevertheless racked up achievements—such as being the first African American deputy attorney general of California—thanks to her indomitable spirit. She was a committed political activist whose legal contributions led the way to decisions like *Brown v. Board of Education.*

In 1938, Pauli Murray, a twenty-eight-year-old Hunter College graduate who had been raised in rural North Carolina, applied to law school at the University of North Carolina and was rejected—on account of her race. Murray was African American—or at least she identified as African American, though with Swedish, French, Irish, and Native American ancestors, she once described her family as a "United Nations in miniature." She subsequently enrolled in the law school at the historically black Howard University, where the faculty included lawyers in the forefront of the National Association for the Advancement of Colored People's (NAACP) legal challenges against racial segregation. Graduating first in her class, she applied to a master's program at Harvard University and was rejected—on account of her gender.

AP Images/Frank C. Curtin

Murray then moved to California and earned a master's degree in law from the University of California, Berkeley. The next year she became the first African American deputy attorney general of California. The National Council of Negro Women and *Mademoiselle* magazine recognized this achievement by naming her Woman of the Year. Such honors, which Murray garnered throughout her life, testified to her talents, and indomitable spirit as well as to the enormous obstacles she confronted as a black female in the United States.

A committed political activist familiar with the passive resistance tactics of India's Mohandas Gandhi, Murray helped stage sit-ins at restaurants in Washington, D.C. In 1940, she and a girlfriend were arrested in Petersburg, Virginia, for sitting in the white section of a segregated bus. Murray began a lifelong correspondence with First Lady Eleanor Roosevelt while leading an unsuccessful campaign to free Odell Waller, a black sharecropper in Virginia accused of killing his white landlord. Her *States' Laws on Race and Color* (1950) became the "bible" for NAACP lawyers who advanced legal challenges culminating in *Brown v. Board of Education*, a landmark U.S. Supreme Court ruling in May 1954 that outlawed racial segregation in public schools.

The *Brown* decision established a crucial legal standard for the postwar "rights revolution." It coincided with a profound and growing revulsion, felt across the United States and around the world, against the Holocaust and other racist acts committed during World War II. The newly established United Nations (UN) put pressure on the United States and other nations to end all forms of discrimination based on race, sex, and religion. More important was the fact that racism in the United States was tarnishing the country's image as the leader of the "free world" in the Cold War fight against communism. To counter Soviet criticism, the U.S. government—for the first time since Reconstruction when the Thirteenth, Fourteenth, and Fifteenth Amendments established the legal basis for nondiscrimination—took a bold step to guarantee the equal treatment of all Americans, thus providing a key element to the civil rights revolution.

How do the many honors that Pauli Murray garnered in her work as a political activist testify to her indomitable spirit—as well as to the obstacles she confronted as a black woman in the United States?

Go to MindTap® to watch a video on Murray and learn how her story relates to the themes of this chapter.

At the same time, a mass movement opposing racial segregation emerged that included visionary leader Martin Luther King Jr., a host of activist organizations with varying strategies and tactics, and an army of everyday people—white and black, male and female. The movement came together to fight against Jim Crow at the ballot box and segregation in public conveyances, restaurants, and the nation's commercial transactions. The Civil Rights Movement, by exposing southern racism to a watchful nation and world community, inspired federal policies and court decisions that dismantled the legal infrastructure of racial discrimination. Murray's career was dedicated to abolishing Jim Crow, but she made sure that the rights revolution also challenged gender discrimination, which she called *Jane Crow*. A founding member of the National Organization for Women, she helped develop the legal arguments for Supreme Court decisions in favor of gender equality.

Yet the new laws and protections were not enough to rectify years of white rule and institutional racism, nor did they relieve the poverty that plagued blacks in the South as well as in the nation's cities. President Lyndon Johnson responded to the crisis of economic inequality by generating the largest expansion of the welfare state since the New Deal. As Murray's critique of Jane Crow attested, civil rights struggles also stimulated the movement for women's rights that pushed for employment equality with men and a critique of the postwar ideal of the happy suburban mother and housewife.

24-1 International Context for Civil and Human Rights

The newly founded UN reacted to the Holocaust and postwar global circumstances by advocating for human rights, a broad notion of universal and inalienable natural rights to nondiscrimination for all peoples and in all places. Here former First Lady Eleanor Roosevelt in 1948 holds up the UN Universal Declaration of Human Rights, which she played a key role in crafting.

Why do you think the UN made human rights one of its first major initiatives? How did World War II change the global demand for protections against vulnerable groups? From what you know of Roosevelt and women's rights activism, can you suggest why she played a key role in promoting human rights? ▶

america.gov

The revolution against white supremacy, evident in global efforts for human rights, was made possible by a sea change in racial beliefs that emerged during and after World War II. Although racial segregation and discrimination remained entrenched in political, economic, and everyday life throughout the United States, war atrocities fostered the spirit of racial equality. The creation of the United Nations boosted racial egalitarianism and marked an important step in the U.S. campaign for civil rights. Although similar to human rights, civil rights in the United States were based not only in a UN treaty but also in U.S. law, particularly the Thirteenth and Fourteenth Amendments. In 1948, President Harry Truman took a major step for civil rights by desegregating the federal government and military personnel. The rise of the Cold War strengthened the momentum for civil rights because Soviet criticism of inequality in U.S. society compelled the leader of the free world to address its racism at home.

☞ As you read, pay attention to the struggle against racial prejudice that emerged in full force after World War II. What domestic and global circumstances enhanced this struggle? Which ones impeded it?

24-1a Legacies of a Race War

> The UN influences civil rights reforms in the United States.

From the beginning, the United Nations exceeded the support for **human rights** contained in the Atlantic Charter and UN preparations at Dumbarton Oaks, and proved a vast improvement from the League of Nations, which had rejected a racial equality clause at its founding in 1919. The UN charter's first article addressed the goal of promoting human rights and fundamental freedoms "for all without distinction to race, sex, language, or religion." Moreover, the first session of the UN's General Assembly approved a resolution opposing the systematic racism faced by Indians in South Africa, thus continuing the struggle for civil rights in that country that Mohandas Gandhi led in the late nineteenth and early twentieth centuries (see Chapter 21). But the United States, Britain, and white British Commonwealth nations (South Africa, Canada, and New Zealand) constituted a visible minority who voted against the resolution. South Africa's UN representative Jan Smuts complained bitterly that the organization had been taken over by "colored peoples" of the world.

The UN in December 1948 confirmed and elaborated its purpose by crafting the **Universal Declaration of Human Rights**, which Eleanor Roosevelt, who chaired the committee that wrote the document, called an "international Magna Carta of all men everywhere." Roosevelt, the former first lady, had been called by the NAACP's Walter White one of only two white American women who understood the experience of black Americans—the other was Pearl S. Buck, a Nobel Prize-winning American writer and avid social justice activist. In the same month as the Universal Declaration of Human Rights was unveiled, the General Assembly voted to make genocide a crime of international law, whether perpetrated during wartime or not. At the same time, however, UN member nations balked at the petition sent by W.E.B. Du Bois and the NAACP proclaiming that racism against African Americans placed the United States in violation of international standards for human rights. Even in defeat, Du Bois revealed that the UN could provide a forum for advancing U.S. civil rights (Table 24.1).

human rights Universal and inalienable natural rights to life, liberty, pursuit of happiness, and nondiscrimination; codified in UN international treaties (unlike civil rights, which have a basis in the U.S. Constitution).

Universal Declaration of Human Rights Statement by the United Nations, approved in 1948, inspiring the proliferation of the principle of nondiscrimination in domestic and international laws around the world.

24-1b U.S. Military and Racial Equality

> U.S. veterans face discrimination that provokes racial reform.

The NAACP's Double-V campaign had asked racial minorities who had served in World War II to fight for victory over enemies abroad and against racism at home. Upon their return to the United States, veterans of color realized that the racial battle at home was far from over. White veterans in Hood River, Oregon, removed the names of sixteen Japanese American servicemen from an American

Table 24.1 UN Actions Promoting Human Rights, 1945–1965

When the fifty-one nations met in San Francisco to establish the United Nations, they made human rights a core reason and purpose for the newly established international body. The following are UN actions concerning human rights, many of which the United States initially did not support.

Year	Action
1945	UN Charter addresses human rights in six different articles
1946	Resolution opposing Discrimination of Indians in South Africa
1946	Commission on Human Rights established to set standards for human rights
1947	Sub-Commission on Prevention of Discrimination and Protection of Minorities established
1948	Universal Declaration of Human Rights
1948	Convention on the Prevention and Punishment of the Crime of Genocide
1956	Supplementary Convention on the Abolition of Slavery, the Slave Trade, and Institutions and Practices Similar to Slavery
1958	Convention Concerning Discrimination in Respect to Employment and Occupation
1960	Resolution opposing colonialism as a violation of human rights and supporting the granting of independence to colonized peoples
1961	Special UN committee to implement the resolution against colonialism
1962	Convention against Discrimination in Education
1965	International Convention on the Elimination of All Forms of Racial Discrimination
1966	International Covenant on Civil and Political Rights

Source: Lauren, Paul Gordon, *Power and Prejudice,* 2nd ed. Boulder, CO: Westview, 1996.

President's Committee on Civil Rights Including members from private industry, labor, and nongovernmental organizations this committee, established in October 1947, recommended sweeping reforms to provide equal opportunity to all races.

Legion honor roll for fallen soldiers, and only restored them in April 1945 after succumbing to intense pressure from Japanese American veterans, military officials, and the national media.

The burial of Felix Longoria, a Mexican American soldier who died in the Philippines, sparked another link between World War II veterans and civil rights activism. In January 1949, the army returned Longoria's body to his hometown of Three Rivers, Texas, where his widow asked the only funeral home in the city to hold a wake for her deceased husband. She was turned away because Longoria was not white. After protests from Mexican Americans, the national press responded by condemning the funeral home's actions as an affront to U.S. patriotism. Although the State Department concurred and privately encouraged the Longoria family to seek redress, the newly elected U.S. senator from Texas, Lyndon Baines Johnson, arranged to have Felix Longoria given a hero's burial at the nation's most hallowed grounds for fallen soldiers, Arlington National Cemetery.

The most consequential racist act targeting a veteran of color involved Isaac Woodard, who in February 1946 got into an argument with a white bus driver after Woodard returned late from a rest stop break. The driver called the South Carolina police and at the next bus stop the officers pulled Woodard off the bus and beat him, leaving the veteran, who was dressed in uniform, permanently blinded. A national outcry encouraged President Truman to order a federal investigation into the incident, which resulted in the indictment of several police officers who were later absolved of all charges by an all-white jury. Deeply upset, Truman established a special commission to investigate the nation's racial problems. The **President's Committee on Civil Rights** in October 1947 published *To Secure These Rights*, a 178-page report declaring that the "separate but equal doctrine is inconsistent with the fundamental equalitarianism of the U.S. way of life in that it marks groups with the brand of inferior status." Based on this report, Truman called on Congress to make lynching a federal crime and to prevent job discrimination, racial segregation, and voting rights infringements. When Congress failed to consider such legislation, the president used an executive order to desegregate the nation's armed forces and to outlaw racial discrimination in both federal employment and all private firms doing business with the government, which composed one-fifth of the U.S. economy by 1952. Although motivated by personal convictions, Truman was also concerned about Soviet criticism of U.S. race relations and winning the northern black vote in the 1948 election.

24-1c Signs of Immigration Reform

Racial reform also influences U.S. immigration policies.

New international responsibilities initially made Congress more responsive to reforming immigration policy than to civil rights. The plight of

MUTO; AL/Corbis

Felix Longoria Funeral at Arlington, 1949 The racist treatment of veterans of color exposed the contradictions of U.S. ideals in fighting World War II to defeat Nazi and Japanese racism. This photo shows the burial of Felix Longoria, a Mexican American killed in the war, who was interred at Arlington Cemetery because his body would not be handled by a segregated Texas mortuary. ◄

Everett Collection Historical/Alamy Stock Photo

Global Americans Born and raised in China, as the daughter of American missionary parents, **Pearl Sydenstricker Buck** was fluent in Chinese and, although a U.S. citizen, she identified with her birth country throughout her life. She is best known for being the third American to win the Nobel Prize for Literature, which was primarily a testament to her best-selling novel set in China, *The Good Earth* (1931). Buck's acceptance speech as a Nobel Laureate focused on the subject of the Chinese novel, explaining that "I am an American by birth and by ancestry," but "my earliest knowledge of story, of how to tell and write stories, came to me in China." In addition to her fiction, Buck also published extensively on current events, especially to correct misunderstandings of Asia and the developing world in general, as well as racial minorities in the United States. NAACP leader Walter White considered her, along with Eleanor Roosevelt, to be a white woman who understood African Americans. In 1949, Pearl Buck established Welcome House Adoption Program to cater to abandoned biracial children who were often the "most cruelly treated child" around the world. Welcome House initially focused on mixed race Asians, who Buck called *Amerasians*, the often unwanted consequence of U.S. military occupations Japan and Korean after World War II and the Korean War. Buck's efforts countered prejudice against mixed-race peoples and established the field of transpacific adoption.

displaced persons after World War II softened the nation's opposition to further immigration. Despite entrenched anti-Semitism in Congress, it would have damaged the nation's international reputation to turn away victims of Nazi persecution and others who had lost everything in the war. U.S. officials also sought to score points against the Soviets by granting asylum to the growing number of anti-Communist refugees fleeing Soviet-controlled Eastern Europe. Congress passed the Displaced Persons Act in June 1948 and a number of subsequent policies that circumvented the nation's restrictive immigration quotas. As a result, more than a million displaced persons and refugees came into the United States between 1945 and 1960.

Although most of the newcomers admitted were European, a smaller number of migrants from Asia reflected a significant transformation in the nation's long-standing policy of Asian exclusion. As an anti-Communist measure, Congress permitted refugees from the People's Republic of China and North Korea to enter the country. Moreover, by granting Japan an immigration quota in 1952 and enabling those immigrants to become U.S. citizens, it continued a trend, started during World War II, of dismantling the systematic discrimination of Asian Americans. Small influxes of Asian immigrants transformed Chinatowns and Filipino communities from bachelor societies to family-based communities, as wives were now able to join overseas husbands. Some of these women were war brides from Japan and Korea married to white U.S. military personnel. Their mixed marriages were a subject of curiosity in all-white communities even though many states, including California and others in the West that had long discriminated against Asian Americans, overturned laws banning miscegenation. These same states, in part due to the influence of the UN Declaration of Human Rights, also repealed discriminatory laws discouraging Asian immigrants from owning or leasing agricultural land. A final telling sign of the abrupt change in attitude toward Asians was the first contingent of "Hiroshima maidens" who came to New York in May 1955 seeking plastic surgery to repair injuries and scars from the atomic bomb. The *Dayton News* revealed the nation's global caretaking role by expressing sympathy toward the bomb survivors: "We're sorry it had to be you—and we want to help you!"

24-1d Anticommunism and Black Loyalty

Racial reforms become decidedly anti-Communist.

A crucial moment in the postwar decline of racial discrimination came in 1947 when Jackie Robinson and Larry Doby broke the barrier against black players in major league baseball. Both players were former American GIs and were chosen because of their baseball talent as well as ability to weather racist taunts and actions on the field. Robinson won Rookie of the Year honors for the Brooklyn Dodgers and within two seasons became the league's Most Valuable Player. Within a couple of years, most major league teams integrated their clubs, although the Boston Red Sox held out until 1959 (see Figure 24.1).

Robinson, it turned out, was perfectly suited to become a symbol for postwar antiracism. In addition to being a four-sport star at UCLA, he had vocally opposed racial segregation and while serving in the military was court-martialed (later rescinded) for refusing to move from the white-only section of an army bus near the base

Jackie Robinson and Larry Doby, 1947 Jackie Robinson receives most of the accolades for breaking the color barrier in major league baseball in 1947. Less remembered is that Larry Doby broke the barrier in the same year and became an all-star for the Cleveland Indians. The next year he and former Negro professional league star pitcher Satchel Paige helped the team win the World Series. ▲

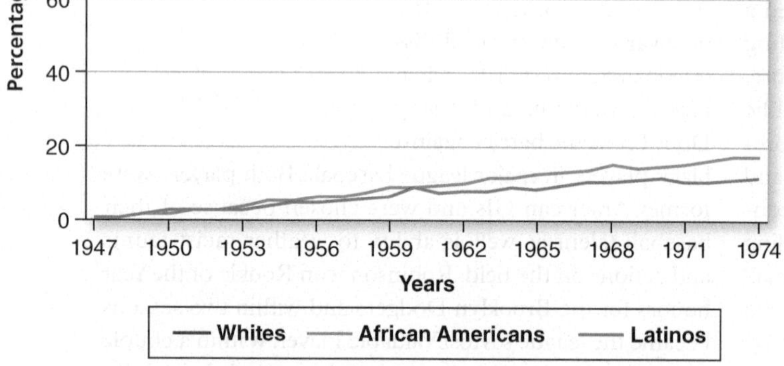

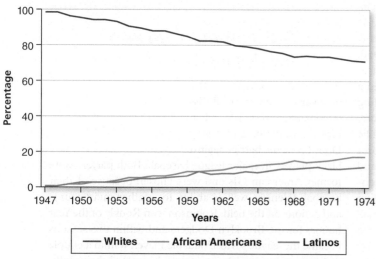

Figure 24.1 Race in Major League Baseball, 1947–1975 When the last Major League team was integrated in 1959, African Americans comprised nearly 9 percent of all rosters, which was almost the same as the proportion of blacks in the United States (10 percent). In the same year, Latino players comprised more than 6 percent of rosters. Such integration put a severe strain on Negro professional baseball, whose national league folded in 1948 while its American league held on for another decade. ▲
Source: Society for American Baseball Research. http://sabr.org/bioproj/topic/baseball-demographics-1947-2012, accessed January 22, 2016.

where he was stationed in Fort Hood, Texas. During the height of Cold War fears, Robinson's anticommunism was also crucial to his becoming an international icon for racial reform. In July 1949, he was called to testify at the HUAC investigation of Paul Robeson, the well-known African American singer and actor who made headlines by saying that blacks would not fight against the Soviet Union because of that nation's opposition to racism (see Global Americans, Chapter 20).

Robeson, like many racial minorities and nationalists in colonized countries in the 1920s and 1930s, had been drawn to the Communist Party's commitment to racial equality. The younger Robinson respected Robeson's many talents, but did not support his views of the Soviet Union. "We [African Americans] can win our fight without the Communists," he told HUAC, "and we don't want their help." At the same hearing, the NAACP's Walter White stressed that the vast majority of African Americans did not share Robeson's views and were solidly anti-Communist. In the end, the Red crusade against Robeson ruined his concert career and caused him in 1958 to flee with his family to Europe, where he was warmly received in the Soviet Union and other Eastern bloc. Robeson preceded his friend W.E.B. Du Bois in escaping political persecution by relocating overseas. His difficulties in the United States reflected the larger McCarthy era purge of leftists in the Communist Party, labor movement, and Hollywood.

24-1e School Desegregation and the Supreme Court

Breakthroughs for racial reform emerge via public education.

While major league baseball was being integrated, civil rights lawyers kept chipping away at Jim Crow in the nation's public schools by adhering to the **NAACP's legal strategy** worked out in the 1930s by Charles Hamilton Houston, dean of Howard University's law school. Houston was one of the reasons why Pauli Murray and other civil rights activists came to study at Howard. He, along with his protégé Thurgood Marshall and a team of other black attorneys, used the courts to require states and school districts to live up to the letter of the *Plessy* decision (1896) by providing fully equal schools for blacks. They believed such a requirement would lead to integration as the cheaper and more expedient option. In 1950, the NAACP team won the *Sweatt v. Painter* case in which the U.S. Supreme Court required integration of the University of Texas law school because the state could not provide an equal education for black students. A year later, the Court handed down a similar ruling with respect to university education in Oklahoma.

Another challenge came with *Mendez v. Westminster*. Gonzalo Mendez, a Mexican American tenant farmer, worked with the **League of United Latin American Citizens (LULAC)**, a Mexican American civil rights organization, to take the school district of Orange Country, California, to federal court so that his children could attend the city of Westminster's all-white schools. The U.S. Court of Appeals for the Ninth Circuit affirmed the lower court ruling upholding Mendez's right to send his daughter to the white school. The California legislature quickly followed the verdict with legislation outlawing the state's segregated schools. California's governor Earl Warren, who approved of this desegregation and signed it into law, would later become chief justice of the U.S. Supreme Court presiding over the landmark ***Brown v. Board of Education of Topeka, Kansas*** (1954), which overturned the long-standing *Plessy decision* (1896) that had sanctioned racial segregation.

Brown originated in 1951 when Oliver L. Brown, an African American welder and assistant pastor at a local church, worked with the NAACP to allow his daughter Linda to attend a white elementary school in Topeka. Unlike earlier test cases, *Brown* directly challenged the constitutionality of *Plessy*'s separate-but-equal doctrine. By 1954, the case, along with four others of its kind, made its way to the Supreme Court, where Chief Justice Warren presided over a unanimous 9-0 decision finding that "Separate education facilities are inherently unequal." In making his decision, Warren was aware of Cold War pressures to improve race relations that the Justice Department emphasized in its friend of the court brief for the Brown case, which included a quote from Secretary of State Dean Acheson lamenting mounting criticism in the foreign press concerning racism within the United States. More explicitly, Warren's decision relied upon studies of racism by social scientists including the psychologists Kenneth and Maime Clark, who showed that racial segregation ruined self-esteem in black children.

The *Brown* decision disappointed President Eisenhower, who supported gradual, not immediate, civil rights. He had nominated Earl Warren as chief justice of the Supreme Court based on the Californian's reputation for law and order that included, when he was the state's attorney general, a racist campaign that advanced Japanese American internment. When Warren came out as the architect of the *Brown* decision, Eisenhower said that nominating him for chief justice was the "biggest damned-fool mistake I ever made."

A year after the *Brown* decision, the Supreme Court moderated its position. It responded to school board requests for relief from the burdens of immediate integration by issuing an ambiguous decision for desegregation to proceed "with all deliberate speed." Known as *Brown II*, this ruling gave school districts the option to initiate a gradual rather than immediate end to segregation. Consequently, many white Southerners were encouraged to slow down the implementation of the *Brown* decision, if not ignore it altogether.

NAACP's legal strategy Approach to fight racial discrimination primarily through the courts.

League of United Latin American Citizens (LULAC) Civil rights organization started in 1929 by Mexican American veterans whose aim was to end the discrimination of Latinos.

Brown v. Board of Education of Topeka, Kansas Landmark U.S. Supreme Court ruling in 1954 overturning the legal precedent for racial segregation in public schools.

The LIFE Picture Collection/Getty Images

Dwight D. Eisenhower Speaks with Earl Warren In talking with Chief Justice Warren (right in photo) as the Supreme Court was considering the *Brown* case, President Eisenhower told him that white segregationists were "not bad people" and that all "they are concerned about is to see that their sweet little girls are not required to sit alongside some big overgrown Negroes." Hoping for a gradual solution, Eisenhower was unhappy with the Court's verdict to end racial segregation in public schools with all deliberate speed. ▲

24-2

Civil Rights Movement and Southern Race Relations

This statue honoring the "A&T Four"—Franklin McCain, Ezell Blair Jr. (later known as Jibreel Khazan), Joseph McNeil, and David Richmond—stands on the campus of North Carolina A&T in Greensboro, North Carolina. As college freshmen in February 1960, these young men protested against racial segregation at a local Woolworth's store lunch counter.

Why do you think these men have been commemorated? What might explain the way in which they are positioned, standing erect and looking straight ahead with arms hanging down on both sides? What does their appearance and dress suggest about the nature of their protest? ▶

Walter Bibikow/Corbis

Highlander Folk School Founded in 1932 by labor organizers, the school trained Martin Luther King Jr., Rosa Parks, and other civil rights leaders in tactics of civil disobedience.

Although civil rights activists, along with the UN, and the U.S. federal government made important progress in countering racial segregation and discrimination after World War II, the pace of change was not fast enough for African Americans who lived with Jim Crow's everyday indignities. Galvanized by the brutal lynching of fourteen-year-old Emmett Till, ordinary people formed the backbone of the Civil Rights Movement that received national attention in 1955 when a prolonged dispute over segregated bus seating in Montgomery, Alabama sparked grassroots protests led by a twenty-six-year-old Baptist minister named Martin Luther King Jr. The movement spread throughout the South requiring federal troops to ensure the integration of an Arkansas high school as well as restaurants, starting in Greensboro, North Carolina. These local struggles awakened the nation and world to the problem of southern race relations, setting in motion a pattern of black protest, white resistance, and federal intervention that would have an impact far beyond the South.

☞ As you read, focus on how the Civil Rights Movement developed over time. What were its key turning points, and why and how did they occur? How did white Southerners and the federal government respond to the Civil Rights Movement? How did their responses shape the course of the movement?

24-2a Emmett Till and the Montgomery Bus Boycott

The vicious murder of a black youth inspires protests that fuel the Civil Rights Movement.

In August 1955, two boys fishing in the Tallahatchie River in Mississippi discovered fourteen-year-old Emmett Till's decomposed body. Three days before, Till, who had been visiting from Chicago, was abducted at gunpoint from his uncle's house by two white men who vowed to get even with the black teenager for allegedly whistling suggestively at the wife of one of the men. Although the idea of sexual relations between black men and white women always had been charged in the South, Till's murder shocked both white and black Southerners. After Till's mother, Mamie Till Bradley, insisted on an open casket funeral, photographs of the boy's bloated and mangled body triggered widespread revulsion. The Soviets, whose crackdown on protests in support of Hungary's independence the U.S. had criticized, used the occasion to denounce the United States as hypocritical. "These accusations ring particularly false," reported *Pravda*, the official Soviet news agency, in referring to the Till case, "because the United States does not protect the elementary rights of man." The outrage over Till's murder reached fever pitch when the accused murderers were acquitted by an all-white jury. Once the two suspects could no longer be tried for the crime, they admitted to killing Till. Jury members said they knew as much, but had acquitted the men to send a message against "sassy niggers making passes at white women."

The racism and miscarriage of justice involving Emmett Till intensified African Americans' demands for an immediate end to white supremacy. Turning her horror at Till's death into action, Rosa Parks, a black seamstress and hospital worker in Montgomery, Alabama, was arrested for refusing to give up her seat on the bus to a white man. An NAACP organizer who had learned Gandhian passive

Grey Villet/Time & Life Pictures/Getty Images

African American Commuters Walk to Work, Montgomery, 1956 As president of the organization behind the Montgomery Bus Boycott, Martin Luther King Jr. backed a federal lawsuit designed to desegregate Montgomery buses and supported a car-pooling system that enabled the boycott to continue throughout the year. Many boycotters also choose to walk instead of ride the bus. ◀

Montgomery Improvement Association Organized by Montgomery's black community leaders and out-of-town black ministers in the wake of Rosa Parks's arrest in December 1955, this association led the famous boycott protesting racial segregation of city buses in Montgomery, Alabama.

White Citizens' Council Network of organizations concentrated in the South prompted by the Brown decision to protest against desegregation mainly in public schools.

Montgomery bus boycott Protest against racial segregation on Montgomery, Alabama, buses and the mistreatment of African American riders.

Southern Christian Leadership Council (SCLC) Organization of African American church leaders, including King, providing provided crucial leadership for the Civil Rights Movement; founded in January 1957.

resistance techniques at the **Highlander Folk School**, Parks was aware of the momentum for desegregation stimulated by the *Brown* decision. But her main motive for getting arrested had to do with the daily indignities that blacks suffered on public transportation. Like Pauli Murray and Jackie Robinson before her, Parks took a stand against this type of abuse: "People always say that I didn't give up my seat because I was tired, but that isn't true. I was not tired physically, or no more tired than I usually was at the end of a working day. . . . No, the only tired I was, was tired of giving in."

After Parks's arrest on December 1, 1955, the Women's Political Council (a leading group of Montgomery's black women), the local NAACP, and prominent out-of-town Christian ministers organized the **Montgomery Improvement Association,** which conducted a massive boycott of city buses, calling for the hiring of African American bus drivers and restraints against the brutal enforcement of racial segregation on public transportation. The association chose as its president Reverend Martin Luther King Jr., the pastor of Dexter Avenue Baptist Church in Atlanta. The city's patience wore thin with the boycott in January as the mayor and city commissioners joined the **White Citizens' Council** of Mississippi, a popular segregationist organization prompted by the *Brown* decision. Soon the police arrested King, and a bomb exploded at his house while he and his family were away. The bombing generated great sympathy and financial contributions from white liberals and cemented King's image as the spokesperson for a broad-based movement for civil rights.

The **Montgomery bus boycott** continued for over a year, ending in December 1956, a month after the U.S. Supreme Court upheld a lower court ruling that declared bus segregation in Alabama violated the Fourteenth Amendment's equal protection clause. The civil rights activists had won an important victory that heightened King's popularity and influence. In January 1957, the Montgomery Improvement Association helped launch the **Southern Christian Leadership Council (SCLC),** a newly established civil rights organization led by black ministers practicing nonviolent means to end all forms of racial segregation. King served as the organization's first president.

24-2b Little Rock and Greensboro

The Civil Rights Movement focuses on implementing desegregation decisions.

The Civil Rights Movement spread to Little Rock, Arkansas, in 1957 when the **Little Rock Nine,** African American teenagers carefully selected by the NAACP, sought to attend a white high school following the *Brown* decision. Arkansas governor Orval Faubus called on the state's National Guard to block the black students from entering Central High School. The move provoked a constitutional crisis that ended in September 1957 when President Eisenhower sent one thousand federal troops to Little Rock to ensure that African Americans could attend the school unharmed. Meanwhile, the president took control of the Arkansas National Guard from Faubus, and for the

History without Borders

Racial, Ethnic, and Caste Discrimination

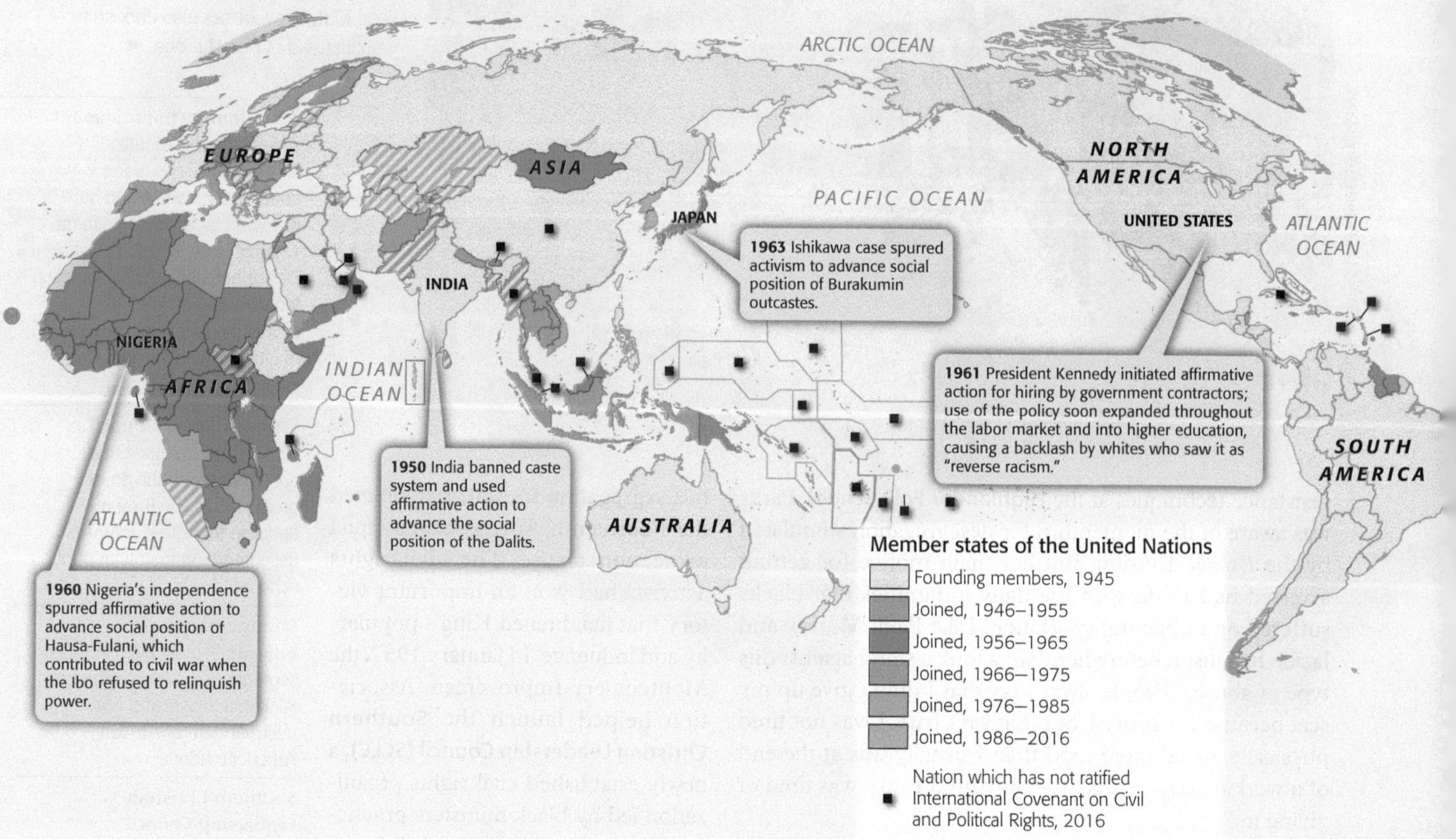
ARCTIC OCEAN
EUROPE
ASIA
NORTH AMERICA
PACIFIC OCEAN
JAPAN
UNITED STATES
ATLANTIC OCEAN
INDIA
NIGERIA
AFRICA
INDIAN OCEAN
SOUTH AMERICA
AUSTRALIA
ATLANTIC OCEAN
1963 Ishikawa case spurred activism to advance social position of Burakumin outcastes.
1961 President Kennedy initiated affirmative action for hiring by government contractors; use of the policy soon expanded throughout the labor market and into higher education, causing a backlash by whites who saw it as "reverse racism."
1950 India banned caste system and used affirmative action to advance the social position of the Dalits.
1960 Nigeria's independence spurred affirmative action to advance social position of Hausa-Fulani, which contributed to civil war when the Ibo refused to relinquish power.
Member states of the United Nations
Founding members, 1945
Joined, 1946–1955
Joined, 1956–1965
Joined, 1966–1975
Joined, 1976–1985
Joined, 1986–2016
Nation which has not ratified International Covenant on Civil and Political Rights, 2016

United Nations Member States, 1945-2016 Based on affirmative action programs practiced in India, Japan, Nigeria, and the United States, the United Nations Committee on Human Rights in 1969 announced that the overwhelming number of nations that had (or would) ratify the International Covenant on Civil and Political Rights must redress various forms of discrimination through special action, such as preferential treatment accorded to underprivileged group. ▲

The shocking murder of the young Emmett Till and other racist crimes committed against African Americans returned global attention to the horror of white supremacy that had killed millions of European Jews and other supposedly inferior racial groups during World War II. Asians and Africans also perpetrated crimes against groups of people based upon inherited ancestry. No country or people in the postwar world held a monopoly on this kind of discrimination.

India, the newly independent nation that impressed the world with its nonviolent revolution, was one of the worst offenders of human rights due to its ancient social hierarchy based on divisions known as "castes." While complex and unique unto itself, the four-tiered caste system in India was similar to the Jim Crow South discrimination in terms of its rigid and inherited ranking of groups, as well as its culturally accepted discrimination and violence perpetrated against the lowest people in the social order. In India these were the Dalits (the oppressed), who did not even have a position in the caste hierarchy—which made them "outcaste" peoples. Mohandas Gandhi bucked tradition in calling them *Harijans* (children of God), and in 1950, India outlawed the caste system and was the first country to use affirmation action policies—in this case to advance Dalit education and social mobility. But as in the United States, change came slowly and with great resistance.

Postwar Japan also made concerted efforts to rectify centuries of discrimination against its own outcastes, known as Burakumin (people of rural hamlets). Although the nation's caste system was abandoned in 1871 with Japan's modernization, and social equality was expanded in the postwar constitution, de jure Burakumin discrimination continued, especially in terms of housing, employment, and marriage. After World War II, the Buraku Liberation League emerged to raise awareness of these problems and fight, along with Japan's Socialist and Communist Parties, for the

Dinodia Photos/Alamy Stock Photo

Gandhi at Bhangi Untouchables Colony, Delhi, India, 1946 Mohandas Gandhi went on hunger strikes to protest the segregation of Indian untouchable castes (Dalit). His activism also involved changing the name of this group to "Harijan," or children of God. Yet Dalits themselves did not always welcome Gandhi's actions on their behalf, with some dubious as to the intentions of the privileged castes. Could a social revolution really come from above, or did it need to be generated from the Dalits themselves? ◄

AP Images/Koichiro Morita

Tokyo Demonstrators Scuffle with Riot Police, Tokyo, 1974 The Kazuo Ishikawa case sparked ongoing protests in Japan when in 1964 he was sentenced to death for the rape and murder of a sixteen-year-old girl. Activists claimed his arrest and conviction were the result of discrimination against his outcaste class, the burakumin. ◄

group's civil rights. One of the major cases centered on the 1963 arrest of Kazuo Ishikawa, a resident of a Burakumin community in Sayama City, who was accused of and sentenced to death for the rape and murder of a high school girl. Activists proclaimed the Ishikawa case was a miscarriage of justice and that he was falsely accused because of his social group status. Ishikawa's sentence was subsequently reduced to life imprisonment, and Japan too went on to enact affirmative action measures designed to promote speedy integration.

When Nigeria became independent in 1960, it too confronted the problem of social hierarchy based on inherited difference. In this case it centered on rival groups of black Africans, especially the Ibos, who descended from the country's southeast, and the Hausa-Fulani, who were based in the north. British colonialism had elevated the Ibos to become an educated, Christianized class who taught school and managed much of the empire's bureaucracy in West Africa, including in northern regions. The Hausa-Fulani, followers of Islam who resisted British missionary education, played little, if any, role in colonial administration. In 1951, only one person out of a northern population of 16 million had a university degree. When independence came, the Hausa-Fulani used affirmative action to advance their uneducated brethren into political positions in the north, while expelling the more qualified Ibo and others. Such ethnic conflict proliferated throughout Nigeria leading to an Ibo-led military coup in which the president, a northerner, was assassinated. Bloody riots erupted against the Ibo in the north that led southerners to secede from the nation, which, in turn, provoked civil war.

To compare struggles against Jim Crow in the U.S. South to simultaneous conflicts over racial, ethnic, and caste discrimination in India, Japan, and Nigeria is in no way to diminish the hateful and unique forms of racism that African Americans experienced. But such a comparison reveals global parallels to U.S. race relations in three ways. First, like the United States, India, Japan, and Nigeria possessed entrenched and rigidly enforced systems of social hierarchy based on inherited characteristics like race, ethnicity, or caste. Second, in the United States, India, Japan, and Nigeria, laws banning discrimination, while symbolically important, were not enough to create equality. Finally, eventually all of these countries used affirmative action programs in order to address past discrimination, and in each case the results were mixed at best.

Critical Thinking Questions

► How did race relations in the American South after World War II compare to social divisions in India, Japan, and Nigeria?

► What solutions did each country try for resolving entrenched discrimination, and what limited their success?

Go to MindTap® to engage with an interactive version of **History without Borders: Racial, Ethnic, and Caste Discrimination.** Learn from an interactive map, view related video, and respond to critical thinking questions.

Bettmann/Corbis

Global Americans **Thurgood Marshall** studied at Lincoln University, a historically black college in Pennsylvania, with the Harlem Renaissance poet Langston Hughes and the Cotton Club musician Cab Calloway. (Ghana's first president Kwame Nkrumah graduated from Lincoln nine years after Marshall.) After graduation, Marshall attended Howard University, where he fell under the influence of its dean, Charles Hamilton Houston, and graduated first in his class in 1933. Marshall went on to join the NAACP and lead its legal strategy to overthrow racial segregation, which included the victory in *Brown v. Board of Education* (1954). In 1967, he was the first African American appointed to the U.S. Supreme Court. Before this, Marshall was invited to newly independent Kenya in 1960 to participate in writing the nation's Bill of Rights. Drawing on the UN Declaration for Human Rights as well as the constitutions of newly independent Nigeria and Malaya, his efforts centered on the legal principle that "All persons are equal before the law and are entitled without discrimination or distinction of any kind . . . to equal protection of the law." As it turned out Kenyans did not follow Marshall's recommendation and did not accord equal protections either to the minority of white settlers who comprised the former colonial ruling class, or long-standing residents from India. Nevertheless, his involvement showed how ideas of American civil rights spread around the world and were adapted, or not, to differing societies and circumstances.

Little Rock Nine African American students enrolled at Little Rock's Central High School whose testing of desegregation orders in 1957 set off a storm of white protests.

remaining eight months of the school year, federal troops protected the Little Rock Nine. Not since Reconstruction had the federal government asserted its constitutional power to enforce civil rights against calls for states' rights.

Eisenhower's intervention in Little Rock stemmed not only from his defense of federal authority over the states, but also from Cold War concerns. He was aware that massive resistance to civil rights was damaging America's global image as a beacon of democracy. The Soviets highlighted U.S. civil rights violations as the sign of a white supremacist society that was ill equipped for world leadership. In a televised address to the nation during the Little Rock crisis, Eisenhower squarely addressed the international implications of American racism in saying, "Our enemies are gloating over this incident and using it everywhere to misrepresent our whole nation. We are portrayed as a violator of those standards of conduct which the peoples of the world united to proclaim in the Charter of the United Nations."

In February 1960, the Civil Rights Movement entered a new phase when four freshmen at North Carolina Agricultural and Technical (A&T) State University in Greensboro, North Carolina, directly confronted racial segregation by sitting down at a lunch counter in a store where they were allowed to buy school supplies but not to

St Petersburg Times/ZUMAPRESS/Newscom

Angry White Mob Protests Little Rock Nine at Central High, 1957 After a three-week standoff with President Eisenhower in September 1957, Arkansas governor Orval Faubus removed the state guardsmen from Little Rock's Central High, allowing an angry mob of white parents and supporters to chase off the black students while beating up seven journalists (three white, four black). This "Black Monday" forced Eisenhower to send in federal troops to thwart massive resistance and allow the Little Rock Nine to attend school. ◄

eat. Their sit-in protest electrified students at black colleges throughout the South. Within two weeks, the lunch-counter struggle had spread to fifteen cities in five states, thus politicizing a new generation of African Americans who were impatient waiting for court victories against segregation to become everyday reality. By August 1960, King and Ella Baker of SCLC worked with young activists to found the **Student Nonviolent Coordinating Committee (SNCC)**, which joined with the Congress of Racial Equality (CORE) to take civil rights struggles in a bolder, more assertive direction.

Established in Chicago in 1942, CORE grew out of the largely white pacifist Fellowship of Reconciliation, which supported conscientious objectors during World War II. One of these was James L. Farmer, an African American who came to embrace nonviolent resistance while studying at Howard University in the late 1930s, just before Pauli Murray entered its law school. A founder of CORE, Farmer and other CORE members took part in some of the first organized sit-in protests when they had successfully integrated Chicago restaurants during World War II. After working for America's Socialist Party, Farmer in the late 1950s returned to civil rights struggles, first with the NAACP and then back at CORE. In 1961, he led an interracial group on a **"freedom ride"** during which they sat in sections reserved for whites while traveling on buses throughout the South. A white mob in Alabama attacked and beat the "freedom riders" while also setting their Greyhound bus ablaze. Freedom riders actually sought to provoke this kind of violence in order to highlight to growing audiences outside the South the failure of southern states to observe Supreme Court rulings, which banned Jim Crow on interstate transportation, bus stops, and train stations, such as the one ending the Montgomery bus boycott.

The youthful SNCC members expanded the freedom ride campaign while at the same time launching a grass roots strategy of empowering rural people to lead their own struggles, rather than simply following the NAACP or King and the SCLC. This "bottom-up" strategy transformed the Civil Rights Movement from a drive for legal and political reform to a call for social revolution.

24-2c Perspectives of Movement Activists

Civil Rights Movement activists express varying positions on strategy, tactics, and leadership.

Since the Montgomery bus boycott, Martin Luther King Jr. remained the movement's most recognized figure. Charismatic and a spell-binding orator, King became celebrated across the nation mainly because his vision of interracial democracy was consistent with postwar sensibilities. Like Walter White and Jackie Robinson, he asserted the loyalty of black Americans and warned that civil rights struggles needed to be ever vigilant against "exploitation by Communist forces." And like Pauli Murray and James L. Farmer, he assured that racial reform was best achieved through nonviolent means. Known as the "American Gandhi," King, along with Rosa Parks and labor activists, had been taught tactics of civil disobedience at the Highlander Folk School. Owing to his Christianity, anticommunism, and nonviolence, King attracted widespread national and global support for the Civil Rights Movement, including sizable financial contributions.

But King was more than just a symbol of the nation's best intentions. Despite his rejection of communism as giving too much power to the state, he did not embrace U.S. capitalism. Privately, he chose the path of democratic socialism that combined the country's commitment to political freedoms with the emphasis on the government's responsibility to respect workers' and poor people's economic rights. His model for democratic socialism was Sweden, not the autocratic socialism of the Soviet Union. King appreciated Gandhi not only for his nonviolent tactics, but also for his rejection of material possessions and identification with outcaste peoples. The preacher's concerns about economic justice also drew him to the black labor organizer A. Philip Randolph, who since the 1920s was a major figure in linking the struggle for civil rights with the U.S. labor movement. Finally, King's interest in socialism put him in good stead with Third World leaders such as Ghana's Kwame Nkrumah and India's first prime minister, Jawaharal Nehru, both of whom advocated non-alignment, refusing to ally with either the Soviet Union or United States in the Cold War. Thus, there were two sides to King: the crusader working to desegregate the South and the radical seeking to transform the entire country into a model of democratic socialism.

King's complex motivations reflected those of the Civil Rights Movement as a whole. The African Americans who risked their lives and livelihoods for the movement were not necessarily in it for the same reasons. King himself recognized differences between middle-class blacks like himself and the working-class blacks who constituted the bulk of the Montgomery boycotters. To the middle class, the boycott was a sign that blacks would no longer tolerate demeaning segregation, while to the workers, it was a way to expose an economic system that exploited black labor. While the middle-class wanted equal respect, the working class wanted equal pay.

The nature of leadership proved another division within the movement. Whereas organizations such as NAACP and SCLC relied on the "talented tenth" of blacks to lead the black masses, SNCC wanted to help them to articulate and advance their own struggles. The talents of someone like King proved crucial for soliciting valuable support from outside the South and inspiring a mass movement. But longtime female

Student Nonviolent Coordinating Committee (SNCC) Founded in August 1960, the committee introduced to the Civil Rights Movement new and more provocative tactics, like sit-in protests.

"freedom ride" Tactic of riding in the whites-only section of segregated interstate buses to provoke violent responses; used effectively by Congress of Racial Equality (CORE) starting in 1961.

activists like Septima Clark and Ella Baker encouraged him to promote a bottom-up approach. Clark asked King "not to lead all the marches himself, but instead to develop leaders who could lead their own marches." Baker pushed him to reach out to rural blacks whom the movement all but ignored. Although neither were able to change SCLC's top-down leadership style, Baker was able to ensure that the young SNCC activists took on the bottom-up priorities that she championed.

Confronting a virtually all-male leadership, Clark and Baker also opposed sexism within the movement. Although King and other civil rights leaders knew that black women were invaluable soldiers for the struggle, they discounted their leadership potential. This was a classic form of male chauvinism, but for black men who had been stripped of their manhood by white racism, it took on special significance. Much of the motivation for the civil rights struggles came from the desire by both men and women to give black men decent jobs so that they could provide for their families. For many black women, an economically stable, male-oriented household, common in white suburbs at the time, would be a welcome step-up on the social ladder. In this way, Murray's criticism of **Jane Crow** did not possess a large appeal in the black community until after the proliferation of feminism in the 1970s.

24-2d Perspectives of White Resisters

Resistance to civil rights reforms reflects growing diversity in the white South.

As with black civil rights activists, the perspectives of white resisters were not all the same. Their response to the movement can be divided into two groups: those who actively resisted integration and those who accepted the inevitability of integration but sought to limit it to superficial levels.

The first group engaged in **massive resistance** to civil rights reforms, and consisted largely of white Southerners. Its leaders included governors such as Alabama's George Wallace and Arkansas's Orval Faubus, and other high-ranking politicians whose electoral base was in rural counties. Immediately after the *Brown* decision, one hundred and one members of Congress signed a **southern manifesto** to "resist forced integration by any lawful means." The resistance coalesced in White Citizens' Councils that with more than two hundred fifty thousand members held significant clout in state and local governments. In addition, at least ten southern states passed **interposition** laws that declared the *Brown* decision unconstitutional in order to prevent racial integration. Schools closed rather than integrate and public funds went to various "academies" that excluded blacks. In addition, the resistance garnered support from the business community, which during the Montgomery bus boycott, for example, put pressure on white employers to fire civil rights activists from their jobs and to cut off supplies and loans to black farmers and businesses that supported the movement. Finally, white resisters did not limit themselves to political and economic tactics, but engaged in repeated and systematic violence, including murder, designed to intimidate civil rights workers. The notoriously racist and nativist Ku Klux Klan, that garnered national attention during Reconstruction as well as during the 1920s, rose again as a vehicle of resistance and terror.

Yet there was another white South that embraced the nation's new postwar economy rather than looking back to the region's segregationist past. Five southern states (Texas, Tennessee, Florida, Maryland, and North Carolina) rejected massive resistance and implemented the *Brown* decision without major incident. Even within those states engaging in massive resistance, some county and city governments, as well as newspapers, adopted a gradual, rather than hostile, approach to integration. In this way, both Little Rock's mayor and its leading newspaper opposed Governor Faubus's showdown at Central High, pleading with Eisenhower to send federal troops.

Southern acceptance of civil rights stemmed from the wave of postwar prosperity that benefited the South and the rest of the nation. Prosperity expanded the South's higher education institutions, white-collar professions, high-tech industries, and suburban neighborhoods. The average Southerner's income rose from 50 percent of the national average in 1940 to 77 percent in 1960. The region's economy attracted waves of northern professionals while the mechanization of the cotton industry and switch to less labor-intensive crops such as soybeans and peanuts sent an equal number of black and white agricultural workers away from the South. Southern suburbanites were most receptive to limited racial reform.

A revealing expression of the post-World War II South was the open-school movement that occurred in Atlanta, Georgia. The struggle pitted white, upper-middle class women against the state's segregationist governor, Ernest Vandiver. Shocked at the resistance to integration in Little Rock, the women established Help Our Public Education (HOPE) and campaigned against Vandiver's reelection in the name of integrating Atlanta schools so that the city would be in compliance with the *Brown* decision. The women framed the issue as in the best interest of white children and the city's overall commerce and industry. In so doing, HOPE gave little, if any, credence to the perspectives of black activists or the social justice reasons for civil rights. HOPE won huge support in urban and suburban Atlanta, forcing Vandiver to give up massive

Jane Crow System of gender and sex segregation in which women suffer discrimination.

massive resistance Fierce public opposition to civil rights struggles and laws by a vocal and active portion of white Southerners.

southern manifesto Document signed by one hundred one members of the U.S. Congress, nearly all from the South, opposing Supreme Court orders to desegregate public places.

interposition Legal theory, often seen as synonymous with nullification, through which a state or group of states has the right to oppose federal rulings.

resistance. But the floodgates to integration did not open; instead, local school boards used a host of mechanisms to severely limit the number of African Americans in formerly all-white schools. This pattern of resistance through tokenization would become the norm throughout the nation as suburbanites in all regions would come to see meaningful racial integration as a threat to property values and the quality of neighborhood schools.

24-3

Enactment of Rights-Based Liberalism

Historical/Corbis

King highlighted the March on Washington in August 1963 with his stirring "I Have a Dream" speech that envisioned an America where persons "will not be judged by the color of their skin but by the content of their character." The signs held by activists in this photograph reveal the breadth of issues subsumed under the rubric of civil rights.

Why do you think that voting rights, jobs, and decent housing were important to civil rights activists? ▶

Go to MindTap® to practice history with the Chapter 24 **Primary Source Writing Activity: Peak of the Civil Rights Movement.** Read and view primary sources and respond to a writing prompt.

The peak of the Civil Rights Movement occurred during the early 1960s when conflict over civil rights at home as well as condemnation of racism around the world pressured Presidents Kennedy and Johnson to ensure the enactment of major civil and voting rights legislation. These were the goals that movement activists had been working toward. Yet because winning political rights did little to help millions of poor, unemployed black Americans within and outside the South, attention turned to securing economic rights. President Johnson urged Congress to enact a historic package of legislation that provided historic social welfare rights, liberalized immigration policy, and offered new federal support for the aged, the natural environment, consumers, and those lacking health care insurance.

☞ As you read, pay attention to the main components of the U.S. "rights-based liberalism." What problems did these rights intend to resolve?

24-3a New Frontiers for Civil Rights

The Civil Rights Movement employs new tactics to encourage major legislation.

The first televised presidential debate in 1960 presented a visual contrast between the youthful good looks of the Democrat candidate John F. Kennedy and the staid and somewhat uneasy appearance of the Republican Richard Nixon. The reality was that both men were ardent cold warriors with weak records on civil rights. Kennedy, who barely won the election, owed his victory to support from crucial southern states that disenfranchised black voters. Because his chances for reelection depended upon votes from white southern Democrats, the new president did not act quickly to fulfill campaign promises he had made to black voters.

Yet mounting international pressure against racial segregation in the United States forced the president's hand. Acknowledging such pressure, Secretary of State Dean Rusk admitted, "The biggest single burden that we carry on our backs in our foreign relations in the 1960s is the problem of racial discrimination." Meanwhile, UN representatives from newly independent African and Asian nations pressured the General Assembly to adopt the Declaration of the Granting of Independence to Colonial Countries and Peoples, which condemned colonialism as a violation of the UN Charter and Declaration of Human Rights, and a threat to world peace. Another sign of the growing power of Afro-Asian nations was the election of U Thant as UN Secretary-General in 1961. Thant, the first nonwhite leader of a major organization of international governance, was a civil servant in Burma's colonial government and major player in the Bandung conference in 1955 that galvanized the nonalignment movement among newly independent nations (such as his own country of

Burma), who chose to ally with neither the United States nor the Soviet Union.

At this moment, many civil rights activists in the United States found common cause with independence movements in Africa and Asia. While most activists, such as King, continued to embrace the example of India's nonviolent revolution, a growing number, given the intransigence of American racism and violent resistance to civil rights, began to embrace more militant models of anticolonial revolution. One such model was Frantz Fanon's *The Wretched of the Earth*, a manifesto for Third World revolutionaries published in 1961 that posed a stunning critique of white racism and its impact on black African colonial subjects. Younger activists in particular were drawn to radical intellectuals such as Fanon, who fought for Algerian independence from French rule, and Ernesto "Che" Guevara, the Latin American revolutionary instrumental in Castro's victory in Cuba. For similar reasons, civil rights activists were drawn to Malcolm X, spokesman for the Nation of Islam, a black Muslim organization in the United States. Rooted in the tradition of Marcus Garvey's "back to Africa movement" of the 1920s, the Nation of Islam saw white racism to be an insurmountable barrier to racial equality in the United States. As a result, they called for blacks to separate from the degrading influence of white America and to develop all-black communities that nurtured and sustained black identity.

By the early 1960s, the national media portrayed Malcolm X as a hate-monger whose racial separatism and condoning of black self-defense "by any means necessary" was in dangerous opposition to King's nonviolent civil disobedience. The reality was more complicated. Like King, Malcolm changed his views over time and in March 1964, Malcolm left the Nation of Islam due to conflict with its leader, Elijah Muhammad, and began to forge ties with whites as well as civil rights organizations such as SNCC. At the time of his assassination in February 1965, Malcolm had been speaking out against the Nation of Islam.

In addition to increasing pressure from abroad and the radicalization of the Civil Rights Movement at home, President Kennedy also faced his own brother, Attorney General Robert Kennedy, who urged him to take progressive action for civil rights. Meanwhile, confrontations in the South grew more violent. Like the freedom rides, James Meredith's attempt to enroll at the all-white University of Mississippi ignited a showdown between Kennedy and white supremacists. The crisis began in September 1962 when the Mississippi governor, backed by an angry mob of white students, defied a federal court order by literally blocking the African American veteran from campus registration. Kennedy responded by sending five hundred federal marshals to protect Meredith in his multiple attempts to enroll, but this was not enough to prevent a violent campus riot that left two persons dead and a large number of the marshals wounded. The president then deployed five thousand army troops to disperse the mob and gain control of the campus. Although order was restored, Meredith required armed guards at Ole Miss until he graduated in August 1963.

A second showdown in Birmingham, Alabama, pushed Kennedy solidly into the civil rights camp. King chose to provoke a confrontation in this large industrial city because it was a bastion of violent racial oppression—the press nicknamed it "Bombingham" because since 1947 the city's civil rights workers had been victimized by fifty "unsolved" bombings. The white segregationist Eugene "Bull" Connor, Birmingham's powerful police chief, turned the Ku Klux Klan loose on freedom riders

Archive Photos/Pictorial Parade/Getty Images

Malcolm X Meets with Saudi Arabian Prince (later King) Faisal al-Saud in Mecca, Saudi Arabia, 1964 Malcolm Little joined the Nation of Islam when he was in prison and after being paroled in 1952, he revealed his devotion to black nationalism by replacing his surname with the letter X, which stood for the African name that had been taken from his ancestors. In 1964, he traveled to the Middle East on a holy pilgrimage and received invitations from pan-African leaders to serve in the governments in Egypt, Ghana, and Algeria. ◀

and closed all of the city's parks, playgrounds, and golf courses when a court ordered their integration. From January to May 1963, SCLC and local civil rights activists engaged in nonviolent resistance, including the acceptance of police brutality and mass incarceration, in order to gain sympathy from a watchful national and world audience. For the first time, the activists deployed a **children's movement** in which hundreds of children and youth marched into the center of the conflict, a deliberate strategy to increase emotional appeal.

Connor arrested hundreds of civil rights protesters including King, who then wrote **Letter from a Birmingham Jail,** an eloquent and widely circulated statement about the necessity to break morally unjust laws. More important, television and still cameras captured images of defenseless movement activists (some of whom were children) being assaulted by high-pressure water cannons and vicious police dogs. This violence, and the international condemnation that the United States received from it, compelled Kennedy to act. In a televised address to the nation, he asked "are we to say to the world, and, much more importantly, for each other, that this is a land of the free except for the Negroes; that we have no second-class citizens except Negroes; that we have no class or caste system, no ghettos, no master race, except with respect to Negroes?"

After the Birmingham crisis, Kennedy promised to push Congress to pass major civil rights legislation to enforce court-ordered integration. King and the labor leader A. Philip Randolph organized a **March on Washington for Jobs and Freedom** in August 1963 to make sure the president lived up to his word. More than one-quarter of a million people rallied at the Lincoln Memorial, including all major civil rights groups (NAACP, SCLC, CORE, and SNCC) together with leading labor unions, and white liberal organizations. The folk singer Joan Baez led the hand-holding crowd in a memorable rendition of "We Shall Overcome," the movement's unofficial theme song. The climax of the day was King's "I Have a Dream" speech in which he shared a vision of a harmonious, interracial United States that would inspire not only Americans but also generations of downtrodden people around the world seeking to become "Free at last!"

Kennedy did not live to see his civil rights bill become law; he was assassinated in November 1963 by Lee Harvey Oswald, a former Marine and outspoken Communist. As the nation mourned, Lyndon Johnson took over as president and forced the bill successfully through Congress as a tribute to Kennedy. The resulting **Civil Rights Act,** signed into law on July 2, 1964, outlawed segregation and discrimination in all businesses involved in interstate commerce. Another part of the act responded to sit-in protests and freedom rides by forbidding racial discrimination in restaurants, hotels, theaters, and other forms of "public accommodation." (An exception, which would later prove important, was made for religious institutions.) The new law also backed the *Brown* decision by disallowing discrimination in any organization that received federal funds, which by the mid-1960s included almost all public school districts. The act's most important protection involved employment discrimination, and the **Equal Employment Opportunity Commission,** a federal investigatory agency, was established to monitor employment practices. Overlooked by many lawmakers who debated it, the Civil Rights Act also included women as a protected class, which meant that for the first time in U.S. history, it was unlawful to discriminate on the basis of sex in public accommodations, federal funded organizations, or any type of employment.

24-3b Johnson and the Election of 1964

Johnson is elected despite infringements on black voting rights in the South.

Although the Civil Rights Act was the most comprehensive civil rights legislation since Reconstruction, movement activists found it difficult to celebrate when the vast majority of southern blacks could not vote (in many states the figure was as low as 23 percent of the eligible black electorate). SNCC and other civil rights workers understood this through their work in rural Mississippi and in the summer of 1964, when nine hundred volunteers, mostly white college students, sought to counteract blacks' disenfranchisement. At the start of the **Mississippi Freedom Summer** program, two white volunteers and one black SNCC activist were killed, drawing international attention to the cause. After they were prevented from registering blacks to vote, the activists organized an alternative "freedom ballot" that elected a slate of almost all African American delegates to the Democratic National Convention held that summer in Atlantic City, New Jersey. These delegates from the **Mississippi Freedom Democratic Party** sought unsuccessfully to replace those from the state's white-only Democratic Party. Johnson, seeking to avoid controversy, brokered a deal in which only two of the Freedom delegates would be seated at the convention. Disillusioned by Johnson, the black activists denounced him and white liberals in general. Fanny Lou Hamer, a cotton

children's movement Civil rights strategy used in Birmingham, Alabama, that gained worldwide sympathy to the cause in Birmingham 1963 by subjecting school children to arrest and violent counter protests.

Letter from a Birmingham Jail Written statement made by Dr. Martin Luther King Jr. in April 1963 about the purpose and necessity of nonviolence resistance.

March on Washington for Jobs and Freedom Massive Washington, D.C., civil rights demonstration in 1963 featuring King's famous "I Have a Dream" speech.

Civil Rights Act Landmark legislation approved in July 1964 outlawing a wide range of discrimination on the basis of race, sex, color, religion, and other forms of prejudice.

Equal Employment Opportunity Commission, Federal body established in 1965 to enforce Civil Rights Act's protections against workplace discrimination regarding race, sex, color, religion, and other forms of prejudice.

Mississippi Freedom Summer SNCC program in the summer of 1964 that recruited white college students from the North to promote black voting in Mississippi.

Mississippi Freedom Democratic Party Alternative Democratic Party in Mississippi whose challenge to the state's white-only Democratic Party created a showdown at the Democratic National Convention in August 1964.

Voting Rights Act Landmark legislation approved in August 1965 guaranteeing the nonrestriction of voting rights based on race, gender, color, and other forms of prejudice.

International Convention on the Elimination of All Forms of Racial Discrimination U.N. treaty approved in 1965 that contributed to the lessening of formal discrimination in the vast majority of nations that signed it.

sharecropper who testified on television about the troubles she faced in trying to register to vote, proclaimed, "We didn't come all this way for no two seats, 'cause all of us is tired."

Johnson, even without the support of either the white or black Mississippi delegates, went on to win the Democratic nomination. The Republican candidate was Arizona senator Barry Goldwater, who strongly opposed the Social Security Act along with other parts of the New Deal welfare state. Goldwater also took a hard-line position against communism, telling a reporter that he would drop a "low-yield atomic bomb" to fight Communists in Vietnam. Goldwater's election slogans tried to appeal to the nation's core anti-Communist sentiment by saying: "In your heart, you know he's right." The Johnson campaign portrayed Goldwater as a dangerous extremist who would start a nuclear war by ignoring the internationalist precedents and organizations established by Truman, Eisenhower, and Kennedy. The Democrats parodied Goldwater's slogan by saying: "In your heart, you know he might."

Johnson won in a landslide, capturing 16 million more votes than Goldwater and winning every state but Arizona and five in the South. In addition, he carried thirty-seven new Democrats to the House of Representatives and two to the Senate, giving the party solid control in both houses. The stage was set for Johnson to forge his own liberal domestic agenda that would exceed Kennedy's and arguably match that of Roosevelt's New Deal.

24-3c Voting Rights

Johnson secures voting rights for southern blacks, but the United States balks at helping the United Nations to secure broad-based human rights.

In 1965, King and the SCLC initiated another confrontation when they came to Selma, Alabama, and marched to Governor George Wallace's office in Montgomery to deliver a list of grievances that called particular attention to voting rights. The Selma march provoked an attack by the local authorities and pressured President Johnson to call for stronger legislation to protect black voters. Raised in segregated Texas, Johnson was personally familiar with the problem of black and Mexican American disenfranchisement. In August 1965, he signed into law the **Voting Rights Act,** another legislative landmark that overruled a jumble of state and local policies preventing southern blacks from voting and, more important, provided federal oversight for voter registration and elections. The act's impact was immediate and striking. Within four years, black voter registration in Mississippi shot up from 7 to 59 percent and in Alabama increased from 23 to 59 percent (Map 24.1).

Not long after the Voting Rights Act, the United Nations, led by the Afro-Asian contingent, also stepped up its opposition to racism by approving the **International Convention on the Elimination of All Forms of Racial Discrimination**. For the first time in history, nations of the world bound themselves by treaty "to adopt all necessary measures for speedily eliminating racial discrimination in all its forms and manifestations, and to prevent and combat racist doctrines and practices in order to promote understanding between races and to build an international community free from all forms of racial segregation and racial discrimination." A handful of countries rejected the convention, including Israel and South Africa, which by this time had implemented a full-scale separation of the races (apartheid). Despite the U.S. government's support for civil and voting rights at home, the Senate did not ratify the UN convention until 1994 due to the nation's reliance on South Africa and its equally white supremacist neighbor Rhodesia for rare raw materials crucial for military weaponry. Until the late 1970s, U.S. Cold War strategy prevented the nation from opposing apartheid and other forms of racism abroad.

It could also be said that Americans were halfhearted in their attempts to eliminate all forms of racism, given the deep structural racism in the United States that was not remedied by civil and voting rights legislation. As the critic Michael Harrington argued in *The Other America* (1962), poverty and racial inequality were built in to the U.S. economy and therefore could not be easily eliminated (see Chapter 23). Women and racial minorities still faced economic, social, and political disadvantages in a society that had been designed to ensure the liberties and social mobility of white men. Massive resistance in the South and racial inequality in the nation's central cities called for a comprehensive government response to rectify decades of structural inequality.

24-3d Great Society Welfare State

Johnson initiates the most expansive social and economic welfare and environmental protections since the New Deal.

As with the Civil Rights Act, Johnson followed Kennedy's initial response to the nation's economic and social crises. A New Deal administrator who had grown up poor, Johnson was already sensitive to the disadvantages of poverty well before Harrington's book influenced a national conversation about it. Johnson closely identified with Franklin Roosevelt. On becoming president, Johnson's

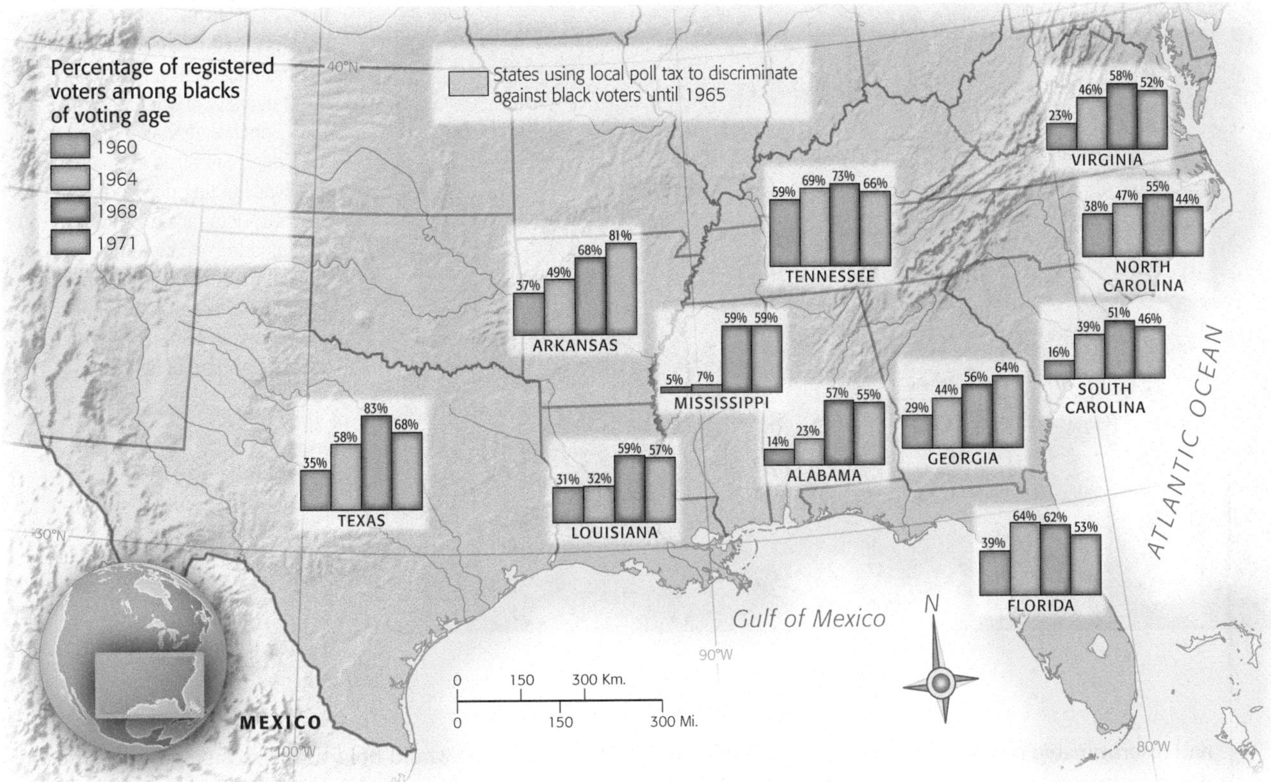

Map 24.1 Black Voting in the South, 1960–1971 In 1960 a majority of African Americans voted in only one (Tennessee) out of eleven states in the South. By 1968, due to compliance with the Voting Rights Act, this was true in all eleven states. ▲

leadership led Congress to pass a wealth of social welfare programs known collectively as the **Great Society**. The centerpiece was the Economic Opportunity Act of 1964, which established the Office of Economic Opportunity (OEO) to oversee the administration's self-declared **War on Poverty**. A major part of OEO's efforts was to increase Social Security benefits for the aged and restore Depression-era programs providing job training, food stamps, and housing assistance. The biggest increase in spending went to Aid to Families with Dependent Children (AFDC), a New Deal welfare program that during the 1960s doubled in size, expanding coverage from 3.1 million to 6.1 million children. Although Johnson was not able to end poverty, his programs helped to cut in half the number of poor people between 1960 and 1970, to just over 10 percent of the nation's population, the lowest level in the twentieth century.

Johnson also spurred Congress to offer federally backed health care to nonveterans for the first time in U.S. history. **Medicare and Medicaid** covered millions of uninsured aged and poor citizens respectively, prompting a historic expansion of the health care industry. The Great Society also provided the first major federal aid for elementary and secondary education in the United States. These funds were given to states based upon their number of poor students, and in order to receive them school districts had to comply with all federal civil rights statutes. As a former teacher, Johnson had an expansive view of educational support that included programs for preschoolers, increased loans for college students, funds for the arts and humanities, and the establishment of the Corporation for Public Broadcasting, which sponsored noncommercial television channels that gave birth to educational programs like kid-favorite *Sesame Street.*

Civil rights leaders compelled Johnson to commit the nation to India's idea of atoning for past inequalities by giving special aid to aggrieved groups. In the United States this **affirmative action** meant that any group either doing business with the federal government or receiving funds from it must have programs giving women and racial minorities an advantage over their competition. The classic case was an elite university that

Great Society Legislation passed under President Johnson expanding and initiating social welfare programs as well as environmental and consumer protections.

War on Poverty An early and crucial part of President Johnson's Great Society addressing widespread poverty through the newly created Office of Economic Opportunity (OEO).

Medicare and Medicaid Federal social insurance programs, established in 1965 as part of the Great Society program, guaranteeing access to health care for the elderly and disadvantaged.

affirmative action Policies that take into account race, sex, class, and other bases of disadvantage as a remedy for racial discrimination and inequality.

LBJ Library photo by Cecil Stoughton.

President Johnson on a Tour of Poverty in Appalachia, 1964 In a commencement address given at the University of Michigan in May 1965, Johnson unveiled his vision of the United States as a "great society" that was not just rich and powerful but that "demands an end to poverty and injustice." Postwar prosperity made him far more confident than Franklin Roosevelt that the nation could provide all citizens with a decent standard of living. ◄

had discriminated against women and racial minorities for decades, changing its admissions standards in order to give preference to applicants based on their race or gender. In an effort to remedy hard-hit central cities, Johnson created Veterans Health Information Systems and Technology Architecture (a VISTA), a domestic equivalent to the Peace Corps that encouraged American youth to devote themselves to their fellow citizens in need. More controversial was the OEO's Community Action Program (CAP). The philosophy behind these programs borrowed from SNCC's goal in the rural South: to help disadvantaged communities by empowering residents to lead themselves. Many young activists from the Civil Rights Movement found their way to one of the one thousand CAP programs around the country. And like SNCC, CAP's bottom-up perspective provoked hostility from competing groups seeking to impose top-down solutions. City officials were the most distrustful of CAP programs, and in one case, the mayor of Los Angeles blamed CAP workers for the violence in the city's Watts neighborhood.

Consumer and environmental crises also encouraged Johnson to expand federal regulations in new directions. Great Society legislation regarding truth in advertising forced cigarette manufacturers to print warnings on their packages about the health risks associated with smoking. He also responded favorably to activist Ralph Nader's campaigns for safer automobiles and children's products by increasing the reach of federal consumer protections. Finally, environmentalists were pleased when the president set aside millions of acres of wilderness from economic development and when his wife Lady Bird Johnson led efforts to clean up and control advertising on federal highways. Younger environmentalists pressured the president to establish clean air and water standards and enforcement agencies that would hold businesses responsible for toxic waste and other dangers to the public's health and the natural environment (see Table 24.2).

The hidden costs of postwar economic development involved environmental and consumer problems that affected rich and poor alike. While Michael Harrington made middle-class Americans feel guilty about their suburban comforts, Rachel Carson's *Silent Spring* (1962) aroused fears that capitalism threatened their health. A biologist who worked for the U.S. Fish and Wildlife Service, Carson targeted agribusinesses and the chemical industry for introducing pesticides and herbicides that were harmful to humans. The title *Silent Spring* referred to a nightmare scenario in which the antimosquito pesticide DDT had the unintended effect of destroying an area's entire bird life and even worse, working its way up the food chain from insects, to fish, birds, other animals, and humans. Carson added that the chemical revolution in agriculture was destroying the beauty of the natural environment by encouraging the development of pesticide-resistant strains of insects and opportunistic weeds. She raised the nation's awareness about the negative effects that came with seemingly benevolent industrial chemicals and brought increased attention to other ways that pollution compromised the nation's health and natural beauty.

The Great Society's gains were real but limited. The nation's income gap did not close as the richest fifth of the population continued to receive 44 percent of total income while the poorest fifth claimed 4 percent. The results regarding race relations were also mixed. Although civil rights protections and affirmative action preferences helped to expand the middle-class in black, Mexican American, and other racial minority communities, these

Table 24.2 Great Society Agencies, Laws, and Programs

If the New Deal built the foundation for U.S. welfare policies, then the Great Society added on to this foundation by eliminating racial discrimination, expanding social and economic rights for the nation's most vulnerable groups, and increasing medical, environmental, educational, and cultural benefits for all Americans.

Year	Legislation	Description
1963	Clean Air Act	Initiated federal attempt to control air pollution
1964	Civil Rights Act	Outlawed discrimination based on race, color, religion, sex, or national origin and established the Equal Employment Opportunity Commission (EEOC) to ensure implementation
1964	Office of Economic Opportunity (OEO)	Implemented and oversaw War on Poverty programs including increases in Social Security benefits, job training, food stamps, assistance for rural families, VISTA, and community action programs (CAP)
1965	Voting Rights Act	Prohibited racial discrimination in voting
1965	Social Security Act	Authorized Medicare and provided federal funding for older people's health care.
1965	Immigration Act	Reformed unequal and discriminatory immigration policy by establishing equal and expanded quotas for all nations outside the Western Hemisphere and for the first time limited immigration from countries there
1965	Elementary and Secondary Education Act	Provided federal funding to public schools, particularly in low-income areas and established a program to prepare low-income children for kindergarten (Head Start)
1965	Higher Education Act	Increased federal funding for enabling low-income persons to enroll in postsecondary and higher education
1965	National Foundation on the Arts and Humanities Act	Established the channels for federal funding of the arts and humanities through the National Endowment for the Arts and National Endowment for the Humanities
1965	Water Quality Act	Required states to set standards for water quality on interstate rivers and other bodies of water
1965	Housing and Urban Development Act	Provided rent subsidies and home ownership aid for low-income Americans
1965	Highway Beautification Act	Limited billboards and other types of advertisements, as well as junkyards, and abandoned vehicles on interstate highways
1966	Highway Safety Act	Established bureau that would become the National Highway Traffic Safety Administration (NHTSA) to reduce highway fatalities and promote safe automobiles
1967	Public Broadcasting Act	Chartered the Corporation for Public Broadcasting as a private, non-profit organization receiving federal funds to promote television programs catering to the public interest.
1968	Fair Housing Act	Banned racial discrimination in housing and provided federal assistance to the rehabilitation of low-income housing

breakthroughs did little to alter persistent structures of disadvantage that plagued the urban and rural poor. For most of those at the bottom of the economic ladder, Great Society programs failed to overcome the inexorable forces of the Cold War economy, which expanded and made more permanent the divide between white suburbs and nonwhite central cities.

24-3e Immigration Reform and Criminalization

A final element of the Great Society was comprehensive immigration reform. Although reforms had begun to take

Although imperfect, immigration reform removes the legacy of racial and national discrimination.

Immigration Act of 1965 Policy shift that proved an unexpected boon to immigration by ending discriminatory national origins quotas and setting preferences for family reunification, job skills, and refugees.

place under Truman, the discriminatory national origins quotas remained in place. Like civil rights legislation, immigration reform reflected the larger rejection of racism operating throughout the world. Canada took the lead in 1962 by removing its own race-based immigration preferences (known as the *"White Canada policy"*) in order to operate more effectively in the United Nations. (Australia all but removed its race-based *"White Australia"* policies in 1966). Immigration reform in the United States, was held up in Congress until the Johnson administration in October 1965 facilitated passage of the **Immigration Act of 1965**. The 1965 act nearly doubled the annual cap on immigration from 155,000 to 290,000. It also eliminated the bias against immigrants from Asia and Eastern and Southern Europe by giving the same yearly quota of twenty thousand immigrants for every nation outside the Western Hemisphere. This was intended to be what one historian calls a "cautious reform." Doubling the annual ceiling on immigration to two hundred ninety thousand still amounted to just one-sixth of 1 percent of the nation's population, a miniscule fraction compared to the more than 10 percent figures for incoming European immigrants in the nineteenth and early twentieth centuries. The Japanese American Citizens League, a prominent Asian American civil rights organization, while accepting the act, criticized its design to preserve the numerical dominance of whites in the United States. And yet, unforeseen by its sponsors, the Immigration Act actually greatly boosted the number of Asian and especially Latino immigrants, which soon became the nation's top two sources of newcomers. The reasons for this unexpected outcome are complicated, but they centered on the preferences established by the Immigration Act, which privileged family reunification, needed workers, and refugees from Communist countries. In gaining access to the United States through one of these preferences, immigrants were able to bring their parents, children, siblings, and other relatives through a process of "chain migration" in which the coming of one led to that of many others.

For Latino immigrants and other peoples in the Western Hemisphere, the Immigration Act was not a cautious reform but a clear setback. When the United States began to protect its borders after World War I, immigrants from North and South America had been exempt from the 155,000 annual ceiling. The 1965 act cancelled this exemption. It limited the number of immigrants from the Americas to no more than 120,000 out of the 290,000 total annual cap. The 120,000 figure represented a 40 percent decline in the pre-1965 level of Western Hemisphere migration. Liberal congressmen expressed equity concerns in seeking to bring in line the nation's two different policies for the Eastern and Western Hemispheres. Was it fair, they asked, for Mexicans (and Canadians) to enjoy unlimited migration while the European nations were limited to 20,000? Conservatives warned about the dramatic increase in Mexican immigrants—a "brown peril" replacing the early twentieth century fear of being flooded by "yellow hordes" from Asia. They also pointed to a rapid population increase throughout Latin America and predicted that the Latino population in the United States would triple in forty-five years (see Figure 24.2).

Mexican immigrants suffered the most from the new limitation. By 1965 with Asian immigration cut off for decades and increasing numbers of whites and blacks heading to cities, Mexicans became the main source of migrant farm labor throughout the Southwest. No immigration policy could stop the demand for Mexican labor. From World War II until 1964, U.S. immigration officials sought to regulate the northward flow of Mexican workers (sometimes for their own good) through *bracero* guest worker programs. But in the end, U.S. farmers kept hiring cheaper and easier to obtain undocumented workers

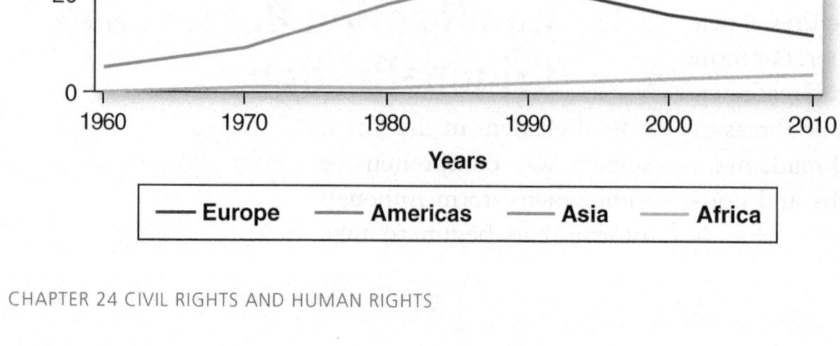

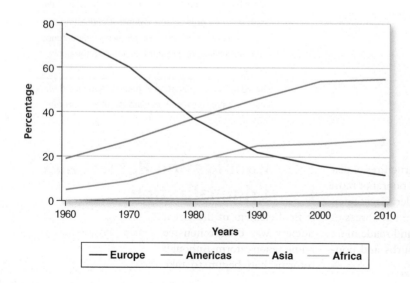

Figure 24.2 U.S. Immigrant Population by World Region, 1960–2010 Even before the Immigration Act of 1965, immigration from Europe was declining while that from the Americas (mainly Mexico) and Asia was rising. The result, as shown here, is that number of immigrants in the United States from these regions dramatically increased as more entered while the older generation of European immigrants passed away. ◀ Source: Migration Policy Institute tabulation of data from the U.S. Census Bureau, including the U.S. Census Bureau's 2006 to 2013 American Community Survey and 2000 Decennial Census. Data for 1960 to 1990 were from Campbell J. Gibson and Emily Lennon, "Historical Census Statistics on the Foreign-born Population of the United States: 1850-1990," U.S. Census Bureau, Population Division, Working Paper No. 29, February 1999.

AP Images/David Kennedy

Global Americans Born in Brownsville, Texas, on the U.S.–Mexico border in 1915, **Américo Paredes** grew up familiar with life in the borderlands between two nations, saluting the American flag in public school during the day, and at night listening to Mexican ballads (*corridos*) and folk tales. While facing discrimination as a Mexican American (his high school counselor assumed that he would not go to college), Paredes found an escape through poetry, which he wrote and published while studying for his degree at junior college. In 1944, he served as an infantryman in the U.S. Army, and after World War II was assigned to the army publication *Stars and Stripes* to cover war crimes trials in Tokyo. Paredes returned to Texas in 1950 after living for five years in East Asia and had a new appreciation for the cultural blending and conflicts that comprised his life experiences on the U.S.–Mexico border. Like the African American writer James Baldwin, his time abroad enabled him to better understand himself, his borderland community, and the peculiarities of racial experience in the United States. A sign of Paredes's connection between Asians and Latinos was his wife Amelia Nagamine, a half-Japanese, half-Uruguayan women he had met while in Japan. Paredes's experience in Japan informed his novels and pioneering research, as a professor at the University of Texas–Austin, on trans-border corridos. His writing and research, especially on the legendary Gregorio Cortez and his heroic victories against U.S. law enforcement (Texas Rangers), revealed how global experiences had reshaped his understanding of local environments.

who crossed the border illegally. The Immigration Act's Western Hemisphere limit added another obstacle preventing Mexicans from working on U.S. farms that led increasing numbers of them to cross the border illegally. In this way, the act (as well as the 1976 imposition of a 20,000 quota for Western Hemisphere nations) criminalized workers for doing what previously had been tolerated if not encouraged.

24-4 Expanded Struggle for Equality

1976 George Ballis/Take Stock/The Image Works

In this photograph, Cesar Chavez (second in line, holding flag) marches in 1965 supporting a strike, or *huelga*, by a union of agricultural workers sponsored by the AFL-CIO. The flags contain the symbol of Chavez's National Farmworkers Association, an eagle whose wings outline steps on a pyramid. The eagle and pyramid harken back to the Meso-American civilizations and are key icons of Mexican history.

Why do you think the farmworkers' protest used the Spanish language and Mexican historical symbols? What advantages and disadvantages might this have in the United States? ▶

Although President Johnson's Great Society took action against racial discrimination, poverty, and a host of other social and environmental problems, it could not anticipate the rise of women's activism and youth protests on college campuses that were beginning to develop at the same time as the Civil Rights Movement. Assumptions about women and their position in the workplace were particularly in flux, and a re-invigorated women's movement pressured the federal government to dismantle the legal structure of gender bias. At the same time, the farmworkers' movement and protests on college and university campuses brought new actors into the civil rights coalition as they used strategies and tactics, as well as the vision of racial and economic justice, learned from black struggles in the South and across the nation.

☞ As you read, consider the Civil Rights Movement's influence on other struggles for social and economic justice. Why did these new movements emerge?

24-4a Postwar Status of Women

After World War II, women continue to seek legal protections and economic equality.

The return of women workers to the labor market because of labor shortages in the booming postwar economy revived the momentum for women's rights. Officials in the federal government's Women's Bureau suggested that employers pay women the same wages for doing work comparable to what men did. The legal concept of **comparable worth** made possible a liberal interpretation of the dollar value of women's work that did not require women to perform the exact same tasks as male coworkers. In this way, a female secretary might get paid the same wages as a male clerk even though they performed different duties.

Although dormant during the Eisenhower administration, equal pay bills in Congress gained new support under Kennedy because of the Democrats' close ties to organized labor. Esther Peterson, a trade unionist and new head of the Women's Bureau, was able to get Congress to consider equal pay legislation. Conservatives managed to water down the bill by, among other things, replacing the concept of comparable worth with a strict definition of equal work that made it much easier for employers to dismiss women's claims to wage equality with men. Even so, the passage of the Equal Pay Act in 1963 was an important step forward for women's rights.

Other moves toward gender equality resulted from Kennedy's December 1961 establishment of the **President's Commission on the Status of Women,** a move reminiscent of Truman's creation of the President's Commission on Civil Rights. Eleanor Roosevelt, who no longer chaired the UN Committee on Human Rights, headed the Kennedy commission and made sure to include her fellow gender activist Pauli Murray as a member. The commission drew attention to the ill effects that women suffered from gender inequality in employment, as well as in civil rights, voting, and property rights; labor legislation; and social insurance and tax laws. But it stopped short of recommending the elimination of legislation designed to protect female workers. Such protective labor laws, considered major victories against the exploitation of women during the Progressive era, required shorter workdays, lighter responsibilities, and other forms of gender difference that prevented working women from earning the same pay as men.

comparable worth Idea that women and men should receive equal pay for jobs at similar skill levels and of similar worth to employers.

President's Commission on the Status of Women Established by President Kennedy in December 1961, the commission highlighted ill effects that women suffered from gender inequality.

feminine mystique Notion originating from Betty Friedan's *The Feminine Mystique* (1963) that being womanly or performing supposed female duties is a noble achievement for women rather than a myth tied to their subordination to men; the concept originated method of subjugation.

24-4b Resurgent Feminism

New ideas of women's equality and the way to obtain it emerge.

Although the Kennedy commission and the Equal Pay Act were early signs of the feminist revival, neither had the force of Betty Friedan's best-selling exposé of U.S. gender norms: *The Feminine Mystique* (1963). Neither the presidential commission nor the Equal Pay Act challenged the traditional and pervasive assumption that women's "maternal functions" made them fundamentally different from men. Friedan, on the other hand, objected to the notion that women's primary function and source of fulfillment was as mothers, wives, and homemakers. Following the French philosopher Simone de Beauvoir's path-breaking analysis of women's subordination, *The Second Sex* (1949), Friedan argued that the idea of the "happy housewife" was a smokescreen or **feminine mystique** that covered up the discrimination and subordination faced by the female half of the population. Friedan concluded that educated, middle-class women were unhappy because their identity was defined by marriage, childrearing, and household management, while their education and aspirations were broader. In addition to being a housewife, Friedan was a left-wing activist who attended the same Highlander Folk School in Tennessee that had served as a catalyst for labor and civil rights leaders including CIO activists, King, and Parks. For nearly a decade after college, Friedan worked as a journalist for a left-wing news service and wrote articles that supported labor unions and civil rights, activities that she kept concealed well beyond the Second Red Scare. The hidden origins of *The Feminine Mystique* revealed the linkage between the labor movement, civil rights activism, and postwar feminism.

Feminist political activism escalated quickly after the publication of Freidan's book. A key achievement was the inclusion of a gender equality clause in the Civil Rights Act of 1964. The clause (which fell under Title VII of the act) was introduced by a segregationist Virginia congressman who hoped to derail the bill by adding sex to its protected categories. But committed feminists such as Murray lobbied vigorously for the bill. "The Negro woman," she wrote, "can no longer postpone or subordinate the fight against discrimination because of sex to the civil rights struggle but must carry on both fights simultaneously." As the Civil Rights Act was being debated, Murray sent a memorandum around Capitol Hill arguing that unless women were included as a protected category, "the civil rights bill would be including only one half of the Negroes." With solid backing from a

Heritage Image Partnership Ltd/Alamy Stock Photo

Women Office Workers, 1968 Most Americans in the 1950s and 1960s did not see a problem with a workplace segregated by sex. Even Martin Luther King Jr. was typical of movement activists in seeing civil rights as key to restoring black men to their "proper" role as breadwinners. ◄

handful of congresswomen, the Senate and House bills were approved with overwhelming support.

The implementation and enforcement of Title VII was left to the Equal Employment Opportunity Commission (EEOC), but this did not mean that the federal government would automatically become a vehicle to advance feminism. Murray and other feminists faced tremendous opposition from the EEOC and the broader civil rights community because gender equality was never their major goal. These activists, like most Americans, had no problem with the segregation of men and women into different jobs, duties, and responsibilities.

24-4c Beginnings of Campus Unrest

Civil rights struggles spark early student protests.

During the early 1960s, radicalism grew on college campuses as an increasing number of white students took on the cause of civil rights, and like their SNCC peers, became impatient with the pace of achieving racial equality. In 1962, **Students for a Democratic Society (SDS)** emerged as the organizing force behind the revival of left-wing, socialist politics on U.S. college campuses. Unlike youth activism of the 1930s, SDS was not closely aligned with the Communist Party or the Soviet Union; and it was not rooted solely in labor and working-class struggles. Indeed, the beginning of the organization's founding manifesto, the **Port Huron Statement,** focused on the era of postwar prosperity: "We are people of this generation, bred in at least modest comfort, housed now in universities, looking uncomfortably to the world we inherit." Like Betty Friedan, the SDS members highlighted negative effects of prosperity and mass society. But instead of focusing on the plight of middle-class mothers, the young radicals were drawn toward struggles for African American freedom, socialism, and nuclear disarmament. One of their main goals was to transform the U.S. government into a "participatory democracy" in which blacks, workers, peace advocates, youth, and other aggrieved groups gained increased power over political and economic decision making.

While SDSers pointed out the differences between their New Left and the Depression-era radicals they called the Old Left, there was one important connection between the two generations of activists. Approximately one-third of the one hundred thousand New Left radicals were "red diaper babies," the children of Popular Front-era socialists and Communists. And as was common in the 1930s, almost two-thirds (60 percent) of New Left activists came for Jewish backgrounds and, although there were exceptions, a much smaller percentage came from Catholic homes.

New Left activism spiked at the University of California–Berkeley in the fall 1964 when the school administration prevented students from promoting civil rights causes on campus. In the eyes of student activists, the administration's actions not only

Students for a Democratic Society (SDS) Organization, established in 1962, by a new generation of radical students, advancing youth protests for civil rights and against the Vietnam War.

Port Huron Statement SDS manifesto promoting "participatory democracy" to increase control over political, economic, and social institutions by everyday people.

Free Speech Movement (FSM) Student activism, inspired by the Civil Rights Movement and beginning at the University of California, Berkeley, in fall 1964, revealing a growing interest on campuses for more student autonomy vis-á-vis the school administrations.

opposed the Civil Rights Movement, but also violated their constitutional right to gather and express opinions. The suspension and arrest of a handful of students who continued campus activism provoked a large student uprising at Berkeley. What started as a campaign to support African American struggles turned into the **Free Speech Movement (FSM)** in which even conservative students stood up for their rights against the university administration. FSM activists such as Mario Savio, who had recently returned from SNCC's Mississippi Freedom Summer, used civil disobedience tactics in taking over the school's main administration building, and, like civil rights activists, allowed themselves to be arrested for the cause. In the end, the administration gave in to FSM demands for greater political expression on campus but not before a good portion of students became politicized about social injustice within and outside their campus, and from there, became involved in movements for peace and the liberation of women and racial minorities.

24-4d Stirrings on the Farms

Farmworkers adapt strategies, tactics, and aims of the Civil Rights Movement to fight labor exploitation.

Another group inspired by labor and civil rights activism was agricultural workers, who as a rule were excluded from the collective bargaining agreements won by industrial labor as well as from most federal protections. Adding to their troubles, many were *braceros* or undocumented workers lacking the rights and protections of U.S. citizenship. Cesar Chavez and Dolores Huerta spoke up for agricultural workers in leading strikes, boycotts, and other forms of protest in Delano, California, part of the extensive grape-growing region in the state's Central Valley. Born in Arizona, Chavez spent much of his youth with his family as migrant farmworkers in California, which prevented him from going to school beyond the eighth grade. After two years in the U.S. Navy, he spent ten years in San Jose, California, learning how to advance progressive social change through community organizing. During this time, he became inspired by Gandhi's writings on nonviolent protest and those by Saint Francis of Assisi on serving the poor.

In 1962, Chavez moved with his wife and children to Delano and immediately organized the National Farm Worker's Association (NFWA), adopting the distinctive flag bearing the Mexican-inspired eagle with the outline of ancient Meso-American pyramids. Despite this symbol and the organization's decidedly Mexican American leadership, Chavez opposed ethnic chauvinism, seeking actively to include African Americans, who composed the bulk of his staff and volunteers. Chavez also relied on support from white students in frequent trips to college campuses to raise awareness of the farmworker struggle. Finally, he and the NFWA made the fateful decision in September 1965 to join Filipino farmworkers in a strike against grape growers. By this time the fledging organization had only 1,700 members distributed over fifty local bodies. They launched a protracted struggle that, like the Montgomery Bus Boycott, would catapult into the nation's spotlight a charismatic new leader for social justice.

Summary

The March on Washington for Jobs and Freedom in 1963 was a powerful example of Americans—"black men and white men, Jews and Gentiles, Protestants and Catholics"— coming together in a way that signaled the dawn of a historic era of the struggle for inclusiveness. In the three decades after World War II, persistent social divisions of race, ethnicity, religion, and sex had softened and the restrictions on black voting and the legal interpretation of civil rights collapsed. The change resulted from two interrelated sources: long-standing domestic protests by the NAACP and other civil rights groups that exploded into mass protests during the age of human rights; and from international pressures against racism in the United States that the U.S. in its drive to win the Cold War was compelled to oblige.

During this period, more Americans than ever achieved newfound rights as racial minorities, women, workers, consumers, voters, and students. At the same time, the nation ended long-standing discriminatory immigration policies. But the surge in freedoms did not make up for decades, and in many instances centuries, of mistreatment and inequality suffered by racial minorities, women, agricultural workers, and the poor. Real social equality, for most disadvantaged Americans, would come gradually, if at all. Although groups and individuals committed to the status quo slowed and stalled expansions of freedoms, the underdevelopment of America's decaying cities created class barriers to social mobility that trapped millions of racial minorities in persistent poverty. For many Americans the revolution in rights and freedoms could not compensate for the economic losses suffered from the wrenching transformation from industrial to postindustrial capitalism.

Thinking Back, *Looking Forward*

As you review, consider how and why the civil rights won by African Americans after the Civil War were taken away from them, and how the civil rights struggles addressed in this chapter were part of a long movement since the end of Reconstruction to get them back. How did World War II and especially the Cold War contribute to civil rights achievements? In the next chapters, pay attention to further expansions of the rights revolution and the negative reaction to them.

To make your study concrete, review the time line and reflect on the entries there. Think about their causes, consequences, and connections. How do they fit with global trends?

Additional Resources

Books

Branch, Taylor. *Parting the Waters: America in the King Years 1954–63*. New York: Simon and Schuster, 1988. ▶ Comprehensive history of the Civil Rights Movement that has become a classic.

Brooks, Charlotte. *Alien Neighbors, Foreign Friends: Asian Americans, Housing, and the Transformation of Urban California*. Chicago, IL: University of Chicago Press, 2009. ▶ Incisive examination tracing the impact of international pressures on the repeal of anti-Asian policies related to housing.

Dudziak, Mary L. *Cold War Civil Rights: Race and the Image of American Democracy*. Princeton, NJ: Princeton University Press, 2000. ▶ Pioneering study connecting America's Cold War imperatives to its civil rights revolution.

Gaines, Kevin K. *American Africans in Ghana: Black Expatriates and the Civil Rights Era*. Chapel Hill: University of North Carolina Press, 2006. ▶ Fascinating social history of black migration to Africa after World War II.

Gutiérrez, David G. *Walls and Mirrors: Mexican Americans, Mexican Immigrants, and the Politics of Ethnicity*. Berkeley: University of California Press, 1995. ▶ Examination of how Mexican immigration has shaped politics in the Southwest for more than a century.

Harrington, Michael. *The Other America: Poverty in the United States*. 1962. Reprint, New York: Touchstone, 1997. ▶ Study of poverty that shocked the nation in 1962 and sparked the War on Poverty.

Isserman, Maurice, and Michael Kazin. *America Divided: The Civil War of the 1960s*, 3rd ed. New York: Oxford University Press, 2007. ▶ Inclusive reader of primary sources on the United States during the 1960s that pays particular attention to race, gender, and civil rights.

Lewis, David Levering. *King: A Biography*, 3rd ed. Urbana: University of Illinois Press, 2013. ▶ Major biography of the civil rights leader.

MacLean, Nancy. *Freedom Is Not Enough: The Opening of the American Workplace*. Cambridge, MA: Harvard University Press, 2008. ▶ Innovative analysis of civil rights and workplace issues that conjoins racial and gender movements and issues.

Ngai, Mae M. *Impossible Subjects: Illegal Aliens and the Making of Modern America*. Princeton, NJ: Princeton University Press, 2004. ▶ Path-breaking study that addresses the politics of the 1965 Immigration Act and the criminalization of undocumented workers in the United States.

Go to the MindTap® for **Global Americans** to access the full version of select books from this Additional Resources section.

Websites

Changing America: The Emancipation Proclamation, 1863, and the March on Washington, 1963. (http://americanhistory.si.edu/changing-america-emancipation-proclamation-1863-and-march-washington-1963) ▶ Smithsonian online exhibit with explanatory text and images of historical artifacts regarding the Emancipation Proclamation and March on Washington.

Civil Rights History Project at the Library of Congress. (http://www.loc.gov/collections/civil-rights-history-project/) ▶ Rich collection of essays and oral history videos about the Civil Rights Movement.

Free Speech Movement Digital Archives. (http://bancroft.berkeley.edu/FSM/) ▶ Collection of primary sources, images, and oral history transcripts with key players in the Berkeley struggles.

History of the United Nations. (http://www.un.org/en/sections/history/history-united-nations/index.html) ▶ Text and some audio/visual materials related to the background and beginning of the United Nations.

The Universal Declaration of Human Rights. (http://www.un.org/en/documents/udhr/index.shtml) ▶ UN Website devoted to the declaration and its history with a page of Web-based resources.

MindTap®

Continue exploring online through MindTap®, where you can:
- **Assess your knowledge with the Chapter Test**
- **Watch historical videos related to the chapter**
- **Further your understanding with interactive maps and timelines**

Civil Rights and Human Rights

1945–1946

October 1945
United Nations is established.

February 1946
Discharged soldier Isaac Woodard is blinded by police in South Carolina.

1947–1948

1947
Jackie Robinson and Larry Doby break the colorline by playing in Major League Baseball.

March 1947
Truman Doctrine commits United States to containing communism.

October 1947
President's Committee on Civil Rights publishes *To Secure These Rights*, recommending elimination of racial discrimination.

December 1948
UN approves Universal Declaration of Human Rights.

1949–1952

1949
French intellectual Simone de Beauvoir publishes *The Second Sex*—kicks off postwar feminism.

January 1949
Funeral home in Texas refuses to bury deceased Mexican American veteran Felix Longoria.

1950
Pauli Murray publishes *States' Laws on Race and Color*, the "bible" for NAACP civil rights lawyers.

India outlaws centuries-old caste system.

June 1950
Korean War begins.

1952
Malcolm Little is paroled from jail, changes name to Malcolm X.

June 1952
Congress ends exclusion of all Asian immigrants and permits their naturalization.

1954–1955

May 1954
U.S. Supreme Court hands down decision in *Brown v. Board of Education*, which overturns the *Plessy* era of segregation.

May 1955
Soviets establish Warsaw Pact to counter NATO.

August 1955
Emmett Till murdered in Mississippi.

December 1955
Montgomery bus boycott erupts in Alabama when Rosa Parks refuses to comply with racial segregation; boycott propels Martin Luther King Jr. into leadership of Civil Rights Movement.

1957–1959

January 1957
Southern Christian Leadership Council (SCLC) is established with Martin Luther King Jr. as president.

March 1957
Ghana becomes independent.

September 1957
President Eisenhower sends troops to Little Rock, Arkansas, to integrate Central High School.

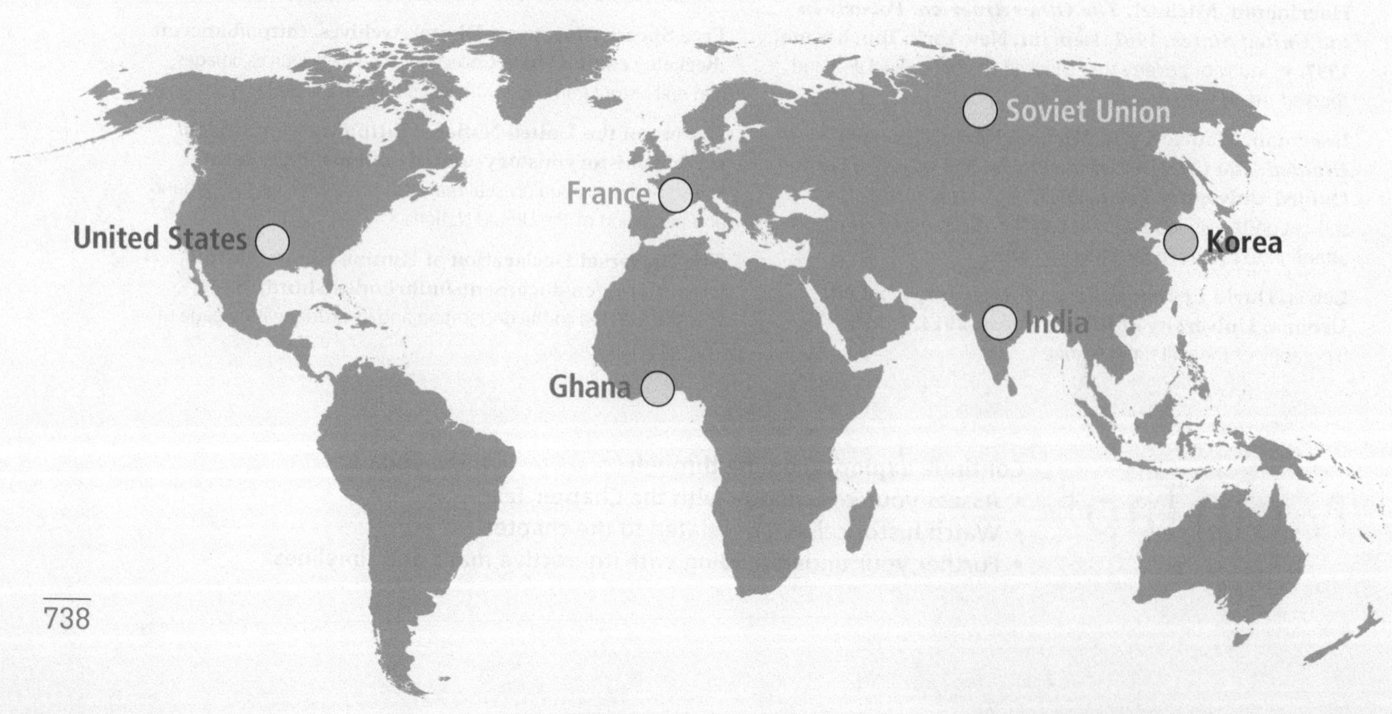

1960

February

Four Greensboro college students spark sit-in protests at lunch counters throughout the South.

August

Student Nonviolent Coordinating Committee (SNCC) is established, bringing new tactics and youth into the civil rights struggle.

September

Richard Nixon and John F. Kennedy engage in first televised political debate.

1961–1962

1961

Frantz Fanon publishes *The Wretched on the Earth.*

James L. Farmer and CORE start "freedom rides" to integrate public transportation in South.

African and Asian nations comprise majority in UN General Assembly.

President Kennedy enters the White House, establishes the President's Commission on the Status of Women; Freedom rides used to integrate inter-state buses and trains.

1962

Rachel Carson's *Silent Spring* generates broad environmental awareness.

Students for a Democratic Society (SDS) is established in Ann Arbor, Michigan.

October 1962

Kennedy sends troops to allow James Meredith to integrate University of Mississippi.

1963

Betty Friedan publishes *The Feminine Mystique*, stimulates new wave of women's activism.

January–May

King and SCLC provoke violent confrontation in Birmingham, Alabama.

King writes "Letter from a Birmingham Jail."

August

March on Washington for Jobs and Freedom assembles massive civil rights demonstration; King delivers "I Have a Dream" speech.

November

Kennedy is assassinated, Lyndon Johnson becomes president.

1964

January

President Johnson declares "War on Poverty" to greatly expand welfare programs.

July

Civil Rights Act is passed.

Summer: Mississippi Freedom Summer strives to re-enfranchise blacks.

August

Congress authorizes greatly increasing U.S. troops in Vietnam.

October–December

Free Speech Movement protests erupt at the University of California, Berkeley.

November

Johnson is elected president to serve first full term in office.

1965

March

King leads marches for voting rights in Selma, Alabama.

July

Equal Employment Opportunity Commission (EEOC) opens for business as federal government agency devoted to upholding Civil Rights Act.

August

Congress passes Voting Rights Act.

Racial uprising erupts in Watts, California.

September

Cesar Chavez and National Farm Workers Association join grape strike in Delano, California.

October

Johnson signs Immigration Act.

December

UN approves the International Convention on the Elimination of All Forms of Racial Discrimination.

25

The Vietnam War Era

1965–1975

After fleeing Cambodia on foot to the Thai border, Dith Pran came to the United States, with the help of friend Sydney Schanberg, to be reunited with his family.

In April 1975, Cambodian journalist Dith Pran chose to remain in his war-torn country while his wife and children fled to safety in the United States. He stayed to document the end of the bloody Cambodian civil war as the Communist Khmer Rouge defeated the regime of U.S.-backed dictator Lon Nol. This victory came after the United States had withdrawn its troops and military support from Vietnam and neighboring Cambodia and Laos. Without the world's greatest superpower to oppose them, Communist parties seized power throughout Indochina.

Jerry Soloway/Corbis

Dith was relieved that the fighting was over and, like his friend and fellow journalist *New York Times* foreign correspondent Sydney Schanberg, was optimistic about Cambodia's future. The victorious Khmer Rouge, however, dashed their hopes. In the name of overthrowing the remnants of capitalism and Western imperialism, the new regime turned on its own people, slaughtering innocent civilians. In reporting on the casualties, Dith and Schanberg rushed to a local hospital, where they were captured by Khmer Rouge soldiers, who, if not for Dith's heroic pleading, would have executed them. Once released, the two found their way to the French embassy, where they created a fake passport so that Dith could flee the country. The scheme failed, forcing Schanberg to return to the United States without his dear friend.

Because the Khmer Rouge sought to "cleanse" the nation of "intellectuals," "foreigners," and Western influences, Dith disguised himself as a peasant taxi driver, threw away his money and material possessions, and concealed the signs of his French education and English-language skills. He ended up in a labor camp where city folk like him were forced to work in rice fields while receiving political indoctrination. Khmer Rouge cruelty seemed to have no bounds as they let "lucky" ones like Dith starve, while butchering 1.5 to 2 million people in what became known as the "killing fields."

After more than three years, Dith was liberated when Vietnam invaded and overthrew the Khmer Rouge regime. But he still was not safe given his earlier connection to the United States, so he fled Cambodia on foot via a harrowing sixty-mile jungle trek to the Thai border. Upon hearing that Dith had made it to freedom, Schanberg, who refused to believe rumors that his friend was dead, immediately flew to Thailand and then brought Dith to the United States where he was reunited with his wife and children, and became a U.S. citizen.

Dith's ordeal had a fortunate ending, but the military conflicts throughout Indochina did not. These wars came at great costs for all parties involved. The Khmer Rouge committed gruesome atrocities in Cambodia. The U.S. withdrawal from the region also sealed the fate of U.S.-backed regimes in South Vietnam and Laos, whose collapse displaced millions of people and subjected those who could not escape to vicious victor's justice. Although North Vietnam effectively won the war against the U.S. enemy and achieved the long- sought

How does Dith Pran's harrowing experience in Cambodia during the Khmer Rouge regime and Vietnam's invasion reflect the tragedies and costs of the region's military conflicts?

Go to MindTap® to watch a video on Dith and learn how his story relates to the themes of this chapter.

goal of reuniting the country, these victories came at the cost of millions of lives, millions of acres of defoliated countryside, and other tragedies that destroyed the promise of Ho Chi Minh's socialist revolution. Fallout from the U.S. war also embroiled Vietnam in further military conflicts against former Cambodian and Chinese allies. The fighting, deaths, and destruction continued in Indochina for almost fifteen years after the Americans left. The region had experienced nearly half a century of continuous warfare.

For the United States, its withdrawal constituted the nation's worst military defeat. More than fifty thousand Americans died, and billions of dollars were spent on a lost cause in which the United States sacrificed much of its prestige as the leader of the "free world." The war also took its toll on two U.S. presidents: Johnson ended his reelection campaign because of military setbacks and domestic opposition, and Nixon was forced to resign from office due to spying on political enemies opposed to the war. Intense antiwar protests revealed how the conflict polarized the nation, as Americans were torn between their sense of patriotism and their own moral conscience. The Vietnam question, furthermore, exacerbated deep race and gender divisions related to the nation's unfinished civil rights agenda, as well as cultural conflicts brought on by the coming-of-age of the baby boomer generation. The violence in Indochina seemed to beget violent conflicts at home.

25-1 U.S. Escalates War in Vietnam

This photograph depicts the reconnaissance in February 1965 of a bridge in North Vietnam destroyed by a U.S bomber. The United States' Operation Rolling Thunder counted on U.S. air supremacy to destroy Hanoi and targets throughout North Vietnam.

How does this image convey a sense of U.S. advantages during the Vietnam War? What other advantages do you think the United States had that are not revealed by this photo? What advantages do you think the North Vietnamese had? ▶

akg-images/Newscom

Vietnam was one of many sites of Cold War conflict in the Third World in which the United States and Soviet Union, as well as China, clashed. America's involvement in Vietnam began during the French war (1950–1954) in which the United States backed and paid for 80 percent of France's war to reclaim its former colony from the newly declared Democratic Republic of Vietnam (North Vietnam) led by the Communist revolutionary Ho Chi Minh. The United States took over from the French after 1954 as the main Western force in Indochina (Vietnam, Cambodia, and Laos), and ensured the establishment of the Republic of Vietnam (South Vietnam) with its capital in Saigon. President Eisenhower sent military advisers and aid to prop up the anti-Communist regime in Saigon. President Kennedy stepped up this support as South Vietnam faced increased threats of invasion from North Vietnam as well as a homegrown insurgency (for U.S. involvement in Vietnam before 1964, see chapter 22). His successor, Lyndon B. Johnson launched an all out war, albeit one that was undeclared.

With air superiority and the world's largest and most sophisticated stockpile of weapons, the United States was poised to overwhelm its smaller and weaker opponents in Vietnam. President Johnson relied on massive aerial bombing to get them to sue for peace, but despite air raids that destroyed Hanoi and killed countless North Vietnamese troops and civilians, the United States was still unable to defeat its opponent. Hanoi's Le Duan, like Johnson, was also seeking total victory. He attacked the Americans and their South Vietnam allies by launching an offensive meant to provoke a popular uprising in the south. But these efforts failed to subdue his enemies. In the first three years of the war, neither side gained a clear advantage.

☞ As you read, pay attention to military conflict in Vietnam. What was the military strategy on both sides of the conflict? Explain why or why not it was effective in the early years of the war?

25-1a Washington's War

U.S. conventional tactics flounder in Vietnam.

Responding to Hanoi's General Offensive-General Uprising (GO-GU) surge in 1964, President Johnson realized that the twenty-three thousand U.S. military advisers and troops in the South were not enough to overcome 170,000 Communist guerillas. When a U.S. naval destroyer clashed with North Vietnamese torpedo boats in August of that year, the president portrayed this skirmish in which both sides were at fault as a call to arms to for the United States to greatly expand its troop strength in Vietnam. Congress obliged with the nearly unanimous **Gulf of Tonkin Resolution**, permitting the president "to take all necessary steps, including the use of armed force, to assist any member or protocol state of the Southeast Asia Collective Defense Treaty requesting assistance in defense of its freedom." Thus began the U.S phase of North Vietnam's war for independence as the number of American troops rose dramatically (see Figure 25.1).

Scholars have debated Johnson's motivations regarding Vietnam, but it is clear that his escalation of the war was in step with the policy goals inherited from the two preceding administrations. In fact, Johnson retained many of Kennedy's military advisers, including Secretary of Defense Robert McNamara. Whereas Kennedy had rejected McNamara's requests to engage in overt warfare, Johnson, once empowered by the Gulf of Tonkin Resolution, approved bombing raids in North Vietnam and the deployment of U.S. ground troops to South Vietnam. The defense secretary and General William C. Westmoreland did not seek to defeat the enemy as much as bring them to the negotiating table. Johnson and his advisers believed that overwhelming U.S. firepower would eventually break the North Vietnamese resolve. They paid close attention to enemy "body counts" on the assumption that a higher death rate would produce a lower motivation to fight.

Johnson's major air offensive, Operation Rolling Thunder, began in March 1965 with assaults designed to destroy Hanoi's supply lines to **National Liberation Front (NLF)** insurgents based in South Vietnam, derisively labeled *Vietcong* (Vietnamese Communists) by their enemies. What started out as targeted bombing of minor sites far from Hanoi, gradually developed into the kind of massive urban bombing campaigns such as those that had leveled Dresden, Tokyo, and Pyongyang during earlier wars. Hanoi was flattened. In addition, the U.S. Air Force defoliated hundreds of square miles of jungles in attempting to interdict what Americans called the **Ho Chi Minh trail**, a number of clandestine transportation routes that snaked through Laos and Cambodia by which North Vietnam sent troops and supplies south to NLF insurgents.

Gulf of Tonkin Resolution Congressional authorization giving the president power to send combat troops to fight Communist forces in Vietnam.

National Liberation Front (NLF) Hidden military force within South Vietnam struggling to overthrow the Saigon regime through an alliance with its North Vietnamese enemies.

Ho Chi Minh trail Path of clandestine routes snaking through neighboring Laos and Cambodia over which North Vietnam supplied NLF insurgents in the south.

By spring 1967, McNamara knew the U.S. war plan was not working. There were not as many targets to bomb in Hanoi because the government had evacuated most of the population and relocated key industries underground or to nearby caves. Organized teams of North Vietnamese civilians quickly rebuilt roads, bridges, and the crucial Ho Chi Minh trail. Moreover, Soviet-supplied fighter planes and surface-to-air missiles enabled the North Vietnamese air force to scuttle numerous bombing raids, preventing total U.S. domination of the skies. While President Johnson kept telling the American public that their country was winning the war, the reality in Vietnam was far from Johnson's claims.

Meanwhile, U.S. ground troops faced a very different challenge than in the Korean War or World War II. The closest precedent was the U.S. repression of Philippine independence after the Spanish–American War. As in the Philippines, U.S. soldiers confronted an enemy of

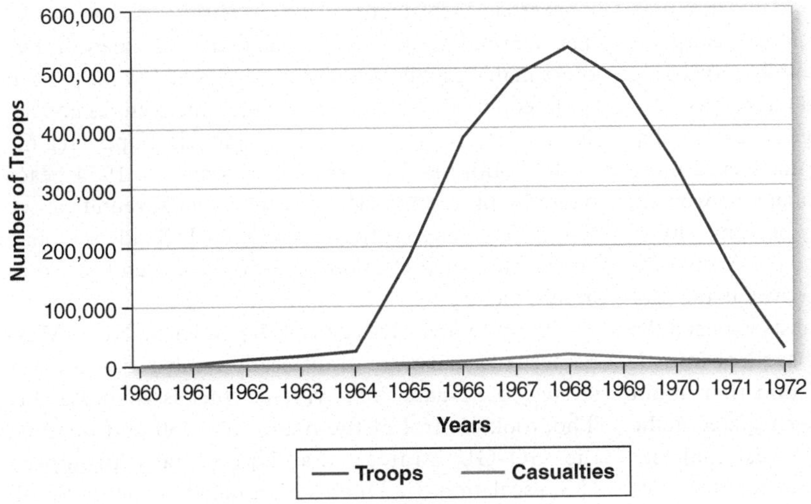

Figure 25.1 Number of U.S. troops in Vietnam and U.S. casualties, by year Following the Gulf of Tonkin Resolution, the presence of U.S. soldiers in South Vietnam increased more than sevenfold in one year to 184,000. By 1968 (the peak of the troop buildup), that figure had nearly tripled, rising to 536,000. The apex of troop numbers corresponded with the peak of U.S. casualties. ◄ Sources: U.S. Census (for data regarding total U.S. troops); National Archives (for data regarding U.S. casualties)

LBJ Library photo by Yoichi Okamoto

President Lyndon B. Johnson with Defense Secretary Robert McNamara, 1967 Using the same type of sophisticated statistical analysis that made his reputation as a corporate "whiz kid," Secretary McNamara calculated precisely how much death and destruction the United States needed to inflict before Hanoi would abandon the war as unwinnable. It turned out that his calculations were wrong and that the U.S. war plan had misjudged the enemy's capacity and resolve. ◀

guerilla fighters who blended into and were supported by local populations. U.S. soldiers implemented pacification strategies seeking to root out insurgent strongholds among South Vietnam's vast rural peasantry while at the same time winning their "hearts and minds" through aid and development programs. At the same time, U.S. troops sprayed 19 million gallons of toxic herbicides, most notably **Agent Orange**, defoliating more than 4 million acres of forest to uncover insurgent hideouts. The chemicals had a devastating human cost as over time both Vietnamese and U.S. veterans suffered elevated cases of cancer, miscarriages, birth defects, and type-2 diabetes.

Soldiers implementing the pacification program pointed out the difficulty in distinguishing friend from foe when securing rural villages from insurgents. They dehumanized the Vietnamese enemy by referring to them as *gooks,* a racialized term derived from earlier U.S. wars in the Philippines and Korea that could stand for any or all Asians (even South Vietnamese allies). The confusion and blind hatred of the enemy that sometimes resulted from pacification campaigns were evident in March 1968 in **My Lai**, a section of the Son My village where "Charlie Company," a one hundred twenty-man U.S. army unit, entered on a mission to root out and destroy insurgents who were planting land mines and stealthily murdering U.S. troops. Unaware that their intended target was actually nowhere nearby and eager to avenge recent combat losses, the soldiers massacred more than five hundred unarmed women, children, and elderly persons. Horrified by the episode, U.S. Army officials attempted to cover it up. But months later, journalists exposed the killings and in a subsequent investigation, the army found that about thirty soldiers had participated in the massacre, while the vast majority watched until U.S. helicopter pilot Hugh Thompson Jr. stopped the rampage by landing his craft between the attackers and victims. My Lai became a powerful symbol of a war that had gone terribly wrong. Although a court-martial court charged fourteen officers as being responsible for the massacre or its cover up, almost all of these cases were dropped, and the one that went to trial was acquitted. William Calley was the only enlisted man, out of twenty-six charged, who was convicted. He received a life sentence for the premeditated murder of no less than twenty persons, but he served only three and a one-half years of house arrest for his crimes. In 1998, thirty years later, Thompson and his crew received the Soldier's Medal for bravery.

Agent Orange Poisonous chemical used by the U.S. military in Vietnam to defoliate jungles in order to expose NLF insurgents.

My Lai Site in central Vietnam of a massacre in March 1968 perpetrated by U.S. troops that when exposed the next year, became a symbol of an immoral war.

25-1b Hanoi's War

North Vietnam overestimates its strengths against the Americans.

The North Vietnamese had learned from the French War that the longer their troops held out, the more public opinion abroad would sour on the war. As it turned out, their forces could hang on much longer than McNamara's statistical analyses had predicted. The men and women loyal to Hanoi not only knew the territory in this guerilla war, they were charged by the passion for freedom. They characterized the Americans as imperialists who were propping up an illegitimate puppet regime in the South that had refused to honor the 1954 peace treaty by preventing elections for national reunification. South Vietnamese officials, and their U.S. advisers, had known that such elections, if held, would end in Communist victory.

Despite their desire for independence, North Vietnamese officials were of different minds regarding war strategy. Le Duan, along with his chief assistant Le Duc Tho, took control of the nation in 1960 and pursued the GO-GU strategy that had initially prompted U.S. escalation. Le Duan's plan failed to topple South

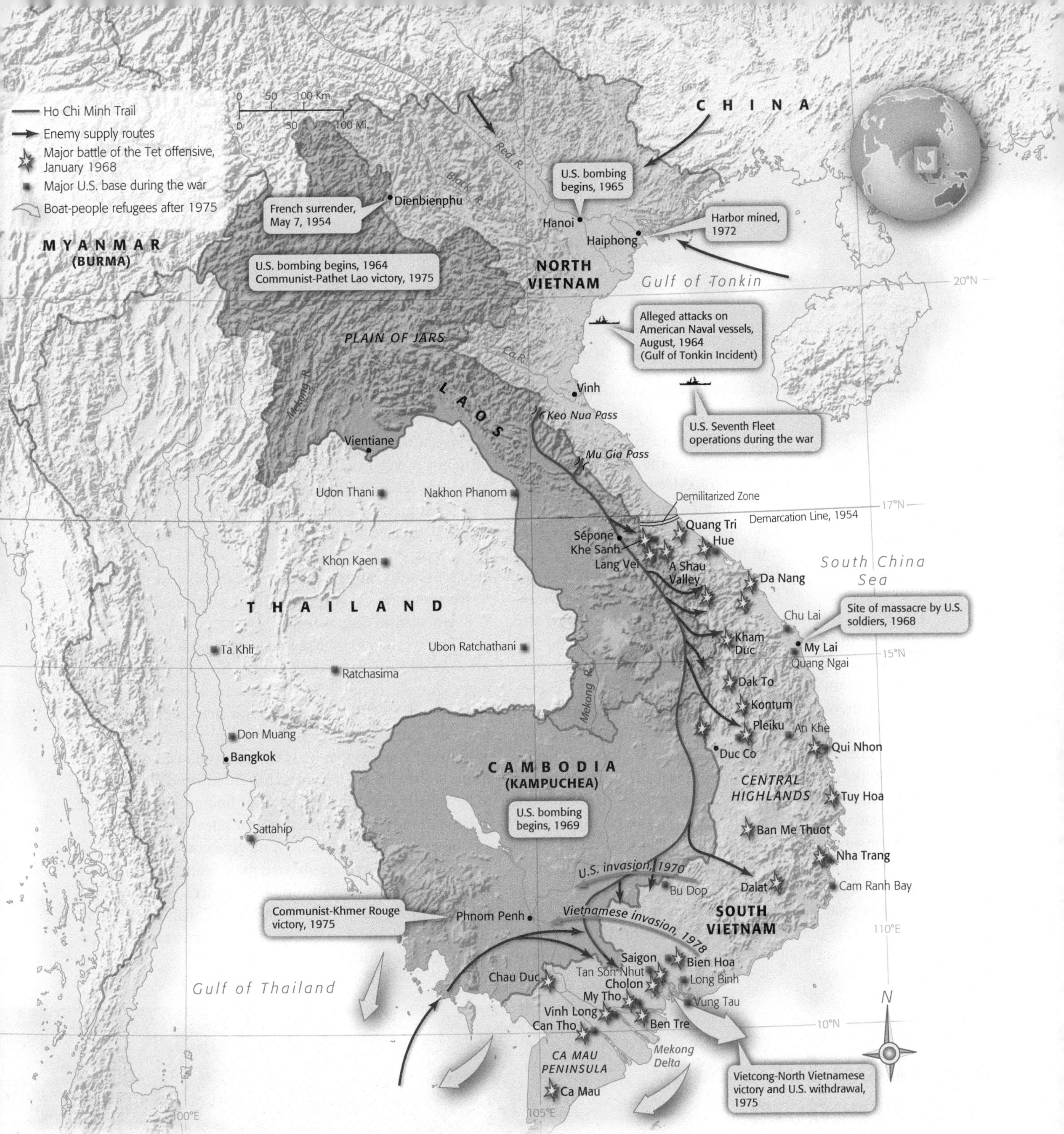

Map 25.1 The U.S. War in Vietnam and Indochina Compelled by the French surrender in 1954, U.S. military involvement in Vietnam escalated greatly a decade later with congressional backing in the form of the Gulf of Tonkin Resolution. U.S. attempts to interdict the movement of enemy troops and supplies from north to south via the Ho Chi Minh trail expanded the war to neighboring Laos and Cambodia. ▲

Vietnam, which not only triggered the massive U.S. response, but also failed to incite a general uprising among the South Vietnamese. As a result, Le Duan's critics, including Ho Chi Minh, did not want to rely exclusively on the GO-GU plan, proposing, instead, prolonged **guerilla warfare** to wear the enemy down (see Map 25.1).

guerilla warfare Military strategy that employs small-scale surprise attacks rather than large-scale direct combat; it is often used by weaker powers to gain an advantage over strong ones and to prolong conflict.

Eddie Adams/Corbis

South Vietnamese Shooting NLF Insurgent at Close Range, 1968 This is a Pulitzer Prize–winning photograph of South Vietnamese police chief General Nguyen Ngoc Loan executing an NLF insurgent during the Tet Offensive. General Loan had witnessed the insurgent kill one of his fellow officers along with the officer's wife and three children. Taken out of context, the photograph was seen as an example of South Vietnamese cold-hearted brutality, and fueled global antiwar protests. ◀

Tet Offensive Major offensive launched by North Vietnam in tandem with insurgents in South Vietnam who were defeated but caused the U.S. public's faith in their leaders and the overall war effort to falter.

Le Duan, in turn, silenced his critics to pave the way for an even larger GO-GU attack. He secured his power by purging North Vietnam of political dissent, causing Ho Chi Minh to flee to China, ostensibly for health reasons. But Le Duan, the leader of the Vietnamese Worker's Party, still had to contend with his allies, who also opposed the GO-GU strategy. The Soviets, fearful that U.S. involvement would lead to nuclear warfare, were pushing Hanoi to come to terms with the United States. The Chinese, on the other hand, supported Ho Chi Minh's idea of extending the war indefinitely through the use of guerilla warfare. In response, Le Duan brilliantly exploited Soviet–Chinese tensions to his advantage by securing continued military aid and support from both by threatening to side with one Communist superpower over the other. This kept the Soviets and Chinese in check because neither wanted to be shut out from the biggest showdown of the Cold War.

The road was clear for Le Duan to implement a second GO-GU plan in January 1968 during Tet, Vietnam's lunar New Year holidays. The **Tet Offensive**, the largest of the war to that point, sent eighty thousand troops in three different waves to attack the U.S.-backed Saigon regime in South Vietnam. But, again, the plan failed to provoke a general uprising and proved a military setback for both North Vietnam and the NLF insurgency. Tet's main damage was psychological; U.S. citizens, who had been repeatedly told their country was winning the war, were shocked to see television coverage of NLF insurgents invading the U.S. embassy in Saigon.

The world's first televised war, the Vietnam conflict drew more staff from the major U.S. networks than any place outside of New York City and Washington, D.C. After the Tet Offensive, respected news anchor Walter Cronkite came to see the war as unwinnable, reporting to millions of viewers that he was "disappointed by the optimism of the U.S. leaders, both in Vietnam and Washington, to have faith any longer in the silver linings they find in the darkest clouds." But the impact of television on the war can be exaggerated. Although news accounts focused on U.S. soldiers, they rarely showed their deaths and suffering at close range. Moreover, public support for the war had been dropping even before the Tet Offensive. Fall 1967 polls revealed that a majority of Americans saw the Vietnam War as a "mistake."

25-2

Fighting for Peace and Freedom

The escalation of U.S. troop numbers in Vietnam provoked antiwar protests at home, beginning on college campuses but eventually including politicians, religious leaders, homemakers, and even Vietnam War veterans. In this photograph, taken in August 1968, a young, unarmed woman, holding a flower and sign reading "Stop the War," confronts a guardsman wearing a helmet and a gas-mask who is pointing a bayonet at her.

How does this photo reveal the tension between the state (police) and antiwar protesters? ▶

Paul Sequeira/Getty Images

An antiwar movement in the United States gained momentum in 1968 after the Tet Offensive, as doubts about the war pushed the nation to a crisis point in that year's presidential election. The negative public reaction to Tet ruined President Johnson's reelection campaign, and he refused to seek a second term. Although both Democratic and Republican candidates called for peace in Vietnam, many young antiwar protesters supported neither party and sought instead to stop the war through civil disobedience, draft resistance, and even violence. Such protests meshed with increasingly radical calls for equal rights for African Americans and other racial minorities, women of all races, the New Left, and sexual minorities. The increased radicalism sparked a conservative resurgence that enabled Republican Richard Nixon to win the White House. Nixon, along with National Security Adviser Henry Kissinger, transformed the war strategy in Vietnam by seeking total victory in renewing attacks in Laos and broadening the conflict to Cambodia.

☞ As you read, focus on the impact that the Vietnam War had on the U.S. home front. How did various Americans respond to the war? How did the issues raised by this response change U.S. political culture?

25-2a War at Home

The peace movement combines with the youth movement during the Vietnam War.

The conflict in Vietnam ignited the largest groundswell of antiwar sentiment in U.S. history. Longtime peace activists such as Quakers and the Women's International League for Peace and Freedom joined with newer ones such as the Committee for a SANE Nuclear Policy and Women Strike for Peace in opposition to the Vietnam War. The Civil Rights Movement also brought forth new voices, rationales, and tactics to peace activism. But the main catalysts of the antiwar movement were America's youth, especially college students. Many of them had already been active in politics through campus protests and civil rights organizing. Young people were at the forefront of a mass movement for peace, as many men who deferred military conscription by pursuing undergraduate or graduate degrees joined the antiwar cause. Major centers of peace activism included the University of California–Berkeley, University of Wisconsin–Madison, Harvard University, and Columbia University.

No youth group was more active in the antiwar struggle than Students for a Democratic Society (SDS), which in May 1965 joined ten thousand antiwar protesters at a demonstration in Washington, D.C. The organization's three hundred fifty chapters called for the withdrawal of U.S. troops, protested against military conscription and recruitment, and demanded that universities sever ties to the military by ending ROTC programs and weapons research. By the fall of 1967, students engaged in seventy-one antiwar demonstrations on sixty-two campuses across the nation. Following the Tet offensive in the winter of 1968, these figures rose to two hundred twenty-one demonstrations on one hundred one campuses.

The antiwar message also spread through the **counterculture**, a youthful alternative to mainstream authority and respectability emerging from centers in New York City and San Francisco but arising at the same time throughout the U.S., Canada, Great Britain, Western Europe, Japan, Australia, and New Zealand. The counterculture was a global transformation of social values and lifestyles that pitted baby boomers against their parents' generation. The icon of the counterculture was the "hippie," a young man or woman dressed in faded blue jeans, tie-dyed T-shirt, beaded necklaces, and long natural hair. Hippies experimented with LSD, marijuana, peyote, and other mind-altering substances; they embraced the sexual revolution, collective living and ownership of property, Eastern religions and spirituality, and a new form of rock 'n' roll music rooted in radical politics and psychedelic states of consciousness. One of the legendary hippie experiences was the Woodstock Festival where for three days in August 1969 four hundred thousand youths descended on a dairy farm in upstate New York to hear the leading acts of psychedelic and folk rock.

counterculture Reaction to and rejection of the normative culture that embodies a wide range of alternative cultural forms and lifestyles through music, art, literature, film, collective housing, communities, and use of hallucinogenic drugs.

Despite the counterculture's popularity and attention-getting tactics, slogans, and demonstrations, a large percentage of young people continued to support the war in Vietnam. The majority of Americans who served overseas, after all, volunteered for duty. Although many did so for practical reasons, such as to gain preferential placement in military units, most of them, especially early in the war, believed wholeheartedly in the U.S. government's anti-Communist campaign and the virtues of military honor and sacrifice. Others serving in Vietnam were drafted. These included men who were at least age eighteen and were not married with children or enrolled in higher education or technical training programs. U.S. enlisted men were disproportionately from poor and lower income backgrounds because these groups were least likely to qualify for a college deferment from the draft.

25-2b Transition from Civil Rights to Black Nationalism

The Civil Rights Movement adopts antiwar protests and divides over black nationalism and the use of violent tactics.

In April 1967, Martin Luther King Jr. paused from domestic causes to speak out against the U.S. war in Vietnam: "I knew that I could never again raise my voice against the violence

History without Borders

Asian Religions, the Beatles, and Kung Fu

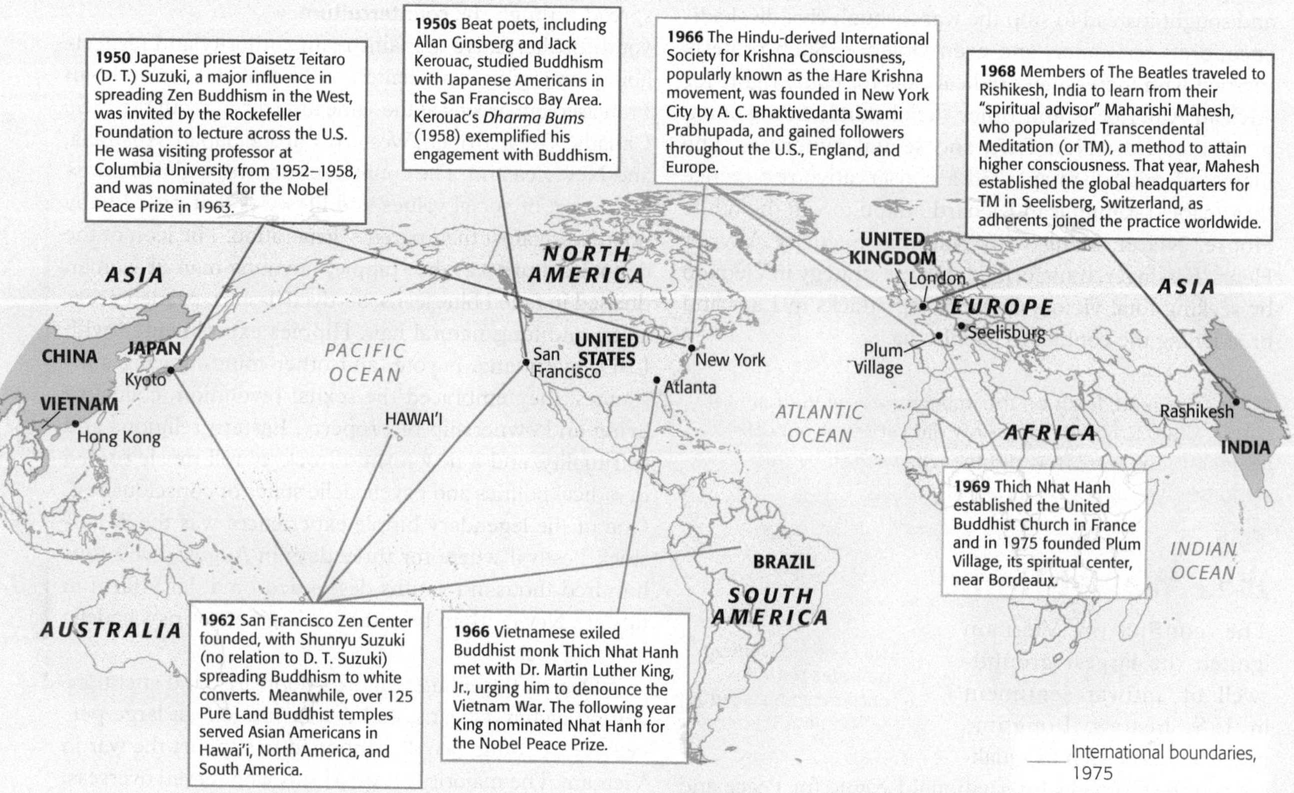

1950 Japanese priest Daisetz Teitaro (D. T.) Suzuki, a major influence in spreading Zen Buddhism in the West, was invited by the Rockefeller Foundation to lecture across the U.S. He wasa visiting professor at Columbia University from 1952–1958, and was nominated for the Nobel Peace Prize in 1963.
1950s Beat poets, including Allan Ginsberg and Jack Kerouac, studied Buddhism with Japanese Americans in the San Francisco Bay Area. Kerouac's *Dharma Bums* (1958) exemplified his engagement with Buddhism.
1966 The Hindu-derived International Society for Krishna Consciousness, popularly known as the Hare Krishna movement, was founded in New York City by A. C. Bhaktivedanta Swami Prabhupada, and gained followers throughout the U.S., England, and Europe.
1968 Members of The Beatles traveled to Rishikesh, India to learn from their "spiritual advisor" Maharishi Mahesh, who popularized Transcendental Meditation (or TM), a method to attain higher consciousness. That year, Mahesh established the global headquarters for TM in Seelisberg, Switzerland, as adherents joined the practice worldwide.
ASIA
NORTH AMERICA
UNITED KINGDOM
London
EUROPE
Seelisburg
ASIA
CHINA
JAPAN
Kyoto
VIETNAM
Hong Kong
PACIFIC OCEAN
San Francisco
UNITED STATES
New York
Atlanta
Plum Village
HAWAI'I
ATLANTIC OCEAN
AFRICA
Rashikesh
INDIA
1969 Thich Nhat Hanh established the United Buddhist Church in France and in 1975 founded Plum Village, its spiritual center, near Bordeaux.
INDIAN OCEAN
BRAZIL
SOUTH AMERICA
AUSTRALIA
1962 San Francisco Zen Center founded, with Shunryu Suzuki (no relation to D. T. Suzuki) spreading Buddhism to white converts. Meanwhile, over 125 Pure Land Buddhist temples served Asian Americans in Hawai'i, North America, and South America.
1966 Vietnamese exiled Buddhist monk Thich Nhat Hanh met with Dr. Martin Luther King, Jr., urging him to denounce the Vietnam War. The following year King nominated Nhat Hanh for the Nobel Peace Prize.
International boundaries, 1975

The Spread of Eastern Religions, 1950-1975 The U.S. attraction to Eastern religions reflected larger religious trends. Always a multireligious nation, the United States, according to Gallup polling, experienced a dramatic rise in non-Christian religions (including atheists who did not claim any religion) during the half century from 1958 to 2008, a period in which the proportion of Protestants declined from 92 to 77 percent. ▲

The Vietnam War, more than any previous event, raised awareness of Buddhism and other Asian religions little-known to Western audiences. While self-immolating Buddhists protesting religious persecution in South Vietnam had left a lasting impression on world opinion, Martin Luther King Jr. came to appreciate the prospects for world peace through discussions with Thich Nhat Hanh, an exiled scholar and peace activist whom the civil rights leader called a "gentle Buddhist monk from Vietnam." In 1967, King used his privilege as a Nobel Peace Prize winner to nominate Thich Nhat Hanh for the award. "Here is an apostle for peace and non-violence," King wrote, "cruelly separated from his own people while they are oppressed by a vicious war which has grown to threaten the sanity and security of the entire world." Although no award was given that year (King had violated Nobel protocol in making his nomination public), Thich Nhat Hanh's following in the West grew. As a formal representative to the Paris peace talks, he supported neither side in the war. But still North Vietnam, after it won the war in 1975, permanently exiled him, causing the monk to establish headquarters for a global peace movement in France.

Meanwhile, one of the first Buddhist training monasteries outside of Asia was being established in San Francisco, where Japanese Zen Buddhist priest Shunryu Suzuki developed an enthusiastic following consisting of Beat poet Allan Ginsberg and counterculture youth looking to get beyond conventional Christianity. Zen Center, founded in San Francisco's youth-oriented Haight-Ashbury district in 1969, spawned a growing interest in Buddhism

Hulton Archive/Getty Images

Beatles in India with Maharishi Mahesh, 1968 Maharishi Mahesh, guru to the world's most popular rock band, the Beatles, embodied the kind of non-Western religions that had a long history in the United States, Great Britain, and Western Europe, but reached its zenith of popularity as a result of the age of experimentation during the 1960s. Thus was born the "new age" spirituality and healing. Mahesh (center back) is seated behind Paul McCartney (left) and George Harrison (right). ▲

Dave Pickoff/AP Images

Thich Nhat Hanh Calls for Peace in Vietnam, 1966 Thich Nhat Hanh spoke at a press conference in New York City upon returning to the United States, where he earlier had studied at Princeton University. By this time, the Vietnamese monk had been exiled from South Vietnam for leading a peace movement among his students to stop the Vietnam War. ▲

throughout the nation, especially among intellectuals and artists.

Other Asian religions also gained an audience in the West, including Hinduism, Sufism, Islam, and various sects of Buddhism from Tibet, Thailand, Nepal, and other places. Hinduism was one of the most popular Asian religions in the West due to the influence of celebrities like the Beatles who turned for inspiration to Indian guru Maharishi Mahesh. In 1966, Beatle George Harrison said "he believed much more in the religions of India than anything he ever learned in Christianity." By the mid-1970s, Maharishi Mahesh, whom *The New York Times* called "chief guru to the Western world," had founded a university in Iowa and three hundred seventy centers around the United States for teaching transcendental meditation designed to relieve stress while promoting health and peaceful well-being.

The fascination with Asian spirituality overlapped with the rising interest in Asian martial arts. Many Westerners attributed North Vietnam's ability to withstand U.S. superior firepower not only to the tactics of guerilla warfare, but mysterious Asian fighting techniques. Outside of Asian immigrant communities, Americans knew little about such skills until Bruce Lee, a Chinese American martial arts champion and actor from Hong Kong, launched the genre of Kung Fu films. The success of Lee's Hollywood premiere, *Enter the Dragon* (1973), inspired the proliferation of Kung Fu–themed movies and television shows, from Chuck Norris adventures to the family favorite *Karate Kid*, that inspired a generation of Americans to embrace Asian martial arts.

Critical Thinking Questions

▶ What factors influenced the spread of Asian religions and martial arts in the West?

▶ What impact do you think they have on U.S. views of Asia and Asian peoples?

of the oppressed in the ghettos without having first spoken clearly to the greatest purveyor of violence in the world today: my own government." According to King, Johnson's war was wrong on two counts: It opposed the legitimate national liberation of the Vietnamese people, and, by overwhelming the U.S. budget, prevented the full implementation of the president's War on Poverty. Here King expanded his focus on civil and voting rights for African Americans in seeking to resolve problems of economic inequality for all races. Like socialist critic Michael Harrington, King called on the federal government to radically transform the economic and social conditions that made it nearly impossible for poor people to achieve the American Dream. To this end, he criticized institutional racism, police brutality, and the undemocratic power of corporations. He also promoted affirmative action, full-employment policies, and raising the minimum wage as a means to ending the cycle of poverty that offered little hope of escape.

Seeking economic justice, King went to Memphis, Tennessee, in April 1968 to support striking African American sanitation workers. It was there that white segregationist James Earl Ray shot and killed the civil rights leader. King's assassination sparked another wave of urban unrest as blacks in more than one hundred cities rose up against the kind of economic and racial injustice that King had been opposing in Memphis and throughout the nation. Race riots the year before had spurred President Johnson to appoint the **Kerner Commission** to investigate the nation's racial problems. In February 1968, the commission produced a widely circulated report warning "our nation is moving toward two societies, one black, one white—separate and unequal."

King sought solutions to poverty through a racially inclusive poor people's movement, but others advocated empowering African Americans through the radical strategies of black nationalism. In 1966, SNCC adopted the practice of racial separatism by having its chapters sever ties with white liberal organizations. In a speech at Greenwood, Mississippi, SNCC leader Stokely Carmichael defended Malcolm X and the Nation of Islam, dismissing the image perpetuated by the mainstream media of them as antiwhite racists who threatened to destroy the nation's interracial goodwill. The only way for blacks to make it in America, Carmichael maintained, was to come together as a newly independent nation-within-a-nation with its own identity, culture, and economic self-sufficiency. Carmichael called this kind of racial nationalism **black power**. The phrase stuck and became a rallying cry for racial minorities who began to see integration as a dead end. King's assassination by a white man seemed to prove to many activists and disgruntled ghetto dwellers that the United States was still not ready for interracial democracy. A year later, Carmichael expatriated to Guinea and eventually changed his name to Kwame Ture in honor of pan-African leaders Kwame Nkrumah (Ghana) and Ahmed Sekou Toure (Guinea). The activist then traveled to North Vietnam, China, Cuba, and throughout Africa preaching revolution against racist imperialism.

Kerner Commission Presidential committee whose report warned about the nation's growing racial schism that pitted poor blacks against affluent whites.

black power Slogan used by African American social activists based on the strategy of racial separatism and total liberation from white racism and its legacy.

Black Panther Party Radical organization begun in 1965 that used humanitarian and violent means to liberate African Americans from poverty and racial discrimination.

At the same time, Muhammad Ali, the world's heavyweight boxing champion, refused to be inducted when drafted into the U.S. Army. A follower of the Nation of Islam, Ali, like other black Muslims, declared conscientious objector status and refused to fight because of his faith and his racial solidarity with the nonwhite enemy, saying "no Vietcong ever called me nigger." As a result, he was arrested, found guilty of draft evasion, and stripped of his boxing titles. It took four years for the champ to clear his name in a 1971 Supreme Court decision that allowed him to resume his legendary boxing career.

The African American organization most identified with radicalism was the **Black Panther Party**. The first chapter began in New York City in 1965, but it was the second chapter—established the next year in Oakland, California, by Huey Newton and Bobby Seale—that garnered national attention for its use of guns and violence in the name of black self-defense and the struggle to overthrow American capitalism. In this sense, Newton and Seale combined the racial separatism of Malcolm X with the revolutionary socialism of Karl Marx, Vladimir Lenin, and Mao Zedong. Like Ali, the Panthers opposed the Vietnam War as an act of imperialist aggression in which Americans of color fought and died in disproportionate numbers.

While the Panthers pushed black power to revolutionary extremes, African Americans also revealed a willingness to work within the political system toward black nationalist ends. In 1967 the New York City Board of Education experimented with an alternative to school integration that enabled a version of black power to influence the curriculum of public schools in Brooklyn's Ocean Hill and Brownsville neighborhoods. With support from the New York City mayor and funds provided by the Ford Foundation, the people in these largely black neighborhoods were able to control local schools by electing their own school officials. The new black-run school board fired several unionized Jewish American teachers, provoking a series of teachers' strikes against the Ocean Hill and Brownsville schools that doomed the short-lived experiment in "community control." The conflict revealed the limits of civil rights reforms and strained the black-Jewish coalition that had collaborated in earlier civil rights struggles.

William P. Straeter/AP Images

Black Panthers' Free Breakfast Program, 1969 In addition to its militant black nationalism and opposition to the Vietnam War, the Black Panthers provided free meals and other services to the black poor, and they worked to forge a broad-based revolutionary movement that reached out to a wide variety of radical groups within and outside the United States. ▲

25-2c 1968

Domestic upheavals in 1968 enable the Republicans to gain the White House.

The simultaneous rise of black nationalism, race riots, and antiwar protests reached a crisis point in the presidential election of 1968. In November 1967, Eugene McCarthy entered the presidential race as an antiwar candidate seeking to unseat the incumbent Johnson as the Democratic Party nominee. McCarthy (not to be confused with the anti-Communist crusader Joseph McCarthy) was a U.S. senator from Minnesota with a long history of supporting liberal domestic and international causes, and his candidacy became a barometer measuring the nation's response to Johnson's Vietnam War. In March 1968, after McCarthy defeated Johnson in the New Hampshire primary, Senator Robert Kennedy, President John Kennedy's brother, also entered the race as an antiwar Democrat challenging Johnson. With mounting political opposition and serious health problems, the president announced that he would not run for reelection and would begin peace talks with the North Vietnamese. McCarthy and Kennedy then battled for the Democratic nomination as Vice President Hubert Humphrey also announced his candidacy. In June, after winning the California primary, Kennedy was assassinated by a Christian Palestinian who was upset about the candidate's support for Israel. But this did not clear the way for McCarthy. After the Republicans nominated Richard Nixon as their candidate, Humphrey beat out McCarthy at the Democratic National Convention in Chicago in August 1968.

The Chicago convention proved to be a turning point for the Democratic Party and the antiwar movement. Thousands of activists from the New Left, counterculture, and black power movement came to the city to oppose Humphrey's nomination. They organized large demonstrations before and during the DNC convention. Humphrey had the support of the party's old guard, especially labor unions and big-city bosses such as Chicago mayor Richard Daley, who comprised the heart of the New Deal coalition. While the convention was deciding on the nominee, Mayor Daley's police cracked down on antiwar protests to prevent them from disrupting the proceedings. Dressed in riot gear, the police used tear gas and billy clubs against the demonstrators, some who returned fire by throwing rocks, bottles, and broken glass. As millions of Americans viewed the clashes on television, the youth chanted the "the whole world is watching."

The win by Humphrey, who had supported Johnson's war as his vice president, was a bitter pill for antiwar activists to swallow. The antiwar movement responded to the "days of rage" in Chicago by increasing the volume and volatility of their protests. Students at the University of Akron, for example, shouted down Richard Nixon in a campus election speech, yelling "Ho, Ho, Ho Chi Minh, Ho Chi Minh is gonna win" (they did not know that the legendary Vietnamese leader was but a figurehead at this

Prague Spring Dramatic although temporary loosening of political restrictions in Czechoslovakia under the new leadership that inspired global protests before the Soviets invaded and ended the opposition's movements.

silent majority Nixon's term for potential mainstream Republican voters who did not agree with noisy protests during the 1960s but were quiet about their convictions.

southern strategy Tactics designed to attract southern Democratic voters to the Republican Party used in 1964 by presidential candidate Barry Goldwater and four years later by Nixon.

Vietnamization Nixon's plan to shift the burden of fighting in Vietnam from Americans to South Vietnamese.

point). A number of Vietnam veterans began to openly oppose the war and spoke out about the atrocities they saw and even committed in the defense of "freedom." Even more dramatic was the surge in student protests around the world. Antiwar sentiment in France spawned popular student strikes in Paris that generated violent clashes with police. West German students called for its government to take full responsibility for the Holocaust and to stop another genocide in Vietnam. Antiwar demonstrations in Japan combined with student strikes and radical opposition to the nation's security alliance with the United States. At the same time, students propelled revolutionary impulses in Eastern bloc countries such as Czechoslovakia in which leader Alexander Dubcek responded to university strikes by experimenting with a less repressive form of communism dubbed "socialism with a human face." This **Prague Spring** lasted seven months until Soviet leaders stopped the experiment by invading Czechoslovakia. Violent government crackdowns also produced misery for Mexican university students who opposed the 1968 Olympic Games to be held in Mexico City, chanting "No queremos Olimpiadas, queremos revolución" ("We do not want Olympic Games, we want revolution").

Back in the United States, Nixon, the Republican presidential candidate, emphasized the importance of law and order and appealed to what he called the **silent majority** of loyal, law-abiding Americans. Nixon also distanced himself from the third-party candidacy of segregationist George Wallace, the Alabama governor who engaged in massive resistance to civil and voting rights reforms. Instead of attacking such reforms, Nixon, following a script from Barry Goldwater, the 1964 Republican presidential candidate, deployed a **southern strategy** that emphasized the importance of states rights in order to woo southern whites to his campaign. The strategy worked, and Nixon defeated Humphrey by a large number of electoral votes but only a fraction of the popular vote to become the thirty-seventh president (see Map 25.2).

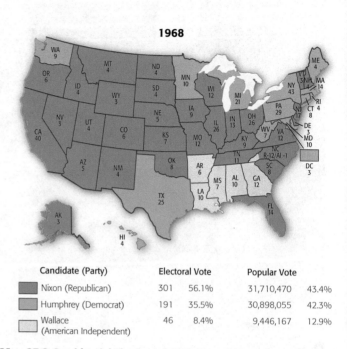

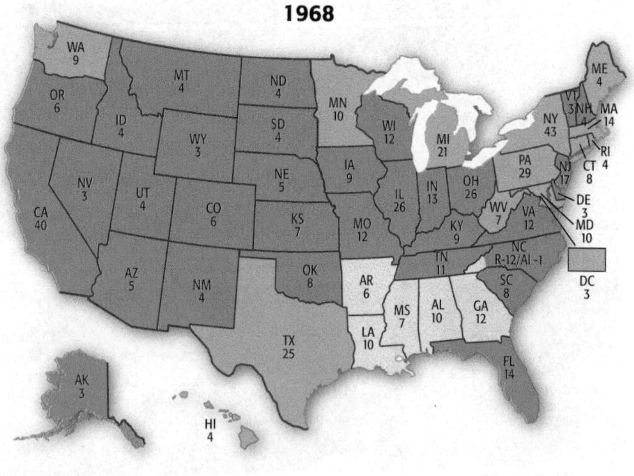

Candidate (Party)	Electoral Vote		Popular Vote	
Nixon (Republican)	301	56.1%	31,710,470	43.4%
Humphrey (Democrat)	191	35.5%	30,898,055	42.3%
Wallace (American Independent)	46	8.4%	9,446,167	12.9%

Map 25.2 Presidential Election of 1968 The solid Democratic South was no more in 1968 as only Texas voted for Hubert Humphrey, while the rest of the states split between Nixon and Wallace. Although Wallace won electoral votes from five southern states (an impressive showing for a third-party candidate), Nixon's southern strategy also netted him five states in the South, continuing Republican inroads into this heavily Democratic region and revealing the weakening of the New Deal coalition. ▲

25-2d Nixon and Kissinger's War

Nixon expands the Vietnam war into Laos and Cambodia.

Nixon came to the presidency with a mandate to bring U.S. troops home from Vietnam and spoke publicly about achieving "peace with honor." Together with his trusted military adviser Henry Kissinger, he developed a four-pronged strategy for ending the war. First was to use North Vietnam's superpower allies, the Soviets and Chinese, to pressure Le Duan to reach a negotiated settlement. Second was to reduce the number of U.S. troops by empowering the South Vietnamese military to fight the southern insurgency on its own—what Nixon called **Vietnamization**. Third was to engage in formal peace negotiations that would build on Johnson's 1968 agreement reached with North Vietnam to stop U.S. bombings. Nixon's Vietnamization and peace negotiations represented a new kind of thinking that appealed to the war-weary American public. But like Johnson, who did not want to be the first president to lose a foreign war, the new president was seeking a total victory that would give the United States the upper hand at the bargaining table. This led to the secret implementation of the fourth part of his war strategy. In March 1969, while Americans were being told that the war was winding down, Nixon ordered airstrikes against Communist strongholds in ostensibly neutral Laos and Cambodia in order to interdict troop movement and destroy the Ho Chi Minh trail.

The Geneva Accords in 1954 granted Laos independence, and the United States supported the anti-Communist Laotian government while North Vietnam-backed Pathet Lao revolutionaries who controlled the mountain regions that contained and concealed the supply lines feeding NLF insurgents from North Vietnam. Beginning in the early 1960s, the Central Intelligence Agency (CIA) recruited a secret army of mountain peoples known as the Hmong to help defeat North Vietnam and their Pathet Lao allies. The forty-five thousand Hmong fighters represented roughly 10 percent of the total population of this minority group in Laos. The majority, who had earlier fought with the Viet Minh against the French, sided with North Vietnam.

Like Laos, Cambodia had received independence after the French left Indochina in 1954. The widely popular Prince Norodom Sihanouk took over as head of state and steered the small nation on the difficult path of nonalliance, seeking to protect his country from being overpowered by neighboring Thailand, as well as by North and South Vietnam. In 1965, the prince broke off diplomatic relations with the United States because of its support for South Vietnam. At the same time, he reached secret agreements allowing Chinese war supplies to be shipped to North Vietnam and NLF insurgents via Cambodian ports and the "Sihanouk trail" into South Vietnam. When Nixon learned about such shipments, he expanded the war into Cambodia and ordered massive bombings to interdict the Sihanouk trail in successive attacks—Operations Breakfast, Lunch, Snack, Supper, Dessert—that became known collectively as *Operation Menu*. In 1970, a U.S.-backed coup forced Sihanouk into exile and ushered in the aggressively anti-Communist regime of Lon Nol, who purged Cambodia of Communists and consented to a U.S. ground invasion of his country.

Nixon's bombings in Laos and Cambodia confirmed Le Duan's fear that the U.S. would remain committed to total victory in Vietnam. In Nixon and Kissinger, Le Duan and Le Duc Tho now had counterparts who were equally adept at silencing dissent within their governments, while stubbornly waiting for an opportunity to land a knock-out punch to end the war. Ho Chi Minh's death in 1969 added to Le Duan's concerns about the war by casting a pall across North Vietnam even though the beloved revolutionary leader had long been a mere figurehead. The failure of the Tet invasion combined with the rejuvenation of U.S. war effort under Nixon pushed Le Duan to change his war strategy from toppling the Saigon regime to obtaining favorable peace terms that would require the United States to leave Indochina.

Nixon's new strategy in Indochina also had an impact at home. In May 1970, when the news media reported that U.S. soldiers had invaded Cambodia, antiwar activists across the United States protested Nixon's widening of the war. Amidst angry clashes at Kent State University in Ohio and the historically black Jackson State College in Mississippi, six students were shot and killed by law enforcement officers. In 1971, Nixon received another blow when former defense analyst Daniel Ellsberg leaked the Pentagon Papers, a top-secret Defense Department study revealing that previous administrations had misled the nation about the government's involvement in Vietnam. In the *Sullivan* decision, the Supreme Court overruled Nixon's attempts to prevent *The New York Times* and other major newspapers from publishing the documents. It was a landmark decision affirming the freedom of the press. Illegal actions taken by Nixon aides attempting to discredit Ellsberg became part of the major scandal that later doomed Nixon's presidency.

Bettmann/CORBIS

Henry Kissinger and Le Duc Tho at Paris Peace Talks for War in Vietnam, 1972 The United States and North Vietnam entered into peace talks in May 1968 with neither side ready to give up the war effort. In addition to the four-party peace talks occurring in Paris between representatives from the United States, North Vietnam, South Vietnam, and the southern (NLF) insurgents, Henry Kissinger (left) and Le Duc Tho (right) held secret two-party talks starting in August 1969 in order to get around the interests of South Vietnam, which opposed peace on any terms. ◄

AP Images/Dang Ngoc Khoa

Global Americans In 1970, **Le Ly Hayslip** married a U.S. civilian worker in Vietnam and eventually left her country to join him in starting a new life with her two sons in San Diego, California. She was twelve when the war came to her village of Ky La in central Vietnam. Both sides of the conflict recruited children to serve as spies and saboteurs; Hayslip fell in with NLF insurgents. Within two years, she was caught for holding "revolutionary sympathies" and tortured at a South Vietnamese prison. After being released, she was then accused by NLF insurgents of being a traitor, raped, and sentenced to death. Although members of Hayslip's family fought on both sides of the conflict, she was more concerned about surviving the war than taking sides. She managed to evade the NLF death sentence and flee to Saigon where she became a housekeeper for a wealthy Vietnamese family. She was fired after becoming pregnant by her employer. After working in the black market as a drug courier and prostitute, Hayslip met and married Ed Munro, the American who would bring her and her children (one of them his) to San Diego. A year after Munro died in 1973, Le Ly Hayslip married Dennis Hayslip and bore a third son. The marriage, however, ended in divorce as she charged her husband with domestic abuse. Le Ly Hayslip would eventually write two books that documented her ability to survive horrifying challenges in Vietnam and the United States. Such suffering, she wrote in her memoir *When Heaven and Earth Changed Places*, taught her "how to be strong while we are weak, how to be brave when we are afraid, how to be wise in the midst of confusion, and how to let go of that which we can no longer hold. In this way, anger can teach us forgiveness, hate can teach us love, and war can teach us peace."

25-3
Rights Revolution

The push to legalize abortion was part of the expansion of rights that many activists called for during the turbulent Vietnam War era. In this photograph, demonstrators marched to the U.S. Capitol in Washington, D.C. where they met a counterprotest by anti-abortion forces.

Why was the right to abortion considered an important part of the movement for women's equality? Why would groups oppose the right to abortion? ▶

Go to MindTap® to practice history with the Chapter 25 **Primary Source Writing Activity: Protest Movements.** Read and view primary sources and respond to a writing prompt.

AP Images

The proliferation of antiwar and black power protests inspired a wide array of activists to assert their own causes and claims on the state. While many had already been working to expose and eliminate discrimination against women, young people, African Americans, Latinos, Asian Americans, Native Americans, and sexual minorities, the "war at home" provided an opportunity to broaden support for their causes by joining together with antiwar and black power activists to create a broad coalition for political and social change. The coalition included both liberal reformers and radical extremists who criticized the status quo but often disagreed over strategies, tactics, and goals. President Nixon and most conservatives were especially alarmed by leftist extremists, who proclaimed violence to be a legitimate means of protest. As a result, the FBI closely monitored dissent and cracked down on those deemed most threatening.

☞ As you read, notice the differences between liberal and radical views about society and its problems. How and why were these expressed within the antiwar movement as well as struggles seeking social justice for women, racial minorities, and sexual minorities?

25-3a Third World Movements in the United States

Black power thrived on many college and university campuses, and given the prominence of youth radicalism in the San Francisco Bay Area, it was not surprising that the agitation for black nationalist university courses and service programs began there. In winter 1968, racial minority students at San Francisco State College and the University of California–Berkeley waged general strikes that pressured these schools to establish departments of black studies along with programs run by Native Americans, Mexican Americans, and Asian Americans. **Ethnic studies** departments created classes to counteract what they viewed as the damaging psychological effects of living in a fundamentally racist society that devalued the experiences and contributions of nonwhites. The idea of ethnic studies quickly spread and inspired cultural heritage movements that included the invention of Kwanza, a seven-day holiday offering a noncommercial alternative to Christmas drawing on African traditions to build black unity, pride, and economic and cultural self-sufficiency.

Black nationalism influences other racial minorities.

As the strikes for ethnic studies revealed, the notion of black power resonated with other racial minority groups. Native Americans faced the same urban ghetto conditions as blacks as a result of federal Indian relocation programs that encouraged them to leave reservations. In the late 1960s, nearly one in three Indian youths in Minneapolis dropped out of school, and while Native Americans made up only 10 percent of the city's population, they comprised 70 percent of its prison inmates. The **American Indian Movement (AIM)**, a national struggle to advance Native American economic and cultural autonomy, grew out of these dire conditions. To draw attention to their cause, AIM occupied Alcatraz Island, protested at historic sites such as Mount Rushmore and a replica of the *Mayflower* ship, and took over the headquarters of Bureau of Indian Affairs in Washington, D.C. In 1973, these protests culminated in the occupation of Wounded Knee, the historic site on the Pine Ridge Indian reservation in South Dakota where the U.S. military had massacred families of Lakota Siouxs in 1890.

Mexican Americans also embraced the spirit of racial nationalism. While older civil rights organizations such as the League of United Latin American Citizens (LULAC) and the G.I. Forum relied on the courts to fight discrimination, radical Chicanos such as the paramilitary Brown Berets took the Black Panthers' revolutionary stance. This was not surprising given that Mexican American communities experienced many of the same urban problems as African Americans and Native Americans. The **Chicano movement** emerged within rapidly growing Mexican American urban ghettos, or *barrios*. The Brown Berets sought to provide "self-defense" against police brutality, protested against the disproportionate death rate of Latino soldiers in the Vietnam War, and encouraged "blowouts" in which thousands of high school students, starting in March 1968, walked out of public schools in the East Los Angeles area to protest poor educational conditions. Meanwhile, activists in Texas sought to improve *barrio* conditions by running candidates for public office from

ethnic studies Academic interdisciplinary study of race and ethnicity that emerged from racial protest movements inspired by black power and antiwar protest.

American Indian Movement (AIM) Social movement to liberate and empower Native Americans catalyzed by black power and antiwar movements.

Chicano movement Social movement to liberate and empower Mexican Americans inspired by black power and antiwar movements.

JIM MONE/AP Images

Resolution of the Siege at Wounded Knee, 1973 This photograph captures a peace-pipe ceremony between leaders of the American Indian Movement (AIM) and a representative from the U.S. government (seated at right). The ceremony marked the end of AIM's ten-week seizure of the town of Wounded Knee. The takeover was part of a militant struggle by Native American activists to reclaim land, independence, and dignity that was the birthright of their ancestors. ◀

Obama Presidential Campaign/AP Images

Global Americans In the fall of 1972, **Stanley Ann Dunham** enrolled in a master's of arts program at the University of Hawai'i's East-West Center, a magnet for international students, as well as Americans like Dunham who were drawn toward cross-cultural relations. Her two husbands had each come to the center from newly independent Third World countries—the first from Kenya, and the second from Indonesia. Dunham herself was transplanted to Honolulu, having moved there with her parents after living in Kansas, California, Oklahoma, Texas, and Washington state. As a result of her marriages and birth of her two biracial children, she embodied the kind of open-minded race and culture mixing upon which the center, and Hawai'i as a whole, had built its reputation. Dunham also stood out for academic reasons. Having lived and taught in Indonesia for eleven years and being fluent in the language and folk arts, she was seen as a promising scholar of development programs in that country. Her research and activities were supported by the UN's International Labour Organization, the United States Agency for International Development (USAID), the Ford Foundation, the World Bank, and the Indonesian government. But while she would become a respected anthropologist, it was through her son, President Barack Obama, that the world would come to know about her—a white, single mother from Kansas whose internationalism epitomized the growing significance of the Asia-Pacific region during America's Vietnam War era.

United Farm Workers Labor union for agricultural workers in California led by Cesar Chavez and Dolores Huerta.

Asian American movement Social operation to liberate and empower Asian Americans spurred by black power and antiwar movements.

the *La Raza Unida* (the unified race) political party. On college and university campuses, student groups such as *Movimiento Estudiantil Chicano de Aztlan* (MEChA) established Chicano and Chicana feminist studies to foster a separatist identity rooted in a sense of Mexican peoplehood.

The most widely known Latino protests were Cesar Chavez's efforts on behalf of agricultural workers in California. Together with Dolores Huerta and Filipino farmworkers like Philip Vera Cruz, Chavez led a successful boycott of California table grapes in 1966 leading to America's first collective bargaining agreement in agriculture later that year. The charismatic, Gandhi-like Chavez garnered widespread notoriety for engaging in marches and hunger strikes to provide the civil and economic rights for one of the most aggrieved groups of workers in U.S. society. His **United Farm Workers**' (UFW) union expanded the California cause throughout the nation and enabled millions of migrant laborers for the first time to receive the job protections and security of a union contract.

The Filipino Americans who helped found the UFW revealed that Asian Americans, who comprised less than one percent of the U.S. population in 1970, were also swept up in the activist spirit. Yet the **Asian American movement** derived from the growing Chinese and Japanese American middle classes. "Yellow power" activists established social service programs in Chinatowns, Little Tokyos, and Little Manilas that drew inspiration from both the Black Panthers' free breakfast programs and Mao Zedong's mandate to "serve the people." The movement's antiwar protests emphasized U.S. racism against the Vietnamese and even against Asian American soldiers whose own U.S. officers and unit-mates sometimes confused as enemy "gooks." Asian American studies programs emerged on college and university campuses to counteract the ignorance and invisibility of Asians within the mainstream curriculum. Of all the struggles, the most well-known was the demand for redress for the internment of Japanese Americans during World War II. Movement activists pushed the community's established civil rights organization, the Japanese American Citizens League, to raise awareness about the injustice of internment, and began the campaign that culminated in 1988 with Congress issuing an official apology, along with awarding each living survivor of the forced relocation $20,000.

25-3b Women's Rights

> A new generation of feminists win economic and reproductive rights.

The women's movement, like other protest movements during the Vietnam Era, experienced divisions between radical separatists and liberal reformists. Liberals were represented by Betty Friedan and other feminists who joined the National Organization of Women (NOW) and worked to gain equal rights through the courts and the federal government's Equal Employment Opportunity Commission (EEOC). By 1968, the EEOC began to back away from its position of treating male and female workers differently in order to protect women from doing "men's work." NOW feminists saw such protection as gender discrimination that prevented women from working the same hours as men. Wracked by indecisiveness, the EEOC referred many of these cases to the courts, and in the *Weeks* decision in

Table 25.1 Equal Employment Opportunity Commission (EEOC) Milestones, 1964–1973

One of the main achievements of the Civil Rights Movement, the EEOC began its mission with a decided focus on racial discrimination and only a token interest in gender equality. But it became a major player in creating new economic opportunities for both women and racial minorities.

Year	Milestone
1964	Civil Rights Act (Title VII) establishes the EEOC to eliminate unlawful employment discrimination.
1965	EEOC begins with a budget of $2.25 million and 100 employees to investigate charges of unlawful employment practices and if found to be true, to try to reach a voluntary agreement to rectify the problem. The EEOC cannot bring its own lawsuits, but it can support individuals who sue.
1965	EEOC maintains that businesses cannot fire female employees when they marry.
1966	EEOC gets 111 businesses, mostly in the South, to desegregate employee facilities such as cafeterias, restrooms, and showers and locker rooms.
1966	EEOC requires 50 percent of the nation's private employers to report on their workers and work conditions regarding women and racial minorities.
1966	EEOC issues its guidelines on employment testing procedures used for hiring purposes, which can intentionally or unintentionally discriminate against women and racial minorities.
1966	EEOC issues guidelines on discrimination because of religion.
1967	EEOC holds public hearings about employment discrimination in the textile industry, the largest of complaints.
1968	EEOC has a budget of approximately $6.5 million and 380 employees to investigate a record 15,058 complaints filed that year.
1968	EEOC issues revised guidelines on sex discrimination to ban widespread help-wanted advertisements that use "*male*" and "*female*" column headings.
1968	EEOC decides that policies designed to protect women workers in 43 states constituted unlawful sex discrimination.
1968	EEOC holds public hearings on employment discrimination in white-collar employment.
1969	EEOC holds public hearings on employment discrimination in the aerospace, motion picture, radio, television, and financial services industries.
1970	EEOC issues guidelines on discrimination because of language or national origin.
1972	Congress amends Title VII allowing the EEOC to bring a lawsuit against nongovernment employers.
1972	EEOC issues revised guidelines on sex discrimination to prohibit employers from requiring pregnant employees from taking a mandatory leave of absence or firing them because of their pregnancy.
1973	EEOC joins with the Department of Labor, Department of Justice to require that AT&T, the nation's largest private employer, eliminate discriminatory recruiting, hiring, and promotion practices against women and racial minorities. The company agrees to provide $15 million in back-pay to 13,000 women and 2,000 men of color, and $30 million in immediate pay raises to 36,000 employees.
1973	EEOC has a $43 million budget, 2,000 employees, and a backlog of 80,000 cases awaiting investigation.

Source: Milestones in the History of the U.S. Equal Employment Opportunity Commission, http://www.eeoc.gov/eeoc/history/35th/milestones/index.html.

1969, the Supreme Court overturned protective labor legislation, which allowed women to work at jobs that had been reserved for men, such as those requiring the lifting of heavy objects. By the late 1960s, feminists had succeeded in getting the EEOC to collaborate openly with NOW in challenging sex segregation in the workplace. They pushed to make child care an essential right for working women, but the campaign for a national policy fell short, leaving it to businesses to develop child care programs on their own accord. Feminists also sought to define sexual harassment as workplace discrimination. In June 1972, they welcomed passage of **Title IX**, an amendment to the Education Act that barred gender discrimination in all federally funded school programs and activities. As a result, collegiate women's athletics blossomed as colleges and universities were required to provide equal opportunities and financial support for female student athletes (see Table 25.1).

Title IX Amendment to Education Act requiring gender equity in all schools that receive federal funding.

reproductive rights Legal empowerment of women to have ultimate control over whether to become pregnant or to abort a pregnancy.

Roe v. Wade Landmark U.S. Supreme Court decision legalizing abortion and establishing guidelines for when and under what conditions it can be performed.

sexist Term used by the women's liberation movement to characterize gender bias and discrimination, as in "sexist pig."

male chauvinism Term used especially by the women's liberation movement for biased and discriminatory views about women that men held.

homophile Term connoting a positive view of homosexuality that gay and lesbian activists in the United States commonly used during the 1950s and 1960s.

Not all women benefited equally from obtaining economic rights. As was the case for racial minorities, affirmative action for jobs and college admissions offered the greatest benefits to those with the most educational and class privileges. Moreover, the elimination of protective labor legislation, which viewed women as equal to men, did unexpected damage to women who relied on welfare programs. In 1967, Congress revised the Social Security Act to reflect the new view of women as independent workers rather than dependent on a male breadwinner. This revision required mothers receiving Aid to Families with Dependent Children (AFDC) to get a job rather than receive benefits for staying at home with their children. Although appreciating being treated as independent women, many preferred the older protections that did not require them to leave the home for work.

Feminism at this time also concerned **reproductive rights**. During the 1950s and early 1960s, practicing birth control became legal in most states, which the Supreme Court confirmed in the landmark *Griswold v. Connecticut* case (1965) upholding the right to privacy of married couples to obtain birth control counseling and prescriptions from a Planned Parenthood clinic in New Haven, Connecticut. The decision struck down the last remaining state laws against birth control, and in 1972, the Court found that unmarried couples too could practice birth control.

The next step for reproductive rights advocates was to challenge laws that banned abortion in forty-six states and Washington, D.C. In 1970, Norma McCovey provided two young lawyers, Sara Weddington and Linda Coffee, with a test case for challenging the constitutionality of the Texas ban on abortion, which only exempted cases when it was necessary to preserve a mother's life. McCovey had been unable to obtain an abortion in Texas, and subsequently asked Weddington and Coffee to represent her in challenging the law. The case made its way to the Supreme Court, which in January 1973 ruled in favor of McCovey (named as plaintiff under the pseudonym "Jane Roe") and other defendants added to the case as part of a class action suit. The ***Roe v. Wade*** decision, as did *Griswold*, turned on the right to privacy, which in the former decision was counterbalanced by the state's concerns about a woman's health and the potential for human life.

Roe v. Wade divided the term of pregnancy into three parts (trimesters) and held that preventing abortion during the first trimester violated a woman's right to privacy between her and the attending physician—a point that abortion opponents insisted disregarded Christian principles for the "right to life." Though weakened and under continuous threat of being overturned, *Roe v. Wade* continues to stand as a hallmark to postwar feminism.

25-3c Radical Feminism and Gay Liberation

Protests push for radical understanding of gender and sexual equality.

While feminists worked to gain equal rights through the courts and the EEOC, a younger generation, inspired by antiwar and black power struggles, lost hope in the nation's ability to reform itself through the regular political process. These radical feminists separated themselves from male activists in order to better empower women. Such an approach saw **sexist** laws, **male chauvinism**, and gender-biased hiring practices as merely symptoms of more fundamental social, cultural, and psychological problems relating to women's oppression. Radical organizations such as Redstockings, Cell 16, The Feminists, and New York Radical Feminists forced liberal organizations such as NOW to move farther to the left. Betty Friedan herself called on NOW to form political alliances with the younger activists to stage a national women's strike that called for twenty-four-hour child care centers, unlimited access to abortion, and equal employment and educational opportunities for women.

But both radical and liberal feminists in many cases balked at the place of sexual minorities within the movement. Friedan called lesbians a "lavender menace" that threatened to damage the reputation of the feminist movement by associating it with a stigmatized sexuality. Others dismissed lesbians as re-enacting, and thus supporting, male power dynamics through their relations with other women. Lesbian activists countered these claims by asserting themselves as the true feminists because they, unlike others who dated and married men, identified exclusively with women. Despite these pleas, the feminist movement in the early 1970s was not able yet to accept homosexuality as readily as it did youth radicalism.

The marginalization of sexual minorities from activist organizations, combined with their stigmatization throughout U.S. society, laid the foundation for the gay liberation movement. Beginning in 1950, **homophile** organizations including Mattachine and the Daughters of Bilitis had mobilized to resist the inequities of the McCarthy-era lavender scare largely through education campaigns. But in the late 1960s, a new generation of radical activists rejected the reformist strategies of the homophile groups. The spark for gay liberation ignited in June 1969 at the Stonewall Inn in New York City, where a routine police raid of the unlicensed bar induced a riot by its gay, lesbian, transvestite, and transsexual patrons. Influenced by black power, a crowd of roughly four hundred resisted police

Fred W. McDarrah/Premium Archive/Getty Images

Gay Pride March, 1969 One month after the Stonewall Rebellion, gay rights activists marched in New York City. By 1973 almost eight hundred lesbian, gay, bisexual, and transgender (LGBT) organizations had been established, and LGBT bars, restaurants, churches, synagogues, health clinics, community centers, and other businesses and nonprofits had opened across the country. Gay pride marches began in a number of cities to commemorate the Stonewall Rebellion as a new beginning for gay liberation. ◄

arrest, shouting chants of "gay power." A larger mob returned the next night, engaging in another round of clashes with the police that would be known as the **Stonewall Rebellion**. The rioters paid a high price as those arrested had their names printed in newspapers and many lost their jobs during a time when homosexuality was criminalized in most states and people could be involuntarily hospitalized on the mere suspicion of same-sex attraction. After the Stonewall Rebellion, calls significantly increased to bring the lesbian, gay, bisexual, and transgender (LGBT) community "out of the closet" and into the plain sight of mainstream America.

25-3d Extremism and Government Repression

Political conflicts become violent when some radicals become armed revolutionaries, and the U.S. government counterattacks them.

In December 1969, the most extreme members of SDS dissolved the organization and advocated the use of violence to promote a revolution in the United States that would eliminate race, sex, and economic inequality, as well as end "imperialist" wars in Vietnam and around the world. They were known as the *Weathermen*, a name taken from lyrics of a popular Bob Dylan song. The group later changed its name to the gender-neutral **Weather Underground**, reflecting its fugitive status as well as commitment to women's empowerment. Group members were largely white leftist revolutionaries from middle-class backgrounds who became utterly disillusioned with the status quo while at the same time convinced that their violent acts would incite a general uprising among the country's poor to overthrow the government. They were wrong. From 1969, when they blew up a statue paying tribute to Chicago police, until the mid-1970s, when most of its founding members were arrested, the group engaged in seventeen acts of domestic terrorism, mostly bombing government buildings such as the Senate wing of the U.S. Capitol and the ROTC building at the University of Washington. They identified with revolutionaries in Japan, France, Mexico, Algeria, Germany, and other nations.

Stonewall Rebellion June 1969 riot at a New York City gay bar kicking off the movement for gay liberation.

Weather Underground Revolutionary organization that splintered off from SDS and used violence, such as bombing government buildings, as a means of protest.

COINTELPRO Counterintelligence program through which the U.S. government repressed radical protest groups such as the Black Panthers.

Meanwhile, the FBI was engaged in covert operations to counteract extremist organizations on the left and right, including the Black Panthers, AIM, the Ku Klux Klan, and antiwar protesters. The plan began in 1956 as a counterintelligence program known by its acronym, **COINTELPRO**, to spy on the Communist Party and later expanded to include civil rights groups like SCLC, SNCC, and the NAACP. By December 1969, the program had engaged in secret acts of violent repression, including the murder of Chicago Black Panther leader Fred Hampton and the sowing of internal discord within the Panthers and between its members and rival black militants and street gangs. In this way, the FBI played a key role in the decline of the Panthers. One of the last gasps of left extremism was the Symbionese Liberation Army (SLA), a revolutionary terrorist group headed by an escaped convict who identified with the violent wing of the black power movement. SLA members, most of whom were white, murdered two people, engaged in bank robberies, and, most famously, kidnapped Patty Hearst —the heiress to the Hearst newspaper fortune—and coerced her to join their acts of urban guerilla warfare. SLA terrorism ended in 1975 with the killing of many group leaders in a police shootout in southern California and the subsequent capture and arrest of Hearst and other SLA members.

25-4

Nixon Triumphs and Then Resigns

Fotosearch/Getty Images

President Nixon and First Lady Pat Nixon toured the Great Wall of China in February 1972, as Nixon and Mao Zedong re-established relations between their countries. Nixon sought to create a friendship between the two superpowers in part to compel China to stop supporting North Vietnam.

Can you identify the Americans in this photo by their clothing? What do the differences in dress reveal about the differences between China and the United states at that time? ▶

desegregation busing Program backed by the federal government that uses buses to bring racial minorities to all-white schools.

Swann v. Charlotte-Mecklenburg Board of Education U.S. Supreme Court ruling that upheld the constitutionality of school busing for purposes of desegregation.

Nixon's reelection by a landslide in 1972 revealed the continuing rise of a new brand of conservatism that stood for law and order at the time of increasingly violent political protest. Nixon transformed the nation's Cold War stance by thawing relations with the Soviets through arms control agreements and with the Chinese by re-establishing diplomatic relations. These international breakthroughs were part of the president's successful strategy to pressure North Vietnam to negotiate an end of the Vietnam War. In 1973, both combatants reached a peace agreement that ended the war and brought U.S. troops home. Their withdrawal spelled doom for South Vietnam and pro-American regimes in Cambodia and Laos. Meanwhile, at home, Nixon confronted his own crisis involving unlawful wiretaps of his political enemies that became a major scandal, ultimately forcing him to resign from office, which in turn created a historic loss of faith in U.S. public officials. The simultaneous collapse of the nation's global economic supremacy gave the public a rather glum outlook on the future.

☞ As you read, focus on Nixon's second term as president. What were his successes? What were his failures? How did his failures contribute to a pessimistic outlook for the nation as a whole?

25-4a Republicans and the New Conservatives

Nixon advances civil rights reforms within limits.

The nation's growing antiwar sentiment had little impact on Nixon's bid for reelection in 1972. The incumbent routed George McGovern, the Democratic challenger, to keep the Republican momentum going strong. The party's success was driven by the transformation of American conservatives who, after Barry Goldwater's trouncing in the 1964 presidential election, softened their Cold Warrior stance on foreign policy while moving away from the white supremacist stance of segregationist George Wallace. Nixon came to epitomize conservatives' openness to cautious racial reform in advancing desegregation; on his watch, the overwhelming number of school districts in the South turned away from Jim Crow. The Nixon administration also was the first to sanction the use of racial quotas to promote affirmative action in the workplace.

But the president drew the line at **desegregation busing** programs designed to transport racial minorities out of poor, inner-city neighborhoods to predominantly white suburban schools. Soon after the Civil Rights Act (1964), many cities such as New York and Boston relied upon school busing to quickly integrate public schools. Such programs met stiff resistance from white parents who not only held racial stereotypes about nonwhites but also were convinced that integration devalued their children's education and their property values. Nixon sided with the white parents in opposing the U.S. Supreme Court's decision in ***Swann v. Charlotte-Mecklenburg Board of Education*** (1970). Rooted in the same desegregationist logic of the original Brown decision, the *Swann* ruling ordered the North Carolina school district involved to use busing as a weapon against the legacy of Jim Crow, paving the way for similar programs in Los Angeles, Boston, Cleveland, and Indianapolis. In 1972, a public opinion poll revealed that 70 percent of Americans opposed race-based school busing, and a later poll found that the nation was more concerned about busing than abortion. One victory for the antibusing proponents was the Supreme Court's decision in *Milliken v. Bradley* (1974) to prevent school busing programs in Michigan that crossed from one school district to another.

Opponents of desegregation busing found ingenious ways to delay or defeat racial integration. In 1969, after courts ordered school districts to speed up the pace of desegregation, many whites removed their children from public schools and enrolled them in private schools that were beyond the purview of the government's orders. The stunning increase in private school enrollment was revealed in the huge growth of non-Catholic private schools in Mississippi: from seventeen schools with a combined total of 2,362 students in 1964 to one hundred fifty-five schools enrolling 42,000 students in 1970. The "white flight" from public schools was in no way limited to the South as parents in all parts of the country got around court-ordered busing. By the 1970s, few Americans championed the racism of segregationists such as George Wallace, let alone extremist organizations including the KKK. Instead, these Americans resisted desegregation busing by arguing, in ostensibly nonracial terms, that the federal government had overstepped its authority and interfered with the right of their children to a good education. In this way, racial segregation lived on even after the passage of civil rights laws.

25-4b Grand Strategy for U.S. Foreign Policy

Nixon and Kissinger relax tensions with China and the Soviet Union.

Despite the war in Vietnam, the Cold War competition with the Soviet Union continued to preoccupy U.S. officials. In 1969, Nixon had enjoyed a welcome victory in the race to land on the moon. In 1961, Soviet cosmonaut Yuri Gargarin was the first human to orbit the Earth, but eight years later, Americans Neil Armstrong and Buzz Aldrin were the first to walk on the moon as part of NASA's successful **Apollo program** that fulfilled President Kennedy's goal.

From the start of the Nixon administration, the president and Kissinger adopted a realist approach to foreign policy that emphasized pragmatism over ideology. In an effort to ease international tensions, they crafted a grand strategy called **détente**, a French term for the relaxation of a drawn bow and arrow. Their first efforts at détente involved the People's Republic of China (PRC). Although the United States had yet to establish formal diplomatic relations with the PRC, a country founded in 1949, the vehemently anti-Communist Nixon believed that he could approach China without his political rivals accusing him of being soft on communism. The Chinese government, reeling from the internal tumult unleashed by the Cultural Revolution (1966–1976) and unsettled by recent military clashes along its 4,150-mile border with the Soviets, proved receptive to Nixon and Kissinger's overtures.

A major breakthrough occurred in April 1971, after Chinese Premier Zhou Enlai directed the Chinese national table tennis team to invite its U.S. counterpart to play a series of matches in Beijing. In February 1972, Nixon and Kissinger (along with First Lady Pat Nixon) traveled to China. The men met privately with Mao and Zhou. Although they failed to resolve differences over Taiwan, both sides agreed that no nation should seek to establish hegemony over the Asian Pacific region. After the historic exchange, the Chinese gave the First Lady a pair of panda bears as a symbol of friendship (President Nixon reciprocated with a gift of two musk oxen).

Apollo program NASA space flight project committed to having an American be the first human to land on the moon.

détente Foreign policy strategy designed to advance the interests of a state through de-escalating conflict with among major superpowers.

Strategic Arms Limitation Talks (SALT) Breakthrough arms control agreement between the United States and Soviet Union signed in May 1972.

Improving relations with the Soviet Union was the second component of Nixon and Kissinger's détente. After the 1962 Cuban Missile Crisis, the Soviets had made a concerted effort to match U.S. nuclear capabilities. By 1970, they had achieved a 1,140 to 1,054 advantage over the United States in intercontinental ballistic missiles (ICBMs), but the huge arms buildup was severely straining the Soviet economy. The Soviets also had feared that their deteriorating relationship with the PRC could trigger a war. The two behemoths had long vied for leadership of the Communist world and the loyalty of nations recently liberated from colonialism. To capitalize on the Sino-Soviet split, Nixon and Kissinger pursued a triangular diplomacy that used a combination of incentives and penalties to play the Chinese and Soviets off against the other.

The strategy worked. After Nixon's trip to China, the Soviets—troubled at the prospect of a Sino–American partnership—made concessions in long-stalled **Strategic Arms Limitation Talks (SALT)**. During a May 1972 visit to Moscow, Nixon and General Secretary Leonid Brezhnev signed two SALT agreements, one restricting each superpower to two hundred antiballistic missiles (ABMs) and the other freezing the development of offensive missiles for a five-year period. In addition to the SALT pacts, Brezhnev and Nixon agreed to avoid direct military confrontations and to prevent nuclear war. Although ambiguous and unenforceable, this code of conduct reflected a new spirit of optimism in Soviet–U.S. relations.

25-4c U.S. Withdraws from Indochina

The U.S. and North Vietnam sign a peace agreement after each fails to achieve total victory.

Despite historic breakthroughs with China and the Soviet Union, Nixon's quest for total victory in Vietnam by stepping up bombings in Laos and Cambodia failed to induce Le Duan to give up the strategy of "talking while fighting." In fact, the North's victory over South Vietnamese forces in Laos gave Le

Bettmann/CORBIS

Global Americans In 1966, during his last year at Yale University, **John Kerry** both enlisted in the U.S. Navy and criticized America's war in Vietnam as a speaker for his class graduation. After completing officer training, he volunteered to serve on a patrol boat in Vietnam, thinking that it would keep him away from military action. As it turned out, he was assigned to a region in the Mekong Delta that was in the thick of conflict. Within two years of service, Kerry was wounded three times in battle, receiving three Purple Hearts along with Silver and Bronze star medals. In spring 1969, he returned to the United States where he joined nearly a thousand Vietnam veterans in discarding their service medals on the steps of the U.S. Capitol. Kerry also testified against the war before the Senate Foreign Relations Committee, where he was asked the now memorable question: "How do you ask a man to be the last man to die for a mistake?" In 1972, Kerry lost an election to serve as a representative to U.S. Congress from Massachusetts. Twelve years later he would arrive on Capitol Hill as a U.S. senator. In 2004, he lost the presidential election as the Democratic candidate. In 2009 he then served as secretary of state.

Easter Offensive Last failed attempt by North Vietnam at the GO-GU plan in March 1972 that caused Le Duan to make a serious push for a peace settlement.

Operation Linebacker One of the last attempts by the United States to gain a total victory in Vietnam whose failure, as well as the failure of a second attempt (Operation Linebacker II), pushed Nixon to accept a negotiated peace settlement.

Duan a boost of confidence that encouraged him to give the GO-GU strategy another try. Worried that Nixon and Kissinger's grand strategy would convince the Soviets and Chinese to end their support of the war in Vietnam, North Vietnamese leaders launched a new attack on South Vietnam in March 1972. But the **Easter Offensive** failed; for the third time, the North Vietnamese were repelled and no general uprising emerged. In addition, China and the Soviet Union, neither of whom supported the offensive, began limiting military support to North Vietnam.

Nixon responded to the Easter Offensive by waging **Operation Linebacker**, which for the first time since Johnson's no-bombing agreement in 1968, engaged in a barrage of aerial assaults on Hanoi and other northern cities. At this point, Le Duan admitted the failure of the GO-GU plan and had no choice but to take the ongoing peace talks seriously. Still hopeful for total victory, Nixon launched Operation Linebacker II during Christmas 1972. But this attempt failed again to bring Hanoi to its knees and, in the end, stirred up world opinion against the United States to a fever pitch. This proved to be Nixon's breaking point, as he too was now prepared for a negotiated peace.

On January 27, 1973, the United States, North Vietnam, South Vietnam, and the provisional government representing NLF insurgents signed a peace treaty in Paris that officially ended the war. The Paris Peace Treaty called for the withdrawal of American troops, the end of U.S. bombings, dismantling of mines in North Vietnamese waters, a cease-fire between the insurgents and South Vietnam military, and the return of prisoners of war. The United States, after blocking democratic elections in Vietnam since 1954, consented to holding elections regarding the reunification of North and South Vietnam. The long-term dream of a united and independent Vietnam was finally possible, while South Vietnam's fear of being abandoned by the United States was realized.

By April 1975, with U.S. troops gone, North Vietnam toppled the South Vietnamese government, and Saigon was renamed Ho Chi Minh City. Lacking both U.S. and South Vietnamese support, the anti-Communist regimes in Cambodia and Laos fell to the Khmer Rouge and Pathet Lao, respectively. In this sense, domino theory predictions were correct that a Communist victory in Vietnam would cause other Indochinese nations to follow suit, but the chain reaction did not spread beyond Laos and Cambodia. If anything, the removal of the U.S. threat in Indochina also revealed deep conflicts among the Communist regimes. The reunified Vietnam soon clashed with China, resuming a long-standing enmity that had been papered over by their alliance against the United States. Vietnam also invaded Cambodia in part because of the Khmer Rouge's close ties to the Chinese. In return, China invaded Vietnam in February 1979 and engaged in three weeks of hostilities before withdrawing.

In the end, the U.S. war in Indochina proved to be the nation's longest military endeavor and its worst defeat. Over 50,000 Americans had died trying to prevent the reunification of Vietnam under Communist rule. The overall death rate for Vietnamese civilians and troops (both North and South) has been variously reported from 800,000 to more than 3 million. The Laotian war dead numbered about 60,000. The death toll in Cambodia is estimated to have been around 250,000, not including the 1.7 million victims of the Khmer Rouge genocide. In proportion to the country's overall population, the Cambodian genocide was more devastating than the mass murders and starvation committed under Hitler, Stalin, or Mao.

After U.S. troops went home leaving behind thousands missing in action, the 5 million veterans of the former South Vietnamese military suffered at the hands of their former enemies. They represented half of the 1 million people forced to leave Saigon to work on rural land development projects. Many other veterans were among the 300,000 "enemies of the people" sent to re-education camps. The fortunate few former South Vietnamese military were among the 125,000 South Vietnamese refugees who were airlifted out of Saigon before reunification. Thousands of other refugees fled Cambodia and Laos.

Later on, a second and larger wave of refugees began to flee Vietnam through perilous journeys by sea on makeshift boats. These so-called **boat people** joined hundreds of thousands of "land people" fleeing persecution in Cambodia and Laos to create a humanitarian crisis throughout the region. Refugee camps in Thailand, Malaysia, Singapore, Hong Kong, and the Philippines overflowed with occupants, some of whom were forced to return to their home countries. The United States responded to the crisis by taking in an additional 400,000 refugees from Indochina. Although this figure was more than half of the total number of refugees, smaller nations such as Canada, Australia, France, and Germany stepped up by accepting as many or even more refugees than the United States in per capita terms. In addition, China gave asylum to 265,000 ethnic Chinese from Vietnam.

25-4d Watergate

A major scandal forces Nixon to resign the presidency and diminishes U.S. citizens' faith in their government.

Before entering the White House, Richard Nixon had a reputation for being a no-holds barred political fighter; to him, politics was war. After winning the presidency in 1968, Nixon was planning for reelection by using the power of his administration, as well as the CIA, FBI, Internal Revenue Service (IRS), and other federal agencies to discredit two hundred political opponents, including another Kennedy younger brother, Massachusetts congressman Edward M. "Ted" Kennedy. Added to this "enemies list" was Daniel Ellsberg, the defense department official who in 1971 had leaked the Pentagon Papers that aided the antiwar movement. Nixon authorized a team of special agents to discredit the whistle-blower by breaking into his psychiatrist's office to obtain personal records. White House tape recordings later revealed that the president justified the illegal actions by saying, "We're up against an enemy conspiracy. They're using any means. We're going to use any means."

The "dirty tricks" used to attack Nixon's political opponents included accusations of sexual improprieties, financial misconduct, and the falsification of State Department records. But the most notorious campaigns came from Nixon's own Committee to Reelect the President (CRP). Known as CREEP by its opponents, this fund-raising organization run by high-level White House officials waged a covert offensive against the Democratic Party and the campaign of its 1972 presidential candidate George McGovern. In the early morning of May 28, 1972, covert operatives connected to the White House including former CIA agent E. Howard Hunt and former New York district attorney G. Gordon Liddy, broke into the headquarters of the Democratic National Committee at the **Watergate**, an office complex in Washington, D.C., to wiretap phones, photograph documents, and plant listening devices. Some of the burglars—known as "plumbers" because of their role in closing leaks to the media of confidential information damaging to Nixon—returned on June 17 to fix an improperly planted bug and were caught by a security guard. One of the men arrested carried a phone number that was traced back to the White House.

boat people Refugees fleeing Southeast Asia after the end of the Vietnam War who did not have the means or connections to leave by airplane or automobile. Instead they left by boat.

Watergate Washington, D.C., hotel and office complex where covert operatives sent by the White House broke into the headquarters of the Democratic National Committee, the crime whose subsequent exposure led to the Watergate scandal that eventually forced Nixon to resign from office.

Nixon's staff promptly denied that he or his administration had any connection to what the president's press secretary dismissed as a "third-rate burglary attempt." Meanwhile, *Washington Post* reporters Bob Woodward and Carl Bernstein began to uncover the relationship between the arrested plumbers and Nixon's reelection committee. The reporters received tips from the FBI's number two officer W. Mark Felt, known only as "Deep Throat" at the time and for thirty years after the Watergate scandal broke. Felt passed on top-secret information to the reporters because he worried that the FBI was becoming the personal spy agency for the White House.

In January 1973, after Nixon was reelected, the arrested plumbers went on trial and, when faced with harsh prison sentences, began to reveal their ties to the White House. The Senate then launched a formal investigation into the Watergate scandal and aired its hearings on live television with damaging results for the Nixon administration. The president, then, faced his toughest challenge when Archibald Cox, the independent prosecutor looking into the scandal, discovered that Nixon had installed a system that generated audio recordings of all phone calls and conversations in the Oval Office. Both Cox and the Senate investigating committee pressed hard to gain access to the recordings that could link Nixon to the Watergate break-ins and their cover-up.

In October 1973, Nixon responded to Cox's demands for the White House tapes by having him fired. The move revealed the withering of support for Nixon as both the president's attorney general and his assistant resigned in protest over Cox's removal. By July 1974, Nixon's refusal to turn over the Oval Office recordings set up a constitutional showdown between the president and Congress. Nixon claimed that it was his executive privilege to withhold evidence, and Congress charged him with obstruction

Archive Photos/Getty Images

Impeach Nixon Protest in Front of White House Protests to impeach President Nixon, such as this one in front of the White House in 1974, revealed a deep disillusionment among Americans about the nature of their government. It would take more than the pardon of Nixon for Americans to recover from the shock of Watergate. America's faith in their public officials, already battered and bruised by the Vietnam War, had been reduced to a new low in U.S. history. ◄

War Powers Act
Congressional act passed in November 1973 that made it illegal after forty-eight days for a president to engage in an undeclared war.

of justice. The conflict was settled by the U.S. Supreme Court, which required Nixon to turn over the Oval Office tapes to the new independent prosecutor, Leon Jaworski.

Next, the House of Representatives voted to impeach Nixon on three counts: obstruction of justice, contempt of Congress, and abuse of power (charges of tax evasion and concealment from Congress of the secret war in Cambodia were not approved). Nixon, however, resigned from office on August 8, 1974, before he could be impeached; he was the only president to do so. Gerald R. Ford, Nixon's vice president, took over as president. Two years earlier, Ford, a House representative from Michigan, had been appointed vice president, replacing Spiro Agnew who had resigned from office due to a tax evasion scandal. Ford was the only person to serve as president and vice president without being elected by the electoral college. His first action in the White House was to pardon Nixon of all crimes related to the Watergate scandal and to put to rest the nation's "long national nightmare" (see Table 25.2).

During the Watergate scandal, Congress pushed to reassert the authority of the legislative branch by limiting the president's authority to conduct foreign affairs. The **War Powers Act**, passed over Nixon's veto in November 1973, sought to prevent another Vietnam fiasco by making it illegal for the president to carry on an undeclared war for more than forty-eight days and giving to Congress the power to shut down the president's military engagement if it is not adequately apprised on the situation. In addition, Congress strengthened the Freedom of Information Act (1974), guaranteeing citizens' access to federal records. The Ethics in Government Act (1978) sought to clean up corruption by requiring public officials to disclose their financial information, and in response to Nixon's firing of special investigator Archibald Cox, Congress established the Office of Independent Counsel. Finally, the Foreign Intelligence Surveillance Act (1978) made it unlawful for federal officials to engage in domestic wiretapping without a warrant.

Despite these protections against government intrusion, the fallout from Watergate and the Vietnam War lived on in the disillusionment experienced by many Americans who no longer assumed the U.S. government to be a force of good at home and in the world. Nixon retired to California, and although he enjoyed moments of renewed appreciation, his misdeeds were forever etched into U.S. consciousness by the naming of any scandal in government, business, and even entertainment and sports with the suffix *gate* as in Iran-Contragate or Deflategate.

25-4e Collapse of Postwar Prosperity

The end of two decades of continuous economic growth reveals major shortcomings of the U.S. economy.

The shock of Watergate and the embarrassment of Vietnam occurred at the same time as United States dominance in the global economy ceased. While the U.S. in 1964 enjoyed a trade surplus of 6.8 billion dollars with the rest of the world, this declined by 1971 to a trade deficit, and for the first time in the twentieth century, U.S. merchandise imports exceeded exports. The transition resulted mainly from foreign competition in the steel, textiles, transportation equipment, and electronics industries. Yet U.S. officials also were convinced that the rapid swing in world trade reflected a disadvantage in the Bretton-Woods monetary system that

Table 25.2 Watergate-Related Chronology

November 1968	Nation elects Richard Nixon president.
June 1971	*New York Times* and *Washington Post* begin publishing Pentagon Papers, a Defense Department secret history of the Vietnam War smuggled by former defense analyst Daniel Ellsworth.
September 1971	White House "plumbers" break into psychiatrist's office searching for files on Ellsworth.
May 1972	Plumbers break into Democratic National Committee headquarters, at Watergate hotel and office complex.
June 1972	Arrests made in second Watergate break-in to fix listening device; one plumber is tied to White House; Nixon denies any connection to plumber.
October 1972	*Washington Post* reports from secret information gained from the FBI that the Watergate break-in was part of orchestrated campaign of spying and sabotage by Nixon reelection committee.
November 1972	Nixon is reelected as president in a landslide.
January 1973	Five of the plumbers plead guilty to Watergate break-in; the two who refused to do so were convicted of conspiracy, burglary, and wiretapping.
April 1973	Nixon issues statement saying that he had no prior knowledge of Watergate break-in.
May 1973	Senate Committee begins televised hearings on the Watergate affair.
May 1973	Justice Department appoints Archibald Cox as special investigator for Watergate scandal.
June 1973	Former White House Counsel John Dean testifies to the Senate Committee that Nixon was involved in the cover-up of the Watergate break-in.
July 1973	Senate Committee and Archibald Cox demand that Nixon hand over tape recordings of Oval Office conversations; Nixon refuses, setting up a constitutional showdown.
October 1973	Vice President Spiro Agnew resigns amid a scandal involving tax evasion; Gerald Ford appointed in his place.
October 1973	Nixon orders Attorney General Elliot Richardson to fire special investigator Archibald Cox; Richardson resigns in protest and new attorney general fires Cox.
November 1973	Leon Jaworski becomes Justice Department's new special investigator.
April 1974	Jaworski subpoenas Nixon to surrender 64 White House tapes; Nixon refuses but provides edited transcripts of them.
May 1974	Impeachment hearings begin in House Judiciary Committee.
July 1974	Supreme Court issues order for Nixon to surrender White House tapes.
July 1974	House Judiciary Committee adopts three articles to impeach Nixon.
August 1974	Nixon releases transcripts of tapes that prove he was involved in Watergate cover-up; Nixon resigns from office and Gerald Ford becomes president.
September 1974	Ford pardons Nixon.

allowed every nation except the United States to devalue their currency. A strong U.S. dollar meant that it was cheaper for Americans to buy foreign goods while more difficult to sell U.S. products abroad. In 1971, attempting to prop up U.S. exports, President Nixon surprised the world by abolishing the global system of exchange rates to allow the dollar to weaken in order to boost U.S. exports. Since then, there have been no stable exchange rates as all currencies, including the U.S. dollar, have been allowed to fluctuate.

Floating exchange rates, however, did little (if anything) to prop up the U.S. economy. The problems went deeper. The productive capacity of workers in both Germany and Japan had more than tripled the U.S. rate from 1950–1973. On top of this, U.S. companies paid much higher salaries and benefits to workers than their foreign counterparts. Thus, while the U.S. economy grew "fat and content," the foreign competition became "leaner and meaner" by investing in new, more efficient technologies and keeping labor costs low (see Figure 25.2).

In addition, the nation's depletion of natural resources, especially oil, ensured that it would remain a debtor nation for all but two years from 1973 to 2010. From 1890 to 1940, America's natural resources abundance made it the world's largest exporter of minerals. But this changed as lead, zinc, and copper imports climbed in the late 1940s, and iron ore deposits dwindled in the 1950s. By the 1980s, the U.S. imported most minerals from abroad. The same

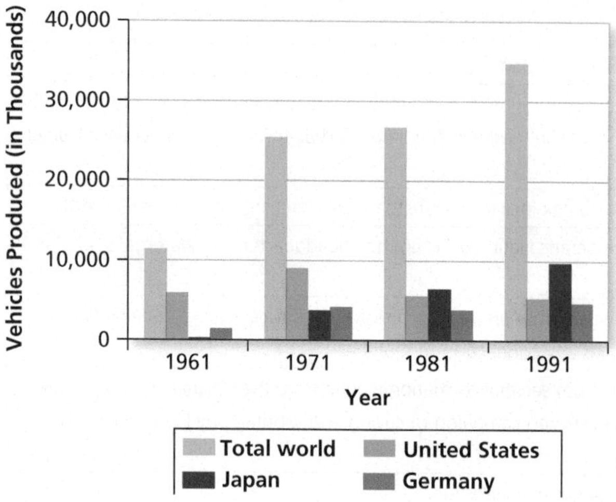

Figure 25.2 Global Automobile Production, 1961–1991 Foreign economic competition began to catch up to the U.S. manufacturers by the 1970s. This emerged most strikingly in the tremendous increase in Japanese and German automobile production. In 1950, U.S. firms produced 85 percent of the world's automobiles, but two decades later the Germans and Japanese were catching up, and by 1981, the Japanese overtook the Americans to become the world's largest car manufacturer. ◀ Source: U.S. Department of Transportation, http://www.rita.dot.gov/bts/sites/rita.dot.gov.bts/files/publications/national_transportation_statistics/html/table_01_23.html_mfd.

Organization of Petroleum Exporting Countries (OPEC) A group of oil-producing nations, mainly in the Middle East, agreeing to collude on the price and supply of oil in order to gain control over the global petroleum market.

trend of declining supplies was true for the nation's oil reserves. This contrasted with the abundant and cheap supplies of oil in the Persian Gulf. In 1960, this region surpassed the United States as the world's leader in oil production.

To offset this disadvantage, U.S. officials and oil executives, beginning in the 1940s, brokered deals with Middle Eastern nations that put much of the region's oil fields under U.S. control. In 1959, Congress imposed a limit on the importation of foreign oil in order to forestall the inevitable dominance of the Middle East. A year later, in an effort to obtain more control and profit from their oil supplies, Saudi Arabia, Iran, Iraq, Kuwait, Venezuela, and other oil-rich nations came together to form the **Organization of Petroleum Exporting Countries (OPEC)**. The first sign of OPEC's influence came in June 1967 with the return of Arab–Israeli warfare. In June, conflicts between Israel and its neighbors erupted into the Six Day War in which the Jewish state quickly defeated combined Arab nations to claim the Gaza Strip and Sinai Peninsula from Egypt, the West Bank and East Jerusalem from Jordan, and the Golan Heights from Syria. OPEC's Arab nations responded by cutting off the supply of oil to Israel and its U.S. ally. The oil embargo, however, failed as non-Arab nations including Indonesia and Venezuela stepped up production.

By 1973, increasing global demand for oil strengthened the position of the Persian Gulf nations. The price of oil tripled to $10 per barrel between 1970 and 1974, and

Long Lines for Gasoline, OPEC Embargo, 1973 Many of the iconic images of the 1970s were of gasoline stations feeling the ill-effects of an OPEC embargo, which twice during the decade caused consumers to suffer bouts of high prices, long lines, and short supplies. Pain at the gas pumps, however, did not reveal the whole economic picture, as the United States suffered an overall loss of competitiveness in the global economy.

AP Images

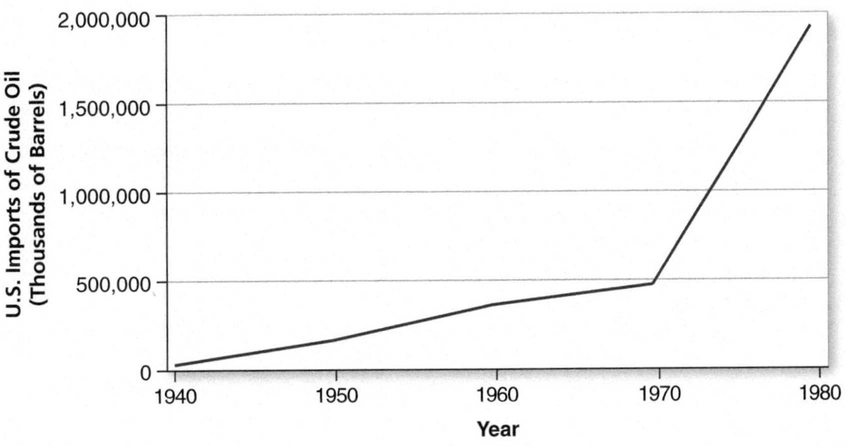

Figure 25.3 Oil Imports in U.S., 1940–1980 The spike in oil imports to the United States reflected the huge rise in worldwide demand for oil. Between 1948 and 1972, U.S. consumption of oil tripled, Western Europe's increased sixteen times, and Japan's skyrocketed one hundred thirty-seven times. Most of this growth came from the proliferation of automobiles, increasing more than eight times worldwide during the postwar era. Another reason for U.S. dependency on foreign oil was the discovery of abundant oil reserves in the Persian Gulf region.
◀ Source: U.S. Energy Information Administration

during this time the United States—which consumed an astonishing 40 percent of world petroleum—ended its restrictive quota on foreign oil imports. Within a few months, U.S. purchases of foreign oil doubled. Oil-rich Middle Eastern nations finally became cash rich and enjoyed the market power that their natural abundance all but guaranteed. They renegotiated unfavorable deals with U.S. and European oil companies to gain nearly total control of their own oil fields and, just as important, OPEC won the right to set the price of oil. OPEC's newfound power became apparent when the return of Arab-Israeli warfare in October 1973 pushed it to declare a second oil embargo on nations friendly to the Jewish state. In one fell swoop, OPEC raised the price of a barrel of oil by 70 percent and removed 14 percent of the world's oil production. Given the heightened global demand for oil, the **OPEC oil embargo** this time had a devastating impact on world economies. A third embargo after the Iranian Revolution in 1979 had an even more powerful impact. Consequently, OPEC had become a political as well as economic powerhouse (see Figure 25.3).

OPEC oil embargo Ceasing of oil exports by OPEC nations in 1967, 1973, and 1979 as a result of Middle Eastern affairs that produced energy crises in the United States and around the world.

The new competitiveness of Germany and Japan combined with dependence on Middle Eastern oil sent the U.S. economy into a tailspin for most of the 1970s. The U.S. economy, which had been growing at an annual rate of 3 percent since World War II, slowed to 1.6 percent for nearly two decades after 1973.

Summary

The Vietnam War was a watershed in U.S. history. The nation's most devastating military defeat significantly lowered America's reputation around the world. At home, the conflict provoked the country's largest antiwar protests, while heightening the militancy of black power, as well as social movements by feminists; Native, Latino, and Asian Americans; and sexual minorities. At the same time, the war exposed the secretive and deceptive ways that the president and military leaders manipulated Congress as well as the public to gain consent for their policies and practices. The Pentagon Papers and Watergate scandal were the two most obvious examples of how the public lost respect for President Nixon and public officials in general. The simultaneous collapse of the U.S. postwar economic supremacy added energy, trade, and financial crises to an already bleak political and social environment.

The Vietnam War was also a watershed for Southeast Asian and world history. Its scale of death and destruction was unprecedented in Indochina, delaying postcolonial economic development and sacrificing the promise of North Vietnam's social revolution. The region's numerous wars also meant decades of political repression, civil wars, and regional instability. Yet for the world as a whole, the war influenced a positive transformation in superpower relations when the United States engaged in détente with both the Soviet Union and China. Although the Cold War continued, the odds of global nuclear destruction lessened considerably.

<Thinking Back, *Looking Forward*>

As you review the Vietnam War era, think about how World War I, World War II, and then the Cold War gave hope for national independence to the Vietnamese and other colonized peoples. Also consider how civil rights reforms, and the U.S. urban crisis, encouraged the demand for even more radical social equality within the United States. In the coming chapters, look for the consequences of the Vietnam War for U.S. politics, society, and international relations. How did the war's legacy continue to influence Americans for decades after the conflict ended?

To make your study concrete, review the timeline and reflect on the entries there. Think about their causes, consequences, and connections. How do they fit with global trends?

Additional Resources

Books

Bloom, Joshua, and Waldo Martin. *Black against Empire: The History and Politics of the Black Panther Party*. Berkeley: University of California Press, 2013. ▶ Definitive study of this influential black nationalist organization.

Borstelmann, Thomas. *The 1970s: A New Global History from Civil Rights to Economic Inequality*. Princeton, NJ: Princeton University Press, 2012. ▶ Far-reaching study of this understudied but crucial decade.

Echols, Alice. *Daring to Be Bad: Radical Feminism in America 1967–1975*. Minneapolis: University of Minnesota Press, 1989. ▶ Important study of the radicalization of the women's rights movement.

Karnow, Stanley. *Vietnam: A History*. 1983. Reprint, New York: Penguin, 1997. ▶ Widely regarded history of the war that served as the foundation for the thirteen-hour, award-winning PBS video series on the subject.

Kutler, Stanley I. *Wars of Watergate: The Last Crisis of Richard Nixon*. New York: W. W. Norton, 1992. ▶ One of the major studies of the subject by a historian who has contributed to public release of Nixon's White House tapes.

Maeda, Daryl J. *Chains of Babylon: The Rise of Asian America*. New Brunswick, NJ: Rutgers University Press, 2009. ▶ Study of political, social, and cultural activism of the Asian American movement.

Means, Russell. *Where White Men Fear to Tread: The Autobiography of Russell Means*. New York: St. Martins Press, 1995. ▶ Autobiography of one of the American Indian Movement's leading figures involved in the siege at Wounded Knee.

Muñoz, Carlos. *Youth, Identity, Power: The Chicano Movement*. 1989. Reprint, New York: Verso, 2007. ▶ Classic account that has been updated and expanded.

Nguyen, Lien-Hang T. *Hanoi's War: An International History of the War for Peace in Vietnam*. Chapel Hill: University of North Carolina Press, 2012. ▶ Important rethinking of the war based on North Vietnamese documents and perspectives.

Ung, Loung. *First They Killed My Father: A Daughter of Cambodia Remembers*. New York: Harper Perennial, 2006. ▶ Powerful first-hand account of the genocide in Cambodia.

Go to the MindTap® for **Global Americans** to access the full version of select books from this Additional Resources section.

Websites

Cambodian Genocide Project at Yale University. (http://www.yale.edu/cgp/index.html) ▶ Descriptions, photos, maps, chronology, resources, and searchable database of information regarding the genocide and subsequent war crimes tribunal.

Experiencing War: Vietnam War Looking Back, part 1. (http://www.loc.gov/vets/stories/ex-war-vietnam50.html) ▶ Part of Library of Congress project collection of texts, photos, and oral interviews with U.S. veterans (parts 2–4 of same series on Vietnam War veterans).

FBI Records: The Vault (https://vault.fbi.gov/) ▶ A library of sixty-seven thousand primary sources gained through the Freedom of Information Act related to FBI activity concerning many radical organizations and individuals including Malcolm X, Stokely Carmichael, Abbie Hoffman, the Black Panther Party, and the Weather Underground.

Fiftieth Anniversary of the Equal Opportunity Employment Commission (EEOC). (http://www.eeoc.gov/eeoc/history/50th/) ▶ In-depth chronology of EEOC milestones, text of laws and executive orders related to employment discrimination, and a twenty-four-minute video regarding EEOC history.

The Price of Freedom: Americans at War. (http://amhistory.si.edu/militaryhistory/printable/section.asp?id=12&sub=1) ▶ Smithsonian exhibition with many exceptional photographs of the Vietnam War.

MindTap®

Continue exploring online through MindTap®, where you can:

- **Assess your knowledge with the Chapter Test**
- **Watch historical videos related to the chapter**
- **Further your understanding with interactive maps and timelines**

The Vietnam War Era

1964–1965

August 1964

Congress approves Gulf of Tonkin Resolution.

1965

United States has 184,000 U.S. troops deployed fighting in Vietnam.

February 1965

President Johnson approves Operation Rolling Thunder.

March 1965

President Johnson escalates U.S. aerial assaults on enemy targets in Vietnam.

1966

SNCC practices racial separatism and proclaims "black power."

Cesar Chavez and farm workers' union strike expands to boycott grapes.

October

Black Panther Party for Self Defense is established in Oakland, CA.

1967

April

Martin Luther King Jr. opposes Vietnam War.

June

Arab members of OPEC cut off supply of oil to U.S. in protest of its position on Six Day War between Israel and the neighboring states of Egypt, Jordan, and Syria.

1968

January

Prague Spring begins amid liberalization in Czechoslovakia.

United States has 543,000 troops deployed in Vietnam.

North Vietnam and NLF insurgents launch Tet Offensive.

March

President Johnson announces that he will not seek second term.

Mexican American youth in Los Angeles walk out of classes to protest substandard schooling.

1968

April

King is assassinated in Memphis.

May

North Vietnam and United States begin peace talks in Paris.

June

Robert Kennedy is assassinated in Los Angeles.

August

Protests erupt into riots against police during the Democratic National convention in Chicago.

October

Mexican students clash with organizers of Olympic Games held in Mexico City.

1969

January

Nixon becomes president and promises to end the war in Vietnam while renewing bombing in Laos and expanding war to Cambodia.

March

Weeks decision removes sexual discrimination in employment.

June

Stonewall Rebellion sparks gay liberation movement.

November

Public learns of U.S. massacre at My Lai.

December

FBI murders Black Panther Fred Hampton.

Weather Underground is formed; SDS dissolves.

1970–1971

May 1970

Ohio National Guard shoots antiwar protesters at Kent State University.

1971

U.S. has trade deficit for first time in twentieth century.

June 1971

Excerpts of Pentagon Papers are published in *The New York Times*.

1972

February

Nixon and First Lady visit China.

May

U.S. and Soviet Union sign SALT arms reduction agreement.

Five men are caught breaking into DNC headquarters at the Watergate hotel.

1973

U.S. trade deficit is $6 billion.

January

Nixon begins second term as president.

Peace treaty ends Vietnam War, U.S. withdraws from Vietnam, Cambodia, and Laos.

Roe v. Wade decision legalizes abortion.

February–May

American Indian Movement occupies Wounded Knee historical site.

October

OPEC implements second OPEC oil embargo against the U.S. to protest its position on another Arab–Israeli war between Israel and a coalition of Arab states led by Syria and Egypt.

1974–1975

August 1974

Nixon resigns from presidency; Gerald Ford takes over.

April 1975

North Vietnamese troops and NLF insurgents topple Saigon regime, and Vietnam is reunited.

Khmer Rouge topples Lon Nol regime in Cambodia and starts genocide.

May 1975

Pathet Lao comes to power in Laos.

Go to MindTap® to engage with an interactive version of the timeline. Analyze events and themes with clickable content, view related videos, and respond to critical thinking questions.

26

The Global Conservative Shift

1975–1988

Fifty years after having immigrated to Detroit to pursue her American Dream, Lily Chin returned to her homeland of China, her faith in the U.S. justice system destroyed.

26-1
Shifts in Global Dynamics

26-1a Latin America and the Middle East
26-1b Iranian Revolution and Hostage Crisis
26-1c End of Détente
26-1d Political Upheaval and Immigration

26-2
Economic Transformations

26-2a Energy Shocks and Economic Stagnation
26-2b Challenges and Opportunities for U.S. Business, Industry, and Labor
26-2c Resurgent Environmentalism
26-2d Rise of the Free Market Economy

26-3
Private Lives and Public Debates

26-3a Changes for Families and Women
26-3b Lesbian, Gay, Bisexual, and Transgender Rights Movement
26-3c Religious Revivalism
26-3d Global Fundamentalism

26-4
Triumph and Travail on the Right

26-4a Mobilization on the Right
26-4b The Reagan Revolution
26-4c Divisions Deepen
26-4d Confrontations with Communism and Terrorism
26-4e Cold War's Final Phase

Lily Chin's American Dream imploded on June 23, 1982, the day her son Vincent died. A Chinese American, he had been assaulted by two men who mistook him for Japanese and blamed him for the depressed state of the U.S. auto industry. Her story intersects the economic struggles and racial divisions in American society in the late 1970s and 1980s.

Bettmann/Getty Images

Lily Chin leaving the courthouse after hearing the verdict in the trial of the two men who beat her son to death. ▲

Lily was an unlikely public figure. She was born Lilly Yee in 1920 in Canton, China, the only child of a successful merchant. Her youth was scarred by the Sino-Japanese War and World War II. In 1947, friends told her about David Bing Hing Chin, the son of her grandmother's neighbor who emigrated to the United States twenty-five years earlier. The next year, despite only knowing David from a photograph, Lily moved to Detroit and married him.

Lily's father was displeased by the union and worried for his daughter because his grandfather, who had temporarily worked in the United States building rail lines, had told stories of American racism and discrimination against the Chinese. Lily tried to calm her father's fears and promised she would return home to visit. But after the Communists won control of China in 1949, she was unable to see her family for decades.

The Chins worked hard to build a life in Detroit, despite the racial tensions that escalated as U.S. auto manufacturing declined and thousands were out of work. They took jobs in laundries, restaurants, and factories. Unable to have children of their own, they adopted Vincent from a Chinese orphanage when he was six years old. After completing his education, Vincent worked full-time as a draftsman and part-time as a waiter to help his mother, recently widowed, and to save money for his coming wedding.

On June 19, 1982, three of Vincent's friends took him to a Detroit strip club to celebrate his bachelor party. Ronald Ebens, a plant supervisor at Chrysler, and his stepson Michael Nitz, an unemployed autoworker, sat nearby. Soon they started muttering racial epithets, engaging in the Japan-bashing that was common in Detroit where laid-off workers blamed Japanese automakers for their lost jobs and homes. A scuffle ensued, and Vincent and his friends left the bar, but Ebens and Nitz followed. In a McDonald's parking lot, Nitz pinned Vincent down while Ebens beat him with a baseball bat. Vincent died four days later. He was twenty-seven years old. The case drew little attention until Judge Charles Kaufman sentenced Ebens and Nitz on March 18, 1983. Having pled guilty to killing Vincent, the pair each received three years of probation and $3,780 in fines and court costs. "These are not the kind of men you send to jail," Kaufman explained. "You fit the punishment to the criminal, not the crime."

Vincent Chin's murder catapulted Asian Americans into political action. Joining across ethnic lines, they held rallies across the nation protesting Kaufman's lenient sentence and accusing him of racial bias in the case.

How does the Vincent Chin case reflect the deep divisions among Americans in the post-Vietnam War Era?

Go to MindTap® to watch a video on Lily Chin and learn how her story relates to the themes of this chapter.

Although she spoke little English, Lily also demanded justice for her son. These efforts resulted in federal charges against Ebens and Nitz for criminal violations of Vincent Chin's civil rights, the first such case involving an individual of Asian descent. The June 1984 trial drew international attention and sparked bitter debates over whether Asian Americans faced racial discrimination equivalent to that experienced by other minorities. Although Nitz was acquitted and Ebens's twenty-five year sentence was overturned on appeal in May 1987, the Vincent Chin case was a critical turning point in the Asian American civil rights movement. In September 1987, Lily Chin won a $1.5 million civil judgment against Ebens, but he made few payments and then disappeared without a trace. Her faith in the U.S. justice system destroyed, Lily returned to China after spending fifty years in the United States.

The Vincent Chin case reflected the deep divisions among Americans in the post-Vietnam War era. Politicians battled over taxes and the proper role of government. Economic changes triggered by structural shifts in the U.S. economy, increased foreign competition, and free market reforms created both opportunity and hardship. Women and lesbian, gay, bisexual, and transgender (LGBT) people pushed for inclusion and equal treatment while political conservatives and religious fundamentalists mobilized in defense of more traditional notions of family and morality. Confronted with a wave of immigration that included people from many nations traditionally underrepresented in the United States, Americans both embraced and resisted their country's increasing diversity.

Throughout the era, Americans contended with shifting dynamics of international relations and the resurgence of religious fundamentalism. In the United States and many other nations, conservatives gained political power. New nonstate actors pushed governments to protect human rights. In the late 1970s, upheavals in the developing world and the escalating nuclear arms race unraveled détente, and Cold War tensions escalated. By the early 1980s, millions feared that a superpower confrontation would spark a nuclear holocaust. But the convergence of a new Soviet leader intent on reforming his ailing nation and a president willing to alter his assumptions about his adversary soon transformed Soviet–American relations and set the stage for the Cold War's end.

26-1

Shifts in Global Dynamics

After a revolution deposed the Shah of Iran, Mohammad Reza Pahlavi, protestors stormed the U.S. Embassy in Tehran and seized dozens of American hostages on November 4, 1979. Images of the blindfolded captives being paraded before crowds of angry Iranians stunned millions in the United States.

Why do you think that images like this shocked Americans? How had the U.S. been involved in establishing the Shah's regime in 1953? What are some of the reasons that anti-American protestors might target a U.S. Embassy? ▶

AP Images

In the aftermath of the Vietnam War, U.S. global power declined, and the superpowers' attempts in the third phase of the Cold War to create a more stable and cooperative relationship collapsed. In the final phase of this global struggle, Cold War competition intensified, especially in the volatile developing world. Millions of people were uprooted by wars and political upheavals, and many fled their homelands. At the same time, heightened concerns about human rights violations inspired transnational activism and policy change.

Throughout his successful 1976 presidential campaign against incumbent Gerald Ford, Democrat Jimmy Carter capitalized on the Republicans' damaged reputation in the wake of Watergate. He promised to make significant changes to U.S. foreign policy and to stop supporting foreign leaders who violated human rights. He vowed to reduce military spending, U.S. foreign arms sales, and nuclear proliferation. He hoped to prioritize global economic inequities over traditional Cold War concerns.

But as president, Carter's actions were riddled with contradictions. He cut U.S. aid to some foreign dictators but continued to support others. Rather than slash defense spending and arms sales abroad, he increased both significantly. Although Carter enjoyed some diplomatic successes in the Middle East and Central America, the Iranian Revolution and the Soviet invasion of Afghanistan forced him to confront new threats posed by radical Islamists and renewed Cold War tensions. His critics charged that rather than restoring America's international status and confidence in the post-Vietnam War era, Carter only further weakened the U.S. position in the world.

☞ As you read, pay attention to the ways in which Carter attempted to modify U.S. foreign relations. What were his major aims? What were his major successes and failures?

26-1a Latin America and the Middle East

Carter tries to lessen anti-Americanism in Latin America and to facilitate peace in the Middle East.

A man whose deep religious convictions and integrity had helped him win the presidency, Carter pursued an active agenda in Latin America to improve U.S. relations with countries there. In Panama, he opted to end U.S. control over the ten-mile-wide Canal Zone, which it had held since 1903. The Canal Zone bisected Panama, and under U.S. jurisdiction, Panamanians within it could be jailed under U.S. laws by U.S. courts using English, a language few natives understood. Most Panamanians had low-paying, unskilled jobs. None had high-level jobs operating the locks or piloting ships through the canal. In 1977, Carter negotiated two treaties with Panama. The first increased the share of canal revenue Panamanians received, voided the 1903 agreement granting the United States legal jurisdiction, and ceded U.S. operation of the canal to Panama effective December 31, 1999. The second extended indefinitely the U.S. right to keep the canal neutral. Carter won praise for his efforts to generate goodwill in the Western Hemisphere, but critics who viewed the Panama Canal as U.S. property denounced the treaties. In 1978, after a protracted debate, the Senate voted sixty-eight to thirty-two to approve both treaties—only one vote more than the minimum required for ratification.

Carter's diplomatic overtures elsewhere in the region had mixed results. He suspended U.S. military aid to Guatemala and Bolivia because of human rights violations and persuaded right-wing dictatorships in Haiti, Argentina, and the Dominican Republic to free political prisoners. But talks aimed at normalizing U.S.–Cuban relations failed because of Cuba's support for leftist rebels in Angola and Ethiopia. In April 1980, after ten thousand Cubans seeking asylum flooded the Peruvian Embassy in Havana, Fidel Castro announced that anyone who wished to leave Cuba could do so, and a mass exodus from the port of Mariel ensued. By late October, one hundred twenty-five thousand Cuban refugees in seventeen hundred vessels of varying seaworthiness had landed on U.S. shores. The "freedom flotillas" sometimes overwhelmed the U.S. Coast Guard, and twenty-seven migrants died en route.

Upon their arrival, the **Marielitos** were placed in crowded camps and stadiums until they could be processed. U.S. officials were dismayed to discover that as many as forty thousand of the migrants were criminals and mental patients whom Castro had released to purge his nation of "undesirables." Although fewer than twenty-eight hundred refugees were denied U.S. citizenship because they were classified as violent criminals, negative stereotypes of the Marielitos persisted.

Carter's efforts to mediate the Arab–Israeli conflict were more successful. When Egyptian–Israeli diplomatic talks to resolve disputes stemming from the Six Day War stalled, Carter tried to re-ignite the process by inviting Egypt's Anwar el-Sadat and Israel's Menachem Begin to the presidential retreat in Camp David, Maryland, in September 1978. For two weeks, the president brokered discussions, which eventually resulted in two significant agreements. The first called for negotiations concerning self-government for Palestinians living in the West Bank and Gaza. In the second, Israel vowed to withdraw its troops from the Sinai Peninsula in exchange for Egyptian recognition of Israel as a sovereign nation. After Israel and Egypt formalized these agreements in a March 1979 treaty, the signatories were surprised when no other Arab nation—not even Jordan and Saudi Arabia, both U.S. allies—joined the peace process. Instead, many Arabs denounced the treaty for its failure to grant autonomy to the Palestinians. Syrian-backed troops of the **Palestinian Liberation Organization (PLO)**—then a paramilitary organization fighting for the

Marielitos Cuban immigrants who departed from the port of Mariel in a mass exodus to the United States in 1980.

Palestinian Liberation Organization (PLO) Established in 1964, uses a variety of tactics to defend Palestinian nationalism. Defined by the United States and Israel as a terrorist group until 1991.

creation of a Palestinian homeland—began attacking Israeli forces based in Lebanon. Other Arab states ostracized Egypt where serious internal tensions arose. The conflicts did not bode well for a sustainable peace in the volatile region.

26-1b Iranian Revolution and Hostage Crisis

U.S. policy makers confront anti-Americanism, an Islamic revolution, and a hostage situation in Iran.

Carter's most vexing foreign policy problems arose in Iran. Placed in power by U.S. and British intelligence operatives during a 1953 coup, Shah Mohammed Reza Pahlavi was a loyal ally who allowed the United States to use his nation as a base for electronic surveillance of the Soviet Union. He also continued U.S. oil sales when all other OPEC nations imposed a 1973 embargo. But the 1970s petroleum boom triggered high inflation and exacerbated the economic gap between Iran's rich and poor. The Shah and his family kept billions of dollars in national oil revenues for themselves. Oil companies imported tens of thousands of foreign skilled workers instead of employing Iranians. Rather than address unemployment, housing shortages, and poverty, the Shah spent $19 billion on U.S. weapons and military equipment between 1973 and 1978.

The Shah's extravagance and efforts to westernize and secularize Iran outraged Muslim clerics, students, merchants, and workers. These disparate groups began protesting the Shah's rule and his close ties to the United States. In response, SAVAK, the Iranian secret police, brutally suppressed demonstrations and arrested thousands. By 1977, Amnesty International, a nongovernmental organization focused on human rights, estimated that SAVAK had incarcerated as many as fifty thousand political dissidents.

Despite this repression and his own professed commitment to human rights, Carter supported the Shah. In a 1977 visit to Tehran, Carter praised him for creating "an island of stability in one of the most troubled areas of the world." Although the Shah ordered the release of some dissidents and permitted the Red Cross to treat prisoners, he did not institute political or economic reforms. After his diagnosis with inoperable cancer, he became even less attuned to the simmering discontent in his country.

Throughout 1978, massive demonstrations and riots rocked Iran. After the Shah declared martial law in September, his security forces shot and killed dozens of protestors. In October, a general strike paralyzed the entire country. Ayatollah Ruhollah Khomeini, an eighty-year-old **Shi'ite** cleric leading the Iranian revolution from France after the Shah exiled him, called for the Shah's removal and the establishment of an Islamic **theocracy**. For months, U.S. officials vacillated between supporting the Shah and urging him to resign so Iran's autocratic monarchy could be replaced with a civilian government.

On January 16, 1979, after naming a prime minister, the Shah and his wife fled to Egypt. Two weeks later, Ayatollah Khomeini returned to Iran. He rejected the new regime and appointed his own competing government. Denouncing the Shah and characterizing the United States as the **"Great Satan,"** Khomeini tried to capitalize on anti-Americanism and to undermine moderates battling Islamists for control over the government. At the same time, the deposed Shah moved from Egypt to Morocco, to the Bahamas, to Mexico in an unsuccessful quest for asylum. In late October 1979, Carter reluctantly permitted him to come to New York for cancer treatment.

The move triggered enormous demonstrations in Iran. On November 1, three million people protested outside the U.S. Embassy in Tehran. Three days later, hundreds of militants stormed the compound and seized sixty-nine Americans. Although they released sixteen hostages, the captors proclaimed they would not release the other fifty-three until the Shah returned to Iran for trial. In the United States, television viewers were stunned by images of the blindfolded captives being paraded through the streets in front of hostile crowds. Each evening, a U.S. news program called *America Held Hostage* (later renamed *Nightline*) provided updates on the crisis. Millions of Americans tied yellow ribbons around trees in a gesture of support for the hostages' safe return.

Carter quickly froze $8 billion of Iranian assets held in U.S. banks and asked the Shah to leave the United States. But as the hostage crisis dragged on, it consumed Carter's presidency. On April 7, 1980, after several failed secret overtures, the United States severed diplomatic relations with Iran. Carter then approved a covert rescue mission that failed after a helicopter and a C-130 military transport aircraft collided during a heavy dust storm in the staging area outside Tehran. Eight U.S. servicemen died. The Iranian captors then scattered the fifty-three hostages, making another rescue attempt impossible. Iran did, however, release one of the hostages after he became seriously ill with multiple sclerosis.

But subsequent events resolved the hostage crisis. In late July 1980, the Shah died in Egypt. Shortly thereafter, the Islamic clerics consolidated their control over the Iranian parliament and decided that the hostages no longer had political value. In September, after Iraq's Saddam Hussein attacked Iranian oil fields and threatened the Khomeini regime, Iran redirected its energies toward marshaling allies and funding for war against the Iraqis that ultimately lasted for eight years. Two months later, Ronald Reagan defeated Carter in the 1980 presidential election. In the final weeks of his term, Carter negotiated

Shi'ite Also called *Shi'a*, the second-largest branch of Islam whose adherents believe that the Prophet Muhammad's proper successor was his son-in-law and cousin Ali ibri Abi Talib.

theocracy System of government that places supreme civil authority in a religious deity and whose officials are regarded as agents of that deity.

"Great Satan" Derogatory term used by some Iranians to describe the United States that first came to prominence during the Iranian Revolution in the late 1970s.

the hostages' release in exchange for unfreezing Iranian assets. On January 20, 1981, in a final insult to Carter, the Iranians waited until after Reagan had been sworn in before allowing the Americans to leave Iranian airspace. After a four hundred forty-four-day ordeal, the hostages joyfully returned to the United States.

26-1c End of Détente

Détente helps de-escalate Cold War tensions in Europe but unravels in the developing world.

Throughout the mid-1970s, détente—the de-escalation of superpower tensions initiated by Nixon and Secretary of State Henry Kissinger—had mixed results. In Africa, leftist rebels backed by the Soviet Union or Cuba battled U.S.-sponsored forces in Angola, Ethiopia, and Somalia. In Europe, under a variant of détente called **Ostpolitik** (German for "new eastern policy"), East Germany and West Germany expanded trade and travel between the two nations. In July 1975, representatives from thirty-five countries gathered in Helsinki, Finland, and signed an agreement recognizing existing European boundaries, accepting territorial adjustments in Germany and Eastern Europe that had been made in the late 1940s. The conferees pledged to uphold détente and to support human rights. As newly created Helsinki Watch groups monitored the compliance of all signatories, organizations like Czechoslovakia's Charter 77 and Poland's Solidarity pushed for political and civil rights behind the Iron Curtain. Such dissidents later played a critical role in bringing down Communist regimes in 1989.

But détente generated passionate criticism in the United States. Conservatives remained suspicious of Soviet intentions and argued that maintaining nuclear superiority was essential to U.S. security. Liberals condemned increases in U.S. arms sales abroad and continued U.S. support for regimes that violated human rights. In 1976, attacks on détente grew so intense that Ford barred his aides from using the term.

Carter's contradictory policies toward the Soviet Union further eroded détente. Sensitive to any perceived insult to their superpower status, the Soviets objected when Carter attempted to modify previously agreed-upon arms limitations. The aging Kremlin leadership seemed blind to how provocative U.S. policy makers found Soviet actions in the Middle East, Africa, and Asia. To put the Soviets on the defensive, Carter formally recognized China on January 1, 1979, thereby completing the reconciliation begun by Nixon and Mao.

Despite the tense atmosphere, the Soviet Union and the United States signed the SALT II agreement in June 1979. The pact limited nuclear warheads and granted each side the right to verify the other's compliance. When Carter submitted the treaty to the Senate for ratification, critics of détente led by Democrat Henry "Scoop" Jackson of Washington vociferously opposed it. They argued that any nuclear arms agreement should be contingent on Soviets' respect for human rights and abandonment of their support for Communist revolutionaries in the developing world. Carter tried to mollify his critics by approving the installation of five hundred seventy-two Pershing-II missiles in Western Europe to counter recently deployed Soviet SS-20 missiles.

Attacks on détente intensified after Cuba and the Soviet Union began backing leftist uprisings in Central America. Cognizant of the region's severe economic inequality and political repression, U.S. policy makers were forced to balance human rights concerns and fears that communism would spread in a region deemed vital to national security. In 1979, after a junta seized power in El Salvador, U.S. officials provided military aid for its internal war against leftist insurgents.

In Nicaragua, Carter took the opposite approach and supported the leftist **Sandinistas** when they overthrew dictator Anastasio Somoza Debayle in July 1979. After decades of his family's corrupt and brutal rule, Somoza fled the country, but Sandinista assassins killed him in Paraguay a year later. Despite Republican charges that he was abetting the spread of communism in Central America, Carter continued economic aid to Nicaragua, a practice Reagan stopped when he became president.

The Soviet invasion of Afghanistan ended any pretense of a Soviet–U.S. détente. In December 1979, fifty thousand Soviet troops crossed into Afghanistan to prop up a faltering Marxist regime and to stem the spread of Islamic fundamentalism in Central Asia. Carter portrayed the Soviet invasion as the first step of a master plan to dominate oil supplies. He withdrew the SALT II treaty from Senate consideration, halted U.S. grain and technology sales to the Soviet Union, and removed the United States from the 1980 Summer Olympics to be held in Moscow. He also called for a massive $1.2 trillion expansion in defense spending over the next five years and ordered the reinstitution of draft registration. Privately, he directed the CIA to increase its covert aid to the Afghan Islamist resistance. On January 24, 1980, the president announced that the United States would protect its "vital interests" against any "outside force" attempting to gain control over the Persian Gulf region. The **Carter Doctrine** sent a strong warning to the Soviets that reflected escalating Cold War tensions.

Carter's tough stance did little to improve his standing at home and abroad. His critics saw Communist gains in Latin America, the Iranian hostage crisis, and the Soviet invasion of Afghanistan as proof that the international reputation of the United States was declining. Carter's own inconsistencies worsened his political problems. His diplomatic successes in the Egyptian–Israeli peace process, Panama, and China were not enough to convince voters to support him for a second term.

Ostpolitik Instigated by West German politician Willy Brant in the late 1960s, policy aimed at improving diplomatic and trade relations with the Communist nations of Eastern Europe.

Sandinistas Members of the Sandinista National Liberation Front, a left-wing Nicaraguan political group that overthrew the long-time dictatorship of the Somoza family in 1979.

Carter Doctrine Policy issued in 1980 warning that foreign incursions in the Persian Gulf region threatened U.S. national security and would be repelled.

26-1d Political Upheaval and Immigration

Cold War politics and global conflicts shaped U.S. immigration policies. Under the Immigration Act of 1965, less than 10 percent of visas had been reserved for refugees. As a result of this cap, many families displaced by wars languished in refugee camps, sometimes for years, awaiting sponsorship from relatives, churches, or humanitarian organizations. In 1975, when Congress refused to provide additional visas for those displaced by the wars in Indochina, President Ford used his executive parole powers to admit more refugees. But many others were fleeing political upheavals in the Middle East, Central America, and Africa.

Global conflicts contribute to changes in U.S. immigration laws.

In response, Congress passed the Refugee Act of 1980, a law that systemized procedures for resettling refugees and raising annual refugee admissions from seventeen thousand four hundred to fifty thousand. Once in the United States, many refugees gravitated to immigrant enclaves such as those formed by Somalis and Hmong in Minneapolis and Arabs in Detroit. Not all prospered in the United States. Many struggled with the English language and languished in poverty. Vietnamese American fishermen clashed with local residents in coastal communities in Texas and Louisiana. Many Americans welcomed refugees, but others viewed them as another strain on a weak economy that Carter had done little to fix.

26-2 Economic Transformations

Library of Congress Prints and Photographs Division Washington, D.C.[LC-DIG-ppmsca-03433]

Drivers in Maryland wait to purchase gas during the 1979 oil shock. High gasoline prices prompted many Americans to purchase more fuel-efficient vehicles such as the Datsun (later renamed Nissan) truck shown. Rising sales of Japanese cars contributed to a major downturn in the U.S. automobile industry that had devastating economic consequences for many communities. As the U.S. manufacturing sector declined, unions struggled to protect wages and benefits and battled conservatives intent on weakening organized labor.

How do you think that gas lines like this affected Americans' attitudes toward the U.S. economy and their political leaders? ▶

The onset of a global recession in 1973 had ended nearly three decades of unprecedented prosperity and growth of the middle class in the United States. Energy crises, foreign competition, and high inflation severely strained the U.S. economy. As the manufacturing sector of the economy declined, American workers moved to new service-oriented jobs, many of which paid far less than positions in heavy industry. Influenced by an international network of economic theorists, the federal government reduced its regulation of private business. The resulting free market reforms generated unprecedented wealth and economic growth but also undermined organized labor and exacerbated the income gap between the rich and poor. At the same time, a transnational environmental movement pushed for population control and more cautious stewardship of natural resources.

☞ As you read, pay attention to the factors that created the economic downturn of the 1970s. What were some of the reasons that the United States lost its global economic dominance in the 1970s? What were some of the ways that people attempted to restore prosperity?

26-2a Energy Shocks and Economic Stagnation

The shock of the 1973 OPEC oil embargo was only the beginning of the struggle over energy consumption that created political and economic vulnerabilities for the nation. Although the United States contained only 6 percent of the world's population, it used

Dependency on oil imports, increased foreign competition, and inflation impede the U.S. economy.

40 percent of the world's petroleum. Cheap energy had been a vital component of the abundance and prosperity most Americans had enjoyed after World War II. In the course of the 1970s, a sixfold increase in petroleum prices imperiled U.S. standards of living built on inexpensive gasoline, heating, and air conditioning.

The 1973 oil shock had global ramifications. Many nations were even more oil dependent than the United States. In 1970, Europe had derived 60 percent of its energy from imported foreign petroleum. In response to the 1973 OPEC embargo and rising international prices, some countries expanded their domestic oil production and exploration. In 1977, the United States greatly increased its domestic production as oil began flowing from the northern slopes of Alaska through a 789-mile pipeline to the ice-free port at Valdez. Meanwhile, the Soviet Union drilled additional wells in Siberia. After the discovery in 1969 of large oil fields under the North Sea, a part of the Atlantic Ocean linking Britain, Western Europe, and Scandinavia, oil companies built offshore drilling platforms and a European oil and natural gas boom ensued despite the hazards of oil extraction in such a harsh environment.

But the energy crisis was only one of the economic challenges facing the United States in the 1970s. As the costs of defense and social welfare programs expanded, the federal budget shifted from a $3.2 budget surplus in 1969 to annual deficits as high as $73.7 billion over the next decade. Global food shortages triggered by world population increases and poor harvests led to rising food prices. Health care and housing costs were increasing. Buffeted by high unemployment and inflation combined with a stalled economy (a phenomenon termed **stagflation** by economists), the typical U.S. family income rose only $36 from 1973 to the late 1970s. At the same time, ninety-eight nations had higher rates of economic growth than the United States.

Presidents Gerald Ford and Jimmy Carter attempted to redress the nation's economic travails. In 1975, Ford persuaded Congress to pass a $23 billion federal tax reduction in order to stimulate the economy, but the recession continued into Carter's presidency. In 1979, the situation worsened when the Iranian Revolution led to a second, deeper oil shock. When Iran's oil production plummeted by 90 percent, the price of crude oil doubled from $18 to $36 per barrel. U.S. gasoline prices spiked to more than $1 per gallon, triple the 1973 average cost. Having quintupled its petroleum imports since 1970, the United States felt the effects of restricted international oil production almost immediately. More than 50 percent of U.S. gas stations temporarily closed because supplies were limited.

Continued inflation also hindered economic recovery. After annual price increases averaging 2.5 percent throughout the 1960s, U.S. prices rose an average of 6.6 percent each year from 1973 to 1980 when inflation peaked at 13.5 percent. Britain's inflation rate was even worse, averaging 15.6 percent over the same period. Facing the biggest economic crisis since the Great Depression, U.S. and British policy makers concluded that Keynesian economic policies no longer seemed to increase standards of living and reduce rates of inequality. Seeking alternatives, officials began adopting ideas espoused by a transatlantic network of **neoliberal** economists, journalists, think tanks, and politicians calling for less intervention in the economy.

In August 1979, Carter appointed Paul Volcker to chair the Federal Reserve Board. A **monetarist**, Volcker abandoned the long-held practice of supporting a specific interest rate through the purchase and sale of government securities. Instead, he set strict new targets to control the amount of currency in circulation and allowed interest rates to fluctuate. But Volcker's tight money policies did not immediately stop the recession. As unemployment and interest rates rose, voters blamed Carter for the nation's deepening economic travails.

26-2b Challenges and Opportunities for U.S. Business, Industry, and Labor

Economic changes result in job losses and lower wages but also prompt innovation and migration.

Throughout the 1970s, foreign competition seriously eroded the global economic supremacy that the United States had enjoyed since World War II. In the mid-1950s, U.S. manufacturers produced half of the world's goods, including 75 percent of all automobiles and more than 50 percent of global steel supplies. But over time, foreign countries began to dominate highly profitable, technologically advanced fields such as aerospace, consumer electronics, and machine tools. In addition, American and even Japanese companies shifted low-skill production work to such places as South Korea, Taiwan, Hong Kong, Singapore, and Indonesia where goods could be produced more cheaply because of lower wage scales and limited worker protections. As many as 30 million U.S. jobs—most of them in manufacturing—disappeared as a result of such **outsourcing**. If U.S. displaced workers found new jobs, they often had to accept lower-paying positions. The growth of the postindustrial service economy ballooned, and by 1980, 70 percent of Americans

stagflation Term coined in the 1970s to describe a combination of rising prices, high unemployment, and slow economic growth.

neoliberal Calls for smaller government and expansion of the private sector through deficit reduction, tax reforms, fluctuating exchange rates, privatization of public enterprises, free trade, and deregulation.

monetarism Developed by Milton Friedman, economic theory that argues that overproduction of money leads to increased inflation. Calls for close government oversight over cash supply.

outsourcing Assigning core functions of a company to a contractor or subcontractor or obtaining goods or services from an outside vendor as a cost-saving strategy.

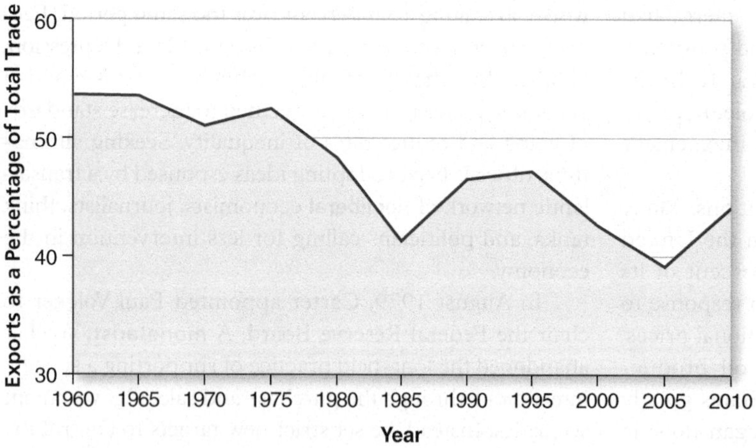

Note: Less than 50 percent indicates an export deficit and above 50 percent indicates an export surplus.

Figure 26.1 U.S. Trade Balance, 1960–2003 In the late 1960s, foreign competition began to erode U.S. economic dominance. Manufacturing declined in the United States, and consumers began importing many products such as cars and electronics. By the early 1970s, the United States had developed a trade deficit, importing more than it exported—a trend that has continued at differing levels ever since. ◀ Source: U.S. Census Bureau, Economic Indicator Division, https://www.census.gov/foreign-trade/statistics/historical/gands.pdf.

worked in the **service sector**. Rather than producing tangible goods, such workers provided a wide array of services including sales, housekeeping, health care, education, and financial consulting.

These trends had a devastating impact on the U.S. automobile industry. As oil prices increased, so had U.S. consumer demand for more fuel-efficient vehicles. German and Japanese automakers captured one-fifth of the U.S. market by 1977. Already struggling to meet new federal safety and emissions guidelines, U.S. companies including Ford and General Motors raced to retool production facilities to build smaller cars with higher gas mileage. In September 1979, Congress approved a $1.5 billion loan that enabled the Chrysler Corporation to avert bankruptcy (see Figure 26.1).

The shift toward a service economy dramatically affected organized labor in the United States. After impressive wages and benefits from their employers in the 1950s, unions in manufacturing industries like steel and automobiles lost membership as foreign competition rose. Public sector employees fared better. In 1962, John F. Kennedy issued an executive order allowing federal employees to bargain collectively and public unions grew as the Great Society programs of the Johnson administration led to expansion of government, social welfare, and teaching jobs. But total U.S. union membership fell from 1970 to 1981, dropping from 25 percent to 16 percent of the civilian workforce.

In the face of these trends, many workers wondered whether the American Dream was slipping away. Popular culture of the era reflected these fears in songs like Johnny Paycheck's "Take This Job and Shove It" (1977) and Bruce Springsteen's "The River" (1980). The film *Saturday Night Fever* (1977) popularized disco but also told the story of a white working-class man's efforts to escape a life of dead-end, low-wage work.

service sector Portion of economy that produces intangible goods such as investment management, retail, food service, scientific and technological expertise, health care, housekeeping, and entertainment.

Despite (or sometimes because of) the sluggish economy of the 1970s, entrepreneurship flourished in the era. Facing rising overhead and increased competition, investors were willing to back innovators offering cost- and time-saving efficiencies. After making Wal-Mart a publicly traded company in 1970, Sam Walton built a nationwide chain of "big-box" stores promising "the lowest prices, anytime, anywhere" and used computers to track sales and inventory—a practice then rare in the retail industry. The computing industry also transformed as small desktop or personal computers joined (and in many cases replaced) large mainframe computers that had descended from the army's ENIAC (1946). Bill Gates and Paul Allen started the company Micro-Soft in April 1975 and soon created MS-DOS, a computer operating system that required users to type in specific command codes. In 1976, Steve Jobs and Steve Wozniak formed Apple Computer to market the Apple II, widely considered the first personal computer suited for business tasks. In 1984, Apple revolutionized desktop computing by creating the Macintosh computer which allowed users to make commands by pointing and clicking on the screen through the combination of a graphical user interface and a "mouse." A year later, Gates's company, now known as Microsoft, came out with its own operating system (Windows) also based on the use of a mouse interface.

The wave of technological advances accelerated the demographic shift in the United States toward the Sunbelt. Many technology start-up companies were located near universities in California, North Carolina, and Texas. Other corporations were drawn to the South and the West by the regions' right-to-work laws, weak unions, warm climates, and skilled workforces. As workers fled the urban decay and unemployment of northern and midwestern rust-belt industrial cities, the Sunbelt prospered (see Map 26.1).

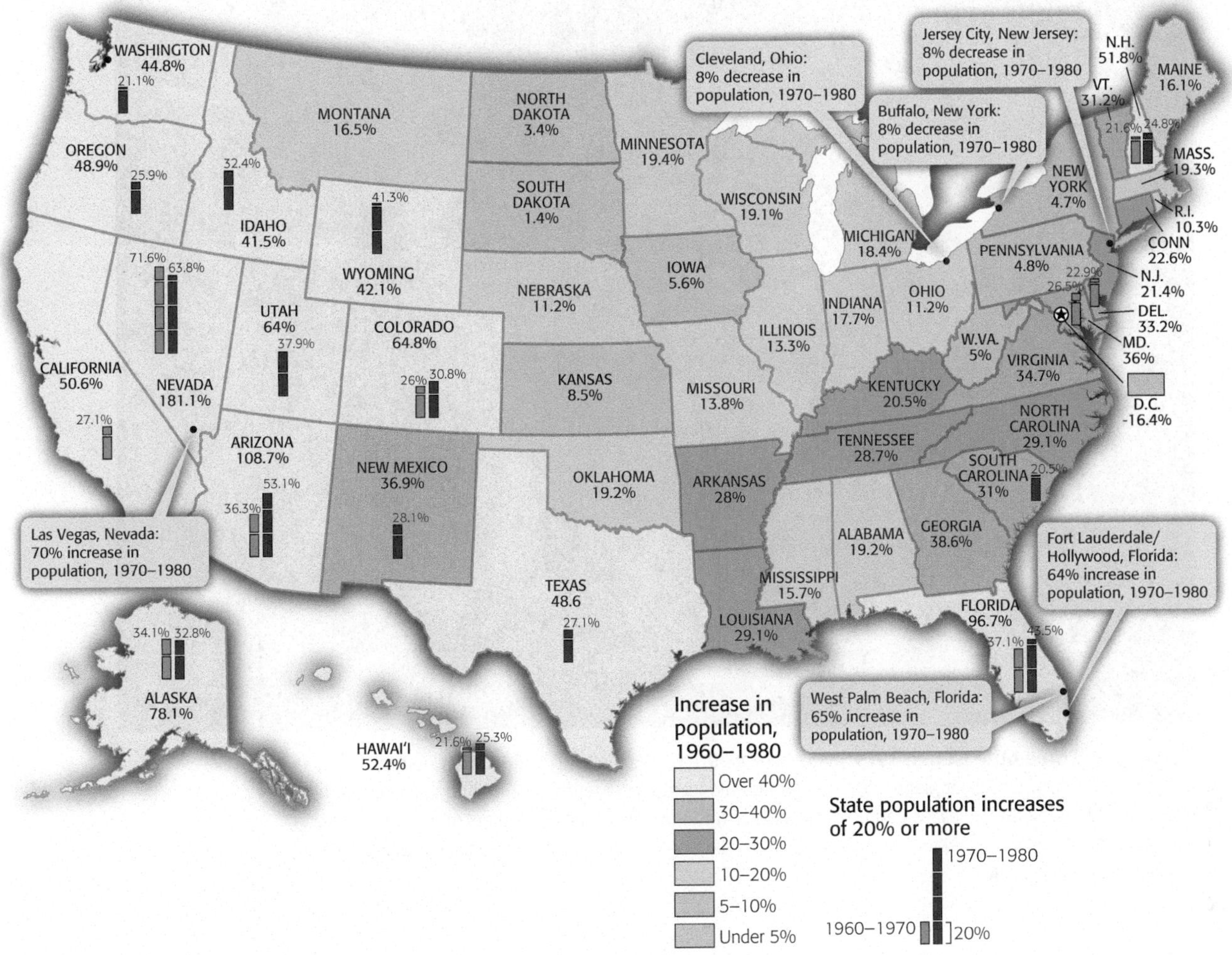

Map 26.1 Relocation in the Sunbelt Since the 1960s, the Sunbelt has witnessed a surge in its population fueled by people seeking warmer climates, comfortable retirement communities, and well-paying jobs in the defense, aerospace, and petroleum industries. Tourism and agriculture also contributed to the economic success of the region. While the Sunbelt boomed, many urban areas of the northern United States experienced economic decline and population loss. ▲

26-2c Resurgent Environmentalism

> A burgeoning global population, economic challenges, and limited natural resources fuel a transnational environmental movement.

Throughout the 1970s, many nations began trying to find the best ways to control pollution and to safeguard natural resources and wildlife without restricting economic growth. Developing nations ("the South") pushed wealthier, industrialized countries ("the North") to increase their foreign assistance programs, cut their tariffs, and share power in international organizations like the World Bank. In many areas of the developing world, droughts, pollution, and shortages of land and fertilizer resulted in mass hunger. Rising birth rates and falling death rates intensified the scramble for natural resources. In 1975, after the global population reached 4 billion, the United States and other developed nations expanded their international family planning, nutrition, and health initiatives. In 1979, following a twelve-year global campaign, the World Health Organization (WHO) announced that smallpox, one of the world's deadly diseases, had been completely eradicated.

The economic challenges of the 1970s provided new incentives for Americans to adopt more environmentally conscious practices and policies. In 1975, Congress instituted the first federal fuel-efficiency standards and fines for auto manufacturers that failed to meet them. Between 1974 and 1989, the average mileage per gallon of gasoline rose from 13.8 to 27.5. As the price of oil rose, many drivers stopped buying gas-guzzling cars, a trend that later reversed when fuel prices declined in the mid-1980s

Cleanup at Three Mile Island, 1979 In October 1979, a crew cleans up radioactive contamination at the Three Mile Island nuclear plant. Although Three Mile Island's containment building remained intact and its small radioactive releases had no detectable health impacts on plant workers or nearby residents, the accident prompted sweeping changes to commercial nuclear emergency response planning, training, and federal oversight. ▲

Three Mile Island A nuclear reactor near Middletown, Pennsylvania, that experienced a partial meltdown in March 1979, the worst nuclear accident in U.S. history.

Chernobyl Soviet-run nuclear power plant in the Ukraine, site of the world's worst nuclear accident in April 1986.

deregulation Removal or reduction of government oversight over an industry, usually aimed at fostering economic competition.

when the popularity of large vehicles including SUVs and trucks soared. Communities instituted recycling programs. Design changes made homes and appliances more energy-efficient. Environmentalists advocated alternative sources of energy such as solar, wind, and hydroelectric power.

The era also witnessed renewed discussions about nuclear energy. Nuclear power plants did not release carbon or other "greenhouse" gases into the atmosphere, by-products scientists later linked to increases in global warming. But nuclear reactors produced waste that remained radioactive for hundreds of years, prompting fierce debates over how and where to store such materials. Popular anxieties about nuclear energy skyrocketed in March 1979 after a cooling system malfunction and human errors triggered the partial meltdown of a nuclear reactor at the **Three Mile Island** plant outside Harrisburg, Pennsylvania. In 1986, an even more devastating nuclear accident at the **Chernobyl** plant in the Soviet Union forced the permanent evacuation of three hundred thousand people. Although antinuclear protests led to the premature closure of some facilities and cancellation of dozens of plant construction projects, the U.S. government tightened safety guidelines, and the production of nuclear-generated electricity more than tripled over the next three decades.

26-2d Rise of the Free Market Economy

Advocates of free market doctrines deregulate private industries, lower taxes, and cut government spending.

The 1970s marked the beginning of a major shift toward a free market economy (see **free enterprise**). Influenced by economists like Friedrich von Hayek and Milton Friedman, advocates of free-market doctrines believed that economic regulations limited innovation and wealth creation. They strongly opposed socialist or Communist command economies in which the state controlled production, wages, and prices. Such collective decision making, they argued, violated individual freedoms. Instead, they called for a system of economics that minimized (or outright abolished) taxes, subsidies, and regulations, thus allowing unrestricted competition among private businesses to determine wages and prices. As bipartisan support for **deregulation** increased, the

Keystone/Hulton Archive/Getty Images

Global Americans **Milton Friedman** (1912–2006) was an economist renowned for his theories on monetary policy. After completing a doctorate at Columbia University in 1946, he accepted a professorship at the University of Chicago and became part of a transatlantic network of experts challenging the prevailing macroeconomic theories of John Maynard Keynes. Since the 1930s, Keynesians had argued that government spending provided a corrective to economic downturns. Friedman's monetarist theories rejected the Keynesians' reliance on government spending and instead advocated controlling the amount of money in circulation to combat inflation and ensure economic stability. His ideas gained worldwide exposure though his prolific publications. In 1976, the same year he retired from the University of Chicago, Friedman was awarded the Nobel Prize in Economics. In the late 1970s, President Jimmy Carter, influenced by Friedman's views, began deregulating banking and transportation and appointed Paul Volcker, a monetarist, to chair the Federal Reserve. British prime ministers Harold Wilson and James Callaghan also embraced some of Friedman's ideas and made deep cuts in government spending to control inflation.

A key adviser to Reagan and British Prime Minister Thatcher, Friedman called for a free market with minimal government intervention. His ideas on taxation, deregulation, and privatization shaped government policies around the world. Near the end of his life, Friedman advocated the legalization of drugs, prostitution, and same-sex marriage—positions consistent with his lifelong belief in limiting the role of government to protect individual freedoms. He is widely considered one of history's most influential economists.

federal government shifted from interventionist policies instituted in the Progressive era and by the New Deal and the Great Society.

To foster competitive pricing in transportation, both Ford and Carter decreased the power of the Interstate Commerce Commission. Private railroad and trucking companies were granted more control over rates and routes, a move especially valuable to firms using **containerization** to ship standardized containers of goods across land and sea. In 1978, Congress passed legislation disbanding the Civil Aeronautics Board and permitting airlines more autonomy in setting prices. The move generated intense competition among carriers and resulted in more passengers flying at much lower fares.

Deregulation swept other industries too. Looser federal rules on telecommunications led to increased competition and significantly lower rates on telephone calls. Relaxed regulation of the New York Stock Exchange sparked more competitive stock prices and much higher trade volume. New banking rules enabled small investors to put their money in Treasury bills and mutual funds, financial instruments with higher yields than traditional savings accounts. In 1978, the Supreme Court ruled that credit card companies could base themselves in states with low interest rates and continue to market their products nationwide. The decision made credit cards more accessible to U.S. consumers than ever before. As the free market took hold worldwide, its supporters lauded the rapid growth of individual and corporate wealth that it created. Critics, however, blamed the introduction of less restricted forms of capitalism for a deepening of global income inequality and erosion of worker protections in the years that followed.

The United States was not alone in implementing free market reforms in the 1970s. Troubled by rising unemployment and declining economic growth, many Western Europeans challenged their governments to cut generous social welfare benefits such as pensions and health care. Great Britain made a significant political shift to the right after Margaret Thatcher, leader of the Conservative Party, won the general election in May 1979. As prime minister, she advocated deregulation, restricting trade unions, privatizing state-owned companies, reducing taxes, and cutting government spending on social services such as housing and education.

Even some Communist nations instituted free market reforms. In 1979, a new Chinese regime led by Deng Xiaoping introduced limited forms of capitalism in order to rebuild a society shattered by the Cultural Revolution. "Poverty is not socialism," Deng declared. "To get rich is glorious." While still defining itself as Communist or socialist, the government opened China to foreign trade, dismantled the commune system, and allowed some private ownership and market competition. In coming years, China had one of the fastest growing economies in world history, and hundreds of millions of Chinese were lifted out of poverty. In the mid-1980s, both Vietnam and the Soviet Union emulated China's attempt to blend Communist and free market principles.

containerization Shipping method that uses standardized freight containers that do not have to be unloaded and are transferred with cranes from one means of transport to another.

26-3

Private Lives and Public Debates

This 1976 *Time Magazine* cover reflects some of the ways that changes in women's lives had great ripple effects through American society and culture in the post-Vietnam era.

What do these images suggest about the changing professional and personal lives of women in the 1970s? Why was it significant for *Time* to devote this issue to "Women of the Year?" ▶

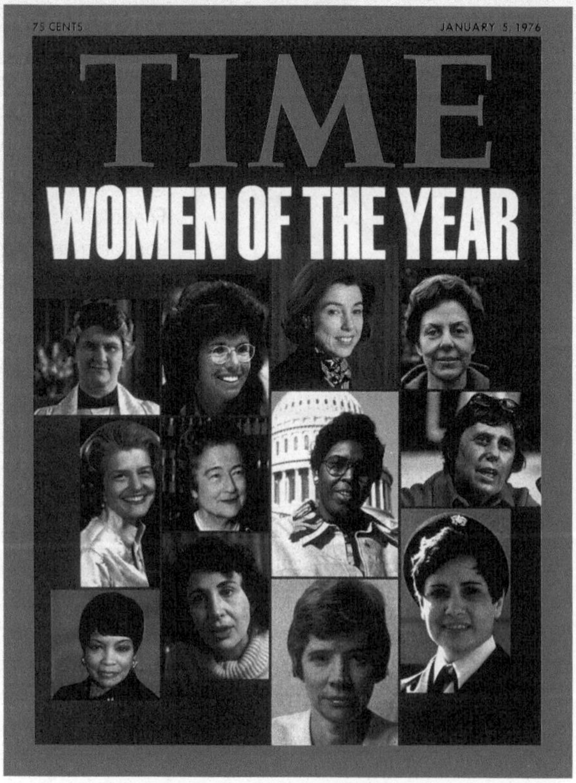

Go to MindTap® to practice history with the Chapter 26 **Primary Source Writing Activity: Private Lives and Public Debates.** Read and view primary sources and respond to a writing prompt.

In the 1970s, economic imperatives, social movements, and individual decisions contributed to significant changes in the private lives of most Americans. As more women joined the workforce, more families became two-income households. Divorce rates soared. Unmarried couples cohabited. Men and women alike pursued sexual liberation. Lesbian, gay, bisexual, and transgender (LGBT) Americans shattered stereotypes and demanded equal rights. At the same time, a multifaceted religious revival swept the United States and other nations. Echoing earlier responses to modernity in the 1920s, many Americans embraced faith as a source of stability and community in an age of rapidly changing social mores and rising individualism. In some nations, religious fervor fueled political activism and catapulted religious figures into political power. Newly politicized American social conservatives defended their ideals of family, gender, and sexuality and helped reshape the Republican Party.

☞ As you read, think about the roots and impact of shifting family dynamics and views of morality on American society as a whole. What were the major changes in individuals' lives during this era? How and why did they become politically and socially divisive?

26-3a Changes for Families and Women

Family structures change as women's economic status increases and rates of divorce and single parenthood climb.

Family life changed dramatically in the 1970s. Inspired by economic imperatives and broader acceptance of white women employed outside the home, more married women with children under eighteen joined the workforce, and the number of two-income households increased. With rising rates of divorce, unmarried cohabitation, and single parenthood, fewer and fewer U.S. families resembled the nuclear family ideal.

Divorces climbed sharply from the late 1960s through the 1970s. Following California's adoption of the nation's first "no-fault" divorce law, forty-six states adopted similar statutes allowing spouses to dissolve their legal unions on the basis of incompatibility instead of the previously required charges of spousal neglect, cruelty, or disloyalty. More than 1 million couples divorced in 1975 alone. In the early 1980s, the divorce rate leveled at about 50 percent of all marriages, but an increasing number of people waited longer to get married or chose not to at all (see Figure 26.2).

As women's economic status rose, U.S. birth patterns also shifted. After the postwar baby boom ended in the mid-1960s, fertility rates dropped during the 1970s from 2.5 to 1.7 per woman of childbearing age, levels comparable to the pre-World War II era. Simultaneously, more women over the age of thirty began having children, and an increasing number of single women became mothers.

Other nations experienced similar shifts. In 1980, unmarried women in Sweden accounted for almost 40 percent of all live births—more than double the rate in the United States. But Western Europe, Canada, and Japan had far fewer single-parent households than the 1980 U.S. rate of nearly 20 percent. In the 1970s, many Roman Catholic nations in Europe including Spain, Portugal, and Italy legalized divorce. Echoing trends in the United States, the divorce rate in many industrialized nations rose as more women secured economic autonomy, families had fewer children, and divorce became more readily available and socially acceptable.

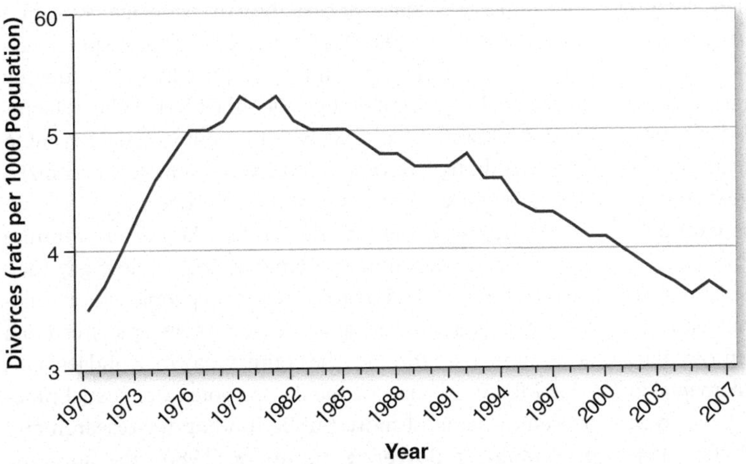

Note: Includes reported annulments and some estimated state figures for all years.

Figure 26.2 U.S. Divorce Rates, 1970–2007
Divorce rates in the United States escalated in the 1970s, peaking at nearly 50 percent, or half of all marriages. Divorce rates are inexact, however, because they are based on the number of people marrying every year, and some states stopped gathering divorce statistics in the 1980s. It is also difficult to discern how rates of divorce differ among different racial and cultural groups, ages, and educational and income levels. ▶ Source: U.S. National Center for Health Statistics, Vital Statistics of the United States, National Vital Statistics Reports (NVSR), http://www.cdc.gov/nchs/nvss.htm.

During the same years, dramatic changes in the lives of American women occurred. Inspired by feminism, economic needs, or individual aspirations, women continued to rapidly enter the workforce. Female employees secured more than 60 percent of the 19 million jobs created during the decade, most of which were low-paying, entry-level positions. Even with two incomes, many families struggled to make ends meet because of high inflation and economic stagnation.

But women also made important breakthroughs. Centuries-old employment barriers fell, and women became corporate executives, small business owners, law enforcement officers, firefighters, and construction workers. In 1976, the nation's military academies became coed. The numbers of women attending medical and law schools rose significantly. In 1981, Sandra Day O'Connor won confirmation as the first female justice to sit on the Supreme Court.

Some obstacles proved more difficult to surmount. Many working women remained in traditional **"pink-collar" jobs** such as nursing, office administration, and teaching— positions with little chance of upward mobility. Despite civil rights protections backed by the Equal Opportunity Employment Commission (EEOC), women who entered better-paying corporate or professional jobs often hit the **glass ceiling**, discriminatory barriers that prevented women and nonwhite men from reaching the highest levels of compensation and responsibility. A **wage gap** between the sexes also persisted. After hovering at about 60 percent since the mid-1950s, the ratio of women's to men's median pay for full-time employment began to rise in the late 1970s and reached about 70 percent by 1990. Despite this gain, the gender disparities in pay and rising divorce rates that often removed the male breadwinner from the family economy helped to explain the disproportionate percentage of women among America's poor, a trend described as the **feminization of poverty**. Burdened by racial and language barriers in addition to gender-based obstacles, African American and Latina single mothers experienced the highest rates of poverty.

26-3b Lesbian, Gay, Bisexual, and Transgender Rights Movement

The LGBT rights movement becomes more visible and pushes for civil rights.

In the years following the June 1969 Stonewall Riots, the lesbian, gay, bisexual, and transgender (LGBT) rights movement made impressive gains. Police harassment of LGBT establishments declined. Half of the states repealed their **sodomy laws**. In 1974, the American Psychiatric Association removed homosexuality from its list of mental disorders, and the following year, the U.S. Civil Service Commission lifted its ban on the employment of gay men and lesbians by the federal government. Several dozen cities, including Detroit, Boston, Los Angeles, San Francisco, and Houston, incorporated sexual orientation into their municipal nondiscrimination protections in housing, public accommodations, and employment. Across the country, openly gay candidates ran for public office and heterosexual candidates sought political support from the LGBT community. In 1980, the Democratic Party included a gay rights plank in its national platform for the first time.

Such advances were echoed in many nations. In the 1970s, Austria, Costa Rica, Finland, Norway, Malta, Cuba, and Spain decriminalized homosexuality. In 1977, Quebec became the world's first jurisdiction larger than a municipality to outlaw discrimination based on sexual orientation. In 1978, the International Lesbian

"pink-collar" jobs Positions traditionally held by women such as secretary, nurse, or telephone operator, juxtaposed to blue-collar jobs involving manual labor and "white-collar" jobs in management.

glass ceiling Perceived or actual barrier that prevents women and minorities from obtaining the best-paying, highest-ranking jobs in a specific industry or company.

wage gap Statistical indicator of women's average yearly pay expressed as a percentage of men's average annual earnings.

feminization of poverty Disproportionate representation of women among the world's poor as a result of low average annual incomes and gender biases.

sodomy laws Statutes defining certain sexual acts as criminal that were found to be unconstitutional in *Lawrence v. Texas* (2003).

Bowers v. Hardwick U.S. Supreme Court five-to-four ruling upholding a Georgia law barring private, consensual oral or anal sex between men.

and Gay Association, an advocacy organization aimed at securing LGBT rights worldwide, was formed.

But these changes triggered fierce opposition. In 1977, after Dade County, Florida, outlawed discrimination on the basis of sexual orientation, Anita Bryant—best-known as a beauty pageant queen, singer, and spokesperson for the Florida Citrus Commission—led a coalition called Save Our Children that successfully pushed for the repeal of the ordinance. The campaign drew on fundamentalist Christian doctrine that equated homosexuality with sin and claimed that homosexuals "recruited" and molested children. It proved instrumental in persuading the Florida legislature to prohibit gays from adopting children, a ban that was not lifted until 2008. Following her victories in Florida, Bryant led successful efforts to repeal gay rights ordinances in Eugene, Oregon, and Wichita, Kansas. But her supporters failed to win passage of the Briggs Initiative (Proposition 6), a California ballot measure that would have barred LGBT teachers or anyone who supported LGBT equality from working for the state's public schools. Harvey Milk, an openly gay man elected to the San Francisco Board of Supervisors in 1977 and later assassinated by a colleague, played a leading role in the initiative's defeat.

Bryant was a polarizing national figure. Some Americans praised her work, but others declared her a dangerous extremist. Many of her detractors boycotted orange juice, and gay bars across North America swapped orange juice and vodka "screwdriver" cocktails with "Anita Bryants" made of vodka and apple juice. In 1979, stung by the national boycott of orange juice, the Florida Citrus Commission allowed its contract with the controversial Bryant to expire. Although Bryant faded from public life, organized efforts to block gay rights continued for decades.

U.S. Postal Service Commemorates Harvey Milk, 2014 This U.S. postage stamp honors Harvey Milk, one of the nation's first openly gay elected officials. While serving on the San Francisco Board of Supervisors, he played critical roles in the passage of a nondiscrimination ordinance and in the successful campaign to defeat a statewide ballot initiative that sought to bar LGBT teachers from California's public schools. Following his death by assassination in 1978, Milk became a worldwide symbol of LGBT equality. ▲

With the onset of the AIDS (Acquired Immune Deficiency Syndrome) epidemic in 1981, many gay men encountered harsh discrimination from people who erroneously believed it was a "gay disease." As the epidemic cut a devastating path through the country, gay men and lesbians joined forces to care for the ill, promote safer sexual practices, and demand more public funding for research and prevention. In ***Bowers v. Hardwick*** (1986), the Supreme Court handed gays a major setback by upholding sodomy laws barring consensual sex between homosexuals in private. Already reeling from the impact of AIDS on their community, gays escalated their efforts to secure civil rights.

26-3c Religious Revivalism

A multifaceted religious revival has great social and political effects.

As in the 1920s and the 1950s, a strong wave of religious revivalism occurred during the 1970s. While most worshippers embraced monotheistic faiths such as Christianity, Judaism, and Islam, alternative spiritual practices including Buddhism, Native American traditions, and New Age also gained adherents. Some of the religious enthusiasm found expression in cults and pseudo-faiths like the Church of Scientology (founded by science fiction writer L. Ron Hubbard in 1952), Reverend Sun Myung Moon's Unification Church (whose followers were sometimes called "Moonies"), and Reverend Jim Jones's People's Temple. In the summer of 1977, Jones abruptly moved his congregation from San Francisco to a compound named *Jonestown* in the jungles of Guyana. In November 1978, his guards shot and killed Congressman Leo Ryan and four others engaged in a fact-finding mission to investigate allegations of human rights abuses at Jonestown. Jones then ordered his followers to drink cyanide-laced grape drink. Nine hundred and nine people, including more than three hundred children, died in the mass suicide. The phrase "drinking the Kool-Aid" became a synonym for blind devotion to a destructive cause or leader.

Fundamentalism and evangelicalism were much more common expressions of the wave of religiosity. Fundamentalists strictly adhere to religious orthodoxy and rigorously defend their view of religious truth against secularism. Protestant fundamentalism in the United States arose in the late nineteenth century and is characterized by beliefs in the inerrancy of the Bible and in the possibility of personal atonement through acceptance of Jesus Christ. Many fundamentalist Christians reject the scientific doctrine of evolution and instead embrace the biblical story of Creation. Fundamentalists are part of a larger group of evangelicals who share

AP Images/Carl R. Battreall

Global Americans

Bill Bright (right) was an American evangelical and founder of Campus Crusade for Christ. Born in Oklahoma in 1921, he graduated from Northeastern State University and moved to California. After becoming an evangelical Christian in 1944, he attended Princeton and Fuller Theological Seminaries but did not graduate from either. In 1951, he and his wife Vonette founded Campus Crusade for Christ (now known as *Cru* in the United States) to preach to students at UCLA. Over the next five decades, it went on to become the biggest Christian ministry in the world with over 27,000 staff members and 225,000 volunteers working in 190 countries.

In 1956, Bright published "The Four Spiritual Laws," a pamphlet offering guidance on how to establish a personal connection to Jesus Christ. It is perhaps the most widely distributed religious publication in history, with 2.5 billion copies disseminated in two hundred languages. Building a global network worth more than $500 million, Bright wrote more than 100 publications and reached hundreds of millions through radio broadcasts, television, films, billboards, the Internet, and training conferences. In 1994, he co-founded Alliance Defending Freedom, a conservative Christian nonprofit organization supporting litigation aimed at protecting the religious provisions of the First Amendment. Two years later, Bright won the $1.1 million Templeton Prize for Progress in Religion, donating the proceeds to publicizing the spiritual value of prayer and fasting. Although unfamiliar to many Americans, Bright was an essential figure in the expansion of American evangelicalism's influence on U.S. politics, business, and culture in the post-World War II era.

a belief in individual conversion through a direct relationship with God but who interpret the Bible less literally and are more willing to associate with people who have different religious faiths in the greater cause of bringing people to Christ.

Fundamentalists and evangelicals both played important roles in a broad movement of conservatives that dramatically changed modern U.S. politics. As the booming post-1945 economy lifted many evangelicals into the middle-class, some abandoned their traditional detachment from politics. Evangelicals joined anti-Communist organizations that criticized the official atheism and repressive practices of the Soviet Union. Others became politically engaged after the U.S. Supreme Court declared mandatory school prayers and school-sanctioned Bible readings unconstitutional.

By the mid-1970s, more than 70 million Americans described themselves as "born-again" Christians who had established a direct personal relationship with Jesus. Christian evangelicals owned their own businesses and operated their own schools and universities including Oral Roberts University in Tulsa, Oklahoma, and Liberty Baptist College (later renamed Liberty University) in Lynchburg, Virginia. Televangelists including Pat Robertson, Jimmy Swaggert, and Jim and Tammy Faye Bakker built huge domestic and international audiences for their television and radio ministries.

Jimmy Carter, a southern Baptist and self-described "born-again" Christian, won the presidency in 1976 with the support of many evangelical voters. His public discussion of his faith was unusual among public officials of the era and garnered widespread media attention. But Carter's liberal views on women's liberation, abortion, and other social issues alienated more conservative evangelicals. So did a 1978 ruling by the Internal Revenue Service stripping racially segregated Christian academies of their tax-exempt status. Distressed by a culture they perceived as increasingly immoral and godless, the **Christian Right** began mobilizing politically.

Christian Right Social conservatives of several faiths that mobilized politically in the late 1970s.

Moral Majority Founded in 1979 by Reverend Jerry Falwell, political organization that mobilized social conservatives. Major influence on the Republican Party throughout the 1980s.

Jerry Falwell, a fundamentalist minister in Virginia, launched the **Moral Majority**. Founded in 1979, the organization paired support for free market capitalism and a strong U.S. presence in global affairs with opposition to abortion, divorce, feminism, and homosexuality. It intentionally adopted a platform that would draw conservatives from many faiths including evangelical Protestants, Catholics, Jews, and Mormons. Moral Majority chapters around the nation registered millions of voters and urged them to support like-minded political candidates running for local, state, and federal offices. These voters played a significant role in Reagan's 1980 presidential victory.

Conservative people of faith were also instrumental in the defeat of the Equal Rights Amendment (ERA). First introduced in Congress in 1923, the proposed amendment read, "Equality of rights under the law shall not be denied or abridged by the United States or by any state on account of sex." Support for it had languished for many years, but the revitalization of the women's movement prompted the House of Representatives to pass it by a vote of three hundred fifty-four to twenty-three in October 1971. Five months later, the Senate approved the ERA by a vote of eighty-four to eight, and the process of ratification began. Within a year, twenty-two of the required thirty-eight states ratified the amendment. With prominent supporters including Nixon and his successors Ford and Carter (and their wives Betty and Rosalyn, respectively) and celebrities such as Alan Alda, Phil Donahue, and Valerie Harper, passage of the ERA within the allotted seven-year period seemed assured.

But the ERA soon met passionate opposition. Led by long-time conservative activist Phyllis Schlafly, the STOP

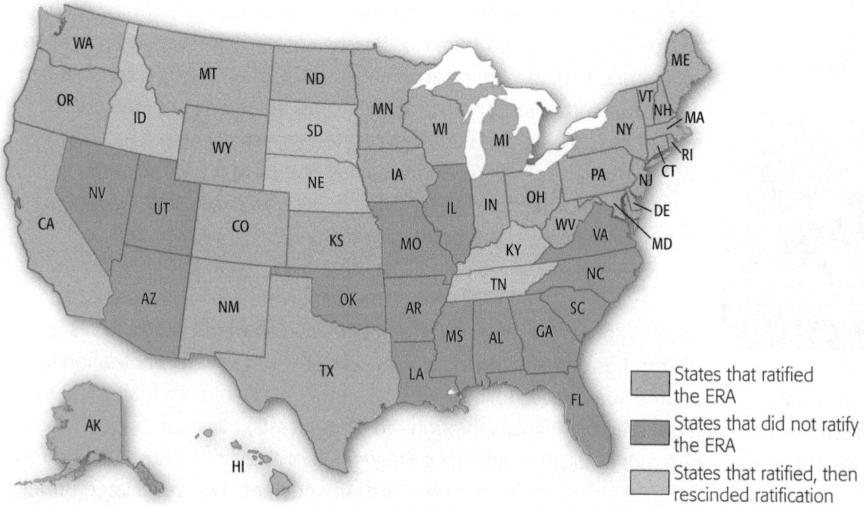

Map 26.2 Struggle for the Equal Rights Amendment First introduced in 1923, the Equal Rights Amendment (ERA) passed Congress in 1972. While 22 of the necessary 38 states quickly ratified the amendment, progress stalled as ERA opponents mobilized. Pro-ERA forces, despite massive lobbying and public education campaigns, proved unable to secure enough popular support to win ratification before the extended ratification deadline of June 30, 1982. Since then, pro-ERA advocates have adopted different strategies for securing ratification, but none has succeeded so far. ◀

ERA campaign rapidly gained supporters who viewed the amendment as an assault on traditional womanhood. They claimed that the ERA would lead to the legalization of same-sex marriage, the conscription of women into the armed forces, and the establishment of mandatory unisex restrooms and taxpayer-funded abortions. They feared that the ERA would free men from their legal and financial responsibilities as husbands and fathers. As popular backing for the ERA began to erode, Congress extended the ratification deadline by three years. Nonetheless, in 1982, the ERA fell three states short of ratification after failing to win support in much of the South (see Map 26.2).

26-3d Global Fundamentalism

> In an age of great flux, religious belief gives millions refuge but also generates conflict.

Throughout the era, religious conservatives were also gaining power internationally. In 1978, traditional Catholics welcomed the election of Archbishop Karol Wojtyla of Cracow, Poland, to the papacy. The first non-Italian Pope in four hundred fifty-five years, he adopted the name John Paul II and energetically promoted Catholicism around the world. He improved the Church's relations with Jews, Muslims, and Anglicans. He strongly defended the all-male, celibate priesthood and condemned artificial contraception and abortion. He attacked the godlessness and human rights abuses of Communist regimes.

A new generation of Israeli Jews vigorously defended their faith too. Shaken by Israel's near defeat in the October War of 1973, a radical right-wing movement called the *Gush Emunim* (or *Bloc of the Faithful*) arose. Its supporters—to the dismay of Israeli authorities—established Jewish settlements in the West Bank, the Gaza Strip, and the Golan Heights, all then occupied by Palestinian Arabs. Gush Emunim believed that, according to the Torah, God had granted Jews these lands. In 1977, such views gained more influence when the religiously conservative Likud party defeated the long-ruling Labor Party. Although Gush Emunim's influence declined, its aggressive Zionism and claims to the Occupied Territories affected Israeli politics for decades.

Islamism Muslim revivalist movement that seeks to reorder government and society to support moral conservatism and a literal interpretation of the Koran.

Because Judaism, Christianity, and Islam traced their origins to the "Holy Land," religion as well as geopolitics shaped connections between the United States and Israel. As the Soviets forged alliances with Arab states including Iraq and Syria, U.S. officials drew closer to the anti-Communist, democratic Israelis. Abandoning their historic anti-Semitism, fundamentalist Christian Americans embraced Israel as the site of the Battle of Armageddon described in the Book of Revelation, the conflict in which God defeats the Antichrist and Satan prior to the Second Coming of Christ. Jewish American support for Israel also intensified.

The 1970s Muslim fundamentalism also surged around the globe. One variant stemmed from the teachings of Hasan al-Banna, an Egyptian who began calling for renewed dedication to the Koran as a means of reinvigorating Muslim communities undermined by Western colonialism and cultural domination. In 1928, al-Banna established the Muslim Brotherhood, an educational organization dedicated to these principles. In subsequent decades, it clashed violently with secular rulers promoting socialism and modernization.

But the Egyptian government's harsh repression of the Muslim Brotherhood did little to stop the spread of Islamic fundamentalism throughout the Middle East. Demoralized by the Israeli victory over Syria, Egypt, and Jordan in the Six-Day War (1967) and frustrated by the limited economic opportunities under authoritarian, secular governments, many educated young people gravitated toward religious critics of these repressive regimes. Some embraced **Islamism**, a political ideology calling for the creation of governments based on Sharia (Islamic law).

In the late 1970s, Islamism gained momentum in Afghanistan. Electrified by the Iranian Revolution, Islamist rebels called the *mujahidin* (soldiers of God) won U.S. backing in their war against the Communist regime that took power in Afghanistan in late 1978. At the time, America's Cold War rivalry with the Soviet Union obscured the possible ramifications of arming Islamic militants with deep contempt for Western values.

26-4 Triumph and Travail on the Right

David Hume Kennerly/Getty Images

Reagan's presentation of proposed tax reduction legislation was televised in July 1981.

How would you describe Reagan's presentation and demeanor in this photograph? Why do you think his advisers thought it was important for him to have a chart? ▶

In the late 1970s, a powerful alliance of social and fiscal conservatives reshaped the Republican Party and propelled Ronald Reagan to victory in the presidential election of 1980. Dismayed by the weak economy and a growing federal bureaucracy, he slashed government programs, cut taxes, and instituted market-based reforms that empowered the private sector. To some Americans, he was a hero who reinvigorated a nation demoralized by war, social upheaval, and economic stagnation. To others, he was a reckless ideologue who amassed huge budget deficits and harmed the poor and disfranchised.

To combat Communist gains in the developing world, Reagan adopted strongly anti-Communist rhetoric and embarked on a major defense buildup. He hoped to pressure the Soviets into making concessions and cutting nuclear arsenals, but the deaths of a succession of Soviet leaders undermined his attempts at negotiations, and an enormous antinuclear movement mobilized worldwide. U.S.–Soviet relations were fraught with distrust. At the same time, the rise of Islamist militancy exacerbated tensions in the already volatile Middle East and presented U.S. policy makers with escalating dangers of global terrorism.

Although dogged by scandal during his second term, Reagan simultaneously responded to changes in the Soviet Union that dramatically affected the Cold War. In March 1985, the Soviets selected Mikhail Gorbachev as general secretary of the Communist Party. He and Reagan forged a partnership that produced historic arms control agreements. Gorbachev's internal reforms and Reagan's openness to them ushered in the Cold War's mostly peaceful end.

☞ As you read, consider how and why conservatives in the 1980s influenced U.S. domestic and foreign policies. What were Reagan's major initiatives? Were they successful? Explain why or why not.

26-4a Mobilization on the Right

Fiscal and social conservatives join forces and transform U.S. politics.

In the 1970s, a diverse coalition of conservatives arose and quickly gained momentum. The **New Right** included businesspeople, white Southerners, evangelical Christians, Catholics, and others who supported a smaller federal government, greater economic competition, and traditional morality. The movement originated in the early 1960s when grassroots conservatives backed Arizona Senator Barry Goldwater. Goldwater called for cuts in social welfare spending and claimed that big government threatened individual liberties and inhibited economic growth. Undeterred by Goldwater's loss in the 1964 presidential race, conservatives positioned themselves for future electoral victories. Through innovative use of direct mail, the New Right developed strong communications and fund-raising networks. They established conservative think tanks and lobbying firms. They cultivated leaders who supported a strong national defense, traditional values, and limited government.

Reagan exemplified the new conservative ideal. Once a New Deal Democrat, he switched parties as the Cold War arose in the late 1940s. A popular actor, Reagan became a spokesman for the General Electric Company, touring the nation making speeches extolling **free enterprise** and attacking communism. After winning acclaim for a speech he made at the 1964 Republican convention, Reagan successfully ran for governor of California two years later and easily won reelection to a second term. In 1976, he nearly defeated Ford in the Republican presidential primaries. A moderate, Ford

New Right Diverse coalition of fiscal and social conservatives that arose in the late 1970s and played a major role in defining the modern Republican Party.

free enterprise Economic system permitting private businesses to compete with little or no government intervention.

Proposition 13 Ballot initiative approved by California voters in 1978 that lowered property taxes significantly and helped make tax reduction a key element of modern U.S. conservatism.

supply-side economics Theory that lower taxes inspire corporate investment, higher production, and lower prices, thus elevating the economy as a whole.

had alienated his party's growing right wing by continuing the Nixon administration's détente policy. Once he secured the nomination, Ford placated conservatives by dropping liberal Nelson Rockefeller as his running mate and supporting a platform mostly written by North Carolina senator Jesse Helms, a Reagan ally and the leading social conservative in Congress. Ford's subsequent loss to Carter catapulted Reagan to Republican front-runner status for the 1980 election.

A revolt against high tax rates also fueled the New Right. In 1978, California voters approved **Proposition 13**, a referendum that lowered property taxes statewide. Conservative activists realized that tapping into popular resentment of paying taxes provided a way to win support for reducing the size of government without targeting individual programs that had vocal constituencies. The antitaxation message became an effective political tool for conservatives across the country.

All of these factors converged in Reagan's victory in the 1980 presidential race. His optimism contrasted sharply with Carter's focus on "a crisis of confidence" plaguing the nation. Although Reagan was not a particularly religious man, he convinced evangelical voters to abandon Carter, a devout Christian. Despite his close ties to the wealthy, he appealed to working-class people. Some "Reagan Democrats" even crossed party lines to vote for him.

AP Images/FILE

Howard Jarvis Campaigns for Proposition 13, 1978 This 1978 photograph from the *Los Angeles Times* shows tax cut advocate Howard Jarvis promoting Proposition 13. ▲

Reagan capitalized on the fact that many Americans blamed Carter for a decline in U.S. international prestige and an economy hobbled by high interest rates, unemployment, and inflation. When Reagan asked potential voters "Are you better off than you were four years ago?" few could answer affirmatively. The Iranians' seizure and long captivity of fifty-two U.S. hostages and the recent Soviet invasion of Afghanistan provided fodder for Reagan's attacks on Carter's foreign policy. Winning forty-four states (but only 51 percent of the popular vote), Reagan trounced Carter and helped Republicans gain control of the Senate for the first time since 1954.

26-4b The Reagan Revolution

U.S. conservatives and their counterparts abroad limit the role of government and adopt free market policies.

On taking office in January 1981, Reagan promised Americans the most sweeping changes in the federal government since the New Deal. "In this present crisis, government is not the solution to our problem," Reagan declared; "government is the problem." Fueled by the president's charisma and communications skills, the "Reagan Revolution" fell short of its most grandiose aims but profoundly altered the U.S. economic and political landscape.

Building on the neoliberal reforms launched by Carter, the Reagan administration instituted a vigorous economic agenda built on belief in the supremacy of the free market. Government officials expanded Carter's deregulation initiatives, opened public lands to private development, and adopted looser interpretations of federal environmental protections. At Reagan's urging, Congress passed several bills reducing taxes, closing tax loopholes, and eliminating many tax deductions. By 1987, the highest income tax rate was capped at 28 percent, down from 70 percent in 1980. Reagan's advisers argued that their **supply-side economics** (or "Reaganomics") would result in increased investment by wealthier people, creating more jobs. The resulting prosperity would then "trickle-down" to people lower on the income scale.

In August 1981, Reagan's response to a strike by federal air traffic controllers had long-term ramifications for workers in the United States and abroad. Formerly president of the Screen Actors' Guild, Reagan supported federal employees' right to bargain collectively for improved pay and benefits. But after negotiations with the Federal Aviation Administration stalled, about sixteen thousand members of the Professional Air Traffic Controllers Organization (PATCO) went on strike. Two days later, calling the work stoppage a violation of federal law, Reagan fired nearly all of the PATCO strikers. His unprecedented dismissal of skilled laborers encouraged private employers to hire replacement workers rather than bargain with strikers and later inspired calls for dismantling public employee unions—a position that Reagan himself never adopted (see Figures 26.3 and 26.4).

Figure 26.3 U.S. and Global Union Membership Although the decline of U.S. manufacturing and the passage of state right-to-work laws have contributed to a decrease in unionization among private sector employees, protections for collective bargaining by federal workers and an expansion of government programs have stablized rates among public employees including civil servants and teachers. Overall union membership, however, has trended downward for decades. ▼

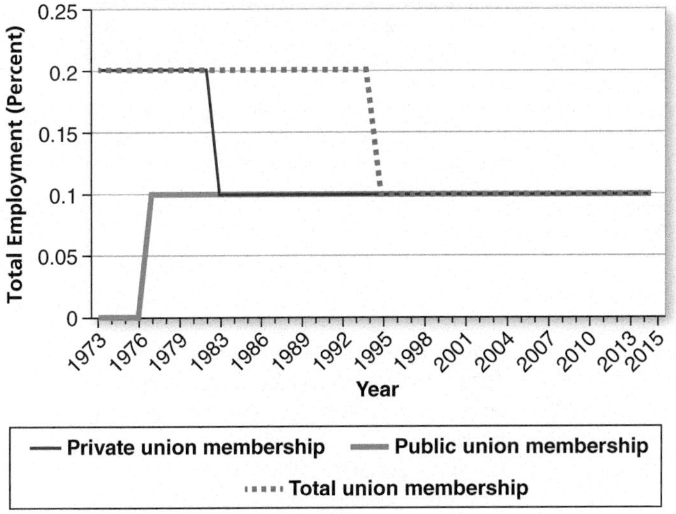

Figure 26.3(a) U.S. Union Membership, 1973–2015

Sources: For the years 1973–1981, the May Current Population (CPS), and for the years 1983–2015, the CPS Outgoing Rotation Group (ORG) Earnings Files, http://www.unionstats.com/. © 2016 by Barry T. Hirsch and David A. Macpherson.

Notes: No union questions were in the 1982 CPS. The definition of union membership was expanded in 1977 to include "employee associations similar to a union."

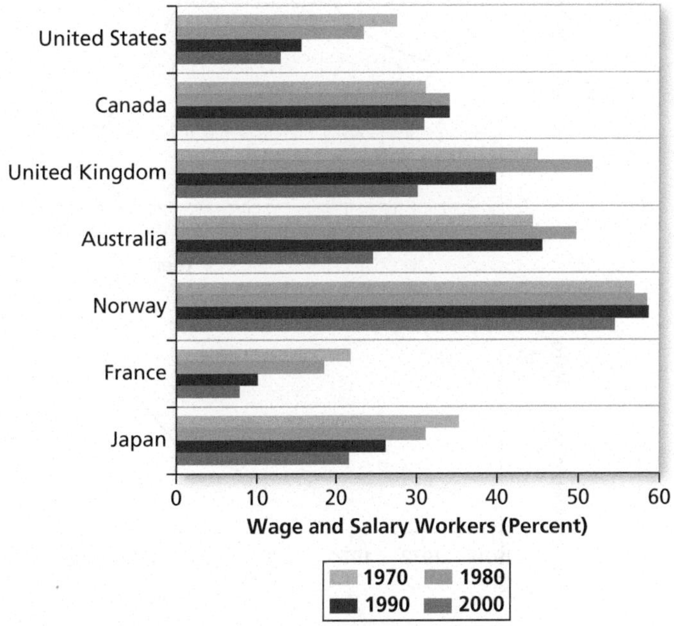

Figure 26.3(b) Union Membership Worldwide, 1970–2000

Source: Visser, Jelle. Data Base on Institutional Characteristics of Trade Unions, Wage Setting, State Intervention and Social Pacts, 1960–2011 (ICTWSS), vers 4.0, April 2013.

Reagan's supply-side policies were echoed in several other nations. Australia's economic rationalists and proponents of New Zealand's Rogernomics also favored deregulation, privatization of state-owned industries, reduction of the welfare state, and lower direct taxes. Inspired by Reagan's firing of the PATCO strikers, British prime minister Thatcher vigorously assaulted trade unions and launched more free market reforms. Thatcher's supporters credited her policies with transforming Britain's stagnant economy and re-establishing the nation as a world power, but critics blamed her for increasing social unrest, poverty, and unemployment.

Reductions in the size of the federal bureaucracy and cuts in many federal programs were core elements of Reagan's economic plans. Claiming that welfare created dependency and eroded individual initiative, the administration reduced spending on child care subsidies for low-income families, food stamps, child nutrition initiatives, job training, child abuse prevention programs, and mental health services. It also slashed funding for consumer protections, workplace safety, housing assistance, and agricultural subsidies. At the same time, Reagan argued that détente had weakened the United States internationally and pushed for a huge expansion of the defense

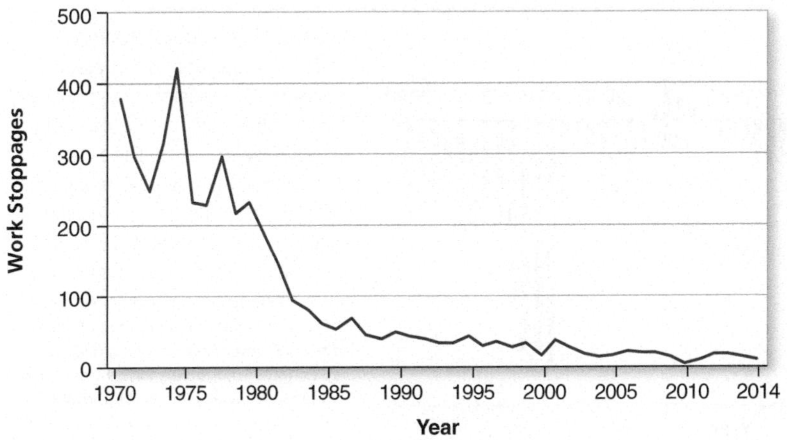

Figure 26.4 U.S. Work Stoppages, 1970–2014 Although strikes by public employees including teachers, police officers, and firefighters spiked in the 1970s, the number of work stoppages markedly declined after the early 1980s. In the aftermath of Reagan's dismissal of thirteen thousand striking federal air traffic controllers, a number of private employers began hiring replacement workers rather than negotiating with unionized workers who went on strike. ◀ Source: U.S. Bureau of Labor Statistics, http://www.bls.gov/news.release/wkstp.t01.htm.

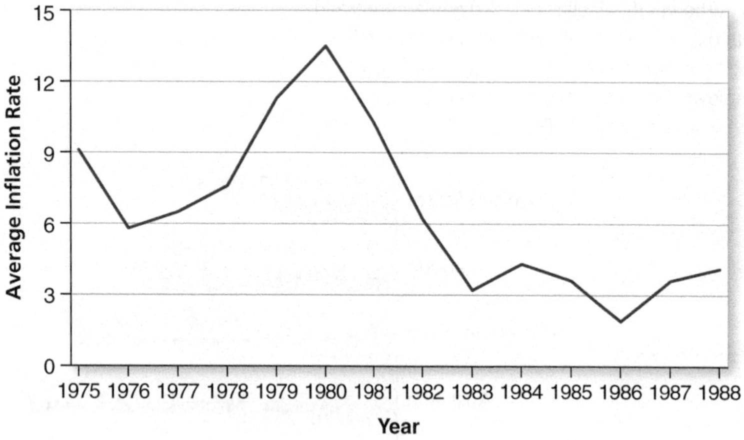

Figure 26.5 U.S. Inflation Rates, 1975–1988 U.S. inflation rates demonstrated a great deal of volatility in the Carter and Reagan years. In 1979, Federal Reserve Chairman Volcker instituted strict monetarist policies designed to lower inflation. Within three years, inflation rates had fallen from their 13.5 percent peak in 1980 to an annual average of about 4 percent. Economists' views on whether monetarist policies were responsible for the decline differ. ◀ Source: U.S. Inflation Calculator, U.S. Historical Inflation Rates, 1914–2015, http://www.usinflationcalculator.com/inflation/historical-inflation-rates/.

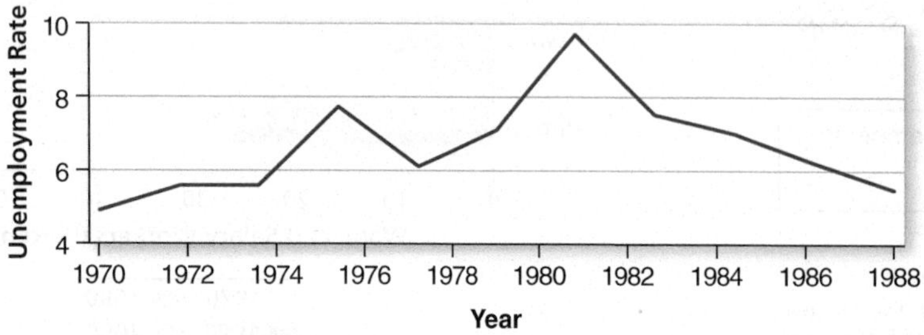

Figure 26.6 U.S. Unemployment Rate, 1970–1988 Energy shocks, foreign competition, outsourcing, and economic stagnation led to a marked increase in unemployment rates in the late 1970s, peaking at 10.8 percent in November 1982, the highest level of unemployment in the United States since 1940. ◀ Source: U.S. Department of Labor, Bureau of Labor Statistics, stats.bls.gov.

budget. U.S. military spending rose from $153.8 billion to $281.8 billion (22.69 percent and 26.48 percent of annual public expenditures, respectively).

Reaganomics did not have an immediate impact, and the recession deepened through 1982. Interest rates hit 20 percent. In November 1982, unemployment reached 10.8 percent, its highest level since 1940. In early 1983, Reagan's approval ratings plummeted to 35 percent and his chances of reelection seemed slim.

But as a combination of loosening the money supply, tax cuts, and defense spending stimulated the economy, the recession gradually ended. Inflation fell from 10 percent in 1981 to an annual average of less than 4 percent in 1983. Unemployment fell to 7.25 percent. Declaring it "morning in America" thanks to the reinvigorated national economy, Reagan crushed Democrat Walter Mondale in the 1984 presidential race (see Figures 26.5 and 26.6).

26-4c Divisions Deepen

Debt, class and racial tensions, and inner city turmoil spark criticisms of Reagan's policies.

Critics claimed that Reagan's policies created only the illusion of recovery. Because large tax cuts and defense expenditures were not offset by commensurate spending cuts, the national debt rose from $900 billion in 1981 to $2.8 trillion in 1988. Cuts to farm subsidies and high mortgage interest rates contributed to a wave of family farm foreclosures. Rising housing prices, cuts in federal welfare spending and housing assistance, the de-institutionalization of the mentally ill, and the decline of well-paying unskilled jobs led to a rapid spike in homelessness in the nation's cities (see Figure 26.7).

The federal "war on drugs" also reflected growing social divides. In the early 1980s, a cartel in Medellin,

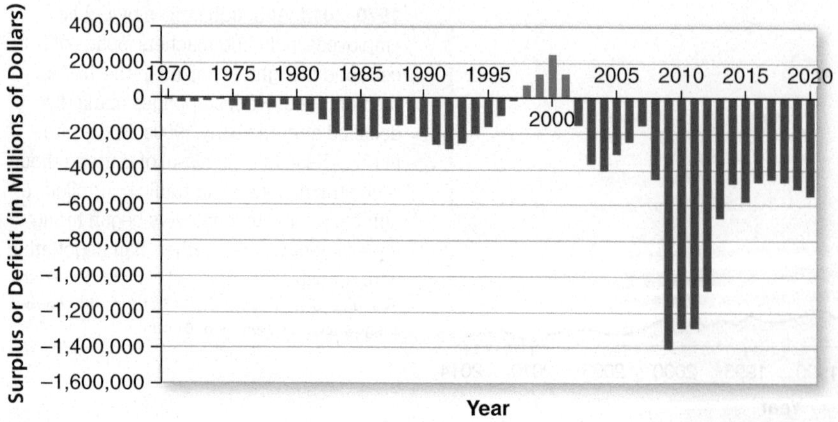

Figure 26.7 Federal Budget Deficits, Historic and Projected, 1970–2022 A federal budget deficit occurs when government spending exceeds tax revenues. The federal government then borrows money to offset the shortfall, thus increasing the national debt. This chart shows the long-range trend of deficit spending since 1970 and projections. ◀ Source: Office of Management and Budget, *Budget of the U.S. Government, FY 2013; Historical Tables,* Table 1.1, February 2012, https://www.whitehouse.gov/omb/budget/Historicals/.

"STRANGE HOW SOME CHOOSE TO LIVE LIKE THAT
INSTEAD OF CHOOSING TO BE RICH LIKE US"
©1984 HERBLOCK

Herblock Parodies Reagan Economic Policies, 1984
This February 1984 political cartoon by Herbert Block (Herblock) reflects some of the criticisms aimed at the Reagan administration's supply-side economic policies. ▲

Colombia, began shipping cocaine into the United States first via Panama and Miami and later through Mexico. Americans created "crack," an inexpensive, cooked form of powder cocaine, a drug formerly accessible only to the wealthy, which reached the masses, leaving a trail of broken families and drug-related violence in its wake.

In response, Reagan signed the Anti-Drug Abuse Act of 1986. The bill appropriated $1.7 billion for interdiction. Under the law's new sentencing guidelines for selling or possessing narcotics, a conviction for possession of twenty-eight grams of crack or five hundred grams of powder cocaine received the same mandatory five-year penalty—a policy that disproportionately affected the poor, blacks, Latinos, and women. Between 1986 and 2000, the U.S. prison population rose from 300,000 to 2 million—an incarceration rate second only to Russia on a global per capita basis.

The era's uneasy political climate intensified debates about immigration. Experts disagreed on whether the costs of social services used by immigrants such as education, welfare, and health care exceeded the taxes they contributed to the U.S. economy. Although numerous businesses such as meatpacking, construction, and agriculture heavily depended on Latino immigrant labor, some economists claimed that these immigrants displaced U.S. workers, depressed wage scales, and lacked the education and job skills necessary for upward mobility. Latinos made educational and economic gains in the 1980s, but fewer than one-half graduated from high school (the highest dropout rate among U.S. minorities), and many remained mired in low-paying jobs.

In 1986, concerns over undocumented Mexican immigrants prompted Reagan to sign the Immigration Reform and Control Act. The law criminalized knowingly recruiting or hiring undocumented workers for the first time in U.S. history. It introduced the **I-9 form** requiring job applicants to provide proof of their eligibility for legal employment and the **H1B visa**, allowing U.S. companies to temporarily employ foreign workers in specialized professions. The law also granted amnesty to immigrants who illegally entered the country before January 1, 1982, and had continuously resided there for at least five years if they admitted their guilt, paid a fine and back taxes, had no criminal record, and possessed basic knowledge of U.S. history and government and the English language. Approximately 3 million undocumented immigrants secured legal status under this policy. But weak employer penalties, poor enforcement, and the ease of obtaining fraudulent documents for the I-9 verification undermined the reform effort, and the number of people immigrating illegally, particularly from Mexico and Central America, continued to rise.

The era's popular culture reflected the nation's increasing polarization. Originating in the South Bronx, hip-hop blended innovative musical techniques with spoken word rhymes. Songs like Grandmaster Flash's "The Message" (1982) offered searing commentary about urban crime, drugs, and poverty and reached both radio and television audiences, thanks to MTV, a cable network devoted to music videos launched in 1981. While television programs *Dynasty* and *Dallas* celebrated the lifestyles of the rich, Oliver Stone's film *Wall Street* (1986) and Tom Wolfe's novel *The Bonfire of the Vanities* (1987) offered more cautionary tales about corruption and excess.

As probusiness books like Donald Trump's *The Art of the Deal* (1987) topped the best-selling lists, the rise of the low-grade, risky "junk bond" market and an unprecedented wave of mergers and acquisitions made Wall Street speculators and "corporate raiders" folk heroes to millions. But after the New York Stock Exchange's Dow Jones industrial average plummeted five hundred eight points on October 19, 1987 (a 22.6 percent decline in stock values), several Wall Street firms laid off employees. Although the market recovered quickly, the 1987 crash and the prosecution of once-venerated financial figures like Michael Milken and Ivan Boesky for illegal trading practices tarnished Wall Street's reputation.

I-9 form Federal document used by employers to verify employees' eligibility to work in the United States.

H1B visa Allows foreigners with certain professional skills to work in the United States for a maximum of six years.

AP Images/Carlos Rene Perez

Global Americans On a November evening in 1982, **Samantha Smith**, a ten-year-old girl from Manchester, Maine (population two thousand), wrote a letter to the new Soviet general secretary Yuri Andropov. She inquired whether he was planning to launch a nuclear attack on the United States. If that was not his intention, Samantha asked, "How you are going to help to not have a war?"

In April 1983, a time of heightened Soviet–U.S. tensions, Andropov wrote Samantha and assured her of the Soviets' peaceful intentions. Eager to score a propaganda victory in the Cold War, he invited Samantha and her parents to visit his nation. At the time, most tourists were only able to enter the Soviet Union with visas and itineraries provided by the state travel agency.

That July, the Smiths visited the Soviet Union for two weeks. Their hosts carefully shielded them from evidence of the country's chronic shortages of food and consumer products. Although illness forced Andropov to cancel his meeting with Samantha, she nonetheless told reporters "not a single Soviet person, neither old, nor young, wants war." After returning to the United States, the Smiths admitted that both U.S. and Soviet intelligence operatives had monitored their trip and acknowledged they had not been shown the worst aspects of the Soviet Union. But they defended Samantha's "propaganda mission" for "peace and kindness." In 1985, she and her father co-authored *Journey to the Soviet Union*, a nonfiction account of their visit. Later that year, they both died in a plane crash, but their story illustrates the important role of U.S.–Soviet cultural exchanges during the Cold War.

26-4d Confrontations with Communism and Terrorism

Tensions with the Soviet Union escalate, and the threat of terrorism intensifies.

Intent on restoring U.S. power and prestige throughout the world, Reagan adopted harsh anti-Communist rhetoric and demonized the Soviet Union. In his first press conference, the president accused the Soviets of using détente as a means of promoting "world revolution." Soviet leaders, Reagan alleged, "reserve to themselves the right to commit any crime, to lie, to cheat…." In a 1983 speech, he evocatively described the Soviet Union as "the focus of evil in the modern world."

At the same time, the United States embarked on the biggest peacetime defense buildup in its history. Adding another $400 billion to the $1.2 trillion military expansion begun by Carter, Reagan supported the development of new weapons including the B-2 (Stealth) bomber and the MX missile and called for the extension of the U.S. fleet from four hundred fifty-six to six hundred vessels. After Congress authorized Reagan's plans, military appropriations increased by 50 percent, hitting $294.7 billion by 1985—an average of $28 million per hour.

Reagan vowed that he would not negotiate with the Soviets until the United States had overwhelmingly superiority in conventional and nuclear arms, an approach he described as "peace through strength." His tough stance alarmed Soviet leaders who believed that the United States was preparing to launch a preemptive nuclear strike on the Soviet Union. Their anxieties deepened in March 1983 when Reagan announced plans to develop the **Strategic Defense Initiative (SDI)**, an atmosphere-based defensive shield that could intercept and destroy nuclear missiles before they struck U.S. soil. Although few experts thought that SDI was technologically feasible, Reagan's statement nonetheless exacerbated Soviet fears.

Superpower relations deteriorated even further in late 1983. In September, a Soviet pilot shot down a South Korean civilian airliner that had inadvertently strayed into Soviet airspace. All two hundred sixty-nine passengers, including sixty-one Americans, died. Reagan denounced the incident as "an act of barbarism." The Soviets' failure to demonstrate much remorse and unsubstantiated claims that the airliner had been engaged in espionage heightened tensions. In December, the Soviets withdrew from arms control negotiations in protest of the recent NATO deployment of Pershing II and Cruise missiles in Western Europe. For the first time since 1972, U.S. and Soviet officials were not engaged in any diplomatic talks.

The collapse of détente and the escalation of the nuclear arms race inspired a resurgence of transnational antinuclear activism. Throughout the early 1980s, millions of Europeans and Americans participated in massive antinuclear rallies. Scientists including Carl Sagan predicted that the debris thrown into the atmosphere by a nuclear conflict would cause temperatures to plummet, creating a **nuclear winter** that would destroy all life on Earth. Although severe restrictions on freedom of speech limited antinuclear protests behind the Iron Curtain, isolated dissidents such as Soviet physicist Andrei Sakharov spoke out against nuclear proliferation.

Strategic Defense Initiative (SDI) Antiballistic missile system proposed by Reagan in 1983 to guard the United States from nuclear missile attacks. Never implemented.

nuclear winter Scientific theory positing that a nuclear war would have devastating environmental consequences that would imperil most of the living creatures on Earth.

At first dismissive of calls for a **nuclear freeze**, Reagan realized that intensifying popular opposition to his military policies might jeopardize his reelection. Accordingly, he softened his position and introduced a new framework for nuclear disarmament talks with the Soviets. He also carefully avoided direct U.S. military confrontation with Communist states. One exception occurred in October 1983 when he authorized the U.S. invasion of Grenada after a Communist regime took power on the tiny Caribbean island. After six thousand marines quickly defeated Grenada's six hundred-man army and ousted the Marxist leader, Americans cheered a decisive victory in an era of so much international uncertainty.

The 1985 **Reagan Doctrine** more closely resembled the president's preferred approach to combatting international communism. Under this policy, the United States provided financial support and military equipment to anti-Communist insurgents resisting Soviet-supported regimes throughout the world. With congressional approval, the CIA engaged in covert operations aiding anti-Communist rebels in Angola, Cambodia, Afghanistan, and Ethiopia. In Nicaragua, U.S.-backed **contras**—whom Reagan described as "freedom fighters . . . the moral equal of the Founding Fathers"—began mining harbors, sabotaging crops and infrastructure, and raiding Sandinista strongholds. In October 1984, disturbed by the contras' brutality toward civilians and wary of another entanglement resembling the Vietnam War, Congress passed the **Boland Amendment** barring any U.S. government agency from providing financial assistance to the Nicaraguan rebels. Undeterred, presidential aides continued supporting the contras—a decision that had serious consequences during Reagan's second term (see Map 26.3).

Tumult in the Middle East tested U.S. policy makers throughout Reagan's presidency. They closely monitored the implementation of the 1979 Israeli–Egyptian treaty negotiated by Carter. At first, implementation of the agreement appeared to be proceeding smoothly. In April 1982, Israel withdrew its troops from the Sinai Peninsula. But Arabs and Jews continued to differ on the question of a Palestinian homeland. Israel expanded settlements on the West Bank, an area long claimed by Palestinians. In protest, PLO forces based in southern Lebanon launched raids against Israel. On June 6, 1982, Israel retaliated by attacking PLO camps in Lebanon.

To quell the violence, the United States joined a multinational peacekeeping force to oversee the evacuation of the PLO to Tunisia and the withdrawal of Israeli troops.

nuclear freeze A transnational movement that arose in the 1980s calling for the United States and the Soviet Union to stop testing and producing nuclear weapons.

Reagan Doctrine Proclamation pledging U.S. overt and covert support for rebels resisting Communist tyranny around the world.

contras Nicaraguan counterrevolutionaries who opposed the left-wing Sandinistas in a civil war from 1979 to 1990, received U.S. covert aid.

Boland Amendment Three legislative addenda passed from 1982 to 1984 prohibiting U.S. support to contra forces seeking to overthrow the Sandinista government in Nicaragua.

Map 26.3 United States in the Caribbean and Central America Determined to quash the leftist insurgencies that swept the Caribbean and Central America as the détente policy collapsed and Cold War tensions intensified, the Reagan administration extensively intervened in the region, using a combination of overt and covert financial, military, and political tactics.▼

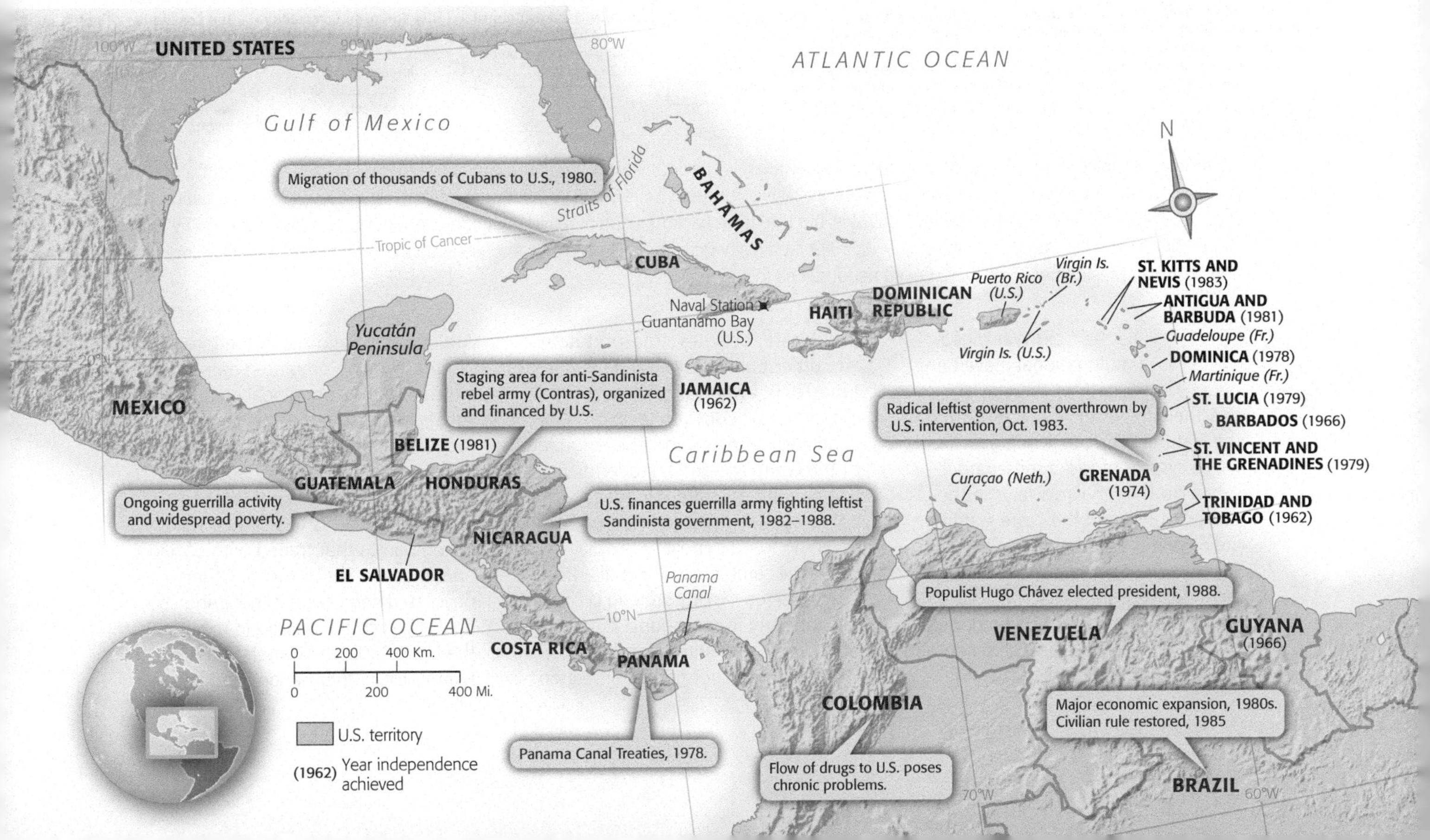

History without Borders

The Global Anti-Apartheid Movement

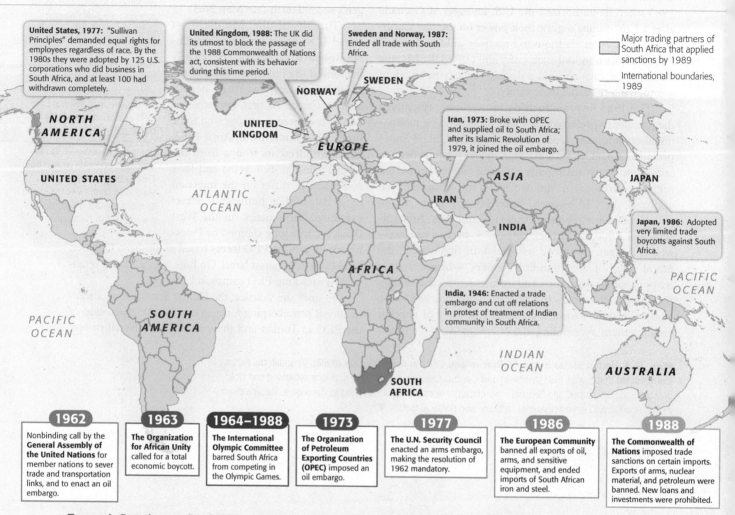

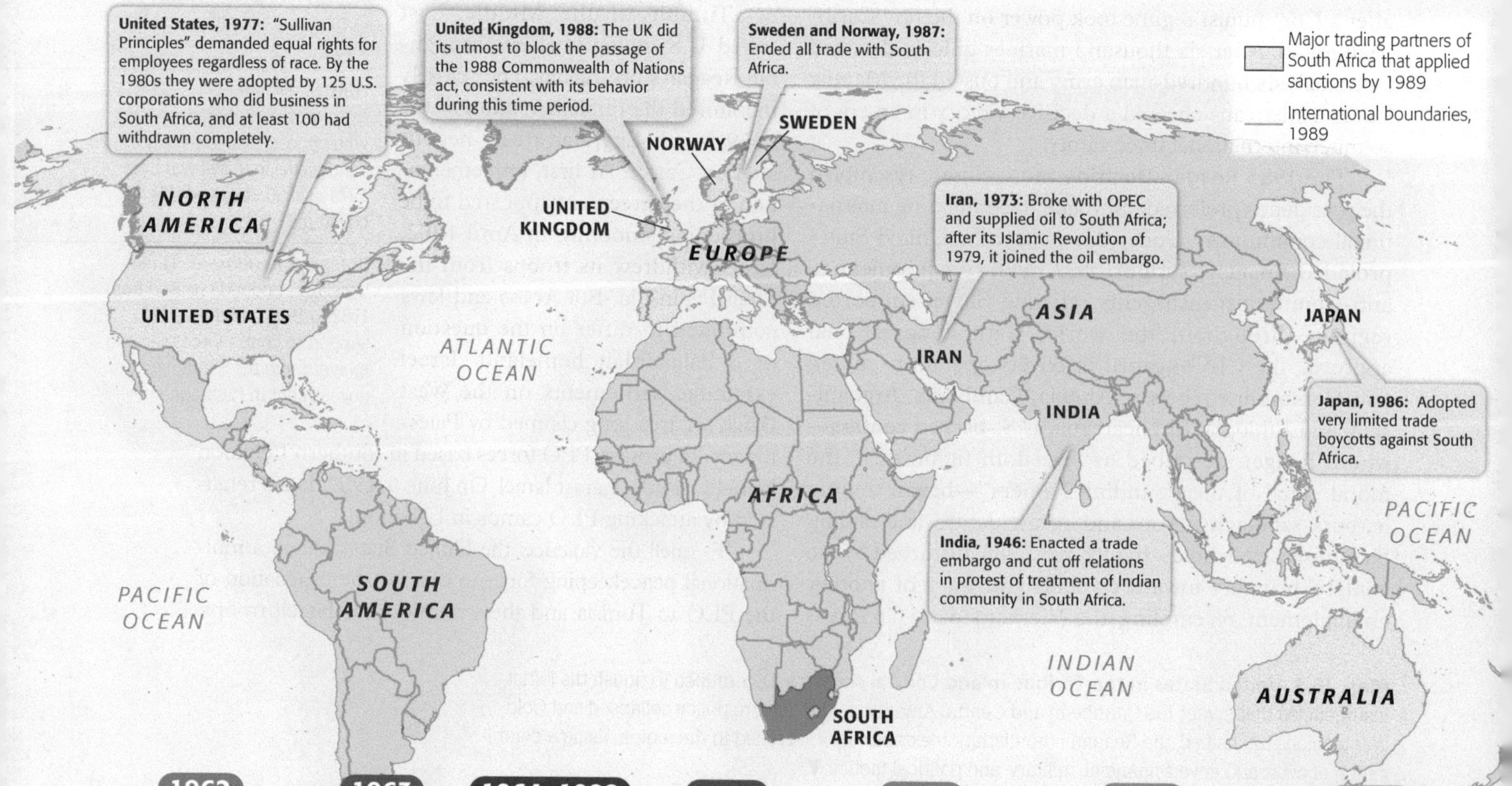

United States, 1977: "Sullivan Principles" demanded equal rights for employees regardless of race. By the 1980s they were adopted by 125 U.S. corporations who did business in South Africa, and at least 100 had withdrawn completely.
United Kingdom, 1988: The UK did its utmost to block the passage of the 1988 Commonwealth of Nations act, consistent with its behavior during this time period.
Sweden and Norway, 1987: Ended all trade with South Africa.
Major trading partners of South Africa that applied sanctions by 1989
International boundaries, 1989
SWEDEN
NORWAY
NORTH AMERICA
UNITED KINGDOM
EUROPE
Iran, 1973: Broke with OPEC and supplied oil to South Africa; after its Islamic Revolution of 1979, it joined the oil embargo.
UNITED STATES
ASIA
JAPAN
ATLANTIC OCEAN
IRAN
INDIA
Japan, 1986: Adopted very limited trade boycotts against South Africa.
AFRICA
PACIFIC OCEAN
India, 1946: Enacted a trade embargo and cut off relations in protest of treatment of Indian community in South Africa.
SOUTH AMERICA
PACIFIC OCEAN
INDIAN OCEAN
AUSTRALIA
SOUTH AFRICA

1962 Nonbinding call by the **General Assembly of the United Nations** for member nations to sever trade and transportation links, and to enact an oil embargo.

1963 **The Organization for African Unity** called for a total economic boycott.

1964–1988 **The International Olympic Committee** barred South Africa from competing in the Olympic Games.

1973 **The Organization of Petroleum Exporting Countries (OPEC)** imposed an oil embargo.

1977 **The U.N. Security Council** enacted an arms embargo, making the resolution of 1962 mandatory.

1986 **The European Community** banned all exports of oil, arms, and sensitive equipment, and ended imports of South African iron and steel.

1988 **The Commonwealth of Nations** imposed trade sanctions on certain imports. Exports of arms, nuclear material, and petroleum were banned. New loans and investments were prohibited.

Economic Sanctions on South Africa in the late 1980s While activists within South Africa risked their lives in anti-apartheid protests, foreigners organized economic sanctions and boycotts against the South African government. In the late 1980s, the white regime brutally repressed anti-apartheid activities, but the move backfired and inspired even more stringent sanctions imposed by the United States and the European community. In 1989, facing severe economic problems and isolation from the international community, South African president F.W. de Klerk began negotiations to end apartheid.

While the Cold War raged, a multinational movement pushed for the end of apartheid in South Africa. Instituted by the National Party in 1948, apartheid was a system of racial segregation similar to the Jim Crow laws in the United States and the caste system in India. Under apartheid, the Afrikaner white minority severely restricted the legal rights of the black majority. By 1970, the government had stripped nonwhites of their citizenship and had segregated the nation's education, health care, beaches, transportation, and other public services and venues. In June 1976, after the government mandated that all educational instruction be conducted in Afrikaans (the language of the white minority), students in Soweto demonstrated. In response, police opened fire and killed up to seven hundred people.

At the same time, a global anti-apartheid movement grew in scope and intensity. Transnational networks of churches and faith-based groups, students, and labor unions protested. Athletic associations and the International Olympic Committee barred South African teams from global competitions. Artists, writers, and actors campaigned for cultural boycotts. Divestment activists successfully persuaded colleges, universities, and local and state governments to sell their holdings in companies that traded with or had operations in South Africa. Others boycotted companies conducting business with the apartheid regime. By the late 1980s, the United States and twenty-four other nations had imposed

AP Images/Catharine Krueger

Anti-apartheid Protest at the University of California, Berkeley, March 1986 U.S. college students played an important role in the global movement against apartheid. In 1977, students at Haverford College persuaded administrators to sell the school's stock in companies that did business with the South African regime. Similar calls quickly arose on other campuses and by 1988, one hundred fifty-five universities had at least partially divested. President Barack Obama later called his participation in an anti-apartheid rally while attending California's Occidental College his "very first political action." ▲

AP Images/Ron Edmonds

Singer Stevie Wonder Arrested in an Anti-apartheid Demonstration at the South African Embassy in Washington, D.C., February 1985 In 1965, after the South African government prohibited multiracial performances, the United Nations Special Committee against Apartheid recommended a cultural boycott, a plea subsequently honored by many governments, organizations, and individuals. Alarmed by its increasing isolation, the South African government relaxed some rules and offered entertainers generous financial incentives. But many performers escalated their anti-apartheid protests. In early 1985, upon winning the Academy Award for Best Song, Stevie Wonder dedicated the prize to Nelson Mandela. ▲

trade sanctions on South Africa, resulting in approximately $35 billion in lost revenue from 1986 to 1989.

In the mid-1980s, massive demonstrations and political violence in South Africa escalated. The government issued state of emergency decrees giving the president, the police, and the military sweeping powers. Media outlets were heavily censored, and thousands of anti-apartheid protestors were arrested. After government agents tortured and killed suspected members of the African National Congress (ANC) and Pan Africanist Congress (PAC) both at home and abroad, the organizations retaliated by bombing restaurants, stores, and public buildings.

In February 1990, with South Africa's international reputation and economy in tatters and its domestic politics in chaos, President F.W. de Klerk announced that he would repeal racially discriminatory laws and lift the thirty-year ban on anti-apartheid groups including the ANC and PAC. He offered to work with black leaders to devise a new constitution under which all races would share power. On February 11, 1990, ANC leader Nelson Mandela was freed after more than twenty-seven years of imprisonment. In 1993, de Klerk and Mandela jointly won the Nobel Peace Prize for moving South Africa toward democracy. On April 27, 1994, 20 million South Africans voted in the nation's first racially inclusive elections and elected Mandela the nation's first black president. His government adopted a new constitution and established a Truth and Reconciliation Commission to address the crimes and heal the wounds of the apartheid era. With the repeal of economic sanctions, companies that had divested returned to South Africa. The efforts of activists both within South Africa and all over the globe had succeeded in ending one of the most repressive forms of institutionalized racism ever created. Divestment remains a powerful tool for prodemocracy, workers' rights, and environmental activists.

Critical Thinking Questions

▶ What do you think motivated people around the world to join forces to oppose apartheid? What do you believe were the most effective strategies these activists used to pressure the South African government?

▶ Why do you believe that the South African government finally abandoned apartheid?

terrorism Use of coercion and violence as a means of advancing political goals.

Hezbollah Literally "Party of God," a radical Shi'ite Muslim organization that arose in Lebanon in 1982. Took responsibility for several terrorist incidents in the 1980s.

Iran-Contra affair Elaborate scheme orchestrated by members of the Reagan administration in which funds raised by illicit arms sales to Iran were channeled illegally to Nicaraguan counterrevolutionaries.

But the decision embroiled U.S. troops in the bloody civil war between the Christian-dominated Lebanese government and Muslims who opposed the regime's pro-Western policies. After erroneously concluding that the neutral U.S. Marines were aligned with the Christian government, Muslim troops began firing on American soldiers. When members of Congress urged Reagan to withdraw the vulnerable U.S. peacekeepers, he claimed the troops were necessary to protect Lebanon from an attack by Soviet-backed Syria.

The decision had deadly ramifications as a wave of terrorism engulfed the region. Used by a variety of states and groups across the political spectrum, **terrorism** usually involves violent acts that are perpetrated for a religious, political, or ideological goal and often intentionally aimed at noncombatants to maximize their emotional impact. In 1982, **Hezbollah**, a Shi'a Islamic militant group, began kidnapping Westerners in protest of U.S. involvement in Lebanon, seizing approximately 96 people from 21 nations over the next decade. In April 1983, 63 people died in a bombing of the U.S. Embassy in Beirut. Then, on October 23, 1983, two truck bombs struck barracks housing American and French troops, killing 241 U.S. and 57 French servicemen. Although Reagan withdrew U.S. forces in February 1984, Islamist militants continued targeting Westerners.

AP Images/Catharine Krueger

Aftermath of Suicide Bombing in Beirut, 1983 U.S. marines and local Beirut residents search for survivors of a terrorist bombing of a barracks in October 1983. ▲

The Reagan administration blamed the incidents on Libya's Muammar el-Qaddafi. A radical Islamist who seized power in a 1969 coup, Qaddafi financed terrorist activities around the world. In response, U.S. officials severed diplomatic ties with Libya and imposed a trade embargo. In April 1986, in retaliation for Libyan-backed bombings of European airports and a Berlin nightclub, U.S. planes bombed Qaddafi's residence and air bases. Although the raids failed to kill Qaddafi, dozens died, and the Libyan air force was destroyed. But terrorist incidents escalated in the years to come.

26-4e Cold War's Final Phase

President Reagan and Soviet Premier Gorbachev dramatically change the nature of the Cold War.

During Reagan's second term, his controversial policies in Nicaragua and the Middle East became intertwined and resulted in the **Iran-Contra affair**, the biggest scandal of his presidency. In 1985, National Security Advisor Robert McFarlane secretly approached the Iranians with a bold proposal: If Iran would persuade terrorists thought to be sympathetic to Ayatollah Khomeini to release six U.S. hostages being held in Lebanon, the United States would sell Iran antitank missiles, which it desperately needed in its war against Iraq. McFarlane directed Lt. Col. Oliver North, an aide at the National Security Council, to work with CIA director William Casey in implementing the arms-for-hostages plan. Casey convinced Reagan to approve the missile shipments to Iran despite the fact that the United States had severed its diplomatic ties to Iran in 1978 amid the Iranian Revolution and the fleeing of the Shah. Violating the Boland Amendment and the Constitution's separation of powers, North helped Israeli and private arms merchants ship hundreds of missiles and aircraft parts to Iran. He then directed the money from the arms sales to the contras in Nicaragua.

After the media broke the story of the arms-for-hostage deal, a congressional commission investigated the Iran-Contra affair. It could not determine whether Reagan had authorized the illegal diversion of funds to the contras, but it faulted him for not being more aware of the activities of his subordinates. Several top administration officials, including North and John Poindexter (who succeeded McFarlane as national security adviser), were indicted or convicted of illegalities. A federal appeals court later overturned the convictions of North and Poindexter because they had been granted immunity in exchange for testifying before Congress.

The fallout from the Iran-Contra affair, the biggest government scandal since Watergate, did not preclude Reagan from making historic changes in the U.S. relationship with the Soviet Union. After Leonid Brezhnev died

"What do I know...And when will I know it?"

Political Cartoon on the Iran-Contra Affair As depicted in this political cartoon, the Iran-Contra affair harmed Reagan's reputation. The final report of the committee that investigated the scandal did not find conclusive proof that Reagan had ordered his subordinates to violate the law, but it criticized his lack of awareness of actions that others were committing in the name of his administration. ◄

Perestroika Russian for "restructuring," policy implemented by Mikhail Gorbachev aimed at reforming the Soviet political and economic systems.

Glasnost Russian for "openness," policy instituted by Mikhail Gorbachev loosening Soviet restrictions on political speech and the press.

in 1982, the deaths of his successors, Yuri Andropov and Konstantin Chernenko, quickly followed. But in 1985, Gorbachev, a fifty-four-year-old reformer, became general secretary. Tackling the economic stagnation and social apathy plaguing his nation, Gorbachev instituted two major initiatives, perestroika (restructuring) and glasnost (openness). **Perestroika** introduced some aspects of capitalism into the Soviet economy. **Glasnost** loosened state restrictions on freedom of speech and of the press. To ease the crushing economic burden created by the nuclear arms race, Gorbachev also sought to improve relations with the West in order to free resources for his proposed domestic reforms.

A staunch anti-Communist, Reagan was at first wary of Gorbachev but later embraced him. After a contentious first meeting in Geneva in November 1985, the two men met again the following October in Reykjavik. They came incredibly close to agreeing to abolish their respective nuclear stockpiles, but Reagan's refusal to abandon SDI scuttled the deal. Nonetheless, superpower relations continued to improve. Gorbachev dropped his insistence that the United States abandon SDI as a prerequisite for any arms reductions. In December 1987, Reagan and Gorbachev signed the Intermediate Nuclear Forces (INF) Treaty, a landmark agreement that abolished an entire class of nuclear weapons. The U.S Senate quickly ratified the pact, which led to the destruction of eighteen hundred forty-six Soviet and eight hundred forty-six U.S. nuclear weapons over a three-year period and granted each side unprecedented inspection of the other's missile sites.

Cold War tensions continued to dissipate in 1988, Reagan's final year in office. Gorbachev began withdrawing Soviet troops from the costly and inconclusive war in Afghanistan and pressured his Cuban allies into withdrawing from Angola. In August, U.S. and Soviet diplomats jointly persuaded Iran and Iran to agree to a cease-fire after an eight-year war. Just months later, as a result of events unleashed by Gorbachev and Reagan, the decades-long Cold War would also reach its end.

Soviet Leader Mikhail Gorbachev and President Ronald Reagan Meet in Moscow, 1988 Gorbachev and Reagan in Red Square during Reagan's May 1988 visit to Moscow. At first wary of one another, the men developed a warm friendship as they forged agreements that led to the end of the Cold War. ▲

Summary

Over the course of the 1970s, Americans struggled with a loss of faith in government following Watergate and the Vietnam War and the collapse of the economic supremacy that the United States had enjoyed since World War II. Fluctuations in the international price per barrel of petroleum made the highly oil-dependent U.S. economy quite unstable. High inflation constricted families' earning power. Rising foreign competition undercut U.S. manufacturing. Organized labor lost power. Activists and public officials raised awareness about the planet's finite resources. Despite these obstacles, entrepreneurship thrived as new business opportunities created by technological innovations and increasing global interconnectedness emerged. To stimulate economic growth, advocates of free market doctrines pushed for tax cuts, privatization, deregulation, and cuts in public spending.

In the late 1970s, détente unraveled and superpower dynamics shifted. The Carter administration's efforts to promote human rights collided with difficult political realities and anti-Americanism in the developing world. A revolution in Iran had ripple effects throughout the Middle East. The Soviet invasion of Afghanistan re-ignited Cold War tensions. Determined to restore U.S. stature in the world and to put the Soviets on the defensive, the Reagan administration dramatically increased military spending. An intensification of superpower rivalries in the early 1980s generated mass anxieties about nuclear war, and emerging threats posed by terrorism and religious radicalism signaled new dangers that would punctuate the post-Cold War era.

American society changed significantly. The number of two-income households rose. Increasing rates of unmarried cohabitation, single parenthood, and divorce reshaped norms of family life. Some women remained mired in poverty, but others broke gender barriers and enjoyed great professional and economic success. LGBT people became more open and made political gains, sparking intense opposition from those who believed that homosexuality was immoral.

An international wave of religious revivalism arose. Some worshippers gravitated to mainstream faiths such as Christianity, Islam, and Judaism. Others adopted alternative spiritualities. A resurgence of fundamentalism had enormous political and societal ramifications in the United States, Iran, and other nations. Governments responded to powerful blocs demanding the preservation of traditional gender roles and strict adherence to religious doctrines.

The same years witnessed the rise of political conservatives who celebrated a free market economy and who sought to dismantle the social welfare programs of the New Deal and the Great Society. As the U.S. government curtailed its regulation of the private sector and slashed spending, some Americans amassed unprecedented wealth while others languished in poverty. Conservatives in other nations adopted similar agendas.

Although the Iran-Contra affair overshadowed much of his second term, Ronald Reagan forged a remarkable partnership with Soviet Premier Mikhail Gorbachev. As Gorbachev tried to reform an economically stagnant and politically repressive Soviet Union, Reagan moved from initial skepticism about his Communist rival's professed desire to de-escalate U.S.–Soviet tensions toward negotiating agreements that helped end the Cold War entirely.

<Thinking Back, *Looking Forward*>

As you review this chapter, contemplate how the legacies of the Vietnam War, Watergate, and the social movements of 1960s shaped the post-1975 era. How did free market reforms affect workers in capitalist and Communist nations? How and why did the United States and the Soviet Union evolve from the mid-1970s to the late 1980s? What roles did nonstate actors play in drawing attention to human rights and global concerns? What triggered the resurgence of religious fundamentalism and conservatism in the United States and elsewhere? In future chapters, assess how and why global dynamics shifted in the aftermath of the Cold War.

To make your study concrete, review the chapter timeline and reflect on the entries there. Think about their causes, consequences, and connections. How do they fit with global trends?

Additional Resources

Books

Borstelmann, Thomas. *The 1970s: A New Global History from Civil Rights to Economic Inequality*. Princeton, NJ: Princeton University Press, 2012. ▶ Synthesis of the 1970s placing the United States in transnational context.

Brands, H.W. *Reagan: The Life*. New York: Doubleday, 2015. Engaging and exhaustive biography written by a celebrated historian.

Chang, Jeff. *Can't Stop Won't Stop: A History of the Hip-Hop Generationz*. New York: Picador, 2005. ▶ Journalist's account of origins and impact of hip-hop on U.S. history and culture.

Cowie, Jefferson. *Stayin' Alive: The 1970s and the Last Days of the Working Class*. New York: The New Press, 2010. ▶ Examination of how political and economic changes during the 1970s affected working-class Americans.

Farber, David. *Taken Hostage: The Iran Hostage Crisis and America's First Encounter with Radical Islam*. Princeton, NJ: Princeton University Press, 2004. ▶ Gripping history of the hostage crisis and its connection to the current war on terrorism.

Iriye, Akira, Petra Goedde, and William I. Hitchcock, eds. *The Human Rights Revolution: An International History*. New York: Oxford University Press, 2012. ▶ Collection of essays on human rights activism from 1945 to the present.

Jones, Daniel Steadman. *Masters of the Universe: Hayek, Friedman, and the Birth of Neoliberal Politics*. Princeton, NJ: Princeton University Press, 2012. ▶ Brilliant analysis of the origins and impact of transatlantic neoliberalism.

Moreton, Bethany. *To Serve God and Wal-Mart: The Making of Christian Free Enterprise*. Cambridge, MA: Harvard University Press, 2009. ▶ Fascinating history of Wal-Mart's interconnections between evangelicalism and capitalism.

Rossinow, Doug. *The Reagan Era: A History of the 1980s*. New York: Columbia University Press, 2015. ▶ Synthesis of the political, cultural, economic, and international dimensions of the 1980s.

Wilson, James Graham. *The Triumph of Improvisation: Gorbachev's Adaptability, Reagan's Engagement, and the End of the Cold War*. Ithaca, NY: Cornell University Press, 2014. ▶ Study of leadership and decision making based on newly declassified materials.

Go to the MindTap® for **Global Americans** to access the full version of select books from this Additional Resources section.

Websites

Cold War International History Project. https://www.wilsoncenter.org/program/cold-war-international-history-project ▶ Rich array of multinational publications and primary sources related to the Cold War.

Jimmy Carter Presidential Museum and Library. http://www.jimmycarterlibrary.gov/ ▶ Research and teaching sources on Jimmy Carter's presidency and postpresidential activities.

Like Totally 80s. http://www.liketotally80s.com/ ▶ Fun, exhaustive collection of blog posts and news stories on the history of 1980s popular culture.

PBS *American Experience:* "The Presidents." http://www.pbs.org/wgbh/americanexperience/collections/presidents/ ▶ Excellent primary sources and film documentaries on Jimmy Carter and Ronald Reagan.

Ronald Reagan Presidential Library and Museum. http://www.reagan.utexas.edu/ ▶ Collection of textual, audiovisual, and photographic sources on the Reagan presidency.

MindTap®

Continue exploring online through MindTap®, where you can:

- **Assess your knowledge with the Chapter Test**
- **Watch historical videos related to the chapter**
- **Further your understanding with interactive maps and timelines**

The Global Conservative Shift

1975–1976

April 1975
Gates founds software company Micro-Soft.

July 1975
Delegates from thirty-five nations sign the Helsinki Accords.

July 1976
Bicentennial celebrations in the United States.

November 1976
Carter defeats Ford in presidential race.

1978

Deng Xiaoping launches economic reforms in China.

June
California voters approve Proposition 13, a statewide ballot initiative slashing property taxes.

September
Carter brokers the Camp David Accords between Israel and Egypt.

November
Nine hundred members of the People's Temple commit mass suicide in Jonestown, Guyana.

San Francisco supervisor Harvey Milk and mayor George Moscone are assassinated by their colleague Dan White.

1979

March
Partial nuclear meltdown occurs at Three Mile Island in Pennsylvania.

May
Thatcher is elected Britain's first woman prime minister.

August
Carter appoints Volcker to chair the Federal Reserve Board.

November
Islamic radicals in Tehran seize Americans

U.S. gas prices exceed $1 per gallon for the first time.

December
Soviet forces invade Afghanistan to bolster a faltering Communist regime.

1980

January
United States imposes grain and technology embargo on Soviet Union in retaliation for Soviet invasion of Afghanistan.

March
Carter signs Refugee Act, permits immigration of refugees for humanitarian purposes.

April
U.S. effort to rescue fifty-three Americans being held hostage in Tehran fails.

U.S. Olympic Committee votes to boycott 1980 Summer Olympics in Moscow.

November
Reagan defeats Carter by a landslide in presidential race.

1981

January
Reagan inaugurated.

U.S. hostages in Iran freed.

March
Reagan shot in an assassination attempt, recovers.

August
Reagan fires striking air traffic controllers.

September
Sandra Day O'Connor sworn in as first female U.S. Supreme Court justice.

October
Egyptian president Anwar el-Sadat assassinated by Islamic extremists in Cairo.

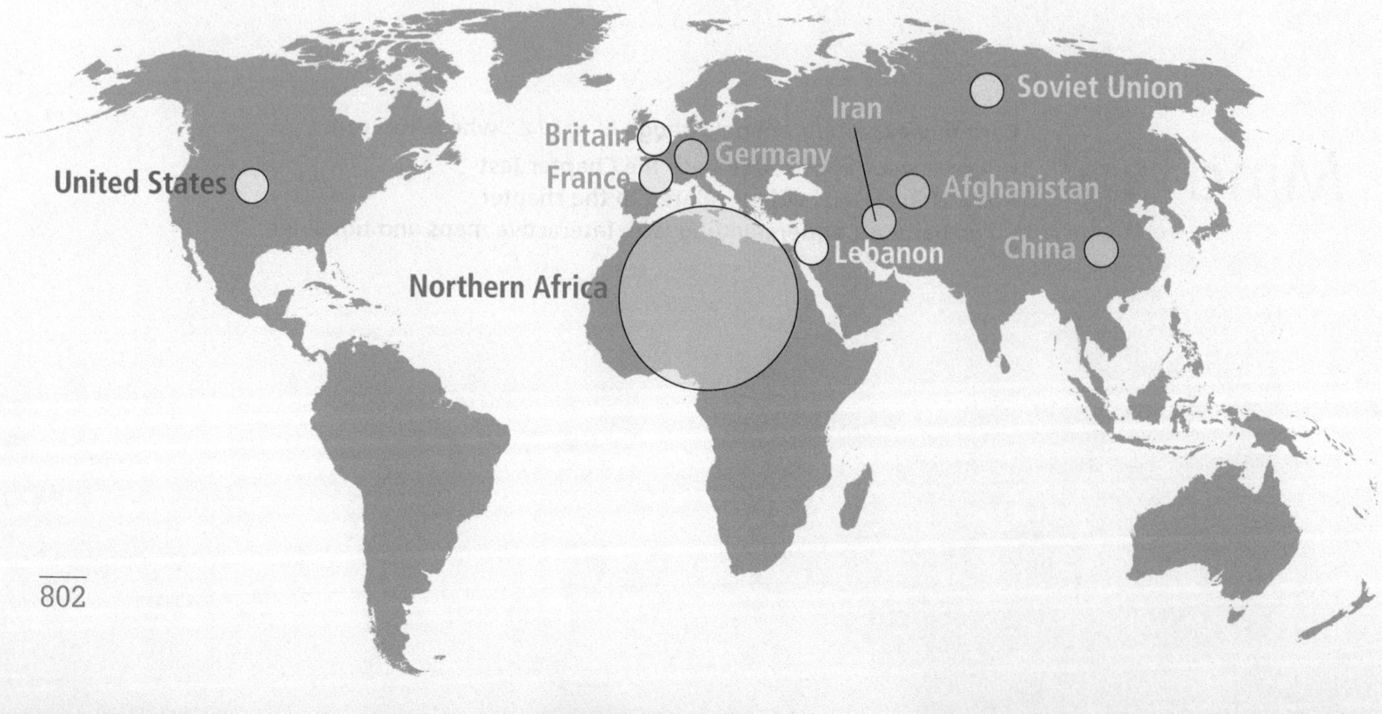

1983

March
Reagan gives fiercely anti-Soviet "evil empire" speech before the National Association of Evangelicals.

April
U.S. Embassy in Beirut bombed.

September
Soviets shoot down Korean civilian airliner, killing two hundred sixty-nine passengers and crew.

October
U.S. Marines and French paratroopers die in suicide bombing of a barracks in Beirut, Lebanon.

U.S. forces invade Grenada to oust a Marxist regime.

1984

October
Congress passes the Boland Amendment.

November
Reagan defeats Mondale, wins second term.

1985

March
Gorbachev becomes leader of the Soviet Union.

November
Reagan and Gorbachev meet in Geneva, and agree to resume arms reduction talks.

1986

April
In retaliation for sponsoring terrorism, United States launches air raids on Libya.

World's worst nuclear accident occurs at Soviet Chernobyl plant, and radioactive contamination spreads to Western Europe.

October
Reagan signs Anti-Drug Abuse Act imposing mandatory minimum sentences for drug possession and selling narcotics.

November
Lebanese magazines reveal U.S. weapons-for-hostages deal, Iran-Contra affair begins.

1987

February
Tower Commission condemns Ronald Reagan for failing to monitor subordinates' activities in the Iran-Contra affair.

June
Reagan speaks in West Berlin, challenges the Soviets to destroy the Berlin Wall.

December
Intermediate Nuclear Forces Treaty signed in Moscow.

Go to MindTap® to engage with an interactive version of the timeline. Analyze events and themes with clickable content, view related videos, and respond to critical thinking questions.

27 Closer Together, Further Apart

1988–2000

In 1976, Linda Alvarado launched Alvarado Construction. She initially submitted bids signed only with her initials in order to conceal her gender from potentially sexist readers.

27-1
Victories Abroad and Challenges at Home

27-1a Polarization of Politics
27-1b End of the Cold War
27-1c Rise of Regional Conflicts
27-1d Domestic Struggles

27-2
A Changing Population

27-2a Debating Multiculturalism
27-2b Demographic Trends
27-2c Global Population Control and Transnational Adoption

27-3
The Clinton Years

27-3a Ambitious Agenda
27-3b Partisan Backlash
27-3c Confronting the Post-Cold War World
27-3d Scandal, Impeachment, and the Election of 2000

27-4
Global Village

27-4a Proliferation of Intergovernmental and Nongovernmental Organizations
27-4b The Digital Revolution and Its Critics
27-4c Americanization of Global Culture

In 1992, Linda Alvarado became the first Latina and only the second woman—the first was Cincinnati Reds owner Marge Schott—to buy a stake in a major league sports team, the Colorado Rockies. Part of a wave of entrepreneurs who capitalized on opportunities created by the economic shifts of the 1970s and the women's and civil rights movements, Alvarado reached the highest echelons of American business. Her career is a microcosm of the great demographic and economic changes characterizing U.S. society in the 1980s and 1990s.

Denver Post/Getty Images

Born in Albuquerque in 1952, Alvarado was the only daughter in a family of eight. She and her brothers lived with their parents in a three-room adobe house without indoor heating or plumbing. Undaunted by their difficult living conditions, the Alvarado children embraced their mother's optimistic worldview—*empieza pequeña, pero piensa muy grande* ("start small, but think big"). In 1969, Alvarado accepted an academic scholarship to Pomona College. To help pay expenses, she applied for a part-time job on an all-male landscaping crew. When the supervisor asked, "What are you doing here? Don't you understand that all the girls work in food service?" she refused to leave until he hired her.

After graduating with an economics degree, she became a contract administrator on a construction site. Despite harassment from some of her male coworkers, she learned the estimating, blueprinting, and computer scheduling techniques that were transforming the construction industry. Deciding to launch her own company, she drew up a business plan and sought financing from six banks, but none was willing to issue a loan to a Latina in a male-dominated business. Her parents took out a $2,500 mortgage on their home that she combined with aid from the Small Business Administration to launch Alvarado Construction in 1976. To conceal her gender from potentially sexist readers, she initially submitted bids signed only with her initials. After proving its skills on small structures like bus shelters, the firm won contracts for shopping centers, hotels, sports facilities, and other multimillion-dollar projects in the United States and several foreign countries. In the early 1980s, Alvarado founded Palo Alto, Inc., a fast-food franchise company. By 2002, it operated more than one hundred fifty Taco Bell, Kentucky Fried Chicken, and Pizza Hut restaurants. She serves as president, and her husband Robert is CEO.

Alvarado has spent many years working as a mentor for women, minorities, and youth. She has received many awards. She plays an active role in the United States Hispanic Chamber of Commerce and travels the world giving lectures about leadership. She has served on the boards of several multinational corporations including 3M Company and Pepsi Bottling Company. A mother of three, she lauds her husband's vital role in helping her balance professional and family responsibilities. When she

Linda Alvarado embraced her mother's world view "start small, but think big," and reached the highest echelons of business. In what ways does her career trajectory illustrate the transformations in American society during the 1980s and 1990s?

Go to MindTap® to watch a video on Alvarado and learn how her story relates to the themes of this chapter.

attended Career Day at her son Rob's kindergarten, his teacher asked him, "Don't you want to be a contractor like your mother . . . and build high-rises, schools, and sports facilities?" He replied, "No. That's women's work." His nonchalant answer spoke volumes about how much pathbreakers like his mother had helped transform daily life in the United States.

As Alvarado built her business career, U.S. society became more inclusive and diverse. But the transition was not an easy one, and Americans often intensely battled matters of identity, politics, and culture. New campaign techniques and ideologically charged media outlets amplified these debates. A new wave of immigrants, largely from Asia and Latin America, shifted the demographics of the U.S. population. The Cold War's end added both hope and uncertainty to international relations. Although President George H.W. Bush won praise for his foreign policy acumen, more conservative Republicans criticized his moderate positions on social and fiscal issues. Victory in the Persian Gulf War sent Bush's approval ratings to record highs, but an economic recession helped Democrat Bill Clinton prevail in the 1992 presidential race.

As Clinton attempted to implement centrist policies, a polarized political system complicated efforts to redress economic inequities and social problems. Yet the era also witnessed a communications revolution triggered by the Internet, fostering greater interconnectivity among the world's peoples. Fueled by technological innovations, the U.S. economy experienced its most vigorous growth since the 1960s. But in spectacularly dramatic fashion, the election of 2000 demonstrated the depth of American political divides at the beginning of the twenty-first century.

27-1

Victories Abroad and Challenges at Home

The 1988 presidential race pitted Vice President George H.W. Bush against Massachusetts governor Michael Dukakis and witnessed an intensification of the media's scrutiny of political candidates. In October 1987, the same week that Bush announced his candidacy, *Newsweek* ran a cover story called "The Wimp Factor." To offset the damage, Bush's team highlighted his participation in traditionally masculine pursuits (see top photo). In September 1988, during a campaign stop at a defense contractor, Dukakis donned a helmet while riding in an M1A1 Abrams tank (see bottom photo). This photo sparked widespread ridicule. Even today, many political candidates refuse to wear headgear in public because of it.

What messages about themselves do you think that George H.W. Bush and Michael Dukakis hoped these photographs would convey? Why do you think each succeeded or failed? How does media coverage of politics shape our views of those seeking or holding public office? ▶

AP Images/Eric Gay

AP Images/Michael E. Samojeden

After prevailing in one of the most negative political campaigns in U.S. history, George H.W. Bush faced an increasingly polarized electorate and large federal budget deficits from the Reagan era that forced him to break a no-tax pledge. Although he scored domestic policy victories with passage of a landmark disability rights law and new environmental protections, he clashed with more conservative members of his own party. As the Cold War ended and a regional conflict arose in the Persian Gulf, Bush confronted complicated global dynamics and won praise for his foreign policy acumen. But when the nation experienced an economic downturn, he discovered that his international accomplishments were not enough to guarantee reelection.

☞ As you read, contemplate why and how the end of the Cold War changed international relations. Do you think that President Bush was right to respond cautiously to the rapidly changing events in Eastern Europe and the Soviet Union? Explain your answer. Why was success in foreign policy not enough to win him a second term?

27-1a Polarization of Politics

The 1988 presidential race ushers in an era of negative campaigning and increasing political divisions.

In 1988, both parties hoped to prevail in an electoral contest marked by increasing reliance on political consultants, "sound bites," and "photo ops." George H.W. Bush entered the presidential race as the Republican frontrunner. A former World War II aviator and Texas oilman, Bush had been a successful congressman, U.S. ambassador to the United Nations, director of the Central Intelligence Agency, and Ronald Reagan's vice president. Despite this distinguished record, some observers characterized Bush as a "wimp" and believed that his privileged background (son of a U.S. senator from Connecticut) would not resonate with voters. After several leading Democrats either declined to run or dropped out of the primaries, little-known Massachusetts governor Michael Dukakis secured enough delegates to capture the Democratic nomination. Civil rights leader Jesse Jackson won the second-highest delegate count, becoming the nation's most successful African American presidential candidate to date. Attempting to mobilize a **Rainbow Coalition** of racial minorities, farmers, gays, working-class, and poor people, Jackson had campaigned on a very liberal platform that aimed to unite an increasingly diverse society and to mitigate racial and economic disparities that had deepened during the Reagan years.

Upon discovering that Dukakis had an unexpected seventeen-point lead, the Bush campaign defied conventional wisdom and focused on defining Dukakis rather than trumpeting Bush's achievements. "You gotta go negative. You just gotta," explained political strategist Lee Atwater. Although Bush had promised a "kinder, gentler America," he ran one of the nastiest campaigns in U.S. history, reshaping politics for years afterward. Bush supporters produced an ad attacking Dukakis's record on crime by featuring Willie Horton, an African American man who raped a white woman during a prison furlough in Massachusetts. Critics blasted the commercial's racist overtones and its failure to mention that Dukakis had not created the prison furlough program. Simultaneously, Bush operatives made *liberal* an epithet by assaulting Dukakis's membership in the American Civil Liberties Union (ACLU), a political organization committed to defending the Bill of Rights. Refusing to engage in reciprocal mudslinging, Dukakis ran an uninspired campaign. In November, Bush carried 53 percent of the popular vote and won forty states.

The race coincided with a seismic shift in the media landscape. In 1987, the Federal Communications Commission repealed the **Fairness Doctrine**, a policy it had introduced in 1949 mandating that broadcast licensees cover both sides of controversial issues in an honest, balanced way. The decision opened the airwaves to much more ideologically charged programming, and stations could now align themselves with one political perspective or another. Conservatives, long convinced of liberal media bias, pounced at the chance to promote their views. In August 1988, Rush Limbaugh launched a nationally syndicated talk radio program just weeks before the Republican National Convention. He quickly became the nation's most popular talk radio host and his audience—composed mainly of white men like Limbaugh—delighted in his withering, often humorous, jibes at liberals. He and other conservative radio commentators soon wielded great influence in Republican politics.

27-1b End of the Cold War

Communism collapses in Eastern Europe and the Soviet Union but endures in China.

Bush's foreign policy expertise served him well as a series of momentous events ended the Cold War and China transformed its economy. In December 1988, Soviet general secretary Mikhail Gorbachev traveled to Washington for a final meeting with Reagan and President-Elect Bush. During this trip, Gorbachev appeared before the United Nations and announced that he was cutting 500,000 troops from the Soviet armed forces and removing and disbanding six tank divisions from East Germany, Czechoslovakia, and Hungary. Because of the growing trust between the superpowers, Gorbachev asserted, the entire world could "breathe a sigh of relief."

Gorbachev's glasnost policy removed restrictions on the press and freedom of speech in the Soviet Union and Eastern Europe, but the Communist government of the Peoples Republic of China (PRC) was more cautious in embracing reforms. Following the chaotic and economically disastrous Cultural Revolution (1966–1971) and especially the death of Mao Zedong in 1976, the PRC under Mao's revolutionary comrade Deng Xiaoping began liberalizing the state-controlled economy by including key elements of a capitalist free market such as foreign

Rainbow Coalition Nonprofit political alliance of minorities and groups who are disadvantaged founded by Jesse Jackson in 1984.

Fairness Doctrine Introduced in 1949, policy of the Federal Communications Commission requiring publicly licensed broadcasters to devote equal time to both sides of controversial issues.

The Fall of the Berlin Wall, 1989 On November 9, 1989, after hearing the announcement that citizens of the GDR were free to cross the country's borders, hundreds of thousands of East and West Berliners flocked to the Berlin Wall, launching what one journalist called "the greatest street party in the history of the world." Between 1961 and 1989, armed East German guards killed at least one hundred seventy-one people trying to cross the Wall, but more than five thousand managed to reach the West. ▶

Patrick PIEL/Getty images

investment, competition, and a global business outlook. But China's second generation of Communist leaders stopped short of removing restrictions on the press despite the pleas of the liberal general secretary of the Communist Party Hu Yaobang. After Hu was deposed and executed in April 1989, thousands of university students and other prodemocracy activists occupied Beijing's Tiananmen Square and demanded more political openness, freedom of expression, and better economic opportunities for highly educated citizens. The activists constructed a Goddess of Democracy statute loosely modeled on the Statue of Liberty. With millions of people watching the protests on the Cable News Network (CNN), the aging Chinese rulers decided that the peaceful demonstrations presented an unacceptable challenge to their authority. On the night of June 3, Deng Xiaoping deployed soldiers and tanks to crush the protests. By the next morning, hundreds of demonstrators lay dead and thousands were arrested.

Although the brutal crackdown sparked international outrage, President Bush rejected calls for sanctions against the PRC. Convinced that severing U.S.–Chinese ties would be detrimental to global security, he maintained China's most-favored nation trade status while privately pressuring the Chinese to improve their record on human rights. The Chinese government continued to oppose political reforms, but country's economy grew at the astonishing rate of 10 percent per year, and its exports to the United States soared. In years to come, it became increasingly difficult for U.S. policy makers to balance America's economic reliance on China with their desire to promote a more democratic Chinese society.

Throughout 1989, a series of independence movements swept Eastern Europe. Gorbachev refused to use military force to stop them in stark contrast to his predecessors' responses to the 1956 Hungarian Revolution and the 1968 Prague Spring. By 1990, Poland, Hungary, Czechoslovakia, Bulgaria, Romania, East Germany, Yugoslavia, and Albania overthrew or transformed their Communist governments. All regained their national sovereignty, established democracies, and adopted capitalism.

Nothing exemplified the stunning shift more than the opening of the Berlin Wall on November 9, 1989. A huge global audience watched television coverage of East and West Germans celebrating the collapse of the twenty-eight-mile long concrete barrier that was both a literal and figurative reflection of Cold War divides. In October 1990, the Communist German Democratic Republic (GDR) ceased to exist, and Germany became a unified nation for the first time since 1945.

The political earthquake soon reverberated in the Soviet Union. By July 1990, the Soviet republics of Lithuania, Estonia, Latvia, and Ukraine declared independence. By the end of 1991, following the failure of a coup that sought to reverse Gorbachev's policies, the Soviet Union had disintegrated into fifteen separate nations, and the Soviet Communist Party disbanded (see Map 27.1). Russia, the largest of the former Soviet republics, declared its independence and formed a new government led by Boris Yeltsin. On December 25, 1991, the Soviet Union formally ceased to exist. Gorbachev, having unwittingly unleashed forces that destroyed the Soviet empire, resigned. The Cold War came to an abrupt, mostly peaceful, end. For the first time in nearly five decades, the world was not split along capitalist and Communist lines.

27-1c Rise of Regional Conflicts

A multinational coalition forces Iraq to withdraw from Kuwait.

While some observers viewed the collapse of communism as the inevitable triumph of liberal democracy and free market capitalism,

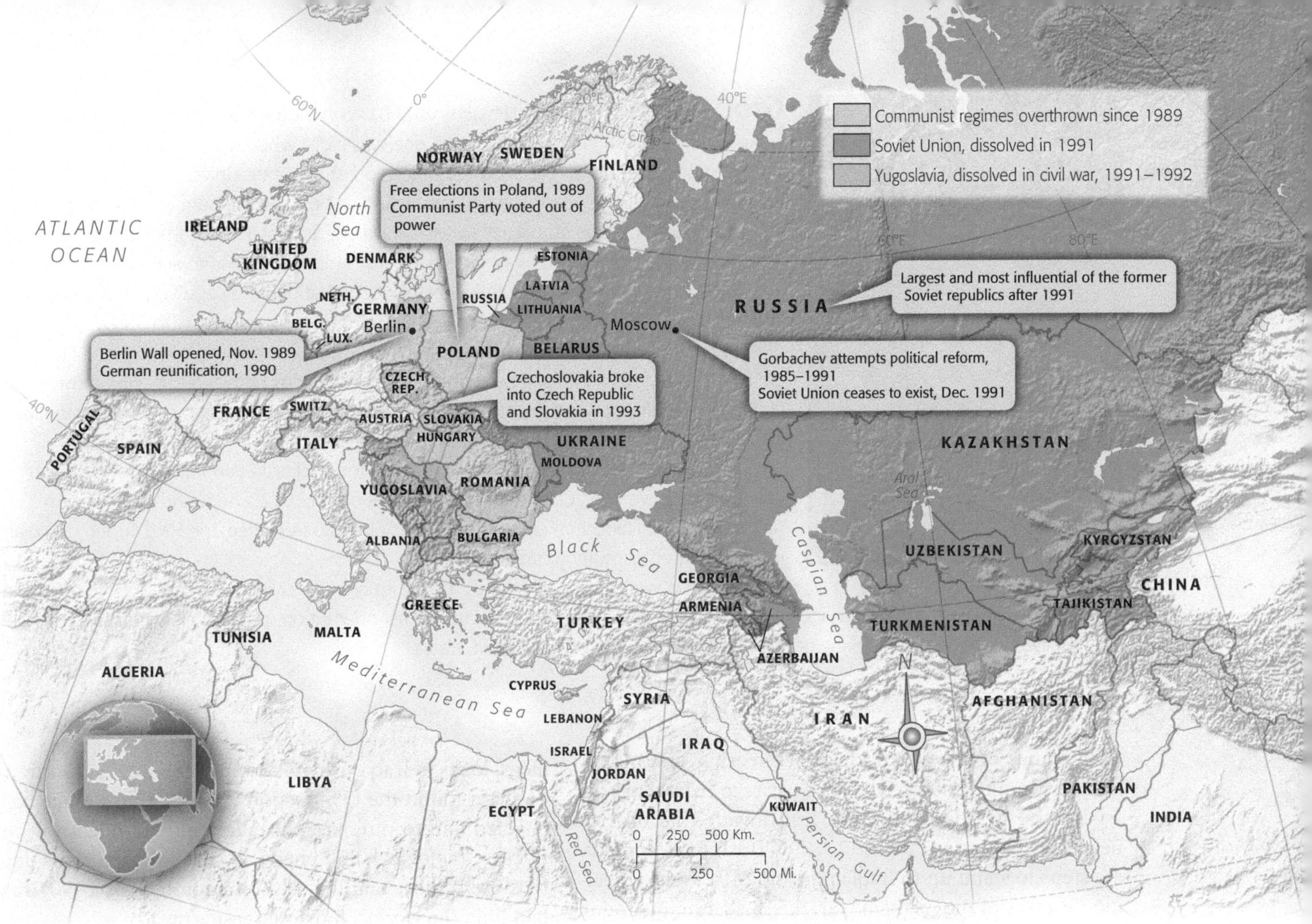

Map 27.1 Map of Europe at the End of the Cold War Between 1989 and 1993, the end of the Cold War transformed the map of Europe as nations formerly part of the Eastern bloc regained their independence and transformed their governments and economies. The Soviet Union's dissolution into separate countries changed the geographic landscape even more. Most nations transitioned from communism relatively peacefully, but Yugoslavia fragmented into four different states and degenerated into civil war. ▲

others predicted that a "clash of civilizations" between different cultural and religious groups would arise in the post-Cold War era. Although few Americans advocated a complete U.S. retreat from global affairs, many hoped that the United States would slash military spending and use the resulting "peace dividend" to address pressing domestic issues. But a series of regional conflicts signaling new dangers in an unstable, multipolar world soon consumed the attention and resources of U.S. policy makers.

Ignoring calls to celebrate the U.S. victory in the Cold War, President Bush responded cautiously to the rapidly changing political events in the Soviet Union and Eastern Europe. At a summit in Washington in June 1990, Bush and Gorbachev signed two treaties significantly reducing their respective nuclear arsenals. Bush encouraged the International Monetary Fund (IMF) and private investors to support Russia's difficult transition to a free market economy. He was also instrumental in gaining Soviet support for the inclusion of a reunified Germany in the NATO alliance.

In some places, ethnic and religious tensions that had been suppressed under communism exploded. Czechoslovakia split into separate Czech and Slovak republics. After Yugoslavia fragmented into four different republics, a civil war ensued in which Serbian soldiers killed as many as twenty thousand, mostly Muslim, civilians in Bosnia and Herzegovina. While urging European nations to send humanitarian aid to Sarajevo, the capital of Bosnia-Herzegovina, the Bush administration refused to intervene militarily in the Balkan conflict.

The end of the Cold War prompted a reassessment of U.S. policies throughout the Western Hemisphere. In Nicaragua, Bush ended U.S. support for the contras after the Sandinistas agreed to free elections. U.S. officials worked closely with the IMF to cut Latin American debt. To curb the illegal drug trade (and aware that voracious U.S. demand helped fuel it), U.S. policy makers aided regional counternarcotic operations. The booming drug trade also played a role in a December 1989 U.S. invasion of Panama to capture dictator Manuel Noriega. After his extradition to the United States, Noriega was convicted on

Wayne Scarberry/Getty Images

Global Americans **Urvashi Vaid** has committed her life to working for social justice. Born in 1958 in New Delhi, India, she was eight when her family moved to the United States after her father accepted a position at the State University of New York in Potsdam. Within three years, she was protesting against the Vietnam War. After graduating from Vassar College and Northeastern University School of Law, she worked as a staff attorney for the American Civil Liberties Union's National Prisons Project.

In 1989, she became executive director of the National Gay and Lesbian Task Force (NGLTF). In keeping with her belief that LGBT rights are interwoven with other human rights struggles, she spoke out for reproductive justice and strongly opposed the Persian Gulf War. She amplified her views on the interconnections between the LGBT movement and larger familial and social institutions in her book *Virtual Equality: The Mainstreaming of Gay and Lesbian Liberation* (1995).

After leaving NGLTF in 2001, Vaid worked for the Ford Foundation and spent five years as executive director of the Arcus Foundation. In 2012, she founded the nation's first lesbian political action committee, LPAC. She also launched The Vaid Group, a social justice-oriented consulting firm.

Vaid has won several awards for her writing and activism. She continues to advocate a more inclusive society that values all people equally, regardless of race, class, sexual orientation, physical ability, or age. Her multifaceted identity is emblematic of the increasing diversity of the United States.

eight counts of drug trafficking, racketeering, and money laundering and sentenced to thirty years in federal prison.

In the Middle East, after Iraq invaded its oil-rich neighbor Kuwait on August 2, 1990, Bush took immediate steps to stand up to Iraqi aggression. To avoid repeating mistakes of the Vietnam War, the Bush administration embraced the **Powell Doctrine,** a policy articulated by chairman of the Joint Chiefs of Staff Colin Powell that called for the use of overwhelming force and a clear exit strategy to ensure that regional conflicts were brief and decisive. After Bush won support for stationing U.S. troops in Saudi Arabia, Osama Bin Laden, a thirty-three-year-old Islamic fundamentalist who had fought against the Soviets in Afghanistan, accused the Saudi government of desecrating Muslim holy sites, and its regime imprisoned him.

On August 7, two hundred thousand U.S. troops began arriving in Saudi Arabia to guard petroleum supplies from potential Iraqi attack. Two months later, the U.S. force exceeded more than 500,000. By that time, the United Nations Security Council had imposed harsh economic sanctions and passed twelve resolutions demanding that the Iraqis withdraw from Kuwait by January 15, 1991. Through adroit diplomacy, Bush built a multinational coalition of 700,000 troops from thirty countries. Many Arab nations and even the Soviet Union, Iraq's long-time military sponsor, joined the partnership.

Powell Doctrine Named after General Colin Powell, policy calling for U.S. military intervention only after all nonviolent strategies have failed and there are clear and attainable goals.

Operation Desert Storm Code name for the combat phase of the U.S.-led United Nations mission to liberate Kuwait after its occupation by Iraq.

The global outrage surprised Saddam Hussein, Iraq's president since 1979. He viewed the dispute with Kuwait as a local affair. Because the United States had provided intelligence and helped to broker secret and illegal loans to Iraq during its 1980–1988 war against Iran, Saddam found the U.S. response baffling. The loans had enabled him to purchase $2 billion in equipment for his nuclear, biological, and chemical weapons programs and to support more than 1 million Iraqi troops. By 1990, Iraq had built the world's fourth largest army.

Whatever their previous relationship with Saddam, U.S. officials were not willing to imperil the Persian Gulf's oil supplies. After diplomacy failed to resolve the crisis, Bush asked for congressional authorization to use military force under the terms of the UN Security Council's resolutions. Despite large antiwar demonstrations held across the country, the war resolution won majority support in both houses.

On January 16, 1991, eighteen hours after the passage of the UN deadline, coalition troops began **Operation Desert Storm** and unleashed an aerial assault on Iraq and Kuwait (see Map 27.2). Millions watched CNN's live coverage of "smart bomb" raids, but Pentagon officials, cognizant of the negative impact of news coverage of the Vietnam War, carefully controlled images of the death and destruction. On February 23, coalition ground forces entered Kuwait and eastern Iraq, meeting virtually no resistance. Four days later, Bush announced that the coalition had achieved its aims of liberating Kuwait and compelling Iraq to accept a cease-fire.

Rather than risk a bloody and long U.S. occupation of Baghdad, Bush allowed Saddam to remain in power. Within days after the cease-fire, the Iraqi Republican Guard crushed rebellions among Shi'a in the south and Kurds in the north. Although Bush had encouraged Iraqis to rise up against Saddam during the war, he denied that insurgents were promised U.S. aid. Subsequently, critics attacked Bush's decision not to oust Saddam. Bush and his aides remained unrepentant, insisting that their decision

AP Images/Peter Dejong

The Persian Gulf War, Saudi Arabia, January 31, 1991. A U.S. Marine Corps Cobra helicopter flies over Iraqi and coalition ground forces approaching the Saudi-Kuwait border during the battle for Khaf ji. ◀

saved U.S. lives and a weakened Iraq could have been captured by neighboring Iran. In the aftermath of the war, Osama Bin Laden fled to Sudan, vowing to exact revenge on the United States for defiling sacred Muslim land.

The Persian Gulf conflict left at least 20,000 Iraqi troops and 2,300 civilians dead and much of Iraq in ruins. Despite predictions of high casualties, only 303 U.S. soldiers died. But approximately 250,000 of the 697,000 Gulf War veterans later developed **Gulf War Syndrome**, a chronic medical condition linked to exposure to toxic nerve agents such as sarin gas. Coalition partners provided more than $35 billion to reimburse the United States for its costs in the war.

Gulf War Syndrome Medical condition found among veterans of 1991 Gulf War. Symptoms include chronic fatigue, migraine, and respiratory problems. Possible origins in anthrax vaccines or chemical exposure.

Map 27.2 Gulf War This map shows the progression of major Allied military operations during the Gulf War as well as the location of Allied military forces and Iraqi missile targets. The path of Kurds seeking refuge from the conflict is also shown. ▼

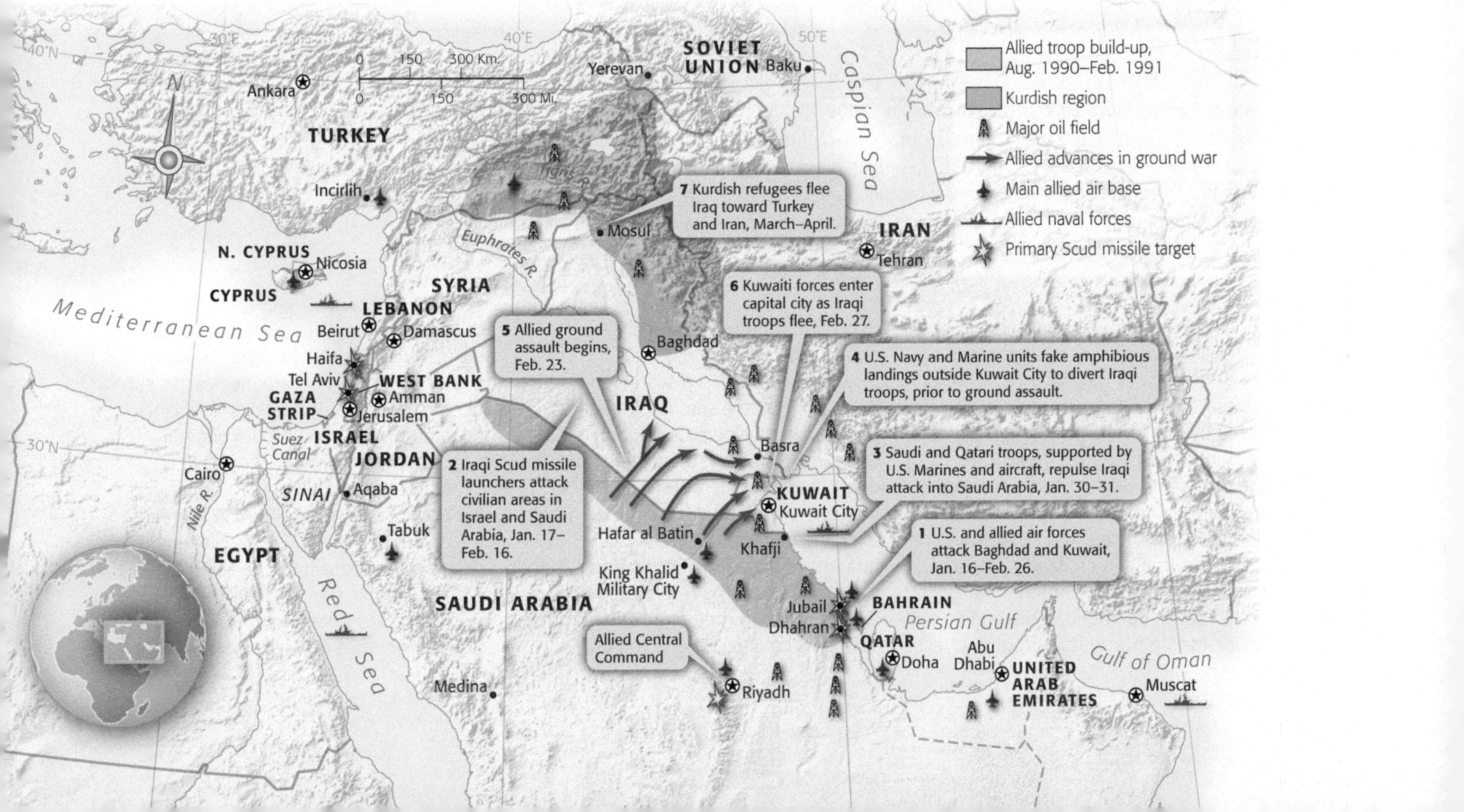

History without Borders

HIV/AIDS

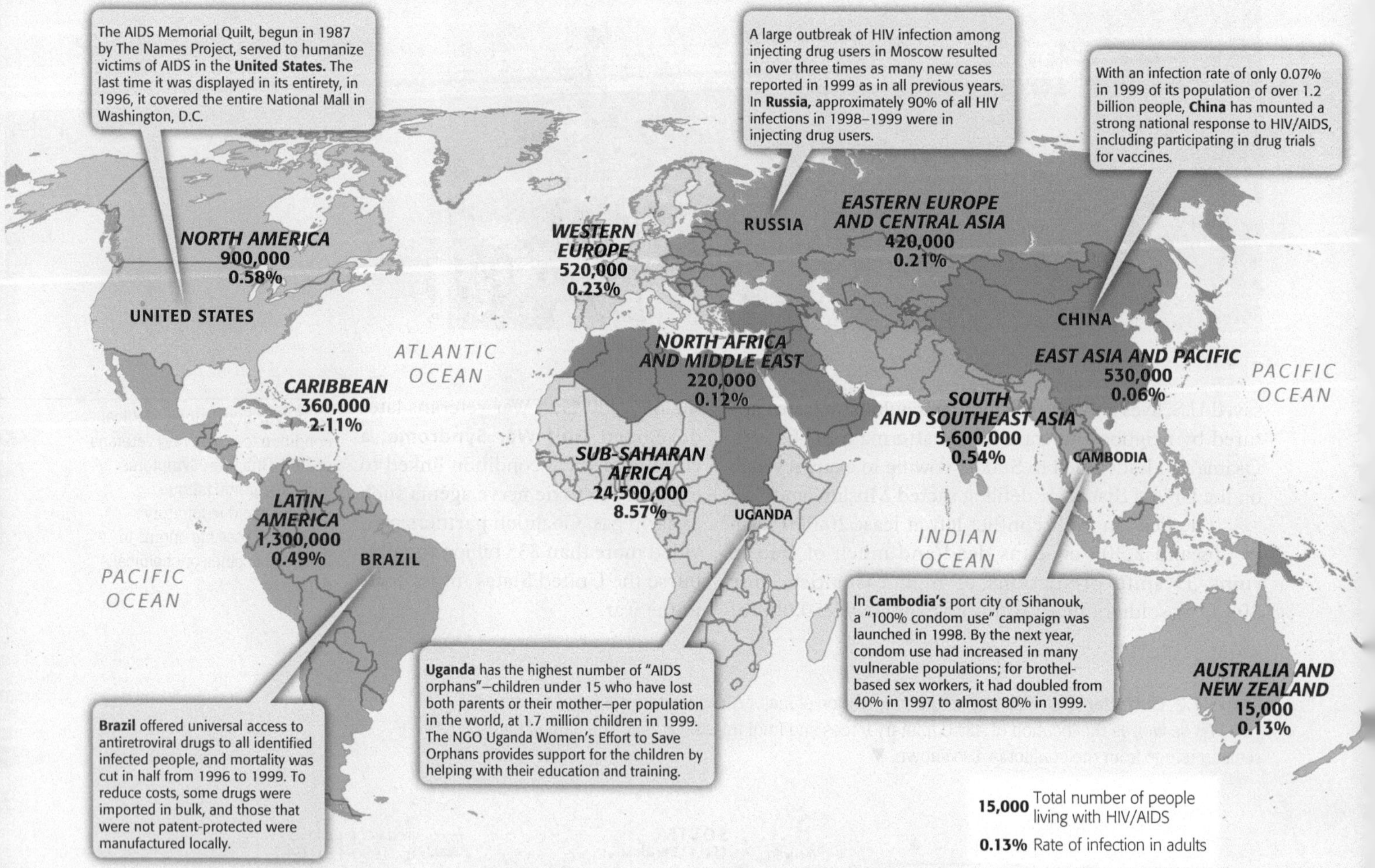

The AIDS Memorial Quilt, begun in 1987 by The Names Project, served to humanize victims of AIDS in the United States. The last time it was displayed in its entirety, in 1996, it covered the entire National Mall in Washington, D.C.
A large outbreak of HIV infection among injecting drug users in Moscow resulted in over three times as many new cases reported in 1999 as in all previous years. In Russia, approximately 90% of all HIV infections in 1998–1999 were in injecting drug users.
With an infection rate of only 0.07% in 1999 of its population of over 1.2 billion people, China has mounted a strong national response to HIV/AIDS, including participating in drug trials for vaccines.
NORTH AMERICA 900,000 0.58%
UNITED STATES
WESTERN EUROPE 520,000 0.23%
RUSSIA
EASTERN EUROPE AND CENTRAL ASIA 420,000 0.21%
CHINA
ATLANTIC OCEAN
NORTH AFRICA AND MIDDLE EAST 220,000 0.12%
EAST ASIA AND PACIFIC 530,000 0.06%
PACIFIC OCEAN
CARIBBEAN 360,000 2.11%
SOUTH AND SOUTHEAST ASIA 5,600,000 0.54%
CAMBODIA
SUB-SAHARAN AFRICA 24,500,000 8.57%
UGANDA
LATIN AMERICA 1,300,000 0.49%
BRAZIL
INDIAN OCEAN
PACIFIC OCEAN
In Cambodia's port city of Sihanouk, a "100% condom use" campaign was launched in 1998. By the next year, condom use had increased in many vulnerable populations; for brothel-based sex workers, it had doubled from 40% in 1997 to almost 80% in 1999.
AUSTRALIA AND NEW ZEALAND 15,000 0.13%
Uganda has the highest number of "AIDS orphans"—children under 15 who have lost both parents or their mother—per population in the world, at 1.7 million children in 1999. The NGO Uganda Women's Effort to Save Orphans provides support for the children by helping with their education and training.
Brazil offered universal access to antiretroviral drugs to all identified infected people, and mortality was cut in half from 1996 to 1999. To reduce costs, some drugs were imported in bulk, and those that were not patent-protected were manufactured locally.
15,000 Total number of people living with HIV/AIDS
0.13% Rate of infection in adults

People Living with HIV/AIDS Worldwide, 2000 By 2000, 18.8 million people around the world had died from AIDS-related complications. Nearly twice that many—34.3 million—were living with HIV, the virus that causes AIDS. A few sub-Saharan African nations successfully stabilized their HIV infection rates, but most did not. Efforts to control the global AIDS epidemic were complicated by the difficulty of persuading people to modify risky personal behaviors and the economic and logistical obstacles to providing antiretroviral drugs. ▲

Human immunodeficiency virus infection/acquired immunodeficiency syndrome (HIV/AIDS) is a disease of the immune system triggered by infection with the human immunodeficiency virus (HIV). While the disease itself is not fatal, it makes people much more susceptible to certain types of cancers and opportunistic infections that can be deadly. HIV is transmitted primarily through unprotected sex or contaminated syringes, but it can also be transmitted from mother to child in pregnancy, delivery, and by breastfeeding.

Although experts disagree on the origins of HIV, the spread of the virus unquestionably increased with globalization. Some medical researchers think the disease originated in central Africa in the early twentieth century when a virus affecting wild chimpanzees passed to humans engaged in hunting and eating these creatures. The researchers believe that the virus mutated into HIV and then spread as colonialism and the growth of large African cities increased sexual promiscuity and prostitution. Another theory posits that unsafe medical practices used in post-World War II vaccination campaigns exposed the general population to HIV.

Although isolated cases of what was later confirmed to be HIV/AIDS appeared as early as 1959, it did not reach epidemic proportions until the 1980s. In early 1981, the Centers for Disease Control (CDC) noted an unusually high number of cases of Pneumocystis carinii

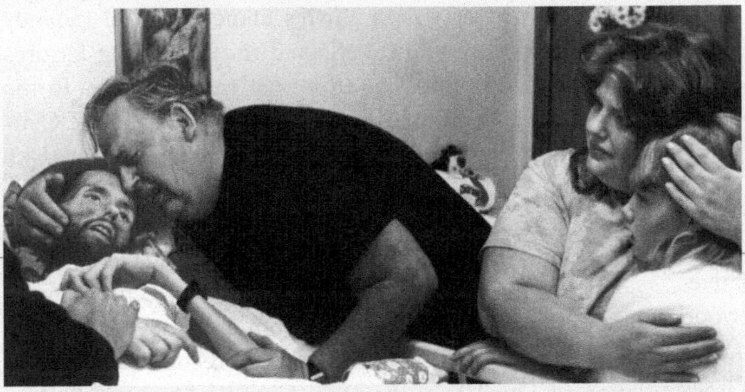

The Advertising Archives/Alamy Stock Photo

David Kirby, AIDS Patient, 1990 In May 1990, graduate student and hospice volunteer Therese Frare took a black and white photograph of David Kirby surrounded by his family shortly before he died of AIDS-related complications at age thirty-two. In November 1990, *Life* magazine published the image, and it later appeared in hundreds of newspapers, magazines, and televised stories around the world. In 1992, with the permission of Kirby's family, the clothier Benetton launched a controversial advertising campaign using a colorized version of the photo to generate awareness of the disease. ◄

Malcolm Linton/Liaison/Getty Images

Billboard for HIV/AIDS Educational Campaign, Kampala, Uganda, February 1, 1997 At a time when many African leaders refused to speak publicly about HIV/AIDS, Ugandan president Yoweri Museveni earned worldwide acclaim for his response to the disease. Shortly after taking office in 1986, he launched a three-pronged AIDS prevention campaign calling for abstinence from premarital sexual activity, monogamy within marriage, and condom use as a last resort (shorthanded as "ABC"). HIV infection rates dropped from about 15 percent in 1991 to approximately 6 percent in 2007. ◄

pneumonia (PCP) and Kaposi's sarcoma (KS) among gay men in New York and Los Angeles. Doctors also reported cases among heterosexual drug users, hemophiliacs, and Haitian refugees. At the same time, African physicians noted striking medical parallels between the U.S. cases and nondrug-using, heterosexual patients in Zaire. Despite the obviously diverse group of people contracting the strange ailments, the CDC called the disease *gay-related immune disorder* (GRID) until August 1982 when the agency quietly adopted the new name AIDS—Acquired Immune Deficiency Syndrome. Throughout this period, scientific and health communities worked with no knowledge of the disease's origins or means of transmission. They had no idea how many people were infected. They only knew the disease was lethal.

By 1983, with more than one thousand cases in the United States alone, it was no longer possible to ignore the possible worldwide impact of AIDS. Much of the international scientific community refused to accept claims that HIV could be contracted heterosexually even as the World Health Organization estimated that approximately six hundred twenty thousand Africans had been infected between 1980 and 1997, and a total social breakdown consumed sub-Saharan Africa.

The politics of the Reagan administration exacerbated this already grave situation. Because the disease initially struck marginalized populations like gay men and drug users, officials were reluctant to provide research funding or public information. Erroneous reports that AIDS could be spread through casual contact generated widespread panic. In 1984, French and U.S. doctors identified HIV, the virus that causes AIDS and is passed through blood, saliva, and semen. But the discovery did little to mitigate the stigma and discrimination people with HIV and AIDS faced.

Enraged by the government's indifference to the devastating impact of AIDS on their community, gay men and lesbians began raising public awareness about the disease and providing services for people with AIDS. In 1987, the playwright Larry Kramer and others founded AIDS Coalition to Unleash Power (ACT UP), a direct action group whose confrontational tactics and motto ("Silence = Death") inspired the opening of chapters around the world.

Advocacy and education helped foster greater compassion toward people living with HIV/AIDS, but the disease reached pandemic proportions as it spread quickly and globally. In 1995, the introduction of antiretroviral therapy was a major medical breakthrough that enabled people to live with HIV/AIDS for years. But the expense and complexity of the treatment made it inaccessible to many in the developing world. In December 2000, UNAIDS estimated that 36.1 million people were living with HIV/AIDS worldwide and that approximately 21.8 million people had died of AIDS since the epidemic began.

Critical Thinking Questions

▶ Why do you think this photograph of David Kirby had such a powerful effect on people's attitudes toward those with HIV/AIDS? Why was the use of the image in an advertising campaign so provocative?

▶ What were some of the factors that made combatting HIV/AIDS particularly difficult in the early stages of the epidemic? Why does globalization both complicate and help the world community's ability to respond to public health emergencies?

Go to MindTap® to engage with an interactive version of **History without Borders: HIV/AIDS.** Learn from an interactive map, view related video, and respond to critical thinking questions.

27-1d Domestic Struggles

Bush addresses difficult economic problems while trying to advance a multifaceted domestic policy agenda.

Although Bush's approval ratings reached 90 percent in the days following the Gulf War, a troubled economy soon diminished his popularity. On accepting the Republican presidential nomination in 1988, Bush—eager to win backing from conservatives wary of his moderate views—invoked a Clint Eastwood movie and declared: "The Congress will push me to raise taxes, and I'll say no . . . and they'll push again, and I'll say to them, 'Read my lips, no new taxes.'" The pledge came back to haunt Bush when he began focusing on serious economic problems created in the Reagan years. These issues included a crisis spawned by deregulation of savings and loan institutions and a federal budget deficit that had tripled to $220 billion since 1980.

Aware of the possible political consequences, Bush supported what became a $500 billion federal bailout of the savings and loan industry and worked with the Democrat-controlled Congress on a budget deal that would have combined tax increases and spending cuts to slash the deficit by one-half trillion dollars over a six-year period. When his Republican colleagues balked at his violation of his no-tax pledge and killed the deal, Bush was forced to accept a Democratic counterproposal that included even higher taxes and spending *increases*. The deficit rose to $269 billion in 1991 and to $290 billion the following year. Bush never regained the trust of conservative Republicans, but supporters praised his courage in adopting policies that saved Reagan's political legacy and set the stage for booming economic growth for much of the 1990s.

While fending off criticisms from the right wing of his party, Bush increased federal spending on education, highway improvements, and technological research. He signed the Radiation Exposure Compensation Act providing monetary assistance to those suffering health problems resulting from exposure to irradiated materials during nuclear tests or uranium mining. In 1990, Bush signed the **Americans with Disabilities Act (ADA),** a landmark bill that expanded accessibility requirements and civil rights protections for disabled persons and those debilitated by HIV/AIDS. It culminated decades of work by people with disabilities and their allies who had challenged discrimination in employment, housing, education, transportation, and public spaces. Responding to the environmental damage caused when the tanker *Exxon Valdez* ran aground and spilled millions of gallons of oil on the Alaskan coast, warnings about climate change, and increased rates of air pollution, Bush backed the Federal Clean Air Act, a law originally passed in 1970, but was allowed to lapse under the Reagan administration.

Americans with Disabilities Act (ADA) 1990 federal civil rights law outlawing discrimination in employment, transportation, public spaces, and housing.

Hill–Thomas hearings October 1991 hearings before the Senate Judiciary Committee in which law professor Anita Hill accused Supreme Court justice nominee Clarence Thomas of sexual harassment.

A controversy over Bush's choice to fill a vacancy on the Supreme Court reflected the deepening fissures in American political culture over race and sex. In the fall of 1991, Bush nominated federal appeals judge Clarence Thomas to succeed Thurgood Marshall on the U.S. Supreme Court. Thomas's confirmation seemed assured until Anita Hill, a University of Oklahoma law professor who had worked with Thomas at the U.S. Department of Education and the Equal Employment Opportunity Commission (EEOC), accused him of sexual harassment. Because sexual harassment had been recognized as a violation of Title VII of the 1964 Civil Rights Act following a ruling in *Meritor Savings Bank v. Vinson* (1986), Hill's allegations enraged civil rights and feminist groups who were already lobbying against Thomas's confirmation because of his opposition to affirmative action. In three days of televised testimony, Hill, Thomas, and several witnesses addressed Hill's claims. Members of the all-white male Judiciary Committee grilled Hill, an African American woman, while Thomas, an African American man, denounced the proceedings as "a high-tech lynching." The hearings became a lightning rod for national attitudes about racism and sexism. On October 15, the Senate confirmed Thomas with a 52-48 vote. In the aftermath of the **Hill–Thomas hearings,** employers across the nation implemented antiharassment codes and diversity training. Hill's harsh treatment by the all-male Judiciary Committee inspired dozens of women to run for public office, and a record twenty-nine women were elected to Congress in 1992.

Earlier that year, Bush's reelection seemed assured. His approval ratings remained high. Interest and inflation rates were low. But by mid-year, the outsourcing of jobs overseas, the savings and loan bailout, the Gulf War, and rising health care costs contributed to a recession. Retail and housing sales nose-dived, and unemployment reached 7.4 percent. States cut social welfare spending in response to budget shortfalls.

When Bush refused to extend unemployment benefits for fear of increasing the budget deficit, many voters found him out of touch with their financial realities. While fellow Republican and conservative pundit Pat Buchanan attacked Bush for raising taxes, Democratic nominee Bill Clinton, the five-term governor of Arkansas, adopted the informal slogan "It's the economy, stupid" and put forth a program of economic growth and job creation that attracted some voters even as revelations of his draft evasion, marijuana use, and adultery repelled others.

The late entry of H. Ross Perot added drama to the race. A billionaire businessman with no previous political experience, Perot spoke directly to potential voters and announced on CNN's *Larry King Show* that he would run for president if supporters got him added to the ballot in all fifty states. Rejecting the tactics and fund-raising of both mainstream parties, Perot ran as an independent and self-financed 90 percent of his campaign. Instead of the usual political ads, he bought thirty-minute blocs of television time and used charts, an easel, and a pointer to illustrate his protectionist and isolationist views. His ideas and unconventional style resonated with voters frustrated with mainstream politics and the sputtering economy. Although many polls showed him leading Bush and Clinton, Perot unexpectedly dropped out of the race in July, only to re-enter it in October.

The following month, Clinton won with 43 percent of the popular vote to Bush's 38 percent. Perot won 19 percent of the vote, the highest showing by a third-party candidate since Teddy Roosevelt ran as a Progressive in 1912 (see Map 27.3). Clinton's victory also helped the Democrats regain control of both houses of Congress for the first time since Jimmy Carter was in the White House. Like the previous three presidential races, the 1992 elections reflected a gender gap in which a higher percentage of women than men preferred the Democratic candidate, a political trend that continues to the present day (see Table 27.1).

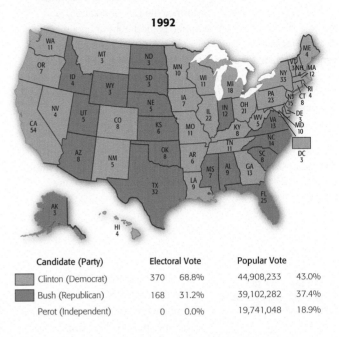

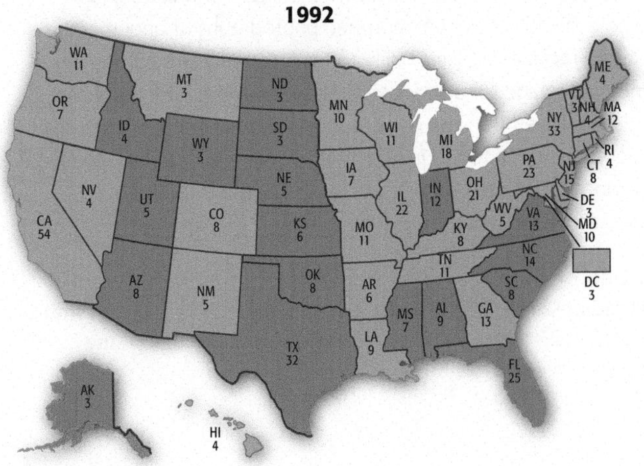

Map 27.3 Election of 1992 Ross Perot's unexpectedly strong third-party run, a stream of damaging revelations about Bill Clinton, and an electorate frustrated by an economic recession made the 1992 presidential race especially unpredictable. Although commentators such as Rush Limbaugh allege that Ross Perot cost George H.W. Bush a second term, political experts refute those claims, pointing to data showing that Perot drew voters away from both Bush and Clinton and that Bush lagged behind Clinton throughout the entire race. ▶

Candidate (Party)	Electoral Vote		Popular Vote	
Clinton (Democrat)	370	68.8%	44,908,233	43.0%
Bush (Republican)	168	31.2%	39,102,282	37.4%
Perot (Independent)	0	0.0%	19,741,048	18.9%

Table 27.1 Gender Gap and Presidential Elections, 1980–2012

Since the 1980 presidential race, political experts have noted differences in the political views and voting choices of women and men. In general, women tend to support a more activist government, federal social welfare programs such as Medicaid, and gun control—a trend that has favored Democratic candidates.

Year	Presidential Candidates	Women Voters (percentage)	Men Voters (percentage)	Gender Gap (percentage points)	Information Source
2012	Barack Obama (D)	55%	45%	10	Edison Research
	Mitt Romney (R)	44%	52%		
2008	Barack Obama (D)	56%	49%	7	Edison Media Research and Mitofsky International
	John McCain (R)	43%	48%		
2004	George W. Bush (R)	48%	55%	7	Edison Media Research and Mitofsky International
	John Kerry (D)	51%	41%		
2000	George W. Bush (R)	43%	53%	10	Voter News Service
	Al Gore (D)	54%	42%		
	Ralph Nader (Green)	2%	3%		
1996	Bill Clinton (D)	54%	43%	11	Voter News Service
	Bob Dole (R)	38%	44%		
	Ross Perot (Reform)	7%	10%		
1992	Bill Clinton (D)	45%	41%	4	Voter News Service
	George H.W. Bush (R)	37%	38%		
	Ross Perot (Reform)	17%	21%		
1988	George H.W. Bush (R)	50%	57%	7	CBS News/*New York Times*
	Michael Dukakis (D)	49%	41%		
1984	Ronald Reagan (R)	56%	62%	6	CBS News/*New York Times*
	Walter Mondale (D)	44%	37%		
1980	Ronald Reagan (R)	46%	54%	8	CBS News/*New York Times*
	Jimmy Carter (D)	45%	37%		
	John Anderson (I)	7%	7%		

Source: Center for the American Woman and Politics, Fact Sheet on The Gender Gap: Voting Choices in Presidential Elections, http://www.cawp.rutgers.edu/sites/default/files/resources/ggpresvote.pdf.

27-2
A Changing Population

Since the mid-1970s, changes in immigration trends, birth rates, and life expectancy have transformed the U.S. population. In November 1993, Ted Thai morphed photographs of people of different racial and ethnic backgrounds to create this computer-generated image for a special issue of *Time Magazine*. Some readers believed that the photo echoed demeaning presentations of people of color found in late nineteenth-century publications and world's fairs, but others saw it as a beautiful reflection of American multiculturalism.

How does this image reflect some of the ways that U.S. society has changed over the last few decades? Why do you think that readers had such diverging responses to this image of "the new face of America"? ▶

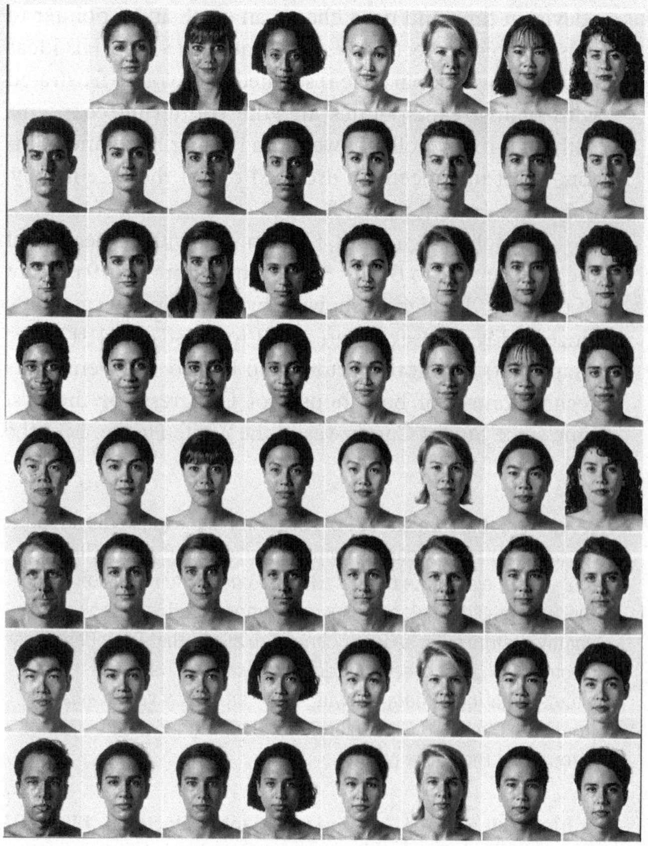

The LIFE Picture Collection/Getty Images

multiculturalism Coexistence of differing races, ethnicities, cultures, and religion in a single society.

English-only laws Statutes mandating the use of the English language in government documents and interactions with public officials.

In the late twentieth century, the United States became a larger, older, and more racially and ethnically diverse nation. The Immigration Act of 1965 had ended the discriminatory national origin quota system by raising the annual quota of immigrants legally permitted to enter the United States and admitting those from Africa, the Middle East, and Asia in equal proportion to those from Europe. Medical advances enabled people to live longer, and the nation's median age began to rise. A wave of births beginning in the early 1980s produced the nation's second-largest generation ever. Many nations experienced similar trends, and concerns about the economic and environmental implications of the globe's burgeoning population fueled international population control efforts.

☞ As you read, closely note changing demographics of the United States. What factors increased the diversification of the nation's population?

27-2a Debating Multiculturalism

> The first large wave of immigrants since the early twentieth century transforms U.S. society.

In the late twentieth century, the United States became more diverse as immigration surged and the number of nonwhite Americans increased. Although rates of immigration had declined during the economic downturn of the 1970s, more than 7 million immigrants arrived in the 1980s and another 9 million came in the 1990s. Between 1970 and 1990, the percentage of whites in the U.S. population dropped from 87.6 percent to 83.9 percent. By 2000, 31.1 million Americans—11.1 percent of the total U.S. population of 281.4 million—were foreign born.

These trends ignited debates over **multiculturalism.** For reasons that varied from nation to nation, Canada, Australia, and several European countries made the recognition of cultural and racial diversity an official government policy. For example, Canada adopted the Canadian Multiculturalism Act (1988) to ensure mutual respect among the nation's different ethnic, religious, and linguistic subgroups. The United States—a multicultural society from its inception—did not adopt similar laws. But racial minorities successfully pushed for the inclusion of nonwhite and non-European perspectives in school curricula and programming. In the 1980s, critics attacked these initiatives as "political correctness" and claimed that multicultural education would erode America's cohesive civic identity. Several states passed **English-only laws** requiring the use of the English language in all government operations and publications.

These tensions coexisted with a shortage of skilled U.S. workers that prompted Congress to pass the Immigration Act of 1990 (see Table 27.2). The law increased annual caps on immigrants and simplified requirements for proving English competency and establishing permanent residency. It provided legal sanctuary for those fleeing violence and war and expanded the number of H1B visas available to skilled workers seeking permanent residence in the United States from fifty thousand to one hundred forty thousand per year. To obtain such visas, U.S. employers

Keith Birmingham/ZUMA Press/Newscom

Global American In December 1978, **David Tran**, a former major in the South Vietnamese army, joined more than thirty-three hundred refugees fleeing Vietnam on a Taiwanese freighter. One of thousands of boat people displaced by the Vietnam War, he eventually came to Los Angeles. To support himself, he began making Sriracha, a hot sauce blended from serrano peppers (later switched to red jalapeños), vinegar, garlic, and salt. Naming his business Huy Fong Foods after the ship that took him out of Southeast Asia, he packaged his Sriracha in green-topped clear plastic bottles marked with a rooster, the Vietnamese zodiac sign for the year of his birth, 1945. Text in five languages (Vietnamese, English, Chinese, French, and Spanish) identifies the sauce's contents. By 1987, sales were so good that the company moved to a 68,000 square-foot facility in Rosemead, California.

Although the company has never advertised its products, Sriracha has become a culinary phenomenon. After *Bon Appétit* magazine chose Sriracha as its Ingredient of the Year for 2010, the company sold 20 million bottles. By 2012, annual sales were more than $60 million. The subject of documentaries, festivals, and cookbooks, Sriracha is now found in hamburgers, potato chips, popcorn, candy, ice cream, vodka, and beer. Tran trademarked his distinctive rooster logo and bottle but not his hot sauce. He insists he does not mind that it has inspired countless imitators, and he does not charge royalty fees for those who legitimately license products using Sriracha. He has not only succeeded in his adopted country but also added to its diet.

had to attest that no Americans with comparable skills were available to fill specific positions. The Immigration Act helped professionals including doctors, scientists, educators, and athletes move to the United States permanently. But as non-English speaking, nonskilled workers exploited loopholes in the law, controversies over border control and deportation continued.

Debates about undocumented immigrants often obscured the fact that the majority of immigrants came to the United States legally. During the 1980s, the rate of Asian immigrants from China, South Korea, Vietnam, the Philippines, and India rose dramatically. Sometimes called "model minorities," many Asian Americans excelled academically and economically. They completed high school and college and earned professional degrees in the highest percentages of any minority, and their national income was 20 percent above the national average in 2004. Yet many Southeast Asian refugees (especially rural groups

Table 27.2 Major U.S. Immigration Laws, 1965–1990

Year	Legislation	Description
1965	Immigration and Nationality Act (Hart-Cellar Act)	Abolishes national origin quota system and replaces it with a system admitted immigrants based on relationships with a U.S. citizen, employer, or legal resident. Sets annual caps on total number of immigrants permitted with the exception of "immediate relatives" (spouses, parents, or minor children).
1975	Indochina Migration and Refugee Assistance Act	Expands the legal category of *refugee* to include those fleeing violence and persecution in Cambodia and Vietnam.
1980	Refugee Act	Creates a new system for processing and admitting refugees and asylum seekers. Legally defines *a refugee* as someone unable or unwilling to return to his or her country of origin because of maltreatment or possible persecution on the basis of race, religion, social group, or political opinion.
1986	Immigration Reform and Control Act (IRCA)	Increases number of border patrol agents by 50 percent. Penalizes employers who knowingly hire or recruit undocumented workers. Provides a path to legal citizenship for unauthorized immigrants who entered the United States prior to 1982. Allows unauthorized immigrants in certain agricultural jobs to apply for permanent resident status.
1988	Anti-Drug Abuse Act (ADAA)	Allows the deportation of resident aliens found guilty of murder or trafficking drugs or weapons.
1990	Immigration Act	Increases number of legal immigrants permitted by 50 percent, loosens regulations on temporary foreign workers, and expands grounds for deportation for immigrants committing aggravated felonies.

Source: Migration Policy Institute, Fact Sheet, http://www.migrationpolicy.org/research/timeline-1790.

deindustrialization Economic and social changes resulting from the removal or decline of well-paying factory jobs.

Los Angeles riots. Three days of destruction, looting, and arson following the April 1992 acquittal of four white police officers in a highly publicized police brutality case.

al-Qaeda Founded by Osama bin Laden in 1998, militantly anti-Western radical Sunni Muslim organization responsible for numerous terrorist incidents around the world.

such as the Hmong) struggled with poverty, welfare dependency, cultural alienation, and the persistent effects of war trauma. Some youth joined urban street gangs and became embroiled in the competition and violence of the drug trade.

At the same time, socioeconomic stratification divided the African American community. The number of black women graduating from college steadily increased throughout the 1980s while the number of men declined. The number of black-owned businesses rose, and African Americans broke into the ranks of corporate executives as celebrities like singer Michael Jackson and talk show host Oprah Winfrey amassed fortunes worth hundreds of millions of dollars. But the black community was also hit hard by changes in the U.S. economy.

The continuing crisis in America's central cities, descending back to the Watts Riots in 1965, decimated black working-class communities, and now included a large and fast-growing population of Latinos. **Deindustrialization** resulted in the loss of millions of well-paying industrial and manufacturing jobs in urban areas with high black populations. Faced with declining tax revenue, many cities reduced spending on education and public services at the same time that the Reagan administration cut budgets for federal job training and urban development programs. In some inner-city neighborhoods, African American unemployment rates exceeded 40 percent and poverty, addiction, and violence tore formerly tight-knit communities apart. Arrest rates soared as police cracked down on drug trafficking. By 2000, half of the nation's 2 million prisoners were African American, and one-third of all black men in their twenties were incarcerated, on parole or probation, or awaiting criminal sentencing.

Such harsh realities inspired a subgenre of hip-hop music called *gangsta rap*. Emerging in Los Angeles, gangsta rap lyrics were often violent, misogynistic, and profane, but also vividly reflected inner-city life. N.W.A.'s "F— tha Police" (1988) and "Cop Killer" (1990), penned by Body Count lead vocalist Ice-T, offered scathing critiques of police brutality—a phenomenon that gripped the world's attention after four white Los Angeles police officers arrested Rodney King, an African American man, for reckless driving on March 3, 1991. Pulling King from his vehicle, the officers forced him to the ground and beat him fifty-six times with their batons. A bystander filmed the episode on a video camera and released the footage to the media (a rare occurrence in an age before smart phones), sparking outrage in the black and Latino communities of Los Angeles over long-standing patterns of excessive force and racial profiling by local law enforcement.

In April 1992, after the four police officers were acquitted, racial tensions exploded during the **Los Angeles riots.** Unleashing rage at deepening economic disparities and a criminal justice system perceived to be biased, African Americans and Latinos destroyed property and looted stores, most owned by whites and Asian Americans. The three-day disturbance left fifty-five people dead and $1 billion in property damage. Law enforcement advocates and politicians suggested that gangsta rap encouraged urban violence but proved less able to redress inner city economic and racial inequalities.

Terrorism highlighted other divisions in American society. In February 1993, after Islamic radicals linked to **al-Qaeda** bombed the World Trade Center in New York City, killing six people and wounding more than one thousand, many U.S. citizens' suspicions of Arab Americans and Islam intensified, complicating some Arab Americans' pursuit of a better life in the United States.

AP Images/JOHN GAPS III

Armed Volunteers at a Korean American–Owned Market, Los Angeles, May 1992 In South Central Los Angeles, Korean Americans call the May Los Angeles riots "Sa-I-Gu" (Korean for "four-two-nine," the date the unrest began). During the disturbance, more than twenty-two hundred Korean American-owned stores were burned or looted by largely African American and Latino rioters, resulting in more than $400 million in damage. Korean immigrants, many of them armed, tried to protect Koreatown, their ethnic enclave. Since the riots, the Korean American community in Los Angeles has become more visible and politically powerful. ▶

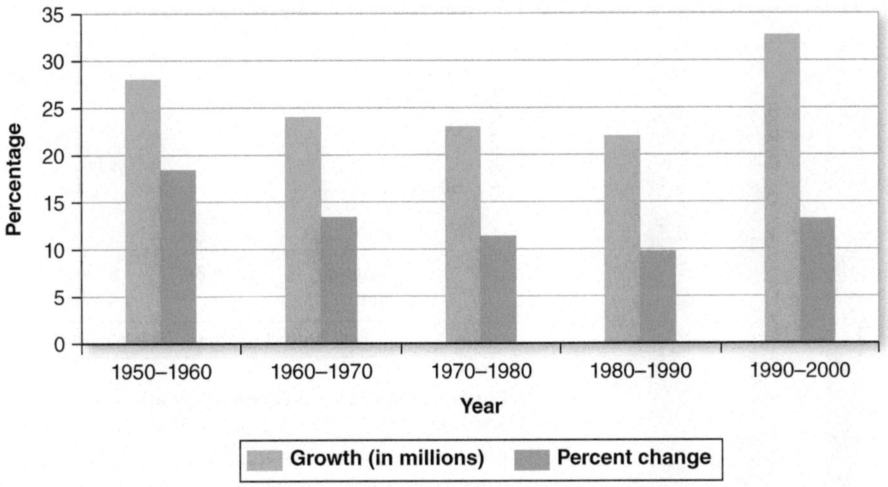

Figure 27.1 U.S. Population Growth, 1950–2000 Fueled by the birth of the so-called Millennial generation, the U.S. population increased 13.2 percent between 1990 to 2000, from 248.7 million to 281.4 million—the largest census increase in U.S. history. Thanks to the post-1965 wave of immigration, the Millennials were more ethnically diverse than the Baby Boomers. Nearly 20 percent were of Hispanic origin, almost double the proportion among the Boomers. Source: U.S. Census Bureau, *Census 2000 Brief*, https://www.census.gov/prod/2001pubs/c2kbr01-2.pdf. ◀

27-2b Demographic Trends

During the twentieth century, the U.S. population changed dramatically. From 1900 to 2000, it almost quadrupled, increasing from 76 million in 1900 to 200 million in 1968 to 281.4 million in 2000 (see Figure 27.1). The population concentrated in urban areas and by 1990, 78 percent of Americans lived in cities. As the shift westward and southward continued, California and Texas became the two most populous U.S. states. From 1982 to 2003, 80 million so-called Millennials were born, making them a generation as proportionally large as the Baby Boomers.

The U.S. population grows as the birth rate spikes and people live longer.

Fueled by post-1965 immigration trends and the Millennial generation, the United States was becoming more racially diverse. In 2000, whites composed 69.1 percent of total U.S. population, but rising numbers of Asian and Latino Americans signaled that nonwhites would become the majority as early as 2043 (see Figure 27.2). More Americans also began to identify as multiracial. In 1997, after becoming the youngest and first person of color to win the prestigious Masters golf tournament, Tiger Woods—who is half-Asian (Thai, Chinese), one-quarter African American, one-eighth Native American, and one-eighth Dutch—described himself as "Cablinasian" as a way of honoring all the elements of his racial and cultural heritage. To acknowledge Americans with such complex identities, Congress passed the "Tiger Woods bill" adding a multiracial option on the U.S. census effective in the year 2000.

At the same time, medical advances increased the percentage of the U.S. population over age sixty-five. In the first half of the twentieth century, immigration, relatively high fertility rates, and declining infant mortality gave the

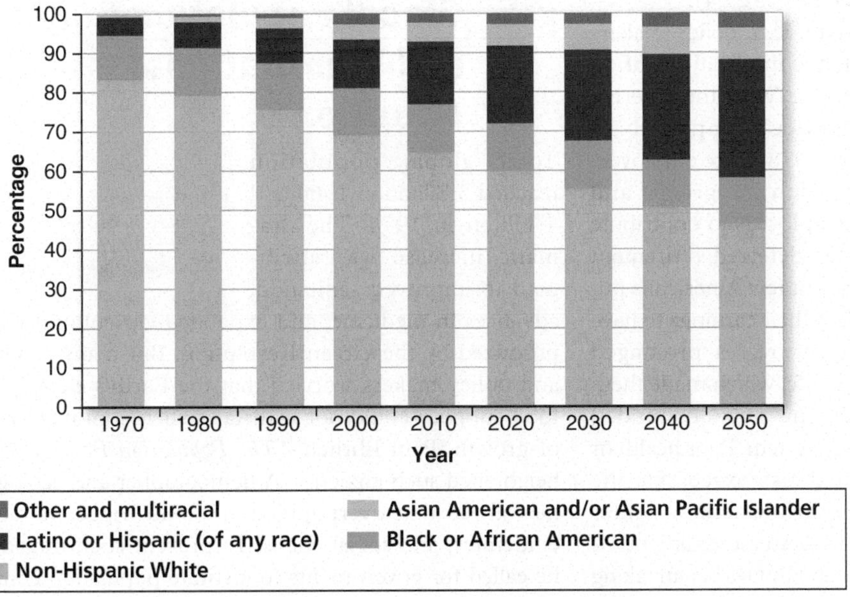

Figure 27.2 Racial and Ethnic Composition of the United States, 1970–2050 Racial and ethnic demographics of the United States have changed a great deal since 1970 and are projected to shift dramatically by 2050. Because the U.S. Census Bureau has used different racial categories over time, some changes are difficult to trace. In 2000, for example, the categories "Native Hawaiian or Other Pacific Islander" and "Two or More Races" were used for the first time, enabling people to self-identify differently than they might have previously. Sources: Data for 1970 and 1980 from Statistical Abstract of the United States. Data for 1990, 2000, and 2010 from the U.S. Census Bureau. Data for 2020 through 2050 from the U.S. Census Bureau Population Projections by Race and Ethnicity (2008). ◀

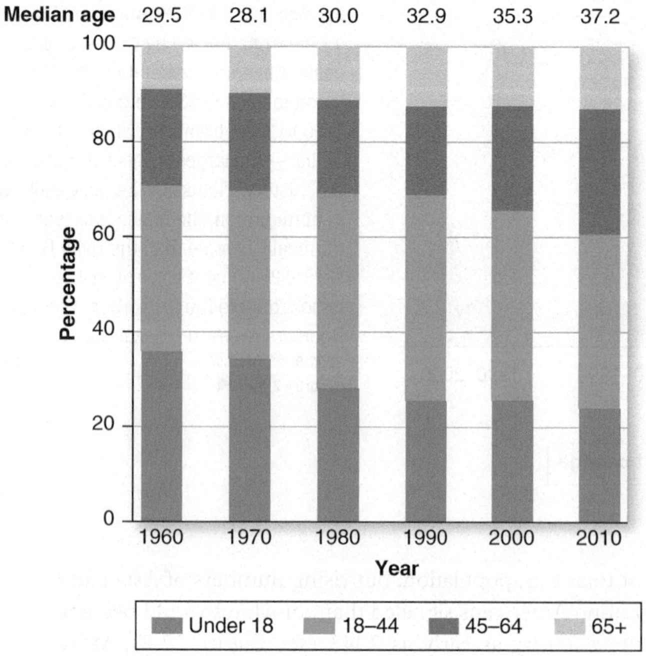

Figure 27.3 U.S. Age Distribution and Median Age, 1960–2010 Thanks to improvements in medical care and pharmaceuticals, Americans are living longer than in previous times. With longer average survival rates than men, women over age eighty composed 4.3 percent of the total U.S. population in 2000 compared to only 2.2 percent of men. Some experts predict that by 2050, people over age eighty will be the nation's largest age group. Source: United States Census Bureau, "Age and Sex Composition: *2010," 2010 Census Briefs*, http://www.census.gov/prod/cen2010/briefs/c2010br-03.pdf. ▲

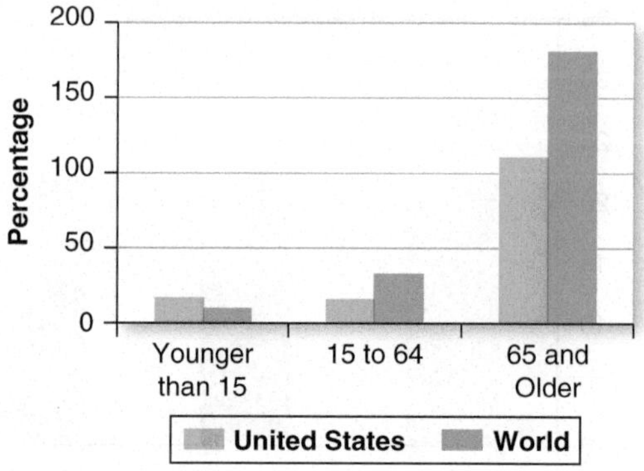

Figure 27.4 U.S. and Global Population by Age, 2010–2050 Demographers predict that the number of people over age sixty-five worldwide will triple by 2050, a trend particularly strong in developed nations like the United States, Japan, South Korea, and Germany. Younger workers in these countries may have to support older family members in addition to their own children. As a consequence of falling birth rates, the global population of people under age fifteen is projected to increase by only 10 percent over the same period. Source: United Nations, Department of Economic and Social Affairs, World Population Prospects: 2012 Revision, June 2013, http://esa.un.org/unpd/wpp/index/htm. ▲

United States an overall young population. But as Americans lived longer, the median age rose from 29.5 in 1960 to 35.3 in 2000 (see Figure 27.3). These trends were even more pronounced in Japan, South Korea, and Germany. Demographers predict that the global population of people over sixty-five will reach 1.5 billion in 2050, almost triple the 531 million in 2010 (see Figure 27.4).

Like their counterparts abroad, U.S. policy makers wrestled with the possible economic implications of an aging population. With the Internal Revenue Service's approval of **401(k) plans** in 1978, more employers curtailed pension programs and encouraged employees to contribute to the new tax-deferred retirement savings plans. But few Americans put aside enough of their earnings to have income security over a prolonged postretirement life, which made them rely more on the publicly funded Social Security system. Poor health or disability could also exacerbate the financial precariousness of older Americans' lives. An increasing number of American families began taking care of elderly parents or struggling to absorb often exorbitant costs of placing a parent in a long-term care facility. Hamstrung by a gridlocked political system, politicians proved unwilling to confront the challenge of adjusting Social Security or Medicare to meet the needs of a population with a higher proportion of senior citizens, many of whom lived longer than people in previous generations. Advocacy organizations like the **Gray Panthers** and the **American Association of Retired Persons (AARP)** pushed for public policies that protected senior citizens, and older voters tended to be much more politically engaged than their younger counterparts.

401(k) plans Established by the Internal Revenue Service in 1978, defined contribution pension plan in which an employee applies a portion of salary toward retirement savings.

Gray Panthers Social justice organization founded in 1970 by Maggie Kuhn in response to her forced retirement at age sixty-five.

American Association of Retired Persons (AARP) Founded in 1958, leading U.S. lobbying and educational organization working on behalf of people age fifty and older.

27-2c Global Population Control and Transnational Adoption

Fears that the Earth will not sustain a rapidly growing population prompt international action.

Total global population reached 3 billion in 1960 and 4 billion in 1974. The dramatic increase was attributed to improved sanitation, advances in medicine, and expanded agricultural yields produced by the Green Revolution. But many scholars and policy makers worried that the Earth's energy and food supplies could not withstand such continued rates of growth. Paul Ehrlich's *The Population Bomb* (1968) heightened such anxieties. A demographer and ecologist, he warned that overpopulation would trigger famines, epidemics, and social chaos. To prevent such tragedies, he called for governments to institute population control programs.

Although few of Ehrlich's most dire predictions came to pass, his views influenced population control initiatives in many nations. In 1970, Congress enacted **Title X of the Public Health Service Act,** a measure providing birth control counseling and supplies to people with low incomes. Title X became a vital source of funding for reproductive health clinics across the United States and made contraception accessible for millions of Americans.

But some countries resorted to more coercive methods. In April 1976, India adopted a forced sterilization policy that used propaganda and financial incentives to persuade people to undergo vasectomies or tubal ligations. The program generated an intense backlash against family planning with aftereffects enduring for decades. In 1979, China instituted a policy permitting most Chinese couples to have only one child. Although the **one-child policy** prevented at least 250 million births over the next thirty years, local officials also invasively tracked women's fertility, forcing abortions and compulsory sterilizations on those who failed to comply. Because of the cultural value placed on boys, many families elected to terminate pregnancies if tests indicated that a fetus was female. Girl babies were abandoned and even murdered. Although the government banned prenatal sex screening in 1994, a striking gender imbalance emerged among those under age twenty with boys outnumbering girls by as many as 32 million. Fearful that there would not be enough young people to care for the elderly or to resolve China's labor shortage, government officials abolished the one-child policy in 2015.

International population control efforts met opposition. The Roman Catholic Church protested the promotion of birth control and condemned sterilizations and abortion. At the 1984 United Nations International Conference on Population in Mexico City, Ronald Reagan announced that the U.S. Agency for International Development would not fund non-governmental organizations (NGOs) that promoted or performed abortions "as a method of family planning" anywhere in the world. The **Mexico City policy** became a political football in years to come as Democratic presidents rescinded it and Republican presidents reinstituted it. Critics charged that the policy limited the ability to dispense birth control and accurate medical information. Supporters viewed it as a vital component of the transnational pro-life movement.

Title X of the Public Health Service Act Established in 1970, federal grant program for comprehensive family planning and reproductive health services.

one-child policy Enacted in the late 1970s, official Chinese policy of permitting families to have only one child. Abolished in 2015.

Mexico City policy Intermittent U.S. policy of barring NGOs that perform abortions or provide abortion counseling from receiving federal funds that Republican administrations upheld and Democratic ones repealed.

This era also witnessed an increase in the number of transnational adoptions by which an individual or couple from one nation adopts a child or children from a different country. Between 1982 and 2004, annual international adoptions to the United States nearly quadrupled from 5,749 to 22,991. Most of these children originated from China (overwhelmingly girls abandoned as a result of the one-child policy), Ethiopia, Russia, South Korea, and Guatemala (see Figure 27.5). In 1993, The Hague Adoption Convention (1993) protected children from traffickers and promoted transparency and legal documentation of the adoption process. In 2000, Congress passed the Child Citizenship Act, automatically granting U.S. citizenships to foreign-born children when at least one adoptive parent is a U.S. citizen.

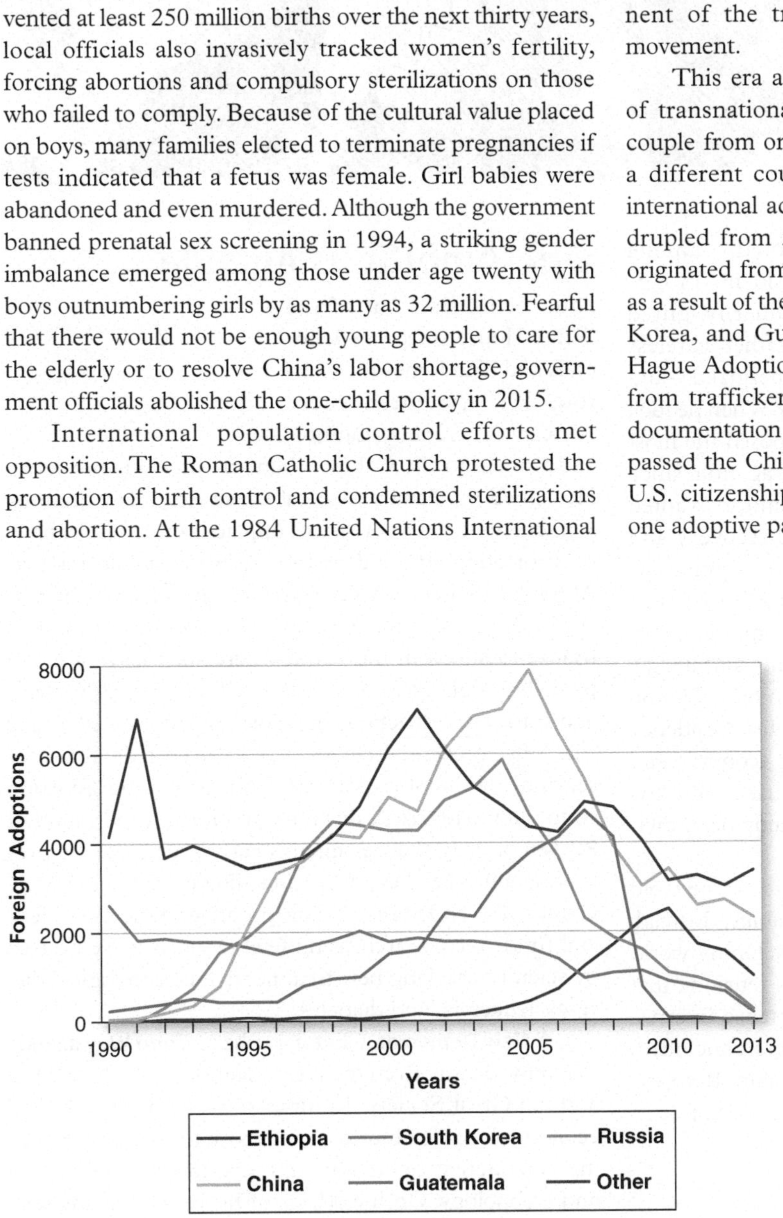

Figure 27.5 International Adoption in the United States by Selected Countries, 1990–2013 After peaking in 2004, the number of foreign-born children adopted by U.S. citizens began to decline. The U.S. government halted adoptions from Cambodia and Guatemala and restricted adoptions from Nepal in response to kidnapping and baby selling. China, once the largest source of transnationally adopted children, instituted strict qualifications for foreign parents seeking to adopt. In 2013, after a U.S. couple returned their adopted Russian child, the Russian government outlawed adoptions to the United States. Source: Johnston's Archive, http://www.johnstonsarchive.net/policy/adoptionstatsintl.html. ◀

27-3

The Clinton Years

Editorial cartoonist Mike Luckovich speculates on how the Clinton presidency might be remembered.

Why is it significant that this cartoon includes Bill Clinton among the presidents etched on Mt. Rushmore? Which of the images of President Clinton, the "statesman" or the "frat boy," do you think will prove the more enduring? Why? ▶

Mike Luckovich/Atlanta Journal-Constitution/Creators Syndicate

Family Medical Leave Act Legislation that permits workers up to twelve weeks of unpaid leave after the birth of a child or to care for a sick family member.

RU-486 Trademark name for mifepristone, a drug that can terminate a pregnancy of less than seven weeks.

New Democrat Centrist faction of the Democratic Party that emerged after Michael Dukakis lost the 1988 presidential race.

Third Way Centrist political philosophy attempting to fuse right-wing economic ideas and left-wing social policies.

Clinton was undoubtedly among the most colorful presidents in U.S. history. An extraordinarily gifted politician though a rather careless individual, Clinton energized—and polarized—the country. When he took office in 1993, he proposed the most ambitious legislative agenda since the Great Society. Clinton wanted to focus on economic recovery and health care reform, but missteps and scandals jeopardized his political goals. Repeatedly outmaneuvering his political rivals and surviving a failed effort to impeach him, Clinton remained popular, and his presidency ended with a booming economy and federal budget surpluses. But the 2000 presidential election revealed continuing deep divisions among Americans.

Contrary to initial predictions, the end of the Cold War did not usher in an age of peace and stability. Instead, it highlighted ongoing struggles in the developing world and exposed bitter ethnic and nationalist tensions that sometimes erupted into violence. Such a tense international landscape, the nation's policy makers concluded, demanded active and engaged U.S. leadership. Both triumph and tragedy would punctuate the new U.S. role as the world's only remaining superpower.

☞ As you read, consider the domestic politics of the Clinton era. How and why did politics become more polarized? How did this polarization affect the Clinton presidency?

27-3a Ambitious Agenda

Clinton tries to advance policy goals despite missteps and political opposition.

After being shut out of the White House since 1980, liberals had high hopes for Clinton. He appointed more African Americans, Latinos, and women to the Cabinet than any previous president. He signed the **Family Medical Leave Act**, a law granting workers up to twelve weeks of unpaid leave to tend a newborn or adopted child or to care for an ailing relative. Although 35 million Americans took advantage of the new law by 2001, the United States was one of the only industrialized nations in the world where such leave was not paid. Through executive orders, Clinton lifted Reagan- and Bush-era restrictions on abortion. He revoked a "gag rule" that prevented clinics that received federal aid for serving low-income patients from providing abortion counseling. He struck down a ban on the importation of **RU-486,** a drug that terminates early pregnancy by preventing a fertilized egg from attaching to the uterine wall. Clinton also ended restrictions prohibiting the use of federal funds for research using fetal tissue, a move praised by scientists seeking new treatments for neurological diseases, leukemia, and diabetes.

A **New Democrat,** Clinton pushed a **Third Way** agenda that moved away from the Keynesianism of the New Deal and the Great Society. To jump-start the nation's stalled economy, he called for tax increases on the wealthy, spending cuts, deficit reduction, and investment in education and technology. On the advice of his economic advisers, Clinton dropped a campaign promise to cut taxes for the middle class. After intense debate, his budget plan very narrowly passed Congress—significantly without a single

Republican vote. The Deficit Reduction Act of 1993 raised taxes on the wealthiest 1.2 percent of taxpayers while expanding the **Earned Income Tax Credit** for 15 million Americans and reducing taxes for 90 percent of small businesses. Through spending cuts and tax increases, it slashed the budget deficit by $496 billion over five years. The act put the nation on course for debt reduction and budget surpluses, but the Democrats would pay a high political price for increasing taxes.

Clinton's efforts to honor a campaign pledge to allow gays and lesbians to serve openly in the U.S. armed forces met a fusillade of opposition from military leaders and conservatives. In June 1993, he struck a compromise that barred the military from inquiring about soldiers' sexual orientation and prevented soldiers from disclosing their sexual orientation. The "don't ask, don't tell" policy (DADT) resulted in the involuntary discharges of more than thirteen thousand troops before Congress repealed the policy in December 2010. Although many LGBT Americans lambasted the DADT compromise, they applauded President Clinton for making the first-ever appointments of openly gay people to administrative positions, expanding federal funding for the treatment and prevention of HIV/AIDS, and issuing an executive order allowing qualified LGBT people to receive federal security clearances—a move that ended a policy enacted at the height of the Lavender Scare in the early 1950s.

When Clinton introduced a sweeping proposal for national health insurance in response to skyrocketing health care costs and rising number of uninsured Americans, his decision to make Hillary Clinton its point person riled critics who thought such a high-profile public policy role was inappropriate for a first lady. A graduate of Wellesley and Yale Law School, Mrs. Clinton impressed supporters with her mastery of the thirteen hundred-page plan's intricacies. But the proposal drew widespread criticism. Conservatives objected to its expansion of the role of government and restriction of patient options. The health insurance industry launched ads criticizing its highly bureaucratized structure. In September 1994, after a year of contentious debate and the Clintons' refusal to accept alternatives, the Democratic-controlled Congress abandoned the complicated legislation.

President Clinton also launched major initiatives aimed at reducing crime and improving education. Gun control advocates cheered his signing of the **Brady Bill,** a federal law mandating a five-day waiting period and criminal background checks for handgun purchases, and a federal ban on assault weapons. In 1994, Congress approved his $30.2 billion plan expanding community policing and crime prevention programs. While experts differed in their views on what caused the trend, the overall national crime rate soon dropped to its lowest level since 1973. Clinton expanded federal funding for **Head Start** and K-12 education. To expand access to higher education and foster civic engagement, Clinton established **AmeriCorps,** a program in which people work as community service volunteers to earn college aid. Within five years, almost 200,000 young Americans were enrolled. He increased **Pell Grants** for low-income college students and supported the **Federal Direct Loan Program** that made student loans more accessible and affordable.

Earned Income Tax Credit Federal tax credit benefiting low-to-moderate income families, especially those with children.

Brady Bill Named after former Reagan press secretary and gun control advocate James Brady, 1993 federal law instituting background checks on those who buy firearms.

Head Start Federal program founded in 1965 that provides early childhood education and health and nutrition programs to low-income children and their families.

AmeriCorps Created by the Clinton administration in 1993, the federal community service program fostering volunteerism and viewed as the domestic counterpart of the Peace Corps.

Pell Grants Need-based federal aid to low-income college students that does not have to be repaid.

Federal Direct Loan Program National program that simplified student loans and removed private intermediaries to save money for both students and the federal government.

AP Images/Doug Mills

Hillary Clinton Testifying to Congress on Health Care Reform, 1993 While heading the Task Force on National Health Care Reform, Clinton drew criticism for the secrecy of the committee's proceedings but won praise for her ability to explain the administration's complex proposals. Although that initiative failed, she continued her health care advocacy, promoting a program that raised childhood immunization rates to 90 percent and working to secure passage of the State Children's Health Insurance Program providing federally funded health care to 6 million children. ◄

27-3b Partisan Backlash

Republicans capitalize on opposition to Clinton's policies and win historic electoral gains.

The Clinton administration drew passionate detractors. On April 19, 1993, after a fifty-one-day standoff, federal agents used tear gas to expel members of the Branch Davidians, a religious group, from their compound in Waco, Texas. A fire erupted, and eighty-six people perished. Many Americans criticized the use of military force on civilians, and the incident fueled antigovernment extremism. In May 1994, the president's troubles mounted when Paula Jones, a former Arkansas state employee, filed a sexual harassment lawsuit against him. A few weeks later, Congress held hearings on Whitewater, a failed Arkansas real estate development project in which both Clintons had invested.

Contract with America Blueprint for Republican legislative agenda once the party gained control of Congress and signed on the Capitol steps in September 1994.

Republicans won a landslide victory in the 1994 midterm elections that was enabled by Clinton's legal challenges and mixed domestic record. For the first time in forty years, the GOP controlled both houses of Congress. Newt Gingrich (Republican from Georgia) became Speaker of the House and vowed to enact the **Contract with America,** a conservative plan for balancing the federal budget, reforming the welfare system, reducing government regulations, and cutting taxes. With notable discipline, House Republicans passed most of the Contract's agenda but it met staunch opposition in the Senate. Rather than be cowed by the Gingrich juggernaut, Clinton stuck to his Third Way principles and moved to the right as the political center shifted. In late 1995, after Clinton and the House reached an impasse over Republican proposals to cut taxes on the wealthy and to slash federal spending on education and health care, the federal government shut down twice. Voters blamed Gingrich, and the Speaker's popularity tumbled.

Clinton and the Republicans found common ground in responding to terrorism. In April 1995, on the second anniversary of the Waco incident, Timothy McVeigh detonated a truck filled with five thousand pounds of ammonium nitrate and racing fuel in front of the Alfred P. Murrah Federal Building in Oklahoma City. One hundred sixty-eight people, including nineteen children, died

Murrah Federal Building after the Oklahoma City Bombing, 1995 Motivated by their hatred of the U.S. government, Timothy McVeigh and Terry Nichols orchestrated the bombing of a federal building in Oklahoma City. The huge explosion killed one hundred sixty-eight people and damaged or destroyed more than three hundred nearby structures. The community's immediate and overwhelming humanitarian response set what became known as "the Oklahoma standard" for dealing with disaster. McVeigh was sentenced to death and executed in 2001. Nichols is serving a life sentence without the possibility of parole. ▼

AP Images

in the massive explosion, the worst act of domestic terrorism in U.S. history. Some initial media reports speculated that Islamic radicals were responsible for the Oklahoma City bombing, but upon arrest, McVeigh, a U.S. citizen and Army veteran, stated that his actions were motivated by hatred of the federal government. In April 1996, Clinton signed a $1 billion antiterrorism bill permitting deportation of noncitizens suspected of terrorism and barring fundraising by terrorist groups.

Clinton deprived the Republicans of a powerful campaign issue by keeping his promise to "end welfare as we know it." In August 1996, he signed legislation overhauling welfare policies enacted during the New Deal that had guaranteed federal support for families with dependent children. The new law required welfare recipients to find work within two years and placed a five-year cap on total lifetime benefits. By 2001, the number of federal welfare recipients had dropped by 50 percent and most of those on public assistance had found jobs.

In September 1996, Clinton dealt LGBT Americans a major blow when he supported the **Defense of Marriage Act (DOMA).** The bill was introduced after a Hawai'i Supreme Court ruling sparked fears that the state might legalize same-sex marriages and that the **full faith and credit clause** of the U.S. Constitution would require other states to recognize them. To prevent such a scenario, Republicans introduced legislation defining marriage as a union of one man and one woman and barring married same-sex couples from receiving federal benefits (although no state legalized same-sex marriage until Massachusetts did so in 2004). Just weeks before the 1996 presidential elections, the legislation sped through Congress and passed both chambers with veto-proof majorities. Clinton called the legislation "divisive and unnecessary" but signed it into law, enraging many of his LGBT supporters.

A strategy of maintaining control of the political center enabled Clinton to win reelection in 1996. He faced Senator Robert Dole, Republican from Kansas, who ran on a platform combining supply-side economics with social conservatism. While deflecting charges of fundraising improprieties, Clinton emphasized the nation's booming economy. On Election Day, Clinton won with 49 percent of the popular vote to Dole's 41 percent. Ross Perot, who mobilized his 1992 supporters in the new Reform Party, won 8 percent. In his January 1997 State of the Union address, Clinton proclaimed "the era of big government is over." Four months later, Tony Blair, a New Labour politician who also ascribed to the Third Way, became Britain's prime minister after a landslide victory. Inspired by Clinton's centrism, Blair introduced market-based reforms in education and health care, revamped the welfare system, and advocated tough antiterrorism legislation.

Clinton pursued a modest second-term agenda aimed at helping the middle class. In 1997, he signed legislation to balance the federal budget and implement $152 billion in tax cuts by 2002. The bill also instituted new tax credits for child care and college expenses. In 1998, he announced that the United States had a budget surplus for the first time since 1969, and his next three budgets also ran surpluses, all used to pay $452 billion in public debt. Persuaded by neoliberal arguments that additional banking deregulation would help U.S. financial institutions compete with their European counterparts, Clinton in 1998 supported the repeal of the Glass-Steagall Act, a 1933 law mandating the separation of commercial and investment banking.

The Clinton years coincided with the longest period of economic expansion in U.S. history. More than 22.5 million jobs were created. Unemployment fell from 6.9 percent in 1993 to 4.0 percent in 2001, and inflation dropped from 4.7 to 2.5 percent, the lowest rates since the 1960s. Over the same period, poverty rates declined significantly, and home ownership rates exceeded 67 percent, the highest rate in U.S. history. But critics noted that rising levels of employment coexisted with dramatically increasing levels of corporate executive pay and that 16 million Americans had lost their jobs when companies downsized their workforces. Although many found new employment, they often earned lower wages, one of many factors exacerbating income inequality in the 1990s.

27-3c Confronting the Post-Cold War World

After the Cold War ends, U.S. policy makers foster free trade and encounter new global challenges.

In his January 1993 inaugural address, Clinton declared, "There is no longer a clear division between what is foreign and what is domestic. The world economy, the world environment, the world AIDS crisis, the world arms race: they affect us all." With the Cold War's end, Clinton warned, "The new world is more free, but less stable." As commerce and technology increasingly interconnected the global population, U.S. officials set new priorities and met new adversaries.

Clinton made free trade an integral element of his global policy. Although some Americans feared that easier access to cheaper foreign products would result in the loss of U.S. jobs, Clinton saw free trade as a means of increasing American exports and compelling antidemocratic nations to embrace human rights and economic reforms. Eager to compete with the **European Union**—a partnership of European states established in 1993 that were linked by a common currency called the

Defense of Marriage Act (DOMA) Federal law defining marriage as between one man and one woman and granting states permission not to recognize same-sex marriages performed in other jurisdictions.

full faith and credit clause Provision outlined in Article IV of the U.S. Constitution mandating that states recognize the acts, records, and legal proceedings of other states.

European Union Established in 1993, grouping of European countries operating as a single economic unit.

euro—and to decrease the $150 billion U.S. trade deficit, he won bipartisan support for the **North American Free Trade Agreement (NAFTA)**, a pact in which the United States, Mexico, and Canada created a trade bloc. In 1994, the Senate ratified a modification of the **General Agreement on Tariffs and Trade (GATT)**, approving the most significant restructuring of international trade regulations since the 1944 Bretton Woods Agreement. Designed to gradually eliminate obstacles to global free trade, the revised GATT established the **World Trade Organization (WTO)** to enforce its provisions. In 1999, Clinton brokered a landmark trade deal with China. The following year, despite concerns about China's human rights record and the possible implications of expanding Chinese imports to the United States, Congress ratified the agreement, thus paving the way for China's acceptance in the WTO. While many Americans enjoyed the lower prices and increased product selection these trade agreements facilitated, others linked free trade to worker exploitation, environmental degradation, and political repression.

Trade played an important role in the re-establishment of U.S.–Vietnamese relations. In February 1994, after the Vietnamese government provided photographs and data that accounted for the last two thousand two hundred sixty-five U.S. soldiers still listed as missing in action in the Vietnam War, Clinton lifted the trade embargo that the United States had placed on Vietnam in 1975. Eager to compete with foreign rivals in the thriving Vietnamese market, U.S. companies such as PepsiCo, General Electric, and Mobil began operating in the Socialist Republic of Vietnam (SRV). In July 1995, Clinton formally recognized the SRV and appointed Pete Peterson as U.S. ambassador, a Vietnam veteran and former Air Force pilot who spent more than six years in a North Vietnamese prison after his plane was shot down.

At the same time, economic issues strained U.S.–Japanese relations. By 1990, Japanese investors owned almost half of downtown Los Angeles, and Sony's acquisitions of CBS Records and Columbia Pictures made it a powerhouse in the U.S. entertainment industry. A wave of Japan-bashing like the one in which Vincent Chin was murdered in 1982 (see Chapter 26) began as Americans worried about Japanese economic and cultural domination. Such fears subsided in the 1990s, however, when Japan experienced a prolonged recession triggered by financial and ethical scandals that paralyzed its huge conglomerates and its business culture struggled to adapt to the rapidly globalizing economy. Although the Japanese maintained large trade surpluses in the United States, Tokyo's stock exchange, the Nikkei, lagged far behind the New York Stock Exchange. In 1997 and 1998, Japanese banks were hit hard when a financial crisis swept much of Asia. Despite their sometimes contentious economic relations, the United States and Japan remained close military allies who shared the costs of supporting tens of thousands of U.S. troops stationed in Japan and worked cooperatively to check North Korean nuclear ambitions and Chinese threats to Taiwan.

In the aftermath of the Cold War, many U.S. leaders hoped to help war-torn and underdeveloped societies, but their experiences in Somalia revealed that **nation-building** activities could have unanticipated consequences. A vital U.S. ally in battles against communism on the Horn of Africa during the late 1970s, Somalia degenerated into famine and civil war after the overthrow of its long-time dictator in 1991. In December 1992, George H.W. Bush sent more than twenty-eight thousand U.S. troops to Somalia to aid **Operation Restore Hope,** a UN coalition mission that rebuilt roads and bridges and protected relief workers.

Foreign intervention triggered the ire of a local warlord, and his soldiers killed several UN peacekeepers. After efforts to apprehend the warlord failed, Clinton deployed four hundred elite Army Rangers and Delta Force operatives to Somalia. In early October 1993, these soldiers and accompanying UN troops encountered fierce resistance in Mogadishu. After armed Somalis shot down two U.S. Black Hawk helicopters, soldiers sent to rescue the crews got locked in an overnight firefight that left eighteen U.S. troops dead and seventy-four wounded. Up to two thousand Somalis, mostly civilians, were also killed and injured. Television footage of cheering Somalis dragging the corpse of a U.S. soldier through the streets outraged Americans. Stung by the failure of the mission, Clinton announced that all U.S. combat troops would be withdrawn from Somalia by April 1994 and issued strict new guidelines on U.S. participation in future peacekeeping operations. The UN mission ended in defeat, and Somalia remained mired in violence and poverty for years afterward.

The debacle in Somalia shaped the global response to an outbreak of horrific violence that engulfed the east African nation of Rwanda. In April 1994, the deaths of the presidents of Rwanda and Burundi—both members of the Hutu majority—in a suspicious plane crash sparked mass killings of members of the Tutsi minority. Up to 1 million people were murdered over an eighty-nine-day period—the fastest pace of genocide in world history.

Reluctant to enter the fray of another complicated African conflict, the UN Security Council directed UN peacekeepers in Rwanda to evacuate foreign nationals and to begin withdrawing. Clinton rejected calls for U.S. intervention. Fearful of Tutsi retribution, about 2 million Hutus fled the country and poured into neighboring countries. In

North American Free Trade Agreement (NAFTA) Implemented in 1994, free trade agreement abolishing most tariffs between the United States, Mexico, and Canada.

General Agreement on Tariffs and Trade (GATT) 1948 international law aimed at fostering free trade in the aftermath of World War II replaced by the World Trade Organization in 1995.

World Trade Organization (WTO) Created in 1995, the only international organization that regulates trade between nations, tries to foster trade stability and openness. Target of antiglobalization protests.

nation-building Umbrella term for policies designed to make citizens embrace a commonality of interests, goals, and identities with their compatriots.

Operation Restore Hope Code name for a UN humanitarian relief operation in Somalia led by the United States from December 1992 to May 1993.

July, after the violence ended, the United States sent troops to Rwanda on a three-month mission to help with the refugee crisis. On a 1998 trip to Rwanda, Clinton apologized for failing to do "as much as we could have and should have done" to limit what U.S. officials had earlier refused to label as genocide.

Ethnic violence also consumed Yugoslavia. Although most of the former Soviet satellite states had transitioned to non-Communist governments peacefully, Yugoslavia disintegrated into the most devastating conflict in Europe since 1945. Serbs took up arms against their Muslim neighbors in campaigns of "ethnic cleansing" marked by murder, atrocities, detentions, and mass rapes. In 1995, after Clinton had hesitated for months to get involved in what he called "a problem from hell," U.S. diplomats helped broker accords ending the Serbs' campaign against the Croats and Bosnians. The United States contributed twenty thousand troops to a NATO contingent charged with implementing the agreement, providing humanitarian aid, and disposing of weapons and unexploded ordinance. More than 200,000 people were killed during the war, and 1.8 million became refugees.

In 1999, another Balkan crisis erupted after the Serbs launched a campaign of genocide against ethnic Albanians living in Kosovo. When the Serbs ignored calls for withdrawal, U.S. and NATO forces commenced seventy-eight days of bombing raids throughout Yugoslavia. A monstrous refugee crisis ensued as 800,000 people fled Kosovo for neighboring Albania and Macedonia. In June 1999, the Serbs agreed to remove their troops from Kosovo and to accept the terms of a cease-fire. Several top Serbian leaders were charged with crimes against humanity and extradited to stand trial at The Hague, the headquarters of United Nations International Court of Justice located in a coastal city in the western Netherlands.

Throughout the 1990s, the Clinton administration dealt with ramifications of the Persian Gulf War. Left in control of Iraq, Saddam continued to bedevil U.S. policy makers. Although UN economic sanctions created mass suffering among the Iraqi populace, Saddam repeatedly obstructed UN weapons inspectors searching for hidden stores of chemical and biological weapons. In 1996, Clinton ordered missile strikes on Iraq in retaliation for Saddam's attacks on Kurds. Two years later, a joint U.S.–British force bombed suspected Iraqi military sites. But Clinton rejected calls to overthrow Saddam.

International terrorism also escalated. In June 1996, members of Hezbollah, a Shi'a Islamist militant group financed by Iran, killed nineteen U.S. airmen and wounded hundreds more in a truck bombing at Khobar Towers, a U.S. military housing complex in Dharan, Saudi Arabia. In August 1998, Osama bin Laden's terrorist group Al-Qaeda launched simultaneous truck bombings at the U.S. embassies in Nairobi, Kenya, and Dar es Salaam, Tanzania, that left two hundred people dead and wounded more than four thousand. In retaliation, Clinton ordered air strikes on sites in Sudan and Afghanistan allegedly linked to al-Qaeda. In October 2000, an al-Qaeda suicide attack on the *U.S.S. Cole* killed seventeen sailors in the port of Aden in Yemen. The bombings signaled escalating dangers to national security posed by terrorist networks that were extremely difficult to track and combat.

27-3d Scandal, Impeachment, and the Election of 2000

Surviving a failed impeachment, Clinton leaves office with high approval ratings and a flourishing economy.

Allegations of sexual impropriety overshadowed much of Clinton's second term. In January 1998, attorneys representing Paula Jones announced plans to depose Monica Lewinsky, a twenty-four-year-old former White House intern, about an alleged affair with the president. Although a judge dismissed Jones's lawsuit three months later, Kenneth Starr, the independent counsel whom Congress had appointed to examine the Whitewater real estate scandal, broadened his inquiry and convinced former White House staff member Linda Tripp to secretly record her conversations with Lewinsky. As a result of Starr's investigation, eleven people were convicted of fraud and other crimes related to Whitewater. Critics blasted Starr's tactics and close ties to the Republican Party.

In January 1998, news of Clinton's alleged affair with Lewinsky became public. He denied the claim, memorably declaring, "I did not have sexual relations with that woman." In August 1998, after Clinton was forced to testify to a grand jury, he gave a nationally televised speech admitting having had a sexual relationship with Lewinsky. While the legal proceedings unfolded, Lewinsky became the subject of intense media scrutiny and ridicule on the Internet. In September, Starr submitted a four hundred forty-five-page report to Congress offering salacious details about Clinton and Lewinsky's sexual encounters and accusing Clinton of perjury, obstruction of justice, witness tampering, and abuse of power. On October 8, 1998, the Republican-controlled House of Representatives voted two hundred fifty-eight to one hundred seventy-six to conduct impeachment hearings. Two months later, the House approved two articles of impeachment for perjury and obstruction of justice. In February 1999, the Senate acquitted Clinton. In September 2000, Robert Ray, Starr's successor as independent counsel, closed the $50 million Whitewater investigation after finding insufficient evidence to merit criminal charges against the president or the first lady.

Although the Lewinsky scandal markedly harmed Clinton's reputation, it also hurt the Republicans. In the 1998 elections, the Democrats gained five congressional seats—a testament to voters' satisfaction with a thriving economy and disdain for the partisanship driving the impeachment process. Ironically, two Republicans, not Clinton, were pushed from office. First, Newt Gingrich

red states and blue states Term taken from the color code on television news maps indicating which states vote Republican or Democratic and used to describe prevailing political and cultural views.

resigned as Speaker of the House after the disappointing election returns and allegations of fund-raising improprieties. Then Bob Livingston, a Republican from Mississippi who was Gingrich's designated successor, resigned when reporters exposed his own marital infidelity. Clinton, meanwhile, retained a 59 percent approval rating.

The changing nature of the media helped to fuel partisanship. In October 1996, Australian media mogul Rupert Murdoch hired former NBC executive and Republican operative Roger Ailes as CEO of Fox News, a twenty-four-hour cable news channel. By 2000, Fox was reaching 56 million homes nationwide, experiencing a 440 percent increase in viewers, and becoming a highly influential platform for conservative politics. So did the *Drudge Report*, a Web-based news aggregator that gained nationwide attention for breaking the story of the Lewinsky scandal in 1998.

Despite the increasingly partisan political culture, no one could have predicted the drama of the 2000 presidential elections. With a booming economy, the Democrats expected their nominee, Vice President Al Gore, to win election easily. The Republicans picked George W. Bush, two-term governor of Texas and son of former president George H.W. Bush. Both Gore and Bush ran as centrists but differed in their views on the best uses for projected federal budget surpluses and the proper role of the federal government. Bush advocated large tax cuts, partial privatization of Social Security, and government-funded vouchers for private education. Gore supported putting the surpluses into Social Security and Medicare. Bush was pro-life; Gore was pro-choice. Although Pat Buchanan ran as the Reform Party nominee and Ralph Nader represented the Green Party, neither won significant national support.

The election itself was a forty-two-day roller coaster ride. Senate elections resulted in a fifty-fifty Democratic-Republican split. Early on election night, commentators declared Gore winner of Florida. Later, they claimed Bush had won. Then they said that the race was too close to call. Returns from the rest of the nation gave Gore a 337,000 lead in the popular vote and two hundred sixty-seven electoral votes. Carrying the South and much of the Midwest, Bush had two hundred forty-six electoral votes. Because neither had the two hundred seventy electoral votes needed to win, the outcome of the election hinged on Florida's twenty-five electoral votes. Television commentators used map graphics highlighting states that Bush won in red and those voting for in Al Gore in blue. **Red states and blue states** quickly became a shorthand way to describe the partisan and cultural differences among Americans.

In Florida, mandatory recounts began. Voters protested unclear "butterfly ballots," "under votes," antiquated voting machines, and unhelpful poll officials. With the nation's attention riveted on his state, Governor Jeb Bush, brother of George W. Bush, tried to keep order as his state's voting irregularities were exposed. Baffled officials tried to interpret ballots with pregnant, dimpled, and hanging "chads," the cardboard removed when punching a ballot. On November 27, Florida secretary of state Katherine Harris, a leader in the state Bush campaign organization, ended the recounts and certified Bush the winner by five hundred thirty-seven votes. After Gore won an appeal to the Florida Supreme Court demanding a statewide hand recount, the Bush campaign appealed to the U.S. Supreme Court, insisting that the recounts be stopped. On the evening of December 12, the U.S. Supreme Court issued a 5-4 decision ordering the completion of all recounts by December 13—a deadline that was obviously impossible to meet. The four opposing justices issued blistering dissents to the *Bush v. Gore* ruling. Despite winning the popular vote by a 540,000 margin, Gore lost the electoral vote, two hundred sixty-seven to two hundred seventy-one. Bush became the nation's forty-third president (see Map 27.4). While some Americans cheered the end of the political chaos and welcomed Bush's victory, others were dismayed by the politicization of the Supreme Court. One protestor held a poster that read, "The people have spoken—all five of them." It was only one sign of the many ways that Americans had grown more politically divided during the Clinton years.

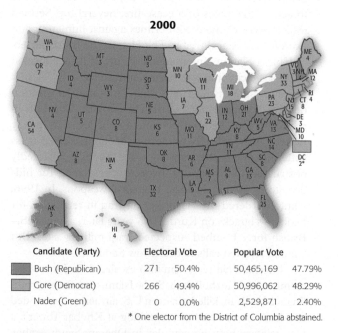

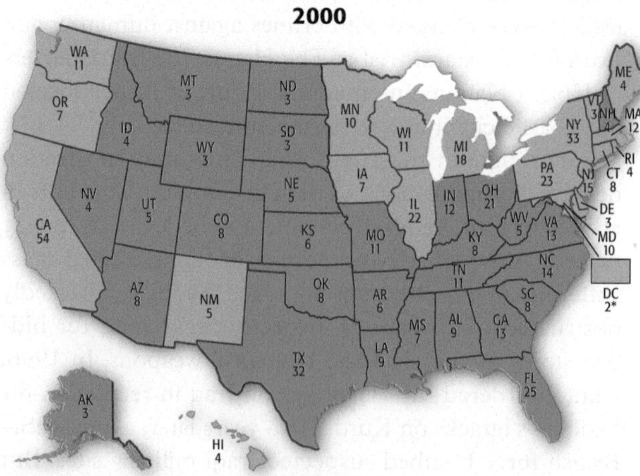

Candidate (Party)	Electoral Vote		Popular Vote	
Bush (Republican)	271	50.4%	50,465,169	47.79%
Gore (Democrat)	266	49.4%	50,996,062	48.29%
Nader (Green)	0	0.0%	2,529,871	2.40%

* One elector from the District of Columbia abstained.

Map 27.4 Election of 2000 After forty-two days of recounts, legal challenges, and a Supreme Court ruling, George W. Bush was declared the winner of the 2000 presidential race, winning 271–261 in the electoral vote but trailing Democratic challenger Al Gore by 540,000 votes in the popular vote. ▲

27-4

Global Village

In the late twentieth century, globalization generated anxieties about U.S. cultural domination.

What does this cartoon suggest about the artist's views about globalization and the United States? Why do you think he used imagery evoking the D-Day invasion of World War II? ▶

Andy Singer

Go to MindTap® to practice history with the Chapter 27 **Primary Source Writing Activity: The Americanization of Global Culture.** Read and view primary sources and respond to a writing prompt.

The post-1975 era witnessed remarkable transformations in the ways people across the globe communicated, learned, shopped, worked, and played. Intergovernmental and nongovernmental organizations proliferated. Corporations expanded their operations across national borders. The Internet, facsimile (fax) machines, and mobile phones made keeping in touch with transnational friends, family, and business associates much easier. Technological innovations drove an economic boom and created a new class of billionaire entrepreneurs.

But the revolution created new challenges as well. Some foreign audiences objected to the ubiquity of U.S. products and culture. Technology changed the nature of personal relationships and notions of privacy. As the amount of readily available information exploded, distinguishing legitimate facts from satire or misinformation became more difficult. Criminals found new tactics for victimizing others and disseminating illegal goods and services. Multinational corporations could locate their operations in nations that did not guard the rights of workers or protect the environment. Although the overall effects of these trends were disputed, there was no denying that the pace and scope of change was profound.

☞ As you read, evaluate the impacts of globalization. How and why was the world more interconnected in 2000 than it was in 1975? What do you think are the most positive and negative aspects of globalization?

27-4a Proliferation of Intergovernmental and Nongovernmental Organizations

Nonstate actors play an increasing role in addressing global problems.

In the late twentieth century, **globalization**, the process of integrating people culturally, politically, and economically across national lines, expanded dramatically. The increasing number of nonstate actors engaging international issues illustrated this trend. In the 1970s, as détente eased superpower tensions and economic stagnation and public distrust limited governmental power, intergovernmental (IGOs) and nongovernmental organizations (NGOs) tackled problems that states were either unable or unwilling to address. Others worked together to challenge sovereign countries to improve how they treated their own citizens or addressed societal and economic problems. The number of **intergovernmental organizations** (groups, such as the UN, that were comprised of member states) grew from 280 in 1972 to 1,530 by 1984. Over the same period, the number of NGOs increased from 2,795 to 12,686. They took on a wide array of causes including human rights, humanitarian relief, disarmament, and environmental protection.

A flurry of organizers championed women's rights. In 1975, the UN General Assembly launched the International Decade of Women that began with an international congress of women in Mexico City. It inspired transnational campaigns aimed at improving women's status throughout the world. In 1979, one hundred eighty-seven nations signed a UN convention outlawing discrimination against women, but only twenty countries ratified the treaty, and it was hampered by differing interpretations of its provisions and weak enforcement mechanisms.

globalization International interconnectedness created by the global exchange of ideas, products, services, and culture.

intergovernmental organizations Body composed of at least two separate nations.

Transnational organizations also increased global awareness of crimes against women and gender inequality. In 1994, the U.S. State Department's annual human rights reports began documenting crimes against women including forced abortions and involuntary sterilizations in China, sexual slavery in Thailand, and "dowry killings" of women in India. In 1996, the United States granted asylum to Fauziya Kassindja, who had escaped from Togo fleeing female genital mutilation (FGM) and a forced marriage. The ruling helped to highlight the plight of an estimated 2 million women worldwide still subjected to ancient rituals involving the removal of portions of their genitalia as a means of ensuring chastity or marking adulthood, a practice that can have serious health consequences.

At the Fourth World Conference on Women held in Beijing in 1995, First Lady Hillary Clinton proclaimed "women's rights are human rights"—a call to action echoed by governments and transnational organizations that intensified their efforts to combat global women's poverty. In much of the developing world, social and cultural taboos restricted women's labor opportunities outside the home and limited their economic power within their households. Illiteracy; lack of access to health care, land, inheritance, and credit; and inadequate supplies of food and water created additional economic and physical hardships for many of these women. In 2000, the United Nations estimated that the majority of the 1.5 billion people in the world living on less than $1 a day were female. Worldwide, women's incomes averaged about half those of men. The provision of small loans—sometimes called **microcredit**—has proved a particularly successful strategy for eradicating women's poverty.

NGOs played a vital role in responding to famines, epidemics, natural disasters, and civil strife. One of the most influential was Doctors without Borders (Médecins Sans Frontières) founded in France in 1971. Its medical professionals helped refugees displaced by the Indochina wars and conflicts in Africa and aided victims of earthquakes and floods. In war zones such as Somalia and the Balkans, relief workers sometimes became targets of violence.

Other transnational activists worked to protect endangered species and the environment. NGOs such as the World Wildlife Fund and Friends of the Earth mobilized campaigns to safeguard whales, elephants, and other animals. In 1989, eighty-six nations pledged to phase out the use of chlorofluorocarbons (CFCs) that were damaging the ozone layer. In 1997, the United States and one hundred ninety other nations signed the **Kyoto Protocol** requiring industrialized countries to lower their production of greenhouse gases linked to global warming. But the United States rejected other environmental initiatives. Although it joined one hundred sixty-seven nations in signing a 1992 convention on biological diversity, the U.S. Senate refused to ratify the treaty.

microcredit Small, low-interest loans made to help people, especially women, in developing nations establish businesses and become economically self-sufficient.

Kyoto Protocol International agreement brokered by the United Nations to address global climate change by reducing carbon emissions around the world.

27-4b The Digital Revolution and Its Critics

Digital technologies spark a communications revolution that changes personal interactions, business practices, and consumerism.

In the late twentieth century, digital computing and communications technology changed daily life in much of the world. Developed in the 1940s, computers were originally large machines using vacuum tubes, relays, and large bundles of wires. Within twenty years, the federal government, businesses, and universities were using more than thirty thousand mainframe computers. In 1971, Intel's introduction of the microprocessor greatly expanded the possible applications of computers. Six years later, Steven Jobs and Stephen Wozniak released the Apple II, the first personal computer (PC). In 1981, International Business Machines (IBM) released its own PC. Between 1989 and 2000, the number of U.S. households that owned at least one PC rose from 15 percent to 51 percent. Computers and digital technologies transformed banking, publishing, medicine, and many other industries.

The digital revolution fueled the development of the Internet, a worldwide system of interconnected computer networks. In the 1960s, the U.S. Department of Defense established Arpanet, a network linking computers at federally funded research facilities. Information-sharing applications for the system such as electronic mail (e-mail) and file transfer protocol (FTP) soon emerged. Packet-switching technology enabled computers that were not directly wired together to exchange large amounts of information. Centralized communications circuits routed messages to individual computers. In the early 1980s, as the number of computers linked by Arpanet grew, the Department of Defense withdrew from the project because of security concerns, and Arpanet was renamed the Internet. As private companies and government agencies poured resources into the Internet, it expanded rapidly. In 1989, Tim Berners-Lee and his colleagues in Geneva developed the World Wide Web (WWW), a system that allowed users to access the vast amount of documents on the Internet by means of electronic tags called *hyperlinks*. In 1993, Marc Andreessen and others at the University of Illinois released Mosaic (later called *Netscape*), the first widely used Web browser that greatly simplified the retrieval, transfer, and display of Internet files. The same year, the federal government approved the use of the Internet by commercial e-mail services. President Clinton directed all federal agencies to use information technologies to make the U.S. government more accessible to its citizens and launched an educational technology initiative that significantly expanded Internet access at schools and libraries. Between 1984 and 1994, the number of computers linked to the Internet rose from less than 1,000 to 6 million. In 2001, the total reached 400 million, including 130 million in the United States.

Digital technology spawned thousands of new businesses and products. In the 1970s, the success of Atari's *Pong*, a simulated table tennis game, inspired a thriving video gaming industry. Hit arcade games such as *Space Invaders* (1978) and *Pac-Man* (1980) were adapted for home computers and helped drive PC sales. Nintendo's Entertainment System (1987), Sony's PlayStation (1994), and Microsoft's X-Box (2001) made video gaming a multibillion-dollar, transnational industry drawing people together in both the real and virtual worlds.

The music industry changed dramatically in this era too. In the 1980s, digital compact discs (CDs) supplanted analog vinyl records and cassettes. At the same time, foreign-owned media conglomerates bought most U.S. record companies and began to dominate the production and distribution of music. To recoup the costs of mergers and acquisitions, these companies privileged homogenized, marketable music and artists often found that concert tours were their only means of earning money. In the 1990s, computer-formatted MP3 files that compress sound (primarily music) for digital transmission and storage began supplanting CD. In 1999, Shawn Fanning launched Napster, a peer-to-peer file-sharing program that allowed individuals to swap selections from their personal digital music collections. As Napster became the fastest-growing application in Internet history, the music industry sued Fanning for copyright infringement and forced the site's closure in 2001.

The digital revolution also transformed the film, television, camera, and telecommunications industries. With the introduction of the digital video disc (DVD) in 1997, sales of analog videocassettes and players began to decline. In 1990, the first digital cameras were marketed in the United States and led to major changes in how people took, processed, and shared photographs. The following year, the first digital cellular phones were sold commercially, and the number of cell phone subscribers increased from 12.4 million in 1990 to 1.2 billion in 2002, nearly 20 percent of the world's population.

The digital revolution contributed to tremendous growth in the U.S. economy for much of the 1990s. Corporations maximized profits through mergers, reduction of labor costs, and restructuring. The "New Economy" created thousands of jobs. Many entrepreneurs gravitated to the Internet, and national interest in "dot-coms" and "e-commerce" appeared boundless. Enthusiasm for technology stocks lifted the Dow Jones Industrial Average over eleven thousand, its highest rate ever, and spawned the NASDAQ, a stock exchange exclusively for technology shares. Productivity and incomes soared as unemployment and inflation remained low. But in March 2000, the dot-com bubble burst as investors began rejecting overvalued technology stocks. By October 2002, technology companies had lost $5 trillion in market value and many "dot-bombs" had failed, but many Internet-based businesses regrouped and became highly profitable.

The digital revolution had both positive and negative aspects. It became harder for totalitarian regimes to suppress information. Small businesses could reach huge markets. People had access to an astonishing array of entertainment, news, products, and services. Individuals and organizations could create and share information with a global audience at a negligible cost. But the sheer amount of information could be overwhelming, and the Internet created new ways for predators to find victims. Spreading

Seattle Police Pepper Spray Antiglobalization Protestors, 1999 In November 1999, during the World Trade Organization's ministerial conference in Seattle, Washington, approximately forty thousand antiglobalization protestors demonstrated in the streets. The participants included NGOs and local activists from a variety of political perspectives and causes. Some used nonviolent techniques to protest specific WTO policies or to advocate more broadly for labor rights or environmental protections. Others, many of them anarchists, tried to disrupt the meetings by blocking roads, disrupting proceedings, and destroying property. ▶

Christopher J. Morris/Corbis

cyber-espionage Use of computer networks to gain access to confidential information held by governments or corporations.

inaccurate or libelous material and entrapping people in financial scams became much easier, and digital communication could exacerbate social isolation. Fears arose about possible misuse of the vast amount of personal data being collected by governments and businesses. Businesses faced new threats of piracy, copyright infringement, hacking, and **cyber-espionage.** In 2000, a single computer virus resulted in $15 billion in damage in the United States alone after Filipino hackers released ILOVEYOU, a computer worm that infected more than 45 million Windows-based computers in only ten days. To protect their systems, the Pentagon, the CIA, the British Parliament, and most major corporations temporarily disabled their e-mail systems.

As the digital revolution transformed economic and cultural interactions, criticisms of the labor and environmental aspects of globalization intensified. In November 1999, antiglobalization protests at the WTO meeting in Seattle, Washington, drew international attention. Ironically, many of those demonstrators had used the Internet, itself a tool of globalization, to mobilize supporters. Approximately forty thousand people gathered in Seattle to stage a variety of mostly peaceful protests accusing the WTO of displacing local cultures, exploiting workers, and undermining environmental protection. But violent factions clashed with police who responded with tear gas and rubber bullets. By the time the WTO meeting had ended, Seattle had sustained more than $3 million in property damage. Similar demonstrations engulfed meetings of the World Bank and IMF held in Washington, D.C., and Genoa, Italy. To avoid more protests, IMF and World Bank delegates met in more isolated locations.

27-4c Americanization of Global Culture

U.S. culture and products are welcomed, re-interpreted, and rejected abroad.

Globalization renewed debates over the "Americanization" of the world first voiced by the British journalist William Stead in 1901. But Stead, who died in the sinking of the *Titanic* in 1912, never lived to see how air travel, multinational corporations, and technology expanded the international reach of U.S. cultural power. Nor could he have predicted how foreign audiences would embrace, reject, and transform the avalanche of U.S. products and ideas they encountered.

Film and television became major vehicles for exposing foreign audiences to U.S. clothing, interior design, and verbal expressions. Hollywood films became hugely popular overseas and earned most of their profits in foreign markets. International broadcasts and distribution made U.S. television shows, such as *Baywatch* and *The Simpsons*, global hits. Foreign listeners bought millions of albums from American musicians including Michael Jackson and Madonna, and global tours by U.S. bands became commonplace. U.S.-based multinational companies such as Coca-Cola, McDonald's, Starbucks, and Apple opened outlets around the world.

Yet the increased visibility and presence of American cultural exports and businesses abroad did not equate to total U.S. control of global culture and commerce. In the 1970s, European and Japanese investments in the United States expanded and continued to rise. Two decades later, China began buying U.S. Treasury bonds and eventually became the world's largest holder of U.S. debt. In the 1990s, U.S. companies including Wal-Mart increased

McDonald's in Seoul, South Korea
In 1967, McDonald's opened its first two international franchises in British Columbia and Costa Rica. By 1996, when it opened a location in Belarus, it had expanded into one hundred countries. As a reflection of McDonald's international scope, *The Economist* magazine publishes an annual "Big Mac index" using the price of the famous hamburger as a light-hearted way to gauge the comparative purchasing power of global currencies. ▶

Chung Sung-Jun/Getty Images

Manny Millan/Getty Images

Global Americans **Michael Jordan** dominated the National Basketball Association (NBA) from the mid-1980s to the late 1990s. After three years playing for the University of North Carolina, he left school and was drafted by the Chicago Bulls. Jordan led them to six national championships, earning the NBA Most Valuable Player Award five times. In 1984 and 1992, he played on gold medal–winning U.S. Olympic basketball teams. In 1996, Jordan starred in *Space Jam*, a mixed live action and animation film that paired him with legendary cartoon characters Bugs Bunny and Daffy Duck.

Although basketball is not played in much of the world, Jordan's endorsements for Nike made him internationally famous. In 1984, the company offered him a five-year contract worth $500,000 annually plus royalties, an astonishing sum at the time. Largely because of sales of its Air Jordans—basketball shoes emblazoned with an iconic image of Jordan dunking a basketball—Nike's sales hit nearly $10 billion in the mid-1990s. Even though Jordan had retired from the NBA a decade earlier, the 2013 Air Jordan 10 Powder Blue retro sneaker generated $2.25 billion in U.S. sales alone, earning Jordan $90 million.

In the late 1990s, however, Nike and Jordan came under fire when activists exposed child labor, $2 daily wages, and physical abuse of workers among Nike's subcontractors in Asia. Facing boycotts and eager to protect its brand, Nike took steps to ensure more equitable conditions at its production facilities abroad. The same forces of globalization that made Nike and Jordan millions also created tools for activists to expose injustice.

importation of products from China. Companies like Nike and General Motors displaced U.S. workers by outsourcing production to subcontractors in Indonesia, Vietnam, and Mexico. India's Bollywood produced more films than Hollywood. Even in markets saturated with U.S. television programs and music, foreign audiences continued to watch locally produced shows and to support their own artists. Foreign opponents of Americanization objected when U.S. restaurants and advertising appeared in historic neighborhoods. In August 1999, a French sheep farmer became a folk hero when he bulldozed a McDonald's in protest of its "McDomination" of small agricultural producers and regionally distinctive cuisines.

Rather than unilaterally impose their goods and practices on foreign markets, U.S. companies adjusted to local mores, tastes, competition, and criticism. McDonald's, for example, modified its menu for specific countries. In Germany, its restaurants sell beer. In Japan, it offers a shrimp burger. In predominately Hindu India, it does not serve beef. As digital technologies transformed the media, U.S. news outlets faced new competitors such as Al Jareeza, an Arabic current affairs satellite network launched in Qatar in 1996. In the late 1990s, under fierce international criticism for the working conditions and low pay at facilities of its foreign subcontractors, Nike created the Fair Labor Association, an international collaboration of corporations and human rights activists devoted to ensuring safe working conditions and equitable pay for laborers around the world. Some observers claim that the United States is uniquely suited to tailor its products, services, and entertainment to diverse audiences because of its own multicultural society. "In the end, American mass culture has not transformed the world into a replica of the United States," notes cultural historian Richard Pells, "Instead, America's dependence on foreign cultures has made the United States a replica of the world."

Summary

The election of 1988 signaled the rise of a more negative style of political campaigning. The victorious candidate, George H.W. Bush made tough, politically costly fiscal choices. While trying to advance civil rights and environmental protections at home, he responded cautiously to a tense international landscape. But Bush failed to translate his foreign policy achievements into a successful 1992 reelection bid.

Changes in immigration law and birth patterns made the United States a more populated and ethnically diverse nation. As medical advances prolonged life, people over age sixty-five composed an increasing percentage of the total population. The rapidly rising global population generated concerns about the limits of natural resources and governments' ability to meet basic needs for burgeoning and diversifying populaces.

Although Clinton helped to usher in one of the greatest periods of economic growth in U.S. history, his efforts to institute national health insurance triggered a conservative backlash that enabled the Republicans to win control of Congress. Clinton outmaneuvered his rivals by adopting more moderate positions on issues such as welfare reform, but scandal and a failed impeachment attempt plagued his second term. At the same time, U.S. policy makers adjusted to the complexities of an increasingly unstable global environment. The presidential elections of 2000 highlighted how polarized Americans had become.

Technological and communications innovations significantly increased the ways that people could connect across national boundaries. Nonstate actors played a larger role in humanitarian relief, human rights, disarmament, and environmental protection. Multinational corporations maximized profits by expanding their operations into countries with lower labor and production costs but met controversy when such efforts displaced U.S. workers, exploited foreign workers, or harmed the environment.

The digital revolution transformed daily life. People could create and share information globally, a trend that frightened totalitarian governments, aided social justice advocates, and greatly altered journalism and entertainment. The rise of the Internet not only generated astounding opportunities for business innovation but also created new opportunities for criminals to find victims and for governments and corporations to intrude on private lives.

Globalization compounded and complicated long-standing fears about the ubiquity of American culture and products abroad. Although foreigners undoubtedly embraced U.S. goods, services, and entertainment, they did not reject their local cultures and proved that not even a country as diverse as the United States could supplant individuals' cultural and national identities.

<Thinking Back, *Looking Forward*>

As you review this chapter, compare post-1965 migration patterns to previous waves of immigration in U.S. history. How and why did the composition of the U.S. population change, and what were the political consequences? How did globalization and technology affect communications, commerce, and culture? In the last chapter, pay attention to how globalization and technology have influenced and accelerated developments with deep historical roots: terrorism and income inequality.

To make your study concrete, review the timeline and reflect on the entries there. Think about their causes, consequences, and connections. How do they fit with global trends?

Additional Resources

Books

Boys, James D. *Clinton's Grand Strategy: US Foreign Policy in a Post-Cold War World*. London, U.K.: Bloomsbury Academic, 2015. ▶ Assessment of key ideas, individuals, and events shaping U.S. strategies.

Briggs, Laura. *Somebody's Children: The Politics of Transracial and Transnational Adoption*. Durham, NC: Duke University Press, 2012. ▶ Examination of transnational adoption in the United States since 1945.

Connelly, Matthew. *Fatal Misconception: The Struggle to Control World Population*. Cambridge, MA: Belknap Press, 2008. ▶ Multinational, archival history of population control programs.

Harris, John F. *The Survivor: Bill Clinton in the White House*. New York: Random House, 2006. ▶ Political reporter's account of the Clinton presidency.

Harrison, Colin. *American Culture in the 1990s*. Edinburgh, UK: Edinburgh University Press, 2010. ▶ Synthesis that places major cultural trends of the decade into historical context.

Iriye, Akira. *Global Interdependence: The World after 1945*. Cambridge, MA: Belknap Press, 2014. ▶ Massive collection on international, environmental, cultural, political, and economic trends.

Isaacson, Walter. ***The Innovators: How a Group of Hackers, Geniuses, and Geeks Created the Digital Revolution*****. New York: Simon and Schuster, 2014.** ▶ Best-selling author traces the evolution of computers and the Internet.

Meacham, Jon. ***Destiny and Power: The American Odyssey of George Herbert Walker Bush*****. New York: Random House, 2015.** ▶ Pulitzer Prize–winning author's biography based on extensive interviews and archival sources.

Pells, Richard. ***Not Like Us: How Europeans Have Loved, Hated, and Transformed American Culture since World War II*****. New York: Basic Books, 1997.** ▶ Entertaining and persuasive history of U.S. cultural transmission and reception.

Thompson, Graham. ***American Culture in the 1980s*****. Edinburgh, UK: Edinburgh University Press, 2007.** ▶ Overview of the decade's films, television programs, art, music, and literature.

Go to the MindTap® for **Global Americans** to access the full version of select books from this Additional Resources section.

Websites

Computer History Museum. http://www.computerhistory.org/ ▶ Exhibits, archival materials, and teaching resources on the history of computing and the Digital Revolution.

George Bush Presidential Library and Museum. http://bush41.org/ ▶ Extensive collection of teaching resources and textual, audio, video, and photographic primary sources related to George H.W. Bush.

PBS *American Experience*: "The Presidents." http://www.pbs.org/wgbh/americanexperience/collections/presidents/ ▶ Excellent documentaries on George H.W. Bush and Bill Clinton plus teaching resources.

PBS *Frontline:* "The Gulf War." http://www.pbs.org/wgbh/pages/frontline/gulf/ ▶ Collection of oral histories, video clips, and teaching resources.

William J. Clinton Presidential Library and Museum. http://www.clintonlibrary.gov/ ▶ Research and teaching materials on Clinton's presidency and postpresidential activities.

MindTap®

Continue exploring online through MindTap®, where you can:

- **Assess your knowledge with the Chapter Test**
- **Watch historical videos related to the chapter**
- **Further your understanding with interactive maps and timelines**

Closer Together, Further Apart

1989

January

George H.W. Bush is inaugurated as president.

March

Exxon Valdez oil spill occurs in Prince William Sound, Alaska.

June

Chinese authorities crush pro-democracy protests in Beijing.

December

The Simpsons debuts on FOX television.

Romanian dictator Nicolae Ceausescu and his wife are executed.

1990

February

Sandinistas lose free elections in Nicaragua, coalition government takes power.

May

Latvia declares independence from the Soviet Union.

June

President Bush accepts tax increases in budget deficit reduction plan.

August

Iraq invades Kuwait.

October

Germany reunites.

1991

February

UN coalition forces oust Iraq from Kuwait.

August

World Wide Web is publicly launched.

October

Clarence Thomas wins confirmation as Supreme Court justice.

December

Soviet Union dissolves, Cold War ends.

1992

April–May

Riots in Los Angeles result in more than fifty deaths.

November

Bill Clinton wins 1992 presidential race.

1993

February

Terrorist bombing at the World Trade Center kills six, injures thousands.

April

Stand-off ends between federal agents and Branch Davidians in Waco, Texas, and eighty-six people perish.

June

Clinton accepts "Don't ask, don't tell" compromise.

1994

January
North American Free Trade Agreement goes into effect.

April
Nelson Mandela is elected president of South Africa.

April–July
Genocide occurs in Rwanda.

November
Republicans win control of both chambers of Congress.

1995

March
Religious terrorists launch sarin attacks on Tokyo railway.

April
Terrorist bombing of federal building in Oklahoma City kills one hundred sixty-eight people.

July
Bosnian Serbs massacre 8,000 Muslim men and boys in Srebrenica.

September
Online auction site eBay is launched.

October
Former NFL star O.J. Simpson is acquitted of murder, millions watch verdict.

December
Dayton Agreement ends more than three years of war in Bosnia.

1998

January
Hillary Clinton denounces "vast right-wing conspiracy" against her husband.

July
In Rome, 120 countries vote to create permanent International Criminal Court.

August
Al-Qaeda operatives bomb U.S. embassies in Kenya and Tanzania.

September
Larry Page and Sergey Brin, Stanford PhD students, found Google.

September
Kenneth Starr issues his report.

October
Gay college student Matthew Shepard is tortured and killed near Laramie, Wyoming.

1999

February
Clinton is acquitted in impeachment proceedings.

October
World population reaches 6 billion, up from 4 billion in 1974.

2000

May
ILOVEYOU virus causes Internet havoc, costing millions to repair.

October
U.S.S. Cole is bombed while in port in Yemen.

December
George W. Bush is declared winner of disputed U.S. presidential election.

28 Global Americans Today

2000–2016

Young religious seeker John Walker Lindh left home to become an Islamic scholar, and in the fall of 2000 made the fateful decision to venture into Afghanistan to join the Taliban.

In December 2001, John Walker Lindh returned to the United States, the country where he was born and held citizenship but no longer considered home. The American public received the twenty-one-year-old with scorn and disbelief: How could a young, white man from an affluent suburb take up arms against U.S.-backed allies in Afghanistan? Pundits condemned his supposedly overly permissive "hippie" parents for encouraging their son's journey into the Islamic faith, which led him to study Arabic in Yemen and to fight for the Taliban in Afghanistan. Upon closer look, however, Lindh's route to becoming the "American Taliban" was more complex than it seemed.

AP Images

A brainy and sickly kid who repeatedly changed schools and eventually studied at home with a tutor, he had a difficult childhood and adolescence. After seeing a popular feature film about the radical black nationalist Malcolm X, he began to study Muslim websites and converted to Islam at age sixteen. His newfound spirituality pleased his parents because, in their eyes, he had finally found a community where he belonged—and a wholesome one with strictures against alcohol and drugs. After Lindh completed high school, he studied in Yemen, fulfilling his dream of becoming an Islamic scholar.

The young religious seeker, however, grew frustrated with education in Yemen, where classes welcomed women and classmates repeatedly violated Islamic protocols. He kept searching for more orthodox religious training, a quest that brought him to a village in Pakistan where he memorized one-third of the Muslim holy book, the Koran. In the fall of 2000, Lindh made the fateful decision to venture into nearby Afghanistan to join its government (the Taliban) in fighting against an internal rebellion by the Northern Alliance. In November 2001, U.S. forces seeking revenge on the Taliban for sheltering the terrorists responsible for the September 11, 2001 attacks, captured Lindh. Filthy and wounded, Lindh insisted he had joined the Taliban for religious reasons, not to harm Americans, a fact that later made it possible for him to avoid conviction for treason. He accepted a plea bargain in which the U.S. government charged him with the lesser offense of "supplying services to the Taliban." In exchange, Lindh dropped charges that he had been tortured while in U.S. custody. He was sentenced to twenty years in prison and remains a devout Muslim.

His odyssey from suburban misfit to "American Taliban" revealed the changing historical circumstances that empowered and confounded Americans in the early twenty-first century. With the Cold War's end, the United States and its allies confronted religious and ethnic tensions, economic shifts, and environmental challenges. On September 11, 2001, al-Qaeda

How does John Walker Lindh's odyssey from suburban misfit to "American Taliban" reveal the changing historical circumstances that empowered and confounded Americans in the early twenty-first century?

Go to MindTap® to watch a video on Lindh and learn how his story relates to the themes of this chapter.

attacked the United States, killing over three thousand people and demonstrating the threat to global security posed by radical Islamic terrorism. The attack shocked the entire world and transformed the presidency of newly elected George W. Bush, son of former President George H.W. Bush.

The 9/11 attacks and the aftermath occurred in an era of broad economic and technological changes that enabled Lindh, an isolated young man, to join a virtual community sharing his religious views. With unprecedented speed, the Internet became the greatest connector of, and resource for, humans around the world. It was the centerpiece of an information and communication revolution that altered the structure of the global economy, which had expanded to include 30 million people in China, India, Russia, and other nations formerly closed to trade during the Cold War. More people than ever were linked in a single global trading network, but not everyone benefited equally. As with the industrial revolution in the late nineteenth century and the postindustrial revolution after World War II, the new global economy exacerbated social divisions between rich and poor. The rapid industrialization of China and other developing countries due to globalization also contributed to climate changes with the potential to wreak worldwide environmental and human destruction.

With the expansion of the global economy came an accompanying economic downturn in 2007. The United States and the world plunged into recession, the deepest since the Great Depression of the 1930s. Risky financial products and practices, deregulation, and a collapse of the housing market threw both the U.S. and global economies into turmoil. During this crisis, Barack Obama was elected as the first African American president in an era of highly polarized domestic politics. In the early twenty-first century, the United States was more connected to the world than ever but also an extremely divided society.

28-1 National Security and the Global Order

Seattle Post Intelligencer

On the first anniversary of 9/11, David Horsey, an editorial cartoonist for the *Seattle Post-Intelligencer*, portrays the impact of the terrorist attacks on Americans.

How does the cartoonist contrast U.S. society before and after the 9/11 attacks? What are some of the ways he suggests that the United States changed in the year following the assaults? ▶

Go to MindTap® to practice history with the Chapter 28 **Primary Source Writing Activity: War on Terrorism**. Read and view primary sources and respond to a writing prompt.

After his contested victory in the 2000 presidential election, George W. Bush took office intending to focus on domestic affairs. But after over three thousand people died in orchestrated terrorist attacks on the United States on September 11, 2001, Bush shifted his attention to foreign policy and built a multinational coalition to wage what he dubbed the "War on Terror." In the fall of 2001, U.S. and British forces invaded Afghanistan in pursuit of the Islamic radicals responsible for the 9/11 attacks. In March 2003, the Bush administration mobilized international support for a controversial invasion of Iraq followed by a protracted process of pacification and reconstruction.

Upon winning the presidency in 2008, Obama vowed to withdraw U.S. troops from the unpopular war in Iraq, to expand military operations in Afghanistan, and to continue the global war on terrorism. When a wave of mass protests swept much of the Arab world in early 2011, it appeared that democracy might supplant authoritarianism there. But devastating civil wars in Libya and Syria and a powerful new radical Islamic insurgency soon dimmed those hopes.

☞ As you read, consider how and why the 9/11 attacks changed U.S. foreign policy and American daily life. Has the United States prevailed in the fight against terrorism? Explain your answers.

28-1a 9/11 and War on Terrorism

The 9/11 attacks on the United States reorder global diplomatic relations.

After his inauguration in January 2001, President Bush began limiting U.S. commitments abroad. At the UN, he refused to grant the International Criminal Court jurisdiction over U.S. soldiers accused of violating international law while participating in multinational peacekeeping operations. Most controversially, Bush abandoned ratification of the Kyoto Protocol, an international treaty signed by one hundred eighty nations to reduce global warming by setting limits on industrial emissions. Accustomed to a more collaborative approach to international affairs, such moves alarmed domestic critics and foreign allies.

Sergey Komarov-Kohl/Alamy Stock Photo

Thomas Franklin, *Flag-Raising at Ground Zero*, September 11, 2001 Thomas Franklin's photograph of firefighters Dan McWilliams, George Johnson, and Billy Eisengrein raising the U.S. flag over the rubble of the World Trade Towers became a symbol of hope and heroism on a day of horrific violence. First responders and cleanup crews worked at the site for five months following the 9/11 attacks. Many later experienced serious health complications as a result of exposure to highly toxic dust. ▲

September 11, 2001 changed the global landscape. That morning, four commercial jets departed from East Coast cities. Shortly after each reached cruising altitude, hijackers killed or disabled the pilots and steered the planes toward their intended targets. At 8:48 a.m., the first— American Airlines flight 11 from Boston— hit the North Tower of New York's World Trade Center. At 9:03 a.m., United flight 175, which also departed from Boston, struck the South Tower. Less than two hours later, both one hundred ten-story buildings collapsed. At 9:37 a.m., American 77, scheduled to travel from Dulles International Airport to Los Angeles, collided into the south wall of the Pentagon. At 10:03 a.m., passengers aboard United flight 93, who had received word of the other three hijackings shortly after taking off from Newark, almost overpowered their attackers before the hijackers crashed the plane in a field outside Shanksville, Pennsylvania, thwarting another planned assault on the nation's capital. All 246 people aboard the planes perished. Another 2,753 died at the World Trade Center, including 343 firefighters and 72 law enforcement officers among the first responders to the attacks. Another 184 died at the Pentagon. Citizens of more than eighty nations were among the casualties of 9/11.

Globally, millions watched these events unfold on live television. For weeks afterward, news stations repeatedly showed footage of the explosions, people jumping to their deaths to escape flames and smoke, and the Towers' collapse. Commentators interviewed anguished family members seeking answers about the fate of their loved ones and hailed the courage of police officers and firefighters helping with rescue efforts. Swept up in a wave of patriotism, Americans rushed to buy flags, give blood, enlist in the armed forces, and volunteer for relief organizations. U.S. charities received $1 billion in donations. Vigils for the victims were held all over the world.

Within days, the nineteen Saudi hijackers were identified and linked to Osama bin Laden, the fundamentalist Muslim leader of the al-Qaeda terrorist network. Many of the hijackers had lived and worked in the United States for years, blending in inconspicuously while awaiting directives from al-Qaeda. A few took flying lessons from U.S. schools, requesting instruction on flying large planes but expressing no interest in mastering takeoffs or landings—demands their teachers found puzzling. Al-Qaeda chose its targets precisely, aiming for maximum symbolism and physical damage to centers of U.S. finance, militarism, and politics. In the weeks immediately preceding 9/11, CIA director George Tenet and other counterterrorism experts presented evidence of an al-Qaeda plot to use commercial aircraft as missiles, but neither President Bush nor National Security

Richard Drew, *The Falling Man*, September 11, 2011
At 9:41 a.m. on 9/11, Associated Press photographer Richard Drew took twelve shots of a man falling from the North Tower of the World Trade Center, one of an estimated two hundred people who either fell or jumped from the upper floors to escape smoke and flames. When Drew's image appeared in newspapers around the world, it prompted a huge outcry and was pulled from circulation. The falling man's identity has never been confirmed. ▲

Taliban Political movement in Afghanistan based in Islamic fundamentalism and a strict obedience to Islamic law (*Sharia*) that is particularly restrictive for women and girls.

drone attacks Missile strikes by unmanned, remote controlled aircraft used in risky areas of combat for surveillance and attack.

enemy combatants Detainees, mainly from al-Qaeda or the Taliban held by the United States who were not subject to international rules governing prisoners of war.

USA Patriot Act U.S. counterterrorism legislation enhancing government surveillance, antimoney-laundering policies, border security, and information sharing among federal agencies and between the United States and other nations.

Advisor Condoleezza Rice gave the briefings much credence.

But after the attacks, the Bush administration reacted decisively. The president vowed to capture bin Laden "dead or alive" and warned nations of dire consequences if they assisted terrorists. To explain what motivated the attackers, Bush posed the question "Why do they hate us?" and answered "They hate our freedoms: our freedom of religion, our freedom of speech, our freedom to vote and assemble and disagree with each other." The president described Islam as a peaceful religion that forbids the killing of innocents and condemns suicide, but some Americans found it difficult to distinguish nonviolent Muslims from Islamic radicals who called for a holy war, *jihad*, against the United States. Although critics called the president's rhetoric jingoistic, his popular approval ratings soared to 90 percent.

Bush demanded that the **Taliban**, the Islamist regime ruling Afghanistan, surrender bin Laden, who ran al-Qaeda training camps there. In October 2001, after the Taliban refused to comply, U.S. and U.K. pilots began bombing Afghanistan. With the assistance of anti-Taliban forces, U.S. ground troops gained control of Afghan cities and captured John Walker Lindh, an American fighting with the Taliban. In early December, the Taliban collapsed, but bin Laden, likely with the aid of allies in Pakistani intelligence, escaped. In 2003, a coalition force representing forty-seven nations began battling a Taliban insurgency. Although vastly outnumbered and outgunned, the Taliban fought back to regain influence in rural areas. Fighting soon spilled over into neighboring Pakistan where the Pakistani Army clashed with local tribes who aided Taliban and al-Qaeda rebels. In response, the United States launched unmanned **drone attacks** on enemies in Pakistan. Afghani civilians struggled as reconstruction efforts faltered.

While waging war in Afghanistan, U.S. soldiers and intelligence operatives backed by a multinational coalition pursued al-Qaeda across the globe. By 2003, more than 2,700 suspected terrorists in 98 countries had been abducted or killed. Because captives were not seized during an officially declared war against any nation's armed forces, the Bush administration made the controversial decision to characterize them as **enemy combatants** who were not protected by either the U.S. Constitution or the Geneva Conventions. Seven hundred and seventy-five alleged terrorists, 420 of whom were eventually released without charge, were sent to a newly created U.S. prison camp at Guantánamo Bay, Cuba. Bin Laden, however, remained at large.

At home, the war on terror produced tremendous changes (see Table 28.1). Expanded security procedures transformed air travel and the postal service. Enacted in October 2001, the **USA Patriot Act** granted law enforcement officials sweeping new powers to detain and deport suspected terrorists, to use wiretapping and other surveillance tools on U.S. citizens, and to conduct searches without warrants. In November 2002, Congress approved the **Department of Homeland Security**, a consolidation of twenty-two federal agencies charged with responding to terrorism, man-made accidents, and natural disasters.

28-1b War in Iraq

The Bush administration launches a controversial war in Iraq.

In the aftermath of 9/11, the Bush administration reshaped U.S. foreign policy. Abandoning Cold War-era policies of collective security and deterrence, President Bush and his aides developed a doctrine of preemptive self-defense in which the United States used overwhelming military superiority to defend itself against emerging as well as imminent threats. In place of permanent regional alliances, the **Bush Doctrine** called for

Table 28.1 Selected Global Terrorist Attacks, 1972–2015

Originating in the term *terrorisme* used to describe violence practiced by the French government during the 1793–1794 Reign of Terror, *terrorism* refers to acts perpetrated by states or nonstate groups that harm and frighten civilians or non-combatants in order to further ideological, racial, ethnic, religious, political, or nationalistic goals. This chart documents many of the varied terrorist acts that have occurred globally since 1972.

Date	Location	Description
July 1972	Belfast, Ireland	Irish Republican Army attacked British government and citizens, killing 11 and injuring 130 on "Bloody Friday"
September 1972	Munich, Germany	12 Israeli athletes killed by Black September (Palestinian group) at the Olympic Games
April 1983	Beirut, Lebanon	Islamic Jihad bombed U.S. embassy, killing 63 and injuring 120
October 1983	Beirut, Lebanon	Islamic Jihad attacked French and U.S. embassies, killing 301 and injuring 161
December 1988	Lockerbie, Scotland	Libyan government agents bombed, in mid-air, Pam-Am flight, killing 270 and injuring 12
February 1993	New York, NY	Islamic terror cell used truck bomb to attack World Trade Center, killing 6 and injuring 1,040
March 1993	Mumbai (Bombay), India	Dawood Ibrahim implemented 15 simultaneous bombings, killing 317 and injuring 1,400
March 1995	Tokyo, Japan	Aum Shinrikyo attacked subway with sarin nerve gas, killing 12 and injuring 5,511
April 1995	Oklahoma City, OK	Timothy McVeigh bombed a federal building, killing 169 and injuring 675
June 1996	Dhahran, Saudi Arabia	Hezbollah bombed U.S. military base, killing 18 and injuring 515
August 1998	Nairobi, Kenya and Dar es Salaam, Tanzania	Al-Qaeda bombed U.S embassies, killing 244 and injuring 4,877
September 2001	Washington, DC; New York, NY; Shanksville, PA	Al-Qaeda attacked U.S., killing 2,993 and injuring 8,900
October 2002	Moscow, Russia	Chechen separatists attack and take hostages, killing 170 and injuring 656
March 2004	Madrid, Spain	Al-Qaeda bombs 4 trains, killing 191 and injuring 1,876
September 2004	Beslan, Russia	Chechen separatists attack and take hostages at a school, killing 372 and injuring 747
July 2005	London, England	Islamic extremists bomb 3 subways and a bus, killing 56 and inuring 784
July 2006	Mumbai (Bombay), India	Lashkar-e-Taiba bombs 7 commuter trains, killing 209 and injuring 714
January 2012	Kano, Nigeria	Boko Haram attacks multiple sites, killing 178 and injuring 50
April 2015	Garissa, Kenya	Al-Shabaab attacks college campus, killing 152 and injuring 79

Sources: http://fas.org/irp/threat/terror_chron.html; http://www.johnstonsarchive.net/terrorism/wrjp255i.html

selective cooperation with foreign allies while emphasizing U.S. willingness to act unilaterally to build democratic states. In January 2002, Bush reiterated his intention to punish nations who sponsored terrorism, singling out Iran, Iraq, and North Korea as an "axis of evil, arming to threaten the peace of the world. " Many people around the world who had expressed solidarity with the United States on 9/11 now criticized Bush's unapologetic embrace of unilateral action.

Iraq soon became the test case for the new doctrine. Accusing Iraqi dictator Saddam Hussein of secretly possessing **weapons of mass destruction (WMD)** and having ties to al-Qaeda, Bush called for "regime change" and demanded that Iraq allow UN weapons inspections for the first time since 1998. While fending off more hawkish members of the Bush administration calling for a U.S. invasion of Iraq, Secretary of State Colin Powell tried to build a UN coalition. In October 2002, persuaded by Bush's claims that Saddam was attempting to acquire fissile materials to build nuclear weapons, the

Department of Homeland Security Executive department resulting from the merger of twenty-two federal agencies to better coordinate the U.S. government's counterterrorism programs.

Bush Doctrine Foreign policy paradigm calling for the United States to act alone (unilaterally) in striking against threats outside its borders.

weapons of mass destruction (WMD) Nuclear, chemical, biological, or other type of weapons that can kill or bring great harm to a large number of human beings.

Operation Iraqi Freedom Name given by George H. Bush to U.S. war in Iraq to remove Saddam Hussein from power and to capture his reported arsenal of weapons of mass destruction.

Republican-led House voted two hundred ninety-six to one hundred thirty-three, and the Democrat-led Senate voted seventy-seven to twenty-three to grant Bush authorization to use force in Iraq. British Prime Minister Tony Blair, alone among America's closest allies, endorsed Bush's call for Saddam's ouster. Although the UN redeployed inspectors to Iraq, they failed to find stores of biological, chemical, or nuclear weapons. At Bush's insistence, Powell—despite his reservations about the intelligence being used to justify U.S. intervention—then made the case for war at the Security Council. On February 15, 2003, more than 10 million people participated in antiwar demonstrations in six hundred cities around the world, the largest peace demonstrations ever. Later that month, the UN defeated the war resolution by a large margin. Undaunted, Bush prepared to attack Iraq.

On March 20, 2003, **Operation Iraqi Freedom** began with U.S. airstrikes on Baghdad, and two hundred forty thousand U.S. and U.K. ground troops invading Iraq (see Map 28.1). Within five weeks, the Saddam regime collapsed and coalition forces controlled Iraq. Saddam himself eluded capture until December, when U.S. commandos

STEPHEN JAFFE/AFP/Getty Images

President George W. Bush on the U.S.S. *Abraham Lincoln*, May 1, 2003 On May 1, 2003, Bush, a former pilot in the Air National Guard, landed a fighter on the aircraft carrier USS *Abraham Lincoln*. Standing before a banner reading "Mission Accomplished," Bush announced that major combat operations in Iraq were over and vowed to continue the search for banned weapons there. To critics of the war, the banner later symbolized the flawed assumptions the Bush administration made about Iraq before the invasion and during the occupation. ▲

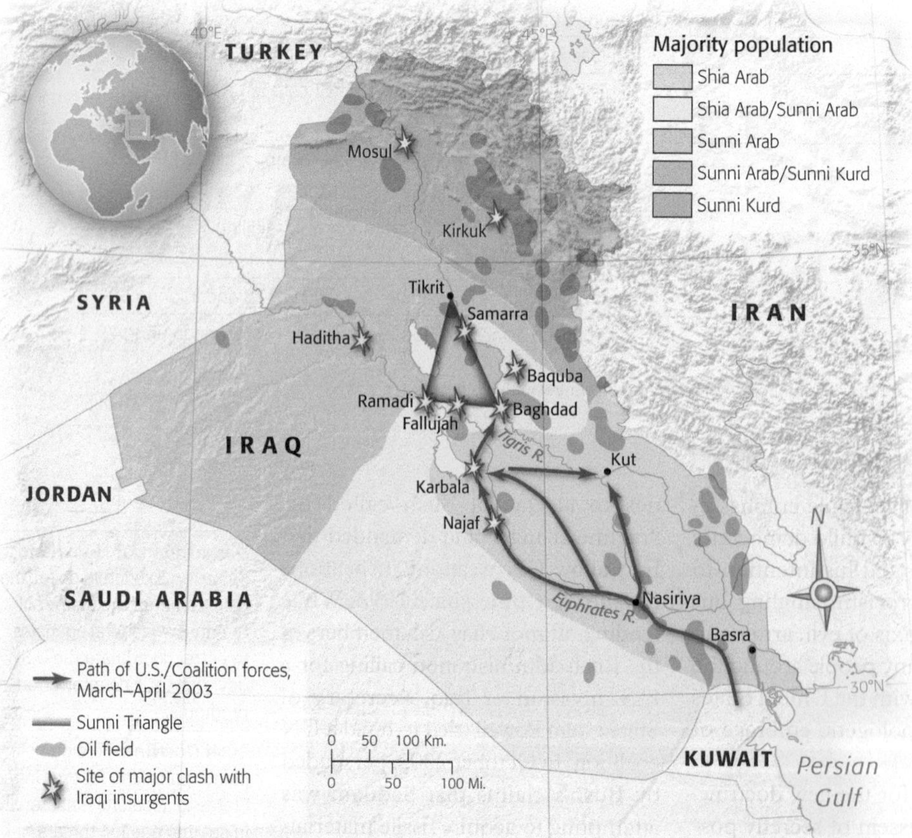

Map 28.1 Iraq in Transition, 2003–2008 This map details the trajectory of the initial U.S.-led invasion of Iraq and sites of subsequent battles between U.S. forces and Iraqi insurgents. Ethnic and religious factionalism greatly complicated U.S. efforts to unite and rebuild Iraq. ◀

AP Images/Tulsa World

Global Americans Born near Miami, Oklahoma, in 1970, **Fern Holland** graduated from the University of Oklahoma and then volunteered in children's hospitals in South Africa and Russia. In 1999, three years after finishing law school at the University of Tulsa, she left her law practice and joined the Peace Corps to work in Namibia as an HIV/AIDS educator. Returning to the United States after 9/11, she entered the LLM program at Georgetown Law Center and developed a program to train journalists, lawyers, and judges in Africa. But she interrupted her studies to aid victims of sexual exploitation in Guinea.

In July 2003, Holland was hired by the U.S. Agency for International Development (USAID) to investigate human rights abuses under the Saddam Hussein regime. She then joined the Coalition Provisional Authority to help Iraqis establish democracy. Determined to help women in a society that had rendered them powerless, Holland instituted centers where Iraqi women learned about representative government, drafted portions of the Iraqi interim constitution that protected women's rights, and demanded that women hold one-quarter of the seats in the National Assembly.

On March 9, 2004, on the road between Karbala and Al Hillah, Holland, her Iraqi counterpart, Salwa Ali Oushami, and CPA press liaison Robert Zangas were assassinated by insurgents. Holland and Zangas were the first U.S. civilians to die in the Iraq War. She exemplified the millions of aid workers and ordinary citizens who believe that democracy can supplant autocracy in the Middle East.

captured him. Three years later, he was executed after an Iraqi tribunal found him guilty of crimes against humanity.

The process of democratizing and rebuilding a shattered Iraq proved challenging and costly. Contrary to Vice President Richard "Dick" Cheney's assertion that U.S. forces would be "greeted as liberators," many Iraqis harbored great bitterness about prior U.S. support of Saddam's dictatorial regime. Jettisoning plans for a brief occupation and quick transfer of power to a provisional government led by Iraqi exiles, Bush created the U.S-led Coalition Provisional Authority (CPA). In the United States, many Americans remained skeptical about Bush's rationale for intervention, and support for the war in the world community eroded as investigators found no evidence that Iraq possessed WMD, had attempted to acquire unenriched uranium to build nuclear weapons, or collaborated with the 9/11 attackers.

The situation in Iraq deteriorated. U.S. soldiers faced suicide bombers and **improvised explosive devices (IEDs)**. Many troops, including those in the Reserves and National Guard, endured multiple tours of duty and mounting casualties. Repeated deployments added hardships for military families separated for months at a time and increased the likelihood of soldiers experiencing post-traumatic stress disorder (PTSD).

By 2007, almost 2 million Iraqis were displaced by violence and became refugees. Sabotage, unemployment, corruption, and outdated infrastructure undermined efforts to jump-start the Iraqi economy. Factionalism between Shi'ite (Shi'a) and **Sunni** Muslims and Kurdish demands for independence complicated efforts to create a stable Iraqi government.

In April 2004, tensions in Iraq heightened after CBS News broadcast graphic photographs of U.S. soldiers abusing Iraqis held in **Abu Ghraib** prison, sparking widespread condemnation of some of the Bush administration's policies in the war on terror. The International Red Cross and Amnesty International challenged U.S. officials' claims that the incidents at Abu Ghraib were an aberration and pointed to a broader pattern of brutality at U.S. overseas detention centers in Iraq, Afghanistan, and Guantánamo Bay. In late 2004, after the release of memos detailing the administration's approval of "enhanced interrogation techniques" like prolonged sleep deprivation, restraining prisoners in positions that maximized physical discomfort, and using waterboarding to simulate drowning, a debate over the efficacy and morality of such tactics arose. These discussions intensified when the media reported on secret CIA prisons and the agency's use of **extraordinary renditions** where "high-value detainees" were shipped to nations that subjected them to torture, a practice intended to distance the Bush administration from human rights abuses. In *Hamdan v. Rumsfeld* (2006) and other cases, the U.S. Supreme Court rejected the administration's characterization of the prisoners at Guantánamo as enemy combatants and ruled that the detainees there were fully protected by the Constitution and the Geneva Conventions. While critics claimed that the U.S. tactics in the war on terrorism were exacerbating anti-Americanism and Islamist radicalism, supporters argued that extreme measures were

improvised explosive devices (IEDs) Bombs made and deployed in nonstandard ways for military combat, linked to over 50 percent of deaths among U.S. and allied forces during the Iraq War.

Sunni Largest of two major branches of Islam, Sunnis contend that the Muslim community was to select the Prophet's successor (caliph), whereas Shi'a believe the Prophet chose his his son-in-law, Ali, as his successor.

Abu Ghraib Jail located west of Baghdad used by U.S. forces and their allies during the Iraq War to hold military captives and political enemies.

extraordinary renditions Covert abduction of persons for the purpose of torture that is conducted in countries that permit such human rights abuse.

Courtesy Wikipedia/ZUMA Press/Newscom

Prisoner at Abu Ghraib, 2003 A hooded prisoner at Abu Ghraib stands on a box with electrical wires used to shock him attached to his hands. Investigations revealed widespread human rights violations including physical and sexual abuse, torture, rape, sodomy, and murder. Eleven U.S. soldiers were court-martialed and dishonorably discharged for dereliction of duty, mistreatment, and aggravated assault and battery. Specialists Charles Graner and Lynndie England were sentenced to imprisonment for ten and three years, respectively. ▲

merited in obtaining information about those who engaged in terrorist activities.

Despite these controversies, Bush narrowly defeated Democratic nominee John Kerry in the 2004 presidential election, and democratization efforts in Iraq continued. In January 2005, six months after the CPA ended its formal occupation, Iraq had its first free elections in fifty years and voters adopted a new constitution soon after. But the elections did not stem the insurgency, which grew increasingly sectarian during 2005 and witnessed Sunni insurgents targeting Shi'ite and Kurdish civilians in suicide bombings. One hundred thirty thousand U.S. troops remained in Iraq, and costs of the war soared to $5 billion per month. In November 2006, with Bush's approval ratings below 40 percent, the Democrats regained control of both houses of Congress.

In January 2007, responding to mounting criticism of the war effort and the fragile Iraqi political situation, Bush announced a new multinational "surge" of thirty thousand additional advisers and trainers to help the Iraqis. In December 2008, Bush and Iraqi prime minister Nouri al-Maliki agreed on a December 31, 2011, deadline for the complete withdrawal of U.S. combat forces.

The war in Iraq was only part of the expansion of U.S. defense and intelligence capabilities. To confront global terrorists and the regimes that supported them, the Pentagon constructed a string of new military facilities in the Middle East, Central Asia, and Africa. U.S. defense spending rose from $304 billion in 2001 to $696 billion in 2008—far more than any other nation in the world. As it had done since initiating the Marshall Plan, the United States promoted economic development and political stability by expanding the U.S. foreign aid budget from $13 billion in 2000 to $34 billion in 2008. In 2003, similar motives inspired Bush to create the President's Emergency Plan for AIDS Relief (PEPFAR), a $15 billion campaign to combat HIV/AIDS in selected developing nations, the largest commitment ever by a nation to fight a single disease.

28-1c U.S. Troops Leave Iraq and Afghanistan

The Obama administration withdraws U.S. forces from Iraq and Afghanistan but continues war on terrorism.

After defeating Senator John McCain in the 2008 presidential election, Obama, a biracial American and self-described "citizen of the world" with a Kenyan father and a white American mother, promised a less confrontational approach to international affairs. In June 2009, Obama gave a speech in Cairo calling for "a new beginning between the United States and Muslims around the world, one based upon mutual interest and mutual respect."

The Obama administration used a mix of military power and diplomacy. He pursued nuclear nonproliferation agreements with Iran and North Korea. In 2010, he signed a major nuclear arms reduction treaty with Russia, but U.S.–Russian relations soon deteriorated over crises in Georgia and Ukraine. In pursuit of al-Qaeda and its affiliates, Obama increased counterinsurgency aid to the Pakistani government and escalated the use of drones in Pakistan, Yemen, and Somalia. From 2009 to 2015, an estimated 2,464 people, including more than 300 noncombatants and four American aid workers, were killed in U.S. drone strikes, more than nine times the drone casualties of the Bush era.

Facing an intensifying insurgency in Afghanistan, Obama escalated the war (see Map 28.2). Bolstered by a "surge" of thirty thousand additional U.S. troops, coalition forces captured and killed hundreds of Taliban. In May 2011, Obama scored a political and military victory when U.S. Navy SEALs found Osama bin Laden in a compound in Abbottabad, Pakistan. The result of months of careful intelligence analysis and planning, the raid resulted in bin Laden's death and seizure of valuable al-Qaeda materials. In June 2013, the United States and Afghanistan signed a bilateral security agreement, and

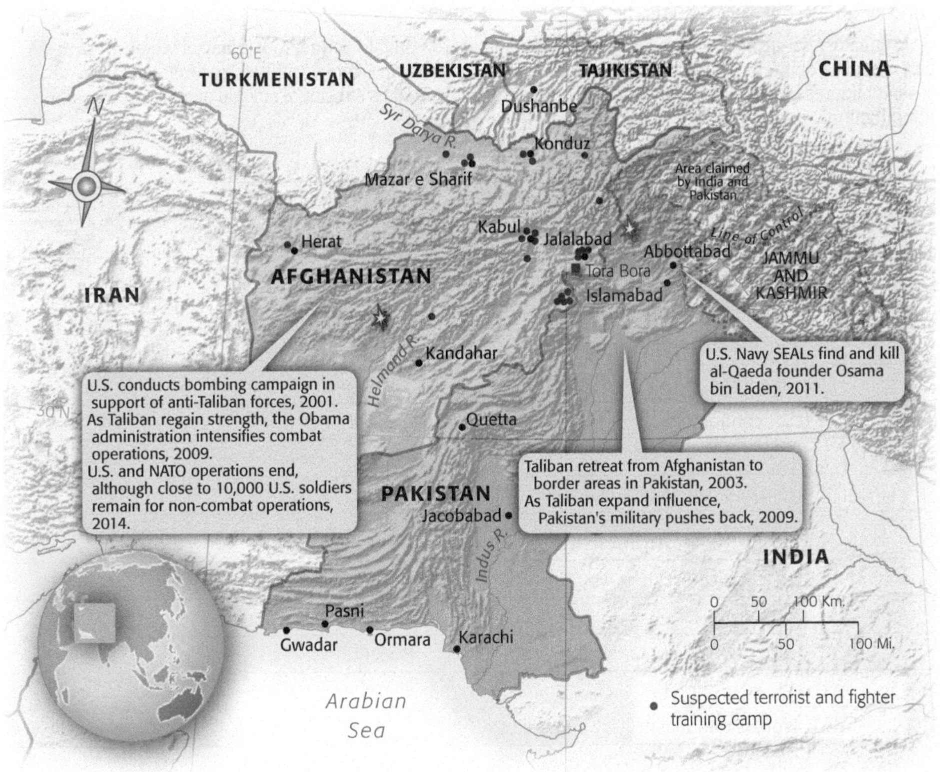

Map 28.2 War in Afghanistan, 2001–2014 After U.S. and British troops invaded Afghanistan in October 2001 to punish the Taliban for harboring terrorists and to capture those responsible for 9/11, they ousted the Taliban quickly. But it proved quite difficult to stabilize and reconstruct Afghanistan. Multinational forces battled a Taliban insurgency that soon spread into neighboring Pakistan. After U.S. commandos killed Osama bin Laden in May 2011, the United States and NATO began a gradual withdrawal from Afghanistan. ◄

U.S. military leaders began transferring combat operations to their Afghani counterparts. U.S. and NATO combat operations ended in late 2014, but ninety-eight hundred U.S. soldiers remained behind to conduct military training and counterinsurgency operations.

In Iraq, Obama reaffirmed the December 31, 2011, troop withdrawal deadline agreed upon by the Bush administration and the Iraqi government. Obama and al-Maliki outlined plans for postwar cooperation on trade, energy, economic development, and security. The United States maintained its embassy in Baghdad and consulates in Basra, Mosul, and Kirkuk. On December 15, 2011, the United States formally ended its mission in Iraq and withdrew its last five hundred troops.

U.S. intervention in Iraq and Afghanistan had high human and financial costs. Two thousand three hundred and fifty seven U.S. troops died in Afghanistan and another 4,489 died in Iraq (see Table 28.2). The United States spent $1.65 trillion on the Afghan conflict and another $1.71 trillion on the Iraq war. Experts predicted that care for U.S. veterans of both wars could cost as much as $4.3 trillion by 2054. More than fifty thousand U.S. soldiers were wounded in the two conflicts. But not all injuries were immediately apparent or occurred on the battlefield. By 2015, the Veterans Administration (VA) had approved more than six hundred seventy-five thousand disability claims for conditions such as physical trauma, brain injury, and post-traumatic stress disorder (PTSD). High rates of suicides among veterans and sexual assaults of female soldiers by male comrades sparked calls for improved mental health services and policy reforms to help the nation's warriors.

Throughout his presidency, civil liberties groups assailed Obama's continuation of government surveillance programs established in the aftermath of 9/11. Beginning in 2011, the website WikiLeaks began to release, amid the protests of the U.S. government, hundreds of thousands of classified State Department documents. In June 2013, Edward Snowden, a contractor for the National Security Agency, leaked a huge cache of classified materials about the agency's worldwide collection of electronic data to reporters. The scope and targets of the program outraged Americans and foreigners alike. To avoid prosecution for violating the Espionage Act, Snowden fled first to Hong Kong then to Russia and began seeking permanent asylum in nations without extradition treaties with the United States. A polarizing figure, Snowden was seen by some as a patriotic whistleblower who exposed a dangerous expansion of government intrusion into private lives. Others saw him as a traitor who gravely damaged intelligence-gathering capabilities. In June 2015, as a result of Snowden's revelations and federal cases challenging the constitutionality of the bulk collection of Americans' phone records, Congress added new limits on electronic surveillance of U.S. citizens when it reauthorized several provisions of the Patriot Act.

Obama defended the National Security Agency's (NSA's) data-gathering practices and made little progress in reigning in the excesses of the war on terror. Although the administration announced that it would no longer define detainees at Guantánamo Bay as enemy combatants, its efforts to close the prison and to prosecute suspect terrorists in civil courts instead of military tribunals ran

Table 28.2 Casualties in Iraq and Afghanistan, 2001–2015

The Pentagon has carefully tracked U.S. military deaths in the wars in Iraq and Afghanistan, but private contractors (many of whom were not U.S. citizens) and soldiers fighting on behalf of international coalition partners and the Afghan and Iraqi security forces (military and police) have also perished. These casualty figures do not include soldiers and contractors who died as a result of suicide or risky behaviors associated with PTSD after completing their military tours.

Iraq		
Affiliation	**Description**	**Deaths**
Nonaffiliated	Iraqi civilians	137,000–165,000[a]
Opposition	Opposition combatants	36,400[a]
Allied armed forces	U.S. armed forces	4,424[b]
Allied armed forces	Iraqi national military and police	12,000[a]
Allied armed forces	Other (non-U.S.) armed forces	319
Allied civilians	U.S. contractors	3,481
Allied civilians	Journalists	221
Allied civilians	Humanitarian and NGO workers	62
Afghanistan		
Affiliation	**Description**	**Deaths**
Nonaffiliated	Afghani civilians	26,000[a]
Opposition	Opposition combatants	35,000[a]
Allied armed forces	U.S. armed forces	2,215[c]
Allied armed forces	Afghani national military and police	23,470
Allied armed forces	Other (non-U.S.) armed forces	1,114
Allied civilians	U.S. contractors	3,401
Allied civilians	Journalists	25
Allied civilians	Humanitarian and NGO workers	331

[a] Indicates rounded figures.

[b] Includes 14 Department of Defense civilian employees.

[c] Includes 4 Department of Defense civilian employees.

Sources: http://www.defense.gov/casualty.pdf; http://watson.brown.edu/costsofwar/files/cow/imce/figures/2015/SUMMARY%20CHART%20-%20Direct%20War%20Death%20Toll%20to%20April%202015.pdf; https://www.iraqbodycount.org/database/.

into congressional opposition. By 2011, the global war on terrorism had resulted in 119,044 arrests and 35,117 convictions in sixty-six countries.

28-1d Revolutions and Negotiations

U.S. officials confront insurgencies in the Arab world and reach out to old adversaries.

In late 2010, popular revolutions erupted throughout the Arab world, inspiring hopes that democracy could prevail over Islamic radicalism and authoritarianism. After the government in Tunisia was overthrown in January 2011, demonstrations arose in Oman, Yemen, Syria, and Morocco. In Cairo, thousands of protestors gathered in Tahrir Square to demand the resignation of Egyptian president Hosni Mubarak. On February 11, with his international and domestic support collapsing, Mubarak stepped down. Four days later, demonstrations against Muammar Qaddafi erupted in Libya. Throughout the **Arab Spring**, prodemocracy activists spread their calls for freedom around the world via YouTube videos, tweets, and Facebook posts—a potent illustration of the political power of the Internet, mobile technology, and smart phones.

Arab Spring Wave of revolutionary protests throughout the Arab world from December 2010 to mid-2012 that pushed rulers out of power in Tunisia, Egypt, Libya, and Yemen.

In March 2011, after Qaddafi used violence to crush a burgeoning civil war in Libya, the UN Security Council voted to establish an arms embargo, a no-fly zone, and a naval blockade to protect civilians. While the Obama administration refused to provide ground troops to the NATO-led coalition that enforced the UN sanctions, the United States provided air and naval support. In August, after rebel forces seized Tripoli, Qaddafi was ousted from power. On October 23, three days after rebels captured and killed Qaddafi, their governing committee declared an end to the Libyan civil war.

But democracy and peace in the region proved short lived. In July 2013, after months of increasing popular unrest, Mohammed Morsi, Egypt's recently elected president, was ousted in a military coup. Syrian president Bashar al-Assad unleashed a violent crackdown and used chemical weapons on rebel forces. In August 2013, a multinational coalition prepared to intervene militarily but cancelled operations after Russia persuaded the Syrian government to destroy its chemical weapons. A horrific civil war nonetheless ensued. More than two hundred thousand Syrians died, and a refugee crisis spilled into neighboring nations. On September 11, 2012, Islamic militants in Libya attacked the U.S. Consulate in Benghazi and killed U.S. ambassador Christopher Stevens and three other Americans. The Obama administration's shifting explanations of the attackers' motives and security lapses at the compound prompted a series of congressional investigations. In 2014, tensions between rival military and Islamist factions plunged Libya back into civil war.

Nothing better exemplified the ongoing challenges of the global war on terrorism than the rise of the **Islamic State (IS)**. In 2014, the Sunni militants started capturing territory in Iraq and Syria. Through social media and propaganda, they publicized their destruction of cultural antiquities and beheadings of aid workers, soldiers, and journalists. Muslim clerics around the world condemned these actions and more than sixty nations declared IS terrorists. A U.S.-led coalition began launching manned and unmanned attacks against IS strongholds in Iraq and Syria.

Islamic State (IS) Offshoot of al-Qaeda also known as *ISIS*, *ISIL*, and *Daesh*; fundamentalist Islamist terrorist group that began capturing territory in Iraq and Syria in 2014.

While confronting new adversaries like IS, Obama normalized U.S. relations with former Cold War adversary Cuba. In July 2015, Cuba and the United States restored full diplomatic relations, severed since 1961. Some issues remained unresolved, such as whether the U.S. would lift its fifty-three-year trade embargo on Cuba and whether Cuba would agree to improve its human rights record.

28-2
Global Capitalism

In 2011, protesters dressed as corpses lie prone in front of a Hong Kong computer store dressed up as high tech workers. The skull and crossbones on a mock computer product represent dangerous working conditions at a U.S. supplier in China, while slogans and the face of Apple Computer head Steve Jobs hold the U.S. firm responsible.

Why did a U.S. company like Apple rely on workers in China to build its products, and how was this possible given the distance from its headquarters in California? ▶

AP Images/Kin Cheung

America's post-9/11 conflicts coexisted with a major economic transformation that began decades earlier. After World War II, developed nations like the United States grew increasingly multinational as companies reduced labor costs by relocating manufacturing operations to countries where wages were lower. The end of the Cold War greatly accelerated this process by enabling three of the world's largest nations—China, India, and Russia—to participate fully in the global economy. At the same time, technological breakthroughs, such as the Internet and wireless technology, further shrank the world by dramatically increasing the speed of global business transactions and, more importantly, empowering individuals to communicate with any person, government, business, or organization around the world. Like industrialization and postindustrialization, globalization also had a downside as nations struggled to maintain economic autonomy, and workers in the developed world fought to keep jobs while those in developing countries fought to improve pay and labor conditions. The interconnected global economy became vulnerable to local shocks anywhere in the world. Moreover, in many nations, the expansion of global capitalism did not reduce poverty or underdevelopment, and the increase in manufacturing and living standards in the developing world heightened global environmental hazards.

☞ As you read, pay attention to the conditions that gave rise to the spreading of global capitalism as well as its impact on U.S. economic and social trends. In what ways did the world become smaller? What impact did this have on consumers, workers, and businesses?

28-2a Economic Integration

The removal and lowering of trade barriers creates an expansive global economy.

Capitalism reached a new stage of development after World War II with the Bretton Woods economic system, which included the creation of the International Monetary Fund, World Bank, and General Agreements on Trade and Tariffs (GATT). The World Trade Organization (WTO), founded in 1995 by one hundred twenty-five nations that controlled 90 percent of world trade, grew by 2015 to include one hundred sixty-one nations, including free market Communist states like China and Vietnam. The WTO remains an engine of neoliberal economic theory that sees open borders to trade as the best possible opportunity for sustained global economic growth and development. A stunning example is China, home to the world's largest population (1.3 billion in 2013). Eight years after joining the WTO in 2001, China became the world's leading exporting nation, rising from .75 percent of global exports in 1978 to over 9 percent in 2009. At the same time, foreign investments exploded from $3 billion in 1983 to $94 billion in 2008. In 2010, China surpassed Japan to become the second largest economy in the world and in late 2014, according to the IMF, surpassed the U.S. to lead the world in gross domestic product (GDP). Given the nation's stunning growth rate of 10 percent per year since Deng Xiaoping's economic reforms took hold in the 1980s, there is little chance that the United States can reclaim the top spot even though China's growth slowed to 7 percent in 2014 (compared to the U.S. rate of 2.2 percent).

India, the only nation with a population rivaling China's, also experienced swift economic ascent, and, according to the IMF, is the only nation that over the long-term can surpass China's GDP. After gaining independence in 1947, India had the most restricted economy in the non-Communist world. But in 1991, it began drastically reducing tariffs, deregulating businesses, and encouraging foreign investment. The effect was particularly pronounced in high-tech industries as Bangalore became India's Silicon Valley and Hyderabad turned into "Cyberbad." Between 1991 and 2001, sales in India's computer industry increased from $150 million to $9.6 billion. India also became a major hub for a wide range of global business services that operated over the telephone and Internet, including call centers and medical recordkeeping. In less than two decades, the rapid economic ascent of China and India revealed how much globalization had changed the world.

The development of China and India continued the economic ascendance of the Asia-Pacific region. The process began with Japan's economic takeoff and was followed by the rise of many other economies including South Korea, Singapore, Hong Kong, Taiwan, and then China and India (see Map 28.3). In October 2015, eleven nations, including the United States and Japan but excluding China, signed the Trans-Pacific Partnership (TPP), a historic agreement to lower or remove trade barriers for the Asia-Pacific region similar to the European Union and the smaller-scale North American Free Trade Agreement (NAFTA). Americans, however, were divided about whether the of elimination of tariffs on Asian imports (like Japanese automobiles) and U.S. exports to Asia like beef and rice benefits U.S. corporations more than consumers. Organized labor and many members of President Obama's own Democratic Party opposed the TPP that his administration spent seven years negotiating. The TPP was part of the economic side of Obama's "pivot to East Asia," a new foreign policy program designed to shift attention and U.S. military resources from Europe and the Middle East to Asia in order to offset China's growing military power and its impact throughout the Asia-Pacific region.

Money sharma/EPA/Newscom

Call Center in Bangalore, India, 2012 Initially motivated mainly by low labor costs, many multinational companies began outsourcing call center jobs to India. But in response to customer complaints about Indians' English accents and idioms, some U.S. companies like J.P. Morgan Chase, AT&T, and Expedia moved their operations to the Philippines, now the world's biggest call center hub. Realizing cost savings was only part of successful globalization, employers were willing to pay higher wages in exchange for more Americanized workers. ◄

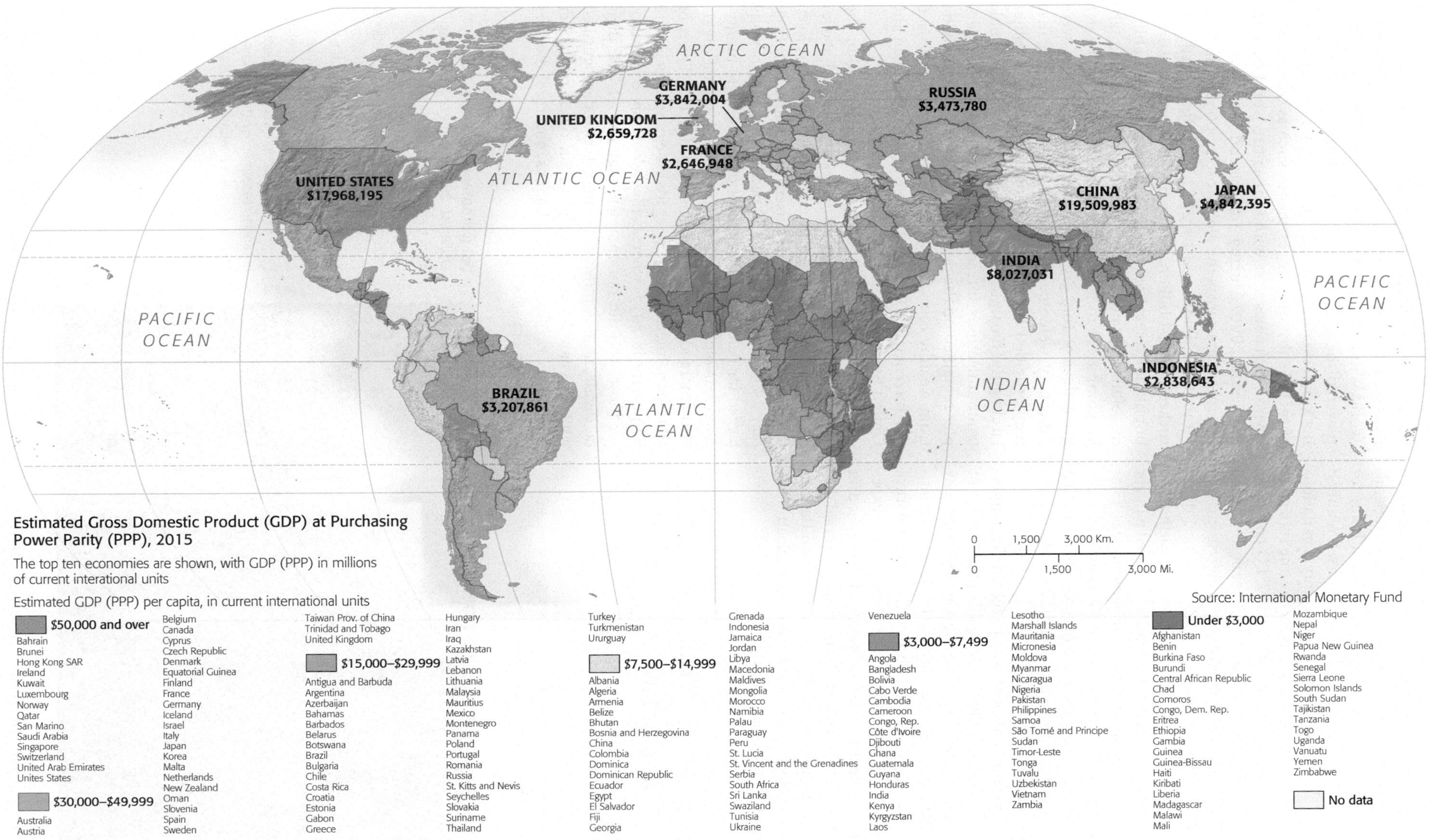

Map 28.3 Global Distribution of Wealth, 2004 Despite neoliberalism and globalization, a major division of wealth between nations above (the Global North) and below the equator (the Global South) still exists. In 2004, one billion people owned 80 percent of the world economy, while another billion earned merely one dollar per day. ▲

digital divide Division between peoples and countries who do and do not have reliable access to digital technologies linked to economic opportunities and improved quality of life.

While economic integration from the perspective of neoliberalism was supposed to be a boon for the entire global economy, it required diminishing sovereignty for nations as their economies became subject to standards set by the WTO and other international bodies. Proponents of neoliberalism worried that globalization made it nearly impossible to protect economies from external shocks—such as natural disasters, wars, and financial crises. A devastating earthquake and tsunami that hit Japan in March 2011 caused a major slowdown in the global production of automobiles. Globalization increased the risk of worldwide economic meltdown by making it possible for any economy, including weak and poorly managed ones, to start a calamitous chain reaction leading to depression.

Under globalization, poor nations feared rich nations as well. While China and India exemplified the benefits of neoliberalism, the majority of the developing world saw little or no improvement in economic standing under globalization. People in the Middle East, Northern Africa, and sub-Saharan Africa with few exceptions did not experience improvement in their standards of living, and in many cases, suffered a decline. Poorer nations decried that richer ones were using the WTO, IMF, and World Bank to bully them into opening up their economies while protecting their own from global competition.

28-2b Innovation and Infrastructure

Technology accelerates global commerce and changes the nature of business.

Debates over inequality in the global economy occurred at the same time as new technologies were leveling the playing field for nations, companies, and individuals to compete for its riches. The invention of the Internet browser made the World Wide Web an "information superhighway" that powered the expansion of global business. The Internet's potential to revolutionize global communication attracted substantial investments, such as transoceanic fiber optic cables that wired the entire world between 1995 and 2000. During this period the number of Internet users across the globe rose 2,000 percent from 20 to 400 million, and by 2012, that figure had skyrocketed to 2.4 billion, nearly one-third of the world's population (see Figure 28.1). The expanded ability of cellular phones and other mobile devices like tablet computers to access the Internet accounted for a great deal of this growth. Mobile technologies were especially welcomed in developing nations because they provided Internet and phone access via satellites circling the Earth to places otherwise lacking a reliable communications infrastructure. But many poor peoples remained on the opposite side of the **digital divide** from wealthy ones. Only 15 percent of Africans used the Internet in 2012 compared to 83 percent in the United States.

New technologies generated divisions within the United States. Older persons (age sixty-five and above) lagged behind younger age groups in Internet usage. Even though usage rate by senior citizens rose dramatically from only 14 percent in 2000 to 58 percent in 2015, they still lagged far behind the 96 percent of eighteen- to twenty-nine-year-olds who used the Internet. A digital divide also emerged between persons with differing levels of education. Internet usage rates for college graduates were 95 percent in 2015, whereas they were only 65 percent for those who did not complete high school. The digital divide, although less pronounced, also distinguished whites, Asian Americans, and urban dwellers (higher Internet users) from blacks, Latinos, and rural dwellers (lower Internet users).

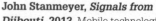

JOHN STANMEYER/National Geographic Creative

John Stanmeyer, *Signals from Djibouti*, 2013 Mobile technologies have transformed global communications, making it possible to connect with people even from remote locations. This award-winning photograph shows Somali migrants living in Djibouti trying to catch an inexpensive cellular signal from their neighboring homeland. Each evening, people visit the beach, hoping to reconnect with their loved ones or to make business and financial transactions. ◄

Bloomberg/Getty Images

Global Americans Born in Moscow in 1973, **Sergey Brin** was part of a stream of Jews fleeing the Soviet Union during the late twentieth century. Most went to Israel, but in 1979, at age six, he came with his parents and grandmother to the United States. Michael and Eugenia Brin both held degrees in mathematics from the prestigious Moscow State University and lived in relative comfort but bristled at anti-Semitic restrictions and sought a better life for Sergey. With the help of a former professor, Michael joined the mathematics faculty at the University of Maryland, and the family settled nearby with Eugenia finding employment at NASA as a research scientist.

Given his family's background and emphasis on academics, it was not surprising that Sergey breezed through the University of Maryland in three years as an award-winning honors student in math and computer science. He went on to study for a Ph.D. in computer science at Stanford University, where in 1998 he dropped out to start a company named Google (with Larry Page) that revolutionized search engines on the emerging World Wide Web. After Google's initial public offering of stock in 2004, Brin became one of the wealthiest and most powerful players in Silicon Valley. Ten years later, he was named the eighteenth richest person in the world, and Google was a titan of the global economy. Brin's story reveals how the "brain drain" from the Soviet Union (as well as China, India, and other nations) has powered the U.S. digital economy.

In the early years, the Internet retained an antimaterialist spirit that was evident through such practices as free "open-source" software but soon businesses exerted powerful control. In the wake of the **dot.com bust**, the technology-heavy NASDQ stock exchange lost 78 percent of its value from 2000 to 2002. But online retailers like Amazon.com and the auction site eBay rebounded and grew rapidly, raising the question of whether "brick-and-mortar" stores would become obsolete. At the same time, Internet service providers made huge profits, and free "social networking" websites like Facebook as well as the search engine Google became publicly traded corporations with revenues generated largely through advertising.

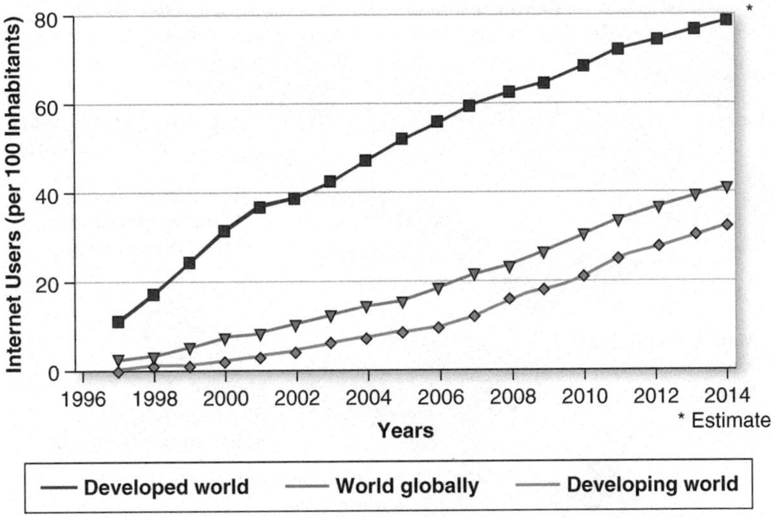

Figure 28.1 Global Internet Usage, 1996–2014 The blue line on this chart displays the growth of Internet users around in the world, which increased from an average of two to forty users per one hundred people from 1997 to 2014. In addition, comparing the purple and orange lines reveals the digital divide between the developed and developing world that was not lessened during the same seventeen-year period. ▲ Source: https://en.wikipedia.org/wiki/Internet_users_per_100_inhabitants_ITU.svg.

28-2c Production, Work, and Climate

The new economy creates a global marketplace that empowers individuals but exploits vulnerable workers.

U.S. consumers, including millions shopping on the Internet, were some of the biggest beneficiaries of globalization. *Newsweek* reported that between 1996 and 2005, the United States, which comprised 20 percent of the world's total economic worth, generated 45 percent of its growth in consumer spending. But because Americans spent much more for imports than they made on exports, more consumption increased the U.S. trade deficit from around $96 million in 1995 to almost $560 million in 2011 (see Figure 28.2).

One of the main reasons for cheaper products was the liberalization of rules regarding foreign investment that enabled U.S. manufacturers to use much cheaper labor in China, India, and other developing countries. As a result, more products than ever emerged from a "global assembly line." A Boeing 787 commercial airplane was produced from parts made across four different continents (see Figure 28.3). The three major parts composing the front, mid, and center fuselage alone originated from Kansas, Japan, and Italy, respectively. Improvements in technology and communication made this process much faster and more

dot.com bust Major downturn in the formally skyrocketing stock prices of technology firms largely connected to the World Wide Web.

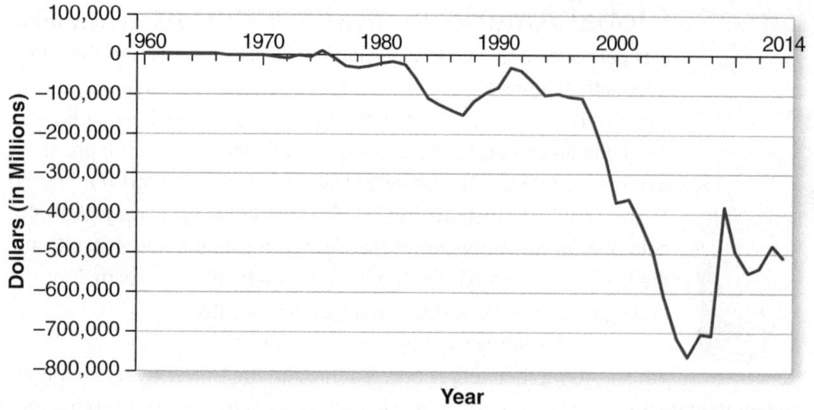

Figure 28.2 U.S. Trade Deficit Until the early 1980s, the U.S. maintained a balance between exports and imports, but since then imports have dominated and the balance, with some exceptional years, turned into deeper deficit. ◀ Source: Data presented on a balance of payment (BOP) basis. Information on data sources and methodology are available at United States Census, Foreign Trade Statistics, http://www.census.gov/foreign-trade/guide/sec2.html#bop

global supply chains High-tech system through which a product moves from manufacturing to consumer that balances supply and demand for a given product, benefiting consumers and businesses alike.

efficient so that major retailers like Walmart created a sophisticated system of **global supply chains** enabling its stores to calibrate stock to meet shifting consumer demand. A shortage of a particular item would immediately activate the entire global assembly line to produce more of it.

During the late twentieth and early twenty-first centuries, more companies switched from being domestic firms with some international branches to transnational firms with multiple headquarters around the world and a vision of a single, global market. As a result, businesses required new types of managers who could communicate in more than one language, deal effectively with cultural diversity, and have a stateless view of the world. Following businesses, universities responded to globalization by integrating global perspectives and experiences by admitting increasing numbers of international students and building satellite campuses in China,

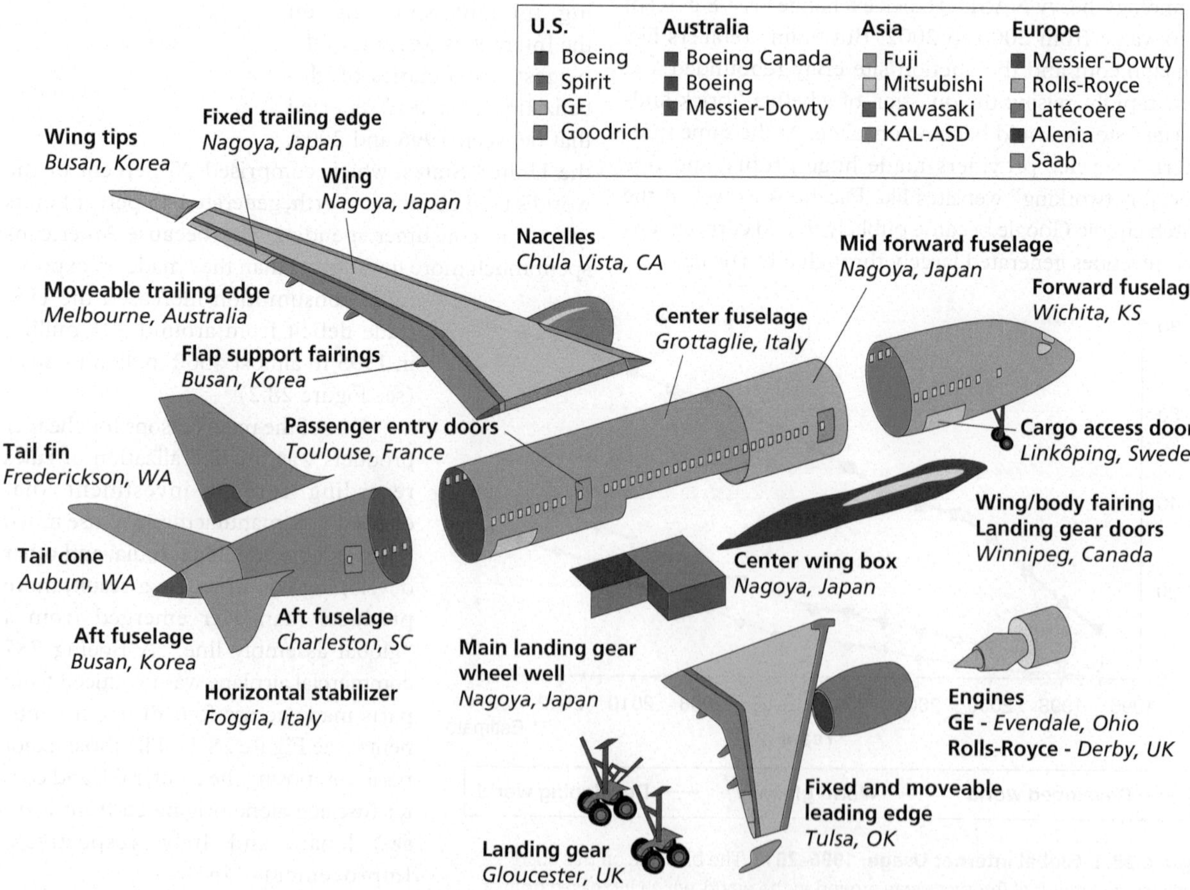

Figure 28.3 Global Supply Chain for the Boeing 787, 2012 The expansion of the global economy meant that manufacturing various parts for a product could be achieved in places around the world that produce high-quality items for the lowest cost. The Boeing airplane was produced from parts made across four different continents. ▲ Source: http://aerospacereview.ca/eic/site/060.nsf/eng/00040.html

the Middle East, and other fast-developing areas. The global economy generated millions of jobs in developing nations and in so doing expanded the middle class and increased consumer demand for services, information, and education.

In the United States and other developed countries, new job opportunities emerged in high-tech industries, especially in the areas of management, research, and design. High-tech companies like Apple and Google filled their ranks with recent university graduates. But manufacturing jobs in the United States suffered great insecurity as firms moved factories **offshore** to countries with cheaper labor, lower taxes, and less restrictive labor and environmental regulations. The relatively high cost of U.S. labor made it more attractive for businesses to relocate overseas.

In a neoliberal global economy that encouraged offshoring and other means of sending work overseas, the power of U.S. labor unions fell to an all-time low since union membership peaked during the 1950s, when almost 30 percent of all employed Americans were union members. By 2003, this figure shrank to less than 7 percent. The decline of unions, which had been evident since President's Reagan's firing of striking federal air traffic controllers in 1981, corresponded with millions of U.S. workers being forced to accept less pay and benefits or risk losing their jobs. In 1998, the California Labor Commissioner said, "Global competition results in a feeding frenzy in which local producers compete against one another and against foreign factories in a brutal race to the bottom." One of the few signs of hope for labor unions came in Los Angeles in the mid-1990s with the organization of seventy-four thousand home care workers, mostly women of color, by the Service Employees International Union (SEIU). Since then, some of labor's biggest victories involved making union members out of immigrants and racial minorities who were previously deemed "unorganizable."

offshore Relocation of a business process from one country to another to take advantage of more efficient production, lower labor costs, and less costly environmental restrictions.

In global areas of manufacturing, labor problems were often more severe than in the United States. In places like Guangdong province in China, a manufacturing hub for both the nation and the world, workers had little power to demand better wages and working conditions. In 2009, an employee at Foxconn, a Taiwan-based firm that manufactured electronics such as Apple's iPhone, committed suicide in order to draw attention to exploitative labor practices at the company's plant. After more worker suicides followed, the company was forced to raise the monthly wage by 30 percent. While human rights activists had successfully pressured Nike to improve labor conditions for thousands of workers in the developing world making its shoes and apparel, most workers in developing nations were not fortunate enough to have their cause taken up by outside activists. Labor disputes spread to other manufacturers in China including Japanese automakers Honda and Toyota.

The transformation of work and production were part of a sea change in the global economy that had powerful implications for society. Many saw the wonders of instant communication and information accessed almost anywhere and at any time as the sign of progress in human civilization portending a bright future. Others were less certain and instead focused on the digital divide by which the poor and disadvantaged in the United States and around the world lacked access to new technology and economic opportunities. Such differences were part of the uneven experience of globalization.

MUNIR UZ ZAMAN/Stringer/AFP/Getty Images

Savar Building Collapse, Dhaka, Bangladesh, 2013 On April 24, 2013, an eight-story building containing a bank, shops, and a garment factory collapsed in Dhaka, killing one thousand one hundred twenty-nine people and leaving two thousand five hundred fifteen injured. The accident highlighted disjunctures in working conditions and safety standards across the supply chains used by multinational corporations. In June 2015, Bangladeshi police filed murder charges against forty-one people, including the building's owner and several government officials, for failing to close the plant despite warnings about its serious structural flaws. ◄

global warming Long-term transformation of the Earth's atmosphere generating a rise in temperatures, triggering severe droughts and hurricanes, a rise in oceans leading to flooding, and extinction of animal species.

The global economy had far-reaching environmental effects as well. The rapid industrialization in the developing world stimulated the growth of a new, global middle class that consumed goods and pursued lifestyles much like Americans had done during their country's middle-class expansion for two decades after World War II. From 1993 to 2011, automobile ownership increased almost ten times in three Chinese cities (Beijing, Shanghai, and Guangdong), adding more than 100 million new cars and trucks to cities that struggled to accommodate them. The growing global middle class also led to a construction boom that saw the building of millions of new homes in urban and suburban locations greatly increase demand for water and fossil fuels.

The population generated by globalization and the demands of the global middle class have had a negative impact on the Earth's climate, leading to **global warming**. The burning of fossil fuels (coal, natural gas, and oil) and automobile exhaust release carbon dioxide into the air, changing the Earth's upper atmosphere such that more heat is trapped, as in a greenhouse, thus warming up the planet's surface. This results in increasingly severe weather events like droughts and hurricanes. It also melts glaciers and sea ice leading to rising ocean levels and contributing to flooding. Global warming also changes habitats, triggering the extinction of many animal species and new infestations of pests. Between 1970 and 2013, the United States was the world's leading producer of the "greenhouse gases" responsible for global warming, but China and India have now taken the lead and face pressure from the United States and other developed nations to reduce their emissions.

Scientists, government officials, and a wide range of advocates mobilized to educate the U.S. public about the pending disasters of climate change. President Obama made climate change a major part of his agenda and through executive action, enacted a host of measures designed to reduce the consumption of fossil fuels including tougher standards against carbon pollution, incentives to research and deploy environmentally friendly technologies (such as solar and wind energy), and the highest-ever fuel economy requirements for automobiles. Environmental advocates claimed that Obama's efforts fell well short of what was needed to reduce global warming. Yet some Americans who denied a causal link between human behavior and climate change attacked Obama's actions as expensive and unnecessary. In December 2015, one hundred eighty-eight nations, including the United States, agreed to an important UN treaty to prevent the worst possible scenarios due to climate change. This was a major step forward, but it is unclear whether the Republican-controlled U.S. Senate will ratify the accord.

28-3 Twenty-First Century America

In the early twenty-first century, a highly segmented news media and the Internet made it easier for people to ignore perspectives different from their own. National politicians, especially those on the far right, became less willing to compromise for fear of attacks from members of their own base, a trend that worsened legislative gridlock. In this April 2015 drawing, Pulitzer Prize–winning cartoonist Nick Anderson offers a liberal perspective on Republican responses to President Barack Obama.

What does this cartoonist suggest are the root causes of Republican opposition to Obama? Is the cartoon a fair reflection of U.S. partisan politics? Why or why not? ▶

Nick Anderson/Cartoonist Group

Despite the contested election of 2000, President George W. Bush pursued a vigorous agenda of tax cuts, educational reforms, and new drug benefits for older people. But spiraling costs of the wars in Afghanistan and Iraq limited his legislative successes in his second term. Then a collapse of the nation's housing market combined with risky, unregulated practices in the financial sector triggered a banking crisis that imperiled the global economy.

Governments around the world tried to lessen the impact of the crisis on their economies, but it took years before most countries slowly emerged from the recession.

Americans reacted to the economic downturn in a variety of ways. Some benefited from the new economy while others languished. In 2008, the election of Obama as the nation's first African American president generated great optimism about a more unified populace. But those hopes quickly ebbed as a controversial plan to expand federal health coverage sparked intense conservative opposition. New grassroots movements appeared on both the right and the left, each with profoundly different views of the proper role of government. Americans also battled over changing social mores and race relations. By 2016, the United States found itself a very divided nation.

☞ As you read this section think about the kinds of issues that divided Americans. What were the major reasons that Americans were so polarized in the early twentieth-first century? Can you imagine a way in which these issues could be resolved and consensus developed?

28-3a Divided Government

George W. Bush wins policy victories in his first term but meets resistance after reelection.

Upon taking office in 2001, George W. Bush embarked on an ambitious domestic agenda. Avidly pro-life, he emulated Ronald Reagan and George H.W. Bush in blocking federal financing of international family planning programs that provided abortions or abortion counseling. George W. Bush also limited federally funded stem cell research to extant cell lines already extracted from human embryos and signed legislation banning late-term abortions, the first federal law to ban an abortion procedure since *Roe v. Wade* (1973). An evangelical Christian, Bush also created the new Office of Faith-Based and Community Initiatives that made it easier for religious organizations to secure federal funds for humanitarian work at home and abroad.

With the economy in recession because of the dot .com bust and a $237 billion federal budget surplus, Bush won congressional support for $1.35 trillion in tax cuts over the next eleven years, one of the largest tax reductions in U.S. history. In May 2003, backed by a Republican majority that defied historic trends and increased its margin in the House of Representatives and regained control of the Senate in the midterm elections, he won approval of a second $350 billion tax cut, although Congress slashed his original $674 billion proposal by almost one-half because of escalating costs of the wars in Afghanistan and Iraq.

Later that year, Bush signed into law a major Medicare reform that included a new $400 billion prescription drug provision. In 2002, although he had shifted the focus of his presidency to foreign affairs after 9/11, Bush signed the **No Child Left Behind Education Reform Act** instituting new performance and testing standards for public schools.

With rising poverty rates, a rapidly increasing national debt, and an erosion of public support for the war in Iraq, Bush enjoyed less legislative success in his second term. In 2005, after he proposed partially privatizing Social Security, he met intense political opposition from Democrats and advocates for senior citizens. In August, the administration drew widespread criticism for its response to massive destruction and flooding in New Orleans after Hurricane Katrina hit the southern coast. Scenes of poor, mostly African American residents of the city stranded atop their homes and in chaotic conditions at inadequately

No Child Left Behind Education Reform Act Federal law intended to improve public education by requiring annual assessment tests in a wide variety of subjects, higher teaching qualifications, and school performance standards.

New Orleans Police Rescue Residents of the Lower Ninth Ward, New Orleans, August 29, 2005 Although Hurricane Katrina was only a Category 3, poorly engineered levees in New Orleans burst and 80 percent of the city flooded. One hundred twelve thousand of almost five hundred thousand residents had not evacuated because they did not have access to cars. The Federal Emergency Management Agency's delayed, disorganized response to the crisis left thousands without food, water, or medical attention for days. The storm killed nearly two thousand people and left over $100 million in damage in its wake ►.

Marko Georgiev/Getty Images

subprime mortgage Variable-interest loan given to a person with poor credit history who normally would not be able to qualify for a mortgage.

underwater Condition when one's home loan is higher than the value of the property, making it impossible to repay the loan even upon selling the house.

prepared shelters highlighted deepening economic and racial disparities in the United States.

Bush's second term also witnessed intensifying political polarization. Bush's successful appointments of John Roberts and Samuel Alito to the Supreme Court shifted its ideological balance to the right. But in November 2006, Democrats recaptured control of both houses of Congress. When they attempted to expand the federal health care benefits to children of low-income families, Bush vetoed the legislation, deriding it as socialism.

28-3b Economic Reckoning

The collapse of the U.S. housing market triggers a devastating global economic crisis.

Throughout much of the early twenty-first century, recession hobbled the U.S. economy. The dot.com bust, 9/11, and a wave of corporate scandals impeded recovery. To stimulate growth and consumer spending, the Federal Reserve (the Fed) repeatedly lowered interest rates, eventually setting them at 1 percent in June 2003—the lowest rate since 1958. Capitalizing on easy credit, Americans racked up debt on cars and other major purchases. Many sold and bought homes, eager to take advantage of rapidly increasing housing values. The market boomed after President Bush, working with Congress, signed legislation that made homeownership available to a wider swath of Americans, much like Franklin Roosevelt's Federal Housing Administration and G.I. Bill initiatives had done.

The combination of low interest and federal incentives triggered a **subprime mortgage** frenzy where lenders approved even borrowers with no income, no job, and no assets (so-called NINJA loans). Investment banks in turn bundled these mortgages into complex stock instruments that were traded on financial markets. At the same time, the Securities and Exchange Commission allowed five major investment banks to lessen their capital reserve requirements, meaning the firms could leverage investments worth up to forty times more than their liquid assets. In 2004, after the Fed started raising interest rates and U.S. homeownership peaked at 70 percent, housing prices began to tumble. Unable to pay higher interest and often **underwater** on mortgages higher than the worth of the house, many subprime borrowers defaulted and a number of lenders filed bankruptcy (see Figure 28.4).

The housing collapse put severe stress on the nation's shadow banking system. Beginning in the late 1970s, as the U.S. government loosened banking regulations, investment banks and hedge funds began issuing credit but were not subject to federal disclosure rules. In 2007, with trillions of dollars invested in subprime loans that were failing, panic began to sweep Wall Street. By March 2008, crushed by billions of dollars of bad mortgages, investment bank Bear Stearns was perilously close to bankruptcy, creating great market volatility. In a stunning departure from the neoliberalism of the last three decades, Federal Reserve Chairman Ben Bernanke, a former Princeton University economist who was an expert on the Great Depression, orchestrated a deal in which the commercial bank JPMorgan acquired Bear Stearns and received $30 billion from the federal government to cover the firm's toxic assets. The move discomforted conservatives like Secretary of the Treasury Henry Paulson, a former Goldman Sachs executive, who feared government intervention in the free market would encourage firms to take on excessive financial risks for which someone else bore the burden. But on September 7, 2008, Paulson himself brokered a deal in which the federal government took over quasifederal mortgage giants Fannie Mae and Freddie Mac.

The move encouraged executives at Lehman Brothers, the nation's fourth largest investment bank, who were

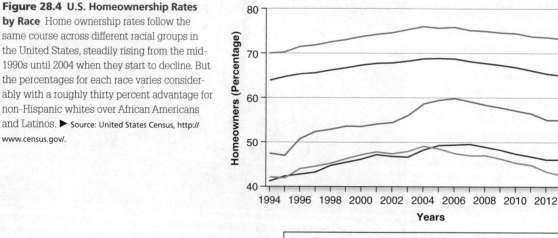

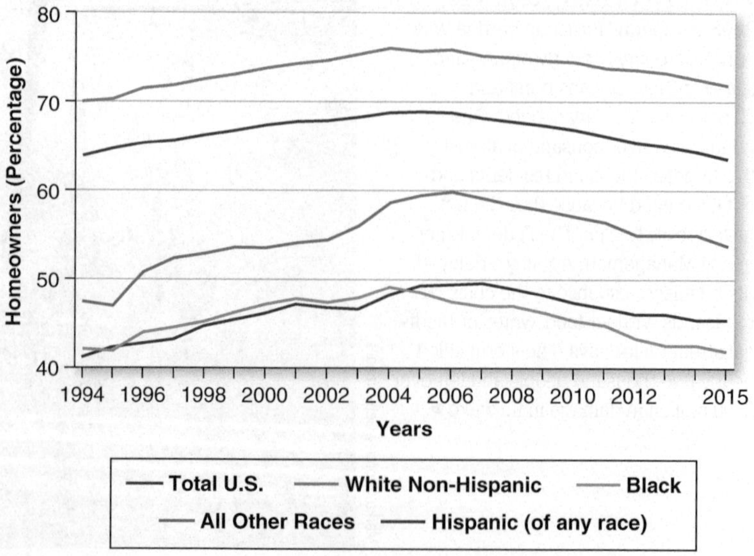

Figure 28.4 U.S. Homeownership Rates by Race Home ownership rates follow the same course across different racial groups in the United States, steadily rising from the mid-1990s until 2004 when they start to decline. But the percentages for each race varies considerably with a roughly thirty percent advantage for non-Hispanic whites over African Americans and Latinos. ▶ Source: United States Census, http://www.census.gov/.

also on the brink of bankruptcy. The firm had leveraged its assets by borrowing more money than it had to back up the debt and then used the loans to overinvest in the subprime mortgage market. Opposed to more government bailouts, conservative Republican leaders urged Paulson to let Lehman Brothers fail. On September 15, after Paulson proved unable to persuade another bank to buy Lehman, the company filed the biggest bankruptcy in history. Its demise sent shockwaves throughout global financial markets. On October 2, persuading horrified lawmakers of the risk of a total economic meltdown, Bernanke and Paulson won congressional passage of the Emergency Economic Stabilization Act, creating a $700 billion **Troubled Asset Relief Program (TARP)** under which the federal government purchased distressed securities (most related to subprime mortgages). Nonetheless, by the end of October, the value of U.S. companies' stocks had fallen by an astonishing $10 trillion, 50 percent of the total worth. It was the worst recession since the Great Depression of the early 1930s.

The global downturn had a dramatic impact on the auto industry. Prior to the **Great Recession**, the U.S. "Big Three" automakers, Ford, General Motors, and Chrysler, were flailing as high fuel prices combined with their overproduction of fuel-guzzling models led to lower sales. The task of solving the crisis fell to President Obama after he took office. In early 2009, to prevent catastrophic U.S. job losses, he continued a process initiated by the Bush administration and worked with Congress on a $79.6 billion bailout of the auto industry to help it cover costs and avoid bankruptcy. Only Ford did not take the bailout money. Chrysler filed for bankruptcy protection. By late 2014, the industry had recovered and the automakers had repaid the government all but $9.3 billion of the total bailout costs, a far smaller loss than economists had predicted five years earlier.

The low point of the recession came in spring 2009, and it hit globally. The European Union economy shrank by 4 percent with unemployment reaching 10 percent on average with countries such as Greece, Ireland, Spain, Portugal, and Italy hit the hardest. Global trade decreased by 13 percent. Exports by the United States, Japan, China, and Germany each decreased by about 20 percent.

Globally, Keynesian economic principles were employed as governments pumped money into their economies to jump-start them, a dramatic shift from neoliberal policies that proliferated throughout the late twentieth and early twenty-first centuries. The United States spent $787 billion, the European Union $634 billion, China $586 billion, and Japan $486 billion in economic stimulus. In the United States, the money was used to help rebuild infrastructure. The Chinese Communist Party went much further and used its significant government resources to push the Chinese economy ahead of all other industrializing economies. In July 2010, Congress passed the **Dodd-Frank Act**, enacting regulatory reforms aimed at preventing a recurrence of a similar financial crisis.

28-3c Protesting Inequality

Grassroots movements protest the widening global income gap and institutionalized racism.

The Great Recession hit average Americans hard. Between June 2007 and November 2008, they lost more than $6 trillion of their net worth as home equity values and retirement assets plummeted. At the peak of the crisis in 2010, almost 4 million homes were in foreclosure. Many owners just walked away from their homes and sent a "jingle mail" (mailed the keys) to the bank. Unemployment rose to 6.1 percent and was disproportionately higher among blacks and Hispanics. In some urban areas, African American unemployment peaked at almost 16 percent in the summer of 2010, a year after the recession had supposedly ended, and it remained that high nationwide through 2011. Many Americans felt great bitterness that they had lost homes and jobs while banks and businesses deemed by the government to be "too big to fail" received government bailouts.

The Bush tax cuts were set to expire in 2013 and became an important political issue during the 2012 presidential campaign as partisan conflict about growing income inequality intensified. But in January 2013, after Obama won reelection over Republican challenger Mitt Romney, he made a budget deal with the Republican-controlled Congress in which most of the tax cuts were made permanent with the American Taxpayer Relief Act of 2012.

The combination of the tax cuts, decreased spending on social services, and the Great Recession created an economy based on a record-high level of income inequality. In 2009, one in seven people were living below the poverty line. Young children were the hardest hit with nearly one in four children under the age of six classified as poor. Historically, racial and ethnic minority families have been more likely to be living in poverty than white non-Hispanic families, regardless of whether the economy was in an expansion or recession phase. During the Great Recession, these trends were particularly pronounced and roughly one in four Hispanics and African Americans were living in poverty (see Figure 28.5).

The issue of income equality was also a problem globally with the gap between rich and poor around the world increasing dramatically. In October 2013, the international bank, Crédit Suisse, reported that people with a net worth of more than $1 million represented just 0.7 percent of the global population but they held 41 percent of the world's wealth. Meanwhile, those with a net

Troubled Asset Relief Program (TARP) Authorized U.S. government purchase of bad assets from financial institutions in order to prevent bankruptcies that would ripple through the national and global economy.

Great Recession Major economic downturn in the global economy starting with the subprime mortgage crisis in December 2007 and continuing for almost two years until June 2009.

Dodd-Frank Act Most comprehensive regulation of financial markets since the Great Depression, increased transparency of financial products, ensured financial institutions could withstand market shocks, and strengthened consumer protections.

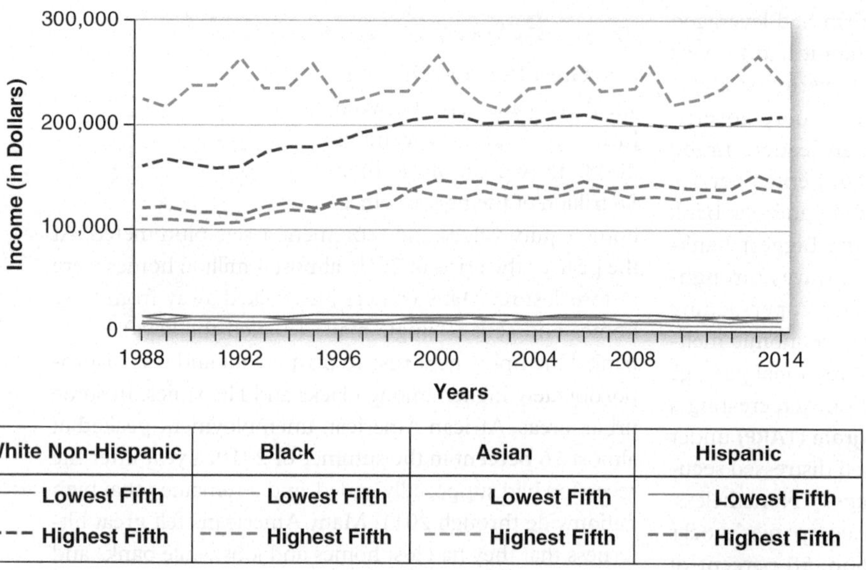

Figure 28.5 Income Inequality in the United States Differences between income in the U.S. have varied significantly by race judging by the highest twenty percent of earners. Asian Americans and whites have earned at least $50,000 more on average than African Americans and Latinos. But there is no income gap by race for the poorest twenty percent of these groups. ◀ Source: http://www.census.gov/hhes/www/income/data/historical/inequality/

worth of less than $10,000 (far below the U.S. poverty line) represented 69 percent of the global population but held just 3 percent of global wealth. Economists, like Thomas Pikkety and Paul Krugman, pointed out that the income inequality was greater in the 2010s than it had been during the Gilded Age in the era of so-called Robber Barons.

Many people globally, particularly the younger generation, protested the negative impact of the recession, income inequality, and the globalization of capital. Inspired by the Arab Spring and antiausterity protests in Spain, the **Occupy Movement** launched into the public view in September 2011, taking its first aim at Wall Street, where its members protested the government bailout of faltering banks as well as banks' unfair treatment of failing homeowners and students mired in debt. Occupy decried the fact that Wall Street bonuses in 2010 alone outstripped the wages of all minimum wage workers in the United States. Using the slogan "We are the 99%," in reference to the fact that 1 percent of the world's people held the majority of the wealth, the movement focused on income and wealth inequality and spread nationally and globally through the use of social media to organize protests in cities across the world.

The Occupy Movement tapped into unrest not only about income inequality but also about the place of the younger generation, the **Millennials**, in the global economy. Both this generation and their parents worried that as a

Occupy Movement Grassroots protests against economic inequality and undemocratic power of large corporations starting near Wall Street in New York City in September 2011 and spreading globally.

Millennials Generation of Americans born since the 1980s and raised during a period of more uneven economic growth than experienced by Generation X (1960s–1980s) or the Baby Boomers (1940s–1960s).

Occupy Wall Street Protest, New York City, New York, October 2011 In September 2011, a protest movement called Occupy Wall Street began in Zuccotti Park near New York City's Wall Street financial district. Adopting the slogan "We are the 99%" to emphasize disparities between the wealthiest 1 percent and the rest of the population, the movement spread rapidly across the United States. Although Occupy lost its momentum, it inspired campaigns for a $15 per hour minimum wage, divestment from private prisons, and student loan relief. ▶

Mario Tama/Getty Images

class, this group would not have the same upward mobility as earlier generations had. The Occupy Movement tapped into the feelings of fatigue and disillusion that young Americans felt about the economy, the relentless war on terrorism, and political gridlock.

Anger at institutionalized racism and police brutality fueled another mass movement called **Black Lives Matter**. In July 2013, after the acquittal of George Zimmerman, a neighborhood watch coordinator who shot and killed Trayvon Martin, an unarmed African American teenager, protesters created the hashtag #BlackLivesMatter and inspired hundreds of protest rallies across the nation. In 2014, the movement gained momentum after the deaths of several African Americans at the hands of law enforcement officers under questionable circumstances. Black Lives Matter criticized the militarized police response to popular uprisings in Ferguson, Missouri, and Baltimore, Maryland. At the same time, other civil rights activists denounced new state laws requiring voter identification and restricting voting periods. After the Supreme Court's ruling in *Shelby County v. Holder* (2013) struck down portions of the Voting Rights Act of 1965, fears of minority voter suppression intensified.

28-3d Polarized Politics

The election of Obama further divides Americans along partisan lines.

In 2008, Obama ran on a platform that pushed for universal health care, immigration reform, and economic stimulus to boost the economy. John McCain, the Republican candidate, emphasized deficit reduction, free trade, and national security. In a surprise move, McCain chose Sarah Palin, a little-known, first-term governor from Alaska, as his running mate. Her rise in national politics during and after the 2008 election mirrored the shift to the right in Republican politics for the next eight years.

In January 2009, enormous, joyous crowds attended Obama's inauguration, but that buoyant optimism proved difficult to sustain as the president encountered intense personal and political opposition. Some Americans questioned Obama's U.S. citizenship, demanding that he release his long-form birth certificate. Others erroneously claimed he was a Muslim, although he attended a Christian church regularly.

But Obama's governing philosophy and legislative agenda drew the strongest criticism. In February 2009, with the nation still mired in the Great Recession, Obama signed a $787 billion economic stimulus bill that not a single Republican member of Congress supported. In March 2010, after months of lobbying efforts, Obama won congressional passage of the Patient Protection and Affordable Care Act (ACA), a sweeping national health insurance program soon known as *Obamacare*. While the Democratic majority hailed the law as a landmark achievement that had taken decades to bring to fruition, no Republican voted in favor of the bill.

Fueled by frustration about the health care law and skyrocketing national debt (see Figure 28.6), a grassroots movement on the right arose. On Tax Day (April 15) 2009, supporters of the **Tea ("Taxed Enough Already") Party** staged rallies all over the country. Groups tied to David and Charles Koch, billionaire co-owners of Koch Industries, the nation's second-largest privately held company, played a key role in the Tea Party. It opposed the bailout of banks and corporations as well as the economic stimulus package that the Obama administration adopted to address the Great Recession. Tea Party leaders, however, rarely said anything about the Bush administration's earlier relief package or the cost of the Iraq War, giving it a partisan slant that opposed the Democrats. The Tea Party aimed to tap into the anger that some Americans felt about the sinking economy and the liberal leanings of President Obama. They adopted their name to evoke the colonists'

Black Lives Matter Mass movement arising in 2013 to challenge police brutality, mass incarceration of African Americans, and institutionalized racism.

Tea ("Taxed Enough Already") Party Conservative political movement rising in 2009 to oppose Obama's economic and health care agenda and to advocate lower taxes and smaller government.

Figure 28.6 U.S. National Debt National debt measures the balance between the amount a government spends versus the amount it receives as revenue. Since the early 1980s, the United States has dramatically increased spending mainly for health care, social security, defense, and interest payments on treasury bonds. The increase was not offset by a corresponding rise in income taxes or social security payments, the main sources of revenue. ▶

Source: TreasuryDirect, http://www.treasurydirect.gov/govt/reports/pd/histdebt/histdebt.htm.

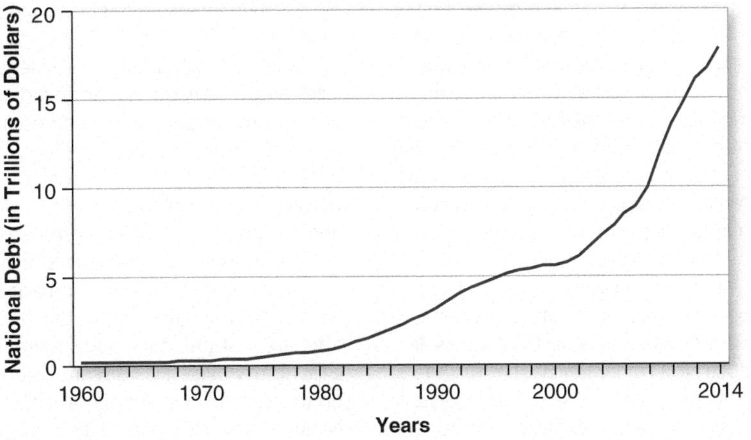

History without Borders

Same-Sex Marriage

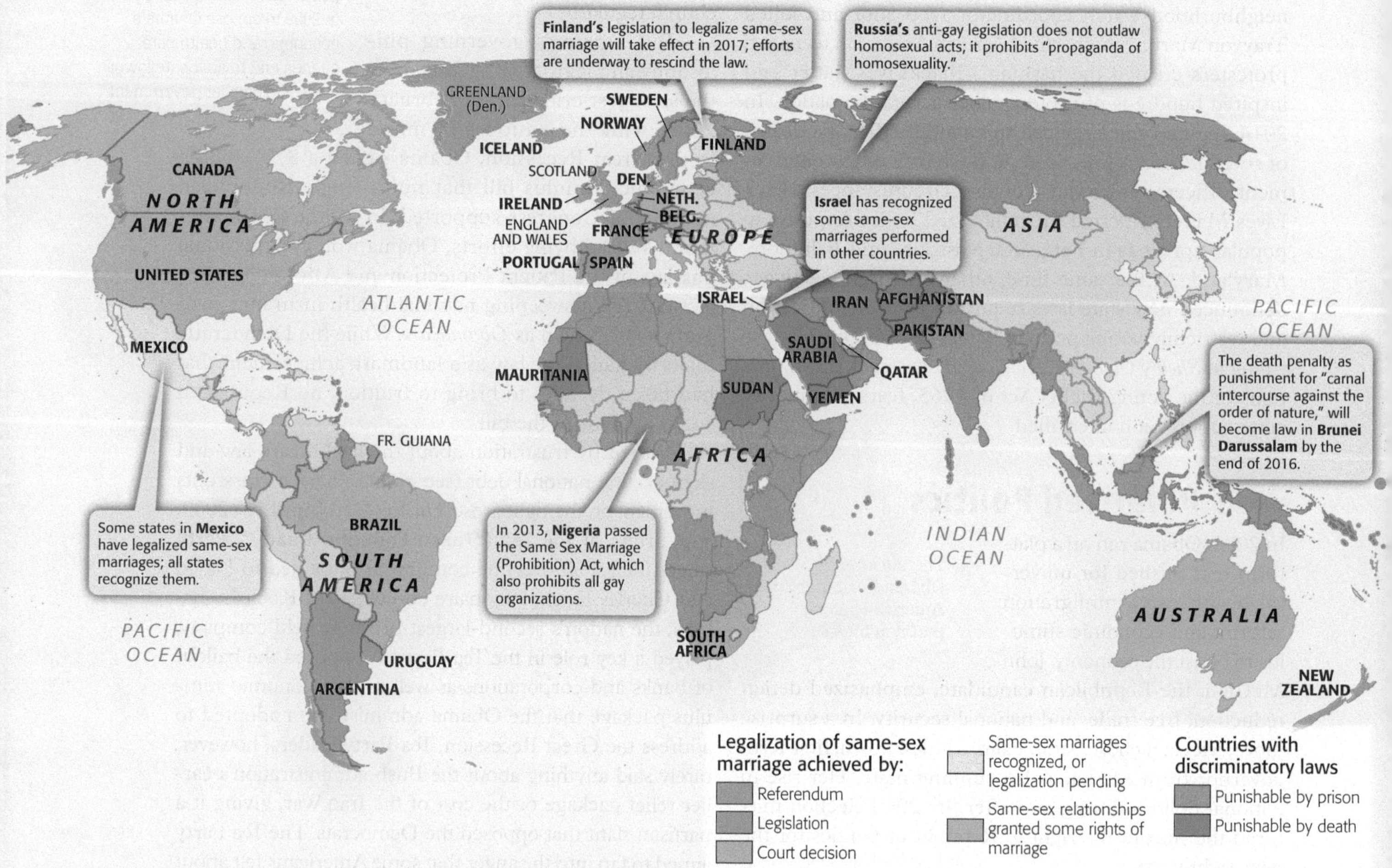
Finland's legislation to legalize same-sex marriage will take effect in 2017; efforts are underway to rescind the law.
Russia's anti-gay legislation does not outlaw homosexual acts; it prohibits "propaganda of homosexuality."
GREENLAND (Den.)
SWEDEN
NORWAY
FINLAND
ICELAND
SCOTLAND
DEN.
CANADA
NORTH AMERICA
IRELAND
NETH.
BELG.
ENGLAND AND WALES
FRANCE
EUROPE
Israel has recognized some same-sex marriages performed in other countries.
ASIA
PORTUGAL
SPAIN
UNITED STATES
ISRAEL
IRAN
AFGHANISTAN
ATLANTIC OCEAN
PAKISTAN
PACIFIC OCEAN
MEXICO
SAUDI ARABIA
QATAR
The death penalty as punishment for "carnal intercourse against the order of nature," will become law in Brunei Darussalam by the end of 2016.
MAURITANIA
SUDAN
YEMEN
FR. GUIANA
AFRICA
BRAZIL
INDIAN OCEAN
Some states in Mexico have legalized same-sex marriages; all states recognize them.
SOUTH AMERICA
In 2013, Nigeria passed the Same Sex Marriage (Prohibition) Act, which also prohibits all gay organizations.
AUSTRALIA
PACIFIC OCEAN
SOUTH AFRICA
URUGUAY
ARGENTINA
NEW ZEALAND
Legalization of same-sex marriage achieved by:
Referendum
Legislation
Court decision
Same-sex marriages recognized, or legalization pending
Same-sex relationships granted some rights of marriage
Countries with discriminatory laws
Punishable by prison
Punishable by death

Nations with Legalized Same-Sex Marriage, 2015 By late 2015, eighteen nations had legalized same-sex marriage. Several states in Mexico perform same-sex marriages that are recognized in all thirty-one states. Finland's same-sex marriage law goes into effect in 2017. ▲

Same-sex marriage moved swiftly to prominence in national and international politics, growing out of civil rights activism and changing ideas about the hierarchical nature of marriage itself. In the late twentieth century, a few nations began granting same-sex couples the rights accorded married opposite-sex couples in matters such as taxes, inheritance, and health care decisions. In 1989, Denmark became the first country to permit civil partnerships for same-sex couples. In 2001, the Netherlands went further, becoming the first nation to legalize same-sex marriages. As of late 2015, eighteen countries recognize same-sex marriages.

Same-sex marriage has been legalized through a combination of legislative action, judicial rulings, and popular referenda. Each nation's experience differs. On July 20, 2005, Canada became the fourth country in the world and the first country in the Americas to legalize same-sex marriage after the Civil Marriage Act defined marriage in gender-neutral terms. In South Africa, after a Constitutional Court's ruling that existing marriage laws discriminated on the basis of sexual orientation, the National Assembly passed legislation making South Africa the first and so far only African nation to legalize same-sex marriage. In July 2010, Argentina became the first Latin American country to legalize same-sex marriage.

In April 2013, the Socialist-led National Assembly and upper house of Parliament voted to legalize same-sex marriage in France. Opponents of same-sex marriage violently clashed with police in Paris and Lyon. After a failed legal challenge of the bill's constitutionality, President François Hollande signed it into law on May 18, 2013.

On May 22, 2015, after 62 percent of voters supported the measure,

AP Images/Thibault Camus

Same-Sex Marriage Opponents March, in Paris, March 2013 In early 2013, as the French National Assembly and Parliament prepared to vote on whether or not to legalize same-sex marriage, hundreds of thousands of French citizens rallied in opposition to allowing same-sex couples to wed or adopt children legally. ◄

AP Images/Pablo Martinez Monsivais

Supporters of Same-Sex Marriage Celebrate, Washington, D.C., June 2015 In June 2015, the U.S. Supreme Court ruled in *Obergefell v Hodges* that a state's failure to recognize the same-sex marriage of a couple in another state violated the Fourteenth Amendment's due process of law and equal protections clauses. Same-sex marriage thus became legal in all fifty states. Here, supporters of the ruling celebrate outside the Supreme Court. ◄

Ireland became the first country in the world to approve same-sex marriage in a nationwide referendum. A month later, the U.S. Supreme Court ruled 5-4 in *Obergefell v. Hodges* that states could not prohibit the issuing of marriage licenses to same-sex couples or deny recognition of lawfully performed out-of-state marriage licenses to same-sex couples, thus striking down same-sex marriage bans in thirteen states and certain U.S. territories.

With the exceptions of South Africa and Israel, no country in Africa or Asia currently recognizes same-sex marriage. While proponents see same-sex marriage as a civil right essential to the dignity and protection of gay and lesbian people and their families, opponents view such unions as an affront to their religious beliefs or cultural practices. There are seventy-six nations where homosexuality itself is criminalized. Several African and Eastern European nations and Russia have recently passed laws that impose severe penalties on same-sex relationships.

The world's largest religions vary widely in their views on same-sex marriage. The Roman Catholic Church officially opposes same-sex marriage, as do the Orthodox Church, a majority of Muslims, and Orthodox Jews. But many faith communities around the world support same-sex marriage or conduct religious ceremonies solemnizing same-sex marriage including U.S. Episcopalians, Presbyterians, Congregationalists, Native American religions with a two-spirit tradition, and Reform Jews, the United Protestant Church in Belgium, and the Protestant Church in the Netherlands.

Critical Thinking Questions

► How and where has same-sex marriage been legalized around the world?

► What societal factors do you think have contributed to legalization? Do you believe that same-sex marriage will be legalized worldwide? Why or why not?

revolt against British taxation in 1773 when they dumped British tea into Boston Harbor.

The Tea Party was not an organized third party, and some considered it to be a re-branding of the conservative wing of the Republican Party. Not only did leaders such as Sarah Palin oppose the Democratic policies such as extending social services, reforming immigration laws, and using Keynesian economic principles to stimulate the economy but they also usually stood in opposition to Republican moderates, leaving the GOP fragmented through much of the second decade of the twenty-first century. In 2010, successful Tea Party candidates helped the Republicans regain control of the House of Representatives in midterm elections, but they often challenged their party leadership and brought the legislative process to a standstill over formerly routine matters like raising the debt ceiling or approving the budget. They filed numerous legal challenges to the Affordable Care Act and repeatedly led unsuccessful attempts to repeal the law—an impossibility as long as Obama was in office and sure to veto any such measure. Critics accused Tea Party supporters of valuing ideology more than the best interests of the nation.

The rise of the Tea Party deepened long-standing partisan differences on the issue of immigration reform with immigration from Mexico and Central America a particular flashpoint. In the summer of 2001, Mexican President Vicente Fox and President Bush were set to negotiate major immigration reform that would have allowed for a path to citizenship for undocumented immigrants already in the United States, a guest worker program, as well as tightened security along the U.S.–Mexican border to stem the drug trade. As governor of Texas, George W. Bush had been a proponent of immigration and free trade between his state and Mexico. But after the attacks on 9/11, the opportunity for immigration reform was lost as most Americans were unwilling to consider the possibilities of more open borders.

In 2005 and 2006, each house of Congress passed an immigration bill, but no law resulted as the two bills could not be reconciled and the parties could not agree on a compromise package that balanced secure borders with fair treatment of undocumented immigrants who had been working as law-abiding guests in the United States. The Great Recession exacerbated these tensions as many Americans accused immigrants of taking jobs away from U.S. citizens.

Secure Fence Act Policy approved in 2006 to strengthen the U.S.–Mexico border by building seven hundred miles of secure fencing to keep out drug traffickers, security threats, and illegal immigrants.

One of the most potent reflections of the debate over border control was the building of a security fence between the United States and Mexico. In 2006, the **Secure Fence Act** appropriated monies to better secure the border. More than $1 billion dollars was set aside to build an actual wall. While there is not and probably never will be a wall extending along the one thousand nine hundred fifty-one-mile-long border between the United States and Mexico, by 2010, the Department of Homeland Security estimated that it had more than six hundred miles of fence in place along the highest trafficked areas. The wall, better security technology, and efforts by citizen vigilante groups like the Minutemen Project shut off what had been a regular ebb and flow of immigrants across the border. The result was that many immigrants who otherwise would have returned home instead stayed in the United States for fear of being unable to return or having to pay a prohibitively higher fee to coyotes who brought them across the border. The fence also made the crossings more perilous as immigrants had to choose paths that went through dangerous deserts in order to evade the increased border security.

In 2009, the Obama administration called on Congress to pass legislation that included better border and interior enforcement of laws, more flexible allocation of visas to adjust with the changing economic climate, and a path to U.S. citizenship for those who had been living as law-abiding but undocumented persons. Congress was unable to enact any legislation because of partisan gridlock. Some states reacted to the Obama administration's perceived leniency toward immigrants. In 2009, the Arizona state legislature passed SB 1070. It allowed state and local police to stop anyone who had a reasonable suspicion of being an illegal immigrant. Critics charged that this amounted to racial profiling or "Driving while Brown." A national boycott of the state ensued and eventually the state legislature amended the bill to tone down its language. Nevertheless, across the country, anti-immigrant, and what many perceived as anti-Latino, sentiment was on the rise.

In 2012, with the failure of Congress to pass any legislation and state initiatives to block any reform, the Obama administration put in place the Deferred Action for Childhood Arrivals (DACA or Dreamers) policy. This allowed children under the age of sixteen whose parents had brought them into the United States illegally to remain in the country and to apply for citizenship. Subsequent expansions of DACA, however, led to political pushback from Congress as well as injunctions from the federal courts. In 2013, a bipartisan group of senators, who became known as the *Gang of Eight*, passed an immigration bill that was widely viewed as promising. The bill, however, languished in the House of Representatives. The politically polarizing issue of immigration further solidified the Latino vote for Democrats while the Republicans continued to use anti-immigrant rhetoric.

In November 2012, Obama defeated Mitt Romney and was re-elected president. He continued to lead a nation beset by stark contrasts in Americans' views on

Brad Barket/Getty Images

Global Americans The nature of Christianity among American Latinos has changed dramatically in the last half century as they shift from Catholicism to Evangelicalism. Much of that change is due to ministers such as **Luis Palau**, who was born in Argentina. Palau migrated to the United States as a young man after hearing Billy Graham, the American evangelist, give a sermon broadcast over the radio to his hometown. Palau moved to Oregon, earned a degree in Biblical Studies, and began working for Billy Graham as a translator. With both mentoring and financial aid from Graham, Palau launched his own ministry, which has grown exponentially as he aims his ministry to draw in younger people.

Palau spread his teachings through old-fashioned tent revivals that drew thousands of worshippers, and in his hometown of Portland, Oregon, which is not known for its ties to religion, he drew one hundred forty thousand people for a weekend event. His popularity and appealing message of service and hope were so striking that George W. Bush asked Palau to accompany him on his visit to China where he and Bush visited one of the few Christian churches in Beijing, and Palau preached. In an interview Palau gave in 2007, he claimed to have reached over 25 million people globally with his message of service to others, particularly the homeless and addicted. Today, Palau draws thousands to his tent revivals from Central Park in New York City to the cornfields of Nebraska and can be heard on twenty-six hundred radio stations across forty-two countries in both English and Spanish.

race relations, income inequality, reproductive justice, climate change, same-sex marriage, and immigration. This divide was quite apparent in how different groups of Americans got their information and news. The advent of the Internet and the domination of cable news opened the door to partisan news reporting such as *The Drudge Report* and *The Huffington Post* as well as FOX News and MSNBC. While younger Americans relied more on the Internet to obtain news, older Americans still relied largely on televised newscasts. The biggest demographic shift in news culture came with the rise of news parody programs such as *The Daily Show with Jon Stewart* and *The Colbert Report*, popular among young viewers. Critics worried that the polarization of media outlets combined with the comedic news contributed to cynicism and apathy among young voters.

But other forces united Americans with fellow citizens and foreigners. One of the major social and political phenomena to coalesce in the early twenty-first century was the place of Protestant evangelicalism in both U.S. and global society. Between one-quarter and one-third of all Americans identified themselves as Protestant evangelicals. They found their religious homes in small congregations as well as in the growing megachurches, defined as churches that have more than two thousand attendees in any given week and generate more than $25,000 in television revenue for their congregations. The largest megachurch in the United States is Lakewood Church in Houston, Texas, which boasts a congregation of more than forty thousand. However, only one of the ten largest megachurches in the world is located in the United States. Five are in South Korea and the rest are in Africa, Latin America, and one in India. Some U.S.-based megachurches, like Rick Warren's Saddleback Churches, have international branches in Argentina, South Korea, and Hong Kong. The Republican Party has capitalized on these organizations to make them the core of their political base since the late 1970s.

By the middle of the second decade, mass mobilization campaigns on both sides of the political spectrum combined with the expansion of political action committees (PACs) who financed campaigns behind a veil of secrecy significantly shifted the nature of U.S. politics. In 2010, the U.S. Supreme Court held in ***Citizens United v. FEC*** that corporations, like individuals, could assert First Amendment rights of free speech. This opened the door for unlimited funds to be spent on campaigns without any restrictions. Although Democrats and Republicans called for campaign finance reform, none came about, and the costs of political campaigns and ballot initiatives skyrocketed and led to further polarization.

Citizens United v. FEC U.S. Supreme Court decision ruling that the federal government cannot limit campaign spending by organizations, upholding the influence of big money on elections.

Summary

The 9/11 terrorist attacks fundamentally reshaped U.S. foreign policy and society. The United States built a multinational coalition to wage a global "War on Terror" and adopted controversial tactics against suspected terrorists. New security procedures affected Americans' daily lives and the government expanded its surveillance operations. In October 2001, U.S. and allied forces invaded Afghanistan to punish the regime that harbored those responsible for 9/11. In March 2003, driven by a new doctrine of preemption, the Bush administration launched a controversial and costly war in Iraq.

In early 2011, popular protests in the Arab world generated optimism that democracy would supplant dictatorships there, but such hopes quickly unraveled as civil wars and Islamic radicalism engulfed the region.

Furthermore, the globalization of the world's economy created vast amounts of wealth for some in the United States and around the world while impoverishing and limiting the economic chances of many others who remained on the poor side of the global economy and the digital divide. Meanwhile the entire planet felt the negative effects of global warming as many parts of the Earth experienced their hottest-ever recorded temperatures. Climate change demanded responses that twenty-first century governments seemed disinclined or unable to provide.

The cost of war combined with the Great Recession created the conditions for a political and cultural polarization as red states and blue states squared off on taxes, government spending, health care, labor unions, and abortion. These issues combined with increasingly vitriolic responses to immigration polarized the nation's politics as other Americans sought other venues for compromise and protest.

Thinking Back

As you review this chapter, think about the collapse of the Cold War global order in the face of a world economy in which the former Communist enemies (Russia and China) of the United States were fundamental players. Also consider the new challenges faced by the United States in a world in which it existed as the main military and economic power. How did nonstate actors confront U.S. power? What did the United States do to thwart such confrontations? Finally, consider how the post-9/11 global role of the United States and the new global economy affected its society. What were the forces and issues that united and divided Americans?

To make your study concrete, review the timeline and reflect on the entries there. Think about their causes, consequences, and connections. How do they fit with global trends?

Additional Resources

Books

Alexander, Michelle. *The New Jim Crow: Mass Incarceration in the Age of Colorblindness*. New York: The New Press, 2010. ▶ Civil rights advocate's provocative depiction of the War on Drugs as systematized racial subjugation.

Bravin, Jess. *The Terror Courts: Rough Justice at Guantánamo Bay*. New Haven, NJ: Yale University Press, 2014. ▶ Legal reporter's narrative of war on terror's military tribunals.

Chandrasekaran, Rajiv. *Imperial Life in the Emerald City: Inside Iraq's Green Zone*. New York: Knopf, 2006. ▶ Journalist's account of the U.S. administration of postwar Iraq.

Finkel, David. *The Good Soldiers*. New York: Sarah Crichton Books, 2009. ▶ Award-winning recounting of a Ranger battalion during a fifteen-month deployment in Iraq.

Jones, Seth G. *In the Graveyard of Empires: America's War in Afghanistan*. New York: W.W. Norton, 2009. ▶ A military policy analyst's assessment of the U.S. war against the Taliban.

Lewis, Michael. *The Big Short: Inside the Doomsday Machine*. New York: W.W. Norton & Company, 2010. ▶ Gripping account of the housing and credit bubble in the 2000s.

Packer, George. *The Assassins' Gate: America in Iraq*. New York: Farrar, Straus and Giroux, 2005. ▶ Nonfiction book detailing the U.S. invasion of Iraq and its aftermath.

Go to the MindTap® for **Global Americans** to access the full version of select books from this Additional Resources section.

Websites

National September 11 Memorial & Museum. (http://www.911memorial.org/museum) ▶ Collection of exhibits, photographs, and primary sources on 9/11 and its aftermath.

Costs of War Project. (http://watson.brown.edu/costsofwar/) ▶ Human, economic, and political costs of the post-9/11 wars in Afghanistan, Iraq, and Pakistan.

PBS *Frontline*: "Inside the Meltdown." (http://www.pbs.org/wgbh/pages/frontline/meltdown/) ▶ Documentary, interviews, timeline, and teacher's guide on the global financial crisis that began in 2007.

Occupy Archive. (http://occupyarchive.org/) ▶ Repository of first-hand accounts, photographs, and videos of Occupy protests.

The State of Working America. (http://stateofworkingamerica.org/about/) ▶ Published by the Economic Policy Institute, a nonpartisan think take that collects statistics about workers in the United States.

MindTap®

Continue exploring online through MindTap®, **where you can:**

- **Assess your knowledge with the Chapter Test**
- **Watch historical videos related to the chapter**
- **Further your understanding with interactive maps and timelines**

Global Americans Today

2000–2001

December 2000

George W. Bush is declared winner over Al Gore in contested presidential election.

March 2001

Bush abandons ratification of the Kyoto Protocols aimed at reducing global warming.

June 2001

Bush signs $1.35 trillion tax cut into law.

September 2001

Nineteen Saudi hijackers linked to al-Qaeda attack the World Trade Center and the Pentagon.

October 2001

In pursuit of Osama bin Laden and al Qaeda, U.S. and U.K. forces attack Afghanistan.

USA Patriot Act becomes law.

2002–2003

January 2002

Bush signs the No Child Left Behind Act, a major education reform.

March 2003

U.S. and U.K. troops invade Iraq.

April 2003

Saddam regime collapses, coalition forces capture Iraq.

October 2003

Chief U.S. weapons inspector reports his team's failure to find chemical, biological, or nuclear weapons in Iraq.

2004

April

CBS News releases photographs of U.S. soldiers abusing prisoners at Abu Ghraib.

May

Massachusetts becomes first U.S. state to legalize same-sex marriage.

June

U.S. ends formal occupation of Iraq and grants interim Iraqi government sovereignty.

November

Bush defeats Kerry and wins second term as president.

2005–2006

August 2005

Hurricane Katrina strikes the Gulf Coast, New Orleans floods.

2006

U.S. trade deficit hits all-time high of $761 billion.

October 2006

To deter illegal immigration, Bush signs legislation approving construction of a seven hundred-mile fence along the U.S.-Mexican border.

November 2006

Democrats recapture control of both houses of Congress in midterm elections.

December 2006

After being found guilty of crimes against humanity by an Iraqi tribunal, Saddam Hussein is hanged.

2007–2008

January 2007

Vietnam joins the WTO.

December 2007

Great Recession begins.

October 2008

Bush signs Troubled Assets Relief Program (TARP).

November 2008

Barack Obama defeats John McCain in 2008 presidential election.

WTO's Doha Round of talks breaks down.

2009–2010

April 2009
Tea Party emerges as a viable political force.

March 2010
Obama signs Patient Protection and Affordable Care Act into law. No Republican member of Congress votes for the bill.

November 2010
Republicans regain control of the U.S. House of Representatives in midterm elections.

December 2010
Arab Spring begins with revolution in Tunisia.

2011

May
U.S. special forces assassinate Osama bin Laden in Pakistan.

September
Occupy Movement begins in New York City.

2012–2013

2012
One-third of world's population (2.4 billion people) use the Internet.

November 2012
Defeating Mitt Romney, Obama wins reelection as president.

August 2013
Google stock trades above $870 per share, a 900 percent rise from its initial offering price ($85) in 2004.

2014

September
Multinational coalition launches air strikes in Syria.

October
IMF reports that China has the world's largest economy, surpassing the United States.

November
In midterm election, Republicans win the Senate and control of both houses of Congress.

2015

May
Walmart owns more stores abroad (6,283) than it does in the U.S. (5,212).

July
Countries using the euro, for the third time, bail out Greece, preventing it from going bankrupt and leaving the Eurozone.

U.S. and Iranian negotiators announce nuclear deal.

United States and Cuba resume diplomatic relations for the first time since 1961.

Go to MindTap® to engage with an interactive version of the timeline. Analyze events and themes with clickable content, view related videos, and respond to critical thinking questions.

Appendix

The Declaration of Independence

In Congress, July 4, 1776

The Unanimous Declaration of the Thirteen United States of America

When in the Course of human events it becomes necessary for one people to dissolve the political bands which have connected them with another, and to assume among the Powers of the earth, the separate and equal station to which the Laws of Nature and of Nature's God entitle them, a decent respect to the opinions of mankind requires that they should declare the causes which impel them to the separation.

We hold these truths to be self-evident, that all men are created equal, that they are endowed by their Creator with certain unalienable Rights, that among these are Life, Liberty and the pursuit of Happiness. That to secure these rights, Governments are instituted among Men, deriving their just Powers from the consent of the governed. That whenever any Form of Government becomes destructive of these ends, it is the Right of the People to alter or to abolish it, and to institute new Government, laying its foundation on such principles and organizing its Powers in such form, as to them shall seem most likely to effect their Safety and Happiness. Prudence, indeed, will dictate that Governments long established should not be changed for light and transient causes; and accordingly all experience hath shewn, that mankind are more disposed to suffer, while evils are sufferable, than to right themselves by abolishing the forms to which they are accustomed. But when a long train of abuses and usurpations, pursuing invariably the same Object evinces a design to reduce them under absolute Despotism, it is their right, it is their duty, to throw off such Government, and to provide new Guards for their future security. Such has been the patient sufferance of these Colonies; and such is now the necessity which constrains them to alter their former Systems of Government. The history of the present King of Great Britain is a history of repeated injuries and usurpations, all having in direct object the establishment of an absolute Tyranny over these States. To prove this, let Facts be submitted to a candid world.

He has refused his Assent to Laws, the most wholesome and necessary for the public good.

He has forbidden his Governors to pass Laws of immediate and pressing importance, unless suspended in their operation till his Assent should be obtained; and when so suspended, he has utterly neglected to attend to them.

He has refused to pass other Laws for the accommodation of large districts of people, unless those people would relinquish the right of Representation in the Legislature, a right inestimable to them and formidable to tyrants only.

He has called together legislative bodies at places unusual, uncomfortable, and distant from the depository of their Public Records, for the sole Purpose of fatiguing them into compliance with his measures.

Text is reprinted from the facsimile of the engrossed copy in the National Archives. The original spelling, capitalization, and punctuation have been retained. Paragraphing has been added.

He has dissolved Representative Houses repeatedly, for opposing with manly firmness his invasions on the rights of the People.

He has refused for a long time, after such dissolutions, to cause others to be elected; whereby the Legislative Powers, incapable of Annihilation, have returned to the People at large for their exercise; the State remaining in the mean time exposed to all the dangers of invasion from without, and convulsions within.

He has endeavoured to prevent the Population of these States; for that purpose obstructing the Laws for Naturalization of Foreigners; refusing to pass others to encourage their migrations hither, and raising the conditions of new Appropriations of Lands.

He has obstructed the Administration of Justice, by refusing his Assent to Laws for establishing Judiciary Powers.

He has made Judges dependent on his Will alone, for the tenure of their offices, and the amount and payment of their salaries.

He has erected a multitude of New Offices, and sent hither swarms of Officers to harass our People, and eat out their substance.

He has kept among us, in times of peace, Standing Armies without the Consent of our legislatures.

He has affected to render the Military independent of and superior to the Civil Power.

He has combined with others to subject us to a jurisdiction foreign to our constitution, and unacknowledged by our laws; giving his Assent to their Acts of pretended Legislation: For Quartering large bodies of armed troops among us: For protecting them, by a mock Trial, from Punishment for any Murders which they should commit on the Inhabitants of these States: For cutting off our Trade with all parts of the world: For imposing Taxes on us without our Consent: For depriving us in many cases, of the benefits of Trial by Jury: For transporting us beyond Seas to be tried for pretended offences: For abolishing the free System of English Laws in a neighbouring Province, establishing therein an Arbitrary government, and enlarging its Boundaries so as to render it at once an example and fit instrument for introducing the same absolute rule into these Colonies: For taking away our Charters, abolishing our most valuable Laws, and altering fundamentally the Forms of our Governments: For suspending our own Legislatures, and declaring themselves invested with Power to legislate for us in all cases whatsoever.

He has abdicated Government here, by declaring us out of his Protection, and waging War against us.

He has plundered our seas, ravaged our Coasts, burnt our towns, and destroyed the lives of our people.

He is at this time transporting large Armies of foreign Mercenaries to compleat the works of death, desolation and tyranny, already begun with circumstances of Cruelty and perfidy scarcely paralleled in the most barbarous ages, and totally unworthy the Head of a civilized nation.

He has constrained our fellow Citizens taken Captive on the high Seas to bear Arms against their Country, to become the executioners of their friends and Brethren, or to fall themselves by their Hands.

He has excited domestic insurrections amongst us, and has endeavoured to bring on the inhabitants of our frontiers, the merciless Indian Savages, whose known rule of warfare, is an undistinguished destruction of all ages, sexes and conditions.

In every stage of these Oppressions We have Petitioned for Redress in the most humble terms: Our repeated Petitions have been answered only by repeated injury. A Prince, whose character is thus marked by every act which may define a Tyrant, is unfit to be the ruler of a free People.

Nor have We been wanting in attentions to our British brethren. We have warned them from time to time of attempts by their legislature to extend an unwarrantable jurisdiction over us. We have reminded them of the circumstances of our emigration and settlement here. We have appealed to their native justice and magnanimity, and we have conjured them by the ties of our common kindred to disavow these usurpations, which, would inevitably interrupt our connections and correspondence. They too have been deaf to the voice of justice and of consanguinity. We must, therefore, acquiesce in the necessity, which denounces our Separation, and hold them, as we hold the rest of mankind, Enemies in War, in Peace Friends.

We, therefore, the Representatives of the United States of America, in General Congress, Assembled, appealing to the Supreme Judge of the world for the rectitude of our intentions, do, in the Name, and by Authority of the good People of these Colonies, solemnly publish and declare, That these United Colonies are, and of Right ought to be Free and Independent States; that they are Absolved from all Allegiance to the British Crown, and that all political connection between them and the State of Great Britain, is and ought to be totally dissolved; and that, as Free and Independent States, they have full Power to levy War, conclude Peace, contract Alliances, establish Commerce, and to do all other Acts and Things which Independent States may of right do. And for the support of this Declaration, with a firm reliance on the protection of divine Providence, we mutually pledge to each other our Lives, our Fortunes and our sacred Honor.

The Constitution of the United States of America

We the People of the United States, in Order to form a more perfect Union, establish Justice, insure domestic Tranquility, provide for the common defence, promote the general Welfare, and secure the Blessings of Liberty to ourselves and our Posterity, do ordain and establish this Constitution for the United States of America.

Article I

SECTION 1. All legislative Powers herein granted shall be vested in a Congress of the United States, which shall consist of a Senate and House of Representatives.

SECTION 2. The House of Representatives shall be composed of Members chosen every second Year by the People of the several States, and the Electors in each State shall have the Qualifications requisite for Electors of the most numerous Branch of the State Legislature.

No Person shall be a Representative who shall not have attained to the Age of twenty five Years, and been seven Years a Citizen of the United States, and who shall not, when elected, be an Inhabitant of that State in which he shall be chosen.

Representatives and direct Taxes[1] shall be apportioned among the several States which may be included within this Union, according to their respective Numbers, which shall be determined by adding to the whole Number of free Persons, including those bound to Service for a Term of Years, and excluding Indians not taxed, three fifths of all other Persons.[2]

The actual Enumeration shall be made within three Years after the first Meeting of the Congress of the United States, and within every subsequent Term of ten Years, in such Manner as they shall by Law direct. The Number of Representatives shall not exceed one for every thirty Thousand, but each State shall have at Least one Representative; and until such enumeration shall be made, the State of New Hampshire shall be entitled to chuse three; Massachusetts eight; Rhode Island and Providence Plantations one; Connecticut five; New York six; New Jersey four; Pennsylvania eight; Delaware one; Maryland six; Virginia ten; North Carolina five; South Carolina five; and Georgia three.

When vacancies happen in the Representation from any State, the Executive Authority thereof shall issue Writs of Election to fill such Vacancies.

The House of Representatives shall chuse their Speaker and other Officers; and shall have the sole Power of Impeachment.

SECTION 3. The Senate of the United States shall be composed of two Senators from each State, chosen by the Legislature thereof, for six Years; and each Senator shall have one Vote.[3]

Immediately after they shall be assembled in Consequence of the first Election, they shall be divided as equally as may be into three Classes. The Seats of the Senators of the first Class shall be vacated at the Expiration of the second Year, of the second Class at the Expiration of the fourth Year, and of the third Class at the Expiration of the sixth Year, so that one third may be chosen every second Year; and if Vacancies happen by Resignation, or otherwise, during the

---

Text is from the engrossed copy in the National Archives. Original spelling, capitalization, and punctuation have been retained.

[1] Modified by the Sixteenth Amendment.

[2] Replaced by the Fourteenth Amendment.

[3] Superseded by the Seventeenth Amendment.

Recess of the Legislature of any State, the Executive thereof may make temporary Appointments until the next Meeting of the Legislature, which shall then fill such Vacancies.[4]

No Person shall be a Senator who shall not have attained to the Age of thirty Years, and been nine Years a Citizen of the United States, and who shall not, when elected, be an Inhabitant of that State for which he shall be chosen.

The Vice President of the United States shall be President of the Senate, but shall have no Vote, unless they be equally divided.

The Senate shall chuse their other Officers, and also a President pro tempore, in the Absence of the Vice President, or when he shall exercise the Office of President of the United States.

The Senate shall have the sole Power to try all Impeachments. When sitting for that Purpose, they shall be on Oath or Affirmation. When the President of the United States is tried, the Chief Justice shall preside: And no Person shall be convicted without the Concurrence of two thirds of the Members present.

Judgment in Cases of Impeachment shall not extend further than to removal from Office, and disqualification to hold and enjoy any Office of honor, Trust or Profit under the United States: but the Party convicted shall nevertheless be liable and subject to Indictment, Trial, Judgment and Punishment, according to Law.

SECTION 4. The Times, Places and Manner of holding Elections for Senators and Representatives, shall be prescribed in each State by the Legislature thereof, but the Congress may at any time by Law make or alter such Regulation, except as to the Places of chusing Senators.

The Congress shall assemble at least once in every Year, and such Meeting shall be on the first Monday in December, unless they shall by Law appoint a different Day.[5]

SECTION 5. Each House shall be the Judge of the Elections, Returns and Qualifications of its own Members, and a Majority of each shall constitute a Quorum to do Business; but a smaller Number may adjourn from day to day, and may be authorized to compel the Attendance of absent Members, in such Manner, and under such Penalties as each House may provide.

Each House may determine the Rules of its Proceedings, punish its Members for disorderly Behaviour, and, with the Concurrence of two thirds, expel a Member.

Each House shall keep a Journal of its Proceedings, and from time to time publish the same, excepting such Parts as may in their Judgment require Secrecy; and the Yeas and Nays of the Members of either House on any question shall, at the Desire of one fifth of those Present, be entered on the Journal.

Neither House, during the Session of Congress, shall, without the Consent of the other, adjourn for more than three days, nor to any other Place than that in which the two Houses shall be sitting.

SECTION 6. The Senators and Representatives shall receive a Compensation for their Services, to be ascertained by Law, and paid out of the Treasury of the United States. They shall in all Cases, except Treason, Felony and Breach of the Peace, be privileged from Arrest during their Attendance at the Session of their respective Houses, and in going to and returning from the same; and for any Speech or Debate in either House, they shall not be questioned in any other Place.

No Senator or Representative shall, during the Time for which he was elected, be appointed to any civil Office under the Authority of the United States, which shall have been created, or the Emoluments whereof shall have been encreased during such time; and no Person holding any Office under the United States, shall be a Member of either House during his Continuance in Office.

---

[4] Modified by the Seventeenth Amendment.

[5] Superseded by the Twentieth Amendment.

SECTION 7. All Bills for raising Revenue shall originate in the House of Representatives; but the Senate may propose or concur with Amendments as on other Bills.

Every Bill which shall have passed the House of Representatives and the Senate shall, before it become a Law, be presented to the President of the United States; If he approve he shall sign it, but if not he shall return it, with his Objections to that House in which it shall have originated, who shall enter the Objections at large on their Journal, and proceed to reconsider it. If after such Reconsideration two thirds of that House shall agree to pass the Bill, it shall be sent, together with the Objections, to the other House, by which it shall likewise be reconsidered, and if approved by two thirds of that House, it shall become a Law. But in all such Cases the Votes of both Houses shall be determined by yeas and Nays, and the Names of the Persons voting for and against the Bill shall be entered on the Journal of each House respectively. If any Bill shall not be returned by the President within ten Days (Sundays excepted) after it shall have been presented to him, the Same shall be a Law, in like Manner as if he had signed it, unless the Congress by their Adjournment prevent its Return, in which Case it shall not be a Law.

Every Order, Resolution, or Vote to which the Concurrence of the Senate and House of Representatives may be necessary (except on a question of Adjournment) shall be presented to the President of the United States; and before the Same shall take Effect, shall be approved by him, or being disapproved by him shall be repassed by two thirds of the Senate and House of Representatives, according to the Rules and Limitations prescribed in the Case of a Bill.

SECTION 8. The Congress shall have power To lay and collect Taxes, Duties, Imposts and Excises, to pay the Debts and provide for the common Defence and general Welfare of the United States; but all Duties, Imposts and Excises shall be uniform throughout the United States; To borrow Money on the credit of the United States; To regulate Commerce with foreign Nations, and among the several States, and with the Indian Tribes; To establish an uniform Rule of Naturalization, and uniform Laws on the subject of Bankruptcies throughout the United States; To coin Money, regulate the Value thereof, and of foreign Coin, and fix the Standard of Weights and Measures; To provide for the Punishment of counterfeiting the Securities and current Coin of the United States; To establish Post Offices and post Roads; To promote the Progress of Science and useful Arts, by securing for limited Times to Authors and Inventors the exclusive Right to their respective Writings and Discoveries; To constitute Tribunals inferior to the supreme Court; To define and punish Piracies and Felonies committed on the high Seas, and Offences against the Law of Nations;

To declare War, grant Letters of Marque and Reprisal, and make Rules concerning Captures on Land and Water; To raise and support Armies, but no Appropriation of Money to that Use shall be for a longer Term than two Years; To provide and maintain a Navy; To make Rules for the Government and Regulation of the land and naval Forces; To provide for calling forth the Militia to execute the Laws of the Union, suppress Insurrections and repel Invasions; To provide for organizing, arming, and disciplining, the Militia, and for governing such Part of them as may be employed in the Service of the United States, reserving to the States respectively, the Appointment of the Officers, and the Authority of training the Militia according to the discipline prescribed by Congress; To exercise exclusive Legislation in all Cases whatsoever, over such District (not exceeding ten Miles square) as may, by Cession of particular States, and the Acceptance of Congress, become the Seat of the Government of the United States, and to exercise like Authority over all Places purchased by the Consent of the Legislature of the State in which the Same shall be, for the Erection of Forts, Magazines, Arsenals, dock-Yards, and other needful Buildings;—And To make all Laws which shall be necessary and proper for carrying into Execution the foregoing Powers, and all other Powers vested by this Constitution in the Government of the United States, or in any Department or Officer thereof.

SECTION 9. The Migration or Importation of such Persons as any of the States now existing shall think proper to admit, shall not be prohibited by the Congress prior to the Year one thousand eight hundred and eight, but a Tax or duty may be imposed on such Importation, not exceeding ten dollars for each Person.

The Privilege of the Writ of Habeas Corpus shall not be suspended, unless when in Cases of Rebellion or Invasion the public Safety may require it.

No Bill of Attainder or ex post facto Law shall be passed.

No Capitation, or other direct, Tax shall be laid, unless in Proportion to the Census or Enumeration herein before directed to be taken.

No Tax or Duty shall be laid on Articles exported from any State.

No Preference shall be given by any Regulation of Commerce or Revenue to the Ports of one State over those of another: nor shall Vessels bound to, or from, one State, be obliged to enter, clear, or pay Duties in another.

No Money shall be drawn from the Treasury, but in Consequence of Appropriations made by Law, and a regular Statement and Account of the Receipts and Expenditures of all public Money shall be published from time to time.

No Title of Nobility shall be granted by the United States: And no Person holding any Office of Profit or Trust under them, shall, without the Consent of the Congress, accept of any present, Emolument, Office, or Title, of any kind whatever, from any King, Prince, or foreign State.

SECTION 10. No State shall enter into any Treaty, Alliance, or Confederation; grant Letters of Marque and Reprisal; coin Money; emit Bills of Credit; make any Thing but gold and silver Coin a Tender in Payment of Debts; pass any Bill of Attainder, ex post facto Law, or Law impairing the Obligation of Contracts, or grant any Title of Nobility.

No State shall, without the Consent of the Congress, lay any Imposts or Duties on Imports or Exports, except what may be absolutely necessary for executing its inspection Laws: and the net Produce of all Duties and Imposts, laid by any State on Imports or Exports, shall be for the Use of the Treasury of the United States; and all such Laws shall be subject to the Revision and Controul of the Congress.

No State shall, without the Consent of Congress, lay any Duty of Tonnage, keep Troops, or Ships of War in time of Peace, enter into any Agreement or Compact with another State, or with a foreign Power, or engage in War, unless actually invaded, or in such imminent Danger as will not admit of delay.

Article II

SECTION 1. The executive Power shall be vested in a President of the United States of America. He shall hold his Office during the Term of four Years, and, together with the Vice President, chosen for the same Term, be elected, as follows: Each State shall appoint, in such Manner as the Legislature thereof may direct, a Number of Electors, equal to the whole Number of Senators and Representatives to which the State may be entitled in the Congress: but no Senator or Representative, or Person holding an Office of Trust or Profit under the United States, shall be appointed an Elector.

The Electors shall meet in their respective States, and vote by Ballot for two Persons, of whom one at least shall not be an Inhabitant of the same State with themselves. And they shall make a List of all the Persons voted for, and of the Number of Votes for each; which List they shall sign and certify, and transmit sealed to the Seat of the Government of the United States, directed to the President of the Senate. The President of the Senate shall, in the Presence of the Senate and House of Representatives, open all the Certificates, and the Votes shall then be counted. The Person having the greatest Number of Votes shall be the President, if such Number be a Majority of the whole Number of Electors appointed; and if there be more than one who have such Majority, and have an equal Number of Votes, then the House of Representatives shall immediately chuse by Ballot one of them for President; and if no Person have a Majority, then from the five highest on the List the said House shall in like Manner chuse the President. But in chusing the President, the Votes shall be taken by States, the Representation from each State having one Vote; A quorum for this Purpose shall consist of a Member or Members from two thirds of the States, and a Majority of all the States shall be necessary to a Choice. In every Case, after the Choice of the

President, the Person having the greatest Number of Votes of the Electors shall be the Vice President. But if there should remain two or more who have equal Votes, the Senate shall chuse from them by Ballot the Vice President.[6]

The Congress may determine the Time of chusing the Electors, and the Day on which they shall give their Votes; which Day shall be the same throughout the United States.

No Person except a natural born Citizen, or a Citizen of the United States, at the time of the Adoption of this Constitution, shall be eligible to the Office of President, neither shall any Person be eligible to that Office who shall not have attained to the Age of thirty five Years, and been fourteen Years a Resident within the United States.

In Case of the Removal of the President from Office, or of his Death, Resignation, or Inability to discharge the Powers and Duties of the said Office, the Same shall devolve on the Vice President, and the Congress may by Law provide for the Case of Removal, Death, Resignation or Inability, both of the President and Vice President, declaring what Officer shall then act as President, and such Officer shall act accordingly, until the Disability be removed, or a President shall be elected.[7]

The President shall, at stated Times, receive for his Services, a Compensation, which shall neither be encreased nor diminished during the Period for which he shall have been elected, and he shall not receive within that Period any other Emolument from the United States, or any of them.

Before he enter on the Execution of his Office, he shall take the following Oath or Affirmation:—"I do solemnly swear (or affirm) that I will faithfully execute the Office of President of the United States, and will to the best of my Ability, preserve, protect and defend the Constitution of the United States."

SECTION 2. The President shall be Commander in Chief of the Army and Navy of the United States, and of the Militia of the several States, when called into the actual Service of the United States; he may require the Opinion, in writing, of the principal Officer in each of the executive Departments, upon any Subject relating to the Duties of their respective Offices, and he shall have Power to grant Reprieves and Pardons for Offences against the United States, except in Cases of Impeachment.

He shall have Power, by and with the Advice and Consent of the Senate, to make Treaties, provided two thirds of the Senators present concur; and he shall nominate, and by and with the Advice and Consent of the Senate, shall appoint Ambassadors, other public Ministers and Consuls, Judges of the supreme Court, and all other Officers of the United States, whose Appointments are not herein otherwise provided for, and which shall be established by Law; but the Congress may by Law vest the Appointment of such inferior Officers, as they think proper, in the President alone, in the Courts of Law, or in the Heads of Departments.

The President shall have Power to fill up all Vacancies that may happen during the Recess of the Senate, by granting Commissions which shall expire at the End of their next Session.

SECTION 3. He shall from time to time give the Congress Information of the State of the Union, and recommend to their Consideration such Measures as he shall judge necessary and expedient; he may, on extraordinary Occasions, convene both Houses, or either of them, and in Case of Disagreement between them, with Respect to the Time of Adjournment, he may adjourn them to such Time as he shall think proper; he shall receive Ambassadors and other public Ministers; he shall take Care that the Laws be faithfully executed, and shall Commission all the Officers of the United States.

SECTION 4. The President, Vice President and all civil Officers of the United States, shall be removed from Office on Impeachment for, and Conviction of, Treason, Bribery, or other high Crimes and Misdemeanors.

---

[6] Superseded by the Twelfth Amendment.

[7] Modified by the Twenty-fifth Amendment.

Article III

SECTION 1. The judicial Power of the United States, shall be vested in one supreme Court, and in such inferior Courts as the Congress may from time to time ordain and establish.

The Judges, both of the supreme and inferior Courts, shall hold their Offices during good Behaviour, and shall, at stated Times, receive for their Services, a Compensation, which shall not be diminished during their Continuance in Office.

SECTION 2. The judicial Power shall extend to all Cases, in Law and Equity, arising under this Constitution, the Laws of the United States, and Treaties made, or which shall be made, under their Authority;—to all Cases affecting Ambassadors, other public Ministers and Consuls;—to all Cases of admiralty and maritime Jurisdiction;—to Controversies to which the United States shall be a Party;—to Controversies between two or more States;—between a State and Citizens of another State;[8]—between Citizens of different States,—between Citizens of the same State claiming Lands under Grants of different States, and between a State, or the Citizens thereof, and foreign States, Citizens or Subjects.

In all Cases affecting Ambassadors, other public Ministers and Consuls, and those in which a State shall be Party, the supreme Court shall have original Jurisdiction. In all the other Cases beforementioned, the supreme Court shall have appellate Jurisdiction, both as to Law and Fact, with such Exceptions, and under such Regulations as the Congress shall make.

The Trial of all Crimes, except in Cases of Impeachment, shall be by Jury; and such Trial shall be held in the State where the said Crimes shall have been committed; but when not committed within any State, the Trial shall be at such Place or Places as the Congress may by Law have directed.

SECTION 3. Treason against the United States, shall consist only in levying War against them, or in adhering to their Enemies, giving them Aid and Comfort. No Person shall be convicted of Treason unless on the Testimony of two Witnesses to the same overt Act, or on Confession in open Court.

The Congress shall have Power to declare the Punishment of Treason, but no Attainder of Treason shall work Corruption of Blood, or Forfeiture except during the Life of the Person attainted.

Article IV

SECTION 1. Full Faith and Credit shall be given in each State to the public Acts, Records, and judicial Proceedings of every other State. And the Congress may by general Laws prescribe the Manner in which such Acts, Records and Proceedings shall be proved, and the Effect thereof.

SECTION 2. The Citizens of each State shall be entitled to all Privileges and Immunities of Citizens in the several States.

A Person charged in any State with Treason, Felony, or other Crime, who shall flee from Justice, and be found in another State, shall on Demand of the executive Authority of the State from which he fled, be delivered up, to be removed to the State having Jurisdiction of the Crime.

No Person held to Service or Labour in one State, under the Laws thereof, escaping into another, shall, in Consequence of any Law or Regulation therein, be discharged from such Service or Labour, but shall be delivered up on Claim of the Party to whom such Service or Labour may be due.

SECTION 3. New States may be admitted by the Congress into this Union; but no new State shall be formed or erected within the Jurisdiction of any other State, nor any State be formed by the Junction of two or more States, or Parts of States, without the Consent of the Legislatures of the States concerned as well as of the Congress.

[8] Modified by the Eleventh Amendment.

The Congress shall have Power to dispose of and make all needful Rules and Regulations respecting the Territory or other Property belonging to the United States; and nothing in this Constitution shall be so construed as to Prejudice any Claims of the United States, or of any particular State.

SECTION 4. The United States shall guarantee to every State in this Union a Republican Form of Government, and shall protect each of them against Invasion; and on Application of the Legislature, or of the Executive (when the Legislature cannot be convened) against domestic Violence.

Article V

The Congress, whenever two thirds of both Houses shall deem it necessary, shall propose Amendments to this Constitution, or, on the Application of the Legislatures of two thirds of the several States, shall call a Convention for proposing Amendments, which, in either Case, shall be valid to all Intents and Purposes, as Part of this Constitution, when ratified by the Legislatures of three fourths of the several States, or by Conventions in three fourths thereof, as the one or the other Mode of Ratification may be proposed by the Congress; Provided that no Amendment which may be made prior to the Year One thousand eight hundred and eight shall in any Manner affect the first and fourth Clauses in the Ninth Section of the first Article; and that no State, without its Consent, shall be deprived of its equal Suffrage in the Senate.

Article VI

All Debts contracted and Engagements entered into, before the Adoption of this Constitution, shall be as valid against the United States under this Constitution, as under the Confederation.

This Constitution, and the Laws of the United States which shall be made in Pursuance thereof; and all Treaties made, or which shall be made, under the Authority of the United States, shall be the supreme Law of the Land; and the Judges in every State shall be bound thereby, any Thing in the Constitution or Laws of any State to the Contrary notwithstanding.

The Senators and Representatives before mentioned, and the Members of the several State Legislatures, and all executive and judicial Officers, both of the United States and of the several States, shall be bound by Oath or Affirmation, to support this Constitution; but no religious Test shall ever be required as a Qualification to any Office or public Trust under the United States.

Article VII

The Ratification of the Conventions of nine States, shall be sufficient for the Establishment of this Constitution between the States so ratifying the Same.

Done in Convention by the Unanimous Consent of the States present the Seventeenth Day of September in the Year of our Lord one thousand seven hundred and Eighty seven and of the Independence of the United States of America the Twelfth. In witness whereof We have hereunto subscribed our Names,

Articles in Addition to, and Amendment of, the Constitution of the United States of America, Proposed by Congress, and Ratified by the Legislatures of the Several States, Pursuant to the Fifth Article of the Original Constitution.

Amendment I[9]

Congress shall make no law respecting an establishment of religion, or prohibiting the free exercise thereof; or abridging the freedom of speech, or of the press; or the right of the people peaceably to assemble, and to petition the Government for a redress of grievances.

---

[9]The first ten amendments were passed by Congress September 25, 1789. They were ratified by three-fourths of the states December 15, 1791.

Amendment II

A well regulated Militia, being necessary to the security of a free State, the right of the people to keep and bear Arms shall not be infringed.

Amendment III

No Soldier shall, in time of peace, be quartered in any house, without the consent of the Owner, nor in time of war, but in a manner to be prescribed by law.

Amendment IV

The right of the people to be secure in their persons, houses, papers, and effects, against unreasonable searches and seizures, shall not be violated, and no Warrants shall issue, but upon probable cause, supported by Oath or affirmation, and particularly describing the place to be searched, and the persons or things to be seized.

Amendment V

No person shall be held to answer for a capital or otherwise infamous crime, unless on a presentment or indictment of a Grand Jury, except in cases arising in the land or naval forces, or in the Militia, when in actual service in time of War or public danger; nor shall any person be subject for the same offence to be twice put in jeopardy of life or limb; nor shall be compelled in any criminal case to be a witness against himself, nor be deprived of life, liberty, or property, without due process of law; nor shall private property be taken for public use, without just compensation.

Amendment VI

In all criminal prosecutions, the accused shall enjoy the right to a speedy and public trial, by an impartial jury of the State and district wherein the crime shall have been committed, which district shall have been previously ascertained by law, and to be informed of the nature and cause of the accusation; to be confronted with the witnesses against him; to have compulsory process for obtaining witnesses in his favor, and to have the Assistance of Counsel for his defence.

Amendment VII

In suits at common law, where the value in controversy shall exceed twenty dollars, the right of trial by jury shall be preserved, and no fact tried by a jury, shall be otherwise reexamined in any Court of the United States, than according to the rules of the common law.

Amendment VIII

Excessive bail shall not be required, nor excessive fines imposed, nor cruel and unusual punishments inflicted.

Amendment IX

The enumeration in the Constitution, of certain rights, shall not be construed to deny or disparage others retained by the people.

Amendment X

The powers not delegated to the United States by the Constitution; nor prohibited by it to the States, are reserved to the States respectively, or to the people.

Amendment XI[10]

The Judicial power of the United States shall not be construed to extend to any suit in law or equity, commenced or prosecuted against one of the United States by Citizens of another State, or by Citizens or Subjects of any Foreign State.

Amendment XII[11]

The Electors shall meet in their respective States and vote by ballot for President and Vice-President, one of whom, at least, shall not be an inhabitant of the same State with themselves; they shall name in their ballots the person voted for as President, and in distinct ballots the person voted for as Vice-President, and they shall make distinct lists of all persons voted for as President, and of all persons voted for as Vice-President, and of the number of votes for each, which lists they shall sign and certify, and transmit sealed to the seat of the government of the United States, directed to the President of the Senate;—The President of the Senate shall, in the presence of the Senate and House of Representatives, open all the certificates and the votes shall then be counted;—The person having the greatest number of votes for President, shall be the President, if such number be a majority of the whole number of Electors appointed; and if no person have such majority, then from the persons having the highest numbers not exceeding three on the list of those voted for as President, the House of Representatives shall choose immediately, by ballot, the President.

But in choosing the President, the votes shall be taken by states, the representation from each state having one vote; a quorum for this purpose shall consist of a member or members from two-thirds of the states, and a majority of all the states shall be necessary to a choice. And if the House of Representatives shall not choose a President whenever the right of choice shall devolve upon them, before the fourth day of March next following, then the Vice-President shall act as President, as in the case of the death or other constitutional disability of the President.—The person having the greatest number of votes as Vice-President, shall be the Vice-President, if such number be a majority of the whole number of Electors appointed, and if no person have a majority, then from the two highest numbers on the list, the Senate shall choose the Vice-President; a quorum for the purpose shall consist of two-thirds of the whole number of Senators, and a majority of the whole number shall be necessary to a choice. But no person constitutionally ineligible to the office of President shall be eligible to that of Vice-President of the United States.

Amendment XIII[12]

SECTION 1. Neither slavery nor involuntary servitude, except as a punishment for crime whereof the party shall have been duly convicted, shall exist within the United States, or any place subject to their jurisdiction.

SECTION 2. Congress shall have power to enforce this article by appropriate legislation.

Amendment XIV[13]

SECTION 1. All persons born or naturalized in the United States, and subject to the jurisdiction thereof, are citizens of the United States and of the State wherein they reside. No State shall make or enforce any law which shall abridge the privileges or immunities of citizens of the United States; nor shall any State deprive any person of life, liberty, or property, without due process of law; nor deny to any person within its jurisdiction the equal protection of the laws.

[10] Passed March 4, 1794. Ratified January 23, 1795.

[11] Passed December 9, 1803. Ratified June 15, 1804.

[12] Passed January 31, 1865. Ratified December 6, 1865.

[13] Passed June 13, 1866. Ratified July 9, 1868.

SECTION 2. Representatives shall be apportioned among the several States according to their respective numbers, counting the whole number of persons in each State, excluding Indians not taxed. But when the right to vote at any election for the choice of electors for President and Vice-President of the United States, Representatives in Congress, the Executive and Judicial officers of a State, or the members of the Legislature thereof, is denied to any of the male inhabitants of such State, being twenty-one years of age, and citizens of the United States, or in any way abridged, except for participation in rebellion, or other crime, the basis of representation therein shall be reduced in the proportion which the number of such male citizens shall bear to the whole number of male citizens twenty-one years of age in such State.

SECTION 3. No person shall be a Senator or Representative in Congress, or elector of President and Vice-President, or hold any office, civil or military, under the United States, or under any State, who, having previously taken an oath, as a member of Congress, or as an officer of the United States, or as a member of any State legislature, or as an executive or judicial officer of any State, to support the Constitution of the United States, shall have engaged in insurrection or rebellion against the same, or given aid or comfort to the enemies thereof. But Congress may by a vote of two-thirds of each House, remove such disability.

SECTION 4. The validity of the public debt of the United States, authorized by law, including debts incurred for payment of pensions and bounties for services in suppressing insurrection or rebellion, shall not be questioned. But neither the United States nor any State shall assume or pay any debt or obligation incurred in aid of insurrection or rebellion against the United States, or any claim for the loss or emancipation of any slave; but all such debts, obligations, and claims shall be held illegal and void.

SECTION 5. The Congress shall have the power to enforce, by appropriate legislation, the provisions of this article.

Amendment XV[14]

SECTION 1. The right of citizens of the United States to vote shall not be denied or abridged by the United States or by any State on account of race, color, or previous conditions of servitude—

SECTION 2. The Congress shall have power to enforce this article by appropriate legislation.

Amendment XVI[15]

The Congress shall have power to lay and collect taxes on incomes, from whatever source derived, without apportionment among the several States, and without regard to any census or enumeration.

Amendment XVII[16]

The Senate of the United States shall be composed of two Senators from each State, elected by the people thereof, for six years; and each Senator shall have one vote. The electors in each State shall have the qualifications requisite for electors of the most numerous branch of the State legislatures.

When vacancies happen in the representation of any State in the Senate, the executive authority of such State shall issue writs of election to fill such vacancies: Provided, That the legislature of any State may empower the executive thereof to make temporary appointments until the people fill the vacancies by election as the legislature may direct.

---

[14] Passed February 26, 1869. Ratified February 2, 1870.

[15] Passed July 12, 1909. Ratified February 3, 1913.

[16] Passed May 13, 1912. Ratified April 8, 1913.

This amendment shall not be so construed as to affect the election or term of any Senator chosen before it becomes valid as part of the Constitution.

Amendment XVIII[17]

SECTION 1. After one year from the ratification of this article the manufacture, sale, or transportation of intoxicating liquors within, the importation thereof into, or the exportation thereof from the United States and all territory subject to the jurisdiction thereof for beverage purposes is hereby prohibited.

SECTION 2. The Congress and the several States shall have concurrent power to enforce this article by appropriate legislation.

SECTION 3. This article shall be inoperative unless it shall have been ratified as an amendment to the Constitution by the legislatures of the several States, as provided in the Constitution, within seven years from the date of the submission hereof to the States by the Congress.

Amendment XIX[18]

The right of citizens of the United States to vote shall not be denied or abridged by the United States or by any State on account of sex.

Congress shall have power to enforce this article by appropriate legislation.

Amendment XX[19]

SECTION 1. The terms of the President and Vice-President shall end at noon on the 20th day of January, and the terms of Senators and Representatives at noon on the 3d day of January, of the years in which such terms would have ended if this article had not been ratified; and the terms of their successors shall then begin.

SECTION 2. The Congress shall assemble at least once in every year, and such meeting shall begin at noon on the 3d day of January, unless they shall by law appoint a different day.

SECTION 3. If, at the time fixed for the beginning of the term of the President, the President elect shall have died, the Vice-President elect shall become President. If a President shall not have been chosen before the time fixed for the beginning of his term, or if the President elect shall have failed to qualify, then the Vice-President elect shall act as President until a President shall have qualified; and the Congress may by law provide for the case wherein neither a President elect nor a Vice-President elect shall have qualified, declaring who shall then act as President, or the manner in which one who is to act shall be selected, and such person shall act accordingly until a President or Vice-President shall have qualified.

SECTION 4. The Congress may by law provide for the case of the death of any of the persons from whom the House of Representatives may choose a President whenever the right of choice shall have devolved upon them, and for the case of the death of any of the persons from whom the Senate may choose a Vice-President whenever the right of choice shall have devolved upon them.

SECTION 5. Sections 1 and 2 shall take effect on the 15th day of October following the ratification of this article.

SECTION 6. This article shall be inoperative unless it shall have been ratified as an amendment to the Constitution by the legislatures of three-fourths of the several States within seven years from the date of its submission.

[17] Passed December 18, 1917. Ratified January 16, 1919.

[18] Passed June 4, 1919. Ratified August 18, 1920.

[19] Passed March 2, 1932. Ratified January 23, 1933.

Amendment XXI[20]

SECTION 1. The eighteenth article of amendment to the Constitution of the United States is hereby repealed.

SECTION 2. The transportation or importation into any State, Territory, or possession of the United States for delivery or use therein of intoxicating liquors, in violation of the laws thereof, is hereby prohibited.

SECTION 3. This article shall be inoperative unless it shall have been ratified as an amendment to the Constitution by conventions in the several States, as provided in the Constitution, within seven years from the date of the submission hereof to the States by the Congress.

Amendment XXII[21]

No person shall be elected to the office of the President more than twice, and no person who has held the office of President, or acted as President, for more than two years of a term to which some other person was elected President shall be elected to the office of the President more than once.

But this Article shall not apply to any person holding the office of President when this Article was proposed by the Congress, and shall not prevent any person who may be holding the office of President, or acting as President, during the term within which this Article becomes operative from holding the office of President or acting as President during the remainder of such term.

Amendment XXIII[22]

SECTION 1. The District constituting the seat of Government of the United States shall appoint in such manner as the Congress may direct: A number of electors of President and Vice President equal to the whole number of Senators and Representatives in Congress to which the District would be entitled if it were a State, but in no event more than the least populous State; they shall be in addition to those appointed by the States, but they shall be considered, for the purposes of the election of President and Vice President, to be electors appointed by the State; and they shall meet in the District and perform such duties as provided by the twelfth article of amendment.

SECTION 2. The Congress shall have power to enforce this article by appropriate legislation.

Amendment XXIV[23]

SECTION 1. The right of citizens of the United States to vote in any primary or other election for President or Vice President, or for Senator or Representative in Congress, shall not be denied or abridged by the United States or any State by reason of failure to pay any poll tax or other tax.

SECTION 2. The Congress shall have power to enforce this article by appropriate legislation.

Amendment XXV[24]

SECTION 1. In case of the removal of the President from office or of his death or resignation, the Vice President shall become President.

SECTION 2. Whenever there is a vacancy in the office of the Vice President, the President shall nominate a Vice President who shall take office upon confirmation by a majority vote of both Houses of Congress.

---

[20] Passed February 20, 1933. Ratified December 5, 1933.

[21] Passed March 12, 1947. Ratified March 1, 1951.

[22] Passed June 16, 1960. Ratified April 3, 1961.

[23] Passed August 27, 1962. Ratified January 23, 1964.

[24] Passed July 6, 1965. Ratified February 11, 1967.

SECTION 3. Whenever the President transmits to the President pro tempore of the Senate and the Speaker of the House of Representatives his written declaration that he is unable to discharge the powers and duties of his office, and until he transmits them a written declaration to the contrary, such powers and duties shall be discharged by the Vice President as Acting President.

SECTION 4. Whenever the Vice President and a majority of either the principal officers of the executive department or of such other body as Congress may by law provide, transmit to the President pro tempore of the Senate and the Speaker of the House of Representatives their written declaration that the President is unable to discharge the powers and duties of his office, the Vice President shall immediately assume the powers and duties of the office of Acting President.

Thereafter, when the President transmits to the President pro tempore of the Senate and the Speaker of the House of Representatives his written declaration that no inability exists, he shall resume the powers and duties of his office unless the Vice President and a majority of either the principal officers of the executive department or of such other body as Congress may by law provide, transmit within four days to the President pro tempore of the Senate and the Speaker of the House of Representatives their written declaration that the President is unable to discharge the powers and duties of his office. Thereupon Congress shall decide the issue, assembling within forty-eight hours for that purpose if not in session. If the Congress, within twenty-one days after receipt of the latter written declaration, or, if Congress is not in session, within twenty-one days after Congress is required to assemble, determines by two-thirds vote of both Houses that the President is unable to discharge the powers and duties of his office, the Vice President shall continue to discharge the same as Acting President; otherwise, the President shall resume the powers and duties of his office.

Amendment XXVI[25]

SECTION 1 The right of citizens of theUnited States,who are eighteen years of age or older, to vote shall not be denied or abridged by the United States or by any State on account of age.

SECTION 2. The Congress shall have power to enforce this article by appropriate legislation.

Amendment XXVII[26]

No law, varying the compensation for the service of the Senators and Representatives, shall take effect, until an election of Representatives shall have intervened.

[25] Passed March 23, 1971. Ratified July 5, 1971.

[26] Passed September 25, 1789. Ratified May 7, 1992.

Admission of States

Order of admission	State	Date of admission	Order of admission	State	Date of admission
1	Delaware	December 7, 1787	26	Michigan	January 26, 1837
2	Pennsylvania	December 12, 1787	27	Florida	March 3, 1845
3	New Jersey	December 18, 1787	28	Texas	December 29, 1845
4	Georgia	January 2, 1788	29	Iowa	December 28, 1846
5	Connecticut	January 9, 1788	30	Wisconsin	May 29, 1848
6	Massachusetts	February 6, 1788	31	California	September 9, 1850
7	Maryland	April 28, 1788	32	Minnesota	May 11, 1858
8	South Carolina	May 23, 1788	33	Oregon	February 14, 1859
9	New Hampshire	June 21, 1788	34	Kansas	January 29, 1861
10	Virginia	June 25, 1788	35	West Virginia	June 20, 1863
11	New York	July 26, 1788	36	Nevada	October 31, 1864
12	North Carolina	November 21, 1789	37	Nebraska	March 1, 1867
13	Rhode Island	May 29, 1790	38	Colorado	August 1, 1876
14	Vermont	March 4, 1791	39	North Dakota	November 2, 1889
15	Kentucky	June 1, 1792	40	South Dakota	November 2, 1889
16	Tennessee	June 1, 1796	41	Montana	November 8, 1889
17	Ohio	March 1, 1803	42	Washington	November 11, 1889
18	Louisiana	April 30, 1812	43	Idaho	July 3, 1890
19	Indiana	December 11, 1816	44	Wyoming	July 10, 1890
20	Mississippi	December 10, 1817	45	Utah	January 4, 1896
21	Illinois	December 3, 1818	46	Oklahoma	November 16, 1907
22	Alabama	December 14, 1819	47	New Mexico	January 6, 1912
23	Maine	March 15, 1820	48	Arizona	February 14, 1912
24	Missouri	August 10, 1821	49	Alaska	January 3, 1959
25	Arkansas	June 15, 1836	50	Hawai'i	August 21, 1959

Population of the United States

Year	Total population	Number per square mile	Year	Total population	Number per square mile	Year	Total population	Number per square mile
1790	3,929	4.5	1828	12,237		1866	36,538	
1791	4,056		1829	12,565		1867	37,376	
1792	4,194		1830	12,901	7.4	1868	38,213	
1793	4,332		1831	13,321		1869	39,051	
1794	4,469		1832	13,742		1870	39,905	13.4
1795	4,607		1833	14,162		1871	40,938	
1796	4,745		1834	14,582		1872	41,972	
1797	4,883		1835	15,003		1873	43,006	
1798	5,021		1836	15,423		1874	44,040	
1799	5,159		1837	15,843		1875	45,073	
1800	5,297	6.1	1838	16,264		1876	46,107	
1801	5,486		1839	16,684		1877	47,141	
1802	5,679		1840	17,120	9.8	1878	48,174	
1803	5,872		1841	17,733		1879	49,208	
1804	5,065		1842	18,345		1880	50,262	16.9
1805	6,258		1843	18,957		1881	51,542	
1806	6,451		1844	19,569		1882	52,821	
1807	6,644		1845	20,182		1883	54,100	
1808	6,838		1846	20,794		1884	55,379	
1809	7,031		1847	21,406		1885	56,658	
1810	7,224	4.3	1848	22,018		1886	57,938	
1811	7,460		1849	22,631		1887	59,217	
1812	7,700		1850	23,261	7.9	1888	60,496	
1813	7,939		1851	24,086		1889	61,775	
1814	8,179		1852	24,911		1890[1]	63,056	21.2
1815	8,419		1853	25,736		1891	64,361	
1816	8,659		1854	26,561		1892	65,666	
1817	8,899		1855	27,386		1893	66,970	
1818	9,139		1856	28,212		1894	68,275	
1819	9,379		1857	29,037		1895	69,580	
1820	9,618	5.6	1858	29,862		1896	70,885	
1821	9,939		1859	30,687		1897	72,189	
1822	10,268		1860	31,513	10.6	1898	73,494	
1823	10,596		1861	32,351		1899	74,799	
1824	10,924		1862	33,188		1900	76,094	25.6
1825	11,252		1863	34,026		1901	77,585	
1826	11,580		1864	34,863		1902	79,160	
1827	11,909		1865	35,701		1903	80,632	

Figures are from *Historical Statistics of the United States, Colonial Times to 1957* (1961), pp. 7, 8; *Statistical Abstract of the United States: 1974*, p. 5, Census Bureau for 1974 and 1975; and *Statistical Abstract of the United States: 1988*, p. 7.

Note: Population figures are in thousands. Density figures are for land area of continental United States.

[1] Indians living in Indian Territory or on reservations were not included in the population count until 1890.

Population of the United States *(continued)*

Year	Total population	Number per square mile	Year	Total population[1]	Number per square mile	Year	Total population[1]	Number per square mile
1904	82,165		1941	133,894		1978	218,717	
1905	83,820		1942	135,361		1979	220,584	
1906	85,437		1943	137,250		1980	226,546	64.0
1907	87,000		1944	138,916		1981	230,138	
1908	88,709		1945	140,468		1982	232,520	
1909	90,492		1946	141,936		1983	234,799	
1910	92,407	31.0	1947	144,698		1984	237,001	
1911	93,868		1948	147,208		1985	239,283	
1912	95,331		1949	149,767		1986	241,596	
1913	97,227		1950	150,697	50.7	1987	234,773	
1914	99,118		1951	154,878		1988	245,051	
1915	100,549		1952	157,553		1989	247,350	
1916	101,966		1953	160,184		1990	250,122	70.3
1917	103,414		1954	163,026		1991	254,521	
1918	104,550		1955	165,931		1992	245,908	
1919	105,063		1956	168,903		1993	257,908	
1920	106,466	35.6	1957	171,984		1994	261,875	
1921	108,541		1958	174,882		1995	263,434	
1922	110,055		1959	177,830		1996	266,096	
1923	111,950		1960	178,464	60.1	1997	267,901	
1924	114,113		1961	183,642		1998	269,501	
1925	115,832		1962	186,504		1999	272,700	
1926	117,399		1963	189,197		2000	282,172	80.0
1927	119,038		1964	191,833		2001	285,082	
1928	120,501		1965	194,237		2002	287,804	
1929	121,700		1966	196,485		2003	290,326	
1930	122,775	41.2	1967	198,629		2004	293,046	
1931	124,040		1968	200,619		2005	295,753	
1932	124,840		1969	202,599		2006	298,593	
1933	125,579		1970	203,875	57.5[2]	2007	301,580	
1934	126,374		1971	207,045		2008	304,375	
1935	127,250		1972	208,842		2009	307,007	
1936	128,053		1973	210,396		2010	308,746	87.4
1937	128,825		1974	211,894		2011	311,588	
1938	129,825		1975	213,631		2012	313,914	
1939	130,880		1976	215,152		2013	316,439	
1940	131,669	44.2	1977	216,880				

[1] Figures after 1940 represent total population including armed forces abroad, except in official census years.

[2] Figure includes Alaska and Hawai'i, were territories through 1950, and were first included in the United States in the 1960 census.

Presidential Elections

Year	Number of states	Candidates[1]	Parties	Popular vote	Electoral vote	Percentage of popular vote[2]
1789	11	**George Washington**	No party designations		69	
		John Adams			34	
		Minor Candidates			35	
1792	15	**George Washington**	No party designations		132	
		John Adams			77	
		George Clinton			50	
		Minor Candidates			5	
1796	16	**John Adams**	Federalist		71	
		Thomas Jefferson	Democratic-Republican		68	
		Thomas Pinckney	Federalist		59	
		Aaron Burr	Democratic-Republican		30	
		Minor Candidates			48	
1800	16	**Thomas Jefferson**	Democratic-Republican		73	
		Aaron Burr	Democratic-Republican		73	
		John Adams	Federalist		65	
		Charles C. Pinckney	Federalist		64	
		John Jay	Federalist		1	
1804	17	**Thomas Jefferson**	Democratic-Republican		162	
		Charles C. Pinckney	Federalist		14	
1808	17	**James Madison**	Democratic-Republican		122	
		Charles C. Pinckney	Federalist		47	
		George Clinton	Democratic-Republican		6	
1812	18	**James Madison**	Democratic-Republican		128	
		DeWitt Clinton	Federalist		89	
1816	19	**James Monroe**	Democratic-Republican		183	
		Rufus King	Federalist		34	
1820	24	**James Monroe**	Democratic-Republican		231	
		John Quincy Adams	Independent Republican		1	
1824	24	**John Quincy Adams**	Democratic-Republican	108,740	84	30.5
		Andrew Jackson	Democratic-Republican	153,544	99	43.1
		William H. Crawford	Democratic-Republican	46,618	41	13.1
		Henry Clay	Democratic-Republican	47,136	37	13.2
1828	24	**Andrew Jackson**	Democratic	647,286	178	56.0
		John Quincy Adams	National Republican	508,064	83	44.0

[1]Before the passage of the Twelfth Amendment in 1804, the Electoral College voted for two presidential candidates; the runner-up became vice president. Figures are from *Historical Statistics of the United States, Colonial Times to 1957* (1961), pp. 682–83; and the U.S. Department of Justice.

[2]Candidates receiving less than 1 percent of the popular vote have been omitted. For that reason the percentage of popular vote given for any election year may not total 100 percent.

Presidential Elections *(continued)*

Year	Number of states	Candidates	Parties	Popular vote	Electoral vote	Percentage of popular vote[1]
1832	24	**Andrew Jackson**	Democratic	687,502	219	55.0
		Henry Clay	National Republican	530,189	49	42.4
		William Wirt	Anti-Masonic		7	
		John Floyd	National Republican	33,108	11	2.6
1836	26	**Martin Van Buren**	Democratic	765,483	170	50.9
		William H. Harrison	Whig		73	
		Hugh L. White	Whig	739,795	26	
		Daniel Webster	Whig		14	
		W. P. Mangum	Whig		11	
1840	26	**William H. Harrison**	Whig	1,274,624	234	53.1
		Martin Van Buren	Democratic	1,127,781	60	46.9
1844	26	**James K. Polk**	Democratic	1,338,464	170	49.6
		Henry Clay	Whig	1,300,097	105	48.1
		James G. Birney	Liberty	62,300		2.3
1848	30	**Zachary Taylor**	Whig	1,360,967	163	47.4
		Lewis Cass	Democratic	1,222,342	127	42.5
		Martin Van Buren	Free Soil	291,263		10.1
1852	31	**Franklin Pierce**	Democratic	1,601,117	254	50.9
		Winfield Scott	Whig	1,385,453	42	44.1
		John P. Hale	Free Soil	155,825		5.0
1856	31	**James Buchanan**	Democratic	1,832,955	174	45.3
		John C. Frémont	Republican	1,339,932	114	33.1
		Millard Fillmore	American	871,731	8	21.6
1860	33	**Abraham Lincoln**	Republican	1,865,593	180	39.8
		Stephen A. Douglas	Democratic	1,382,713	12	29.5
		John C. Breckinridge	Democratic	848,356	72	18.1
		John Bell	Constitutional Union	592,906	39	12.6
1864	36	**Abraham Lincoln**	Republican	2,206,938	212	55.0
		George B. McClellan	Democratic	1,803,787	21	45.0
1868	37	**Ulysses S. Grant**	Republican	3,013,421	214	52.7
		Horatio Seymour	Democratic	2,706,829	80	47.3
1872	37	**Ulysses S. Grant**	Republican	3,596,745	286	55.6
		Horace Greeley	Democratic	2,843,446	[2]	43.9
1876	38	**Rutherford B. Hayes**	Republican	4,036,572	185	48.0
		Samuel J. Tilden	Democratic	4,284,020	184	51.0

[1] Candidates receiving less than 1 percent of the popular vote have been omitted. For that reason the percentage of popular vote given for any election year may not total 100 percent.

Presidential Elections *(continued)*

Year	Number of states	Candidates	Parties	Popular vote	Electoral vote	Percentage of popular vote[1]
1880	38	**James A. Garfield**	Republican	4,453,295	214	48.5
		Winfield S. Hancock	Democratic	4,414,082	155	48.1
		James B. Weaver	Greenback-Labor	308,578		3.4
1884	38	**Grover Cleveland**	Democratic	4,879,507	219	48.5
		James G. Blaine	Republican	4,850,293	182	48.2
		Benjamin F. Butler	Greenback-Labor	175,370		1.8
		John P. St. John	Prohibition	150,369		1.5
1888	38	**Benjamin Harrison**	Republican	5,477,129	233	47.9
		Grover Cleveland	Democratic	5,537,857	168	48.6
		Clinton B. Fisk	Prohibition	249,506		2.2
		Anson J. Streeter	Union Labor	146,935		1.3
1892	44	**Grover Cleveland**	Democratic	5,555,426	277	46.1
		Benjamin Harrison	Republican	5,182,690	145	43.0
		James B. Weaver	People's	1,029,846	22	8.5
		John Bidwell	Prohibition	264,133		2.2
1896	45	**William McKinley**	Republican	7,102,246	271	51.1
		William J. Bryan	Democratic	6,492,559	176	47.7
1900	45	**William McKinley**	Republican	7,218,491	292	51.7
		William J. Bryan	Democratic; Populist	6,356,734	155	45.5
		John C. Wooley	Prohibition	208,914		1.5
1904	45	**Theodore Roosevelt**	Republican	7,628,461	336	57.4
		Alton B. Parker	Democratic	5,084,223	140	37.6
		Eugene V. Debs	Socialist	402,283		3.0
		Silas C. Swallow	Prohibition	258,536		1.9
1908	46	**William H. Taft**	Republican	7,675,320	321	51.6
		William J. Bryan	Democratic	6,412,294	162	43.1
		Eugene V. Debs	Socialist	420,793		2.8
		Eugene W. Chafin	Prohibition	253,840		1.7
1912	48	**Woodrow Wilson**	Democratic	6,296,547	435	41.9
		Theodore Roosevelt	Progressive	4,118,571	88	27.4
		William H. Taft	Republican	3,486,720	8	23.2
		Eugene V. Debs	Socialist	900,672		6.0
		Eugene W. Chafin	Prohibition	206,275		1.4
1916	48	**Woodrow Wilson**	Democratic	9,127,695	277	49.4
		Charles E. Hughes	Republican	8,533,507	254	46.2
		A. L. Benson	Socialist	585,113		3.2
		J. Frank Hanly	Prohibition	220,506		1.2

[1] Candidates receiving less than 1 percent of the popular vote have been omitted. For that reason the percentage of popular vote given for any election year may not total 100 percent.

[2] Greeley died shortly after the election; the electors supporting him then divided their votes among minor candidates.

Presidential Elections *(continued)*

Year	Number of states	Candidates	Parties	Popular vote	Electoral vote	Percentage of popular vote[1]
1920	48	**Warren G. Harding**	Republican	16,143,407	404	60.4
		James N. Cox	Democratic	9,130,328	127	34.2
		Eugene V. Debs	Socialist	919,799		3.4
		P. P. Christensen	Farmer-Labor	265,411		1.0
1924	48	**Calvin Coolidge**	Republican	15,718,211	382	54.0
		John W. Davis	Democratic	8,385,283	136	28.8
		Robert M. La Follette	Progressive	4,831,289	13	16.6
1928	48	**Herbert C. Hoover**	Republican	21,391,993	444	58.2
		Alfred E. Smith	Democratic	15,016,169	87	40.9
1932	48	**Franklin D. Roosevelt**	Democratic	22,809,638	472	57.4
		Herbert C. Hoover	Republican	15,758,901	59	39.7
		Norman Thomas	Socialist	881,951		2.2
1936	48	**Franklin D. Roosevelt**	Democratic	27,752,869	523	60.8
		Alfred M. Landon	Republican	16,674,665	8	36.5
		William Lemke	Union	882,479		1.9
1940	48	**Franklin D. Roosevelt**	Democratic	27,307,819	449	54.8
		Wendell L. Willkie	Republican	22,321,018	82	44.8
1944	48	**Franklin D. Roosevelt**	Democratic	25,606,585	432	53.5
		Thomas E. Dewey	Republican	22,014,745	99	46.0
1948	48	**Harry S. Truman**	Democratic	24,105,812	303	49.5
		Thomas E. Dewey	Republican	21,970,065	189	45.1
		J. Strom Thurmond	States' Rights	1,169,063	39	2.4
		Henry A. Wallace	Progressive	1,157,172		2.4
1952	48	**Dwight D. Eisenhower**	Republican	33,936,234	442	55.1
		Adlai E. Stevenson	Democratic	27,314,992	89	44.4
1956	48	**Dwight D. Eisenhower**	Republican	35,590,472	457	57.6
		Adlai E. Stevenson	Democratic	26,022,752	73	42.1
1960	50	**John F. Kennedy**	Democratic	34,227,096	303	49.9
		Richard M. Nixon	Republican	34,108,546	219	49.6
1964	50	**Lyndon B. Johnson**	Democratic	43,126,506	486	61.1
		Barry M. Goldwater	Republican	27,176,799	52	38.5
1968	50	**Richard M. Nixon**	Republican	31,785,480	301	43.4
		Hubert H. Humphrey	Democratic	31,275,165	191	42.7
		George C. Wallace	American Independent	9,906,473	46	13.5
1972	50	**Richard M. Nixon**	Republican	47,169,911	520	60.7
		George S. McGovern	Democratic	29,170,383	17	37.5
1976	50	**Jimmy Carter**	Democratic	40,827,394	297	50.0
		Gerald R. Ford	Republican	39,145,977	240	47.9

[1] Candidates receiving less than 1 percent of the popular vote have been omitted. For that reason the percentage of popular vote given for any election year may not total 100 percent.

Presidential Elections *(continued)*

Year	Number of states	Candidates	Parties	Popular vote	Electoral vote	Percentage of popular vote[1]
1980	50	**Ronald W. Reagan**	Republican	43,899,248	489	50.8
		Jimmy Carter	Democratic	35,481,435	49	41.0
		John B. Anderson	Independent	5,719,437		6.6
		Ed Clark	Libertarian	920,859		1.0
1984	50	**Ronald W. Reagan**	Republican	54,281,858	525	59.2
		Walter F. Mondale	Democratic	37,457,215	13	40.8
1988	50	**George H. Bush**	Republican	47,917,341	426	54
		Michael Dukakis	Democratic	41,013,030	112	46
1992	50	**William Clinton**	Democratic	44,908,254	370	43.0
		George H. Bush	Republican	39,102,343	168	37.4
		Ross Perot	Independent	19,741,065		18.9
1996	50	**William Clinton**	Democratic	45,628,667	379	49.2
		Robert Dole	Republican	37,869,435	159	40.8
		Ross Perot	Reform	7,874,283		8.5
2000	50	**George W. Bush**	Republican	50,456,062	271	47.9
		Albert Gore	Democratic	50,996,582	266	48.4
		Ralph Nader	Green	2,858,843		2.7
2004	50	**George W. Bush**	Republican	62,040,606	286	51
		John F. Kerry	Democratic	59,028,109	252	48
		Ralph Nader	Green/Independent	411,304		1
2008	50	**Barack Obama**	Democratic	66,882,230	365	53
		John McCain	Republican	58,343,671	173	46
2012	50	**Barack Obama**	Democratic	65,917,258	332	51
		Mitt Romney	Republican	60,932,235	206	47

[1]Candidates receiving less than 1 percent of the popular vote have been omitted. For that reason the percentage of popular vote given for any election year may not total 100 percent.

Presidents and Vice Presidents

Term	President	Vice President
1789–1793	George Washington	John Adams
1793–1797	George Washington	John Adams
1797–1801	John Adams	Thomas Jefferson
1801–1805	Thomas Jefferson	Aaron Burr
1805–1809	Thomas Jefferson	George Clinton
1809–1813	James Madison	George Clinton (d. 1812)
1813–1817	James Madison	Elbridge Gerry (d. 1814)
1817–1821	James Monroe	Daniel D. Tompkins
1821–1825	James Monroe	Daniel D. Tompkins
1825–1829	John Quincy Adams	John C. Calhoun
1829–1833	Andrew Jackson	John C. Calhoun (resigned 1832)
1833–1837	Andrew Jackson	Martin Van Buren
1837–1841	Martin Van Buren	Richard M. Johnson
1841–1845	William H. Harrison (d. 1841) John Tyler	John Tyler
1845–1849	James K. Polk	George M. Dallas
1849–1853	Zachary Taylor (d. 1850) Millard Fillmore	Millard Fillmore
1853–1857	Franklin Pierce	William R. D. King (d. 1853)
1857–1861	James Buchanan	John C. Breckinridge
1861–1865	Abraham Lincoln	Hannibal Hamlin
1865–1869	Abraham Lincoln (d. 1865) Andrew Johnson	Andrew Johnson
1869–1873	Ulysses S. Grant	Schuyler Colfax
1873–1877	Ulysses S. Grant	Henry Wilson (d. 1875)
1877–1881	Rutherford B. Hayes	William A. Wheeler
1881–1885	James A. Garfield (d. 1881) Chester A. Arthur	Chester A. Arthur
1885–1889	Grover Cleveland	Thomas A. Hendricks (d. 1885)
1889–1893	Benjamin Harrison	Levi P. Morton
1893–1897	Grover Cleveland	Adlai E. Stevenson
1897–1901	William McKinley	Garret A. Hobart (d. 1899)
1901–1905	William McKinley (d. 1901) Theodore Roosevelt	Theodore Roosevelt
1905–1909	Theodore Roosevelt	Charles W. Fairbanks
1909–1913	William H. Taft	James S. Sherman (d.1912)
1913–1917	Woodrow Wilson	Thomas R. Marshall
1917–1921	Woodrow Wilson	Thomas R. Marshall
1921–1925	Warren G. Harding (d. 1923) Calvin Coolidge	Calvin Coolidge
1925–1929	Calvin Coolidge	Charles G. Dawes
1929–1933	Herbert Hoover	Charles Curtis
1933–1937	Franklin D. Roosevelt	John N. Garner
1937–1941	Franklin D. Roosevelt	John N. Garner
1941–1945	Franklin D. Roosevelt	Henry A. Wallace
1945–1949	Franklin D. Roosevelt (d. 1945) Harry S Truman	Harry S Truman
1949–1953	Harry S Truman	Alben W. Barkley
1953–1957	Dwight D. Eisenhower	Richard M. Nixon
1957–1961	Dwight D. Eisenhower	Richard M. Nixon
1961–1965	John F. Kennedy (d. 1963) Lyndon B. Johnson	Lyndon B. Johnson
1965–1969	Lyndon B. Johnson	Hubert H. Humphrey, Jr.
1969–1974	Richard M. Nixon	Spiro T. Agnew (resigned 1973); Gerald R. Ford
1974–1977	Gerald R. Ford	Nelson A. Rockefeller
1977–1981	Jimmy Carter	Walter F. Mondale
1981–1985	Ronald Reagan	George Bush
1985–1989	Ronald Reagan	George Bush
1993–1993	George Bush	J. Danforth Quayle III
1993–2001	William Clinton	Albert Gore, Jr.
2001–2005	George W. Bush	Richard Cheney
2005–2009	George W. Bush	Richard Cheney
2009–	Barack Obama	Joseph Biden

Justices of the U.S. Supreme Court

Name	Term of service	Years of service	Appointed by	Name	Term of service	Years of service	Appointed by
John Jay	1789–1795	5	Washington	Robert C. Grier	1846–1870	23	Polk
John Rutledge	1789–1791	1	Washington	Benjamin R. Curtis	1851–1857	6	Fillmore
William Cushing	1789–1810	20	Washington	John A. Campbell	1853–1861	8	Pierce
James Wilson	1789–1798	8	Washington	Nathan Clifford	1858–1881	23	Buchanan
John Blair	1789–1796	6	Washington	Noah H. Swayne	1862–1881	18	Lincoln
Robert H. Harrison	1789–1790	—	Washington	Samuel F. Miller	1862–1890	28	Lincoln
James Iredell	1790–1799	9	Washington	David Davis	1862–1877	14	Lincoln
Thomas Johnson	1791–1793	1	Washington	Stephen J. Field	1863–1897	34	Lincoln
William Paterson	1793–1806	13	Washington	**Salmon P. Chase**	1864–1873	8	Lincoln
John Rutledge[1]	1795	—	Washington	William Strong	1870–1880	10	Grant
Samuel Chase	1796–1811	15	Washington	Joseph P. Bradley	1870–1892	22	Grant
Oliver Ellsworth	1796–1800	4	Washington	Ward Hunt	1873–1882	9	Grant
Bushrod Washington	1798–1829	31	J. Adams	**Morrison R. Waite**	1874–1888	14	Grant
Alfred Moore	1799–1804	4	J. Adams	John M. Harlan	1877–1911	34	Hayes
John Marshall	1801–1835	34	J. Adams	William B. Woods	1880–1887	7	Hayes
William Johnson	1804–1834	30	Jefferson	Stanley Matthews	1881–1889	7	Garfield
H. Brockholst Livingston	1806–1823	16	Jefferson	Horace Gray	1882–1902	20	Arthur
Thomas Todd	1807–1826	18	Jefferson	Samuel Blatchford	1882–1893	11	Arthur
Joseph Story	1811–1845	33	Madison	Lucius Q. C. Lamar	1888–1893	5	Cleveland
Gabriel Duval	1811–1835	24	Madison	**Melville W. Fuller**	1888–1910	21	Cleveland
Smith Thompson	1823–1843	20	Monroe	David J. Brewer	1890–1910	20	B. Harrison
Robert Trimble	1826–1828	2	J. Q. Adams	Henry B. Brown	1890–1906	16	B. Harrison
John McLean	1829–1861	32	Jackson	George Shiras, Jr.	1892–1903	10	B. Harrison
Henry Baldwin	1830–1844	14	Jackson	Howell E. Jackson	1893–1895	2	B. Harrison
James M. Wayne	1835–1867	32	Jackson	Edward D. White	1894–1910	16	Cleveland
Roger B. Taney	1836–1864	28	Jackson	Rufus W. Peckham	1895–1909	14	Cleveland
Philip P. Barbour	1836–1841	4	Jackson	Joseph McKenna	1898–1925	26	McKinley
John Catron	1837–1865	28	Van Buren	Oliver W. Holmes, Jr.	1902–1932	30	T. Roosevelt
John McKinley	1837–1852	15	Van Buren	William R. Day	1903–1922	19	T. Roosevelt
Peter V. Daniel	1841–1860	19	Van Buren	William H. Moody	1906–1910	3	T. Roosevelt
Samuel Nelson	1845–1872	27	Tyler	Horace H. Lurton	1910–1914	4	Taft
Levi Woodbury	1845–1851	5	Polk	Charles E. Hughes	1910–1916	5	Taft

[1] Acting chief justice; Senate refused to confirm appointment.

Note: Chief justices appear in bold type.

Justices of the U.S. Supreme Court *(continued)*

Name	Term of service	Years of service	Appointed by	Name	Term of service	Years of service	Appointed by
Willis Van Devanter	1911–1937	26	Taft	Sherman Minton	1949–1956	7	Truman
Joseph R. Lamar	1911–1916	5	Taft	**Earl Warren**	1953–1969	16	Eisenhower
Edward D. White	1910–1921	11	Taft	John Marshall Harlan	1955–1971	16	Eisenhower
Mahlon Pitney	1912–1922	10	Taft	William J. Brennan, Jr.	1956–1990	34	Eisenhower
James C. McReynolds	1914–1941	26	Wilson	Charles E. Whittaker	1957–1962	5	Eisenhower
Louis D. Brandeis	1916–1939	22	Wilson	Potter Stewart	1958–1981	23	Eisenhower
John H. Clarke	1916–1922	6	Wilson	Byron R. White	1962–1993	31	Kennedy
William H. Taft	1921–1930	8	Harding	Arthur J. Goldberg	1962–1965	3	Kennedy
George Sutherland	1922–1938	15	Harding	Abe Fortas	1965–1969	4	Johnson
Pierce Butler	1922–1939	16	Harding	Thurgood Marshall	1967–1994	24	Johnson
Edward T. Sanford	1923–1930	7	Harding	**Warren E. Burger**	1969–1986	18	Nixon
Harlan F. Stone	1925–1941	16	Coolidge	Harry A. Blackmun	1970–1994	24	Nixon
Charles E. Hughes	1930–1941	11	Hoover	Lewis F. Powell, Jr.	1971–1987	15	Nixon
Owen J. Roberts	1930–1945	15	Hoover	**William H. Rehnquist**	1971–2005	34	Nixon
Benjamin N. Cardozo	1932–1938	6	Hoover	John P. Stevens III	1975–2010	35	Ford
Hugo L. Black	1937–1971	34	F. Roosevelt	Sandra Day O'Connor	1981–2006	25	Reagan
Stanley F. Reed	1938–1957	19	F. Roosevelt	Antonin Scalia	1986–2016	30	Reagan
Felix Frankfurter	1939–1962	23	F. Roosevelt	Anthony M. Kennedy	1988–	—	Reagan
William O. Douglas	1939–1975	36	F. Roosevelt	David Souter	1990–2009	19	Bush
Frank Murphy	1940–1949	9	F. Roosevelt	Clarence Thomas	1991–	—	Bush
Harlan F. Stone	1941–1946	5	F. Roosevelt	Ruth Bader Ginsburg	1993–	—	Clinton
James F. Byrnes	1941–1942	1	F. Roosevelt	Stephen G. Breyer	1994–	—	Clinton
Robert H. Jackson	1941–1954	13	F. Roosevelt	**John G. Roberts, Jr.**	2005–	—	G. W. Bush
Wiley B. Rutledge	1943–1949	6	F. Roosevelt	Samuel Anthony Alito, Jr.	2006–	—	G. W. Bush
Harold H. Burton	1945–1958	13	Truman	Sonia Sotomayor	2009–	—	Obama
Fred M. Vinson	1946–1953	7	Truman	Elena Kagan	2010–	—	Obama
Tom C. Clark	1949–1967	18	Truman				

Note: Chief justices appear in bold type.

Index